To my mother and father,
who made it all possible,

to my wife Beverly *and children,*
Heather, Jennifer, and Jeremy,

and to my grandchildren,
Matthew, Rachel, Gabriella, Ashley, Rebecca, and Elijah,
who make it all so worthwhile,

I dedicate this sixth edition.

FOREWORD

I am very pleased to be invited to offer a foreword to the new sixth edition of *Medical Emergencies in the Dental Office*. In recalling the original publication of 1978, one is impressed with the creative talent and knowledge of the "titans of teaching"—Dr. Frank ("Cap") McCarthy and Dr. Stanley Malamed. They foresaw the need and developed basic logical ways of assessing a patient's physical status when presenting for dental treatment.

Undergraduate dental education often pays limited lip service to our basic concern for the well-being of the total patient as it struggles to teach the many manual and technique-oriented procedures. But we know that the "mouth is really part of the body" and our concerns involve the whole individual, especially one compromised by underlying systemic pathology.

Although a bridge or implant may fail, these are repairable. When a patient sustains a stroke secondary to an unsuspected hypertensive crisis or aspirates a chunk of impression material that blocks breathing, we are faced with a potential tragedy. Learning how to assess the physical and emotional status of each patient provides a hedge against disaster.

I have always believed that the dental undergraduate curriculum should include a better grounding in pathophysiology to provide a basis for practice. The dental profession has moved forward to use blood pressure recording almost routinely, especially in assessing new patients and has moved to require basic life support (BLS) and advanced cardiac life support (ACLS) education for licensure. Further, monitoring devices are now mandated in most states for those dentists who use sedative and anesthetic agents.

It is impressive to see how these teachings have changed over time; important algorithms that were believed to be like gospel have been discarded as more experience is gained. The sixth edition of this book reflects these improvements. These changes mandate that we keep current in our new knowledge and practices.

Some tragedies are inevitable when dealing with patients, but knowing how and when to anticipate and manage them reduces the likelihood of their occurrence. The expense of training the professional and lay public in the recognition and management of emergencies is enormous, but a successful resuscitation, saving the life of a loved one, is worth it.

Norman Trieger, DMD, MD
Chairman Emeritus and Professor
Department of Dentistry
Albert Einstein College of Medicine/Montefiore
Medical Center
Bronx, New York

PREFACE

In December of 1975 I started writing *Medical Emergencies in the Dental Office*. The first edition was published in April of 1978. As I wrote in the preface to that first edition, my primary aim in writing the book was, and still is, to stimulate members of my profession—dentistry: the doctor, dental hygienist, dental assistant, and all other office personnel—to improve and to maintain their skill in the prevention of medical emergencies and in the recognition and management of emergencies that will inevitably occur. This aim is ever more focused in my mind as this, the sixth edition of *Emergencies,* is written in 2007.

Up to three-quarters of medical emergencies occurring in the dental environment may be preventable through implementation of a system of patient evaluation, treatment modification, and management.

Though most medical emergencies may be prevented, many potentially life-threatening situations still occur. I continue to receive letters, telephone calls, and e-mail messages about such situations. I have met with many doctors and other dental personnel who have had real-life experiences with life-threatening medical problems. Virtually all of these have occurred within the dental office. However, a significant number happened outside: on family outings, driving in a car, or at home.

There is a significant need for increased awareness by dental professionals in the area of emergency medicine. Although many states and provinces in North America mandate current certification in basic life support (cardiopulmonary resuscitation [CPR]) for dental licensure, not all states and provinces have as yet addressed this important issue.

As someone with a long-term commitment in the teaching of basic life support (BLS), pediatric advanced life support (PALS), and advanced cardiovascular life support (ACLS), I see an immense value in training all adults in the simple procedures collectively known as *basic life support*. Local and state dental societies, as well as specialty groups, should continue to present courses in BLS or initiate them posthaste.

Progress has been made, yet much remains to be done. The awareness of our profession has been elevated, and laudable achievements continue. (As of 28 February 2006, the Dental Board of Florida has required that every dental office location have an automated external defibrillator [AED] on site. Failure to have an AED available would constitute practicing dentistry below the minimum standard of care.*)

Yet, because of the very nature of the problem, what we in dentistry require is continued maintenance of a high level of skill in the prevention, recognition, and management of medical emergencies. To do so we must all participate in ongoing programs designed by individual doctors to meet the specific needs of their offices. These programs should include: attendance at continuing dental education seminars in emergency medicine; access to up-to-date information on this subject (through the Internet, journals, and text books); semiannual or annual recertification in basic life support, PALS, or ACLS; and in-office practice sessions in emergency procedures with mandatory participation of the entire office staff. Such a program is discussed more completely in Chapter 3. The ultimate goal in the preparation of a dental office for emergencies should be for you, the reader, to be able to put yourself into the position of a victim of a serious medical complication in your dental office, and for you to be confident that your office staff would be able to react promptly and effectively in recognizing and managing the situation.

Emergency medicine is a rapidly evolving medical specialty, and because of this, many changes have occurred since publication of the first edition of this text. My goal now, as it was then, is to enable you to manage a given emergency situation in an effective yet uncomplicated manner. Alternative treatments and alternative drugs, which are also effective, may be advocated by some authors. My goal, as well as theirs, is simply to enable you to keep the victim alive until they either recover or until emergency assistance becomes available to take over management . . . as long as they are better able to manage the situation than are you.

Continual revision and updating of essential material is evident in this sixth edition. Significant changes have been incorporated into Chapter 2 with the introduction of an excellent medical history questionnaire from the University of the Pacific School of Dentistry, while Chapter 4 (Legal Considerations) has undergone a complete rewrite. In response to comments and suggestions from many readers, a new chapter on Pediatric Considerations in emergency medicine (Chapter 31) has been added to this edition.

In December 2005, the American Heart Association and the International Liaison Committee on Resuscitation (ILCOR) published revised guidelines for BLS, ACLS, and PALS.† Recommended changes in both philosophy and technique have been incorporated into appropriate sections of this sixth edition.

The basic format of the text—based on clinical signs and symptoms rather than on a systems-oriented approach—remains quite well received and is continued in this sixth edition. Continued emphasis is placed on the management algorithm for all medical emergencies: **P** . . . position, **A** . . . airway, **B** . . . breathing, **C** . . . circulation, and **D** . . . definitive care. Management of medical emergencies need not, and should not, be complicated. Emphasizing this concept throughout this textbook should make it somewhat easier for the entire office staff to grasp the importance of certain basic steps in life saving (**P, A, B, C, D**).

EVOLVE INSTRUCTOR RESOURCES

New to the sixth edition is an online component available to instructors who wish to further the understanding of this content in their classrooms, or practitioners who wish to utilize electronic resources in the training of their office staff. The Evolve Instructor Resources for *Medical Emergencies in the Dental Office*, available at **www.evolve.elsevier.com/Malamed/emergencies** features three main elements:

- **Outlines of major headings in the text** aid in teaching plans and lecture preparation.
- An **electronic image collection** contains most figures from the text in downloadable formats. The figures can be implemented for study or additional lecture material.
- **More than 300 chapter-specific multiple-choice questions** form a test bank that can be used to

create quizzes or exams for student assessment as a course progresses. These questions are also useful as a training tool to gauge office staff's readiness to respond in emergency situations.

ACKNOWLEDGMENTS

As with earlier editions of this text, I have been quite fortunate to have been associated with a number of persons who helped to make the task of revision somewhat more tolerable and enjoyable. As I have discovered with each previous edition, it is impossible to mention everyone involved in the production of a book. However, I must mention a number of persons without who this volume would not have been completed: Drs. Amy Buehler, Abraham Estess, George Hanna, Amy Durisin, Tran Han, Scott Frederick, as well as Rachel Teixeira, Matthew Boyd, and Sarah Melamed all of whom participated as photographic models and tolerated all sorts of injustices and indignities, all in the name of science and education. Most photographs in this new edition were redone in color, greatly adding to the impact of the materials.

Dr. James (Jimmy) W. Tom, Mr. Andy Nordby, Dr. John Roberson, and Ms. Rose Dodson also provided assistance with photographs and information necessary to upgrade this volume.

Reader input concerning previous editions of this text and suggestions for new items for inclusion in future editions have proved to be of inestimable value. I greatly appreciate, and indeed wish to solicit, future comments from my readers.

Stanley F. Malamed, DDS

*Rule 64B5-17.015, Department of Health, Board of Dentistry, volume 29, number 42, October 17, 2003, Office Safety Requirement, Tallahassee, FL.
†International Liaison Committee on Resuscitation: 2005 International Consensus on Cardiopulmonary Resuscitation and Emergency Cardiovascular Care Science with Treatment Recommendations. *Circulation* 112:I-1–I-187, 2005.

CONTENTS

PART ONE:
PREVENTION, 1

1 Introduction, 3

Morbidity, 4
Death, 7
Risk Factors, 9
    Increased number of older patients, 9
    Medical advances, 11
    Longer appointments, 11
    Increased drug use, 11
Classification of Life-Threatening
    Situations, 12
Outline of Specific Emergency Situations, 13

2 Prevention, 15

Evaluation Goals, 16
Physical Evaluation, 16
    Medical history questionnaire, 16
    Physical examination, 38
    Vital signs, 39
    Visual inspection, 46
    Additional evaluation procedures, 47
    Dialogue history, 47
Anxiety Recognition, 48
    Psychological examination, 48
    Determination of medical risk, 50
    Medical consultation, 53
    Stress-reduction protocol, 54

3 Preparation, 59

General Information, 60
    Geographic requirements for emergency
      training, 60
    Office personnel, 60
    Emergency drugs and equipment, 65
    Commercial versus homemade emergency
      drug kits, 65
Emergency Drug Kits, 67
    Components of the emergency kit, 67
    Administration of injectable drugs, 68
Module One: Critical (Essential) Emergency
    Drugs and Equipment, 70
    Critical injectable drugs, 70
    Critical noninjectable drugs, 73
Module Two: Secondary (Noncritical)
    Emergency Drugs and Equipment, 81
    Secondary injectable drugs, 81
    Secondary noninjectable drugs, 86
    Secondary emergency equipment, 88
Module Three: ACLS, 90

    ACLS essential drugs, 90
Module Four: Antidotal Drugs, 93
    Antidotal drugs, 94
Organization of the Emergency Kit, 96
Appendix: Parenteral Administration of
    Drugs, 101
    IM drug administration, 101
    IV drug administration, 103

4 Legal Considerations, 105

Daniel L Orr II, DDS, MS (anes), PhD, JD, MD

Modern Liability Insurance Crises, 106
Theories of Liability, 106
    Statute violation, 106
    Contract law, 107
    Criminal law, 107
    Tort law, 108
    Duty, 108
    Breach of duty, 108
    Causation, 108
    Damage, 109
    Reasonableness, 109
    Consent, 109
    Statute of limitations, 110
Emergency Situations, 110
    Standard of care during emergencies, 110
    Consent during emergencies, 110
    Defining emergency, 110
    Emergency rescues—Good Samaritan
      statutes, 112
    Relationship between doctor and
      emergency patient, 112
    Foreseeability, 113
Limiting Liability for Emergencies, 113
    Prevention and preparation, 113
    Poor decisions, 113
    Respondeat superior, 113
    Community standards, 114
    Professional relationships, 114
    Collegiality, 114
    Philosophical aspects of treating
      emergencies, 114

PART TWO:
UNCONSCIOUSNESS, 117

5 Unconsciousness: General Considerations, 119

Predisposing Factors, 120
Prevention, 121

Clinical Manifestations, 122
Pathophysiology, 122
    Inadequate cerebral circulation, 122
    Oxygen deprivation, 123
    General or local metabolic changes, 123
    Actions on the central nervous system, 123
    Psychic mechanisms, 123
Management, 124
    Recognition of unconsciousness, 124
    Management of the unconscious
      patient, 124

6 Vasodepressor Syncope, 137

Predisposing Factors, 138
Prevention, 139
    Proper positioning, 139
    Anxiety relief, 139
    Dental therapy considerations, 139
Clinical Manifestations, 140
    Presyncope, 140
    Syncope, 140
    Postsyncope (recovery), 141
Pathophysiology, 141
    Presyncope, 141
    Syncope, 141
    Recovery, 142
Management, 142
    Presyncope, 142
    Syncope, 143
    Delayed recovery, 144
    Postsyncope, 144
    ADDENDUM case report—vasodepressor
      syncope, 144

7 Postural Hypotension, 147

Predisposing Factors, 148
    Drug administration and ingestion, 148
    Prolonged recumbency and
      convalescence, 149
    Inadequate postural reflex, 149
    Pregnancy, 149
    Age, 149
    Venous defects in the legs, 150
    Recovery from sympathectomy for high
      blood pressure, 150
    Addison's disease, 150
    Physical exhaustion and starvation, 150
    Chronic postural hypotension (Shy-Drager
      syndrome), 150
Prevention, 150
    Physical examination, 150
    Dental therapy considerations, 151
Clinical Manifestations, 151
Pathophysiology, 151
    Normal regulatory mechanisms, 151
    Postural hypotension, 152
Management, 153

8 Acute Adrenal Insufficiency, 155

Predisposing Factors, 156
Prevention, 158
    Dialogue history, 159
    Dental therapy considerations, 160
Clinical Manifestations, 161
Pathophysiology, 161
    Normal adrenal function, 161
    Adrenal insufficiency, 163
Management, 165
    Conscious patient, 165
    Unconscious patient, 166

9 Unconsciousness: Differential Diagnosis, 171

Age of Patient, 172
Circumstances Associated with Loss of
    Consciousness, 172
Position of the Patient, 172
Presyncopal Signs and Symptoms, 173
    No clinical symptoms, 173
    Pallor and cold, clammy skin, 173
    Tingling and numbness of the
      extremities, 173
    Headache, 173
    Chest pain, 173
    Breath odor, 174
    Tonic-clonic movements and
      incontinence, 174
    Heart rate and blood pressure, 174
    Duration of unconsciousness and
      recovery, 174

PART THREE:
RESPIRATORY DISTRESS, 177

10 Respiratory Distress: General Considerations, 179

Predisposing Factors, 180
Prevention, 180
Clinical Manifestations, 181
Pathophysiology, 181
Management, 181

11 Foreign Body Airway Obstruction, 185

Prevention, 186
    Rubber dam, 186
    Oral packing, 187
    Chair position, 187
    Dental assistant and suction, 188
    Magill intubation forceps, 188
    Tongue grasping forceps, 188
    Ligature, 188
Management, 190

Recognition of airway obstruction, 191
Basic airway maneuvers, 193
Establishing an emergency airway, 194
Invasive procedures: tracheostomy versus cricothyrotomy, 199

12   Hyperventilation, 209

Predisposing Factors, 210
Prevention, 210
Medical history questionnaire, 210
Physical evaluation, 210
Vital signs, 210
Dental therapy considerations, 210
Clinical Manifestations, 210
Signs and symptoms, 210
Effect on Vital Signs, 211
Pathophysiology, 211
Management, 212

13   Asthma, 215

Predisposing Factors, 216
Extrinsic asthma, 216
Intrinsic asthma, 216
Mixed asthma, 217
Status asthmaticus, 217
Prevention, 217
Dialogue history, 218
Dental therapy considerations, 220
Clinical Manifestations, 221
Usual clinical progression, 221
Status asthmaticus, 222
Pathophysiology, 222
Neural control of the airways, 222
Airway inflammation, 223
Immunologic responses, 223
Bronchospasm, 223
Bronchial wall edema and hypersecretion of mucous glands, 223
Breathing, 224
Management, 225
Acute asthmatic episode (bronchospasm)
Severe bronchospasm, 225

14   Heart Failure and Acute Pulmonary Edema, 233

Predisposing Factors, 235
Prevention, 235
Dialogue history, 237
Physical evaluation, 238
Dental therapy considerations, 239
Clinical Manifestations, 240
Left ventricular failure, 240
Right ventricular failure, 242
Acute pulmonary edema, 242
Pathophysiology, 243
Normal left ventricular function, 244
Heart failure, 245
Management, 246

15   Respiratory Distress: Differential Diagnosis, 251

Medical History, 252
Age, 252
Sex, 252
Related Circumstances, 252
Clinical Symptoms Between Acute Episodes, 252
Position, 252
Accompanying Sounds, 252
Symptoms Associated with Respiratory Distress, 252
Peripheral Edema and Cyanosis, 253
Paresthesia of the Extremities, 253
Use of Accessory Respiratory Muscles, 253
Chest Pain, 253
Heart Rate and Blood Pressure, 253
Duration of Respiratory Distress, 253

**PART FOUR:
ALTERED CONSCIOUSNESS, 255**

16   Altered Consciousness: General Considerations, 257

Predisposing Factors, 258
Prevention, 259
Clinical Manifestations, 259
Pathophysiology, 259
Management, 259

17   Diabetes Mellitus: Hyperglycemia and Hypoglycemia, 261

Acute Complications, 263
Chronic Complications, 263
Predisposing Factors, 264
Classification of Diabetes, 265
Type 1 diabetes mellitus, 265
Type 2 diabetes mellitus, 266
Gestational diabetes mellitus, 267
Impaired glucose tolerance/impaired fasting glucose tolerance, 267
Hyperglycemia, 268
Hypoglycemia, 268
Control of Diabetes, 268
Management of type 1 diabetes mellitus, 269
Management of type 2 diabetes mellitus, 271
Prevention, 273
Dialogue history, 274
Physical examination, 275
Dental therapy considerations, 275

Clinical Manifestations, 276
    Hyperglycemia, 276
    Hypoglycemia, 276
Pathophysiology, 277
    Insulin and blood glucose, 277
    Hyperglycemia, ketosis, and acidosis, 279
    Hypoglycemia, 279
Management, 280
    Hyperglycemia, 280
    Hypoglycemia, 281

18   Thyroid Gland Dysfunction, 287

Predisposing Factors, 288
    Hypothyroidism, 288
    Thyrotoxicosis, 289
Prevention, 289
    Dialogue history, 290
    Physical examination, 291
    Dental therapy considerations, 291
Clinical Manifestations, 292
    Hypothyroidism, 292
    Thyrotoxicosis, 293
Pathophysiology, 295
    Hypothyroidism, 295
    Thyrotoxicosis, 295
Management, 295
    Hypothyroidism, 295
    Thyrotoxicosis, 296

19   Cerebrovascular Accident, 299

Classification, 300
    Lacunar infarction, 300
    Cerebral infarction, 301
    Transient ischemic attack (TIA), 301
    Hemorrhagic stroke: intracerebral
      hemorrhage and subarachnoid
      hemorrhage, 303
Predisposing Factors, 303
Prevention, 304
    Dialogue history, 305
    Physical examination, 306
    Vital signs, 306
    Apprehension, 306
    Dental therapy considerations, 306
Clinical Manifestations, 307
    Transient ischemic attack, 308
    Cerebral infarction, 308
    Cerebral embolism, 308
    Cerebral hemorrhage, 309
Pathophysiology, 309
    Cerebrovascular ischemia and
      infarction, 309
    Hemorrhagic CVA, 310
Management, 310
    Cerebrovascular accident and transient
      ischemic attack, 311

**20   Altered Consciousness:
Differential Diagnosis, 317**

Medical History, 318
Age, 318
Sex, 318
Related Circumstances, 318
Onset of Signs and Symptoms, 318
Presence of Symptoms Between Acute
  Episodes, 318
Loss of Consciousness, 318
Signs and Symptoms, 319
    Appearance of the skin (face), 319
    Obvious anxiety, 319
    Paresthesia, 319
    Headache, 319
    "Drunken" appearance, 319
    Breath Odor, 319
Vital Signs, 319
    Respiration, 319
    Blood pressure, 319
    Heart rate, 319
Summary, 319

PART FIVE:
SEIZURES, 321

21   Seizures, 323

Types of Seizure Disorders, 324
    Partial seizures, 325
    Generalized seizures, 325
Causes, 326
Predisposing Factors, 328
Prevention, 329
    Nonepileptic causes, 329
    Epileptic causes, 329
    Dialogue history, 329
    Physical examination, 330
    Psychological implications of epilepsy, 330
    Dental therapy considerations, 331
Clinical Manifestations, 332
    Partial seizures, 332
    Absence seizure (petit mal), 332
    Tonic-clonic seizure, 333
    Tonic-clonic seizure status (grand mal
      status), 334
Pathophysiology, 334
Management, 335
    Absence seizures and partial seizures, 335
    Tonic-clonic seizures (grand mal), 336
Differential Diagnosis, 341

PART SIX:
DRUG-RELATED
EMERGENCIES, 345

22 Drug-Related Emergencies: General Considerations, 347

Prevention, 348
  Dialogue history, 349
  Care in drug administration, 350
Classification, 350
  Overdose reaction, 351
  Allergy, 351
  Idiosyncrasy, 352
Drug-Related Emergencies, 352
  Drug use in dentistry, 352

23 Drug Overdose Reactions, 359

Local Anesthetic Overdose Reaction, 360
  Predisposing factors, 360
  Prevention, 364
  Clinical manifestations, 371
  Pathophysiology, 374
  Management, 376
Epinephrine (Vasoconstrictor) Overdose
  Reaction, 381
  Precipitating factors and prevention, 381
  *Clinical manifestations and
    pathophysiology, 382*
  Management, 383
Central Nervous System Depressant
  Overdose Reactions, 385
  Predisposing factors and prevention, 385
  Clinical manifestations, 385
  Management, 387
Summary, 391

24 Allergy, 397

Predisposing Factors, 399
  Antibiotics, 399
  Analgesics, 400
  Antianxiety drugs, 400
  Local anesthetics, 401
  Other agents, 402
Prevention, 402
  Dialogue history, 403
  Medical consultation, 404
  Allergy testing in the dental office, 405
  Dental therapy modifications, 405
Management, 406
  Alleged allergy to local anesthetics, 406
  Confirmed allergy to local anesthetics, 408
Clinical Manifestations, 408
  Onset, 409
  Skin reaction, 409
  Respiratory reactions, 409
  Generalized anaphylaxis, 410
Pathophysiology, 411

  Antigens, haptens, and allergens, 412
  Antibodies (immunoglobulins), 412
  Defense mechanisms of the body, 413
  Type I allergic reaction—anaphylaxis, 414
  Respiratory signs and symptoms, 416
  Cardiovascular signs and symptoms, 416
  Gastrointestinal signs and symptoms, 416
  Urticaria, rhinitis, and conjunctivitis, 416
Management, 416
  Skin reactions, 416
  Respiratory reactions, 419
  Epinephrine and allergy, 422
  Generalized anaphylaxis, 423
  Laryngeal edema, 425

25 Drug-Related Emergencies: Differential Diagnosis, 429

Medical History, 430
Age, 430
Sex, 430
Position, 430
Onset of Signs and Symptoms, 430
Prior Exposure to Drug, 430
Dose of Drug Administered, 431
Overall Incidence of Occurrence, 431
Signs and Symptoms, 431
  Duration of reaction, 431
  Changes in appearance of skin, 431
  Appearance of nervousness, 431
  Loss of consciousness, 431
  Presence of seizures, 432
  Respiratory symptoms, 432
Vital Signs, 432
  Heart rate, 432
  Blood pressure, 432
Summary, 432

PART SEVEN:
CHEST PAIN, 435

26 Chest Pain: General Considerations, 437

Predisposing Factors, 438
  Risk factors for atherosclerotic disease, 441
Prevention, 443
Clinical Manifestations, 444
Pathophysiology, 445
  Atherosclerosis, 445
  Location, 446
  Chest pain, 446
Management, 447

27 Angina Pectoris, 451

Predisposing Factors, 452
Prevention, 453
  Dialogue history, 455

Physical examination, 457
Unstable angina pectoris, 457
Dental Therapy Considerations, 457
Length of appointment, 457
Supplemental oxygen, 457
Pain control during therapy, 458
Psychosedation, 459
Additional considerations, 460
Clinical Manifestations, 460
Signs and symptoms, 460
Physical examination, 461
Complications, 461
Prognosis, 461
Pathophysiology, 461
Management, 462
Patient with a history of angina
pectoris, 462
No history of chest pain, 464

**28   Acute Myocardial
Infarction, 467**

Predisposing Factors, 468
Location and extent of infarction, 469
Prevention, 470
Dialogue history, 471
Physical examination, 472
Dental Therapy Considerations, 472
Stress reduction, 473
Supplemental oxygen, 473
Sedation, 473
Pain control, 473
Duration of treatment, 473
Six months after MI, 473
Medical consultation, 473
Anticoagulant or antiplatelet therapy, 473
Clinical Manifestations, 474
Pain, 474
Other clinical signs and symptoms, 474
Physical findings, 475
Acute complications, 475
Pathophysiology, 475
Management, 476
Immediate in-hospital management, 481

**29   Chest Pain: Differential
Diagnosis, 487**

Noncardiac chest pain, 488
Cardiac Chest Pain, 488
Medical history, 488
Age, 489
Sex, 489
Related circumstances, 489
Clinical symptoms and signs, 489
Vital signs, 489
Summary, 490

**PART EIGHT:
CARDIAC ARREST, 491**

30   Cardiac Arrest, 493

Survival from Sudden Cardiac Arrest, 494
Witnessed versus unwitnessed, 495
Initial rhythm, 495
Bystander CPR, 496
Response time, 496
The Chain of Survival, 496
The first link: early access, 496
The second link: early BLS (CPR), 496
The third link: early defibrillation, 497
The fourth link: early ACLS, 497
The Dental Office, 497
Cardiopulmonary Arrest, 498
Pulmonary (respiratory) arrest, 498
Cardiac arrest, 498
Basic Life Support (CPR), 499
Team approach, 500
BLS, 500
Cardiac arrest in the dental office, 500
CPR sequence—adult victim, 502
Beginning and terminating BLS, 510
Transport of victim, 510

31   Pediatric Considerations, 515

Preparation, 516
Basic life support, 516
Emergency team, 517
Access to emergency medical services, 518
Emergency drugs and equipment, 518
Basic Management, 518
Position, 519
Airway and breathing, 519
Circulation, 520
Definitive care, 520
Specific Emergencies, 520
Bronchospasm (acute asthmatic
attack), 520
Generalized tonic-clonic seizure (grand
mal seizure), 520
Sedation overdose, 521
Local anesthetic overdose, 521
Respiratory arrest, 522
Cardiac arrest, 525
CPR sequence—child victim (age 1 year to
the start of puberty), 526

**Appendix:
Quick-Reference Section
to Life-Threatening Situations, 531**

Index, 545

PART 1

PREVENTION

1 Introduction

2 Prevention

3 Preparation

4 Legal Considerations

CHAPTER 1

Introduction

Life-threatening emergencies can and do occur in the practice of dentistry. They can happen to anyone—a patient, a doctor, a member of the office staff, or a person who is merely accompanying a patient. Although the occurrence of life-threatening emergencies in dental offices is infrequent, many factors can increase the likelihood of such incidents. These include (1) the increasing number of older persons seeking dental care, (2) the therapeutic advances in the medical profession, (3) the growing trend toward longer dental appointments, and (4) the increasing use and administration of drugs in dentistry.

Fortunately, other factors minimize the development of life-threatening situations. These include a pretreatment physical evaluation of each patient, consisting of a medical history questionnaire, dialogue history, and physical examination, and possible modifications in dental care to minimize medical risks. McCarthy[1] has estimated that through the effective implementation of stress-reduction procedures, all but about 10% of life-threatening situations in the dental office can be prevented. He said, "10% of all nonaccidental deaths are classified as sudden, unexpected deaths…unpreventable."

■ MORBIDITY

In spite of the most meticulous protocols designed to prevent the development of life-threatening situations, emergencies will still occur. Consider, for example, newspaper articles describing the sudden and unexpected deaths of young, well-conditioned athletes.[2,3] Such emergencies can happen in any environment. The occurrence of such a tragedy inside a dental office is not a surprising event given the stress many patients associate with dental care. In a survey of medical emergencies occurring in dental offices in Scotland, four deaths were reported in persons sustaining cardiac arrest who were listed as "bystanders," that is, persons not scheduled for dental treatment in the office in which they died.[4] This text studies emergency situations that develop in dental practice. However, dental practitioners first must understand that no medical emergency is unique to dentistry. For instance, even local anesthetic overdose is seen outside dentistry in cocaine abuse.

Table 1-1 presents the combined findings of two surveys from the United States, one completed by Fast, Martin, and Ellis[5] in 1985 and the other by Malamed[6] in 1992. A total of 4309 survey respondents from all 50 U.S. states and 7 Canadian provinces reported 30,608 emergencies over 10 years. Of the 4309 respondents, 96.6% answered positively to the following question: "In the past ten years, has a medical emergency occurred in your dental office?" (Doctors used their own definitions of emergency situations.)

About 50% of these emergencies (15,407) were listed as syncope (e.g., fainting), a usually benign occurrence. (Beware the word *benign* in any description of an emergency. When improperly managed, any emergency can turn into a catastrophe. The reader is referred to the addendum to Chapter 6 for an example of this.) On the other hand, a notable portion (25.35%) of reported emergencies were related to the cardiovascular (3381), central nervous (1663), and respiratory (2718) systems, all of which are potentially life threatening.

Table 1-2 summarizes medical emergency situations that occurred at the School of Dentistry clinics at the University of Southern California from 1973 through mid-2004. Although most situations arose while the

TABLE 1-1 Emergencies in private-practice dentistry

Emergency situation	Number reported
Syncope	15,407
Mild allergic reaction	2583
Angina pectoris	2552
Postural hypotension	2475
Seizures	1595
Asthmatic attack (bronchospasm)	1392
Hyperventilation	1326
"Epinephrine reaction"	913
Insulin shock (hypoglycemia)	890
Cardiac arrest	331
Anaphylactic reaction	304
Myocardial infarction	289
Local anesthetic overdose	204
Acute pulmonary edema (heart failure)	141
Diabetic coma	109
Cerebrovascular accident	68
Adrenal insufficiency	25
Thyroid storm	4
TOTAL	**30,608**

N = 4309 reporting dentists. Data combined from Fast TB, Martin MD, Ellis TM: Emergency preparedness: a survey of dental practitioners, *J Am Dent Assoc* 112:499–501, 1986; and Malamed SF: Managing medical emergencies, *J Am Dent Assoc* 124:40–53, 1993.

TABLE 1-2 Emergencies at the University of Southern California School of Dentistry (1973–June 2004)

Emergency situation	Number reported
TYPE	
Seizures	50
Vasodepressor syncope	50
Hyperventilation	44
Hypoglycemia	27
Postural hypotension	21
Mild allergic reaction	17
Angina pectoris	16
Acute asthmatic attack	13
Acute myocardial infarction	1
VICTIM	
Patient (during treatment)	149
Patient (before or after treatment)	53
Dental personnel	26
Other persons (bystanders, patient escort, parents, spouses)	11

patient was undergoing treatment, others developed while the patient was not in the dental chair. Some patients experienced episodes of orthostatic (postural) hypotension in the restroom, several suffered convulsive seizures in the waiting room, and one suffered a seizure just outside the clinic entrance. An adult accompanying a patient developed an allergic skin reaction after ingesting aspirin to treat a headache.[7] In two other instances, a dental student viewing pictures of acute maxillofacial injuries in a lecture hall and a dentist treating a patient suffered episodes of vasodepressor syncope. Such examples merely stress the need for dental practitioners to be prepared in case of emergencies.

Tables 1-3, 1-4, and 1-5 present the results of similar surveys carried out in Australia, New Zealand, and the United Kingdom that sought to determine the incidence of medical emergencies in dental practices.

Although any medical emergency can develop in the dental office, some are seen more frequently than others. Many such situations are stress related (e.g., pain, fear, and anxiety) or involve preexisting conditions that are exacerbated when patients are placed in stressful environments. Stress-induced situations include vasodepressor syncope and hyperventilation, whereas preexisting medical conditions that can be exacerbated by stress include most acute cardiovascular emergencies, bronchospasm (asthma), and seizures. The effective management of pain and anxiety in the dental office is therefore essential in the prevention and minimization of potentially catastrophic situations.

Drug-related adverse reactions make up another category of life-threatening situations that occur more often than dentists expect. The most frequent are associated with local anesthetics, the most commonly used drugs in dentistry. Psychogenic reactions, drug overdose, and drug allergy are just a few of the problems associated with the administration of local anesthetics. The overwhelming majority of such "drug-related" emergencies are stress related (psychogenic); however, other reactions (overdose, allergy) represent responses to the drugs themselves. Most adverse drug responses are preventable. Therefore, thorough knowledge of drug pharmacology and proper drug administration are critical in the prevention of drug-related complications.

Matsuura[8] evaluated medical emergency situations in dental offices in Japan (Tables 1-6 and 1-7). Only 1.5% of the emergency situations occurred in the waiting room. The greatest percentage of medical emergencies, 54.9%, took place during the administration of local anesthesia, which, according to both patients and doctors, is the most stressful procedure performed in the dental office. About 22% of these emergencies developed during dental treatment while 15% occurred in the dental office after completion of treatment. Most such emergencies were orthostatic (postural) hypotension or vasodepressor syncope.

TABLE 1-3 Incidence of medical emergencies in a practicing lifetime—Australian dentists*

Emergency	Number of events	Incidence in a practicing lifetime
Adverse reaction to local anesthesia (LA)	1753[†]	7.0
Grand mal seizure	381	1.52
Angina	252	1.01
Insulin shock	160	0.64, or about 1 in 2 dentists
Severe asthma	88	0.35, or about 1 in 3 dentists
All resuscitations	35	0.14, or about 1 in 7 dentists
Cardiopulmonary resuscitation	20	0.08, or about 1 in 13 dentists
Artificial ventilation[‡]	15	0.06, or about 1 in 17 dentists
Myocardial infarction	19	0.08, or about 1 in 13 dentists
Stroke	12	0.05, or about 1 in 20 dentists
Anaphylactic reaction to penicillin	4	0.016, or about 1 in 60 dentists
Anaphylactic reaction to LA	4	0.016, or about 1 in 60 dentists

*A 40-year period is used to represent a lifetime career in these calculations.
[†]Extrapolated figure based on subsample of 661 responses (82% of total).
[‡]Including expired air respiration (EAR) and use of resuscitation.
From Chapman PJ: Medical emergencies in dental practice and choice of emergency drugs and equipment: a survey of Australian dentists, *Austral Dent J* 42:103–108, 1997.

TABLE 1-4 Incidence of medical emergencies in a practicing lifetime—New Zealand dentists*

Emergency event	Number of dentists reporting episode, 1-year period (%)	Number of dentists reporting episode, 10-year period (%)	Mean number of events per reporting dentist (range)
Faints	120 (61.1)	–	2.8 (1–15)
Hyperventilation	55 (27.8)	–	2.9 (1–30)
Angina	–	29 (14.6)	1.7 (1–5)
Circulatory depression	–	22 (11.1)	1.9 (1–10)
Myocardial infarction	–	5 (2.5)	1.0
Cardiovascular accident	–	5 (2.5)	1.0
Respiratory depression	–	34 (17.2)	6.1 (1–40)
Respiratory obstruction	–	3 (1.5)	1.3 (1–2)
Severe asthma	–	15 (7.6)	2.1 (1–8)
Epilepsy (grand mal)	–	45 (22.7)	1.5 (1–3)
Status epilepticus	–	7 (3.5)	1.1 (1–2)
Allergic reaction to drug	–	60 (30.3)	2.7 (1–10)
Anaphylaxis	–	7 (3.5)	1.1 (1–2)
Hypoglycemia	–	41 (20.7)	3.1 (1–30)
Swallowed or inhaled foreign body	–	41 (20.7)	1.7 (1–5)
Anesthetic overdose	–	10 (5.1)	1.4 (1–2)
Drug interaction	–	11 (5.6)	2.0 (1–6)
Other emergencies	–	18 (9.1)	2.4 (1–10)

*199 respondents to survey.
From Broadbent JM, Thomson WM: The readiness of New Zealand general dental practitioners for medical emergencies, *N Z Dent J* 97:82–86, 2001.

A survey of 1029 dentists in England, Wales, and Scotland demonstrated that most emergencies occurred during dental treatment (36.7%); 23.1% occurred before the start of treatment, 20.1% after the administration of local anesthetic, and 16.4% after completion of the dental procedure.[4]

Approximately 3% of the events in England and Wales and 2.2% of those in Scotland affected persons who were not actually undergoing dental treatment. This group included persons who were accompanying patients, passersby, and five members of the dental staff, including a dentist and a technician.[4]

The nature of the dental care being administered at the time of each emergency is illuminating. In Matsuura's paper, more than 65% of cases developed during two types of dental care—tooth extraction (38.9%) and pulp extirpation (26.9%).[8] In the British paper, 52.2% of events occurred during conservative dental treatment and 23.5% occurred during dentoalveolar surgery.[4] All types of treatment were implicated, with 1.1% occurring during orthodontic treatment.[4] Although information regarding the specific cause of the problem is not always available, these emergencies most likely occurred when the patient experienced sudden, unexpected pain. In one instance in which the cause is known, a local anesthetic was administered to a patient reporting a sensitive tooth (a mandibular molar) and pain control was achieved (lip and tongue got "numb"). After treatment began, the patient experienced an unexpected spasm of intense pain as the drill neared the pulp chamber. In a similar situation, pain control was achieved but the patient felt intense pain as extraction of the tooth began. In both cases the sudden pain triggered the release of the endogenous catecholamines epinephrine and norepinephrine, which in turn added to the creation of an emergency. Thus, the importance of clinically adequate pain control in safe dental care cannot be overstated.

TABLE 1-5 Number of emergency events not associated with general anesthesia (GA) and their frequency*

Event	England and Wales (N = 701)		Scotland (N = 328)	
	Number	Per 40 years	Number	Per 40 years
Fits/seizures	417	2.75	282	4.05
Swallowed object	230	1.52	139	2.00
Asthma events	198	1.31	88	1.26
Diabetic events	155	1.02	72	1.03
Angina pectoris	148	0.98	89	1.28
Drug reactions	135	0.89	45	0.65
Other events	37	0.24	12	0.17
Cardiac arrest	20	0.13	17	0.24
Myocardial infarction	17	0.11	8	0.12
Stroke	14	0.09	4	0.06
Inhaled object	9	0.06	4	0.06

*Expressed per 40 years of practice, reported by the respondents in England and Wales and in Scotland who stated when they commenced working in the General Dental Service.
From Atherton GJ, McCaul JA, Williams SA: Medical emergencies in general dental practice in Great Britain. Part 1: their prevalence over a 10-year period, *Br Dent J* 186:72–79, 1999.

TABLE 1-6 Occurrence of systemic complications

Time of complication	% of total
In waiting room	1.5
During or immediately following local anesthesia	54.9
During treatment	22.0
After treatment (in office)	15.2
After leaving dental office	5.5

Data from Matsuura H: Analysis of systemic complications and deaths during treatment in Japan, *Anesth Prog* 36:219–228, 1990.

TABLE 1-7 Treatment performed at time of complication

Treatment	% of total
Tooth extraction	38.9
Pulp extirpation	26.9
Unknown	12.3
Other treatment	9.0
Preparation	7.3
Filling	2.3
Incision	1.7
Apicoectomy	0.7
Removal of fillings	0.7
Alveolar plastics	0.3

Data from Matsuura H: Analysis of systemic complications and deaths during dental treatment in Japan, *Anesth Prog* 36:219–228, 1990.

■ DEATH

Most emergency situations that occur in dental practice are defined as *potentially* life threatening. Only on rare occasions does a patient actually die in a dental office (Figure 1-1). Although accurate statistics on dental morbidity and mortality are extremely difficult to obtain, various investigators and organizations, including the Southern California Society of Oral and Maxillofacial Surgeons[9,10] and the American Dental Association,[11] have undertaken surveys of dental practices.

In a 1962 American Dental Association survey of nearly 4000 dentists, 45 deaths in dental offices were reported.[11] In addition, 7 such deaths occurred in the waiting room before the patients had been treated. In

Part II / Sunday, August 6, 2006

Patient Has Heart Attack, Dies; Dentist Also Stricken

FIGURE 1-1 A dentist and a patient both are stricken with heart attacks.

a survey of Texas dentists, Bell[12] reported 8 deaths in dental offices, 6 of which occurred in the offices of general practitioners and 2 in oral surgery practices; 1 death occurred in a waiting room before treatment. Only 2 deaths were associated with the administration of general anesthetics.

In 1989, Lytle[10] reported 8 deaths associated with the administration of general anesthesia in a 20-year period (1 death in every 673,000 general anesthetic administrations) and Robinson[13] reported 8 deaths related to the use of anesthetics. In 1985, Adelman[14] documented 3 deaths resulting from aspiration of dental appliances. In fact, any of the emergencies mentioned in the previous section potentially could double or triple these numbers. Failure to properly recognize and treat clinical signs and symptoms can turn a relatively innocuous situation into an office tragedy.

Chapman, in 1997, reporting on emergency preparedness and experiences of 811 Australian dentists, noted that 20 "CPR [cardiopulmonary resuscitation] emergencies were reported and 75% survived."[15] Five patients died. He reported 4 cases of anaphylaxis, 3 of which developed into cardiac arrest, with all patients surviving.

In the British paper, 10 deaths were reported in England and Wales and 10 in Scotland.[4] Table 1-8 summarizes these deaths. Fourteen were listed as cardiac arrest, 4 as myocardial infarction, and 2 as cerebrovascular accident.[4]

Four of the deaths listed in Scotland occurred in passersby, not patients. Taking this into account, fatalities resulted from about 0.7% of emergencies in England, Wales, and Scotland.[4]

In a New Zealand survey of 199 dentists, 2 deaths from cardiac arrest that occurred after acute myocardial infarction were reported over a 10-year study period.[16] One primary cardiac arrest was reported in a patient undergoing general anesthesia. The patient was successfully resuscitated.[16]

Adequate pretreatment physical evaluation, combined with proper use of the many techniques for pain and anxiety control, can help prevent many emergencies and deaths. It is this author's firm belief that all dental practitioners must pursue prevention vigorously. Chapter 2 of this text is devoted to this goal, as are other excellent textbooks.[17]

Unfortunately, even the most stringent precautions and preparation cannot always prevent a death from occurring. Each year in the United States, 10% of all nonaccidental deaths occur suddenly and unexpectedly in relatively young persons believed to be in good health. The cause of death most often is a fatal cardiac dysrhythmia, usually ventricular fibrillation. Preventive measures cannot entirely eliminate this from happening,

TABLE 1-8 Circumstances of deaths reported in the survey

Event (number)	Location	Stage of treatment	Procedure
ENGLAND AND WALES			
Cardiac arrest (1)	Waiting room	Before	Dentures
Cardiac arrest (1)	Surgery	During	Dentures
Cardiac arrest (1)	Waiting room	Before	Scaling
Cardiac arrest (1)	Waiting room	Before	Not stated
Stroke (1)	Waiting room	Before	None
Stroke (1)	Surgery	During	Scaling
Myocardial infarct (2)	Waiting room	Before	Not stated
Myocardial infarct (1)	Outside surgery	Before	None
SCOTLAND			
Cardiac arrest (1)	Waiting room	Before	Impression
Cardiac arrest (1)	Waiting room	Before	None
Cardiac arrest (3)	Waiting room	Before	Not stated
Myocardial infarct (1)	Waiting room	After	Not stated
Cardiac arrest (4)	Passer-by		

From Atherton GJ, McCaul JA, Williams SA: Medical emergencies in general dental practice in Great Britain. Part 1: their prevalence over a 10-year period, *Br Dent J* 186:72–79, 1999.

so the dental profession must be prepared. Successful outcomes are possible when the dental "team" acts quickly to recognize and to manage the situation. The survival rate in cases of "CPR emergencies" in Australia was 75%; an additional 3 patients with cardiac arrest secondary to anaphylaxis survived.[15]

However, not all such deaths occur within the confines of the dental office. The stress associated with dental treatment can potentially trigger events that result in a patient's demise days after their treatment. In the Southern California Society of Oral and Maxillofacial Surgeons survey, 10 such incidents were reported.[9] Of particular interest are 3 deaths secondary to myocardial infarction and 1 secondary to cerebrovascular accident. Another death reportedly was related to an allergic reaction to propoxyphene hydrochloride, which the dentist had prescribed for postoperative pain relief. In Matsuura's study in Japan, 5.5% of all medical emergencies developed "after [the patient had left] the dental office."[8]

■ RISK FACTORS
Increased number of older patients

The life expectancy of persons born in the United States is increasing steadily. In 1900 the life expectancy for a white man was 40 years; for a white woman, 49 years. In 2002, these figures were 75.1 for white men, 80.3 for white women, 68.6 for black men, and 75.6 for black

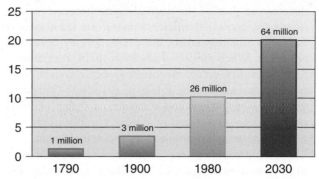

FIGURE 1-2 The most rapidly growing segment of the U.S. population is the group 65 and older because of the large number of aging post–World War II baby boomers.

women (Table 1-9).[18] Aging post–World War II baby boomers have turned the most rapidly growing segment of the U.S. population into those 65 and older (Figure 1-2), and these increasing numbers of older Americans are seeking dental care. The National Vital Statistics Reports in 2004 stated that between 1950 and 2000 the percentage of Americans over the age of 75 years doubled from 3% to 6%. It is projected that this percentage will increase to 12% by 2050.[19]

Although many older patients appear to be in good health, the dental practitioner must always be on the lookout for significant subclinical disease. All major organ systems (cardiovascular, hepatic, renal, pulmonary, endocrine, and central nervous) must be evaluated in older patients, with the cardiovascular system of particular importance. Cardiovascular function and efficiency

TABLE 1-9 Life expectancy in the United States

Year	Total	White men	White women	African-American men	African-American women
2002	77.3	75.1	80.3	68.8	76.0
2000	77.0	74.9	80.1	68.3	75.2
1996	76.1	73.8	79.6	66.1	74.2
1981	74.2	71.1	78.5	64.4	73.0
1975	72.5	68.7	76.5	N/A	N/A
1970	70.8	67.1	74.6	60.0	68.3
1960	69.7	66.6	73.1	N/A	N/A
1950	68.2	66.6	71.1	N/A	N/A
1940	62.9	60.8	65.2	N/A	N/A
1930	59.7	58.1	61.6	N/A	N/A
1920	54,1	53.6	54.6	N/A	N/A
1910	47.3	46.3	48.2	N/A	N/A
1900	n/a	40.0	49.0	N/A	N/A

Data from *National Vital Statistics Reports* 53:33, November 10, 2004.

decrease as part of the normal aging process. In some instances, decreased efficiency manifests itself as heart failure or angina pectoris, but overt signs are not always apparent. When subjected to stress (pain, fear, anxiety, heat, humidity, cold), the cardiovascular system of the older person may not be able to meet the body's demands for increased oxygen and nutrients, a deficit of which may lead to acute cardiovascular complications such as life-threatening dysrhythmias and anginal pain.

Cardiovascular disease is *the* leading cause of death in persons over 65 years in the United States today (Box 1-1).[20] Situations that might have proved innocuous to a person at a younger age may well prove to be harmful 20 years later. This relative inability of older persons to tolerate undue stress was demonstrated in a survey of the effects of age in fatally injured automobile drivers. Baker and Spitz[21] found the proportion of drivers age 60 years or older to be five times as high among those killed as among drivers who survived multivehicle crashes.

Many drivers 60 years and over died after crashes that did not prove fatal to younger drivers. The correlation of age and length of survival suggests that whereas younger drivers recover from injuries, many older drivers die of complications. The aging process involves both physiologic and pathologic changes that may alter the patient's ability to successfully adapt to stress.

Box 1-2 lists changes that older patients frequently encounter. Decrease in tissue elasticity is a major physiologic change that has a significant effect on all the body's organs. For example, in a 75-year-old individual, cerebral blood flow is 80% of what it was at age 30, cardiac output has declined to 65%, and renal blood flow has decreased to 45%. The changes in renal blood flow might affect the actions of certain drugs, primarily those that rely principally on urinary excretion to remove the drug and its metabolites from the body. Penicillin, tetracycline, and digoxin, for example, greatly exhibit increased beta half-lives in older patients.

Decreased tissue elasticity also affects the lungs. Pulmonary compliance decreases with age and can progress to senile emphysema. Long-term exposure to

---

Box 1-1 Top five causes of death by age group in 2003

1–4 YEARS	5–14 YEARS
1. Accidents (unintentional injuries)	1. Accidents (unintentional injuries)
2. Congenital malformations	2. Malignant neoplasms
3. Malignant neoplasms	3. Congenital malformations
4. Assault (homicide)	4. Assault (homicide)
5. Diseases of the heart	5. Intentional self-harm (suicide)

15–24 YEARS	25–44 YEARS
1. Accidents (unintentional injuries)	1. Accidents (unintentional injuries)
2. Assault (homicide)	2. Malignant neoplasms
3. Intentional self-harm (suicide)	3. Diseases of the heart
4. Malignant neoplasms	4. Intentional self-harm (suicide)
5. Diseases of the heart	5. Assault (homicide)

45–64 YEARS	65 YEARS AND OLDER
1. Malignant neoplasms	1. Diseases of the heart
2. Diseases of the heart	2. Malignant neoplasms
3. Accidents (unintentional injuries)	3. Cerebrovascular diseases
4. Diabetes mellitus	4. Chronic lower respiratory diseases
5. Cerebrovascular diseases	5. Alzheimer's disease

Data from Deaths and death rates for the 10 leading causes of death in specific age groups: United States, preliminary 2003; in *National Vital Statistics Reports*, 53:29, February 28, 2005.

Box 1-2 Changes in geriatric patients

CENTRAL NERVOUS SYSTEM
Decreased number of brain cells
Cerebral arteriosclerosis
     Cerebrovascular accident
     Decreased memory
     Emotional changes
Parkinsonism

CARDIOVASCULAR SYSTEM
Coronary artery disease
     Angina pectoris
     Myocardial infarction
     Dysrhythmias
     Decreased contractility
High blood pressure
     Renovascular disease
     Cerebrovascular disease
     Cardiac disease

RESPIRATORY SYSTEM
Senile emphysema
Arthritic changes in thorax
Pulmonary problems related to pollutants
Interstitial fibrosis

GENITOURINARY SYSTEM
Decreased renal blood flow
Decreased number of functioning glomeruli
Decreased tubular reabsorption
Benign prostatic hypertrophy

ENDOCRINE SYSTEM
Decreased response to stress
Type 2 (adult-onset) diabetes mellitus

Modified from Lichtiger M, Moya F: *Curr Rev Nurse Anesth* 1:1, 1978.

TABLE 1-10 Pulmonary changes in patients 65 years and older

Function	Percentage compared with capacity at age 30
Total lung capacity	100
Vital capacity	58
O_2 uptake during exercise	50
Maximum breathing capacity	55

Data from Lichtiger M, Moya F: *Curr Rev Nurse Anesth* 1:1, 1978.

smoke, dust, and pollutants can decrease respiratory function in older patients, producing disorders such as asthma and chronic bronchitis. Pulmonary function in the older patient is considerably diminished compared with that of the younger patient (Table 1-10).[22]

However, within the last two decades, dental practitioners have begun treating more patients older than 60 years who retain most of their natural dentition. These patients require the full range of dental care—periodontics, endodontics, crowns, bridges, restorative work, implants, and oral surgery. Because of their ages and the possibility of preexisting physical disabilities, many of these patients are less able to handle the stress normally associated with dental treatment. This reduced stress tolerance should forewarn the dental practitioner that older patients are at greater risk during dental treatment, even in the absence of clinically evident disease (Box 1-3). In addition, the dental practitioner must take every step to minimize this risk (see stress reduction protocols[4] in Chapter 2).

Medical advances

With age, the incidence of disease rises. Diabetic patients and patients with cardiovascular diseases (heart failure, arteriosclerosis) face significantly longer life expectancies today than they did 25 or 35 years ago. Many patients

who were confined to their homes or who needed to rely on wheelchairs and were unable to work and unlikely to seek dental care now live fairly normal lives because of drug therapy and surgical technique advances. Radiation and chemotherapy enable many patients with cancer to live longer. Surgical procedures, such as coronary artery bypass and graft surgery and heart valve replacement, have become commonplace, permitting previously incapacitated patients to pursue active lifestyles. Single- and multiple-organ transplants have higher success rates and are performed with greater frequency than in past years. Newer and more effective drug therapies are available for the management of chronic disorders such as high blood pressure, diabetes, and human immunodeficiency virus infection.

These medical advances are truly significant. They also mean that dental practitioners must manage the oral-health needs of potentially at-risk patients, many of whom have chronic disorders that are merely being controlled or managed, not cured. McCarthy termed these persons "the walking wounded, accidents looking for a place to happen."[1]

Longer appointments

In recent years many doctors have increased the length of their typical dental appointment. Although appointments of less than 60 minutes are still commonplace, many doctors now schedule 1- to 3-hour treatment sessions.[23] Dental care can be stressful for the patient, for the doctor, and for staff members, and longer appointments naturally create more stress. Medically compromised patients are more likely to react adversely under these conditions than are healthy individuals, but even healthy patients can suffer from stress, which can create unforeseen complications. Stress reduction has become an important concept in the prevention of medical emergencies.

Increased drug use

Drugs play an integral role in contemporary dental practice. Drugs for preventing pain, managing fear, and treating infection are important components of every doctor's armamentarium. However, all drugs exert multiple actions; no drug is absolutely free of risk. Knowledge of the pharmacologic actions of a drug and of proper technique of drug delivery will go far to decrease the occurrence of drug-related emergencies.

In addition, many dental practitioners must work with patients who ingest drugs not prescribed by a doctor. Halpern[24] found that 18% of his patients were taking some form of medication. This incidence rose with age; 41% of patients over 60 years were taking

---

Box 1-3 Factors increasing risk during dental treatment

Increased number of older patients
Medical advances
Drug therapy
Increased number of surgical procedures (e.g., implants)
Longer appointments
Increased drug use
    Local anesthetics
    Sedatives
    Analgesics
    Antibiotics

Modified from Lichtiger M, Moya F: *Curr Rev Nurse Anesth* 1:1, 1978.

one or more medications regularly. Dental practitioners must take special care to anticipate and recognize complications related to either the pharmacologic actions of a drug or the complex interactions between commonly used dental drugs and other medications. For example, orthostatic hypotension is associated with many drugs used in the management of high blood pressure.

Other examples include the potentially fatal interactions between the monoamine-oxidase inhibitors and opioids (e.g., meperidine and fentanyl) or between epinephrine and noncardiospecific β-adrenergic blockers. This text aims, in part, to increase the dental practitioner's awareness of possible high-risk patients so that appropriate modifications may be incorporated into the planned treatment. A second aim is to increase prompt recognition and effective management of such situations, which will continue to occur in spite of the most stringent prevention efforts.

Goldberger[25] wrote, "When you prepare for an emergency, the emergency ceases to exist." The ultimate aim in the management of any emergency is the preservation of life. This primary goal is the thread that holds together each section in this text.

■ CLASSIFICATION OF LIFE-THREATENING SITUATIONS

Several methods are available for the classification of medical emergencies. The traditional approach has been the *systems-oriented classification*, which lists major organ systems and discusses life-threatening situations associated with those systems (Box 1-4).

Although a systems approach is often considered suitable for educational purposes, from a clinical perspective it is lacking. A second classification method divides emergency situations into two broad categories— *cardiovascular and noncardiovascular emergencies*, which both can be broken down further into stress-related and non–stress-related emergencies. This system offers a very general breakdown of life-threatening emergencies that is particularly useful to doctors.* Combining the systems provides two divisions from which to work—cardiovascular versus noncardiovascular and stress-related versus non–stress-related emergencies (Table 1-11).

This classification can assist the doctor in the preparation of a workable treatment protocol for the prevention of such a situation. The risk of developing a stress-related emergency may be reduced through the

---

*The term doctor is applied generically throughout the rest of this text. The term describes the individual charged with the direction and management of emergency situations, often the dentist for the purposes of this text.

Box 1-4 Systems-oriented classification

INFECTIOUS DISEASES
Immune system
  Allergies
  Angioneurotic edema
  Contact dermatitis
  Anaphylaxis

SKIN AND APPENDAGES
EYES
EARS, NOSE, AND THROAT
RESPIRATORY TRACT
Asthma
Hyperventilation

CARDIOVASCULAR SYSTEM
Arteriosclerotic heart disease
Angina pectoris
Myocardial infarction
Heart failure

BLOOD
GASTROINTESTINAL TRACT AND LIVER
OBSTETRICS AND GYNECOLOGY
NERVOUS SYSTEM
Unconsciousness
  Vasodepressor syncope
  Orthostatic hypotension
Convulsive disorders
  Epilepsy
Drug overdose reactions
Cerebrovascular accident
  Endocrine disorders
Diabetes mellitus
  Hyperglycemia
  Hypoglycemia
Thyroid gland
  Hyperthyroidism
  Hypothyroidism
Adrenal gland
  Acute adrenal insufficiency

---

incorporation in dental care of several stress-reducing modifications. Such factors include the use of psychosedative techniques, effective pain control, and limitations on the length of dental treatments. The stress reduction protocol is described in Chapter 2.

Although the cardiovascular emergency system is effective in emergency prevention, doctors need a method that can help them to more easily recognize and manage such situations. Therefore we must abandon classifications based on organ systems. In most real-life clinical situations, doctors are frequently unaware of their patients' underlying pathologic conditions. The doctor needs to recognize and initiate management of potentially life-threatening situations using only the most obvious clinical *signs* and *symptoms* as guides. For

TABLE 1-11 Cardiac-oriented classification

		Noncardiovascular	Cardiovascular
Stress-related		Vasodepressor syncope	Angina pectoris
		Hyperventilation	Acute myocardial infarction
		Seizure	Acute heart failure (pulmonary edema)
		Acute adrenal insufficiency	Cerebral ischemia and infarction
		Thyroid storm	Sudden cardiac arrest
		Asthma (bronchospasm)	
		Orthostatic (postural) hypotension	Acute myocardial infarction
		Overdose (toxic) reaction	Sudden cardiac arrest
Non–stress-related		Hypoglycemia	
		Hyperglycemia	
		Allergy	

this reason a classification of medical emergencies based on *clinical signs and symptoms* has proved useful since the first publication of this book in 1978.

Of necessity, the doctor will base the initial management of most emergency situations on these clinical clues until a more definitive diagnosis is obtained. Commonly seen signs and symptoms include alterations of consciousness (unconsciousness, impaired, or altered consciousness), respiratory distress, seizures, drug-related emergencies, and chest pain. In each situation a successful outcome will depend on the doctor's adherence to a defined treatment protocol. Once these steps have been employed successfully, additional (secondary) steps can direct the doctor toward a more definitive diagnosis, which can help correct the problem.

This text is set up through use of defined protocols and steps of management. Each major section is devoted to a common symptom complex. Each section contains a list of the more common manifestations of that symptom complex. Basic management procedures for the problem are discussed and are followed by a detailed review of that category's more common emergencies. Each section closes with a differential diagnosis (Box 1-5).

These classifications are designed to place each life-threatening situation in the category that most closely represents the usual clinical manifestation of the problem. Several situations could also be included in a classification other than the one in which they have been placed. For example, acute myocardial infarction and cerebrovascular accident are possible causes of unconsciousness, but full discussions of these emergencies are found in their more commonly encountered clinical manifestations—chest pain for myocardial infarction and altered consciousness for cerebrovascular accident.

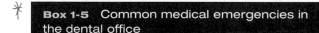

Box 1-5 Common medical emergencies in the dental office

UNCONSCIOUSNESS
Vasodepressor syncope
Orthostatic hypotension
Acute adrenal insufficiency

RESPIRATORY DISTRESS
Airway obstruction
Hyperventilation
Asthma (bronchospasm)
Heart failure and acute pulmonary edema

ALTERED CONSCIOUSNESS
Diabetes mellitus: hyperglycemia and hypoglycemia
Thyroid gland dysfunction (hyperthyroidism and hypothyroidism)
Cerebrovascular accident

SEIZURES

DRUG-RELATED EMERGENCIES
Drug overdose reactions
Allergy

CHEST PAIN
Angina pectoris
Acute myocardial infarction

SUDDEN CARDIAC ARREST

■ OUTLINE OF SPECIFIC EMERGENCY SITUATIONS

In the discussion of each emergency situation, various factors will be presented. Included are the following headings and the aim of each:

1. General considerations: An introductory section presents general information about the situation.

Definitions and synonyms are included when relevant.

2. Predisposing factors: Discussions focus on the incidence and cause of the disorder and those factors that can predispose a patient to experience a life-threatening situation.

3. Prevention: This section builds on previous sections to minimize the occurrence of an acute exacerbation of the disorder. The medical history questionnaire, vital signs, and dialogue history are used to determine a risk category for each patient based on the system developed by the American Society of Anesthesiologists.[26] Suggestions for specific dental treatment modifications complete the discussion.

4. Clinical manifestations: This section focuses on the clinically evident signs and symptoms that foster recognition of the disorder.

5. Pathophysiology: Discussion centers on the pathologic process underlying clinical signs and symptoms. A fuller understanding of the problem's cause can better enable the doctor to manage the situation.

6. Management: The step-by-step management of clinical signs and symptoms is this section's aim.

7. Differential diagnosis: Each section then closes with a chapter devoted to helping the doctor identify the probable cause of that patient's emergency.

REFERENCES

1. McCarthy EM: Sudden, unexpected death in the dental office, *J Am Dent Assoc* 83:1091–1092, 1971.
2. Drooz A: Gathers collapses, then dies, *Los Angeles Times,* March 5, 1990, C-1.
3. Schoolgirl dies during basketball drill, *New York Times,* November 20, 1988.
4. Atherton GJ, McCaul JA, Williams SA: Medical emergencies in general dental practice in Great Britain. Part 1: their prevalence over a 10-year period, *Br Dent J* 186:72–79, 1999.
5. Fast TB, Martin MD, Ellis TM: Emergency preparedness: a survey of dental practitioners, *J Am Dent Assoc* 112:499–501, 1986.
6. Malamed SF: Managing medical emergencies, *J Am Dent Assoc* 124:40–53, 1993.
7. Berkes EA: Anaphylactic and anaphylactoid reactions to aspirin and other NSAIDs, *Clin Rev Allergy Immunol* 24:137–148, 2003.
8. Matsuura H: Analysis of systemic complications and deaths during dental treatment in Japan, *Anesth Prog* 36:219–228, 1990.
9. Lytle JJ: Anesthesia morbidity and mortality survey of the Southern California Society of Oral Surgeons, *J Oral Surg* 32:739–744, 1974.
10. Lytle JJ, Stamper EP: The 1988 anesthesia survey of the Southern California Society of Oral and Maxillofacial Surgeons, *Oral Surg* 47:834–842, 1989.
11. Moen BD, Ogawa GY: The 1962 survey of dental practice, Chicago, American Dental Association, 1963.
12. Bell WH: Emergencies in and out of the dental office: a pilot study of the State of Texas, *J Am Dent Assoc* 74:778–783, 1967.
13. Robinson EM: Death in the dental chair, *J Forensic Sci* 34:377–380, 1989.
14. Adelman GC: Asphyxial deaths as a result of aspiration of dental appliances: a report of three deaths, *J Forensic Sci* 23:389–395, 1985.
15. Chapman PJ: Medical emergencies in dental practice and choice of emergency drugs and equipment: a survey of Australian dentists, *Austral Dent J* 42:103–108, 1997.
16. Broadbent JM, Thomson WM: The readiness of New Zealand general dental practitioners for medical emergencies, *N Z Dent J* 97:82–86, 2001.
17. Little JW, Falace DA, Miller C, Rhodus NL: *Dental management of the medically compromised patient,* ed 6, St. Louis, Mosby, 2002.
18. *National Vital Statistics Reports* 53:33, November 10, 2004.
19. *National Vital Statistics Reports* 53:41, November 10, 2004.
20. Deaths and death rates for the 10 leading causes of death in specified age groups: United States, preliminary 2003, *National Vital Statistics Reports* 53:29, February 28, 2005.
21. Baker SP, Spitz WU: Age effects and autopsy evidence of disease in fatally injured drivers, *JAMA* 214:1079–1088, 1970.
22. Lichtiger M, Moya F: *Curr Rev Nurse Anesth* 1:1, 1978.
23. American Dental Association: 2002 Survey of Dental Practice—Characteristics of Dentists in Private Practice and their Parents. American Dental Association, Chicago, 2004.
24. Halpern IL: Patient's medical status: a factor in dental treatment, *Oral Surg* 39:216–226, 1975.
25. Goldberger E: *Treatment of cardiac emergencies,* ed 5, St. Louis, Mosby, 1990.
26. American Society of Anesthesiologists: New classification of physical status. *Anesthesiology* 24:111, 1963.

CHAPTER 2

Prevention

McCarthy has stated that use of a complete system of physical evaluation for all prospective dental patients would be capable of preventing approximately 90% of life-threatening situations.[1] The remaining 10% will occur in spite of all preventive efforts. Goldberger[2] wrote, "When you prepare for an emergency, the emergency ceases to exist." This is accurate to the extent that adequate preparation for an emergency diminishes the danger or possibility of its resulting in significant morbidity or death. Prior knowledge of a patient's physical condition enables the doctor to incorporate modifications into the dental treatment plan. In other words, "To be forewarned is to be forearmed."

This chapter provides a detailed discussion of the most important components of physical evaluation, which, when used properly, can lead to a significant reduction in the occurrence of acute medical emergencies. (This chapter will be referred to frequently throughout the rest of the text.)

■ EVALUATION GOALS

This section describes a comprehensive but easily employed physical evaluation system. The steps described enable the doctor to accurately assess potential risk (the risk that a potentially life-threatening situation [e.g., medical emergency] might develop during treatment of this patient) before the start of dental treatment. Box 2-1 and the following list present the goals each doctor should pursue:

1. Determine the patient's ability to physically tolerate the stress involved in the planned treatment.
2. Determine the patient's ability to psychologically tolerate the stress involved in the planned treatment.
3. Determine whether treatment modifications are required to enable the patient to better tolerate the stress involved in the planned treatment.
4. Determine whether the use of psychosedation is warranted:
   a. Determine which sedation technique is most appropriate.
   b. Determine whether contraindications exist to any drugs to be used in the planned treatment.

The first two goals involve the patient's ability to tolerate the stress involved in dental treatment. That stress may be either physiologic or psychologic. Many if not most patients with preexisting medical conditions are less able to tolerate the usual levels of stress associated with dental treatment. These patients are more likely to undergo acute exacerbations of their preexisting medical conditions when exposed to such stress. Examples of such preexisting conditions include angina pectoris, epilepsy, asthma, and sickle cell disease. Although most patients are able to tolerate dental treatment, the doctor must determine before treatment begins (1) the potential problem, (2) the level of severity of the problem, and (3) the potential effect on the planned dental treatment.

Excessive stress may also be detrimental to a person who is not medically compromised.[3] Fear, anxiety, and pain—especially sudden, unexpected pain—can lead to acute changes in the body's homeostasis. Many dental patients experience fear-related (psychogenic) emergencies, including hyperventilation and vasodepressor syncope (fainting).

The third goal in physical evaluation is to determine whether the planned dental treatment requires modification to better enable the patient to tolerate the stress. In some instances a healthy patient physically can handle the treatment but is unable psychologically to tolerate it.

The medically compromised patient also benefits from treatment modifications aimed at minimizing stress. Doctors must always remember that medically compromised patients often fear dental treatment, which can increase the risk of a medical emergency when combined with their reduced tolerance for stress. Stress-reduction protocols, which are discussed later in this chapter, aid the doctor in minimizing treatment-related stress. When the patient requires assistance in coping with dental treatment, the doctor may consider psychosedation. Determining the need for these techniques, selecting the most appropriate technique, and choosing the most appropriate drug or drugs for the patient are part of the final goal of the physical evaluation.

■ PHYSICAL EVALUATION

The term *physical evaluation* describes the steps involved in the fulfillment of the aforementioned goals. Physical evaluation in dentistry consists of the medical history questionnaire, physical examination, and dialogue history. Armed with this information, the doctor can better (1) determine the physical and psychologic status of the patient, which enables the doctor to assign that patient a risk factor classification; (2) seek medical consultation; and (3) institute appropriate treatment modifications.

Medical history questionnaire

The use of a written, patient-completed medical history questionnaire is a moral and legal necessity in the health care professions. In addition, a medical history questionnaire provides the doctor with valuable information about the physical and psychological condition of the patient.

Many versions of medical history questionnaires are available. However, there are two basic types: the short-form medical history and the long-form medical history. The short form, usually one page, provides basic information about a patient's medical history and ideally is suited for a doctor who has considerable clinical

---

Box 2-1   Goals of physical evaluation

1. Determine the patient's ability to **physically** tolerate the stress involved in the planned treatment.
2. Determine the patient's ability to **psychologically** tolerate the stress involved in the planned treatment.
3. Determine whether **treatment modifications** are required to enable the patient to better tolerate the stress involved in the planned treatment.
4. Determine whether the use of **psychosedation** is warranted.
   a. Determine which sedation technique is most appropriate.
   b. Determine whether contraindications exist to any of the drugs to be used in the planned treatment.

experience in physical evaluation. To use the short form effectively, the doctor must have a firm grasp of the appropriate dialogue history required to aid in the determination of risk. The doctor also must be experienced in the use and interpretation of physical evaluation techniques. Unfortunately, many doctors employ a short form or a modification primarily as a convenience for their patients. The long form, usually two or more pages, provides a more detailed summary of the patient's past and present physical condition. It is used most often in teaching capacities, for which it is ideal.

Any medical history questionnaire can prove to be extremely valuable or entirely worthless. The ultimate value of the questionnaire resides in the ability of the doctor to interpret the significance of the answers and to elicit additional information through physical examination and dialogue history.

In this edition of *Emergency Medicine* I have included as the prototypical adult health history questionnaire one developed by the University of the Pacific School of Dentistry in conjunction with MetLife (Figure 2-1). Figure 2-2 is an example of a pediatric medical history questionnaire.

This health history has been translated into 36 different languages, comprising the languages spoken by 95% of the people on this planet. The cost of the translation was supported by several organizations, including the California Dental Association, but most extensively by MetLife Dental. The health history (see Figure 2-1), translations of the health history (Figure 2-3), interview sheet (Figure 2-4), medical consultation form (Figure 2-5), and protocols for the dental management of medically complex patients may be found on the University of the Pacific's website, www.dental.pacific. edu, under *Dental Professionals* and then under *Health History Forms*. Protocols for management of medically complex patients can be found at the same website under *Pacific Dental Management Protocols*. Translations of the medical history form can also be found at www.metdental.com under *Resource Center* and then under *Multi-Language Medical Health History Forms Available*.

The health history has been translated, keeping the same question numbering sequence. Thus, a dentist who speaks English and is caring for a patient who doesn't can ask the patient to complete the health history in his or her own language. The dentist then compares the English health history to the patient's translated health history, scanning the translated version for "yes" responses. When a "yes" is found, the dentist can look at the question number and match it to the question number on the English version. For example, the dentist would know that a "yes" response to question 34 on the non-English version is the same as question 34,

concerning high blood pressure, on the English version. Similarly, a Chinese-speaking doctor could also use the multilanguage health history with an English-speaking patient and have the same cross-referenced information. A dentist who speaks Spanish could use the multilanguage health history with a patient who speaks French. With the uniform health history question sequence, these health history translations can serve patients and doctors all around the world.

The health history is divided into sections related to signs and symptoms ("Have you experienced?"), diagnosed diseases ("Do you have or have you had?"), medical treatments (including drugs and other physiologically active compounds), and several other questions.

Although both long- and short-form medical history questionnaires are valuable in determining a patient's physical condition, a criticism of most available health history questionnaires is the absence of questions on the patient's attitudes toward dentistry. It is recommended therefore that one or more questions be included that relate to this all-important subject: (1) Do you feel very nervous about having dentistry treatment? (2) Have you ever had a bad experience in the dental office?

Following is the University of the Pacific's medical history questionnaire, with a discussion of the significance of each:

✎ MEDICAL HISTORY QUESTIONNAIRE

1. Is your general health good?
Comment: A general survey question seeking the patient's general impression of their health. Studies have demonstrated that a "yes" response to this question does not necessarily correlate with the patient's actual state of health.[4]

2. Has there been a change in your health within the last year?

3. Have you been hospitalized or had a serious illness in the last three years? If YES, why?

4. Are you being treated by a physician now? For what? Date of last medical exam? Date of last dental exam?
Comment: Questions 2, 3, and 4 seek information regarding recent changes in the patient's physical condition. In all instances of a positive response, an in-depth dialogue history must ensue to determine the precise nature of the change in health status, type of surgical procedure or illness, and the names of any medications the patient may now be taking to help manage the problem.

5. Have you had problems with prior dental treatment?
Comment: I have found that many adults are reluctant to verbally admit to the doctor, hygienist, or assistant their fears about treatment for fear of being labeled a "baby." This is especially true of young men in their late teens or early 20s; they attempt to "take it like a man" or "grin and bear it" rather than admit their fears. All too often, such macho behavior results in an

MetLife	HEALTH HISTORY	University of the Pacific
	English	

Patient Name:_____   Patient Identification Number:_____

Birth Date:_____

I. CIRCLE APPROPRIATE ANSWER (leave blank if you do not understand question):

1. Yes No Is your general health good?
2. Yes No Has there been a change in your health within the last year?
3. Yes No Have you been hospitalized or had a serious illness in the last three years?
   If YES, why?_____
4. Yes No Are you being treated by a physician now? For what?   _____
   Date of last medical exam?_____Date of last dental exam _____
5. Yes No Have you had problems with prior dental treatment?
6. Yes No Are you in pain now?

II. HAVE YOU EXPERIENCED:

7.	Yes	No	Chest pain (angina)?	18.	Yes	No	Dizziness?
8.	Yes	No	Swollen ankles?	19.	Yes	No	Ringing in ears?
9.	Yes	No	Shortness of breath?	20.	Yes	No	Headaches?
10.	Yes	No	Recent weight loss, fever, night sweats?	21.	Yes	No	Fainting spells?
11.	Yes	No	Persistent cough, coughing up blood?	22.	Yes	No	Blurred vision?
12.	Yes	No	Bleeding problems, bruising easily?	23.	Yes	No	Seizures?
13.	Yes	No	Sinus problems?	24.	Yes	No	Excessive thirst?
14.	Yes	No	Difficulty swallowing?	25.	Yes	No	Frequent urination?
15.	Yes	No	Diarrhea, constipation, blood in stools?	26.	Yes	No	Dry mouth?
16.	Yes	No	Frequent vomiting, nausea?	27.	Yes	No	Jaundice?
17.	Yes	No	Difficulty urinating, blood in urine?	28.	Yes	No	Joint pain, stiffness?

III. DO YOU HAVE OR HAVE YOU HAD:

29.	Yes	No	Heart disease?	40.	Yes	No	AIDS
30.	Yes	No	Heart attack, heart defects?	41.	Yes	No	Tumors, cancer?
31.	Yes	No	Heart murmurs?	42.	Yes	No	Arthritis, rheumatism?
32.	Yes	No	Rheumatic fever?	43.	Yes	No	Eye diseases?
33.	Yes	No	Stroke, hardening of arteries?	44.	Yes	No	Skin diseases?
34.	Yes	No	High blood pressure?	45.	Yes	No	Anemia?
35.	Yes	No	Asthma, TB, emphysema, other lung diseases?	46.	Yes	No	VD (syphilis or gonorrhea)?
36.	Yes	No	Hepatitis, other liver disease?	47.	Yes	No	Herpes?
37.	Yes	No	Stomach problems, ulcers?	48.	Yes	No	Kidney, bladder disease?
38.	Yes	No	Allergies to: drugs, foods, medications, latex?	49.	Yes	No	Thyroid, adrenal disease?
39.	Yes	No	Family history of diabetes, heart problems, tumors?	50.	Yes	No	Diabetes?

IV. DO YOU HAVE OR HAVE YOU HAD:

51.	Yes	No	Psychiatric care?	56.	Yes	No	Hospitalization?
52.	Yes	No	Radiation treatments?	57.	Yes	No	Blood transfusions?
53.	Yes	No	Chemotherapy?	58.	Yes	No	Surgeries?
54.	Yes	No	Prosthetic heart valve?	59.	Yes	No	Pacemaker?
55.	Yes	No	Artificial joint?	60.	Yes	No	Contact lenses?

V. ARE YOU TAKING:

61.	Yes	No	Recreational drugs?	63.	Yes	No	Tobacco in any form?
62.	Yes	No	Drugs, medications, over-the-counter medicines (including aspirin), natural remedies?	64.	Yes	No	Alcohol?

Please list:_____

_____

VI. WOMEN ONLY:

65.	Yes	No	Are you or could you be pregnant or nursing?	66.	Yes	No	Taking birth control pills?

VII. ALL PATIENTS:

67. Yes No Do you have or have you had any other diseases or medical problems NOT listed on this form?

If so, please explain:_____

To the best of my knowledge, I have answered every question completely and accurately. I will inform my dentist of any change in my health and/or medication.

Patient's signature:_____Date:_____

RECALL REVIEW:

1. Patient's signature_____Date:_____

2. Patient's signature_____Date:_____

3. Patient's signature_____Date:_____

The Health History is created and maintained by the University of the Pacific School of Dentistry, San Francisco, California.
Support for the translation and dissemination of the Health Histories comes from MetLife Dental Care.

FIGURE 2-1 University of the Pacific adult health history questionnaire. (Reprinted with permission from University of the Pacific Dental School, San Francisco, California.)

Child's Name: _____ Date of Birth: _____ Age _____ Date: _____

Address: _____ Telephone: ( )

Physician's name (Medical Doctor): _____ Telephone: ( )

Please circle the appropriate answer

1. Does your child have a health problem? .... YES NO
2. Was your child a patient in a hospital? .... YES NO
3. Date of last physical exam: _____
4. Is your child now under medical care? .... YES NO
5. Is your child taking medication now? .... YES NO
   If so, for what? _____
6. Has your child ever had a serious illness or operation? YES NO
7. If so, explain: _____
8. Does your child have (or ever had) any of the following diseases?
   a. Rheumatic fever or rheumatic heart disease ... YES NO
   b. Congenital heart disease .... YES NO
   c. Cardiovascular disease (heart trouble, heart attack, coronary insufficiency, coronary occlusion, high blood pressure, arteriosclerosis, stroke) .... YES NO
   d. Allergy? Food □, Medicine □, Other □ .. YES NO
   e. Asthma □ Hay Fever □ .... YES NO
   f. Hives or a skin rash .... YES NO
   g. Fainting spells or seizures .... YES NO
   h. Hepatitis, jaundice or liver disease .... YES NO
   i. Diabetes .... YES NO
   j. Inflammatory rheumatism (painful or swollen joints) .... YES NO
   k. Arthritis .... YES NO
   l. Stomach ulcers .... YES NO
   m. Kidney trouble .... YES NO
   n. Tuberculosis (TB) .... YES NO
   o. Persistent cough or cough up blood .... YES NO
   p. Veneral disease .... YES NO
   q. Epilepsy .... YES NO
   r. Sickle Cell disease .... YES NO
   s. Thyroid disease .... YES NO
   t. AIDS .... YES NO
   u. Emphysema .... YES NO
   v. Psychiatric treatment .... YES NO
   w. Cleft lip/palate .... YES NO
   x. Cerebral palsy .... YES NO
   y. Mental retardation .... YES NO
   z. Hearing disability .... YES NO
   aa. Developmental disability .... YES NO
       If yes, explain: _____
   bb. Was your child premature? .... YES NO
       If yes, how many weeks _____
   cc. Other: _____

9. Does your child have to urinate (pass water) more than six times a day? .... YES NO
10. Is your child thirsty much of the time? .... YES NO
11. Has your child had abnormal bleeding associated with previous surgery, extractions or accidents? .... YES NO
12. Does he/she bruise easily? .... YES NO

13. Has he/she ever required a blood transfusion? ..... YES NO
14. Does he/she have any blood disorders such as anemia, etc? .... YES NO
15. Has he/she ever had surgery, x-ray or chemotherapy for a tumor, growth, or other condition? .... YES NO
16. Does your child have a disability that prevents treatment in a dental office? .... YES NO
17. Is he/she taking any of the following?
    a. Antibiotics or sulfa drugs .... YES NO
    b. Anticoagulants (blood thinners) .... YES NO
    c. Medicine for high blood pressure .... YES NO
    d. Cortisone or steroids .... YES NO
    e. Tranquilizers .... YES NO
    f. Aspirin .... YES NO
    g. Dilantin or other anticonvulsant .... YES NO
    h. Insulin, tolbutamide, Orinase, or similar drug ... YES NO
    i. Any other? _____
18. Is he/she allergic to, or has he/she ever reacted adversely to, any of the following?
    a. Local anesthetics .... YES NO
    b. Penicillin or other antibiotics .... YES NO
    c. Sulfa drugs .... YES NO
    d. Barbituates, sedatives, or sleeping pills .... YES NO
    e. Aspirin .... YES NO
    f. Any other? _____
19. Has he/she any serious trouble associated with any previous dental treatment? .... YES NO
    If so, please explain: _____
20. Has your child been in any situation which could expose him/her to x-rays or other ionizing radiators? ...... YES NO
21. Last date of dental examination: _____
22. Has he/she ever had orthodontic treatment (worn braces)? .... YES NO
23. Has he/she ever been treated for any gum diseases (gingivitis, periodontitis, trenchmouth, pyorrhea)? .... YES NO
24. Does his/her gums bleed when brushing teeth? .... YES NO
25. Does he/she grind or clench teeth? .... YES NO
26. Has he/she often had toothaches? .... YES NO
27. Has he/she had frequent sores in his/her mouth? .. YES NO
28. Has he/she had any injuries to his/her mouth or jaws? YES NO
    If yes, explain: _____
29. Does he/she have any sores or swellings of his/her mouth or jaws? .... YES NO
30. Have you been satisfied with your child's previous dental care? .... YES NO

ADOLESCENT WOMEN:
31. Are you pregnant now, or think you may be? .... YES NO
32. Do you anticipate becoming pregnant? .... YES NO
33. Are you taking the pill? .... YES NO

To the best of my knowledge, all of the preceding answers are true and correct. If my child ever has a change in his/her health or his/her medicines change, I will inform the doctor at the next appointment without fail.

Parent's Signature: _____ Date _____

MEDICAL HISTORY / PHYSICAL EXAMINATION REVIEW

Date   Addition   Student/Faculty Signatures

_____   _____   _____   _____
_____   _____   _____   _____
_____   _____   _____   _____

FIGURE 2-2 University of Southern California pediatric medical history questionnaire.

episode of vasodepressor syncope. Whereas many such patients do not offer verbal admissions of fear, I have found that these same patients may volunteer the information in writing. (Additional ways a doctor can determine a patient's anxiety are discussed later in this chapter.)

6. Are you in pain now?

Comment: The primary thrust of this question is related to dentistry. Its purpose is to determine what prompted the patient to seek dental care. If pain or discomfort is present, the doctor

may need to treat the patient immediately on an emergency basis, whereas in the more normal situation treatment can be delayed until future visits.

Have You Experienced:

7. Chest pain (angina)

Comment: A history of angina (defined, in part, as chest pain brought on by exertion and alleviated by rest) usually indicates the presence of a significant degree of coronary artery disease with attendant ischemia of the myocardium. The risk factor for

MetLife   **Historia Médica**   **University of the Pacific**
                                            Spanish

Nombre del paciente:_____ No. de Ident. del Paciente: _____
                                                                          Fecha de nacimiento: _____

I. MARQUE CON UN CÍRCULO LA RESPUESTA CORRECTA (Deje en BLANCO si no entiende la pregunta)**:**

  1. Sí No ¿Está en buena salud general?

  2. Sí No ¿Han habido cambios en su salud durante el último año?

  3. Sí No ¿Ha estado hospitalizado/a o ha tenido de una enfermedad grave en los últimos tres años?

        ¿Si Sí, por qué? _____

  4. Sí No ¿Se encuentra actualmente bajo tratamiento médico? ¿Para qué? _____

        Fecha de su último examen médico: _____ Fecha de su última cita dental: _____

  5. Sí No ¿Ha tenido problemas con algún tratamiento dental en el pasado?

  6. Sí No ¿Tiene algún dolor ahora?

II. HA NOTADO:

7.	Sí	No	¿Dolor de pecho (angina)?	18.	Sí No	¿Mareos?
8.	Sí	No	¿Los tobillos hinchados?	19.	Sí No	¿Ruidos o zumbidos en los oídos?
9.	Sí	No	¿Falta de aliento?	20.	Sí No	¿Dolores de cabeza?
10.	Sí	No	¿Reciente pérdida de peso, fiebre, sudor en la noche?	21.	Sí No	¿Desmayos?
11.	Sí	No	¿Tos persistente o tos con sangre?	22.	Sí No	¿Vista borrosa?
12.	Sí	No	¿Problemas de sangramiento, moretes?	23.	Sí No	¿Convulsiones?
13.	Sí	No	¿Problemas nasales (sinusitis)?	24.	Sí No	¿Sed excesiva?
14.	Sí	No	¿Dificultad al tragar?	25.	Sí No	¿Orina con frecuencia?
15.	Sí	No	¿Diarrea, estreñimiento, sangre en las heces?	26.	Sí No	¿Boca seca?
16.	Sí	No	¿Vómitos con frecuencia, náuseas?	27.	Sí No	¿Ictericia?
17.	Sí	No	¿Dificultad al orinar, sangre en la orina?	28.	Sí No	¿Dolor o rigidez en las articulaciones?

III. TIENE O HA TENIDO:

29.	Sí	No	¿Enfermedades del corazón?	40.	Sí No	¿SIDA?
30.	Sí	No	¿Infarto de corazón, defectos en el corazón?	41.	Sí No	¿Tumores, cáncer?
31.	Sí	No	¿Soplos en el corazón?	42.	Sí No	¿Artritis, reuma?
32.	Sí	No	¿Fiebre reumática?	43.	Sí No	¿Enfermedades de los ojos?
33.	Sí	No	¿Apoplejía, endurecimiento de las arterias?	44.	Sí No	¿Enfermedades de la piel?
34.	Sí	No	¿Presión sanguínea alta?	45.	Sí No	¿Anemia?
35.	Sí	No	¿Asma, tuberculosis, enfisema, otras enfermedades pulmonares?	46.	Sí No	¿Enfermedades venéreas (sífilis o gonorrea)?
36.	Sí	No	¿Hepatitis, otras enfermedades del hígado?	47.	Sí No	¿Herpes?
37.	Sí	No	¿Problemas del estómago, úlceras?	48.	Sí No	¿Enfermedades renales (riñón), vejiga?
38.	Sí	No	¿Alergias a remedios, comidas, medicamentos látex?	49.	Sí No	¿Enfermedades de tiroides o glándulas suprarrenales?
39.	Sí	No	¿Familiares con diabetes, problemas de corazón, tumores?	50.	Sí No	¿Diabetes?

VI. TIENE O HA TENIDO:

51.	Sí	No	¿Tratamiento psiquiátrico?	56.	Sí No	¿Hospitalizaciones?
52.	Sí	No	¿Tratamientos de radiación?	57.	Sí No	¿Transfusiones de sangre?
53.	Sí	No	¿Quimioterapia?	58.	Sí No	¿Cirugías?
54.	Sí	No	¿Válvula artificial del corazón?	59.	Sí No	¿Marcapasos?
55.	Sí	No	¿Articulación artificial?	60.	Sí No	¿Lentes de contacto?

V. ESTÁ TOMANDO:

61.	Sí	No	¿Drogas de uso recreativo?	63.	Sí No	¿Tabaco de cualquier tipo?
62.	Sí	No	¿Remedios, medicamentos, medicamentos sin receta (incluyendo aspirina)?	64.	Sí No	¿Alcohol (bebidas alcohólicas)?

Liste por favor:_____

VI. SÓLO PARA MUJERES:

  65. Sí No ¿Está o podría estar embarazada o dando pecho?   66. Sí No ¿Está tomando pastillas anticonceptivas?

VII. PARA TODOS LOS PACIENTES:

  67. Sí No ¿Tiene o ha tenido alguna otra enfermedad o problema médico que NO está en este cuestionario?

Si la respuesta es afirmativa, explique: _____

Que yo sepa, he respondido completamente y correctamente todas las preguntas. Informaré a mi dentista si hay algún cambio en mi salud y/o en los medicamentos que tomo.

    Firma del Paciente _____ Fecha _____

REVISIÓN SUPLEMENTARIA:

  1. Firma del Paciente _____ Fecha _____
  2. Firma del Paciente _____ Fecha _____
  3. Firma del Paciente _____ Fecha _____

The Health History is created and maintained by the University of the Pacific School of Dentistry, San Francisco, California.
Support for the translation and dissemination of the Health Histories comes from MetLife Dental Care.

FIGURE 2-3 University of the Pacific (UOP) Medical History form in Spanish. This form is available in 36 languages on the UOP website or at www.metdental.com. (Reprinted with permission from University of the Pacific Dental School, San Francisco, California.)

MetLife   **HEALTH HISTORY INTERVIEW**   **University of the Pacific**

Patient Name:_____

SIGNIFICANT MEDICAL FINDINGS	DENTAL MANAGEMENT CONSIDERATIONS	DATE

Record below the number and details of any YES
response noted on the Health History, plus details
of any YES response to questions A through F.

A.	yes/no	Cardiovascular
B.	yes/no	Infectious diseases
C.	yes/no	Allergy to medicines
D.	yes/no	Hematologic, bleeding
E.	yes/no	Medications
F.	yes/no	Other medical problems not asked?

_____   _____
Date   Doctor's Signature

This Health History Interview form is created and maintained by the University of the Pacific School of Dentistry, San Francisco, California.
Support for the translation and dissemination of the Health Histories comes from MetLife Dental Care.

FIGURE 2-4 University of the Pacific interview sheet. (Reprinted with permission from University of the Pacific Dental School, San Francisco, California.)

MetLife   **MEDICAL CONSULTATION REQUEST**   **University of the Pacific**

To: Dr._____

_____

_____

RE: _____

_____
Date of Birth

Please complete the form below and return it to

Dr._____

_____

_____

Phone # _____

Fax # _____

Our patient has presented with the following medical problem(s):_____

_____

_____

The following treatment is scheduled in our clinic:_____

_____

Most patients experience the following with the above planned procedures:

bleeding: • minimal (<50ml)   • significant (>50ml)
stress and anxiety: • low   • medium   • high

_____   _____
Dentist signature   Date

PHYSICIAN'S RESPONSE

Please provide any information regarding the above patient's need for antibiotic prophylaxis, current cardiovascular condition, coagulation ability, and the history and status of infectious diseases. Ordinarily, local anesthesia is obtained with 2% lidocaine, 1:100,000 epinephrine. For some surgical procedures, the epinephrine concentration may be increased to 1:50,000 for hemostasis. The epinephrine dose NEVER exceeds 0.2 mg total.

*CHECK **ALL** THAT APPLY*

- **OK** to **PROCEED** with dental treatment; **NO** special precautions and **NO** prophylactic antibiotics are needed.

- Antibiotic prophylaxis **IS** required for dental treatment according to the current American Heart Association and/or American Academy of Orthopedic Surgeons guidelines.

- Other precautions are required (please list):_____

_____

- **DO NOT** proceed with treatment. (Please give reason.)_____

_____

Treatment may proceed on (Date)_____

- Patient has an infectious disease:
  - AIDS (please provide current lab results)
  - TB (PPD+/active)
  - Hepatitis, type _____(acute/carrier)
  - Other (explain)_____

- Requested relevant medical and/or laboratory information is attached.

_____   _____
Physician signature   Date

PATIENT CONSENT

I agree to the release of my medical information to the University of the Pacific School of Dentistry.

_____   _____
Patient signature   Date

This Medical Consultation form is created and maintained by the University of the Pacific School of Dentistry, San Francisco, California. Support for the translation and dissemination of the health histories comes from MetLife Dental Care.

FIGURE 2-5 University of the Pacific consultation form. (Reprinted with permission from University of the Pacific Dental School, San Francisco, California.)

the typical patient with stable angina is class III in the American Society of Anesthesiologists (ASA) Physical Status Classification System.* Stress reduction is strongly recommended in these patients. Patients with unstable or recent-onset angina represent ASA class IV risks.

8. Swollen ankles?

Comment: Swollen ankles (pitting edema or dependent edema) indicate possible congestive heart failure (CHF). However, varicose veins, pregnancy, and renal dysfunction are other causes of ankle edema. Healthy persons who stand on their feet for long periods (e.g., mail carriers and dental staff members) also may develop ankle edema.

9. Shortness of breath?

Comment: Although the patient may respond negatively to the specific questions (questions 29 to 35) in section III regarding the presence of various heart and lung disorders (e.g., angina, heart failure, pulmonary emphysema), clinical signs and symptoms of heart or lung disease may be evident. A positive response to this question does not always indicate that the patient has such a disease. To more accurately determine the patient's status before the start of dental care, further evaluation is suggested.

10. Recent weight loss, fever, night sweats?

Comment: The question refers primarily to an unexpected gain or loss of weight, not intentional dieting. Unexpected weight changes may indicate heart failure, hypothyroidism (increased weight), hyperthyroidism, widespread carcinoma, uncontrolled diabetes mellitus (weight loss), or many other disorders. The presence of fever or night sweats should be pursued to determine whether these symptoms are innocent or perhaps clues to the presence of a more significant problem, such as tuberculosis.

11. Persistent cough, coughing up blood?

Comment: A positive response mandates in-depth dialogue history to determine the cause of the persistent cough or hemoptysis (blood-tinged sputum). The most common causes of hemoptysis are bronchitis/bronchiectasis, neoplasms, and tuberculosis.

A chronic cough can indicate active tuberculosis or other chronic respiratory disorders, such as chronic bronchitis. Cough associated with an upper respiratory tract infection confers an ASA II classification on the patient, whereas chronic bronchitis in a patient who has smoked more than one pack of cigarettes daily for many years may indicate chronic lung disease and confer on the patient an ASA III risk. The doctor must weigh the risks carefully before administering central nervous system (CNS) depressants—especially those such as opioids and barbiturates, which depress the respiratory system more than others—in patients who exhibit signs of diminished respiratory reserve (ASA III and IV).

12. Bleeding problems, bruising easily?

Comment: Bleeding disorders such as hemophilia are associated with prolonged bleeding or frequent bruising, and can lead to modification of certain forms of dental therapy (e.g., surgery and

local anesthetic administration) and must therefore be made known to the doctor before treatment begins. Modifications in the planned dental treatment plan may be necessary when excessive bleeding is likely to be present.

13. Sinus problems?

Comment: Sinus problems can indicate the presence of an allergy (ASA II), which should be pursued in the dialogue history, or upper respiratory tract infection (ASA II), such as a common cold. The patient may experience some respiratory distress when placed in a supine position; distress may also be present if a rubber dam is used. Specific treatment modifications—postponing treatment until the patient can breathe more comfortably, limiting the degree of recline in the dental chair, and forgoing use of a rubber dam—are advisable.

14. Difficulty swallowing?

Comment: Dysphagia, or the inability to swallow, can have many causes. Before the start of any dental treatment, the dentist should seek to determine the etiology and the severity of the patient's symptoms.

15. Diarrhea, constipation, blood in stools?

Comment: Evaluation to determine whether gastrointestinal problems are present, many of which require patients to be medicated. Causes of blood in feces can range from benign, self-limiting events to serious life-threatening disease. Some common causes include anal fissures, aspirin-containing drugs, bleeding disorders, esophageal varices, foreign body trauma, hemorrhoids, neoplasms, use of orally administered steroids, the presence of intestinal polyps, and thrombocytopenia.

16. Frequent vomiting, nausea?

Comment: A multitude of causes can lead to nausea and vomiting. Medications, however, are among the most common causes of nausea and vomiting.[5] Opiates, digitalis, levodopa, and many cancer drugs act on the chemoreceptor trigger zone in the area postrema to induce vomiting. Drugs that frequently induce nausea include nonsteroidal anti-inflammatory drugs, erythromycin, cardiac antidysrhythmics, antihypertensive drugs, diuretics, oral antidiabetic agents, oral contraceptives, and many gastrointestinal drugs, such as sulfasalazine.[5]

Gastrointestinal and systemic infections, viral and bacterial, are probably the second most common cause of nausea and vomiting.

17. Difficulty urinating, blood in urine?

Comment: Hematuria, the presence of blood in the urine, requires evaluation to determine the cause, potentially indicative of urinary tract infection or obstruction.

18. Dizziness?

Comment: A positive response may indicate a patient's chronic postural (orthostatic) hypotension, symptomatic hypotension or anemia, or transient ischemic attack, a form of prestroke. In addition, patients with certain types of seizure disorders, such as the "drop attack," may report fainting or dizzy spells. The doctor may be advised to perform further evaluation, including a consultation with the patient's primary care physician. A transient ischemic attack represents an ASA III risk, whereas chronic postural hypotension is normally an ASA II or III risk.

---

*The ASA physical evaluation system is discussed in detail later in this chapter.

19. Ringing in ears?

Comment: Tinnitus (an auditory sensation in the absence of sound heard in one or both ears, such as ringing, buzzing, hissing, or clicking) is a common side effect of certain drugs, including salicylates, indomethacin, propranolol, levodopa, aminophylline, and caffeine. It may also be seen with multiple sclerosis, tumor, and ischemic infarction.

20. Headaches?

Comment: Presence of headache should be evaluated to determine the cause. Common causes include chronic daily headaches, cluster headaches, migraine headaches, and tension-type headaches. If necessary, consultation with the patient's primary care physician is warranted. The drug or drugs that the patient uses to manage symptoms should be determined because many of these agents can influence clotting.

21. Fainting spells?

Comment: See comment for question 18.

22. Blurred vision?

Comment: Blurred vision is a common finding as the patient ages. Leading causes of blurred vision and blindness include glaucoma, diabetic retinopathy, and macular degeneration. Double vision, or diplopia, usually results from extraocular muscle imbalance, the cause of which must be sought. Common causes include damage to the third, fourth, or sixth cranial nerve secondary to myasthenia gravis, vascular disturbances, and intracranial tumors.

23. Seizures?

Comment: Seizures are common dental emergencies. The most likely candidate for a seizure is the epileptic patient. Even epileptic patients whose condition is well controlled with antiepileptic drugs may sustain seizures in stressful situations, such as might occur in the dental office. The doctor must determine the type, frequency of occurrence, and drug or drugs used to prevent the seizure before the start of dental treatment. Treatment modification using the stress-reduction protocols (discussed later in this chapter) is frequently desirable for patients with known seizure disorders. Epileptic patients whose seizures are under control (i.e., are infrequent) are ASA II risks; those with more frequent occurrence of seizures represent ASA III or IV risks.

24. Excessive thirst?

Comment: Polydipsia, or excessive thirst, is often seen in diabetes mellitus, diabetes insipidus, and hyperparathyroidism.

25. Frequent urination?

Comment: Polyuria, or frequent urination, may be benign (too much fluid intake) or a symptom of diabetes mellitus, diabetes insipidus, Cushing's syndrome, or hyperparathyroidism.

26. Dry mouth?

Comment: Fear is a common cause of a dry mouth, especially in the dental environment. Many other causes of xerostomia exist, including Sjögren's syndrome.

27. Jaundice?

Comment: Jaundice (yellowness of skin, whites of the eyes, and mucous membranes) is due to a deposition of bile pigment resulting from an excess of bilirubin in the blood (hyperbilirubinemia). It is frequently caused by obstruction of bile ducts, excessive destruction of red blood cells (hemolysis), or disturbances in the functioning of liver cells. Jaundice is a sign that might indicate a benign problem, such as a gallstone obstructing the common bile duct, or might be due to pancreatic carcinoma involving the opening of the common bile duct into the duodenum.

28. Joint pain, stiffness?

Comment: A history of joint pain and stiffness (arthritis) may be associated with long-term use of salicylates (aspirin) or other nonsteroidal anti-inflammatory drugs (NSAIDs), some of which may alter blood clotting. Arthritic patients who are receiving long-term corticosteroid therapy may have an increased risk of acute adrenal insufficiency, especially in patients who have recently stopped taking the steroid. Such patients may require a reinstitution of steroid therapy or a modification (increase) in corticosteroid doses during dental treatment so that their body will be better able to respond to any additional stress that might be associated with the treatment.

Because of possible difficulties in positioning the patient comfortably, modifications may be necessary to accommodate the patient's physical disability. Most patients receiving corticosteroids are categorized as ASA II or III risks depending on the reason for the medication and the degree of disability present. Patients with significantly disabling arthritis are ASA III risks.

Do You Have or Have You Had:

29. Heart disease?

Comment: This survey question seeks to detect the presence of any and all types of heart disease. In the presence of a "yes" answer the doctor must seek more specific detailed information on the nature and severity of the problem as well as a list of any medications the patient is taking to manage the condition.

30. Heart attack, heart defects?

Comment: Heart attack is the lay term for a myocardial infarction (MI). The doctor must determine the time that has elapsed since the patient sustained the MI, the severity of the MI, and the degree of residual myocardial damage to decide whether treatment modifications are indicated. Elective dental care should be postponed 6 months after an MI.[6] Most post-MI patients are considered to be ASA III risks; however, a patient who had an MI less than 6 months before the planned dental treatment should be considered an ASA IV risk. Where little or no residual damage to the myocardium is present, the patient is an ASA II risk.

Heart failure: The degree of heart failure (weakness of the "pump") present must be assessed through the dialogue history. When a patient has a more serious condition, such as CHF or dyspnea (labored breathing) at rest, specific treatment modifications are warranted. In this situation the doctor must consider whether the patient needs supplemental O_2 during treatment. Whereas most patients with CHF are classified as ASA II (mild HF without disability) or ASA III (disability developing with exertion or stress) risks, the presence of dyspnea at rest is an ASA IV risk.

Congenital heart lesions: An in-depth dialogue history is required to determine the nature of the lesion and the degree of disability it produces. Patients can represent ASA II, III, or

IV risks. The doctor may recommend medical consultation, especially for the pediatric patient, to judge the lesion's severity. Many dental treatments will require prophylactic antibiotics.

31. Heart murmurs?

Comment: Heart murmurs are common, and not all murmurs are clinically significant. The doctor should determine whether a murmur is functional (nonpathologic or ASA II) or whether clinical signs and symptoms of either valvular stenosis or regurgitation are present (ASA III or IV) and whether antibiotic prophylaxis is warranted. A major clinical symptom of a significant (organic) murmur is undue fatigue. Table 2-1 provides guidelines for antibiotic prophylaxis. These were most recently revised in June 1997.[7,8] Box 2-2 categorizes cardiac problems as to their requirements for antibiotic prophylaxis, and Box 2-3 addresses prophylaxis and dental procedures specifically.

32. Rheumatic fever?

Comment: A history of rheumatic fever should prompt the doctor to perform an in-depth dialogue history for the presence of rheumatic heart disease. If rheumatic heart disease is present, antibiotic prophylaxis can minimize the risk of the patient's developing subacute bacterial endocarditis. Depending on the severity of the disease and the presence of a disability, patients with rheumatic heart disease can be an ASA II, III, or IV risk. Additional treatment modifications may be advisable.

33. Stroke, hardening of arteries?

Comment: The doctor must pay close attention to stroke, cerebrovascular accident (CVA), or "brain attack" (the term being increasingly used to confer on the lay public as well as health care professionals the urgency needed in prompt management of the victim of a CVA). A patient who has had a CVA is at greater risk of suffering another CVA or a seizure should they become hypoxic. If the doctor uses sedation in patient management, only light levels, such as those provided through inhalation sedation or intravenous conscious sedation, are recommended. The doctor should be especially sensitive to the presence of transient cerebral ischemia, a precursor to CVA; this represents an ASA III risk. The post-CVA patient is an ASA IV risk within 6 months of the CVA, becoming an ASA III risk 6 or more months after the incident (if their recovery is uneventful). In rare cases the post-CVA patient can be an ASA II risk.

34. High blood pressure?

Comment: Elevated blood pressure measurements are frequently encountered in the dental environment, primarily as a result of the added stress many patients associate with a visit to the dentist. In patients with a history of high blood pressure the doctor must determine the drugs the patient is taking, the potential side effects of those medications, and any possible interactions with other medications. Guidelines for clinical evaluation of risk (ASA categories) based on adult blood pressure values are presented later in this chapter.

35. Asthma, tuberculosis, emphysema, other lung disease?

Comment: Determining the nature and severity of respiratory problems is an essential part of patient evaluation. Many acute problems developing in the dental environment are stress related, increasing the workload of the cardiovascular system and the oxygen requirements of many tissues and organs in the body. The presence of severe respiratory disease can greatly influence the planned dental treatment.

TABLE 2-1 Prophylactic regimens for dental, oral, respiratory, and esophageal procedures

Situation	Agent	Regimen*
Standard general prophylaxis	Amoxicillin	Adults, 2 g; children, 50 mg/kg orally 1 hour before procedure
Inability to take oral medications	Ampicillin	Adults, 2 g IM or IV; children, 50 mg/kg IM or IV 30 minutes before procedure
Allergy to penicillin	Clindamycin	Adults, 600 mg; children, 20 mg/kg orally 1 hour before procedure
	or	
	Cephalexin[†] or cefadroxil[†]	Adults, 2 g; children, 50 mg/kg orally 1 hour before procedure
	or	
	Azithromycin or clarithromycin	Adults, 500 mg; children, 15 mg/kg orally 1 hour before procedure
Allergy to penicillin and inability to take oral medications	Clindamycin	Adults, 600 mg; children, 20 mg/kg IV 30 minutes before procedure
	or	
	Cefazolin	Adults, 1 g; children, 25 mg/kg IM or IV 30 minutes before procedure

IM, Intramuscular; *IV,* intravenous.
*Total doses for children should not exceed those for adults.
[†]Cephalosporins should not be prescribed for individuals with immediate-type hypersensitivity reactions (e.g., urticaria, angioedema, or anaphylaxis) to penicillins.
Modified from Dajani AS, Taubert KA, Wilson W, et al.: Prevention of bacterial endocarditis: recommendations by the American Heart Association, *J Am Dent Assoc* 128:1142–1151, 1997. © 1997 American Dental Association. Excerpted by the JADA with permission of The Journal of the American Medical Association, *JAMA* 277:1794–1801, 1997; © 1997 American Medical Association. Modified 2007 with permission of the American Dental Association.

Box 2-2 Cardiac conditions associated with endocarditis

ENDOCARDITIS PROPHYLAXIS RECOMMENDED
High-risk category
Prosthetic cardiac valves, including bioprosthetic and homograft valves
Previous bacterial endocarditis
Complex cyanotic congenital heart disease (e.g., single-ventricle states, transposition of great arteries, tetralogy of Fallot)
Surgically constructed systemic pulmonary shunts or conduits

Moderate-risk category
Most other congenital cardiac malformations (other than those listed in this box)
Acquired valvular dysfunction (e.g., rheumatic heart disease)
Hypertrophic cardiomyopathy
Mitral valve prolapse with valvar regurgitation or thickened leaflets*

ENDOCARDITIS PROPHYLAXIS NOT RECOMMENDED
Negligible-risk category (no greater risk than general population)
Isolated secundum atrial septal defect
Surgical repair of atrial septal defect, ventricular septal defect, or patent ductus arteriosus (with no residual effects beyond 6 months)
Previous coronary artery bypass graft surgery
Mitral valve prolapse without valvular regurgitation*
Physiologic, functional, or innocent heart murmurs*
Previous Kawasaki disease without valvular dysfunction
Previous rheumatic fever without valvular dysfunction
Cardiac pacemakers (intravascular and epicardial) and implanted defibrillators

*Prophylaxis is recommended for patients with high- and moderate-risk cardiac conditions.
Modified from Dajani AS, Taubert KA, Wilson W, et al.: Prevention of bacterial endocarditis: recommendations by the American Heart Association, *J Am Dent Assoc* 128:1142–1151, 1997. © 1997 American Dental Association. Excerpted by the JADA with permission of The Journal of the American Medical Association, *JAMA* 277:1794–1801, 1997; © 1997 American Medical Association. Modified 2007 with permission of the American Dental Association.

Box 2-3 Dental procedures and endocarditis prophylaxis

ENDOCARDITIS PROPHYLAXIS RECOMMENDED*
Dental extractions
Periodontal procedures, including surgery, scaling and root planing, probing, and recall maintenance
Dental implant placement and reimplantation of avulsed teeth
Endodontic (root canal) instrumentation or surgery beyond the apex
Subgingival placement of antibiotic fibers or strips
Initial placement of orthodontic bands but not brackets
Intraligamentary local anesthetic injections
Prophylactic cleaning of teeth or implants where bleeding is anticipated

ENDOCARDITIS PROPHYLAXIS NOT RECOMMENDED
Restorative dentistry† (operative and prosthodontic) with or without retraction cord‡
Local anesthetic injections (nonintraligamentary)
Intracanal endodontic treatment and post placement and buildup
Placement of rubber dams
Postoperative suture removal
Placement of removable prosthodontic or orthodontic appliances
Taking of oral impressions
Fluoride treatments
Taking of oral radiographs
Orthodontic appliance adjustment
Shedding of primary teeth

*Prophylaxis is recommended for patients with high- and moderate-risk cardiac conditions.
†Restorative dentistry includes restoration of decayed teeth (filling of cavities) and replacement of missing teeth.
‡Clinical judgment may indicate antibiotic use in selected circumstances that may create significant bleeding.
Modified from Dajani AS, Taubert KA, Wilson W, et al.: Prevention of bacterial endocarditis: recommendations by the American Heart Association, *J Am Dent Assoc* 128:1142–1151, 1997. © 1997 American Dental Association. Excerpted by the JADA with permission of The Journal of the American Medical Association, *JAMA* 277:1794–1801, 1997; © 1997 American Medical Association. Modified 2007 with permission of the American Dental Association.

Asthma (bronchospasm) is marked by a partial obstruction of the lower airway. The doctor must determine the nature of the asthma (intrinsic [allergic] versus extrinsic [nonallergic]), frequency of acute episodes, causative factors, method of management of acute episodes, and drugs the patient may be taking to minimize the occurrence of acute episodes. Stress is a common precipitating factor in acute asthmatic episodes. The well-controlled asthmatic patient represents an ASA II risk, whereas the patient with well-controlled but stress-induced asthma is an ASA III risk. Patients whose acute episodes are frequent or difficult to terminate (requiring hospitalization) are ASA III or IV risks.

With a history of tuberculosis the doctor must first determine whether the disease is active or arrested. (Arrested tuberculosis represents an ASA II risk.) Medical consultation and dental treatment modification are recommended when such information is not easily determined. Inhalation sedation with nitrous oxide and O_2 is not recommended for patients with active tuberculosis (ASA III or IV) because of the likelihood that the rubber goods (reservoir bag and conducting tubing) may become contaminated and the difficulty in their sterilization. However, for doctors who treat many patients with tuberculosis and other infectious diseases, disposable rubber goods for inhalation sedation units are recommended.

Emphysema is a form of chronic obstructive pulmonary disease (COPD), also called chronic obstructive lung disease. The patient with emphysema has a decreased respiratory reserve from which to draw if the body's cells require additional O_2, which they do during stress. Supplemental O_2 therapy during dental treatment is recommended in severe cases of emphysema; however, the severely emphysematous (ASA III, IV) patient should not receive more than 3 L of O_2 per minute.[11] This flow restriction helps to ensure that the doctor does not eliminate the patient's hypoxic drive, which is the emphysematous patient's primary stimulus for breathing. The emphysematous patient is an ASA II, III, or IV risk depending on the degree of the disability.

36. Hepatitis, other liver disease?

Comment: These diseases or problems are transmissible (hepatitis A and B) or indicate the presence of hepatic dysfunction. A history of blood transfusion or of past or present drug addiction should alert the doctor to a probable increase in the risk of hepatic dysfunction. (Hepatic dysfunction is a common finding in the patients who abuse parenteral drugs.) Hepatitis C is responsible for more than 90% of cases of posttransfusion hepatitis, but only 4% of cases are attributable to blood transfusions; up to 50% of cases are related to intravenous drug use. Incubation of hepatitis C virus averages 6 to 7 weeks. The clinical illness is mild, usually asymptomatic, and characterized by a high rate (>50%) of chronic hepatitis.[9]

37. Stomach problems, ulcers?

Comment: The presence of stomach or intestinal ulcers may indicate acute or chronic anxiety and the possible use of medications such as tranquilizers, H_1-inhibitors, and antacids. Knowledge of which drugs are being taken is important before additional drugs are administered in the dental office. A number of H_1-inhibitors are now over-the-counter drugs. Because many patients do not consider such drugs "real" medications, the doctor must specifically question the patient about them. The presence of ulcers does not itself represent an increased risk during treatment. In the absence of additional medical problems, the patient may represent an ASA I or II risk.

38. Allergies to: drugs, foods, medications, latex?

Comment: The doctor must evaluate a patient's allergies thoroughly before administering dental treatment or drugs. The importance of this question and its full evaluation cannot be overstated. A complete and vigorous dialogue history must be undertaken before the start of any dental treatment, especially when a presumed or documented history of drug allergy is present. Adverse drug reactions are not uncommon, but most are labeled by the patient and, on occasion, also by their doctor, as allergic reactions. However, despite the great frequency with which allergy is reported, true documented and reproducible allergic drug reactions are relatively rare. The doctor must thoroughly evaluate all adverse reactions to drugs, especially when the doctor plans to administer or prescribe closely related medications for the patient during dental treatment (see Chapters 22 through 25).

Two questions that must be asked for each alleged allergy are (1) Describe your reaction and (2) How was it managed?

The presence of allergy alone represents an ASA II risk. No emergency situation is as frightening to health care professionals as the acute, systemic allergic reaction known as anaphylaxis. Prevention of this life-threatening situation is ever more gratifying than treatment of anaphylaxis once it develops.

39. Family history of diabetes, heart problems, tumors?

Comment: Knowledge of family history can help determine the presence of many disorders that have some hereditary component.

40. AIDS?

Comment: Patients who have tested positive for human immunodeficiency virus (HIV) are representative of every area of the population. The usual barrier techniques should be employed to minimize risk of cross-infection to both the patient and staff members. Patients who are HIV positive are considered ASA II, III, IV, or V risks depending on the progress of the infection.

41. Tumors, cancer?

Comment: The presence or previous existence of cancer of the head or neck may require specific modification of dental therapy. Irradiated tissues have decreased resistance to infection, diminished vascularity, and reduced healing capacity. However, no specific contraindication exists to the administration of drugs for the management of pain or anxiety in these patients. Many persons with cancer may also be receiving long-term therapy with central nervous system (CNS) depressants, such as antianxiety drugs, hypnotics, and opioids. Consultation with the patient's oncologist is recommended before dental treatment. A past or current history of cancer does not necessarily increase the ASA risk status. However, patients who are cachectic or hospitalized or are in poor physical condition may represent ASA IV or V risks.

42. Arthritis, rheumatism?

Comment: See Comment for question 28.

43. Eye diseases?

Comment: For patients with glaucoma, the need to administer a drug that diminishes salivary gland secretions will need to be addressed. Anticholinergics, such as atropine, scopolamine, and glycopyrrolate, are contraindicated in patients with acute narrow angle glaucoma since these drugs produce an increase in intraocular pressure. Patients with glaucoma are usually ASA II risks.

44. Skin diseases?

Comment: Skin represents an elastic, rugged, self-regenerating, protective covering for the body. The skin also represents our primary physical presentation to the world and as such presents with a myriad of clinical signs of disease processes, including allergic, cardiac, respiratory, hepatic, and endocrine disorders.[10]

45. Anemia?

Comment: Anemia is a relatively common adult ailment, especially among young adult women (iron deficiency anemia). The doctor must determine the type of anemia present. The ability of the blood to carry O_2 or to give up O_2 to other cells is decreased in anemic patients. This decrease can become significant during procedures in which hypoxia is likely to develop.

Although rare, hypoxia is more likely to occur with the use of deeper levels of intramuscular (IM), intranasal (IN), or intravenous (IV) sedation without the concomitant administration of supplemental O_2, which can become an even more serious situation if the patient is anemic. ASA risk factors vary from II to IV depending on the severity of the O_2 deficit.

Sickle cell anemia is seen exclusively in black patients. Periods of unusual stress or of O_2 deficiency (hypoxia) can precipitate a sickle cell crisis. The administration of supplemental O_2 during treatment is strongly recommended for patients with sickle cell disease. Persons with sickle cell trait represent ASA II risks, whereas those with sickle cell disease are II or III risks.

In addition, congenital or idiopathic methemoglobinemia, although rare, is a relative contraindication to the administration of the amide local anesthetic prilocaine.[10]

46. Venereal disease (syphilis or gonorrhea)?

47. Herpes?

Comment: When treating patients with sexually transmitted diseases, dentists and staff members are at risk of infection. In the presence of oral lesions, elective dental care should be postponed. Standard barrier techniques, protective gloves, eyeglasses, and masks provide operators with a degree of (but not total) protection. Such patients usually represent ASA II and III risks but may be IV or V risks in extreme situations.

48. Kidney, bladder disease?

Comment: The doctor should evaluate the nature of the renal disorder. Treatment modifications, including antibiotic prophylaxis, may be appropriate for several chronic forms of renal disease. Functionally anephric patients are ASA IV risks, whereas patients with most other forms of renal dysfunction present as either ASA II or III risks. Box 2-4 shows a sample dental referral letter for a patient on long-term hemodialysis treatment because of chronic kidney disease.

49. Thyroid, adrenal disease?

Comment: The clinical presence of thyroid or adrenal gland dysfunction—either hyperfunction or hypofunction—should prompt the doctor to use caution in the administration of certain drug groups (e.g., epinephrine to hyperthyroid patients and CNS depressants to hypothyroid patients). In most instances, however, the patient has already seen a physician and undergone treatment for their thyroid disorder by the time they seek dental treatment. In this case the patient is in a euthyroid state (normal blood levels of thyroid hormone) because of surgical intervention, irradiation, or drug therapy. The euthyroid state represents an ASA II risk, whereas clinical signs and symptoms of hyperthyroidism or hypothyroidism represent ASA III or, in rare instances, ASA IV risks.

Patients with hypofunctioning adrenal cortices have Addison's disease and receive daily replacement doses of glucocorticosteroids. In stressful situations their body may be unable to respond appropriately leading to loss of consciousness. Hypersecretion of cortisone, Cushing's syndrome, rarely results in a life-threatening situation.

50. Diabetes?

Comment: A positive response to this question requires further inquiry to determine the type, severity, and degree of control of the diabetic condition. A patient with type 1 diabetes mellitus (insulin-dependent diabetes mellitus) or type 2 (non–insulin-dependent diabetes mellitus) is rarely at great risk from dental care or commonly administered dental drugs (e.g., local anesthetics, epinephrine, antibiotics, CNS depressants). Patients with type 2 diabetes are usually an ASA II risk; those with well-controlled type 1 diabetes are an ASA III risk; and those with poorly controlled type 1 diabetes, an ASA III or IV risk.

Box 2-4 Dental referral letter

Dear Doctor:

The patient who bears this note is undergoing long-term hemodialysis treatment because of chronic kidney disease. In providing dental care to this patient, please observe the following precautions:

1. Dental treatment is most safely done 1 day after the last dialysis treatment or at least 8 hours thereafter. Residual heparin may make hemostasis difficult. (Some patients are on long-term anticoagulant therapy.)
2. We are concerned about bacteremic seeding of the arteriovenous shunt devices and heart valves. We recommend prophylactic antibiotics before and after dental treatment. Antibiotic selection and dosage can be tricky in renal failure.

We recommend 3 g of amoxicillin 1 hour before the procedure and 1.5 g 6 hours later. For patients with penicillin allergies, 1 g of erythromycin 1 hour before the procedure and 500 mg 6 hours later is recommended.

Sincerely,

Courtesy Kaiser Permanente Medical Center, Los Angeles, California.

The greatest concerns during dental treatment relate to the possible effects of the dental care on subsequent eating and development of hypoglycemia (low blood sugar). Patients leaving a dental office with residual soft tissue anesthesia, especially in the mandible, usually defer eating until sensation returns, a period potentially lasting 3 to 5 hours (lidocaine, mepivacaine, articaine, prilocaine with vasoconstrictor) or more (bupivacaine with vasoconstrictor). Diabetic patients have to modify their insulin doses if they do not maintain normal eating habits.

Do You Have or Have You Had:

51. Psychiatric care?

Comment: The doctor should be aware of any nervousness (in general or specifically related to dentistry) or history of psychiatric care before treating the patient. Such patients may be receiving several drugs to manage their disorders that might interact with drugs the doctor uses to control pain and anxiety (see Table 2-1). Medical consultation should be considered in such cases. Extremely fearful patients are ASA II risks, whereas patients receiving psychiatric care and drugs represent II or III risks.

52. Radiation treatments?

53. Chemotherapy?

Comment: Therapies for cancer. See Comment for question 41.

54. Prosthetic heart valve?

Comment: Patients with prosthetic (artificial) heart valves are no longer uncommon. The doctor's primary concern is to determine the appropriate antibiotic regimen. Antibiotic prophylactic protocols[8] list these requirements. The doctor should be advised to consult with the patient's physician (e.g., the cardiologist or

American Dental Association, American Academy of Orthopaedic Surgeons: Advisory statement: antibiotic prophylaxis for dental patients with total joint replacements. *JADA* 128:1004–1008, 1997. Copyright © 1997 American Dental Association. All rights reserved. Modified 2007 with permission.

cardiothoracic surgeon) before treatment. Patients with prosthetic heart valves usually represent ASA II or III risks.

55. Artificial joint?

Comment: Approximately 450,000 total joint arthroplasties are performed annually in the United States. An expert panel of dentists, orthopedic surgeons, and infectious disease specialists convened by the ADA and the American Academy of Orthopaedic Surgeons thoroughly reviewed the available data to determine the need for antibiotic prophylaxis to prevent hematogenous prosthetic joint infections in dental patients who have undergone total joint arthroplasties. The panel concluded that antibiotic prophylaxis is not recommended for dental patients with pins, plates, and screws or those who have undergone total joint replacements. However, doctors should consider premedication in a small number of patients who may be at increased risks for the development of hematogenous total joint infection (Box 2-5).[11]

56. Hospitalization?

57. Blood transfusions?

58. Surgeries?

Comment: Determine the cause of the hospitalization, the duration of stay in the hospital, and any medications prescribed that the patient may still be taking.

Determine the reason for the blood transfusion (e.g., prolonged bleeding, accident, type of surgery).

Determine the nature (elective, emergency) and type of surgery (e.g., cosmetic, gastrointestinal, cardiac) and the patient's physical status at the present time.

59. Pacemaker?

Comment: Cardiac pacemakers are implanted beneath the skin of the upper chest or the abdomen with pacing wires extending

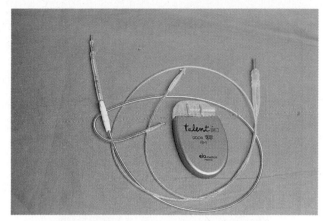

FIGURE 2-6 Diagram of a pacemaker. (From Forbes CD, Jackson WF: *Color atlas and text of clinical medicine,* ed 3, Edinburgh, Elsevier Ltd., 2004.)

into the myocardium (Figure 2-6). The most frequent indication for the use of a pacemaker is the presence of a clinically significant dysrhythmia. Fixed-rate pacemakers provide a regular, continuous heart rate regardless of the heart's inherent rhythm, whereas the much more common demand pacemaker is activated only when the rhythm of the heart falls into an abnormal range. Although there is little indication for the administration of antibiotics in these patients, medical consultation is suggested before the start of treatment to obtain the specific recommendations of the patient's physician. The patient with a pacemaker is commonly an ASA II or III risk during dental treatment.

In recent years persons who represent a significant risk of sudden unexpected death (e.g., cardiac arrest) due to electrical instability of the myocardium (e.g., ventricular fibrillation) have had implantable cardioverter/defibrillators placed below the skin of their chest (Figure 2-7). Medical consultation is recommended strongly for these patients.

60. Contact lenses?

Comment: Contact lenses are commonly worn by persons with vision disturbances. Dental considerations for patients with contact lenses include removal of the lenses during the administration of conscious sedation with techniques such as oral, IM, IN, IV, and inhalation drugs. Sedated patients may not close their eyes as frequently as unsedated patients, thereby increasing the likelihood of irritating the sclera and cornea of the eye.

Are You Taking:

61. Recreational drugs?

Comment: Although some patients may not admit to the use of recreational drugs, it is important to ask the question. This becomes particularly important when the doctor is considering the use of CNS depressant drugs for sedation or local anesthetics with or without a vasoconstrictor such as epinephrine.

62. Drugs, medications, over-the-counter medicines (including aspirin), natural remedies?

Comment: Because many patients distinguish between the terms "drug" and "medication," questionnaires should use both terms to determine what drugs (pharmaceutically active

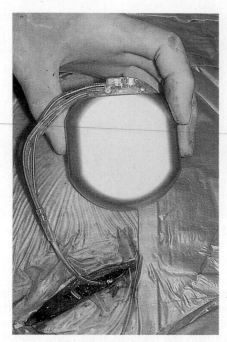

FIGURE 2-7 Implantable cardioverter defibrillator. (From Forbes CD, Jackson WF: *Color atlas and text of clinical medicine,* ed 3, Edinburgh, Elsevier Ltd., 2004.)

substances) a patient has taken. Unfortunately, in today's world the term "drug" often connotes the illicit use of medications (e.g., opioids). In the minds of many patients, people "do" drugs but "take" medications to manage medical conditions. Natural remedies contain many active substances, some of which may interact with drugs commonly used in dentistry.[12,13]

The doctor must be aware of all medications and drugs their patients take to control and to treat medical disorders. Frequently, patients take medications without knowing the condition the medications are designed to treat; many patients do not even know the names of drugs they are taking. It becomes important therefore for doctors to have available one or more means of identifying these medications and of determining their indications, side effects, and potential drug interactions. Many excellent sources are available, including online services such as MD Consult (www.mdconsult.com.) and Epocrates (www.epocrates. com). The *Physicians' Desk Reference* (PDR),[14] both in hard copy and online, offers a picture section that helps identify commonly prescribed drugs. The PDR also offers *Physicians' Desk Reference for Herbal Medicines.*[15] The *ADA Guide to Dental Therapeutics* is also an invaluable reference to drugs commonly used in dentistry and to the medications most often prescribed by physicians. The book stresses potential complications and drug interactions.[16]

Knowledge of the drugs and medications their patients are taking permits doctors to identify medical disorders, possible side effects—some of which may be of significance in dental treatment (e.g., postural hypotension)—and possible interactions between those medications and the drugs administered during dental treatment (Table 2-2).

63. Tobacco in any form?

64. Alcohol?
Comment: Long-term use of tobacco or alcohol can lead to potentially life-threatening problems, including neoplasms, hepatic dysfunction, and, in females, complications during pregnancy.

Women Only:

65. Are you or could you be pregnant or nursing?

66. Taking birth control pills?
Comment: Pregnancy represents a relative contraindication to extensive elective dental care, particularly during the first trimester. Consultation with the patient's obstetrician/gynecologist is recommended before the start of any dental treatment. Although administration of local anesthetics with or without epinephrine is permitted during pregnancy,* the doctor should evaluate the risk versus the benefits to be gained from the use of most sedative drugs. Of the available sedation techniques, inhalation sedation with nitrous oxide and O_2 is recommended. Use of oral, IM, or IV routes is not contraindicated but should be reserved for patients for whom other techniques are unavailable.

All Patients:

67. Do you have or have you had any other diseases or medical problems NOT listed on this form?
Comment: The patient is encouraged to comment on specific matters not previously mentioned. Examples of several possibly significant disorders include acute intermittent porphyria, methemoglobinemia, atypical plasma cholinesterase, and malignant hyperthermia.

To the best of my knowledge, I have answered every question completely and accurately. I will inform my dentist of any change in my health and/or medication.
Comment: This final statement is important from a medical legal perspective because although instances of purposeful lying on health histories are rare, they do occur. This statement must be accompanied by the date on which the history was completed and the signatures of the patient (or the parent or guardian if the patient is a minor or is not legally competent) and of the doctor who reviews the history. This in effect becomes a contract obliging the patient, parent, or guardian to report any changes in the patient's health or medications. Brady and Martinoff[4] demonstrated that a patient's analysis of personal health frequently is overly optimistic and that pertinent health matters sometimes are not immediately reported.

The medical history questionnaire must be updated on a regular basis, approximately every 3–6 months or after any prolonged lapse in treatment. In most instances the entire medical history questionnaire need not be redone. The doctor need ask only the following questions:

1. Have you experienced any change in your general health since your last dental visit?

Text continues on p. 38.

*FDA pregnancy risk categories for local anesthetics: B—lidocaine, prilocaine; C—articaine, bupivacaine, mepivacaine, epinephrine.

TABLE 2-2 Dental drug interactions

Dental drug	Interacting drug	Consideration	Action
Local anesthetics (LAs)	Cimetidine, β-adrenergic blockers (propranolol)	Hepatic metabolism of amide LA may be depressed	Use LAs cautiously, especially repeat dosages
	Antidysrhythmics (mexiletine, tocainide)	Additive CNS, CVS depression	Use LAs cautiously—keep dose as low as possible to achieve anesthesia
	CNS depressants: alcohol, antidepressants, antihistamines, benzo-diazepines, antipsychotics, centrally acting antihypertensives, muscle relaxants, other LAs, opioids	*Possible additive or supra-additive CNS, respiratory depression*	*Consider limiting maximum dose of LAs, especially with opioids*
	Cholinesterase inhibitors: antimyasthenics, antiglaucoma drugs	Antimyasthenic drug dosage may require adjustment because LA inhibits neuromuscular transmission	MD consultation
Vasoconstrictors Epinephrine	α-adrenergic blockers (phenoxybenzamine, prazosin) antipsychotics (haloperidol, entacapone)	Possible hypotensive response following large dose of epinephrine	Use vasoconstrictor cautiously—as low a dose as possible
	Catecholamine-O-methyltransferase inhibitors (tolcapone, entacapone)	May enhance systemic actions of vasoconstrictors	Use vasoconstrictor cautiously—as low a dose as possible
	CNS-stimulants (amphetamine, methylphenidate); ergot derivatives (dihydroergotamine, methylsergide)	↑ effect of stimulant or vasoconstrictor may occur	Use vasoconstrictor cautiously—as low a dose as possible
	Cocaine	*↑ effects of vasoconstrictors; can result in cardiac arrest*	*Avoid use of vasoconstrictor in patient under influence of cocaine*
	Digitalis glycosides (digoxin, digitoxin)	↑ risk of cardiac dysrhythmias	MD consultation
	Levodopa, thyroid hormones (levothyroxine, liothyronine)	Large doses of either (beyond replacement doses) may ↑ risk of cardiac toxicity	Use vasoconstrictor cautiously—as low a dose as possible
	Tricyclic antidepressants (amitriptyline, doxepin, imipramine)	*May enhance systemic effect of vasoconstrictor*	*Avoid use of levonordefrin or norepinephrine; use epinephrine cautiously—as low a dose as possible*
	Nonselective β-blockers (propranolol, nadolol)	May lead to hypertensive responses, especially to epinephrine	Monitor blood pressure after initial LA injection
Benzodiazepines, zolpidem, zaleplon	*Alcohol or CNS depressants*	*Concurrent use may ↑ depressant effects of either drug*	*Observe for ↑ response to CNS depression; ↓ dose of BZD if necessary*
	Chlorpromazine	**With zolpidem, zaleplon:** concurrent use may prolong elimination half-life of chlorpromazine	

Continued

TABLE 2-2 Dental drug interactions—*cont'd*

Dental drug	Interacting drug	Consideration	Action
	Cimetidine	May enhance certain actions of BZD, especially sedation	Monitor for enhanced BZD response
	Disulfiram	May increase CNS depressant action of certain BZD	Monitor for enhanced BZD response
	Erythromycin, clarithromycin, troleandomycin	May ↓ metabolism of certain BZD, ↑ CNS depressant effect	Monitor for enhanced BZD response
	Imipramine	**With zolpidem, zaleplon:** concurrent use may ↑ drowsiness and risk of anterograde amnesia; may also ↓ peak concentrations of imipramine	
	Oral contraceptives	May inhibit metabolism of BZD that undergo oxidation	Monitor for enhanced BZD response
	Theophyllines	May antagonize sedative effects of BZD	Monitor for ↓ BZD response
Barbiturates	Acetaminophen	Risk of ↑ hepatotoxicity may exist with large or chronic barbiturate dose	Monitor liver enzymes. Avoid prolonged high dosage use
	Alcohol	*Concurrent use may ↑ CNS depressant effects of either agent*	*Monitor patient for ↑ CNS depressant effects*
	Anticoagulants	May ↑ metabolism of anticoagulants, resulting in a ↓ response	Barbiturate therapy should not be started or stopped without considering the possibility of readjustment of the anticoagulant dose
	Oral contraceptives	Reliability may be reduced because of accelerated estrogen metabolism caused by barbiturates induction of hepatic enzymes	Suggest alternative form of birth control
	Doxycycline	Phenobarbital ↓ doxycycline's half-life and serum levels	Dose of doxycycline may have to be increased
	MAO-I	MAO-I may enhance sedative effects of barbiturates	Consider reduced dosage of barbiturate
	Metronidazole	Antimicrobial effectiveness of metronidazole may be decreased	Dose of metronidazole may have to be increased
	Narcotics	May ↑ toxicity of meperidine and ↓ effect of methadone	Monitor for excessive meperidine effect; dosage of methadone may have to be increased
	Theophylline	Barbiturates ↓ theophylline levels possibly resulting in ↓ effects	MD consult
	Valproic acid	*Concurrent use may ↓ metabolism of barbiturates resulting in ↑ plasma concentrations*	*Monitor for excessive phenobarbital effect*

TABLE 2-2 Dental drug interactions—*cont'd*

Dental drug	Interacting drug	Consideration	Action
Opioids (used for conscious sedation)	*Benzodiazepines*	↑ *respiratory depression* ↑ *recovery time* ↑ *risk of hypotension*	*Titrate dosages and monitor for excessive sedation*
	Cimetidine	Actions of opioids may be enhanced resulting in toxicity	If significant CNS depression occurs withdraw the drugs; if warranted administer opioid antagonist such as naloxone
	CNS depressants	↑ *CNS depression*	*Monitor for excess sedation*
	Diuretics/antihypertensives	↑ hypotensive effects	Monitor BP
	MAO inhibitors	*With meperidine: agitation, seizures, fever, coma, apnea, death*	*Avoid this combination*
	Phenothiazines	↑ or ↓ effects of opioid analgesic drugs. Hypotension may occur when phenothiazine administered with meperidine	Avoid concurrent use of meperidine and phenothiazines
Chloral hydrate	CNS depressants	Concurrent use may ↑ CNS depressant effects of either drug	Monitor for excess CNS depression
	Anticoagulants, coumarin or indandione-derivative	*Displacement of anticoagulants from its plasma protein ↑ anticoagulant effect*	*Avoid use*
	Catecholamine	Large CH doses may sensitize myocardium to catecholamine	Avoid treating CH overdose with catecholamine
Standard opioids (used for post-operative pain management)	Agonist-antagonist drugs (nalbuphine, butorphanol, pentazocine)	Can lead to withdrawal syndrome or loss of analgesia with hypertension, tachycardia	Never prescribe agonist-antagonist opioids with conventional agonist opioids
	Alcohol	Sedative side effects	Advise patients never to drink alcohol when taking opioids
	Amphetamines	With meperidine: hypotension, respiratory collapse	Do not prescribe meperidine to a patient taking amphetamines
	Anticholinergics	Constipation	Prescribe opioids only for short periods of time; consider MD consultation
	Antidiarrheals	Constipation	Prescribe opioids only for short periods of time; consider MD consultation
	Antihypertensives and vasodilators	Potentiation of hypotensive effects	Advise patients to notify dentist if hypotension or dizziness occurs
	Barbiturates	Sedative side effects	Alert patient to possible additive side effects and to notify dentist if not tolerated

Continued

TABLE 2-2 Dental drug interactions—*cont'd*

Dental drug	Interacting drug	Consideration	Action
	CNS depressants	Sedative side effects	Alert patient to possible additive side effects and to notify dentist if not tolerated
	Hydroxyzine	Sedative side effects	Alert patient to possible additive side effects and to notify dentist if not tolerated
	Hypnotics (sedative)	Sedative side effects	Alert patient to possible additive side effects and to notify dentist if not tolerated
	MAO inhibitors	With meperidine: severe hypertension	Avoid prescribing meperidine to patients taking MAO inhibitors prescribe opioids only for short periods of time; consider MD consultation
	Metoclopramide	Can antagonize metoclopramide	
	Other opioids	Sedative side effects	Avoid prescribing two opioids at one time, unless for chronic pain
NSAIDs	Alcohol	↑ risk of ulceration	Advise patient to avoid if possible
	Oral anticoagulants	↑ risk of bleeding	Advise patient that concurrent use is contraindicated
	Antihypertensives	Effect ↓ by NSAIDs	Monitor BP
	Aspirin	↑ risk of ulceration and bleeding	Advise patient that concurrent use is contraindicated
	NSAIDs other than aspirin	↑ risk of ulceration and bleeding	Avoid this combination
	Corticosteroids	↑ risk of bleeding	Avoid combination, if possible
	Cyclosporin	Can cause nephrotoxicity	Avoid combination, if possible
	Digitalis	↑ digitalis levels	Avoid combination, if possible
	Diuretics (especially triamterene)	Effects ↓ by NSAIDs	Monitor BP/excessive fluid retention
	Heparin	↑ risk of bleeding	Advise patient that concurrent use is contraindicated
	Oral hypoglycemics	Effect ↑ by NSAIDs	Advise patient to monitor blood glucose carefully
	Lithium	Concentration ↑ by NSAIDs	Contraindicated unless approved by MD, so avoid concurrent use
	Potassium supplements	↑ risk of ulceration	Avoid combination, if possible
	Valproic acid	↑ risk of ulceration and bleeding	Avoid combination, if possible
Penicillins and cephalosporins	Allopurinol	Concurrent use with ampicillin, amoxicillin, or amoxicillin with clavulanic acid ↑ incidence of rashes	Monitor for signs of rash and need to change to other antibiotic

TABLE 2-2 Dental drug interactions—*cont'd*

Dental drug	Interacting drug	Consideration	Action
	Oral contraceptives, combined with estrogen and progestin	Sporadic reports of ↓ oral contraceptive effectiveness resulting in unexplained pregnancies	Patient should be advised of the possible ↓ in effectiveness and encouraged to use alternate or additional method of birth control while taking these penicillins
	Probenecid	May ↓ renal tubular secretion of penicillin and cephalosporins resulting in ↑ and prolonged antibiotic blood levels	Monitor patient for any need in adjustment of antibiotic dose
Macrolides	Alfentanil	Prolonged or enhanced respiratory depression with concurrent use of erythromycin	Chronic preoperative and postoperative use of erythromycin contraindicated
	Carbamazepine	↑ risk of ataxia, vertigo, drowsiness, and confusion with concurrent use of erythromycin or clarithromycin	If used concurrently, must be done with great caution
	Cyclosporine	*↑ immunosuppression and nephrotoxicity with concurrent use of erythromycin or clarithromycin*	*Concurrent use of these drugs is contraindicated*
	Digoxin	*Erythromycin can lead to ↑ digoxin blood levels leading to digitalis toxicity with resulting cardiac dysrhythmias*	*Concurrent use of these drugs is contraindicated*
		Clarithromycin is also reported to lead to elevated digoxin levels	
	Felodipine	*↑ risk of hypotension, tachycardia and edema with concurrent use of erythromycin*	*Concurrent use of these drugs is contraindicated*
	Lovastatin	*Muscle pain and skeletal muscle lysis with concurrent use of erythromycin*	*Concurrent use of these drugs is contraindicated*
	Oral contraceptives with estrogen and progestin	Sporadic reports of ↓ oral contraceptive effectiveness resulting in unexplained pregnancies	Patient should be advised of the possible ↓ in effectiveness and encouraged to use alternate or additional method of birth control while taking these macrolides
	Theophylline	*↑ risk of tachycardia, cardiac dysrhythmias, tremors, and seizures reported with concurrent use of erythromycin or clarithromycin*	*Concurrent use of these drugs is contraindicated*

Continued

TABLE 2-2 Dental drug interactions—*cont'd*

Dental drug	Interacting drug	Consideration	Action
	Triazolam or midazolam	*Marked ↑ in blood levels of both BZDs leading to ↑ depth of sedation and duration reported with concurrent use of erythromycin*	*Concurrent use of these drugs is contraindicated*
	Warfarin	Erythromycin and clarithromycin ↓ metabolism of warfarin and may significantly ↑ prothrombin and/or INR times and ↑ risk of serious bleeding in patients receiving anticoagulation therapy	Warfarin dosage adjustments may be necessary during and after therapy, and prothrombin or INR times should be monitored closely
Tetracyclines	Combinations containing any of the following: antacids, calcium, magnesium, aluminum, iron supplements, sodium bicarbonate	Tetracycline molecules chelate divalent and trivalent cations, impairing absorption	Advise patients against taking these medications within 1–3 h of taking oral tetracycline
	Digoxin	*Tetracyclines may lead to ↑ digoxin blood levels, leading to digitalis toxicity with resulting cardiac dysrhythmias* *Clarithromycin has also been reported to result in ↑ digoxin blood levels*	*Concurrent use of these drugs is contraindicated*
	Oral contraceptives, estrogen and progestin combined	Reports of ↓ oral contraceptive effectiveness in women taking tetracyclines resulting in unplanned pregnancy	Patients should be advised of the possible reduction in the effectiveness and encouraged to use an alternate or additional method of contraception while taking tetracyclines
	Warfarin	Tetracycline may ↓ metabolism of warfarin and may significantly ↑ prothrombin and/or INR times and ↑ risk of serious bleeding in patients receiving anticoagulation therapy	Warfarin dosage adjustments may be necessary during and after therapy, and prothrombin or INR times should be monitored closely
Clindamycin	Antidiarrheals	Concurrent use of clindamycin and antidiarrheals containing kaolin or attapulgite may delay absorption of oral clindamycin	Concurrent use is contraindicated; otherwise patients should be advised to take absorbent antidiarrheals not less than 2 h before or 3–4 h after taking oral clindamycin
	Narcotic analgesics	Concurrent use with clindamycin may lead to ↑ or prolonged respiratory depression or apnea	If concurrent use of these drugs is necessary, caution and careful monitoring of respiration are indicated
	Neuromuscular blocking agents	Concurrent use with clindamycin may enhance neuromuscular blockade, resulting in skeletal muscle weakness and respiratory depression or apnea	Avoid concurrent use; if use is necessary, carefully monitor patient for muscle weakness or respiratory depression

TABLE 2-2 Dental drug interactions—*cont'd*

Dental drug	Interacting drug	Consideration	Action
Metronidazole	Alcohol	Combination may produce a disulfiram effect, leading to facial flushing, headache, palpitations, and nausea	Concurrent use is contra-indicated, and use should be delayed at least 1 day after ingestion of alcohol
	Anticoagulants	Coumarin or indandione-derived anticoagulants may be potentiated by metronidazole resulting in ↑ prothrombin or INR times	Anticoagulant adjustments may be necessary in consultation with MD
	Cimetidine, phenobarbital, phenytoin	*Hepatic clearance rates may be affected by concurrent use of metronidazole*	*Concurrent use of these drugs is contraindicated*
	Disulfiram	*In alcoholic patients, psychotic reactions have been reported in concurrent use to within 2 weeks of use of disulfiram*	*Concurrent use of these drugs is contraindicated*
Ciprofloxacin	*Aminophylline, oxtriphylline, or theophylline*	*Concurrent use of these drugs and ciprofloxacin may result in ↑ risk of theophylline-related toxicity with serious life-threatening reactions*	*Concurrent use of these drugs is contraindicated*
	Antacids containing aluminum, calcium, or magnesium; laxatives containing magnesium	*Absorption of ciprofloxacin may be ↓ through chelation by these drugs*	*Concurrent use of these drugs is contraindicated*
	Caffeine	*Concurrent use of caffeine and ciprofloxacin may ↓ the metabolism of caffeine resulting in CNS stimulation*	*Concurrent use of these drugs is contraindicated*
	Cyclosporine	Concurrent use of ciprofloxacin has been reported to ↑ serum creatinine and serum cyclosporine concentrations	Cyclosporine concentrations should be monitored and dosage adjustments may be required
	Vitamin or mineral supplements containing ferrous sulfate or zinc	*Absorption of ciprofloxacin may be ↓ through chelation by these agents*	*Concurrent use of these agents is contraindicated*
	Warfarin	Concurrent use of warfarin and ciprofloxacin has been reported to ↑ the anti-coagulant effect of warfarin, ↑ the risk of bleeding	The prothrombin time or INR of patients receiving warfarin and ciprofloxacin should be carefully monitored
Trimethoprim and sulfamethoxazole	Coumarin or indanedione-derived anticoagulants	Concurrent use may prolong the patients prothrombin time or INR and lead to bleeding	Prothrombin time or INR of patients concurrently taking these drugs should be monitored carefully
	Hydantoin anticonvulsants	*Concurrent use may lead to excessive phenytoin serum levels*	*Concurrent use of these drugs is contraindicated*
	Thiazide diuretics	Elderly patients taking thiazide diuretics have an ↑ risk of thrombocytopenia if these drugs are taken concurrently	If these drugs are taken concurrently, platelet counts and clinical signs of purpura should be carefully monitored

CVS, cardiovascular system; CNS, central nervous system; BP, blood pressure; BZD, benzodiazepine; CH, chloral hydrate; INR, International Normalized Ratio. *Drug-drug interactions of greater clinical significance are italicized and emboldened for emphasis.*
From Ciancio SG: ADA guide to dental therapeutics, 3rd ed, Chicago, American Dental Association, Chicago, 2003. Copyright © 2003 American Dental Association. All rights reserved. Excerpted 2007 with permission.

2. Are you now under the care of a medical doctor? If so, what is the condition being treated?
3. Are you currently taking any drugs, medications, or over-the-counter products?

If any of these questions elicits a positive response, a detailed dialogue history should follow. For example, a patient may answer that no change has occurred in general health but may want to notify the doctor of a minor change in condition, such as the end of a pregnancy or the recent diagnosis of type 2 diabetes or asthma.

In either situation a written record of having updated the history should be entered into the patient's progress notes or on the health history form. When the patient's health status has changed significantly since the last history was completed, the entire history should be redone (e.g., if a patient was recently diagnosed with cardiovascular disease and is managing it with a variety of drugs not previously prescribed).

In reality, most persons do not undergo significant changes in their health with any regularity. Thus, one health history questionnaire can remain current for many years and the ability to demonstrate that a patient's medical history has been updated on a regular basis becomes all the more important.

The medical history questionnaire should be completed in ink. The doctor makes a correction or deletion by drawing a single line through the original entry without obliterating it. The change is then added along with the date of the change. The doctor initials the change. A written notation should be placed in the chart whenever a patient reveals significant information during the dialogue history. As an example, when a patient answers affirmatively to the question about a heart attack, the doctor's notation may read "2006" (the year the myocardial infarction occurred).

Physical examination

As important as the patient-completed medical history questionnaire is in the overall assessment of a patient's physical and psychological status, it does have limitations. For the health history to be of value, patients must (1) be aware of their state of health and of any existing medical conditions and (2) be willing to share this information with their dentist.

Most patients do not knowingly deceive the dentist by omitting important information from their medical history questionnaires. However, such deceptions have been recorded. For example, a patient who sought treatment for an acutely inflamed tooth decided to withhold from his doctor the fact that he had suffered a myocardial infarction 2 months earlier because he knew that to inform the doctor of this would probably mean that the desired treatment would not be carried out.[17]

The more likely cause of unintentional misinformation is that the patient is unaware that a problem exists. Many "healthy" persons do not visit their physicians for regular checkups. In fact, recent information suggests that annual medical visits be discontinued in healthy patients younger than 40 years because the annual physical examination has not proven as valuable an aid in preventive medicine as researchers once believed.[18]

Most people simply do not visit their physicians on a regular basis, doing so only when they feel ill. Therefore, both the patient and the doctor may be unaware of an existing medical disorder. Simply because the person feels good does not mean that he or she is necessarily in good health. Many disorders can be present in subclinical states for months or years without presenting any overt signs or symptoms. When such signs and symptoms, such as shortness of breath or undue fatigue, do occur, patients frequently mistake them for more benign problems.

The first few questions on most history forms establish the length of time since a patient's last physical examination. The doctor can gauge the value of answers to the questions dealing with specific diseases in sections III and IV. The more recent the patient's latest physical examination, the more valuable are the answers on the medical history questionnaire. Because of these problems, patient-completed medical history questionnaires are not always reliable. The doctor must seek additional sources for information concerning the patient's physical status. The physical examination provides much of this information. Physical examination in dentistry consists of the following steps:

- Monitoring of vital signs
- Visual inspection of the patient
- Function tests as indicated
- Auscultation, monitoring (via electrocardiogram), and laboratory tests of the heart and lungs as indicated

Minimal physical evaluation of prospective patients should consist of measurement of the vital signs and a visual inspection of the patient. The primary value of this examination is that it provides the doctor with important current information about the patient's physical status, whereas the questionnaire provides historical, anecdotal information.

Physical examination should be completed at an initial visit before the actual start of dental treatment. Vital signs obtained at this preliminary appointment, known as *baseline* vital signs, serve two functions. First, they help to determine a patient's ability to tolerate the stress involved in the planned treatment. Second, baseline vital signs are used as a standard during the management of emergency situations in comparison with readings obtained during the emergency.

Vital signs

The six vital signs are as follows:

1. Blood pressure
2. Heart rate (pulse) and rhythm
3. Respiratory rate
4. Temperature
5. Height
6. Weight

Baseline vital signs should be obtained before the start of dental treatment. Although the screaming 3-year-old and the difficult-to-manage disabled adult may present difficulties, the doctor should make every effort to record baseline vital signs for each patient.

Blood pressure and heart rate and rhythm always should be recorded when possible. Respiratory rate also should be evaluated whenever possible but usually must be assessed surreptitiously. Temperature recording may be part of the routine evaluation but more often is done in situations in which it is deemed necessary (e.g., when infection is present or the patient appears feverish). Height and weight may be obtained in most instances by asking the patient but should be measured when the response appears inconsistent with visual appearance. Weight is of considerable importance when parenteral (IM or IN) or enteral (oral) sedation is to be used.

The following information provides techniques for the recording and interpretation of vital signs.

Blood pressure

The following technique is recommended for the accurate determination of blood pressure.[19] A stethoscope and sphygmomanometer (blood pressure cuff) are necessary (Figure 2-8). The aneroid manometer, the most frequently used, is calibrated to show results in millimeters of mercury (mm Hg or torr) and is also quite accurate if well maintained. Rough handling of the aneroid manometer can lead to erroneous readings. The aneroid manometer should be recalibrated at least annually, checked against a mercury manometer.

Automatic blood pressure monitoring devices have become available primarily for home monitoring. The earliest such device lacked accuracy, sensitivity, and reliability; however, many newer devices now possess all three qualities. Their costs range from well under $100 (Figure 2-9) to several thousands of dollars (Figure 2-10). (All values are in U.S. dollars.)

For the routine preoperative monitoring of blood pressure, the patient should be seated in an upright position. The patient's arm should rest at the level of the heart, relaxed, slightly flexed, and supported on a firm surface. The patient should be permitted to rest at least

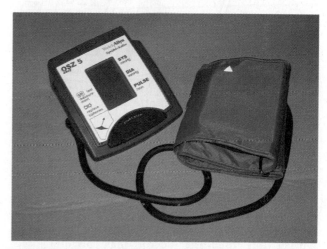

FIGURE 2-9 Automatic blood pressure cuff for home use. (Courtesy Sedation Resource, Lone Oak, Texas, www.sedationresource.com)

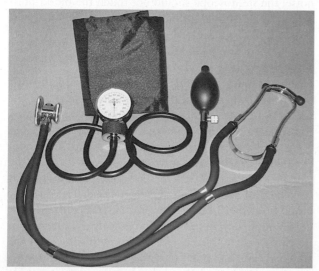

FIGURE 2-8 Aneroid blood pressure cuff and stethoscope. (Courtesy Sedation Resource, Lone Oak, Texas, www.sedationresource.com)

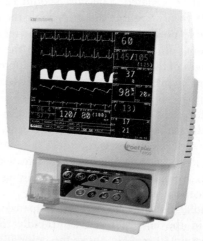

FIGURE 2-10 Monitor used in operating room, includes blood pressure. (Courtesy CritiCare Systems, Inc., Waukesha, Wisconsin.)

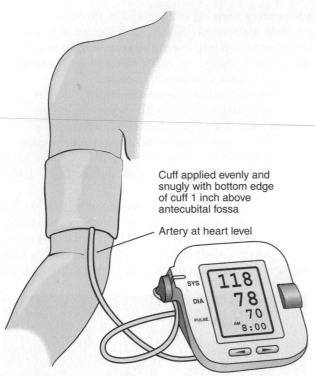

Cuff applied evenly and snugly with bottom edge of cuff 1 inch above antecubital fossa

Artery at heart level

SYS
118
DIA
78
PULSE
70
AM
8:00

FIGURE 2-11 Proper placement of the blood pressure cuff (sphygmomanometer). (Redrawn from Burch GE, DePasquale NP: *Primer of clinical measurement of blood pressure*, St. Louis, Mosby, 1962.)

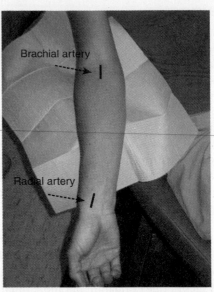

Brachial artery

Radial artery

FIGURE 2-12 Location of the brachial and radial arteries. The brachial artery is located on the medial half of the antecubital fossa, whereas the radial artery is on the lateral volar aspect of the wrist.

5 minutes before the blood pressure is recorded. This permits the patient to relax so that the blood pressure recorded is closer to the patient's usual baseline reading. During this time the doctor may perform other noninvasive procedures, such as a review of the medical history questionnaire.

Before it is placed on the arm, the blood pressure cuff should be deflated. The cuff should be wrapped evenly and firmly around the arm, with the center of the inflatable portion over the brachial artery and the rubber tubing along the medial aspect of the arm. The lower margin of the cuff should be placed approximately 1 inch (2 to 3 cm) above the antecubital fossa. A cuff is too tight if two fingers cannot fit under the lower edge of the cuff. A tight cuff decreases venous return from the arm, which results in erroneous measurements (elevated diastolic pressure). A cuff is too loose (a more frequent problem) if it can be pulled off the arm with only a gentle tug. A slight resistance should be present when a cuff is properly applied (Figure 2-11).

The radial pulse in the wrist is palpated while the pressure in the cuff is increased rapidly to a point approximately 30 mm Hg above the point at which the radial pulse disappears. The cuff should then be deflated slowly at 2 to 3 mm Hg per second until the radial pulse

reappears. This is called *palpatory systolic pressure*. Pressure in the cuff then should be released.

Determination of blood pressure by the more accurate auscultatory method requires palpation of the brachial artery, which is located on the medial aspect of the antecubital fossa (Figure 2-12). The earpieces of the stethoscope should be placed facing forward firmly in the recorder's ears. The diaphragm of the stethoscope must be placed firmly on the medial aspect of the antecubital fossa, over the brachial artery. To reduce noise, the stethoscope should not touch the blood pressure cuff or rubber tubing. The blood pressure cuff should be inflated rapidly to a level 30 mm Hg above the previously determined palpatory systolic pressure. Pressure in the cuff should be released gradually (2 to 3 mm Hg per second) until the first sound is heard through the stethoscope. A light tapping sound is heard as the pressure decreases. This first sound is the systolic blood pressure.

As the cuff deflates further, the sound undergoes changes in quality and intensity (Figure 2-13). As the cuff pressure approaches the diastolic pressure, sounds become dull and muffled and then cease. The diastolic blood pressure can be determined best when the sounds cease completely. In some instances, however, the sounds do not stop completely. Thus, the point at which the sounds become muffled serves as the diastolic pressure. The cuff should be deflated slowly to a point 10 mm Hg beyond the point of disappearance and then totally deflated.

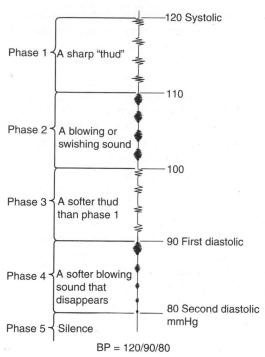

Phase 1 — A sharp "thud" — 120 Systolic

Phase 2 — A blowing or swishing sound — 110

Phase 3 — A softer thud than phase 1 — 100

Phase 4 — A softer blowing sound that disappears — 90 First diastolic

Phase 5 — Silence — 80 Second diastolic mmHg

BP = 120/90/80

FIGURE 2-13 Korotkoff sounds. Systolic blood pressure is recorded during the first phase, and diastolic blood pressure is recorded at the point in which sound disappears (fifth phase). (From Burch GE, DePasquale NP: *Primer of clinical measurement of blood pressure*, St. Louis, Mosby, 1962.)

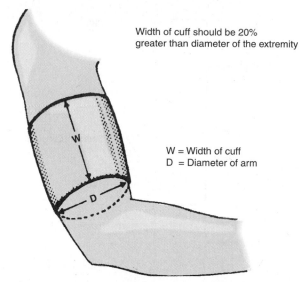

Width of cuff should be 20% greater than diameter of the extremity

W = Width of cuff
D = Diameter of arm

FIGURE 2-14 Determination of the proper size of a blood pressure cuff. (Modified from Burch GE, DePasquale NP: *Primer of clinical measurement of blood pressure*, St. Louis, Mosby, 1962.)

If additional recordings are necessary, at least 15 seconds should elapse before the cuff is reinflated. This time period allows blood trapped in the arm to flow elsewhere, providing a more accurate reading. Blood pressure is recorded on the patient's chart or sedation and anesthesia record as a fraction—130/90 R (right) or L (left) depending on the arm used to obtain the reading.

Awareness of the errors involved in proper blood pressure recording decreases the likelihood of unnecessary medical consultation, which can burden the patient financially and cause patients to lose faith in their dentist. Some relatively common errors associated with the recording of blood pressure include the following:

- Loose application of the blood pressure cuff provides false elevated readings, which are probably the most common errors.
- Use of the wrong cuff size can result in erroneous readings. A normal adult blood pressure cuff placed on an obese patient's arm produces falsely elevated readings. This same cuff applied to the arm of a child or a thin adult produces falsely decreased readings. Sphygmomanometers are available in many sizes. The width of the compression cuff should be approximately 20% greater than the diameter of the extremity on which the blood pressure is being recorded (Figure 2-14). Doctors

may want to keep handy a pediatric cuff and a thigh cuff in addition to the adult cuff.

- An *auscultatory gap* may occur. This gap represents a loss of sound between systolic and diastolic pressures, with the sound reappearing at a lower level (Figure 2-15). For example, systolic sounds are noted at 230 mm Hg; however, the sound then disappears at 198 mm Hg, reappearing at approximately 160 mm Hg. All sound is lost at 90 mm Hg. If the person taking the blood pressure has not palpated (estimated) the systolic blood pressure before auscultation, the cuff may be inflated to some arbitrary pressure, such as 165 mm Hg. At this pressure, no sound is heard because the value lies within the auscultatory gap. Sounds are first noticed at 160 mm Hg and disappear at 90 mm Hg, levels well within treatment limits for adults (Table 2-3). In reality, however, this patient's blood pressure is 230/90, a significantly elevated pressure that represents a greater risk to the patient during dental care. Although the auscultatory gap occurs infrequently, the possibility of error can be eliminated through use of the palpatory technique. A pulse is palpable in the gap even when the sound disappears. Although the auscultatory gap has no pathologic significance, it is found most often in patients with high blood pressure.
- The patient may be anxious. Anxiety can cause transient elevations in blood pressure, primarily systolic pressure. Such an elevation is even more likely in the patient who is scheduled to undergo sedation to manage dental fears. Thus, baseline vital

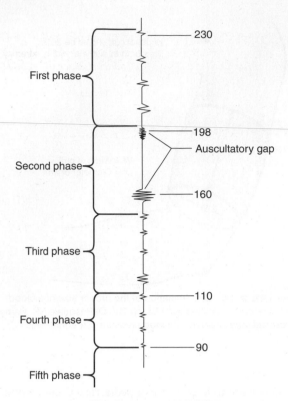

Blood pressure 230/110/90

FIGURE 2-15 Korotkoff sounds, illustrating an auscultatory gap. Sound is heard at 230 mm Hg, disappears at 198 mm Hg, and reappears at 160 mm Hg. All sound is lost (fifth phase) at 90 mm Hg. (From Burch GE, DePasquale NP: *Primer of clinical measurement of blood pressure*, St. Louis, Mosby, 1962.)

signs should be taken during a visit before the start of dental treatment, perhaps at the initial office visit when vital sign measurements should be closer to the patient's "normal."

- Blood pressure is based on the Korotkoff sounds produced by the passage of blood through obstructed, partially obstructed, or unobstructed arteries (see Figure 2-13). Watching a mercury column or needle on an aneroid manometer for pulsations leads to the recording of falsely elevated systolic pressures. These pulsations are observed approximately 10 to 15 mm Hg before the initial Korotkoff sounds are heard.
- Use of the right or left arm produces differences in recorded blood pressure. A difference of 5 to 10 mm Hg exists between the arms, with the left arm producing slightly higher measurements.

Guidelines for clinical evaluation. The University of Southern California (USC) physical evaluation system is based on the ASA physical status classification system,

which classifies patients into five risk categories based on their medical history and physical evaluation (see p. 51). Table 2-3 presents blood pressure recordings by ASA classifications.

Adult patients with blood pressure in the ASA I range (<140/<90 mm Hg) should have their blood pressures re-recorded every 6 months unless specific dental procedures mandate more frequent monitoring. Enteral, parenteral, or inhalation routes of drug administration require more frequent recording of vital signs. Ideally, the administration of local anesthesia should be preceded by monitoring of the blood pressure. Patients whose blood pressure places them into the ASA II, III, or IV categories for blood pressure should be monitored more frequently. Patients with known high blood pressure should have their blood pressure monitored at each dental visit to assess whether the blood pressure is being adequately controlled.

If these recommendations are adhered to, the routine monitoring of blood pressure in all dental patients can minimize the occurrence of acute complications associated with elevations of blood pressure (e.g., CVA and chest pain). When enteral, parenteral, or inhalation sedation techniques or general anesthesia are employed, a greater need exists for baseline and preoperative vital sign recording. A comparison of postoperative and baseline vital signs helps the doctor assess a patient's recovery from the effects of CNS depressants and readiness for discharge.

Yet another reason the routine monitoring of blood pressure should be emphasized relates to the management of medical emergencies. After assessment and management in each emergency are completed, certain specific steps may be necessary for definitive treatment. Primary among these is the monitoring of vital signs, particularly blood pressure. Blood pressure recorded during an emergency situation is an important indicator of the status of the cardiovascular system. However, unless a baseline (nonemergency) blood pressure had been previously recorded, the measurement obtained during the emergency is of less significance. A reading during an emergency of 80/50 mm Hg is less dire if the preoperative blood pressure was 110/70 mm Hg than if it was 190/110 mm Hg. In all situations, absence of a recordable blood pressure is an indication for cardiopulmonary resuscitation.

Normal blood pressure values in younger patients are lower than those in adults. Table 2-4 presents normal ranges of blood pressure for infants and children.

Heart rate and rhythm

Heart rate (pulse) and rhythm can be measured through palpation of any readily accessible artery. Most com-

TABLE 2-3 Guidelines for blood pressure in adults

Blood pressure (mm Hg or torr)	ASA classification	Dental therapy considerations
<140 and <90	I	1. Observe routine dental management. 2. Recheck in 6 months.
140 to 159 and/or 90 to 94	II	1. Recheck blood pressure before dental treatment for three consecutive appointments; if all measurements exceed these guidelines, medical consultation is recommended. 2. Observe routine dental management. 3. Implement stress reduction protocol as indicated.
160 to 199 and/or 95 to 114	III	1. Recheck blood pressure in 5 minutes. 2. If still elevated, perform medical consultation before beginning dental therapy. 3. Observe routine dental therapy. 4. Implement stress reduction protocol.
>200 and/or >115	IV	1. Recheck blood pressure in 5 minutes. 2. Perform immediate medical consultation if pressure is still elevated. 3. Do not perform dental therapy, routine or emergency,* until elevated blood pressure is corrected. 4. Perform emergency dental therapy with drugs (analgesics, antibiotics). 5. Refer to hospital if immediate dental therapy indicated.

[handwritten] 60 + old

[handwritten] ASA (I) w Anxiety / Pregnancy

*When the blood pressure of the patient is slightly above the cutoff for category IV and when anxiety is present, the use of inhalation sedation may diminish the blood pressure (via the elimination of stress) below the 200/115 level. The patient should be advised that if the nitrous oxide and oxygen succeeds in decreasing the blood pressure below this level, the planned treatment can proceed. However, if the blood pressure remains elevated, the planned procedure must be postponed until the elevated blood pressure has been lowered to a more acceptable range.

monly employed for routine (nonemergency) measurement are the brachial artery, located on the medial aspect of the antecubital fossa, and the radial artery, located on the radial and volar aspects of the wrist. Other arteries, such as the carotid and femoral, can also be used but rarely are in routine situations because they are not as accessible. In emergency situations the carotid artery should be palpated in lieu of others because it delivers oxygenated blood to the brain. Prompt and accurate palpation of this artery is essential in emergency situations. (Locating the carotid artery [in the neck] is reviewed in Chapter 5.)

When palpating for a pulse, the doctor should press the fleshy portions of the index and middle fingers onto the patient's skin gently enough to feel the pulsation but not so firmly that the pressure occludes the artery. The thumb should not be used to monitor a pulse because it contains its own artery that pulsates. Situations have arisen in which the measured heart rate has been the doctor's, not the victim's. Furthermore, in the infant the precordium is no longer recommended as the site to determine the presence of an effective heartbeat.[20,21] The brachial artery in the upper arm is the preferred site (see Figure 2-13).[21]

Guidelines for clinical evaluation. The following three factors should be assessed when heart rate and rhythm are monitored:
1. Heart rate (recorded as beats per minute)
2. Heart rhythm (regular or irregular)
3. Pulse quality (thready, strong, bounding, or weak)

The heart rate should be evaluated for a minimum of 30 seconds, ideally for 1 minute. The normal resting heart rate for an adult ranges from 60 to 110 beats per minute. This rate is frequently lower in well-conditioned athletes and elevated in apprehensive patients. However, clinically significant pathologic processes can also produce slow (<60 = bradycardia) or rapid (>110 = tachycardia) heart rates. Any adult heart rate below 60 or above 110 beats per minute should receive further evaluation. When no obvious cause for the deviation in rate is discernible (e.g., the absence of a history of participation in endurance sports or the presence of anxiety), medical consultation should be considered.

The normal heart maintains a relatively regular rhythm, known as a *normal sinus rhythm* or NSR (Figure 2-16). Occasional premature ventricular contractions (PVCs) are so common that they are not necessarily considered abnormal (Figure 2-17). Smoking, fatigue, stress, various

TABLE 2-4 Normal pediatric blood pressure measurements*

Age (yr)	Mean systolic ± 2 SD (mm Hg)	Mean diastolic ± 2 SD (mm Hg)
Newborn	80 ± 16	46 ± 16
6 mo–1 yr	89 ± 29	60 ± 10[†]
1	96 ± 30	66 ± 25[†]
2	99 ± 25	64 ± 25[†]
3	100 ± 25	67 ± 23[†]
4	99 ± 20	65 ± 20[†]
5–6	94 ± 14	55 ± 9
6–7	100 ± 15	56 ± 8
7–8	102 ± 15	56 ± 8
8–9	105 ± 16	57 ± 9
9–10	107 ± 16	57 ± 9
10–11	111 ± 17	58 ± 10
11–12	113 ± 18	59 ± 10
12–13	115 ± 19	59 ± 10
13–14	118 ± 19	60 ± 10

SD, Standard deviation.
*Modified from data in the literature; figures have been rounded off to the nearest decimal place.
[†]In this study the point of muffling was taken as the diastolic pressure.
From Nadas AS, Fyler DC: *Pediatric cardiology,* ed 3, Philadelphia, WB Saunders, 1972.

medications (such as epinephrine), and alcohol can all produce PVCs. However, when PVCs are present at a rate of five or more per minute in a patient with other risk factors for coronary artery disease, medical consultation should be considered. When the pulse is palpated, PVCs are detected clinically as breaks in a generally regular heart rate in which a longer than normal pause (e.g., "my heart skipped a beat") is noted and followed by resumption of normal rhythm.

In reality, a PVC represents contraction of the ventricles (specifically the left ventricle) before enough blood is present in their chambers to produce a pulse wave in a peripheral artery. Unusually frequent PVCs (more than five per minute in a patient with other cardiovascular disease risk factors) indicate myocardial irritability and may presage severe dysrhythmias,* such as ventricular fibrillation (Figure 2-18).

Indeed, patients with more PVCs are considered to be prime candidates for implanted cardioverter/defibrillators.

A second significant disturbance in pulse is *pulsus alternans.* Pulsus alternans is not truly a dysrhythmia but a regular heart rate characterized by a pulse in which strong and weak beats alternate. The alternating contractile force of a diseased left ventricle produces the disturbance. Pulsus alternans is observed frequently in left ventricular failure, severe arterial high blood pressure, and coronary artery disease. When pulsus alternans is present, medical consultation is indicated.

Accurate diagnosis of a cardiac dysrhythmia via palpation of an artery alone is difficult if not impossible. However, consultation with the patient's physician and possible testing (e.g., electrocardiography, Holter monitor) helps to determine the nature of the dysrhythmia and its significance to the planned dental treatment.

The quality of the pulse is commonly described as "bounding," "thready," "strong," or "weak." These adjectives relate to the "feel" of the pulse and are used to describe different conditions. For example, a patient with severe arterial high blood pressure may exhibit a "strong, bounding" pulse, whereas the pulse of a patient with hypotension and signs of shock may be described as "weak and thready." Table 2-5 demonstrates the normal heart rates for children, which are more rapid than those of adults.

Respiratory rate

The respiratory rate must usually be assessed surreptitiously. Patients aware that their breathing is being observed usually do not breathe normally. For that reason, respiration should be monitored immediately after the heart rate is obtained. The person recording vital signs should keep their fingers on the patient's radial or brachial pulse after they have assessed the heart rate counting respirations by observing the rise and fall of the patients chest for a minimum of 30 seconds (ideally for 1 minute).

Guidelines for clinical evaluation. The normal adult respiratory rate is 16 to 18 breaths per minute. Bradypnea (slow rate of breathing) may be produced by opioid administration, while tachypnea (rapid rate of breathing) is seen with fever and alkalosis. The most commonly noted change in breathing in dentistry is hyperventilation, an abnormal increase in both the rate and depth of breathing that almost always is a manifestation of anxiety. Hyperventilation also is seen in patients with diabetic acidosis. Extreme psychologic stress is

---

*The terms *dysrhythmia* and *arrhythmia* are used interchangeably to describe irregularities in the heart's rhythm. In fact, the term *dysrhythmia* is the more correct because the prefix *dys* means "abnormal"; thus, a *dysrhythmia* is an abnormal rhythm. The prefix *a* means the "absence of"; thus, *arrhythmia* describes the absence of a rhythm, or asystole (a flat line on an electrocardiogram).

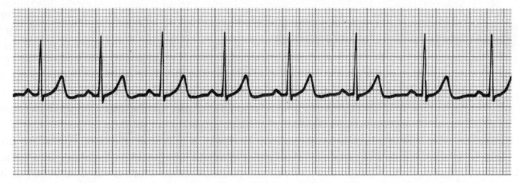

FIGURE 2-16 Normal sinus rhythm. (From Berne RM, Levy MN: *Physiology*, ed 4, St. Louis, Mosby, 1998.)

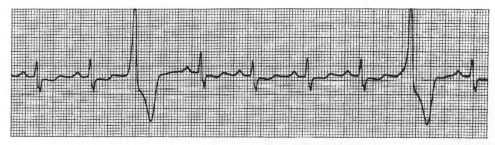

FIGURE 2-17 The third and eighth complexes show unifocal premature ventricular contractions. (From Zalis EG, Conover MH: *Understanding electrocardiography: physiological and interpretive concepts*, St. Louis, Mosby, 1972.)

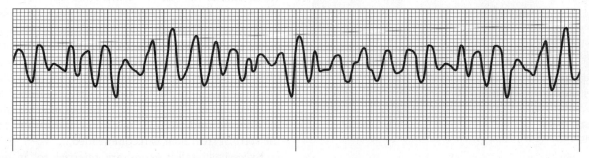

FIGURE 2-18 Ventricular fibrillation. (From McSwain NE: *The basic EMT: comprehensive hospital care,* ed 2, St. Louis, Mosby, 2003.)

TABLE 2-5 Average heart rates for children

Age (yr)	Lower limit of normal	Average	Upper limit of normal
Newborn	70	120	170
1–11 months	80	120	160
2	80	110	130
4	80	100	120
6	75	100	115
8	70	90	110
10	70	90	110

*Heart rates are expressed as beats per minute.
From Behrman RE, Vaughn VC, III: *Nelson textbook of pediatrics,* ed 12, Philadelphia, WB Saunders, 1983.

the most common reason for hyperventilation in dental settings.

Any significant variation in respiratory rate or depth should be fully evaluated before the start of dental treatment. The absence of spontaneous ventilation is always abnormal and is an indication for artificial ventilation. Table 2-6 presents the normal range of respiratory rates for different age groups.

Blood pressure, heart rate and rhythm, and respiratory rate all provide information about the status of the patient's cardiorespiratory system. These measurements should be recorded as an integral part of the routine physical evaluation of all prospective patients. Recording of the remaining vital signs—temperature, height, and weight—is desirable but optional. However, in cases in which parenteral drugs (e.g., CNS depressants, local

TABLE 2-6 Respiratory rates by age

Age (yr)	Breaths/minute
Neonate	40
1 week	30
1	24
3	22
5	20
8	18
12	16
21	12

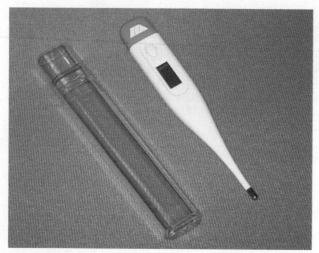

FIGURE 2-19 Digital thermometer. (Courtesy Sedation Resource, Lone Oak, Texas, www.sedationresource.com)

anesthetics) are to be administered, especially in lighter-weight, younger patients, recording a patient's weight is of considerable importance.

Temperature

Temperature should be monitored orally if possible. The thermometer, sterilized and shaken down, is placed under the tongue of the patient, who should not eat, smoke, or drink anything 10 minutes before the recording. The thermometer remains in the closed mouth for 2 minutes before removal. Disposable thermometers and digital thermometers (Figure 2-19) have become more popular and commonplace today.

Guidelines for clinical evaluation. The normal oral temperature of 37° C (98.2° F) is merely an average. The true normal range encompasses 36.1° to 37.5° C (97° to 99.6° F). Body temperature varies slightly, from

0.25° to 1.1° C (0.5° to 2.0° F), throughout the day; temperature is lowest in the early morning and highest in the late afternoon. Fever represents an increase in temperature beyond 37.5° C (99.6° F). Temperatures above 38.3° C (101° F) usually indicate the presence of an active pathologic process.

The cause of the fever must be determined before dental treatment begins. If the fever is thought to be related to a dental infection, immediate treatment and antibiotic and antipyretic therapy are indicated. If the patient's temperature is 40° C (104° F) or higher, prior medical consultation is suggested. With elevated temperature, elective dental care is contraindicated and treatment limited to drug administration (antibiotics and antipyretics) because the patient is less able than usual to tolerate additional stress.

Height and weight

Patients are asked for their height and weight, two variable measurements. Numerous insurance companies have developed charts of normal height and weight ranges available for doctors' offices.

Guidelines for clinical evaluation. Patients at either end of the normal distribution curve for height and weight should be screened carefully. Gross obesity or extreme underweight may indicate the presence of an active pathologic process. Patients with various endocrine disorders, such as Cushing's syndrome, may be obese; those with pulmonary tuberculosis, malignancy, the latter stages of AIDS, and hyperthyroidism may be extremely underweight. In all instances of gross obesity or extreme underweight, medical consultation before the start of treatment is recommended.

Excessively tall persons are referred to as *giants,* whereas persons who are decidedly shorter than normal are called *dwarfs.* In both instances, endocrine gland dysfunction may be present. Medical consultation relative to the planned dental treatment is usually unnecessary.

Visual inspection

Visual observation of the patient can provide the doctor with additional information about the patient's physical status and degree of anxiety. Observation of a person's posture, body movements, speech, and skin may help the doctor detect disorders that may previously have gone unnoticed.

Persons with CHF and chronic pulmonary disorders often must sit more upright in the dental chair than other patients because of severe orthopnea (e.g., three- or four-pillow orthopnea). Arthritic patients with a rigid neck may need to rotate their entire trunk when turning toward the doctor or when viewing an object from the side. Recognition of these factors better enables the doctor to determine necessary treatment modifications.

In addition, involuntary body movements occurring in conscious patients may indicate significant disorders. Tremor may be noted in disorders such as fatigue, multiple sclerosis, parkinsonism, and hyperthyroidism, as well as hysteria and nervous tension (the latter being prominent in dental settings).

The character of a patient's speech may also be significant. A CVA can cause muscle paralysis leading to speech difficulties. Epileptic patients receiving long-term antiepileptic drug therapy may demonstrate sluggish speech patterns. Anxiety about the impending dental treatment also can be detected in speech. Rapid response to questions or nervous voice quivers can indicate increased anxiety and the possible need for sedation during dental treatment.

Other possible disorders can be detected from the presence of specific, nondental odors on the patient's breath. Patients with diabetic acidosis and ketosis often have the sweet, fruity odor of acetone on their breath, whereas uremic patients often emit the smell of ammonia. The most likely breath odor detectable in a dental patient is that of alcohol, the presence of which should alert the doctor to the likely presence of heightened anxiety or of drug abuse.

The feel and color of the patient's skin are other important sources of information. The doctor can learn a great deal by greeting patients with a welcoming handshake. The skin of a very apprehensive person is cold and wet; that of a patient who is hyperthyroid is warm and wet; while that of a patient in diabetic acidosis is warm and dry. The color of a patient's skin also is significant. Pallor (a loss of color) can indicate anemia or heightened anxiety (i.e., presyncope). Cyanosis indicates inadequate oxygenation and may be seen in the presence of heart failure, chronic pulmonary disease, methemoglobinemia, or polycythemia. Cyanosis is most noticeable in the nail beds and mucous membranes (lips). Flushed skin may suggest apprehension, hyperthyroidism, or elevated temperature, whereas the presence of a yellowish cast to the skin (jaundice) may indicate past or present hepatic disease. However, each of these observations may also have a benign explanation that should always be considered.

Additional factors revealed through visual examination include (1) the presence of prominent jugular veins in a patient seated upright, an indication of possible right ventricular failure (or of an overly tight collar on a shirt); (2) clubbing of the fingers, which may indicate chronic cardiopulmonary disease; (3) swelling of the ankles, seen in cases of right ventricular failure, varicose veins, renal disease, and occasionally near-term pregnancy; and (4) exophthalmos, which can indicate hyperthyroidism. (Each such finding is discussed more thoroughly in the prevention section within specific chapters.)

For a more thorough discussion of the art of observation and its importance in medical diagnosis, the reader should consult additional sources.[10,22]

Additional evaluation procedures

After completion of the written medical history questionnaire, recording of vital signs, and physical examination, a more in-depth evaluation of specific medical disorders should be performed. This examination can include auscultation of the heart and lungs, testing of blood glucose levels, retinal examination, function tests for cardiorespiratory status (e.g., the breath-holding test), electrocardiographic examination, and blood chemistries. At present, many such tests are used in dental offices but only irregularly. Explanation and evaluation of many of these tests are beyond the scope of this text, but specific tests (e.g., blood glucose testing and cardiopulmonary function) are referred to in later chapters during the discussion of the management of specific emergency situations.

Dialogue history

Following the gathering of the previously described information regarding the patient's physical condition, the doctor must next determine what significance, if any, these disorders present to the planned dental treatment. (By "significance," this text means the risk that a patient's preexisting medical problem would be acutely exacerbated during or immediately following the dental appointment.) This discussion with the patient is the *dialogue history*, in which the doctor must use all available knowledge of the pathologic process to assess the degree to which the patient is at risk. (Dialogue history is emphasized in each chapter in the discussion on the prevention of specific emergency situations.)

For example, in response to a positive reply in section III to the presence of diabetes, the following questions may be included in the dialogue history:

At what age did you develop diabetes?

Comment: This question is designed to help determine whether the disease manifested itself while the patient was a child or an adult. Diabetes developing when the patient is a child (previously known as juvenile-onset diabetes) is known as type 1 or insulin-dependent diabetes mellitus, whereas adult-onset diabetes more likely represents type 2 or non–insulin-dependent diabetes mellitus.

How do you control your diabetes?

Comment: The answer should provide enough information to determine whether the diabetes is type 1 or type 2 diabetes.

Patients with type 1 diabetes are more likely to develop acute complications associated with diabetes, primarily hypoglycemia.

How often do you monitor your blood sugar, and what are the recordings? (monitoring the degree of control the patient maintains over the disease)

Have you been hospitalized for your diabetic condition? Why?

Comment: A history of hospitalization for low blood (CVM: keep the original text "sugar" glucose (hypoglycemia) may alert the doctor to seek outside assistance more immediately in the event a problem develops with this patient during treatment. Additionally, hospitalization due to the chronic complications of diabetes should prompt the doctor to seek signs and symptoms of cardiovascular system disease.

The following dialogue history may be initiated if a patient records a positive answer for section II for angina pectoris:

What precipitates your angina?
How frequently do you suffer anginal episodes?
How long do your anginal episodes last?
Describe a typical anginal episode.
How does nitroglycerin affect the anginal episode?
Has there been any change in the frequency, intensity, or radiation of pain of your angina in the past several weeks?

(These questions along with possible patient responses are discussed in more detail in Chapter 27.)

■ ANXIETY RECOGNITION

Thus far the primary aim in the evaluation of a prospective patient has been to determine the patient's physical ability to handle the stress of the planned dental treatment. Few questions have been directed at the patient's mental outlook toward dentistry in general and the planned treatment in particular. The traditional (long form) medical history questionnaire asks questions such as "Do you have fainting spells or seizures?" and "Have you had any serious trouble associated with any previous dental treatment?" Most short-form medical histories ignore questions about anxiety.

Heightened anxiety and fear of dentistry can lead to an acute exacerbation of medical problems such as angina, seizures, and asthma, as well as other stress-related problems such as hyperventilation and vaso-depressor syncope. One of the goals in patient evaluation is to determine whether a patient is psychologically capable of tolerating the stress associated with the planned dental treatment. Three methods are available to enable the doctor to recognize the presence of anxiety. The first is the medical history questionnaire; second, the anxiety questionnaire; and third, the art of observation.

Psychological examination
Medical history questionnaire
Earlier in this chapter we discussed the inclusion in the medical history questionnaire of one or more questions relating to the patient's attitudes toward dentistry. Professionals at the USC School of Dentistry have found that patients who will not verbally admit their fears to their doctor oftentimes indicate on the written questionnaire that they are fearful. An affirmative response to any question relating to prior negative dental experiences should alert the doctor to begin a more in-depth dialogue history with the patient to determine the cause or causes of the fear.

Dental anxiety questionnaire
An additional aid in the recognition of anxiety is the dental anxiety questionnaire (Box 2-6) devised by Dr. Norman Corah.[23] Used for more than 30 years at the USC School of Dentistry, this questionnaire has proven to be a reliable aid in the recognition of anxiety. Answers to individual questions are scored 1 through 5 (with "a" being assigned a score of 1 and "e" being assigned a score of 5). The maximum score possible is 20. Scores of 8 or above are associated with higher-than-normal levels of anxiety that should be addressed by the doctor before treatment begins.

Observation
In the absence of such questions on the written medical history questionnaire or absent an affirmative response to such questions, careful observation of the patient may permit the doctor and staff members to recognize unusually anxious patients. Some patients may admit to the doctor and staff that they are quite apprehensive; however, a majority of apprehensive adult patients do everything possible to hide their fear. These patients usually feel that their fear of dentistry is irrational and childish. They do not tell the doctor of their fears because they are afraid of being labeled a "baby." Because of this all too pervasive attitude, dental staff members must be trained to seek out and to recognize clinical signs and symptoms associated with heightened patient anxiety. Whereas a number of levels exist into which anxiety may be subdivided, for the purposes of this discussion two are presented: severe (neurotic) and moderate (more "usual").

Patients with severe anxiety usually make no effort at hiding this fact from their doctor or any member of the office staff. In fact, these patients frequently do anything in their power to avoid dental treatment. It is estimated that between 6% and 14% (14 million to 34 million) of Americans actively avoid dental treatment completely because of fear and that another 20% to 30% dislike it enough to make only occasional visits.[24]

Box 2-6 Anxiety questionnaire

1. **If you had to go to the dentist tomorrow, how would you feel about it?**
   a. I would look forward to it as a reasonably enjoyable experience.
   b. I would not care one way or the other.
   c. I would be very uneasy about it.
   d. I would be afraid that it would be unpleasant and painful.
   e. I would be very frightened of what the dentist might do.
2. **When you are waiting in the dentist's office for your turn in the chair, how do you feel?**
   a. Relaxed
   b. A little uneasy
   c. Tense
   d. Anxious
   e. So anxious that I almost break out in a sweat or almost feel physically sick
3. **When you are in the dentist's chair waiting for him or her to get the drill ready and begin working on your teeth, how do you feel?**
   a. Relaxed
   b. A little uneasy
   c. Tense
   d. Anxious
   e. So anxious that I almost break out in a sweat or almost feel physically sick
4. **You are in the dentist's chair to have your teeth cleaned. While you are waiting and the dentist is getting out the instruments with which to scrape your teeth around the gums, how do you feel?**
   a. Relaxed
   b. A little uneasy
   c. Tense
   d. Anxious
   e. So anxious that I almost break out in a sweat or almost feel physically sick
5. **In general, do you feel uncomfortable or nervous about receiving dental treatment?**
   a. Yes
   h. No

From Corah NL: Development of a dental anxiety scale, *J Dent Res* 48:596, 1969.

Such patients constitute the severe anxiety group. When in the dental office, they may be recognized by the following signs:

- Increased blood pressure and heart rate
- Trembling
- Excessive sweating
- Dilated pupils

Severely anxious patients most commonly appear in the dental office when they have an infection or a severe toothache. Such patients usually say that they have had the problem for quite some time and have tried every available of home remedy (e.g., toothache drops). Their reason for finally coming to the dental office is that they have been unable to sleep for the past few nights because of an intense pain that no home remedy has been able to alleviate. Such patients are compelled to come to the dental office by extreme discomfort. Their usual expectation is that the tooth will have to be removed.

These patients frequently represent behavioral management problems. Although they wish to have their dental problems alleviated, their underlying fear of dentistry often makes it impossible for them to tolerate the procedure when the time comes for the treatment to begin. In addition, the doctor often is faced with the unpleasant prospect of having to either extract an acutely inflamed tooth or to extirpate the pulp of an acutely sensitive tooth, two situations in which achieving clinically adequate pain control in any patient may prove to be a daunting task.

Because of these factors, severely anxious patients usually are candidates for the use of either IV sedation or general anesthesia. Oral, IM, IN, or inhalation sedation, when used as recommended, have but little likelihood of success in this high-fear patient population, primarily because of their limited effectiveness or the constraints that are properly placed on their use. Children with severe anxiety are frequently candidates for either IM or IV (deep) sedation or for general anesthesia.

Therefore, assuming that adult patients may attempt to keep their fears hidden, the doctor and staff members should observe clues before and during the patient's treatment. Front-office personnel, such as the receptionist, may overhear patients in the reception room talk amongst themselves. Patients also may ask significant questions of the receptionist, such as, "Is the doctor gentle?" "Does the doctor give painless 'shots'?" or "Does the doctor use gas?" The receptionist should inform their doctor immediately whenever a patient makes any comment that might indicate an increased level of concern about their impending treatment. All chairside personnel should also be on the lookout for signs of increased anxiety. Greeting the patient with a shake of the hand can help staff members detect signs of anxiety, such as cold, sweaty palms in an office that is not particularly cool.

Discussing with a patient their prior dental experiences may elicit their level of anxiety. A patient with a history of emergency treatments only (e.g., extractions or incision and drainage) and who cancels or does not appear for subsequent appointments may be a high-fear patient. The same may be true for the patient with a history of multiple canceled appointments. The doctor should address this history with the patient to determine the reason for this pattern of treatment (or nontreatment).

Box 2-7 Clinical signs of moderate anxiety

RECEPTION AREA

Questions to receptionist regarding injections or use of sedation

Nervous conversations with other patients in waiting room

History of emergency dental care only

History of canceled appointments for nonemergency treatment

Cold, sweaty palms

IN DENTAL CHAIR

Unnaturally stiff posture

Nervous play with tissue or handkerchief

White-knuckle syndrome

Perspiration on forehead and hands

Overwillingness to cooperate with doctor

Quick answers

Once the patient is seated in the dental chair, the doctor and staff members should watch and listen carefully. Apprehensive patients stay alert and "on guard" at all times. They sit at the edge of the chair, their eyes roaming around the room, taking in everything. They are afraid of being surprised, and their posture appears unnaturally stiff, with tensed arms and legs. They may nervously play with a handkerchief or tissue, occasionally unaware of such actions, perhaps exhibiting the white-knuckle syndrome, in which the knuckles turn white from severe clenching of the armrest of the dental chair. The patient may exclaim, "Gee, it's hot in here!" to explain away diaphoresis (sweating) of the palms or forehead.

The moderately apprehensive patient often is overly willing to oblige the dentist. Actions are carried out quickly, usually without thought. These patients answer the doctor's questions quickly, usually too quickly. Box 2-7 summarizes the clinical signs of moderate anxiety.

Once anxiety is recognized, whether through the questionnaire or observation or both, the patient must be confronted. A straightforward approach is surprisingly successful. The dentist may say, "Mr. Smith, I see from your medical history that you have had several unpleasant experiences in a dental office. Would you kindly describe these to me?" After noticing anxiety, the dentist might say, "Mrs. Smith, you appear to be somewhat nervous today. Is something bothering you?" It has been my experience that patients rapidly drop all pretense at being calm once they realize that their doctor is aware of their fears. They frequently say, "Doctor, I didn't think you could tell." Now that the fears are out in the open, the dentist should seek to determine their cause (e.g., injections or drills). Once the source of a patient's

fears is known, the stress reduction protocol should be used to minimize the likelihood of their becoming a problem during treatment.

A moderately anxious patient is usually treatable. In most instances, conscious sedation can effectively manage these patients. Conscious sedation may involve the use of a drug (pharmacosedation) or nondrug (iatrosedation) technique. General anesthesia is rarely needed in the effective management of the moderately fearful dental patient.

Determination of medical risk

Following completion of the physical examination and a thorough dental exam and deciding on a tentative treatment plan, the doctor must review all of this information to answer the following questions:

- Is this patient capable, both physiologically and psychologically, of tolerating in relative safety the stress involved in the proposed dental treatment plan?
- Is the patient at greater risk (of morbidity or mortality) than usual during the planned dental care?
- If the patient does represent an increased risk what treatment modifications, if any, may be employed to minimize this risk during the planned dental treatment?
- Is the risk too great for the patient to be managed safely in my dental office?

The USC School of Dentistry physical evaluation system has been developed to assist the doctor in assessing patient risk during dental treatment. The system is designed to place each patient into an appropriate risk category so that dental care can be provided with greater comfort and safety. The system is based on the ASA Physical Status Classification System.

ASA physical status classification system

In 1962 the American Society of Anesthesiologists adopted what is now referred to as the ASA Physical Status Classification System.[25] The classification represents a method by which the doctor can estimate the medical risk to a patient who is scheduled to receive "anesthesia" for a surgical procedure. The system was designed primarily for patients who were to receive a general anesthetic, but since its introduction the classification system has been used for all surgical patients regardless of anesthetic technique (e.g., general anesthesia, regional anesthesia, or conscious sedation). The system has remained essentially unchanged and in continuous use since its introduction and has proven a valuable method in the determination of surgical and anesthetic risk before medical and dental procedures.[26,27] The classification system is as follows:

ASA I: A normal, healthy patient without systemic disease

ASA II: A patient with mild systemic disease

ASA III: A patient with severe systemic disease that limits activity but is not incapacitating

ASA IV: A patient with an incapacitating systemic disease that is a constant threat to life

ASA V: A moribund patient not expected to survive 24 hours with or without an operation

ASA E: Emergency operation of any variety, with E preceding the number to indicate the patient's physical status (for example, ASA E-III)

In recent years another category, ASA VI, has been introduced. It is defined as a declared brain-dead patient whose organs are being removed for donor purposes.[28]

When the ASA system was adopted for use in a typical outpatient dental setting, the ASA V classification was eliminated. An effort has been made to correlate the remaining four classifications with possible modifications for dental treatment. Figure 2-4 illustrates the University of the Pacific's physical evaluation record on which a summary of the patient's physical and psychologic status is presented. Each classification is reviewed, and clinical examples of each are listed.

ASA I. ASA I patients are considered normal and healthy. Review of their medical history, physical evaluation, and all other evaluation parameters indicate no abnormalities. Major organs and organ systems—the heart, lungs, liver, kidneys, and CNS—appear to be in good health. ASA I patients are able to walk up one flight of stairs or two level city blocks without distress.* Physiologically, ASA I patients should be able to tolerate whatever stress is associated with their planned dental treatment without added risk of serious complications. Psychologically, such patients also should have little or no difficulty handling the planned treatment. Healthy patients with little or no dental anxiety are assigned an ASA I classification representing a "green light" for treatment. Treatment modification is usually not required for these patients.

ASA II. An ASA II patient has a mild systemic disease or is a healthy (ASA I) patient who demonstrates extreme anxiety and fear in the dental environment. ASA II patients are able to walk up one flight of stairs or two level city blocks before distress causes them to stop.

---

*Shortness of breath, undue fatigue, and chest pain all are signs of distress.

ASA II patients generally are less stress tolerant than ASA I patients; however, they still represent a minimal risk during their dental treatment. Routine (elective) dental care is permitted as long as some thought is given to possible treatment modification or considerations warranted by the patient's medical condition. Examples of such considerations or modifications include the use of prophylactic antibiotics or sedative techniques, limits on the duration of treatment, and possible medical consultation.

An ASA II classification should serve as a "yellow light," a warning to the doctor to proceed, but with caution. Elective dental care is warranted because of the minimal increase in risk to the patient during therapy. Treatment modifications should also be considered.

Examples of ASA II conditions/patients include the following:

- Type 2 diabetes (well controlled)
- Epilepsy (well controlled)
- Asthma (well controlled)
- Hyperthyroid or hypothyroid disorders (well controlled) in which patients are under a physician's care and currently have normal thyroid function (considered euthyroid)
- ASA I patients presenting with upper respiratory tract infections
- Healthy (ASA I) pregnant patient
- Otherwise healthy patients with allergies, especially to drugs
- Otherwise healthy patients with extreme dental fears
- Healthy patients over 60 years of age
- Adults with blood pressures between 140 and 159 mm Hg systolic and/or 90 to 94 mm Hg diastolic

Generally, the ASA II patient is able to perform normal activities without experiencing distress (e.g., undue fatigue, dyspnea, or precordial pain).

ASA III. ASA III patients have a severe systemic disease that limits their activity but is not incapacitating. At rest, ASA III patients do not exhibit signs and symptoms of distress; however, distress is exhibited when patients encounter either physiologic or psychologic stress. For example, an anginal patient may be normal (no chest pain) in the reception area but develops chest pain when placed in the dental chair. ASA III patients are able to negotiate one flight of stairs or two level city blocks, but will have to stop and rest at least once while en route. Like ASA II patients, these are "yellow light" patients (e.g., proceed with caution). Elective dental care is not contraindicated, but this patient's risk during treatment is increased. Serious consideration should be given to the possible use of treatment modifications.

Examples of ASA III conditions/patients include the following:

- Angina pectoris (stable)
- Status post–myocardial infarction: more than 6 months prior to dental appointment and with no significant residual signs or symptoms
- Status post-CVA: more than 6 months prior to dental appointment and with no residual signs and symptoms
- Type 1 diabetes (well controlled)
- Heart failure (HF) with orthopnea and ankle edema
- Chronic obstructive pulmonary disease (COPD): emphysema or chronic bronchitis
- Exercise-induced asthma
- Epilepsy (less well controlled)
- Hyperthyroid or hypothyroid disorders (patient is symptomatic)
- Adults with blood pressures 160 to 199 mm Hg systolic and/or 95 to 114 mm Hg diastolic

ASA III patients can usually perform normal activities without experiencing distress (e.g., undue fatigue, dyspnea, or precordial pain) but will need to stop and rest during an activity should they become distressed.

ASA IV. ASA IV patients have an incapacitating systemic disease that is a constant threat to their lives. They have severe medical problems that are of greater significance to their health than the planned dental treatment. Whenever possible, elective dental care should be postponed until the patient's medical condition has improved at least to an ASA III classification.

ASA IV patients are unable to walk up one flight of stairs or two level city blocks. Distress is present even at rest. These patients present in the dental office exhibiting clinical signs and symptoms of their underlying disease. An ASA IV classification is a "red light," a warning that the risk involved in treatment of the patient is too great to permit elective care. The management of dental emergencies, such as infection and pain, should be treated as conservatively as possible in the dental office until the patient's physical condition improves.

Whenever possible, dental treatment should be non-invasive, consisting of the prescription of medications such as analgesics for pain and antibiotics for infection. In situations in which immediate intervention is deemed necessary (e.g., incision and drainage, extraction, pulpal extirpation), the patient should receive such care within the confines of an acute care facility (i.e., hospital), if possible. Although hospitalized patients are still at risk, their chance of survival may be greater in the event an acute medical emergency arises.

Examples of ASA IV conditions include the following:

- Unstable angina pectoris (preinfarction angina)
- Myocardial infarction: within the past 6 months

- CVA: within the past 6 months
- Adult blood pressure greater than 200 mm Hg or 115 mm Hg
- Severe HF or COPD (requiring O_2 supplementation or confinement in a wheelchair)
- Uncontrolled epilepsy (with a history of hospitalization)
- Uncontrolled type 1 diabetes (with a history of hospitalization)

ASA V. ASA V patients are moribund and are not expected to survive more than 24 hours with or without the planned surgery. ASA V patients almost always are hospitalized*, terminally ill patients. They may be referred to as DNAR (do not attempt resuscitation) or "no code" patients. Resuscitation efforts are not instituted if the patient suffers respiratory or cardiac arrest. Elective dental treatment definitely is contraindicated; however, emergency care in the realm of palliative treatment (that is, relief of pain) may be necessary. An ASA V classification is a "red light" for dental care.

Examples of ASA V conditions include the following:

- End-stage renal disease
- End-stage hepatic disease
- End-stage cancer
- End-stage infectious disease
- End-stage cardiovascular disease
- End-stage respiratory disease

The ASA classification system is not only a helpful means of determining the risk involved in treatment; it is also easy to employ. Assignment of ASA classification is especially easy when a patient is healthy (ASA I) or quite debilitated (ASA IV) or has but one isolated medical problem, such as the previous examples provided with each category. However, many patients will be afflicted with multiple ailments, in which case determination of the appropriate ASA classification will be more difficult. In such situations the doctor must weigh the significance of each disease and choose an appropriate category. Most debate over ASA classification arises when deciding whether a patient represents an ASA II or III. Though heated discussion may ensue, the fact remains that the doctor has (1) recognized that there is a degree of increased risk involved in management of this patient (they are not an ASA I) but that (2) the patient remains treatable (they are not an ASA IV) and that (3) treatment modification should be considered.

The ASA physical status classification system is not meant to be inflexible; rather, it should function as a relative value system based on a doctor's clinical judgment and assessment of the relevant clinical data

---

*This is to mean that the ASA V patient is located within a hospital, nursing home, or hospice facility.

available. When the doctor is unable to determine the clinical significance of one or more disease entities, consultation with the patient's physician or other medical or dental colleague is recommended. In all cases, however, the treating doctor ultimately must decide to either treat or postpone treatment. The ultimate responsibility for the health and safety of a patient rests solely in the hands of the treating doctor.

ASA I, II, and III patients are candidates for both elective and emergency dental treatment. The degree of risk represented by these patients increases with each successive category, as do the indications for treatment modification.

ASA VI - life support; to harvest organs

Medical consultation

A number of steps are involved in the typical medical consultation (Box 2-8). Medical consultation should not be obtained until the patient's dental and physical evaluation has been completed. The dentist should be prepared to discuss fully with the patient's physician the proposed dental treatment plan and any anticipated problems. One of the most important considerations in medical consultation is the determination of the patient's ability to tolerate in relative safety the stress involved

---

Box 2-8 Medical consultation

- Obtain the patient's dental and medical histories.
- Complete the physical examination, including both oral and general examination.
- Provide a tentative treatment plan based on the patient's oral needs.
- Make a general systemic assessment (choose a physical status category).
- Consult the patient's physician, when appropriate, via telephone:
  - Physician's receptionist
    - Introduce yourself and give the patient's name.
    - Ask to speak with the physician.
  - Physician:
    - Introduce yourself.
    - Give the patient's name and the reason for the visit to you.
    - Relate briefly your summary of the patient's general condition.
    - Ask for additional information about the patient.
    - Present your treatment plan briefly, including medications to be used and the degree of stress anticipated.
    - Discuss any problems.
- After consultation:
  - Write a complete report of the conversation for records and obtain a written report from the physician if possible.

Modified with permission from WH Davis, DDS, Bellflower, California.

---

in the proposed dental treatment. The advice of the patient's regular physician should be carefully considered. Whenever doubt remains after a consultation, a second opinion, perhaps from a specialist in the specific area of concern, should be sought. Figure 2-5 is an example of a medical consultation request form.

After receiving the consult, the dentist next must consider implementing steps to minimize any potential risk to the patient. The dentist alone bears the final responsibility for the dental treatment plan and its attendant risks. Risk cannot be shared with the patient's physician. In most cases, medical consultation alters the dental plan minimally or not at all. Specific treatment modifications represent potentially important steps the dentist may undertake to decrease the patient's risk. (Specific modifications are discussed in the following section.)

At this point in the pretreatment evaluation, all relevant history and physical evaluation data have been reviewed and a physical status classification assigned. Most patients are classified as ASA I or II risks, a few as ASA III, and only a very small percentage as ASA IV. The percentages in each category change as the ages of the patients increase. In a study of the health histories and ASA classifications of 4087 dental patients in the Netherlands, percentages of ASA I and II patients decreased and percentages of ASA III and IV patients increased as the ages of the participants increased. Patients completed risk-related, patient-administered questionnaires. Classifications determined (all patients) for ASA I were 63.3%; for ASA II, 25.7%; for ASA III, 8.9%; and for ASA IV, 2.1%.[29]

In a review of 29,424 medical histories of dental patients in the Netherlands, Smeets et al. found an increasing percentage of medically compromised patients with aging.[30]

In the age group from 65 to 74 years, 23.9% of patients were either ASA III or IV, and the percentage increased to 34.9% in patients age 75 years and older.

Most dental procedures can be stressful to patients. Stress may be either physiologic (pain or strenuous exercise) or psychological (anxiety or fear). In either case the body responds to stress with an increased release of catecholamines (epinephrine and norepinephrine) from the adrenal medulla and other tissue storage sites into the cardiovascular system. This results in an increase in cardiovascular workload (increased heart rate, strength of myocardial contraction, and myocardial O_2 requirement).

Although ASA I patients should be able to tolerate such changes in cardiovascular activity, ASA II, III, and IV patients, with cardiovascular problems, are increasingly less able to withstand them safely. For example, patients with angina may respond to increased stress with episodes of chest pain, and various dysrhythmias may develop. Patients with HF may develop acute pulmonary edema. Even patients with noncardiovascular disorders can respond adversely when faced with increased levels of stress. For example, patients with asthma may develop acute episodes of breathing difficulty (bronchospasm), and epileptic patients may suffer seizures.

Unusual degrees of stress in ASA I patients may be responsible for several psychogenically induced emergency situations, such as hyperventilation or vasodepressor syncope.

Interviews with fearful dental patients have demonstrated that many patients start to worry a day or two before their dental appointment. They may have trouble sleeping the night before an appointment, arriving at the dental office fatigued and even less able to tolerate stress. The risk presented by these patients during dental treatment is increased.

Stress-reduction protocol

The stress-reduction protocol[31] listed in Box 2-9 includes two series of procedures that, used individually or collectively, minimize dental treatment–related stress, decreasing the degree of risk to which the patient is exposed. This protocol is predicated on the belief that the prevention or reduction of stress should start before the dental appointment, continue throughout treatment, and follow through into the postoperative period, if necessary.

Recognition of medical risk and anxiety

Recognition of the presence of increased medical risk or dental-related anxiety and fear represents the starting point for the management of stress. Medical risk assessment is determined accurately through strict adherence to the measures previously described in this chapter, including the medical history questionnaire, physical examination, and dialogue history. The recognition of anxiety is often more difficult. As previously discussed, visual observation and verbal communication with the patient can provide the doctor with important clues to the presence of dental anxiety.

Medical consultation

Medical consultation with a patient's primary care physician should be considered in situations in which the doctor is uncertain about the degree to which the patient is at risk. Medical consultation is neither required nor recommended for all patients with medical problems. However, consultation should be sought when the treating doctor is uncertain about the nature of the patient's disorder or the possible interactions between the disorder and the planned dental treatment. The doctor always must remember that a consultation

---

Box 2-9 Stress-reduction protocols

NORMAL, HEALTHY, ANXIOUS PATIENT (ASA I)
Recognize the patient's level of anxiety.
Premedicate the evening before the dental appointment, as needed.
Premedicate immediately before the dental appointment, as needed.
Schedule the appointment in the morning.
Minimize the patient's waiting time.
Consider psychosedation during therapy.
Administer adequate pain control during therapy.
Length of appointment variable.
Follow up with postoperative pain and anxiety control.
Telephone the highly anxious or fearful patient later the same day that treatment was delivered.

MEDICAL RISK PATIENT (ASA II, III, IV)
Recognize the patient's degree of medical risk.
Complete medical consultation before dental therapy, as needed.
Schedule the patient's appointment in the morning.
Monitor and record preoperative and postoperative vital signs.
Consider psychosedation during therapy.
Administer adequate pain control during therapy.
Length of appointment variable; do not exceed the patient's limits of tolerance.
Follow up with postoperative pain and anxiety control.
Telephone the higher medical risk patient later on the same day that treatment was delivered.
Arrange the appointment for the highly anxious or fearful, moderate-to-high-risk patient during the first few days of the week (Monday through Wednesday in most countries; Saturday or Sunday through Monday in many Middle Eastern countries) when the office is open for emergency care and the treating doctor is available.

---

is merely a request for additional information to aid in the determination of the degree of risk present and the possible therapy modifications that might be indicated. The final responsibility for the care and safety of a patient rests with the treating doctor.

Premedication

Many apprehensive patients state that their fear of dental treatment is so great that they are unable to get a good night's sleep the night before their scheduled treatment. These patients arrive at the dental office on the day of their appointment fatigued and even less able to tolerate the additional stresses occurring during treatment. If such patients are also medically compromised, the risk of an acute exacerbation of their medical problem increases. In an ASA I patient, such additional

TABLE 2-7 Oral sedative-hypnotics

Drug	Proprietary name (USA)	Recommended dosage	
		Adult	Pediatric
Alprazolam	Niravam, Xanax	4 mg/day	NE
Diazepam	Valium	2–10 mg	NE
Flurazepam	Dalmane	15–30 mg	NE
Midazolam	Versed	Rarely used	≥6 months NE
			≥6 months 0.25–0.5 mg/kg 30–45 min before surgery
Oxazepam	Serax	10–30 mg	NE
Triazolam	Halcion	125–250 µg	NE
Eszopiclone	Lunesta	2–3 mg	NE
Zaleplon	Sonata	5–10 mg	NE
Zolpidem	Ambien	10 mg	NE

NE, not established.
Data from *ADA guide to dental therapeutics*, ed 3, Chicago, ADA Publishing, 2003, and from www.Epocrates.com.

stress may provoke a psychogenically induced response. Clinical manifestations of increased fatigue include a lowered pain reaction threshold. This patient is more likely to interpret what is usually perceived as a non-painful stimulus as being painful than is a well-rested patient.

The doctor should seek to determine whether a patient's heightened anxiety interferes with their sleep. Oral administration of sedative drugs is one technique a doctor can use to help the patient achieve restful sleep. The doctor may prescribe an antianxiety or sedative-hypnotic drug, such as triazolam, flurazepam, zolpidem, or zaleplon to be taken 1 hour before sleep. The appropriate use of oral antianxiety or sedative-hypnotic drugs is an excellent way to decrease preoperative stress. Other drugs, such as diazepam, oxazepam, hydroxyzine, promethazine, and chloral hydrate, have proved effective in adults and children. The use of barbiturates, such as secobarbital, pentobarbital, and hexobarbital, is not recommended. Recommended dosages of orally administered sedative-hypnotics are presented in Table 2-7.* As the scheduled appointment approaches, the patient's anxiety level becomes heightened. Administration of a CNS-depressant drug (orally) approximately 1 hour prior to the scheduled treatment should decrease the patient's anxiety level to such a degree that the thought of dental treatment is no longer frightening. (Most orally administered CNS-depressant drugs are administered

1 hour prior to the scheduled start of treatment to permit a therapeutic blood level of the drug to be achieved.) It is recommended that orally administered CNS-depressant drugs be administered to the patient in the dental office to avoid dosing errors. However, when the doctor prescribes a CNS-depressant drug to be taken by the patient at home (because it is felt that the intense dental fear might prevent the patient from even coming to the dental office), the doctor must advise the patient against driving a car or operating other potentially hazardous machinery. This admonition MUST be documented in the patient's chart.

Appointment scheduling

Fearful or medically compromised patients (including children) are best able to tolerate stress when they are well rested. The most appropriate time to schedule appointments with these patients is usually earlier in the day. When apprehensive patients have an afternoon appointment, they must contend (mentally) with the ominous specter of the dental appointment, casting a pall over their entire day, giving them more time to worry. The patients become more fearful, which increases the likelihood that adverse psychogenic reactions may develop. An early-morning appointment permits such patients to "get it over with" and then continue to perform their daily activities without the added burden of dental anxiety.

Medically compromised patients face a similar situation. As fatigue sets in during the day, such patients become increasingly less able to tolerate increases in stress. Before their late-afternoon appointment, medically

*For a more in-depth discussion of the use of orally administered sedative-hypnotics, the reader is referred to Malamed SF: *Sedation: a guide to patient management,* ed 4, St. Louis, Mosby, 2002.

compromised patients may have spent many hours at work and driving in traffic, rendering them less able to tolerate the stress of treatment. An earlier appointment provides both the patient and the doctor some degree of flexibility in management.

The doctor also should consider scheduling treatment for the moderately to highly anxious medical risk patient early in the week so that if postoperative complications do arise, the patient can contact and be seen promptly by the treating doctor. In addition, the treating doctor should make it a routine to contact such patients later on the same day of dental treatment to check on their condition. Patients greatly appreciate such personal contact, which also helps to minimize or prevent many post-treatment complications.

Minimized waiting time

The fearful patient should not have to wait for extended periods in the dental office reception room before their treatment begins. Anticipation of a procedure often can induce more fear that the actual procedure itself.[32] Sitting and waiting allow scared patients to smell dental office smells, hear dental office sounds, and fantasize about the "terrible things" that are going to happen to them. Cases of serious morbidity and death have occurred in dental office waiting rooms prior to treatment.[33] Minimal waiting time is of even greater significance for an apprehensive, medically compromised patient.

Vital signs (preoperative and postoperative)

Before beginning any treatment on a medically compromised patient, the doctor should as a routine monitor and record the patient's preoperative vital signs. (A trained dental auxiliary can monitor and record vital signs.) Vital signs recorded should include blood pressure, heart rate and rhythm, and respiratory rate. Comparison of these signs to the patient's baseline values recorded at a prior visit can indicate the patient's physical status at any given appointment. Although vital sign recordings are particularly relevant in patients with cardiovascular disease, they should be taken and recorded on all medically compromised (all ASA III and appropriate ASA II) patients. Postoperative vital signs also should be monitored and recorded in these same patients regularly.

Psychosedation during treatment

If additional stress reduction is required during dental treatment, any technique of sedation or general anesthesia may be used. Nondrug techniques include iatrosedation and hypnosis, whereas more commonly used pharmacosedation techniques include oral, inhalation, IM, and IV sedation. The primary goal of all these techniques is the same—to decrease or eliminate stress in a conscious patient. When appropriate techniques are used properly, this goal is usually achieved without any added risk to the patient. (The use of these techniques in various medical problems is discussed in later chapters.)

Adequate pain control during treatment

Adequate pain control is essential for the reduction of stress. This is especially important in the medically compromised patient. For example, patients with clinically significant heart or blood vessel disease may be affected adversely by endogenously released catecholamines; such patients almost always warrant inclusion of a vasoconstrictor in their local anesthetics. However, the doctor must always use and administer these drugs judiciously. Without adequate control of pain, sedation and stress reduction are impossible to achieve.

Duration of dental treatment

The length of the treatment period is significant to both the medically compromised and the apprehensive patient. Unless the patient's physical condition mandates short visits, the doctor should consider the patient's wishes and decide on an appropriate length.

In many cases fearful patients (ASA I or II) may desire to have as few dental appointments as possible regardless of their length; such patients may prefer to accomplish their dental treatments with 3-hour or longer appointments. However, attempting to satisfy the patient's desire for a longer appointment is inadvisable when the doctor believes that a shorter appointment is warranted. For example, cases of serious morbidity and death have occurred when doctors complied with parents' wishes to complete treatment of their children in one long appointment instead of multiple shorter visits.[34,35]

Unlike the fearful ASA I patient, medically compromised patients should not be subjected to long appointments. For many persons, being seated in a dental chair for 1 hour is quite stressful. Even a "good" ASA I patient may have difficulty tolerating 2- or 3-hour, or longer, dental procedures. Permitting a higher-risk patient to undergo such extended treatment unnecessarily increases the patient's risk. Dental appointments for the medically compromised patient therefore should be shorter, never exceeding the limit of the patient's tolerance. Signs that this tolerance limit has been reached include evidence of fatigue, restlessness, sweating, and discomfort. The most prudent way to manage the patient at this time is to terminate their procedure as expeditiously as possible and reschedule the patient for a later date.

Postoperative control of pain and anxiety

Equally important to preoperative and intraoperative pain and anxiety control is the management of pain and anxiety in the post-treatment period. Post-treatment management is especially relevant in the patient who has undergone a potentially traumatic procedure, such as endodontics, periodontal or oral surgery, extensive oral reconstruction, or restorative procedures. The doctor must consider potential complications that might arise during the 24 hours immediately after dental care, discuss these with the patient, and take steps to assist the patient in their management. These steps may include any or all of the following:

- Be available by telephone 24 hours a day.
- Monitor pain control and prescribe analgesic medication as needed.
- Prescribe antibiotics if a possibility of infection exists.
- Prescribe antianxiety drugs if the patient requires them.
- Prescribe muscle relaxants after prolonged therapy or multiple injections into one area (such as inferior alveolar nerve block).

Availability of the doctor by telephone 24 hours a day has become the standard of care for the health care professional. With cell phones, pagers, and answering services readily available, the patient realistically expects to be able to contact the doctor whenever necessary.

Several studies have demonstrated that patients consider unexpected pain more uncomfortable than anticipated pain.[36] If postoperative pain is a possibility, the doctor should forewarn the patient and prescribe for them an analgesic drug. If the patient experiences post-treatment pain and was not forewarned, the patient may immediately think something has gone wrong. If the doctor had previously discussed the possibility of post-treatment pain and that pain never materializes, the patient remains relaxed and confident in the doctor's abilities.

In addition to these general modifications that are designed to reduce the patient's stress level, the doctor may consider specific treatment modifications for medically compromised patients. Both the general and specific modifications for a given patient should be entered on the patient's permanent record (see Figure 2-4). Examples of specific therapy modifications include the following:

- Humidified oxygen may be administered intraoperatively through a nasal cannula, at a flow of 3 to 4 L per minute (Figure 2-20). This step should be considered for patients with HF or COPD who are judged ASA III risks.

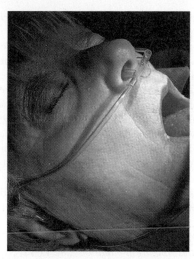

FIGURE 2-20 As a therapy modification for medically compromised patients, the doctor may administer supplemental oxygen through a nasal cannula and humidifier.

- The patient's position during treatment may require modification. Some patients may be unable to tolerate the recommended supine or semisupine position and may require a more upright position. Patients with significant degrees of orthopnea (three or four pillows) may be unable to breathe comfortably in a supine position.
- The doctor may opt not to use a rubber dam when treating patients with latex allergy or certain cardiovascular or respiratory disorders. If a rubber dam cannot be used, the doctor should advise the patient about the danger of swallowing or aspirating a foreign body (for example, a dental instrument) and make a note of this on the patient's chart.

Stress reduction protocols and specific treatment modifications have improved patient management before, during, and after treatment. These protocols have made it possible to manage the dental health needs of a broad spectrum of both fearful and medically compromised patients with a minimum of complications.

REFERENCES

1. McCarthy FM: Sudden, unexpected death in the dental office, *J Am Dent Assoc* 83:1091–1092, 1971.
2. Goldberger E: *Treatment of cardiac emergencies,* ed 5, St. Louis, Mosby, 1990.
3. Montebugnoli L, Servidio D, Miaton RA, Prati C: Heart rate variability: a sensitive parameter for detecting abnormal cardiocirculatory changes during a stressful dental procedure, *J Am Dent Assoc* 135:1718–1723, 2004.
4. Brady WF, Martinoff JT: Validity of health history data collected from dental patients and patient perception of health status, *J Am Dent Assoc* 101:642–645, 1980.

5. Goldman L, editor: *Cecil textbook of medicine*, ed 22, Philadelphia, WB Saunders, 2004.

6. Singleton JK, Sandowski SA, Green-Hernandez C, et al., editors: *Primary care*, Philadelphia, Lippincott Williams & Wilkins, 1999.

7. Dajani AS, Taubert KA, Wilson W, et al.: Prevention of bacterial endocarditis: recommendations by the American Heart Association, *JAMA* 277:1794–1801, 1997.

8. Dajani AS, Taubert KA, Wilson W, et al.: Prevention of bacterial endocarditis: recommendations by the American Heart Association, *J Am Dent Assoc* 128:1142–1151, 1997.

9. Akahane Y, Kojima M, Sugai Y, et al.: Hepatitis C virus infection in spouses of patients with type C chronic liver disease, *Ann Intern Med* 120:748–752, 1994.

10. Seidel HM, Ball JW, Dains JE, et al., editors: *Mosby's physical examination handbook*, St. Louis, Mosby, 2003.

11. American Dental Association, American Academy of Orthopaedic Surgeons: Advisory statement: antibiotic prophylaxis for dental patients with total joint replacements, *J Am Dent Assoc* 128:1004–1008, 1997.

12. DerMarderosian A, Beutler JA, editors: *Review of natural products,* St. Louis, Facts & Comparisons, 2006.

13. Fetrow CH, Avila JR: *Professionals handbook of complementary and alternative medicine,* Philadelphia, Lippincott Williams & Wilkins, 2003.

14. *2005 Physicians' Desk Reference,* ed 52, Oradell, NJ, Medical Economics, 2005.

15. *2005 Physicians' Desk Reference for Herbal Medicines,* Oradell, NJ, Medical Economics, 2005.

16. *ADA guide to dental therapeutics,* ed 3, Chicago, 2003, American Dental Association.

17. Prior AJ, Drake-Lee AB: Auditing the reliability of recall of patients of minor surgical procedures, *Clin Otolaryngol* 16:373–375, 1991.

18. Dorman JM: The annual physical comes of age (editorial), *J Am Coll Health* 38:205–206, 1990.

19. American Heart Association: *Recommendations for human blood pressure determination by sphygmomanometry,* Dallas, American Heart Association, 1967.

20. Cavallaro D, Melker R: Comparison of two techniques for determining cardiac activity in infants, *Crit Care Med* 11:189–190, 1983.

21. American Heart Association: *PALS provider manual,* Dallas, American Heart Association, 2002.

22. Binkley LS, Hoekelman RA: *Bates' guide to physical examination and history taking,* ed 7, Philadelphia, JB Lippincott, 1997.

23. Corah NL, Gale EN, Illig SJ: Assessment of a dental anxiety scale, *J Am Dent Assoc* 97:816–819, 1981.

24. Milgrom P. Weinstein P, Getz T: *Treating fearful dental patients: a patient management handbook,* ed 2, Reston, VA, University of Washington, 1995.

25. American Society of Anesthesiologists: New classification of physical status, *Anesthesiology* 24:111, 1963.

26. Haynes SR, Lawler PG: An assessment of the consistency of ASA physical status classification allocation, *Anaesthesia* 50:195–199, 1995.

27. Forrest JB, Rehder K, Cahalan MK, Goldsmith CH: Multicenter study of general anesthesia. III. Predictors of severe perioperative adverse outcomes, *Anesthesiology* 76:3–15, 1992.

28. Hurford WE, Bailin MT, Davison JK, et al., editors: *Clinical anesthesia procedures of the Massachusetts General Hospital.* Philadelphia, Lippincott Williams & Wilkins, 2003.

29. de Jong KJ, Oosting J, Abraham-Inpijn L: Medical risk classification of dental patients in the Netherlands, *J Public Health Dent* 53:219–222, 1993.

30. Smeets EC, deJong KJ, Abraham-Inpijn L: Detecting the medically compromised patient in dentistry by means of the medical risk-related history. A survey of 29,424 dental patients in the Netherlands, *Prev Med* 27:530–535, 1998.

31. McCarthy FM: Stress reduction and therapy modifications, *J Calif Dent Assoc* 9:41–47, 1981.

32. Gale EN: Fears of the dental situation, *J Dent Res* 51:964–966, 1972.

33. Bell WH: Emergencies in and out of the dental office: a pilot study in the state of Texas, *J Am Dent Assoc* 74:778–783, 1967.

34. deJulien LE: Causes of severe morbidity/mortality cases, *J Cal Dent Assoc* 11:45, 1983.

35. Goodson JM, Moore PA: Life-threatening reactions after pedodontic sedation: an assessment of opioid, local anesthetic, and antiemetic drug interaction, *J Am Dent Assoc* 107:239–245, 1983.

36. Corah N: Development of a dental anxiety scale, *J Dent Res* 48:596, 1969.

CHAPTER 3

Preparation

In spite of efforts to prevent them, life-threatening emergencies can, and do, occur in the practice of dentistry. Prevention, as successful as it may be, is not always enough. The entire dental office staff must be prepared to assist in the recognition and management of any potential emergency situation. If every staff member is not prepared, those few serious emergencies that all doctors will encounter during their career may result in tragedy.

■ GENERAL INFORMATION

Guidelines have been established to help doctors and staff members adequately prepare for the immediate and effective management of life-threatening situations. Most of these guidelines were developed by state boards of dental examiners in connection with the certification of doctors who wish to use parenteral sedation techniques, such as intramuscular (IM) or intravenous (IV) sedation or general anesthesia, in their offices.[1] Of late, many state dental boards have enacted regulations controlling the use of orally administered central nervous system (CNS) depressants. Guidelines for emergency preparedness are included in all of these regulations.[2] Specialty groups, such as the American Association of Oral & Maxillofacial Surgeons,[3] the American Academy of Pediatric Dentistry,[4] and the American Association of Periodontists[5] have developed guidelines for their membership. The American Association of Dental Schools has developed curricular guidelines for the teaching of anesthesia and pain control that include recommendations for emergency preparation.[6]

Those primarily affected by these guidelines are doctors who have received advanced education and training degrees in various techniques of CNS-depressant drug administration. The guidelines provide lists of recommended personnel, equipment, and emergency drugs for the safe and effective management of emergency situations. Many of these guidelines also present protocols for management of specific situations.[3]

Unfortunately, no such guidelines exist for the overwhelming majority of doctors who have not received advanced training in drug administration or who do not belong to these specialty societies. In addition, the level of training in emergency medicine that most health care professionals receive varies considerably. Only a few doctors (DDS, MD, DO) are experts in emergency medicine, whereas most possess no more than basic knowledge of emergency care.

Regardless of a doctor's level of training in emergency medicine, staff members should be equally prepared to manage these situations. The doctor is always expected to initiate emergency management and be capable of sustaining a patient's life through application of the steps of basic life support (BLS [also known as cardiopulmonary resuscitation, or CPR]): **P** (positioning), **A** (airway), **B** (breathing), and **C** (circulation). Management of **D** (definitive treatment), which includes the administration of drugs, will be predicated on the training level of the treating doctor.

Geographic requirements for emergency training

Some doctors will find themselves in special situations that require significantly more training than the basic level recommended in this text. In some parts of the world, including sections of the United States and Canada, sparsely populated areas still exist in which medical care—whether routine or emergency—is not readily available. In my travels, I have met dentists, assistants, and hygienists from rural areas of Montana, North Dakota, eastern Nevada, Arizona, New Mexico, Alaska, and Canada who themselves handle all the urgent health care needs in large geographic areas.

Many of these practitioners state that they are their area's primary source for emergency medical care because the nearest ambulance service is more than 1 hour away. Many of them are trained in advanced cardiovascular life support (ACLS) and certified in advanced trauma life support (ATLS), while others possess varying degrees of training as emergency medical technicians (EMTs) and paramedics. Morrow[7] suggests appropriate levels of emergency training for these doctors and recommends that they have immediate access to emergency kits, the design of which is based on the distance between the dental office and nearest emergency medical facility. The greater this distance and the time needed for travel, the more training and access to emergency drugs the doctor requires.

Office personnel

Because the doctor cannot be with patients from the time they walk through the door to the time they leave the office, all office staff members must be prepared to manage problems and emergencies that might arise in the doctor's absence. Preparation of dental staff members and of the office for medical emergencies should include the following minimal requirements:

1. Staff training should include BLS instruction for all members of the dental office staff, recognition and management of specific emergency situations, and emergency "fire drills."
2. Office preparation should include the posting of emergency assistance numbers and the stocking of emergency drugs and equipment.

Training

Without a doubt, the most important step in the preparation for medical emergencies in the dental office is the training of all office personnel, including nonchairside employees (e.g., receptionists and laboratory technicians), in the recognition and management of emergency situations. This training should include an annual refresher course in emergency medicine that includes all possible conditions, such as seizures, chest pain, and respiratory difficulty, rather than simply a recertification in BLS. Continuing education courses in emergency preparedness and management are presented at most major dental meetings and through most local dental societies. Lists of scheduled courses are available from the American Dental Association and local dental organizations.

The Institute of Medical Emergency Preparedness is a proprietary organization created to better prepare people in the case of a medical emergency.[8] Their "Emergency Response System" consists of comprehensive training manuals, Internet-enabled testing programs, email medical alerts, and a step-by-step Red E Emergency Action Guide designed for placement next to the emergency drug kit, oxygen cylinder, and automated external defibrillator (AED).* The goal is to better prepare the dental office and all staff members to recognize and respond quickly and effectively when medical emergencies develop.

Basic life support

The aforementioned training must include an understanding of, and an ability to perform, BLS (CPR). An understanding of BLS includes intimate knowledge of the P→A→B→C→D protocol.† All office personnel should be required to obtain certification at the level of a BLS health care provider (American Heart Association) or professional rescuer (American Red Cross) at least annually. The mandate for BLS training should be included in every dental staff member's job description.

The ability of all office personnel to administer BLS is *the* most important step in the preparation for emergency management. Initial management of all emergency medical situations includes BLS administration as needed. (Specific BLS components are discussed in detail in Chapters 5, 30, and 31.) Many, if not most, emergency situations in the dental office are readily manageable through the use of these steps alone. Drug therapy is always relegated to a secondary role.

Defibrillation

Interesting and sobering statistics from the American Heart Association and other sources[9,10] have shown that BLS (P→A→B→C) by itself does not provide the patient of an out-of-hospital sudden cardiac arrest a significant chance of survival. Survival rates are less than 5% when P→A→B→C is initiated promptly and efficiently but D (defibrillation) is delayed for more than 10 minutes.[11] A survival rate of less than 5% may seem dismal, but it contrasts dramatically with a 0% survival rate when BLS is not performed. On the other hand, survival rates for patients experiencing out-of-hospital cardiac arrest reached 43% in Seattle, Washington, when rapid implementation of BLS was combined with ready (less than 8 minutes) access to defibrillation.[12]

Studies in Las Vegas, Nevada, have demonstrated survival rates from out-of-hospital cardiac arrest on the casino floor of 78%.[13] Some medical and dental professionals have used these data to argue against the requirement that dentists and physicians be CPR-certified before they can be licensed. This argument is faulty for two reasons:

1. CPR (BLS) is not used solely in situations of cardiac arrest.* In fact, most health professionals working outside the hospital may never need to use all the steps of BLS as they must with cardiac arrest. However, all health care providers, especially dentists, are likely to be required many times in the course of their professional careers to maintain an airway (**A**) and, on fewer occasions, to maintain the patient's breathing (**A** and **B**) in managing medical emergencies other than cardiac arrest.

2. Dentists are one of the few groups of health professionals permitted to learn and administer ACLS. Though the author does not advocate requiring ACLS for all dentists or for all physicians (there are some groups, however, for whom such training should be required, as described shortly), it is a plain and simple fact that ACLS will not be effective in the absence of BLS. Those dentists who practice in remote areas of the country where emergency medical assistance is less readily available should seriously consider receiving training in ACLS.

ACLS training involves the following areas:

1. Adjuncts for airway control and ventilation (including intubation)
2. Patient monitoring and dysrhythmia recognition
3. Defibrillation and synchronized cardioversion
4. Cardiovascular pharmacology
5. Acid-base balance maintenance
6. Venipuncture
7. Resuscitation of infants, including newborns

Although not all dentists need to know these procedures, they are invaluable in emergency situations. ACLS programs are provided by hospitals under the sponsorship of the American Heart Association. Such training is especially valuable to those who use parenteral sedation or general anesthesia in their offices. Local American Heart Association affiliates and in-house

---

*Institute of Medical Emergency Preparedness, 866-729-REDE, www.getrede.com.

†P→A→B→C→D. P = Position; A = airway; B = breathing; C = circulation; D = defibrillation.

*I prefer to call this technique *basic life support* (BLS) instead of *cardiopulmonary resuscitation* (CPR). The term *CPR* conjures up images of a patient suffering cardiac arrest on whom chest compressions are being performed. In reality, airway and breathing doubtless are the components most often used in BLS. A move is under way to change the name *CPR* to *CPCR* (*cardiopulmonarycerebral resuscitation*), a term that more fully describes the primary goal of BLS—the maintenance of normal brain function.

training programs at local hospitals or medical centers can provide additional ACLS information.[*]

For the pediatric dentist, or any dentist treating a significant number of younger patients, training in pediatric advanced life support is recommended.[*] In addition, the American Academy of Pediatric Dentistry (AAPD) sponsors an excellent clinical program in pediatric emergency medicine.[†]

Team management

When office personnel are trained to recognize and manage emergency situations, each person is able to maintain the life of the victim alone or, as is more likely, as a member of a trained emergency team. Although management of most emergencies is possible with a single rescuer (often the doctor), the combined efforts of several trained individuals are usually more efficient. Because most dental offices have more than one staff member present during working hours (when most emergencies occur), a team approach is possible. The emergency team should consist of a minimum of two to three members, each with a predefined role in emergency management. The doctor usually leads the team and directs the actions of the other team members.

Team member 1 is the first person to reach the victim when the emergency occurs. This member's primary task is to initiate BLS ($P \rightarrow A \rightarrow B \rightarrow C \rightarrow D$) as indicated after assessment of the victim. This person also activates the office emergency system by calling (yelling) for help to alert other office personnel to the need for assistance (similar to a "code blue" in a hospital). Member 1 should remain with the victim throughout the emergency unless another team member steps in to relieve them.

Duties of team member 1
- Provide BLS as indicated
- Stay with the victim
- Alert office staff members

Team member 2, on hearing the call for emergency assistance, should gather the emergency kit and portable oxygen (O_2) system and bring them to the site of the emergency. The O_2 delivery system, emergency drug kit, and AED should be stored together in a readily accessible location.

Duties of team member 2
- Bring emergency drug kit, O_2, and AED to emergency site
- Check O_2 daily
- Check emergency kit weekly
- Check AED weekly

[*]www.americanheart.org.
[†]www.aapd.org.

Team member 3 acts as a circulating nurse or assistant. Member 3 may actually be more than one person as these tasks may be delegated. For example, a chairside assistant working alongside the doctor may serve in this capacity if the patient undergoing treatment is the victim of an emergency. In another situation, member 3 may be the next person to come to the aid of member 1. Primary functions of member 3 include assisting member 1 with BLS as required, monitoring vital signs (blood pressure, heart rate and rhythm, respiration), and providing assistance in any way that is needed. For example, member 3 may prepare emergency drugs for administration, occasionally administer drugs, position the victim, loosen a collar or belt, activate the emergency medical services (EMS) number, or perform all such duties.

Member 3 also may keep a written chronological record of all events, including vital signs, drug administration, and patient response to treatment. In a large medical office building, member 3 may be sent to the building's main entrance to meet the emergency medical technicians and lead them to the victim.

Duties of team member 3
- Assist with BLS
- Monitor vital signs
- Prepare emergency drugs for administration
- Activate EMS system
- Assist as needed
- Maintain records
- Meet rescue team at building entrance and escort to office

All office personnel must be able to function in emergency situations. In addition, all team members should be able to perform the duties of every other team member. Thus, practice becomes vitally important.

Dentists do not have to serve in the capacity of team member 1. Duties may be delegated during emergency situations as long as the person or persons carrying out these functions are well trained. If dentists feel that they are better able to carry out a task, then by all means, they should do it themselves. It is the doctor, however, who ultimately bears the responsibility for the overall management and outcome of the emergency situation.

Emergency practice drills

If life-threatening situations occurred with any regularity in dentistry, emergency practice sessions would be unnecessary; team members would receive their training under actual emergency conditions. Fortunately, life-threatening situations occur only infrequently. Therefore, members of the dental office emergency team quickly become "rusty" because they do not receive ample opportunity to practice. Annual refresher courses therefore are invaluable in the maintenance of a functional emergency team.

However, the ability of the team to perform effectively in the office setting is even more important. Periodic in-office emergency drills help to maintain efficient emergency teams in the absence of true emergency situations. All members of the team should respond exactly as they must under true emergency conditions. Some doctors purchase mannequins and hold frequent mandatory practice sessions at which staff members can practice BLS skills. In addition, instructional programs can provide visual examples of proper emergency management in the dental office, including demonstrations in drug preparation and administration.[14]

For instance, the doctor prepares to administer a local anesthetic to a patient. As the syringe is inserted in the patient's mouth, the patient loses consciousness. The doctor (member 1) calls the other team members, using a code word or communication device such as a light or buzzer. Member 2, an assistant working in the back room, fetches the emergency O_2 cylinder, emergency drug kit, and AED and brings them to the site while member 3, the chairside assistant, aids the doctor and victim. Member 1 initiates BLS, positioning the patient and ensuring a patent airway.

Member 3 monitors the victim's vital signs, beginning with the heart rate (carotid, brachial, or radial pulse). Under the doctor's supervision, member 2 prepares the O_2 for possible use and locates the aromatic ammonia vaporoles. If possible, member 3 will record, in chronological fashion, the vital signs and management of this situation (Figure 3-1). If the victim does not regain consciousness in a reasonable short period of time, member 2 or 3 is requested to activate the EMS system, meet the emergency personnel, and escort them to the emergency site. If emergency drug administration is warranted, the doctor should, if possible, administer the drugs. However, when this is not possible, the doctor should assign another team member to administer the drugs under his or her supervision.

In subsequent chapters, dental staff members will be provided with guidelines for the prevention, recognition, and management of emergency situations. However, emergency teams are effective only if team members practice on a regular basis.

Office preparation: emergency medical assistance

Emergency team members must be aware of whom to call when help is needed and when to call them.

Whom to call. Although most office emergencies may be managed efficiently by the office emergency team, some may require additional assistance. The

---

Information to be given to EMS (9-1-1) operator

1. Location of the emergency (with names of cross streets or roads or office or room number, if possible)
2. Telephone number from which the call is being made
3. What happened—heart attack, motor vehicle crash, etc.
4. How many persons need help
5. Condition of the victim(s)
6. What aid is being given to the victim(s) (e.g., "CPR is being performed" or "we're using an AED")
7. Any other information requested

To ensure that EMS personnel have no more questions, the caller should hang up only when instructed to do so by the EMS system operator.

---

doctor must prepare for this before an emergency situation actually develops. Certain emergency telephone numbers should be available, be conspicuously displayed near all office telephones, and be programmed into the telephones "speed dial" system. The doctor may want to include the telephone numbers of local EMS personnel (9-1-1 in the United States and 9-9-9 in Great Britain), a dental or medical professional in close proximity to their office who is well trained in emergency management, an emergency ambulance service, or a nearby hospital emergency department.

Almost all areas in the United States, and an increasing number of countries worldwide, have instituted universal emergency numbers to expedite activation of fire, police, and EMS personnel. Though varying degrees of sophistication exist, this number usually connects the caller to an emergency triage operator who screens the call and activates the appropriate response (fire, police, medical). When emergency medical assistance is required in the dental office, the community EMS (9-1-1) is the preferred source for immediate assistance. Response times for EMS in the United States average slightly more than 9 minutes for urban centers and over 15 minutes for rural areas.[15]

The team member calling EMS must try to remain calm and should clearly provide the EMS operator with all requested information.

The operator will request the nature of the emergency in general terms (e.g., whether the patient is conscious or unconscious or has chest pain or seizures) and the location of the office.* The address of the dental office

---

*More advanced EMS systems automatically provide the address of the caller if the caller remains on the line for a minimum period of time (e.g., 15 seconds). However, address errors have occurred, especially where the address has been changed but the telephone number has not. The caller should confirm the address when placing the emergency call.

**INSTITUTE OF MEDICAL
EMERGENCY PREPAREDNESS**

Emergency Treatment Record

White-File Copy, Yellow-EMS Copy
. Note: Fill out and keep White copy for your files. Give Yellow copy to EMS.

Person's Name: _____ Date: _____ Time: _____

Allergies: _____

List all medications taken prior to emergency: _____

Time	Blood Pressure	Pulse	Resp	Oxygen Saturation %	Oxygen Flow L/min	Medications Administered	Medication Dosage	Medication Route (IV, IM, PO, SL)

Called 911 EMS at (time): _____

EMS arrival at (time): _____

EMS called by (who): _____

Person taken to what hospital: _____

Condition of person when transported from site: _____

_____

EMS personnel: _____

_____

People present: _____

_____

Signature of person recording events: _____ Phone:_____

1.866.729.7333 • www.EmergencyActionGuide.com

FIGURE 3-1 Institute of Medical Emergency Preparedness Carbonless Emergency Treatment Record. (Reprinted with permission, Institute of Medical Emergency Preparedness, Hattiesburg, Mississippi.)

should be posted by every telephone. If the office is located in a large professional building, a team member should wait near the building's main entrance with the elevator available for emergency personnel and escort them to the emergency site.

The doctor may also enlist the assistance of a well-trained dental or medical professional in preparation for an emergency. This arrangement should be finalized before help is actually needed, and the doctor should check to ensure that this professional is available during the doctor's office hours. In my experience, the best-trained individuals in this field are emergency medicine physicians, anesthesiologists (both medical and dental), surgeons (medical), and oral and maxillofacial surgeons (dental).

Unfortunately, emergency medicine specialists and anesthesiologists are hospital based and are not readily available for assistance outside of the hospital. However, most medical and dental surgeons and dental anesthesiologists maintain private practices in the community and may, therefore, be available. Prior arrangement with these individuals can help prevent misunderstandings and increase their usefulness in emergency situations.

Many emergency ambulance services require that their personnel be trained as emergency medical technicians. These individuals can assist the doctor in the absence of additional help. The level of assistance available in this case will vary, ranging from BLS to ACLS.

More and more commonly, the "first responders" (fire fighters, police, and ambulance drivers) to the scene of a medical emergency are trained in BLS, including defibrillation.

The location of a hospital close to the dental office should be determined. This facility should have a 24-hour emergency department staffed with fully trained emergency personnel. Additionally, all office staff members should determine the nearest fully equipped hospital emergency department to their place of residence. The American Heart Association periodically evaluates hospital emergency departments and awards symbols that are prominently displayed outside emergency departments that successfully meet their requirements (Figure 3-2). Evaluations are made for adult and pediatric emergency departments.

Whom to call
- EMS (9-1-1)
- Nearby medical or dental doctor well trained in emergency medicine
- Ambulance service
- Nearby hospital with American Heart Association–approved emergency department

One point worth stressing in an emergency situation is that the telephone number for EMS in most U.S. areas is 9-1-1 (nine-one-one) and not 9-11 (nine-eleven). In moments of panic, callers may become confused and be unable to locate the 11 (eleven) on the telephone keypad. This is especially significant when the person making the call is a child. In a number of recorded incidents, this problem has led to a delayed arrival (or nonarrival) of EMS personnel and the death of the victim.

When to call. The designated team member should call for EMS assistance as soon as the individual responsible for the patient's health and safety (usually the doctor) deems it necessary. Never hesitate to seek assistance if any doubt remains as to the nature of the situation or to its management. The earlier the assistance is sought, the better.

Emergency drugs and equipment

Emergency drugs and equipment must be available in every dental office. In a survey of 2,704 dentists in the United States and Canada, 84% had emergency drugs

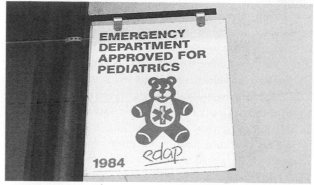

FIGURE 3-2 A, Emergency heart care seal from American Heart Association. **B,** Pediatric emergency care seal.

and equipment available.[16] Although most emergency situations do not demand the administration of drugs, on occasion it may save lives. For example, in anaphylaxis (acute systemic allergy), the administration of epinephrine is critical to the patient's survival. In most other emergency situations, however, drug administration will be secondary in overall management to BLS.

Commercial versus homemade emergency drug kits

A number of emergency kits are produced commercially for sale to dental and medical professionals. Although some proprietary kits are well designed, others contain drugs and equipment of dubious value in a typical medical or dental office. These kits are usually designed by their manufacturer in collaboration with experts in the field of emergency medicine. The drugs and equipment these kits include all too often reflect the expertise of the experts, not the level of training of the doctors for whom they are designed.

The Council on Dental Therapeutics of the American Dental Association issued reports on emergency drug kits in 1973, 1998, and 2002.[17-19] The following statement is from the 2002 report:

In addition, all dental offices should maintain at least the basic recommended emergency equipment and drugs.

The content and design of these kits should be based upon each practitioner's training and individual requirements. Proprietary emergency drug kits are available, but none of these kits is compatible with the needs of all practitioners. The Council on Scientific Affairs does not recommend any specific proprietary emergency drug kit: it does recommend that dentists, after considering their specific training and special needs, design their own individualized emergency kits if proprietary kits do not meet their needs.

The American Dental Association's "Guidelines for the Use of Conscious Sedation, Deep Sedation and General Anesthesia for Dentists"[1] clearly defines the training, emergency drugs and equipment necessary to safely manage emergencies related to those modalities in the dental office. Dental specialty organizations have similar recommendations, and many state Boards of Dental Examiners also have lists of emergency drugs and equipment that are required for dentists to obtain.... All dentists using these techniques are strongly urged to consult their own state's requirements for specific emergency drugs and equipment. Recently, several insurance carriers mandated lists of emergency drugs and equipment that insured practitioners must have available in their offices....

In designing an emergency drug kit, the Council suggests that the following drugs be included as a minimum: epinephrine 1:1000 (injectable), histamine-blocker (injectable), oxygen with positive pressure administration capability, nitroglycerin (sublingual tablet or aerosol spray), bronchodilator (asthma inhaler), sugar and aspirin. Other drugs may be included as the doctor's training and needs mandate. It is particularly important that the dentist be knowledgeable about the indications, contraindications, dosages and methods of delivery of all items included in the emergency kit. Dentists are urged to perform continual emergency kit maintenance by replacing soon-to-be-outdated drugs before their expiration.

For offices in which emergency medical services, or EMS, personnel with defibrillation skills and equipment are not available within a reasonable time frame, the dentist may wish to consider an automated external defibrillator, or AED, consistent with AED training acquired in the BLS section of health care provider courses.

Figures 3-3 through 3-6 illustrate a variety of commercially prepared and self-made emergency drug kits.

The most practical emergency drug kit is one the doctor designs personally that reflects the doctor's special requirements and capabilities. In my experience, proprietary emergency drug kits are quickly placed in storage cabinets, where they remain until an emergency arises. The doctor and staff members spend little, if any, time familiarizing themselves with the contents

FIGURE 3-3 Banyan STAT KIT 700. (Courtesy Banyan International Corporation, Abilene, Texas.)

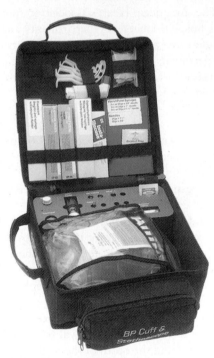

FIGURE 3-4 Banyan CritiKit. (Courtesy Banyan International Corporation, Abilene, Texas.)

of the kit or the indications for the use of its drugs. Worst of all, the doctor may try to use the drugs in the kit without having become familiar with them or with the nature of the patient's problem. The emergency kit quickly becomes a security blanket that provides little security. By preparing an individualized kit, the doctor becomes familiar with all of the drugs and equipment inside. This intimate knowledge benefits both the doctor and the patient in an emergency situation.

Each doctor should select items for the emergency kit based on that doctor's training in emergency medicine,

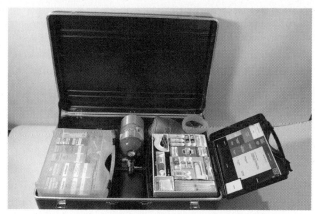

FIGURE 3-5 Healthfirst large kit. (Courtesy Healthfirst Corporation, Edmonds, Washington.)

FIGURE 3-6 Healthfirst minimal kit. (Courtesy Healthfirst Corporation, Edmonds, Washington.)

the importance of the drug in the successful outcome of the situation, and, in some cases, regulations for mandatory drugs and equipment. The latter requirement usually is found in specialty practices such as anesthesiology or parenteral sedation,[2] oral and maxillofacial surgery,[3] pedodontics,[4] and periodontology.[5]

■ EMERGENCY DRUG KITS

The dental office emergency kit need not and indeed should not be complicated. It should be as simple as possible to use. The "KISS" principal is important at this time: "Keep It Simple, Stupid." Pallasch's statement[20]

that "complexity in a time of adversity breeds chaos" is as true today as it was when written in 1976. The doctor should remember three things in preparing and using emergency drug kits:

1. Drug administration is *not* necessary for the immediate management of medical emergencies (BLS is always used, as needed, first).
2. Primary management of ALL emergency situations involves BLS.
3. When in doubt, don't medicate.

The emergency kit described in the following sections is a simple, organized collection of drugs and equipment that has been highly effective in the management of life-threatening situations that occur in dental offices. However, proper management of a patient in almost all emergency situations does not require drug administration. First and foremost in the management of emergency situations are the steps of BLS (P→A→B→C). Only after these steps have been implemented should the doctor consider the administration of drugs. Even in acute anaphylaxis, in which the patient experiences immediate respiratory distress, circulatory collapse, or both, BLS remains the immediate response, followed as rapidly as possible by the administration of epinephrine. Management of all emergency situations follows the P→A→B→C→D protocol (D…definitive management: drugs and EMS).

Components of the emergency kit

The following guidelines are designed to aid in the development of a useful dental office emergency kit. Therapeutic categories for inclusion in the kit are listed, suggestions are offered for specific drugs within each group, and selection criteria for each drug mentioned are explained.

Doctors should consider including items from each therapeutic category in the emergency kit; however, doctors should select only those categories or drugs with which they are familiar and able to use. Preferred drugs are listed, with alternatives suggested in many instances. All doctors must evaluate carefully every item that is included in their emergency drug kit. If a doctor has any doubt about the categories or specific agents, consultation with a physician (preferably a specialist in emergency medicine) or hospital pharmacist is recommended—but above all determine their reason for suggesting a certain drug or drug category over others.

All drugs come with drug-package inserts. Doctors should save this information sheet from each drug included in their kit, read it, and take note of important information about the drug, including its indications, usual doses (pediatric, adult, and geriatric), adverse reactions, and expiration dates. Many doctors transfer this information to an index card for quick reference. The emergency drugs and equipment described in the following sections are presented in four levels, or modules. The design of each module is based on the doctor's level of training and experience in emergency medicine:

- Module one: basic emergency kit (critical drugs and equipment)
- Module two: noncritical drugs and equipment
- Module three: ACLS drugs
- Module four: antidotal drugs

Two categories are described for each module—injectable and noninjectable drugs, as well as emergency equipment. Doctors always must remember that the categories of drugs and equipment included in the emergency kit must conform to the level of training of the office personnel who will use it. Emergency kits should be simple but effective.

A complete discussion of when and how each item should be used can be found in the sections detailing management of specific emergencies. The drugs and equipment in the emergency kit are intended for use in patients of any age (pediatric, adult, or geriatric). Doctors must be aware of the distinction in therapeutic doses between patients of different ages; pediatric (and in many cases, geriatric) doses are smaller than adult doses. Specific drug doses are not emphasized in this chapter but are presented in individual discussions of emergency management.

Most injectable emergency drugs are prepared in a 1-mL glass ampule or vial. The number of milligrams of drug present in 1 mL of solution will vary from drug to drug. For example, for diazepam the amount is 5 mg/mL, whereas for diphenhydramine the amount is 50 mg/mL and for ephedrine, 10 mg/mL. The 1-mL form of the drug is known as its *therapeutic dose,* or *unit dose.* Thus, 1 mL of solution is the usual dose of the drug administered to an adult patient (8 years of age and older or a younger patient weighing in excess of 60 lbs [27 kg]) in an emergency situation. For pediatric patients (age 1 to 8 years), the therapeutic dose of an injectable drug is 0.5 mL, or half the adult dose; for infants (under 1 year), the therapeutic dose is 0.25 mL, or one quarter the adult dose (Table 3-1).

However, epinephrine is the major exception to this basic rule of doses. Although the 1-mL solution of 1:1000 epinephrine is considered the adult therapeutic dose, a smaller initial dose—0.3 mL—is recommended, with subsequent doses based on the patient's response. Initial pediatric and infant epinephrine doses are reduced accordingly (0.15 mL and 0.075 mL of a 1:1000 epinephrine solution).

Noninjectable drugs are usually prepared so that one tablet or metered spray is the adult therapeutic

TABLE 3-1 Injectable drug dosages

	Age range (y)	Solution (mL)	Epinephrine (1:1000 mL)
Infant	<1	0.25	0.075
Child	1–8	0.5	0.15
Adult	8 and older (or >60 lbs)	1.0	0.3

dose. Many noninjectable drugs are also prepared in pediatric forms to simplify administration. Because both adults and children are seen in most dental offices, a doctor treating many children should consider including both drug forms in the emergency drug kit.

Other items of emergency equipment should be available in both adult and pediatric forms. These include face masks and oropharyngeal and nasopharyngeal airways (if warranted by training). Indeed the pediatric dentist (and general dentist who treats many children) must provide a wider range of equipment in both pediatric (for the patient) and adult (for the doctor or staff patient) sizes than the doctor who treats only adults.

Administration of injectable drugs

For a drug to exert a therapeutic effect, a therapeutic blood level must be achieved in the target organ (e.g., the brain for anticonvulsants, the heart for antidysrhythmics) or target system (skin). In other words, enough of the drug must enter the bloodstream and be transported to the part of the body where it exerts its clinical actions. Therefore, the ideal route for emergency drug administration is IV; onset of action is approximately 20 seconds, and the drug effect the most reliable of all routes of administration.

Unfortunately, unless the doctor has established an IV line in the patient prior to the emergency, most doctors may find its venous cannulation to be difficult if not impossible during the emergency. If the doctor is not comfortable with venipuncture, an alternative route of administration should be employed. Emergency drugs may be administered via the IM route into various sites, most often the anterolateral aspect of the thigh (vastus lateralis), the mid-deltoid region of the upper arm, and the upper outer quadrant of the gluteal region. IM drugs have an onset of action of about 10 minutes in the presence of normal tissue perfusion. This will be somewhat slower in the presence of decreased blood pressure (hypotension). Of the three traditional IM injection sites, the mid-deltoid provides the most rapid uptake of most drugs (because of its greater tissue perfusion) and is therefore the site of choice. The vastus

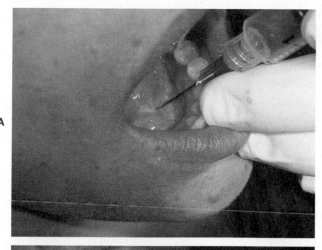

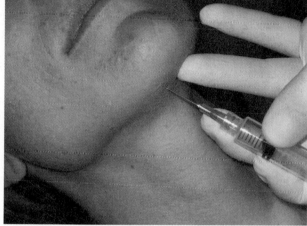

FIGURE 3-7 **A,** Intralingual injection—intraoral approach. **B,** Intralingual injection—extraoral approach.

lateralis is a close second because of its accessibility and anatomic safety. In the smaller pediatric patient, the vastus lateralis is the preferred IM injection site. Emergency drugs should not be administered in the gluteal region because it lacks the vascularity of the other sites. A number of anatomic considerations, especially with pediatric patients, also accompany drug administration into the gluteal region.

One additional site provides an even more effective and rapid uptake than the mid-deltoid region—the tongue. Emergency drugs can be injected either into the body of the tongue (intralingual injection) or sublingually for a more rapid uptake and onset of clinical action. The drug may be administered into the body of the tongue or floor of the mouth, either intraorally (Figure 3-7A) or extraorally (Figure 3-7B). Onset of action is approximately 5 to 10 minutes in the presence of effective circulation, but slower in patients with hypotension.

The steps of BLS must continue, as needed, while the emergency team awaits the onset of the drug's action.

However, in the absence of effective circulation, neither IV nor IM drugs will be effective. In this situation (as in all emergency situations), drugs are secondary to BLS.

In situations where IV access is impossible but a patient has been successfully intubated, the administration of certain drugs (epinephrine, lidocaine, atropine, naxolone, and flumazenil) into the endotracheal tube provides a rapid onset of action as the drug is absorbed from the well-perfused pulmonary vascular bed (Box 3-1).

Parenteral drug administration

Almost all injectable emergency drugs can be purchased in preloaded syringes. I believe strongly that these drugs should not be available in preloaded form in the typical dental office setting because preloaded drugs become too easy to administer. In virtually all emergencies, there is no urgent need to administer any drug to the victim other than O_2.

However, I do recommend preloaded syringes of epinephrine (Adrenalin) because this drug must be administered as quickly as possible when the acute allergic reaction develops. With only epinephrine available in a preloaded form, doctors and staff members are less likely to be confused about which drug to administer in this situation.

Drugs used in ACLS are normally available in preloaded form but should be kept separate from the "basic" emergency drugs.

The time required to load drugs into syringes for administration can be better used in the performance of BLS (P→A→B→C→D). The appendix at the end of this chapter reviews parenteral drug administration.

In dental offices in which the doctor is well versed in emergency drugs and their administration and has a well-trained emergency team, preloaded and labeled syringes of emergency drugs are more appropriate. This situation is most likely when the doctor has been trained in the techniques of general anesthesia or, in certain instances, IV conscious sedation.

TABLE 3-2 Module one—critical (essential) emergency drugs

Category	Generic drug	Proprietary drug	Alternative	Quantity	Availability
INJECTABLE					
Allergy—anaphylaxis	Epinephrine	Adrenalin	None	1 preloaded syringe + 3 x 1-mL ampules	1:1000 (1 mg/mL)
Allergy—histamine-blocker	Chlorpheniramine	Chlor-Trimeton	Diphenhydramine (Benadryl)	3 x 1-mL ampules	10 mg/mL
NONINJECTABLE					
Oxygen	Oxygen	Oxygen		1 "E" cylinder	
Vasodilator	Nitroglycerin	Nitrolingual spray	NitroStat sublingual tablets	1 metered spray bottle	0.4 mg/metered dose
Bronchodilator	Albuterol	Proventil, Ventolin	Metaproterenol	1 metered-dose inhaler	Metered-aerosol inhaler
Antihypoglycemic	Sugar	Orange juice, Nondiet soft drink	Insta-Glucose gel	1 bottle	
Inhibitor of platelet aggregation	Aspirin	Many	None	2 packets	325 mg/tablet

Equipment	Recommended	Alternative	Quantity
Oxygen delivery system	Positive pressure and demand valve	O_2 delivery system with bag-valve-mask device	Minimum: 1 large adult, 1 child
	Pocket mask		1 per employee
Automated electronic defibrillator (AED)	Many		1 AED
Syringes for drug administration	Plastic disposable syringes with needles		3 x 2-mL syringes with needles for parenteral drug administration
Suction and suction tips	High-volume suction	Nonelectrical suction system	Office suction system
	Large-diameter, round-ended suction tips		Minimum 2
Tourniquets	Robber or Velcro tourniquet; rubber tubing	Sphygmomanometer	3 tourniquets and 1 sphygmomanometer
Magill intubation forceps	Magill intubation forceps		1 pediatric Magill intubation forceps

■ MODULE ONE: CRITICAL (ESSENTIAL) EMERGENCY DRUGS AND EQUIPMENT

What should be included in the minimum (absolutely basic) emergency kit for a dental or medical office? As always, BLS training is the most significant asset and the first management technique to be used in all emergencies. However, a number of injectable and noninjectable drugs and items of equipment should also be considered absolutely essential for inclusion in the dental office emergency kit (Table 3-2).

Critical injectable drugs

The following two categories of injectable drugs are considered critical in any emergency kit:
1. Epinephrine
2. Histamine blocker

Both drugs are used in the management of an acute allergic reaction, one of the most feared of all emergency situations faced by the health care professional.

Primary injectable: drug for acute allergic reaction (anaphylaxis)

Drug of choice. Epinephrine

Drug class. Catecholamine

Alternative drug. None

Proprietary. Ana-Guard, EpiPen, EpiPen Jr., Twinject

Epinephrine (Adrenalin) is the most important emergency drug in medicine. Epinephrine is the drug of choice in the management of the acute (life-threatening) allergic reaction. Epinephrine is valuable in the management of both the respiratory and cardiovascular manifestations of acute allergic reactions. Desirable properties of epinephrine include (1) a rapid onset of action; (2) potent action as a bronchial smooth muscle dilator ($\beta 2$ properties); (3) histamine-blocking properties; (4) vasopressor actions; and (5) cardiac effects, which include an increase in heart rate (21%), increased systolic blood pressure (5%), decreased diastolic blood pressure (14%), increased cardiac output (51%), and increased coronary blood flow. Undesirable actions include epinephrine's tendency to predispose the heart to dysrhythmias and its relatively short duration of action.

Therapeutic indications. A 1:1000 concentration of epinephrine should be used to treat cases of acute allergic reaction (anaphylaxis, see Chapter 24) and acute asthmatic attack (bronchospasm, see noninjectable drugs and Chapter 13). A 1:10,000 concentration is recommended in the management of cardiac arrest (ACLS, see Chapter 30).

Side effects, contraindications, and precautions. Tachydysrhythmias, both supraventricular and ventricular, may develop. Epinephrine should be administered with caution to pregnant women because it decreases placental blood flow and can induce premature labor. When it is used, all vital signs should be monitored frequently. In the setting of the dental office, epinephrine will usually be considered for administration in situations felt to be acutely life-threatening, such as anaphylaxis and (possibly) cardiac arrest. In such situations, the advantages of epinephrine administration clearly outweigh any risks. No contraindications exist to epinephrine administration under these conditions.

Availability. Epinephrine for parenteral administration is supplied in either a 1:1000 concentration

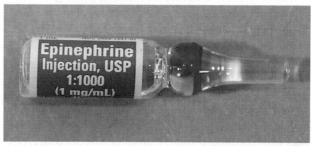

FIGURE 3-8 **A,** Twinject epinephrine syringe. **B,** Epinephrine 1-mL ampule. (A, Copyright Verus Pharmaceuticals, Inc., 2006. Used by permission. Twinject® is a registered trademark of Verus Pharmaceuticals, Inc. All rights reserved.)

(1 g [1000 mg]/L), in which each milliliter contains 1 mg of the agent, or as a 1:10,000 concentration. The 1:1000 concentration is meant for IM and subcutaneous administration only, whereas the 1:10,000 concentration is designed for IV administration. Because the dosage of this drug is critical, it is advisable to have parenteral epinephrine available in preloaded syringe form rather than in a multidose vial. In addition, preloaded syringes permit the drug to be administered quickly, a requirement in the treatment of the acute allergic reaction (Figure 3-8A and B). It is recommended, therefore, that epinephrine be available in preloaded syringes and 1-mL ampules.

Because of its short duration of action and because the dose administered is 0.3 mg, multiple administrations are usually necessary during the management of the acute phase of anaphylaxis. Unit-dose (1-mL) ampules are preferred over multidose vials because the unit-dose form prevents the doctor or other staff member from inadvertently overadministering epinephrine. An overdose of epinephrine can produce significant complications.[21,22]

The drug package insert for epinephrine states that "Overdosage or inadvertent intravenous injection of epinephrine may cause cerebrovascular hemorrhage resulting from the sharp rise in blood pressure."[23]

Dose. Although the 1-mL ampule of 1:1000 epinephrine is considered the adult therapeutic dose, epinephrine is administered via the IM or subcutaneous route in a dose of 0.3 to 0.5 mL of solution with additional doses administered as needed. This break with tradition (1 mL as the adult therapeutic dose of an emergency drug) stems from the fact that although 1 mg of epinephrine is the usual therapeutic dose for anaphylaxis, this dose may be excessive for some patients. For instance, the person with significant cardiovascular disease (for example, American Society of Anesthesiologists [ASA] stage IV, status post–myocardial infarction or high blood pressure, or post–cerebrovascular accident) who suffers an anaphylactic reaction to an insect bite and receives 1 mL of a 1:1000 epinephrine solution probably will not die from the allergic response. However, the possibility that the epinephrine's action on the patient's cardiovascular system can lead to serious adverse consequences is increased.

Unfortunately, in what may be a near-panic situation (anaphylaxis), the doctor may administer to the victim an overly large dose of epinephrine. Preloaded syringes are available that make it impossible to administer in excess of the predetermined dose (see Figure 3-8).[24] The syringe's plunger and guide channel are rectangular. However, at the 0.3-mL mark the rectangle shifts 90 degrees, which makes the administration of more than 0.3 mL (0.3 mg) at a time impossible. The plunger must be rotated to administer an additional dose. Such a syringe is highly recommended for inclusion in all emergency drug kits. Pediatric forms of these syringes that deliver a dose of 0.15 mg also are available.

Suggested for emergency kit. Each kit should have one preloaded syringe (1 mL of 1:1000 [1 mg epinephrine]) and three or four ampules of 1:1000 epinephrine to treat anaphylaxis via an IM or subcutaneous route.

Primary injectable: drug for allergic reaction
Drug of choice. Chlorpheniramine

Proprietary. Chlor-Trimeton

Drug class. Histamine blocker (nonselective antihistamine)

Alternative drug. Diphenhydramine

Antihistamines now are categorized as *histamine-blockers,* a term that better describes their mode of clinical action. Histamine blockers are valuable in the management of the more common delayed allergic response and in the definitive management of the acute allergic reaction (administered after epinephrine has resolved the life-threatening phase of the reaction).

Histamine blockers are competitive antagonists of histamine; they do not prevent the release of histamine from cells in response to injury, drugs, or antigens but do prevent histamine's access to its receptor site in the cell, blocking the response of the effector cell to histamine. Therefore, histamine-blockers are more potent in preventing the actions of histamine than in reversing these actions once they occur. An interesting action of many histamine-blockers is that they are also potent local anesthetics, especially diphenhydramine and tripelennamine.[25,26]

The choice of a specific histamine-blocker for the emergency kit was made after considering that most patients seeking dental care are ambulatory and desire to leave the dental office unescorted (probably to drive a car). However, cortical depression (sedation), a potential side effect of many histamine-blockers, should prevent the patient from being discharged from the dental office unescorted.

Diphenhydramine HCl (Benadryl) causes sedation in nearly 50% of individuals. On the other hand, chlorpheniramine (ChlorTrimeton) produces less sedation (10%) than diphenhydramine with an equivalent histamine-blocking action.

Therapeutic indications. Histamine blockers are recommended in management of delayed-onset allergic reactions, the definitive management of acute allergic reactions, and as local anesthetics when the patient has a history of alleged allergy to local anesthesia (see Chapter 24).

Side effects, contraindications, and precautions. Side effects of histamine-blockers include CNS depression, decreased blood pressure, and thickening of bronchial secretions resulting from the drug's drying action. Because of this drying effect, histamine-blockers are contraindicated in the management of acute asthmatic episodes. *Pt must leave w escort*

Availability. Chlorpheniramine is available as 10 mg/mL in 1- and 2-mL ampules and as 1-mL preloaded syringes. Diphenhydramine is available as 10 mg/mL in 10- and 30-mL multidose vials, 50 mg/mL in 1-mL ampules and 10-mL multidose vials, and 1-mL preloaded syringes.

Suggested for emergency kit. The emergency kit should contain three or four 1-mL ampules of either chlorpheniramine (10 mg/mL) or diphenhydramine (50 mg/mL). Syringes preloaded with histamine-blockers are not recommended because there is never any urgency associated with their administration.

FIGURE 3-9 "E"-sized O_2 cylinder. (From McSwain N: *The basic EMT: comprehensive prehospital care,* ed 2, St. Louis, Mosby, 2003.)

Critical noninjectable drugs

The following five noninjectable drugs are also considered critical:
1. Oxygen
2. Vasodilator
3. Bronchodilator
4. Antihypoglycemic
5. Aspirin

Primary noninjectable: oxygen (O_2)
Drug of choice. Oxygen

Drug class. None

Alternative drug. None

Proprietary. None

Unquestionably the most useful drug in the entire emergency kit is O_2, which is supplied in a variety of sizes of compressed gas cylinders. Recommended is the "E" cylinder, which is quite portable (Figure 3-9). In emergency situations an E cylinder provides O_2 for approximately 30 minutes (when the patient is apneic). Larger cylinders (H cylinders) provide significantly more O_2 but are less portable; smaller cylinders (A through D cylinders) contain too little O_2 to be clinically effective for more than an extremely short duration. O_2 produced through a chemical reaction in small canisters is not

adequate for an emergency kit. A portable E cylinder of O_2 also should be available in offices in which centrally located nitrous oxide and O_2 is available. Because emergencies do occur in areas of the dental office other than in the dental chair, the O_2 delivery system must be portable.

Therapeutic indications. O_2 administration is indicated in any emergency situation in which respiratory distress is evident. Indeed O_2 should never be withheld from a patient during a medical emergency.[*]

Side effects, contraindications, and precautions. None with the emergency use of O_2, although O_2 administration is not indicated in the treatment of hyperventilation.

Availability. Compressed gas cylinders come in a variety of sizes. Portability of the emergency O_2 cylinder is desirable.

Suggested for emergency kit. One E cylinder is the minimum requirement for an emergency kit.

Primary noninjectable: vasodilator
Drug of choice. Nitroglycerin

Proprietary. Nitrolingual spray, Nitrostat tablets

Drug class. Vasodilator

Alternative drug. Amyl nitrite

Vasodilators are used in the immediate management of chest pain as may occur with angina pectoris or acute myocardial infarction. Two varieties of vasodilator are available: (1) nitroglycerin as a tablet and a spray (Figure 3-10) and (2) an inhalant, amyl nitrite. A patient with a history of angina pectoris usually carries a supply of nitroglycerin.

Tablets remain the most used form of the drug by patients, but most prefer the translingual spray once they have used it. During dental care the patient's nitroglycerin source should be readily accessible. Placed sublingually or sprayed onto the lingual soft tissues, nitroglycerin acts in 1 to 2 minutes. The patient's own drug should be used if at all possible, but if it is unavailable or is ineffective, the emergency kit should contain the 0.4-mg formulation.

---

[*]Although O_2 administration is not necessary in the treatment of hyperventilating patients, its administration does not produce a significant adverse reaction.

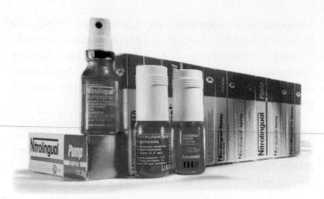

FIGURE 3-10 Nitrolingual spray.

The shelf life of nitroglycerin tablets, once exposed to air, is short (about 12 weeks) when the container is not adequately sealed or the tablets are stored in a pill box. In such cases the active nitroglycerin vaporizes, leaving behind nothing but inert filler. This is not problem for a patient with angina who uses only one bottle with 25 tablets. The typical patient with stable angina uses a bottle within 4 to 6 weeks. Most patients with angina, however, have several opened bottles of nitroglycerin available—in their pockets, cars, offices, and homes. The doctor should not use the patient's drug if doubt exists as to when the bottle was opened. Nitroglycerin deterioration is more likely to occur with a dental office's supply of nitroglycerin, which is used (it is hoped) only rarely.

Nitroglycerin tablets placed sublingually usually produce a bitter taste and impart a sting. When the bitter taste is absent, the doctor should suspect the drug has become ineffective. A translingual nitroglycerin spray introduced in the United States in 1986 has a significantly longer shelf life than sublingual tablets even after being used once or repeated times and is highly recommended for inclusion in the emergency drug kit.

Amyl nitrite, another vasodilator, is available in inhalant form. It is supplied in a yellow vaporole or a gray cardboard vaporole with yellow printing in doses of 0.3 mL, which when crushed between the fingers and held under the victim's nose produces profound vasodilation in about 10 seconds. The duration of action of amyl nitrite is shorter than nitroglycerin, but its shelf life is considerably longer. Side effects occur with all vasodilators (see following section) but are more significant with amyl nitrite.

Therapeutic indications. With chest pain, vasodilators are used as an aid in differential diagnosis and in the definitive management of angina pectoris (see Chapter 27), the early management of acute myocardial infarction (see Chapter 28), and the management of acute hypertensive episodes.

Side effects, contraindications, and precautions. Side effects of nitroglycerin include a transient, pulsating headache; facial flushing; and a degree of hypotension, especially if the patient is in an upright position. Because of its mild hypotensive actions, nitroglycerin is contraindicated in patients who are hypotensive but may be used with some degree of effectiveness in the management of acute hypertensive episodes. Because nitroglycerin as a tablet is an unstable drug (has a short shelf life once opened), it usually must be replaced within 12 weeks after its initial use.

Side effects of amyl nitrite are similar to but more intense than those of nitroglycerin. These include facial flushing, pounding pulse, dizziness, intense headache, and hypotension. Amyl nitrite should not be administered to patients seated in upright positions because significant postural changes develop.

The recent introduction of sildenafil (Viagra), tadalafil (Cialis), and vardenafil (Levitra) to treat erectile dysfunction has created another drug-drug interaction. The combination of these drugs with nitrates may increase the risk of severe hypotension, tachycardia, and cardiovascular collapse, representing a synergistic effect. Men who have received nitroglycerin for the treatment of ischemic heart disease have died after ingesting these drugs.[27-29]

Availability. Nitroglycerin is available in three forms: 0.3-, 0.4-, 0.6-mg doses of sublingual tablets, 0.4- and 0.8-mg/dose translingual spray, and 0.3-mL doses of amyl nitrate yellow vaporoles.

Suggested for emergency kit. Kits should contain one bottle of metered translingual nitroglycerin spray (0.4 mg).

Primary noninjectable: bronchodilator
Drug of choice. Albuterol

Proprietary. Proventil, Ventolin

Drug class. Bronchodilator

Alternative drug. Metaproterenol

Asthmatic patients and patients with allergic reactions manifested primarily by respiratory difficulty require the use of bronchodilators. Although epinephrine remains the drug of choice in the management of bronchospasm, its wide-ranging effects on systems other than the respiratory tract have resulted in the introduction of newer, more specific drugs known as β_2-adrenergic agonists. These drugs, of which albuterol is an example, have specific bronchial smooth muscle-relaxing properties (β_2) with little or no stimulatory

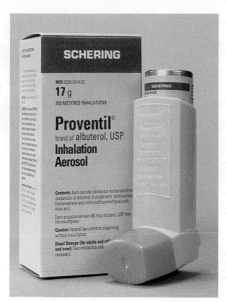

FIGURE 3-11 Bronchodilator. (From McSwain N: *The basic EMT: comprehensive prehospital care,* ed 2, St. Louis, Mosby, 2003.)

action on the cardiovascular and gastrointestinal systems (β_1) (Figure 3-11).

In the dental environment, where the doctor may be unaware of the patient's true cardiovascular status, β_2 agonists appear more attractive for management of acute asthmatic episodes than do drugs with both β_1- and β_2-agonist properties, such as epinephrine and isoproterenol. As with anginal patients, most asthmatic patients carry their medication (in this case, a bronchodilator) with them at all times. In virtually all situations the bronchodilator is an inhaler that dispenses a calibrated dose, which the patient inhales. Inhalation allows the drug to reach the bronchial mucosa, where it acts directly on bronchial smooth muscle.

Before dental treatment begins, asthmatic patients who are at greater risk of bronchospasm (e.g., patients with dental phobia) should be asked to make their bronchodilators available. Bronchodilators must be administered precisely as directed. One or two inhalations every 4 to 6 hours is the recommended dosage for albuterol. Nebulized epinephrine (e.g., Primatene Mist) should be administered at one or two inhalations per hour. In situations in which nebulized agents fail to terminate the attack, other bronchodilators (e.g., epinephrine, aminophylline, isoproterenol) must be administered parenterally (via an IM or subcutaneous route).

Therapeutic indications. Bronchodilators are used to treat bronchospasm (acute asthmatic episodes) (see Chapter 13) and allergic reactions with bronchospasm (see Chapter 24).

Side effects, contraindications, and precautions. Albuterol, like other β_2 agonists, can have clinically significant cardiac effects in some patients. This response is less likely to develop with albuterol than with other bronchodilators, hence its selection for the emergency kit. Metaproterenol, epinephrine, and isoproterenol mistometers are more likely to produce cardiovascular side effects, including tachycardia and ventricular dysrhythmias. Administration of these latter drugs is contraindicated in patients with preexisting tachydysrhythmias from prior use of the drug (see Chapter 13).

Availability. Albuterol inhalers (Ventolin, Proventil), metaproterenol inhalers (Alupent), epinephrine mistometers (Medihaler-Epi; Primatene Mist), and isoproterenol mistometers (Medihaler-Iso).

Suggested for emergency kit. One metered albuterol inhaler.

Primary noninjectable: antihypoglycemic
Drug of choice. Orange juice

Drug class. Antihypoglycemic

Alternative drug. Soft drink (nondiet)

Proprietary. None

Antihypoglycemics are useful in the management of hypoglycemic reactions in patients with diabetes mellitus or nondiabetic patients with hypoglycemia (low blood sugar). The diabetic patient usually carries a sugar source such as a candy bar. The dental office also should have such items available for use in the conscious hypoglycemic patient.

For management of the unconscious hypoglycemic patient, refer to the discussion of secondary injectable drugs in this chapter. In certain well-defined and well-controlled situations, thick nonviscous forms of carbohydrate may be used to manage the unconscious hypoglycemic patient when no injectable source is available and in locations where emergency medical assistance is not readily obtainable. This technique, *transmucosal application of sugar,* is described in Chapter 17.

Therapeutic indications. Hypoglycemic states secondary to diabetes mellitus or fasting hypoglycemia in the conscious patient (Chapter 17); emergency management of unconscious hypoglycemic states in the absence of both parenteral medications and rapid access to emergency medical assistance (Chapter 17).

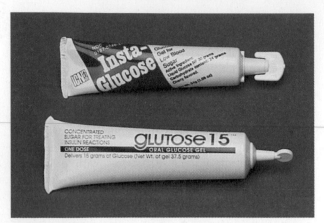

FIGURE 3-12 Oral glucose gels. (From McSwain N: *The basic EMT: comprehensive prehospital care,* ed 2, St. Louis, Mobsy, 2003.)

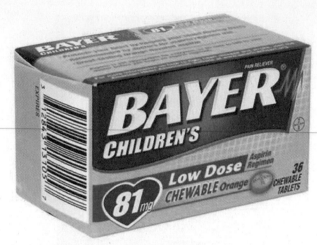

FIGURE 3-13 Chewable children's aspirin are recommended for the emergency kit. (Courtesy Bayer Health Care LLC, Morristown, New Jersey.)

Side effects, contraindications, and precautions. Liquid or viscous oral carbohydrates should not be administered to a patient who does not have an active gag reflex or is unable to drink without assistance. Parenteral administration of antihypoglycemics is recommended in these situations. There are no side effects when oral carbohydrates are administered as directed.

Availability. Antihypoglycemics come in a variety of forms, including Glucola, Gluco-Stat, Insta-Glucose, nondiet cola beverages, fruit juices, granulated sugar, and tubes of decorative icing (Figure 3-12).

Suggested for emergency kit. Any of the previously mentioned sources can be included in the emergency kit.

Primary noninjectable: antiplatelet
Drug of choice. Aspirin

Drug class. Antiplatelet

Alternative drug. None

Aspirin has become a recommended antithrombotic drug in the prehospital phase of suspected myocardial infarction. Considered to be the standard antiplatelet agent, aspirin represents the most cost-effective treatment available for patients with acute ischemic coronary syndromes. Aspirin irreversibly acetylates platelet cyclooxygenase, removing all cyclooxygenase activity for the life span of the platelet (8 to 10 days).[30] Aspirin stops production of proaggregatory thromboxane A_2 and is also an indirect antithrombotic agent. Aspirin also has important nonplatelet effects because it likewise inactivates cyclooxygenase in the vascular endothelium and thereby diminishes formation of antiaggregatory prostacyclin.[30]

The ISIS-2 (Second International Study of Infarct Survival) trial provides the strongest evidence that aspirin independently reduces mortality rates in patients with acute myocardial infarction without additional thrombolytic therapy (overall 23% reduction) and is synergistic when used in combination with thrombolytic therapy (42% reduction in mortality).[31,32] Administration of aspirin is recommended for all patients with suspected acute myocardial infarction or unstable angina.[30] Standard doses range from 160 to 324 mg given orally. Minimal side effects are noted, particularly with the 160-mg dose.

Therapeutic indications. Aspirin is recommended in management of patients with suspected myocardial infarction or unstable angina.

Side effects, contraindications, and precautions. Definite contraindications to aspirin therapy include ongoing major or life-threatening hemorrhage; a significant predisposition to such hemorrhage, such as a recent bleeding peptic ulcer; or a history of aspirin allergy.

Availability. Aspirin is available in 65-, 81-, 162-, and 325-mg tablets under many brand names.

Suggested for emergency kit. The emergency kit should include three or four "baby" chewable aspirin (162 mg) (Figure 3-13). Two tablets should be taken as directed by a doctor if a heart attack is suspected.

Critical emergency equipment
Critical items of emergency equipment include the following:
1. O_2 delivery system
2. Automated external defibrillator

TABLE 3-3 Comparison of ventilation methods

Technique	% oxygen delivered
Mouth-to-mouth	16
Mouth-to-mask	16
Bag-valve-mask	21
Bag-valve-mask + supplemental O_2	>21 to <100
Positive pressure O_2	100

3. Syringes
4. Suction and suction tips
5. Tourniquets : BP cuff
6. Magill intubation forceps

Merely having various items of emergency equipment available does not of itself better equip a dental office or better prepare the staff member for the management of emergency situations. Personnel who are expected to use this equipment must be well trained in its proper use. Unfortunately, many emergency equipment items commonly found in dental and medical offices can be useless and even hazardous if they are used improperly or in the wrong situation. Training in the proper use of equipment, such as the laryngoscope and the oropharyngeal airway, can be achieved best through the care of patients under general anesthesia, a situation not readily available to most dental personnel.

Many items listed in this section are therefore recommended for use only by properly trained individuals. All emergency equipment items classified as secondary and unfortunately several classified as primary (e.g., the O_2 delivery system) require training to be used effectively. Although all doctors should be trained in the use of O_2 delivery systems, courses in which these techniques are taught are particularly difficult to locate. (Readers interested in such hands-on programs should contact their local dental society, dental school, hospital, or American Heart Association affiliate.)

Therefore, dental personnel must use only those pieces of emergency equipment with which they are intimately familiar and have been trained to use properly. The usefulness of the items described here varies with the training of the office personnel. All dental personnel should become proficient in the use of the primary items of equipment.

O_2 delivery system
Table 3-3 compares several methods of ventilation.

Positive pressure. An O_2 delivery system adaptable to the E cylinder allows for the delivery of O_2 under positive pressure to the patient. Examples of this device include the positive-pressure/demand valve (Figure 3-14)

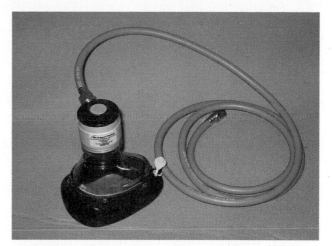

FIGURE 3-14 Positive-pressure demand valve. (Courtesy Sedation Resource, Lone Oak, Texas. www.sedationresource.com)

FIGURE 3-15 Bag-valve-mask. (Courtesy Sedation Resource, Lone Oak, Texas. www.sedationresource.com)

and the reservoir bag on many inhalation sedation units. The devices should be fitted with a clear face mask, allowing for the efficient delivery of 100% O_2 while permitting the rescuer to visually inspect the victim's mouth for the presence of foreign matter (e.g., vomitus, blood, saliva, water). Face masks should be available in child, small-adult, and large-adult sizes.

Bag-valve-mask device. A portable, self-inflating bag-valve-mask device (Ambu-bag, PMR [pulmonary manual resuscitator]; Figure 3-15) is a self-contained unit that may be easily transported to any site within a dental office. This is an important feature since not all emergencies will develop within the dental operatory and it may be necessary to resuscitate a person in other areas, such as the waiting room or restroom. A source of positive-pressure oxygen or ambient air or enriched O_2 (>21%, <100%) attached to an oxygen delivery tube

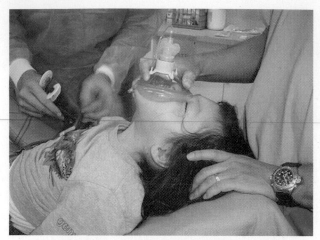

FIGURE 3-16 Holding pocket mask on face.

FIGURE 3-18 Pocket mask inverted on small infant or child. (Courtesy Sedation Resource, Lone Oak, Texas. www.sedationresource.com)

FIGURE 3-17 Pocket mask. (Courtesy Sedation Resource, Lone Oak, Texas. www.sedationresource.com)

should be available in these areas. With either device the rescuer must be able to maintain both an airtight seal and a patent airway with one hand while using the other hand to activate the device and ventilate the victim (Figure 3-16).

Pocket mask. The pocket mask is a clear full-face mask, identical in shape and application to the positive-pressure and bag-valve-mask devices (Figure 3-17). Unlike these devices, however, the rescuer must apply exhaled air ventilation (16% O_2) into the inlet on top of the mask to ventilate the victim. Exhalation occurs passively through a one-way valve located on the side of the mask. In this way, the rescuer does not rebreathe the victim's exhaled air. The pocket mask also is available with a supplemental O_2 port, permitting attachment of the mask to an O_2 tube, and deliver enriched O_2 ventilation.

Small enough to fit easily into a pocket or purse, the pocket mask enables the rescuer to provide mouth-to-

mask ventilation to the apneic victim in place of mouth-to-mouth ventilation. The pocket mask also helps individuals overcome the "yuck" factor, which refers to the fact that a significant percentage of victims requiring artificial ventilation regurgitate, presenting with a pharynx and oral cavity filled with vomitus ("yuck").

The rescuer can also use the pocket mask to ventilate a pediatric patient by simply inverting the mask, holding the narrow nose side of the mask in the cleft of the chin and the wider chin side on the bridge of the child's nose (Figure 3-18). Because of concern in the health professions about the transmission of hepatitis viruses and HIV as a result of direct physical contact with bodily fluids, the pocket mask (or any other mask or "barrier" technique for that matter) is an ideal choice to provide the rescuer positive psychological support. In addition, the low cost of the mask (approximately $20) is another reason that all dental office personnel should have their own pocket mask.

Suggested for emergency kit. One portable O_2 cylinder (E cylinder) with a positive-pressure mask, one portable self-inflating bag-valve-mask device, and one pocket mask for each staff member. Several sizes—child, small-adult, and large-adult—of clear full-face masks also should be available; specialty practices should stock additional mask sizes.

NOTE: *Advanced training is required for the safe and effective use of masks for ventilation.*

Automated external defibrillator
Though rare in the dental environment, sudden cardiac arrest does occur. Successful resuscitation from sudden cardiac arrest depends on many factors collectively

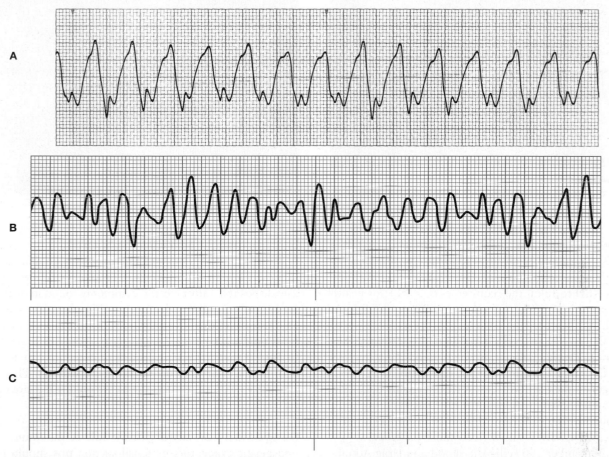

FIGURE 3-19 Dysrhythmias on electrocardiography. **A,** Ventricular tachycardia. **B,** Coarse ventricular fibrillation. **C,** Fine ventricular fibrillation. (From McSwain N: *The basic EMT: comprehensive prehospital care,* ed 2, St. Louis, Mosby, 2003.)

known as the "chain of survival."[33] The adult chain of survival has four links: (1) early access to EMS (9-1-1); (2) early BLS; (3) early defibrillation; and (4) early ACLS.

The most important component in the chain of survival is the elapsed time between collapse and defibrillation.[34-36] The shorter this span of time, the greater the chance of successful resuscitation. The likelihood of successful resuscitation from out-of-hospital sudden cardiac arrest decreases at a rate of approximately 7% to 10% per minute, even if basic life support is administered effectively.[37]

Early defibrillation (shock delivered within 5 minutes of receipt of the EMS call) is a high-priority goal of EMS care.[38] Unfortunately, this goal is only rarely achieved. Large U.S. cities, such as New York, Los Angeles, and Chicago, have EMS response times of 11.4 minutes and 16 minutes, respectively, with depressingly low survival rates from out-of-hospital cardiac arrest (New York 1%, Chicago 1%, Los Angeles 1.4%).[39-41]

Automated external defibrillators are sophisticated, yet simple, battery-operated computerized devices that have been shown to be reliable and easy to operate. Simply stated, AEDs are computers that recognize the two cardiac dysrhythmias, ventricular fibrillation (VF) and pulseless ventricular tachycardia (VT), which may be effectively treated through defibrillation (Figure 3-19).

The directions on the AED advise the rescuer that a shock is (or is not) indicated, but the machine will not deliver the shock without the rescuer's activating the unit (pushing the "Shock" button). AEDs record and analyze the electrocardiography (ECG) signal to determine whether it is consistent with VF/VT.[42] The AED then verbally advises a shock if an ECG signal consistent with these rhythms is detected. The accuracy of these devices in rhythm analysis is extremely high.[43]

Chapter 30 discusses AEDs in detail.

Basic life support (CPR) certification is mandated for dental licensure in many states and provinces. "BLS for health care providers," as now defined by the American

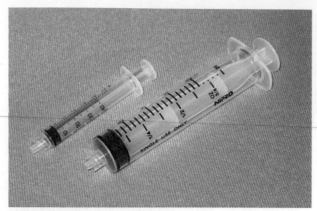

FIGURE 3-20   Plastic disposable syringes (2 mL). (Courtesy Sedation Resource, Lone Oak, Texas. www.sedationresource.com)

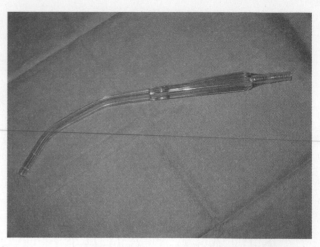

FIGURE 3-21   Aspirator tip.

Heart Association, includes defibrillation (P→A→B→C→D).[44] Therefore, all jurisdictions requiring BLS for dental licensure should mandate the on-site availability of an AED to fulfill the requirements of BLS for health care providers. As of February 28, 2006, the Florida Board of Dentistry has mandated the availability of an AED on-site in every dental office location.[45] The American Dental Association recommends "that dentists consider purchasing an AED for dental offices in which emergency medical services personnel with defibrillation skills and equipment are not available within a reasonable time frame. As of June 2005 six AEDs participate in the ADAs Seal of Acceptance program."[46]

In September 2004, the U.S. Food and Drug Administration approved AEDs for over-the-counter sales.[47] Many AEDs are available for purchase in the United States. It is recommended that the doctor considering purchase of an AED research these devices. The American Dental Association Council on Scientific Affairs may be contacted via e-mail at science@ada.org. A proprietary website that compares many AEDs is www.aedsuperstore.com.

Suggested for emergency kit. One AED.

Syringes

Plastic disposable syringes equipped with an 18- or 21-gauge needle are used in parenteral drug administration. Although many sizes are available, the 2-mL syringe is adequate for the delivery of emergency drugs (Figure 3-20).

Suggested for emergency kit. Two to four 2-mL disposable syringes with 18- or 21-gauge needles.

NOTE: *Before a drug is drawn into the syringe, the needle must be tightened, to ensure no leakage, by turning it in a clockwise manner.*

Suction and aspirating apparatus

A strong suction system and a number of large-diameter suction tips are essential items of emergency equipment. The disposable saliva ejector, commonly found in dental offices, is entirely inadequate in situations in which anything other than the tiniest object must be evacuated from a patient's mouth. Aspirator tips should be rounded to ensure that there is little risk of bleeding should it become necessary to suction the hypopharynx. Plastic evacuators and tonsil suction tips are quite adequate for this purpose (Figure 3-21).

Suggested for emergency kit. A minimum of two plastic evacuators or tonsil suction tips should be available in the emergency kit.

Tourniquets

A tourniquet will be required if IV drugs are to be administered. In addition, three tourniquets are needed to perform a bloodless phlebotomy in the management of acute pulmonary edema (see Chapter 14). A sphygmomanometer (blood pressure cuff) can be used as a tourniquet, as may a simple piece of latex tubing (Figure 3-22).

Suggested for emergency kit. Three tourniquets and a sphygmomanometer should be included in each kit.

Magill intubation forceps   *: suction tube*

The Magill intubation forceps is designed to aid in the placement of an endotracheal tube during nasal intubation. The Magill intubation forceps is a blunt-ended scissors with a right-angle bend (Figure 3-23). This design permits the forceps to grasp objects deep in the hypopharynx such as the endotracheal tube.

Published reports have described the ingestion or aspiration of dental items such as crowns and endodontic files.[48,49] Just before being "swallowed," these

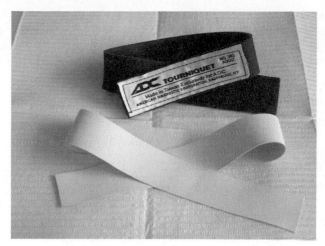

FIGURE 3-22 Variety of tourniquets.

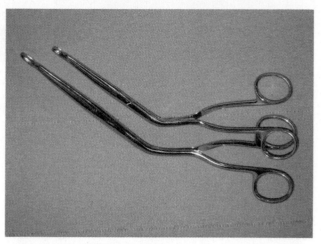

FIGURE 3-23 Magill intubation forceps. (Courtesy Sedation Resource, Lone Oak, Texas. www.sedationresource.com)

items lie in the posterior region of the patient's oral cavity. There is usually nothing readily available on an instrument tray that can be easily used to retrieve such objects. The Magill intubation forceps is designed to perform this function and is highly recommended for inclusion in every emergency kit.

Suggested for emergency kit. One pediatric-size Magill intubation forceps.

■ MODULE TWO: SECONDARY (NONCRITICAL) EMERGENCY DRUGS AND EQUIPMENT

Drugs and equipment included in this module, though important and valuable in the management of emergency situations, are not considered to be as critical as those in the basic office emergency kit. Only doctors who have been trained in the use of these drugs should consider including them in the office kit. Doctors who administer parenteral sedation may be required by their state or specialty organization to maintain many of these drugs in their emergency kits.

Secondary injectable drugs

Seven drug categories are included in this level (Table 3-4):
1. Anticonvulsant
2. Analgesic
3. Vasopressor
4. Antihypoglycemic
5. Corticosteroid
6. Antihypertensive
7. Anticholinergic

Secondary injectable: anticonvulsant
Drug of choice. Midazolam

Proprietary. Versed

Drug class. Benzodiazepine

Alternative drug. Diazepam

Seizure disorders may occur in the dental office under several circumstances, including epileptic seizures, overdose reactions to local anesthetics, obstructed airway in an unconscious patient, hypoglycemia, and febrile convulsions. Only rarely will administration of an anticonvulsant be required to terminate seizure activity. An anticonvulsant should be considered for inclusion in the emergency kit so that is readily available. The choice of an anticonvulsant has become somewhat simpler since the introduction of the benzodiazepines.

Until about 40 years ago, barbiturates were the drugs of choice in the management of acute seizure disorders. With its introduction in 1960, diazepam became the preferred anticonvulsant. Because seizure disorders are characterized by stimulation of the central nervous, respiratory, and cardiovascular systems followed by a period of depression of these same systems, drugs that depress these systems at therapeutic doses are more likely to produce postseizure complications.

When barbiturates are administered to terminate seizure activity, the patient's postseizure depression is more profound and prolonged because of the pharmacologic actions of the barbiturate. When seizure activity is intense, the ensuing postictal period of depression

TABLE 3-4 Module two—secondary (noncritical) drugs and equipment

Category	Generic drug	Proprietary drug	Alternative	Quantity	Availability
INJECTABLE					
Anticonvulsant	Midazolam	Versed	Diazepam	1 x 5-mL vial	5 mg/mL
Analgesic	Morphine sulfate	Generic	Meperidine	3 x 1-mL ampules	10 mg/mL
Vasopressor	Phenylephrine	Generic		3 x 1-mL ampules	10 mg/mL
Antihypoglycemic	50% dextrose		Glucagon	1 vial	50-mL ampule
Corticosteroid	Hydrocortisone sodium succinate	Solu-Cortef	Dexamethasone	2 x 2-mL mix-o-vial	50 mg/mL
Antihypertensive	Esmolol	Brevibloc	Propranolol	2 x 100-mg/mL vial	100 mg/mL
Anticholinergic	Atropine	Generic	Scopolamine	3 x 1-mL ampules	0.5 mg/mL
NONINJECTABLE					
Respiratory stimulant	Aromatic ammonia	Generic		2 boxes	0.3 mL/ Vaporole
Antihypertensive	Nifedipine	Procardia		1 bottle	10 mg/capsule

usually is profound, with compromised respiration and a period of hypotension. When barbiturates are used to terminate seizures, the ensuing depression will likely be intensified, leading to respiratory arrest (apnea) and a profound cardiovascular depression or collapse. If the doctor is not adept at recognizing and managing this situation, the patient can face more risks after the seizure than during it.

Unlike barbiturates, benzodiazepines usually terminate seizure activity without significant depression of the respiratory and cardiovascular systems. For many years, diazepam was the anticonvulsant drug of choice because of its ability to terminate seizures without producing profound postictal depression. Its lack of water solubility, however, limited its use to IV administration. It was highly unlikely that a physician or dentist who was not technically proficient in venipuncture would be able to start an IV line on a patient during a generalized tonic-clonic seizure. Where this was possible, diazepam was the preferred drug.

With the introduction of midazolam, a water-soluble benzodiazepine that is effective as an anticonvulsant in the IV, IM, and intranasal (IN) routes became available. Although IV administration still is preferred, the IM and IN routes are now available (Figure 3-24).

IM or IN midazolam provides clinical action within 10 to 15 minutes. (Time of onset is dependent upon blood pressure and tissue perfusion.)[50–52]

Therapeutic indications. Midazolam is used to treat prolonged seizures (see discussion of status epilepticus in Chapter 21), local anesthetic–induced seizures

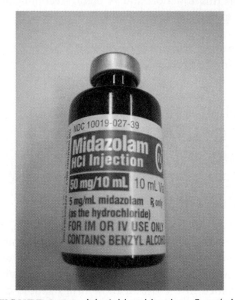

FIGURE 3-24 Injectable midazolam, 5 mg/mL.

(see Chapter 23), hyperventilation (see discussion of sedation in Chapter 12), and thyroid storm (see discussion of sedation in Chapter 18).

Side effects, contraindications, and precautions. The major clinical side effect noted with benzodiazepines when used as anticonvulsants is respiratory depression or arrest. However, with careful titration during administration, this effect is less likely to occur. Compared with the effect of barbiturates, benzodiazepine-induced respiratory depression is considerably more mild.

Availability. Midazolam (Versed [United States], Hypnovel and Dormicum [Europe, Great Britain]) is available as 5 mg/mL in 1-, 2-, 5-, and 10-mL vials and in 2-mL preloaded syringes, and 1 mg/mL in 2-, 5-, and 10-mL vials. Diazepam (Valium) is available as 5 mg/mL in 2-mL ampules and 10-mL vials and in 2-mL preloaded syringes.

Suggested for emergency kit. One 5-mL vial of midazolam (5 mg/mL) (Figure 3-24).

Secondary injectable: analgesic
Drug of choice. Morphine sulfate

Proprietary. None

Drug class. Opioid agonist

Alternative drug. Meperidine; nitrous oxide, and oxygen (N_2O-O_2)

Analgesics are used in emergency situations in which acute pain or anxiety is present. In most instances the pain or anxiety increases the myocardial workload (which increases the myocardial O_2 requirement) which may prove detrimental to the patient's well-being. Two such circumstances include acute myocardial infarction and congestive heart failure. The analgesic drugs of choice include the opioid agonists morphine sulfate and meperidine (Demerol).

Therapeutic indications. Intense, prolonged pain or anxiety; acute myocardial infarction (see Chapter 28); and congestive heart failure (see Chapter 14).

Side effects, contraindications, and precautions. Opioid agonists are potent central nervous and respiratory system depressants. Vigilant monitoring of vital signs is mandatory whenever these drugs are used. Use of opioid agonists is contraindicated in victims of injury and multiple trauma; the drugs should be used with care in any person with compromised respiratory function. (Naloxone can be administered to reverse the respiratory depressant actions of opioid agonists and other opioid-agonist properties and of analgesia [see Module Four: Antidotal Drugs].) Opioid analgesics should be administered through an IV route to victims suspected of having acute myocardial infarction. This group of drugs should not be included in the emergency drug kit unless the doctor and staff members are trained in both IV drug administration and ACLS.

Availability. Morphine sulfate is available as 8, 10, and 15 mg/mL (in 2-mL ampules and 20-mL vials), and meperidine comes in 50- and 100-mg/mL doses (in 1-mL ampules and 20- and 30-mL vials).

Suggested for emergency kit. Emergency kits may contain 10 mg/mL morphine sulfate (two 2-mL ampules) or 50 mg/mL meperidine (2 mL ampules).

NOTE: *In recent years, emergency medical services in many countries have employed mixtures of nitrous oxide (N_2O) and O_2 in place of opioid analgesics in the management of pain associated with acute myocardial infarction.[53] Concentrations of N_2O have varied between 35% and 50%. At these levels a mixture of 35% to 50% N_2O and 50% to 65% O_2 decreases pain, sedates the patient, and provides that patient two and a half to three times ambient levels of O_2 (see Chapter 28). When available, N_2O-O_2 may be used in place of opioid analgesics. This is especially important where IV access is unavailable. In its absence, however, an opioid analgesic should be considered for inclusion in the emergency kit.*

Opioid agonists are schedule II drugs, which means that they must be maintained in a secure location in the dental office. A schedule II classification precludes their physical presence in the emergency drug kit, which should be readily accessible at all times.

Secondary injectable: vasopressor
Drug of choice. Phenylephrine

Proprietary. Many

Drug class. Vasopressor

Alternative drug. None

Although one potent vasopressor—epinephrine—is already included in the emergency kit, most emergencies in the dental office in which a vasopressor is needed will not require epinephrine. Epinephrine is used primarily in the management of acute allergic reactions and is rarely indicated in the management of clinically mild to moderate hypotension. Epinephrine elicits an extreme antihypotensive response. In addition to an increase in blood pressure, this drug increases the heart's workload through its effect on heart rate and strength of cardiac contractions; it also increases the irritability of the myocardium, thereby sensitizing it to dysrhythmias.

In most clinical situations listed below (see Therapeutic Indications), the victim's systolic blood pressure has fallen to about 60 to 80 mm Hg and has not returned to its baseline level in an appropriate time period. A drug should be available to elevate the systolic blood pressure approximately 30 to 40 mm Hg for a sustained period, allowing the body to return to a more normal functional state. Furthermore, in most instances the cardiovascular status of the patient is unknown unless electrocardiographic monitoring is being employed.

For this reason, it is desirable to have available a vaso-pressor that produces a moderate increase in blood pressure without an undue increase in the myocardium's workload.

Phenylephrine produces moderate blood pressure elevations through peripheral vasoconstriction (α-receptor agonists). A 5-mg IM dose of phenylephrine causes the systolic blood pressure to elevate 30 mm Hg and diastolic blood pressure to elevate 20 mm Hg, and the response lasts for 50 minutes. A pronounced and persistent bradycardia is noted (average decline in heart rate from 70 to 44 beats per minute).

Therapeutic indications. Vasopressors are used to manage hypotension, in which the status of the patient's cardiovascular system is unknown and the intent is to raise the blood pressure without undue cardiac stimulation. Possible uses include the following:

- Syncopal reactions (see Part Two)
- Drug overdose reactions (see Chapter 23)
- Postseizure states (see Chapter 21)
- Acute adrenal insufficiency (see Chapter 8)
- Allergy (see Chapter 24)

Side effects, contraindications, and precautions. Parenteral administration of most vasopressors is contraindicated in patients with high blood pressure or ventricular tachycardia. The drugs must be used with extreme caution in patients with hyperthyroidism, bradycardia, partial heart block, myocardial disease, or severe atherosclerosis.

Availability. Phenylephrine is available as 10 mg/mL (1-mL ampules).

Suggested for emergency kit. Phenylephrine, 10 mg/mL (two to three 1-mL ampules).

> NOTE: *Vasopressors are used only infrequently for the management of hypotensive states. Other non-pharmacologic means are available for the elevation of blood pressure, such as the positioning of the patient in the supine position with the feet elevated or the administration of IV fluids (D5&W, lactated Ringers). A number of anesthesiologists have opined that the only vasopressor they administer is epinephrine—and then only when no blood pressure is present.*

Secondary injectable: antihypoglycemic
Drug of choice. Dextrose, 50% solution

Proprietary. None

Drug class. Antihypoglycemic

Alternative drug. Glucagon

In the management of low blood glucose (hypo-glycemia), the mode of treatment depends largely on the patient's level of consciousness. Oral carbohydrate administration is preferred, but when a patient is un-conscious or severely obtunded, 30 mL of a 50% dextrose solution should be administered IV. When the IV route is not available, glucagon may be administered by using IM delivery.

Glucagon, normally produced in the pancreas, elevates the blood glucose level by mobilizing hepatic glycogen and converting it to glucose. Glucagon is effective only when hepatic glycogen is available; it is ineffective in the treatment of starvation or chronic hypoglycemic states. As soon as the patient begins to respond (i.e., regains consciousness and is able to swallow) oral carbohydrates should be administered.

Therapeutic indications. Antihypoglycemics are used in the treatment of hypoglycemia (see Chapter 17) and as a diagnostic aid in unconsciousness or seizures of unknown origin (see Chapter 9).

Side effects, contraindications, and precautions. 50% dextrose solution, which must be administered by the IV route, may produce tissue necrosis if extravascular infil-tration occurs. There are no specific contraindications to the use of 50% dextrose. Administration of a bolus of 50% dextrose to an already hyperglycemic patient does not significantly elevate blood glucose levels. Glucagon administered either via IV or IM routes is contraindicated in patients in starvation states or with chronic hypoglycemia.

Availability. 50% dextrose is available in 30-mL glass ampules, whereas glucagon is available in 1 mg (1 unit) of dry powder with 1 mL of diluent and in 10 mg of dry powder with 10 mL of diluent.

Suggested for emergency kit. 50% dextrose (1-2 vials), if IV route is available or 1 mg/mL (two or three 1-mL vials) of glucagon for IV or IM adminis-tration.

Secondary injectable: corticosteroid
Drug of choice. Hydrocortisone sodium succinate

Proprietary. Solu-Cortef

Drug class. Adrenal glucocorticosteroid

Alternative drug. None

Corticosteroids are used to manage acute allergic reactions, but only after the rescuer has brought the acute, life-threatening phase under control through the use of epinephrine, BLS, and histamine-blockers. Corticosteroids are valuable primarily in the prevention of recurrent anaphylactic episodes. Corticosteroids also are used to manage acute adrenal insufficiency.

The onset of action for corticosteroids is slow, even when the drugs are administered via an IV route.[54] Because maximum effectiveness may not occur for up to 60 minutes after IV administration, many doctors and researchers question the effectiveness of these drugs in the management of allergic reactions in patients with normally functioning adrenal glands. The antiallergic effects of corticosteroids are probably simple manifestations of the nonspecific antiinflammatory action of the adrenal glucocorticoids (hydrocortisone and cortisone). The use of dexamethasone (Decadron) and methylprednisolone sodium succinate (Solu-Medrol) are contraindicated in patients with acute adrenal insufficiency. Therefore, hydrocortisone sodium succinate is the corticosteroid of choice for the dental emergency kit. Corticosteroids are considered second-line drugs primarily because of their slow onset of action.

Therapeutic indications. Corticosteroids are used in the definitive management of acute allergy (see Chapter 24) and in the treatment of acute adrenal insufficiency (see Chapter 8).

Side effects, contraindications, and precautions. There are no contraindications to the administration of corticosteroids in the management of life-threatening medical emergencies. When the drug is administered for nonemergency treatment (e.g., the prevention of edema during surgery or for pruritus), many factors must be considered, such as the presence of a preexisting infection, peptic ulcer, or hyperglycemia.

Availability. Hydrocortisone sodium succinate (Solu-Cortef) is available as 50 mg/mL (2-mL vials).

Suggested for emergency kit. Hydrocortisone sodium succinate (one 2-mL vial).

Secondary injectable: antihypertensive
Drug of choice. Esmolol

Proprietary. Brevibloc

Drug class. β-Adrenergic blocker

Alternative drug. Propranolol

The need to administer drugs to manage a hypertensive crisis (dangerously elevated blood pressure) is extremely uncommon. First, the incidence of extreme acute blood

pressure elevation is rare; second, there are many ways other than the parenteral administration of antihypertensive drugs to decrease a patient's blood pressure. Indeed, in interviews with hundreds of dentists who regularly administer parenteral sedation and general anesthesia, I have not found a single one who has needed to administer a drug to decrease excessively elevated blood pressure. Oral drugs, such as nifedipine and nitroglycerin, may be administered in most situations to decrease blood pressure slightly. The inclusion of an antihypertensive in the emergency drug kit is in response to state requirements for general anesthesia permits (and in a few states for parenteral sedation).

Esmolol (Brevibloc) is a β₁-selective (cardioselective) adrenergic receptor blocking agent with a very short duration of action (elimination half-life [IV] is approximately 9 minutes). Esmolol is indicated for use as an antidysrhythmic agent in patients with paroxysmal supraventricular tachycardia (PSVT) and for the management of intraoperative and postoperative tachycardia and hypertension. When used in management of PSVT, esmolol produced significant drops in blood pressure in 20% to 50% of patients. Hypotension was significant (<90 mm Hg systolic or <50 mm Hg diastolic) in 12% of these patients (mainly diaphoresis or dizziness).[55,56] Owing to the short duration of esmolol (~30 minutes via IV route) this hypotensive effect is short-lived.[55] β-adrenergic and nonselective β-adrenergic receptor-blocking actions. After IV administration, the α- to β-blockade ratio is 1:7. Labetalol produces a dose-related decrease in blood pressure without reflex tachycardia or a significant reduction in heart rate (presumably through its mixture of both α- and β-blockade). Because of its α-blockade, decreases in blood pressure are greater when the patient is standing than when the patient is in a supine position, in which signs of postural hypotension may develop. When administered to patients (who are in supine positions) for the management of severe hypertension, an initial IV dose of 0.25 mg/kg of body weight (17.5 mg for a 70-kg patient), the drug decreases blood pressure by an average of 11/7 mm Hg.[57]

Therapeutic indication. Acute hypertensive episodes.

Side effects, contraindications, and precautions. Esmolol is contraindicated in patients with sinus bradycardia, heart block greater than first degree, cardiogenic shock, or overt heart failure. Potentially significant hypotension can develop with any dose of esmolol, but is more likely to be seen with doses beyond 200 μg/kg per minute. Patients receiving esmolol should be closely monitored. In patients with congestive heart failure, esmolol in higher doses may precipitate more severe cardiac failure. In both situations, hypotension and cardiac failure, discontinuation of esmolol therapy leads to reversal of clinical signs and symptoms within 30 minutes. Extravascular injection of the 20-mg/mL concentration of esmolol may lead to serious localized reactions and skin necrosis. This is less common with the 10-mg/mL solution.

Availability. Esmolol is available as 2.5 g in a 10-mL ampule, which is diluted to a 10-mg/mL concentration prior to infusion, and as a 100-mg/mL solution, which is also diluted to 10-mg/mL prior to administration.

Suggested for emergency kit. Two ampules 100 mg/mL with diluent.

Secondary injectable: parasympathetic blocking agent
Drug of choice. Atropine

Drug class. Anticholinergic

Alternative drug. None

Proprietary. None

Atropine, a parasympathetic blocking agent, is recommended for the management of clinically symptomatic bradycardia (adult heart rate <60 beats per minute). By enhancing discharge from the sinoatrial node, atropine can provoke tachycardia (adult heart rate >110 beats per minute). Atropine is beneficial in situations in which the patient's heart has an overload of parasympathetic activity (more than vagus nerve stimulation). Extremely fearful patients are likely to develop this response. With stimulation, the vagus nerve decreases sinoatrial node activity, which slows the heart rate. When the heart rate becomes overly slow, cerebral blood flow is decreased and clinical signs and symptoms of cerebral ischemia develop. By blocking this vagal effect, atropine acts to maintain adequate cardiac output and cerebral circulation.

Atropine also is considered an essential component of ACLS, in which it is used to manage hemodynamically significant bradydysrhythmias (significant heart block and asystole).

Therapeutic indications. Atropine is used to treat bradycardia and hemodynamically significant bradydysrhythmias (see Chapter 30).

Side effects, contraindications, and precautions. Large doses of atropine (2 mg and above) may produce clinical signs of overdose, including hot, dry skin; headache; blurred nearrightedness; dry mouth and throat; disorientation; and hallucinations. Administra-

tion of atropine is contraindicated in patients with glaucoma or prostatic hypertrophy. However, in life-threatening situations the benefits of atropine administration usually outweigh the possible risks. Atropine can increase the degree of partial urinary obstruction associated with prostatism; the drug also is contraindicated in older patients with narrow-angle glaucoma.

Availability. Atropine is available as 0.5 mg/mL in 1-mL vials and as 1 mg/mL in 10-mL preloaded syringes.

Suggested for emergency kit. Two or three ampules of 0.5 mg/mL (for IM administration) or two 10-mL syringes with 1 mg per syringe (for IV administration).

Secondary noninjectable drugs
Two noninjectable drugs are considered at this level:
1. Respiratory stimulants
2. Antihypertensives

Secondary noninjectable: respiratory stimulant
Drug of choice. Aromatic ammonia

Proprietary. None

Drug class. Respiratory stimulant

Alternative drug. None

Aromatic ammonia is the agent of choice for inclusion in the emergency kit as a respiratory stimulant. It is available in a silver-gray vaporole, which is crushed and placed under the breathing victim's nose until respiratory stimulation is effected (Figure 3-25). Aromatic ammonia has a noxious odor and irritates the mucous membrane of the upper respiratory tract, stimulating the respiratory and vasomotor centers of the medulla. This action in turn increases respiration and blood pressure. Movement of the arms and legs often occurs in response to ammonia inhalation; these movements further increase blood flow and raise blood pressure, especially in the patient who has been positioned properly.

Therapeutic indications. Aromatic ammonia is used to treat respiratory depression not induced by opioid analgesics; vasodepressor syncope (see Chapter 6).

Side effects, contraindications, and precautions. Ammonia should be used with caution in persons with chronic obstructive pulmonary disease or asthma; its irritating effects on the mucous membranes of the upper respiratory tract may precipitate bronchospasm.

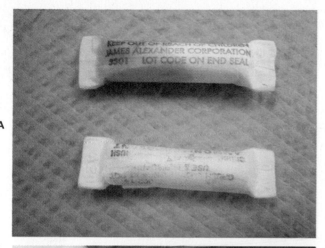

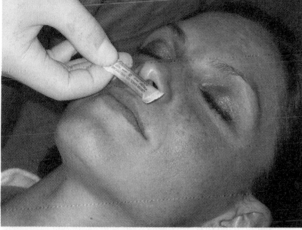

FIGURE 3-25 A, Ammonia vaporole, used *(top),* unused *(bottom).* **B,** Ammonia crushed and held under nose.

Availability. Silver-gray vaporoles containing 0.3 mL of aromatic ammonia.

Suggested for emergency kit. One to two boxes of vaporoles.

> NOTE: *After O$_2$, aromatic ammonia might be the most used drug in the emergency kit. Keep one or two vaporoles within arms reach of every dental unit so that when it is needed, time is not wasted searching for it (Figure 3-26). The vaporoles should be located so that the doctor or staff member can reach them without having to leave the patient. In addition, several vaporoles should be kept in the emergency kit for use in other areas of the dental office.*

Secondary noninjectable: antihypertensive
Drug of choice. Nifedipine

Proprietary. Procardia

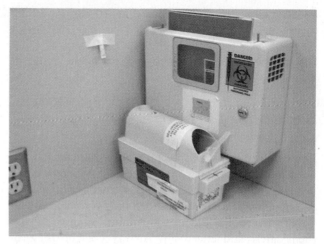

FIGURE 3-26 Ammonia taped on wall or near unit.

Drug class. Calcium channel blocker

Alternative drug. Nitroglycerin

Two drugs that help manage acute elevations in blood pressure—esmolol for parenteral administration and nitroglycerin for sublingual or translingual administration—have previously been discussed. The need for yet another antihypertensive drug is minimal, especially in view of the fact that the need for antihypertensive drug administration in dental office situations is extremely slight.

Nifedipine is used primarily to manage angina, especially vasospastic or Prinzmetal's variant angina. As is seen with nitroglycerin, a modest and usually well-tolerated hypotension commonly is observed as a side effect of nifedipine administration. The occasional patient also may experience excessive and less well-tolerated hypotension, especially if standing or seated upright.

Many doctors and researchers have questioned the use of nifedipine in the treatment of hypertensive events. Grossman and others[58] stated, "Given the seriousness of the reported adverse events, the use of nifedipine capsules for hypertensive emergencies and pseudoemergencies should be abandoned. Adverse events cited include: cerebrovascular ischemia, stroke, numerous instances of severe hypotension, acute myocardial infarction, conduction disturbances, fetal distress, and death."

Therapeutic indications. Hypertension; acute anginal pain (see Chapter 27).

Side effects, contraindications, and precautions. Excessive hypotension may be noted, especially when nifedipine is administered to patients who are already receiving β-blockers and are undergoing anesthesia with high doses of fentanyl.

Availability. Nifedipine comes in 10-mg or 20-mg capsules.

Suggested for emergency kit. One bottle of 10-mg capsules.

Secondary emergency equipment

Items described in this section are adjunctive to the basic techniques of airway management presented in the primary equipment section of this chapter and in Chapter 5. These items are recommended only for persons who have received the advanced training required to use them safely and effectively. Airway control using an invasive device is fundamental to ACLS. Determining rapidly whether the tracheal tube is in the esophagus or trachea should be one of the primary end points of training and clinical use of invasive airway techniques. This key skill is required for the safe and effective use of these devices. Training, frequency of use, and monitoring or success and complications influence the long-term impact of any device more than the choice of the specific device.[59] They are not meant to serve as substitutes for the basic techniques of airway management.

Secondary emergency equipment items include the following:
1. Scalpel or cricothyrotomy needle
2. Artificial airways
3. Laryngoscope and endotracheal tubes
4. Laryngeal mask airway

Scalpel or cricothyrotomy device

When all other noninvasive procedures have failed to secure a patent airway, a cricothyrotomy may have to be performed. The emergency kit should contain an instrument that can be used to create an opening into the trachea below the obstruction. A scalpel or specially designed cricothyrotomy device is recommended (Figure 3-27) (see Chapter 11).

Suggested for emergency kit. One scalpel with a disposable blade and one cricothyrotomy device should be included in the emergency kit.

> NOTE: *Advanced training is required for safe and effective use of these devices.*

Artificial airways

Plastic or rubber oropharyngeal (Figure 3-28) or nasopharyngeal airways (Figure 3-29) are used to assist in the maintenance of a patent airway in the unconscious patient (Figure 3-30). These devices, which lift the base of the tongue off the posterior pharyngeal wall, are

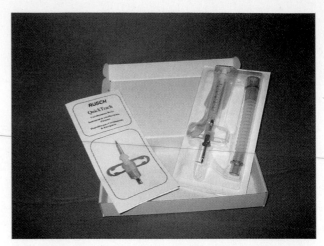

FIGURE 3-27 Cricothyrotomy device. (Courtesy Sedation Resource, Lone Oak, Texas. www.sedationresource.com)

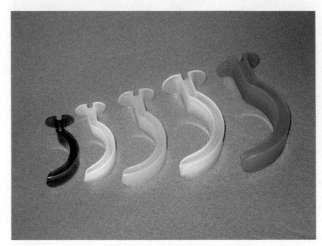

FIGURE 3-28 Oropharyngeal airways. (Courtesy Sedation Resource, Lone Oak, Texas. www.sedationresource.com)

recommended by the American Heart Association only when manual methods in the maintenance of an airway have proved ineffective.[59] Patients who are not deeply unconscious can tolerate the nasopharyngeal airway better, whereas the oropharyngeal airway will induce gagging, regurgitation, or vomiting in patients who are not deeply unconscious. Therefore, the suggested inclusion of the nasopharyngeal airway, in a variety of sizes (e.g., child, small adult, normal adult), for the office emergency kit.

Suggested for emergency kit. At a minimum, the kit should contain one set each of adult and pediatric nasopharyngeal airways.

> NOTE: *Advanced training is required for safe and effective use of oropharyngeal and nasopharyngeal airways.*

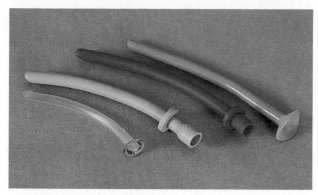

FIGURE 3-29 Nasopharyngeal airways. (From McSwain N: *The basic EMT: comprehensive prehospital care,* ed 2, St. Louis, Mosby, 2003.)

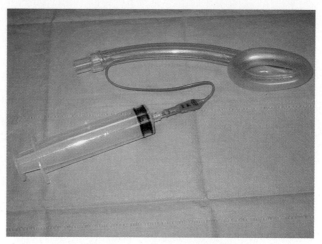

FIGURE 3-31 Laryngeal mask airway.

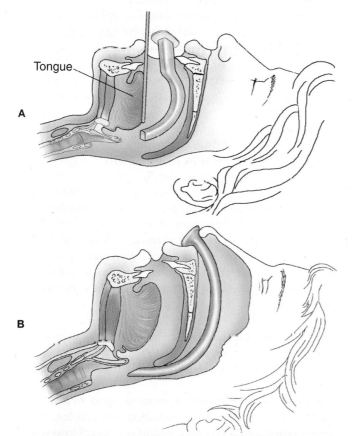

Tongue

A

B

FIGURE 3-30 Plastic or rubber oropharyngeal or nasopharyngeal airways are used to assist in the maintenance of a patent airway in the unconscious patient. (From McSwain N: *The basic EMT: comprehensive prehospital care,* ed 2, St. Louis, Mosby, 2003.)

Advanced airway devices

Many devices are available to aid in the maintenance of a patent airway in the unconscious or semiconscious patient. Among these are the laryngeal mask airway (LMA), laryngoscope, and endotracheal tube. As with the other devices listed in this section, advanced training in the use of each item is absolutely essential.

The LMA has become quite popular for airway management during anesthesia (Figure 3-31).[60,61] The airway is a tube (similar to an endotracheal tube) and a small mask with an inflatable circumferential cuff intended for placement in the victim's posterior pharynx that seals the base of the tongue and laryngeal opening. This device has a very high success rate and low complication rate, both of which are achievable with considerable training.[62,63] The laryngeal mask airway is used in situations in which endotracheal intubation is difficult and increasingly has become the sole means of airway management in many anesthetic procedures.[63]

NOTE: *The LMA is not recommended for inclusion in the emergency kit unless the doctor and staff members have received training in its proper insertion and removal.*

Endotracheal intubation using a laryngoscope to visualize the trachea and an endotracheal tube (Figure 3-32) is a technique of airway maintenance that must be restricted to persons extremely well trained in its use. Realistically, this limits its usefulness to anesthesiologists, anesthetists, trained paramedical personnel, and those dentists and physicians who have received extensive general anesthesia training.

A number of advantages make endotracheal intubation the preferred technique of airway management. These include the isolation of the airway, which prevents aspiration; the facilitation of ventilation and oxygenation; and the provision of an avenue for the administration of emergency drugs (e.g., epinephrine, lidocaine, atropine, naloxone). The most common mistakes in intubation include accidentally intubating the esophagus

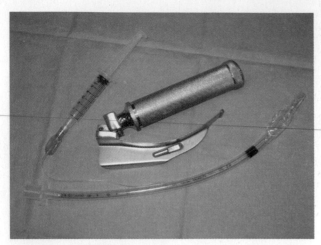

FIGURE 3-32   Endotracheal tube and laryngoscope.

and taking more than 30 seconds to intubate. In addition, improper intubation technique often results in fracture of the maxillary anterior teeth.

When used by properly trained individuals, tracheal intubation is a preferred technique of airway management in the unconscious patient.

Suggested for emergency kit. A minimum of one laryngoscope and a set of spare batteries and assorted adult- and pediatric-size endotracheal tubes may be included in the emergency kits of doctors trained in their use.

> NOTE: *Endotracheal tubes and laryngoscope are not recommended for inclusion in the emergency kit unless the doctor and staff members have received training and are proficient in their use.*

■ MODULE THREE: ACLS

A third category of injectable drugs that should be included in the emergency kit are those classified as essential in the performance of ACLS (Table 3-5). These drugs should be considered for inclusion only by doctors who have completed a course in ACLS.

ACLS essential drugs

In recent years a number of ACLS drugs previously considered essential have been deemphasized. These include sodium bicarbonate, calcium chloride, bretylium tosylate, and isoproterenol. Essential ACLS drugs include the following:

1. Epinephrine
2. Oxygen (O$_2$)
3. Lidocaine

4. Atropine
5. Dopamine
6. Morphine sulfate
7. Verapamil

ACLS essential: cardiac arrest
Drug of choice. Epinephrine

Proprietary. Adrenalin

Drug class. Endogenous catecholamine

Alternative drug. None

Three items form the essentials of ACLS—epinephrine, O$_2$, and defibrillation. Epinephrine (Adrenalin) previously has been discussed as an essential injectable drug in the management of anaphylaxis. Epinephrine is available as a 1-mg dose in preloaded syringes containing either 1 mL (1:1000 concentration) or 10 mL (1:10,000) of solution. The 1:10,000 concentration is for IV or endotracheal administration, whereas the 1:1000 solution is designed for subcutaneous, sublingual, or IM administration.

Epinephrine's importance in cardiac arrest lies in the fact that no other drug can maintain coronary artery blood flow while CPR is in progress, which is essential for preserving a chance of survival in cardiac arrest. Epinephrine also preserves blood flow to the brain. In the absence of drug therapy, cerebral blood flow during CPR is minimal, with most blood entering into the common carotid artery and flowing into the external carotid branch, not into the internal carotid artery.[64] After the administration of a drug such as epinephrine, with α-adrenergic properties, cerebral blood flow increases significantly.[65]

Therapeutic indications. Cardiac arrest (including ventricular fibrillation, pulseless ventricular tachycardia, asystole, and pulseless electrical activity) (see Chapter 30).

Side effects, contraindications, and precautions. In those situations requiring epinephrine, no contraindications to its administration exist. However, doctors should be aware that when large doses are administered to patients not receiving CPR, hypertension frequently results.[66] In addition, epinephrine may induce or exacerbate ventricular ectopy, especially in patients who are receiving digitalis.[67]

Availability. Epinephrine is available at a 1:10,000 concentration in preloaded 10-mL syringes.

Suggested for emergency kit. Two or three preloaded syringes may be included in the kit.

TABLE 3-5   Module three—advanced cardiac life support: essential drugs

Category	Generic drug	Proprietary drug	Alternative	Quantity	Availability
INJECTABLE					
Cardiac arrest	Epinephrine	Adrenalin		3 x 10-mL preloaded syringes	1:10,000 (1 mg/10 mL syringe)
Analgesic	Morphine sulfate		N_2O-O_2	3 x 1-mL ampules	10 mg/mL
Antidysrhythmic	Lidocaine	Xylocaine	Procainamide	1 preloaded syringe and 2 x 5-mL ampules	100 mg/syringe
Symptomatic bradycardia	Atropine		Isoproterenol	2 x 10-mL syringes	1.0 mg/10 mL
Paroxysmal supraventricular tachycardia	Verapamil	Isoptin		2 x 4-mL ampules	2.5 mg/mL
NONINJECTABLE					
Oxygen	Oxygen			1 "E" cylinder	1 "E" cylinder

ACLS essential: O_2

Drug of choice. O_2

Proprietary. None

Drug class. None

Alternative drug. None

O_2 already is included in the emergency kit as an essential noninjectable drug. It is essential in cardiac resuscitation and emergency cardiac care. Although exhaled air ventilation provides 16% to 17% O_2 and ambient air ventilation provides 21% O_2, enriched O_2 ventilation, or 100% O_2 ventilation, precludes the possibility of the development of hypoxia if ventilation is adequate.

Absolutely no contraindications exist to the administration of O_2 in emergency situations. Long-term administration of high O_2 concentrations can produce O_2 toxicity, but the duration required for the development of such a situation far exceeds the duration of almost all emergency situations. O_2 must never be withheld or diluted during resuscitation because of the mistaken belief that it is harmful.[31] (See the discussion of O_2 included in Module One in the section on critical noninjectable drugs for a fuller description of the precautions, availability, and recommendations associated with O_2.)

ACLS essential: antidysrhythmic

Drug of choice. Lidocaine

Proprietary. Xylocaine

Drug class. Local anesthetic, antidysrhythmic

Alternative drug. Procainamide

Lidocaine (Xylocaine) is used extensively in the management of cardiac dysrhythmias, especially those of ventricular origin that develop after acute myocardial infarction. Lidocaine is considered the primary antidysrhythmic drug in ACLS. Procainamide also effectively suppresses ventricular ectopy and is recommended for administration when lidocaine has not effectively suppressed life-threatening ventricular dysrhythmias.[68,69]

Therapeutic indications. Lidocaine is administered when premature ventricular contractions (PVCs) occur more than six times per minute or with the presence of closely coupled PVCs, multifocal PVCs, or those occurring in bursts of two or more in succession. Lidocaine administration also is indicated in sustained ventricular tachycardia (where a palpable pulse is present) and in ventricular fibrillation that is refractory to electrical defibrillation (see Chapter 30).[70]

Side effects, contraindications, and precautions. Excessive doses of lidocaine produce myocardial, circulatory, and CNS depression. Clinical signs and symptoms of lidocaine overdose include drowsiness, paresthesias, and muscle twitching.[71] More severe overdoses may produce tonic-clonic seizure activity.[72] Decreased hepatic function or hepatic blood flow slows the rate of lidocaine biotransformation, producing prolonged elevated blood levels and a greater risk of lidocaine overdose. Impaired hepatic blood flow frequently is observed in the presence of acute reductions in cardiac output (e.g., in myocardial infarction and congestive heart failure).[73]

Availability. Lidocaine is available for IV injection in 5-mL prefilled syringes containing either 50 or 100 mg and in 5-mL ampules of 100 mg.

Suggested for emergency kit. One 100-mg preloaded syringe and one 5-mL ampule.

ACLS essential: symptomatic bradycardia
Drug of choice. Atropine

Proprietary. Atropine

Drug class. Parasympatholytic

Alternative drug. Isoproterenol

Atropine is the drug of choice for hemodynamically significant bradydysrhythmias and also is administered during asystole that is refractory to epinephrine administration. A bradydysrhythmia is considered to be hemodynamically unstable when the following conditions are present:[74]

Symptoms:
1. Chest pain
2. Shortness of breath
3. Decreased level of consciousness
4. Weakness, fatigue
5. Exercise intolerance
6. Lightheadedness, dizziness, and "spells"
Signs:
1. Hypotension
2. Drop in blood pressure upon standing
3. Diaphoresis
4. Pulmonary congestion upon physical examination or chest x-ray
5. Frank congestive heart failure or pulmonary edema
6. Chest pain
7. Acute coronary syndrome (unstable angina, angina, or other symptoms of acute myocardial infarction)
8. PVCs

Isoproterenol is a synthetic sympathomimetic amine with nearly pure β-adrenergic receptor activity. Despite producing a decrease in mean blood pressure, isoproterenol provides increased cardiac output. However, it also markedly increases myocardial O_2 consumption and may therefore induce or exacerbate myocardial ischemia. Although still considered for administration in the management of hemodynamically significant and atropine refractory bradycardia, isoproterenol is no longer the drug of choice. Electronic pacing of the heart has proven more effective than isoproterenol, and does not increase myocardial O_2 requirements. Atropine is one of four drugs that may be administered endotracheally (see discussion on secondary injectable drugs).

ACLS essential: symptomatic hypotension
Drug of choice. Dopamine

Proprietary. Intropin

Drug class. Sympathomimetic amine

Alternative drug. Dobutamine

Dopamine (Intropin) is a chemical precursor of norepinephrine. In large doses it stimulates both α- and β-adrenergic receptors. At lower doses it dilates renal, mesenteric, and cerebral arteries.[75] Dopamine also stimulates the release of norepinephrine; it is indicated for administration in hemodynamically significant hypotension in the absence of hypovolemia. When administered, the dose of dopamine should be kept as low as possible to ensure adequate perfusion of vital organs.

Dobutamine is a synthetic sympathomimetic amine that exerts significant inotropic effects by stimulating β_1- and α-adrenergic receptors in the myocardium.[76] Its β-stimulatory actions greatly outweigh its α-stimulatory actions, usually resulting in a mild vasodilation. In its usual dose, dobutamine is less likely than isoproterenol or dopamine to induce tachycardias. Dopamine is administered via an IV infusion, with the infusion rate altered according to the response of the patient.

Therapeutic indications. The primary therapeutic indication for dopamine is to treat hemodynamically significant hypotension in the absence of hypovolemia.

Side effects, contraindications, and precautions. Because dopamine produces an increase in heart rate, it may induce or exacerbate supraventricular or ventricular dysrhythmias. In addition, dopamine may alter the imbalance between supply and demand of the myocardium for O_2, inducing or exacerbating myocardial ischemia.[76]

Nausea and vomiting frequently are noted with dopamine administration. In patients receiving monoamine oxidase inhibitors (isocarboxazid, pargyline, tranyl-cypromine, or phenelzine), dopamine activity may be augmented. These patients should receive no more than one tenth the usual dose of dopamine.

Availability. Dopamine is available as 200 mg, 400 mg, and 800 mg in 5-mL ampules and syringes.

Suggested for emergency kit. One or two ampules of 400-mg dopamine (80 mg/mL).

ACLS essential: analgesia
Drug of choice. Morphine

Proprietary. Morphine

Drug class. Opioid agonist

Alternative drug. Meperidine
The management of pain and anxiety during ischemic chest pain is a critical part of overall patient care. Although a number of analgesics are available, morphine is the drug of choice (see discussion on secondary injectable drugs).

ACLS essential: paroxysmal supraventricular tachycardia
Drug of choice. Verapamil

Proprietary. Isoptin

Drug class. Calcium channel blocker

Alternative drug. None
Verapamil (Isoptin) is the second calcium channel blocker discussed in this section (nifedipine, discussed as a secondary noninjectable drug for the management of hypertensive situations, is the other). Verapamil is included in the ACLS category because it is extremely effective in the management of supraventricular tachy-

cardia.[77] Verapamil slows conduction through the atrioventricular node, reducing ventricular response to atrial flutter and fibrillation. Although verapamil may be administered orally, in the context of ACLS it should be administered via an IV route.

Therapeutic indications. In emergency cardiac care, verapamil is used primarily to treat paroxysmal supraventricular tachycardia that does not require cardioversion. When verapamil proves ineffective in the management of PSVT, synchronized cardioversion is recommended.

Side effects, contraindications, and precautions. A transient decrease in arterial pressure may be noted because of peripheral vasodilation in response to verapamil.[78] Verapamil is not indicated for ventricular tachycardia; it may induce severe hypotension and predispose a patient to ventricular fibrillation.[76]

Availability. Verapamil is available for injection as 2.5 mg/mL in 2-mL and 4-mL ampules.

Suggested for emergency kit. One or two 4-mL ampules.
For a complete discussion of all aspects of ACLS, the doctor should consult one of the available recommended references.[79,80] In addition, ACLS certification at (minimally) the provider level helps the doctor better understand how properly to use the drugs mentioned in this section.

■ MODULE FOUR: ANTIDOTAL DRUGS

Four categories of injectable drugs are used to manage emergency situations that arise in response to the administration of drugs used primarily for sedation via the IM and IV routes or general anesthesia (Table 3-6).

TABLE 3-6 Module four—antidotal drugs

Category	Generic drug	Proprietary drug	Alternative	Quantity	Availability
INJECTABLE					
Opioid antagonist	Naloxone	Narcan	Nalbuphine	2 x 1-mL ampules	0.4 mg/mL
Benzodiazepine antagonist	Flumazenil	Romazicon	—	1 x 10-mL vial	0.1 mg/mL
Anticholinergic toxicity Antiemergence delirium	Physostigmine	Antilirium	—	3 x 2-mL ampules	1 mg/mL

These drugs should be maintained in the emergency kit only as warranted by the nature of the dental practice. For example, an opioid antagonist is not essential when opioid agonists are not used in patient management.

Antidotal drugs

Categories of antidotal drugs include the following:
1. Opioid antagonist
2. Benzodiazepine antagonist
3. Antiemergence delirium drug
4. Vasodilator

Antidotal drug: opioid antagonist
Drug of choice. Naloxone

Proprietary. Narcan

Drug class. Thebaine derivative

Alternative drug. Nalbuphine

The most significant side effect of parenterally administered opioid agonists is their ability to produce respiratory depression by diminishing the responsiveness of the brain's respiratory centers to arterial carbon dioxide. Thus, the patient's breathing rate is decreased. Opioid antagonists have been available since 1951 (nalorphine, levallorphan). Although these agents reversed opioid-induced respiratory depression, when administered to patients with non–opioid-induced respiratory depression, both nalorphine and levallorphan were able to produce their own respiratory depression and to enhance barbiturate-induced respiratory depression.

Naloxone (Narcan) became available in the late 1960s and today remains the only opioid antagonist free of any agonistic properties. Naloxone also reverses other properties of opioids, namely analgesia and sedation.[81] This action is not entirely innocuous; if opioids are administered for postsurgical analgesia, naloxone administration antagonizes this effect, leaving the patient with unmanaged postsurgical pain. Naloxone may be administered endotracheally in situations in which IV access is not available. Administered via an IV route or endotracheally, improved respiratory function is noted within 2 minutes.

Nalbuphine, an opioid agonist-antagonist, has been used successfully to reverse respiratory depression induced by opioid agonists.[82] Because nalbuphine has its own agonist properties, it provides excellent reversal of opioid-induced respiratory depression, but does not entirely remove postsurgical analgesia or sedation because of its own analgesia-inducing properties.

Therapeutic indications. Naloxone is indicated for use in opioid-induced depression, including respiratory depression (see Chapter 23).

Side effects, contraindications, and precautions. When administered via an IV route or endotracheal tube, naloxone's effects last only 30 minutes. Respiratory depression may recur if the opioid previously administered is of longer duration (e.g., morphine). The IM administration of a second naloxone dose after the IV dose is common. Although this dose is slower in onset, its duration is considerably longer than that of the IV dose. This regimen minimizes a possible recurrence of respiratory depression.

It is important to remember that in the presence of opioid-induced respiratory depression, naloxone administration is neither the most important nor the first step in patient management. Airway patency and ventilation are the prime considerations. Naloxone must be administered with extreme care to persons with known or suspected physical dependence on opioids. Naloxone's abrupt and complete reversal of opioid agonist effects may precipitate acute withdrawal syndrome.

Availability. Naloxone is available for adults as 0.4 mg/mL in 1-mL ampules and 10-mL vials. The drug is available for pediatric administration as 0.02 mg/mL in 2-mL ampules.

Suggested for emergency kit. Two 1-mL ampules of 0.4 mg/mL naloxone.

Antidotal drug: benzodiazepine antagonist
Drug of choice. Flumazenil

Proprietary. Romazicon

Drug class. Benzodiazepine antagonist

Alternative drug. None

Although the benzodiazepines have been described as the most nearly ideal agents for anxiety control and sedation, a number of potential adverse reactions are associated with their administration. Emergence delirium, excessive duration of sedation, and possibly (though unlikely in most instances) significant respiratory depression are but a few side effects. The availability of a specific antagonist for benzodiazepines adds another degree of safety to IV (and to a lesser extent IM) sedation.

Flumazenil (Romazicon) has been demonstrated to produce a rapid reversal of sedation and to improve the patient's ability to comprehend and obey commands.[83]

The duration of anterograde amnesia associated with midazolam was reduced from 121 minutes without flumazenil to 91 minutes with flumazenil.[83,84] Flumazenil also decreased the recovery time from midazolam sedation, increased alertness, and provided a decreased amnesic effect in the geriatric population (72.9 years). Two patients, however, became anxious following flumazenil administration.[85] The availability of flumazenil is recommended wherever benzodiazepines such as diazepam, midazolam, or lorazepam are administered parenterally. Reversal with flumazenil is not effective following the oral administration of benzodiazepines (e.g., triazolam).

Therapeutic indications. Flumazenil is used to reverse the clinical actions of parenterally administered benzodiazepines (see Chapter 23).

Side effects, contraindications, and precautions. Flumazenil has been demonstrated to produce a rebound anxiety state is some patients.[85]

Availability. Flumazenil (Romazicon) is available as 0.1 mg/mL in 5-mL and 10-mL multidose vials.

Suggested for emergency kit. One 10-mL multidose vial of flumazenil.

Antidotal drug: antiemergence delirium drug
Drug of choice. Physostigmine

Proprietary. Antilirium

Drug class. Cholinesterase inhibitor

Alternative drug. None
Several drugs that are commonly employed parenterally to induce sedation have the ability to produce what is known as emergence delirium (anticholinergic syndrome). Scopolamine and the benzodiazepines, diazepam and midazolam, are most likely to produce this phenomenon in which the patient appears to lose contact with reality. There may also be increased muscular movement, and the patient may seem to speak but makes unintelligible sounds. Physostigmine (Antilirium), a reversible cholinesterase with the ability to cross the blood-brain barrier, has become the drug of choice in the management of emergence delirium.[86]
Physostigmine is recommended for inclusion in the emergency drug kit if scopolamine, benzodiazepines, or other drugs that may induce emergence delirium are administered parenterally.

Therapeutic indications. Physostigmine is used to reverse emergence delirium (Chapter 23).

Side effects, contraindications, and precautions. Side effects noted with physostigmine administration are increased salivation, possible emesis, and involuntary urination and defecation. The first two actions are most common. If administered too rapidly, physostigmine can produce the preceding effects as well as bradycardia and hypersalivation, leading to respiratory difficulty. Atropine should always be available whenever physostigmine is administered because it is an antagonist and antidote for physostigmine. Physostigmine should not be administered to patients with asthma, diabetes, cardiovascular disease, or mechanical obstruction of the gastrointestinal or genitourinary tracts.

Availability. Physostigmine is available as Antilirium as 1 mg/mL in 2-mL ampules.

Suggested for emergency kit. Two to three ampules.

Antidotal drug: local anesthetic/vasodilator
Drug of choice. Procaine

Drug class. Local anesthetic

Alternative drug. None
A local anesthetic that also possesses significant vasodilating properties is recommended for inclusion in the emergency kit whenever IM or IV drugs are employed. Indications for the administration of procaine are extravascular injection of an irritating chemical and accidental intraarterial administration of a drug. In both instances the problems are those of localized tissue irritation and compromised circulation in either a localized area (extravascular administration) or a limb (intraarterial administration).
Procaine possesses excellent vasodilating properties along with its anesthetic actions, both of which make it ideal for administration in the aforementioned situations.

Therapeutic indications. Management of vasospasm and compromised circulation following intraarterial injection of a drug. Management of pain and vascular compromise following extravascular administration of irritating drugs

Side effects, contraindications, and precautions. Allergy to ester-type local anesthetics is not uncommon. Do not administer procaine to patients with histories (either documented or alleged) of allergy to "Novocain."

Availability. Procaine is available as a 1% (10 mg/mL) solution in 2-mL and 6-mL ampules.

Suggested for emergency kit. Two 2-mL ampules.

■ ORGANIZATION OF THE EMERGENCY KIT

The emergency drug kit need not and indeed should not be complicated. Adherence to the KISS (Keep It Simple, Stupid) principle is suggested. Four levels or modules of drugs and equipment were presented:

1. Module One: basic emergency kit (critical drugs and equipment)
2. Module Two: noncritical drugs and equipment
3. Module Three: ACLS
4. Module Four: antidotal drugs

Doctors should match their educational backgrounds and clinical experiences with these different levels and

drugs before considering them for inclusion in the office emergency kit. Only those drugs and items of equipment with which the doctor is familiar should be included. Minimally, Module One (critical drugs and equipment) should be available in all offices.

A simple place in which to store emergency drugs and equipment is in a fishing tackle box or plastic box with several compartments (Figure 3-33). Larger kits may be stored in mobile tool cabinets (Figure 3-34). Labels should be applied to each compartment in which a drug is stored, listing the drug's generic and proprietary names to avoid possible confusion during an emergency as well as its dosage emergency indication and expiry date (Box 3-2).

A written record of the expiration dates of each of the drugs in the emergency kit must be kept and the drug replaced prior to that date (Figure 3-35). Expired drugs and empty O_2 cylinders are ineffective in the management of any emergency situation. An office staff member should be assigned to check the emergency drug kit at least once a week and all emergency equipment

FIGURE 3-33 Simple self-made emergency drug kit.

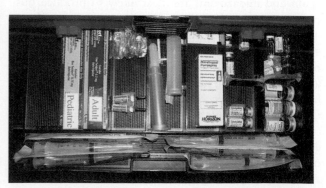

FIGURE 3-34 Large self-made emergency drug kit.

Box 3-2	Sample label for emergency drug

Generic name of drug: Epinephrine
Proprietary name of drug: Adrenalin
Indication for drug: Anaphylaxis
Dosage and how to use: 0.3 mg IM (vastus lateralis)
Expiration date: June 2007

daily—especially the O_2 cylinders—to ensure that all emergency items are ready for use. Records of all emergency drug and equipment inspections should be maintained in a bound (not a loose-leaf) notebook. The emergency kit and equipment must be kept in a readily accessible area. The back of a storage cabinet or a locked closet is not the place for life-saving equipment.

Emergency Drug Checklist

INSTITUTE OF MEDICAL
EMERGENCY PREPAREDNESS

Emergency Drug Checklist

Injectable Drugs

Generic	Trade	Dose	Action	Expire
Diazepam	**Valium**	5–10 mg	Anticonvulsant	_____
or				
Midazolam	**Versed**	2–5 mg	Anticonvulsant	_____
Glucagon	**Glucogen**	1 mg/mL	Antihypoglycemic	_____
or				
Dextrose	**Dextrose**	0.5 g/mL	Antihypoglycemic	_____
Atropine	**Atropine**	0.5–1 mg	Anticholinergic	_____
Lidocaine	**Xylocaine**	1–1.5 mg/kg	Antiarrhythmic	_____
Hydrocortisone	**Solu-Cortef**	100 mg	Anti-inflammatory	_____
Diphenhydramine	**Benadryl**	25–50 mg	Antihistamine	_____
Epinephrine	**Epinephrine**	0.3 mL of 1:1000 3 mL of 1:10,000	Cardiac Stimulant	_____
Morphine	**Morphine**	10 mg	Analgesic	_____
Flumazenil	**Romazicon**	0.2 mg	Benzodiazepine Antagonist	_____
Naloxone	**Narcan**	0.4 mg	Narcotic Antagonist	_____

Other Medications: _____

_____

Noninjectable Drugs

Generic	Trade	Dose	Action	Expire
Aromatic Ammonia	Ammonia	1 ampule	Chemical irritant	_____
Albuterol	**Proventil**	Aerosol 2 puffs	Bronchodilator	_____
Glucose Tabs	Glucose Tabs	3–4 tablets	Antihypoglycemic	_____
Aspirin	Aspirin	325 mg tablet	Antiplatelet	_____
Nitroglycerin	**Nitrostat**	0.4 mg q 5 mins	Coronary Artery Vasodilator	_____
Oxygen	Oxygen	2–6 L/min	Supplement to Airway	

Other: _____

1.866.729.7333 • www.EmergencyActionGuide.com

FIGURE 3-35 Record of each drug with expiration date. (Reprinted with permission, Institute of Medical Emergency Preparedness, Hattiesburg, Mississippi.)

Occasionally, office personnel may run into difficulty purchasing the small quantities of drugs required for the emergency kit. Most drug wholesalers sell these drugs in prepackaged boxes of 12 or 25 units, but in most instances only two or three ampules are required for the office emergency kit. In such cases, office personnel may want to contact a hospital pharmacy, which is more likely to dispense small quantities of the required drugs, or an anesthesia supply house.*

Although this text recommends that each office make its own emergency kit, commercially prepared kits do have one advantage. With most manufacturers, soon-to-be-outdated drugs are automatically replaced (at a cost) by mail. When a doctor does not have easy access to a source for emergency drugs, this service may prove beneficial.

To assess whether your office is prepared to manage life-threatening situations, each emergency team member should ask the following question: "If I were in need of emergency medical care, would I want it to be in my office managed by my dental team?"

REFERENCES

1. American Dental Association: *Guidelines for the use of conscious sedation, deep sedation, and general anesthesia for dentists,* Chicago, American Dental Association, October 2003.
2. Dental Board of California website: www.dbc.ca.gov.
3. American Association of Oral and Maxillofacial Surgeons: *Parameters of care for oral and maxillofacial surgery: a guide for practice, monitoring and evaluation,* Rosemont, Ill, American Association of Oral and Maxillofacial Surgeons, 1995.
4. American Academy of Pediatric Dentistry: *Clinical guideline on the elective use of minimal, moderate, and deep sedation, and general anesthesia for pediatric dental patients,* Chicago, American Academy of Pediatric Dentistry, 2004–2005.
5. Task Force on State and Regional Periodontal Matters, American Academy of Periodontology: The use of conscious sedation by periodontists, *J Periodontol* 74:934, 2003.
6. American Dental Association: *Guidelines for teaching the comprehensive control of pain and anxiety in dentistry,* Chicago, American Dental Association, October 2003.
7. Morrow GT: Designing a drug kit, *Dent Clin North Am* 26:21–33, 1982.
8. Institute of Medical Emergency Preparedness. *Medical emergency book,* Hattiesburg, MS, Institute of Medical Emergency Preparedness, 2004.
9. De Maio VJ: The quest to improve cardiac arrest survival: overcoming the hemodynamic effects of ventilation, *Crit Care Med* 33:898–899, 2005.

10. Bunch TJ, White RD, Gersh BJ, et al.: Does early defibrillation improve long-term survival and quality of life after cardiac arrest? *N Engl J Med* 348:2626–2633, 2003.
11. Caffrey SL, Willoughby PJ, Pepe PE, Becker LB: Public use of automated external defibrillators, *N Engl J Med* 347:1242–1247, 2002.
12. Key CB: Operational issues in EMS, *Emerg Med Clin North Am* 20:913–927, 2002.
13. Sommers AL, Slaby JR, Aufderheide TP: Public access defibrillation, *Emerg Med Clin North Am* 20:809–824, 2002.
14. Malamed SF: Emergency medicine in dentistry, Seattle, WA: HealthFirst Corporation, 2004.
15. Vukmir RB: The influence of urban, suburban, or rural locale on survival from refractory prehospital cardiac arrest, *Am J Emerg Med* 22:90–93, 2004.
16. Malamed SF: Managing medical emergencies, *J Am Dent Assoc* 124:40–53, 1993.
17. American Dental Association Council on Dental Therapeutics: Emergency kits, *J Am Dent Assoc* 87:909, 1973.
18. American Dental Association: *ADA guide to dental therapeutics,* Chicago, American Dental Association, 1998.
19. American Dental Association Council on Scientific Affairs: Office emergencies and emergency kits, *J Am Dent Assoc* 133:364–365, 2002.
20. Pallasch TJ: This emergency kit belongs in your office, *Dent Management* August:43–45, 1976.
21. Woodard ML, Brent LD: Acute renal failure, anterior myocardial infarction, and atrial fibrillation complicating epinephrine abuse, *Pharmacotherapy* 18:656–658, 1998.
22. Cohen M: Epinephrine: tragic overdose, *Nursing* 26:13, 1996.
23. Epinephrine. In: MD Consult, Mosby, 2005.
24. EpiPen. Dey Laboratories, a Division of Merck & Company, Inc. Whitehouse Station, New Jersey.
25. Malamed SF: The use of diphenhydramine HCl as a local anesthetic in dentistry, *Anesth Prog* 20:76–82, 1973.
26. Pollack CV Jr, Swindle GM: Use of diphenhydramine for local anesthesia in "caine"-sensitive patients, *J Emerg Med* 7:611–614, 1989.
27. Israel bans import of sildenafil citrate after six deaths in the US, *BMJ* 316:1625, 1998.
28. Kloner RA: Cardiovascular effects of tadalafil, *Am J Cardiol* 92:37M–46M, 2003.
29. Wysowski DK, Farinas E, Swartz L: Comparison of reported and expected deaths in sildenafil (Viagra) users, *Am J Cardiol* 89:1331–1334, 2002.
30. Opie LH: Pharmacologic options for treatment of ischemic disease. In: Smith TW, editor: *Cardiovascular therapeutics: a companion to Braunwald's heart disease,* Philadelphia, WB Saunders, 1996.
31. ISIS-2 (Second International Study of Infarct Survival) Collaborative Group: Randomised trial of intravenous streptokinase, oral aspirin, both, or neither among 17,187 cases of suspected acute myocardial infarction, ISIS-2, *Lancet* 2:349–360, 1988.
32. Cohen M, Arjomand H, Pollack CV Jr.: The evolution of thrombolytic therapy and adjunctive antithrombotic

*Southern Anesthesia and Surgical Supply, 800-624-5926, www.southernanesthesia.com.

regimens in acute ST-segment elevation myocardial infarction, *Am J Emerg Med* 22:14–23, 2004.

33. *2002 heart and stroke statistical update.* Dallas, American Heart Association, 2002.

34. Calle PA, Verbeke A, Vanhaute O, et al.: The effect of semi-automatic external defibrillation by emergency medical technicians on survival after out-of-hospital cardiac arrest: an observational study in urban and rural areas of Belgium, *Acta Clin Belg* 52:72–83, 1997.

35. Malamed SF: *Handbook of medical emergencies in the dental office*, ed 5, St. Louis, Mosby, 2000.

36. Tan WA, Moliterno DJ: Aspirin, ticlopidine, and clopidogrel in acute coronary syndromes: underused treatments could save thousands of lives, *Cleve Clin J Med* 66:615–618, 621–624, 627–628, 1999.

37. Antiplatelet Trialist's Collaboration. Collaborative overview of randomised trials of antiplatelet therapy, I: prevention of death, myocardial infarction, and stroke by prolonged antiplatelet therapy in various categories of patients, *BMJ* 308:81–106, 1994.

38. Eisenberg MS, Hallstrom AP, Copass MK, et al.: Treatment of ventricular fibrillation: emergency medical technician defibrillation and paramedic services, *JAMA* 251: 1723–1726, 1984.

39. Weaver WD, Copass MK, Bufi D, et al.: Improved neurologic recovery and survival after early defibrillation, *Circulation* 69:943–948, 1984.

40. Eckstein M, Stratton SJ, Chan LS: Cardiac arrest resuscitation in Los Angeles: CARE-LA, *Ann Emerg Med* 45:504–509, 2005.

41. Kannel WB, Schatzkin A: Sudden death: lessons from subsets in population studies, *J Am Coll Cardiol* 5(Suppl):141B–149B, 1985.

42. Cummins RO, Ornato JP, Thies WH, Pepe PE: Improving survival from sudden cardiac arrest: the "chain of survival" concept: a statement for health care professionals from the Advanced Cardiac Life Support Subcommittee and the Emergency Cardiac Care Committee, American Heart Association, *Circulation* 83:1832–1847, 1991.

43. Stapczynski JS, Svenson JE, Stone CK: Population density, automated external defibrillator use, and survival in rural cardiac arrest, *Acad Emerg Med* 4:552–558, 1997.

44. Larson MP, Eisenberg MS, Cummins RO, Hallstrom AP: Predicting survival from out-of-hospital cardiac arrest: a graphic model, *Ann Emerg Med* 22:1652–1658, 1993.

45. Florida Board of Dentistry. Vol 29, 42, October 17, 2003.

46. Council supports AEDs, *ADA News* June 2005.

47. U.S. Food and Drug Administration. AEDs approved for over-the-counter sales, September 2004.

48. Tiwana KK, Morton T, Tiwana PS: Aspiration and ingestion in dental practice: a 10-year institutional review, *J Am Dent Assoc* 135:1287–1291, 2004.

49. Stoffers KW, Gobetti JP: The disappearing tooth: report of a case, *J Mich Dent Assoc* 84:32–35, 2002.

50. Raines A, Henderson TR, Swinyard EA, Dretchen KL: Comparison of midazolam and diazepam by the IM route for the control of seizures in a mouse model of status epilepticus, *Epilepsia* 31:313–317, 1990.

51. Harbord MG: Use of intranasal midazolam to treat acute seizures in paediatric community settings, *J Paediatr Child Health* 40:556–558, 2004.

52. Mahmoudian T: Comparison of intranasal midazolam with intravenous diazepam for treating acute seizures in children, *Epilepsy Behav* 5:253–255, 2004.

53. O'Sullivan IO, Benger J: Nitrous oxide in emergency medicine, *BMJ* 20:214–217, 2003.

54. Streeten DHP: Corticosteroid therapy. I. Pharmacological properties and principles of corticosteroid use, *JAMA* 232:944–947, 1975.

55. Esmolol hydrochloride. In: MD Consult, Elsevier, 2005.

56. Mitchell RG: Esmolol in acute ischemic syndromes, *Am Heart J* 144:E9, 2002.

57. Labetalol hydrochloride. In: MD Consult, Elsevier, 2005.

58. Grossman E, Messerli FH, Grodzicki T, Kowey P: Should a moratorium be placed on sublingual nifedipine capsules given for hypertensive emergencies and pseudo-emergencies? *JAMA* 76:1328–1331, 1996.

59. International Consensus on Science. Guidelines 2000 for Cardiopulmonary Resuscitation and Emergency Cardiovascular Care, *Circulation* (Suppl)102:I-95– I-104, 2000.

60. Brimacombe J: A multicenter study comparing the ProSeal and Classic laryngeal mask airway in anesthetized, non-paralyzed patients, *Anesthesiology* 96:289–295, 2002.

61. Hartmann B: Laryngeal mask airway versus endotracheal tube for outpatient surgery: analysis of anesthesia-controlled time, *J Clin Anesth* 16:195–199, 2004.

62. Pennant JH, White PF: The laryngeal mask airway: its uses in anesthesiology, *Anesthesiology* 79:144–163, 1993.

63. Verghese C, Brimacombe JR: Survey of laryngeal mask airway usage in 11,910 patients: safety and efficacy for conventional and nonconventional usage, *Anesth Analg* 82:129–133, 1996.

64. Paradis NA, Koscove EM: Epinephrine in cardiac arrest: a critical review, *Ann Emerg Med* 19:1288–1291, 1990.

65. Paradis NA: Pressor drugs in the treatment of cardiac arrest, *Cardiol Clin* 20:61–78, 2002.

66. Jacobsen G: Stung postman gets $2.6m for wrong help. *Sydney Morning Herald*, February 1, 2005.

67. Packer M, Gottlieb SJ, Kessler PD: Hormone-electrolyte interactions in the pathogenesis of lethal cardiac arrhythmias in patients with control of arrhythmias, *Am J Med* 80(Suppl 4A):23–29, 1986.

68. Kudenchuk PJ: Advanced cardiac life support anti-arrhythmic drugs, *Cardiol Clin* 20:79–87, 2002.

69. Wyman MG: Prevention of primary ventricular fibrillation in acute myocardial infarction with prophylactic lidocaine, *Am J Cardiol* 94:545–551, 2004.

70. Somberg JC: Intravenous lidocaine versus intravenous amiodarone (in a new aqueous formulation) for incessant ventricular tachycardia, *Am J Cardiol* 90:853–859, 2002.

71. Lidocaine hydrochloride. In: MD Consult, Elsevier, 2005.

72. Auroy Y: Major complications of regional anesthesia in France: The SOS Regional Anesthesia Hotline Service, *Anesthesiology* 97:1274–1280, 2002.

73. Thomson PD, Melmon KL, Richardson JA, et al.: Lidocaine pharmacokinetics in advanced heart failure, liver disease, and renal failure in humans, Ann Intern Med 78:499–508, 1973.

74. *ACLS provider manual, bradycardias (case 7)*, Dallas, American Heart Association, 2001, p 146.

75. Weiner N: Norepinephrine, epinephrine, and the sympathomimetic amines. In: Hardman JG, Limbird LE, editors: *Goodman & Gilman's the pharmacological basis of therapeutics*, ed 9, New York, McGraw-Hill, 1996.

76. Dobutamine hydrochloride. In: MD Consult, Mosby, 2005.

77. Eisenberg MJ: Calcium channel blockers: an update, *Am J Med* 116:35–43, 2004.

78. Verapamil hydrochloride. In: MD Consult, Elsevier, 2005.

79. American Heart Association. *ACLS provider manual*, Dallas, American Heart Association, 2001.

80. Aehlert B: *ACLS quick review study guide*, St. Louis, Mosby, 2002.

81. Pallasch TJ, Gill CJ: Naloxone-associated morbidity and mortality, *Oral Surg* 52:602–603, 1981.

82. Magruder MR, Delaney RD, DiFazio CA: Reversal of narcotic-induced respiratory depression with nalbuphine hydrochloride, *Anesth Rev* 9:34, 1982.

83. Rodrigo MR, Rosenquist JB: The effect of Ro 15-1788 (Anexate) in conscious sedation produced with midazolam, *Anaesth Intensive Care* 15:185–192, 1987.

84. Wolff J, Carl P, Clausen TG, et al.: Ro 15-1788 for postoperative recovery: a randomised clinical trial in patients undergoing minor surgical procedures under midazolam anaesthesia, *Anaesthesia* 41:1001–1006, 1986.

85. Ricou B, Forster A, Bruckner A, et al.: Clinical evaluation of a specific benzodiazepine antagonist (Ro 15-1788): studies in elderly patients after regional anaesthesia under benzodiazepine sedation, *Br J Anaesth* 58:1005–1011, 1986.

86. Physostigmine salicylate. In: MD Consult, Elsevier, 2005.

■ APPENDIX: PARENTERAL ADMINISTRATION OF DRUGS

To prepare an injectable emergency drug for either IM or IV administration, the unit-dose glass ampule is opened by cracking its prescored neck with a gauze pad protecting your finger (Figure 3-36). After the needle is tightened onto the syringe (Figure 3-37), the drug is withdrawn from the ampule. The person administering the drug must always check its printed label to determine the drug's name, dose, and expiration date, especially when administering epinephrine, naloxone, and meperidine, which are available in multiple dosage forms. Furthermore, when the emergency situation is not urgent, the doctor or staff member should label the loaded syringe with the drug's name and concentration (in mg/mL).

IM drug administration

Preferred sites for emergency IM drug administration:
1. Vastus lateralis (Figure 3-38)
2. Mid-deltoid (Figure 3-39)

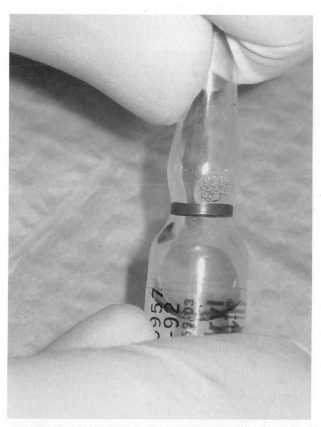

FIGURE 3-36 Open the ampule by breaking at its prescored neck. Use gauze to protect yourself from cuts.

The following steps outline the technique for the intramuscular drug administration:
1. Cleanse the area of needle insertion.
2. Grab the muscle and pull it away from the bone (Figure 3-40).

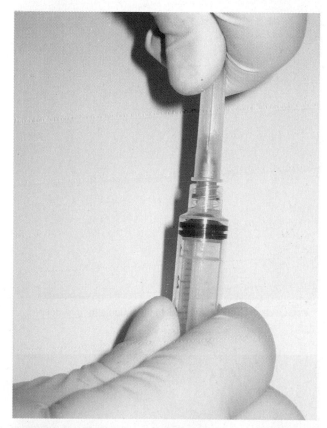

FIGURE 3-37 Needle must be tightened onto syringe to prevent air from leaking in as drug is drawn into syringe.

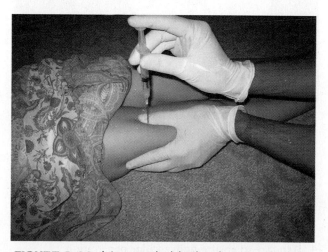

FIGURE 3-38 Intramuscular injection site: vastus lateralis.

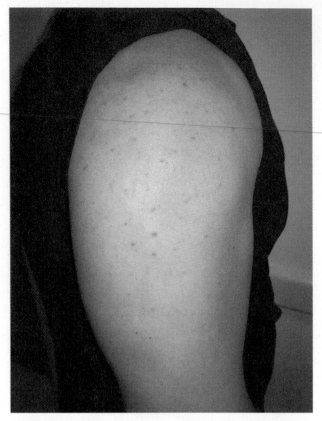

FIGURE 3-39 Intramuscular injection site: mid-deltoid.

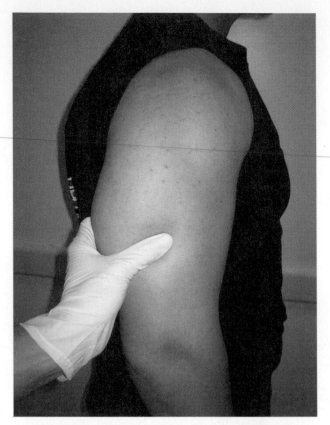

FIGURE 3-40 Muscle is pulled away from bone.

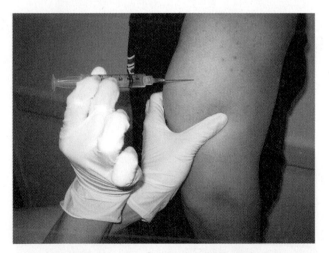

FIGURE 3-41 Syringe is held like a dart.

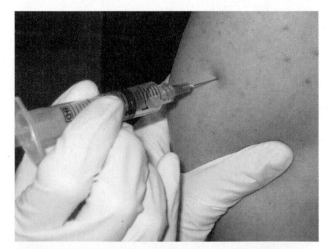

FIGURE 3-42 Needle inserted about 1 inch into muscle.

3. Holding the syringe like a dart, quickly insert the needle into the muscle mass approximately 1 inch (half the length of the needle) (Figures 3-41 and 3-42).

4. Aspirate to ensure nonvascular penetration.

5. Administer the drug.

6. Release pressure on the muscle before removing syringe.

7. Remove the syringe, place, a piece of dry gauze, and apply pressure to the injection site for a minimum of 1 to 2 minutes.

8. Rub the area to increase vascularity and rate of drug absorption.

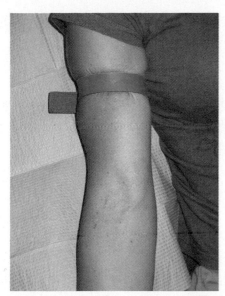

FIGURE 3-43 Tourniquet placed on arm above antecubital fossa.

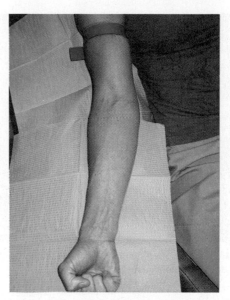

FIGURE 3-44 Veins are distended before venipuncture attempt by patient opening and closing hand.

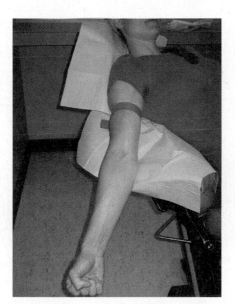

FIGURE 3-45 Hanging arm below level of heart helps distend veins.

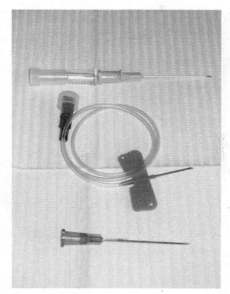

FIGURE 3-46 Indwelling catheter, scalp vein needle, straight needle (top to bottom).

IV drug administration

The following steps outline the technique of venipuncture.

1. Place a tourniquet above the antecubital fossa (Figure 3-43).
2. Have the patient open and close the fist (if possible) to help distend veins (Figure 3-44). Where the patient cannot open and close the fist (as with the unconscious or uncooperative patient), the arm should be placed below the level of the patient's heart to help distend the veins (Figure 3-45).

3. Cleanse and dry the area in which the vein is to be punctured.
4. Angle an indwelling catheter, scalp vein needle, or syringe (Figure 3-46), with the bevel of the needle facing up, at about a 30-degree angle to the vein to be entered (Figure 3-47).
5. Advance the needle into the vein until a return of blood is noted (Figure 3-48).

NOTE: *The return of blood into the needle is the only consistent sign of a successful venipuncture.*

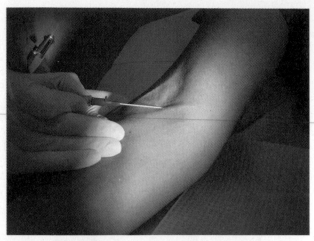

FIGURE 3-47 Penetrate skin with bevel facing up at an angle of approximately 30 degrees.

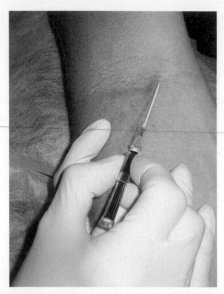

FIGURE 3-48 Advance needle until a return of blood is noted.

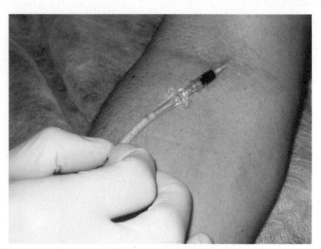

FIGURE 3-49 Tourniquet is removed and intravenous infusion attached.

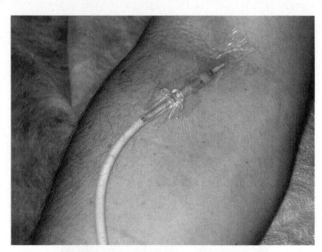

FIGURE 3-50 Needle is secured with tape.

6. Remove the tourniquet and either start the IV infusion (Figure 3-49) or administer the desired drug directly into the vein.
7. Secure the needle with tape to maintain continuous venous access (Figure 3-50). (IM drug administration and venipuncture are reviewed in depth in selected texts.[1])

REFERENCES

1. Malamed SF: *Sedation: a guide to patient management*, ed 4, St. Louis, Mosby, 2003.

CHAPTER 4

Legal Considerations

There is no question that health professionals are faced with onerous requirements based on legal issues as we practice in the 21st century.

The history of liability for alleged medical errors is long, no doubt dating to times before medical records were even written. It is difficult to find "the good old days" when one considers that doctors have been under constraint to perform successfully for millennia. Consider Babylon's Code of Hammurabi (1700 BCE), which codified the laws of the period and contains the first known written record regulating medical practice.[1] The Code provides, for instance, that "If a doctor treats a man with a metal knife for a severe wound, and has caused the man to die, or has opened the man's tumor with a metal knife and destroyed the man's eye, his hands shall be cut off."[1]

■ MODERN LIABILITY INSURANCE CRISES

Experienced practitioners today know that we are in the midst of our third modern "liability crisis." Perhaps a more appropriate term would be "liability insurance crisis." As taxing as liability issues are, it appears that most of today's world has accepted the principle of accepting remuneration rather than a literal pound of flesh for medical errors.

Those who were practicing in the 1970s will recall the first modern liability insurance crisis. Doctors in California went on strike for services other than true emergencies. The result of the strike and other types of health professional activism was MICRA, or California's Medical Insurance Compensation Reform Act of 1975.

MICRA provided a multipronged solution to the crisis at that time and included the following:
1. Limits on noneconomic damages
2. Evidence of collateral sources of payment
3. Limits on attorney's fees
4. Advance notice of a claim
5. Statute of limitations reform
6. Periodic payments for future needs
7. Binding arbitration of disputes

The results of MICRA have been impressive and include such findings as the following:
1. The time to settlement in California is 3 years, while the national average is 4 years.
2. The cost of settlement in California is half that of the national average. Although insurers pay out less, the plaintiffs receive larger average awards during settlement.
3. The cost of liability insurance premiums in California from 1975 to 2000 rose 168%, but nationally premiums rose 505%.

The second modern liability crisis occurred in the 1980s and resulted in many doctors' being economically forced to find alternative liability insurance options. One successful experiment involved forming private offshore insurance companies. Despite the significant legal, temporal, and financial logistics involved, this type of planning was successful, as evidenced by the fact that major carrier insurance rates uniformly decreased nationally as the doctor-owned and -operated companies thrived. Rates decreased in part because when the doctors themselves were managers and shareholders, companies quickly settled meritorious claims and aggressively defended frivolous suits. In addition, many health professionals involved in such planning actually profited financially from well-managed concerns. The profits were significant enough that the traditional insurers re-entered the marketplace and purchased most of the doctor-owned companies.

Unfortunately, the overall national economic boon of the 1980s did not continue into the 1990s. This, coupled with the loss of personally involved doctor-managers and -shareholders, resulted in the third crisis, which continues to this day.

Currently, MICRA is still in place in California and appears to be beneficial. Interestingly, there are over 200,000 attorneys in California[2] and approximately 20,000 dentists. Nationally, 1,100,000 attorneys practice, while the American Dental Association has 170,000 members.

At the time of this writing, tort reform is a major state and national issue. Tort reform involves not only health professionals, but all aspects of society where individuals are accused of breaching a duty to another's disadvantage. The trend at this time is, logically, to revisit California MICRA-based tort reform. MICRA has stood the test of time and has been shown to be of economic benefit to all interested groups, save that of the trial lawyers (both plaintiff and defense).

The nation has seen a dramatic rise in not only tort-based malpractice lawsuits over the past several years but also the predictable sequelae of such legal action. Trauma centers have closed, doctors are actively (and passively, by limiting their practice or opting for early retirement) leaving lawsuit-friendly communities or states, and patient consumers are now starting to directly feel the loss of health professional availability and other consequences of a litigation system that has never been busier.

As states enact MICRA-based reform, constitutional challenges are predictably foisted in the courts. The Wisconsin Supreme Court invoked the relatively rare rational basis legal theory in a four to three decision that eliminated the $350,000 cap on some medical malpractice damages.[3] Time will only tell where the states' machinations lead us, but to many legal commentators it appears that ultimately a federal resolution is necessary.

■ THEORIES OF LIABILITY

There are several legal theories by which plaintiffs can seek redress against health professionals.

Statute violation

Violation of a state or federal statute leads to an assumption of negligence if damage to a patient occurs. In other words, the burden of proof, a significant obligation usually borne by the plaintiff, now shifts to the defendant, who must prove that the statute violation was not such that it caused any damage claimed.

Two basic types of statutes exist, malum in se and malum prohibitum. Malum in se (bad in fact) statutes restrict behavior that in and of itself is recognized as harmful, such as driving while inebriated. Malum prohibitum (defined as bad) conduct in and of itself may not be criminal, reckless, or wanton but is regulated simply to, for instance, promote social order. Driving at certain speeds is an example of a malum prohibitum statute. The difference between legally driving at 15 MPH in a school zone and criminally driving at 16 MPH in a school zone is not the result of a criminal mind but a social regulatory decision.

For instance, if one is speeding while driving, several sequelae may result when that statute violation is recognized. First, the speeder may simply be warned to stop speeding. Second, the speeder may be issued a citation and have to appear in court, argue innocence, pay a fine if found guilty, attend traffic school, and so forth. Third, if the speeder's conduct causes damage to others, additional civil or criminal sanctions may apply. Fourth, the situation may be compounded civilly or criminally if multiple statute violations are present, such as speeding and driving recklessly or driving while intoxicated.

Occasionally statute violation is commendable. For instance, a driver may swerve to the "wrong" side of the centerline to avoid a child who suddenly runs into the street from between parked cars. At times, speeding may be considered a heroic act, such as when a driver is transporting a patient to a hospital during an emergency. However, even if the speeder has felt he is contributing to the public welfare somehow, the statute violation is still subject to review.

For health professionals, the administration of local anesthetic without a current state license or Drug Enforcement Administration certification is probably a violation of statute. If the type of harm sustained by the patient is the type that would have been prevented by obeying the statute, additional liability may attach to the defendant. As an example, someone without a license may be liable for permanent lingual nerve paresthesia[4,5] after the administration of a local block, but probably would not be liable for temporally related appendicitis.

Conversely, an example of a beneficial regulatory violation, and a subsequent positive educational experience for regulatory agency, occurred when a licensee did not fulfill mandatory basic cardiopulmonary resuscitation (CPR) certification but chose to complete advanced cardiac life support (ACLS) certification instead. When admonished by the state board that a violation had occurred, potentially putting the public at greater risk, the licensee pointed out to the regulatory board that ACLS certification is actually more beneficial to the public than CPR. The licensing board then changed the regulation to allow CPR or ACLS certification as a requirement to maintain a license.

Generally, employers are not responsible for statute violations of employees. An exception to this guideline can occur in the health professions. When employees engage in the practice of dentistry or medicine, even without the knowledge or approval of the employer, that employee and the employer may both be held liable for damage. Employer sanctions may be magnified, such as loss of one's professional license, if an employee practices dentistry or medicine with employer knowledge.

Finally, at times some types of specific conduct are defined statutorily as malpractice per se. For instance, unintentionally leaving a foreign body in a patient after a procedure may be deemed malpractice per se. In these types of cases, theoretically simply the plaintiff's demonstration of the foreign body, via radiograph, a secondary procedure to remove the foreign body may be all that is required to establish malpractice.

Contract law

The relationship between a health professional and a patient is first contractual in that services are provided and payment is received. Any remedies the doctor or patient may have against one another in contract are separate and distinct from tort, or malpractice, claims.

Several contractual relationships are possible. The most common interaction is probably the implied contract. In this instance, a patient presents for treatment and fees are not discussed in detail. If a controversy arises, the courts will look to see that the fees charged for the procedures provided were reasonable. Another type of relationship is the express contract, in which the procedures and fees are discussed specifically. Last is a formal written contract regarding services and fees.

A contract is binding whether it is a written agreement, verbal agreement, or implied. Occasionally one will read about a case in which a doctor is sued because a contract principle has allegedly been violated. For instance, "guaranteed results" are a particularly worrisome concept and should be avoided.[6]

Criminal law

Recent history has seen a dramatic increase in the number of suits filed under criminal law theories by government prosecutors. Criminally based suits against health professionals most often fall under three general categories.

The first type of criminal suit is secondary to alleged fraud, particularly involving Medicare or Medicaid.[7]

Second, prosecution for misuse of narcotics is becoming more common. In 2004, John Walters, Chief of the Office of National Drug Control Policy, promised "an unprecedented and comprehensive effort, including increased investigative work by the DEA, to combat the diversion of prescription drugs to the black market."[8]

Third, health professionals are undergoing increased prosecution for plaintiff morbidity or mortality, which previously was considered under tort theory only. "A social intolerance of medical mistakes has caused them to be criminalised."[9] Government criminal prosecutors litigating against health providers must in theory be able to prove that a criminal or guilty mind (mens rea)[10] exists in addition to statute violation. In other words, for an act to be criminal, the act must itself be illegal and accompanied by mens rea. Once a criminal act has been shown, mens rea can be documented by proving intentional or knowing commission of a crime. Additionally, the government may prove its case by convincing a jury that reckless, wanton, or grossly negligent conduct existed even if specific intent to commit a crime is not seen. If the government does not meet these burdens, acquittal should result.[11]

Finally, occasional criminal conduct is reported in the dental arena that may realistically have only a remote relationship to dentistry. For example, consider the arrest of a correctional center dental auxiliary who allegedly conspired to help a convict escape from prison in Nevada by providing a cell phone to the inmate.[12]

Tort law

However, the legal theory covering most health professional activity is that of tort law. A tort is a private, civil wrong not dependent on a contract. A tort allegation may be pursued by a plaintiff citizen (civilly) or by a plaintiff government (criminally). Classically, a viable civil suit in tort requires perfection of four essential elements: duty, a breach of duty, proximate cause, and damage. A health professional may successfully defend a suit in tort by proving that no duty existed, no breach of duty occurred, the health professional's conduct was not the cause of damage, or no damage exists.

Duty

Briefly, the health professional owes a duty to a patient if the health professional's conduct created a foreseeable risk to the patient. Generally, a duty is created when a patient and health professional personally interact for health care purposes. Face-to-face interaction at the practitioner's place of practice would most likely fulfill the requirement of a created duty, while interaction over the telephone or computer may not be as clear-cut regarding establishment of a relationship leading to duty.

Breach of duty

A breach of duty occurs when the health care professional fails to act as a reasonable health care provider. A determination of whether a provider has acted reasonably is contemplated by the jury and involves the battle of the expert witnesses for plaintiff and defendant. A professional has acted reasonably if his or her conduct has been what a comparable professional in the same or similar circumstances would have done.

Exceptions to the rule requiring experts are cases in which no consent was given or obtained for an elective or urgent procedure. Additional exceptions are cases in which the defendant's conduct is obviously erroneous and speaks for itself (res ipsa loquitur),[13] such as wrong-sided surgery. In addition, as noted previously, some complications are defined as malpractice per se by statute (i.e., statute violation), such as unintentionally leaving a foreign body in a patient after a procedure.

The experts testifying as to the alleged breach of duty are arguing about the standard of care. It is often mistakenly assumed that the standard of the practitioner's community is the one to which he or she will be judged. Today, the community standard is the national standard. Additionally, if there are specialists reasonably accessible to the patient, the standard may be the national standard for specialists, regardless of whether the practitioner is a specialist or not.[14–17]

The standard of care may also be illustrated by the professional literature. Health care professionals are expected to be aware of current issues in the literature, such as previously unreported complications to local anesthetics. Often, articles will also proffer preventative suggestions and review treatment options.

A breach of duty is not necessarily indicated simply because an accepted writing recommends conduct other than that which the health care provider used. For instance, specific drug use other than that recommended by the *Physicians' Desk Reference* is commonplace and legally acceptable as long as the health care provider can articulate a reasonable purpose for his or her conduct.[18] Part of this reasoning for off-label drug use may include a benefit-risk analysis for various treatment options for a specific patient. The ordinary standard of care is not necessarily what is statistically most often done by similarly situated health professionals.[19]

Causation

Proximate cause is the summation of the actual cause and legal cause. Actual cause is the cause that exists if a chain of events factually flows from the defendant's conduct to the plaintiff's injury. Legal cause is present if actual cause exists and if the plaintiff attorney can prove that the harm sustained was foreseeable or not highly extraordinary in hindsight.

Damage

Damage, of course, is usually the most obvious of the elements of the tort. Generally, the damage must be physical. For instance, plaintiffs who sue for emotional distress must also show a physical manifestation of the emotional distress. The physical damage to one's patient can lead to damages claimed by another individual, such as a patient's spouse's loss of consortium claim.

Reasonableness

An underlying legal principle in all health care–related discussions is the concept of reasonableness. Legal analysis of a controversy usually involves an evaluation of reasonable care (see preceding discussion of breach of duty and standard of care) and the reasonable man. The reasonable man is a hypothetical person who uses "those qualities of attention, knowledge, intelligence, and judgment which society requires of its members for the protection of their own interest and the interests of others."[20] Depending on the type of case, the reasonableness of a defendant's conduct can be analyzed by the facts as the defendant perceived them, as the defendant should have known them, or as the facts actually existed as analyzed in hindsight in the courtroom.

Consent

Reasonably, the consent process is an essential part of patient treatment for health care professionals. The doctrine of *simple consent* has been recognized since 18th-century English common law. Simple consent can be defined as obtaining permission to perform an act without discussing the ramifications of that act.

The doctrine of consent has historically been well recognized in the United States. In 1914, U.S. Supreme Court Justice Benjamin Cardozo stated, "Every human being of adult years and sound mind has a right to determine what shall be done with his own body; and a surgeon who performs an operation without his patient's consent commits an assault for which he is liable in damages."[21]

Legally, an unauthorized (i.e., without consent) touching of another is a battery and is subject to civil or criminal remedies.

The specific doctrine of informed consent is a modern concept and was developed in California in 1957.[22] Essentially, informed consent involves explaining the following:

1. Nature and purpose of treatment proposed
2. Risks and consequences of the treatment proposed

3. Alternatives to the treatment proposed, including no treatment
4. The prognosis with or without the proposed treatment

Often treatment planning will result in several viable options that may be recommended by the doctor. The patient then makes an informed decision as to which option is most preferable to that patient, and treatment may begin.

Consent is essential because many of the procedures doctors perform would be considered illegal in other settings (i.e., an incision developed by a doctor during surgery versus an equivalent traumatic wound placed during a criminal battery).

Consent may be verbal or written, but when a controversy presents at a later date a written consent is extremely beneficial. In fact, since consent is often a standard of care for a procedure, the lack of a written consent may reduce the fact finding to a "he said/she said" scenario. This circumstance may greatly diminish the plaintiff's burden of proving the allegations and may even shift the burden of proof to the defendant.[23]

When treating mentally challenged persons or children under the age of majority, consent from a legal guardian is necessary for elective procedures.

Consent obtained before one procedure may not be assumed for the same procedure at a different time or a different procedure at the same time. In addition, consent obtained for one health care provider may not be transferable to another health care provider, such as a partner doctor, an employee dental hygienist, or a registered nurse.[24]

It is a recognized legal principle that a patient may not consent to malpractice. The patient who offers to sign a "waiver" in order to convince a practitioner to provide treatment will not likely be held to that waiver if malpractice is adjudicated to exist. However, there are several instances when consent may not be required. The first and second, emergencies and Good Samaritan rescues, are discussed later in this chapter.

A third situation when consent may not be required is the extension doctrine. The extension doctrine generally applies during surgery under general anesthesia. An example of a valid use of the extension doctrine would be the removal of an undiagnosed nonfunctional supernumerary found adjacent to and secondary to a third molar's removal.

Fourth, revisiting the concept of waiver, a patient may knowingly and voluntarily waive the presentation of a portion of the information that would normally be given during the consent process. However, the patient who wishes to waive some consent information can not waive all consent information. The practitioner might consider mentioning at least the most significant adverse possibility, such as central nervous system compromise or death. Also, the patient who elects to waive routine consent information should sign a document stating that the waiver is knowing and voluntary and that the health care provider is ready, willing, and able to provide complete consent.

Finally, the doctrine of therapeutic privilege allows doctors not to provide consent. If, in the doctor's reasonable and objective opinion, the provision of consent to a patient would be detrimental to that patient, therapeutic privilege allows consent not to be perfected.

The author's (Orr) general consent is included (Figure 4-1) in this chapter. In addition to the general consent, which is essentially used for any and all procedures, verbal consent is obtained and occasionally initialed. Finally, specific written consent for singular procedures is at times obtained.

Statute of limitations

Statutes of limitations are laws that fix the time in which the litigants, usually plaintiffs, must seek to avail themselves of legal recourse. After the statute of limitations tolls, the parties are barred from seeking legal recourse.

As mentioned previously, modern tort reform, including MICRA-type laws, usually include statute of limitations clauses. However, statutes of limitations are subject to judicial interpretation and in fact can be predictably extended in certain situations, such as when the plaintiff is a minor or during recalls of hazardous dental devices years after such devices were placed.[25]

■ EMERGENCY SITUATIONS
Standard of care during emergencies

The standard of care during emergencies is the same as during other situations, in that the health care professional must act as a correspondingly qualified health professional would in the same or similar circumstances.

However, by their very nature, emergencies lend themselves to a different analysis of the health professional's conduct. An emergency scenario does not lend itself to typical doctor-patient circumstances. For instance, in an emergency, there is generally no time for leisurely reflection about the problem; consultation with colleagues, the patient, or the patient's family; or even proffering of informed consent, let alone bare consent.

Consent during emergencies

Emergency situations present a different paradigm for consent evaluation. During an emergency, there simply may be no reasonable opportunity to obtain consent.

Defining emergency

It is important in the law and the health professions to consider how words are defined. *Emergency* is derived from the Latin "mergere": "to dip, plunge, inundate, engulf, or overwhelm, or to bury."[26] *Webster* defines an emergency as "1. a sudden, urgent, usually unexpected occurrence or occasion requiring immediate action. 2. a state, especially of need for help or relief, created by some unexpected event."[27]

Black's Law Dictionary defines emergency as "a sudden unexpected happening; an unforeseen occurrence or condition; perplexing contingency or complication of circumstances; a sudden or unexpected occasion for action; exigency; pressing necessity."[28] Notice the iteration of "unforeseen" in this definition relative to the following comments.

Thus, the patient with chronic odontalgia who "just can't stand it anymore" may define the toothache as an emergency. Clearly, a chronic toothache is probably not an emergency because it is, at the least, not sudden or unexpected and most likely does not require immediate action. That patients define emergency differently than health professionals is understandable and in part the fault of the health care industry. For instance, patients often avail themselves of an "emergencies welcome" advertisement at the dentist's office. Is the office that advertises "emergencies welcome" soliciting anaphylaxis, massive oral hemorrhage, or something altogether different, like chronic odontalgia? Also, it is well documented that most patients who present to hospital emergency departments are not actually seen because of an emergency but secondary to convenience, lack of funds, no previous doctor-patient relationship, and so forth.[29]

At www.ada.org, the American Dental Association itself lists the following as dental emergencies: "bitten lip or tongue; broken tooth; cracked tooth; jaw possibly broken; knocked out tooth; objects caught between teeth; toothache."[30] A chronic toothache, per *Webster*, may indeed be an "urgent" situation: "1. compelling or requiring immediate action or attention; imperative; pressing. 2. insistent or earnest in solicitation; importunate. 3. expressed with insistence, as requests or appeals."[31]

But urgencies are not emergencies, although at times the definitions may begin to meld. It is important not to be lulled into a legal confrontation because of a misuse of terms with definitive meanings.

As health professionals, we must recognize how we use the term "emergency," just as we are with the term "allergy" (as opposed to sensitivity or another physiologic phenomenon). For instance, it has been documented that most patients who give a history of penicillin allergy are not in fact allergic to penicillin.[32]

An important aspect of an emergency situation is the element of unexpectedness. Thus, if a certain result is commonly predictable from certain conduct, such as a

ORAL & MAXILLOFACIAL SURGERY CONSENT

The procedures to be performed have been explained to me and I understand what is to be done. This is my consent to the procedures discussed and to any other procedures found to be necessary or advisable in addition to the preoperative treatment plan. I agree to the use of local, sedation, or general anesthesia depending on the judgment of Dr. Daniel L. Orr II.

I have been informed and understand that occasionally there are complications of the surgery, drugs, and anesthesia. The more common complications are pain, infection, swelling, bleeding, bruising and temporary or permanent numbness and/or tingling of the lip, tounge, chin, gums, cheeks, or teeth. I understand that pain, numbness, swelling, and inflammation of veins or other structures may occur from injections. I understand death from other procedures has been estimated at 1/400,000. I understand the possibility of injury to the neck and facial muscles, and changes in the bite or jaw joint. I understand the possibility of injury to the adjacent teeth, restorations, and tissues, reffered pain to other areas of the head and neck, bone fractures or infections, and delayed healing. I understand the combination of anesthesia and surgery may lead to nausea, vomiting, allergic reactions, and other physical or psychological reactions. I understand sinus complications may include an opening into the sinus from the mouth after the removal of teeth. I understand injury may occur when instruments fail. I understand that many other complications not listed may occur. I understand medications, drugs, anesthetics, and prescriptions may cause drowsiness and lack of coordination, which could be increased by the use of alcohol or other drugs; I have been advised not to operate any vehicle or potentially hazardous devices or work while taking such medications and/or drugs or until fully recovered from their effects.

I acknowledge the receipt of and understand the postoperative instructions. I understand that there is no guarantee related to treatment. I understand that most complications can be rectified with proper follow-up care. I agree to follow up as needed or advised for any concerns or complications. I understand I can receive a review of these and other possible risks by asking.

_____

Signature

_____

Signature

_____

Date

FIGURE 4-1 Oral and maxillofacial surgery consent.

toothache due to chronically neglected decay, it would be difficult to truly categorize such a situation as an emergency.

Also, per _Black's Law Dictionary,_ a complication of circumstances may exist. In fact, emergencies often do seem to be secondary to at least a small series of singular circumstances that would not ordinarily be reasonably expected to occur, especially sequentially.[33]

Consider the unexpectedness of a chronic toothache progressing to an acute abscess that is in immanent danger of compromising an airway. It is likely that an emergency exists. Most toothaches are not expected to progress to life-threatening situations in which immediate action is required.

Notice that pain, a widely variable subjective phenomenon, is not part of the discussion. Further, many health professionals would logically not include pain in any definition of emergency, no matter what the lay public feels.

Two caveats warrant mention in the discussion of the term "emergency." First, one's state statutes may define emergency differently than do authoritative dictionaries or health professionals would. Remember that statutes are generally written by lay legislators with significant input from the legal profession. It is important to know how emergencies are defined in one's own jurisdiction.

The second admonition involves the singular situation of the trial. When one is in the courtroom, the jury itself may be allowed the latitude to define an emergency in the case at hand. The jury's definition may not correspond to that outlined by *Webster's*, *Black's*, or statute.

Emergency rescues—Good Samaritan statutes

Generally, emergencies outside healthcare settings also do not require consent secondary to Good Samaritan statutes, which apply to rescues. Rescues involve aiding a victim in serious peril that the rescuer's conduct has not created. Interestingly, an injured rescuer may have legal recourse against an individual who negligently created the peril, including the victim (rescue doctrine).

Again, however, it is wise to know what the statute in one's own jurisdiction iterates. Generally, legislators want to encourage rescues and thus limit potential liability that might be attributed to would-be rescuers. Under the doctrine of imminent or sudden peril, when a potential rescuer is confronted with an emergent or urgent rescue scenario, he or she is not held to the same degree of duty as one who has time to reflect calmly on the scenario. An individual can lose rescuer status by charging a victim a fee.

In addition, some jobs have required duties of rescue. While law enforcement officers are not required to rescue,[34,35] aquatic lifeguards are. Lifeguards, by the very nature of their employment, are required to rescue, while most of society is not. Lifeguards are also held to a higher standard of care, and although a Good Samaritan statute may apply to off-duty professional rescuers, it is less likely that they would receive Good Samaritan protection while on duty.

Statutes in some jurisdictions impose a duty to rescue or perform medical treatment on physicians or other persons employed as professional rescuers.[36]

If a victim is conscious, permission should be sought before aid is rendered. If the victim refuses to allow a rescue, the Good Samaritan has no privilege or duty to attempt a rescue. Unconscious victims require no consent at all. When an emergency victim who is spontaneously or traumatically unconscious is being treated, consent is implied.

Consent may be obtained from a legal guardian. The possibility of obtaining consent from a guardian before a rescue is generally timing dependent. In an urgent situation, time may be available to discuss the rescue with a guardian. However, during a more emergent situation, taking time to discuss options may actually compromise the patient.

Even though most rescue situations are essentially free from potential legal liability flowing from the victim to the rescuer, a source of liability even when being fully qualified as a "Good Samaritan" is reckless conduct. For instance, reckless conduct in a rescue situation would involve electively and knowingly leaving the victim in a situation that is more desperate than when the rescuer found the victim. An example of such conduct might be when a rescuer offers to transport a victim to a hospital for necessary treatment and then abandons the victim farther from a hospital than where the victim was initially found.

Relationship between doctor and emergency patient

The first type of relationship, already discussed, is the Good Samaritan relationship. Generally, any rescuer, including a health professional, is granted wide latitude for conduct as far as reasonableness.

In the second type of emergency situation, based on the doctor-patient relationship, a health provider might find himself or herself called upon to treat a previously unknown patient. An example of this relationship would be when one is called to an emergency department to treat a trauma victim. Often, even a basic history or consent of any type cannot be obtained. Again, doctors are allowed relatively wide latitude in what is reasonable therapeutic intervention in these scenarios. This latitude may even be legislated at times, for instance by granting doctors in these situations sovereign immunity, or the same protection the king (state or federal government) enjoys from prosecution in the promulgation of duties.[37]

The third type of association is the one most relevant to the emergencies presented in this text. Specifically, we need to consider emergencies that present during elective procedures for known patients in the private dental office. Again, the standard of care does not change: one is expected to treat patients in this scenario as another with comparable training would in the same or similar circumstances. However, when the circumstances include an emergency, the guidelines present are less defined because of the unexpected presentation of the problems that need to be immediately addressed.

Foreseeability

Foreseeability is a legal principle that may be used to limit or impose liability for an individual's conduct. A foreseeable result or consequence is one that the reasonable man would expect might occur. Contrarily, an unforeseeable result is one which a reasonable man would not expect to occur. For instance, one might reasonably expect inflammation after a surgical procedure such as the intraoral administration of local anesthetic. However, one would generally not foresee that a patient would typically lose vision after local anesthetic administration for dentistry, although the phenomenon has been reported.[38-40]

The obvious question at hand is whether medical emergencies in the dental office are foreseeable. If adverse consequences are foreseeable, liability may be imposed. If the adverse consequences are not foreseeable, liability may be avoided.

Medical emergencies in the dental office do occur and are generally foreseeable, as evidenced by the publication of the sixth edition of this very text. It has been accurately stated that if one practices long enough, a life-threatening event will occur in one's office. This statement is obviously true, but the mere foreseeability of a single life-threatening event sometime during decades of practice does not make that event, when and if it ultimately occurs, expected. Certainly, if dentists routinely expected to be faced with life-threatening events in their offices, the entire nature of the profession would have to change.

◼ LIMITING LIABILITY FOR EMERGENCIES

Just as injudicious practice protocols will lead to an increased incidence of complications and emergencies, careful practice within the standard of care of the profession will minimize adverse sequelae, including emergencies, in an office practice. However, even the most careful practitioners through no fault of their own will, given a long enough career, experience emergency situations.

So many factors play a part in the judicious practice that it would be impossible to discuss them in a single text, let alone a chapter. Nonetheless, several will be briefly discussed.

Prevention and preparation

Carefully review the prevention and preparation recommendations elsewhere in this text. Following the admonitions therein will do much to maximize the control a practitioner has in reducing the incidence of office emergencies.

Poor decisions

A poor outcome does not necessarily relate to a poor decision. Examples abound wherein reasonable decisions about standard of care were made throughout a case in which a bad result occurred. However, it has been proposed that three basic types of errors can lead to the development of critical situations that otherwise could be avoided.[41]

The first error is lack of experience. Certainly, most doctors do not routinely treat emergencies. But emergencies may occur secondary to doctors who have extended themselves beyond their routine experiences in medical or surgical therapy. It is never optimal to routinely perform surgical or therapeutic procedures one is not thoroughly familiar with. Ideally, extending oneself to the limits of one's abilities occurs very infrequently and not electively. One legitimate circumstance for such an extension would be when dealing with an emergency. If one desires to expand a practice's scope, appropriate continuing education or specialty training may be considered. In fact, even if one simply desires to simply maintain status quo licensure, continuing education is usually mandated by most state professional boards. The lesson to be learned is that if one is not experienced in providing a certain elective treatment, perhaps that treatment should be deferred.

The second commonly found error is a lack of information for the situation at hand. For instance, an incomplete review of a patient's medical history might result in less than optimal treatment for the patient.

The third source of poor decisions is a lack of aggressiveness when something amiss is noted. For example, at what blood pressure does one become concerned enough to alter routine treatment protocol?

Respondeat superior

Respondeat superior (let the superior reply) is the legal doctrine that assigns liability for employee conduct to the employer. If an employee commits a tort against a patient, in some cases the employer doctor will have to assume responsibility for the patient's damage.

Even if the doctor is well trained in dealing with various emergencies, if the staff is not trained for their concomitant duties, optimal emergency treatment will be compromised. Any poor performance by one's staff may be attributed to the supervision of the employer doctor. In addition, peripheral staff, such as answering services, are critical. Perceived or real emergencies may arise after normal office hours, and one must make reasonable arrangements to properly deal with such situations.[42]

Community standards

Today, automated external defibrillators (AEDs) are commonplace in shopping centers and at sporting events. Dentists would be hard pressed to explain convincingly why, as health care providers, their office had no AED when lay providers are so common. Similarly, if one's own lay patients know CPR better than anyone in the practice, such a discrepancy should be addressed.

Professional relationships

It would seem judicious to develop relationships with colleagues, including specialist dentists and physicians, for times when consultation would be helpful. Timely consultations can truncate the development of emergency situations. Similarly, a close affiliation with a local hospital can facilitate patient care should admission of one's own patient be necessary.

As mentioned previously, one is responsible for patients after office hours. Patients reasonably expect to have access to their doctor as necessary for perceived or real emergencies. If the primary caregiver is not going to be available, arrangements with another dentist to take call for the practice are strongly recommended.

Collegiality

Occasionally patients choose not to or are not able to follow up with their original doctor or those designated for follow up as necessary. This situation results in one's patient seeing a new doctor for evaluation and possible treatment.

A common denominator seen in almost all malpractice litigation is criticism, warranted or not, to the patient from another health professional about the original treatment. This criticism is usually proffered without consultation with the original doctor. Unwarranted criticism could be easily eliminated by the second doctor's simply contacting the original health professional in order to compile a more complete history.

Any conduct that promotes frivolous legal action is not in the patient's best interest. A health professional's highest obligation is to patients, but that duty is part and parcel of other ethical obligations, including those owed to one's colleagues.[43-45]

Philosophical aspects of treating emergencies

The primary author, Dr. Malamed, occasionally asks a series of relevant questions, which are addressed in the following section.

Is a dentist absolutely required to manage a potentially life-threatening emergency?

The "duty to rescue" is a wonderful subject for legal analysis. One can easily find eloquent arguments both pro and con the societal duty to rescue. Distilling the question to its elemental issue, does society want to legally mandate rescues or does society want to preserve individual freedom to accept or reject rescue responsibility and potential liability?

Two well-known tragic incidents seemingly compel mandated rescues. In 1964, a resident of New York City screamed for help from the street outside her apartment when attacked by a knife-wielding criminal. It is well documented that many neighbors witnessed the attack and the wounded woman helpless on the sidewalk. No one responded to the cries for help. After the initial attack, seeing no aid proffered, the criminal returned twice to continue the attack, ultimately leading to the victim's death. The second incident occurred in a Massachusetts tavern in 1983. Patrons watched a rape attack for over an hour without intervention or a call for help.

A third similar incident occurred in a case the author was involved in as a forensic expert (*NV v Strohmeyer*, 1997). College student Jeremy Strohmeyer was convicted of the sexual assault and murder of 7-year-old Sherrice Iverson. During the crime, Strohmeyer's friend witnessed a portion of the attack early on as he peered into the bathroom stall Iverson had tried to escape into. A short time later, immediately after Iverson's death, Strohmeyer's friend asked Strohmeyer what happened and Strohmeyer bragged about the assault and homicide. The two friends subsequently drove home. The public reaction to the lack of any rescue effort by Strohmeyer's friend led to a flurry of legislative proposals to legally require rescues.

Such cases in which a life could have likely been saved by minimal intervention regularly present to the legal system. Almost uniformly, courts decline to impose any liability on individuals who decline the responsibility and potential liability involved in a rescue.

However, persons with special relationships to the victim may be required to attempt to effect a rescue.

Some such persons considered to have special relationships include family members; the individual who is the cause of the victim's duress; an employee duty bound to rescue (i.e., a lifeguard); and a property owner who has invited the victim onto the owner's property.

Occasionally, states will consider requiring its citizens to rescue. Currently, only Minnesota and Vermont have statutes requiring rescue under certain circumstances. However, Good Samaritan statutes are found uniformly in state law because legislatures want to encourage rescues by removing potential liability, although some liability may always attach.

Good Samaritan statutes are aptly named and intended by states to promote moral behavior. Religious and philosophical leaders throughout history have championed selfless service to others.[46,47] In the New Testament, Jesus' iteration of the story of the Good Samaritan[48] simply builds on a well-known tenet of the Old Testament,[49] thus reasonably representing and uniting the views of at least the world's Jews, Christians, and Muslims, which all recognize Abraham as a patriarchal ancestor.

Briefly, the Biblical Good Samaritan rescued a victim despite potential physical or legal harm to himself, contrary to existing social mores regarding his nation's sworn enemies, and only after others who might have been expected to give aid refused. Interestingly, the question leading to Jesus Christ's narrative was posed by an adversarial lawyer. The lesson offered is that if the Samaritan can rescue his enemy, we are thus admonished to also serve our neighbor and fellow man.

The American Dental Association's Code of Professional Conduct states an ethical obligation for dentists to "make reasonable arrangement for the emergency care of their patients of record. Dentists shall be obliged when consulted in an emergency by patients not of record to make reasonable arrangements for emergency care."[42]

Thus, it appears after this brief analysis that dentists are probably obligated morally, ethically, and often legally to treat both established and emergency patients who need care.

Is calling 9-1-1 sufficient to fulfill responsibility for the rescue?

Calling 9-1-1 is probably the minimal effort that would be required to fulfill rescue obligations in the dental office and in fact requires no professional expertise whatsoever. Depending on the emergency and the dentist's prior conduct, much more responsibility might be mandated by the body that evaluates the case, be it one's regulatory board or a criminal or civil court. For instance, a known epileptic patient in the waiting room who has a central nervous system seizure would likely be evaluated differently than a child who seizes secondary to an absolute or relative local anesthetic overdose.

What is the dentist's responsibility when another with more emergency expertise arrives?

The dentist who calls 9-1-1 and goes to lunch is in a different position than one who is actively helping treat the emergency by, for instance, maintaining an airway. The dentist who is deciding whether or not to relinquish the emergency care of his patient to another must reasonably weigh the risk and benefit of such conduct. It is possible that emergency medical technicians, oral and maxillofacial surgeons, and some physicians (e.g., anesthesiologists) will have more expertise in maintaining an airway than a general practitioner. Some physicians, such as radiologists, pathologists, or psychiatrists, may have minimal airway training. What reasonably appears to be in the patient's best interests is the correct course of action. Unfortunately, the one considering relinquishing care can be legally liable for damage no matter which decision is made.

Is a dentist legally required to maintain an emergency drug kit and/or CPR certification?

Many dentists are indeed legally required to have an emergency drug kit. Specifically, those who have special general anesthesia or sedation permits issued by the various state boards are required to have such kits.

Dentists who do not have general anesthesia or sedation permits would do well to consider the package inserts from the various local anesthetic solutions, which state that drugs, equipment, and personnel for management of drug-related emergencies must be immediately available.

Such package inserts, coupled with the almost universal state board requirement that licensed dentists must be proficient in CPR, appear to imply that dentists are probably responsible for reasonable efforts in maintaining airways and cardiovascular function in the event of a local anesthetic reaction requiring such.

What drugs should be contained in an emergency kit?

Depending on the patients treated, modalities used, and personal preference, the recommended contents of an emergency kit are myriad.

Dentist anesthesiologist and educator Dr. Ken Reed offers a reasonable suggestion for the basic emergency kit for dental offices utilizing local anesthesia and nitrous oxide.[50] Dr. Reed's basic kit includes oxygen, epinephrine, diphenhydramine, albuterol, aspirin, nitroglycerine, a form of sugar, and an AED.

What is the dentist's ultimate responsibility during a medical emergency in the office?

For years, Dr. Malamed has iterated the reasonable response that the dentist's responsibility is to "keep the victim alive by treating the victim until recovery or until another more qualified individual assumes responsibility for treatment."[51]

REFERENCES

1. Lyons AS, Petrucelli RJ: *Medicine: an illustrated history*, New York, Harry N. Abrams, 1978.
2. McCarthy N: 200,000 lawyers and counting, *California Bar Journal*, February 2005, p 1.
3. Gibeaut J: Med-mal ruling has doctors reeling, *ABA Journal Report*, July 29, 2005, pp 1–4.
4. Pogrel MA, Thamby S: Permanent nerve involvement resulting from inferior alveolar nerve blocks, *J Am Dent Assoc* 131:901–907, 2000.
5. Pogrel MA, Schmidt BL, Sambajon V, Jordan RC: Lingual nerve damage due to inferior alveolar nerve blocks: a possible explanation, *J Am Dent Assoc* 134:195–199, 2003.
6. *Heffner vs Reynolds,* 777 N.E. 2d 312 (OH).
7. *Florida vs Harden,* 2004 FL App. Lexis 623.
8. Kerr JC: Anti-drug strategy to include pain killers, Associated Press, March 1, 2004.
9. Holbrook J: The criminalisation of fatal medical mistakes, *BMJ* 327:1118–1119, 2003.
10. *Barron's law dictionary*, ed 2, Woodbury, NY: Barron's Educational Services, 1984.
11. Jury acquits Pasadena dentist of 60 child endangering charges, Associated Press. March 5, 2002.
12. State news, Nevada. *USA Today,* August 29, 2005.
13. *Barron's law dictionary*, ed 2, Woodbury, NY: Barron's Educational Services, 1984.
14. Pollack BR: *Handbook of dental jurisprudence and risk management*, Littleton, MA, PSG Publishing, 1980.
15. Prosser WL, Keeton WP, Dobbs DB, Keeton RE: *Prosser and Keeton on the law of torts*, St. Paul, MN, West Publishing, 1984.
16. Sandar SS: *Legal medicine*, Philadelphia, Mosby, 2004.
17. Tierney K: *The dental clinics of North America: legal consideration in dentistry*, 26:284–285, 1982.
18. Johnson LJ: Off-label prescribing and the standard of care, *Med Econ* 78:97, 2001.
19. *Williamson vs Elrod,* 72 S.W. 3d 489 (AR 2002).
20. Restatement of Torts 2d, 283(b).
21. *Schloendorff vs Society of New York Hospital*, 105 N.E. 92, 93 (NY 1914).
22. *Salgo vs Leland Stanford, Jr., University Board of Trustees*, 317 P. 2d 170, 181 (CA App. Ct. 1957).
23. Orr DL 2nd, Curtis WJ: Obtaining written informed consent for the administration of local anesthetic in dentistry, *J Am Dent Assoc* 136:1568–1571, 2005.
24. *Starozyntk vs Reich*, Superior Ct. of NJ, Case #A-4706-03T1, *Legal Medicine Perspectives* Sep/Oct 2005, pp 75–76.
25. *Cox vs Paul,* 2005 Ind. LEXIS 575.
26. *The new college Latin & English dictionary*, New York, Bantam Books, 1995.
27. *Webster's encyclopedic unabridged dictionary of the English language*, New York, Gramercy Books, 1996.
28. *Black's Law Dictionary*, ed 5, St. Paul, MN, West Publishing, 1979.
29. Carpenter D: Our overburdened ERs, *Hosp Health Netw* 75:44–47, 2001.
30. American Dental Association. Dental emergencies & injuries, available at www.ada.org/public/manage/emergencies.asp.
31. *Webster's encyclopedic unabridged dictionary of the English language*, New York, Gramercy Books, 1996.
32. Arroliga ME, Wagner W, Bobek MB, et al.: A pilot study of penicillin skin testing in patients with a history of penicillin allergy admitted to a medical ICU, *Chest* 118:1106–1108, 2000.
33. Gaba DM, Fish JK, Howard SK: *Crisis management in anesthesiology*, New York, Churchill Livingstone, 1994.
34. *Weiner v. Metropolitan Authority* and *Shernov v. New York Transit Authority*, 55 N.Y. 2d 175. 948 N.Y.S. 2d l4l.1982
35. *Warren vs District of Columbia*, 444, A. 2d 1.1981
36. *State vs Perry*, 29 Ohio App. 2d 33, 278 N.E. 2d 50, 53.
37. Nevada Revised Statutes, Chapter 41, 2005.
38. Goldenberg AS: Transient diplopia as a result of block injections mandibular and posterior superior alveolar, *N Y State Dent J* 63:29–31, 1997.
39. Penarrocha-Diago M, Sanchis-Bielsa JM: Ophthalmologic complications after intraoral local anesthesia with articaine, *Oral Surg Oral Med Oral Pathol Oral Radiol Endod* 90:21–24, 2000.
40. Sawyer RJ, von Schroeder H: Temporary bilateral blindness after acute lidocaine toxicity, *Anesth Analg* 95:224–226, 2002.
41. Klein G: *Sources of power: how people make decisions*, Cambridge, MA, MIT Press, 2001.
42. *Principles of ethics and code of professional conduct*, Sec. 4.B. Chicago, American Dental Association.
43. *Ethics handbook for dentists*, Gaithersburg, MD, American College of Dentists, 2004.
44. *Code of professional conduct*, Rosemont, IL, American Association of Oral and Maxillofacial Surgeons, V, A.1, 2006.
45. Orr DL: A plea for collegiality, *J Oral Maxillofac Surg* 64:1086–1092, 2006.
46. *The teaching of buddha*, Tokyo, Kosaido Printing Co., 1989.
47. *The analects of confucius*, New York, Harper Collins, 1992.
48. *King James Bible*, Luke 10:25–37.
49. *King James Bible*, Leviticus 19:18.
50. Reed K: Personal communication, 2005.
51. Malamed S: Personal communication, 2005.

UNCONSCIOUSNESS

5 Unconsciousness: General Considerations

6 Vasodepressor Syncope

7 Postural Hypotension

8 Acute Adrenal Insufficiency

9 Unconsciousness: Differential Diagnosis

CHAPTER 5

Unconsciousness

General Considerations

In surveys of dental practices by Fast et al.[1] and Malamed,[2] the loss of consciousness was the most commonly observed emergency situation reported. Vasodepressor syncope (common faint) is the medical emergency most often reported in the dental environment, accounting for more than 50% of all emergencies. Although any number of other causes can lead to a loss of consciousness (Schultz[3] presents 33 potential causes in a differential diagnosis of syncope [Box 5-1]), initial management of the unconsciousness person, regardless of cause, is the same; these steps are directed primarily toward certain basic, life-sustaining procedures: **P** (position), **A** (airway), **B** (breathing), and **C** (circulation).

In most instances the period of unconsciousness will be brief after provision of the aforementioned basic yet crucial procedures. However, some other causes of unconsciousness will require significant additional attention once these steps have been taken (**D** [definitive care]).[*] This section discusses several of the more common emergency situations that may result in the loss of consciousness. Box 5-2 lists terms and definitions associated with unconsciousness and are found in the following chapters.

---

*Throughout this and subsequent chapters, emergency procedures are explained under the assumption that the doctor performs the life-saving duties. However, staff members may assume some or all of those duties if the doctor is unavailable.

Box 5-1 Differential diagnosis of syncope

Neurogenic causes
Breath holding
Carotid sinus disease
Vasovagal syncope
Vasodepressor syncope
Orthostatic hypotension
Glossopharyngeal neuralgia
Seizure disorders
Vascular causes
Cerebrovascular disease
    Tussive (cough) syncope
    Cerebrovascular accident
Pulmonary embolism
Aortic arch syndromes
Endocrinopathies
Hypoglycemia
Addisonian crisis
Pheochromocytoma
Hypothyroidism
Exposure to toxins and drugs
Psychogenic problems
Cardiogenic causes
Valvular heart disease
Dysrhythmia
Myocardial infarction
Certain congenital heart anomalies
Hypertrophic cardiomyopathy
Pacemaker syndrome
Disorders of oxygenation
Anemia
High altitude exposure
Barotrauma
Decompression sickness

Modified from Raven P, editor: *Emergency medicine: concepts and clinical practice,* ed 4, St. Louis, Mosby, 1998.

Box 5-2 Terms associated with unconsciousness

Anoxia: Absence or lack of oxygen

Coma: From the Greek term *koma,* meaning deep sleep; most often used to designate a state of unconsciousness from which the patient cannot be roused even by powerful stimulation (Huff[4] defined coma as "that altered state that exists in a patient manifesting inappropriate responses to environmental stimuli who maintains eye closure throughout the stimuli")

Consciousness: From the Latin term *conscius,* meaning aware; implies that an individual is capable of responding appropriately to questions or commands and that protective reflexes, including the ability of the individual to independently maintain a patent airway, are intact[5]

Faint: Sudden, transient loss of consciousness

Hypoxia: Low oxygen content

Syncope: From the Greek term *synkope;* a sudden, transient loss of consciousness without prodromal symptoms that is followed within seconds to minutes (<30 minutes) by resumption of consciousness, usually with the premorbid status intact[6]

Unconsciousness: A lack of response to sensory stimulation[7]

The terms *syncope* and *faint* commonly are used interchangeably to describe the transient loss of consciousness caused by reversible disturbances in cerebral function. Throughout this text the term *syncope* will be used to describe this occurrence. However, the reader must remember that syncope is only a symptom and that although syncopal episodes may occur in healthy individuals, they may also indicate serious medical disorders. Any loss of consciousness, however brief, represents a potentially life-threatening situation requiring prompt recognition and effective management.

■ PREDISPOSING FACTORS

Table 5-1 outlines possible causes for a patient's loss of consciousness in the dental office and includes their relative frequency. A glance at this list will indicate to the reader that many causes exist for the loss of

consciousness. However, a closer examination reveals three factors that when present increase the likelihood that a patient may experience an alteration in, or loss of, consciousness: (1) stress, (2) impaired physical status, and (3) the administration or ingestion of drugs.

In the dental setting, stress is the primary cause in most cases of unconsciousness. Vasodepressor syncope, *the* most common cause of unconsciousness in dentistry, commonly occurs as a result of unusually high levels of stress. The sudden loss of consciousness (syncope) that occurs during venipuncture or the intraoral injection of a local anesthetic is a classic example of vasodepressor syncope.[8,9]

Impaired physical status (American Society of Anesthesiologists class III or IV) is another factor working to increase the likelihood of syncope. Many of the causes listed in Table 5-1 are not usually associated with the onset of syncope but may progress to unconsciousness if the underlying problem is not recognized promptly or if the patient is debilitated. When patients with impaired physical status are exposed to undue stress, whether physiologic or psychological, the chances are even greater that they may react adversely to the situation. For example, persons with underlying cardiovascular disease may respond with sudden cardiac arrest

TABLE 5-1 Possible causes of unconsciousness in the dental office

Cause	Frequency	Discussion in this text
Vasodepressor syncope (faint)	Most common	Unconsciousness (Part Two)
Drug administration or ingestion	Common	Drug-related emergencies (Part Six)
Orthostatic hypotension	Less common	Unconsciousness (Part Two)
Epilepsy	Less common	Seizures (Part Five)
Hypoglycemic reaction	Less common	Altered consciousness (Part Four)
Acute adrenal insufficiency	Rare	Unconsciousness (Part Two)
Acute allergic reaction	Rare	Drug-related emergencies (Part Six)
Acute myocardial infarction	Rare	Chest pain (Part Seven)
Cerebrovascular accident	Rare	Altered consciousness (Part Four)
Hyperglycemic reaction	Rare	Altered consciousness (Part Four)
Hyperventilation	Rare	Altered consciousness (Part Four)

secondary to acute cardiac dysrhythmias, which are precipitated by the same physiologic stress that may cause vasodepressor syncope in a healthy individual.[10]

A third factor associated with loss of consciousness is the administration or ingestion of drugs. The three major categories of drugs used in dentistry are analgesics (nonopioids, including nonsteroidal antiinflammatory drugs; opioid analgesics; and local anesthetics), anti-anxiety agents (anxiolytics and sedative-hypnotics), and antibiotics. Drugs in the first two categories are central nervous system (CNS) depressants and therefore produce alterations in the level of consciousness (e.g., sedation) or the loss of consciousness. Some of these drugs, primarily the opioid agonists, predispose the ambulatory dental patient to orthostatic (postural) hypotension (see Chapter 7). Opioids and other CNS-depressant drugs, if administered in larger doses, can induce the loss of consciousness as the CNS is progressively depressed to the point at which consciousness is lost.

Local anesthetics represent the most commonly used drugs in dentistry, and because injection is required for them to be effective, local anesthetics play a major predisposing role in the development of syncope. It is conservatively estimated that members of the dental profession in the United States administer more than 1 million injections of local anesthetics each day. Yet reported morbidity and mortality from these drugs remain incredibly low.[11] Life-threatening situations associated with the administration of local anesthetics can and do occur. By far the overwhelming majority of these adverse reactions are stress induced (fear and anxiety);[12] however, reactions directly related to the local anesthetic drug itself are occasionally observed. These include overdose (toxic) reactions and allergy. (Adverse reactions to local anesthetics and other common dental drugs are discussed more fully in Part Four: Altered Consciousness.)

■ PREVENTION

Loss of consciousness can be prevented in many, if not most, instances by a thorough pretreatment medical and dental evaluation of the prospective patient. Important elements of this evaluation include a determination of the patient's ability to tolerate the stresses—both physiologic and psychological—associated with their planned treatment. Use of a medical history questionnaire and physical examination of the patient, followed by a dialogue history, may uncover medical or psychological disabilities that predispose a patient toward syncope. Detection of these factors allows the doctor to modify the planned treatment to better accommodate the patient's physical or psychological status.

Many adult dental patients seek to hide their fears, thereby making a determination of a patient's anxiety towards dental treatment difficult to uncover. For more than 30 years the University of Southern California has successfully used a method to help doctors recognize the fearful patient. This consists of a short anxiety questionnaire (see Chapter 2) included with the medical history that all patients complete before starting their treatment. Modeled after the questionnaire by Corah et al.,[13] it presents the patient a series of questions related to their attitudes toward various components of dental treatment.

Once dental fear and anxiety are confirmed, the dentist has available a number of conscious sedation techniques to minimize a patient's stress during treatment. These include nondrug techniques, such as iatrosedation and hypnosis; pharmacosedative procedures, including oral, rectal, intranasal, and intramuscular sedation; inhalation sedation with nitrous oxide and oxygen; and intravenous sedation. Properly administered, conscious sedation significantly reduces the medical and psychological risks associated with dental treatment. However, as previously mentioned, the use of drugs will always be associated with additional risk factors of which the doctor administering the agents must be aware and be capable of recognizing and managing. Seventy-five percent of the medical emergencies reported by Fast et al.[1] and Malamed[2] were categorized as "stress-related" and might therefore be preventable through the use of appropriate stress-reduction techniques.

A major factor in the prevention of loss of consciousness was the introduction of sit-down dentistry, in which patients are treated while they lie in a supine or only slightly upright position. The supine position (ideally with the feet elevated about 10 to 15 degrees) prevents the drop in cerebral blood pressure that is the most common mechanism producing syncope. Increasing the use of the supine position during dental treatment has the potential to dramatically decreased the number of episodes of syncope occurring during dental treatment.

■ CLINICAL MANIFESTATIONS

The unconscious person may be described as one who does not respond to sensory stimulation (e.g., "shake and shout"; peripheral pain) and has lost protective reflexes (e.g., swallowing or coughing), accompanied by the inability to maintain a patent airway. Primary management of unconsciousness is directed at reversing these clinical manifestations.

Clinical signs and symptoms associated with the incipient loss of consciousness (presyncope) and the actual state of unconsciousness (syncope) can vary depending upon the primary cause of the situation. For this reason, the precise clinical manifestations of presyncope and syncope are discussed in greater detail under specific situations (see Chapters 6 through 9).

■ PATHOPHYSIOLOGY

In his classic test on fainting, Engle[14] classified the mechanisms that produce syncope into four categories (Table 5-2):

1. Reduced cerebral metabolism resulting from inadequate delivery of blood or O_2 to the brain
2. Reduced cerebral metabolism resulting from general or local metabolic deficiencies

TABLE 5-2 Classification by mechanism of the causes of unconsciousness

Mechanism	Clinical example
Inadequate delivery of blood or O_2 to the brain	Acute adrenal insufficiency
	Hypotension
	Orthostatic hypotension
	Vasodepressor syncope
Systemic or local metabolic deficiencies	Acute allergic reaction
	Drug ingestion and administration
	Nitrites and nitrates
	Diuretics
	Sedatives, opioids
	Local anesthetics
Direct or reflex effects on nervous system	Cerebrovascular accident
	Convulsive episodes
Psychic mechanisms	Emotional disturbances
	Hyperventilation
	Vasodepressor syncope

3. Direct or reflex effects on that part of the CNS that regulates consciousness and equilibrium
4. Psychic mechanisms affecting levels of consciousness with their respective mechanism or mechanisms (categories 1 to 3) of action.

Hypotension is the most common cause of loss of consciousness in humans.

Inadequate cerebral circulation

The most common mechanism of syncope is a sudden decrease in the delivery of blood to the brain. Vasodepressor syncope (common faint) and orthostatic hypotension are the most frequently encountered clinical examples of this condition. Physiologic disturbances that decrease the blood supply to the brain include the following:

- Dilation of the peripheral arterioles
- Failure of normal peripheral vasoconstrictor activity (orthostatic hypotension)
- A sharp drop in cardiac output (from heart disease, dysrhythmias, or decreased blood volume)
- Constriction of cerebral vessels as carbon dioxide is lost through hyperventilation
- Occlusion or narrowing of the internal carotid or other arteries to the brain
- Life-threatening ventricular dysrhythmias

The first four factors rarely produce unconsciousness with the patient in the supine position. Management

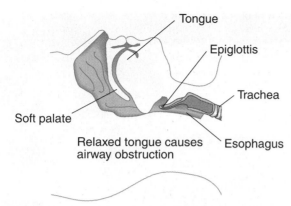

Tongue

Epiglottis

Trachea

Soft palate

Relaxed tongue causes airway obstruction

Esophagus

FIGURE 5-1 In an unconscious victim, the tongue falls backward against the wall of the pharynx, producing airway obstruction. (From Chapleau W: *Emergency first responder: making the difference,* St. Louis, Mosby, 2004.)

of all six factors is directed at an increase in the supply of well-oxygenated blood to the brain.

Oxygen deprivation

A generalized decrease in skeletal muscle tone equivalent to that associated with general anesthesia accompanies the loss of consciousness. The tongue, a mass of skeletal muscle, loses its muscle tone and, as a result of gravity, falls posteriorly into the hypopharynx, producing a complete or partial airway obstruction (Figure 5-1). In the unconscious patient, hypopharyngeal obstruction by the base of the relaxed tongue always occurs when the head is flexed and almost always when the head is maintained in midposition.[15,16] Resuscitation of the unconscious patient focuses primarily on relief of this obstruction. Until the obstruction is removed, the patient continues to receive hypoxic levels of O_2 (partial obstruction) or becomes anoxic (total obstruction), with a decreasing likelihood of successful resuscitation.[15]

The vital importance of airway management and oxygenation in the maintenance of consciousness may be explained as follows: Under normal conditions the brain derives most of its energy from the oxidation of glucose. To maintain this energy source, the brain must receive a continuous supply of glucose and O_2. Without O_2, some glucose can still be metabolized into lactic acid to provide limited energy, but this source cannot fulfill the brain's requirements for more than a few seconds, rapidly leading to the loss of consciousness.

The human brain, accounting for only 2% of total body mass, uses approximately 20% of the total O_2 and 65% of the total glucose the body consumes.[17] To do this, approximately 20% of the total blood circulation per minute must reach the brain. If the supply of either O_2 or glucose is diminished, brain function is rapidly affected. The cerebral blood flow of a normal individual

in the supine position is an estimated 750 mL per minute. Thus, at any given time the blood circulating through the brain contains 7 mL of O_2, an amount adequate to supply the brain's requirements for less than 10 seconds. In a classical experiment, Rossen et al.[18] deprived the human brain of O_2 by a sudden and complete arrest of cerebral circulation. Individuals lost consciousness within 6 seconds.

Complete airway obstruction, in which the victim becomes anoxic, leads to irreversible neurologic damage within 4 to 6 minutes and to cardiac arrest within 5 to 10 minutes. Redding et al.[19] studied asphyxiated dogs. Following 5 minutes of asphyxiation, 50% of those surviving sustained gross brain damage; after 10 minutes, all demonstrated significant brain damage.[19] Periods of anoxia as short as 3 minutes may lead to permanent brain damage.[20] Partial airway obstruction, where the victim receives hypoxic levels of O_2, can produce similar results, although more slowly and through more complex pathways. In either case the doctor and staff members must be able to initiate the steps of basic life support (BLS) rapidly and effectively.

Adequate ventilation has been termed the *sine qua non* of resuscitation.[21] Only once a patient has been secured should the doctor proceed to more definitive life support measures (chest compression or drug administration).

General or local metabolic changes

Changes in the quality of blood perfusion to the brain that are caused by chemical or metabolic derangements may also provoke the loss of consciousness or predispose a patient to its occurrence. The most frequently encountered clinical situations that lead to syncope through this mechanism include hyperventilation, hypoglycemia, the administration or ingestion of drugs, and the acute allergic reaction. In these situations consciousness will not be regained until the underlying chemical or metabolic cause is corrected.

Actions on the central nervous system

Loss of consciousness associated with alterations within the brain itself or through reflex effects on the CNS manifests clinically either as convulsions or a cerebrovascular accident.

Psychic mechanisms

Psychic mechanisms, such as emotional disturbances, are the most common cause of transient losses of consciousness in the dental setting and include several clinical situations discussed previously. Vasodepressor syncope and hyperventilation are included in this category.

■ MANAGEMENT

Immediate management of the unconscious victim is predicated on two objectives:

1. Recognition of unconsciousness
2. Management of the unconscious victim, including the recognition of possible airway obstruction and its management

Recognition of unconsciousness

Step 1: assessment of consciousness. The doctor must first determine whether the victim is conscious or unconscious. Distinguishing between the two is critical since many of the steps of BLS should not be performed on a conscious person. For this reason, the following three criteria based on the previously discussed definition of unconsciousness should be used:

1. Lack of response to sensory stimulation
2. Loss of protective reflexes
3. Inability to maintain a patent airway

The first of these criteria is the most useful to the rescuer, who must rapidly assess a victim's level of consciousness. The latter two—loss of protective reflexes and an inability to maintain a patent airway—are also clinical manifestations of unconsciousness but are used less frequently to initially assess the condition.

The American Heart Association[22] recommends that the rescuer gently shake the victim's shoulder and shout loudly, "Are you all right?" to determine whether the victim lacks a response to sensory stimulation. If the victim does not respond to the shake-and-shout maneuver (Figure 5-2), the rescuer should assume that the victim is unconscious and immediately proceed with the steps of BLS.

Pain is another stimulus that may be used to determine the victim's level of consciousness. The application of peripheral pain, such as pinching of the suprascapular region, usually evokes a motor response from the conscious patient (e.g., deep inhalation, limb movement, forehead furrowing, or spoken words). No response to a painful stimulus indicates unconsciousness (more profound CNS depression). If the victim does not respond to the application of a painful stimulus, the doctor should institute BLS procedures.

Step 2: termination of dental procedure.

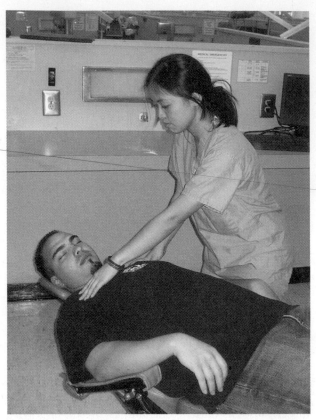

FIGURE 5-2 Unconsciousness is determined by performing the "shake-and-shout" maneuver, gently shaking the shoulders and calling the victim's name.

Step 3: summoning of help. If the victim does not respond to peripheral stimulation, the rescuer calls for assistance immediately by activating the dental office emergency system (see Chapter 3).

Management of the unconscious patient

The loss of consciousness depresses many of the body's vital functions, including its protective reflexes—choking, coughing, sneezing, and swallowing—and the ability of the victim to maintain an open, or patent, airway. The following steps allow the rescuer to maintain these vital functions until the victim either recovers spontaneously or is transported to a hospital for definitive management.

Step 4: P—position victim. As soon as unconsciousness is recognized, the victim is placed into the supine (horizontal) position with the brain at the same level as the heart and the feet elevated slightly (a 10- to 15-degree angle). Rescuers should avoid the head-down (Trendelenburg) position because gravity forces the abdominal viscera superiorly up into the diaphragm,

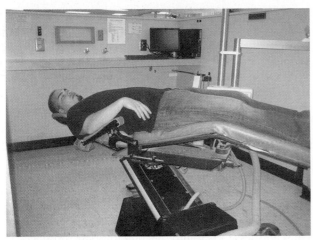

FIGURE 5-3 The unconscious victim should be positioned with the thorax and brain at the same level and the feet elevated slightly (about 10 or 15 degrees). The position aids in the return of venous blood to the heart.

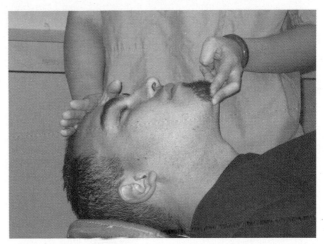

FIGURE 5-5 Head tilt–chin lift: one hand placed on forehead, two fingers under the victim's chin, lifting the chin and rotating the head upward and backward.

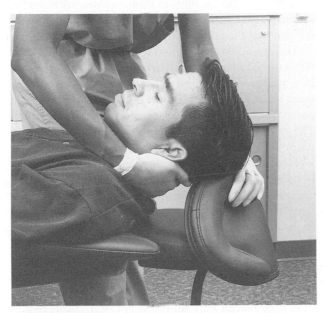

FIGURE 5-4 Any extra head supports, such as pillows, should be removed from the headrest of the dental chair when the victim loses consciousness.

thus restricting respiratory movement and diminishing the effectiveness of breathing.[23] A primary objective in the management of unconsciousness is the delivery of oxygenated blood to the brain, and the supine position best enables the heart to accomplish this goal. A slight elevation of the feet to approximately 10 to 15 degrees further increases the return of blood to the heart. This position is achieved easily in most contoured dental chairs (Figure 5-3). Extra head supports, such as pillows, should be removed from the headrest of the dental chair when the victim loses consciousness (Figure 5-4).

One situation mandating modification of this basic positioning is the loss of consciousness in a pregnant patient near term. Positioning a patient who is in the latter stages of pregnancy in the supine position can actually lead to a decrease in the return of venous blood to the heart, which decreases the blood supply available for delivery to the brain. The gravid uterus may obstruct or diminish blood flow through the inferior vena cava on the right side of the abdomen, preventing large amounts of venous blood from leaving the legs. Normal, healthy pregnant patients have lost consciousness by simply lying on their backs on hard surfaces. If a third-trimester pregnant patient loses consciousness while seated in a dental chair, quickly lower the chair to the supine position, turn the patient onto her right side, and tuck a blanket or pillow under the left side of her back to help her maintain that position.[24] The gravid uterus no longer lies directly over the vena cava, and the return of venous blood from the legs remains unimpeded.

Step 5: A—assess and open airway. In virtually all cases of unconsciousness, some degree of airway obstruction will be present. After the victim is positioned, the next step must be to assess the airway and establish a patent airway, if necessary. Opening of the airway and restoration of breathing are the most basic and most important steps of BLS. These steps can be performed quickly under most circumstances without adjunctive equipment or assistance.

Head tilt–chin lift technique. The head tilt–chin lift procedure is the initial and most important step in the maintenance of a patent airway.

The rescuer performs the head-tilt procedure by placing a hand on the victim's forehead and applying a firm, backward pressure with the palm (Figure 5-5).

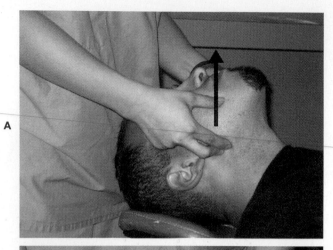

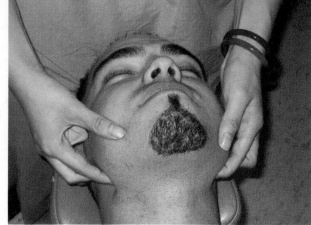

FIGURE 5-6 To perform the jaw-thrust technique, the rescuer must grasp the angles of the mandible with both hands and displace the mandible forward. **A,** Side view. **B,** Front view.

In situations in which the victim retains some degree of muscle, head tilt alone may provide a patent airway. When a lesser degree of muscle tone is present, use of the chin-lift or jaw-thrust technique in conjunction with head-tilt may be necessary.

In performing the chin-lift technique, the rescuer places the tips of two fingers (index and middle) on the symphysis of the mandible, lifting the mandible as the forehead is tilted backward.

Jaw-thrust technique (if necessary). Although head-tilt chin-lift is effective in reestablishing airway patency in most situations, occasionally an airway may remain obstructed. In most of these cases, additional forward displacement of the mandible accomplished with the jaw-thrust maneuver successfully removes this obstruction (Figure 5-6). To perform the jaw-thrust procedure, the rescuer's fingers are placed behind the posterior border of the mandibular ramus; the rescuer then displaces the mandible forward, dislocating it while tilting the head backward. The rescuer's thumbs then retract the lower lip, which allows the victim to exchange air through the mouth and nose. The rescuer must be located behind the top of the supine victim's head to perform this procedure properly. The rescuer's elbows should rest on the surface on which the victim lies.

The jaw-thrust maneuver allows the rescuer to gauge the victim's degree of unconsciousness. As mentioned earlier, peripheral pain is a potent sensory stimulus, and dislocation of the mandible is painful. The victim's response to the jaw-thrust maneuver tells the rescuer how deeply unconscious that victim is. A movement or an audible response is considered a positive sign because the victim is not deeply unconscious. In addition, the ease with which the rescuer can dislocate the mandible is another gauge of the depth of a victim's level of unconsciousness. Profound unconsciousness produces a marked loss of muscle tone throughout the body, with dislocation of the mandible becoming easier to perform. This is in sharp contrast to the doctor's attempt to dislocate the mandible in a patient who is conscious or only slightly unconscious; in these situations the degree of muscle tone makes dislocation of the mandible more difficult and the patient's discomfort more intense.

The modified jaw-thrust technique (without head tilt) is the safest initial approach to opening of the airway of a victim with a suspected neck injury (an unlikely occurrence in the dental office) because the rescuer need not extend the victim's neck to complete the procedure. The rescuer must support the neck carefully without tilting it backward or turning it from side to side.

Head tilt–chin lift technique. To maintain an airway by using the head tilt–chin lift technique (see Figure 5-5), the rescuer places the fingers of one hand under the bony symphysis region of the victim's mandible to lift the tip of the mandible up and bring the chin forward. Because the tongue is attached to the mandible, it is pulled forward and off of the posterior wall of the pharynx. Lifting the mandible forward also tilts the head backward, aiding in head tilt. The tips of the rescuer's fingers should be placed only on bone, not on the soft tissues on the underside of the chin. Compression of these soft tissues increases airway obstruction, pushing the tongue farther upward into the oral cavity. The rescuer should lift the victim's chin, almost bringing the teeth in contact with one another. In addition, the rescuer must try to avoid closing the victim's mouth completely during this procedure.

Research conducted during the past 20 years has provided evidence that the head tilt–chin lift technique of airway management provides the most consistently reliable airway.[25]

All of these head-tilt maneuvers act to stretch the tissues between the larynx and mandible, elevating the base of the tongue and the epiglottis off of the posterior pharyngeal wall. These techniques relieve anatomic

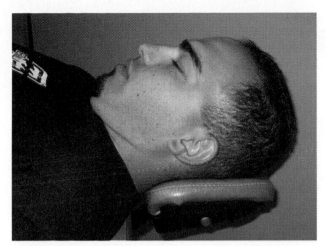

FIGURE 5-7 When the head is not extended, the chin, mandible, and tongue are forced into the airway, producing obstruction.

airway obstruction caused by soft tissues in approximately 80% of unconscious patients.[21]

The rescuer must maintain the victim's head in this position at all times until consciousness returns.

It is important to extend the head sufficiently to lift the tongue and establish a patent airway but to avoid overextension of the head, which will increase the risk of possible damage to the victim's vertebrae and spinal cord. One method by which the rescuer can estimate the appropriate degree of head-tilt is to examine the relationship of the tip of the victim's chin to their earlobes. When the head is not extended, the unconscious victim's airway is obstructed and the tip of the chin lies well below the earlobes (Figure 5-7). With the head extended properly, this relationship is altered so that the tip of the victim's chin points up into the air in line with the earlobes. This line should be perpendicular to the surface on which the victim is lying (Figure 5-8).

In the unconscious adult, it is unlikely that the head will be overextended; the opposite—failure to extend the head far enough—is the more common problem. In the infant or child, however, overextension of the head may produce or exacerbate airway obstruction. Because of anatomic differences in the size of the upper airway and trachea in children and adults, the child's head need not be extended as far in head-tilt as an adult's (Table 5-3). Extension of the child's head to the same degree as that of an adult may lead to airway obstruction as the narrowest portion of the trachea is compressed. Although the degree of extension previously suggested usually produces a patent airway in a child, it must be modified as the need arises.

Step 6a: B—assess airway patency and breathing.
After performing head tilt–chin lift, the

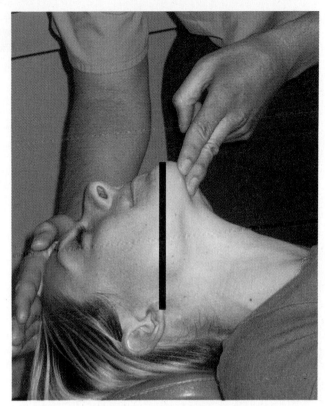

FIGURE 5-8 When the victim's head is extended properly, the tip of the chin points up into the air in line with the earlobes, lifting the mandible and tongue off the pharyngeal wall.

rescuer assesses the patency of the airway (Table 5-4). The victim may be breathing spontaneously or inadequately or may not be breathing at all. During this assessment the rescuer must maintain the victim's head in the extended position previously established by head tilt–chin lift. The rescuer leans over the victim, placing his or her ear 1 inch from the nose and mouth while looking toward the victim's chest (Figure 5-9).

Using this "look-listen-and-feel" technique, the rescuer can determine whether the victim is breathing (e.g., exchanging air). Seeing the chest or abdomen move indicates that the victim is attempting to breathe but not necessarily that air is being effectively exchanged. Feeling or hearing air at the victim's nose and mouth indicates an adequate exchange of air. In addition, if the victim is fully clothed the rescuer may not notice chest or abdominal movement. However, if the rescuer can feel and hear the victim's breath, visual signs of chest movement are not necessary to confirm the adequacy of ventilation.

NOTE: *Seeing the chest move does not guarantee that the person is breathing (exchanging air) but simply that he or she is trying to breathe. Hearing and feeling the*

TABLE 5-3 Anatomic differences between adult and infant airways

Difference	Significance
Infant head larger than adult head	Do not need to elevate infant head to align axes
Infant mouth and nose smaller	Infant requires mouth-to-mouth and mouth-to-nose resuscitation
Infant tongue larger relative to oral cavity	Increases potential for obstruction
At 1 year, tracheal diameter less than the width of a pencil	Increases potential for obstruction
At 2 years the glottic opening only 6.5 mm	Increases potential for obstruction
Cricoid cartilage ring narrowest segment of infant airway; glottic closure narrowest in the adult	Precludes use of cuffed endotracheal tubes in patient younger than 12 years
Infant cricothyroid membrane not palpable	Precludes cricothyrotomy
Air passages in infants smaller than in adults	Decreases airway reserve and increases vulnerability to obstruction: finger sweep contraindicated because increased potential for obstruction

TABLE 5-4 Determination of airway patency and breathing

Clinical signs	Diagnosis	Management
Can feel and hear air at nose and mouth *and* see chest and abdominal movement	Airway patent; patient breathing	Maintain airway
Can feel and hear air at nose and mouth *but* see no chest or abdominal movement	Airway patent; patient breathing	Maintain airway
Cannot feel or hear air at mouth and nose *and* chest and abdominal movements heaving and erratic	Patient attempting to breathe, but airway obstruction still present	Repeat head tilt; if necessary use jaw-thrust technique
Cannot feel or hear air at mouth and nose *and* no chest and abdominal movements evident	Respiratory arrest	Proceed to step 6b; begin artificial ventilation

FIGURE 5-9 The look-listen-feel technique. While maintaining head tilt, the rescuer assesses airway patency by placing their ear 1 inch from the victim's nose and mouth (1) and watching the chest for spontaneous respiratory movements (2).

exchange of air against the rescuer's cheek is a sign that effective spontaneous breathing is present.

If the unconscious person is exchanging air adequately, the airway is managed via head tilt–chin lift and the dental team proceeds with additional management, including the administration of O_2 and monitoring of vital signs (blood pressure, heart rate, and respiratory rate). If no air is felt or heard at the mouth and nose and there is no evidence of chest or abdominal movement, a tentative diagnosis of respiratory arrest is made and artificial ventilation is started immediately (step 6b).

If, in the presence of visible but labored chest or abdominal movements, the rescuer cannot feel or hear airflow at the mouth and nose or detects minimal air exchange along with noisy airflow, airway obstruction, either complete or partial, is present. In this case the rescuer should repeat head tilt–chin lift (see step 5) and reassess the airway (see step 6a). In the presence of

TABLE 5-5 Causes of partial airway obstruction

Sound	Probable cause	Management
Snoring	Hypopharyngeal obstruction by the tongue	Repeat head-tilt; proceed to jaw-thrust maneuver, if necessary
Gurgling	Foreign matter (blood, water, vomitus) in airway	Suction airway
Wheezing	Bronchial obstruction (bronchospasm)	Administer bronchodilator (via inhalation only if patient is conscious; IM or IV delivery if patient is unconscious)
Crowing (high-pitched sound)	Laryngospasm (partial)	Suction airway; positive-pressure oxygen

IM, intramuscular; IV, intravenous.

continued airway obstruction, the rescuer must proceed immediately to the next step of airway maintenance.

If the rescuer discovers evidence of foreign matter in the airway after a check for airway patency, the material must be removed before artificial ventilation is attempted (if necessary). Various causes of partial or complete airway obstruction are associated with sounds that may prove diagnostic (Table 5-5). Partial airway obstruction produces noise; complete airway obstruction produces silence, an ominous "sound." Liquids in the hypopharynx produce a gurgling sound similar to that produced when air is bubbled through water. Common materials present include saliva, blood, water, and vomitus. Regardless of the nature of the material, it must be removed from the airway as quickly as possible. A large volume of foreign matter may lead to complete airway obstruction. In addition, particulate material (vomitus) can enter into the trachea, creating complete obstruction of the airway and leading to the victim's asphyxiation and death unless corrected promptly (see Chapters 10 and 11).

The unconscious person will have previously been placed into the supine position. When the rescuer believes that foreign matter is blocking the airway, the victim should be repositioned even further back so that their head is at a lower level than their heart (the Trendelenburg position) with the head turned to one side (Figure 5-10). Lowering the victim's head to a level below that of the heart allows the foreign material to pool in the upper portions of the airway, which are more readily accessible to suctioning. Turning the victim's head to the side allows the foreign material to pool in the most dependent side of the mouth, facilitating its removal and ensuring that the upper side of the mouth is free of material, thus creating a patent airway.

Breathing, as discussed in this section, refers to the actual exchange of air through the victim's mouth and nose. The rescuer must distinguish this action from chest movement, which occurs during any attempt at breathing. Chest movement may be present in the

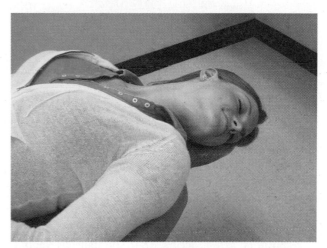

FIGURE 5-10 In the Trendelenburg position, the victim should be tilted back even further in the dental chair so that the head is below the level of the heart and turned to one side.

absence of adequate air exchange through the victim's mouth and nose.

After carrying out these two steps, the rescuer places two fingers (index and middle) in the victim's mouth and removes anything in the oral cavity that can be removed. The sweeping motion of the fingers should begin in the upper portion of the mouth, move posteriorly, and finally move downward and anteriorly (Figure 5-11). A high-volume suction may be used instead of the fingers. Suction devices, if used, should have rounded tips so that they may be placed blindly, if necessary, into the posterior of the mouth or hypopharynx without fear of inducing bleeding (from the delicate and highly vascular pharyngeal mucosa); bleeding can compound airway obstruction. Suctioning should continue until all foreign material is removed from the victim's airway, followed by reapplication of the basic steps of airway maintenance.

Once airway patency and air exchange have been ensured, the rescuer should loosen any constricting

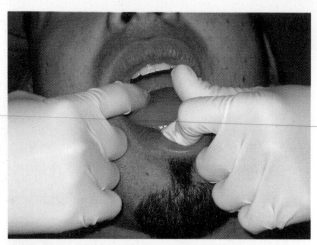

FIGURE 5-11   To remove foreign materials in the mouth, the rescuer must hold the victim's mouth open while using the available fingers to sweep the oral cavity and remove any materials in it. If available, suction may be used.

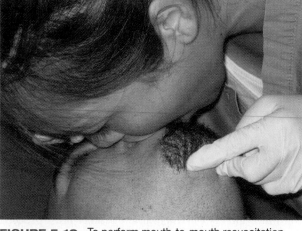

FIGURE 5-12   To perform mouth-to-mouth resuscitation, the rescuer maintains head tilt while pinching the victim's nostrils closed with the thumb and index finger, taking a deep breath, forming a tight seal around the victim's mouth, and blowing air into the mouth. Adequate ventilation is achieved when the victim's chest visibly rises with each ventilatory effort.

clothing, such as belts, ties, or collars, that might interfere with breathing or the circulation of blood. The rescuer should monitor the victim's vital signs and, if available, administer O_2.

Step 6b: B—artificial ventilation (if necessary).

If respiratory arrest occurs or if spontaneous ventilation is inadequate, the dental team must ventilate the victim so that adequate O_2 is available to the brain (see Table 5-4). The victim may receive artificial ventilation in one of three ways:

1. Exhaled air ventilation
2. Atmospheric (ambient) air ventilation
3. O_2-enriched ventilation

Exhaled air ventilation. The rescuer may deliver exhaled air to the victim's lungs as one source of O_2. Exhaled air can deliver 16% to 18% inspired O_2, yielding an arterial O_2 tension (PaO_2) of 88 torr (normal, 75 to 100 torr) at a tidal volume of 1000 to 1500 mL and maintaining an O_2 saturation of 97% to 100%, which is quite adequate to maintain life.[26,27]

Two basic types of exhaled air ventilation are mouth-to-mouth breathing and mouth-to-nose breathing. Because these techniques do not require adjunctive equipment, they can be carried out in any rescue situation. For this reason, they remain the basic techniques of artificial ventilation. Because of the ever-increasing concerns about the possibility of the transfer of infectious agents during ventilation, the use of devices such as the pocket mask have gained popularity.

To adequately perform mouth-to-mouth ventilation, the rescuer uses the head tilt–chin lift position (see

step 5) to maintain the victim's head in an optimal backward tilt. The rescuer's hand on the victim's forehead continues to help maintain a backward tilt while the rescuer's thumb and index fingers pinch the victim's nostrils closed (Figure 5-12). With mouth wide open, the rescuer takes a deep breath, makes a tight seal around the victim's mouth, and blows into the mouth. A rapid and deeply inhaled breath immediately before blowing delivers expired air with the lowest carbon dioxide content.[21]

The first cycle of ventilation consists of two full breaths, with the rescuer allowing 2 seconds per inspiration, taking a breath after each ventilation. Exhalation occurs passively when the rescuer's mouth is removed from the victim's, allowing gravity to deflate the lungs. Artificial ventilation in the adult must be repeated once every 5 to 6 seconds (10 to 12 times per minute) for as long as necessary. The procedure must be repeated once every 3 seconds (20 times per minute) in infants and children.

Adequacy of ventilatory efforts for a victim of any size or age may be assessed by using the following two guides:

1. Feeling the escape of air as the victim passively exhales
2. Seeing the rise and fall of the victim's chest

The latter is the more important of the two. In most adults the volume of air required to produce chest expansion is 800 mL (0.8 L). Adequate ventilation usually need not exceed 1200 mL.[25]

Gastric distention with the subsequent risk of aspiration is potentially the most serious danger of artificial ventilation. The major cause of gastric distention is overinflation during ventilation. This occurs much more commonly in children than in adults. Other causes of gastric distention include ventilation against a partially or totally obstructed airway, which can force air into the esophagus and gastrointestinal tract.

Gastric distention is dangerous both because it increases the incidence of regurgitation during resuscitation and because it increases intraabdominal pressure, which may limit movement of the diaphragm and thereby reduce the ability of the rescuer to ventilate the victim.[28] The rescuer can minimize gastric distention by limiting efforts at ventilation to the point at which the chest rises. Mouth-to-nose ventilation, a discussion of which follows, is associated with a smaller risk of overventilation because the greater resistance to the flow of ventilating gases through the nose decreases the pressure of gases reaching the pharynx. In some instances mouth-to-nose ventilation is more effective than mouth-to-mouth ventilation.[29] This is especially true when the rescuer is unable to open the victim's mouth (e.g., as with trismus or a fractured mandible) to ventilate or seal the mouth adequately.

In the mouth-to-nose technique, the rescuer keeps the victim's head tilted backward with one hand on the victim's forehead; the other hand lifts the victim's mandible, sealing the lips (Figure 5-13). Taking a deep breath, the rescuer then seals his or her lips around the victim's nose and blows until expansion of the victim's lungs is felt and seen. As in mouth-to-mouth ventilation, exhalation is passive. The rescuer uses the same rates—10 to 12 breaths or 20 breaths per minute—in the mouth-to-nose technique for the adult and the child or infant, respectively, as recommended in mouth-to-mouth ventilation.

The rescuer must modify the ventilation technique if the victim is an infant or young child (see previous discussion of the head-tilt procedure). The opening of the airway and method of artificial ventilation are essentially the same in children; however, when the victim is smaller, the rescuer's mouth may cover the child's mouth and nose. The rate of respiration is increased to once every 3 seconds for children age 1 through 8 years and for infants under 1 year, using smaller breaths and less air volume. The same criteria are used for successful ventilation—feeling air escape as the victim passively exhales and seeing the rise and fall of the victim's chest with each inhalation—with infants and small children. In addition, the increased flexibility of the child's neck requires that the rescuer maintain care not to overextend the neck, which can further increase the victim's airway obstruction. When properly performed, artificial ventilation using either method may be continued for long periods without the rescuer becoming fatigued.

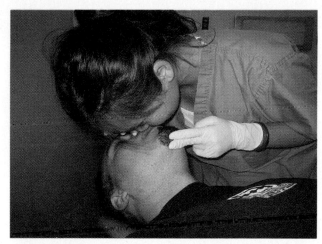

FIGURE 5-13 In mouth-to-nose ventilation, the rescuer maintains head tilt and chin lift, closes the victim's mouth, seals the lips around the victim's nose, and blows air. Adequate ventilation is achieved when the victim's chest visibly rises with each ventilatory effort.

Atmospheric air ventilation. The administration of increased concentrations of O_2 enhances resuscitative efforts. Although exhaled air ventilation, with 16% to 18% O_2, can sustain life, greater O_2 concentrations provide the victim with greater benefits. The air we breathe contains approximately 21% O_2. Devices are available that permit the rescuer to deliver atmospheric air to the victim's lungs; however, all such devices are effective only when basic airway procedures are continually maintained.

Bag-valve-mask (BVM) devices, such as the Ambu-Bag and Pulmonary Manual Resuscitator, usually provide less ventilatory volume than mouth-to-mouth or mouth-to-nose ventilation because of difficulty in maintaining an airtight seal (Figure 5-14). For this reason the International Consensus on Science in 2000 recommended that manually operated, self-inflating BVM devices be used by well-trained and experienced personnel only.[22,30] To use these units properly, the rescuer must be positioned near the top of the victim's head, making it difficult to perform one-rescuer BLS (see Part Seven).

To be considered adequate, a BVM unit must have the following features:[22,30,31]

- A nonjamming valve system that allows a maximum oxygen inlet flow of 30 L/min
- Either no pressure-relief valve or a pressure-relief valve that can be closed or inactivated
- Standard 15-mm/22-mm patient connectors
- An oxygen reservoir to allow delivery of high concentrations of oxygen
- A nonrebreathing valve that cannot be obstructed by foreign material

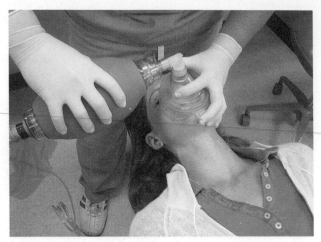

FIGURE 5-14 To administer atmospheric-air ventilation, the rescuer maintains head tilt and hold the face mask securely in place. The victim's chest must rise with each compression of the self-inflating, bag-valve-mask device.

■ Ability to function satisfactorily under common environmental conditions or extremes of temperature.

Before purchasing this device, the doctor should enroll in a program that teaches advanced airway management and become thoroughly trained in the proper use of this and other adjunctive equipment.

Airway adjuncts. Airway adjuncts (oropharyngeal, nasopharyngeal) may be used to assist in airway management but only by persons well trained in their use (Figure 5-15). Airway adjuncts should be used only on deeply unconscious individuals when management of the airway with conventional (manual) techniques is difficult. If used on conscious or stuporous patients, airway adjuncts—especially the oropharyngeal airway— may provoke gagging, vomiting, or laryngospasm, causing a delay in providing adequate ventilation.[32] An oropharyngeal airway must be placed carefully because improper positioning can displace the tongue farther into the pharynx and increase airway obstruction.

The nasopharyngeal airway is used when entry into the patient's mouth is difficult. The nasopharyngeal airway is less likely to stimulate gagging or vomiting in the unconscious patient.[33] Semiconscious and conscious patients are better able to tolerate nasopharyngeal airways than they are oropharyngeal airways. However, insertion of the nasopharyngeal airway is more likely to produce bleeding because it traumatizes the delicate and highly vascular nasal mucosa.

Studies have demonstrated that direct mouth-to-mouth ventilation provides more effective ventilation than that obtained through the use of adjunctive devices.[22,34] Other devices and techniques of airway maintenance, including the laryngeal mask airway and endotracheal intubation, are recommended for use by well-trained personnel only.[32] A pocket mask should always be available so that initial efforts at ventilation need not be through direct mouth-to-mouth contact.[35,36] Dentists properly trained in advanced cardiac life support or anesthesiology may use such devices safely and effectively.

O_2-enriched ventilation. Whenever possible, the rescuer should ventilate with supplemental O_2. Exhaled air ventilation delivers 16% to 18% O_2, whereas atmospheric air provides 21% O_2 (at sea level). Because the object of BLS is to provide the brain with O_2, the use of supplemental O_2 (>21%) is preferred. However, artificial ventilation must never be delayed until supplemental O_2 becomes available. As suggested in Chapter 3, every doctor's office should have available a minimum of one "E" cylinder of O_2. In situations in which artificial ventilation is required, the E cylinder provides approximately 30 minutes of O_2; smaller cylinders (A, B, C, D) provide lesser amounts and are entirely inadequate.

Sources of O_2 available in the dental office may include the portable E cylinder with adjustable O_2 flow (10 to 15 L per minute) and a face mask, an E cylinder with a demand-valve mask unit (Figure 5-16), or an inhalation-sedation unit. If the inhalation-sedation unit is to be used for artificial ventilation, the nasal hood should be removed and replaced with a full-face mask. The reservoir bag on the inhalation sedation unit is squeezed to force O_2 into the victim's lungs. O_2 from sources other than compressed gas cylinders (such as from canisters that produce O_2 via chemical reactions) should not be considered because they are entirely inadequate for artificial ventilation.

Although O_2 is beneficial to the unconscious patient, the doctor should receive adequate training in airway management through mouth-to-mouth and mouth-to-mask ventilation because administration of enriched O_2 is effective only as long as O_2 remains in the compressed gas cylinder. When the O_2 cylinder is empty or if one is not available at the onset of the emergency, the rescuer must revert to the basic technique of artificial respiration.

Step 7: C—assess circulation. After establishing a patent airway, the rescuer must determine the adequacy of the victim's circulation. This includes monitoring of the heart rate and blood pressure. Several sites are available for the recording of heart rate, including the brachial and radial arteries in the arm and the carotid artery in the neck. In nonemergency situations, either artery in the arm adequately indicates the patient's heart rate; however, when a patient is unconscious and particularly when respiratory movements are absent,

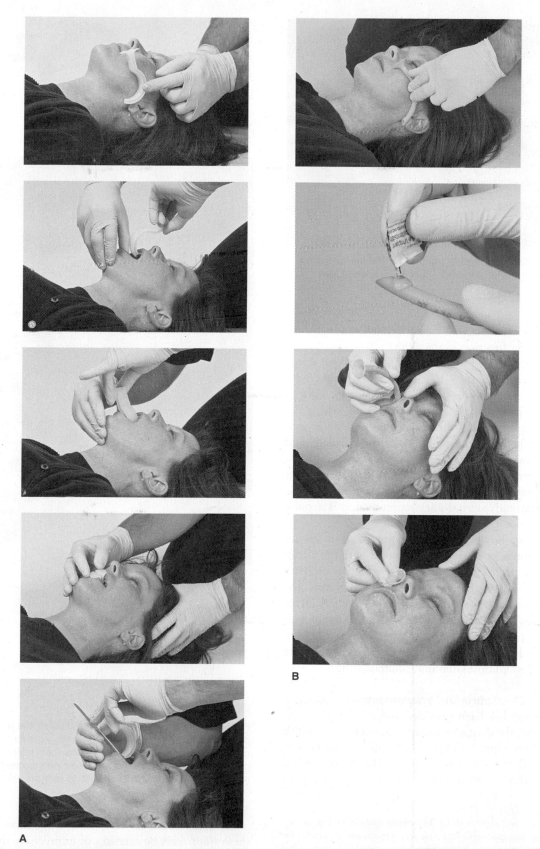

FIGURE 5-15 Insertion of oropharyngeal **(A)** and nasopharyngeal **(B)** airways. Only persons with proper training should insert airway adjuncts.

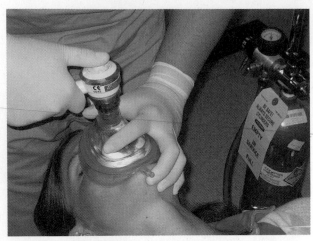

FIGURE 5-16 Enriched-O_2 ventilation. The demand-valve mask unit can provide either a conscious or unconscious patient with up to 100% O_2.

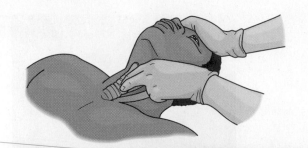

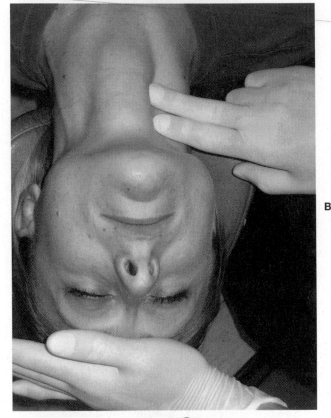

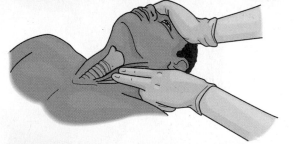

the carotid artery is the most reliable indicator of cardiovascular function in the adult.

The ability of the rescuer to locate the carotid artery properly is vital (Figure 5-17). The rescuer should place the hand supporting the victim's chin onto the thyroid cartilage (Adam's apple). On the side on which the rescuer is positioned, the fingers should slide into the groove between the victim's thyroid cartilage and sternocleidomastoid muscle band in the neck. The carotid artery is located in this groove. The rescuer should allow not more than 10 seconds to feel the pulse before initiating external chest compression if a pulse is absent.[*]

If a pulse, however weak, is present, the rescuer should continue with steps 4 through 6 until the victim recovers or until further medical assistance becomes available. If the victim is a child (age 1 to 8 years), the rescuer also uses the carotid artery, whereas in the infant victim (<1 year) the brachial artery in the upper arm or the femoral artery in the groin is recommended.[38] If a palpable pulse is not present, the rescuer must initiate external chest compression immediately.

Step 8: D—definitive management. Once a patent airway has been provided and adequate circulation ensured, the dental team can proceed with definitive management. (Specific procedures will be discussed in each of the three following chapters.) The steps described in detail in this chapter make up the $P \rightarrow A \rightarrow B$ segments of BLS.

---

[*]Pulse check is performed by healthcare providers but is not expected of lay rescuers. Lay rescuers are taught to check for *signs of circulation* (e.g., normal breathing, coughing, movement) in response to two rescue breaths given to the *unresponsive, nonbreathing victim.*[38]

FIGURE 5-17 To locate the carotid pulse, the rescuer places two fingers (not the thumb) on the victim's thyroid cartilage (Adam's apple) **(A)** and moves them laterally into the groove formed by the sternocleidomastoid muscle **(B and C)**. (A and C from Sorrentino SA: *Assisting with patient care,* ed 2, St. Louis, Mosby, 2004.)

In every instance in which consciousness is lost, these steps must be carried out in precisely the order in which they are described in this chapter. In most cases of unconsciousness, fulfillment of segments $P \rightarrow A$ alone

Box 5-3	Management of unconsciousness

Recognize problem
(lack of response to sensory stimulation)
↓
Discontinue dental treatment
↓
Activate office emergency team
↓
P—Position patient in supine position with feet elevated
↓
A → B → C—Assess breathing, palpate carotid pulse for up to 10 seconds
Provide circulation, if necessary, through chest compression
↓
Activate emergency medical service if recovery not immediate
↓
D—Provide definitive management as needed

A, airway; **B**, breathing; BLS, basic life support; **C**, circulation; **D**, definitive care; IV, intravenous; **P**, position.

or, in fewer cases, segments **P → A → B** of BLS are all the supportive measures required to sustain the victim's life. However, **C** (adequacy of circulation) must always be determined; if a palpable pulse is not present within 10 seconds, the rescuer immediately initiates external chest compression (see Chapter 30).

Box 5-3 summarizes management of the unconscious patient. (Additional airway management procedures are discussed in the section on respiratory difficulty [see Part Three].)

This chapter's discussion was based on the fact that hypopharyngeal obstruction by the tongue is the most common cause of airway obstruction in the unconscious patient.[15] (Lower-airway [tracheal and bronchial] obstruction is discussed in Chapters 10 and 11.)

REFERENCES

1. Fast TB, Martin MD, Ellis TM: Emergency preparedness: a survey of dental practitioners, *J Am Dent Assoc* 112:501–502, 1986.
2. Malamed SF: Back to basics: emergency medicine in dentistry, *J Calif Dent Assoc* 25:285–294, 1997.
3. Schultz KE: Vertigo and syncope. In: Rosen P, editor: *Emergency medicine: concepts and clinical practice*, ed 3, St. Louis, Mosby, 1992, pp. 2165–2173.
4. Huff JS: Coma. In: Rosen P, editor: *Emergency medicine: concepts and clinical practice*, ed 3, St. Louis, Mosby, 1992, pp. 2106–2118.
5. American Dental Association Council on Dental Education: *Guidelines for teaching the comprehensive control of pain and anxiety in dentistry*, Chicago, American Dental Association, 1987.
6. Martin GJ, Adams SL, Martin HG, et al.: Prospective evaluation of syncope, *Ann Emerg Med* 13:499–504, 1984.
7. American Dental Association Council on Dental Education: Guidelines for teaching the comprehensive control of pain and anxiety in dentistry, *J Dent Educ* 36:62–67, 1972.
8. Selcuk E, Erturk S, Afrashi A: An adverse reaction to local anaesthesia: report of a case, *Dent Update* 23:345–346, 1996.
9. Boorin MR: Anxiety: its manifestation and role in the dental patient, *Dent Clin North Am* 39:523–539, 1995.
10. van der Burg AE, Baxx JJ, Boersma E, et al.: Standardized screening and treatment of patients with life-threatening arrhythmias: the Leiden out-of-hospital cardiac arrest evaluation study, *Heart Rhythm* 1:51 57, 2004.
11. Malamed SF: Systemic complications. In: Malamed SF, editor: *Handbook of local anesthesia*, ed 5, St. Louis, Mosby, 2005, pp. 303–332.
12. Chapman PJ: Medical emergencies in dental practice and choice of emergency drugs and equipment: a survey of Australian dentists, *Austral Dent J* 42:103–108, 1997.
13. Corah NL, Gale EN, Illig SJ: Assessment of a dental anxiety scale, *J Am Dent Assoc* 97:816–819, 1978.
14. Engle LL: *Fainting*, ed 2, Springfield, Ill, Charles C Thomas, 1962.
15. Safar P: From control of airway and breathing to cardiopulmonary-cerebral resuscitation, *Anesthesiology* 95:789–791, 2001.
16. Gabrielli A, Layon AJ, Wentzel V, et al.: Alternative ventilation strategies in cardiopulmonary resuscitation, *Curr Opinion Crit Care* 8:199–211, 2002.
17. Salins PC, Kuriakose M, Sharma SM, et al.: Hypoglycemia as a possible factor in the induction of vasovagal syncope, *Oral Surg Oral Med Oral Pathol* 74:544–549, 1992.
18. Rossen R, Kabat H, Anderson JP: Acute arrest of the cerebral circulation in man, *Arch Neurol Psychiatr* 50:510, 1943.
19. Redding JS, Pearson JW: Resuscitation from asphyxia, *JAMA* 182:283–286, 1962.
20. Lim C, Alexander MP, LaFleche G, et al.: The neurological and cognitive sequelae of cardiac arrest, *Neurology* 63:1774–1778, 2004.
21. Safar P: Ventilatory efficacy of mouth-to-mouth artificial respiration: airway obstruction during manual and mouth-to-mouth respiration, *JAMA* 167:335–341, 1958.
22. American Heart Association in Collaboration with the International Liaison Committee on Resuscitation [ILCOR]: guidelines 2000 for cardiopulmonary resuscitation and emergency cardiovascular care, *Circulation* 102: I-1–I-384, 2000.
23. Erie JK: Effect of position on ventilation. In: Faust RJ, editor: *Anesthesiology review*, New York, Churchill Livingstone, 1991.
24. Wright KE Jr, McIntosh HD: Syncope: a review of pathophysiological mechanisms, *Progr Cardiovasc Dis* 13:580–594, 1971.
25. Melker R: Recommendations for ventilation during cardiopulmonary resuscitation: time for change? *Crit Care Med* 13:882–883, 1985.

26. Gordon AS, Frye CW, Gittelson L, et al.: Mouth-to-mouth versus manual artificial respiration for children and adults, *JAMA* 167:320–328, 1958.

27. Safar P, Escarraga LA, Elam JO: A comparison of the mouth-to-mouth and mouth-to-airway methods of artificial respiration with the chest-pressure arm-lift methods, *N Engl J Med* 258:671–677, 1958.

28. Zwillich CW, Pierson DJ, Creagh CE, et al.: Complications of assisted ventilation. A prospective study of 354 consecutive episodes, *Am J Med* 57:161–170, 1974.

29. Ruben HM, Elam JO, Ruben AM, Greene DG: Investigation of upper airway problems in resuscitation, *Anesthesiology* 22:271–279, 1961.

30. Hess D, Baran C: Ventilatory volumes using mouth-to-mouth, mouth-to-mask, and bag-valve-mask techniques. Am J Emerg Med 3:292–296, 1985.

31. American Heart Association. *BLS for healthcare providers*. Dallas, American Heart Association, 2001.

32. American Heart Association in Collaboration with the International Liaison Committee on Resuscitation [ILCOR]: guidelines 2000 for cardiopulmonary resuscitation and emergency cardiovascular care. Part 6: advanced cardiovascular life support: section 3: adjuncts for oxygenation, ventilation and airway control. *Circulation* 102:I95–I104, 2000.

33. Cummins RO, editor: *ACLS provider manual*, Dallas, American Heart Association Subcommittee on Advanced Cardiac Life Support, 2001.

34. Elling R, Politis J: An evaluation of emergency technicians' ability to use manual ventilation devices, *Ann Emerg Med* 12:765–768, 1983.

35. Safar P: Pocket mask for emergency artificial ventilation and oxygen inhalation, *Crit Care Med* 2:273–276, 1974.

36. Malamed SF: Emergency medicine: preparation and basics of management, *Dent Today* 20:66–67, 2001.

37. American Heart Association: *Handbook of emergency cardiovascular care for healthcare providers*. Dallas, American Heart Association, 2004.

38. Cavallaro D, Melker R: Comparison of two techniques for determining cardiac activity in infants, *Crit Care Med* 14:189–190, 1983.

CHAPTER 6

Vasodepressor Syncope

Vasodepressor syncope—also known as *vasovagal syncope* but more often referred to as *common faint*—is a frequently observed, usually benign, and self-limiting process that if not managed correctly is life-threatening. In two surveys of medical emergencies in dental offices, vasodepressor syncope was the most frequently observed emergency, accounting for approximately 53% of all reported emergencies.[1,2] Fainting has been associated with all forms of dental care, but most specifically with tooth extraction and other types of surgery, procedures such as venipuncture and, most frequently with the administration (injection) of local anesthetics. Fainting has occurred upon being seated in the dental chair and even when an individual first entered the dental office.[3–6]

<table>
<tr><td colspan="2">**Box 6-1** Synonyms for syncope</td></tr>
<tr><td>Atrial bradycardia</td><td>Simple faint</td></tr>
<tr><td>Benign faint</td><td>Swoon</td></tr>
<tr><td>Neurogenic syncope</td><td>Vasodepressor syncope</td></tr>
<tr><td>Psychogenic syncope</td><td>Vasovagal syncope</td></tr>
</table>

Box 6-2 Predisposing factors for vasodepressor syncope

PSYCHOGENIC FACTORS
Fright
Anxiety
Emotional stress
Receipt of unwelcome news
Pain, especially sudden and unexpected
Sight of blood or surgical or other dental instruments
  (e.g., local anesthetic syringe)

NONPSYCHOGENIC FACTORS
Erect sitting or standing posture
Hunger from dieting or a missed meal
Exhaustion
Poor physical condition
Hot, humid, crowded environment
Male gender
Age between 16 and 35 years

Syncope is a general term referring to a sudden, transient loss of consciousness that usually occurs secondary to a period of cerebral ischemia. Box 6-1 lists some of the synonyms that describe syncope. *Vasodepressor syncope,* the most descriptive and accurate of these terms, is the name by which this condition is referred throughout the text.

Ordinarily, vasodepressor syncope is a relatively harmless situation during which the victim either falls gently to the floor or is laid down by a second party. The individual regains consciousness almost immediately upon restoration of blood flow to the brain, and within a short period appears to have recovered completely. Statistics from Great Britain confirm the relatively benign nature of this situation. During World War II, more than 25,000 blood donors fainted, and all recovered.[7] Yet despite its seemingly innocuous nature, any loss of consciousness, however brief, produces physiologic changes and can place the victim's life in danger.[8] Examples include cardiopulmonary changes that occur secondary to hypoxia or anoxia, both of which are produced by airway obstruction in the unconscious patient. Although vasodepressor syncope is a fairly common emergency situation, it is usually preventable. When syncope is recognized promptly and managed properly, few individuals experience serious complications.[9]

■ PREDISPOSING FACTORS

Factors that can precipitate vasodepressor syncope are classified into two groups. The first group consists of psychogenic factors, such as fright, anxiety, emotional stress, and receipt of unwelcome news.[10] Two other factors in this group are pain—especially sudden and unexpected pain—and the sight of blood or surgical or dental instruments (e.g., the local anesthetic syringe). These factors lead to the development of the "fight-or-flight" response and, in the absence of muscular movement by the patient, produce the transient loss of consciousness known as *vasodepressor syncope.*

The second group consists of nonpsychogenic factors. These include sitting in an upright position or standing, which permits blood to pool in the periphery, decreasing cerebral blood flow below critical levels (for maintenance of consciousness); hunger from dieting or missed meals, which decreases the glucose supply to the brain to below critical levels; exhaustion; poor physical condition; and hot, humid, crowded environments.

Although incidents of vasodepressor syncope are not limited to any one age group, young adults faint more often than other age groups. In addition, men experience vasodepressor syncope more than women; indeed, men between 16 and 35 years may be the most likely candidates for the development of vasodepressor syncope. Society's view of the male as someone who can "take it" (the pain, the fear, the stress) without exhibiting emotion may explain this gender gap.[11] The fear of injury, coupled with the expectation by peers to act courageously, sets the scene for the escape mechanism of fainting.

In a prospective study of patients who fainted, Martin et al.[12] demonstrated that the average age of those who fainted was 35.5 years. On the other hand, vasodepressor syncope is rare in pediatric patients. Children do not hide their fears; they yell, cry, and move about, unlike the more mature and typically more inhibited adult male. The diagnosis of vasodepressor syncope in the younger pediatric patient or an adult older than 40 years (especially if it develops without prodromal symptoms) should be seriously questioned.[12]

Within dental settings, the most common precipitating factors of vasodepressor syncope are psychogenic (Box 6-2). The dental situation most likely to result in vasodepressor syncope is the administration of a local anesthetic by a female doctor to an anxious "macho" male patient under 35 years of age seated upright in the dental chair who attempts to keep his fear hidden.

■ PREVENTION

Prevention of vasodepressor syncope is directed at eliminating those factors that predispose an individual to faint. Most dental offices are not hot, humid, or crowded. Adequate air conditioning eliminates the heat factor. Patient hunger, a result of dieting or a missed meal before the dental appointment, also should be considered; all patients, but especially those who are anxious, should be requested to eat a light snack or meal before their dental appointment to minimize the risk of developing hypoglycemia in addition to a psychogenic response (see Chapter 17). An individual classified by the American Society of Anesthesiologists (ASA) Physical Status Classification System with impaired physical status (ASA III or greater) has a greater likelihood of developing a life-threatening situation.

Psychological stress, which in individuals without cardiovascular problems may induce fainting, may precipitate sudden death secondary to life-threatening dysrhythmias in those with preexisting cardiac disorders.[11] Modifications in dental treatment should be seriously considered for the more medically compromised patient.

Proper positioning

Probably the most important contributing factor in most cases of vasodepressor syncope is the patient's position in the dental chair. The risk of vasodepressor syncope is greatly increased in an apprehensive patient who is either standing or seated upright during treatment. With the introduction of the contour dental chair and the advent of sit-down dentistry, most patients no longer are treated in upright positions. Today, patients will be placed in a supine or semisupine (30- to 45-degree) position, a practice that has prevented many instances of vasodepressor syncope in the dental chair.

The dentist who seats patients in the upright position and is unable to make the change to sit-down dentistry still may be able to minimize the risk of vasodepressor syncope. Injection of local anesthetics is *the* procedure most often precipitated with vasodepressor syncope. If the dentist can administer the local anesthetic to a patient who is in the supine position, syncope (the actual loss of consciousness) will rarely, if ever, occur. Following the uneventful administration of the local anesthetic the patient may be repositioned, if necessary, for the dental treatment.

Anxiety relief

Most instances of vasodepressor syncope in the dental office involve psychogenic factors. Each potential patient must be evaluated for the presence of dental anxiety. If the patient is overly anxious, dental treatment should be modified to minimize or to eliminate it.

Unfortunately, adult anxiety often is difficult to recognize. The discussion in Chapter 2 established that many men and women do not consider an admission of fear as the "adult" thing to do. Corah's questionnaire[13] is a great asset in the recognition of anxiety (see Chapter 2). Although many patients do not admit their fears in oral interviews, experience with the anxiety questionnaire has shown that they are more likely to express their feelings in writing. The inclusion of this survey or of several questions appended to the medical history questionnaire is worthwhile.

Conversely, the presence of anxiety and fear in children usually is not difficult to recognize. Children, not having the inhibitions that adults do, usually make their feelings quite well known to the doctor and to all others present in the office. It is for this reason that healthy children rarely develop vasodepressor syncope.

 MEDICAL HISTORY QUESTIONNAIRE

The University of the Pacific School of Dentistry medical history questionnaires (see Figure 2-1) provides the doctor with some information about patient anxiety. The following questions may help uncover potential problems:

Question 5: Have you had problems with prior dental treatment?

Question 6: Are you in pain now?
Comment: These questions allow the patient to voluntarily provide information about prior dental treatment experiences. An affirmative response to either or both questions should lead to a thorough dialogue history and to possible treatment modifications aimed at decreasing the patient's dental fears.

Dental therapy considerations

Once anxiety is recognized it should be managed. Combined with placement of patients in a supine or reclined position, the use of psychosedation should be considered. Increased use of psychosedation has decreased the incidence of vasodepressor syncope and other psychogenically induced emergencies during dental treatment. Commonly employed routes of drug administration for conscious sedation include oral, intranasal, intramuscular; inhalation (with nitrous oxide [N_2O] and oxygen [O_2]), and intravenous.

Psychosedation is but one of a number of stress-reducing factors discussed in Chapter 2. The concept of total patient care has led to the development of specific stress reduction protocols and has been responsible for the decreasing number of stress-related, life-threatening situations arising in dentistry. Use of these protocols can nearly eliminate all occurrences of vasodepressor syncope and other psychogenically induced emergencies in dental offices.

■ CLINICAL MANIFESTATIONS

Clinical signs and symptoms of vasodepressor syncope usually develop rapidly in the presence of an appropriate stimulus; however, the actual loss of consciousness does not normally occur immediately. Thus, individuals who experience vasodepressor syncope while alone rarely are injured seriously. There is usually sufficient time for them to sit or lie down before they lose consciousness. The clinical manifestations of vasodepressor syncope can be grouped into three definite phases: presyncope, syncope, and postsyncope (recovery period).[14,15]

Presyncope

The prodromal manifestations of vasodepressor syncope are well known. The patient, in the erect or sitting upright position, reports a feeling of warmth in the neck and face, loses color (pale or ashen-gray skin color), and becomes bathed in a cold sweat (noted primarily on the forehead). During this time the patient usually reports feeling "bad" or "faint" and may also become nauseous. The blood pressure at this time is maintained at or near the baseline level, whereas the heart rate increases significantly (e.g., from 80 to 120 or more beats per minute).[16]

As presyncope continues, pupillary dilation, yawning, hyperpnea (increased depth of respiration) and coldness in the hands and feet are noted. Both the blood pressure and heart rate become acutely depressed (hypotension and bradycardia) just before loss of consciousness.[4,8,17] At this time the patient experiences disturbed vision and becomes dizzy, and syncope occurs.

As syncope develops, the individual usually exhibits warning symptoms for several minutes before losing consciousness (Box 6-3).[12] If the patient is in an upright position, presyncope may lead to unconsciousness in a relatively short time (approximately 30 seconds), whereas if the patient is supine, presyncope may never reach the point at which consciousness is lost.

Syncope

With the loss of consciousness breathing may (1) become irregular, jerky, and gasping; (2) become quiet, shallow, and scarcely perceptible; or (3) cease entirely (respiratory arrest or apnea). The pupils dilate, and the patient

Box 6-3 Presyncopal signs and symptoms
EARLY Feeling of warmth Loss of color; pale or ashen-gray skin tone Heavy perspiration Reports of "feeling bad" or "feeling faint" Nausea Blood pressure at baseline level or slightly lower Tachycardia **LATE** Pupillary dilation Yawning Hyperpnea Cold hands and feet Hypotension Bradycardia Visual disturbances Dizziness Loss of consciousness

takes on a deathlike appearance. Convulsive movements and muscular twitching of the hands, legs, or facial muscles are common when patients lose consciousness and their brains become hypoxic, even for periods as short as 10 seconds.

Bradycardia, which develops at the end of the presyncopal phase, continues. A heart rate of less than 50 beats per minute is common during syncope. In severe episodes, periods of complete ventricular asystole have been recorded, even in normally healthy individuals. Findler and Galili[6] reported syncope in two young healthy patients who experienced asystole for more than 40 seconds followed by spontaneous uneventful recovery. The blood pressure, which falls precipitously to an extremely low level (30/15 mm Hg being common), also remains low during this phase and often is difficult to obtain. The pulse becomes weak and thready. Loss of consciousness is also associated with a generalized muscular relaxation that commonly leads to partial or complete airway obstruction. Fecal incontinence may occur, particularly when systolic blood pressure falls below 70 mm Hg.

Once the patient is placed in the supine position, the duration of syncope is extremely brief, ranging from several seconds to several minutes. If the patient remains unconscious for more than 5 minutes after proper positioning and management are achieved, or if the patient does not undergo a complete clinical recovery in 15 to 20 minutes, causes other than syncope should be considered. Such causes are important, especially if the patient is older than 40 years of age and does not exhibit prodromal symptoms before losing consciousness.[12]

Postsyncope (recovery)

With proper positioning, recovery (return of consciousness) is rapid. In the postsyncopal phase the patient may demonstrate pallor, nausea, weakness, and sweating, all of which can last from a few minutes to several hours. Occasionally, symptoms persist for 24 hours.[18] During the immediate postsyncopal phase, the patient may experience a short period of confusion or disorientation. Arterial blood pressure begins to rise at this time; however, it may not return to the baseline level until several hours after the syncopal episode. The heart rate, which is depressed, also returns slowly toward the baseline level, and the pulse becomes stronger.

In addition, a point worth stressing is that once a patient loses consciousness, the tendency for that patient to faint again may persist for many hours if the patient assumes a sitting position or stands too soon or quickly.

■ PATHOPHYSIOLOGY

Vasodepressor syncope is most commonly precipitated by a decrease in cerebral blood flow below a critical level and usually is characterized by a sudden drop in blood pressure and a slowing of the heart rate.[19] When such predisposing factors occur, a certain pattern of events usually develops.

Presyncope

Stress, whether emotionally triggered (as with fear) or sensorially triggered (unexpected pain), causes the body to release into the circulatory system increased amounts of the catecholamines epinephrine and norepinephrine. Their release is part of the body's adaptation to stress, commonly called the "fight-or-flight" response. This increase in catecholamines results in changes in tissue blood perfusion designed to prepare the individual for increased muscular activity (fight or flight).

Among the many responses to catecholamine release are a decrease in peripheral vascular resistance and an increase in blood flow to many tissues, particularly the peripheral skeletal muscles. In situations in which this anticipated muscular activity occurs, the blood volume that was diverted to the muscles in preparation for this movement is returned to the heart by the pumping action of the muscles. In this case peripheral pooling of blood does not occur; the blood pressure remains at or above the baseline level, and signs and symptoms of vasodepressor syncope do not develop.

In contrast, in situations in which the planned for muscular activity does not occur (e.g., sitting still in the dental chair and "taking it like a man"), the diversion of large volumes of blood into skeletal muscles causes a significant pooling of blood in these muscles with an associated decrease in the volume of blood being returned to the heart. This leads to a relative decrease in circulating blood volume, a drop in arterial blood pressure, and a decrease in cerebral blood flow. Presyncopal signs and symptoms are related to decreased cardiac output, diminished cerebral blood flow, and other physiologic alterations.[4,18]

As blood pools in peripheral vessels and arterial blood pressure begins to fall, compensatory mechanisms are activated that attempt to maintain adequate cerebral blood flow. These mechanisms include baroreceptors, which reflexly constrict peripheral blood vessels, increasing the return of venous blood to the heart, and the carotid and aortic arch reflexes, which increase the heart rate. These mechanisms work to increase the cardiac output and the maintenance of a close to normal blood pressure, all of which are seen during the early presyncopal period.

However, if the situation goes unmanaged, these compensatory mechanisms fatigue (decompensate), which is manifested through the development of a reflex bradycardia. Slowing of the heart rate to less than 50 beats per minute is common and leads to a significant drop in cardiac output, which is associated with a precipitous fall in blood pressure to levels below those critical for the maintenance of consciousness. In such cases, cerebral ischemia results and the individual loses consciousness.

Syncope

The critical level of cerebral blood flow for the maintenance of consciousness is estimated to be about 30 mL of blood per 100 g of brain tissue per minute. The human adult brain weighs approximately 1360 g (young adult male of medium stature). The normal value of cerebral blood flow is 50 to 55 mL per 100 g per minute. In a fight-or-flight situation in which muscular movement is absent with the patient maintained in the upright position, the heart's ability to pump this critical volume of blood to the brain is impaired and the minimal cerebral blood flow is not reached, leading to syncope. In a normotensive individual (systolic blood pressure below 140 mm Hg), this minimal blood flow is equivalent to an approximate systolic blood pressure of 70 mm Hg. For patients with atherosclerosis or high blood pressure, this critical level for cerebral blood flow may be reached with a systolic pressure considerably above 70 mm Hg. Clinically, systolic blood pressure may descend to as low as 20 to 30 mm Hg during the syncopal episode, with periods of asystole (systolic blood pressure of 0) occurring.[6]

Convulsive movements, such as tonic or clonic contractions of the arms and legs or turning of the head, may occur with the onset of syncope. Cerebral ischemia lasting only 10 seconds can lead to seizure activity in patients with no prior histories of seizure disorders.[20] The degree to which the individual moves during the seizure usually depends on the degree and duration of the cerebral ischemia. When present, these muscular movements are usually of brief duration and are rather mild.

Recovery

Recovery is usually hastened by placing the victim in the supine position with their legs elevated slightly, improving venous return to the heart and increasing blood flow to the brain so that cerebral blood flow once again exceeds the critical level necessary for maintenance of consciousness. Signs and symptoms, such as weakness, sweating, and pallor, may persist for hours. The body is fatigued and may require as long as 24 hours to return to its normal functioning state after a syncopal episode.[21] In addition, removal of any factor that might have precipitated the episode (e.g., a syringe or blood-soaked gauze) will help speed recovery.

① may continue Tx if pt ok
② pt ok to leave if fully recovered

■ MANAGEMENT

Management of syncopal patients differs depending on the signs and symptoms the individual exhibits. This section deals with the management of four separate stages of syncope: presyncope, syncope, delayed recovery, and postsyncope.

Presyncope

Step 1: P (position).
As soon as presyncopal signs and symptoms appear, the procedure should be halted and the patient placed into the supine position with the legs slightly elevated. This position change usually halts the progression of symptoms. Muscle movement also helps increase the return of blood from the periphery. If patients can move their legs vigorously, they are less likely to experience significant peripheral pooling of blood, minimizing the severity of the reaction.

Step 2: A→B→C (airway-breathing-circulation).
The fairly common practice (outside of medical or dental offices) of placing the victim's head between his or her legs when presyncopal signs and symptoms develop should be discontinued. Bending over to such an extreme degree may actually further impede the return of blood from the legs through a partial obstruction of the inferior

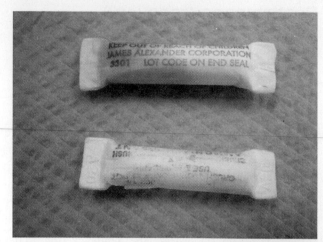

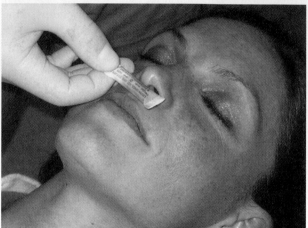

FIGURE 6-1 A, An aromatic ammonia vaporole respiratory stimulant. Color changes to pink when opened. **B,** An aromatic ammonia vaporole is crushed between the rescuer's fingers and held near the patient's nose to stimulate movement.

vena cava, resulting in a greater decrease in blood flow to the brain. Furthermore, if patients lose consciousness while placing their head between their legs, this position (e.g., face down or prone) does not facilitate proper airway management.

O_2 may be administered through use of a full-face mask, or an ammonia ampule may be crushed under the patient's nose to speed recovery (Figure 6-1).

Step 3: D (definitive care).
Following management of presyncope, attempts should be made to determine the cause of the episode while the patient recovers. Modifications in future dental treatment should be considered to minimize the risk of recurrence.

The planned dental treatment may proceed only if both the doctor and the patient feel it is appropriate. If either party remains doubtful, the treatment should be postponed.

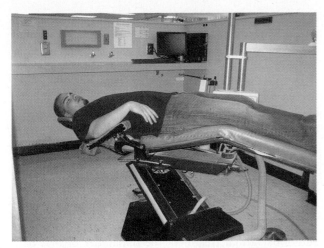

FIGURE 6-2 Placement of unconscious patient in the supine position with feet elevated slightly.

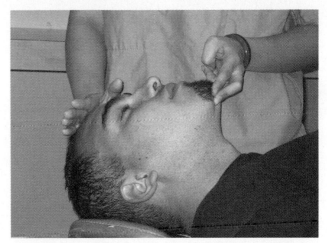

FIGURE 6-3 Airway patency may be obtained through use of the head tilt–chin lift method.

Syncope

Proper management of vasodepressor syncope follows the basic management recommended for all unconscious patients: **P→A→B→C**.[22] This discussion presents a summary of the proper procedures.

Step 1: assessment of consciousness. The patient (victim) suffering vasodepressor syncope demonstrates a lack of response to sensory stimulation ("shake and shout").

Step 2: activation of the dental office emergency system. Office team members should perform their assigned duties.

Step 3: P. The first and most important step in the management of syncope is the placement of the victim in the supine position. In addition, a slight elevation of the legs helps increase the return of blood from the periphery. This step is so vital because the overwhelming majority of the observed clinical manifestations during syncope are the result of inadequate cerebral blood flow. Failure to place the victim in the supine position may result in death or permanent neurologic damage secondary to prolonged cerebral ischemia (see Addendum at the end of this chapter). This damage can occur in as little as 2 to 3 minutes if the victim maintains an upright position.

The ancient Roman practice of crucifixion is an example of death from vasodepressor syncope; individuals who were forced to maintain upright positions eventually died from the mechanisms described previously. The supine position therefore is the preferred position for the management of unconscious patients (Figure 6-2). However, females in the latter stages of

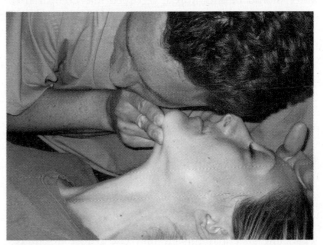

FIGURE 6-4 The adequacy of an airway may be determined through use of the "look, listen, feel" technique.

pregnancy who lose consciousness represent the one important exception to this basic position (see Chapter 5). (Other possible modifications of this positioning will be discussed in later sections.)

Step 4: A→B→C (basic life support, as needed). The victim must be assessed immediately and a patent airway ensured. In most instances of vasodepressor syncope, the head tilt–chin lift procedure successfully establishes a patent airway (Figure 6-3).

Assessment of airway patency and adequacy of breathing constitute the next actions. An adequate airway is present when the patient's chest moves and exhaled air can be heard and felt (Figure 6-4). Spontaneous respiration usually is evident during syncope; however, artificial ventilation may be necessary on those few occasions in which spontaneous breathing ceases. Positioning of the victim and establishment of a patent airway usually lead to the rapid return of consciousness.

To assess circulation, the carotid pulse must be palpated. Though rare, brief periods of ventricular asystole can develop during syncope. In most circumstances, however, a weak, thready pulse is palpable in the neck. The heart rate is commonly quite low. More frequently, however, the victim has begun to regain consciousness by the time the pulse is evaluated.

Step 5: D (definitive care).
Step 5a: administration of O₂.
Step 5a: administration of O$_2$.   O$_2$ may be administered to the syncopal or postsyncopal patient at any time during the episode.

Step 5b: monitoring of vital signs.
Step 5b: monitoring of vital signs.   Vital signs, including blood pressure, heart rate, and respiratory rate, should be monitored, recorded and compared to the patient's preoperative baseline values to determine the severity of the reaction and the degree of recovery.

Step 5c: additional procedures.
Step 5c: additional procedures.   These procedures include the loosening of binding clothes such as ties, collars (which can decrease blood flow to the brain), and belts (which can decrease return of blood from the legs) and the use of a respiratory stimulant, such as aromatic ammonia. To use the ammonia vaporole, the rescuer should crush it between the fingers and allow the patient to inhale it. Ammonia, which has a noxious odor, stimulates both increased breathing and muscular movement.

If the doctor keeps vaporoles handy near the dental chair, the syncopal episode may end before it requires further assistance. A cold towel may be placed on the patient's forehead or blankets can be provided if the victim reports feeling cold or is shivering. If bradycardia persists, an anticholinergic, such as atropine, may be administered either intravenously or intramuscularly.

As the victim regains consciousness, it is important that the doctor and emergency team maintain their composure. In addition, the stimulus that precipitated the episode (e.g., a syringe, an instrument, or a piece of bloody gauze) must be removed from the patient's field of vision. The presence of a terrified dental staff member or the precipitating factor may induce a second episode of syncope.

Delayed recovery

If the victim does not regain consciousness after the previous steps have been performed or does not recover completely in 15 to 20 minutes, a different cause for the syncopal episode should be considered and the emergency medical service (EMS) system activated. Indeed, the doctor may wish to activate the EMS system at any time during the syncopal episode and should continue the administration of the indicated steps of basic life support while awaiting the arrival of the EMS team. If another cause of unconsciousness (e.g., hypoglycemia) becomes obvious, the doctor may initiate definitive management. In the absence of an obvious cause, however, the doctor should continue basic life support and if possible start an intravenous infusion (see Chapter 3).

Postsyncope

After recovery from a period of syncope (loss of consciousness of any duration), patients should not undergo additional dental treatment the remainder of that day. The possibility of a second syncopal episode is greater during the postsyncopal phase; research has demonstrated that the body requires up to 24 hours to return to its normal state.[17,18]

Prior to dismissal of the patient from the dental office, the doctor should determine the primary precipitating event and any other factors (e.g., hunger or fear) that might have contributed to it. This information should be used to formulate a plan for future treatment that can avoid additional syncopal episodes.

Arrangements must be made for a person with a vested interest in the health and safety of the patient (e.g., family member) to take the patient home. Allowing the patient to leave the office unescorted and drive a car puts that patient, and potentially others, at risk because of the possibility of recurrent syncopal episodes. Providing an escort is mandatory whenever an individual has lost consciousness.

Box 6-4 summarizes the management of vasodepressor syncope. In addition, the following items may prove helpful:
- Drugs used in management: O$_2$, ammonia, and atropine.
- Medical assistance: Assistance rarely is required because consciousness normally returns rapidly when the individual is positioned properly and when airway, breathing, and circulation are managed. A delayed recovery of consciousness or a delayed return to normal central nervous system status mandates EMS activation.

ADDENDUM case report—vasodepressor syncope

A 15-year-old patient was scheduled for the extraction of a broken-down mandibular molar under local anesthesia. Because she was somewhat fearful, the dentist orally sedated the patient before the start of the surgery. The sedation was only partially successful.

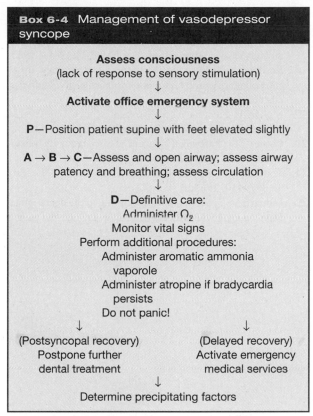

Box 6-4 Management of vasodepressor syncope

Assess consciousness
(lack of response to sensory stimulation)
↓
Activate office emergency system
↓
P—Position patient supine with feet elevated slightly
↓
A → B → C—Assess and open airway; assess airway patency and breathing; assess circulation
↓
D—Definitive care:
Administer O₂
Monitor vital signs
Perform additional procedures:
Administer aromatic ammonia vaporole
Administer atropine if bradycardia persists
Do not panic!
↓   ↓
(Postsyncopal recovery)   (Delayed recovery)
Postpone further   Activate emergency
dental treatment   medical services
↓
Determine precipitating factors

A, airway; **B,** breathing; **C,** circulation; **D,** definitive care; **P,** position.

The patient was placed in the dental chair in an upright position to receive an inferior alveolar nerve block (lidocaine 2% with epinephrine 1:100,000). As the needle approached the patient's mouth, the doctor and assistant noted that "her eyes rolled up into her head" (she fainted).

The dentist immediately asked the staff to get the portable oxygen cylinder and the aromatic ammonia vaporoles. These items were delivered promptly to the doctor, who crushed the vaporole, held it beneath the patient's nostrils, and turned on a flow of about 10 L of oxygen per minute, holding the mask near the patient's face.

A mild seizure was observed, at which time the dentist had the staff call 911. The EMS team arrived in the dental office within 6 minutes of the call's being received. Finding an unconscious patient upright, the EMS squad promptly moved the patient to the supine position and assessed **A→B→C,** finding the patient to be in cardiorespiratory arrest.

Basic life support (BLS) was instituted, and the patient was defibrillated three times unsuccessfully. Epinephrine (1:10,000 intravenously) was administered, followed by BLS and a second round of three (unsuccessful) defibrillations. Additional epinephrine was administered, followed again by BLS and successful defibrillation. The patient was stabilized and transported to a local hospital emergency department.

The patient recovered from the cardiopulmonary arrest with a degree of moderate global myocardial damage; however, because of the length of time that her brain had been deprived of oxygenated blood, she suffered severe (permanent) neurologic damage. At the time of the writing of this chapter (August 2005) the patient is 21 years of age chronologically. Her developmental (mental) age is but 3 years and is unlikely to ever change.

Fainting (vasodepressor syncope) is the most common medical emergency in dentistry. All dentists are likely to encounter it on multiple occasions over the course of a dental career. Fainting is an easy situation to manage if one does not panic, which is something that is not easily taught.

The preceding case vividly illustrates the extreme importance of proper positioning in the management of all medical emergencies, but especially in situations in which the victim is unconscious. Consciousness is usually lost because the brain is not receiving an adequate supply of oxygenated blood. Placing the victim into a supine position is frequently all that is needed to bring about a return of consciousness.

Placing the dental patient into a supine position before their receiving a local anesthetic injection is frequently all that is needed to prevent vasodepressor syncope.

REFERENCES

1. Fast TB, Martin MD, Ellis TM: Emergency preparedness: a survey of dental practitioners, *J Am Dent Assoc* 112:499–501, 1986.

2. Malamed SF: Beyond the basics: emergency medicine in dentistry, *J Am Dent Assoc* 128:843–854, 1997.

3. Locker D, Shapiro D, Liddell A: Overlap between dental anxiety and blood-injury fears: psychological characteristics and response to dental treatment, *Behav Res Ther* 35:583–590, 1997.

4. Leonard M: An approach to some dilemmas and complications of office oral surgery, *Aust Dent J* 40:159–163, 1995.

5. Tizes R: Cardiac arrest following routine venipuncture, *JAMA* 236:1846–1847, 1976.

6. Findler M, Galili D: Cardiac arrest in dental offices. Report of six cases, *J Israel Dent Assoc* 19:79–87, 2002.

7. Ebert RV: Response of normal subjects to acute blood loss, *Arch Intern Med* 68:578, 1941.

8. Wright KE, McIntosh HD: Syncope: a review of pathophysiological mechanisms, *Prog Cardiovasc Dis* 13:580–594, 1971.

9. Soteriades ES, Evans JC, Larson MG, et al.: Incidence and prognosis of syncope, *N Engl J Med* 347:878–885, 2002.

10. Feinberg AN: Syncope in the adolescent, *Adolesc Med* 13:553–567, 2002.

11. Engel GL: Psychologic stress, vasodepressor (vasovagal) syncope, and sudden death, *Ann Intern Med* 89:403–412, 1978.

12. Martin GJ, Adams SL, Martin HG, et al.: Prospective evaluation of syncope, *Ann Emerg Med* 13:499–504, 1984.

13. Corah NL: Development of a dental anxiety scale, *J Dent Res* 48:596, 1969.

14. Brignole M: Neurally-mediated syncope, *Ital Heart J* 6:249–255, 2005.

15. Benditt DG, van Dijk JG, Sutton R, et al.: Syncope, *Curr Probl Cardiol* 29:152–229, 2004.

16. Reuter D: Common emergent pediatric neurologic problems, *Emerg Med Clin North Am* 20:155–176, 2002.

17. Glick G, Yu PN: Hemodynamic changes during spontaneous vasovagal reactions, *Am J Med* 34:42–51, 1963.

18. Friedberg CK: Syncope: pathological physiology, differential diagnosis, and treatment, *Mod Concepts Cardiovasc Dis* 40:55–60, 1971.

19. Mohan L, Lavania AK: Vasovagal syncope: an enigma, *J Assoc Physicians India* 52:301–304, 2004.

20. Cutino SR: Vasovagal syncope associated with seizure activity, *Gen Dent* 42:342–343, 1994.

21. Thomas JE, Rooke ED: Fainting, *Mayo Clin Proc* 38:397–410, 1963.

22. Leonard M: Syncope: treating fainting in the dental office, *Dent Today* 15:72–73, 1996.

CHAPTER 7

Postural Hypotension

Postural hypotension, also known as *orthostatic hypotension*, is the second-leading cause of transient loss of consciousness (syncope) in dental settings. *Postural hypotension* is defined as a disorder of the autonomic nervous system in which syncope occurs when the patient assumes an upright position. Postural hypotension may also be defined as a drop in systolic pressure of 30 mm Hg or greater or a 10–mm Hg or greater fall in diastolic pressure that occurs on standing.[1-3] Postural hypotension is a result of a failure of the baroreceptor reflex–mediated increase in peripheral vascular resistance in response to positional changes.[4]

Postural hypotension differs in several important respects from vasodepressor syncope and is only infrequently associated with fear and anxiety. Awareness of predisposing factors allows the dentist to prevent this condition, which can be dangerous, from developing. An example of injury arising as a result of postural hypotension occurring in a dental office follows:

> A 45-year-old healthy male patient was placed in a semireclined position for the administration of a local anesthetic prior to the start of dental treatment. After administering several maxillary infiltrations (1.5 anesthetic cartridges), the doctor remained with the patient for several minutes to ensure the adequacy of the anesthesia. Then, 2 minutes after the injection the doctor left the room, leaving the patient with a dental assistant, who was busy preparing instruments and materials for the upcoming procedure.
>
> The assistant left the room several minutes later. The patient then began to feel "funny" and called for assistance. When no one responded to his calls the patient sat up in the chair, legs dangling over the side, and leaned forward to get up out of the chair.
>
> Seconds later, the doctor and staff members heard a crashing sound come from the room and immediately ran to help. There, they found the patient lying unconscious on the floor next to the dental chair, bleeding on the face. The patient suffered a broken nose and fractured his clavicle and forearm.

Two more examples of postural hypotension episodes that occurred in dental offices include the following:

- Syncope developed in a 76-year-old woman whose recumbent blood pressure was 180/100 mm Hg and dropped to 100/50 mm Hg immediately after she rose from the dental chair.
- A 35-year-old man lost consciousness after lying in the dental chair in the supine position for 1 hour. He stood up and walked to the reception desk to schedule another appointment. When he reached the front desk and stopped moving, he felt "faint" and lost consciousness.

■ PREDISPOSING FACTORS

Many factors have been identified as causes of postural hypotension; several have possible dental implications. These include the following:

- Administration and ingestion of drugs[5,6]
- Prolonged period of recumbency or convalescence[7]

- Inadequate postural reflex
- Late-stage pregnancy[8]
- Advanced age[9]
- Venous defects in the legs (e.g., varicose veins)
- Recovery from sympathectomy for "essential" hypertension
- Addison's disease
- Physical exhaustion[10] and starvation
- Chronic postural hypotension (Shy-Drager syndrome)

The incidence of postural hypotension increases with age.[9,10] In a group of 100 ambulatory patients age 65 years and older, 31% demonstrated decreases in systolic blood pressure of 20 mm Hg or more when they stood, whereas 16% suffered diastolic drops of 10 mm Hg or more. In addition, 12% experienced significant drops in both systolic pressure and diastolic pressures.[11] Although the incidence of postural hypotension increases with age, it is relatively uncommon in infants and children.[12]

Drug administration and ingestion

Probably the most frequently encountered cause of postural hypotension in the dental office is in response to the use of drugs. The dentist may administer these drugs before, during, or after the dental treatment, or the patient's primary care physician may prescribe them for the management of specific physical or psychological disorders. These drugs fall into the broad categories of antihypertensives, especially the sodium-depleting diuretics, calcium channel blockers, and ganglionic-blocking agents; psychotherapeutics (sedatives and tranquilizers); opioids; histamine-blockers; and levo-dopa, used in the management of Parkinson's disease. In general, drugs produce postural hypotension by diminishing the body's ability to maintain blood pressure (and in turn adequate cerebral perfusion) in response to the increased influence of gravity that occurs when the patient rises suddenly. An exaggerated blood pressure response is observed.

Drugs used to manage fear and anxiety are capable of inducing postural hypotension, especially with parenteral administration (via intramuscular, intranasal, intravenous, or inhalation routes). Those drugs most often used in dentistry include nitrous oxide and oxygen (inhalation); diazepam (intravenous); midazolam (intramuscular, intranasal, or intravenous); meperidine; and fentanyl and its congeners—alfentanil and sufentanil (intravenous, intramuscular). Positional changes should be made slowly and carefully in patients receiving these drugs (Box 7-1).

> **Box 7-1** Drugs and drug categories producing postural hypotension
>
> **CATEGORY**
> Vasodilators
> α-adrenergic receptor antagonists
> β-adrenergic receptor antagonists
> Central α-adrenergic receptor agonists:
> Clonidine, guanabenz, guanfacine
> Cyclic antidepressants
> Phenothiazines

Prolonged recumbency and convalescence

Patients confined to bed for as little as 1 week have an increased risk of postural hypotension.[7] This is one reason that hospitalized patients are encouraged to ambulate as soon as possible after undergoing surgical procedures. Although dental patients are not confined for periods up to a week, longer dental appointments have gained popularity in recent years. Patients may remain recumbent in the dental chair for treatment lasting as long as 2 or 3 hours. In these circumstances, postural hypotension may develop when the dental chair is returned quickly to the upright position or the patient stands. When dental treatment combines long periods of recumbency with the use of psychosedative drugs, the risk of postural hypotension increases.

Inadequate postural reflex

Healthy young people may faint when forced to stand motionless for prolonged periods, such as during school assemblies, religious services, or parades. Syncope also can develop when a patient is seated upright in the dental chair for a prolonged period. This situation is more likely to occur in a hot environment, which produces concomitant peripheral vasodilation. The following example, excerpted from the *Los Angeles Times*,[13] illustrates one U.S. government agency's response to this physiologic occurrence:

How to faint by the numbers

VANCOUVER (UPI)—The order has gone out: Canadian troops may no longer faint in a slovenly or unseemly way while on parade. Soldiers disobeying the order will be put on report. The memo said: "To avoid the possibility of fainting, a soldier should make sure he has had breakfast on the morning of parade day. If worse comes to worst and he must faint, a soldier should fall to the ground under control. To do so, he must turn his body approximately 45 degrees, squat down, roll to the left, and retain control of his weapon to prevent personal injury and minimize damage to the weapon. We must ensure that soldiers who have not complied with the above instructions be charged."

Pregnancy

Pregnant patients may demonstrate two forms of hypotension. In the first, the woman experiences postural hypotension during the first trimester; this usually occurs when she rises from bed in the morning but does not recur during the day. The precise cause of this phenomenon is not known.

The second form, known as the *supine hypotensive syndrome of pregnancy*, occurs late in the third trimester if the woman remains in the supine position for more than 3 to 7 minutes.[14] Signs and symptoms of syncope become evident during this period, and the woman loses consciousness shortly thereafter. It has been demonstrated that the flaccid, gravid uterus compresses the inferior vena cava, decreasing venous return from the legs. If the woman alters her position to the lateral seated, or standing position, the weight of the uterus no longer creates this pressure on the vena cava and the clinical symptoms of syncope rapidly reverse.

Age

The incidence of postural hypotension shows a very definite increase with increasing age and proves to be a major problem in the aged population.[9–11,15,16] Patients who demonstrated a drop in both diastolic and systolic pressures were more likely to have had a fall during the year before the evaluation and decreased functional abilities compared with those patients who did not experience postural hypotension.[2] The mean incidence of falls in nursing homes is 1.5 falls per bed per year (range, 0.2 to 3.6 falls).[17]

Campbell et al.[18] studied 761 individuals 70 years or older and discovered that 507 had fallen during the year before monitoring began. Although many patients had multiple risk factors for falls, postural hypotension was frequently present. Macrae and Bulpitt[19] evaluated blood pressure changes in older patients in the morning and afternoon. Elderly patients experienced the greatest decrease—9.3 mm Hg—in systolic pressure in the morning, approximately 30 seconds after first standing, and returned to normal within 2 minutes. In contrast, diastolic pressure rose a maximum of 9.7 mm Hg in those 2 minutes. When doctors measured these individuals' blood pressures in the afternoon after lunch, the decrease ($n = 13$) was significantly greater across the board—20.8 mm Hg ± 3.6 mm Hg—compared with 7.1 mm Hg ± 2.0 mm Hg in the morning ($p = 0.01$).

Venous defects in the legs

Postural hypotension also occurs in patients with varicose veins and other vascular disorders of the legs. These disorders permit excessive pooling of blood in these patients' legs.

Recovery from sympathectomy for high blood pressure

Surgical procedures designed to lower blood pressure and improve circulation to the legs may result in a greater incidence of postural hypotension. Such cases usually occur immediately after surgery, with the symptoms usually declining spontaneously with time.

Addison's disease

Postural hypotension frequently occurs in patients with chronic adrenocortical insufficiency. The doctor may manage this condition through the administration of corticosteroids (see Chapter 8).

Physical exhaustion and starvation

When syncope occurs during a period of physical exhaustion or starvation, the cause is usually postural hypotension. Such causes are rarely the case in dental offices. Patients should be advised to eat before their dental appointments to reduce the possibility of postural hypotension unless eating is specifically contraindicated for the planned procedure (e.g., general anesthesia).

Chronic postural hypotension (Shy-Drager syndrome)

Shy-Drager syndrome, also known as *idiopathic postural hypotension* or *multiple systems atrophy,* is an uncommon disorder, the cause of which is unknown.[20] Its course is progressive; severe disability or death usually occurs within 5 to 10 years of onset. Patients who suffer from Shy-Drager syndrome are usually in their 50s and initially experience postural hypotension, urinary and fecal incontinence, sexual impotence (males), and anhidrosis (lack of sweating) in the lower trunk.

■ PREVENTION

Awareness of a patient's medical history may help the doctor prevent episodes of postural hypotension. Pre-

vention is based on the (1) medical history, (2) physical examination, and (3) dental treatment modifications. The first two steps are designed to identify patients with potential problems, whereas the third factor helps ensure that those patients do not lose consciousness.

4 stages to raise chair

 MEDICAL HISTORY QUESTIONNAIRE

Section V, Are You Taking:

Question 61: drugs, medications, over-the-counter medicines (including aspirin), natural remedies?
Comment: Postural hypotension is a side effect of many commonly used medications. The drug package insert or drug reference sources, such as Epocrates.com, MDConsult, and Mosby's Drug Consult, should be consulted (see Box 7-1).

Section II, Have You Experienced:

Question 18: Dizziness

Question 21: Fainting spells

Question 23: Seizures
Comment: A history of frequent fainting spells may indicate postural hypotension. A thorough dialogue history should be conducted to determine what factors are involved and whether prodromal signs and symptoms are associated with these syncopal episodes.

For patients with postural hypotension, the names of any medications the patient may be taking to assist in the maintenance of adequate blood pressure should be obtained. Patients often take ephedrine, up to 75 mg orally per day. Fludrocortisone acetate in doses of 0.1 mg or more daily is also effective.[21] If the patient does not know the name of a drug prescribed, the doctor should have a text available that contains illustrations of many common medications, such as *Physician's Desk Reference* or *Mosby's GenRx,* so that the patient can identify the medication causing a delay in treatment.

Physical examination

An integral part of the pretreatment evaluation for all potential patients is the recording of vital signs, including blood pressure, heart rate and rhythm (pulse), respiratory rate, temperature, height, and weight. Postural hypotension may be detectable if the patient's blood pressure and heart rate are recorded in both the supine and standing positions, something that is rarely done in most medical or dental practices. The doctor should record the first blood pressure reading after the patient has been in a supine position for 2 to 3 minutes and the second after the patient has been standing for 1 minute.[22] The normal response of this type of two-prong reading is a standing systolic blood pressure within 10 mm Hg (higher or lower, but usually higher) of the supine blood pressure. The heart rate normally accelerates when the individual stands and generally remains about 5 to 20 beats per minute faster than in the supine position.

> **Box 7-2**   Clinical criteria for postural hypotension
>
> Symptoms develop when individual stands
> Standing pulse increases at least 30 beats per minute
> Standing systolic blood pressure decreases at least 25 mm Hg
> Standing diastolic blood pressure decreases at least 10 mm Hg

If severe clinical symptoms develop, the test for postural hypotension is positive and the patient should lie down immediately. Other criteria that indicate postural hypotension include a rise in the standing pulse of at least 30 beats per minute or a decrease of more than 25 mm Hg in systolic and 10 mm Hg in diastolic blood pressure simultaneous with the appearance of symptoms (Box 7-2). The doctor should recheck the patient's blood pressure in each position; if the patient still exhibits this differential, medical consultation should be considered before dental treatment is initiated.

Dental therapy considerations

Adherence to certain basic precautions will decrease the likelihood of hypotensive episodes either during or after positional changes in the following types of dental patients:

- Patients with histories of postural hypotension
- Patients receiving sedation (inhalation, intravenous, intranasal, or intramuscular) during dental treatment
- Patients who have been reclined in the dental chair for a long period

Patients who have been in a supine or semisupine position throughout long appointments should be cautioned against rising too rapidly. These patients should resume an upright position slowly at the conclusion of treatment. To elevate the patient it is suggested that the position of the dental chair be changed (brought more upright) slowly over about 1 minute, changing the chair position two or three times before moving the chair into the upright position. Allow the patient to remain at each incremental level until any potential dizziness abates.

As the patient stands, the doctor may want to be located in front of the chair until the patient is able to stand without feeling dizzy. If the patient does become weak or faint, however, dental staff members are there to prevent the patient from falling and being injured. These precautions, restated in the following list, are especially important when (older) patients remain reclined for long periods.

Dental therapy considerations: postural hypotension

- Slowly reposition patient upright.
- Stand nearby as the patient stands after treatment.

CLINICAL MANIFESTATIONS

Patients with chronic postural hypotension can experience precipitous drops in blood pressure and lose consciousness whenever they stand or sit upright; frequently they do not exhibit any of the prodromal signs and symptoms of vasodepressor syncope (lightheadedness, pallor, dizziness, blurred vision, nausea, and diaphoresis). These patients also may lose consciousness rapidly, or may merely become lightheaded, or develop blurred vision but not actually lose consciousness. Clinical signs and symptoms more often are seen in patients with other predisposing factors for postural hypotension, such as the administration of drugs, and may include some or all of the usual prodromal signs and symptoms of vasodepressor syncope before consciousness is lost.

Blood pressure during the syncopal period of postural hypotension is quite low, as it is during vasodepressor syncope. Unlike vasodepressor syncope, during which individuals exhibit bradycardia, the heart rate during postural hypotension remains at the baseline level or somewhat higher (>30 beats per minute above baseline). The patient with postural hypotension exhibits all the clinical manifestations of unconscious patients (see Chapters 5 and 6). If unconsciousness persists for 10 or more seconds, the patient may exhibit minor convulsive movements.[23] Consciousness returns rapidly once the patient is returned to the supine position.

PATHOPHYSIOLOGY
Normal regulatory mechanisms

When the patient changes from a supine to an upright position, the influence of gravity on the cardiovascular system intensifies. Blood pumped from the heart must now move upward, against gravity, to reach the cerebral circulation to supply the brain with the O_2 and glucose it needs to maintain consciousness. On the other hand, with the patient in the supine position the force of gravity is distributed equally over the entire body and blood flows more readily from the heart to the brain. With other positions (e.g., semisupine, Trendelenburg), gravity's effect is usually such that systolic blood pressure decreases by 2 mm Hg for each 25 mm (1 inch) that the patient's head is situated above the level of the heart; for each 25 mm (1 inch) that the head is situated below

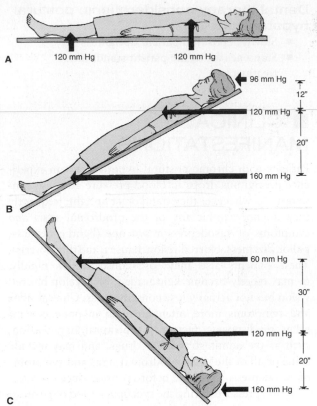

FIGURE 7-1 The effect of gravity on blood pressure. **A,** In the supine position, the effect of gravity is equalized over the entire body. The blood pressures in the legs, heart, and brain are approximately equal. **B,** In the semiupright position, pressure is decreased by 2 mm Hg for each inch the individual remains above the level of the heart. **C,** In the Trendelenburg (head down) position, blood pressure increases 2 mm Hg for each inch the individual is situated below the level of the heart. (Modified from Enderby GE: Postural ischaemia and blood-pressure, *Lancet* 266:185–187, 1954.)

the level of the heart, blood pressure increases by 2 mm Hg (Figure 7-1).

A number of intricate mechanisms have evolved to protect the brain and ensure that it receives an adequate supply of O$_2$ and glucose.[24] These include the following:

- A reflex arteriolar constriction mediated through baroreceptors (pressure receptors) located in the carotid sinus and aortic arch
- A reflex increase in heart rate, which occurs simultaneously with the increase in arteriolar tone and is mediated through the same mechanisms
- A reflex venous constriction that increases the return of venous blood to the heart, mediated both intrinsically and sympathetically
- An increase in muscle tone and contraction in the legs and abdomen—the so-called venous pump—facilitating the return of venous blood (of vital

importance because at least 60% of circulating blood volume at any given moment is in venous circulation)
- A reflex increase in respiration, which also aids in the return of blood to the right side of the heart via changes in intraabdominal and intrathoracic pressures
- The release into the blood of various neurohumoral substances, such as norepinephrine, antidiuretic hormone, renin, and angiotensin

The usual (normal) reaction of the cardiovascular system when an individual is tilted from the supine into the upright sitting position is an immediate drop in systolic blood pressure from 5 to 40 mm Hg; this drop is followed by an equally rapid rise so that within 30 seconds to 1 minute the systolic blood pressure is equal to or slightly higher than that recorded in the supine position. Thereafter, the systolic blood pressure tends to remain within 10 mm Hg higher or lower (usually higher) of the supine recording. The diastolic blood pressure rises approximately 10 to 20 mm Hg. Heart rate (pulse) increases approximately 5 to 20 beats per minute when the patient is standing.

Postural hypotension

One or more of the adaptive mechanisms fails in the patient with postural hypotension, preventing their body from adapting adequately to the increased effects of gravity. Dramatic blood pressure changes accompany positional changes. Blood pressure drops rapidly when the patient moves into an upright position with systolic pressure sometimes approaches 60 mm Hg in less than 1 minute. Diastolic blood pressure also drops precipitously. The heart rate, however, changes only slightly or not at all; the cardiovascular system is unable to respond normally to the blood pressure depression. This combination of signs (rapid decrease in blood pressure, no change in heart rate) is pathognomonic of postural hypotension.

In addition, many patients do not exhibit any of the usual prodromal signs seen in vasodepressor syncope. These patients may lose consciousness when cerebral blood flow drops below the critical level (approximately 30 mL of blood per minute per 100 g of brain), equivalent to a systolic blood pressure at heart level of approximately 70 mm Hg in a normotensive person. Syncope is short-lived once the patient is placed into the supine position because of reestablishment of adequate cerebral blood flow. Table 7-1 compares the postural responses in blood pressure and heart rate of individuals with postural hypotension with responses in normal individuals.

TABLE 7-1 Cardiovascular response to positional change

Change (at 60 sec) after sudden elevation	Normal	Postural hypotension
Systolic blood pressure	Baseline or ± 10 mm Hg	Decrease >25 mm Hg
Diastolic blood pressure	Increase of 10–20 mm Hg	Decrease >10 mm Hg
Heart rate	5–20 beats per minute above baseline	Baseline or higher (>30 beats per minute)

■ MANAGEMENT

Management of postural hypotension parallels that of vasodepressor syncope.

Step 1: assessment of consciousness. The patient may or may not demonstrate a lack of response to sensory stimulation.

Step 2: activation of the office emergency system.

Step 3: P (position). The unresponsive patient is placed into the supine position with the feet elevated slightly. This position immediately enhances cerebral perfusion, and, in most instances, the individual regains consciousness within a few seconds.

Step 4: A→B→C (airway-breathing-circulation). In the unlikely situation in which the patient has not immediately regained consciousness following positioning, a patent airway must be established. Head tilt–chin lift usually is successful. In addition, the "look, listen, feel" technique should be used to detect any obstruction to breathing, and the carotid pulse palpated to determine adequacy of circulation.

Step 5: D (definitive care).
Step 5a: administration of O₂. The syncopal patient may receive O_2 at any time during or after the episode.

Step 5b: monitoring of vital signs. The patient's vital signs—blood pressure, heart rate, and respiratory rate—should be monitored and compared with preoperative baseline values to determine the severity of the hypotensive reaction and the degree of recovery.

The patient's position also should be noted with each recording of vital signs.

Step 6: subsequent management. After an episode of postural hypotension, the now-supine patient usually feels almost normal, experiencing little or no postsyncopal feelings of exhaustion or malaise—symptoms that frequently develop in patients after episodes of vasodepressor syncope.

Most important, changes in position from supine to upright must occur slowly. The patient should be repositioned approximately 22.5 degrees, with sufficient time for accommodation before being raised to approximately 45 degrees. After making this height adjustment, the patient then should be raised to about 67.5 degrees, allowed to accommodate, before finally being raised to the fully upright position of 90 degrees. All signs and symptoms of hypotension must be resolved before the patient assumes the upright position. As a final precaution, the blood pressure should be checked and compared with baseline before permitting the patient to stand. Finally, the doctor or assistant should help the patient rise from the chair and be available for support, if necessary.

Step 6a: delayed recovery. If hypotensive episodes continue to occur when the patient resumes the upright position (an unlikely event), the doctor should consider seeking outside medical assistance to definitively manage the problem.

Step 7: discharge. A patient with chronic postural hypotension or postural hypotension resulting from a prescribed medication (e.g., an antihypertensive) may leave the dental office and drive a motor vehicle only if the doctor deems that the patient has recovered sufficiently from the incident. This judgment may be based on a return of vital signs to approximately baseline levels and the ability of the patient to walk freely without experiencing any clinical signs and symptoms of hypotension (e.g., lightheadedness, pallor, or dizziness). When the patient's history suggests that a prescribed drug may have been responsible for the hypotensive episode, the doctor should consider consulting the patient's primary care physician if episodes recur.

Patients experiencing postural hypotensive episodes who do not have prior histories of such occurrences or patients who experience such episodes after the administration of drugs should recover in the dental office while arrangements are made for a responsible adult* to

---

*A responsible adult may be defined as a person with a vested interest in the health and safety of the patient.

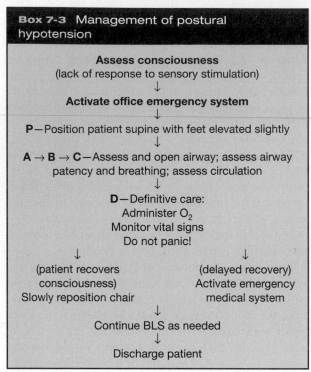

> **Box 7-3** Management of postural hypotension
>
> **Assess consciousness**
> (lack of response to sensory stimulation)
> ↓
> **Activate office emergency system**
> ↓
> **P**—Position patient supine with feet elevated slightly
> ↓
> **A → B → C**—Assess and open airway; assess airway patency and breathing; assess circulation
> ↓
> **D**—Definitive care:
> Administer O_2
> Monitor vital signs
> Do not panic!
> ↓   ↓
> (patient recovers   (delayed recovery)
> consciousness)   Activate emergency
> Slowly reposition chair   medical system
> ↓
> Continue BLS as needed
> ↓
> Discharge patient

A, airway; *B,* breathing; *BLS,* basic life support; *C,* circulation; *D,* definitive care; *P,* position.

escort the patient home or for emergency personnel to escort the patient to an acute-care facility. Consultation with the patient's primary care physician should be considered in cases in which the patient has no prior history of postural hypotension.

Box 7-3 summarizes the proper management of postural hypotension.

- Drugs used in management: O_2
- Medical assistance required: Such assistance usually is not required. Most individuals regain consciousness rapidly upon being properly positioned. When consciousness does not return promptly or recurrent hypotensive episodes develop after repositioning, emergency medical assistance should be considered.

REFERENCES

1. Consensus statement on the definition of orthostatic hypotension, pure autonomic failure, and multiple system atrophy, *J Neurol Sci* 144:218–219, 1996.
2. Thijs RD, Benditt DG, Mathias CJ, et al.: Unconscious confusion—a literature search for definitions of syncope and related disorders, *Clin Auton Res* 15:35–39, 2005.
3. Simon RP: Syncope, In: Goldman L, editor: *Cecil textbook of medicine,* ed 22, Philadelphia, WB Saunders, 2004, pp. 2020–2029.
4. Weimer LH, Williams O: Syncope and orthostatic intolerance, *Med Clin North Am* 87:835–865, 2003.
5. Atkins D, Hanusa B, Sefcik T, Kapoor W: Syncope and orthostatic hypotension, *Am J Med* 91:179–185, 1991.
6. Coperchini ML, Kreeger LC: Postural hypotension from topical glyceryl trinitrate ointment for anal pain, *J Pain Symptom Manage* 14:263–264, 1997.
7. Akhtar M, Jazayeri M, Sra J: Cardiovascular causes of syncope: identifying and controlling trigger mechanisms, *Postgrad Med* 90:87–94, 1991.
8. Ikeda T, Ohbuchi H, Ikenoue T, Mori N: Maternal cerebral hemodynamics in the supine hypotensive syndrome, *Obstet Gynecol* 79:27–31, 1992.
9. Sherman FT: Syncop.aging. n. The art and science of syncope in the aged, *Geriatrics* 58:12, 15, 2003.
10. Yang TM, Chang MS: The mechanism of symptomatic postural hypotension in the elderly, *Chung Hua I Hsueh Tsa Chih* 46:147–155, 1990.
11. Susman J: Postural hypotension in elderly family practice patients, *J Am Board Fam Pract* 2:234–237, 1989.
12. de Jong-de Vos van Steenwijk CC, Harms MP, Wesseling KH: Variability of near-fainting responses in healthy 6-16-year-old subjects, *Clin Sci (Colch)* 93:205–211, 1997.
13. United Press International: How to faint by the numbers, *Los Angeles Times,* February 23, 1975.
14. Lanni SM, Tillinghast J, Silver HM: Hemodynamic changes and baroreflex gain in the supine hypotensive syndrome, *Am J Obstet Gynecol* 187:1636–1641, 2002.
15. Wing LM, Tonkin AL: Orthostatic blood pressure control and aging, *Aust N Z J Med* 27:462–466, 1997.
16. Mukai S, Lipsitz LA: Orthostatic hypotension, *Clin Geriatr Med* 18:253–268, 2002.
17. Rubenstein LZ, Josephson KR, Osterweil D: Falls and fall prevention in the nursing home, *Clin Geriatr Med* 12:881–902, 1996.
18. Campbell AJ, Borrie MJ, Spears GF: Risk factors for falls in a community-based prospective study of people 70 years and older, *J Gerontol* 44:M112–M117, 1989.
19. Macrae AD, Bulpitt CJ: Assessment of postural hypotension in elderly patients, *Age Ageing* 18:110–112, 1989.
20. Biaggioni I, Robertson RM: Hypertension in orthostatic hypotension and autonomic dysfunction, *Cardiol Clin* 20:291–301, 2002.
21. Bradley JG, Davis KA: Orthostatic hypotension, *Am Fam Physician* 68:2393–2398, 2003.
22. Weimer LH: Syncope and orthostatic intolerance for the primary care physician, *Prim Care Clin Office Pract* 31:175–199, 2004.
23. Cutino SR: Vasovagal syncope associated with seizure activity, *Gen Dent* 42:342–343, 1994.
24. Petrella RJ, Cunningham DA, Smith JJ: Influence of age and physical training on postural adaptation, *Can J Sport Sci* 14:4–9, 1989.

CHAPTER 8

Acute Adrenal Insufficiency

A third potentially life-threatening situation that may result in the loss of consciousness is *acute adrenal insufficiency,* or *adrenal crisis.* Of the three conditions discussed in this section—vasodepressor syncope, postural hypotension, and acute adrenal insufficiency—the last is, by far, the least likely to be seen in the dental office. The condition is uncommon, is potentially life-threatening, but is readily treatable.

The adrenal gland is an endocrine gland that is actually a combination of two glands: the cortex and the medulla, which, though fused, remain distinct and identifiable entities. The adrenal cortex produces and secretes more than 30 steroid hormones, most of which do not aid in the performance of any important, currently identifiable biological activity.[1] Cortisol, a glucocorticoid, is widely considered the most important product of the adrenal cortex; cortisol helps the body adapt to stress and is thereby extremely vital to survival. *fight or Flight*

Hypersecretion of cortisol leads to increased fat deposition in certain areas, such as the face and back (often called a "buffalo hump"); elevates blood pressure; and alters blood cell distribution (eosinopenia and lymphopenia).[2] Cortisol hypersecretion usually does not result in the acute, life-threatening situation that is noted with acute cortisol deficiency. Clinically, cortisol hypersecretion is referred to as *Cushing's syndrome,*[3] a condition that can normally be corrected through surgical removal of part or all of the adrenal gland.[4] Today, renal and adrenal surgery are important factors in the development of primary adrenocortical insufficiency.[5]

On the other hand, cortisol deficiency can lead to a relatively rapid onset of clinical symptoms, including loss of consciousness and possible death. Adrenal insufficiency first was recognized by Addison in 1844; thus, primary adrenocortical insufficiency is called *Addison's disease,* an insidious and usually progressive condition.[6] The incidence of Addison's disease, estimated as 0.3 to 1 case per 100,000 individuals, occurs equally in both sexes and among all age groups, including infants and children.[7] Although all corticosteroids may be deficient in this disease state, administration of physiologic doses of exogenous cortisol can correct most pathophysiologic effects associated with Addison's disease.[8]

Clinical manifestations of adrenocortical insufficiency usually do not develop until at least 70% to 80% of the adrenal cortex is destroyed.[9] Because this destruction usually progresses slowly, several months may pass before a diagnosis of adrenocortical insufficiency is made and therapy (exogenous cortisol) is instituted. During this time, the patient will remain in constant jeopardy of developing acute adrenal insufficiency. The patient is capable of maintaining levels of endogenous cortisol adequate to meet the requirements of day-to-day living; however, in stressful situations (e.g., a dental appointment for a fearful patient), the adrenal cortex is unable to produce the additional quantity of cortisol needed to adapt to the stress, and signs and symptoms of acute adrenal insufficiency develop.

The administration of exogenous glucocorticosteroids to a patient with functional adrenal cortices may produce a second form of adrenocortical hypofunction. Glucocorticosteroid drugs are widely prescribed in pharmacologic doses to relieve the symptoms of a wide variety of disorders (Box 8-1). When used in this manner, exogenous glucocorticosteroid administration produces a disuse atrophy of the adrenal cortex, diminishing the ability of the adrenal cortex to increase corticosteroid levels in response to stressful situations. This in turn leads to the development of signs and symptoms associated with acute adrenal insufficiency. Today, secondary adrenal insufficiency is a greater potential threat than Addison's disease in the development of acute adrenal crisis.[10] Acute adrenal insufficiency is a true medical emergency in which the victim is in immediate danger because of glucocorticoid (cortisol) insufficiency. Peripheral vascular collapse (shock) and ventricular asystole (cardiac arrest) are the usual cause of death.[11,12]

The dentist is in the unenviable position of being a major stress factor in the lives of many patients. Therefore, all dental office personnel must become capable of recognizing and managing acute adrenal crises; even more important, staff members must be able to prevent this situation from developing.

■ PREDISPOSING FACTORS

Before the availability of exogenous glucocorticosteroid therapy, acute adrenal insufficiency was the terminal stage of Addison's disease. With exogenous glucocorticosteroid therapy, however, patients with this disease can lead relatively normal lives. Unusually stressful situations require that the patient modify their steroid dose to prevent the development of acute adrenal insufficiency. Lack of glucocorticosteroid hormones is the major predisposing factor in all cases of acute adrenal insufficiency; this deficiency develops through the following six mechanisms:

Mechanism 1: After the sudden withdrawal of steroid hormones in a patient who suffers primary adrenal insufficiency (Addison's disease)

Mechanism 2: After the sudden withdrawal of steroid hormones from a patient with normal adrenal cortices but with a temporary insufficiency resulting from cortical suppression through prolonged exogenous glucocorticosteroid administration (secondary insufficiency)

Patients with primary and secondary adrenocortical insufficiency are dependent on exogenous steroids. Abrupt withdrawal from therapy leaves patients with a deficiency of glucocorticosteroid hormones, making them unable to adapt normally to stress (they become stress-intolerant). Evidence indicates that it may take up to 9 months to fully recover adrenal function following prolonged exogenous steroid therapy in patients with normal cortices.[13] Others have estimated that normal function may not return for as long as 2 years.[14]

Box 8-1 Clinical indications for glucocorticosteroid use

ALLERGIC DISEASES
Angioedema
Asthma, acute and chronic
Dermatitis, contact
Dermatitis venenata
Insect bites
Pollinosis (hay fever)
Rhinitis, allergic
Serum reaction, drug and foreign, acute and delayed
Status asthmaticus
Transfusion reactions
Urticaria

CARDIOVASCULAR DISEASES
Postpericardiotomy syndrome
Shock, toxic (septic)

EYE DISEASES
Blepharoconjunctivitis
Burns, chemical and thermal
Conjunctivitis, allergic, catarrhal
Corneal injuries
Glaucoma, secondary
Herpes zoster
Iritis
Keratitis
Neuritis, optic, acute
Retinitis, centralis
Scleritis; episcleritis

GASTROINTESTINAL DISEASES
Colitis, ulcerative
Enteritis, regional
Hepatitis, viral
Sprue

GENITOURINARY DISEASES
Hunner's ulcer
Nephrotic syndrome

HEMATOPOIETIC DISORDERS
Anemia, acquired hemolytic
Leukemia, acute and chronic
Lymphoma
Purpura, idiopathic thrombocytopenic

INFECTIONS AND INFLAMMATIONS
Meningitis
Thyroiditis, acute
Typhoid fever
Waterhouse-Friderichsen syndrome

INJECTED LOCALLY
Arthritis, traumatic
Bursitis
Osteoarthritis
Tendinitis

MESENCHYMAL DISEASES
Arthritis, rheumatoid
Dermatomyositis
Lupus erythematosus, systemic
Polyarteritis
Rheumatic fever, acute

METABOLIC DISEASES
Arthritis, gouty acute
Thyroid crisis, acute

MISCELLANEOUS CONDITIONS
Bell's palsy
Dental surgical procedures

PULMONARY DISEASES
Emphysema, pulmonary
Fibrosis, pulmonary
Sarcoidosis
Silicosis

SKIN DISEASES
Dermatitis
Drug eruptions
Eczema, chronic
Erythema multiforme
Herpes zoster
Lichen planus
Pemphigus vulgaris
Pityriasis rosea
Purpura, allergic
Sunburn, severe

Patients with Addison's disease require the administration of glucocorticosteroids for as long as they live. Withdrawal from exogenous steroid therapy of patients who do not suffer Addison's disease should occur gradually; in this way the adrenal glands can increase production of endogenous glucocorticoids as the levels of exogenously administered steroids decrease. The time required for the return to normal adrenocortical functioning varies and is influenced by a number of factors (Box 8-2). Predesigned protocols help withdraw patients

Box 8-2 Factors influencing the return of adrenocortical function after exogenous glucocorticosteroid therapy

Dose of glucocorticosteroid administered
Duration of course of therapy
Frequency of administration
Time of administration
Route of administration

from long-term glucocorticosteroid therapy with a minimum of side effects and with relative convenience and safety.[15]

The widespread use of glucocorticosteroids in patients who do not have Addison's disease has become the most common cause of adrenal insufficiency. The hypothalamic-pituitary-adrenocortical axis generally is not suppressed unless exogenous steroid therapy has continued over long periods, in nonphysiologic doses, or both. Most of the indications for glucocorticosteroids in Box 8-1 require pharmacologic doses; these generally are much greater than physiologic doses.*

Mechanism 3: After stress, either physiologic or psychological.

Physiologic stress can include traumatic injuries, surgery (including oral, periodontal, or endodontic), extensive dental procedures, infection, acute changes in environmental temperature, severe muscular exercise, or burns. Psychological stress, such as that seen in the fearful dental patient, may also precipitate adrenal crisis.

In stressful situations, there is normally an increased release of glucocorticoids from the adrenal cortices. The hypothalamic-pituitary-adrenocortical axis mediates this increase, which normally results in a rapid elevation of glucocorticosteroid blood levels. If the adrenal gland cannot meet this increased demand, clinical signs and symptoms of adrenal insufficiency develop. In dental settings, stress is the most common immediate precipitating factor producing acute adrenal insufficiency.

Mechanism 4: After bilateral adrenalectomy or removal of a functioning adrenal tumor that was suppressing the other adrenal gland

Mechanism 5: After the sudden destruction of the pituitary gland

Mechanism 6: After both adrenal glands are injured through trauma, hemorrhage, infection, thrombosis, or tumor

The last three causes of adrenal crisis occur most commonly in hospitalized patients and therefore are not of immediate concern in most dental offices. The first three precipitating factors, however, are the primary factors in the development of acute adrenal insufficiency in dental settings. (These factors will be discussed more fully in later sections of this chapter.)

Stress is a precipitating factor in a majority of cases of acute adrenal insufficiency. Factors that may precipitate stress include surgery, anesthesia, psychological stress, alcohol intoxication, hypothermia, myocardial infarction, diabetes mellitus, intercurrent infection, asthma, pyrogens, and hypoglycemia.[16–19]

---

*Physiologic, or replacement, doses equal the normal daily production of functioning adrenal cortex—approximately 20 mg cortisol. Pharmacologic doses are commonly four or five times greater.

■ PREVENTION

Acute adrenal insufficiency can best be managed through its prevention, which is based on the medical history questionnaire and ensuing dialogue history between the doctor and patient. In many instances, specific dental therapy modifications will be necessary for the patient at risk for acute adrenal insufficiency.

✎ MEDICAL HISTORY QUESTIONNAIRE

Section V, Are You Taking:

Question 62: Drugs, medications, over-the-counter medicines (including aspirin), natural remedies (within the past two years)?

Comment: Table 8-1 lists many of the generic and proprietary names of commonly prescribed corticosteroid drugs. In many instances the patient may know only the proprietary name of the drug. In such cases the doctor must have available a list such as this or an appropriate drug reference;[20,21] these texts can aid in identification of the drug and help the doctor minimize potential problems. The doctor might consider adding the phrase "during the past 2 years" to this question because of the possibility that an individual may develop varying degrees of adrenocortical suppression with long-term pharmacologic doses of glucocorticosteroids.

Section IV, Do You Have or Have You Had:

Question 32: Rheumatic fever?

Question 35: Asthma, TB (tuberculosis), emphysema, other lung diseases?

Question 38: Allergies to: drugs, foods, medications, latex?

 TABLE 8-1 Systemic corticosteroids

Generic name	Proprietary name
Cortisone	Cortone
Dexamethasone	Decadron
Fludrocortisone	Florinef-Acetate
Hydrocortisone	Cortef Solu-Cortef
Methylprednisolone	Depo-Medrol Medrol Solu-Medrol
Prednisolone	Deltasone Orapred Pediapred Prelone Sterapred Sterapred DS
Triamcinolone	Aristocort

Data obtained from Epocrates.com on August 27, 2005.

Question 42: Arthritis, rheumatism?

Comment: The specific diseases or medications listed above represent only a small number of the clinical uses of glucocorticosteroids (see Box 8-1). With each of these drugs, pharmacologic doses—doses many times greater than the adrenal gland's normal daily output—are administered.

Dialogue history

If the patient responds positively to any of the preceding questions, the doctor must vigorously pursue a dialogue history for additional facts, including the following vital drug information:

- Drugs used to manage the disorder
- Drug dose
- Route of administration
- Duration of drug therapy
- Length of time elapsed since drug therapy ended

What drugs did you use to manage the disorder?

Comment: Physicians frequently manage the conditions listed in Section IV in part through the administration of glucocorticosteroids. However, the doctor first must determine the name of the specific drugs involved in the patient's treatment (see Box 8-1 and Table 8-1).

What was your daily drug dose?

Comment: The specific dose of glucocorticosteroid is an important measure of the degree of cortical suppression. The equivalent therapeutic doses of glucocorticosteroids vary from drug to drug (Table 8-2). For example, 20 mg hydrocortisone is equivalent to 5 mg prednisolone, prednisone, and methylprednisone; to 4 mg methylprednisolone and triamcinolone; and to 0.75 mg dexamethasone.

Patients with primary adrenocortical insufficiency (Addison's disease) receive physiologic (replacement) doses of glucocorticosteroids.

TABLE 8-2 Equivalent doses of glucocorticosteroids

Duration/preparation	Corticosteroid potency	Equivalent dose (mg)
SHORT-ACTING		
Hydrocortisone (cortisol)	1	20
Cortisone	0.8	25
INTERMEDIATE-ACTING		
Prednisone	4	5
Prednisolone	4	5
Methylprednisolone (Medrol)	5	4
LONG-ACTING		
Dexamethasone (Decadron)	30	0.75
Betamethasone (Celestone)	25	0.6

Such doses usually mandate daily administration of approximately 15 to 25 mg hydrocortisone orally in two divided doses—two thirds in the morning and the remaining third in the late afternoon or early evening. Many patients, however, do not retain salt sufficiently and require 0.05 to 0.3 mg oral fludrocortisone supplementation daily or every other day.[22] These doses satisfactorily replace the normal output of the adrenal cortex (approximately 20 mg cortisol daily).

Patients receiving glucocorticosteroid therapy for symptomatic treatment of disorders (see Box 8-1) commonly receive large pharmacologic, or therapeutic, doses. For example, patients with rheumatoid arthritis frequently receive daily oral doses of 10 mg prednisone;[23] this dose is equivalent to approximately 50 mg cortisone. Increasingly, individuals whose acute asthmatic attacks do not respond readily to bronchodilator therapy receive prednisone orally.[24] These doses are divided and total 40 to 60 mg per day; this is equivalent to 200 to 300 mg cortisone. Doses such as these can cause suppression of the normal adrenal cortex if continued for long periods. Although admittedly conservative, the "rule of twos" (Box 8-3) is helpful in determining the risk factors for patients who are taking or recently have taken a course of glucocorticosteroid therapy.[25] The first of the three factors in the rule of twos is the daily administration of 20 mg or more of cortisone or its equivalent.

By what route did you take the drug?

Comment: Glucocorticosteroids may be administered via a variety of routes. Parenteral (intramuscular [IM], intravenous [IV], or subcutaneous [SC]) or enteral administration (oral) may result in the suppression of a normal adrenal cortex with a decrease in production of endogenous corticosteroids. Drugs administered topically (ophthalmic, dermatologic, intranasal, tracheobronchial [inhalation], vaginal, or rectal administration) and via intraarticular application normally do not result in clinically significant cortical suppression because these routes provide relatively poor systemic absorption.

How long did your glucocorticosteroid therapy last?

Comment: Although the exact length of time required for the development of significant cortical suppression varies from patient to patient, it has been demonstrated that uninterrupted glucocorticosteroid therapy for as little as 2 weeks may induce suppression.[26] Any patient who has received glucocorticosteroid therapy continuously for 2 weeks or longer risks developing adrenal insufficiency. This is the second important factor in the rule of twos.

How long ago did you stop receiving glucocorticosteroid therapy?

Comment: This question is applicable to patients who had normal, functional adrenal cortices at the onset of glucocorticosteroid

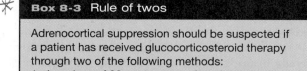

Box 8-3 Rule of twos

Adrenocortical suppression should be suspected if a patient has received glucocorticosteroid therapy through two of the following methods:
1. In a dose of 20 mg or more of cortisone or its equivalent
2. Via the oral or parenteral route for a continuous period of 2 weeks or longer
3. Within 2 years of dental therapy *(any true)*

therapy, underwent therapy (probably at pharmacologic dose levels) until the underlying medical condition was controlled, and then were gradually withdrawn from the drugs. The atrophic adrenal cortex does not function normally for a variable period after withdrawal from exogenous glucocorticosteroid therapy. During this time the cortex usually can produce minimal daily levels of endogenous corticosteroids; however, in stressful situations it may be incapable of meeting the increased demand, leading to the development of signs and symptoms of acute adrenal insufficiency.

The length of time required for full regeneration of normal cortical function varies according to the dosage and length of therapy but is normally at least 9 to 12 months.[11] Instances of acute adrenal insufficiency lasting as long as 2 years after termination of therapy have been reported. The third factor in the rule of twos relates to patients who have received glucocorticosteroid therapy with 2 years of dental treatment. The rule of twos allows the doctor to predict with a degree of reliability those patients at increased risk for acute adrenal insufficiency.

Dental therapy considerations

Patients who are currently receiving glucocorticosteroid therapy or have recently received such therapy and meet the criteria of the rule of twos may require dental treatment modifications. In such circumstances a complete medical and dental evaluation should be completed, a provisional treatment plan established, and the patient's primary care physician consulted before the start of dental treatment. A patient with Addison's disease or a patient receiving long-term pharmacologic doses of glucocorticosteroid therapy usually is classified as an American Society of Anesthesiologists (ASA) II or III risk.

Glucocorticosteroid coverage

Since patients with adrenocortical insufficiency are physiologically less able to adapt to stress in a normal manner, they require the administration of glucocorticosteroids before, during, and possibly after the stressful situation to increase their blood steroid levels. The choice of a therapeutic regimen will depend on the primary care physician's evaluation of the patient's physical status and on the dentist's evaluation of the stress involved in the planned treatment.

Many primary care physicians underestimate the degree of stress associated with nonsurgical dental treatment. Thus, the dentist must evaluate this factor carefully. In an extreme instance, such as a fearful patient with Addison's disease, the patient may require hospitalization and receive 200 to 500 mg cortisone per day, which is equivalent to the maximal response of the normal pituitary-adrenal system to extreme stress.

Card for Patient on Corticosteroid Therapy

Mr.
Mrs.
Miss _____ is being treated for ___(disorder)___ with __(corticosteroid)__ in a dose of _____(dose)_____. In the event of "stress," the steroid dosage should be increased thus:

1. *Mild "Stress"* (e.g., common cold, single dental extraction, mild trauma): use double doses daily.
2. *Moderate "Stress"* (e.g., flu, surgery under local anesthesia, several dental extractions): use hydrocortisone, 100 mg, or prednisolone, 20 mg, or dexamethasone, 4 mg daily.
3. *Severe "Stress"* (e.g., general surgery, pneumonia or other systemic infections, high fever, severe trauma): use hydrocortisone, 200 mg, or prednisolone, 40 mg, or dexamethasone 8 mg daily.

When vomiting or diarrhea precludes absorption of oral doses, give dexamethasone 1 to 4 mg intramuscularly every 6 hours.

(Signed) _____ M.D.
(Address) _____

FIGURE 8-1 Sample corticosteroid coverage protocol for a patient receiving exogenous glucocorticosteroid therapy. (From Streeten DHP: Corticosteroid therapy. I. Pharmacological properties and principles of corticosteroid use, *JAMA* 232:944–947, 1975.)

The requirement for increased glucocorticosteroid therapy decreases in individuals who are only moderately fearful and undergoing dental procedures that are only mildly stressful (as most dental procedures are classified). Usually a twofold or fourfold increase in glucocorticosteroid dosage on the day of the dental treatment prepares the patient adequately. The adrenal cortices of normal adults secrete about 20 mg cortisol daily-the daily maintenance level required by most patients with Addison's disease. Figure 8-1 is a sample of a corticosteroid coverage protocol.

Stress reduction protocol

In addition to medical consultation and possible premedication with glucocorticosteroids prior to dental treatment, the stress reduction protocol (see Chapter 2) will be an extremely valuable tool in the management of patients with adrenocortical insufficiency.

Additional considerations

Patients with Addison's disease may wear an identification bracelet (e.g., Med-Alert) stating the patients' name and the names and telephone numbers of the primary care physician and a close relative. The bracelet will state: "I have adrenal insufficiency. In any emergency involving injury, vomiting, or loss of consciousness, the hydrocortisone in my possession should be injected under my skin, and my physician notified." These patients carry small, clearly labeled kits containing 100 mg hydrocortisone phosphate solution in a sterile syringe ready for use. These kits serve as a constant reminder to such patients that their survival may depend on the timely administration of this drug. During dental treatment the drug should be readily available.

TABLE 8-3 Clinical features of adrenal insufficiency

Symptom, sign, or laboratory finding	Frequency (%)
SYMPTOM	
Weakness, tiredness, fatigue	100
Anorexia	100
Gastrointestinal symptoms	92
Nausea	86
Vomiting	75
Constipation	33
Abdominal pain	31
Diarrhea	16
Salt craving	16
Postural dizziness	12
Muscle or joint pain	6–13
SIGN	
Weight loss	100
Hyperpigmentation	94
Hypotension (<110 mm Hg systolic)	88–94
Vitiligo	10–20
Auricular calcification	5
LABORATORY FINDING	
Electrolyte disturbance	92
Hyponatremia	88
Hyperkalemia	64
Hypercalcemia	6
Azotemia	55
Anemia	40
Eosinophilia	17

From: Larsen PR: *Williams' textbook of endocrinology*, ed 10, St. Louis, Elsevier, 2003.

■ CLINICAL MANIFESTATIONS

In potentially stressful situations such as dental procedures, patients with hypofunctioning adrenal cortices may exhibit clinical signs and symptoms of acute glucocorticosteroid insufficiency. The result of this acute insufficiency may be the loss of consciousness and possible coma. Table 8-3 lists the clinical signs and symptoms of adrenal insufficiency.

Individuals with acute adrenal insufficiency almost universally exhibit lethargy, extreme fatigue, and weakness. In extreme cases the weakness can be so pronounced that even speaking may be difficult.[27] Hyperkalemia may also develop; if severe, this condition can lead to skeletal muscle paralysis.[28] Most deaths and major morbidity that accompany adrenal insufficiency are secondary to hypotension or hypoglycemia.

In addition, most patients with Addison's disease demonstrate hypotension with systolic blood pressures less than 110 mm Hg. Of 108 patients with Addison's disease studied, only 3% had systolic blood pressures greater than 125 mm Hg.[29] Mucocutaneous hyperpigmentation is present in more than three fourths of patients with Addison's disease.[29,30] Melanin deposits usually occur in areas of trauma or friction, such as the palms, soles, elbows, knees, buccal mucosa, and old scars.[31]

Patients with adrenal insufficiency may also suffer orthostatic hypotension with episodes of postural syncope (Chapter 7). More than half of such patients also exhibit nausea, vomiting, and other nonspecific gastrointestinal symptoms.[30] Anorexia is present almost universally and results in the weight loss that inevitably accompanies chronic adrenal insufficiency.[31] Two thirds of patients with adrenal insufficiency have hypoglycemia.[29,30] Symptoms are those normally associated with hypoglycemia (see Chapter 17), including tachycardia, perspiration, weakness, nausea, vomiting, headache, convulsions, and coma.[32] Electrolyte disturbances are almost always evident in these patients, including hyponatremia in 88% of cases, hyperkalemia in 64% of cases, and hypercalcemia in 6% to 33% of cases.[29,30,33,34]

In the dental setting, the acute episode will be marked most notably by a progressively severe mental confusion. The individual also experiences intense pain in the abdomen, lower back, and legs, and the cardiovascular system progressively deteriorates. This latter symptom may result in a loss of consciousness and onset of coma. (Coma is a state in which a patient is totally unresponsive or is unresponsive to all except very painful stimuli; the patient in such a state immediately returns to the state of unresponsiveness when the stimulus is removed.)

If not managed properly, acute adrenal insufficiency may result in death. Mortality is usually secondary to hypoglycemia or hypotension. Most individuals do not lose consciousness immediately. The progressive mental confusion and other clinical symptoms usually permit the prompt recognition of the problem and the immediate initiation of proper management.

■ PATHOPHYSIOLOGY
Normal adrenal function

Adrenocortical steroid hormones affect all bodily tissues and organs helping keep the body's internal environment constant (a condition known as *homeostasis*) through their actions on the metabolism of carbohydrates, fats, proteins, water, and electrolytes. The body provides a minimal supply of corticosteroid hormones (approximately 20 mg cortisol daily in nonstressed adults[35]) through the actions of adrenocorticotropic hormone (ACTH), which is released by the anterior portion of the pituitary gland. ACTH levels in the blood control the adrenal cortex and the production of all steroids except aldosterone.

In nonstressed situations the level of circulating cortisol regulates the rate of ACTH secretion; a high level suppresses ACTH secretion, whereas a low circulating cortisol level permits its more rapid secretion (Figure 8-2A and B). The mechanism is relatively slow acting and does not account for the rapid increase in

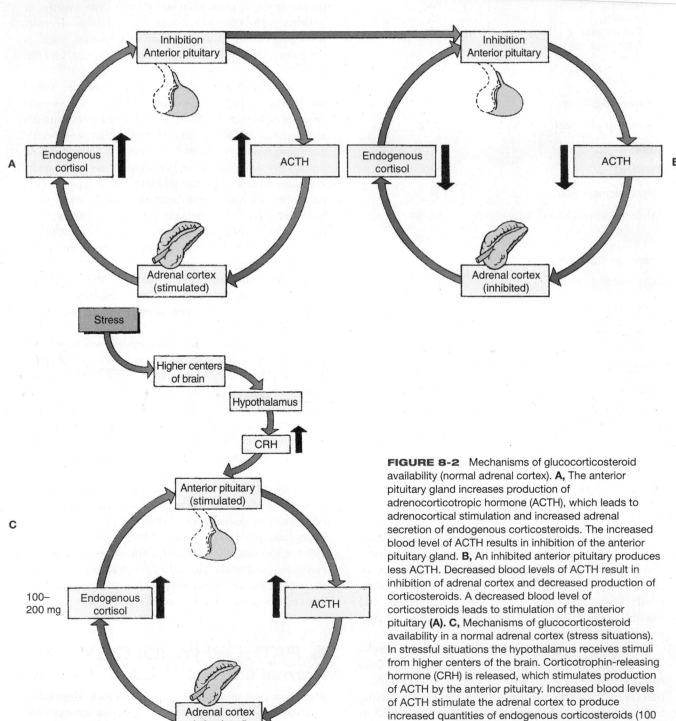

FIGURE 8-2   Mechanisms of glucocorticosteroid availability (normal adrenal cortex). **A,** The anterior pituitary gland increases production of adrenocorticotropic hormone (ACTH), which leads to adrenocortical stimulation and increased adrenal secretion of endogenous corticosteroids. The increased blood level of ACTH results in inhibition of the anterior pituitary gland. **B,** An inhibited anterior pituitary produces less ACTH. Decreased blood levels of ACTH result in inhibition of adrenal cortex and decreased production of corticosteroids. A decreased blood level of corticosteroids leads to stimulation of the anterior pituitary **(A). C,** Mechanisms of glucocorticosteroid availability in a normal adrenal cortex (stress situations). In stressful situations the hypothalamus receives stimuli from higher centers of the brain. Corticotrophin-releasing hormone (CRH) is released, which stimulates production of ACTH by the anterior pituitary. Increased blood levels of ACTH stimulate the adrenal cortex to produce increased quantities of endogenous corticosteroids (100 to 200 mg cortisol) required for stress adaptation.

blood ACTH levels observed during stressful situations. A second factor regulating the secretion of ACTH is the individual's sleep schedule. Plasma ACTH levels begin to rise at 2 a.m. in individuals who sleep at night, reaching peak levels at the time of awakening. They fall during the day, reaching their ebb during the evening. These fluctuations in cortisol blood levels, a process known as *diurnal variation,* is reversed in individuals who work at night and sleep during the day.

In stressful situations, the pituitary gland rapidly increases the release of ACTH, and the adrenal cortex responds within minutes by synthesizing and secreting increased amounts of various corticosteroids. This increased steroid production prepares the body to successfully manage the stressful situation; it increases the metabolic rate and the retention of sodium and water, while making small blood vessels increasingly responsive to the actions of norepinephrine.

To rapidly raise the levels of corticosteroids in the blood, a third mechanism must be activated (Figure 8-2C). When the central nervous system receives stressful stimuli, these stimuli reach the level of the hypothalamus, which releases a substance known as *corticotrophin-releasing hormone* (CRH). The hypothalamic-hypophyseal portal venous system transports CRH to the anterior lobes of the pituitary gland, where it stimulates the secretion of ACTH into the circulation, which then allows the adrenal cortex to increase its secretion of corticosteroids. Cortisol secretion begins within minutes and continues for as long as the plasma ACTH level is maintained. Once ACTH secretion ceases (e.g., when the stressor is removed), plasma ACTH concentration has a half-life of 10 minutes; once cortisol secretion ceases, the plasma cortisol level drops during a half-life of 1 to 2 hours.

Adrenal insufficiency

Patients with primary adrenocortical insufficiency (Addison's disease) have hypofunctioning adrenal cortices and cannot produce the blood levels of corticosteroids necessary to maintain life even at nonstressful levels. For this reason either oral or parenteral glucocorticosteroid replacement therapy is required.

Figure 8-3 shows the feedback mechanisms operating in the patient with Addison's disease. Corticosteroid blood levels are fixed, depending on the total milligram dose administered during the day. As a general rule, a normal adult secretes 20 mg cortisol per day; thus replacement therapy for patients with Addison's disease is approximately 20 mg exogenous cortisol (hydrocortisone) daily. The drug may be administered orally or parenterally in single or, more commonly, in divided doses. The hypofunctioning adrenal cortex cannot respond

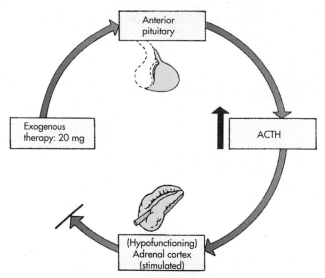

FIGURE 8-3 Corticosteroid levels in an individual with primary insufficiency (Addison's disease). The anterior pituitary gland secretes adrenocorticotropic hormone (ACTH), which stimulates the adrenal cortex. A hypofunctioning adrenal cortex cannot synthesize and secrete the required level of cortisol. Blood levels of corticosteroids do not fluctuate in response to ACTH levels; they are fixed by exogenous doses of approximately 20 mg cortisol daily.

to increases or decreases in blood levels of ACTH, which the anterior pituitary continues to secrete.

In the patient with a normal adrenal cortex who is receiving glucocorticosteroid therapy for a non–endocrine-related disorder, the total amount of endogenous and exogenous steroid determines the blood level of cortisol. Initially, the adrenal cortex continues to secrete approximately 20 mg cortisol daily, to which may be added doses of more than 50 mg exogenous glucocorticosteroids. The effect of this elevation of glucocorticosteroid levels in the blood is to inhibit ACTH secretion, which in turn inhibits the adrenal cortex from secreting cortisol.

As glucocorticosteroid therapy continues, the ability of the adrenal glands to produce endogenous glucocorticoids decreases and a variable degree of disuse atrophy develops (Figure 8-4A). If exogenous therapy is stopped abruptly, or on rare occasions even after a gradual withdrawal, the blood level of cortisol falls; this stimulates the anterior pituitary to produce increased blood levels of ACTH, which in turn stimulates production of cortisol by the adrenal cortex.

At this time ACTH and endogenous corticosteroid levels may prove deficient (see Figure 8-4B). The adrenal cortex cannot produce the required cortisol levels, and a hypoadrenal state ensues. Any increased requirement for cortisol, such as occurs in a stressful situation, may provoke acute adrenal insufficiency. Although the adrenal cortex usually returns to normal function within

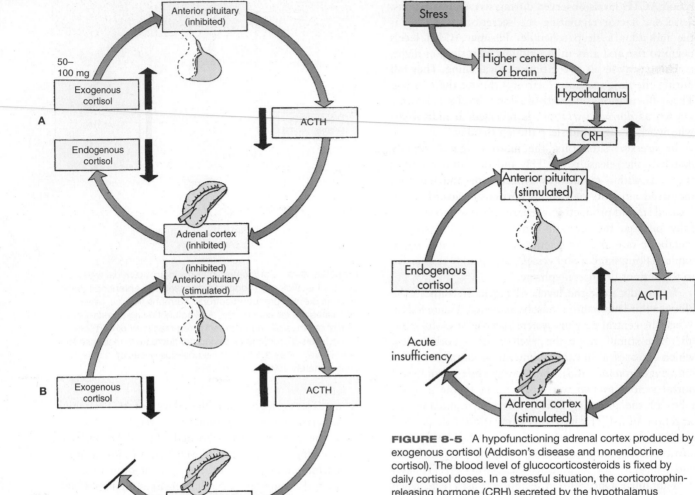

FIGURE 8-4 Glucocorticosteroid levels in an individual with secondary insufficiency due to exogenous therapy. **A,** If additional exogenous glucocorticosteroids are administered to an individual with a normal adrenal cortex, blood levels are increased significantly. Adrenocorticotropic hormone (ACTH) production by the anterior pituitary is inhibited, resulting in inhibition of adrenal cortical function. Inhibition of both ACTH and corticosteroid production continues for the duration of the exogenous therapy. **B,** After a prolonged period of exogenous therapy (2 weeks or longer), disuse atrophy of the adrenal cortex and anterior pituitary develops. After therapy is terminated, blood levels of corticosteroids fall, stimulating the anterior pituitary to produce ACTH. ACTH production may be subnormal; even if it is normal, the adrenal cortex's response may be inadequate. Blood cortisol levels are inadequate, and the patient enters a stress-intolerant state.

FIGURE 8-5 A hypofunctioning adrenal cortex produced by exogenous cortisol (Addison's disease and nonendocrine cortisol). The blood level of glucocorticosteroids is fixed by daily cortisol doses. In a stressful situation, the corticotrophin-releasing hormone (CRH) secreted by the hypothalamus induces adrenocorticotropic hormone (ACTH) secretion by the anterior pituitary, which in turn stimulates the adrenal cortex. The anterior pituitary or the adrenal cortex may not be able to function properly, leading to inadequate cortisol blood levels for stress adaptation. Acute insufficiency results.

A patient with adrenal hypofunction—either primary (Addison's disease) or secondary (exogenous glucocorticosteroid therapy)—receives a fixed level of glucocorticosteroids during therapy (Figure 8-5). In stressful situations the patient cannot increase this level in response to the increasing ACTH levels in the blood, produced as a result of CRH released from the hypothalamus; thus, the clinical manifestations of acute adrenal insufficiency develop. Management of this situation requires replacement and augmentation of low blood levels of steroids.

Hypotension observed in patients with adrenal insufficiency is the result of several mechanisms. A deficiency in cortisol can lead to hypotension even in patients who have normal volumes of circulating blood. Direct depression of myocardial contractility and reduction in

2 to 4 weeks of cessation of glucocorticosteroid therapy, in some instances it may require more than a year.[13] As a general rule, the longer the duration of glucocorticosteroid therapy and the larger the doses during therapy, the longer the recovery period.

myocardial responsiveness to catecholamines together produce hypotension.[36,37]

About two thirds of individuals who demonstrate adrenal insufficiency become hypoglycemic. Glucose levels are less than 45 mg/dL. Hypoglycemia is the result of a decrease in gluconeogenesis and increased peripheral use of glucose secondary to lipolysis.[38,39]

In addition, hyperpigmentation is common in patients with chronic primary adrenal insufficiency and is produced by compensatory secretion of ACTH and melanin-stimulating hormone.[29,30] The condition develops over a period of several months when relative adrenal insufficiency is present; individuals with secondary adrenal insufficiency do not exhibit hyperpigmentation.

■ MANAGEMENT

Acute adrenal insufficiency is a life-threatening situation. Effective management requires that the doctor follow the steps of basic life support (BLS) and administer glucocorticosteroids. Glucocorticoid deficiency, depletion of extracellular fluid, and hyperkalemia place the patient in immediate danger. Treatment is predicated on the prompt correction of these conditions.

Conscious patient

Step 1: termination of dental treatment. As soon as the individual exhibits signs and symptoms of possible acute adrenal insufficiency, dental treatment should cease. Acute adrenal insufficiency should be suspected in patients who exhibit mental confusion, nausea, vomiting, and abdominal pain and who currently are receiving glucocorticosteroids or have received 20 mg or more cortisone (or its equivalent) via oral or parenteral administration for 2 weeks or longer within the past 2 years (Box 8-4).

Step 2: P (position). If the patient appears mentally confused, wet, and clammy (signs and symptoms of hypotension), he or she should be placed in the supine position with the legs elevated slightly. If the patient does not exhibit any of these signs and symptoms, comfort should determine the position.

supine or comfortable

Step 3: A→B→C (airway-breathing-circulation [BLS]), as needed. In the conscious patient, A→B→C are assessed but need not be employed.

Step 4: D (definitive care).
Step 4a: monitoring of vital signs. The blood pressure and heart rate should be monitored at 5-minute intervals throughout the episode. The individual usually

Box 8-4 Criteria for a determination of adrenal insufficiency
History of current or recent long-term steroid use Mental confusion Nausea and vomiting Abdominal pain Hypotension

exhibits hypotension with an increased heart rate (tachycardia).

Step 4b: summoning of medical assistance. The appropriate team member should seek medical assistance as soon as possible. Because the victim is still conscious, it may be wise to contact the patient's primary care physician, if this can be accomplished expeditiously. In most cases emergency personnel will transport the patient immediately to the emergency department of a hospital where more definitive management may be instituted. If hospitalization is required, the doctor should accompany the patient.

Step 4c: emergency kit and oxygen (O₂). The appropriate team member should obtain the emergency kit and portable O_2 immediately. O_2 may be administered via a full-face mask or nasal hood at a flow of approximately 5 to 10 L per minute. *or 4-6 L/min*

Step 4d: administration of glucocorticosteroid. The corticosteroid (if available) and a plastic disposable syringe should be removed from the emergency kit. If the patient has a history of chronic adrenal insufficiency, the doctor may administer the patient's own corticosteroid medication (using the patient's emergency syringe). A corticosteroid is not considered a critical (essential) emergency drug because the incidence of acute adrenal insufficiency is low, and medical assistance is usually available within a relatively short period.

If the patient is known to suffer chronic adrenal insufficiency, the administration of 100 mg hydrocortisone sodium succinate is the next immediate step. The drug should be readministered every 6 to 8 hours.[40] Hydrocortisone sodium succinate (Solu-Cortef) is available as an unmixed powder and liquid in a 2-mL Mix-o-vial (Figure 8-6). When the solution is mixed, each milliliter contains 50 mg hydrocortisone. To mix the solution, the top plastic cap is removed and the rubber plunger is depressed. This combines the powder and liquid. The vial is then mixed until a clear solution forms. The syringe then is inserted through the rubber stopper and 2 mL of solution withdrawn. If possible, the 100 mg

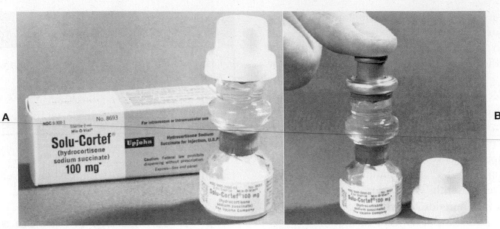

FIGURE 8-6 **A,** Corticosteroid. **B,** Preparation of corticosteroid for use. Depression of the plunger mixes the powder and liquid so that fresh solution is immediately available for use.

hydrocortisone should be administered intravenously over a period of 30 seconds. However, the IM route may be used with 100 mg (2 mL) injected into the vastus lateralis or mid-deltoid areas.

If the patient neither has a prior history of adrenal insufficiency nor is using glucocorticosteroids, the dentist should manage the patient as described in steps 1 through 4c and await the arrival of emergency personnel.

However, as the immediate diagnosis of acute adrenal insufficiency is empiric (based on the presenting signs and symptoms), it is often recommended that corticosteroid therapy be initiated immediately, even before the diagnosis is confirmed by laboratory testing (ACTH stimulation test).* In the office of a doctor with proper training and experience, 4 mg dexamethasone phosphate should be administered through the IV route every 6 to 8 hours while awaiting the ACTH stimulation test.[41] Dexamethasone is approximately 100 times more potent than cortisol.

Step 5: additional management. In most cases of adrenal insufficiency in which the patient retains consciousness, the administration of BLS as needed, O_2, and glucocorticosteroids is adequate to stabilize the patient. Emergency medical personnel will establish an IV line when they arrive and administer additional drugs after confirming the diagnosis. These additional drugs include IV fluids to counteract depletion of the body's circulating fluid (hypovolemia) and hypotension,

which are usually present in adrenal insufficiency. A patient with Addison's disease may be up to 20% volume depleted.[41]

Unless it is contraindicated by the patient's cardiovascular condition, 1 L of normal saline should be infused in the first hour. A 5% dextrose solution usually is added next to help combat the hypoglycemia. The individual may require up to 3 L of fluid over the first 8 hours. Hypoglycemia must also be treated immediately and aggressively. If the individual is symptomatic or if a finger-stick blood glucose test demonstrates low glucose levels (45 mg/dL), 50 to 100 mL of a 50% dextrose solution should be administered. If an IV line is unavailable, 1 to 2 mg glucagon may be administered through an IM route.

Unconscious patient

When a patient loses consciousness, the doctor may not, at the outset, be aware of the patient's medical history of adrenal insufficiency or glucocorticosteroid therapy.

Step 1: recognition of unconsciousness. The shake-and-shout method—yelling "Are you all right?"—is used to determine the individual's level of consciousness. Unconsciousness is determined by a lack of response to this sensory stimulation.

Step 2: P. The patient should be placed in the supine position with the legs elevated slightly.

Step 3: A→B→C (BLS). Immediately implement the steps of BLS (see Chapter 5). These include use of head tilt–chin lift, assessment of the airway and breathing, artificial ventilation (if necessary), and assessment of circulation.

---

*In the ATCH stimulation test, 0.25 mg cosyntropin, a synthetic ACTH, is administered at time 0. To measure the patient's cortisol level, serum samples are drawn at time 0, then in 1 hour, and finally in 6 to 8 hours. Normal adrenal glands respond with increases in cortisol of at least 10 mg/fl, or three times the baseline level.

In most instances of acute adrenal insufficiency, the victim demonstrates depressed respiration and blood pressure and a rapid but weak (thready) pulse. Airway maintenance and O_2 administration are necessary in virtually all cases. In the unlikely occurrence of an absent pulse, external chest compression must be initiated immediately and continued until assistance arrives or a palpable pulse returns spontaneously.

Step 4: D (definitive care).

Step 4a: emergency kit and O_2. The designated team member should bring the office kit and O_2 to the site of the emergency. O_2 may be administered through a positive-pressure face mask or nasal hood. Aromatic spirits of ammonia may also be used because differentiation between acute adrenal insufficiency and other, more common causes of unconsciousness (e.g., vasodepressor syncope) may be difficult at this early stage. The patient with adrenal insufficiency will not respond to the inhalation of aromatic ammonia.

Positioning of the patient, maintenance of an adequate airway, and use of aromatic ammonia and O_2 will not lead to a noticeable improvement of the patient suffering acute adrenal insufficiency. Where the patient's condition does not improve, additional steps should be considered:

Step 4b: summoning of emergency medical assistance. If the patient remains unconscious after the preceding steps are implemented, the unconsciousness is most likely not caused by one of the more commonly encountered conditions, such as vasodepressor syncope or orthostatic hypotension. At this point the appropriate team member should summon emergency medical assistance.

Step 4c: evaluation of medical history. While BLS is being administered and emergency assistance is on the way, a member of the emergency team should review the patient's medical history for clues to a possible cause. If the cause is not obvious, the dental office team should continue to implement the steps of BLS until emergency assistance arrives. If evidence exists that glucocorticosteroid insufficiency may be the cause of unconsciousness, treatment should proceed to step 4d.

Step 4d: administration of glucocorticosteroid. Individuals with suspected adrenal insufficiency should receive 100 mg hydrocortisone via IV or IM administration. If possible, 100 mg should be injected by the IV route over a period of 30 seconds. An IV infusion should be started, and an IV solution to which 100 mg of hydrocortisone is added should be administered over 2 hours. If the IV route is unavailable, the individual may receive 100 mg hydrocortisone intramuscularly.

Step 4e: additional drug therapy. If hypotension also is present, an IV infusion of 1 L of normal saline or a 5% dextrose solution should be administered over 1 hour while awaiting emergency assistance.

Step 5: transfer to hospital. After emergency personnel arrive, they will stabilize the victim before transferring him or her to a medical facility, where emergency physicians obtain blood specimens and correct existing electrolyte imbalances, such as hyperkalemia and hypoglycemia.

Definitive therapy is designed to meet the needs of the individual patient but consists initially of large IV doses of glucocorticosteroids followed by additional doses of oral or IM steroids, or both. Again, if the possibility exists that the loss of consciousness is related in any way to corticosteroid deficiency, the immediate administration of 100 mg hydrocortisone succinate may save the patient's life. If no such indications exist, the doctor should continue with the steps of BLS until the arrival of emergency personnel.

Boxes 8-5 and 8-6 summarize the management of acute adrenal insufficiency. In addition, the following facts may prove helpful:

- **Drugs used in management:** O_2 and glucocorticosteroids

Box 8-5 Management of adrenal insufficiency: the conscious patient

ASSESS CONSCIOUSNESS
CONSCIOUS
(victim responds to stimulation)
↓
Terminate dental treatment
↓
P—Position patient comfortably if asymptomatic;
supine with feet elevated slightly, if symptomatic
↓
A → B → C—Provide BLS as needed
↓
D—Definitive care:
Monitor vital signs
Summon medical assistance
Obtain emergency kit and O_2
Administer glucocorticosteroid, if available, and if
history of adrenal insufficiency exists
↓
Consider additional management:
Provide BLS as needed
Provide O_2 as needed
Provide glucocorticosteroid as needed
Establish IV access

A, airway; **B**, breathing; BLS, basic life support; **C**, circulation;
D, definitive care; IV, intravenous; **P**, position.

Box 8-6 Management of adrenal insufficiency: the unconscious patient

ASSESS CONSCIOUSNESS
UNCONSCIOUS
(victim unresponsive to sensory stimulation)
↓
P—Position patient supine with feet elevated slightly, if symptomatic
↓
A → B → C—Provide BLS as needed
↓
D—Definitive care:
Summon medical assistance
Obtain emergency kit and O$_2$
Evaluate medical history
Monitor vital signs
↓
Consider additional management:
Provide BLS as needed
Provide O$_2$
Provide glucocorticosteroid as needed
Establish IV access if possible
↓
Transfer to hospital

A, airway; **B**, breathing; BLS, basic life support; **C**, circulation; **D**, definitive care; IV, intravenous; **P**, position.

■ **Medical assistance required:** Yes, if patient is unconscious; yes, if conscious patient with history of adrenal insufficiency shows clinical signs and symptoms of acute insufficiency

REFERENCES

1. Guyton AC: The adrenocortical hormones, In: Guyton AC, editor: *Human physiology and mechanisms of disease*, ed 5, Philadelphia, WB Saunders, 1992.
2. Findling JW: Cushing's syndromes: an enlarged clinical spectrum, *N Engl J Med* 321:1677–1678, 1989.
3. O'Riordain DS, Farley DR, Young WF Jr, et al.: Long-term outcome of bilateral adrenalectomy in patients with Cushing's syndrome, *Surgery* 116:1088–1093, 1994.
4. Zeiger MA, Nieman LK, Cutler GB, et al.: Primary bilateral adrenocortical causes of Cushing's syndrome, *Surgery* 110:1106–1115, 1991.
5. Dahlberg PJ, Goellner MH, Pehling GB: Adrenal insufficiency secondary to adrenal hemorrhage: two case reports and a review of cases confirmed by computed tomography, *Arch Intern Med* 150:905–909, 1990.
6. Vallotton MB: Endocrine emergencies: disorders of the adrenal cortex, *Baillieres Clin Endocrinol Metab* 6:41–56, 1992.
7. Oelkers W: Adrenal insufficiency, *N Engl J Med* 335:1206–1212, 1996.
8. Streeten DHP: Corticosteroid therapy. I. Pharmacological properties and principles of corticosteroid use, *JAMA* 232:944–947, 1975.
9. Kountz DS, Clark CL: Safely withdrawing patients from chronic glucocorticoid therapy, *Am Fam Phys* 55:521–525, 1997.
10. Cronin CC, Callaghan N, Kearney PJ, et al.: Addison disease in patients treated with glucocorticoid therapy, *Arch Intern Med* 157:456–458, 1997.
11. O'Donnell M: Emergency! addisonian crisis, *Am J Nurs* 97:41, 1997.
12. Bruton-Maree N, Maree SM: Acute adrenal insufficiency: a case report, *CRNA* 4:128–132, 1993.
13. Graber AL, Ney RL, Nicholson WE, et al.: Natural history of pituitary-adrenal recovery following long-term suppression with corticosteroids, *J Clin Endocrinol Metab* 25:11–16, 1965.
14. Streeten DHP: Corticosteroid therapy. II. Complications and therapeutic indications, *JAMA* 232:1046–1049, 1975.
15. Byyny R: Withdrawal from glucocorticoid therapy, *N Engl J Med* 295:30–32, 1976.
16. von Werder K, Stevens WC, Cromwell TH, et al.: Adrenal function during long-term anesthesia in man, *Proc Soc Exp Biol Med* 135:854–858, 1970.
17. Sachar EJ: Psychological factors relating to activation and inhibition of the adrenocortical stress response in man: a review. *Prog Brain Res* 32:216–324, 1970.
18. Bellet S, Roman L, DeCastro O, Herrera M: Effect of acute ethanol intake on plasma 11-hydroxycorticosteroid levels. *Metabolism* 19:664–667, 1970.
19. Jacobs HS, Nabarro JDN: Plasma 11-hydroxycorticosteroid and growth hormone levels in acute medical illnesses, *Br Med J* 2:595–598, 1969.
20. *Physicians' desk reference*, ed 59, Oradell, NJ, Medical Economics, 2005.
21. American Dental Association: *ADA guide to dental therapeutics*, ed 3, Chicago, American Dental Association, 2003.
22. Fitzgerald PA: Endocrinology. In: Tierney LM Jr., McPhee SJ, Papadakis MA, editors: *Current medical diagnosis & treatment*, ed 45, McGraw-Hill Medical, New York, 2006, pp. 1098–1193.
23. Hellmann DB, Stone JH: Arthritis and musculoskeletal disorders. In: Tierney LM Jr., McPhee SJ, Papadakis MA, editors: *Current medical diagnosis & treatment*, ed 45, McGraw-Hill Medical, New York, 2006, pp. 807–864.
24. Sertl K, Clark T, Kaliner M, editors: Corticosteroids: their biologic mechanisms and application to the treatment of asthma (symposium), *Am Rev Respir Dis* 141(suppl:1S, entire issue), 1990.
25. McCarthy FM: Adrenal insufficiency. In: McCarthy FM, editor: *Essentials of safe dentistry for the medically compromised patient*, Philadelphia, WB Saunders, 1989, pp. 171–173.
26. Melby J: Systemic corticosteroid therapy: pharmacology and endocrine considerations, *Ann Intern Med* 81:505–512, 1974.
27. Torrey SP: Recognition and management of acute adrenal emergencies, *Emerg Med Clin North Am* 23:687–702, 2005.

28. Bell H, Hayes W, Vosburgh J: Hyperkalemic paralysis due to adrenal insufficiency, *Arch Intern Med* 115:418–420, 1965.

29. Nerup J: Addison's disease—clinical studies: a report of 108 cases, *Acta Endocrinol* 76:127—141, 1974.

30. Dunlop D: Eighty-six cases of Addison's disease, *Br Med J* 2:887–891, 1963.

31. Kozak G: Primary adrenocortical insufficiency (Addison's disease), *Am Fam Physician* 15:124–135, 1977.

32. Vesely DL: Hypoglycemic coma: don't overlook adrenal crisis, *Geriatrics* 37: 71–73, 76–77, 1982.

33. Jorgensen H: Hypercalcemia in adrenocortical insufficiency, *Acta Med Scand* 193:175–179, 1973.

34. Walser M, Robinson BHB, Duckett JWL: The hypercalcemia of adrenal insufficiency, *J Clin Invest* 42:456–465, 1963.

35. Stewart PM: The adrenal cortex. In: Larsen PR, editor: *William's Textbook of Endocrinology*, ed 10, Philadelphia, WB Saunders, 2003, pp. 491–551.

36. Webb WR, Degerli IU, Hardy JD, Unal M: Cardiovascular responses in acute adrenal insufficiency, *Surgery* 58:273–282, 1965.

37. Ramey ER, Goldstein MS: The adrenal cortex and the sympathetic nervous system, *Physiol Rev* 37:155–195, 1957.

38. Liddle G: The adrenals. In: Williams RH, Foster DW, Kronenberg HM, et al., editors: *Williams' textbook of endocrinology*, Philadelphia, WB Saunders, 1981, pp. 869–880.

39. Szwed JJ, White C: Normokalemic nonazotemic adrenal insufficiency, *South Med J* 76:919–920, 1983.

40. Leshin M: Acute adrenal insufficiency: recognition, management and prevention, *Urol Clin North Am* 9:229–235, 1982.

41. Wogan JM: Endocrine disorders. In: Marx J, editor: *Rosen's emergency medicine: concepts and clinical practice*, ed 5, St. Louis, Mosby, 2002, pp. 1770–1785.

CHAPTER 9

Unconsciousness:

Differential Diagnosis

Unconsciousness, whatever its cause, must be recognized quickly and managed effectively. When unconsciousness occurs, the proximate cause may not always be immediately obvious; indeed, at the onset of unconsciousness the cause is not the primary concern. In all cases in which loss of consciousness occurs, several basic steps—those described in the preceding chapters on vasodepressor syncope, postural hypotension, and acute adrenal insufficiency—must be implemented as soon as possible. These steps comprise the primary phase of assessment and management (Box 9-1).

After implementing these steps successfully and while awaiting the arrival of emergency personnel (if necessary), dental office team members should proceed to the secondary steps of assessment and management, also termed *definitive management*. The information in this chapter will aid the team in the differential diagnosis of the cause of unconsciousness. Several clinical factors presented here may help establish a diagnosis (see Table 5-1 for common causes of loss of consciousness).

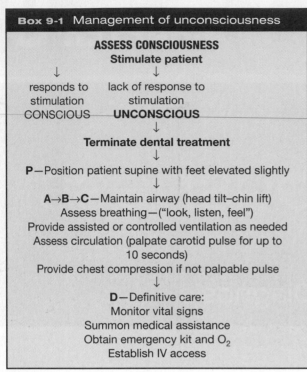

Box 9-1 Management of unconsciousness

ASSESS CONSCIOUSNESS
Stimulate patient

responds to stimulation — lack of response to stimulation

CONSCIOUS — **UNCONSCIOUS**
↓
Terminate dental treatment
↓
P—Position patient supine with feet elevated slightly
↓
A→**B**→**C**—Maintain airway (head tilt–chin lift)
Assess breathing—("look, listen, feel")
Provide assisted or controlled ventilation as needed
Assess circulation (palpate carotid pulse for up to 10 seconds)
Provide chest compression if not palpable pulse
↓
D—Definitive care:
Monitor vital signs
Summon medical assistance
Obtain emergency kit and O₂
Establish IV access

A, airway; *B*, breathing; *C*, circulation; *D*, definitive care; *IV*, intravenous; *P*, position.

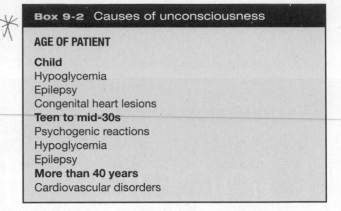

Box 9-2 Causes of unconsciousness

AGE OF PATIENT

Child
Hypoglycemia
Epilepsy
Congenital heart lesions
Teen to mid-30s
Psychogenic reactions
Hypoglycemia
Epilepsy
More than 40 years
Cardiovascular disorders

syncope) in children are infrequent because children are extremely vocal in expressing their feelings toward dentistry, releasing their tensions, and producing muscular movements: in short, they just act like children (Box 9-2)!

■ CIRCUMSTANCES ASSOCIATED WITH LOSS OF CONSCIOUSNESS

Stress, whether psychological (anxiety) or physiologic (pain), is a precipitating factor in most cases of unconsciousness that occur in dental offices. Instances in which stress may be a precipitating factor in the loss of consciousness include vasodepressor syncope, adrenal insufficiency, cerebrovascular accident, hypoglycemia, epilepsy, cardiac arrest, and myocardial infarction. However, patients may still lose consciousness in the absence of obvious stress. Postural (orthostatic) hypotension is the most common non–stress-related cause of unconsciousness; other non–stress-related causes leading to the loss of consciousness include allergic reactions, hyperglycemia (diabetic coma), and the administration or ingestion of drugs (Box 9-3).

■ POSITION OF THE PATIENT

The patient's position when unconsciousness occurs may aid in the differential diagnosis. Syncope, or the transient loss of consciousness, rarely develops when the patient is in the supine position.

However, certain instances do exist in which a patient in the supine position may lose consciousness. These include unconsciousness that occurs secondary to (1) the administration of drugs; (2) seizures in epileptic

■ AGE OF PATIENT

The age of the patient may assist in the differential diagnosis of unconsciousness. Unconsciousness occurring in a dental office in normal healthy patients in their mid- to late teens to late thirties will in almost all instances be related to psychogenic responses such as vasodepressor syncope. Two other possible causes of unconsciousness in patients under 40 years are hypoglycemia and seizures. These conditions normally are easy to differentiate from the more common causes of unconsciousness. (Other sections of this text will discuss these conditions in detail.)

In patients older than 40 years, cardiovascular complications, such as acute myocardial infarction, cerebrovascular accident, valvular lesions (e.g., aortic stenosis), or acute cardiac dysrhythmias, are more likely to precipitate unconsciousness (see Part Seven). Patients in this age group experience unconsciousness occurring secondary to psychogenic reactions much less frequently because they are more likely to have adapted to their dental fears.

Unconsciousness rarely occurs in younger children, except in the presence of specific disease states, such as diabetes mellitus (hypoglycemia), epilepsy, and congenital heart lesions. Psychogenic reactions (vasodepressor

> **Box 9-3** Circumstances associated with the loss of consciousness
>
> **STRESS PRESENT**
> Vasodepressor syncope
> Hypoglycemia
> Epilepsy
> Myocardial infarction
> Cerebrovascular accident
> Adrenal insufficiency
>
> **STRESS ABSENT**
> Postural hypotension
> Ingestion of drugs
> Allergic reactions
> Hyperglycemic reactions

> **Box 9-4** Position of patient at time syncope occurs
>
> **UPRIGHT**
> Vasodepressor syncope
> Hyperventilation (unlikely)
>
> **SUPINE TO UPRIGHT**
> Postural hypertension
>
> **SUPINE**
> Drug administration
> Seizures
> Hypoglycemia or hyperglycemia
> Cardiovascular causes

patients; (3) seizures that develop with hypoglycemic reactions; (4) hyperglycemia; (5) acute adrenal insufficiency; (6) cardiovascular disorders, including valvular disorders, dysrhythmias, myocardial infarction, and cardiac arrest; and (7) cerebral vascular accident. In such circumstances, placing the patient in the supine position does not always help the patient to regain consciousness since the primary causative factor is not related to a deficit in cerebral blood flow. Definitive management is required in all such cases.

Patients suffering from postural hypotension do not experience syncopal episodes in the supine position; however, signs and symptoms of hypotension develop rapidly when such patients assume a more upright position and reverse just as rapidly when they are returned to the supine position. Hyperventilation only rarely progresses to the loss of consciousness—and then only when the patient remains untreated in the upright position for an extended period. More commonly, hyperventilation produces a state of mental confusion, often characterized as lightheadedness and dizziness (Box 9-4).

■ PRESYNCOPAL SIGNS AND SYMPTOMS

No clinical symptoms

Rapid loss of consciousness in the absence of prodromal symptoms leads to a presumptive diagnosis of postural hypotension if the episode occurs immediately after a change in the patient's position (supine to upright). Certain drugs used in dentistry can increase the likelihood of postural hypotension (see Box 7-1). In addition, syncope secondary to cardiac dysrhythmias and heart block is usually of sudden onset and may occur without warning signs or symptoms. It may develop whether the patient is sitting or standing. On rare occasion, cardiac arrest may lead to a patient's unconsciousness without any prodromal signs and symptoms (instantaneous death); diagnosis of this situation will be established as the steps of basic life support are implemented.

Pallor and cold, clammy skin

Restlessness, pallor (loss of normal skin color), clammy (moist) skin, nausea, and vomiting are classic prodromal signs of fainting. They usually are seen in cases of vasodepressor syncope; however, individuals experiencing hypoglycemic reactions, adrenal insufficiency, and myocardial infarction also may exhibit these signs.

Tingling and numbness of the extremities

Hyperventilation, although rarely leading to syncope, may do so if the patient remains untreated and seated upright for an extended period during the episode. Hyperventilation is recognized readily through alterations in the rate (increased) and depth (increased) of breathing, as well as by the clinical symptoms of tingling and numbness of the fingers, toes, and perioral areas.

Headache

Many patients develop an intense headache at the outset of a cerebrovascular accident, especially of the hemorrhagic type. CVA

Chest pain

Chest pain or discomfort may precede the loss of consciousness in cases of angina pectoris (in which unconsciousness rarely occurs), myocardial infarction (in which cardiac arrest and loss of consciousness are more likely), or hyperventilation (rarely).

Breath odor

The smell of alcohol on the dental patient's breath is not uncommon; alcohol is probably the most frequently self-administered drug among patients trying to reduce their dental stress. The presence of alcohol on the breath should prompt the doctor to evaluate the patient for dental fears and anxieties; the doctor also should exercise caution in the use of drugs known to produce further central nervous system depression, including local anesthetics.

The loss of consciousness, under such situations, may be due to psychogenic factors or to profound central nervous system depression produced by one drug or a combination of various drugs.

The sweet, fruity odor of acetone is noticeable on the breath of patients who are hyperglycemic and ketoacidotic. In most instances, these patients will be known to have (through their medical history) type 1 diabetes.

Tonic-clonic movements and incontinence = epilepsy

Anyone who loses consciousness may exhibit tonic-clonic movements of the upper and lower extremities. This is especially likely to be noted in unconscious patients who are maintained in an upright position. Seizure-like movements in such situations are due to decreased cerebral perfusion.

Inadequate airway management, regardless of the patient's position, also induces tonic-clonic movements secondary to cerebral hypoxia (or anoxia).

Although tonic-clonic movements can occur during vasodepressor syncope, they occur only rarely if proper positioning and airway management are provided. Hypoglycemic patients also may exhibit tonic-clonic movements; in this situation, the movements are secondary to inadequate cerebral blood glucose levels. Seizures caused by nonepileptic factors are usually mild and are rarely associated with sphincter-muscle relaxation. However, a diagnosis of epilepsy is strongly suggested in most cases of seizure activity in which the patient exhibits urinary or fecal incontinence and tongue biting.

Heart rate and blood pressure

In most instances of unconsciousness, the heart rate rises above its baseline level while blood pressure decreases. For example, the blood pressure may be quite low during a hypoglycemic or hyperglycemic reaction while the heart, attempting to compensate for the decrease in blood pressure, accelerates its rate of contraction. However, vasodepressor syncope, postural

TABLE 9-1 Vital signs during unconsciousness

Cause of unconsciousness	Heart rate	Blood pressure
Hypoglycemia or hyperglycemia	↑	↓
Vasodepressor syncope	↓	↓
Postural hypotension	Baseline	↓
Cerebrovascular accident (hemorrhagic)	Variable	↑
Clinically significant dysrhythmias	Variable	↓

hypotension, and cerebrovascular accident are exceptions to these changes in vital signs.

In vasodepressor syncope, both the blood pressure and the heart rate usually decrease. A heart rate of 50 beats per minute or less is common during the syncopal phase of vasodepressor syncope. The heart rate during postural hypotension remains at approximately the baseline level, although the blood pressure drops precipitously. The pulse, as monitored in the radial, brachial, or carotid artery, is usually described as weak or thready in persons whose blood pressures are low. On the other hand, the blood pressure in the case of a hemorrhagic cerebrovascular accident may be elevated significantly (systolic pressure elevated more than diastolic pressure) and the pulse described as strong, or bounding.

In cases of clinically significant dysrhythmias, the heart rate may be variable (bradycardic, tachycardic, or baseline), but the functional output of the heart decreases to a level at which it adversely affects peripheral perfusion. The blood pressure is almost always depressed in such situations (Table 9-1).

Duration of unconsciousness and recovery

The response or lack of response of the patient to the basic steps (P→A→B→C [position→airway→breathing →circulation]) of emergency management can provide a wealth of significant diagnostic information. Unconsciousness produced by vasodepressor syncope is usually reversed within a few seconds once the patient is placed into the supine position (Box 9-5). In the recovery period, the patient does not return to a normal state rapidly. More frequently, signs and symptoms of shivering, sweating, headache, and fatigue are present.

Patients who suffer postural hypotension normally regain consciousness rapidly after assuming the supine position. Recovery from postural hypotension is more

> **Box 9-5** Duration of syncope with basic life support
>
> **SHORT**
> Postural hypotension
> Vasodepressor syncope
> Cardiac dysrhythmias
>
> **PROLONGED**
> Hypoglycemia
> Hyperglycemia
> Adrenal insufficiency
> Cardiac dysrhythmias

thorough and rapid than recovery from vasodepressor syncope; residual signs and symptoms are entirely absent or much less intense.

Syncope secondary to cardiac dysrhythmias also reverses quickly following correction of the underlying rhythm disturbance; the patient usually is alert on recovery. The duration of syncope is related to the duration of the dysrhythmia.

Syncope produced through a mechanism other than a lack of adequate cerebral blood flow is not readily reversed with changes. Epileptic patients' seizures usually terminate after a few moments; however, these patients may remain somnolent and often develop intense headaches during recovery. Significant tonic-clonic seizure activity does not usually occur during vasodepressor syncope or postural hypotension, although this may occur in isolated instances.

Basic life support alone will not reverse unconsciousness secondary to alterations in the blood's composition, such as that after drug administration, hypoglycemia, hyperglycemia, or adrenal insufficiency (see Box 9-6). Although proper implementation of these steps (basic life support) is absolutely critical to the patient's survival, definitive management involving specific drug therapy is necessary in each case for the patient to regain consciousness. (These situations will be described in detail in subsequent chapters.)

PART 3

RESPIRATORY DISTRESS

10   Respiratory Distress: General Considerations

11   Foreign Body Airway Obstruction

12   Hyperventilation

13   Asthma

14   Heart Failure and Acute Pulmonary Edema

15   Respiratory Distress: Differential Diagnosis

Respiratory Distress:

General Considerations

To a conscious person, difficulty with breathing is very disconcerting. This section focuses on several common causes of respiratory distress, including hyperventilation, asthma (bronchospasm), and pulmonary edema.

Because the person in respiratory distress usually remains conscious throughout the episode, this section also discusses the extremely important psychological aspects of patient management. Box 10-1 lists terms and definitions relevant to the discussion of respiratory distress.[1]

In almost all medical emergencies involving the loss of consciousness, some degree of airway obstruction is present. The primary cause of airway obstruction is mechanical—the tongue falling into the hypopharynx as skeletal muscle tone is lost. Two steps of basic life support—**A** (airway) and **B** (breathing)—are designed to manage this problem. (Chapter 11 expands on the management of airway obstruction.)

■ PREDISPOSING FACTORS

Table 10-1 lists potential causes of acute respiratory distress.[1] In most of these situations a patient does not exhibit respiratory distress unless an underlying medical disorder becomes acutely exacerbated. Acute myocardial infarction, anaphylaxis, cerebrovascular accident, hyperglycemia, and hypoglycemia are examples.

Awareness of all medical disorders the patient has helps the doctor to modify treatment so as to prevent or minimize exacerbation of that underlying condition. However, in some situations, such as asthma and heart failure, in which the patient suffers from chronic respiratory problems. Patients with these disorders, particularly heart failure, may experience difficulty breathing at all times. In such cases the doctor's role in preventing the worsening of these disorders during dental treatment becomes vitally important.

A major factor leading to the exacerbation of respiratory disorders is undue stress, either physiologic or psychological. Indeed, hyperventilation and vasodepressor syncope—among the most frequently encountered emergency situations in dentistry—are almost exclusively manifestations of extreme psychological stress. Psychological stress associated with dental treatment is a primary factor in exacerbation of preexisting medical problems. Although respiratory distress in pediatric patients rarely is attributable to hyperventilation or vasodepressor syncope, children with asthma may exhibit acute episodes of bronchospasm when they are faced with stressful situations, such as dental treatment.

Box 10-1 Terms related to respiratory distress

Anoxia: Absence of oxygen (O_2).

Apnea: Absence of respiratory movement.

Dyspnea: A subjective sense of shortness of breath; a difficulty in breathing often referred to as "air hunger."

Hyperpnea: Greater-than-normal, per-minute ventilation that just meets metabolic demands.

Hyperventilation: Ventilation that exceeds metabolic demands; $PaCO_2$ less than 35 torr.

Hypoventilation: Ventilation that does not meet metabolic demands; $PaCO_2$ more than 45 torr.

Hypoxia: Deficiency of O_2 in inspired air.

Orthopnea: Inability to breathe except in the upright position.

$PaCO_2$: Arterial carbon dioxide tension (normal, 35 to 45 torr).

PaO_2: Arterial O_2 tension (normal [air], 75 to 100 torr).

Respiration: Process of gas exchange whereby the body gains O_2 and loses carbon dioxide.

Tachypnea: Greater than normal respiratory rate.

Torr Unit of pressure equal to 1 mm Hg (named for Torricelli).

Ventilation, alveolar: Volume of air exchanged per minute.

$$\frac{Volume}{Breath} - Dead\ space \times Respiratory\ rate$$

■ PREVENTION

Adequate pretreatment medical and dental evaluations can prevent development of some respiratory problems.

TABLE 10-1 Potential causes of respiratory distress

Cause	Frequency	Text discussion
Hyperventilation	Most common	Respiratory distress (Part Three)
Vasodepressor syncope	Most common	Unconsciousness (Part Two)
Asthma	Common	Respiratory distress (Part Three)
Heart failure	Common	Respiratory distress (Part Three)
Hypoglycemia	Common	Altered consciousness (Part Four)
Overdose reaction	Less common	Drug-related emergencies (Part Six)
Acute myocardial infarction	Rare	Chest pain (Part Seven)
Anaphylaxis	Rare	Allergy (Chapter 24)
Angioneurotic edema	Rare	Allergy (Chapter 24)
Cerebrovascular accident	Rare	Altered consciousness (Part Four)
Epilepsy	Rare	Seizures (Chapter 21)
Hyperglycemia	Rare	Altered consciousness (Part Four)

If the doctor is aware of existing medical disorders that may result in respiratory distress, modifications in patient management can minimize the risk that these conditions may worsen. For example, where dental anxiety is a major factor, psychosedative procedures and other stress reduction techniques should be considered.

■ CLINICAL MANIFESTATIONS

Clinical manifestations of respiratory distress vary according to the degree of breathing difficulty present. In most cases the patient remains conscious throughout the acute episode. Although retention of consciousness is a positive sign, indicating that the patient is receiving at least the minimum amount of blood and O_2 required for normal cerebral function, it does create an additional problem—acute anxiety. For this reason the doctor managing the situation must appear calm and in control of the situation at all times.

The clinical symptoms of breathing difficulty and the sounds associated with it will vary according to the cause of the problem. Asthmatic patients often exhibit characteristic wheezing sounds produced by turbulent airflow through partially occluded bronchioles. Individuals suffering heart failure often cough and produce other sounds associated with pulmonary venous congestion. (Later chapters will discuss this in more detail, along with the differential diagnosis.)

■ PATHOPHYSIOLOGY

The syndromes responsible for respiratory distress involve various segments of the respiratory system. Bronchioles are the primary site of involvement in acute asthma. In asthmatic patients, bronchi become highly reactive, demonstrating significant smooth muscle reactivity (bronchospasm) in response to various stimuli. Clinical signs and symptoms exhibited during an acute asthmatic attack are related in large part to the restricted exchange of O_2 and carbon dioxide in the lungs.[2,3]

Patients with heart failure usually mention respiratory distress as one of their first symptoms. The chronic inability of the lungs to adequately oxygenate venous blood and the accompanying overuse of the available O_2 produces respiratory distress during heart failure.[4] This type of respiratory distress is related to an engorgement of the pulmonary veins with fluid exuding into alveolar air sacs, preventing portions of the lung from participating in ventilation (removal of carbon dioxide and absorption of O_2) and leading to many of the signs and symptoms associated with heart failure.[5]

Hyperventilation is more of a generalized problem. The primary site of this disorder is the mind (brain) of the patient, and its clinical signs and symptoms are produced by an alteration in the chemical composition of the blood. The rapid breathing (tachypnea) associated with hyperventilation results in the elimination of an excessive amount of carbon dioxide, leading to respiratory alkalosis; this, in turn, produces many of the clinical signs and symptoms exhibited in hyperventilation.[6] Successfully managed hyperventilation has no residual effect. However, heart failure and asthma, which are chronic disorders, may induce permanent changes in the respiratory system.[5,7] Therefore, patients who are at risk for acute exacerbations of asthma (bronchospasm) or heart failure (pulmonary edema) usually require special management considerations during all phases of dental treatment.

Acute foreign body (lower) airway obstruction is a potentially life-threatening situation in which a foreign body becomes impacted in the respiratory tract. The level at which the airway is obstructed determines the severity of the situation and, to some degree, the manner in which it is managed. If the object enters into either the right or left main-stem bronchus, the resulting situation is critical but not immediately life threatening. Foreign bodies most often enter the right main-stem bronchus because of the angle at which this bronchus branches off the trachea.[9] In this situation, all or part of the right lung is excluded from ventilation, but the patient can still maintain adequate ventilation with the left lung. The patient requires hospitalization, but the condition usually is not immediately life-threatening.[10]

In contrast, if the foreign object becomes impacted in the trachea, total airway obstruction ensues—an acutely life-threatening situation.[11] Immediate recognition and management are essential to prevent permanent neurologic damage or death. Figure 10-1 illustrates the sites of origin of the various respiratory disorders.

■ MANAGEMENT

Definitive management of respiratory distress depends on the doctor's prompt recognition of the problem and a determination of its probable cause (Box 10-2). This chapter focuses on the basic steps common to the management of most cases of respiratory distress.

Step 1: recognition of respiratory distress. Many respiratory disorders are associated with characteristic sounds, such as the wheezing of bronchospasm and the cough and crackling respirations (rales) of pulmonary edema. By contrast, hyperventilation does not usually produce a characteristic sound; however,

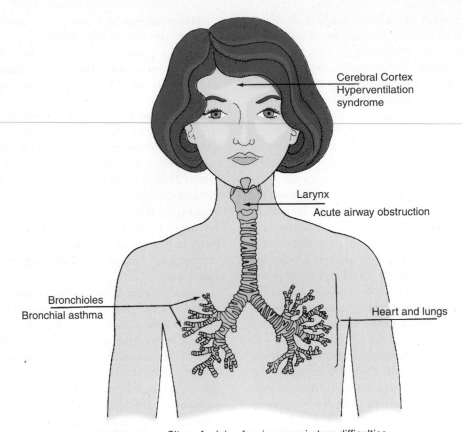

FIGURE 10-1 Sites of origin of various respiratory difficulties.

Cerebral Cortex
Hyperventilation syndrome

Larynx
Acute airway obstruction

Bronchioles
Bronchial asthma

Heart and lungs

Box 10-2 Management of respiratory distress

Recognize respiratory distress
Sounds: wheeze, cough, crackling, abnormal rate or depth of breathing
↓
Discontinue dental treatment
↓
P—Position patient in supine, if unconscious or comfortably (usually upright) if conscious
↓
A → B → C—Assess and provide basic life support, as needed
↓
D—Monitor vital signs: blood pressure, heart rate, respiratory rate
Manage patient's anxiety
Provide definitive management of respiratory distress
Activate emergency medical services as needed

A, airway; **B,** breathing; **C,** circulation; **D,** definitive care; **P,** position

---

hyperventilating patients appear—and actually are—acutely anxious and unable to control their breathing.

Step 2: discontinue dental procedure. Dental treatment should cease as soon as respiratory distress is recognized. Because stress is a primary precipitating factor in most respiratory-related situations, the cessation of treatment may improve the patient's clinical signs and symptoms significantly.

Step 3: P (position) the patient. In conscious patients experiencing respiratory distress, positioning is based on the comfort of the patient. In the presence of near-normal or slightly elevated blood pressure (as is almost always the case in situations of respiratory distress), most persons feel more in control of their breathing in an upright (sitting or standing) position. However, patients can be maintained in this position only as long as they remain conscious.

Step 4: A-B-C (airway-breathing-circulation), basic life support, as needed. Patients in respiratory distress often experience two major problems—primary breathing difficulty initially induced by their fear of dentistry and the added problem of increased anxiety produced by their inability to breathe normally. In the unlikely event that respiratory distress leads to unconsciousness, the patient must be placed immediately into the supine position and the steps in the management of unconsciousness followed.

Step 5: D (definitive care). Response of the victim to the steps of basic life support determines additional management.

Step 5a: monitoring of vital signs. The individual's blood pressure, heart rate (pulse), and respiratory rate should be measured at frequent intervals (every 5 minutes, if possible) throughout the episode and recorded in a permanent record.

Step 5b: definitive management of anxiety. The doctor should keep the patient as comfortable as possible and begin to manage anxiety by speaking calmly but firmly to the patient. The patient's collar or other tight garments may be loosened, enabling the patient to breathe more easily (even if the "ease" in breathing is purely psychological).

Step 5c: definitive management of respiratory distress. After assessing the patient's cardiovascular status, the doctor may begin to manage the cause of the patient's breathing problem. (The following chapters will focus in large part on such management procedures and on the most common causes of respiratory distress.)

Step 5d: activate emergency medical service as needed. At any time during the episode of respiratory distress the doctor may activate emergency medical services, if indicated.

REFERENCES

1. Simon AH: *Elsevier's dictionary of medicine*. St. Louis, Elsevier, 2004.
2. Frieri M: Asthma concepts in the new millennium: update in asthma pathophysiology, *Asthma Allerg Proc* 26:83–88, 2005.
3. Agrawal DK, Bharadwaj A: Allergic airway inflammation, *Curr Allerg Asthma Reports* 5:142–148, 2005.
4. Wang CS, Fitzgerald JM, Schulzer M, et al.: Does the dyspneic patient in the emergency department have congestive heart failure? *JAMA* 294:1944–1956, 2005.
5. Apstein CS, Lorell BH: The physiological basis of left ventricular diastolic dysfunction, *J Card Surg* 3:475–485, 1988.
6. Masaoka Y, Jack S, Warburton CJ, Homma I: Breathing patterns associated with trait anxiety and breathlessness in humans, *Jpn J Physiol* 54:465–470, 2004.
7. Djukanovic R, Roche WR, Wilson JW, et al.: Mucosal inflammation in asthma, *Am Rev Respir Dis* 142:434–457, 1990.
8. Kay M, Wyllie R: Pediatric foreign bodies and their management, *Gastroenter Rep* 7:212–218, 2005.
9. Bhatia PL: Problems in the management of aspirated foreign bodies, *West Afr J Med* 10:158—167, 1991.
10. Uremura MC: Foreign body ingestion in children, *Am Fam Physician* 72:287–291, 2005.
11. Heimlich HJ, Patrick EA: The Heimlich maneuver: best technique for saving any choking victim's life, *Postgrad Med* 87:38–48, 53, 1990.

CHAPTER 11

Foreign Body Airway Obstruction

Because of its frequently sudden and critical nature, acute foreign body airway obstruction must be recognized and managed quickly.

During dental treatment there is great potential for objects to fall into the posterior portion of the oral cavity and subsequently into the pharynx. Indeed, a variety of devices and objects are recovered from the throats of patients each year.[1-4] I am aware of the recovery of the head of a pedodontic handpiece, mouth mirror heads, and gold crowns—either orally or from stool specimens—after they had been swallowed accidentally. Published reports have documented the retrieval of rubber dam clamps, endodontic instruments, teeth, a post and core, and a crucifix.[1,5-8]

In the conscious dental patient, chances are that any object lost in the pharynx will be swallowed and pass into the esophagus or will be recovered after being coughed up, so that the actual incidence of acute airway obstruction or aspiration into the trachea and lung is low. A high probability also exists that any object entering into the airway is small enough in diameter to pass through the larynx (the narrowest portion of the upper airway in the adult) without causing an obstruction. In this situation the object continues through the trachea (if gravity assists) and comes to rest in a portion of one of the main-stem bronchi or smaller bronchioles in the lung.

While an acutely life-threatening situation does not immediately exist, certain important steps must be initiated immediately to ensure removal of the object within a reasonable time to avoid serious consequences. The possibility does exist, however, that a foreign object may become lodged in the larynx and obstruct the trachea. Therefore, all dental office personnel must become familiar with proper management of acute upper-airway obstruction.

The National Safety Council reported that 4313 individuals in the United States died as a result of acute airway obstruction in 2000.[9] More than 90% of deaths from foreign body aspiration in the pediatric age group occur in children younger than 5 years; 65% of those deaths occur in infants.[10] Commonly aspirated items include hot dogs, rounded candies, nuts, grapes, coins, toys, and other hard, colorful objects.[11-14] Baby aspirin, with a diameter of 7.5 mm, has obstructed airways and caused subsequent deaths in several young children.[15] (The diameter of the glottic opening is about 6.5 mm in a 2-year-old.[16])

Following evaluation of clinical research, the American Heart Association published recommendations for techniques of management of the obstructed airway in infants, children, and adults.[10] This chapter presents these recommendations.

In most cases the foreign body causing the acute airway obstruction is lodged firmly in the airway where it can neither be seen nor felt through the mouth without the use of special equipment, such as a laryngoscope or a pair of Magill intubation forceps (items that are not normally available in the dental office). The doctor therefore must be able to recognize the problem instantly and act rapidly to dislodge the object.

Acute airway obstruction is the major cause of nontraumatic cardiac arrest in infants and children.[17] Survival rates from cardiac arrest in infants and children are low (2% to 17%),[18] and a majority of survivors are neurologically devastated.[19]

■ PREVENTION

In spite of the best efforts at prevention, small objects, such as inlays, alloy, burs, or pieces of debris, may fall into the oropharynx of a patient and may subsequently be swallowed or aspirated. The introduction of sit-down dentistry, in which the patient is placed in a semisupine or supine position during treatment, has increased the likelihood of such an incident occurring.

When objects are swallowed, they usually enter the gastrointestinal (GI) tract. During the act of swallowing, the epiglottis seals the tracheal opening so that liquid and solid materials do not enter the trachea. The esophagus is the most likely site in the GI tract for objects to become impacted because of its nature—the esophagus is a collapsed tube through which liquids and solids are forced (Figure 11-1).[20] More than 90% of swallowed foreign objects that successfully pass through the esophagus into the stomach and intestines pass completely through the GI tract without complications.[21]

However, complications are associated with both swallowed and aspirated objects. Swallowed objects entering the GI tract have produced GI blockage, peritoneal abscess, perforation, and peritonitis.[22] Objects aspirated into either the right or left main-stem bronchus can produce infection, lung abscess, pneumonia, and atelectasis.[23] In a discussion of prevention of aspiration, Barkmeier et al.[24] urged the use of two major preventive measures—a rubber dam and oral packing. These measures significantly minimize the occurrence of swallowed foreign objects. Other preventive measures include patient positioning, the dental assistant, suction, Magill intubation forceps, and the use of ligature (Box 11-1).

Rubber dam

A rubber dam effectively isolates the operative field from the oral cavity and airway, preventing foreign objects from being swallowed (Figure 11-2). The use of rubber dams is recommended in all possible situations. Unfortunately, use of the rubber dam during many dental procedures, such as periodontics and surgery, is not feasible.

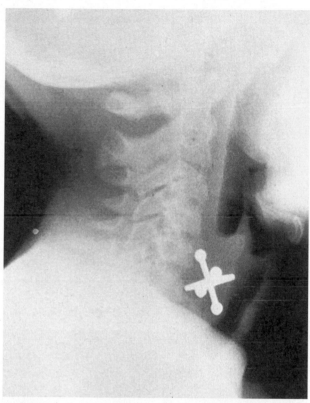

FIGURE 11-1 Radiograph of a child with a metal jack in the esophagus.

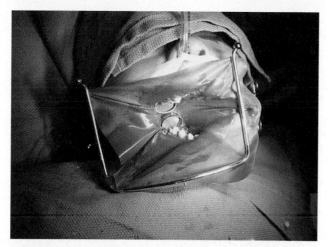

FIGURE 11-2 The use of a rubber dam helps prevent foreign objects from entering the airway.

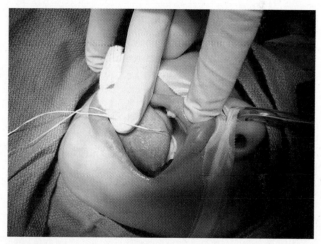

FIGURE 11-3 A pharyngeal curtain, created by spreading 3-inch by 3-inch gauze pads across the posterior portion of the oral cavity effectively prevents small particles or liquids from entering the airway.

Box 11-1 Instruments and techniques used to prevent aspiration and swallowing of objects
Rubber dam Oral packing Chair position Dental assistant Suction Magill intubation forceps Ligature (dental floss)

Oral packing

A pharyngeal curtain, created by the spreading of 4-inch by 4-inch gauze pads across the posterior portion of the oral cavity, effectively prevents small particles or liquids from entering into the airway (Figure 11-3). The pharyngeal curtain is especially useful for patients who are sedated (oral, intramuscular, intranasal, or intravenous sedation) or receiving general anesthesia in whom protective airway reflexes may be compromised. The unsedated patient does not normally tolerate oral packing because it may interfere with swallowing or restrict the volume of air that can be inhaled through their mouth.

Chair position

The supine position, which is recommended as a means of preventing syncope, becomes detrimental to a patient who must use the body of the tongue when a foreign object is being held tenuously by the tongue against the roof of the mouth. Gravity acts to force the object posteriorly into the pharynx. If equipment is not readily available chairside to aid in the retrieval of the object, the patient should be turned onto his or her side and leaned into a head-down (Trendelenburg*) position with the upper body over the side of the dental chair

---

*The Trendelenburg position is one in which the patient's head is placed low and the body and legs are placed on an elevated or inclined plane.

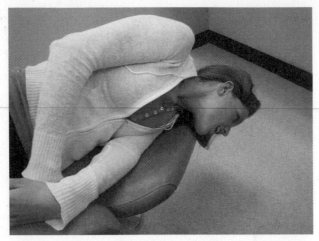

FIGURE 11-4 The patient should turn to the side and bend into a head-down position with the upper body over the side of the dental chair in cases of a swallowed object.

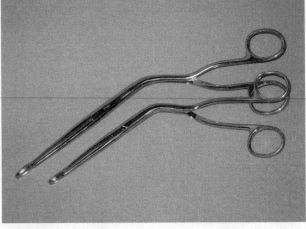

FIGURE 11-5 Magill intubation forceps should be included in the office emergency kit.

(Figure 11-4). This position uses gravity to the patient's advantage, allowing the object to fall from the patient's mouth.

Dental assistant and suction

In most offices a dental assistant is seated across from the doctor. When an object falls free and is in danger of being swallowed, the assistant may have available one or more devices with which to retrieve it, such as pickup forceps and a hemostat. If nothing is readily available, a high-volume, large-diameter suction tip may be used to remove the object from the patient's mouth. A trap on the suction line permits quick retrieval of the object.

Saliva ejectors are not always useful in foreign body removal because the force of the suction may not be great enough to grasp the object. When available, a Magill intubation forceps permits the assistant to more easily retrieve objects from the posterior part of the oral cavity.

Magill intubation forceps

The Magill intubation forceps (Figure 11-5), which is included in the basic emergency kit, is designed to permit retrieval of large and small objects from the distal regions of the oral cavity and pharynx (Figure 11-6). The right-angled bend in the Magill forceps permits a comfortable hand position for the user while its blunt-ended beaks permit easy grasping of the object. No other device, including pickup forceps (cotton pliers) or hemostats, is designed for this purpose (Figure 11-7).

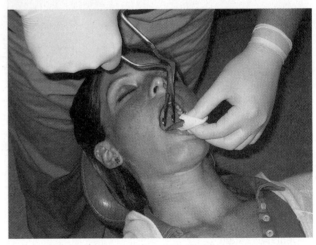

FIGURE 11-6 Proper use of the Magill intubation forceps.

Tongue grasping forceps

A tongue grasping forceps (Figure 11-8) has serrations that allow the tongue to be grasped firmly and pulled forward without causing iatrogenic injury.

Ligature

The use of ligature or dental floss can aid in the prevention of aspirated or swallowed objects and in their retrieval from the distal regions of the oral cavity and pharynx. Dental floss should be secured to rubber dam clamps, endodontic instruments, cotton rolls, gauze pads; around pontics in fixed bridges; or to other small objects placed in the oral cavity during dental treatment (Figures 11-9 and 11-10). The presence of dental floss

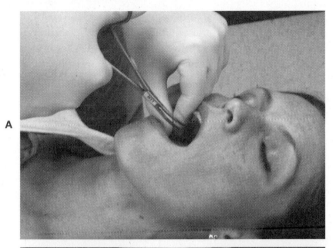

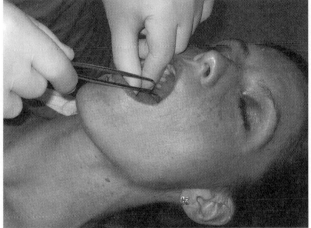

FIGURE 11-7 Hemostat **(A)** and cotton **(B)** pliers are not designed for easy use in the retrieval of objects.

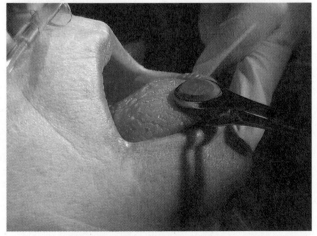

FIGURE 11-8 Tongue-grasping forceps.

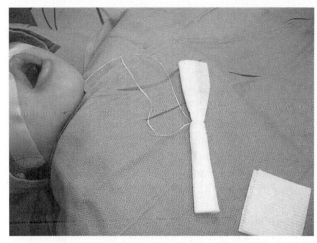

FIGURE 11-9 Dental floss is tied to an object to allow quick retrieval.

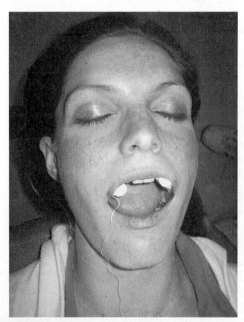

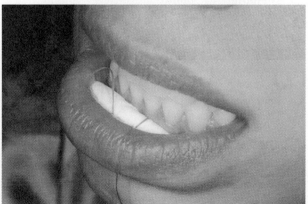

FIGURE 11-10 **A,** Cotton roll without floss. **B,** Cotton roll with floss.

lessens the possibility that a patient may swallow an object or inadvertently leave the dental office with a cotton roll remaining in the buccal fold.

■ MANAGEMENT

When an object enters the oropharynx of a patient lying in the supine or semisupine position, do not allow the patient to sit up. The chair should be moved into a more reclined position (e.g., into the Trendelenburg position, if possible) while the assistant picks up the Magill intubation forceps. Placing the patient into the Trendelenburg position allows gravity to move the object closer to the oral cavity where it may be visible, aiding in its retrieval with the Magill intubation forceps (Box 11-2).

If the object cannot be seen (i.e., if the patient "swallows" it), radiographs are warranted to determine its location; the patient should not be permitted to leave the office without arrangements being made for these radiographs. Because clinical signs and symptoms do not always indicate whether the object has entered the GI or respiratory tract, the doctor should escort the patient (if possible) to the emergency department of a local hospital or to a radiology laboratory. In most instances the radiologist recommends a flat plate of the abdomen or an anteroposterior view of the chest (Figure 11-11), or a lateral view of the chest.

It is hoped that if the object is found, it will be seen on the abdominal radiograph rather than on the chest radiographs within, for example, a bronchus. In any situation in which a foreign object is located within the GI or respiratory tracts, assistance must be sought from the appropriate medical specialty—gastroenterology, pulmonology, or anesthesiology. Subsequent management will usually be directed by the attending physician. If the object's location is not apparent on the radiograph or if any question exists as to its location or any potential complications, immediate medical consultation is warranted (Box 11-3).[25]

Usually, the signs and symptoms that the patient exhibits help determine whether an object has entered into the trachea. Signs and symptoms include the sudden onset of coughing, choking, wheezing, and shortness of breath. More than 90% of patients who aspirate exhibit these signs and symptoms within 1 hour of aspiration. A few patients may experience a time lag as long as 6 hours before symptoms become evident.[26] Depending on the severity of the episode, apnea may follow immediately in as many as one third of these patients. Symptoms may progress to cyanosis and other signs of serious hypoxemia.[27]

In situations in which the foreign body presumably enters the trachea, a well-defined protocol should be

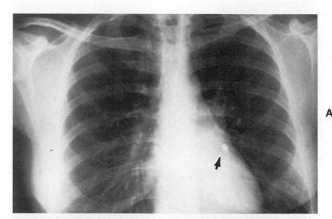

A

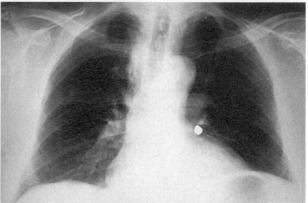

B

FIGURE 11-11 A, Anteroposterior view of the chest demonstrating a rubber prophylaxis cup *(arrow).* **B,** Gold crown that was aspirated into the left lung of the patient.

Box 11-2 Management of visible objects

If assistant is present

Place patient into supine or Trendelenburg position
↓
Use Magill intubation forceps or suction to remove foreign body

If assistant is NOT present

Instruct patient to bend over arm of chair with their head down
↓
Encourage patient to cough

Box 11-3 Management of swallowed objects

Consult radiologist
↓
Obtain appropriate radiographs to determine location of object
↓
Initiate medical consultation with appropriate specialist

followed, beginning with ensuring that the patient does not sit up (sitting up may propel the object deeper into the trachea or bronchi). The patient should be placed into the left lateral decubitus position with the head down (Figure 11-12). The patient may cough spontaneously; if not, coughing should be encouraged to aid in retrieval of the object. The normal cough reflex is powerful and in many cases adequate to expel the aspirated object.

Should the patient cease coughing and state that the object has been swallowed, that patient still should not be permitted to leave the office until a physician or radiographer locates the object to ensure that it is not located within the tracheobronchial tree. Only if the object is recovered should the patient be discharged before a radiograph has been obtained.

In addition, before the patient leaves the office, medical consultation should be sought from an appropriate specialist (e.g., a pulmonologist) to discuss the prevention, recognition, and management of post-aspiration complications. If the object is not recovered, the doctor should accompany the patient to the emergency department of an acute-care facility for definitive diagnosis and management (Box 11-4).

If it is determined that the object is in the tracheobronchial tree, its most likely location is in the right bronchus. Compared with the left bronchus, the right main-stem bronchus takes a more direct path at the bifurcation of the trachea. The right main bronchus branches off the trachea at a 25-degree angle, whereas the left main bronchus branches off at a 45-degree angle. Retrieval of the object from the bronchus may involve the use of a fiberoptic bronchoscope to locate (visualize) the object and bronchoscopy to retrieve it.[28-30] If

bronchoscopy is unsuccessful (a rare occurrence), a surgical procedure known as *thoracotomy* may be necessary.

An immediate life-threatening emergency does not exist in the situations just described. However, the patient should not be allowed to leave the office unless the aspirated object is retrieved. Additional medical management will be necessary to prevent the development of serious consequences.

Recognition of airway obstruction

Acute upper-airway obstruction in the conscious patient occurs most often while the patient is eating. In adults, meat is the most common cause of obstruction.[14,31] Several common factors are identified in cases of the so-called cafe coronary syndrome, including (1) large, poorly chewed pieces of food; (2) elevated blood alcohol levels; (3) laughing or talking while eating; and (4) upper or lower dentures.[31] A higher incidence of cafe coronaries is noted in patients receiving drugs with anticholinergic actions.[32] Other causes of airway obstruction include the following:

- Congenital structural abnormalities of the airway[33]
- Infections, such as acute epiglottitis[34,35]
- Tonsillitis[36-38]
- Retropharyngeal abscesses[39]
- Ludwig's angina[40] and laryngitis[11]
- Trauma[41]
- Tumors and hematomas[42,43]
- Vocal cord pathologic processes, including laryngospasm and paralysis

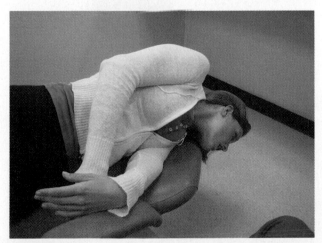

FIGURE 11-12 The patient should be placed in the left lateral decubitus position with the head down when an object enters the trachea.

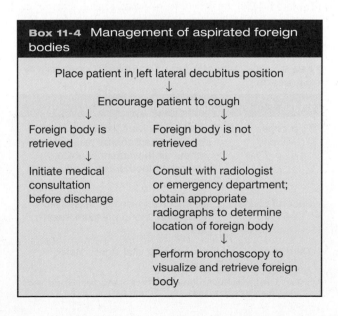

Box 11-4 Management of aspirated foreign bodies

Place patient in left lateral decubitus position
↓
Encourage patient to cough
↓   ↓
Foreign body is   Foreign body is not
retrieved   retrieved
↓   ↓
Initiate medical   Consult with radiologist
consultation   or emergency department;
before discharge   obtain appropriate
                                       radiographs to determine
                                       location of foreign body
                                       ↓
                                       Perform bronchoscopy to
                                       visualize and retrieve foreign
                                       body

- Inflammatory processes, such as angioneurotic edema and anaphylaxis,[11] ingestion of corrosives and toxins,[36] and thermal burns[44]
- Sleep apnea[11]

Foreign body airway obstruction is divided into two categories: complete and partial obstruction. For management purposes, partial obstruction is subdivided into two categories: partial obstruction with good air exchange or partial obstruction with poor air exchange.

Complete airway obstruction

Researchers have documented in dogs the physiologic events that occur with asphyxia (complete obstruction).[45] Several phases of physiologic change are noted before death occurs as a result of acute airway obstruction. Initially, sympathetic outflow increases markedly, increasing blood pressure, heart rate, and respiratory rate. As a result of the increased work of breathing, PaO_2 (arterial oxygen [O_2] tension) decreases, $PaCO_2$ (arterial carbon dioxide [CO_2] tension) increases, and pH falls. At 3 to 4 minutes, blood pressure and heart rate drop precipitously and respiratory efforts diminish. Blood gases deteriorate even further. At 8 to 10 minutes, vital signs disappear as the electrocardiogram degenerates from a sinus to a nodal bradycardia, then to idioventricular rhythms; the electrocardiogram then terminates in ventricular fibrillation or asystole.[45]

If the obstruction is relieved within the initial 4 to 5 minutes, all monitored parameters usually return to normal quickly along with a return of consciousness. However, humans, especially those who are medically compromised, do not tolerate asphyxia as well as in the dog model described in the aforementioned findings. Dailey[46] divided the clinical features of acute upper-airway obstruction in humans into three phases (Table 11-1).

The first phase is the initial 3 minutes of obstruction. The patient is conscious but in obvious distress, demonstrating struggling paradoxical respirations and increased blood pressure and heart rate. The patient often grasps at their throat in the so-called choking sign (Figure 11-13). Although respiratory efforts are evident, no air is being exchanged and no voice sounds produced. Supraclavicular and intercostal retraction is evident, breath sounds are absent in the chest, and the patient becomes cyanotic.

Minutes 2 through 5 make up the second phase. The victim loses consciousness, and respiratory efforts cease. Initially, blood pressure and pulse are present.

Phase three begins after 4 or 5 minutes. After a short period the blood pressure and pulse disappear as electromechanical dissociation leads to full cardiorespiratory arrest (Box 11-5).

Partial airway obstruction

A forceful cough often may be elicited from a victim with good air exchange. Wheezing may be noted between coughs. The victim with partial obstruction and good air exchange should be allowed to continue coughing and to breathe without any physical intervention by rescuers.[47]

TABLE 11-1 Assessment of complete upper-airway obstruction

Phase	Signs and symptoms
First phase (1–3 min)	Conscious; universal choking sign; struggling paradoxical respirations without air movement or voice; increased blood pressure and heart rate
Second phase (2–5 min)	Loss of consciousness; decreased respiration, blood pressure, heart rate
Third phase (>4–5 min)	Coma; absent vital signs; dilated pupils

Modified from Dailey RH: Acute upper airway obstruction, *Emerg Med Clin North Am* 1:261–277, 1983.

FIGURE 11-13 The victim clutches the neck, demonstrating the recommended universal distress signal for an obstructed airway. (From Chapleau W: *Emergency first responder: making the difference,* St. Louis, Mosby, 2004.)

Box 11-5 Signs of complete airway obstruction

Inability to speak
Inability to breathe
Inability to cough
Universal sign for choking
Panic

Those with poor air exchange exhibit weak, ineffectual cough reflexes and a characteristic "crowing" sound during inspiration. The degree of paradoxical respiration is related to the degree of airway obstruction. Voice sounds may be absent or altered because the vocal cords cannot appose normally. The inspiratory phase of breathing is markedly prolonged. Patients with poor air exchange exhibit cyanosis, lethargy, and disorientation if severe hypoxia and hypercarbia are present; these victims must be treated as though their airways were completely obstructed (Box 11-6).[47]

Basic airway maneuvers

Once a patient with an obstructed airway loses consciousness, basic life support, including airway maintenance, is initiated immediately (see Chapter 5). These steps are designed to manage the most common cause of airway obstruction, the tongue. Performance of these steps permits the rescuer to determine whether the tongue is the cause of the airway problem or whether additional steps of airway management are required. In those instances in which a lower-airway obstruction is obvious (e.g., airway obstruction developing immediately after the individual swallows a crown or dental instrument), the steps of basic life support are bypassed and the rescuer immediately proceeds to establish an emergency airway.

Step 1: P (position). The patient should be placed into the supine position with the feet elevated slightly (Figure 11-14).

Step 2: head tilt–chin lift. The patient's neck tissues are extended through the head tilt–chin lift technique (Figure 11-15). In 80% of instances in which the tongue is the cause of the airway obstruction, this procedure effectively opens the airway.[48]

Box 11-6 Signs of partial airway obstruction
INDIVIDUALS WITH GOOD AIR FLOW Forceful cough Wheezing between coughs Ability to breathe
INDIVIDUALS WITH POOR AIR EXCHANGE Weak, ineffectual cough "Crowing" sound on inspiration Paradoxical respiration Absent or altered voice sounds Possible cyanosis Possible lethargy Possible disorientation

Step 3: A + B (look, listen, feel). The rescuer's ear is placed 1 inch (2.5 cm) from the victim's mouth and nose; the rescuer listens and feels for the passage of air while looking toward the victim's chest and watching for spontaneous respiratory movement (Figure 11-16).

Step 3a: jaw-thrust maneuver, if indicated. The rescuer places his or her fingers behind the posterior

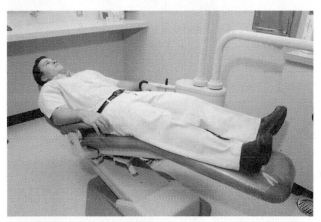

FIGURE 11-14 The patient who loses consciousness should be placed in the supine position with the feet slightly elevated.

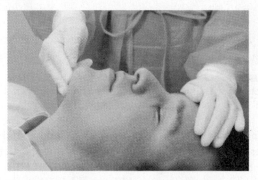

FIGURE 11-15 The head tilt–chin lift technique.

FIGURE 11-16 The "look, listen, feel" technique.

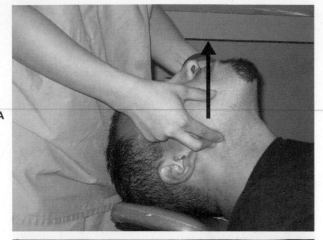

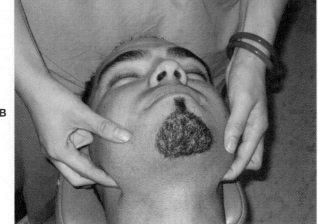

FIGURE 11-17   The jaw-thrust maneuver: **A,** Side view.
B, Front view. The mandible is displaced anteriorly (arrows).

border of the ramus of the victim's mandible and displaces the mandible anteriorly while tilting the victim's head backward and opening the mouth (Figure 11-17).

Dislocation of the mandible is a painful procedure. Therefore, the jaw-thrust maneuver gives the rescuer a sense of the depth of the victim's unconsciousness. If the victim does not respond to this maneuver, the level of unconsciousness is fairly deep, whereas if the victim does respond (e.g., by grimacing, phonating, or moving), the level of unconsciousness is not as deep.

Step 4: A + B.   Repeat step 3 (look, listen, and feel), if necessary.

Step 5: rescue breathing, if indicated.   When the tongue is the cause of airway obstruction, performance of the preceding steps usually reestablishes the airway. When these steps are performed properly but the airway remains obstructed (diagnosed by aphonia, and suprasternal retraction, and continued absence of "hearing and seeing"), the rescuer should consider the

probability that the obstruction is located in the lower airway (larynx or trachea) and proceed immediately to establish an emergency airway.

Establishing an emergency airway

When a patient's airway is obstructed, establishment of a patent airway becomes the immediate goal of treatment. A variety of procedures exist to accomplish this goal. Two procedures—tracheostomy[49–51] and cricothyrotomy[52–54]—require surgical intervention and thus considerable knowledge and technical skill to be carried out effectively. A third procedure, which is nonsurgical, is the procedure of choice for the initial management of all obstructed airways when basic life support techniques prove inadequate. This is the external subdiaphragmatic compression technique, known as the *abdominal thrust,* or the *Heimlich maneuver.*[55–61] Because this procedure is nonsurgical, serious complications are, though possible, less likely to occur, which makes the maneuver particularly attractive for use in the dental office.[62–64] The American Heart Association and American Red Cross recommend the abdominal thrust when lower-airway obstruction is a possibility,[10] a situation responsible for 4313 deaths in 2000.[9]

Noninvasive procedures

When a foreign object enters the tracheobronchial tree, a potentially life-threatening situation exists. Obstruction of the airway may be partial or complete. Management varies according to the degree of obstruction present and the effectiveness of the patient's cough reflex. Manual, noninvasive procedures are used whenever possible. Surgical procedures, used as a last resort, are also within the doctor's expertise. (These techniques are described later in the chapter.)

A victim of a partial airway obstruction who is capable of forceful coughing and is breathing adequately (i.e., with no evidence of cyanosis or duskiness) should be left alone. Although wheezing may be evident between coughs, a forceful cough is highly effective in removing foreign objects. This victim should be left alone. If the victim of partial airway obstruction initially demonstrates poor air exchange or if previously good air exchange becomes ineffective, the victim must be managed as though the airway is completely obstructed.

Victims of complete airway obstruction are unable to speak or make any sounds (aphonia), breathe, or cough. The victim remains conscious as long as the cerebral O_2 level of the blood is sufficiently high. Victims may remain conscious for 10 seconds to 2 minutes, depending on whether the obstruction occurred during inspiration (when the blood has more O_2) or expiration (when the blood has less O_2). Fortunately, most airway obstruction occurs during inhalation; in this way the lungs are inflated and filled with O_2, with the victim remaining conscious longer. The victim also may clutch the neck (see Figure 11-13), the universal sign for choking. Prompt management is critical because the victim will lose consciousness and die unless a patent airway is reestablished immediately.

Several manual, noninvasive procedures are available for use in acute airway obstruction. Each technique will be described, followed by the recommended sequencing of these techniques in actual situations. The techniques are as follows:

- Back blows
- Manual thrust
- Abdominal thrust (Heimlich maneuver)
- Chest thrust
- Finger sweep

Back blows

Back blows have formed an integral part of previous regimens for the removal of foreign objects from the airway.[65] However, data presented at the 1985 National Conference on Cardiopulmonary Resuscitation and Emergency Cardiac Care suggested that back blows used as the sole method of treatment may not be as effective in adults as the Heimlich maneuver.[57] In addition, clinical data on choking demonstrate the feasibility and effectiveness of back blows or "slaps,"[66,67] abdominal thrusts,[68-70] and chest thrusts.[71,72] For simplicity in training, the 2005 American Heart Association Guidelines for electrocardiography and basic life support recommend the abdominal thrust be applied in rapid sequence until the obstruction is relieved. If this approach is ineffective, the rescuer may consider chest thrusts. Abdominal thrusts are not recommended for infants younger than 1 year of age because thrusts may cause injuries to the liver.[73]

However, back blows, now termed *back slaps*, still remain an integral part of the protocol for obstructed-airway management in the infant. When back slaps are performed on the infant, the infant is straddled over the rescuer's arm with the head lower than the trunk and with the head supported by the rescuer's firm hold on the infant's jaw. Using the heel of the hand, the rescuer delivers up to five back slaps forcefully between the infant's shoulder blades while resting the other hand on the thigh (Figure 11-18).

Manual thrusts

Manual thrusts consist of a series of thrusts to the upper abdomen (Heimlich maneuver or abdominal thrust) or to the lower chest (chest thrust). They are designed

FIGURE 11-18 The rescuer uses the heel of one hand to deliver up to five back slaps forcefully between the shoulder blades of an infant. (From Chapleau W: *Emergency first responder: making the difference,* St. Louis, Mosby, 2004.)

to produce a rapid increase in intrathoracic pressure, acting as an artificial cough that can help dislodge a foreign body. The objective of each single thrust should be to relieve the obstruction. Studies have demonstrated that no significant differences exist between abdominal and chest thrusts in the amount of air flow, pressure, and volume.[74,75]

Special situations do exist in which one technique is preferable. The chest thrust is recommended for patients in advanced stages of pregnancy and for those who are markedly obese. Chest thrust is less likely to cause regurgitation than is abdominal thrust. Additionally, chest thrusts are recommended for infants because abdominal thrusts are more likely to cause organ damage (e.g., to the liver or spleen).[73] The Heimlich maneuver is recommended especially for older patients, whose more brittle ribs are more likely to be fractured in the chest thrust, and for children.

Internal injuries are always possible whenever an abdominal or chest thrust is used. Injuries to the thoracic and abdominal organs, including the liver, spleen, and stomach, have been documented.[62-64,76-78] Proper hand placement can minimize occurrence of these potentially serious side effects. The rescuer must never place his or her hands over the xiphoid process or the lower margins of the rib cage. In the Heimlich maneuver the rescuer places the hands below this area, whereas in chest thrust the hands are placed above it.

After successful application of any manual thrust technique to relieve acute airway obstruction, medical or paramedical personnel should evaluate the patient for evidence of secondary injury, such as abdominal bleeding, before discharging the patient.[79]

Heimlich maneuver

The Heimlich maneuver, also known as the *subdiaphragmatic abdominal thrust* or *abdominal thrust*, was first

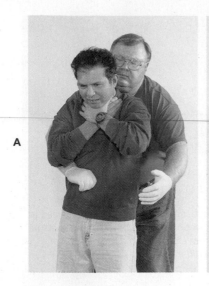

A   B

FIGURE 11-19 The proper technique for an abdominal thrust. (From Chapleau W: *Emergency first responder: making the difference,* St. Louis, Mosby, 2004.)

described in 1975 by Dr. Henry J. Heimlich.[55] Today this maneuver is the recommended primary technique for relief of foreign body airway obstruction in adults and children.[79]

Conscious victim: If the patient is conscious and either standing or sitting, the following recommended steps should be performed after the rescuer confirms that the airway is obstructed by asking "Are you choking?":

1. Stand behind the victim and wrap your arms around the waist and under the arms.
2. Grasp one fist with the other hand, placing the thumb side of the fist against the victim's abdomen. The hand should rest in the midline, slightly above the umbilicus and well below the tip of the xiphoid process (Figure 11-19).
3. Perform repeated inward and upward thrusts until the foreign body is expelled or the victim loses consciousness (Figure 11-20).

The successfully treated victim should be evaluated for the possibility of complications before dismissal from the office.

Unconscious victim: If the victim is unconscious, the following protocol should be performed:

1. Place the victim in the supine position.
2. Open the victim's airway by using the head tilt–chin lift technique and turn the head up into the so-called neutral position. The head is turned into the neutral position to avoid airway obstruction, facilitate foreign body movement up the airway, and allow the foreign body to be visualized.
3. Whenever possible, the rescuer should straddle the victim's legs or thighs (Figure 11-21). Unfortunately, this position is virtually impossible to achieve when the patient is in the dental chair. An alternative to the straddle position places the rescuer alongside the

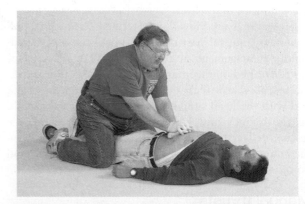

FIGURE 11-20 An abdominal thrust in a conscious victim. (From Chapleau W: *Emergency first responder: making the difference,* St. Louis, Mosby, 2004.)

FIGURE 11-21 When performing the Heimlich maneuver on the floor, the rescuer should straddle the victim's legs. (From Chapleau W: *Emergency first responder: making the difference,* St. Louis, Mosby, 2004.)

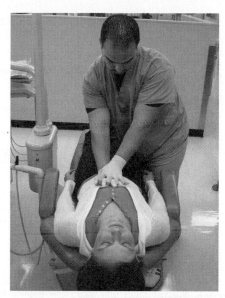

FIGURE 11-22 As an alternative to the straddle position during an abdominal thrust, the rescuer may stand astride the victim in the dental chair. The victim's head should be in the neutral position.

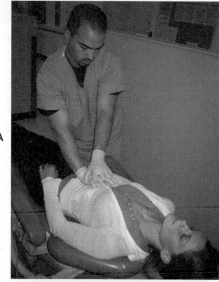

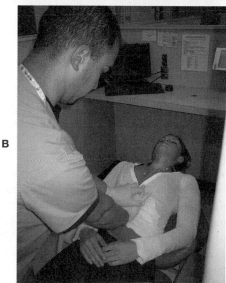

FIGURE 11-23 **A,** The rescuer performs an abdominal thrust while astride the victim, who is in the dental chair. **B,** The force of the compression must be in an upward, not a lateral, direction. The victim's head remains in the neutral position.

victim. The rescuer's knees rest close to the victim's hips on either the right or left side (Figure 11-22). This position is useful when the victim is in the dental chair (Figure 11-23).

4. Place the heel of one hand against the victim's abdomen, in the midline slightly above the umbilicus and well below the tip of the xiphoid process.
5. Place the second hand directly on top of the first hand.
6. Press into the victim's abdomen with a quick inward and upward thrust. (Do not direct the force laterally.)
7. Perform up to five abdominal thrusts.
8. Open the victim's mouth, look to see if the object has been dislodged and is visible. New guidelines do not recommend a blind finger sweep. If the object is visible it should be removed.
9. Repeat steps 2 through 8 until the obstruction is dislodged.

Properly performed, the Heimlich maneuver is exclusively a soft tissue procedure. No bony structures, such as ribs or sternum, are involved. In all cases the rescuer must apply pressure with the heel of the hand *below* the rib cage. The Heimlich maneuver is not a "bear hug"; if performed that way, damage to the intra-abdominal organs, such as the liver and spleen, or to the sternum and ribs could occur. After successful completion of the procedure, the appropriate team member should summon emergency personnel to evaluate the patient before discharge from the office.

Chest thrust

The chest thrust is an alternative—in special situations only—to the Heimlich maneuver as a technique for opening an obstructed airway. There is no substantial difference in the effectiveness of these techniques when performed properly. Box 11-7 lists the indications and contraindications for the chest thrust.

Conscious victim: If the victim is conscious and either standing or sitting, the following steps should be performed:

1. Stand behind the victim and place the arms directly under the armpits, encircling the chest (Figure 11-24).

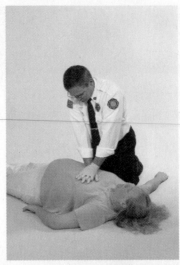

FIGURE 11-25 A chest thrust on an unconscious victim. (From Chapleau W: *Emergency first responder: making the difference,* St. Louis, Mosby, 2004.)

FIGURE 11-24 A chest thrust on a pregnant patient. (From Chapleau W: *Emergency first responder: making the difference,* St. Louis, Mosby, 2004.)

2. Grasp one fist with the other hand, placing the thumb side of the fist on the middle of the sternum, not on the xiphoid process or the margins of the rib cage.
3. Perform backward thrusts until the foreign body is expelled or the victim loses consciousness.

Unconscious victim: If the victim is unconscious, the following steps should be performed:

1. Place the victim in the supine position.
2. Using the head tilt–chin lift, open the victim's airway and place the head into the neutral position.
3. Either straddle or stand astride the victim, as described for the Heimlich maneuver.
4. Place the heel of one hand on the lower half of the sternum with the second hand on top of it, but not on the xiphoid process (Figure 11-25). (The hand position and technique for chest thrust are identical to those of adult closed-chest cardiac compression [see Chapter 30].)
5. Perform up to five quick, downward thrusts to compress the chest cavity.
6. Open the victim's mouth and perform the finger sweep.

Finger sweep

In the conscious victim it is quite difficult for the rescuer to remove foreign bodies from the airway with the

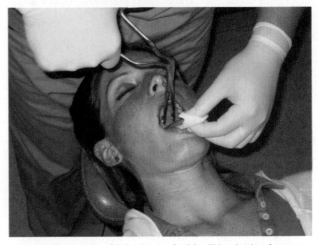

FIGURE 11-26 Clinical use of a Magill intubation forceps.

fingers. With loss of consciousness, muscles relax and it is considerably easier to open the victim's mouth to seek and remove foreign objects with ones fingers. The rescuer must take special care when probing an infant's or small child's airway with a finger so as not to inadvertently force the foreign body deeper into the airway. Therefore, blind finger sweeps are not recommended in any clinical situation, be the victim an infant, child or adult. The rescuer may, however, remove foreign bodies from the airway by this technique if the object is located above the level of the epiglottis and is visualized. Finger sweeps should be performed in unconscious victims only.

A Magill intubation forceps is an integral part of the dental office emergency kit (Figure 11-26). This instrument can aid in the removal of foreign objects from the airway. However, use of the Magill intubation forceps

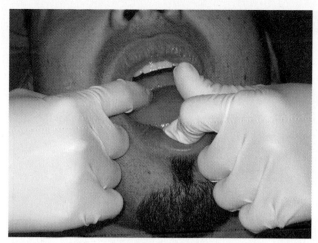

FIGURE 11-27 Use of the crossed-finger technique aids in opening the unconscious victim's mouth.

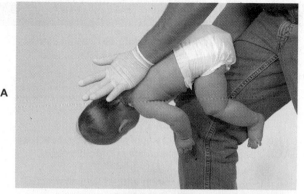

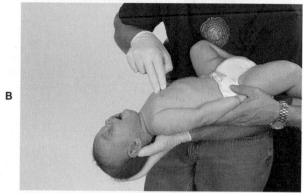

FIGURE 11-28 Technique for an infant with an obstructed airway. **A,** The infant should be supported by the rescuer's forearm with the head lower than the rest of the body for performance of back blows. **B,** The infant is turned over, supported by the rescuer's arms. Using two fingers, the rescuer applies chest thrusts. (From Chapleau W: *Emergency first responder: making the difference,* St. Louis, Mosby, 2004.)

should be limited to situations in which the object is visible to the rescuer.

The finger sweep is performed as follows:
1. The victim is placed into a supine position with the head in the neutral position.
2. The rescuer should open the victim's mouth by using the crossed-finger technique (Figure 11-27). Open the victim's mouth by crossing the index finger and thumb between the teeth and forcing the teeth apart. The tongue-jaw lift technique is no longer taught.
3. To perform a finger sweep, place the index finger of the other hand along the inside of the victim's cheek and advance it deeply into the pharynx at the base of the tongue. Using a hooking movement, try to dislodge the foreign body and move it into the mouth, where either suction or the Magill intubation forceps can remove it. Take care not to force the object more deeply into the airway.

Box 11-8 outlines the American Heart Association's recommended sequence for the removal of airway obstruction.[10]

Procedures for obstructed airways in infants and children

Airway obstruction in children age 1 year to the onset of puberty should be managed in a manner similar to that used for adults—the Heimlich maneuver as the primary technique. However, the combination of back slaps and chest thrusts is still the recommended protocol for the infant under 1 year (Figure 11-28). Box 11-9 reviews the basic rescue procedures for infants.

The rescuer should repeat the sequences presented in this chapter for an infant, child, or adult with an upper-airway obstruction until the foreign matter is successfully removed or until the rescuer judges that time has been exhausted. At this time cricothyrotomy

should be seriously considered—if the rescuer possesses the proper knowledge and training and has the necessary equipment available.

Invasive procedures: tracheostomy versus cricothyrotomy

The previously described noninvasive techniques are highly successful in the removal of foreign bodies from the airway of most victims. However, situations do occur in which noninvasive techniques are ineffective (e.g., in the removal of a dental cotton roll from a victim's airway). In this situation and others, such as when the airway obstruction is caused by the swelling of tissues (edema of the larynx or epiglottis) due to allergy or illness, invasive procedures may be required if the victim is to survive.

Surgical opening of the airway may be performed in several ways. Two of the most commonly used are tracheostomy[49-51] and cricothyrotomy.[52-54] Each technique has advocates and critics within the medical community, but

Box 11-8 Recommended sequences for removing airway obstruction in adults or children

11-8A: CONSCIOUS victim with obstructed airway
Identify complete airway obstruction...ask:
"Are you choking?"
↓
Apply abdominal thrusts until foreign body is expelled
or the victim becomes unconscious
↓
Have medical or paramedical personnel evaluate the
patient for complications prior to dismissal

**11-8B: CONSCIOUS victim with known obstructed
airway who loses consciousness**
Place victim in supine position with head
in neutral position
Call for help!
↓
Activate emergency medical system (i.e., call 9-1-1)
if a second person is available
↓
Maintain airway
(head tilt–chin lift)
↓
Look in mouth for foreign object prior to ventilation
Attempt to ventilate;
if INEFFECTIVE:
↓
Perform abdominal thrust, repeating until object is
expelled or the victim becomes unresponsive
↓
Check for foreign body
If visible, perform finger sweep to remove
↓
Attempt to ventilate;
if INEFFECTIVE
↓
Repeat abdominal thrusts;
If visible, perform finger sweep to remove and
attempt ventilation until effective
↓
Have medical or paramedical personnel evaluate
patient for complications prior to dismissal
or hospitalization

11-8C: UNCONSCIOUS victim, cause UNKNOWN
Rescuer manages unconscious victim
in usual manner:
Assess unresponsiveness
↓
P—Position victim supine with feet elevated slightly
↓
Activate dental office emergency team
↓
A—Open airway (head tilt–chin lift)
↓
B—Assess breathing (look, listen, feel) and
↓
Attempt to ventilate;
if INEFFECTIVE:
↓
Reposition head and attempt to ventilate;
If still INEFFECTIVE:
↓
Activate emergency medical system (i.e., call 9-1-1) and
↓
Look in mouth for foreign object prior to ventilation
Perform abdominal thrusts:
(5 abdominal thrusts)
↓
Check for foreign body
If visible, perform finger sweep to remove
↓
Attempt to ventilate;
if INEFFECTIVE:
↓
Repeat Heimlich maneuver, visualization and finger
sweeps (if visible), and ventilation, until successful

each is equally important for they ensure that the victim's lungs receive O_2. Invasive procedures should be performed only by persons trained in the techniques and only when proper equipment is available.

Tracheostomy has been performed for more than 2000 years, yet its role in the management of acute airway obstruction has changed in recent decades.[80] Tracheostomy once was considered the primary technique for the relief of acute airway obstruction. For a variety of reasons, cricothyrotomy is now considered by many to be the surgical procedure of choice for sudden airway obstruction.[53,81] In the typical dental

setting almost no indications exist for the use of tracheostomy.

Tracheostomy is a surgical procedure currently used most often for long-term airway management and—with a few exceptions, such as direct laryngeal fracture[82] and emergency airway management in infants—is not well suited for most emergency airway management situations. The tracheostomy site contains numerous important anatomic structures, such as the isthmus of the thyroid gland and several large and important blood vessels and nerves.[83] The potential also exists for accidental perforation of the esophagus.

Box 11-9 Recommended management of airway obstruction in infants

11-9A: UNCONSCIOUS victim

Assess unresponsiveness
↓
P—Position victim supine with feet elevated slightly
↓
Activate dental office emergency team
and emergency medical system
↓
A—Open airway (head tilt–chin lift)
↓
B—Assess breathing (look, listen, feel) and
look in mouth for foreign object prior to ventilation
↓
Attempt to ventilate;
if INEFFECTIVE:
↓
Reposition head and attempt to ventilate;
If still INEFFECTIVE:
↓
Manage airway obstruction
(see Box 11-8B and 11-8C)
↓
C—Check pulse;
If NO pulse:
↓
Perform 30 chest compressions

11-9B: CONSCIOUS victim

Back slaps:
1. Supporting the head and neck with one hand, place the infant face down with his or her head lower than the trunk. The infant should straddle the rescuer's forearm and remain supported on the rescuer's thigh (see Figure 11-28)
↓
2. Using the heel of the hand, deliver up to 5 back slaps forcefully in the middle of the back between the shoulder blades
↓

11-9B: CONSCIOUS victim—cont'd

Chest thrusts:
1. While supporting the head and neck, sandwich the infant between the hands and hold the infant face up with the head lower than the trunk
↓
2. Deliver up to 5 chest thrusts in the same location as chest compressions—just below the nipple line—at a rate of about 1 per second
↓
3. Repeat the sequence of up to 5 back slaps and up to 5 chest thrusts until the object is removed or the infant becomes unresponsive

11-9C: Obstructed airway in INFANT—unconscious

Perform the following steps when basic procedures (Box 11-9B) have proved INEFFECTIVE:
Heimlich maneuver:
1. Kneel at infant's feet if infant is on the floor, or stand at infant's feet if child is on a table or in the dental chair
↓
2. Open the infant's airway and look for a foreign object in the pharynx. If it's visible, remove it. DO NOT PERFORM A BLIND FINGER SWEEP
↓
3. Begin BLS (**A → B → C**) with 1 additional step: every time the airway is opened (head tilt–chin lift), look for a foreign object in the back of the throat. If visible, remove it. DO NOT PERFORM A BLIND FINGER SWEEP
↓
4. After 5 cycles (2 minutes) of basic life support, activate emergency medical service

Complications occur more commonly with tracheostomy even when it is performed slowly and meticulously under controlled conditions, such as in an oxygenated, well-ventilated patient in an operating theater, than occur with cricothyrotomy.[82] Hemorrhage and pneumothorax are major complications of tracheostomy. In addition, there is a risk of accidental penetration of the isthmus of the thyroid gland.[84] In most cases the bleeding associated with tracheostomy is a major surgical complication that the dental office may not be equipped to handle satisfactorily.

Cricothyroid membrane puncture (cricothyrotomy) involves establishment of an opening in the airway at the level of the cricothyroid membrane and is an accepted means of emergency airway access. Cricothyrotomy is easier and quicker than tracheostomy, and the incidence of complications is significantly lower.[81] In addition, no significant anatomic structures are found near the cricothyroid membrane.

Cricothyrotomy has been said to provide the most accessible point of entry into the respiratory tree inferior to the glottis.[85] Incision is made through skin, adipose tissue, and fascia. Aside from minor bleeding from the skin incision, major blood loss is seldom associated with cricothyrotomy. Because the cricoid cartilage has an intact posterior segment, inadvertent perforation of the posterior wall of the trachea and laceration of the underlying esophagus are lesser risks (Figure 11-29). An incision into the cricothyroid membrane begins to heal within a few days of removal of the airway.

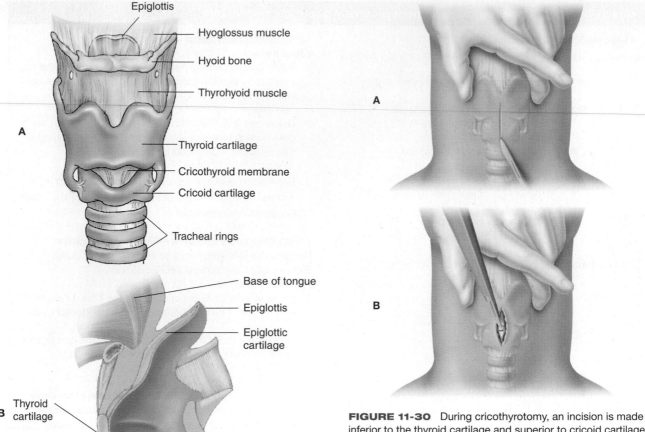

FIGURE 11-29   Important anatomic relationships in cricothyrotomy. **A,** Frontal view. **B,** Side view. (From McSwain N: *The basic EMT: comprehensive prehospital care,* ed 2, St. Louis, Mosby, 2003.)

FIGURE 11-30   During cricothyrotomy, an incision is made inferior to the thyroid cartilage and superior to cricoid cartilage. (From Custalow C: *Color atlas of emergency department procedures,* Philadelphia, Saunders, 2005.)

The ability to rapidly locate the proper site for cricothyrotomy is critical. The rationale behind any emergency surgical airway procedure is that any opening being made must lie below the obstruction in order for the procedure to be effective. Thus, a vital consideration is where a foreign body is most likely to become lodged in the trachea.

Anatomy

The narrowest portion of the adult trachea is located at the larynx. Most objects capable of producing obstruction come to rest in this area. Objects small enough to pass through the larynx and enter into the trachea usually pass into one of the main-stem bronchi (usually

the right), creating an occlusion of one lung or a significant portion of one lung. As discussed previously, this does not represent an immediate threat to the victim's life, although hospitalization and surgery to remove the foreign object may be required.

The narrowest portion of the trachea in children under 3 to 5 years is found a short distance below the vocal cords at the cricoid cartilage.[86] Obstruction is most likely to occur at this site, making cricothyrotomy ineffective. Thus, tracheostomy is the preferred emergency surgical airway procedure in the 3- to 5-year age group, but only individuals experienced in performing tracheostomy on infants and children should attempt it.[86] (Immediate management of this situation in clinical situations in which surgical techniques are unavailable requires the use of nonsurgical procedures, such as inverting the infant and the use of manual thrusts and back blows.)

The thyroid cartilage, the largest of the tracheal cartilages, and the cricoid cartilage (the second tracheal cartilage) represent the anatomic landmarks for cricothyrotomy (Figures 11-29 and 11-30). The thyroid and cricoid are the only two tracheal cartilages that are complete rings; the other tracheal "rings" are open on their posterior aspects. A membranous structure, the cricothyroid membrane forms the anterior connection between these two cartilaginous rings and is the precise site for cricothyrotomy. The membrane is approximately 10 mm high and 22 mm wide.[87] It may be readily located by placing a finger on the laryngeal prominence (Adam's apple) of the thyroid cartilage and moving the finger inferiorly until reaching a slight depression. The cricothyroid membrane is approximately one to one-half of a finger breadth below the laryngeal prominence in the midline of the neck.[52] The prominence of the cricoid cartilage is inferior to this depression. The cricoid cartilage lies inferior to the incision site, whereas the thyroid cartilage and vocal cords lie superior to it.

Equipment

A scalpel with a straight (no. 11) blade may be used in an emergency cricothyrotomy for both the skin incision and the membrane incision. Alternatively, a 13-gauge, 12-inch needle may be used.

Use of a scalpel

Step 1: preparation of the neck.
If enough time exists (it usually does not), the patient's neck should be prepared surgically. However, in emergency situations, antiseptic may be poured over the neck before the incision is made.

The patient's neck should be hyperextended (head tilt) to allow easy identification of the thyroid and cricoid cartilages and cricothyroid membrane. A roll of towels or other material placed under the neck aids hyperextension.

Step 2: identification of landmarks.
The right-handed operator should stand on the patient's right side so that the left hand can immobilize the larynx and help identify landmarks while the right hand is used to perform the cricothyrotomy. In clinical practice the right hand often is used initially to identify landmarks, after which the index finger of the left hand should be placed on the cricothyroid membrane.

Step 3: immobilization of the larynx.
Walls[52] wrote that the importance of this step cannot be overstated. The larynx must be immobilized so that the landmarks are not lost during the actual procedure. Immobilization of the larynx is easy to accomplish; it must be done before the incision is made and maintained until an airway is obtained successfully. The right-handed operator uses the thumb and middle finger of the left hand to grasp the upper poles of the thyroid cartilage, allowing the index finger of the left hand to rest on the membrane (Figure 11-31). Once the larynx

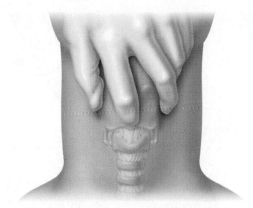

FIGURE 11-31 To stabilize the larynx, the thumb and middle finger stabilize the cartilage while the index finger rests in the cricothyroid membrane. (From Custalow C: *Color atlas of emergency department procedures,* Philadelphia, Saunders, 2005.)

is immobilized, the index finger of the left hand can be used again to palpate the thyroid cartilage, membrane, and cricoid cartilage.

Step 4: incision of the skin.
The skin incision must be vertical and in the midline; it should be approximately 2 to 3 cm long. The vertical incision minimizes the possibility of significant vascular problems during the procedure,[88] whereas a horizontal incision is more likely to result in bleeding. The vertical incision should be made to the depth of the thyroid cartilage, membrane, and cricoid cartilage. Minor bleeding as a result of the skin incision may occur and can be ignored. The establishment of a patent airway is the primary concern; once this task is accomplished, any bleeding can be managed.

Step 5: reidentification of the membrane.
The index finger of the left hand should be reinserted into the incision to reidentify the cricothyroid membrane. The finger is then quickly moved up to the thyroid and down to the cricoid cartilages to ensure proper identification of the cricothyroid membrane. The fingertip may remain in the incision, but should rest on the most inferior border of the thyroid cartilage to provide a point of reference without interfering with the incision into the membrane.

Step 6: incision of the membrane.
The incision into the membrane should be horizontal, using a no. 11 scalpel blade in the lower third of the cricothyroid space. This area is the least vascular part of the membrane. The horizontal incision in the midline should be at least 1.5 cm long to facilitate airway placement.

Upon entry into the airway, bubbling will be visible (if spontaneous respiratory efforts are still present).

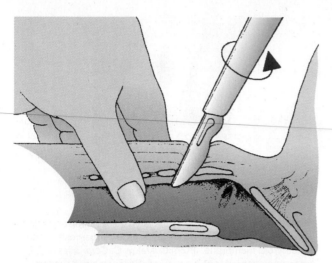

FIGURE 11-32 The handle of the scalpel is inserted into the incision and rotated 90 degrees to enlarge the airway opening.

The scalpel should be withdrawn and the index finger of the left hand reinserted into the cricothyroid space to identify the incision and verify its correct placement. This finger is again moved to the inferior portion of the thyroid cartilage as a guide in airway insertion.

Step 7: dilation of the incision. At this point the cricothyroid space should be enlarged. The handle of the scalpel should be inserted into the horizontal incision and rotated 90 degrees to open the airway (Figure 11-32).

Step 8: insertion of the tube. A cricothyroid or tracheotomy tube may be inserted temporarily, if one is available.

A properly performed cricothyrotomy can be completed in 15 to 30 seconds. Anesthesia is unnecessary because the patient is unconscious and thus does not respond to the stimulus of the scalpel incision.

> NOTE: *The patient may suffer a coughing episode once the trachea is entered.*

Use of a 13-gauge needle for cricothyrotomy

When a 13-gauge, 12-inch needle is used, the tissue is prepared and the thyroid cartilage stabilized the same as with the scalpel, using the index finger to identify the cricothyroid membrane. The needle is inserted through this area and directed toward the chest until it enters the tracheal lumen. Entry into the trachea is confirmed by the sound and feel of air entering and leaving, coughing, and bubbling of fluids. The cartilaginous posterior wall of the cricoid cartilage prevents overinsertion of the needle and perforation of the tracheoesophageal wall.

If spontaneous respiratory movements are present, the victim may regain consciousness but still be unable to speak because of the continued presence of the obstruction at the larynx. Once consciousness returns, the opening into the trachea cannot be closed before the obstruction is removed. If spontaneous respiratory movements are absent, artificial ventilation via the cricothyrotomy should be performed to ensure adequate oxygenation of the blood. Circulatory adequacy then may be determined through palpation of the carotid artery.

Once a patent airway is established, the victim may receive O_2. A cannula or face mask may be placed over the tracheal opening. In addition, the appropriate team member must summon medical assistance to transfer the patient to an emergency medical facility for follow-up management (e.g., removal of the foreign object or closure of the tracheal opening) and observation.

Contraindications to cricothyrotomy

Although a useful and life-saving technique, cricothyrotomy is not recommended in all cases of upper-airway obstruction. The following are examples of a few such exceptions:

- Cricothyrotomy should not be performed without significant trepidation in children under 10 years and probably should not be performed at all in children under 5 years.[38] Although tracheostomy is the preferred emergency airway procedure in young patients, needle cricothyrotomy is more desirable in younger patients.[89]
- Preexisting pathologic processes in the larynx (e.g., in the epiglottitis), chronic inflammation, or cancer make cricothyrotomy more difficult.
- Lack of familiarity with the technique and its complications is a major contraindication to cricothyrotomy. Inexperience may be the single largest factor involved in cricothyrotomy complications.[90]
- Anatomic barriers, such as trauma to the neck region, should warn against performance of this technique.
- When uncontrolled hemorrhage is a possibility, the benefits of cricothyrotomy should be weighed carefully against its risks.

Acute, total airway obstruction is very rare in dental offices. However, when it does occur, signs and symptoms must be recognized instantly with proper management initiated immediately. Thus, all office staff members should receive training in the Heimlich maneuver. Non-invasive procedures for the maintenance of emergency airways are preferred over surgical solutions, but surgical techniques serve as vital last resorts when all else has failed.

REFERENCES

1. Cameron SM, Whitlock WL, Tabor MS: Foreign body aspiration in dentistry: a review, *J Am Dent Assoc* 127:1224–1229, 1996.
2. Tokar B, Ozkan R, Ilhan H: Tracheobronchial foreign bodies in children: importance of accurate history and plain chest radiography in delayed presentation, *Clin Radiol* 59:609–615, 2004.
3. Shinhar SY, Strabbing RJ, Madgy DN: Esophagoscopy for removal of foreign bodies in the pediatric population, *Int J Pediatr Otorhinolaryn* 67:977–979, 2003.
4. Tan HK, Brown K, McGill T, et al.: Airway foreign bodies (FB): a 10-year review, *Int J Pediatr Otorhinolaryn* 56:91–99, 2000.
5. Worthington P: Ingested foreign body associated with oral implant treatment: report of a case, *Int J Oral Maxillofac Implants* 11:679–681, 1996.
6. Lambrianidis T, Beltes P: Accidental swallowing of endodontic instruments, *Endod Dent Traumatol* 12:301–304, 1996.
7. Brunello DL, Mandikos MN: A denture swallowed: case report, *Aust Dent J* 40:349–351, 1995.
8. Ulku R, Baskan Z, Yavuz I: Open surgical approach for a tooth aspirated during dental extraction: a case report, *Austral Dent J* 50:49–50, 2005.
9. National Safety Council: *Injury facts,* Chicago, National Safety Council, 2003.
10. American Heart Association, Emergency Care Committee and Subcommittees: Guidelines for cardiopulmonary resuscitation and emergency cardiac care, *Circulation* 112:IV1–IV187, 2005.
11. Fitzpatrick PC, Guarisco JL: Pediatric airway foreign bodies, *J La State Med Soc* 150:138–141, 1998.
12. Rimell FL, Thome A Jr, Stool S, et al.: Characteristics of objects that cause choking in children, *JAMA* 274:1763–1766, 1995.
13. Karakoc F, Karadag B, Akbenlioglu C, et al.: Foreign body aspiration: what is the outcome? *Pediatr Pulmonol* 34:30–36, 2002.
14. Enwo ON, Wright M: Sausage asphyxia, *Int J Clin Pract* 55:723–724, 2001.
15. Abman SH, Fan LL, Cotton EK: Emergency treatment of foreign-body obstruction of the upper airway in children, *J Emerg Med* 2:7–12, 1984.
16. Netter FH: *Atlas of human anatomy,* ed 2, East Hanover, NJ, Novartis, 1997.
17. Sirbaugh PE, Pepe PE, Shook JE, et al.: A prospective, population-based study on the demographics, epidemiology, management, and outcome of out-of-hospital pediatric cardiopulmonary arrest, *Ann Emerg Med* 33:174–184, 1999.
18. The American Heart Association in collaboration with the International Liaison Committee on Resuscitation: Guidelines 2000 for cardiopulmonary resuscitation and emergency cardiovascular care. Part 10: pediatric advanced life support, *Circulation* 102:I291–I342, 2000.
19. Cote CJ, Rodrea ID, Goudsouzian NG, Ryan JF: *A practice of anesthesia for infants and children,* ed 3, Philadelphia, WB Saunders, 2001.
20. Odelowo EO, Komolafe OF: Diagnosis, management and complications of oesophageal and airway foreign bodies, *Int Surg* 75:148–154, 1990.
21. Storey PS: Obstruction of the GI tract, *Am J Hosp Palliat Care* 8:5, 1991.
22. Weissberg D: Foreign bodies in the gastrointestinal tract, *South Afr J Surg* 29:150–153, 1991.
23. Mu L, He P, Sun D: The causes and complications of late diagnosis of foreign body aspiration in children: report of 210 cases, *Arch Otolaryngol Head Neck Surg* 117:876–879, 1991.
24. Barkmeier WW, Cooley RL, Abrams H: Prevention of swallowing or aspiration of foreign objects, *Am J Dent Assoc* 97:473, 1978.
25. Milton TM, Hearing SD, Ireland AJ: Ingested foreign bodies associated with orthodontic treatment: report of three cases and review of ingestion/aspiration incident management, *Br Dent J* 190:592–596, 2001.
26. Muth D, Scafermeyer RW: All that wheezes, *Pediatr Emerg Care* 6:110–112, 1990.
27. Lumpkin J: Airway obstruction, *Top Emerg Med* 2:15, 1990.
28. Kumar P, Athanasiou T, Sarkar PK: Inhaled foreign bodies in children: diagnosis and treatment, *Hosp Med (London)* 64:218–222, 2003.
29. Erikci V, Karacay S, Arikan A: Foreign body aspiration: a four-year experience, *Turkish J Trauma Emerg Surg* 9:45–49, 2003.
30. Bodart E, de Bilderling G, Tuerlinckx D, Gillet JB: Foreign body aspiration in childhood: management algorithm, *Eur J Emerg Med* 6:21–25, 1999.
31. Jacob B, Wiedbrauck C, Lamprecht J, Bonte W: Laryngologic aspects of bolus asphyxiation—bolus death, *Dysphagia* 7:31–35, 1992.
32. Craig TJ, Richardson MA: "Café coronaries" in psychiatric patients (letter), *JAMA* 248:2114, 1982.
33. Landing BH, Dixon LG: Congenital malformations and genetic disorders of the respiratory tract, *Am Rev Respir Dis* 120:151–185, 1979.
34. Munoz A, Ballesteros AI, Brandariz Castelo JA: Primary lingual abscess presenting as acute swelling of the tongue obstructing the upper airway: diagnosis with MR, *Am J Neuroradiol* 19:496–498, 1998.
35. Mayo-Smith MF, Spinale JW, Donskey CJ, et al.: Acute epiglottitis: an 18-year experience in Rhode Island, *Chest* 108:1640–1647, 1995.
36. Mavrinac JM, Dolan RW: Acute lingual tonsillitis, *Am J Emerg Med* 15:308–309, 1997.
37. Deeb ZE: Acute supraglottitis in adults: early indicators of airway obstruction, *Am J Otolaryngol* 18:112–115, 1997.
38. Sdralis T, Berkowitz RG: Early adenotonsillectomy for relief of acute upper airway obstruction due to acute tonsillitis in children, *Int J Pediatr Otorhinolaryngol* 35:25–29, 1996.
39. Hamer R: Retropharyngeal abscess, *Ann Emerg Med* 11:549–552, 1982.
40. Spitalnic SJ, Sucov A: Ludwig's angina: case report and review, *J Emerg Med* 13:499–503, 1995.

41. Bavitz JB, Collicott PE: Bilateral mandibular subcondylar fractures contributing to airway obstruction, *Int J Oral Maxillofac Surg* 24:273–275, 1995.

42. Myatt HM: Acute airway obstruction due to primary thyroid lymphoma, *Rev Laryngol Otol Rhinol (Bord)* 117:237–239, 1996.

43. Mordenfeld A, Andersson L, Bergstrom B: Hemorrhage in the floor of the mouth during implant placement in the edentulous mandible: a case report, *Int J Oral Maxillofac Implants* 12:558–561, 1997.

44. Watts AM, McCallum MI: Acute airway obstruction following facial scalding: differential diagnosis between a thermal and infective cause, *Burns* 22:570–573, 1996.

45. Kristoffersen MB, Rattenborg CC, Holaday PA: Asphyxial death: the roles of acute anoxia, hypercarbia, and acidosis, *Anesthesiology* 28:488–497, 1967.

46. Dailey RH: Acute upper airway obstruction, *Emerg Med Clin North Am* 1:261–277, 1983.

47. American Heart Association. Part 4: Adult basic life support. Guidelines for CR and ECC, *Circulation* 112: IV27–IV28, 2005.

48. Arnold DN: Airway review, *Am Acad Gnathol Orthop* 7:4–7, 11, 1990.

49. Powell DM, Price PD, Forrest LA: Review of percutaneous tracheostomy, *Laryngoscope* 108:170–177, 1998.

50. Wood DE: Tracheostomy, *Chest Surg Clin North Am* 6:749–764, 1996.

51. Hamilton PH, Kang JJ: Emergency airway management, *Mt Sinai J Med* 64:292–301, 1997.

52. Walls RM: Cricothyroidotomy, *Emerg Med Clin North Am* 6:725–736, 1988.

53. Tobias JD: Airway management for pediatric emergencies, *Pediatr Ann* 25:317–20, 323–8, 1996.

54. Bennett JD: High tracheostomy and other errors—revisited, *J Laryngol Otol* 110:1003–1007, 1996.

55. Heimlich HJ: A life-saving maneuver to prevent food-choking, *JAMA* 234:398–401, 1975.

56. Committee on Emergency Medical Services, Assembly of Life Sciences, National Research Council: *Report of emergency airway management,* Washington, DC, National Academy of Sciences, 1976.

57. Day RL, Crelin ES, DuBois AB: Choking: the Heimlich abdominal thrust vs back blows—an approach to measurement of inertial and aerodynamic forces, *Pediatrics* 70:113–119, 1982.

58. Heimlich HJ, Hoffman KA, Canestri FR: Food-choking and drowning deaths prevented by external subdiaphragmatic compression: physiologic basis, *Ann Thorac Surg* 20:188–195, 1975.

59. Heimlich HJ, Uhtley MH, Netter FH: The Heimlich maneuver, *Clin Symp* 31:1–32, 1979.

60. Patrick EA: Choking: a questionnaire to find the most effective treatment, *Emergency* 12:59, 1980.

61. Heimlich HJ: Pop goes the cafe coronary, *Emerg Med* 6:154, 1979.

62. Visintine RE, Baick CH: Ruptured stomach after Heimlich maneuver, *JAMA* 234:415, 1975.

63. Palmer E: The Heimlich maneuver misused, *Curr Prescribing* 154:155, 1979.

64. Gallardo A, Rosado R, Ramirez D, et al.: Rupture of the lesser curvature after a Heimlich maneuver. *Surg Endoscop* 17:1495, 2003.

65. American Heart Association and National Academy of Sciences, National Research Council: Standards and guidelines for cardiopulmonary resuscitation (CPR) and emergency cardiac care (ECC), *JAMA* 244:453–509, 1980.

66. Vilke GM, Smith AM, Ray LU, et al.: Airway obstruction in children aged less than 5 years: the prehospital experience, *Prehosp Emerg Care* 8:196–199, 2004.

67. Ingalls TH: Heimlich versus a slap on the back, *N Engl J Med* 300:990, 1979.

68. Heimlich HJ: First aid for choking children: back blows and chest thrusts cause complications and death, *Pediatrics* 70:120–125, 1982.

69. Heimlich HJ: Death from food-choking prevented by a new life-saving maneuver, *Heart Lung* 5:755–758, 1976.

70. Brauner DJ: The Heimlich maneuver: procedure of choice? *J Am Geriatr Soc* 35:78, 1987.

71. Redding JS: The choking controversy: critique of evidence on the Heimlich maneuver, *Crit Care Med* 7:475–497, 1979.

72. Skulberg A: Chest compressions—an alternative to the Heimlich manoeuver? (letter), *Resuscitation* 24:91, 1992.

73. Fink JA, Klein RL: Complications of the Heimlich maneuver, *J Pediatr Surg* 24:486–487, 1989.

74. Gordon AS, Belton MK, Ridolpho RF: Emergency management of foreign body airway obstruction. In: Safar P, Elam J, editors: *Advances in cardiopulmonary resuscitation,* New York, Springer-Verlag, 1977.

75. Guildner CW, Williams D, Subitch T: Airway obstructed by foreign material: the Heimlich maneuver, *J Am Coll Emerg Phys* 5:657–677, 1976.

76. Ayerdi J, Gupta SK, Samspson LN, Deshmukh N: Acute abdominal aortic thrombosis following the Heimlich maneuver, *Cardiovasc Surg* 10:154–156, 2002.

77. Tung PH, Law S, Chu KM, et al.: Gastric rupture after Heimlich maneuver and cardiopulmonary resuscitation, *Hepatogastroenterology* 48:109–111, 2001.

78. Wolf DA: Heimlich trauma: a violent maneuver, *Am J Forensic Med Pathol* 22:65–67, 2001.

79. American Heart Association. Part 4: Adult basic life support. Guidelines for BLS and ECC, *Circulation* 112: IV-18–IV-34, 2005.

80. Ward RF: Current trends in pediatric tracheotomy, *Pediatr Pulmonol Suppl* 16:290–291, 1997.

81. Boyd AD, Romita MC, Conlan AA, et al.: A clinical evaluation of cricothyroidotomy, *Surg Gynecol Obstet* 149:365–368, 1979.

82. Walls RM: Airway. In: Mary JA, Hockberger RS, Walls RM, editors: *Rosen's emergency medicine: concepts and clinical practice,* ed 5, St. Louis, Mosby, 2002, pp. 1–20.

83. Morris IR: Functional anatomy of the upper airway, *Emerg Med Clin North Am* 6:639–670, 1988.

84. Gilmore BB, Mickelson SA: Pediatric tracheostomy, *Otolaryngol Clin North Am* 19:141, 1986.

85. Weiss S: A new instrument for emergency cricothyrotomy, *J Am Coll Emerg Phys* 23:331, 1973.

86. Barkin RM: Pediatric emergency management, *Emer Med Clin North Am* 6:687, 1988.

87. DiGiacomo C, Neshat KK, Angus LD, et al.: Emergency cricothyrotomy, *MilMed* 168:541–544, 2003.

88. Narrod JA, Moore EE, Rosen P: Emergency cricothyrostomy: technique and anatomical considerations, *J Emerg Med* 2:443–446, 1985.

89. McLaughlin J, Iserson KV: Emergency pediatric tracheostomy: a usable technique and model for instruction, *Ann Emerg Med* 15:463–465, 1986.

90. McGill J, Clinton JE, Ruiz E: Cricothyroidotomy in the emergency department, *Ann Emerg Med* 11:361–364, 1982.

CHAPTER 12

Hyperventilation

Hyperventilation is defined as ventilation in excess of that required to maintain normal blood PaO_2 (arterial oxygen [O_2] tension) and $PaCO_2$ (arterial carbon dioxide [CO_2] tension).[1] It is produced by an increase in the frequency or depth of respiration, or both. Although the term *hyperventilation* is of recent origin, evidence of the syndrome dates back throughout history.[2] The term *vapors* appeared in 18th- and 19th-century literature to refer to the symptomatic manifestations of anxiety.[3] In Sir William Osler's time (1849–1919), the terms *neurasthenia* or *psychasthenia* described the condition. During World War I, the terms *effort syndrome* and *soldier's heart* were used to describe the symptoms of anxiety encountered in the trenches of Europe.

Hyperventilation, a common emergency occur in the dental office, almost always is a result of extreme anxiety. However, organic causes for hyperventilation do exist; these include pain, metabolic acidosis, drug intoxication, hypercapnia, cirrhosis, and organic central nervous system disorders.[4] In most instances the hyperventilating patient remains conscious throughout the episode. Loss of consciousness secondary to hyperventilation is extremely rare. Hyperventilation more commonly produces an altered level of consciousness; the victim reports feeling faint, lightheaded, or both but does not lose consciousness.

■ PREDISPOSING FACTORS

Acute anxiety is the most common predisposing factor for hyperventilation. In dentistry, hyperventilation most often occurs in apprehensive patients who hide their fears from their doctors and attempt to "tough it out." Hyperventilation rarely occurs in adult patients who freely admit their fears, allowing their doctors to employ stress-reducing techniques. Hyperventilation is rarely encountered in children, primarily because children usually make no attempt to hide their fears. Instead, apprehensive children voice uncertainties in rather obvious ways—crying, biting, kicking. Where the patient's anxieties are released, hyperventilation and vasodepressor syncope rarely occur.

Likewise, patients older than 40 years do not experience hyperventilation and vasodepressor syncope as often as younger age groups; these patients are usually able to cope with the stress of dental treatment and to admit their fears to the doctor. In my experience, hyperventilation most often occurs in patients 15 to 40 years of age. In addition, it has been stated that hyperventilation occurs more frequently in women;[5] however, recent reports and my experience have demonstrated that the condition occurs almost equally across the sexes.[6]

■ PREVENTION
Medical history questionnaire

Hyperventilation can be prevented most effectively through the prompt recognition and management of anxiety. An anxiety questionnaire (see Chapter 2) may be included as part of the medical history the patient completes before the doctor begins treatment. Treatment can then be modified to accommodate the patient's fears. The stress reduction protocol is an invaluable asset in this quest. Though there are no specific questions on the long- or short-form medical histories that relate to hyperventilation, question 5 (Have you had problems with prior dental treatment?) offers a patient the opportunity to mention prior bad dental office experiences or dental fears.

Physical evaluation

Through careful examination it is usually possible to detect a patient's anxiety. Shaking hands with the patient provides valuable information. Cold, wet (clammy) hands usually indicate apprehension. In extreme instances a mild tremor of the hands may be obvious. The patient may appear either flushed or pale; in either case the forehead is usually bathed with perspiration, the patient may remark that the office is unusually warm, regardless of its actual temperature. Fearful patients simply appear uncomfortable when they sit in dental chairs and are overly concerned with the goings-on around them.

Vital signs

The vital signs of apprehensive patients may deviate from the normal, or baseline, values for that individual. Blood pressure is elevated, with the systolic pressure rising more than the diastolic. The heart rate is increased, potentially to a degree significantly higher than the baseline for that patient. In addition, the patient's respiratory rate increases above the normal adult rate of 14 to 18 breaths per minute, whereas the depth of respiration may be either deeper or more shallow than normal.

The vital signs that are recorded on the patient's first visit to the dental office serve as baseline levels for all future readings. Therefore, every effort should be made to minimize any anxiety at this initial visit. Indeed these efforts at anxiety reduction should continue at all times during treatment. To obtain more realistic baseline vital signs through stress reduction, the patient should be allowed to rest for a few minutes before vital signs are taken. An easy way to accomplish this is to start a review of the medical history questionnaire (dialogue history) and then, after 5 minutes, measure the vital signs.

Another important factor to consider is that the recording of baseline vital signs at a visit during which no dental treatment is to be performed is often the best, and only, opportunity to obtain "normal" values. The patient in this situation is better able to relax and the vital signs may be closer to their normal (non–dental office) values. At subsequent visits, monitoring of vital signs may reflect the patient's increased apprehension toward impending treatment.

Dental therapy considerations

The stress reduction protocol outlined in Chapter 2 is the primary means of preventing hyperventilation. Care taken by the dental office staff to make every dental visit a pleasant one leads to the reeducation of the fearful patient and to a decrease in dental anxieties. Stress reduction is one of the most important factors in proper patient management.

■ CLINICAL MANIFESTATIONS
Signs and symptoms

At the onset of hyperventilation, which is frequently precipitated by the fear associated with receiving a local anesthetic injection, the patient may report chest tightness and a feeling of suffocation but may be entirely unaware of that they are overbreathing. As hyperventilation continues, the chemical composition of the blood changes and the patient begins to feel lightheaded or giddy, which enhances their apprehension even more. Increased apprehension leads to an increase in the severity of the episode, and a vicious cycle begins. Hyperventilation caused by dental anxiety leads to even further increased anxiety when the patient becomes aware of their hyperventilation, then to an even further increase in hyperventilation because of the increased anxiety. The goal in management of the situation is to break this cycle.

At the onset of hyperventilation symptoms related to the cardiovascular system and gastrointestinal tract often appear. These symptoms include palpitation (a subjective feeling of a pounding of the heart that is perceptible to the patient), precordial discomfort, epigastric discomfort, and globus hystericus (a subjective feeling of a lump in the throat).

Left untreated, hyperventilation may last for relatively long periods. Patients have hyperventilated for 30 minutes or longer and have suffered several episodes per day. In instances in which hyperventilation continues for prolonged periods, the patient may experience tingling or paresthesias of the hands, feet, and perioral regions. Patients often describe these feelings as sensations of numbness or coldness.

As hyperventilation continues, the patient may develop muscular twitching and carpopedal tetany, a syndrome manifested by flexion of the wrist and ankle joints, muscular twitching and cramps, and convulsions. If the hyperventilating patient is not managed promptly and precisely, syncope may result. Table 12-1 summarizes the signs and symptoms associated with hyperventilation.

Effect on vital signs

Respiratory changes (both the rate and depth) are the primary clinical manifestation of hyperventilation. Normal respiratory rate for the adult is 14 to 18 breaths per minute. During hyperventilation the respiratory rate may exceed 25 to 30 breaths per minute. Not only does the rate of breathing increase, but the patient also usually exhibits an increase in the depth of breathing. To the person who has never seen or experienced hyperventilation, the nature of the patient's breathing may look like to that of someone who has just finished strenuous exercise (e.g., when a runner stands bent over and panting).

In the case of the runner, both the rate and the depth of breathing increase. These increases are normal physiologic responses to an increased metabolic rate as the body works to eliminate excessive CO_2 (produced during the exercise). Although the nature of a hyperventilating patient's breathing is similar to that

TABLE 12-1 Clinical manifestations of hyperventilation

System	Signs and symptoms
Cardiovascular	Palpitations
	Tachycardia
	Precordial "pain"
Neurologic	Dizziness
	Lightheadedness
	Disturbance of consciousness
	Disturbance of vision
	Numbness and tingling of the extremities
	Tetany (rare)
Respiratory	Shortness of breath
	Chest "pain"
	Dryness of mouth
Gastrointestinal	Globus hystericus
	Epigastric pain
Musculoskeletal	Muscle pain and cramps
	Tremor
	Stiffness
	Carpopedal tetany
Psychological	Tension
	Anxiety
	Nightmares

of the athlete, it represents an abnormal physiologic response to the presence of anxiety because there is no elevation of CO_2 levels in the blood.

As previously stated, episodes of hyperventilation are most common in overtly apprehensive patients; however, many other patients may appear calm and totally unaware that they are hyperventilating.

■ PATHOPHYSIOLOGY

Several distinct conditions—anxiety, respiratory alkalosis, an increase in the blood catecholamine level, and a decrease in the level of ionized calcium in the blood—produce the spectrum of signs and symptoms associated with hyperventilation.[7,8]

Anxiety is responsible for both the increase in respiratory rate and depth and the increase in the levels of the catecholamines, epinephrine and norepinephrine, in the blood (a result of the "fight or flight" response). The body's primary response to these respiratory changes is an increased exchange of O_2 and CO_2 by the lungs, which results in an excessive "blowing off" of CO_2. The

$PaCO_2$ decreases from a normal level of 35 to 45 torr to below 35 torr (hypocapnia, or hypocarbia); the decreased CO_2 level produces an increase in the blood's pH to 7.55 (normal, 7.35 to 7.45), a condition known as *respiratory alkalosis*.

However, this same situation—increased ventilation—at the end of strenuous exercise does not produce respiratory alkalosis because exercise increases the body's rate of metabolism, producing an increased blood $PaCO_2$. Increased breathing in this case leads to the restoration of normal CO_2 blood levels. In the patient who starts with normal levels of CO_2, hyperventilation reduces the $PaCO_2$ to an abnormally low level (hypocapnea).

Hypocapnea and respiratory alkalosis are the result of hyperventilation in an individual who has not exercised. Hypocapnea produces vasoconstriction in cerebral blood vessels, leading to a degree of cerebral ischemia, and helping to explain the lightheadedness, dizziness, and giddiness associated with hyperventilation.[9] The degree of cerebral ischemia is usually insufficient to produce the loss of consciousness, although this may occur on rare occasions.[10–12] Many hyperventilating patients describe a "feeling of tightness" in the chest. In certain situations, differentiation of this chest "pain" from that of angina pectoris may be difficult.

Anxiety also produces increased blood levels of catecholamines, which may be responsible for the palpitations, precordial oppression, trembling, and diaphoresis frequently reported with spontaneously hyperventilating patients. It is interesting to note that volunteers who were asked to hyperventilate did not exhibit these symptoms, which are thought to be produced by catecholamine release although the symptoms related to increased rates and depths of breathing (e.g., lightheadedness and faintness) are still present.[13]

Respiratory alkalosis also affects the level of calcium in the blood. As blood pH rises from a normal of about 7.4 to approximately 7.55 in hyperventilation, calcium metabolism is disturbed. Although the total serum level of calcium remains approximately normal, the level of ionized calcium in the blood decreases as the blood's pH increases. Decreases in ionized calcium in the blood result in increased neuromuscular irritability and excitability, which, if permitted to progress, can result in a variety of symptoms, including tingling and paresthesia of the hands, feet, and perioral regions; carpopedal tetany; cramps; and possible convulsions.

■ MANAGEMENT

The management of hyperventilation is directed at correcting the respiratory problem and reducing the patient's anxiety level.

Hyperventilation in the dental environment is almost always produced by dental fears that have been well hidden by the patient. The subsequent inability of the patient to control the breathing further increases those fears. The doctor and staff members must initially attempt to calm the patient; they themselves must remain calm throughout the episode so that they do not exacerbate the situation.

Step 1: termination of the dental procedure. The presumed cause of the episode (e.g., a syringe, dental handpiece, or pair of forceps) should be removed from the patient's line of vision.

Step 2: P (position). The hyperventilating patient is conscious and will exhibit varying degrees of difficulty in breathing. The preferred position for this patient is usually upright. The supine position is normally uncomfortable for such patients because of the diminished ventilatory volume caused by the impingement of the abdominal viscera on the diaphragm and the perceived loss of control patients have over their body when lying down. Most hyperventilating patients will be comfortable sitting fully or partially upright.

Step 3: A-B-C (airway-breathing-circulation), basic life support as needed. Hyperventilating individuals rarely require basic life support. Such victims are conscious and breathing efficiently (indeed, they are overventilating), and the heart is quite functional.

Step 4: D (definitive care):
Step 4a: removal of materials from the mouth. All foreign objects, such as a rubber dam, clamps, and partial dentures, should be removed from the patient's mouth and any tight bindings (e.g., a tight collar, tie, or blouse), which may restrict breathing, loosened.

Step 4b: calming of the patient. Reassure the patient that all is well in a calm and relaxed manner. Attempt to help the patient regain control of their breathing by speaking calmly. Have the patient breathe slowly and regularly at a rate of about 4 to 6 breaths per minute, if possible. This will allow the $PaCO_2$ to increase, reducing the pH of the blood to near normal and eliminating (slowly) any symptoms produced by respiratory alkalosis. In many cases of hyperventilation these are the only steps necessary to terminate the episode.

Step 4c: correction of respiratory alkalosis. When the preceding steps are ineffective, helping the patient to increase their blood's $PaCO_2$ level is our next concern. The patient may be instructed to breathe

FIGURE 12-1 The hyperventilating victim cups the hands together in front of the mouth and nose as a means of increasing the arterial carbon dioxide tension ($PaCO_2$).

a gaseous mixture of 7% CO_2 and 93% O_2, which is supplied in compressed gas cylinders but is highly unlikely to be available in a dental office. More realistically, the patient will be told to rebreathe exhaled air, which contains an increased concentration of CO_2.

The most practical method of increasing $PaCO_2$ levels in the blood is to instruct the hyperventilating victim to cup their hands in front of the mouth and nose and to breathe in and out of this reservoir of CO_2-enriched exhaled air (Figure 12-1). In addition to elevating $PaCO_2$ levels, the warm exhaled air against their cold hands will warm the patient, alleviating one of the more frightening symptoms of hyperventilation. A full-face mask from an O_2 delivery unit may also be used. However, care must be taken not to administer O_2 to the hyperventilating patient. The patient should breathe into the full-face mask, which is held gently but firmly over the face. The use of a paper bag, into which the victim breathes while it is held over their mouth and nose, is no longer recommended.

One hundred percent O_2 is *not* indicated during management of hyperventilation because the symptoms of hyperventilation are produced, in part, by the decrease in the blood level of CO_2, not by a decrease in O_2 levels. The blood's pH rises (respiratory alkalosis), and the symptoms noted above may be observed. For this reason a major goal of management of hyperventilation is to produce an increase, actually a return to normal, in the blood level of CO_2. The administration of 100% O_2 or of any enriched O_2 mixture further decreases the $PaCO_2$ level, delaying return to normal. The administration

of O_2, though not indicated, will not harm the hyperventilating patient. The administration of 100% O_2 will not resolve the clinical problem but might lead to a further progression of the clinical manifestations. A basic rule of thumb in the administration of O_2 is the following: If ever a patient's condition worsens when receiving 100% O_2, the O_2 flow should be terminated and the patient allowed to breathe ambient air.

Step 4d: drug management, if necessary. If the previously discussed steps fail to terminate an episode of hyperventilation—an exceedingly unlikely situation—parenteral drug administration may be necessary to relieve the patient's anxiety and slow the rate of breathing. The drugs of choice in this situation are the benzodiazepines, diazepam, or midazolam. If possible, the drug is administered intravenously, in which case it is titrated (at 1 mL per minute) until the patient's anxiety is visibly reduced and the patient is able to control breathing.

When the intravenous route is unavailable, 10 mg diazepam or 3 to 5 mg midazolam may be administered intramuscularly. Midazolam is preferred because diazepam is not water soluble and burns when injected intramuscularly. If diazepam is used, however, the drug should be injected deep into the muscle mass and the area massaged. Oral administration of diazepam may also be considered because the latent period for diazepam is actually longer after intramuscular administration than after oral administration.[14] An oral dose of 10 to 15 mg diazepam usually terminates hyperventilation within 30 minutes. It must be emphasized that drug therapy for the termination of hyperventilation is rarely required.

Step 5: subsequent dental treatment. Once the episode of hyperventilation is ended, with all clinical signs and symptoms resolved, the dentist must determine the cause of the hyperventilation. Like vasodepressor syncope, hyperventilation is often the first clinical manifestation of a deep-seated dental fear. Dental treatment may continue at this time if both the doctor and the patient are comfortable in doing so. However, subsequent dental treatment should be modified and the stress reduction protocol consulted to prevent a recurrence of hyperventilation.

Step 6: discharge. After the episode has ended and all signs and symptoms are resolved, the patient may be discharged from the office as usual. If the doctor has any uncertainty about the patient's recovery, a person with a vested interest in the health and safety of the patient, such as a friend or relative, should be called to take the patient home. An entry about the

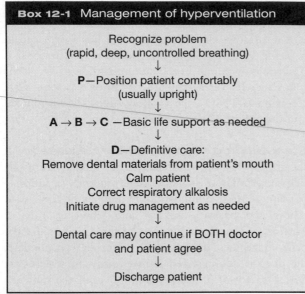

Box 12-1 Management of hyperventilation

Recognize problem
(rapid, deep, uncontrolled breathing)
↓
P—Position patient comfortably
(usually upright)
↓
A → **B** → **C** —Basic life support as needed
↓
D—Definitive care:
Remove dental materials from patient's mouth
Calm patient
Correct respiratory alkalosis
Initiate drug management as needed
↓
Dental care may continue if BOTH doctor
and patient agree
↓
Discharge patient

A, airway; **B,** breathing; **C,** circulation; **D,** definitive care; **P,** position.

episode and its management should be placed in the dental progress notes.

Box 12-1 summarizes the management of hyperventilation.

- **Drugs used in management:** No drugs are usually required in the management of hyperventilation. However, the rare patient who does not respond to conservative management may require the administration of either diazepam or midazolam.
- **Medical assistance required:** None.

Like vasodepressor syncope, hyperventilation should not occur a second time in the same patient. Proper management of the fearful patient through the use of psychosedation can eliminate the recurrence of these two anxiety-produced, potentially life-threatening situations.

REFERENCES

1. Anderson KN: *Mosby's medical, nursing, & allied health dictionary,* ed 5, St. Louis, Mosby, 1998.
2. Paulley JW: Hyperventilation, *Recenti Prog Med* 81: 594–600, 1990.
3. Dalessio DJ: Hyperventilation: the vapors, effort syndrome, neurasthenia—anxiety by any other name is just as disturbing, *JAMA* 239:1401–1402, 1978.
4. Dailey RH: Difficulty in breathing. In: Schwartz GR, editor: *Principles and practice of emergency medicine,* ed 3, Philadelphia, Lea & Febiger, 1992.
5. Sama A, Meikle JC, Jones NS: Hyperventilation and dizziness: case reports and management, *Br J Clin Pract* 49:79–82, 1995.
6. Lum LC: Hyperventilation: the tip and the iceberg, *J Psychosom Res* 19:375–383, 1975.
7. Folgering H: The pathophysiology of hyperventilation syndrome, *Mondali Arch Chest Dis* 54:365–372, 1999.
8. Foster GT, Vaziri ND, Sassoon CS: Respiratory alkalosis, *Respir Care* 46:384–391, 2001.
9. Gardner WN: The pathophysiology of hyperventilation disorders, *Chest* 109:516–534, 1996.
10. Edmeads J: Understanding dizziness: how to decipher this nonspecific symptom, *Postgrad Med* 88:255–258, 263–268, 1990.
11. Neill WA, Hattenhauer M: Impairment of myocardial O_2 supply due to hyperventilation, *Circulation* 52:854–858, 1975.
12. Wheatley CE: Hyperventilation syndrome: a frequent cause of chest pain, *Chest* 68:195–199, 1975.
13. Beck JG, Berisford MA, Taegtmeyer H: The effects of voluntary hyperventilation on patients with chest pain without coronary artery disease, *Behav Res Ther* 29: 611–621, 1991.
14. Divoll M, Greenblatt DJ, Ochs HR, Shader RI: Absolute bioavailability of oral and intramuscular diazepam: effect of age and sex, *Anesth Analg* 62:1–8, 1983.

CHAPTER 13

Asthma

Asthma was defined in 1830 by Eberle, a Philadelphia physician, as "paroxysmal affection of the respiratory organs, characterized by great difficulty of breathing, tightness across the breast, and a sense of impending suffocation, without fever or local inflammation."[1] Today, *asthma* is defined as "a chronic inflammatory disorder that is characterized by reversible obstruction of the airways."[2]

Asthma affects an estimated 5% of adults and approximately 10% of children in the United States[3] and between 3% and 20% worldwide.[4] Approximately 17 million Americans, and more than 100 million persons worldwide, suffer from asthma.[5] A typical asthmatic patient is usually free of symptoms between acute episodes but exhibits varying degrees of respiratory distress during the acute episode. Although the degree of respiratory distress (dyspnea) is usually moderate, asthma represents the third leading cause of emergency department visits (>2 million annually)[6] and preventable hospitalizations (470,000 annually) in the United States.[7] Forty percent of all adults with asthma visit an emergency department at least once a year with an acute exacerbation.[8] It is estimated that asthma is responsible for 5000 to 6000 deaths in the United States annually.[6] A majority of these deaths occur in adults.[9]

Asthma is primarily a disease of young people; half of all cases develop before the individual reaches 10 years of age, and another third before age 40 years.[10] Asthma is also the most chronic disease of childhood. Asthmatic children account for a significant number of children who visit emergency rooms and up to 8% of all admissions at one large children's hospital.[11] Asthma occurs more frequently and with increased severity in minority and inner-city African-American and Hispanic populations.[11] Acute asthmatic episodes are usually self-limiting; however, a clinical entity termed *status asthmaticus* is characterized by a persistent exacerbation of asthma.[12] Status asthmaticus is an acute exacerbation of asthma that remains unresponsive to initial treatment with bronchodilators. Status asthmaticus can vary from a mild to a severe form with bronchospasm, airway inflammation, and mucus plugging that can cause difficulty breathing, carbon dioxide retention, hypoxemia, and respiratory failure. The typical clinical presentation involves persistent wheezing with sternal retractions.[13]

■ PREDISPOSING FACTORS

Asthma is usually classified according to causative factors into two major categories: extrinsic (allergic asthma) and intrinsic (nonallergic asthma, idiosyncratic asthma, nonatopic asthma) (Box 13-1). Individuals with extrinsic asthma have histories of atopy (a type I hypersensitivity or allergic reaction for which there is a genetic component), whereas those with intrinsic asthma do not. One factor, however, is common in all asthmatic patients—extreme sensitivity of the airways. This sensitivity is characterized not only by an increased contractile response of airway smooth muscle but also by an abnormal generation and clearance of secretions and an abnormally sensitive cough reflex.

Extrinsic asthma

Extrinsic asthma, also known as *allergic asthma,* affects 50% of patients with asthma and occurs more often in children and younger adults. Most patients with this form of asthma demonstrate an inherited allergic

Box 13-1 Causative factors for acute asthma
Allergy (antigen-antibody reaction)
Respiratory infection
Physical exertion
Environmental and air pollution
Occupational stimuli
Pharmacologic stimuli
Psychological factors

predisposition. The inhalation of specific allergens may precipitate acute asthmatic episodes. The allergens may be airborne, such as house dust, feathers, animal dander, furniture stuffing, fungal spores, or a wide variety of plant pollens.[14] Foods and drugs may also precipitate allergic asthma. Highly allergenic foods include cow's milk, eggs, fish, chocolate, shellfish, and tomatoes. Penicillin,[15] vaccines, aspirin,[16] and sulfites[17,18] are examples of drugs and chemicals that often induce asthmatic episodes. Bronchospasm usually develops within minutes after exposure to the allergen (antigen). This response is called a type I hypersensitivity reaction in which immunoglobulin E (IgE) antibodies are produced in response to the allergen (see Chapter 24).

Acute episodes of extrinsic asthma usually occur with diminishing frequency and severity during middle and late adolescence and may disappear entirely later in life. Approximately 50% of asthmatic children become asymptomatic before reaching adulthood.[19] It is possible, however, for extrinsic asthma to become chronic in some individuals. This appears to be more common when asthma originally develops in early childhood and is associated with eczema.

Intrinsic asthma

The second major category, which affects the other half of asthmatic patients, is intrinsic asthma. Intrinsic asthma usually develops in adults older than age 35 years. Nonallergic factors—respiratory infection,[20] physical exertion,[21,22] environmental and air pollution,[23,24] and occupational stimuli[25]—precipitate these episodes. Intrinsic asthma is also called *nonallergic asthma, idiopathic asthma,* and *infective asthma.* Individuals who suffer this condition usually have negative histories to allergy, and the results of allergy testing (e.g., skin tests) usually are negative.

Viral infection of the respiratory tract is the most common causative factor. Viral infections are known to enhance airway reactivity in both asthmatic[26] and non-asthmatic[27] patients. Individuals with exercise-induced asthma experience symptoms within 6 to 10 minutes after the start of the exercise, followed by a more severe delayed phase of bronchospasm that develops after the individual has completed the activity. The entire episode, which individuals in all age groups and both sexes experience, classically lasts 30 to 60 minutes.[21]

Psychological and physiologic stress can also contribute to asthmatic episodes in susceptible individuals.[28] Acute asthmatic episodes occur frequently in children during or after a disciplinary session with a parent.[29] The dental office is another common site for asthmatic attacks.[30,31] Simply walking into the treatment room may induce an acute episode in an asthmatic child.

Acute signs and symptoms usually resolve dramatically by simply removing the child from the treatment room into a less threatening environment, such as the reception area.[32] Psychological factors may also be important in adult asthma. Stressful situations, such as dental appointments, produce symptoms in many adults with asthma. I have observed dental students with well-controlled asthma experience periods of chronic bronchospasm during final examination week.

Figure 13-1 illustrates a simplified view of the mechanisms involved in asthma. Acute episodes of intrinsic asthma usually are more fulminant and severe than those of allergic (extrinsic) asthma. The long-term prognosis of intrinsic asthma is also less optimistic because the disease usually becomes chronic and the patient eventually exhibits clinical signs and symptoms (e.g., cough and sputum production) in the intervals between acute episodes.[33]

Mixed asthma

Mixed asthma refers to a combination of extrinsic and intrinsic asthma. The major precipitating factor in this form of asthma is the presence of infection, especially respiratory tract infection.

Status asthmaticus

Status asthmaticus is the most severe clinical form of asthma. Individuals who suffer from status asthmaticus experience wheezing, dyspnea, hypoxia, and others symptoms that are refractory to two to three doses of β-adrenergic agents.[34,35]

Status asthmaticus represents a true medical emergency. If not managed adequately and promptly, the patient in status asthmaticus may die as a result of the respiratory changes that develop secondary to respiratory distress. These changes include hypotension and respiratory acidosis secondary to hypoxemia and hypercapnia.

Table 13-1 presents a classification of asthma based on the severity of signs and symptoms, while Box 13-2 presents the long-term and immediate management protocols for each asthma category.

■ PREVENTION

The primary care physician's goal in the long-term management of asthma is to maintain the patient's pulmonary status as close to normal as possible for as long as possible (Table 13-2). With the advent of newer and longer-acting medications, this goal is more realistic. A second factor that has helped to further this goal is the recognition that the pulmonary status of most asthmatic patients is far from normal in the period between acute episodes. Thus, the goal in dental management of the asthmatic patient is the prevention of acute episodes, an end best accomplished through use of the information obtained from the patient's medical history and the dialogue history between the doctor and patient.

MEDICAL HISTORY QUESTIONNAIRE

The University of the Pacific medical history questionnaire contains several questions that relate to a prior history of asthma, hay fever, and allergy.

Question 35: Do you have or have you had: asthma, tuberculosis, emphysema, other lung diseases?
Comment: A positive response to any part of this question should prompt the doctor to conduct a more in-depth dialogue history to find out what the specific problem is and if it is asthma, to determine how severe it is.

Question 38: Do you have or have you had: allergies to: drugs, foods, medications, latex?
Comment: Approximately 50% of asthmatic patients have extrinsic asthma, acute episodes of which are precipitated by an allergen. Common allergens precipitating bronchospasm include tobacco smoke, dust mites, animal fur, cockroaches, pollens, molds, and other airborne irritants (including acrylic and other aerosolized dental materials).[31,36,37]

Question 62: Are you taking: drugs, medications, over-the-counter medicines (including aspirin), natural remedies?
Comment: Many patients with asthma, especially children, take oral drugs in the period between acute episodes to prevent or reduce the frequency of recurrence. Categories of commonly used drugs include inhaled short-acting β-adrenergic agonists, inhaled corticosteroids, cromolyn and nedocromil, leukotriene antagonists, theophylline, anticholinergics (ipratropium bromide),

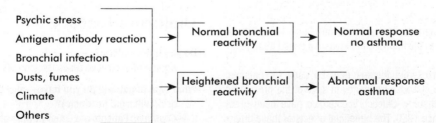

FIGURE 13-1 Predisposing factors for asthma. (From Pain MC: The treatment of asthma, *Drugs* 6:118–126, 1973.)

TABLE 13-1 Asthma classification by severity

Classification	Symptoms	Nighttime symptoms	Lung function
Mild intermittent	Symptoms ≤2 times a week Asymptomatic and normal PEF between exacerbations Exacerbations brief (from a few hours to a few days); intensity may vary	≤2 times a month	FEV$_1$ or PEF 80% predicted PEF variability <20%
Mild persistent	Symptoms >2 times a week but ≤ once per day Exacerbations may affect activity	>2 times a month	FEV$_1$ or PEF ≥80% predicted PEF variability, 20–30%
Moderate persistent	Daily symptoms Daily use of inhaled short-acting β$_2$-agonist Exacerbations affect activity Exacerbations ≥2 times a week; may last days	>1 time a week	FEV$_1$ or PEF >60% ≤80% predicted PEF variability >30%
Severe persistent	Continual symptoms Limited physical activity Frequent exacerbations	Frequent	FEV$_1$ or PEF ≤60% predicted PEF variability >30%

FEV$_1$, forced expiratory volume in 1 second; PEF, peak expiratory flow.
Modified from National Heart, Lung, and Blood Institute: *Expert Panel report 2. Guidelines for the diagnosis and management of asthma.* Baltimore, U.S. Department of Health and Human Services, Public Health Service, National Institutes of Health, National Heart, Lung, and Blood Institute, 1997. NIH publication no. 4051.

Box 13-2 Medical management of asthma: treatment goals

Prevent chronic and troublesome symptoms (e.g., coughing or breathlessness in the night, in the early morning, or after exertion)

Maintain (near) "normal" pulmonary function

Maintain normal activity levels (including exercise and other physical activity)

Prevent recurrent exacerbations of asthma and minimize the need for emergency department visits or hospitalizations

Provide optimal pharmacotherapy with minimal or no adverse effects

Meet patients' and families' expectation of and satisfaction with asthma care

From National Heart, Lung, and Blood Institute: *Expert Panel report 2. Guidelines for the diagnosis and management of asthma.* Baltimore, U.S. Department of Health and Human Services, Public Health Service, National Institutes of Health, National Heart, Lung, and Blood Institute, 1997, NIH publication no. 4051.

---

systemic corticosteroids, and epinephrine (Table 13-3). These drugs usually have little impact on the planned dental treatment.

Long-term glucocorticosteroid therapy may be used for patients who experience acute episodes frequently in spite of the previously mentioned forms of therapy. Glucocorticosteroids have been used to manage asthma since 1950. The beneficial effects of these drugs are most likely related to their antiinflammatory actions because they have little or no direct bronchodilating activity.[38] Patients receiving long-term glucocorticosteroid therapy should be evaluated carefully for possible adrenocortical insufficiency.

Cromolyn sodium (Intal), a mast cell stabilizer, is used in the preventive management of acute asthmatic episodes, primarily in patients with allergic (extrinsic) asthma. The drug is effective only during periods of remission to prevent recurrences and decrease the patient's corticosteroid requirement. Cromolyn sodium is available as an inhalant in a micronized powder. Nedocromil sodium is an antiinflammatory drug that inhibits mediator release and reduces airway hyperreactivity.[39]

In addition, most asthmatic patients carry a "rescue" drug used to terminate the acute episode of bronchospasm. Most commonly employed is albuterol.

Alternative medicines, such as *Ocimum sanctum* Linn (Tulsi),[40] Chinese herbal formula MSSM-002,[41] and dried ivy (*Hedera helix L.*),[42] have been shown in some studies to provide decreased airway resistance and improved asthma control. However, many of these products, which have been widely used, have "an astonishing and perhaps frightening lack of information about the safety of these remedies."[43,44]

Dialogue history

Do you have asthma?
Comment: A positive response prompts further questioning.

What type of asthma do you have—allergic (extrinsic) or nonallergic (intrinsic)?
Comment: Patients are usually aware of the type of asthma from which they suffer.

TABLE 13-2 Medical management of asthma: drug therapies

Classification	Long-term control	Immediate management of acute episodes
Mild intermittent	None needed	Short-acting bronchodilator: inhaled β_2-agonists as needed for symptoms
Mild persistent	Daily medication: Antiinflammatory: either inhaled corticosteroids (low doses) or cromolyn, or nedocromil Sustained-release theophylline as alternative Leukotriene modifiers considered for patients ≥12 years of age	Short-acting bronchodilator: inhaled β_2-agonists as needed for symptoms
Moderate persistent	Daily medication: Either Antiinflammatory: inhaled corticosteroid (medium dose) OR Inhaled corticosteroid (low-medium dose) and addition of long-acting bronchodilator, especially for nighttime symptoms: either long-acting inhaled β_2-agonist, sustained-release theophylline, or long-acting β_2-agonist tablets. If needed: Antiinflammatory inhaled corticosteroids (medium-high dose) AND Long-acting bronchodilator	Short-acting bronchodilator: inhaled β_2-agonists as needed for symptoms
Severe persistent	Daily medications: Antiinflammatory: inhaled corticosteroid (high dose) AND Long-acting bronchodilator: either long-acting inhaled β_2-agonist, sustained-release theophylline, and/or long-acting β_2-agonist in tablet or syrup form AND Corticosteroid in tablet or syrup form, long term	Short-acting bronchodilator: inhaled β_2-agonists as needed for symptoms

Modified from National Heart, Lung, and Blood Institute: *Expert Panel report 2. Guidelines for the diagnosis and management of asthma.* Baltimore, U.S. Department of Health and Human Services, Public Health Service, National Institutes of Health, National Heart, Lung, and Blood Institute, 1997. NIH publication no. 4051.

At what age did you first develop asthma?

Comment: Allergic asthma most often develops in children and younger adults, whereas nonallergic asthma more commonly develops in individuals older than 35 years.

How often do you develop acute episodes?

Comment: The more frequently these episodes occur, the greater the likelihood that an episode will develop during dental treatment.

What precipitates your acute asthmatic attacks?

Comment: Awareness of the factors involved in a patient's acute episodes helps in their prevention during treatment. Stress is a particularly important factor in precipitating both extrinsic and intrinsic asthma. The patient's attitude toward dentistry must be determined and appropriate steps taken to ensure as stress-free an appointment as possible. The stress reduction protocol is an invaluable tool (see Chapter 2).

How do you manage your acute asthmatic attacks?

Comment: Determine which drugs are used by the patient to terminate acute episodes. Most patients keep their medications with them at all times. The doctor should ask to see these medications, note them in the patient's chart, and request that the patient bring them to each visit (with frequent reminders). These medications, usually nebulized β_2-adrenergic agonists, should be kept close to the patient throughout the appointment.

Have you ever required emergency care or hospitalization for your acute asthmatic episodes?

Comment: This question seeks to determine the severity of the acute episodes. Although bronchodilator administration readily terminates most episodes, status asthmaticus is refractory to the usual β-adrenergic therapy. Hospitalization of the patient is normally required in such instances. With a history of prior need for emergency medical assistance or hospitalization, the dentist would be more likely to seek out such assistance earlier in an acute asthmatic episode than in a situation in which an asthmatic patient has never required emergency care. Forty percent of the estimated 17 million American asthmatic patients visit the hospital emergency department at least once a year with an acute exacerbation.[9]

TABLE 13-3 Commonly prescribed drugs for the management of obstructive airway disease

Category	Generic	Proprietary
BRONCHODILATOR		
Sympathomimetic	Albuterol	Proventil, Ventolin, Volmax, VoSpire
	Salmeterol	Serevent
	Metaproterenol	Alupent
	Levalbuterol	Xopenex
	Pirbuterol	Maxair
	Terbutaline	Brethine
	Isoetharine	Bronkometer, Bronkosol
	Isoproterenol	Isuprel
	Epinephrine	MicroNefrin, Primatene Mist
	Tiotropium	Spiriva
	Formoterol	Foradil
Anticholinergic	Ipratropium	Atrovent
Theophylline	Theophylline	Theo-24, Theolair, Uniphyl
	Aminophylline	Generic
CORTICOSTEROID		
	Beclomethasone	Beclovent, Qvar
	Triamcinolone acetonide	Azmacort
	Flunisolide	aeroBid
	Mometasone	Asmanex
	Fluticasone	Flovent
	Budesonide	Pulmicort
ANTIMEDIATOR		
	Cromolyn sodium	Intal
	Nedocromil sodium	Tilade

Dental therapy considerations

Modifications to dental treatment depend on the severity of the patient's asthma. Acute episodes precipitated by emotional stress in a patient with many fears of dentistry require judicious handling by the doctor to prevent further recurrences. Use of the stress reduction protocol minimizes the likelihood of acute episodes.

No contraindications exist to the use of any conscious sedation technique in fearful asthmatic patients; some drug groups, such as barbiturates or opioids (especially meperidine), should not be administered. Barbiturates and opioids may increase the risk of bronchospasm in susceptible patients. Opioids produce histamine release, which may provoke bronchospasm.[45] Barbiturates may sensitize the respiratory reflexes, increasing the risk of bronchospasm.[46] Both drug groups are relatively contraindicated in asthmatic patients. Inhalation sedation with nitrous oxide and oxygen; oral sedation with benzodiazepines; and parenteral sedation via intravenous (IV), intranasal, or intramuscular routes are not contraindicated in the fearful asthmatic patient.

On rare occasion the patient's primary care physician may advise the dentist that nitrous oxide administration is contraindicated. This statement is unfounded. Inhalation anesthetic agents, such as ether, that irritate the respiratory mucosa are capable of inducing bronchospasm in these patients.[47] Nitrous oxide does not irritate the respiratory mucosa, is an excellent antianxiety agent, does not provoke bronchospasm, and is absolutely indicated for the management of dental fears in almost all asthmatic patients.[48] An asthmatic patient who also happens to be claustrophobic may be at increased risk for asthmatic episodes if the nasal hood is used for delivery of anesthetic gases. Although it is no longer a recommended means of nitrous oxide and O_2 delivery, a nasal cannula may be used instead.

Between 3% and 19% of asthmatic patients are sensitive to aspirin administration.[49,50] However, the incidence rises to 30% to 40% in patients who have nasal polyps and pansinusitus.[51] Substitutes for these drugs may be prescribed, but because there is considerable cross-sensitivity between aspirin and other nonsteroidal antiinflammatory drugs (NSAIDs), special care must be exercised when analgesics are prescribed. (NSAIDs include naproxen, flurbiprofen, valdecoxib, celecoxib, sulindac, oxaprozin, diclofenac, diflunisal, salsalate, etodolac, piroxicam, fenoprofen, ibuprofen, nabumetone, ketoprofen, mefenamic acid, tolmetin, ketorolac, and rofecoxib).[52]

The food industry has used sulfur dioxide and other sulfiting agents for years in the preservation of foods from oxidation (the sliced apple being an example of a food that oxidizes rapidly when exposed to air). Reports have documented numerous cases of death and other severe reactions predominantly among individuals with asthma or a sensitivity to sulfites after eating such foods and drinks at restaurants.[53-56] Reactions included urticaria, gastrointestinal upset, bronchospasm, and anaphylactic shock.[17]

TABLE 13-4 American Society of Anesthesiologists classification for asthma

ASA Classification	Description	Treatment modifications
II	Typical asthma—extrinsic or intrinsic	Use stress reduction protocol as needed
	Infrequent episodes	Determine triggering factors
	Easily managed	Avoid triggering factors
	No need for emergency care or hospitalization	Keep bronchodilator available during appointments
III	Patient with exercise-induced asthma	Follow ASA II modifications and administer sedation—N_2O-O_2 or oral benzodiazepines—as needed
	Fearful asthmatic patient	
	Asthmatic patient with prior need for emergency care or hospitalization	

ASA, American Society of Anesthesiologists (Physical Status Classification System).

Sulfiting agents, such as sodium metabisulfite, are added to certain drugs and chemicals as antioxidants. Individuals have experienced asthmatic reactions (bronchospasm) when they inhaled the bronchodilators isoetharine (Bronkosol)[57] and isoproterenol (Isuprel).[58] Local anesthetic cartridges with vasopressors (e.g., epinephrine and levonordefrin) all contain bisulfites to prevent the oxidation of the vasopressor.[59,60] Although the volume of bisulfite in the local anesthetic cartridge is minimal, bisulfite-sensitive patients have suffered acute asthmatic attacks after administration of these drugs.[60,61] The use of local anesthetics containing bisulfites (i.e., all local anesthetics containing vasopressors) is absolutely contraindicated in these patients.[62] However, in other situations, the contraindication may be only relative, with bisulfite containing local anesthetics administered safely.[63] Local anesthetics that do not contain vasopressors (e.g., lidocaine plain, mepivacaine plain, and prilocaine plain) may be used instead.

Table 13-4 classifies asthma according to the American Society of Anesthesiologists (ASA) Physical Status Classification System. The patient with well-controlled, easily managed asthma represents an ASA II risk during dental treatment. Asthmatic patients who experience acute episodes precipitated by stress or exercise or who have required emergency medical care or hospitalization to terminate an acute episode are ASA III risks; the few asthmatic patients exhibiting clinical symptoms while at rest are ASA IV risks.

■ CLINICAL MANIFESTATIONS

Signs and symptoms of an acute asthmatic attack range in severity from episodes consisting of shortness of breath, wheezing, and cough, followed by complete remission (ASA II or III), to more chronic states in which clinical signs and symptoms, varying in intensity, are

Box 13-3 Signs and symptoms of acute asthma

Feeling of chest congestion
Cough, with or without sputum production
Wheezing
Dyspnea
Patient wants to sit or stand up
Use of accessory muscles of respiration
Increased anxiety and apprehension
Tachypnea (>20 to >40 breaths per minute in severe cases)
Rise in blood pressure
Increase in heart rate (>120 beat per minute in severe episodes)
Diaphoresis
Agitation
Somnolence
Confusion
Cyanosis
Supraclavicular and intercostal retraction
Nasal flaring

present almost continuously (ASA IV). Because the inability to breathe normally may terrify the individual, a large psychological component is present in most episodes of asthma. Symptoms of acute asthma classically consist of a triad: cough, dyspnea, and wheezing.

Usual clinical progression

Signs and symptoms of acute asthma may develop gradually or suddenly (Box 13-3). In the typical episode the patient becomes aware of a sensation of thickness or congestion in the chest. This is usually followed by a coughing spell, which may or may not be associated with sputum production,[64] and wheezing, which is audible during both inspiration and expiration. These signs and symptoms tend to increase in intensity as the episode continues. The patient experiences a variable degree of dyspnea, and in most episodes the asthmatic patient sits up as if fighting for air. Although the expiratory phase of the respiratory cycle is actually more difficult than the inspiratory phase for most asthmatic patients, many patients report that inspiration is more difficult and frequently state that they do not know where their next breath is coming from. Air trapping within the lungs occurs during the acute episode, and asthmatic patients will sit up and use accessory muscles of respiration (i.e., the sternocleidomastoid and scalenus muscles) to lift the entire rib cage cephalad and generate high negative intrapleural pressures, thus increasing the work involved in breathing.[65]

Wheezing does not by itself denote the presence, severity, or duration of asthma.[66] The degree of wheezing or its absence varies according to the radius of the bronchial tube. Mild wheezing is an audible, low-pitched, coarse, discontinuous noise, whereas increased airway obstruction produces a more high-pitched and musical wheeze but remains a low-intensity sound. Wheezing vanishes in individuals suffering severe airway obstruction because there is insufficient air movement velocity to produce sound.[67,68]

As the degree of dyspnea increases, so do the levels of anxiety and apprehension. Breathing during an acute asthmatic attack is labored, with the respiratory rate increasing to more than 20 breaths per minute in most episodes and to more than 40 breaths per minute during more severe episodes. This increased rate may be the result of apprehension, airway obstruction, or a change in blood chemistry.

Blood pressure may remain at approximately baseline levels during milder episodes, but usually rises during acute asthmatic attacks. The rise reflects the increased levels of catecholamines in the blood as a result of increased anxiety. In addition, the heart rate increases. A rate of more than 120 beats per minute is common in cases of severe asthma.

Other clinical signs and symptoms may be present during an acute episode that are not diagnostic of asthma but are noted with respiratory distress. Such symptoms include diaphoresis, agitation, somnolence or confusion, cyanosis, soft tissue retraction in the intercostal and supraclavicular regions, and nasal flaring.[69]

If untreated, the acute asthmatic episode previously described may last minutes or hours. Termination of an episode is usually heralded by a period of intense coughing with expectoration of a thick, tenacious mucus plug. This is followed immediately by a sensation of relief and a clearing of the air passages. Prompt management with an aerosol spray usually aborts the attack within seconds.

Regardless of the precipitating cause, acute asthma is characterized by respiratory smooth muscle spasm, airway inflammation with edema, and mucus hypersecretion. Respiratory smooth muscle spasm most likely accounts for the rapidly reversible types of airway obstruction, whereas inflammatory edema and mucus plugging in the airways account for the more unresponsive forms of asthma.[70]

Status asthmaticus

Status asthmaticus is a clinical state in which a patient with moderate to severe bronchial obstruction does not respond significantly to the rapid-acting β-agonist agents administered in the initial treatment protocol. In this situation, bronchospasm may continue for hours or even days without remission.[71]

Patients in status asthmaticus most commonly exhibit signs of extreme fatigue, dehydration, severe hypoxia, cyanosis, peripheral vascular shock, and drug intoxication as a result of intensive pharmacologic therapy.[72,73] The blood pressure may be at or below baseline levels, and the heart rate quite rapid. The status asthmaticus patient requires hospitalization because the condition is life-threatening. Chronic partial airway obstruction may lead to patient death as a result of muscle fatigue of the muscles of respiration and respiratory acidosis. Status asthmaticus may develop in any asthmatic.

■ PATHOPHYSIOLOGY

Regardless of the type of asthma present, one finding common to all asthmatic patients is an extreme sensitivity of the airways characterized not only by increased contractile response of the airway smooth muscle but also by an abnormal generation and clearance of secretions and an abnormally sensitive cough reflex.[68]

Neural control of the airways

The autonomic nervous system significantly influences airway reactivity. Stimulation of the vagus nerve releases acetylcholine, which produces maximal constriction of the airways with an initial diameter of 3 to 5 mm.[74] Acetylcholine also increases glandular or goblet cell secretion and dilates pulmonary vessels.[75] This vagally mediated reflex bronchoconstriction may result from stimulation of the receptors in the larynx and lower airways, chemoreceptors, and subepithelial irritant receptors.[76]

In the adrenergic nervous system, stimulation of β-receptors results in dilation of the airway smooth muscle and bronchial and pulmonary vascular beds. Additionally, ion and water transport into the airway lumen is facilitated, and glandular secretion is likewise stimulated.[76,77] Stimulation of sympathetic nerves innervating the proximal airways has been shown to provide minimal bronchodilation.[75] Therefore, the preponderance of the β_2-adrenergic airway receptor stimulation most likely occurs as a result of systemic catecholamine release from the adrenal medulla.[78] Stimulation of α-adrenergic receptors results in bronchial smooth muscle constriction; however, significant α-adrenergic contractile effects do not occur clinically except under conditions of β-blockade.[78]

The neural component in the pathogenesis of airway hyperreactivity may be summarized as follows.[68] Vagal sensory receptors in airways with increased bronchomotor responses (as a result of viral respiratory tract infections and exposure to oxidant air pollutants) are stimulated and produce constriction. As a result the normal homeostatic dilator responses (for example, a β_2-blockade provoking bronchoconstriction in asthmatic patients but not in healthy persons) may fail.

Airway inflammation

Airway inflammation is another important factor in the production of increased airway responsiveness. Inflammation may occur as a result of either immunologic or nonimmunologic airway insults, which produce airway edema and the immigration of inflammatory cells into the lumen through the epithelium.[68] Inflammation is associated with an opening of tight cellular junctions and an increase in mucosal permeability, which provides access from the lumen to the airway smooth muscle, submucosal mast cells, and irritant subepithelial receptors.[79] This access may provide an environment that induces multiple methods of airway obstruction, including a direct effect on smooth muscle, a stimulation of mast cells, or vagal reflexes.[68]

Immunologic responses

It is thought that allergic or presumed allergic factors are involved in the majority of asthma cases.[64] These factors may induce bronchial hyperreactivity, trigger acute asthmatic episodes, or both. Extrinsic asthma is classified as a type I immune reaction, an immediate allergic reaction in which an antigen combines with an IgE antibody on the surface of pulmonary mast cells in the submucosa of small peripheral airways and in larger central areas at the luminal surface interdigitating with the epithelium.[80] The reaction causes mast cell degranulation and the release or formation of a number of chemical mediators, including histamine, prostaglandins, acetylcholine, bradykinin, eosinophilic chemotactic factors, and leukotrienes (LT).[81]

In addition, slow-reacting substance of anaphylaxis (SRS-A) has been shown to be composed of the leukotrienes LTC, LTD, and LTE. In humans, LTC and LTD are the most potent bronchoconstrictors—approximately 1000 times more potent than histamine[82]—with a duration of effect from 15 to 20 minutes.[83] (The physiologic actions of these mediators are presented in Chapter 24.)

Once mast cells release the mediators, their pharmacologic activities develop rapidly so that clinical symptoms and signs of an acute asthmatic reaction manifest themselves quickly. Type I allergic reactions are characterized by the rapidity of the reaction time (within 15 to 30 minutes after exposure to the allergen) and are associated with IgE. Clinical examples of the type I immune response include asthma, anaphylaxis, and hay fever.

Bronchospasm

Smooth muscle is present throughout the entire tracheobronchial tree.[84] Bronchial smooth muscle tone is regulated by the vagus nerve, which, when stimulated, causes constriction (bronchospasm), and by the sympathetic nervous system, which produces dilation (bronchodilation).[68]

In nonasthmatic patients, bronchial smooth muscle protects the lungs from foreign stimuli; the airways narrow (bronchial smooth muscle constriction) in response to the foreign stimulus. In the asthmatic patient, however, the response is exaggerated (increased constriction), producing clinical signs and symptoms of respiratory distress. Constriction is most prominent in the small bronchi (0.4 to 0.1 cm in diameter) and bronchioles (0.15 to 0.1 cm in diameter); however, smooth muscle constriction may occur wherever smooth muscle is present.

The site of the asthmatic reaction can vary, depending on the anatomic location of the stimulated bronchial smooth muscle. Stimulation of irritant receptors by foreign particles (e.g., gases, pollens, and chemical mediators) initiates an autonomic, or vagal, reflex. The stimulus is carried by the afferent fibers in the vagus nerve to the central nervous system and then by the efferent fibers, again in the vagus nerve, returning to the lungs; there the efferent fibers terminate on bronchial smooth muscle, producing muscle constriction.

Bronchial wall edema and hypersecretion of mucous glands

In gross and microscopic sections of the lungs of patients who die during asthmatic episodes (usually status asthmaticus), many changes become evident, including mucosal and submucosal edema and thickening of the basement membrane, infiltration by leukocytes (primarily eosinophils), intraluminal mucous plugs, and bronchospasm (see Box 13-2).[14] In cross-section, the lungs appear overdistended, and mucous plugs occlude many of the smaller bronchi. Despite the appearance of overinflation, the lungs of these patients exhibit areas of hyperinflation alternating with areas of atelectasis produced by mucous plugs.

All of these factors act to decrease the size of the airway lumen, increase airway resistance, producing the clinical signs and symptoms of bronchospasm (relative to the degree of airway narrowing). Airway resistance varies inversely to the fourth power of its radius. Therefore, cutting the radius of an airway in half leads to a 16-fold increase in airway resistance (according to Poiseuille's approximation).[85] The result of this increased resistance is increased difficulty in gas exchange and ultimately in alterations of blood chemistry and pH.

Breathing

Breathing is composed of two phases—inspiration and expiration. The inspiratory phase is an active process; thoracic volume increases as the diaphragm and other inspiratory muscles function. As volume increases, the intrapleural pressure increases in negativity (from 2 to 6 torr), and the lungs expand to fill the increasing chest volume. The body then draws air into the lungs until these pressures are equalized.[86]

The expiratory phase normally is a passive process that does not require the individual to expend muscular energy. As the respiratory muscles relax, the elastic tissues of the lungs, which were stretched during inspiration, are able to return to their normal unstretched state in a process termed *elastic recoil*. This shortening of fibers forces air from the lungs, which permits the thorax to return to its normal resting state.

The asthmatic patient experiences varying degrees of airway obstruction that may produce large increases in airway resistance compromising airflow during both inspiration and expiration. To accommodate the increased resistance during inspiration, the workload of the respiratory muscles increases in order to produce a greater degree of chest expansion to permit more air into the lungs.

The deleterious effects of increased airway resistance occur during the expiratory phase of respiration in the majority of asthmatic patients. Elastic recoil of the lungs during expiration is no longer adequate to expel air against the increased airway resistance, and air becomes trapped in the lungs, producing hyperinflation.[87] To minimize hyperinflation, the normally passive expiratory phase becomes active, with both the respiratory and

accessory muscles being used to expel air from the lungs.[87] In addition, the increased resistance impairs ventilation, or the quantity of air exchanged per unit of time, which results in an increase in the rate of breathing (tachypnea).

As the asthmatic episode progresses and airway obstruction worsens, the expiratory phase of respiration becomes longer and air increasingly is trapped in the lungs. The alveoli hyperinflate, producing both an increase in airway diameter from the increased tension and an increase in energy use. The increased use of energy is necessary during the inspiratory phase to overcome the tension of the already stretched elastic lung tissues and allow air into the lungs.

Therefore, if an acute asthmatic episode progresses unresolved, much of the body's energy is expended on respiration. The muscles of respiration eventually become fatigued, further decreasing respiratory efficiency and leading to alveolar hypoventilation.[88] Clinical manifestations at this stage include increased dyspnea, tachypnea, and possible cyanosis. Severe alveolar hypoventilation produces carbon dioxide retention (hypercarbia), which is exhibited as an increase in the rate and depth of respiration (hyperventilation) and a further increase in the work of breathing. Sweating, or diaphoresis, is another clinical sign of hypercarbia.

The process is self-limiting. If airway obstruction worsens and the patient's efforts at breathing increase, the increased hypercarbia and hypoxemia lead to acute respiratory acidosis. Box 13-4 lists the signs and symptoms associated with hypoxemia and hypercarbia. Respiratory failure may occur with the patient requiring mechanical ventilation. Mortality rates at this stage are high.

Box 13-4 Clinical signs and symptoms of hypoxia and hypercarbia

HYPOXIA
Restlessness, confusion, anxiety
Cyanosis
Diaphoresis (profuse sweating)
Tachycardia, cardiac dysrhythmias
Coma
Cardiac and/or renal failure

HYPERCARBIA
Diaphoresis
Hypertension (converting to hypotension, if progressive)
Hyperventilation
Headache
Confusion, somnolence
Cardiac failure

TABLE 13-5 Physiologic changes that develop during moderate and severe asthma

Severity of airway obstruction	PaO$_2$	PaCO$_2$	pH	Base excess
Mild	WNL	L	I	Respiratory alkalosis
Moderate	LL	WNL or L	WNL or I	Normal
Severe	LLL	I	L	Metabolic acidosis Respiratory acidosis

I, increased; L, lowered; PaCO$_2$, arterial carbon dioxide tension; PaO$_2$, arterial O$_2$ tension; WNL, within normal limits.
From Barkin RM, Rosen P: *Emergency pediatrics,* ed 6, St. Louis, Mosby, 2004.

The following is a review of the pathophysiology of mild and severe acute asthmatic episodes (Table 13-5):

- During the mild asthmatic episode, produced primarily by bronchospasm, moderate airway obstruction leads to a decrease in blood oxygenation. The ensuing hypoxia and increased work of breathing result in a heightened level of anxiety, producing hyperventilation. Hyperventilation produces a decrease in the blood's level of carbon dioxide (hypocapnia) and subsequent respiratory alkalosis (see Chapter 12).
- In the more severe asthmatic episode (greater influence of airway inflammation) or in status asthmaticus, the greater degree of bronchial obstruction results in a more profound decrease in blood oxygenation. The respiratory workload increases; however, the body's responses soon prove ineffective as the obstruction becomes greater, leading to inadequate ventilation and carbon dioxide retention, or hypercapnia. Hypercapnia causes respiratory acidosis and may lead to respiratory failure.

■ MANAGEMENT
Acute asthmatic episode (bronchospasm)

Management of an acute asthmatic episode requires prompt and specific drug therapy and symptomatic management (Box 13-5).

Step 1: termination of the dental procedure. Treatment should cease immediately when the individual exhibits signs of an acute asthmatic attack.

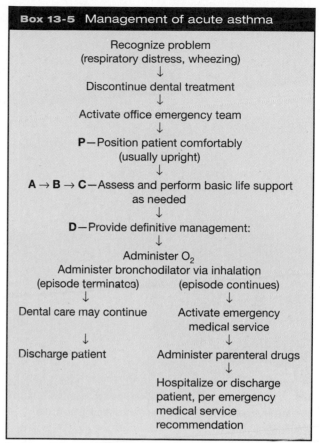

Box 13-5 Management of acute asthma

Recognize problem (respiratory distress, wheezing)
↓
Discontinue dental treatment
↓
Activate office emergency team
↓
P—Position patient comfortably (usually upright)
↓
A → B → C—Assess and perform basic life support as needed
↓
D—Provide definitive management:
↓
Administer O$_2$
Administer bronchodilator via inhalation
(episode terminates)   (episode continues)
↓   ↓
Dental care may continue   Activate emergency medical service
↓   ↓
Discharge patient   Administer parenteral drugs
    ↓
Hospitalize or discharge patient, per emergency medical service recommendation

A, airway; **B,** breathing; **C,** circulation; **D,** definitive care; **P,** position.

Step 2: P (position). The patient is positioned comfortably as soon as signs become evident. The position almost always involves sitting, with the arms thrown forward (Figure 13-2). Other positions are equally acceptable, based upon the comfort and preference of the patient.

Step 3: removal of dental materials. All dental materials or instruments should be removed from the patient's mouth immediately.

Step 4: calming of the patient. Many asthmatic patients, especially those with histories of easily managed bronchospasm, will remain calm throughout the episode. Others, primarily those with acute episodes that have been more difficult to terminate, may exhibit varying degrees of apprehension. Dental personnel must always remain calm themselves as they attempt to calm anxiety-ridden patients.

Step 5: A-B-C (airway-breathing-circulation), basic life support as needed. During the acute asthmatic episode the patient remains conscious, is

FIGURE 13-2 Position for a patient suffering an acute asthmatic attack.

FIGURE 13-3 A patient demonstrates the use of an aerosol inhaler with a spacer attached.

breathing (with a partially obstructed airway), and usually has an increased blood pressure and heart rate.

Step 6: D (definitive care):

Step 6a: administration of O_2. O_2 should be administered during any acute asthmatic episode through a full-face mask, nasal hood, or nasal cannula. (If a nasal cannula is used, a flow of 5 to 7 L per minute is adequate.) The presence of any clinical signs and symptoms of hypoxia and hypercarbia are indications for O_2 administration (see Box 13-4). 10 mL

Step 6b: administration of bronchodilator. Before dental treatment on the asthmatic patient begins, the patient's bronchodilator aerosol inhaler should be placed within easy reach. This medication then should be used to manage an acute episode (Figure 13-3).

Bronchodilators are the drugs used to manage acute bronchospasm. The most potent and effective dilators of bronchial smooth muscle are the β_2-adrenergic agonists, such as epinephrine (Adrenalin), albuterol (Proventil, Ventolin), isoproterenol (Isuprel), and metaproterenol (Alupent) (Figure 13-4). These drugs are agonists of β_2-receptors in the bronchial smooth muscle and relax bronchial, vascular, and uterine smooth muscle. In addition, β_2-stimulation inhibits histamine

release from mast cells, antibody production by lymphocytes, and enzyme release from polymorphonuclear leukocytes.[89]

These agents may be administered orally or sublingually, via aerosol inhalation, or by injection. Although subcutaneous injection of epinephrine produces a rapid onset of relief, it is also associated with many other systemic actions, including dysrhythmias and hypertensive reactions; these reactions occur especially in patients receiving monoamine-oxidase inhibitors or tricyclic antidepressants.[90] Clinically, the best way to achieve bronchial smooth muscle relaxation is to administer β-adrenergic agonists via the inhalation of aerosolized sprays. This method provides an onset of action equal to injection but minimizes systemic absorption and side effects.[91] Aerosolized adrenergic bronchodilators are as effective as those administered via an IV route but have much less potential for serious side effects.[92]

The patient should be given the inhaler and instructed to take the usual dose to terminate the acute episode. Before ever needing to administer a bronchodilator, both the patient and the doctor should read the package insert to determine the maximum dose that may be administered safely in a given period.

Undesirable reactions associated with the use of these drugs relate primarily to the β_1- and α-receptor–stimulating actions of epinephrine and isoproterenol. Metaproterenol is a partially selective β_2-agonist with little or no β_1- and α-stimulating properties. The incidence of side effects (e.g., tachycardia, 4%) is minimal.[93] Albuterol is a selective, fast-acting bronchodilator that lasts a long time and produces minimal side effects.[94] (It was selected by this author as the bronchodilator of choice for inclusion in the office emergency kit.) Epinephrine and isoproterenol produce palpitations,

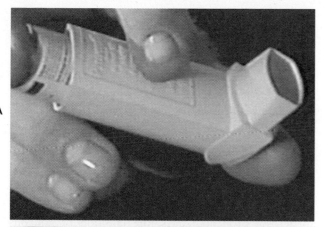

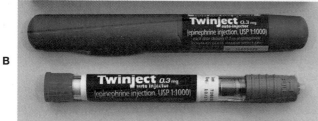

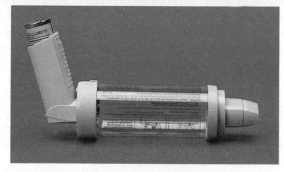

FIGURE 13-4 **A,** Aerosol inhaler (left) and parenteral bronchodilator. **B,** Parenteral bronchodilator. Epinephrine (Adrenalin) may be administered via either an intravenous or intramuscular route. **C,** A spacer device used with an inhaler increases the amount of medication going to the lungs. (Part C from Chapleau W: *Emergency first responder: making the difference,* St Louis, Mosby, 2004.)

tachycardia, and disturbances of cardiac rhythm and rate. In addition, epinephrine may produce headache and increased anxiety. Epinephrine is contraindicated in asthmatic patients with concomitant high blood pressure, diabetes mellitus (because epinephrine induces hyperglycemia), hyperthyroidism, and ischemic heart disease. Albuterol more frequently is recommended to treat acute asthma in patients with concomitant medical problems.[95]

Another factor that should be considered is that prolonged use of these medications (months or years) may result in a state of refractoriness, which leads to prolonged episodes that are more difficult to terminate (status asthmaticus). Therefore, these highly beneficial drugs must be used judiciously.

Aerosolized bronchodilators usually operate via a Freon-pressurized canister that dispenses a metered dose; only about 10% of the dose actually is inhaled.[96] The remaining amount becomes impacted in the oropharynx, but most is swallowed and biotransformed upon passage through the liver.

Proper use of the aerosol inhaler is described in Box 13-6. The onset of action of aerosolized bronchodilators is rapid, with improvement often noted within 15 seconds. To optimize inhalation of the aerosolized bronchodilator, the use of a spacer is recommended.[97] The spacer serves as a reservoir into which the aerosolized bronchodilator is delivered and from which the drug is inhaled. Because the drug is not delivered to the patient rapidly, a greater percentage of the drug reaches the affected bronchi.

Step 7: subsequent dental care. Once the acute episode is terminated, the doctor should determine the cause of the attack. Appropriate steps in the stress reduction protocol should be considered as a means to diminish the risk of future episodes. The planned dental treatment may continue at this visit if both the patient and the doctor feel that it is appropriate.

Step 8: discharge. Following resolution of the acute asthmatic episode, the doctor may discharge the patient from the dental office without an escort if the doctor believes that the patient is in stable condition. Such discharge is not usually a problem in cases of acute episodes that are terminated quickly with bronchodilator therapy. *No cl to driving if pt feels ok to drive*

Severe bronchospasm

Management of the more severe acute asthmatic attack initially mimics the milder episode. However, more intensive treatment often must be used.

Step 1: termination of dental therapy.

Step 2: P. The patient should be placed in the most comfortable position.

Step 3: removal of dental materials from mouth.

Step 4: calming of the patient.

Step 5: A-B-C, basic life support as needed.

Step 6: D (definitive care).
Step 6a: administration of O$_2$.

Box 13-6 Proper use of aerosol inhalers

Getting ready:
1. Take off the cap and shake the inhaler
2. Breathe out all the way
3. Hold your inhaler as directed by physician

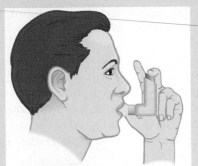

A. Hold inhaler 1 to 2 inches in front of your mouth (about the width of two fingers).

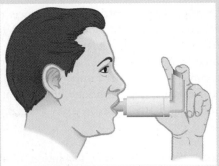

B. Use a spacer/holding chamber. These come in many shapes and can be useful to any patient.

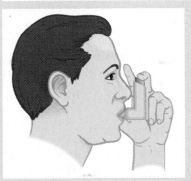

C. Put the inhaler in your mouth. Do not use for steroids.

Breathe in slowly:
4. As you start breathing in **slowly** through your mouth, press down on the inhaler one time. (If using a holding chamber, press first down on the inhaler. Within 5 seconds, begin to breathe in slowly.)
5. Keep breathing in **slowly**, as deeply as you can.

Hold your breath:
6. Hold your breath as you count to 10 slowly, if you can.
7. For inhaled quick-relief medicine (β_2-agonists), wait about 1 minute between puffs. There is no need to wait between puffs for other medicines.

Modified from: National Heart, Lung, and Blood Institute: *Expert Panel report 2. Guidelines for the diagnosis and management of asthma.* Baltimore, MD, U.S. Department of Health and Human Services, Public Health Service, National Institutes of Health, National Heart, Lung, and Blood Institute, 1997, NIH publication no. 4051.

Step 6b: administration of bronchodilator. In situations in which three doses of the aerosolized bronchodilator fail to resolve the acute episode, additional steps of management should be considered.

Step 6c: call for assistance. When aerosolized bronchodilators fail to resolve bronchospasm, the appropriate team member should seek medical assistance (such as 9-1-1).

Step 6d: administration of parenteral bronchodilators. In the management of more severe asthmatic episodes or in milder episodes that prove refractory to aerosol bronchodilators, the injection of aqueous epinephrine may be indicated. Epinephrine is available in a preloaded syringe containing 0.3 ml of a 1:1000 dilution in the basic emergency kit, whereas other, more advanced kits, may contain epinephrine in a 1:10,000 concentration (in a 10-mL syringe) (see Figure 13-4). The usual subcutaneous dose of epinephrine (1:1000 dilution) in an adult patient is 0.3 mL. If a 1:10,000 solution is used, 3 mL is administered intravenously. This dose may be repeated as needed every 30 to 60 minutes. Epinephrine 1:1000 is never administered intravenously.[98,99]

Asthmatic children often cease exhibiting acute symptoms when they are removed from the treatment environment. If this simple measure proves ineffective, an aerosolized bronchodilator (e.g., albuterol) should be administered. Only when this measure fails to resolve the bronchospasm should a 0.15- to 0.3-mg dose of epinephrine be considered.

Step 6e: administration of IV medications (optional). Patients whose condition proves refractory to the commonly used bronchodilators require additional drug therapy to terminate the acute episode. Drugs recommended for such patients include isoproterenol hydrochloride and corticosteroids (i.e., hydrocortisone sodium succinate, 100 to 200 mg via an IV route). Systemic corticosteroids are the only proven treatment for the inflammatory component of asthma, but the onset of their antiinflammatory effects is 6 to 12 hours after administration.[100,101] If the doctor possesses advanced training in emergency medicine and is able to start an IV infusion, these drugs should be considered for inclusion in the office emergency kit.

Glucocorticosteroids have been considered important in the management of severe acute asthma for more than 40 years. Although their direct bronchodilating activity is minimal, their antiinflammatory properties may make early administration of these drugs beneficial. After IV glucocorticosteroid administration, pulmonary function improves within 1 hour, usually peaking at 6 to

12 hours.[100,101] The general consensus is that "the early administration of steroids, even orally, is perhaps the most important therapeutic measure to be taken in severe and resistant asthma, and they should be prescribed early in this situation and in higher doses."[102–104]

Step 6f: additional considerations. Because asthmatic patients are usually quite anxious during acute attacks, the use of sedative drugs should be considered. However, the more severe the asthmatic attack, the more potentially dangerous the administration of any drugs that depress the central nervous or respiratory systems becomes. These drugs are absolutely contraindicated in cases of status asthmaticus or very severe asthma when any indication of carbon dioxide retention is present. Potential respiratory depression produced by sedative agents may be accentuated by concurrent hypoxia, and respiratory arrest may occur. In less severe episodes the judicious use of sedatives (e.g., 5 mg diazepam intramuscularly or via an IV route [preferred], titrated) may be indicated to decrease concomitant anxiety; however, their administration is rarely indicated. O_2 may be administered freely at any time during the asthmatic episode.

Step 7: disposition of patient.

After the resolution of an acute episode of bronchospasm severe enough to require administration of parenteral drugs, the patient frequently requires hospitalization so that the patient's long-term asthma therapy can be reevaluated. In other situations the emergency personnel may determine that the patient does not need hospitalization. In such cases a decision about how and when the patient may leave the office (i.e., alone or escorted) should be made before the emergency personnel depart.

Box 13-5 summarizes the steps in the management of mild and severe asthmatic episodes. In addition, the following facts may prove helpful:

- **Drugs:** O_2, β-adrenergic agonists (epinephrine or albuterol) via aerosol, and glucocorticosteroids (through an IV or oral route) are used to manage severe acute attacks.
- **Medical assistance required:** No assistance is required if the attack is mild or easily terminated with aerosol therapy. However, if the attack is severe or refractory to aerosol therapy, the appropriate emergency team member should seek assistance.

REFERENCES

1. Eberle J: *A treatise on the practice of medicine,* vol 2, Philadelphia, John Grigg, 1830.
2. Merck Medicus. Asthma. Available at www.merckmedicus.com, March 2001.
3. Sveuem RJ: Childhood asthma. Balancing efficacy and adherence for optimum treatment, *Postgrad Med* 118: 43–50, 2005
4. Yang KD: Asthma management issues in infancy and childhood, *Treat Respir Dis* 4:9–20, 2005.
5. Kemp JP: Recent advances in the management of asthma using leukotriene modifiers, *Am J Respir Med* 2:139–156, 2003.
6. Division of Data Services: *New asthma estimates: tracking prevalence, health care, and mortality.* Hyattsville, MD, National Center for Health Statistics, 2001
7. National Center for Health Statistics: Health, United States, 2006. www.cdc.gov/nchs/hus.htm
8. Conner B: Asthma education: areas of proper concern, *Asthma Care Educator* 1:81–82, 1999.
9. Sims J: Guidelines for treating asthma, *Dim Crit Care Nurs* 22:247–250, 2003.
10. Kasper DL, Braunwald E, Fauci AS, et al., editors: *Harrison's principles of internal medicine,* ed 16, New York, McGraw-Hill, 2005.
11. Warner JO, Naspitz CK: Third International Pediatric Consensus statement on the management of childhood asthma, *Pediatr Pulmonol* 25:1–17, 1998.
12. Bone RC, Burch SG: Management of status asthmaticus, *Ann Allergy* 67:461–469, 1991.
13. Schwartz A, Lieh-Lai MW: Status asthmaticus, *WebMD,* June 2004
14. Daniele RP: Pathophysiology of asthma. In: Fishman AP, editor: *Pulmonary diseases and disorders,* ed 2, New York, McGraw-Hill, 1988.
15. Kamada MM, Twang F, Leung DY: Multiple antibiotic sensitivity in a pediatric population, *Allergy Proc* 12: 347–350, 1991.
16. Morwood K, Gillis D, Smith W, Kette F: Aspirin-sensitive asthma, *Intern Med J* 35:240–246, 2005.
17. Food and Drug Administration: Sulfite update, *FDA Drug Bull* 14:24, 1984.
18. Van Schoor J, Joos GF, Pauwels RA: Indirect bronchial hyperresponsiveness in asthma: mechanisms, pharmacology and implications for clinical research, *Eur Respir J* 16:514–533, 2000.
19. Levin RH: Advances in pediatric drug therapy of asthma, *Nurs Clin North Am* 26:263–272, 1991.
20. Hudgel DW, Langston L Jr., Selner JC, et al.: Viral and bacterial infections in adults with chronic asthma, *Am Rev Respir Dis* 120:393–397, 1979.
21. Wilkerson LA: Exercise-induced asthma, *J Am Osteopath Assoc* 98:211–215, 1998.
22. Lucas SR, Platts-Mills TA: Physical activity and exercise in asthma: relevance to etiology and treatment, *J Allergy Clin Immunol* 115:928–934, 2005.
23. Hijazi Z: Environmental pollution and asthma, *Pediatr Pulmonol Suppl* 16:205–207, 1997.
24. Trasande L, Thurston GD: The role of air pollution in asthma and other pediatric morbidities, *J Allergy Clin Immunol* 115:689–699, 2005.
25. Murphy RH: Industrial disease with asthma. In: Weiss E, Segal MS, editors: *Bronchial asthma: mechanisms and therapeutics,* Boston, Little, Brown, 1976.

26. Gern JE, Rosenthal LA, Sorkness RL, Lemanske RF Jr.: Effects of viral respiratory infections on lung development and childhood asthma. *J Allergy Clin Immunol* 115:668–674, 2005.

27. Empey DW, Laitinen LA, Jacobs L, et al.: Mechanisms of bronchial hyperreactivity in normal subjects after upper respiratory tract infection, *Am Rev Respir Dis* 113:131–139, 1976.

28. Goodwin RD: Asthma and anxiety disorders, *Adv Psychosom Med* 24:51–71, 2003.

29. Hamlett KW, Pellegrini DS, Katz KS: Childhood chronic illness as a family stressor, *J Pediatr Psychol* 17:33–47, 1992.

30. Fast TB, Martin MD, Ellis TM: Emergency preparedness: a survey of dental practitioners, *J Am Dent Assoc* 112: 499–501, 1986.

31. Steinbacher DM, Glick M: The dental patient with asthma. An update and oral health considerations, *J Am Dent Assoc* 132:1229–1239, 2001.

32. McCarthy FM: *Essentials of safe dentistry for the medically compromised patient,* Philadelphia, WB Saunders, 1989.

33. Ulrik CS, Backer V, Dirksen A: Mortality and decline in lung function in 213 adults with bronchial asthma: a ten-year follow-up, *J Asthma* 29:29–38, 1992.

34. Soler M, Imhof E, Perruchoud AP: Severe acute asthma: pathophysiology, clinical assessment, and treatment, *Respiration* 57:114–121, 1990.

35. Lencher KI, Saltoun C: Status asthmaticus, *Allergy Asthma Proc* 25(4Suppl 1):S31–S33, 2004.

36. National Heart, Lung, and Blood Institute and World Health Organizartion: NHLBI/WHO Global Strategy for Asthma Management and Prevention workshop: Asthma management and prevention—a practical guide. Washington, DC: National Institutes of Health; 1994. NIH publication 96-3659-A.

37. Nadel JA, Busse WW: Asthma, *Am J Respir Crit Care Med* 157:S130–S138, 1998.

38. Kussin PS: Pathophysiology and management of life-threatening asthma, *Respir Care Clin North Am* 1:177–192, 1995.

39. Toogood JH: Complications of topical steroid therapy for asthma, *Am Rev Respir Dis* 141(part 2):89–96, 1990.

40. Prakash P, Gupta N: Therapeutic uses of Ocimum sanctum Linn (Tulsi) with a note on eugenol and its pharmacological actions: a short review, *Ind J Physiol Pharmacol* 49:125–131, 2005.

41. Li XM, Zhang TF, Sampson H, et al.: The potential use of Chinese herbal medicines in treating allergic asthma, *Ann Allergy Asthma Immunol* 93(2 Suppl 1):S35–S44, 2004.

42. Hofmann D, Hecker M, Volp A: Efficacy of dry extract of ivy leaves in children with bronchial asthma—a review of randomized controlled trials, *Phytomed* 10:213–220, 2003.

43. Gyorik, SA, Brutsche MH: Complementary and alternative medicine for bronchial asthma: is there new evidence? *Curr Opin Pulm Med* 10:37–43, 2004.

44. Passalacqua G, Compalati E, Schiappoli M, Senna G: Complementary and alternative medicine for the treatment and diagnosis of asthma and allergic diseases, *Monaldi Arch Chest Dis* 63:47–54, 2005.

45. Ennis M, Schneider C, Nehring E, Lorenz W: Histamine release induced by opioid analgesics: a comparative study using porcine mast cells, *Agents Actions Suppl* 33:20–22, 1991.

46. Skidmore-Roth L: *Mosby's drug guide for nurses with 2006 update,* ed 6, St. Louis, Mosby, 2006.

47. Tobias JD, Hirshman CA: Attenuation of histamine-induced airway constriction by albuterol during halothane anesthesia, *Anesthesiology* 72:105–110, 1990.

48. Little JW, Falace D, Miller C, Rhodus NL: *Dental management of the medically compromised patient,* ed 6, St. Louis, Mosby, 2002.

49. Sonneveille A: Asthma and aspirin. *Allerg Immunol (Paris)* 30:117–119, 1998.

50. McDonald JR, Mathison DA, Stevenson DD: Aspirin intolerance in asthma, *J Allergy Clin Immunol* 50: 198–207, 1972.

51. Nagy GB: Acute severe asthma, *Acta Microbiol Immunol Hung* 45:147–152, 1998.

52. Simon RA: Treatment of patients with respiratory reactions to aspirin and nonsteroidal anti-inflammatory drugs, *Curr Allergy Asthma Reports* 4:139–143, 2004.

53. Vally H, Thompson PJ: Allergic and asthmatic reactions to alcoholic drinks, *Addict Biol* 8:3–11, 2003.

54. Vally H, Thompson PJ: Role of sulfite additives in wine induced asthma: single dose and cumulative dose studies, *Thorax* 56:763–769, 2001.

55. Asmus MJ, Sherman J, Hendeles L: Bronchoconstrictor additives in bronchodilator solutions, *J Allergy Clin Immunol* 104(2 Pt 2):S53–S60, 1999.

56. Vally H, Carr A, El-Saleh J, Thompson P: Wine-induced asthma: a placebo-controlled assessment of its pathogenesis, *J Allergy Clin Immunol* 103(1 Pt 1):41–46, 1999.

57. Twarog FJ, Laung DYM: Anaphylaxis to a component of isoetharine (sodium bisulfite), *JAMA* 249:2030–2031, 1982.

58. Koepke JW, Staudenmayer H, Selner JC: Inhaled metabisulfite sensitivity, *Ann Allergy* 54:213–215, 1985.

59. Shojaie AR, Haas DA: Local anesthetic cartridges and latex allergy: a literature review, *J Can Dent Assoc* 68:622–626, 2002.

60. Haas DA: An update on local anesthetics in dentistry, *J Can Dent Assoc* 68:546–551, 2002.

61. Wright W, Zhang YG, Salome CM, Woolcock AJ: Effect of inhaled preservatives on asthmatic subjects: I. sodium metabisulfite, *Am Rev Respir Dis* 141:1400–1404, 1990.

62. Seng GF, Gay BJ: Dangers of sulfites in dental local anesthetic solutions: warnings and recommendations, *J Am Dent Assoc* 113:769–770, 1986.

63. Perusse R, Goulet JP, Turcotte JY: Sulfite, asthma and vasoconstrictors, *J Can Dent Assoc* 55:55–56, 1989.

64. Saunders NA, McFadden ER: Asthma: an update, *Dent Management* 24:1–49, 1978.

65. McFadden ER, Kiser R, DeGroot WJ: Acute bronchial asthma: relationships between clinical and physiologic manifestations, *N Engl J Med* 288:221–225, 1973.

66. McCombs RP, Lowell FC, Ohman JL: Myths, morbidity and mortality in asthma, *JAMA* 242:1521–1524, 1979.

67. McFadden ER, Feldman NT: Asthma, pathophysiology and clinical correlates, *Med Clin North Am* 61:1229–1238, 1977.

68. Nowak RM: Acute adult asthma. In: Marx J, Hockberger MD, Walls R, editors: *Rosen's emergency medicine,* ed 6, St. Louis, Mosby, 2006, pp. 1078–1096.

69. Barkin RM, Rosen P: Pulmonary disorders. In: Barkin RM, Rosen P, editors: *Emergency pediatrics,* ed 6, St. Louis, Mosby, 2004, pp. 781–816.

70. Hogg JC: The pathophysiology of asthma, *Chest* 82:8S–12S, 1982.

71. Higgins JC: The "crashing asthmatic," *Am Fam Phys* 67:997–1004, 2003.

72. Groneberg DA, Wagner U, Chung KF: Mucus and fatal asthma, *Am J Med* 116:66–67, 2004.

73. Rodrigo GJ, Rodrigo C, Hall JB: Acute asthma in adults: a review, *Chest* 125:1081–1102, 2004.

74. Olsen CR, et al.: Motor control of pulmonary airways studied by nerve stimulation, *J Appl Physiol Respir Environ Exercise Physiol* 20:202, 1965.

75. Cabezas GA, Graf PD, Nadel JA: Sympathetic versus parasympathetic nervous regulation of airways in dogs, *J Appl Physiol* 31:651–655, 1971.

76. Nadel JA: Airways: autonomic regulation and airway responsiveness. In: Weiss EB, Segal MS, editors: *Bronchial asthma: mechanisms and therapeutics,* Boston, Little, Brown, 1976.

77. Richardson JB: Nerve supply to the lungs, *Am Rev Respir Dis* 119:785–802, 1979.

78. Leff AR, Munoz MN: Interrelationship between alpha- and beta-adrenergic agonists and histamine in canine airway, *J Allergy Clin Immunol* 68:300–309, 1981.

79. Nadel JA: Inflammation and asthma, *J Allergy Clin Immunol* 73:651–653, 1984.

80. Guerzon GM, Pare PD, Michoud MC, Hogg JC: The number and distribution of mast cells in monkey lungs, *Am Rev Respir Dis* 119:59–66, 1979.

81. Bisgaard H: Leukotrienes and prostaglandins in asthma, *Allergy* 39:413–420, 1984.

82. Peters-Golden M, Canetti C, Mancuso P, Coffey MJ: Leukotrienes: underappreciated mediators of innate immune responses, *J Immunol* 174:589–594, 2005.

83. Weis JW, Drazen JM, McFadden ER Jr., et al.: Comparative bronchoconstrictor effects of histamine, leukotriene C, and leukotriene D in normal human volunteers, *Trans Assoc Am Physicians* 95:30–35, 1982.

84. Tortola GJ: The respiratory system. In: Tortola GJ, editor: *Principles of human anatomy,* ed 10, Hoboken, NJ, J. Wiley, 2005.

85. Hlastala MP, Berger AJ: Mechanical factors in breathing. In: Hlastala MP, Berger AJ, editors: *Physiology of respiration,* New York, Oxford University Press, 2001.

86. Zamel N: Normal lung mechanics. In: Baum GL, Crapo JD, Celli BR, Karlinsky JB, editors: *Textbook of pulmonary diseases,* ed 6, Philadelphia, Lippincott-Raven, 1998.

87. Zakynthinos SG, Koulouris NG, Roussos C: Respiratory mechanics and energetics. In: Mason RJ, Murray JF, Broaddus VC, Nadel JA, editors: *Murray & Nadel's textbook of respiratory medicine,* ed 4, St. Louis, Elsevier, 2005.

88. Lemanske RF Jr, Busse WW: Asthma, *J Allergy Clin Immunol* 111(2 Suppl):S502–S519, 2003.

89. Walters EH, Walters JA, Gibson PW: Regular treatment with long acting beta agonists versus daily regular treatment with short acting beta agonists in adults and children with stable asthma. *Cochrane Database of Systematic Reviews*: CD003901, 2002.

90. Yagiiela JA: Adverse drug interactions in dental practice: interactions associated with vasoconstrictors, *J Am Dent Assoc* 130:701–709, 1999.

91. Pliss LB, Gallagher EJ: Aerosol vs. injected epinephrine in acute asthma, *Ann Emerg Med* 10:353–355, 1981.

92. Williams SJ, Winner SJ, Clark TJH: Comparison of inhaled and intravenous terbutaline in acute severe asthma, *Thorax* 36:629–631, 1981.

93. Shim C, Williams MH: Bronchial response to oral versus aerosol metaproterenol in asthma, *Ann Intern Med* 93:428–431, 1980.

94. Godfrey S: Worldwide experience with albuterol (salbutamol), *Ann Allergy* 47:423, 1981.

95. Lotvall J: The long and short of beta$_2$-agonists, *Pulmon Pharmacol Therapeut* 15:497–501, 2002.

96. Newman SP, Pavia D, Moren F, et al.: Deposition of pressurized aerosols in the human respiratory tract, *Thorax* 36:52–55, 1981.

97. Dolovich M, Ahrens RC, Hess DR, et al.: Device selection and outcomes of aerosol therapy: evidence-based guidelines: American College of Chest Physicians/American College of Asthma, Allergy, and Immunology, *Chest* 127:335–371, 2005.

98. Arfi AM, Kouatli A, Al-Ata J, et al.: Acute myocardial ischemia following accidental intravenous administration of epinephrine in high concentration, *Ind Heart J* 57:261–264, 2005.

99. Jaconsen G: Stung postman gets $2.6m for wrong help, *Sydney Morning Herald* February 5, 2005.

100. Gibbs MA, Camargo CA Jr, Rowe BH, Silverman RA: State of the art: therapeutic controversies in severe acute asthma, *Acad Emerg Med* 7:800–815, 2000.

101. ECC Committee, Subcommittees and Task Forces of the American Heart Association. Part 10.5: Near-fatal asthma. In: 2005 American Heart Association guidelines for cardiopulmonary resuscitation and emergency cardiovascular care, *Circulation* 112:IV-139– IV-142, 2005.

102. Rowe BH, Keller JL, Oxman AD: Effectiveness of steroid therapy in acute exacerbations of asthma: a meta-analysis, *Am J Emerg Med* 10:301–310, 1992.

103. Scarfone RJ, Fuchs SM, Nager AL, Shane SA: Controlled trial of oral prednisone in the emergency department treatment of children with acute asthma, *Pediatrics* 2:513–518, 1993.

104. Connett GJ, Warde C, Wooler E, Lenney W: Prednisolone and salbutamol in the hospital treatment of acute asthma, *Arch Dis Child* 70:170–173, 1994.

CHAPTER 14

Heart Failure and Acute Pulmonary Edema

Heart failure is generally described as the inability of the heart to supply sufficient oxygenated blood for the body's metabolic needs.[1] Congestion from fluid accumulates in the pulmonary circulation, systemic circulation, or both. Heart failure is a principal complication of virtually all forms of heart disease.[2]

Heart failure is a complex clinical syndrome that can result from any structural or functional cardiac disorder that impairs the ability of the ventricle to fill with or eject blood. Cardinal manifestations of heart failure are dyspnea and fatigue, which may limit exercise tolerance, and fluid retention, which may lead to pulmonary congestion and peripheral edema. Both abnormalities can impair the functional capacity and quality of life of affected individuals.[2] Because not all patients have volume (fluid) overload at the time of initial or subsequent evaluation, the term *heart failure* is preferred over the older term *congestive heart failure*.[3]

When heart failure occurs solely in the left ventricle, signs and symptoms are related to congestion of the pulmonary vasculature, whereas with right ventricular failure signs and symptoms of systemic venous and capillary congestion predominate. Left and right ventricular failure may develop independently or occur simultaneously. *Acute pulmonary edema* is the most dramatic symptom of left-heart failure.[4,5] It is a life-threatening condition marked by an excess of serous fluid in the alveolar spaces or interstitial tissues of the lungs accompanied by extreme difficulty in breathing. It leads to a sensation of suffocation and oppression in the chest, intensifying the patient's fright, and elevates the heart rate and blood pressure, further restricting ventricular filling. The increased discomfort and work of breathing place additional load on the heart, leading to a further decrease in cardiac function due to hypoxia. If this vicious circle is not interrupted, it may lead rapidly to death.[2]

The human heart is a pump, supplying the tissues and organs of the body with blood, which contains oxygen and nutrients sufficient to meet their metabolic requirements both at rest and during activity. When viewed as a pump, the heart is remarkable not only for its ability to adjust rapidly to the varying metabolic requirements of the body but also for its extreme durability. The heart literally lasts a lifetime.

As durable as it is, the heart is vulnerable to a large number of disorders—congenital, metabolic, inflammatory, and degenerative—that can affect its ability to pump blood. Cardiac dysfunction usually manifests itself clinically in one of two ways. First, signs and symptoms of dysfunction may occur directly at the site of the heart. These include chest pain and palpitation, represented clinically as angina pectoris (see Chapter 27), myocardial infarction (see Chapter 28), and cardiac dysrhythmias. The second manifestation of cardiac dysfunction includes signs and symptoms that are extracardiac. These originate in organs of the body that are either hyperperfused (congested) or hypoperfused (ischemic) with blood. Heart failure is a clinical expression of the former.

Under normal circumstances, the right ventricle should outperform and outlast the left ventricle. The left ventricle is more vulnerable to heart disease and to disorders in its blood supply than is the right ventricle. The patient usually notes the first signs and symptoms of heart failure in the left ventricle. Isolated right ventricular failure is extremely rare; usually the right ventricle fails shortly after, and as a result of, left ventricular failure. (Cardiac function, both normal and pathologic, is discussed further in later sections of this chapter.)

Heart failure therefore represents a clinical diagnosis that is applied to a group of signs and symptoms developing when the heart is unable to fulfill its function as a pump, thus depriving the various tissues and organs of an adequate supply of O_2 and nutrients. The degree of heart failure may vary dramatically: patients may exhibit only mild clinical signs and symptoms that arise only on exertion, whereas patients with more severe heart failure may demonstrate signs and symptoms at all times.

All patients with heart failure are at increased risk during dental treatment. The dental treatment plan may require modification to accommodate varying degrees of cardiac dysfunction. Patients with more advanced heart failure or those with moderate degrees of heart failure who face physiologic or psychological stress, or both, may experience exacerbation of their heart failure. This can lead to acute pulmonary edema, in which the patient exhibits extreme degrees of respiratory distress. Acute pulmonary edema is a life-threatening medical emergency requiring quick and aggressive management.

According to 2002 statistics, approximately 4.9 million Americans have heart failure (2.3% of the U.S. population).[6,7] Prevalence of heart failure increases with age. Heart failure is present in 6.2% of men and 4.1% of women between 65 and 74 years of age (Figure 14-1).

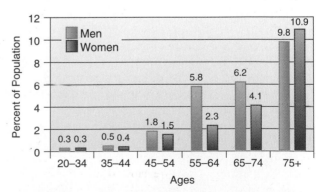

FIGURE 14-1 Prevalence of heart failure by sex and age. (From American Heart Association: *Heart disease and stroke statistics–2006 update.* Dallas, American Heart Association, 2006.)

Over age 75 years, the percentages increase to 9.8% for men and 10.9% for women.[6,7] In 2002, 57,828 persons in the United States died of heart failure, while 970,000 patients were discharged from a hospital with a primary diagnosis of heart failure, up from 377,000 in 1979.[7]

Unfortunately, the prognosis for patients with heart failure is poor. According to a 44-year follow-up of the National Heart, Lung, and Blood Institute's Framingham Heart Study, 80% of men and 70% of women younger than age 65 years who have heart failure will die within 8 years.[8] Following diagnosis of heart failure, survival is poorer in men than in women, but fewer than 15% of women survive more than 8 to 12 years. The 1-year mortality rate is high, with 1 in 5 dying.[8] In persons diagnosed with heart failure, sudden cardiac death occurs at six to nine times the rate of the general population.[9] From 1992 to 2002, overall deaths from heart failure increased 35.3%. Over the same time period, the overall death rate increased 7.7%.[7]

Most individuals with progressive cardiovascular disease develop some degree of heart failure at some stage of their lives. (Chapter 26 discusses etiologic factors found in a majority of cardiovascular diseases.) The dentist must be prepared to manage the dental needs of patients with varying degrees of heart failure. Most important, patients must be evaluated adequately before treatment actually starts. In this way measures may be taken to prevent acute episodes of heart failure (acute pulmonary edema).

■ PREDISPOSING FACTORS

The tendency of heart failure to begin as left ventricular failure relates to the disproportionate workload of, and the prevalence of cardiac disease in, the left ventricle. Disease produces heart failure in one of the two basic ways:

1. Increasing the workload of the heart. For example, high blood pressure increases resistance to the ejection of blood from the left ventricle, increasing the workload of the myocardium.
2. Damaging the muscular walls of the heart through coronary artery disease or myocardial infarction.

Other causes of increased cardiac workload include cardiac valvular deficiencies (e.g., stenosis or insufficiency of the aortic, mitral, tricuspid, or pulmonary valves); increases in the body's requirement for O_2 and nutrients (e.g., pregnancy, hyperthyroidism, anemia, Paget's disease); and hypertension, which is responsible for more than 75% of all cases of heart failure.[7]

Left ventricular failure is the leading cause of right ventricular failure. Other causes of isolated right ventricular failure include mitral stenosis, pulmonary vascular or parenchymal disease, and pulmonary valvular stenosis, all of which significantly increase the workload of the right ventricle.

Any factor that increases the workload of the heart may precipitate an acute exacerbation of preexisting heart failure, which may result in acute pulmonary edema. Acute pulmonary edema may occur at any time, but most often at night, after the individual has been asleep for a few hours. (This latter point will be discussed in more detail in later sections of this chapter.) Other factors that may increase cardiac workload include physical, psychological, and climatic stress. Dental offices may easily precipitate such stress.

In pediatric patients, heart failure may be produced by an obstruction to the outflow of blood from the heart (e.g., coarctation of the aorta or pulmonary stenosis). Of all children who develop heart failure, 90% do so within the first year of life secondary to congenital heart lesions.[10] Older children may also develop heart failure as a result of congenital heart lesions; however, much more common causes include disease acquired from cardiomyopathy, bacterial endocarditis, or rheumatic carditis.

■ PREVENTION

The medical history questionnaire and the dialogue history are the best forms of prevention.

✎ MEDICAL HISTORY QUESTIONNAIRE

Section II, Have You Experienced:

Question 8: Swollen ankles?
Comment: In response to a positive answer, the time of night or day that the swelling develops should be determined. Dependent edema occurs late in the day after many hours of standing in most patients with right ventricular failure. This sign may also be seen in other clinical states, such as the later stages of pregnancy, varicose veins, or renal failure.

Question 9: Shortness of breath?
Comment: Shortness of breath that develops after mild exercise, termed *exertional dyspnea*, is an early sign of left ventricular failure.

Section III, Do You Have or Have You Had:

Question 29: Heart disease?
Comment: A survey question seeking the presence of any cardiovascular problem. Positive response indicates need for further dialogue history to determine the nature of the problem(s).

Question 30: Heart attack, heart defects?
Comment: Following myocardial infarction a degree of heart failure may develop dependent upon the severity of the

myocardial infarction. Heart failure may be a clinical component of many congenital cardiac defects.

Question 31: Heart murmur?

Question 32: Rheumatic fever?

Comment: A positive response to any of the aforementioned conditions should prompt further questioning via dialogue history to determine the degree of severity and other relevant factors concerning the disease. All the conditions listed in Questions 30, 31, and 32 can lead to the development of heart failure.

Section IV, Do You Have or Have You Had:

Question 56: Hospitalization?

Comment: Another survey question, a positive response to which requires further exploration via dialogue history to determine the nature of the hospitalization.

Section V, Are You Taking:

Question 62: Drugs, medications, over-the-counter medicines (including aspirin), natural remedies?

Comment: Persons with heart failure commonly receive a variety of medications, the ultimate goal of which is to improve cardiac function.

TABLE 14-1 Drug therapy in heart failure

Drug class	
Diuretics	Loop diuretics
	Thiazides
	Potassium sparing
	Type I (mineralocorticoid) receptor antagonists
	Carbonic anhydrase inhibitors (acetazolamide)
Vasodilators	Nitrovasodilators
	"Direct-acting" or unknown mechanism vasodilators
	Calcium channel blockers
	Natriuretic peptides (nesiritide)
Positive inotropic agents	Digitalis derivatives
	β-adrenergic receptor agonists
	Phosphodiesterase inhibitors
	Phosphodiesterase inhibitors with calcium sensitizer action
Neurohumoral inhibitors	Angiotensin-converting enzyme inhibitors
	Angiotensin receptor blockers
	β-adrenergic receptor blocking agents

Modified from Bristow MR, Linas S, Port DJ: Drugs in the treatment of heart failure. In: Braunwald E, Zipes DP, Libby P, Bonow R, editors: *Braunwald's heart disease: a textbook of cardiovascular medicine,* ed 7, Philadelphia, WB Saunders, 2004.

One or more of the following are commonly employed: diuretics, positive inotropic agents such as digitalis, medications for high blood pressure, vasodilators, and neurohumoral inhibitors (Tables 14-1 and 14-2).

Diuretics are often the first line of defense in the treatment of heart failure. This class of drugs suppresses renal tubular reabsorption of sodium and helps in the management of diseases associated with excessive sodium and fluid retention. Several groups of diuretics are available, including thiazide, loop, and potassium-sparing diuretics (see Table 14-2).

Positive inotropic agents, with the exception of digitalis, are reserved for the treatment of acute pulmonary edema and refractory heart failure in hospitalized patients. These include dopamine,[11] dobutamine,[12] amrinone,[13] milrinone,[13,14] and aminophylline.

The fundamental action of digitalis glycosides is to increase the force and velocity of cardiac contraction, regardless of whether

TABLE 14-2 Drugs used in the management of heart failure

Class	Category	Drug
Diuretics	Thiazides	Hydrochlorothiazide
		Chlorthalidone
		Metazolone
	Loop diuretics	Furosemide
		Bumetanide
		Ethacrynic acid
	Potassium-sparing diuretics	Spironolactone
		Triamterene
		Amiloride
Positive inotropics		Digoxin
		Dobutamine
		Dopamine
		Inamrinone
		Milrinone
Vasodilators	Nitrates	Nitroglycerin
		Isosorbide
Neurohumoral inhibitors	Angiotensin-converting enzyme inhibitors	Captopril
		Enalapril
		Lisinopril
		Ramipril
		Quinapril
		Trandolapril
	β-blocking agents	Propranolol
		Metoprolol
		Bisoprolol
		Carvedilol
		Bucindolol
		Nebivolol

the heart is failing, through their positive inotropic action. In heart failure, digitalis significantly increases cardiac output, decreases right atrial pressure, decreases venous pressure, and increases the excretion of sodium and water, thus correcting some of the hemodynamic and metabolic alterations that occur in heart failure. Digitalis decreases heart rate and increases the demand of the myocardium for O_2. Although digitalis is still considered an important therapeutic modality for heart failure, more and more frequently vasodilators, diuretics, and inotropic agents are replacing it (see Table 14-2).

High blood pressure is one of the leading causes of left ventricular failure. *Antihypertensive drugs* are frequently prescribed for heart failure patients. Knowledge of which drugs the patient takes helps the doctor to better understand the degree of cardiac dysfunction. This knowledge also enables the doctor to prevent the occurrence of certain side effects associated with many antihypertensive drugs.

Vasodilators have been demonstrated to be well tolerated and effective in improving symptoms in patients with heart failure[15] (see Table 14-2). Depending on whether a drug is a venodilator or arteriodilator or possesses mixed properties, heart failure treatment can be tailored for the individual patient after a consideration of several factors, including blood pressure, degree of pulmonary congestion, degree of peripheral edema, concomitant presence of angina pectoris, renal hypoperfusion, heart rate, and likelihood of patient adherence.

Neurohumoral inhibitors, "agents that inhibit harmful neurohumoral systems that are activated to support the failing heart," are "without question, the greatest advance in the treatment of chronic heart failure."[16,17] Included in this group are the angiotensin-converting enzyme inhibitors and β-blockers (see Table 14-2).

Dialogue history

After reviewing the medical history questionnaire, the dialogue history is used to gather additional information concerning the severity of the heart failure.

Can you carry out your normal daily activities without becoming unduly fatigued?

Comment: This question considers the presence of undue fatigue while at rest, not during exercise. Undue fatigue is a common symptom of left or right ventricular failure, or both. Fatigue and general weakness are usually the first clinical manifestations of heart failure.

Can you climb a normal flight of stairs or walk two level city blocks without distress?

Comment: As it relates to the preceding question, the inability to climb a normal flight of stairs or walk two level city blocks without distress signals an inefficient cardiorespiratory system.

The following categories, based on the American Society of Anesthesiologists (ASA) Physical Status Classification System, may indicate a patient's status in relation to this question (Figure 14-2):

- ASA I patients (that is, normal, healthy patients) can climb one flight of stairs or walk two level city blocks without having to pause because of shortness of breath, undue fatigue, or chest pain.
- ASA II patients can climb one flight of stairs or walk two level city blocks without distress but must stop once they complete either task because of distress. Patients with heart failure most likely experience shortness of breath or undue fatigue.
- ASA III patients can climb one flight of stairs or walk two city blocks but must stop and rest before completing the task because of distress.
- ASA IV patients cannot negotiate a flight of stairs or walk two level city blocks because of shortness of breath or undue fatigue present at rest.

Have you ever awakened at night short of breath?

Comment: Paroxysmal nocturnal dyspnea, awakening at night short of breath, is observed in more advanced left ventricular failure. Medical consultation should be seriously considered before starting any dental treatment.

Do you use more than two pillows to sleep?

Comment: Orthopnea is dyspnea occurring while the patient is in the supine position; elevation of the trunk relieves this condition.[18,19] Clinically, patients cannot breathe comfortably while lying down, requiring three or more pillows to elevate the back and enable them to breathe more easily, a condition termed *three-pillow orthopnea.* In severe cases the patient may rest or sleep only while in an upright position. Orthopnea is a sign of left ventricular failure. Modifications in patient positioning in the dental chair may be required during treatment.

Have you lost or gained more than 10 pounds in the past year?

Comment: A gain of more than 10 pounds—especially if the gain occurred rapidly or without an apparent reason—may indicate the development of heart failure. Fluid retention is a significant factor in the development of heart failure. An in-depth dialogue history must be performed to determine whether other reasons might explain the weight gain.

What is the cause of your child's heart failure?

Comment: Pediatric patients with heart failure secondary to other diseases have a history of congenital or other heart problems. In such cases the parent or guardian should discuss the child's health status with the doctor. Consultation with the patient's primary care physician is also warranted in cases of pediatric heart failure. In the first year of life, 90% of children developing heart failure do so because of congenital heart disease. Older children may also develop heart failure as a result of congenital heart disease, but they more commonly suffer acquired heart failure secondary to cardiomyopathy, bacterial endocarditis, or rheumatic carditis.[10]

FIGURE 14-2 The American Society of Anesthesiologists classification for heart failure. (Courtesy Dr. Lawrence Day.)

In addition, patients may be encountered who appear to have heart failure but provide negative responses to the preceding questions. The doctor must always remember that most individuals accommodate their lifestyles to adapt to varying degrees of physical disability. For example, persons unable to climb a flight of stairs or walk two level city blocks may never try; they can use elevators or motor vehicles instead. The observant doctor always is on the lookout for clinical clues.

Physical evaluation

Added to the steps outlined thus far, physical evaluation of the patient enables the doctor to determine the patient's current state of health more accurately than the medical history questionnaire or the dialogue history.

Vital signs

The patient's vital signs are monitored and recorded, including blood pressure, heart rate and rhythm (pulse), respiratory rate, and weight. Patients with heart failure may demonstrate the following:

- The blood pressure may be elevated, with the increase in diastolic pressure greater than that in systolic pressure. The *pulse pressure* (the difference between the systolic and diastolic pressures) is narrowed. For example, a normal blood pressure of 130/80 mm Hg yields a pulse pressure of 50; in contrast, a blood pressure of 130/100 mm Hg, as seen in cases of heart failure, yields a pulse pressure of 30.
- The heart rate (pulse) and respiratory rate usually increase. Tachycardia is present because of the increased adrenergic activity, a principal compensatory mechanism for support of circulation in the presence of reduced cardiac output.[20] Tachypnea is evident early in the progression of heart failure as the severity of dyspnea increases.
- Any recent, unexplained, large weight gain (more than 3 pounds in a 7-day period) may indicate the onset of acute heart failure. If such a gain occurs in conjunction with clinical signs of dependent edema (e.g., ankle swelling), dental treatment should be postponed pending completion of a more extensive medical evaluation.

Physical examination

The following areas should undergo careful inspection:

- *Skin and mucous membrane color:* Skin color of a patient with more severe heart failure may appear ashen-gray while mucous membranes may be grayish-blue. Although skin color is important, perhaps more attention should be given to the patient's mucous membranes, particularly the nailbeds and lips. Cyanosis (a bluish tinge) indicates

underoxygenation of the blood, and its presence should indicate the possibility of heart failure. Nail polish and lipstick may mask these areas, but the color of the intraoral mucous membranes can always be observed.

- *Neck:* Jugular vein distention develops in patients with right ventricular failure. When such patients are upright or in a semisupine position, their jugular veins may remain visible. In patients without heart failure, jugular vein pressure is negative in the upright position and the jugular veins are collapsed and not visible. However, in individuals with heart failure whose central venous pressures are elevated, jugular veins remain visible while the patient is upright.

Prominent, visible, jugular veins are normal when patients are in a supine position, but they gradually disappear as the patient slowly assumes a more upright position. At approximately a 30-degree angle or more upright, jugular veins should collapse and be undetectable (Figure 14-3). To determine increased jugular vein pressure, the distance that the jugular veins are distended

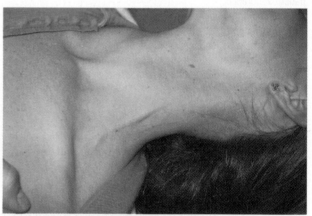

FIGURE 14-3 **A,** Prominent jugular veins. **B,** When the individual is positioned upright, the jugular vein collapses (disappears).

is measured vertically above the sternal angle of Louis; to this distance is added 5 cm for the distance to the atrium. The patient should be situated in a 45-degree upright position and the right jugular vein evaluated.[21] Normally this distance is not less than 10 cm H_2O (the unit of measurement). The causes of elevated jugular vein pressure include right ventricular failure, pulmonic and tricuspid valve stenosis, pulmonary hypertension, right ventricular hypertrophy, and constrictive pericarditis.

■ *Ankles:* Ankle edema, also known as *pitting* or *dependent edema,* may occur in patients with right ventricular failure, pregnancy, varicose veins, and renal failure. It occurs in the more dependent parts of the body, where systemic venous pressures rise to their highest levels. If the patient follows a normal pattern of sleeping at night and staying awake during the day, ankle edema develops in the afternoon and disappears overnight.

Edematous tissue may be differentiated from adipose tissue by a simple test. Pressure placed on edematous tissue for 30 seconds results in a "pitting" effect as the pressure forces the edema fluid from the area (Figure 14-4). This pitting gradually disappears once pressure is released and fluid returns. In contrast, adipose or normal tissues return to their original shape immediately after the individual release of the pressure. As the severity of heart failure intensifies, edema progresses, ascending to involve the legs, thighs, genitalia, and abdominal wall.[18]

Dental therapy considerations

The doctor now must examine all available information to determine the degree of risk that the patient with heart failure represents during dental treatment. The New York Heart Association[22] developed a functional classification of patients with heart disease based on the relationship between the symptoms and the amount of effort required to provoke them (Box 14-1).

The ASA physical status classification for heart failure, which follows, mimics the New York Heart Association's categorization: *may have high BP*

■ ASA I: The patient does not experience dyspnea or undue fatigue with normal exertion.
Comment: If all items of the medical history are negative, this patient may be considered normal and healthy. No special modifications in dental treatment are indicated. Patients with heart failure are not ASA I risks.

■ ASA II: The patient experiences mild dyspnea or fatigue during exertion.
Comment: As with the ASA I patient, the ASA II patient may be managed normally if the rest of the medical history and physical examination prove to be noncontributory. In addition, use of the stress reduction protocol should be considered if any physical or psychologic stress is evident or anticipated.

■ ASA III: The patient experiences dyspnea or undue fatigue with normal activities.
Comment: This patient is comfortable at rest in any position but may demonstrate a tendency

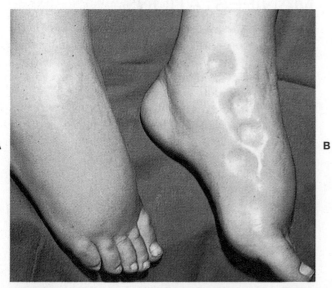

FIGURE 14-4 Ankle with dependent edema. **A,** The clinical appearance of an ankle before pressure is applied with a finger. **B,** Pressure on the right side of the ankle produces "pitting." (From Bloom A, Ireland J: *Color atlas of diabetes,* ed 2, London, Mosby-Wolfe, 1992.)

Box 14-1 Functional classification for patients with heart disease

Class I: No limitation
Ordinary physical activity does not cause undue fatigue, dyspnea, or palpitation.

Class II: Slight limitation of physical activity
The patient is comfortable at rest. Ordinary physical activity results in fatigue, palpitation, dyspnea, or angina.

Class III: Marked limitation of physical activity
Although the patient is comfortable at rest, less than ordinary activity produces symptoms.

Class IV: Inability to carry on any physical activity without discomfort
The patient experiences symptoms of heart failure even while resting. Any physical activity produces increased discomfort.

From Criteria Committee, New York Heart Association: *Diseases of the heart and blood vessels: nomenclature and criteria for diagnosis,* ed 6, Boston, Little, Brown, 1964.

toward orthopnea and have a history of paroxysmal nocturnal dyspnea. The ASA III patient with heart failure is at increased risk during dental treatment. Before starting any treatment, medical consultation and use of the stress reduction protocol and other specific treatment modifications should be given serious consideration.

- ASA IV: The patient experiences dyspnea, orthopnea, and undue fatigue at all times.
  Comment: The ASA IV patient represents a significant risk. Even at rest this patient's heart cannot meet the body's metabolic requirements. Any degree of stress further increasing metabolic demand may exacerbate the condition and possibly provoke acute pulmonary edema. Invasive dental care should be withheld for all elective procedures until the patient's cardiovascular status improves or is controlled. Dental emergencies (e.g., pain or infection) should be managed with medication; if physical intervention becomes necessary, this patient should be treated in a controlled environment, such as in a hospital dental clinic, and be under a physician's care before, during, and immediately following the dental procedure.

The stress reduction protocol indicates the following general treatment modifications for patients with heart failure:

- *Supplemental O_2:* In patients with any degree of heart failure—indeed those with any cardiovascular disorder (e.g., angina pectoris or myocardial infarction)—no contraindication exists to the administration of O_2 during treatment. A nasal cannula or nasal hood from an inhalation sedation unit may be used. A flow rate of 3 to 5 L per minute usually is adequate, but the flow rate may be adjusted in accordance with individual patient comfort (Figure 14-5).
- *Positioning of the patient:* Positioning of the patient with heart failure for dental treatment may require modification. If the patient finds it difficult to breathe while in the supine position, chair position must be modified until the patient is comfortable. Respiratory distress while reclined is known as *orthopnea* and usually indicates a class III risk for which medical consultation before dental treatment is strongly suggested. Use of a rubber dam may be contraindicated as it may severely restrict the already limited ability of this patient to obtain an adequate volume of air.

In 2001 the American College of Cardiology and the American Heart Association published guidelines for the evaluation and management of chronic heart failure in the adult. The guidelines included a staging system for heart failure (Table 14-3) that recognized that there

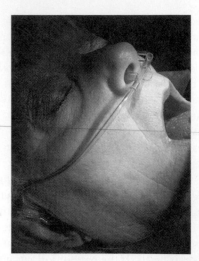

FIGURE 14-5 The patient with congestive heart failure may receive supplemental O_2 via nasal cannula or the nasal hood (not shown) of an inhalation sedation unit.

were established risk factors and structural prerequisites for the development of heart failure, that therapeutic interventions initiated before the onset of left ventricular dysfunction or symptoms can reduce morbidity and mortality, that patients generally progress from one stage to the next unless disease progression is slowed or stopped by treatment, and that all patients benefit from risk factor modification.[3]

■ CLINICAL MANIFESTATIONS

Clinical manifestations of heart failure relate to the specific portion of the heart that is failing. Individuals have varying degrees of heart failure—not all patients exhibit all the symptoms and signs described in this chapter. In addition, most patients exhibit combined failure of the left and right ventricles.

Clinical signs and symptoms are presented individually for each ventricle, followed by a description of acute pulmonary edema. Left ventricular failure (LVF) is manifested clinically primarily by symptoms associated with pulmonary congestion, whereas right ventricular failure is dominated by signs of systemic venous congestion and peripheral edema. Undue fatigue and weakness are prominent symptoms present in both types of heart failure.

Left ventricular failure

Clinical manifestations of LVF are associated primarily with respiratory distress; the severity of distress is related to the degree of heart failure.

TABLE 14-3 Stages of heart failure

Stage	Description	Examples
A	At high risk of developing HF because of the presence of conditions that are strongly associated with the development of HF	Systemic hypertension Coronary artery disease Diabetes mellitus
	No identified structural or functional abnormalities of the pericardium, myocardium, or cardiac valves	History of cardiotoxic drug therapy History of alcohol abuse
	No history of signs or symptoms of HF	Family history of cardiomyopathy
B	Presence of structural heart disease that is strongly associated with the development of HF	Left ventricular hypertrophy or fibrosis Left ventricular dilation or dysfunction
	No history of signs or symptoms of HF	Asymptomatic valvular heart disease Previous myocardial infarction
C	Current or prior symptoms of HF associated with underlying structural heart disease	Dyspnea or fatigue due to left ventricular systolic dysfunction Asymptomatic patients receiving treatment for prior symptoms of HF
D	Advanced structural heart disease and marked symptoms of HF at rest despite maximal medical therapy	Frequent HF hospitalizations and cannot be discharged In the hospital awaiting heart transplant
	Require specialized interventions	At home with continuous inotropic or mechanical support In hospice setting for management of HF

HF, heart failure.
From Hunt SA, Abraham WT, Chin MH, et al.: ACC/AHA 2005 Guidelines Update for the Diagnosis and Management of Chronic Heart Failure in the Adult: a report of the American College of Cardiology/American Heart Association Task Force on Practice Guidelines (Writing Committee to Update the 2001 Guidelines for the Evaluation and Management of Heart Failure); developed in collaboration with the American College of Chest Physicians and the International Society for Heart and Lung Transplantation; endorsed by the Heart Rhythm Society. *Circulation* 112:e154–e235, 2005.

Weakness and *undue fatigue* are usually the first symptoms that the patient with LVF notices. The patient becomes aware of these symptoms when becoming fatigued during a level of physical activity that previously caused no fatigue. As heart failure progresses, the patient becomes fatigued with less and less exertion until fatigue exists even at rest.

Breathlessness, which is a cardinal manifestation of LVF, may arise with progressively increasing severity as (1) exertional dyspnea,[2] (2) orthopnea, (3) paroxysmal nocturnal dyspnea, (4) dyspnea at rest, and (5) acute pulmonary edema.[2]

Dyspnea, or difficulty in breathing, is usually evident on exertion. It is commonly accompanied by an increased rate of breathing (tachypnea). Cough and expectoration are present, related to reflexes produced by the congested lungs and bronchi. The patient with early LVF may report an increased frequency of urination at night (nocturia), a symptom produced by the rediffusion of edema fluid in the extremities from extracellular sites back into the systemic circulation.

Orthopnea and *paroxysmal dyspnea* are later, more ominous signs related to severe LVF. Orthopnea is dyspnea that occurs soon after the patient lies flat and disappears soon after the patient sits up. The patient with orthopnea can alleviate the breathing difficulty by elevating the head and thorax with more than two pillows. As the degree of LVF progresses, this patient may have to remain in the upright position (e.g., by sitting in a chair) even during sleep. Positioning of this patient for dental treatment may prove difficult. If present, orthopnea and paroxysmal dyspnea confer upon the patient an ASA III medical risk and require specific modifications in treatment.

When orthopnea and paroxysmal dyspnea are severe, the patient may require the use of supplemental O_2 24 hours a day (ASA IV risk); such patients carry portable O_2 cylinders with a nasal cannula. They cannot lie down while sleeping but must sleep in an upright position. Paroxysmal dyspnea in resting patients usually occurs at night, thus the term *paroxysmal nocturnal dyspnea*. The patient with this condition awakens from sleep, often quite suddenly and with a feeling of severe anxiety and suffocation, sits bolt upright, and gasps for breath. Bronchospasm, which may be caused by congestion of the bronchial mucosa and interstitial pulmonary edema compressing smaller airways, is a common complicating factor. The association of wheezing with paroxysmal nocturnal dyspnea is responsible for the alternate name of the condition: *cardiac asthma*. Patients with paroxysmal nocturnal dyspnea sit upright at the side of their bed with legs dependent. Unlike orthopnea, which may be relieved immediately on positioning, attacks of paroxysmal nocturnal dyspnea may require 30 minutes or longer in this position for relief.

The patient with moderate to severe LVF appears pale and diaphoretic. Their skin is cool to the touch, and the observer has no difficulty noticing dyspnea, or difficulty in breathing. Monitoring vital signs almost always demonstrates an increase in blood pressure, with diastolic pressure elevated more than systolic pressure. The pulse pressure (systolic pressure minus diastolic pressure) therefore narrows. Heart rate increases. *Pulsus alternans,* the appearance of alternating strong and weak heart beats, may be detected, even though the basic rhythm of the heart remains normal; this condition occurs frequently during the later stages of heart failure. Tachypnea, or an increased rate of breathing, and hyperventilation, an increased depth of breathing, are common signs of LVF as a consequence of pulmonary congestion. Acute pulmonary edema will be discussed later in this chapter.

Right ventricular failure

Right ventricular failure (RVF) usually develops after left ventricular failure has been present for a variable length of time. Signs of systemic venous congestion primarily characterize RVF. The patient first notices signs of peripheral edema. Swelling of the feet and ankles develops during the day, subsiding overnight. This condition is referred to as *dependent,* or *pitting*, edema. If the patient is bedridden for extended periods, the edema fluid relocates into the sacral region. Dependent edema is a characteristic feature of RVF. *Pitting* refers to the depression, or pit, that remains in the tissue after pressure is applied to and removed from the area and is comparable to the impression that the foot leaves in wet sand when an individual walks on the beach. Within seconds the fluid returns, and the pit disappears.

As with LVF, individuals who have RVF experience *weakness* and *undue fatigue*, which are produced by the deficient supply of O_2 and nutrients to the tissues of the body. In addition, this O_2 deficit produces *cyanosis*, which is prominent especially in mucous membranes (such as in the nailbeds and lips). Cyanosis is produced by the removal by the tissues of a greater-than-normal amount of O_2 from the arterial blood in an effort to compensate for the decreased volume of circulating blood. This decreased blood supply is also the cause of the *coolness* often noted in the extremities.

Another sign of RVF is the presence of prominent jugular veins in the neck. In normal individuals the jugular veins are not visible in an upright position, except during moments of emotional or physical stress or exertion; however, as the right ventricle fails, systemic venous blood cannot be delivered to the heart normally and the jugular veins become engorged.

Engorgement of the liver (hepatomegaly) and spleen (splenomegaly) also occur. On examination, an enlarged liver may be palpated.[21] In normal situations, the lower border of the liver is not palpable beneath the right lower costal margin. With hepatomegaly, the liver may become palpable from one to four fingerbreadths below the right costal margin. This procedure evokes a degree of tenderness in the area of palpation. As RVF progresses, the edematous areas enlarge so that the legs, thighs, and eventually the abdomen (ascites) demonstrate clinical edema. Congestion of the gastrointestinal tract also occurs and is associated with clinical signs of anorexia, nausea, and vomiting. Signs of edema in the central nervous system include headache, insomnia, and irritability.

In LVF and RVF, the patient will frequently be quite anxious. Once the patient first experiences difficulty in breathing, hyperventilation often follows. Indeed, patients with heart failure may hyperventilate to the point of inducing respiratory alkalosis, with clinical symptoms of lightheadedness, coldness in the hands, and tingling in the fingers (see Chapter 12). In response to this anxiety the workload of the heart is increased even further, adding to the degree of heart failure.

Acute pulmonary edema

Acute pulmonary edema is a life-threatening situation in which a sudden and rapid transudation of fluid occurs from the pulmonary capillary bed into the alveolar spaces of the lungs.[2,4,5] Often, stressful situations—either physical or psychologic—precipitate this condition, but a salty meal, nonadherence with medications, or infection may also induce acute pulmonary edema.

The onset of symptoms is usually acute. A slight, dry cough is often the initial symptom; acute pulmonary edema may represent a direct extension of paroxysmal nocturnal dyspnea. Asthmatic-type wheezing (i.e., cardiac asthma) may occur. Extreme dyspnea and orthopnea are commonly present. As the episode progresses, the patient experiences a feeling of suffocation and an acute sense of anxiety that further increases the rate and difficulty of breathing. Patients also may experience a sense of oppression in the chest. Physical signs evident at this time include tachypnea, dyspnea, and cough. If auscultated, the lungs demonstrate moist rales at their bases that progressively extend upward as the episode worsens.

TABLE 14-4 Clinical manifestations of heart failure and acute pulmonary edema

Signs	Symptoms
HEART FAILURE	
Pallor, cool skin	Weakness and undue fatigue
Sweating (diaphoresis)	Dyspnea on exertion
Left ventricular hypertrophy	Hyperventilation
Dependent edema	Nocturia
Hepatomegaly and splenomegaly	Paroxysmal nocturnal dyspnea
Narrow pulse pressure	Wheezing (cardiac asthma)
Pulsus alternans	
Ascites	
ACUTE PULMONARY EDEMA	
All of the above signs of heart failure, plus:	All of the above symptoms of heart failure, plus:
Moist rales at the lung bases	Increased anxiety
Tachypnea	Dyspnea at rest
Cyanosis	
Frothy pink sputum	

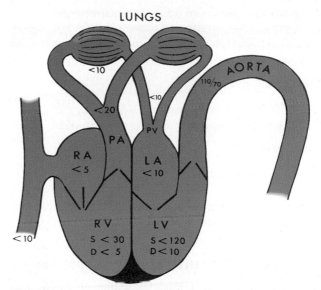

FIGURE 14-6 Average blood pressures in various components of the circulatory system. LA, left atrium; LV, left ventricle; PA, pulmonary arteries. (Modified from Wylie WD, Churchill-Davidson HC: *A practice of anaesthesia*, ed 3, London, Lloyd-Luke, 1972.)

In more severe episodes, patients exhibit pallor, sweating, cyanosis, and a frothy, pink (blood-tinged) sputum. Acute pulmonary edema is common during the period immediately after myocardial infarction if the degree of left ventricular myocardial damage is significant. Most individuals resist attempts at recumbency, may panic, and often remain uncooperative (Table 14-4).

■ PATHOPHYSIOLOGY

To view heart failure in its proper perspective, it is necessary to first review the function of the healthy human heart both at rest and during physical activity. The mechanisms of cardiac dysfunction then become more obvious.

The heart is designed to propel unoxygenated blood to the lungs and oxygenated blood to the peripheral tissues in accordance with their metabolic needs.[23] The human heart is composed of two individual pumps that work together (Figure 14-6). The right side of the heart receives venous (unoxygenated) blood from the body's systemic circulation and pumps this blood through pulmonary arteries to the lungs, where it undergoes oxygenation. From the lungs oxygenated (arterial) blood is delivered to the left atrium and then to the left ventricle, where it is pumped into the systemic circulation.

The amount of work that each ventricle requires to perform its task is considerably different. The right side of the heart may be considered a low-pressure system. An average right ventricular pressure of 25 mm Hg is required to pump blood into the pulmonary artery, the only artery normally containing unoxygenated blood. In contrast, the left side of the heart is a high-pressure system; left intraventricular pressure is approximately 130 mm Hg during systole (contraction). Thus, the left ventricle performs the lion's share of the actual work of the heart. Before birth, both ventricles work equally because they bear the same pressure loads. After birth, pulmonary arterial pressure falls, the workload of the right ventricle decreases, and its walls become thin; conversely, the workload of the left ventricle increases, and its muscular walls enlarge.

The primary function of the heart is to serve as a pump, supplying oxygenated blood and nutrients to the body's tissues and cells. Table 14-5 lists minimal O_2 requirements per minute for the average adult performing various activities. If the heart cannot provide the body with its needed O_2, shortness of breath (dyspnea) and undue fatigue result. These signs normally appear when O_2 transport per minute falls below 1000 to 1250 mL per minute. At this level a person can usually perform a light job and enjoy light recreation and sport

TABLE 14-5   Minimum adult O_2 requirements

Activity	O_2 utilization (mL/min)
At rest	250
Standing	375
Walking	400–1000
Light work and exercise	750–1250
Intense exercise	≥4000

without discomfort; the same individual cannot, however, perform more strenuous activities without distress.

Normal left ventricular function

The left ventricle is a thick muscular organ. At rest (diastole), left intraventricular pressure is approximately 8 mm Hg, whereas the diastolic pressure in the aorta is approximately 70 mm Hg. For blood to be expelled from the left ventricle into the aorta, intraventricular pressure must exceed aortic blood pressure so that the aortic valves can open, permitting blood to exit the heart into the aorta. The following description outlines the normal sequence of left ventricular function when an individual is at rest.

Maximal left ventricular filling, termed *end-diastolic volume,* occurs at the instant just before the start of systole. At this moment the muscles of the ventricle begin to contract, but blood is not yet ejected from the ventricle. Instead, the size of the ventricular cavity is rapidly decreasing, producing a sharp increase in intraventricular pressure. This interval, termed the *isovolemic period of systole,* normally lasts 50 milliseconds (ms), or about 0.050 second.

In a short time when intraventricular pressure exceeds diastolic aortic blood pressure (70 mm Hg), the aortic valves are forced open and the ejection of blood into the arterial circulation begins. The ventricle continues to contract for a period of time (systole), after which relaxation occurs. The blood pressure within the left ventricle drops rapidly as the ventricle relaxes. Once the blood pressure in the left ventricle drops below that of the aorta, the aortic valve closes, signaling the end of systole and the beginning of diastole. During diastole, intraaortic blood pressure exceeds that of the ventricle, permitting the ventricle to refill with blood.

When the aortic valves close left ventricular volume is at its lowest level. The difference in blood volume between end-diastolic volume (maximum volume) and end-systolic volume (minimum volume) is termed the *ejection fraction.* In a normal heart at rest, the ejection fraction is 0.56 to 0.78; in other words, 56% to 78%

of the blood present in the left ventricle at the end of diastole is ejected into the aorta during systole. As LVF develops, the ejection fraction decreases and may reach levels as low as 0.1 to 0.2 in severe heart failure.[24] Although this mechanism functions in normal situations, the demands on the heart change from second to second. The heart therefore must be able to respond rapidly to these ever-changing demands by increasing or decreasing the volume of blood it ejects per stroke (stroke volume).

Three factors—preload, afterload, and contractility—help enable the heart to meet its obligations to the body's tissues. Preload is the end-diastolic volume. The greater the preload, the more the myocardial muscle fibers stretch. According to the Frank-Starling relationship,[25,26] the greater the myocardial muscle stretches in diastole, the greater it will contract in systole; this is similar to the stretching of a rubber band. For example, with a preload of 100 mL of blood and an ejection fraction of 0.6 (60%), the stroke volume is 60 mL. If the preload increases to 140 mL and the ejection fraction remains 0.6, the stroke volume increases to 84 mL. In the same manner, decreased preload results in diminished stroke volume.

Afterload may be defined as the pressure that resists left ventricular ejection (aortic blood pressure). Increased afterload therefore the heart's attempt to eject a normal stroke volume more difficult. For example, if the aortic blood pressure (afterload) rises rapidly (as it may under extreme stress) from 120/80 to 200/120 mm Hg, intraventricular pressure must first rise to 120 mm Hg (the aortic diastolic pressure) before the aortic valve can open, allowing blood to exit the heart. The aortic valve will remain open for only a brief period before the aortic pressure once again exceeds that of the ventricle and the valve closes. The ejection fraction in this instance is very low (0.1 to 0.2).

Such a small stroke volume, if continued indefinitely, is inadequate to support the body's requirements. Fortunately, the normal heart can compensate for this inadequate stroke volume. The end-systolic volume is larger than normal (because of the large nonejected fraction of blood). To this is added the normal blood volume from the left atrium. This increase in preload (normal volume plus large end-systolic volume) causes increased stretch of the myocardial fibers, which results in a more forceful contraction with the next beat (the Frank-Starling relationship). Within several beats the left ventricle can adjust the stroke volume to compensate for the increase in aortic diastolic blood pressure from 120/80 to 200/120 mm Hg.

Limits to the Frank-Starling relationship do exist, however, in that excessive stretch or a sudden increase in afterload cannot be not met by an ever-increasing contraction of the myocardium. If the preload and afterload of the heart are permitted to remain the same, it is still possible for stroke volume to increase. Contractility is a basic property of cardiac muscle. The sympathetic nervous system can increase the heart's contraction through the release of epinephrine and norepinephrine. These catecholamines, which are released in increasing amounts under stress, increase the degree of myocardial fiber contraction, thus increasing the ejection fraction (from 0.6 to 0.8), resulting in an increase of stroke volume.

Heart failure

Heart failure may develop whenever the heart labors for extended periods of time against increased peripheral resistance (increased afterload), such as occurs with high blood pressure or valvular defects (stenosis or insufficiency), or prolonged, continuous demands for increased cardiac output (as occurs in hyperthyroidism). These conditions, which demand a chronic increase in cardiac workload, lead to structural changes in the myocardium that eventually progress to muscular weakness and produce the clinical signs and symptoms of heart failure.

Another major cause of myocardial weakness is the presence of a disease state that directly attacks the myocardium (e.g., coronary artery disease and myocarditis). In these conditions, cardiac muscle cannot respond normally to increases in afterload. The increase in fiber length that occurs as a result of increased ventricular filling is not met with the usual increase in stroke volume, and clinical heart failure results.

The chronic progression of heart failure is best illustrated by following the cardiac changes that develop in patients with high blood pressure, one of the primary causes of heart failure. In response to a sustained elevation of blood pressure (afterload), the myocardium must contract more forcefully for an extended period to maintain an acceptable stroke volume. As with any muscle doing increased work for extended periods, the myocardial fibers hypertrophy, or increase in diameter and length. This response occurs primarily in the left ventricle and leads to the development of the first sign of heart failure, left ventricular hypertrophy (LVH).

A normal heart weighs approximately 250 to 350 g. In patients with mild heart failure the heart may weigh up to 500 g; in more severe cases of heart failure, the heart may weigh up to 1000 g. LVH may be present for many years before being discovered, generally during routine electrocardiography or chest radiography. Another important feature of hypertrophy is that along with the increased size of left ventricular muscle fibers there is not a corresponding increase in the number of capillaries to deliver blood to them; thus, myocardial

blood supply becomes increasingly compromised as hypertrophy progresses. Because of the compromised blood supply seen in LVH, a point is reached at which hypertrophy alone can no longer maintain an adequate stroke volume during a sustained increase in blood pressure.

At this point a second mechanism, called dilation, helps to maintain normal stroke volume. Dilation is an increase in the capacity of the left ventricle and is brought about by an elongation of the myocardial fibers. The force of ventricular contraction of these elongated myocardial fibers increases through the Frank-Starling relationship, thus maintaining a normal stroke volume. However, both end-diastolic (increased total blood volume in the ventricle) and end-systolic (increased residual blood after contraction) volumes are increased, and the ejection fraction of the left ventricle is decreased (<0.56). As end-diastolic volume increases, the heart's workload increases, thereby increasing myocardial O_2 requirement. In the presence of coronary artery disease or LVH this increased O_2 demand may not be met, resulting in increasingly severe heart failure, angina pectoris, or myocardial infarction. As with LVH, dilation is evident on an electrocardiogram or chest radiograph.

If blood pressure continues to rise or if the myocardium weakens, hypertrophy and dilation cannot maintain a stroke volume adequate to supply peripheral tissues with their required amounts of O_2 and nutrients. As this situation develops, the patient first begins to experience undue fatigue and dyspnea during exertion as the left ventricle becomes unable to increase its output in response to exercise. As LVF intensifies, dyspnea develops with less and less exertion (progressing from ASA II to III to IV risk levels).

LVF also occurs at night when the individual lies down. At this time total blood volume increases as venous return from the lower extremities improves because of the diminished effect of gravity on the legs. To breathe comfortably, patients must elevate their head and thorax at night with extra pillows. The elevation is necessary because the now-increased fluid volume begins to produce respiratory distress (e.g., orthopnea) as fluid from the cardiovascular bed diffuses into alveolar sacs in the lungs, preventing the normal exchange of O_2 and carbon dioxide.

Blood volume increases in another, perhaps more important, manner that involves the kidneys. Decreased stroke volume leads to a decrease in renal blood flow and glomerular filtration rate (GFR), thereby decreasing the excretion of sodium. In fact, tubular reabsorption of sodium is actually stimulated through the increased secretion of renin and its attendant chemical reactions (secondary to a decreased GFR). Increased sodium retention prompts the pituitary gland to secrete decreased amounts of antidiuretic hormone, which is responsible for further water retention. These mechanisms result in a further increase in total blood volume (hypervolemia).

Hypervolemia produces increased hydrostatic pressure within the capillaries, leading at first to interstitial edema and then to an actual transudation of fluid into tissues with decreased tissue pressure. Edema of the ankles and lower extremities develops during the day when the individual is upright, because of the downward effect of gravity; it develops in the sacral region when the individual is recumbent, either at night or for long periods during illness or convalescence. Clinical signs and symptoms of LVF become more prominent at night, when most individuals assume recumbent positions for sleep. During the day, when an individual is in an erect position, the force of gravity causes the excessive fluid volume to be deposited into the subcutaneous tissues in the most dependent portions of the body (e.g., the ankles), producing signs of right ventricular failure.

When an individual assumes the supine position, the edematous fluid in the dependent portions of the body is reabsorbed into the cardiovascular system, leading to an increase in blood volume and venous return to the heart. This increase may result in overdistention of an already weakened left ventricle, producing an acute reduction in cardiac output and a large increase in the end-diastolic and end-systolic volumes. As a result the end-diastolic pressure may also rise. A normal end-diastolic pressure of 8 mm Hg may rise to 30 to 40 mm Hg or greater. Increased left ventricular pressure leads to increased pressure in the left atrium. The Frank-Starling relationship enables the left atrium to accommodate this increasing pressure, and after a few heartbeats the pressure in the left atrium increases to 30 to 40 mm Hg or above, remaining elevated for as long as the left ventricle is failing. This increased left atrial pressure is next transmitted backward to the pulmonary veins and capillaries so that the pulmonary capillary pressure also increases to 30 to 40 mm Hg. When this occurs, water and solutes diffuse from the capillaries into the alveolar air sacs, producing paroxysmal nocturnal dyspnea, acute pulmonary edema, or both.

When the alveolar air sacs contain fluid, O_2 and carbon dioxide cannot be exchanged and dyspnea results. Bronchospasm (cardiac asthma) is a common complicating factor of paroxysmal nocturnal dyspnea. Positional changes (e.g., from the supine to upright position) commonly produce dramatic relief from symptoms of LVF by causing fluid to move from the alveolar sacs and concentrate in the base of the lungs.

Right ventricular and atrial failure occur shortly after LVF as the increased pressure in the left side of the heart continues to back up, resulting in signs and symptoms of systemic venous and capillary congestion. As this increase in pressure develops, fluid leaves the blood vessels in dependent parts of the body (ankles and feet). In addition, venous return from the head and upper extremities is compromised because of elevated right atrial pressure, and the jugular veins become engorged and visible. Impaired venous return from the lower portions of the body is evident through engorgement of the liver (hepatomegaly) and spleen (splenomegaly) with blood.

Nocturia, or increased frequency of urination at night, is yet another sign of heart failure. During the day, when the individual is awake, renal function is poor because the individual's activities increase the degree of heart failure. Therefore less urine is produced during the day. At night cardiac and renal functions improve. Increased glomerular filtration produces more urine, and nocturia results.

One final sign of heart failure is cyanosis, which is most evident in mucous membranes and is produced by the heart's failure to provide an adequate stroke volume. To secure an adequate O_2 supply, the body's tissues extract more O_2 than normal from the capillary blood. Therefore the red blood cells within the capillaries and veins are poorly oxygenated and appear darker in color, which is clinically manifested as cyanosis.

■ MANAGEMENT

The patient suffering acute pulmonary edema represents a true medical emergency requiring immediate management. The protocol outlined below should be followed to treat the dental patient who has a history of heart failure (Box 14-2):

Step 1: termination of the dental procedure. Treatment should cease as soon as the patient begins to exhibit signs and symptoms of respiratory distress

Step 2: P (position). As with patients suffering other forms of acute respiratory distress, the patient suffering acute pulmonary edema usually remains conscious. This patient may appear panicky and uncooperative.[1] The patient should be positioned comfortably, which in most cases will be the upright position. This position allows excess fluid within the alveolar sacs to concentrate at the bases of the lungs, permitting a greater exchange of O_2. If at any time the patient loses consciousness, that individual must be placed in the supine position.

Step 3: removal of dental materials. All dental materials or instruments should be removed from the patient's mouth immediately.

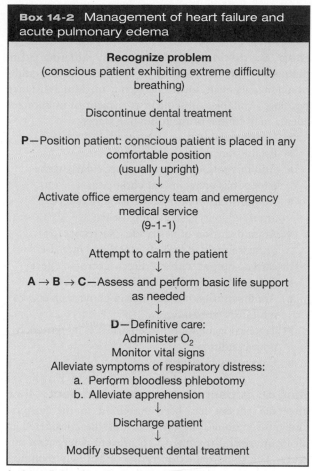

Box 14-2 Management of heart failure and acute pulmonary edema

Recognize problem
(conscious patient exhibiting extreme difficulty breathing)
↓
Discontinue dental treatment
↓
P—Position patient: conscious patient is placed in any comfortable position
(usually upright)
↓
Activate office emergency team and emergency medical service
(9-1-1)
↓
Attempt to calm the patient
↓
A → **B** → **C**—Assess and perform basic life support as needed
↓
D—Definitive care:
Administer O₂
Monitor vital signs
Alleviate symptoms of respiratory distress:
a. Perform bloodless phlebotomy
b. Alleviate apprehension
↓
Discharge patient
↓
Modify subsequent dental treatment

A, airway; **B,** breathing; **C,** circulation; **D,** definitive care; **P,** position.

Step 4: activate office emergency team and summons emergency medical services. At the onset of acute respiratory distress in a patient with preexisting heart failure, the appropriate office team member should contact emergency medical services (9-1-1) immediately. The patient usually requires immediate emergency treatment and hospitalization. Further medical management in the hospital may include phlebotomy, O_2, and drug therapy, such as digitalis and diuretics.

Step 5: calming of the patient. Dental personnel must reassure the patient that they are making every effort to manage the problem and that they have summoned emergency personnel.

Step 6: A-B-C (airway-breathing-circulation), basic life support as needed. In acute pulmonary edema the airway, breathing, and circulation are (usually) adequately maintained by the patient.

Step 7: D (definitive care):

Step 7a: administration of O_2. O_2 should be administered to all patients who demonstrate signs of acute pulmonary edema or severe heart failure. Patients require high concentrations at high flow rates to prevent or alleviate hypoxia. Face masks should be used with a flow rate of 10 L or more of O_2 per minute.

Step 7b: monitoring of vital signs. Vital signs, including blood pressure, heart rate and rhythm, and respiratory rate, should be monitored and recorded every 5 minutes. The blood pressure, heart rate, and respiratory rate increase in patients with acute heart failure; these changes demonstrate the presence of extreme apprehension and cardiac and pulmonary congestion.

Step 7c: alleviation of symptoms. The immediate goal in the management of acute pulmonary edema is to alleviate the patient's breathing difficulties. Proper positioning (per patient wishes, but usually upright) is extremely important. If respiratory distress is still evident, however, additional steps may be required. In cases of acute pulmonary edema, the heart cannot adequately handle the quantity of blood being delivered to it.

Step 7d: bloodless phlebotomy. Phlebotomy is a procedure that may be performed in the hospital. Approximately 400 to 500 mL of blood is removed from the patient.[26] Phlebotomy is sometimes rapidly effective in the reduction of respiratory symptoms because venous return to the right side of the heart is reduced while the left side drains some excess fluid from the lungs.

Phlebotomy in the dental office is not often indicated. However, a bloodless phlebotomy may achieve a similar effect. Bloodless phlebotomy can temporarily remove approximately 12% of circulating blood volume, or 700 of 6000 mL in the average man, permitting the heart to function more effectively and dyspnea to be alleviated.[28] Tourniquets or blood pressure cuffs are applied to three extremities, using wide, soft, rubber tubing for the tourniquets. The tourniquets are placed approximately 6 inches below the groin and approximately 4 inches below the shoulders. Tourniquets are applied to only three extremities at a time. Every 5 to 10 minutes, one of the tourniquets is released and applied to the free extremity. The tourniquets (or blood pressure cuffs) should be applied at a pressure less than the systolic blood pressure but greater than the diastolic pressure. An arterial pulse should be palpable distal to each tourniquet or cuff.

Bloodless phlebotomy actually leads to a total reduction in the circulating blood volume. While trapped in the extremities, a protein-poor filtrate is forced out of the capillaries into the tissues, where it remains for a period even after the tourniquet is removed.

Step 7e: administration of a vasodilator.

The administration of vasodilators in the management of heart failure and acute pulmonary edema has gained popularity.[29] Venodilators, such as nitroglycerin, reduce the preload (the filling pressure) but not the systemic pressure (afterload). Nitrates are predominantly venodilators. Side effects associated with their administration include headache, dizziness, hypotension, and flushing. Between 0.8 and 1.2 mg (two to three tablets or sprays) every 5 to 10 minutes may be administered in the rapid treatment of acute pulmonary edema.[29] Onset of action is within 2 minutes, and the duration is about 15 to 30 minutes. When sublingual nitroglycerin tablets are used, the patient should be asked whether the tablet tingles as it dissolves to ensure the potency of the preparation. The use of nitroglycerin should be considered only when the systolic blood pressure is above 90 mm Hg.

The angiotensin-converting enzyme inhibitors, such as captopril and enalaprilat, are now standard therapy for the treatment of heart failure.[28] These drugs, administered either sublingually or intravenously, act to decrease afterload.

Step 7f: alleviate apprehension.

Most patients suffering acute pulmonary edema are extremely apprehensive, bordering on panic. Increased apprehension leads to increases in cardiac and respiratory workloads, both of which are absolutely contraindicated in these patients. For this reason dental personnel must take special care to eliminate patient anxiety.

If the preceding steps diminished the degree of respiratory distress, the patient may no longer be apprehensive. However, in the presence of continued respiratory distress and anxiety, drug therapy should be considered. Administration of an opioid agonist, such as morphine (2 to 4 mg intravenously, subcutaneously, or intramuscularly, repeated every 15 minutes as needed), is a possibility. (These suggested doses are for adult patients only. Pediatric doses of morphine in the treatment of pulmonary edema are 0.1 to 0.2 mg intravenously per kilogram of body weight.) Morphine acts to reduce anxiety and agitation as well as producing vasodilation, leading to decreased venous return and decreased systemic resistance.[30] Absolute contraindications to these drugs in the management of heart failure include the clinical presence of hypoxia (see Table 13-3) with cyanosis or of mental confusion or delirium. Opioids further depress respiration in these individuals, who already suffer severely compromised respiratory function.

Naloxone, an opioid antagonist, must be available whenever opioid agonists are administered.

Step 8: discharge.

The patient suffering acute pulmonary edema requires hospitalization for additional management. Once emergency medical assistance becomes available, subsequent treatment of pulmonary edema may consist of the following steps:

- Continuous cardiac monitoring
- Establishment of an IV line
- Administration of nitrates, particularly if the patient has concomitant chest pain
- Administration of nitroprusside to reduce afterload in hypertensive patients
- Administration of nesiritide (Natrecor) to decrease preload and afterload and increase cardiac output without direct inotropic effects
- Administration of morphine (see above)
- Administration of angiotensin-converting enzyme inhibitors (see above)
- Tracheal intubation if the patient is in extremely poor condition
- Emergency transport

Step 9: subsequent dental treatment.

Even after the patient has been stabilized in the hospital and returns home, the episode must be considered in all future dental treatments to prevent a repeat occurrence. The stress reduction protocol can help minimize future risk. Consultation with the patient's primary care physician is essential in the development of a reasonable plan for dental treatment.

- **Drugs used in management:** O_2, at high flow rate; nitroglycerin (sublingual) or nifedipine; and morphine (optional) are used in the management of heart failure and acute pulmonary edema.
- **Medical assistance required:** Yes. Emergency assistance is required in the treatment of patients suffering heart failure.

REFERENCES

1. Stirling EL: Congestive heart failure. In: Marx JA, Hockberger RS, Walls RM, et al., editors: *Rosen's emergency medicine: concepts and clinical practice,* ed 5, St. Louis, Mosby, 2002, pp. 1110–1130.
2. Givertz MM, Colucci WS, Braunwald E: Clinical aspects of heart failure; pulmonary edema, high-output failure. In: Braunwald E, Zipes DP, Libby P, Bonow R, editors: *Braunwald's heart disease: a textbook of cardiovascular medicine,* ed 7, Philadelphia, WB Saunders, 2004.
3. Hunt SA, Baker DW, Chin MH, et al.: ACC/AHA guidelines for the evaluation and management of chronic

heart failure in the adult: Executive summary. A Report of the American College of Cardiology/American Heart Association Task Force on Practice Guidelines (Committee to Revise the 1995 Guidelines for the Evaluation and Management of Heart Failure), *Circulation* 104: 2996–3007, 2001.

4. Gandhi SK, Powers JC, Nomeir AM, et al.: The pathogenesis of acute pulmonary edema associated with hypertension, *N Engl J Med* 344:17–22, 2001.

5. Edoute Y, Roguin A, Behar D, Reisner SA: Prospective evaluation of acute pulmonary edema, *Crit Care Med* 28:330–335, 2000.

6. National Center for Health Statistics. Health, United States, 2006. www.cdc.gov/nchs/hus.html

7. American Heart Association, *Heart disease and stroke statistics–2005 Update.* Dallas, American Heart Association, 2005.

8. Levy D, Larson MG, Vasan RS, et al.: The progression from hypertension to congestive heart failure, *JAMA* 275:1557–1562, 1996.

9. Ho KK, Anderson KN, Kannel WB, et al.: Survival after the onset of congestive heart failure in Framingham Heart Study subjects, *Circulation* 88:107–115, 1993.

10. Barkin RM, Rosen P: Congestive heart failure. In: Barkin RM, Rosen P, editors: *Emergency pediatrics: a guide to ambulatory care,* ed 6, St. Louis, Mosby, 2003, pp. 149–158.

11. Scholz H: Inotropic drugs and their mechanism of action, *J Am Coll Cardiol* 4:389–397, 1984.

12. Lowes BD, Tsvetkova T, Eichhorn EJ, et al.: Milrinone vs. dobutamine in heart failure subjects treated chronically with carvedilol, *Int J Cardiol* 81:141–149, 2001.

13. Bayram M, De Luca L, Massie MB, Gheorghiade M: Reassessment of dobutamine, dopamine, and milrinone in the management of acute heart failure syndromes, *Am J Cardiol* 96:47G–58G, 2005.

14. Dec GW: Digoxin remains useful in the management of chronic heart failure, *Med Clin North Am* 87:317–337, 2003.

15. Cohn JN, Archibald DG, Ziesche S, et al.: Effect of vasodilator therapy on mortality in chronic congestive heart failure. Results of a Veterans Administration Cooperative Study, *N Engl J Med* 314:1547–1552, 1986.

16. Bristow MR, Linas S, Port JD: Drugs in the treatment of heart failure. In: Braunwald E, Zipes DP, Libby P, Bonow R, editors: *Braunwald's heart disease: a textbook of cardiovascular medicine,* ed 7, Philadelphia, WB Saunders, 2004.

17. Bristow MR: β-Adrenergic receptor blockade in chronic heart failure, *Circulation* 101:558–569, 2000.

18. Zoorob RJ: Acute dyspnea in the office, *Am Fam Phys* 68:1803–1810, 2003.

19. Duguet A, Tantucci C, Lozinguez D, et al.: Expiratory flow limitation as a determinant of orthopnea in acute left heart failure, *J Am Coll Cardiol* 35:690–700, 2000.

20. Bristow MR, Kantrowitz NE, Ginsburg R, Fowler MB: β-Adrenergic function in heart muscle disease and heart failure, *J Mol Cell Cardiol* 17(suppl2):41–52, 1985.

21. Braunwald E: The physical examination. In: Braunwald E, Zipes DP, Libby P, Bonow R, editors: *Braunwald's heart disease: a textbook of cardiovascular medicine,* ed 7, Philadelphia, WB Saunders, 2004.

22. Criteria Committee, New York Heart Association *Diseases of the heart and blood vessels: nomenclature and criteria for diagnosis,* ed 6, Boston, Little, Brown, 1964.

23. Braunwald E, Sonnenblick EH, Ross J Jr: Contraction of the normal heart. In: Braunwald E, Zipes DP, Libby P, Bonow R, editors: *Braunwald's heart disease: a textbook of cardiovascular medicine,* ed 7, Philadelphia, WB Saunders, 2004.

24. Nohria A, Mielniczuk LM, Stevenson LW: Evaluation and monitoring of patients with acute heart failure syndromes, *Am J Cardiol* 96:32G–40G, 2005.

25. Frank O: Zur Dynamik des Herzmuskels, *Z Biol* 32:370, 1895.

26. Starling EH: *Linacre lecture on the law of the heart, 1915,* London, Longmans, Green, 1918.

27. Green B: Porphyrias and specific therapy. In: Schwartz GR, Hanke BK, Mayer TA, et al., editors: *Principles and practice of emergency medicine,* ed 4, Baltimore, Lippincott Williams & Wilkins, 1999.

28. McCarthy FM: Cardiovascular disease. In: McCarthy FM: *Essentials of safe dentistry for the medically compromised patient,* Philadelphia, WB Saunders, 1989.

29. Ferri FF: Pulmonary edema. In: Ferri FF, editor: *Ferri's clinical advisor: instant diagnosis and treatment,* St. Louis, Mosby, 2006, p. 704.

30. Michael KA, Parnell KJ: Innovations in the pharmacologic management of heart failure, *AACN Clin Issues* 9: 172–191, 1998.

CHAPTER 15

Respiratory Distress:

Differential Diagnosis

In most clinical situations, the cause of acute respiratory distress will be readily evident, thereby expediting its definitive management. However, situations do exist in which the cause of respiratory distress is less than obvious. In these cases consideration of the following factors may assist the doctor in determining the cause of the clinical problem, thereby permitting definitive therapy to proceed expeditiously.

■ MEDICAL HISTORY

Patients suffering acute respiratory distress almost always retain consciousness throughout the episode. Advantage may be taken of this by asking the patient about any previous similar episodes. In addition, the medical history questionnaire includes questions about respiratory problems, such as asthma, heart failure, or a history of hyperventilation, thus helping facilitate a differential diagnosis. If at any time consciousness is lost, management proceeds to follow the protocol for management of the unconscious patient (see Part II: Unconsciousness).

■ AGE

Respiratory distress in younger patients (under the age of 10) most commonly is related to asthma (usually allergic asthma); hyperventilation and heart failure are significantly less common in this age group (children with severe, uncorrected, congenital heart defects may demonstrate respiratory distress, but their medical history will have provided the doctor with this information). Hyperventilation is more likely to be the cause of respiratory distress for individuals between 12 and 40 years of age. Asthma may also occur in this age group, but in most instances patients already know if they suffer from this condition. Clinically significant heart failure is rarely seen before the age of 40 years. The peak incidence of heart failure in men is between 50 and 60 years; in women, the peak falls between 60 and 70 years.

■ SEX

The incidence of hyperventilation, asthma, and heart failure does not differ markedly between males and females, although the incidence of heart failure is slightly greater among males in that age group than in females under the age of 70 years.

■ RELATED CIRCUMSTANCES

Stress, whether physiologic or psychological, is present in most instances of respiratory distress and increases in severity as the episode progresses. In the dental environment, hyperventilation is precipitated almost exclusively by extreme apprehension. Stressful situations may acutely exacerbate asthma, especially in children, regardless of the type of asthma (intrinsic or extrinsic). In addition, stress causes the physical conditions of patients with heart failure to progressively deteriorate.

■ CLINICAL SYMPTOMS BETWEEN ACUTE EPISODES

The patient with heart failure may exhibit clinical signs and symptoms at all times, either during physical activity or at rest. Orthopnea, dependent edema, peripheral cyanosis, dyspnea, and undue fatigue may be evident in the patient during dental appointments, depending on the degree of pump failure. Asthmatic patients may be asymptomatic between acute episodes; however, noisy breathing and chronic coughs may be present while at rest. No clinical signs and symptoms of hyperventilation are present between episodes.

■ POSITION

The position of the patient at the onset of clinical symptoms is most relevant in patients with heart failure. Respiratory distress becomes progressively more severe as the dental chair is reclined toward the supine position. Symptoms can often be dramatically relieved by simply allowing the patient to sit upright. Signs and symptoms of asthma and hyperventilation do not respond to repositioning, although most patients in respiratory distress can breathe more easily in an upright position.

■ ACCOMPANYING SOUNDS

Wheezing is usually present in patients with asthma. Wheezing may also be present in paroxysmal nocturnal dyspnea and pulmonary edema (cardiac asthma), although in these circumstances it is associated with other signs and symptoms of heart failure. Partial obstruction of the trachea or bronchi by a foreign object may also produce wheezing. Individuals with heart failure may also exhibit moist, wet respirations, especially those suffering acute pulmonary edema, which is often associated with a frothy, pink-tinged sputum and cough. Hyperventilating individuals breathe deeper and more rapidly than normal, but produce no accompanying abnormal sounds.

■ SYMPTOMS ASSOCIATED WITH RESPIRATORY DISTRESS

Most individuals in respiratory distress experience shortness of breath. In cases of heart failure, shortness of breath progressively worsens as the patient reclines (orthopnea) and increases with exertion. Shortness of breath during episodes of hyperventilation is related to anxiety and a feeling of suffocation; it is not related to exertion. In addition, hyperventilation is not associated with cough. Asthmatic patients exhibit shortness of breath associated with episodic wheezing during acute periods. Some asthmatic patients are asymptomatic between acute episodes.

■ PERIPHERAL EDEMA AND CYANOSIS

Patients with heart failure may exhibit peripheral edema and cyanosis. Other possible causes of peripheral edema include renal disease, varicose veins, and pregnancy, whereas cardiorespiratory disease and polycythemia vera are possible causes of cyanosis. In cases of severe asthma with hypoxia or hypercarbia, cyanosis may be present; however, peripheral edema is not noted. Neither peripheral edema nor cyanosis usually accompanies hyperventilation.

■ PARESTHESIA OF THE EXTREMITIES

Tingling and numbness of the fingers, toes, and perioral regions are experienced during hyperventilation. These symptoms may also be present, but much less commonly, in milder episodes of asthma and heart failure, produced by hyperventilation secondary to acute anxiety.

■ USE OF ACCESSORY RESPIRATORY MUSCLES

The patient with acute asthma uses accessory muscles of respiration (abdominal, back, and neck muscles) in an effort to breathe adequately. This may also be noted with acute pulmonary edema.

■ CHEST PAIN

Hyperventilating patients often experience chest pain, describing it as a "weight," a "pressing" sensation, or as a "shooting" or "stabbing" feeling. However, these patients rarely exhibit other clinical manifestations of cardiac disease. The age of the hyperventilating patient (under 35 years) is usually below that at which cardiovascular disease normally occurs. Patients suffering asthma usually do not experience chest pain along with their other clinical symptoms. When chest pain occurs in a patient with preexisting heart failure, it might be associated with a concurrent acute myocardial infarction.

■ HEART RATE AND BLOOD PRESSURE

Both heart rate and blood pressure usually increase during periods of respiratory distress. This elevation occurs in hyperventilation and during acute asthmatic episodes as a result of anxiety. In these cases the blood pressure (both systolic and diastolic) and heart rate are elevated.

Although both the systolic and the diastolic pressures increase in during heart failure, diastolic blood pressure is usually elevated to a greater degree; therefore, the pulse pressure (systolic–diastolic) narrows (to 40). Heart rate increases in heart failure. $\frac{S}{D}$ average ≤ 30

■ DURATION OF RESPIRATORY DISTRESS

Respiratory distress associated with heart failure often improves dramatically with repositioning (when the patient sits upright). However, when pulmonary edema is present, respiratory distress does not improve until definitive management is initiated.

Most asthma attacks will not resolve for a considerable period without drug management; therefore, bronchodilator therapy is employed as soon as it is available. Status asthmaticus requires more definitive management, including hospitalization.

Hyperventilation is usually manageable without drug intervention and rarely, if ever, requires the help of additional personnel or hospitalization.

(An algorithm for the diagnosis and management of respiratory difficulty appears in Box 10-2.)

PART 4

ALTERED CONSCIOUSNESS

16 Altered Consciousness: General Considerations

17 Diabetes Mellitus: Hyperglycemia and Hypoglycemia

18 Thyroid Gland Dysfunction

19 Cerebrovascular Accident

20 Altered Consciousness: Differential Diagnosis

CHAPTER 16

Altered Consciousness:

General Considerations

In this section we are dealing with the brain, the central nervous system (CNS), and alterations in functioning of the CNS.

A state of altered consciousness (a conscious person acting "strangely") may represent a clinical manifestation of any number of systemic medical conditions. Almost every one of the situations that commonly produce alterations in consciousness can also lead to the loss of consciousness, which is really just another clinical expression of altered consciousness (Table 16-1). However, in most situations, prompt recognition of clinical signs and symptoms and the equally prompt institution of corrective measures enables the victim to retain consciousness until definitive management becomes available. Box 16-1 lists some of the terms and definitions frequently associated with altered consciousness.

Altered consciousness may be the first clinical sign of a serious medical problem requiring immediate and intensive therapy. The doctor must be aware of the patient's medical history prior to starting any treatment so that prompt recognition and management are possible. Such knowledge will also help in the modification of future dental treatment to prevent episodes.

TABLE 16-1　Causes of altered consciousness

Cause	Frequency	Text discussion
Drug overdose (CNS depressants, insulin)	Most common	Drug-related emergencies (Part Six)
Hyperventilation	Common	Respiratory distress (Part Three)
Hypoglycemia	Common	Altered consciousness (Part Four)
Hyperglycemia	Less common	Altered consciousness (Part Four)
CVA, transient ischemia attack	Less common	Altered consciousness (Part Four)
Hyperthyroidism	Rare	Altered consciousness (Part Four)
Hypothyroidism	Rare	Altered consciousness (Part Four)

CNS, central nervous system; CVA, cerebrovascular accident.

Box 16-1　Definition of terms

Confusion: A mental state marked by the mingling of ideas with consequent disturbances in comprehension and understanding, which eventually leads to bewilderment

Delirium: A mental disturbance marked by illusions, delusions, cerebral excitement, physical restlessness, and incoherence

Dizziness: A disturbed sense of relationship to space; a sensation of unsteadiness accompanied by a feeling of movement within the head

---

■ PREDISPOSING FACTORS

The most common cause of altered consciousness in a dental setting is the ingestion or administration of drugs. With the current increased popularity of pharmacosedation, dentists are more likely to encounter reports of inadvertent overadministration of, or overreaction to, these drugs. Knowledge of drug pharmacology and proper use of such drugs can help to minimize, but not entirely prevent, these incidents.

One particular psychosedative, rarely prescribed by doctors, may be a drug that dental patients most commonly use—alcohol. Most dentists have, at one time or another, had to manage the dental needs of a patient who has accidentally (or in some instances intentionally) ingested an overdose of alcohol; in other words, the patient is intoxicated.

Other drugs, including orally administered benzodiazepines such as triazolam (Halcion) may produce similar undesirable effects.

In any situation in which a patient is suspected of being "under the influence," dental treatment should be postponed and the patient strictly admonished against the self-administration of drugs. The doctor needs to determine the patient's reasons for having taken this drug or drugs and, if appropriate, initiate steps to alleviate the patient's dental anxiety. The administration of additional drugs (e.g., local anesthetics or sedatives) that further depress the CNS of a patient who has already ingested an unknown quantity of an unknown drug that also possesses CNS-depressant properties invites serious and often dire consequences.

Hyperventilation is the most common nondrug cause of altered consciousness in dentistry. Although hyperventilation rarely leads to the loss of consciousness, this may occur if recognition and management are delayed. Fear and anxiety are the primary precipitating factors in almost all cases of hyperventilation in the dental setting, which occurs predominantly in adolescents and young adults. Patients less than 40 years of age make up the majority of cases of hyperventilation in dental settings (see Chapter 12).

This section discusses three other systemic problems that present clinically as alterations in consciousness—diabetes mellitus, cerebrovascular ischemia and infarction, and thyroid gland dysfunction. *Diabetes mellitus* and its acute clinical complication, hypoglycemia, are not encountered frequently in dental patients, though hypoglycemia was the ninth most common emergency situation in two surveys of North American dentists.[1,2] However, inadequate medical management of diabetes and the presence of additional stress rapidly may result in an altered state of consciousness and possibly in the loss of consciousness. Nondiabetic individuals may also develop hypoglycemia under certain circumstances. *Cerebrovascular ischemia* and *infarction* (also known as *stroke* or *brain attack*) are (happily) much less common but potentially more serious causes of altered consciousness. Proper management of the post–cerebrovascular accident (CVA) patient greatly reduces the risk that dental treatment may precipitate a second acute episode. A prodromal form of cerebrovascular ischemia, known as *transient ischemic attack,* is also discussed.

Thyroid gland dysfunction can also lead to altered consciousness. Although acute clinical complications resulting from thyroid gland hypofunction or hyperfunction are extremely rare in dental settings, the doctor must be aware of a patient's thyroid gland dysfunction and be able to recognize those signs and symptoms associated with them. Even more important, the doctor must be aware of the increased incidence of cardiovascular disease that is associated with thyroid gland dysfunction.

In all of these situations, increases in physiologic or psychological stress occurring during dental treatment increases the potential for an acute exacerbation of the patient's underlying medical condition.

■ PREVENTION

Recognition of unusually high levels of apprehension in a prospective patient can lead to modifications in dental treatment and a decreased incidence of vasodepressor syncope and hyperventilation; the proper use of pharmacosedative techniques can help prevent treatment-related drug overdose. In addition, a patient's medical history permits the doctor to modify the treatment plan to minimize any risk to the patient. The medical history questionnaire, dialogue history, physical examination, and monitoring of vital signs are invaluable in the proper pretreatment assessment of a patient; specific questions and examinations should be used as references before treatment begins.

■ CLINICAL MANIFESTATIONS

A spectrum of signs and symptoms may be present in patients with altered consciousness: the cold and wet appearance, mental confusion, and bizarre behavior of the hypoglycemic patient contrasts markedly with the hot, dry, florid appearance of the patient who is hyperglycemic. The presence of the fruity-sweet smell of acetone on the breath further aids in the clinical recognition of hyperglycemia (ketoacidosis).

CVAs may develop with a sudden loss of consciousness (associated with an extremely grave prognosis) or with a more gradual onset of signs and symptoms related to CNS dysfunction. These may include a variable degree of derangement in speech, thought, motion, sensation, or vision. The state of consciousness may remain unimpaired, or the patient may demonstrate varying degrees of altered consciousness, ranging from headache, dizziness, and drowsiness to mental confusion.

Hypothyroidism, left untreated, may produce weakness, fatigue, lethargy, and slow speech, among other signs and symptoms. By contrast, untreated hyperthyroidism causes restlessness, nervousness, and irritability, as well as degrees of motor incoordination that range from fine, mild tremulousness to gross tremors. Thyroid storm, or thyroid crisis, is an example of a serious consequence of unmanaged hyperthyroidism. Thyroid storm may arise spontaneously but more commonly follows a period of sudden stress in persons who are clinically hyperthyroid. The death rate associated with thyroid storm is significant.

■ PATHOPHYSIOLOGY

In all three situations discussed in this section, the clinical signs and symptoms are manifested systemically even though they are produced by a very specific factor. In diabetes and thyroid gland dysfunction it is not the *quantity* of blood flowing to the brain that is altered but the *quality* of the blood. A blood glucose level that is either too high or too low causes most of the signs and symptoms associated with acute diabetic complications. Although diabetes is frequently considered a disease of impaired carbohydrate utilization, it is also, and significantly, a blood vessel disease. Diabetic patients exhibit a greater incidence of cardiovascular disease than persons without diabetes. A change in the quality of circulating blood is responsible for most of the acute clinical complications of diabetes.

Signs and symptoms of thyroid gland dysfunction are related clinically to the circulating blood level of thyroid hormone (thyroxine) and its pharmacologic actions on other parts of the body. In a manner similar to blood sugar levels in diabetes, overly high or overly low blood levels of thyroid hormone produce a spectrum of undesirable clinical signs and symptoms.

Decrease of the volume (quantity) of blood flowing to the brain also produces signs and symptoms of altered consciousness. A temporary blood volume insufficiency leads to transient ischemic attack (akin to angina pectoris in the heart; see Chapter 27) while more prolonged insufficiency results in permanent neurologic changes, termed cerebrovascular infarctions (strokes) (akin to acute myocardial infarction in the heart; see Chapter 28).

■ MANAGEMENT

On recognition of altered consciousness several basic steps must be carried out immediately (Box 16-2). (Subsequent chapters in this section will discuss definitive management of those specific emergencies.)

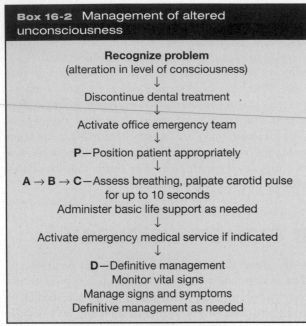

Box 16-2 Management of altered unconsciousness

Recognize problem
(alteration in level of consciousness)
↓
Discontinue dental treatment
↓
Activate office emergency team
↓
P—Position patient appropriately
↓
A → B → C—Assess breathing, palpate carotid pulse
for up to 10 seconds
Administer basic life support as needed
↓
Activate emergency medical service if indicated
↓
D—Definitive management
Monitor vital signs
Manage signs and symptoms
Definitive management as needed

A, airway; **B,** breathing; **C,** circulation; **D,** definitive care; **P,** position.

Step 1: recognition of altered consciousness.

Changes in the level of consciousness of a patient during dental treatment should alert the doctor to terminate treatment. (Subsequent chapters describe specific signs and symptoms.) In most cases changes in the level of consciousness occur gradually (over hours [hypoglycemia] to weeks or longer [thyroid dysfunction]), so the change in a patients level of consciousness may be obvious to the doctor and office staff prior to the start of dental treatment.

Step 2: termination of dental treatment and activate office emergency team

Step 3: P (position).   Proper positioning for patients

with altered levels of consciousness varies according to the underlying cause. In most instances the patient will remain conscious; therefore, any position the patient finds most comfortable is appropriate (supine, semisupine, or erect positions all are acceptable). However, if consciousness is ever lost, initial management must follow the protocol for the treatment of unconsciousness with the patient placed, at least initially, in the supine position with their feet elevated slightly (see Box 5-3).

CVAs are often associated with extreme elevations of blood pressure, especially systolic. In such a situation, a nonrecumbent (nonsupine) position is important; in the upright position, cerebral blood pressure will be somewhat reduced by the effect of gravity. If CVA

leads to a rapid loss of consciousness and is associated with significant elevation of the blood pressure, positioning of the victim is altered slightly. Because the supine position causes an increase in cerebral blood pressure that will not be beneficial at this time, the patient should be placed in a modified supine position with their head and thorax elevated slightly.

Step 4: A-B-C (airway-breathing-circulation), basic life support as needed.   The steps of basic

life support should be initiated as soon as possible:

- Assessment of airway patency and airway maintenance, if needed
- Assessment of spontaneous breathing and artificial ventilation, if needed
- Assessment of circulatory adequacy and artificial circulation, if needed

Step 5: D (definitive care):

Step 5a: monitoring of vital signs.   The blood pressure, heart rate and rhythm, and respiratory rate are monitored and recorded approximately every 5 minutes throughout the episode. A permanent record should also be retained.

Step 5b: management of signs and symptoms.   Clinical signs and symptoms are treated in an effort to increase patient comfort. Blankets should be available if the patient is shivering, and tight garments should be loosened or removed to allow the patient easier breathing.

Step 5c: activation of emergency medical service, if indicated.   If the doctor feels it necessary, emergency medical assistance should be sought immediately.

Step 5d: definitive management.   At this point a decision must be made as to the definitive management of the problem. In-office management ranges from basic life support (CVA) to the administration of drugs to terminate the episode (hypoglycemia), to seeking emergency medical assistance. (The following chapters will describe in detail the management recommended for each situation.)

REFERENCES

1. Fast TB, Martin MD, Ellis TM: Emergency preparedness: a survey of dental practitioners, *J Am Dent Assoc* 112:499–501, 1986.
2. Malamed SF: Managing medical emergencies, *J Am Dent Assoc* 124:40–53, 1993.

CHAPTER 17

Diabetes Mellitus:

Hypoglycemia and Hyperglycemia

Diabetes is the most common endocrine disease.[1] It is a group of diseases marked by high levels of blood glucose resulting from defects in insulin production, insulin action, or both.[1] Approximately 135 million individuals worldwide (a figure estimated to reach 300 million cases by 2025)[2] and 20.8 million Americans (7% of the U.S. population) have diabetes mellitus.[3] Although diabetes has been diagnosed in 14.6 million of these Americans, 6.2 million individuals are unaware that they have the disease. In 2002, diabetes was diagnosed in approximately 1,500,000 Americans over age 20 years.[3]

Among persons in the United States over age 20 years, diabetes is present in 9.6% of the population (20.6 million); in those over age 60 years, the prevalence increases to 20.9% (10.3 million).[3] The prevalence of diabetes in men over age 20 years is slightly greater than that in women: 10.5% versus 8.8%.

Among ethnic groups age 20 years and older in the United States, 8.7% of all non-Hispanic white persons and 13.3% of all non-Hispanic black persons have diabetes. Non-Hispanic black persons are 1.8 times as likely to have diabetes as non-Hispanic white persons. Figure 17-1 presents age-adjusted prevalence rates of diabetes in persons 20 years of age and older by race and ethnicity in the United States.[3]

In addition, diabetes is prevalent in children, with type 1 diabetes diagnosed in about 1 in every 400 to 600 children and adolescents.[2,3] About 176,500 people in the United States under 20 years of age have diabetes (0.22% of all people in this age group).

Diabetes was the sixth leading cause of death in the United States in 2002.[4] This is based on the 73,429 death certificates in which diabetes was listed as the underlying cause of death. According to death certificate reports, diabetes contributed to a total of 224,092 deaths in 2002.[4] Overall, the risk for death among diabetic patients is about twice that of people without diabetes of a similar age.[3]

Diabetes is associated with significant complications. It is a leading cause of both death and early disability. Diabetes is the leading cause of blindness (diabetic retinopathy) among working-age adults (12,000 to 24,000 new cases annually in United States), of end-stage renal disease (44% of all new cases of kidney failure in 2002 occurred in diabetic patients), and of nontraumatic limb amputations (82,000 amputations in 2002 in diabetic patients; >60% of total nontraumatic amputations).[3] Diabetes increases the risk of cardiac, cerebral, and peripheral vascular disease two- to seven-fold and in the obstetric setting is a major contributor to neonatal morbidity and death.[2]

Heart disease and cerebrovascular accidents (CVA) (stroke) account for about 65% of deaths in diabetic persons. Adults with diabetes have rates of death from heart disease about two to four times higher than do nondiabetic adults. The risk of CVA is also two to four times higher among diabetic persons.[3]

About 73% of adults with diabetes in the United States have blood pressure greater than 130/80 mm Hg or use prescription medications to manage high blood pressure.[3] Nervous system disease, of varying severity, is present in about 60% to 70% of diabetic patients. This includes altered sensation in hands or feet (almost 30% of diabetic patients in the United States over age 40 years have impaired sensation in their feet) and other neurologic problems.[3] Diabetic patients have increased risk of periodontal disease, estimated at twice the risk of those without diabetes.[3] The prevalence of diabetes increases with age.[3] Figure 17-2 illustrates the incidence of diabetes and its relationship to age group.

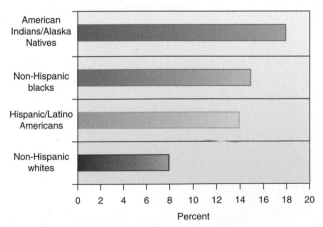

FIGURE 17-1 Estimated age-adjusted total prevalence of diabetes in people age 20 years and older, by race/ethnicity, United States, 2005. (From Centers for Disease Control and Prevention: *National diabetes fact sheet: general information and national estimates on diabetes in the United States, 2005,* Atlanta, GA, U.S. Department of Health and Human Services, Centers for Disease Control and Prevention, 2005.)

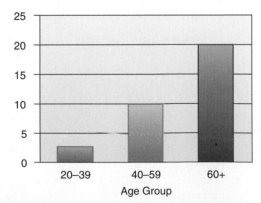

FIGURE 17-2 Estimated total prevalence of diabetes in people age 20 years or older by age group, United States, 2005. (From Centers for Disease Control and Prevention: *National diabetes fact sheet: general information and national estimates on diabetes in the United States, 2005,* Atlanta, GA, U.S. Department of Health and Human Services, Centers for Disease Control and Prevention, 2005.)

ACUTE COMPLICATIONS

Acute complications of diabetes mellitus include hypoglycemia, diabetic ketoacidosis, and hyperglycemic hyperosmolar nonketotic coma.[1] *Hyperglycemia*, or high blood sugar, and its sequelae represent one of two clinically significant complications for the doctor who is called upon to manage the dental needs of the diabetic patient. The second and more acutely life-threatening complication is *hypoglycemia,* or low blood sugar. Hypoglycemia may be present in diabetic and nondiabetic individuals. Blood glucose levels below 50 mg per 100 mL (venous blood) usually indicate hypoglycemia in adults, whereas blood glucose values less than 40 mg per 100 mL indicate hypoglycemia in children.[5] The estimated incidence of hypoglycemia in diabetic patients is 9 to 120 episodes per 100 patient-years.[6–8] Signs and symptoms of hypoglycemia may become evident within minutes, leading rapidly to the loss of consciousness; or, more commonly, they may develop gradually, leading to progressive alterations in consciousness.

Hyperglycemia may also result ultimately in the loss of consciousness (diabetic coma), but this usually represents the end of a much longer process. (The time elapsed from the onset of symptoms to the loss of consciousness is usually at least 48 hours.) Loss of consciousness due to hyperglycemia is an extremely unlikely occurrence in the dental office. Conversely, low blood sugar is significantly more likely to lead to profound changes in levels of consciousness or to the loss of consciousness. Regardless of cause, the doctor must be able to recognize the clinical problem and initiate the proper management protocol. To aid in the differential diagnosis of diabetic complications, this chapter stresses the differences between hyperglycemia and hypoglycemia.

CHRONIC COMPLICATIONS

Long-term complications of diabetes mellitus include disorders of the microvasculature, cardiovascular system, eyes, kidneys, and nerves.[1] Most cases of morbidity and death in diabetic patients results from these chronic complications (Table 17-1).

Three major categories of diabetic complications exist: large blood vessel disease, small blood vessel disease (microangiopathy), and increased susceptibility to infection. Large blood vessel disease, such as arteriosclerosis, frequently occurs in nondiabetic individuals; however, it is more common in diabetic patients and develops at an earlier age (diabetic patients are two

to four times more likely to have heart disease than persons without diabetes).[9] Clinical manifestations are related to an inadequate blood supply to the heart (angina pectoris, myocardial infarction, sudden cardiac arrest), the brain (cerebrovascular ischemia or infarction [again, diabetic patients are two to four times more likely to have cerebrovascular disease]), the kidneys (glomerulosclerosis), and the lower extremities (infection and gangrene). High blood pressure also occurs more frequently and at an earlier age in the diabetic patient.[10,11] Death from heart disease is two to four times more likely in diabetic than in nondiabetic persons.

Diabetic microangiopathy, or small blood vessel disease, is related to disorders affecting arterioles, venules, and capillaries. It is thought that the disease is specific, occurring only in patients with diabetes mellitus. Clinical manifestations of microangiopathy most often appear in the eye (diabetic retinopathy),[12]

TABLE 17-1 Chronic complications of diabetes mellitus

Affected body part or condition	Complications
Vascular system	Atherosclerosis
	Large vessel disease
	Microangiopathy
Kidneys	Diabetic glomerulonephritis
	Arteriolar nephrosclerosis
	Pyelonephritis
Nervous system	Motor, sensory, and autonomic neuropathy
Eyes	Retinopathy
	Cataract formation
	Glaucoma
	Extraocular muscle palsies
Skin	Diabetic xanthoma
	Necrobiosis lipoidica diabeticorum
	Pruritus
	Furunculosis
	Mycosis
Mouth	Gingivitis
	Increased incidence of dental caries and periodontal disease
	Alveolar bone loss
Pregnancy	Increased incidence of large babies, stillbirths, miscarriages, newborn deaths, and congenital defects

kidney (arteriolar nephrosclerosis),[13] and lower extremities (gangrene).[14] The cause of diabetic microangiopathy is not yet entirely clear, but two interpretations are most often accepted. In the first, the cause is related to the carbohydrate intolerance associated with diabetes mellitus. However, documented instances do exist in which microangiopathy develops in the absence of carbohydrate intolerance. A second theory links microangiopathy to a genetic factor that also manifests as diabetes.

Regardless of its cause, diabetic microangiopathy may represent a more serious disease than carbohydrate intolerance itself. Studies have not yet demonstrated that careful control of blood glucose levels decreases or retards small vessel disease. The extent of diabetic microangiopathy is such that approximately 58% to 80% of diabetic patients have diabetic retinopathy within 5 to 10 years of diagnosis.[15] Diabetic retinopathy is the leading cause of new blindness in individuals 20 and 74 years of age.[16]

Approximately 60% to 70% of diabetic patients have mild to severe forms of diabetic nerve damage (neuropathy), which in severe forms can lead to lower-limb amputation. Diabetes is the most frequent cause of nontraumatic lower-limb amputation. The risk of a leg amputation is 15 to 40 times greater for an individual with diabetes. In 2002, 82,000 Americans lost their feet or legs to diabetes.[3]

Diabetic patients are more prone to infections than persons without diabetes. Although the precise cause is yet undetermined, the propensity for infection is most likely related to the combination of vascular lesions and infections.[17] Patients with uncontrolled diabetes also suffer inflammatory periodontal diseases with increased frequencies, but the extent of such diseases is no greater than in patients with well-controlled diabetes.[18] To prevent severe infection, diabetic patients must practice scrupulous personal hygiene.

About 20% to 40% of diabetic patients will develop renal disease (diabetic nephropathy), a major cause of illness and death, particularly in female diabetic patients.[19,20] Diabetic nephropathy may be related to high glucose levels in the urine, which serves as an excellent growth medium for microorganisms. Microangiopathy of diabetic renal disease occurs in two thirds of diabetic patients 20 years after the onset of the disease; microangiopathy generally causes proteinuria.[1] Within 5 years of the onset of proteinuria, uremia may ensue. Diabetic nephropathy is the most common cause of end-stage renal disease, a condition that necessitates dialysis or a kidney transplant for survival.[19,20] In 2002, 44,400 people with diabetes began treatment for end-stage kidney disease in the United States and Puerto Rico.[3] Erectile dysfunction, secondary to diabetic neuro-

pathy or blood vessel blockage, occurs in 40% to 60% of men with diabetes.[21]

The doctor called upon to treat the dental needs of a diabetic patient must be aware of the acute complications of diabetes (i.e., hypoglycemia and hyperglycemia) and take measures to avoid their occurrence. That doctor must also seek out any chronic complications associated with diabetes that may increase the patient's medical risk during dental treatment. In such cases modifications in the planned treatment are likely to be required.

■ PREDISPOSING FACTORS

Type 1 diabetes results from an interplay of genetic, environmental, and autoimmune factors that selectively destroy insulin-producing β cells.[2,22]

- *Genetic factors:* The role of genetic factors in the development of type 1 diabetes has been clearly demonstrated.[23]
- *Environmental factors:* Environmental factors such as diet and toxins have been proposed as triggers of diabetes.[2,24] Recently, scientific attention has focused on viruses as a cause. Epidemics of mumps, congenital rubella, and coxsackievirus have been associated with infrequency of type 1 diabetes. If viruses are involved in the etiology of type 1 diabetes, it is thought that they act by triggering an autoimmune response.
- *Autoimmune factors:* It is felt that type 1 diabetes is a chronic autoimmune disease with acute manifestations.[2,25] About 80% of patients with new-onset type 1 diabetes have islet cell antibodies.[2] The likelihood of type 1 diabetes is greater than 50% if autoantibodies are present to more than one β-cell antigen. If antibodies appear at a young age, the risk for clinical diabetes is particularly high.[2]

Type 2 diabetes probably results from complex genetic interactions, the expression of which is modified by environmental factors such as body weight and exercise. Persons with type 2 diabetes consistently demonstrate three cardinal abnormalities: (1) resistance to the action of insulin in peripheral tissues, particularly muscle and fat, but also liver; (2) defective insulin secretion, particularly in response to a glucose stimulus; and (3) increased glucose production by the liver.[26]

- *Genetic factors:* Type 2 diabetes shows a clear familial aggregation, but it appears that the disease is a result of a combination of genetic defects or the simultaneous presence of multiple susceptibility genes in the presence of predisposing environmental factors.[27,28]

- *Insulin secretion:* Fasting insulin levels in type 2 diabetes are generally normal or elevated, yet they are relatively low given the degree of coexisting hyperglycemia. As type 2 diabetes progresses, with increasing hyperglycemia, basal insulin levels fail to keep up and may even decline.[29]
- *Insulin resistance:* Type 2 diabetes is characterized by impaired insulin action (decreased insulin sensitivity) along with a decreased maximum response, particularly in the setting of severe hyperglycemia.[29,30] The mechanism responsible for reduced insulin sensitivity is poorly understood at present.
- *Obesity:* The association of obesity with type 2 diabetes has been well known for decades.[31] A close relationship between obesity and insulin resistance is seen in all ethnic groups and across the full range of body weights, across all ages, and in both sexes.[31–34]
- *Adipocyte-derived hormones and cytokines:* Adipocytes, once thought of as inert fat storage cells, are now known to produce many metabolically active hormones, such as leptin and adiponectin, that may affect insulin sensitivity.[2] Adipose tissue is an abundant source of cytokine tumor necrosis factor-α, which is known to inhibit muscle glucose metabolism.[27,35] The precise role of these factors in the development of insulin resistance in type 2 diabetes has yet to be established.

Risk factors for the development of type 2 diabetes mellitus are presented in Box 17-1.

■ CLASSIFICATION OF DIABETES

Diabetes is defined by the American Diabetes Association as follows:

- A casual blood glucose level of 200 mg/dL or greater with symptoms of diabetes (polyuria, polydipsia, and weight loss), or
- A fasting glucose of 126 mg/dL or greater (no caloric intake for more than 8 hours), or
- A 2-hour postprandial glucose level greater than 200 mg/dL

The diagnosis must be confirmed by a second measurement on a separate day.[36]

Until recently, classifications of diabetes were based on (1) the age of onset of the disease (*adult-onset* and *juvenile-onset diabetes*) and (2) whether the condition required an injection of insulin in its management (*insulin-dependent diabetes mellitus* and *non–insulin-dependent diabetes mellitus*).

Box 17-1 Epidemiologic determinants of and risk factors for type 2 diabetes

GENETIC FACTORS
Genetic markers, family history, "thrifty gene(s)"

DEMOGRAPHIC CHARACTERISTICS
Sex, age, ethnicity

BEHAVIORAL AND LIFESTYLE-RELATED RISK FACTORS
Obesity (including distribution of obesity and duration)
Physical inactivity
Diet
Stress
Westernization, urbanization, modernization

METABOLIC DETERMINANTS AND INTERMEDIATE RISK CATEGORIES OF TYPE 2 DIABETES
Impaired glucose tolerance
Insulin resistance
Pregnancy-related determinants (parity, gestational diabetes, diabetes in offspring of women with diabetes during pregnancy, intrauterine malnutrition or overnutrition)

From Zimmet P, Alberti KG, Shaw J: Global and societal implications of the diabetes epidemic, *Nature* 414:782–787, 2001.

Age of onset and insulin dependency are no longer considered criteria for classification of the disease. Instead, in 1979 the National Diabetes Data Group recommended a therapeutic classification, subsequently endorsed by the American Diabetes Association.[36] Box 17-2 outlines this classification, and Table 17-2 compares and contrasts the types of diabetes.

Four major types of diabetes mellitus are described: type 1 diabetes mellitus, type 2 diabetes mellitus, gestational diabetes, and impaired glucose tolerance/impaired fasting glucose.[36] The terms *insulin-dependent diabetes mellitus* and *non–insulin-dependent diabetes mellitus* have been discontinued because they are confusing and clinically inaccurate. The National Diabetes Data Group also recommended that the Arabic numerals 1 and 2 be used to replace the roman numerals I and II in the designations of types "one" and "two."[36]

Type 1 diabetes mellitus

This form of diabetes is predominantly genetic, or hereditary. Between 85% and 90% of patients with type 1 diabetes demonstrate evidence of one or more autoantibodies implicated in the cellular-mediated autoimmune destruction of the β cells of the pancreas. This autoimmune destruction has multiple genetic predispositions and may also be related to undefined environmental insults.[36] Approximately 10% of diabetic

Box 17-2 Classification of diabetes mellitus and other categories of glucose intolerance

DIABETES MELLITUS
Type 1 (or type I, formerly "insulin-dependent" or "juvenile onset")
Immune mediated
Idiopathic

Type 2 (or type II, formerly "non–insulin-dependent" or "adult onset")

Other specific types
Genetic defects of β-cell function
Genetic defects of insulin action
Diseases of exocrine pancreas
Drug- or chemical-induced
Infections
Uncommon forms of immune-mediated diabetes
Other genetic syndromes sometimes associated with diabetes

GESTATIONAL DIABETES MELLITUS
IMPAIRED GLUCOSE TOLERANCE
IMPAIRED FASTING GLUCOSE

Modified from: Report of the Expert Committee on the Diagnosis and Classification of Diabetes Mellitus, *Diabetes Care* 20:1183–1197, 1997.

TABLE 17-2 Comparison of type 1 and type 2 diabetes mellitus

Factor	Type 1	Type 2
Frequency (% of total diabetic population)	10%	90%
Age at onset (years)	15	≥40
Body build	Normal to thin	Obese
Severity	Severe	Mild
Use of insulin	Almost all	20–30%
Response to oral hypoglycemic agents	Very few respond	50% respond
Ketoacidosis	Common	Uncommon
Complications	90% in 2 years	Less common than type 1
Rate of clinical onset	Rapid	Slow
Stability	Unstable	Stable
Family history of diabetes	Common	Less common than type 1
HLA and abnormal autoimmune reactions	Present	Not present
Insulin receptor defects	Usually not found	–

HLA, human lymphocyte antigen.
From Little JW, Falace DA: *Dental management of the medically compromised patient,* ed 5, St. Louis, Mosby, 1997.

patients in the United States have type 1 diabetes mellitus.[37] It is a more severe form of diabetes, characterized in its untreated state by ketoacidosis (diabetic ketoacidosis). Type 1 diabetes mellitus can occur at any age but is more common among children and young adults. The peak age on onset of type 1 diabetes mellitus is 10 to 14 years. Type 1 diabetes mellitus is characterized by insulin deficiency (insulinopenia). Affected persons characteristically have wide fluctuations in their blood sugars, abrupt critical onset, a tendency to ketosis even in the basal state, and a dependency on parenteral insulin to sustain life.[1]

In type 1 diabetes, circulating insulin is essentially absent, plasma glucagon levels are elevated, and pancreatic β cells do not respond to all insulinogenic stimuli. Patients with type 1 diabetes require exogenous insulin to reverse this catabolic state, prevent diabetic ketoacidosis, reduce hyperglucagonemia, and reduce elevated blood glucose levels. Studies have demonstrated that the incidence of type 1 diabetes is linked to the presence or absence of certain genetically determined cell surface antigens found on lymphocytes. Human lymphocyte antigens, which are located on the sixth human chromosome adjacent to the immune response genes, are closely associated with the development of type 1 diabetes.[38]

Type 2 diabetes mellitus

Type 2 diabetes mellitus is a heterogeneous group composed of milder forms of diabetes that occur most frequently in adults and, in recent years, increasingly in younger age groups.[39,40] More than 90% of all persons with diabetes in the United States have type 2 diabetes.[41,42] Circulating endogenous insulin blood levels are adequate to prevent ketoacidosis (insulinoplethoric) in the resting state, but are subnormal or inadequate to meet the individual's increased needs, which are caused by insensitivity of the tissues.

Type 2 diabetes mellitus is a nonketotic form of diabetes that is not linked to human lymphocyte antigen markers on the sixth chromosome; it has no islet cell antibodies. There is a high incidence of obesity in type 2 diabetes mellitus. Most, but not all, patients with type 2 diabetes do not require exogenous insulin therapy to sustain life. Regardless of body weight, the tissues of patients with type 2 diabetes demonstrate a degree of insensitivity to insulin, which is produced by a lack of insulin receptors in peripheral tissues or an insensitivity of the existing receptors.[43]

TABLE 17-3 Risk factors for diabetes and metabolic syndrome

Diabetes risk factors	Metabolic syndrome characteristics
Age ≥45 years	
Body mass index ≥25 kg/m^2	Waist >40 inches in men or >35 in women
First-degree relative with diabetes	
Habitual physical inactivity	
High-risk ethnicity (African American, Hispanic American, Native American, Asian American, Pacific Islander)	
History of child weighing >9 pounds at birth	
History of gestational diabetes	
Hypertension (blood pressure ≥140/90 mm Hg)	SBP >130 or DBP >85 mm Hg
Triglycerides ≥250 mg/dL	Triglycerides ≥150 mg/dL
HDL cholesterol ≥35 mg/dL	HDL cholesterol <40 mg/dL in men and <50 mg/dL in women
History of polycystic ovarian syndrome	
Prediabetes on previous testing	Fasting plasma glucose >110 mg/dL
History of vascular disease	

DBP, diastolic blood pressure; HDL, high density lipoprotein; SBP, systolic blood pressure.
The American Diabetes Association recommends screening everyone older than 45 years at least every 3 years. It further suggests screening earlier and perhaps more frequently in younger patients with a body mass index > 25 kg/m^2 and any risk factor.
The National Cholesterol Education Program suggests evaluating these characteristics in people who have uncertain cardiovascular disease risk who have one or more of the listed features and suggests that the presence of the metabolic syndrome is suggested by having three or more of the five listed features.

Gestational diabetes mellitus

Gestational diabetes mellitus is characterized by an abnormal result on the oral glucose tolerance test taken during pregnancy that either reverts back to normal in the postpartum period or remains abnormal. The clinical pathogenesis of gestational diabetes mellitus is similar to that of type 2 diabetes mellitus, while the clinical presentation is usually nonketotic hyperglycemia during pregnancy. Undiagnosed and untreated gestational diabetes mellitus carries significant risks of perinatal illness and death in all levels of disease severity, which may not be apparent in nondiabetic patients and those whose gestational diabetes mellitus is diagnosed and treated in a timely and effective manner.[44,45]

Impaired glucose tolerance/ impaired fasting glucose tolerance

The fourth category of diabetes mellitus is impaired glucose tolerance and its analog, impaired fasting glucose tolerance.[36] These conditions are found in 10% to 15% of adults in the United States.[46]

Persons with impaired glucose tolerance have plasma glucose levels between 140 and 199 mg/dL after a 2-hour oral glucose tolerance test. These levels are higher than normal but not high enough to be classified as diabetic.[3] Persons with impaired glucose tolerance are at increased risk for the development of future diabetes and cardiovascular disease.[1] Atherogenesis is thought to be related to insulin resistance.[36]

In impaired fasting glucose tolerance, the fasting blood sugar level is 100 to 125 mg/dL after an overnight fast, a level higher than normal but not high enough to be classified as diabetic.[3]

Clinical presentation of these conditions is usually nonketotic hyperglycemia, insulin resistance, hyperinsulinism, and, frequently, obesity.[1] Impaired glucose tolerance and impaired fasting glucose tolerance differ from other forms of diabetes mellitus in that they are not usually associated with the complications of diabetes mellitus.[47] Many patients with impaired glucose tolerance and impaired fasting glucose tolerance spontaneously revert to normal glucose tolerance.

Table 17-3 presents risk factors for diabetes mellitus and for metabolic syndrome.[48]*

---

*The National Cholesterol Education Program has defined a "metabolic syndrome." An estimated 40 million Americans meet the criteria for the metabolic syndrome. These persons are at increased risk of cardiovascular disease, defined as vascular disorders of the coronary, cerebral, or peripheral beds.

■ HYPERGLYCEMIA

Any of the following factors, all of which increase the body's demand for insulin, may precipitate hyperglycemia:

- Weight gain
- Cessation of exercise
- Pregnancy
- Hyperthyroidism or thyroid medication
- Epinephrine therapy
- Corticosteroid therapy
- Acute infection
- Fever

Although hyperglycemia does not by itself usually lead to an acute, life-threatening emergency, if left untreated it may progress to diabetic ketoacidosis and subsequent diabetic coma, both of which are life-threatening. Diabetic ketoacidosis most often occurs in patients with type 1 diabetes and is associated with inadequate administration of insulin, infection, or myocardial infarction. Diabetic ketoacidosis can occur in patients with type 2 diabetes and may be associated with any kind of medication, epinephrine therapy, or stress.[49] Infection and a secondary disease state also are common causes of hyperglycemia in diabetics. Diabetic ketoacidosis develops slowly, producing 1 day to 2 weeks of malaise, nausea, polydipsia, polyuria, and polyphagia in younger individuals.[50] In such situations, it is not uncommon for the patient to experience vomiting and shortness of breath. It is highly unlikely that diabetic ketoacidosis will present as an acute medical emergency in the dental office environment.

■ HYPOGLYCEMIA

Unlike hyperglycemia, hypoglycemia may develop rapidly, especially in patients receiving injectable insulin therapy who may lose consciousness within minutes after insulin administration. In patients receiving oral hypoglycemic agents, the onset of symptoms is slower, usually developing over several hours.

The following factors decrease the body's requirement for insulin:

- Weight loss
- Increased physical exercise
- Termination of pregnancy
- Termination of other drug therapies (e.g., epinephrine, thyroid, or corticosteroid)
- Recovery from infection and fever

Administration of the "usual" dose of insulin at this time is associated with an increased risk of hypoglycemia. Common causes of hypoglycemia include

TABLE 17-4 Causes of 240 consecutive cases of hypoglycemia in diabetic patients*

Cause	%
Inadequate food (carbohydrate intake)	66
Excessive insulin dose	12
Sulfonylurea therapy	12
Strenuous exercise	4
Ethanol intake	4
Other (kidney failure, liver failure, decrease in corticosteroid dose)	2

*Patients were observed at Grady Memorial Hospital Emergency Clinic from 1973 to 1975.
Modified from Davidson JK: Hypoglycemia. In: Schwartz GR, Safar P, Stone JH, et al., editors: *Principles and practice of emergency medicine*, Philadelphia, WB Saunders, 1978.

the omission or delay of meals, excessive exercise before meals, or increasing insulin dosage (Table 17-4). Hypoglycemia may also occur in the absence of any likely cause (Box 17-3).

Dental treatment poses a potential threat to diabetic patients and to their control of the disease. Stress—physiologic and psychological—increases the body's requirement for insulin, which increases the diabetic dental patient's chance of developing hyperglycemia. (Both the doctor and the patient must be aware of this possibility so that management can be modified and, if necessary, the patient's insulin dose to preclude a progression into diabetic coma.) In addition, dental treatment may necessitate alterations in patients' normal eating habits for variable lengths of time: Some patients purposefully avoid eating before dental appointments so that their teeth are "clean"; the doctor, out of necessity, may need to schedule a treatment appointment during a normal lunch or dinner hour, forcing the patient to delay or miss a meal. The dental procedure may also delay the patient's ingestion of food. Prolonged anesthesia after treatment and extensive dental procedures (e.g., periodontal or oral surgery or endodontics), use of long-acting local anesthetics, such as bupivacaine, may delay the patient's next meal, increasing the risk of hypoglycemia.

■ CONTROL OF DIABETES

Diabetes is a fascinating disease in that it produces a myriad of clinical signs and symptoms. In addition, many factors affect control of the disease on a daily basis. For these reasons, diabetic patients must be

---

Box 17-3 Precipitants of hypoglycemia in diabetic patients

Addison's disease	Malnutrition
Akee fruit	Old age
Anorexia nervosa	Oral hypoglycemic agents
Decrease in usual food intake	Overaggressive treatment of diabetic ketoacidosis and hyperglycemic hyperosmolar nonketotic coma
Ethanol	Pentamidine
Factitious hypoglycemia	Phenylbutazone
Hepatic impairment	Propranolol
Hyperthyroidism	Recent change in dose or type of insulin or oral hypoglycemic
Hypothyroidism	Salicylates
Increase in usual exercise	Sepsis
Insulin	Some antibacterial sulfonylureas
Islet cell tumors	Worsening renal insufficiency
Malfunctioning, improperly adjusted, or incorrectly used insulin pump	

From Cydulka RK, Siff J: Diabetes mellitus and disorders of glucose homeostasis. In: Marx JA, Hockberger RS, Walls RM, editors, *Rosen's emergency medicine: concepts and clinical practice,* ed 5, St. Louis, Mosby, 2002, pp. 1635–1664.

Box 17-4 Diabetes Control and Complications Trial

In the study, 1441 patients with type 1 diabetes in 29 U.S. centers reported that near-normalization of blood glucose resulted in a delay in the onset and a major slowing of the progression of established microvascular and neuropathic complications during a follow-up as long as 10 years. In addition, the following facts characterized smaller groups of patients who received differing treatments:

- The intensively treated group received multiple insulin injections (66%) or insulin pumps (34%). Conventionally treated groups received no more than two insulin injections. The goal was clinical well-being.
- About 50% of patients receiving intensive therapy achieved a mean blood glucose level of 155 mg/dL. Conventionally treated groups averaged a blood glucose level of 225 mg/dL.
- Over a study period that lasted 7 years, there was an approximately 60% reduction in risk between the two groups with regard to diabetic retinopathy, nephropathy, and neuropathy.
- Intensively treated patients experienced greater tendencies toward weight gain and threefold greater risks for serious hypoglycemia.

Data from DTTC Research Group: The effect of intensive treatment of diabetes on the development and progression of long-term complications in insulin-dependent diabetes mellitus, *N Engl J Med* 329:977–986, 1993.

---

able to monitor the status of their disease and initiate modifications in its management. To manage diabetes mellitus, the patient must learn to control the disease. Treatment does not cure diabetes; therefore, the patient must continue to monitor and manage diabetes mellitus for life. Long-term adherence to management regimens is a major problem that diabetic patients and individuals with other controllable, but not curable, conditions such as high blood pressure often find difficult to maintain.

Diabetes mellitus is a chronic disease requiring ongoing medical care and patient and family education to prevent acute illness and reduce the risk of long-term complications. These goals should not unduly restrict the individual's quality of life. However, the dramatic results of the Diabetes Control and Complications Trial indicate that the therapeutic objective of diabetes control is the restoration of known metabolic derangements to as close to normal as possible to prevent and delay the progression of diabetic complications (Box 17-4). This objective should be approached while every effort is made to avoid severe hypoglycemia.[51]

Management of type 1 diabetes mellitus

Treatment of type 1 diabetes requires a precise balancing of insulin administered with carbohydrate intake and activity. Two approaches are commonly employed:

- In the classic approach to management of diabetes mellitus, health care providers have prescribed very regular lifestyles in the form of restrictive meal plans, as well as fixed insulin doses to match that lifestyle. Most patients cannot adhere to such consistent lifestyle plans over periods of weeks, months, and years.[52]
- Currently, most authorities advocate an approach whereby patients can make fairly unrestricted lifestyle choices, adjusting insulin doses to match those choices by using a multiple daily injection technique.[52] This technique is an alternative to insulin pump therapy (see below), which does not provide the flexibility necessary in some patients. The multiple daily injection technique is described in Box 17-5.

Box 17-5 Management of type 1 diabetes mellitus: the multiple daily injection technique

In the multiple daily injection (MDI) technique, insulin glargine (Lantus) is often used to provide the basal insulin needed to prevent hepatic glucose overproduction and a rise in glucose between meals. Basal insulin requirements are about 50% of total daily insulin requirements. In approximately 10% of patients, the duration of glargine is inadequate and glucose levels will rise just before the injection; in such patients it is sometimes possible to inject glargine about 3 hours after supper and provide a bit of extra insulin with supper to compensate or to just split the glargine into two injections. The dose of glargine is titrated aiming for a normal fasting glucose in the morning and stable blood glucose throughout the night.

Meal-related insulin requirements are approximately 50% of total daily insulin requirements and allow clearance of meal-related carbohydrate from the circulation; this is usually provided in the form of lispro (Humalog) or aspart (NovoLog) insulin given just before or immediately after meals by using a dietary technique called carbohydrate counting. The carbohydrates in the diet include starchy vegetables (potatoes, corn, peas), grains, fruit, milk, and sugary snacks and beverages. There are approximately 15 g of carbohydrate in each American Diabetes Association exchange. Most patients need about 1 unit of insulin for every 15 g of carbohydrate in their diet; a more precise estimate of the "insulin-to-carbohydrate ratio" (the number of grams that 1 unit of insulin would cover) can be obtained by dividing the number 500 by the patient's total daily insulin dose, which is expressed as 1 unit per "x" g carbohydrate.

Adding up the grams of carbohydrate in a meal and dividing by the insulin-to-carbohydrate ratio determines the appropriate insulin dose for a given meal. This part of the insulin regimen can be fine-tuned by having patients check blood glucose 2 hours after meals. When meal-related insulin is appropriately dosed, the glucose level should not rise by more than 40 mg/dL 2 hours after the meal.

Adjustments can be made for glycemic excursion, which occurs as a result of unplanned snacks or miscalculations based on the "rule of 1,500." Basically, it is an empirically derived observation that for every unit of additional regular insulin provided, the glucose falls, on average, by a quantity equal to: 1,500 ÷ total daily insulin dose. This "insulin sensitivity factor" can be used to derive a simple formula to adjust insulin dose based on pre-meal glucose values such as: correction dose = (current glucose − target glucose) ÷ by the insulin sensitivity factor. The adequacy of this estimate can be assessed by examining whether the glucose returns to target values by the next meal.

So, in the multiple daily injection technique, patients are liberated from a stringent meal plan and administer rapid-acting insulin at each meal based on the food that they consume at that meal and the level of glucose at the time of the meal. Because they are taking insulin with each meal, they can also make adjustments for activity, decreasing the insulin dose when prolonged or strenuous activity is planned. Many diabetes educators are quite facile with this technique and can be exceptionally helpful in training, troubleshooting, and dose titrating.

From Buse JB: Diabetes mellitus in adults. In: Rakel RE, Bope ET, editors: *Conn's Current Therapy,* ed 57, Philadelphia, WB Saunders, 2005.

Multiple daily injection regimens and insulin pumps are generally appropriate for all patients with type 1 diabetes mellitus as well as for many with type 2 diabetes mellitus. Such intensive therapy has demonstrated tremendous benefits in patients with errant glucose control, severe hypoglycemia, recurrent diabetic ketoacidosis, irregular lifestyles, serious exercise programs, and pregnancy.[52]

Patients with type 1 and those with 2 diabetes use at-home self-monitoring of blood glucose to aid in the day-to-day management of diabetes mellitus. This has allowed for greater flexibility in the management of diabetes while achieving improved glycemic control. This improved control is especially important for patients with type 1 diabetes trying to achieve "tight" metabolic control. Portable glucose monitors are small battery-operated devices (Figure 17-3).

To test blood glucose with the typical glucose meter, a small drop of capillary blood is obtained from a finger prick and placed onto a disposable test strip (Figure 17-4), which is placed into the meter (Box 17-6). Newer glucose meters allow blood testing from alter-

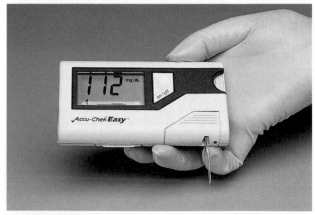

FIGURE 17-3 Example of a portable glucose monitor. (From Perry AG, Potter PA: *Clinical nursing skills and technique,* ed 5, St. Louis, Mosby, 2002.)

native sites, such as the upper arm, forearm, base of the thumb, and thigh. Test strips are coated with chemicals, such as glucose oxidase, dehydrogenase, or hexokinase, that react with glucose in the blood specimen. The meter

FIGURE 17-4 The blood sample is then applied to the test strip and removed at the proper time.

Box 17-6 General instructions for use of self-monitoring blood glucose meters

1. Wash hands with soap and water and dry completely or clean the area with alcohol and dry completely
2. Prick the finger with a lancet
3. Hold the hand down and hold the finger until a small drop of blood appears; catch the blood with the test strip
4. Follow the instructions for inserting the test strip and using the self-monitoring blood glucose meter
5. Record the test result

From www.fda.gov/diabetes/glucose.html#6

---

then measures the amount of glucose in the blood. Several methods are used to determine the blood level: some measure the amount of electric current passing through the sample; others measure the amount of light reflected from the sample. The blood glucose level is displayed as a number (mg/dL). Many newer blood glucose meters are able to store test results, which can then, in some cases, be downloaded to computers or printed.[53]

Self-monitoring of blood glucose is important for all diabetic patients, but especially for those who cannot maintain a stable blood sugar level and exhibit extremes of both hyperglycemia and hypoglycemia despite therapy, women trying to maintain ideal glycemic control during pregnancy, and individuals with little or no warning of impending hypoglycemic episodes. This type of self-monitoring has proved a safe and reliable clinical tool in adherent diabetic patients. Most glucose meters are able to measure glucose levels over a range from 0 to 600 mg/dL.

Glucose levels in blood plasma are usually about 10% to 15% higher than glucose levels in whole blood.

(After eating, this discrepancy can be even greater.) The distinction is important since most home blood glucose meters record glucose levels in whole blood, while most clinical blood laboratories report plasma glucose levels. Many home glucose-monitoring devices now give results as plasma equivalent.

Newer technologies, termed *minimally invasive glucose monitors,* are being developed to avoid the need for fingersticks. The Guardian RT Continuous Glucose Monitoring System* provides the patient with updated blood glucose measurements every 5 minutes and alerts the patient when glucose levels become too low or too high.[54,55] A small plastic catheter is inserted under the skin in an almost painless process. It measures real-time glucose levels in interstitial fluid and is used as an adjunct to fingerstick measurements. Through a radiofrequency transmitter in the sensor, blood sugar measurements are sent wirelessly to the monitor worn by the patient.

A Food and Drug Administration–approved non-invasive monitoring system is the Cygnus GlucoWatch Biographer.† GlucoWatch is worn on the patient's forearm like a wristwatch.[56,57] Through the process of reverse iontophoresis, a low-level electric current pulls small volumes of fluid through the skin into gel discs of the device, allowing measurement of glucose in the fluid without puncturing the skin. The device requires 3 hours to warm up before being placed on the wrist. Once applied, the GlucoWatch can obtain up to three blood sugar measurements per hour for 12 hours. The device has a built-in alarm that can be programmed to alert the user when blood sugar measurements fall below preset low levels and above preset high levels. GlucoWatch is not recommended as a replacement for standard finger-stick tests, but it is helpful in detecting and evaluating episodes of hypoglycemia and hyperglycemia.

Management of type 2 diabetes mellitus

Patients with type 2 diabetes can be managed by maintaining control over diet and physical activity and administering oral antidiabetic drugs and insulin, as needed. Many patients with type 2 diabetes use the combination of weight loss, exercise, and diet control. However, when this regimen fails, as unfortunately it frequently does, oral antidiabetic drugs must be prescribed (Table 17-5). Sulfonylurea agents (such as tolbutamide, tolazamide, chlorpropamide, and acetohexamide) and newer second-generation sulfonylurea drugs (glyburide

---

*Guardian® RT Continuous Glucose Monitoring System. www.minimed.com
†GlucoWatch® Automatic Glucose Biographer. www.glucowatch.com

TABLE 17-5   Classification of oral agents used to treat type 2 diabetes

Class of drug	Example	Mechanism of action
Biguanides	Metformin (Glucophage)	Decrease hepatic glucose production; increase insulin sensitivity
Thiazolidinediones	Rosiglitazone (Avandia), pioglitazone (Actos)	Increase insulin sensitivity
Sulfonylureas	Glipizide (Glucotrol), glyburide (Micronase), tolbutamide (Orinase)	Stimulate insulin secretion
Meglitinides	Repaglinide (Prandin)	Stimulate insulin secretion
Glucosidase inhibitors	Acarbose (Precose)	Decrease hydrolysis and adsorption of complex carbohydrates

From American Diabetes Association: Type 2 diabetes in children and adolescents, *Pediatrics* 105:671–680, 2000.

TABLE 17-6   Currently available insulin preparations

Classification	Generic (brand name)	Onset	Peak effect (hr)	Duration (hr)
Rapid-acting	Lispro (Humalog), Aspart (Novolog)	<15 min	1–2	3–4
Regular (short)-acting	(Humulin R, Novolin R, ReliOn)	0.5–1 hr	2–3	3–6
Intermediate-acting	NPH (Humulin N, Novolin N, ReliOn)	2–4 hr	4–10	10–16
Long-acting	Insulin glargine (Lantus)	2–4 hr	Peakless	20–24

From Grady R, editor: *Diabetes forecast, 2006.* American Diabetes Association, 59:19, 2006.

and glipizide) remain the most widely prescribed oral drugs for the treatment of hyperglycemia.[58–61] Glyburide and glipizide are 100-fold more potent than the earlier oral antidiabetic agents, such as tolbutamide.[62]

In December 1994, the Food and Drug Administration approved the use of metformin, a biguanide drug, for clinical use as an oral antidiabetic agent. Unlike the sulfonylureas, which work by stimulating the pancreas to secrete more insulin, metformin decreases hyperglycemia via other mechanisms. The drug is an "insulin-sparing" drug that does not causes weight gain in treated diabetic patients. It reduces both the fasting level of blood glucose and the degree of postprandial hyperglycemia in patients with type 2 diabetes; however, the drug does not affect fasting blood glucose in persons without diabetes.

Patients with type 1 diabetes require insulin to manage blood glucose levels. In addition, more nonobese patients with type 2 diabetes whose hyperglycemia does not respond to diet therapy either alone or in combination with oral antidiabetic drugs require insulin. Until recently, diabetic patients received insulin extracted from the pancreas of the cow and pig. A risk of adverse reactions accompanied administration of this bovine or porcine insulin, including both localized allergy and systemic allergy, immune insulin resistance, and localized lipoatrophy at the injection site. Improvements in the purification of beef and pork insulin have minimized the occurrence of serious adverse reactions in most patients with type 1 diabetes. In 1983, genetically designed human insulin became available.[63] This insulin is synthesized in a non–disease-producing special laboratory strain of *Escherichia coli* that has been genetically altered by the addition of the human gene for insulin production. Although the risk of serious adverse reaction is diminished, reports of such responses still appear.[64]

Insulin is available in several preparations that differ in their onset and duration of action (Table 17-6). They are characterized as rapid-acting, intermediate-acting, regular (or short-acting), and long-acting insulin. Regular insulin is absorbed rapidly and is administered before meals, whereas neutral protamine Hagedorn (NPH) and Lente preparations are intermediate acting and are administered once a day. Long-acting insulin (protamine) preparations are available, but are rarely required.

Pramlintide (Symlin), a synthetic form of the hormone amylin, which is produced in the β cells of the pancreas along with insulin, has been approved by the Food and Drug Administration for use by patients with type 1 and type 2 diabetes who are not achieving the goal hemoglobin A_{1c} levels.[65,66] Amylin, insulin, and glucagon work in an interrelated manner to maintain normal blood glucose levels. Pramlintide injections administered with meals have been demonstrated to modestly improve hemoglobin A_{1c} levels without causing increased hypoglycemia or weight gain or even promoting modest weight loss. Its primary side effect is nausea, which improves with time.

Patients requiring insulin therapy are initially regulated under conditions of optimal diet and normal daily activities. If "tight" control (near-normalization of blood glucose levels) is the goal, at least three measurements of capillary blood glucose are required daily to prevent frequent hypoglycemic reactions.

A typical initial dose schedule for a 70-kg patient taking 2200 kcal divided into six or seven feedings may be 10 units of regular and 15 units of NPH insulin in the morning, followed by 5 units each of regular and NPH insulin in the evening. Diabetic patients are taught to adjust insulin intake by observing their pattern of glycemia and correlating it with the approximate duration of action and the time of peak effect after injection of the various insulin preparations.

When intensive insulin therapy is deemed necessary (when conventional split doses of insulin mixtures fail to maintain near-normalization of blood glucose without hypoglycemia), multiple insulin injections may be required. A popular regimen consists of decreasing the evening dose of intermediate insulin and adding a portion of it at bedtime. The administration of three smaller doses of regular insulin (before meals) and one injection of long-acting insulin at bedtime is yet another possible regimen.[47]

Other options available today include the use of continuous subcutaneous infusions with portable insulin pumps, which require subcutaneous needle insertion only every 48 hours (Figure 17-5). Insulin doses are divided into basal rates, bolus doses, and correction or supplemental doses. Basal insulin is delivered continuously over 24 hours. The insulin pump can be programmed to deliver varying doses of insulin at different times of day or night. Bolus doses of insulin are administered to cover hyperglycemia associated with meals and snacks, while supplemental doses are used if blood levels are elevated before eating. Insulin pumps have the advantage of eliminating the requirement for injections of insulin, delivering insulin doses more accurately, improving hemoglobin A_{1c} measurements, minimizing episodes of severe hypoglycemia, and generally improving quality of life for diabetic patients.[67,68] Use of an insulin pump can lead to weight gain and can

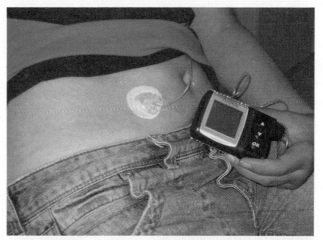

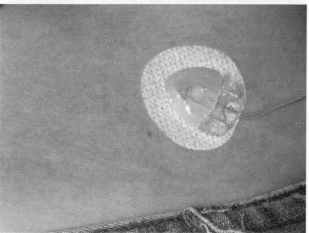

FIGURE 17-5 Insulin pump.

produce diabetic ketoacidosis if the catheter becomes displaced.

■ PREVENTION

Adequate patient evaluation can help avert the occurrence of acute complications associated with diabetes. In addition, the dental health professional is in a position to aid in the detection of previously undiagnosed diabetes (approximately 6.2 million persons with undiagnosed diabetes live in the United States).[3] Relevant questions from the medical history questionnaire and the ensuing dialogue history may lend some insight.

MEDICAL HISTORY QUESTIONNAIRE

Section I, Circle Appropriate Answer:

Question 2: Has there been a change in your health within the last year?

Question 3: Have you been hospitalized or had a serious illness in the last 3 years?

Question 4: Are you being treated by a physician now? For what?

Comment: These are general survey question designed to detect known diseases and other significant medical problems. If diabetes is mentioned, then a thorough dialogue history must follow.

Section II, Have You Experienced:

Question 10: Recent weight loss, fever, night sweats?

Comment: An affirmative response to unexplained weight loss may indicate the presence of previously undetected diabetes mellitus.

Question 24: Excessive thirst?

Question 25: Frequent urination?

Question 26: Dry mouth?

Comment: Although these symptoms are not specific for diabetes mellitus, they can lead to a presumptive diagnosis of the disease. The classical triad of diabetic symptoms—the three P's: polydipsia (increased thirst), polyphagia (increased appetite), and polyuria (increased frequency of urination)—when accompanied by unexpected weight loss should alert the doctor to the possible presence of diabetes.

Section III, Do You Have or Have You Had:

Question 39: Family history of diabetes, heart problems, tumors?

Comment: Both type 1 and type 2 diabetes have a significant genetic component.

Question 50: Diabetes?

Comment: Dialogue history required to determine significant information.

Section V, Are You Taking:

Question 62: Drugs, medications, over-the-counter medicines (including aspirin), natural remedies?

Comment: Dialogue history required to determine significant information.

Dialogue history

If the patient responds negatively to questions 39 or 50 but positively to any or all of questions 24, 25, or 26, the following dialogue history should be considered:

Questions: Are you frequently thirsty?

Are you hungry much of the time?

Do you wake up at night to void (urinate) frequently?

Have you gained or lost weight recently without dieting; if so, how many pounds?

Comment: If the response to questions 39 or 50 in the medical history questionnaire are negative but responses to the dialogue questions are positive, the doctor should continue with the preliminary medical and dental examination and consult the patient's primary care physician before initiating dental treatment.

If the response to question 50 is positive, the doctor should conduct the following dialogue history:

Question: How long have you had diabetes, and what type of treatment do you use to control it?

Comment: The severity of the diabetes and the potential for the development of its acute complications are increased in patients with type 1 or 2 diabetes who manage the disease through injectable insulin or diet control. Patients who successfully control their blood glucose levels through diet alone or through diet and oral hypoglycemic agents (patients with type 2 diabetes) usually retain some pancreatic function; these patients are more resistant to diabetic ketoacidosis (see Table 17-5).

Question: How often do you monitor your urine or blood glucose levels? What have your results shown over the past few days? What is your most recent hemoglobin A_{1c} measurement?

Comment: Diabetic patients self-monitor blood glucose levels at home. Capillary blood glucose testing is a more sophisticated and logical extension of tests usually performed by physicians and laboratories. Many proprietary home blood glucose testing kits are available, several of which provide a digital readout of the patient's blood glucose level within 60 seconds. In recent years, a blood test for glycosylated hemoglobin (glycohemoglobin, hemoglobin A_{1c}), commonly called A_{1c}, has been available to give a patient an average of their hemoglobin A_{1c} level over a 2- or 3-month period.[68] In the presence of hyperglycemia, glucose enters red blood cells and links up (glycates) with hemoglobin. The higher the blood sugar level, the more hemoglobin becomes glycated and the higher the A_{1c} measurement. The hemoglobin A_{1c} value is used to monitor the glucose control of diabetic patients over time. In general, diabetic patients requiring injections of insulin (or use a pump) have their hemoglobin A_{1c} levels monitored 4 times a year. Diabetics not requiring insulin are testing twice a year.

A nondiabetic individual has a 5% hemoglobin A_{1c} level. Diabetic patients and persons with elevated blood glucose levels have higher values. A 1–percentage point change in hemoglobin A_{1c} reflects a change of about 30 mg/dL in average blood glucose. A hemoglobin A_{1c} value of 6% corresponds to an average glucose level of 135 mg/dL, while a hemoglobin A_{1c} value of 9% corresponds to a blood glucose level of 240 mg/dL. The goal in management of blood sugar is to maintain a hemoglobin A_{1c} level of 6% or below. It has been demonstrated that as hemoglobin A_{1c} levels decrease, so does the risk of complications.[69] Table 17-7 presents evaluation of hemoglobin A_{1c} levels.

TABLE 17-7 Hemoglobin A_{1c} values and their meaning

Hemoglobin A_{1c} value (%)	Degree of control
<6.5	Normal
6.5–7.5	Excellent
7.5–8.5	Good
8.5–9.5	Fair

From www.endocrineweb.com

Table 17-8 summarizes the optimal American Society of Anesthesiologists physical classification for type 1 and type 2 diabetes, and Table 17-9 presents modifications in these optimal classifications based on blood glucose or hemoglobin A_{1c} levels.

Question: How frequently (if ever) do you experience hypoglycemic episodes?

Comment: Awareness of a diabetic patient's predisposition to acute episodes of low blood sugar better prepares the doctor to manage it. Patients with frequently low blood glucose readings are more likely to become hypoglycemic.

Physical examination

After completing the medical history questionnaire and dialogue history, the diabetic patient should be evaluated carefully for signs and symptoms of secondary disease, particularly of the cardiovascular system. Vital signs should be recorded before and after all dental treatments.

The skin of a diabetic patient may indicate the possible presence of acute complications associated with overly high or low blood sugar levels. Hyperglycemic patients appear flushed and their skin dry (absence of sweating because of dehydration), whereas hypoglycemic patients appear cold and wet (clammy). Patients with diabetic ketoacidosis exhibit the characteristic smell of acetone (a sweet, fruity odor) on the breath.

The blood pressure of the hyperglycemic, ketoacidotic patient is decreased because of hypovolemia, with a compensatory tachycardia. Hypoglycemic patients exhibit increased blood pressures as well as tachycardia (increased sympathetic response).

Dental therapy considerations

Oral complication of uncontrolled diabetes mellitus can include xerostomia, infection, poor healing, increased incidence and severity of caries, candidiasis, gingivitis, periodontal disease, periapical abscesses, and burning mouth syndrome.[70,71]

After the medical and dental evaluations are completed, patient management must be considered. If any doubt exists about the patient's medical status, consultation with the patient's primary care physician is warranted.

Patients with type 2 diabetes are usually less prone to acute fluctuations in blood glucose levels and are better able to tolerate all forms of dental treatment, including general anesthesia, parenteral sedation, and local anesthesia, with minimally increased concern. Basic dental treatment modifications may be considered with patients who have type 1 diabetes (who are prone to diabetic ketoacidosis) through use of the stress reduction protocol. Patients should also be advised to try to maintain normal dietary habits by taking their usual insulin dose and eating a normal breakfast before a dental appointment. Scheduling dental appointments earlier in the day also helps minimize episodes of hypoglycemia. The use of appropriate local anesthetics (e.g., shorter-acting [mepivacaine plain] versus longer-acting [bupivacaine with epinephrine]) minimizes posttreatment eating impairment. If the nature of the dental procedure is likely to hamper the patient's normal eating habits either before (intravenous [IV] sedation) or after surgery (the surgery itself), the insulin dose should be

TABLE 17-8 Optimal physical status classifications for diabetic patients

Type of diabetes	Management	Optimal ASA physical status
Type 1 or 2	Insulin plus diet	III
Type 2	Oral medication plus diet	II

ASA, American Society of Anesthesiologists.

TABLE 17-9 Physical status classification for diabetes mellitus

Hemoglobin A_{1c} measurement (%)	Blood glucose (mg/dL)	Change in physical status from optimal (Table 17-10)	Comment
	<70	+1	May accept for treatment but increased likelihood of hypoglycemia
<6.5	70–110	0	May accept for treatment
6.5–7.5	110–175	0	May accept for treatment
7.5–8.5	175–240	+1	Evaluate carefully before treatment
8.5–9.5	240	+1	Evaluate carefully before treatment; medical consultation suggested
>9.5	>400	+2	Medical consultation before treatment; elective dental care not indicated; emergency care only

adjusted accordingly.[72] In addition, medical consultation should be considered for patients with type 1 diabetes who require large doses of insulin to maintain blood glucose levels (>40 units daily) or in any case in which doubt remains about adjustment of the patient's insulin dose.

The dentist should encourage diabetic patients to bring their glucose meter with them to dental appointments. Where a dentist treats many diabetic patients, it is suggested that a glucose meter be purchased, enabling the doctor to check the patients' blood and receive an accurate measurement (glucose meters are accurate within 5%) within 1 minute. If blood levels are low or at the lower end of the normal fasting blood glucose range (80 to 120 mg/dL), a fast-acting carbohydrate may be administered prior to the start of dental treatment.[70]

Diabetic patients are better able to tolerate transient periods of hyperglycemia than periods of hypoglycemia. After extensive dental procedures (e.g., oral or periodontal surgery), reconstruction, or endodontics, patients with type 1 diabetes should be instructed to check their blood glucose levels more frequently for the next few days. If glucose or ketone levels become elevated, the patient should change the insulin dose and contact the primary care physician. A diabetic patient who has the disease under tight control generally does not require antibiotics following surgical procedures.[70] Antibiotic coverage in the postsurgical period is appropriate, particularly if there is significant infection, pain, or stress[70] (Table 17-10).

■ CLINICAL MANIFESTATIONS
Hyperglycemia

Hyperglycemia, or high blood sugar, may manifest itself in different ways depending on the severity of the diabetes. It may be evident in patients with previously undiagnosed diabetes or in those with known diabetes who neglect their therapeutic regimens. Patients with type 2 diabetes may not exhibit any clinical signs or symptoms of hyperglycemia. Quite commonly, this form of diabetes is detected during a routine physical examination through evidence of elevated blood glucose levels. Generally, diabetes mellitus is first diagnosed after a clinical episode brought about by an advanced degree of atherosclerosis associated with the disease. Myocardial infarction in a younger man or woman or development of peripheral vascular insufficiency at an early age may also prompt the doctor to suspect diabetes. Other indicators for further evaluation for the presence of diabetes include obesity, age older than

TABLE 17-10 Diabetes mellitus—dental therapy considerations

ASA physical status	Treatment considerations
II	Follow usual ASA II considerations, plus the following:
	Eat a normal breakfast and take usual insulin dose in morning, if possible
	Avoid missing meals before and after surgery, if possible
	If missing meal is unavoidable, consult physician or decrease insulin dose by half
III	Follow usual ASA III considerations, plus the following:
	Monitor blood glucose levels more frequently for several days following surgery or extensive procedure; modify insulin doses accordingly
	Consider medical consultation
IV	Follow usual ASA IV considerations, plus the following:
	Consult a physician before beginning dental treatment.

ASA, American Society of Anesthesiologists.

40 years, delivery of babies weighing more than 10 pounds, spontaneous abortion or stillbirth, or diabetic relatives.[73]

Patients with type 1 diabetes presents a more severe clinical picture of hyperglycemia. The classic diabetic triad—polydipsia, polyphagia, and polyuria—is evident for a day or more and is associated with a marked loss of weight, fatigue, headache, blurred vision, abdominal pain, nausea and vomiting, constipation, dyspnea, and mental stupor, which can progress into a state of unconsciousness known as *diabetic coma*.[74]

Clinical signs of hyperglycemia include a florid appearance of the face (bright red color) associated with hot and dry skin, signs of dehydration. Respirations are commonly deep and rapid (signs of Kussmaul's respiration), with a fruity, sweet smell of acetone evident if diabetic ketoacidosis is present. Heart rate is rapid, whereas blood pressure is lower than normal. This combination of tachycardia and hypotension is yet another indication of dehydration and salt depletion (Table 17-11).

Hypoglycemia

Hypoglycemia, the second and much more common acute complication of diabetes mellitus, may progress

TABLE 17-11 Clinical manifestations of hyperglycemia

	Type 1 diabetes	Type 2 diabetes
Polyuria	++	+
Polydipsia	++	+
Polyphagia with weight loss	++	–
Recurrent blurred vision	+	++
Vulvovaginitis or pruritus	+	++
Loss of strength	++	+
Nocturnal enuresis	++	–
Absence of symptoms	–	++

Other symptoms type 1 diabetes	Other symptoms type 2 diabetes
Repeated skin infections	
Marked irritability	Decreased vision
Headache	Paresthesias
Drowsiness	Loss of sensation
Malaise	Impotence
Dry mouth	Postural hypotension

–, not usually present; +, occasionally present; ++, usually present.
Modified from Karan JH: Diabetes mellitus and hypoglycemia. In: Tierney LM Jr, McPhee SJ, Papadakis MA, editors: *Current medical diagnosis and treatment*, ed 35, Stamford, CT, Appleton & Lange, 1996; and Little JW, Falace DA: *Dental management of the medically compromised patient*, ed 5, St. Louis, Mosby, 1997.

Box 17-7 Clinical manifestations of hypoglycemia

EARLY STAGE—MILD REACTION
Diminished cerebral function
Changes in mood
Decreased spontaneity
Hunger
Nausea

MORE SEVERE STAGE
Sweating
Tachycardia
Piloerection
Increased anxiety
Bizarre behavioral patterns
Belligerence
Poor judgment
Uncooperativeness

LATER SEVERE STAGE
Unconsciousness
Seizure activity
Hypotension
Hypothermia

rapidly to loss of consciousness, or it may take a relatively mild form, representing a less ominous clinical picture. Episodes of hypoglycemia usually develop when the patient has not eaten for several hours. Initially, hypoglycemia usually manifests as diminished cerebral function, such as the inability to perform simple calculations, decreased spontaneity of conversation, and change in mood (for example, lethargy). Throughout this text, I have categorized these symptoms as altered consciousness.

Signs and symptoms of central nervous system involvement include hunger, nausea, and an increase in gastric motility. This is followed by a phase of sympathetic hyperactivity, marked clinically by signs of increased epinephrine activity that include sweating, tachycardia, piloerection, and increased anxiety. Skin is cold and wet, in marked distinction to the hot, dry skin of hyperglycemia. The individual is conscious but may exhibit bizarre behavioral patterns that often lead onlookers to suspect alcohol or drug intoxication. If the condition progresses, the hypoglycemic patient may lose consciousness, and seizures may develop (Box 17-7).

Because hypoglycemia is a more acute problem than hyperglycemia, diabetic patients always carry with them a source of carbohydrate, such as a packet of sugar or hard candy. Tablets containing 3 g of glucose (Dextrosol) are available. It is also recommended that every diabetic patient receiving insulin therapy be given an ampule of glucagon (1 mg), and that their primary care physician instruct family and friends on intramuscular (IM) injection technique in case the patient loses consciousness or refuses food. In addition, the state of altered consciousness produced by hypoglycemia may mimic drug intoxication; thus, diabetic patients may not be able to respond rationally to questioning. For this reason, diabetic individuals wear either a MedicAlert bracelet* or pendant (Figure 17-6) or carry a card stating the individual's condition and primary care physician's number and asking the reader to call in an emergency (Figure 17-7).

■ PATHOPHYSIOLOGY
Insulin and blood glucose

Glucose is a major fuel and energy source for all the body's cells. In fact, glucose is the only fuel that the brain can use to replenish its continuous need. Blood

*MedicAlert Foundation International, 2323 Colorado Avenue, Turlock, CA 95382, 888.633.4298, www.medicalert.org.

A

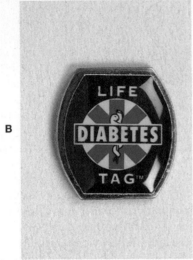

B

FIGURE 17-6   A and B, MedicAlert bracelet and necklace. The bracelet and pendant are engraved with a membership identification number, primary medical condition(s), and a 24-hour emergency response center telephone number. (From www.medicalert.org)

I Am a Diabetic and Take Insulin

If I am behaving peculiarly but am conscious and able to swallow, give me sugar or hard candy or orange juice slowly. If I am unconscious, call an ambulance immediately, take me to a physician or a hospital, and notify my physician. *I am not intoxicated.*

My name _____

Address _____

Telephone _____

Physician's name _____

Physician's address _____

Telephone _____

FIGURE 17-7   Identification card carried by many diabetic patients.

sugar that is too high (hyperglycemia) or too low (hypoglycemia) produces varying degrees of central nervous system dysfunction (altered consciousness). The body's homeostatic mechanisms are targeted at maintaining the blood glucose level within a range of 50 to 150 mg/dL of blood. The mean blood glucose level in normal individuals who fast overnight is 92 to 100 mg/dL, with a range of 78 to 115 mg/dL. The minimal blood glucose level that the brain requires to maintain normal cerebral function is 50 mg/dL. When blood glucose levels exceed the saturation point of renal reabsorption (approximately 180 mg/dL), glucose "spills" into the urine, resulting in loss of energy (glucose is fuel) and water.

Insulin is the most important factor in the regulation of the blood glucose level. It is synthesized in β cells of the pancreas and rapidly secreted into the blood in response to elevations in blood sugar levels (e.g., after a meal). The half-life of insulin in the blood is 3 to 10 minutes, with biotransformation occurring in the liver and kidneys. Insulin promotes the uptake of glucose into the body's cells and its storage in the liver as glycogen; it also promotes the uptake of fatty acids and amino acids into cells and their subsequent conversion into storage forms (triglycerides and proteins). In this way, insulin produces a decrease in the blood glucose level, preventing its loss through urinary excretion.

Without insulin, the cell membranes of many cells are impermeable to glucose. Muscle and adipose cells are insulin dependent; they require its presence to enable glucose to cross the cell membrane, even in hyperglycemic states.[75] In the absence of insulin, these cells break down triglycerides into fatty acids, which the body can use as an alternative energy source. This process gives rise to the hyperglycemic state known as diabetic ketoacidosis. Other tissues and organs, such as nerve tissue (including the brain), the kidneys, and hepatic tissue, are not insulin dependent. These tissues can transfer glucose across cell membranes without insulin.

In the fasting stage, decreased blood sugar levels (hypoglycemia) inhibit insulin secretion. The body's cells still require glucose, however, and several mechanisms exist through which it is made available. The goal of these mechanisms is to provide the central nervous system with the minimal glucose level required to maintain normal function. The body breaks down glycogen stores in the liver into glucose through a process called *glycogenolysis,* while amino acids are converted into glucose through a process known as *gluconeogenesis.* This newly formed glucose is available principally to the central nervous system; in fact, insulin-dependent cells actually suffer a decreased uptake of glucose. Fuel for these cells (e.g., muscle and adipose) is provided through the breakdown of triglycerides, the storage form of fat, into free fatty acids.

Thus, insulin is a signal to the body that it has been fed as well as a means of maintaining glucose homeostasis. After a meal, the high blood level of insulin tells the body's cells to absorb and store any fuel that is not immediately required for metabolic needs. In the fasting state, low insulin levels tell the body that no food is entering and that storage forms of nutrients should be utilized for fuel.

Hyperglycemia, ketosis, and acidosis

After the diabetic or nondiabetic individual eats a meal, hyperglycemia develops. However, the diabetic patient's blood glucose level remains elevated for a prolonged period because of a lack of insulin (type 1) or because of a lack of response by tissues to circulating insulin (type 2). Other factors increasing blood glucose levels include an increase in the hepatic production of glucose from glycogenolysis and a decreased uptake of glucose by the peripheral insulin-dependent tissues (muscle and adipose).

Glucose appears in the urine when the blood glucose level exceeds the renal reabsorption threshold of approximately 180 mg/100 mL. The presence of glucose in the urine is called *glycosuria.* Because of its large molecular size, glucose in the urine, through osmosis, carries with it large volumes of water as well as the electrolytes sodium and potassium. This, in addition to the presence of ketones, which also increase the secretion of sodium and potassium in the urine, helps produce the clinical symptoms of polyuria (an increased frequency of urination) and the dehydrated state of the hyperglycemic patient, which is characterized by a florid appearance, dry skin, and polydipsia (increased thirst).

Weight loss accompanying a normal or increased appetite is a common feature of type 1 diabetes mellitus. Weight loss initially is due to depletion of water, glycogen, and triglyceride stores. In addition, muscle mass is lost as amino acids are converted into glucose and ketone bodies. Without insulin, most of the body's cells cannot use the large quantities of glucose in the blood. The fasting state mechanisms previously described respond to the call for required energy. Glycogen in

the liver and muscle is converted to glucose via glycogenolysis, and proteins are broken down into their component amino acids, which are subsequently converted into glucose through gluconeogenesis in the liver. The body also converts triglycerides into free fatty acids in the liver. In the absence of glucose, the body's muscles use these free fatty acids, primarily acetoacetate and β-hydroxybutyrate (ketone bodies), as fuel. The metabolism of acetoacetate creates acetone as a by-product, which is responsible for the characteristic fruity, sweet breath odor noted in this stage, called diabetic ketoacidosis.

If the insulin deficiency is severe, gluconeogenesis and ketogenesis continue to increase, regardless of the blood glucose level. However, the tissues decrease their use of ketones over time so that blood levels of acetoacetate and β-hydroxybutyrate increase. This leads to a decrease in the blood's pH, a condition known as *metabolic acidosis (ketoacidosis).* As blood levels of ketones increase, the renal threshold quickly becomes exceeded and ketones become detectable in the urine. Ketoacidosis depresses cardiac contractility and decreases the response of arterioles to the catecholamines epinephrine and norepinephrine.

More significant perhaps is the effect of metabolic acidosis on blood pH and respiration. As the blood level of ketoacids rises, the blood's pH drops below 7.3. This level induces hyperventilation, the body's attempt to raise the pH by means of respiratory alkalosis (see Chapter 12). When severe, this breathing is called *Kussmaul's respirations,* a very deep, gasping type of respiration that may be slow or rapid. When severe, this type of breathing may cause the individual to lose consciousness, as in a hyperglycemic or diabetic coma. Hyperglycemic coma is associated with either severe insulin deficiency (diabetic ketoacidosis) or mild to moderate insulin deficiency (hyperglycemic non-ketotic hyperosmolar coma). Poor patient adherence is one of the most common causes of ketoacidosis, particularly when episodes are recurrent.

Hypoglycemia

Hypoglycemia is the most commonly encountered acute complication of diabetes; patients without diabetes also may develop this condition. Approximately 70% of cases of nondiabetic hypoglycemia are caused by functional hyperinsulinism, a condition related to an over-secretion of insulin by β cells in the pancreas because of an exaggerated response to glucose absorption, muscular exertion, pregnancy, or anorexia nervosa, all of which increase insulin requirements.

Whatever its cause, diabetic or nondiabetic, the clinical manifestations of hypoglycemia are the same. By arbitrary definition, hypoglycemia in adults is equated with blood glucose values below 50 mg/dL, whereas a blood sugar level of 40 mg/dL defines the condition in children.[76] Hypoglycemia is characterized by varying degrees of neurologic dysfunction, may occur with or without signs of epinephrine overactivity, and is responsive to the administration of glucose. Although the definition of hypoglycemia indicates a blood glucose level less than 50 mg/dL, hypoglycemic reactions may occur in individuals with normal or higher than normal blood glucose levels. Indeed, published reports of hypoglycemic reactions in diabetic patients document blood sugar levels ranging from 82 to 472 mg/dL, with reactions developing within 40 minutes of IV insulin administration.[77] On the other hand, blood glucose levels of 25 to 30 mg/dL have been reported in patients who exhibit no clinical evidence of hypoglycemia.[78]

One of the most important factors precipitating clinical hypoglycemia is the rate at which the blood glucose level drops. After the administration of insulin, signs and symptoms of hypoglycemia may develop within a few minutes and progress rapidly to the loss of consciousness. In diabetic patients receiving oral hypoglycemic agents, the onset of signs and symptoms is normally more gradual, developing over a period of hours. Clinical signs and symptoms of hypoglycemia are similar to those exhibited by individuals during acute anxiety states or after the administration of excessive doses of epinephrine ("epinephrine reaction"), except for the mental disorientation seen in hypoglycemia.

The lack of adequate blood glucose levels alters the normal functioning of the cerebral cortex and manifests clinically as mental confusion and lethargy. Lack of glucose further manifests itself in the increased activities of the parasympathetic and sympathetic nervous systems. Part of this response is mediated by increased epinephrine secretion, which produces increases in the systolic and mean blood pressures, increases sweating, and produces tachycardia. When the blood sugar level drops even further, consciousness may be lost, the patient entering a state of hypoglycemic coma, or insulin shock. During this stage, diabetic patients frequently experience tonic-clonic convulsions, which may lead to permanent cerebral dysfunction if not treated promptly.

■ MANAGEMENT

Prompt recognition of diabetes-related complications is vital. Equally important is the doctor's ability to differentiate between hyperglycemia and hypoglycemia. Because of the differing rates of onset of these acute complications, diabetic patients who exhibit behavioral changes, behave strangely, or lose consciousness should be managed as if they were hypoglycemic until proved otherwise.

Hyperglycemia and ketoacidosis usually develop over a period of many hours or days, and the diabetic patient appears and behaves chronically ill. Another important factor in differential diagnosis is the hot, dry appearance seen in hyperglycemia, which contrasts to the cold, wet look of hypoglycemia. The odor of acetone on the breath further confirms a diagnosis of hyperglycemia. When doubt remains as to the cause of the condition, supportive therapy (**P-A-B-C** [position-airway-breathing-circulation]) is indicated until additional medical assistance becomes available.

Hyperglycemia

Definitive management of hyperglycemia, ketosis, and acidosis consists of the administration of insulin to normalize the body's metabolism, restoration of fluid and electrolyte deficiencies, determination of the precipitating cause, and avoidance of complications. Diabetic ketoacidosis is a life-threatening medical emergency with a mortality rate just under 5%. It is most common in type 1 diabetes mellitus; cases of severe stress, such as sepsis, may result in diabetic ketoacidosis in type 2 diabetes mellitus. Dental office management of patients who are hyperglycemic or ketoacidotic is supportive in nature.

The following signs serve as diagnostic clues to the presence of hyperglycemia and its emergency manifestations, diabetic ketoacidosis and diabetic coma:

- Hyperglycemia (>250 mg/dL)
- Acidosis with blood pH 7.3
- Dry, warm skin
- Kussmaul's respirations
- Fruity, sweet breath odor
- Rapid, weak pulse
- Normal to low blood pressure
- Altered level of consciousness

Hyperglycemia—conscious patient
The dental patient presenting for treatment exhibiting signs and symptoms of hyperglycemia represents an American Society of Anesthesiologists IV risk and should not receive any dental treatment until a physician is consulted. In most cases, medical consultation results in the scheduling of an immediate appointment between patient and physician or hospitalization.

NOTE: *Emergency medical technicians (EMTs) are trained to regard any unknown diabetic emergency as hypoglycemia until shown otherwise. If the patient is awake and alert, the EMT may administer oral glucose;*

if the patient's level of consciousness is altered, glucose paste may be used while monitoring airway management.[79] The reason for this is that if hypoglycemia is not treated rapidly, the patient is more likely to die or suffer serious neurologic damage. In contrast, death or permanent disability usually takes longer to develop in hyperglycemic patients.[80]

Hyperglycemia—unconscious patient

Step 1: termination of dental therapy.
Step 1a: activation of dental office emergency team.

Step 2: P. Unconscious patients should be placed into the supine position with their legs elevated slightly.

Step 3: removal of dental materials from mouth.

Step 4: A-B-C (basic life support), as needed. If the diabetic patient loses consciousness in the dental office, the doctor must initiate basic life support (BLS) quickly (check airway, check breathing, and check the pulse), thus ensuring adequate oxygenation and cerebral blood flow. However, this patient will remain unconscious until the underlying metabolic cause (e.g., hyperglycemia, metabolic acidosis) can be determined. The only steps of BLS usually required in diabetic coma are positioning and airway management. Breathing is usually spontaneous, deep, and either rapid or slow. It may be possible to detect the sweet, fruity odor of acetone. Adequate circulation will usually be present.

Step 5: D (definitive care)
Step 5a: summoning of medical assistance. Medical assistance should be sought if any unconscious person does not demonstrate improvement after the steps of BLS are initiated.

Step 5b: IV infusion (if available). An IV infusion of 5% dextrose and water or of normal saline may be started before emergency personnel arrive. Access to a patent vein facilitates subsequent patient management. Insulin has no place in the office emergency kit (unless the doctor or staff member has diabetes and must take insulin). Insulin must be administered carefully and blood tests performed to monitor its effect on blood glucose. The patient requires hospitalization to correct the hyperglycemia and other deficits that occur.

Step 5c: administration of oxygen. Oxygen may be administered at any time during this emergency.

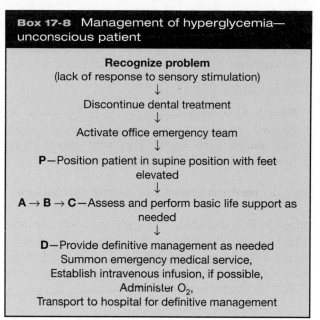

Box 17-8 Management of hyperglycemia—unconscious patient

Recognize problem
(lack of response to sensory stimulation)
↓
Discontinue dental treatment
↓
Activate office emergency team
↓
P—Position patient in supine position with feet elevated
↓
A → B → C—Assess and perform basic life support as needed
↓
D—Provide definitive management as needed
Summon emergency medical service,
Establish intravenous infusion, if possible,
Administer O$_2$,
Transport to hospital for definitive management

A, airway; **B,** breathing; **C,** circulation; **D,** definitive care; **P,** position.

Although oxygen will not help this patient recover, no harm can result from its administration.

Step 5d: transportation of the patient to the hospital. As soon as emergency personnel arrive and stabilize the patient, they will transport the patient to the emergency department of a local hospital for definitive diagnosis (if in doubt) and treatment (Box 17-8).

Hypoglycemia

Management of hypoglycemia yields more dramatic results than hyperglycemia; most individuals experience a rapid relief from symptoms in a short period of time. The method of management depends on the patient's level of consciousness.

The following signs provide diagnostic clues to the presence of hypoglycemia, also known as *insulin shock*:

- Weakness, dizziness
- Pale, moist skin
- Normal or depressed respirations
- Headache
- Altered level of consciousness

Hypoglycemia—conscious and responsive patient

Step 1: recognition of hypoglycemia. Bizarre behavior or changes in personality (if the patient's breath does not smell of alcohol) and other clinical signs of possible glucose insufficiency should prompt the doctor to suspect hypoglycemia. Hypoglycemia may develop in both diabetic and nondiabetic individuals. If the patient is diabetic, the doctor should determine how long ago the patient ate or injected a dose of insulin.

> NOTE: *Hypoglycemic patients may be unable to respond rationally to such questions (concerning diet and insulin) even though they may appear to be functioning normally.*

Step 2: termination of the dental procedure.

Step 3: P (position).
As with any conscious individual during an emergency, positioning is dictated by the person's comfort. In most situations the hypoglycemic patient prefers to sit upright. Depending on the patient's wishes, the doctor may vary the position.

Step 4: A-B-C (BLS, as indicated).
The conscious patient should be capable of maintaining adequate control over airway, breathing, and circulation.

Step 5: D (definitive care).
Step 5a: administration of oral carbohydrates.
If the patient is conscious and cooperative but still demonstrates clinical symptoms of hypoglycemia, an oral carbohydrate is the treatment of choice. The emergency kit should contain sugar, which can be dissolved and ingested by the patient. Other available items might include orange juice, soft drinks, and candy bars. A 6- to 12-ounce portion of soft drink contains 20 to 40 g of glucose. The carbohydrate should be administered in 3- or 4-ounce doses every 5 to 10 minutes until the symptoms disappear.

Step 6: recovery.
The patient should be observed for approximately 1 hour before being permitted to leave the office. The patient may leave the office unescorted if the dentist believes the patient has recovered completely from the episode. If the doctor harbors any doubts about recovery, the patient should remain in the office longer or arrangements should be made for an adult relative or friend to escort the patient home. In addition, the doctor should determine whether the patient ate before the appointment and reaffirm the importance of eating before each dental visit.

Hypoglycemia—unresponsive conscious patient
If the patient does not respond to oral glucose or cooperate in ingesting the glucose, the doctor continues with the management. Steps 1 through 5a refer to the preceding management protocol for the conscious-responsive hypoglycemic patient.

Step 1: recognition of hypoglycemia.

Step 2: termination of the dental procedure.

Step 3: P (position).

Step 4: A-B-C (BLS, as needed).

Step 5: D (definitive care).
Step 5a: administration of oral carbohydrates.

Step 5b: summoning of medical assistance.
When oral carbohydrates prove ineffective, outside medical assistance should be summoned immediately.

Step 5c: administration of parenteral carbohydrates.
If oral carbohydrates do not reverse the signs and symptoms of hypoglycemia or if the individual declines to ingest the oral carbohydrate, parenteral drug administration must be considered. Glucagon, 1 mg, may be administered intramuscularly or intravenously, or if available, 50 mL of a 50% dextrose solution may be administered intravenously over 2 to 3 minutes (Figure 17-8). The patient usually responds within 10 to 15 minutes after IM injection of glucagon and within 5 minutes following IV administration of 50% dextrose. Oral carbohydrates should be started as soon as tolerated by the patient.

Step 5d: monitoring of the patient.
Vital signs should be monitored and recorded at least every 5 minutes during the episode until medical assistance becomes available.

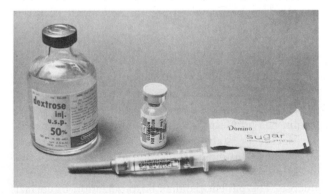

FIGURE 17-8 Antihypoglycemic agents. The 50% dextrose solution must be administered via an intravenous route, but glucagon and epinephrine may be administered either intramuscularly or intravenously. Sugar is administered orally to the conscious patient.

Step 6: discharge and subsequent dental treatment. Emergency medical services personnel will provide definitive care either in the dental office or during transfer to a hospital. In most instances the patient will be hospitalized, at least until blood sugar levels return to normal. Before scheduling subsequent dental appointments, the doctor should discuss with the patient possible reasons that the episode may have occurred and seek ways in which its recurrence can be prevented.

Hypoglycemia—unconscious patient

Step 1: termination of the dental procedure.

Step 2: P (position). Unconscious patients are placed in the supine position with their legs elevated slightly.

Step 3: A-B-C (BLS, as needed). If a diabetic patient loses consciousness in the dental office, the doctor should quickly implement the steps of BLS, thus ensuring the maintenance of adequate oxygenation and cerebral blood flow. However, hypoglycemic patients will remain unconscious until their underlying metabolic problem (low blood sugar) is corrected. The only step of BLS that such patients usually require is airway management. Breathing is spontaneous, and circulation adequate.

Step 4: D (definitive care):
Step 4a: summoning of medical assistance.
If the unconscious patient fails to respond to the steps of BLS, medical assistance should be sought.

Step 4b: administration of carbohydrates. An unconscious patient with a history of diabetes mellitus should be presumed to be hypoglycemic unless other obvious causes of unconsciousness exist. Definitive management of the unconscious diabetic patient requires the administration of carbohydrates via the most effective route available. In most instances this is the IV injection of a 50% dextrose solution or IM injection of glucagon or epinephrine. (All patients with type 1 diabetes should carry glucagon.) Unconscious patient must never receive via mouth any liquid or other substance that can run into their throat because this increases the possibility of airway obstruction, pulmonary aspiration, or both.

Administration of glucagon (1 mg intramuscularly or intravenously) leads to an elevation of blood glucose via the breakdown of glycogen stores in the liver. The response to glucagon varies,[81] with an onset of action in approximately 10 to 20 minutes and a peak response in 30 to 60 minutes.[82] If neither glucagon nor a 50% dextrose solution is available, 0.5 mg of a 1:1000 epinephrine concentration may be administered via the subcutaneous or IM route and repeated every 15 minutes, as needed. Epinephrine increases blood glucose levels but should be used with caution in patients with known cardiovascular disease. Once consciousness is restored, the patient should receive fruit juice or soft drinks orally.

In the absence of the parenteral route or of parenteral drugs, the doctor should maintain BLS until medical assistance arrives. Although liquids should never be placed in the mouth of an unconscious or stuporous patient (the risk of aspiration or airway obstruction is too great) a thick paste of concentrated glucose may be used with a high degree of safety. A small amount of honey or syrup may be placed into the patient's buccal fold.[83] Perhaps even more effective for use in a dental office is a small tube of decorative icing designed for bakers; its consistency is similar to or thicker than that of toothpaste. A very small, very thin veneer of this icing may be placed in the patient's maxillary and mandibular buccal folds in the anterior sextant only. Onset is not rapid (usually 30 to 40 minutes), but the blood sugar level will slowly rise; during this wait BLS should continue, and the oral cavity should be evaluated and suctioned every 5 minutes, if necessary.

NOTE: *Previous editions of this text have recommended the transmucosal application of sugar in certain clinical situations. Because of its slow onset of action and the ready access to emergency medical care available to most individuals in the United States and Canada, transmucosal application of sugar is now recommended for use only when access to assistance is considerably delayed (e.g., more than 40 minutes).*

Although not applicable in many dental settings, the rectal administration of honey or syrup (30 mL per 500 mL of warm water), the so-called honey bear enema, is another effective method in the management of hypoglycemia.[83]

Step 5: recovery and discharge. The unconscious hypoglycemic patient recovers consciousness when the blood glucose level becomes elevated, as long as no additional damage has occurred (e.g., from hypoxia). Once the patient is conscious, oral carbohydrates, such as fruit juice or soft drinks, may be administered to the patient. On arrival, emergency medical service personnel ensure BLS, establish an IV line, and administer any necessary drugs. Once stabilized, the patient then is transported to a hospital for definitive care and observation.

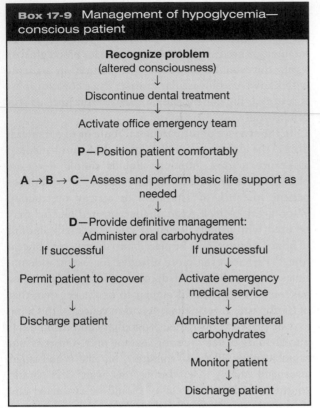

Box 17-9 Management of hypoglycemia—conscious patient

Recognize problem
(altered consciousness)
↓
Discontinue dental treatment
↓
Activate office emergency team
↓
P—Position patient comfortably
↓
A → B → C—Assess and perform basic life support as needed
↓
D—Provide definitive management:
Administer oral carbohydrates

If successful	If unsuccessful
↓	↓
Permit patient to recover	Activate emergency medical service
↓	↓
Discharge patient	Administer parenteral carbohydrates
	↓
	Monitor patient
	↓
	Discharge patient

A, airway; **B**, breathing; **C**, circulation; **D**, definitive care; **P**, position.

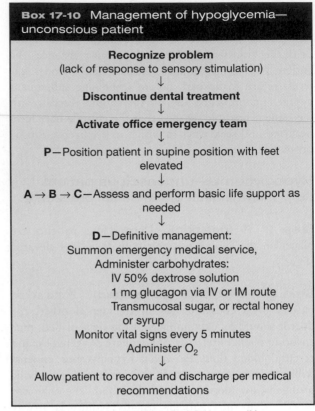

Box 17-10 Management of hypoglycemia—unconscious patient

Recognize problem
(lack of response to sensory stimulation)
↓
Discontinue dental treatment
↓
Activate office emergency team
↓
P—Position patient in supine position with feet elevated
↓
A → B → C—Assess and perform basic life support as needed
↓
D—Definitive management:
Summon emergency medical service,
Administer carbohydrates:
IV 50% dextrose solution
1 mg glucagon via IV or IM route
Transmucosal sugar, or rectal honey or syrup
Monitor vital signs every 5 minutes
Administer O$_2$
↓
Allow patient to recover and discharge per medical recommendations

A, airway; **B**, breathing; **C**, circulation; **D**, definitive care; IM, intramuscular; IV, intravenous; **P**, position.

Another important point to remember is that severe hypoglycemia may be associated with the development of generalized tonic-clonic seizures. Management of hypoglycemia-induced seizures follows the guidelines discussed in the section on seizure disorders (see Chapter 21). However, seizures induced by hypoglycemia may persist until the blood glucose level increases.

Boxes 17-9 and 17-10 outline the management of hypoglycemia. In addition, the following facts may prove helpful in its treatment:

■ **Drugs:** The conscious patient may receive oral forms of sugar. For the unconscious patient, administration of a 50% dextrose solution intravenously, glucagon intramuscularly or intravenously, sugar paste transmucosally, or syrup or honey rectally is recommended.

■ **Medical assistance:** If the individual suffers only a mild alteration of consciousness, no assistance is required. However, if the diabetic patient loses consciousness or does not respond to the administration of sugar, emergency assistance should be summoned at once.

REFERENCES

1. Cydulka RK, Siff J: Diabetes mellitus and disorders of glucose homeostasis. In: Marx JA, Hockberger RS, Walls RM, editors: *Rosen's emergency medicine: concepts and clinical practice,* ed 5, St. Louis, Mosby, 2002, pp. 1635–1664.
2. Sherwin RS: Diabetes mellitus. In: Goldman L, Ausiello D, editors: *Cecil textbook of medicine,* ed 22, Philadelphia, WB Saunders, 2003.
3. Centers for Disease Control and Prevention: National diabetes fact sheet: general information and national estimates on diabetes in the United States, 2005, Atlanta, GA, U.S. Department of Health and Human Services, Centers for Disease Control and Prevention, 2005.
4. American Heart Association: *2005 Heart and stroke facts,* Dallas, TX, American Heart Association, 2005.
5. Cranston I, Lomas J, Maran A, et al.: Restoration of hypoglycaemia awareness in patients with long-duration insulin-dependent diabetes, *Lancet* 344:283–287, 1994.
6. Bell DS, Cutter G: Characteristics of severe hypoglycemia in the patient with insulin-dependent diabetes, *South Med J* 87:616–620, 1994.
7. DCCT Research Group. Epidemiology of severe hypoglycaemia in the Diabetes Control and Complications Trial, *Am J Med* 90:450–459, 1991.

8. Mulhausser I, Berger M, Sonnenberg G: Incidence and management of severe hypoglycemia in 434 adults with insulin-dependent diabetes mellitus, *Diabetes Care* 8:268–273, 1985.

9. Pyoeralae K: Diabetes and coronary heart disease: what a coincidence, *J Cardiovasc Pharmacol* 16(suppl 9):S8, 1990.

10. Douglas JG: Hypertension and diabetes in blacks, *Diabetes Care* 13:1191–1195, 1990.

11. Hamilton BP: Diabetes mellitus and hypertension, *Am J Kidney Dis* 16(suppl 4)1:20–29, 1990.

12. Davis MD: Diabetic retinopathy, *Diabetes Care* 15: 1844–1874, 1992.

13. Humphrey LL, Ballard DJ: Renal complications in non-insulin-dependent diabetes mellitus, *Clin Geriatr Med* 6:807–825, 1990.

14. Fylling CP, Knighton DR: Amputation in the diabetic population: incidence, causes, cost, treatment, and prevention, *J Enterostomal Ther* 16:247–255, 1989.

15. Jawa A, Kcomt J, Fonseca VA: Diabetic nephropathy and retinopathy, *Med Clin North Am* 88:1001–1036, 2004.

16. Tielsch JM, Sommer A, Witt K, et al.: Blindness and visual impairment in an American urban population. The Baltimore Eye Survey, *Arch Ophthalmol* 108:286–290, 1990.

17. Rosenberg CS: Wound healing in the patient with diabetes mellitus, *Nurs Clin North Am* 25:247–261, 1990.

18. Wilson TG Jr: Periodontal diseases and diabetes, *Diabetes Educ* 15:342–345, 1989.

19. Thorp ML: Diabetic nephropathy: common questions, *Am Fam Physician* 72:96–99, 2005.

20. Rabkin R: Diabetic nephropathy, *Clin Cornerstone* 5:1–11, 2003.

21. Hijazi RA, Betancourt-Albrecht M, Cunningham GR: Gonadal and erectile dysfunction in diabetics, *Med Clin North Am* 88:933–945, 2004.

22. Eisenbarth GS, Polonsky KS, Buse JB: Type 1 diabetes mellitus. In: Larsen PR, Kronenberg HM, Melmed S, Polonsky KS, editors: *Williams textbook of endocrinology,* ed 10, Philadelphia, WB Saunders, 2003, pp. 1485–1509.

23. Thorsby E: Invited anniversary review: HLA associated diseases, *Hum Immunol* 53:1–11, 1997.

24. Vaarala O: Environmental causes: dietary causes, *Endocrinol Metab Clin North Am* 33:17–26, 2004.

25. Robles DT, Eisenbarth GS: Type 1 diabetes induced by infection and immunization, *J Autoimmun* 16:355–362, 2001.

26. Bach JF: Etiology and pathogenesis of human insulin-dependent diabetes mellitus. In: Volpe R, editor: *Contemporary endocrinology: autoimmune endocrinopathies.* Totowa, NJ, Humana Press, 1999, pp. 293–307.

27. Buse JB, Polonsky KS, Burant CF: Type 2 diabetes mellitus. In: Larsen PR, Kronenberg HM, Melmed S, Polonsky KS, editors: *Williams textbook of endocrinology,* ed 10, Philadelphia, WB Saunders, 2003, pp. 1427–1484.

28. Almind K, Doria A, Kahn CR: Putting the genes for type II diabetes on the map, *Nat Med* 7:277–279, 2001.

29. Bell GI, Polonsky KS: Diabetes mellitus and genetically programmed defects in beta-cell function, *Nature* 414: 788–791, 2001.

30. Warram JH, Martin BC, Krowelski AS, et al.: Slow glucose removal rate and hyperinsulinemia precede the development of type II diabetes in the offspring of diabetic parents, *Ann Intern Med* 113:909–915, 1990.

31. Lillioija S, Mott DM, Howard BV, et al.: Impaired glucose tolerance as a disorder of insulin action: longitudinal and cross-sectional studies in Pima Indians, *N Engl J Med* 318:1217–1225, 1988.

32. Fujioka S, Matsuzawa Y, Tokunaga K, Tarui S: Contribution of intra-abdominal fat accumulation to the impairment of glucose and lipid metabolism in human obesity, *Metabolism* 36:54–59, 1987.

33. Brambilla P, Manzoni P, Sironi S, et al.: Peripheral and abdominal adiposity in childhood obesity, *Int J Obes Relat Metab Disord* 18:795–800, 1994.

34. Berman DM, Rodriguez LM, Nicklas BJ, et al.: Racial disparities in metabolism, central obesity, and sex hormone binding globulin in postmenopausal women, *J Clin Endocrinol Metab* 86:97–103, 2001.

35. Hotamisligil GS, Spiegelman BM: Tumor necrosis factor alpha: a key component of the obesity-diabetes link, *Diabetes* 43:1271–1278, 1994.

36. American Diabetes Association: Report of the Expert Committee on the Diagnosis and Classification of Diabetes Mellitus, *Diabetes Care* 20:1183–1197, 1997.

37. Bernal-Mizrachi E, Bernal-Mizrachi C: Diabetes mellitus and related disorders. In: Green GB, Harris IS, Lin GA, Moylan KC, editors: *The Washington manual of medical therapeutics,* Philadelphia, Lippincott Williams & Wilkins, 2004, pp. 470–487.

38. Goldstein S: Cellular and molecular biological studies on diabetes mellitus, *Pathol Biol (Paris)* 32:99–106, 1984.

39. Macaluso CJ, Bauer UE, Deeb LC: Type 2 diabetes mellitus among Florida children and adolescents, 1994 through 1998, *Public Health Rep* 117:373–379, 2002.

40. Neufeld ND, Raffel LF, Landon C: Early presentation of type 2 diabetes in Mexican-American youth, *Diabetes Care* 21:80–86, 1998.

41. King H, Aubert RE, Herman WH: Global burden of diabetes. 1995-2025: prevalence, numerical estimates, and projections, *Diabetes Care* 21:1414–1431, 1998.

42. Zimmet P. Alberti KG, Shaw J: Global and societal implications of the diabetes epidemic, *Nature* 414:782–787, 2001.

43. Perez MI, Kohn SR: Cutaneous manifestations of diabetes mellitus, *Am Acad Dermatol* 30:519–531, 1994.

44. Langer O, Yogev Y, Most O, Xenakis EMJ: Gestational diabetes: the consequences of not treating, *Am J Obstet Gynecol* 192:989–997, 2005.

45. Turok DK: Management of gestational diabetes mellitus, *Am Fam Physician* 68:1767–1772, 2003.

46. Rao SS: Impaired glucose tolerance and impaired fasting glucose, *Am Fam Physician* 69:1961–1968, 2004.

47. Sumner CJ: The spectrum of neuropathy in diabetes and impaired glucose tolerance, *Neurology* 60:108–111, 2003.

48. Tonstad S, Svendsen M: Premature coronary heart disease, *Am J Cardiol* 96:1681–1685, 2005.

49. Kitabchi AE, Wall BM: Diabetic ketoacidosis, *Med Clin North Am* 79:9–37, 1995.

50. Fleckman AM: Diabetic ketoacidosis, *Endocrinol Metab Clin North Am* 22:181–207, 1993.

51. DTTC Research Group: The effect of intensive treatment of diabetes on the development and progression of long-term complications in insulin-dependent diabetes mellitus, *N Engl J Med* 329:977–986, 1993.

52. Buse JB: Diabetes mellitus in adults. In: Rakel RE, Bope ET, editors: *Conn's current therapy,* ed 57, Philadelphia, WB Saunders, 2005.

53. Glucose meters and diabetes management. Food and Drug Administration. www.fda.gov/diabetes/glucose.html#2.

54. Kaufman FR, Gibson LC, Halvorson M, et al.: A pilot study of the continuous glucose monitoring system: clinical decisions and glycemic control after its use in pediatric type 1 diabetic subjects, *Diabetes Care* 24:2030–2034, 2001.

55. Bode B, Gross K, Rikalo N, et al.: Alarms based on real-time sensor glucose values alert patients to hypo- and hyperglycemia: the guardian continuous glucose monitoring system, *Diabetes Technol Ther* 6:105–113, 2004.

56. Potts RO: Glucose monitoring by reverse iontophoresis, *Diabetes Metab Res Rev* 17(suppl 2):s1–s6, 2001.

57. Pitzer K, Desai S, Dunn T, et al.: Detection of hypoglycemia with the GlucoWatch Biographer, *Diabetes Care* 24:881–885, 2001.

58. Meinert CL, Knatterud GL, Prout TE, Klimt CR: Effects of hypoglycemic agents on vascular complications in patients with adult-onset diabetes. II. Mortality results, *Diabetes* 19:789–830, 1970.

59. University Group Diabetes Program: Effects of hypoglycemic agents on vascular complications in patients with adult-onset diabetes. V. Evaluation of phenformin therapy, *Diabetes* 24:65–184, 1975.

60. University Group Diabetes Program: Effects of hypoglycemic agents on vascular complications in patients with adult-onset diabetes. VI. Supplementary report on nonfatal events in patients treated with tolbutamide, *Diabetes* 25:1129–1153, 1976.

61. Knatterud GL, Klimt CR, Levin ME, et al.: Effects of hypoglycemic agents on vascular complications in patients with adult-onset diabetes. VIII. Mortality and selected nonfatal events with insulin treatment, *JAMA* 240:37–42, 1978.

62. Glyburide and glipizide. *Med Lett Drugs Ther* 26:79–80, 1984.

63. Human insulin: *Med Lett Drugs Ther* 25:63–64, 1983.

64. Grammer LC, Metzger BE, Patterson R: Cutaneous allergy to human (recombinant DNA) insulin, *JAMA* 251:1459–1460, 1984.

65. Uwaifo GI, Ratner RE: Novel pharmacological agents for type 2 diabetes, *Endocrinol Metab Clin North Am* 34:155–197, 2005.

66. Davis T, Edelman SV: Insulin therapy in type 2 diabetes, *Med Clin North Am* 88:865–895, 2004.

67. Fox LA, Buckloh LM, Smith SD, et al.: A randomized controlled trial of insulin pump therapy in young children with type 1 diabetes, *Diabetes Care* 28:1277–1281, 2005.

68. Fiallo-Scharer R: Eight-point glucose testing versus the continuous glucose monitoring system in evaluation of glycemic control in type 1 diabetes, *J Clin Endocrinol Metab* 90:3387–3391, 2005.

69. Havas S, Donner T: Tight control of type 1 diabetes: recommendations for patient. *Am Fam Physician* 74:971–978, 2006.

70. Vernillo AT: Diabetes mellitus: relevance to dental treatment, *Oral Surg Oral Med Oral Pathol Oral Radiol Endod* 91:263–270, 2001.

71. Little JW, Falace DA: Diabetes. In: Little JW, Falace DA, Miller C, Rhodes NL, editors: *Dental management of the medically compromised patient,* ed 5, St Louis, Mosby, 1997, pp. 387–409.

72. Rees TD: Periodontal management of the patient with diabetes mellitus, *Periodontology* 23:63–72, 2000.

73. Andreani D, DiMario U, Pozzilli P: Prediction, prevention, and early intervention in insulin-dependent diabetes, *Diabetes Metab Rev* 7:61–77, 1991.

74. Nabarro JD: Diabetes in the United Kingdom: a personal series, *Diabetic Med* 8:59–68, 1991.

75. Garland PB, Newsholm EA, Randle PJ: Regulation of glucose uptake by muscle, *Biochem K* 93:665, 1964.

76. Sperling MA: Hypoglycemia. In: Behrman RE, Kliegman RM, Jenson HB, editors: *Nelson Textbook of Pediatrics,* ed 17, Philadelphia, WB Saunders, 2004, pp. 505–518.

77. Hepburn DA, Deary IJ, Frier BM, et al.: Symptoms of acute insulin-induced hypoglycemia in humans with and without IDDM: factor-analysis approach, *Diabetes Care* 14:949–957, 1991.

78. Arogyasami J, Conlee RK, Booth CL, et al.: Effects of exercise on insulin-induced hypoglycemia, *J Appl Physiol* 69:686–693, 1990.

79. Pollakoff J, Pollakoff K: *EMT's guide to treatment,* Los Angeles, Jeff Gould, 1991.

80. Pollakoff J: Diabetes. In: *EMT news update,* Pacoima, CA, Poicoma Skills Center, 1989.

81. Vermeulen MJ, Klompas M, Ray JG, et al.: Subcutaneous glucagon may be better than oral glucose for prehospital treatment of symptomatic hypoglycemia, *Diabetes Care* 26:2472–2473, 2003.

82. Cryer PE, Davis SN, Shamoon H: Hypoglycemia in diabetes, *Diabetes Care* 26:1902–1912, 2003.

83. Karam JH: Diabetes mellitus and hypoglycemia. In: Tierney LM Jr, McPhee SJ, Papadakis MA, editors: *Current medical diagnosis & treatment,* ed 35, Stamford, CT, Appleton & Lange, 1996, pp. 1069–1109.

CHAPTER 18

Thyroid Gland Dysfunction

The thyroid gland is composed of two elongated lobes on either side of the trachea that are joined by a thin isthmus of thyroid tissue located at or below the level of the thyroid cartilage.[1] The thyroid gland produces and secretes three hormones that are vital in the regulation of the level of biochemical activity of most of the body's tissues. These hormones are thyroxine (T_4), triiodothyronine (T_3), and calcitonin. Proper functioning of the thyroid gland from the time of birth is vital for normal growth and metabolism.

Thyroid gland dysfunction may occur either through overproduction (thyrotoxicosis) or underproduction (hypothyroidism) of thyroid hormone. In both instances the observed clinical manifestations may encompass a broad spectrum, ranging from subclinical dysfunction to acutely life-threatening situations. Most patients with thyroid dysfunction exhibit milder forms of the disease.

Like adrenal insufficiency, thyroid gland dysfunction presents initially as a slow, insidious process in which nonspecific signs and symptoms develop over months or years and then are acutely exacerbated by intercurrent stress. Thyroid dysfunction is relatively uncommon, and the characteristic symptoms are not easy to recognize. Both thyroid conditions are potentially fatal if untreated and constitute medical emergencies in their extreme stages.[2]

This chapter focuses primarily on the detection of clinical signs and symptoms of thyroid gland dysfunction. In addition, parts of the discussion consider the life-threatening situations myxedema coma and thyroid "storm," or crisis—both of which are extremely rare.

Hypothyroidism is a clinical state in which the body's tissues do not receive an adequate supply of thyroid hormones. Clinical signs and symptoms of hypothyroidism relate to the age of the patient at the time of onset and to the degree and duration of the hormonal deficiency. A deficiency of thyroid hormone during fetal or early life can produce a clinical syndrome known as *cretinism* in infants and children.[3] Severe hypothyroidism that develops in an adult is called *myxedema* and refers to the appearance of nonpitting, gelatinous, mucinous infiltrates beneath the skin.[4] Severe, unmanaged hypothyroidism ultimately may induce the loss of consciousness, a condition known as *myxedema coma.* The mortality rate in myxedema coma is high (up to 50%) even with optimal treatment.[5,6]

Thyrotoxicosis is also known by several other names, including *hyperthyroidism, toxic goiter (diffuse or nodular), Basedow's disease,*[7] *Graves' disease,*[8] *Parry's disease,* and *Plummer's disease.* It is a state of heightened thyroid gland activity associated with the production of excessive quantities of the thyroid hormones T_4 and T_3. Because the thyroid hormones affect the cellular metabolism of virtually all organ systems, signs and symptoms of thyrotoxicosis may be noted in any part of the body. Left untreated, thyrotoxicosis may lead to an acute life-threatening situation known as *thyroid storm,* or *thyroid crisis,* which manifests as severe hypermetabolism, including high fever, and cardiovascular, neurologic, and gastrointestinal dysfunction.[9] Although uncommon today, thyroid storm still has a high mortality rate.

■ PREDISPOSING FACTORS

Dysfunction of the thyroid gland is a relatively common medical disorder. Excluding diabetes mellitus, the most common endocrine disorder, thyroid gland dysfunction accounts for 80% of all endocrine disorders.

Hypothyroidism

Thyroid failure usually occurs as a result of diseases of the thyroid gland (primary hypothyroidism), pituitary gland (secondary), or hypothalamus (tertiary).[2] Secondary failure accounts for less than 4% of cases,[10] whereas tertiary failure is even less common. Primary thyroid disease causes the remaining cases. Adult hypothyroidism usually develops as a result of idiopathic atrophy of the thyroid gland, which many researchers currently believe occurs via an autoimmune mechanism.[11] Other causes of hypothyroidism include total thyroidectomy or ablation after radioactive iodine therapy, both of which are used commonly to manage thyroid gland hyperfunction, and chronic thyroiditis. Thyroid hypofunction occurs 3 to 10 times more frequently in females than males,[12] with the greatest incidence in the seventh decade of life.[13] Myxedema coma, the end stage of untreated hypothyroidism, carries a mortality rate of up to 50% but is seen infrequently clinically.[5,6] Myxedema coma is associated with severe hypothermia,[10] hypoventilation, hypoxia, hypercapnia, and hypotension.[14] Box 18-1 lists possible causes of hypothyroidism.

The dentist should be aware of patients who may have hypothyroidism because if medically untreated or inadequately managed, they represent increased risks during dental treatment. The clinically hypothyroid

---

Box 18-1   Causes of hypothyroidism

PRIMARY
Autoimmune hypothyroidism
Idiopathic causes
Postsurgical thyroidectomy
External radiation therapy
Radioiodine therapy
Inherited enzymatic defect
Iodine deficiency
Antithyroid drugs
Lithium, phenylbutazone

SECONDARY
Pituitary tumor
Infiltrative disease (sarcoid) of pituitary

Modified from Wogan JM: Selected endocrine disorders. In: Marx JA, Hockberger RS, Walls RM, editors: *Rosen's emergency medicine concepts and clinical practice,* ed 5, St. Louis, Mosby, 2002, pp. 1770–1784.

patient is unusually sensitive to most central nervous system (CNS)–depressant drugs, including sedatives, opioids, and antianxiety drugs, which are commonly used in dentistry. Commonly employed sedative doses of these drugs can result in extreme overreactions in clinically hypothyroid individuals.

Thyrotoxicosis

Like hypothyroidism, thyrotoxicosis, also known as *hyperthyroidism,* begins insidiously and may progress, resulting in the more severe form of the disorder, thyroid storm, or thyroid crisis, if left untreated.

Approximately 3 of 10,000 adults develop thyroid gland hyperfunction each year; diagnosis occurs in eight females for every male.[15] Thyrotoxicosis occurs most often in patients between 20 and 40 years of age.[16] By far the most common form of thyrotoxicosis is that associated with diffuse enlargement of the thyroid gland and the presence of antibodies against different fractions of the thyroid gland. This autoimmune thyroid disorder, called *Graves' disease (Basedow's disease* in Europe and Latin America), has a familial tendency. Box 18-2 lists other causes of thyrotoxicosis.

Although rare, thyroid storm, or thyroid crisis, occurs in patients with untreated or incompletely treated thyrotoxicosis. Only about 1% to 2% of patients with thyrotoxicosis progress to thyroid storm.[17] On rare occasion thyroid storm may occur suddenly in a patient who has not previously been diagnosed with thyrotoxicosis. More commonly, however, thyroid storm follows a long history of uncomplicated thyrotoxicosis. The patient usually experiences 6 to 8 months of milder symptoms and may have developed thyrotoxicosis as long as 2.5 to 5 years previously.[17,18] Thyroid storm represents a sudden and severe exacerbation of the signs and symptoms of thyrotoxicosis, usually accompanied by hyperpyrexia (elevated body temperature) and precipitated by some form of stress, intercurrent disease, infection, trauma, thyroid surgery, or radioactive iodine administration.

Patients who are clinically hyperthyroid tend to be unusually sensitive to catecholamines, such as epinephrine, responding to their administration with hypertensive episodes, tachycardia, or significant dysrhythmias. In addition, hyperthyroid patients may seem apprehensive, which may suggest the need for sedation during dental treatment. However, sedation may prove a futile exercise in these patients, whose "anxiety" is not psychological but hormonally induced.

Both thyrotoxicosis and hypothyroidism are associated with an increased incidence of cardiovascular disease.[19,20]

Milder forms of both types of dysfunction may go easily unnoticed. Although both thyrotoxicosis and hypothyroidism can potentially create increased risks during dental treatment, the more severe, undiagnosed, or untreated patient presents the greatest risk. The doctor must be able to recognize each form of thyroid dysfunction and take the steps necessary to decrease potential risks.

■ PREVENTION

Two goals are essential in the management of patients with thyroid dysfunction:

1. Prevention of the occurrence of the life-threatening situations myxedema coma and thyroid storm
2. Prevention of the exacerbation of complications associated with thyroid dysfunction, notably cardiovascular disease

---

Box 18-2   Causes of hyperthyroidism

Toxic diffuse goiter (Graves' disease)
Toxic multinodular goiter
Toxic uninodular goiter
Factitious thyrotoxicosis
T_3 thyrotoxicosis
Thyrotoxicosis associated with thyroiditis
Hashimoto's thyroiditis
Subacute (de Quervain's) thyroiditis
Jod-Basedow phenomenon
Metastatic follicular carcinoma
Malignancies with circulating thyroid stimulators
TSH-producing pituitary tumors
Struma ovarii with hyperthyroidism
Hypothalamic hyperthyroidism

T_3, triiodothyronine; TSH, thyroid-stimulating hormone.
From Wogan JM: Selected endocrine disorders. In: Marx JA, Hockberger RS, Walls RM, editors: *Rosen's emergency medicine: concepts and clinical practice,* ed 5, St. Louis, Mosby, 2002, pp. 1770–1784.

✎ MEDICAL HISTORY QUESTIONNAIRE

Question 49 on the University of the Pacific School of Dentistry medical history refers specifically to thyroid disease. However, other questions may provide important information about potential thyroid gland dysfunction.

Section III, Do You Have or Have You Had:

Question 49: Thyroid, adrenal disease?

Section I, Questions 1 to 4

Question 1. Is your general health good?

Question 2. Has there been a change in your health within the last year?

Question 3. Have you been hospitalized or had a serious illness in the last three years? If YES, why?

Question 4. Yes/No: Are you being treated by a physician now? For what? Date of last medical exam?

Comment: Patients with a known history of thyroid gland dysfunction most often mention the problem in one or more of these questions.

Section II, Have You Experienced:

Question 10: Recent weight loss, fever, night sweats?

Comment: Unexplained weight loss in a patient with a ravenous appetite should alert the doctor to the possible presence of thyrotoxicosis. Conversely, an unexplained increase in weight accompanied by other clinical signs and symptoms may indicate hypothyroidism.

Section IV, Have You Experienced:

Question 52: Radiation treatments?

Question 10: Recent weight loss, fever, night sweats?

Question 58: Surgeries?

Comment: Thyroid dysfunction is frequently discovered during routine palpation of the patient's neck; the condition often manifests itself as a lump or bump. Question 58 prompts the individual to explain the type of thyroid dysfunction and mode of treatment. Subtotal thyroidectomy is a common surgical treatment for thyroid hyperfunction. Surgical intervention is especially common in patients whose glands develop benign or malignant thyroid nodules. Irradiation with radioactive iodine (iodine-131) is another common technique in the destruction of hyperactive thyroid tissue.

Section V, Are You Taking:

Question 62: Drugs, medications, over-the-counter medicines (including aspirin), natural remedies?

Comment: Patients with thyroid gland hypofunction receive thyroid extract or a synthetic preparation.[21] The most frequently used drug, which is also the drug of choice, is L-thyroxine sodium (Synthroid). Other drugs commonly used in management of thyroid hypofunction include liotrix (Euthyroid, Thyrolar) and dextrothyroxine sodium (Choloxin). The goal in thyroid dysfunction management is to maintain normal blood levels of thyroid hormones, known as the *euthyroid* state.

Hyperthyroid patients receive treatment aimed at halting the excessive secretion of thyroid hormone. Three methods—drug therapy, subtotal thyroidectomy, and radioactive iodine ablation of the gland—help to achieve this goal.[22] Frequently prescribed antithyroid drugs include propylthiouracil (Propyl-Thyracil) and methimazole (Tapazole).[23] Propranolol (Inderal), dexamethasone, and lithium also are used to manage thyrotoxicosis (Table 18-1).[23]

Dialogue history

If the patient indicates on Question 49 of the health history questionnaire a positive history of thyroid disease, an in-depth dialogue history is indicated.

Question: What is the nature of the thyroid dysfunction—hypofunction or hyperfunction?

Question: How do you manage the disorder?

Comment: These questions prompt the individual to disclose general information about their thyroid problem.

A physical examination should be performed next to uncover any clinical evidence of thyroid dysfunction. In most instances the patient is in a euthyroid state and will represent a normal risk during dental treatment. According to the American Society of Anesthesiologists (ASA) physical classification system, the euthyroid patient is an ASA II risk.

However, when no history of thyroid dysfunction is disclosed but clinical evidence leads to a suspicion of its presence, the following dialogue history is warranted.

Question: Have you unexpectedly gained or lost weight recently?

Comment: Recent weight gain (10 or more pounds) is noted commonly in clinically hypothyroid individuals, whereas persons who are hyperthyroid frequently lose weight in spite of an increase in appetite. Note, however, that many other medical conditions, including diabetes, heart failure, and malignancy, can also induce weight gain or loss.

Question: Are you unusually sensitive to cold temperatures or pain-relieving medications?

Comment: Individuals with a hypofunctioning thyroid often exhibit these symptoms.

TABLE 18-1 Medications used to manage hypothyroidism and thyrotoxicosis (hyperthyroidism)

Hypothyroidism		Thyrotoxicosis	
Generic	**Proprietary**	**Generic**	**Proprietary**
Thyroid USP (desiccated)	Armour Thyroid, Thyrar, Thyroid Strong, Westhroid	Propylthiouracil	Propyl-Thyracil
Levothyroxine (T_4)	Leo-T, Levoxine, Synthroid, Eltroxin	Methimazole	Tapazole
Liothyronine (T_3)	Cytomel	Carbimazole	
Liotrix	Euthyroid, Thyrolar	Propranolol	Inderal

USP, U.S. Pharmacopoeia.

Question: Are you unusually sensitive to heat?

Question: Have you become increasingly irritable or tense?

Comment: Patients with a hyperfunctioning thyroid gland frequently exhibit the previous two symptoms. The patient might be more aware of their sensitivity to temperature but be less aware of changes in temperament, whereas a close acquaintance (e.g., a spouse) is more likely to notice subtle changes in temperament.

Physical examination

In most cases in which patients report a history of thyroid gland dysfunction, they have received or are currently receiving treatment. These persons are usually in an euthyroid state (a condition of normal thyroid hormone levels) and do not represent an increased risk during dental treatment.

On the other hand, patients with previously undetected thyroid dysfunction possibly represent a significant risk during dental treatment. Fortunately, the presence of clinical signs and symptoms enable the doctor to recognize thyroid dysfunction and to modify treatment accordingly. Clinically hypothyroid patients may have a large, thick tongue with atrophic papillae and thick edematous skin with puffy hands and face. Their skin is dry, and they do not sweat. Blood pressure is close to normal (for the patient), with diastolic pressure elevated slightly, and the heart rate slow (bradycardia). The hypothyroid patient appears lethargic and speaks slowly.

Hyperthyroid patients often appear nervous, with warm, sweaty hands that may tremble slightly. Blood pressure is elevated (systolic more than diastolic), with the heart rate markedly increased (tachycardia). It may be quite difficult to distinguish between thyrotoxicosis and acute anxiety. One possible clue is that the patient with thyrotoxicosis has warm, sweaty palms, whereas acutely anxious individuals' palms frequently are cold and clammy.

Dental therapy considerations

Euthyroid

Patients with thyroid gland dysfunction who are receiving or have received therapy to treat the condition (e.g., surgery, medication, or irradiation), have normal levels of circulating thyroid hormone, and have no symptoms are considered euthyroid. They represent ASA II risks and may be managed normally during dental treatment. In addition, if mild clinical manifestations of either hyper- or hypothyroidism are present, elective dental treatment may proceed, although certain treatment modifications should be considered. These patients represent ASA III risks.

Hypothyroid

If clinical hypothyroidism is suspected, certain precautions are recommended. Medical consultation with the patient's primary care physician should be considered prior to the start of any dental treatment. In addition, caution must be exercised when prescribing any CNS-depressant drugs. Of particular concern are the sedative-hypnotics (barbiturates), opioid analgesics, and other antianxiety drugs. Because hypothyroid patients demonstrate hypersensitivity to CNS-depressant drugs, administration of a "normal" dose may produce an overdose (known as a *relative* overdose), leading to respiratory or cardiovascular depression, or both.[24]

Furthermore, an increased incidence of cardiovascular disease is associated with the hypothyroid state. In 1976, Barnes and Barnes[25] theorized that thyroid hypofunction produced most instances of cardiovascular disease and that correction of thyroid deficiency leads to the elimination of cardiovascular disease. A history of thyroid gland hypofunction should direct the doctor to seek other possible signs and symptoms of cardiovascular disease. In an individual with more intense signs and symptoms of thyroid hypofunction (e.g., mental apathy, drowsiness, or slow speech), dental treatment should be postponed until consultation with the patient's primary care physician or definitive management of the clinical disorder is achieved.

Hyperthyroid

Mild degrees of thyroid hyperfunction may pass for acute anxiety, with little increase in clinical risk. However, various cardiovascular disorders, primarily angina pectoris, are exaggerated in cases of thyrotoxicosis. If, in the course of the dental treatment, the patient develops one or more of these cardiovascular disorders, the management protocol for that specific situation should be followed (see Part Seven: Chest Pain).

Patients exhibiting severe hyperfunction should receive immediate medical consultation. Dental care should be postponed until the patient's underlying metabolic disturbance is corrected. Worth remembering is that psychological or physiologic stress may precipitate thyroid crisis in the untreated or incompletely treated hyperthyroid individual.

Furthermore, use of atropine, a vagolytic drug (i.e., one that inhibits the vagus nerve, which decelerates the heart) should be avoided. Atropine causes an increase in heart rate and may be a factor in precipitating thyroid storm. In addition, epinephrine and other vasopressors should be used with caution in clinically hyperthyroid patients. Vasopressors stimulate the cardiovascular system and can precipitate cardiac dysrhythmias, tachycardia, and thyroid storm in hyperthyroid patients, whose cardiovascular systems have already been sensitized.

TABLE 18-2   Physical status classifications of thyroid gland dysfunction

Degree of thyroid dysfunction	ASA physical status	Considerations
Hypofunctioning or hyperfunctioning patient receiving medical therapy; no signs or symptoms of dysfunction evident	II	Usual ASA II considerations
Hypofunction or hyperfunction; signs and symptoms of dysfunction evident	III	Usual ASA III considerations, including avoidance of vasopressors (hyperfunction) or CNS depressants (hypofunction) Evaluation for cardiovascular disease

ASA, American Society of Anesthesiologists; CNS, central nervous system.

However, local anesthetics with vasoconstrictors may be used when the following precautions are taken:

- Use the least-concentrated effective solution of epinephrine (1:200,000 is preferred to 1:100,000, which is preferred to 1:50,000)
- Injecting the smallest effective volume of anesthetic/vasopressor
- Aspiration prior to every injection (see Chapter 23)

Of greater potential risk, however, is racemic epinephrine impregnated cord used for gingival retraction. This form of epinephrine is more likely to precipitate unwanted side effects, especially in the presence of clinical thyrotoxicosis. The use of racemic epinephrine is absolutely contraindicated in a clinically hyperthyroid patient.

Mildly hyperthyroid patients may easily be mistaken for those who are apprehensive. Use of conscious sedation is not contraindicated; however, because the apparent nervousness of the hyperthyroid individual is hormonally induced, not fear related, sedative drugs may prove to be less than effective (the patient requiring larger than normal doses to achieve any degree of sedation).

Hypothyroid or hyperthyroid patients who have been treated and are currently euthyroid are ASA II risks, whereas patients who exhibit clinical manifestations of thyroid dysfunction are ASA III risks (Table 18-2).

■ CLINICAL MANIFESTATIONS

Hypothyroidism

Hypothyroidism is a state in which all bodily functions progressively slow down, a process caused by an insufficient supply of the thyroid hormones. When this deficiency occurs during childhood, the syndrome is termed *cretinism* and the child exhibits alterations in growth and development. Children who suffer cretinism

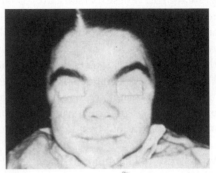

FIGURE 18-1   A clinical picture of an individual with cretinism demonstrates the characteristic flat nose and broad, puffy face.

lack the necessary thyroid hormone in utero or shortly after birth, which retards the child's entire physical and mental development. Ossification of bone is delayed, tooth development is poor, tooth eruption is delayed, and permanent neurologic damage is evident. Clinically, the infant is dull and apathetic, and their body temperature is usually subnormal. Physically, the tongue is enlarged, the skin and lips are thick, the face is broad and puffy, and the nose is flat (Figure 18-1).

When hypothyroidism develops in the adult, the onset is usually insidious. A friend or spouse often persuades the individual to seek medical assistance because of noticeably increased weakness and fatigue, sudden weight gain (usually about 7 or 8 pounds) not associated with an increased appetite,[26] or cold intolerance, present in half the cases.[27] Frequently, the patient is unaware of these changes.

As hypothyroidism progresses, the patient may demonstrate slowing of the speech, hoarseness, absence of sweating, moderate weight gain, constipation (in 25% of cases), decreased sense of taste and smell, peripheral nonpitting edema, dyspnea, and anginal pain. Clinical signs include puffiness of the face and eyelids,[28] carotenemic (orange-red) skin color and rosy cheeks, thickened tongue, and thickened edematous skin (nonpitting).

Blood pressure remains approximately normal, with the potential for slight elevation of the diastolic pressure;[13] however, the heart rate decreases (sinus bradycardia being the most common dysrhythmia in individuals who have a hypofunctioning thyroid). Patients with severe, untreated hypothyroidism may develop heart failure with pulmonary congestion.

Pseudomyotonic deep tendon reflexes and paresthesias are extremely common (almost 100% occurrence) in hypothyroid patients. Pseudomyotonic deep tendon reflexes are characterized by a prolonged relaxation phase, which is confirmed through testing of the Achilles tendon reflex while the patient kneels on a chair. The relaxation phase is at least twice as long as the contraction phase in these patients.[29] About 80% of cases include paresthesias,[30] in which the median nerve in carpal tunnel syndrome is the most common.

The most severe complication of hypothyroidism, however, is myxedema coma. This condition has a high mortality rate and is marked by hypothermia (29.5°C to 30°C), bradycardia, hypotension, and intense cerebral obtundation (loss of consciousness). Myxedema coma is rare, occurring in only 0.1% of all cases of hypothyroidism, and extremely rare in patients younger than 50 years; the condition is most common in elderly women.[28] About 80% of patients with myxedema experience hypothermia, some with recorded temperatures as low as 24°C.[10]

Symptoms that are essential to a diagnosis of hypothyroidism include weakness, fatigue, cold intolerance, constipation, menorrhagia, and hoarseness. Signs necessary for diagnosis include dry, cold, yellow, puffy skin; scant eyebrows; thick tongue; bradycardia; and the delayed return of deep tendon reflexes (Table 18-3).[31]

Thyrotoxicosis

Like hypothyroidism, thyrotoxicosis is rarely severe at its time of onset. In most cases, questioning of the patient reveals clinical evidence of the dysfunction over a period of months before its "discovery." As with hypofunction, the individual who actually discovers the disease frequently is a spouse or friend, someone who notices subtle changes in the habits and personality of the patient. Nervousness, increased irritability, and insomnia are usually the first clinical signs to be noted. Other clinical manifestations include an increased intolerance to heat; hyperhidrosis, or a marked increase in sweating; overactivity, including quick, uncoordinated movements that range from mild to gross tremors; and rapid speech. Unexplained weight loss accompanied by an increased appetite is another important signal. Up to half of all patients seen in an emergency department with thyroid storm have lost more than 40 pounds.[18]

TABLE 18-3 Clinical manifestations of hypothyroidism

Symptoms or Signs (10% or greater incidence)	% manifestation
SYMPTOMS	
Paresthesias	92
Loss of energy	79
Intolerance to cold	51
Muscular weakness	34
Pain in muscles and joints	31
Inability to concentrate	31
Drowsiness	30
Constipation	27
Forgetfulness	23
Depressed auditory acuity	15
Emotional instability	15
Headaches	14
Dysarthria	14
SIGNS	
"Pseudomyotonic" reflexes	95
Change in menstrual pattern	86
Hypothermia	80
Dry, scaly skin	79
Puffy eyelids	70
Hoarse voice	56
Weight gain	41
Dependent edema	30
Sparse axillary and pubic hair	30
Pallor	24
Thinning eyebrows	24
Yellow skin	23
Loss of scalp hair	18
Abdominal distention	18
Goiter	16
Decreased sweating	10

Modified from Wogan JM: Selected endocrine disorders. In: Marx JA, Hockberger RS, Walls RM, editors: *Rosen's emergency medicine: concepts and clinical practice*, ed 5, St. Louis, Mosby, 2002, pp. 1770–1784.

Hyperthyroid patients become fatigued easily and may note heart palpitations.

Clinical signs include excessive sweating; the skin of a hyperthyroid individual feels warm and moist to the touch. The extremities, especially the hands, exhibit varying degrees of tremulousness. When thyrotoxicosis results from Graves' disease, ophthalmopathy may be noted, the severity of which does not parallel the

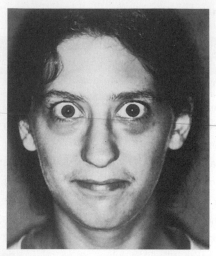

FIGURE 18-2 Hyperthyroid patient exhibiting exophthalmos.

intensity of the thyroid gland dysfunction. Werner[32,33] classified the clinical manifestations of ophthalmopathy in hyperthyroid patients, including upper-lid retraction, staring, lid lag, proptosis, exophthalmos (Figure 18-2), and extraocular muscle palsies.[34] Cardiovascular manifestations of thyrotoxicosis vary, from an increase in blood pressure (systolic pressure increasing more than diastolic pressure), widening of the pulse pressure, sinus tachycardia (more common during sleep), and on occasion paroxysmal atrial fibrillation and heart failure. In addition, hyperthyroid individuals experience mitral valve prolapse significantly more does than the general population.[16]

Untreated thyrotoxicosis may eventually result in thyroid storm, an acute life-threatening emergency. Extremely rare today, thyroid storm is an acute exacerbation of the signs and symptoms of thyrotoxicosis manifested by signs of severe hypermetabolism. Clinical manifestations include hyperpyrexia; excessive sweating, nausea, vomiting, abdominal pain, cardiovascular disturbances (such as tachycardia and atrial fibrillation), and heart failure with possible pulmonary edema. CNS manifestations usually start as mild tremulousness with the patient then becoming severely agitated and disorientated, which leads to psychotic behavior, stupor (partial unconsciousness), and eventual coma. Thyroid storm is associated with a high mortality rate, often even with proper management.

Symptoms necessary for the diagnosis of thyrotoxicosis include weakness, sweating, weight loss, nervousness, loose stools, and heat intolerance. Signs include warm, thin, soft, moist skin; exophthalmos; staring; and tremors (Table 18-4).[31,35]

TABLE 18-4 Clinical manifestations of hyperthyroidism

Symptoms or Signs (10% or greater incidence)	% manifestation
SYMPTOMS	
Common	
Weight loss	
<20 lb	72–100
20–40 lb	Up to 14
>40 lb	27–36
Palpitations	23–45
Nervousness	
Tremor	
Less common	
Chest pain	
Dyspnea	
Edema	
Psychosis	
Disorientation	
Diarrhea/hyperdefecation	
Abdominal pain	
SIGNS	
Fever	100
Temperature <103°F	57–70
Temperature >103°F	30–43
Tachycardia	100
100–139 beats/min	24
140–169 beats/min	62
170–200 beats/min	14
Sinus tachycardia	67
Dysrhythmias	37
Wide pulse pressure	86–100
40–59 mm Hg	38
60–100 mm Hg	62
Tremor	73
Thyrotoxic stare and eyelid retraction	60
Hyperkinesis	55
Heart failure	50
Weakness	23
Coma	18–23
Tender liver	17
Infiltrative ophthalmopathy	17
Somnolence or obtundence	14–46
Psychosis	9–29
Jaundice	9–24

Modified from Wogan JM: Selected endocrine disorders. In: Marx JA, Hockberger RS, Walls RM, editors: *Rosen's emergency medicine: concepts and clinical practice,* ed 5, St. Louis, Mosby, 2002, pp. 1770–1784.

PATHOPHYSIOLOGY
Hypothyroidism

Insufficient levels of circulating thyroid hormone produce the signs and symptoms of hypothyroidism. All the body's functions in effect slow down. In addition, mucopolysaccharides and mucoproteins progressively infiltrate the skin of individuals with chronic hypofunction, lending the skin its characteristic puffy appearance. This hard, nonpitting, mucinous edema, called *myxedema,* is characteristic of hypothyroidism. Initially, the edema does not appear in dependent areas.[28]

Myxedema may also cause significant cardiac enlargement leading to pericardial and pleural effusions and to the cardiovascular and respiratory difficulties associated with hypothyroidism.[25,36] Research has demonstrated that coronary artery disease is often accelerated in clinically hypothyroid patients.[19]

Myxedema coma is the end point of the progression of severe hypothyroidism. The loss of consciousness may be produced by hypothermia, hypoglycemia, or carbon dioxide retention, all of which are present in this clinical condition.

Thyrotoxicosis

Thyrotoxicosis is the result of excessive production of endogenous thyroid hormone by the thyroid gland or excessive administration of exogenous thyroid hormone (as in treatment of hypothyroid states). Clinically observed signs and symptoms relate to the level of these hormones in the blood. Thyroid hormones increase the body's energy consumption and elevate the basal metabolic rate. This increased energy use results in fatigue and weight loss.

Cardiovascular findings in thyrotoxicosis are related to the direct actions of thyroid hormones on the myocardium. They are characterized by a hyperdynamic, electrically excitable state. These findings include an elevated heart rate and increased myocardial irritability. The increased incidence of cardiac problems (e.g., angina pectoris and heart failure) and cardiac symptoms (e.g., palpitations, dyspnea, chest pain) in hyperthyroid individuals is most likely related to the increase in cardiac workload.[18,20] Subclinical cardiac disease may have been present prior to the onset of the hyperthyroid state or in the hypothyroid state before the start of therapy; however, clinically significant cardiac disease becomes evident with the addition of thyroid hormone, which creates the increase in the heart's workload and myocardial oxygen requirement.

In addition, thyrotoxicosis decreases liver function. Jaundice may appear but is readily eliminated through treatment of thyrotoxicosis.[37] Because of the variable degree of liver dysfunction associated with thyrotoxicosis, all drugs and medications metabolized primarily in the liver should be administered judiciously and in smaller than normal doses. Because of the effects of atropine and epinephrine on the heart and cardiovascular systems, their use is contraindicated in severely hyperthyroid individuals.

Thyroid storm, or crisis, is the end point of untreated thyrotoxicosis. The primary difference between thyroid storm and severe thyrotoxicosis is the presence of hyperpyrexia; if left untreated, the body's temperature may reach a lethal level (105°F [40.5°C] or higher) within 24 to 48 hours. In this severe hypermetabolic state, the body's demand for energy overtaxes the cardiovascular system, leading to the production of the clinical signs and symptoms of cardiac dysrhythmia, heart failure, and acute pulmonary edema. Thyroid storm also produces profound delirium, vomiting, diarrhea, and dehydration.

MANAGEMENT

Acute thyroid-related emergencies are unlikely to develop during dental treatment of patients with thyroid disease. When loss of consciousness does occur, management is essentially supportive.

Hypothyroidism

No specific management is necessary for most patients who exhibit clinical evidence of thyroid hypofunction. If the doctor has doubts or concerns after a complete medical and dental evaluation, medical consultation with the patient's primary care physician is warranted before treatment begins.

It is worth noting that hypothyroid patients may be unusually sensitive to the following categories of drugs:

- Sedatives and anxiolytics (e.g., barbiturates, benzodiazepines)
- Opioids (e.g., meperidine and codeine)
- Most other CNS depressants, such as histamine-blockers (antihistamines).

Moderate to severe overdose reactions may develop following administration of "normal" doses of these drugs.

Effective management of the hypothyroid patient is normally achieved through oral administration of desiccated thyroid hormone. In almost all cases, therapy continues for the remainder of the patient's life. Within 30 days of the start of therapy, the patient usually returns to a normal body weight, with all clinical signs and symptoms disappearing. On the whole, the prognosis for treated hypothyroidism is a return to normal health.

Diagnostic clues to the presence of hypothyroidism include

- Cold intolerance
- Weakness
- Fatigue
- Dry, cold, yellow, puffy skin
- Thick tongue

Unconscious patient with history of hypothyroidism

The possibility that the undiagnosed, untreated, clinically hypothyroid patient may lose consciousness and not respond to resuscitative measures is extremely unlikely. More likely is the possibility that a patient may lose consciousness because of a fear of dental treatment. In this situation the individual usually regains consciousness after the steps in the management protocol for any unconscious patient are performed.

Step 1: termination of the dental procedure.

Step 2: P (position).
The unconscious patient is placed in the supine position with the legs elevated slightly.

Step 3: A-B-C (airway-breathing-circulation), basic life support (BLS), as needed.
If a hypothyroid patient loses consciousness, the possibility of myxedema coma must be considered. Management of this situation includes establishment of a patent airway (head tilt–chin lift), assessment of breathing, administration of O_2, and assessment of the adequacy of circulation.

Step 4: D (definitive care):
Step 4a: summoning of medical assistance.
Because the underlying cause of unconsciousness is not a lack of cerebral blood flow or O_2, the hypothyroid patient will not regain consciousness after BLS is initiated. Medical assistance should be sought immediately whenever a patient does not regain consciousness after implementation of BLS.

Step 4b: establishment of an intravenous (IV) line (if available).
If available, an IV infusion of 5% dextrose and water or normal saline may be started before the arrival of emergency personnel. Availability of a patent vein facilitates subsequent medical management of this patient.

Step 4c: administration of O_2.
O_2 may be administered at any time during this emergency. Although O_2 administration will not lead to the recovery of consciousness, no harm can result.

Box 18-3 Management of the unconscious patient with thyroid disease

Hypothyroid patient (myxedema coma)
Hyperthyroid patient (thyroid storm)
Recognize problem
↓
Discontinue dental treatment
↓
Activate office emergency team
↓
P—Position patient supine with feet elevated
↓
A → B → C—Assess and perform basic life support as needed
↓
D—Definitive management:
Activate emergency medical service if recovery not immediate
Establish IV access, if possible
Administer O_2
↓
Discharge or hospitalization of patient as per emergency medical technicians

A, airway; **B,** breathing; **C,** circulation; **D,** definitive care; IV, intravenous; **P,** position.

Step 4d: definitive management.
Definitive management of myxedema coma includes the transport of the individual to a hospital emergency department, the administration of massive IV doses of thyroid hormones (e.g., T_3 or T_4) for several days, and the reversal of hypothermia. Additional therapy may vary according to the patient's clinical state. The mortality rate associated with myxedema coma is high (40%), even with proper, rigorous management (Box 18-3).

Thyrotoxicosis

Hyperthyroid patients often appear nervous and apprehensive. If clinical symptoms are so intense that the doctor remains doubtful as to the nature of the patient's problem, medical consultation is indicated before the start of dental treatment. Although the risk of thyroid storm is minimal, undue stress can induce this acute life-threatening situation. In addition, the use of certain drugs, particularly atropine and epinephrine, may precipitate thyroid crisis; therefore, these drugs should not be administered to clinically hyperthyroid individuals.

The following are diagnostic clues that may prompt a suspicion of thyrotoxicosis:

- Sweating
- Heat intolerance
- Tachycardia
- Warm, thin, soft, moist skin

- Exophthalmos
- Tremor

Unconscious patient with history of thyrotoxicosis

As with the hypothyroid patient, the undiagnosed, untreated, clinically hyperthyroid patient is unlikely to lose consciousness to the point at which resuscitation is impossible. Vasodepressor syncope is a much more likely cause of unconsciousness. In this situation the patient should regain consciousness rapidly after implementation of the basic steps in the management of an unconscious patient.

Step 1: termination of the dental procedure.

Step 2: P (position). The patient is placed in the supine position with the legs elevated slightly.

Step 3: A-B-C or BLS as needed. If a hyperthyroid patient loses consciousness, the possibility of thyroid storm must be seriously considered, especially if the body temperature is elevated. Management of this situation includes implementing the steps of BLS, including establishment of a patent airway, assessment of breathing and circulation, and administration of O_2, as needed.

Step 4: D (definitive care):
Step 4a: summoning of medical assistance.
Because the underlying cause of unconsciousness is not a lack of cerebral blood flow or O_2, the hypothyroid patient will not regain consciousness after these basic procedures are implemented. Medical assistance should be sought immediately whenever the patient does not regain consciousness after the steps of BLS have been performed.

Step 4b: establishment of an IV line (if available). An IV infusion of a 5% solution of dextrose and water or normal saline may be established before emergency personnel arrive. Availability of a patent vein facilitates subsequent medical management of this patient.

Step 4c: administration of O_2. O_2 may be administered at any time during the emergency. Although its administration does not lead to recovery, O_2 cannot harm the individual.

Step 4d: definitive management. Definitive management of thyroid storm includes transport of the patient to a hospital emergency department and administration of large doses of antithyroid drugs (e.g.,

propylthiouracil). Additional therapy includes administration of propranolol to block the adrenergic-mediated effects of thyroid hormones and large doses of glucocorticosteroids to prevent acute adrenal insufficiency. Other measures may include O_2, cold packs, sedation, and careful monitoring of hydration and electrolyte balance. The prognosis is poor for individuals with thyroid storm.

Box 18-3 outlines the management of an unconscious patient with thyroid disease. In addition, the following information may prove useful:

- **Drugs used in management:** No drugs are used to manage thyroid disease in the dental office.
- **Medical assistance required:** If the hyperthyroid or hypothyroid individual loses consciousness, medical assistance is required.

REFERENCES

1. Larsen PR, Davies TF, Schlumberger MJ, Hay ID: Thyroid physiology and diagnostic evaluation of patients with thyroid disorders. In: Larsen PR, Kronenberg HM, editors: *Williams textbook of endocrinology*, ed 10, Philadelphia, WB Saunders, 2003, pp. 331–373.
2. Wogan JM: Selected endocrine disorders, In: Marx JA, Hockberger RS, Walls RM, editors: *Rosen's emergency medicine: concepts and clinical practice*, ed 5, St. Louis, Mosby, 2002, pp. 1770–1784.
3. Wong SC: Children with congenital hypothyroidism are at risk of adult obesity due to early adiposity rebound, *Clin Endocrinol (Oxf)* 61:441–446, 2004.
4. Ord WM: On myxedema, a term proposed to be applied to an essential condition in the cretinoid affection occasionally observed in middle-aged women, *Med Chir Trans London* 61:57, 1877.
5. Jordan RM: Myxedema coma: pathophysiology, therapy and factors affecting prognosis, *Med Clin North Am* 79:185–194, 1995.
6. Rodriguez I, Fluiters E, Perez-Mendez LF, et al.: Factors associated with mortality of patients with myxedema coma: prospective study in 11 cases treated in a single institution, *J Endocrinol* 180:347–350, 2004.
7. von Basedow CA: *Exophthalmos durch Hypertrophie des Zellgewbes in der Augenhohle, Wochenschrift fur die gesammte Heilkunde*, Berlin, 1840. Reprinted in Major RH: *Classic descriptions of disease*, Springfield, IL, Charles C Thomas, 1978.
8. Graves RJ: Newly observed affection of the thyroid gland in females, *London Med Surg J* 7:516–517, 1835. Reprinted in Major RH: *Classic descriptions of disease*, Springfield, IL, Charles C Thomas, 1978.
9. Fliers E, Wiersinga WM: Myxedema coma, *Rev Endocr Metab Disord* 4:137–141, 2003.
10. Pimentel L, Hansen KN: Thyroid disease in the emergency department: a clinical and laboratory review, *J Emerg Med* 28:201–209, 2005.
11. Ai J, Leonhardt JM, Heymann WR: Autoimmune thyroid

diseases: etiology, pathogenesis, and dermatologic mani-festations, *J Am Acad Dermatol* 48:641–659, 2003.

12. Flynn RW, MacDonald TM, Morris AD, et al.: The thyroid epidemiology, audit, and research study: thyroid dysfunction in the general population, *J Clin Endocrinol Metab* 89:3879–3884, 2004.

13. Diez JJ, Iglesias P: Spontaneous subclinical hypothyroidism in patients older than 55 years: an analysis of natural course and risk factors for the development of overt thyroid disease, *J Clin Endocrinol Metab* 89:4890–4897, 2004.

14. Sarlis NJ, Gourgiotis L: Thyroid emergencies, *Rev Endocr Metab Disord* 4:129–136, 2003.

15. Reid JR, Wheeler SF: Hyperthyroidism: diagnosis and treatment, *Am Fam Physician* 72:623–630, 2005.

16. McKeown NJ, Tews MC, Gossain VV, Shah SM: Hyper-thyroidism, *Emerg Med Clin North Am* 23:669–685, 2005.

17. Goldberg PA, Inzucchi SE: Critical issues in endocrinology, *Clin Chest Med* 24:583–606, 2003.

18. Dillmann WH: Thyroid storm, *Curr Ther Endocrinol Metab* 6:81–85, 1997.

19. Imaizumi M, Akahoshi M, Ichimaru S, et al.: Risk for ischemic heart disease and all-cause mortality in subclinical hypothyroidism, *J Clin Endocrinol Metab* 89:3365–3370, 2004.

20. Donatelli M, Assennato P, Abbadi V, et al.: Cardiac changes in subclinical and overt hyperthyroid women: retrospective study, *Int J Cardiol* 90:159–164, 2003.

21. Kaplan MM, Sarne DH, Schneider AB: In search of the impossible dream? Thyroid hormone replacement therapy that treats all symptoms in all hypothyroid patients, *J Clin Endocrinol Metab* 88:4540–4542, 2003.

22. Pearce EN, Braverman LE: Hyperthyroidism: advantages and disadvantages of medical therapy, *Surg Clin North Am* 84:833–847, 2004.

23. American Academy of Family Physicians: Information from your family doctor. Treating hyperthyroidism, *Am Fam Physician* 72:635–636, 2005.

24. Urbanic RC, Mazzaferri EL: Thyrotoxic crisis and myxedema coma, *Heart Lung* 7:435–447, 1978.

25. Barnes BO, Barnes CW: *Solved: the riddle of heart attacks,* Fort Collins, CO, Robinson, 1976.

26. Gaitan E, Cooper DS: Primary hypothyroidism, *Curr Ther Endocrinol Metab* 6:94–98, 1997.

27. Hierholzer K, Finke R: Myxedema, *Kidney Int Suppl* 9:S82–S89, 1997.

28. Pittman CS, Zayed AA: Myxedema coma, *Curr Ther Endocrinol Metab* 6:98–101, 1997.

29. Khaleeli AA, Griffith DG, Edwards RHT: The clinical presentation of hypothyroid myopathy, *Clin Endocrinol (Oxf)* 19:365–376, 1983.

30. Tsitouras PD: Myxedema coma, *Clin Geriatr Med* 11:251–258, 1995.

31. Singer PA: Hypothyroidism. In: Rakel RE, Bope ET, editors: *Conn's current therapy,* ed 57, Philadelphia, WB Saunders, 2005, pp. 760–763.

32. Werner SC: Classification of the eye changes in Graves' disease, *Am J Ophthalmol* 68:646–648, 1969.

33. Werner SC: Modification of the classification of eye changes in Graves' disease, *Am J Ophthalmol* 83:725–727, 1977.

34. Perros P, Crombie AL, Matthews JNS, et al.: Age and gender influence the severity of thyroid-associated ophthal-mopathy: a study of 101 patients attending a combined thyroid-eye clinic, *Clin Endocrinol* 38:367–372, 1993.

35. Bartalena L, Marcocci C, Pinchera A: Treating severe Graves' ophthalmopathy, *Baillieres Clin Endocrinol Metab* 11:521–536, 1997.

36. Gomberg-Maitland M, Frishman WH: Thyroid hormone and cardiovascular disease, *Am Heart J* 135:187–196, 1998.

37. Tews MC, Shah SM, Gossain VV: Hypothyroidism: mimicker of common complaints, *Emerg Med Clin North Am* 23:649–667, 2005.

CHAPTER 19

Cerebrovascular Accident

Stroke (cerebrovascular accident [CVA]) is the third leading cause of death in the United States and the leading cause of adult disability.[1] It afflicts over 700,000 patients per year (500,000 first strokes, 200,000 recurrent), with an in-hospital mortality of almost 15% and a 30-day mortality of 20% to 25%.[2-4] Even among survivors, over half are left with a permanent disability and one third need assistance in the activities of daily living.[5] Almost 2% of all 9-1-1 calls and 4% of hospital admissions from the emergency department involve patients with potential strokes.[6,7]

CVA can be defined as any vascular injury that reduces cerebral blood flow to a specific region of the brain, causing neurologic impairment. The onset of symptoms may be sudden or slow and may result in transient or permanent loss of neurologic function. Eighty-eight percent of all strokes are ischemic, caused by an occlusion of the cerebral vessel.[3,4] The rest are hemorrhagic strokes caused by rupture of the blood vessel into the parenchyma of the brain (intracerebral hemorrhage) (9%) or into the subarachnoid space (subarachnoid hemorrhage) (3%).[8]

CVA is a focal neurologic disorder caused by destruction of brain substance as a result of intracerebral hemorrhage, thrombosis, embolism, or vascular insufficiency. It is also known as *stroke, cerebral apoplexy*, and *"brain attack."*[9] The term *brain attack* has gained popularity in recent years in order to stress the need of patients with CVA to receive immediate emergency medical care; the parallel to the term *heart attack* is intentional.

Although mortality rates for the different forms of CVA vary considerably, the overall death rate is relatively high. In 2003, 157,804 individuals in the United States died as a result of CVA, making it the third-leading cause of death in the country, behind only cancer (second) and heart disease (first).[1,10] Most stroke victims survive, but they often have significant disability. The frequency with which CVAs occur is emphasized by the fact that approximately 25% of routine autopsies demonstrate evidence of CVA, even though the patient may never have exhibited evidence of stroke.

CVA is the most common form of brain disease. The average age of an individual at the time of the first CVA is approximately 64 years. In addition, 28% of all CVAs occur in individuals under 65 years. Approximately 3% to 4% of all strokes occur in patients between ages 15 and 45 years.[8]

The incidence of stroke in children age 1 to 14 years is approximately 2.7 per 100,000 per year.[11] Although stroke can occur at any age between infancy and childhood, such episodes occur most frequently between 1 and 5 years.[12] Cyanotic heart disease is the most common underlying systemic disorder that predisposes children to stroke. Sickle cell disease is the most important cause of ischemic stroke among African-American children.[13]

In 2003, stroke accounted for about 1 in 5 deaths in the United States, with about 50% of these deaths occurring out of the hospital.[1] Eight percent to 12% of ischemic strokes and about 38% of hemorrhagic strokes result in death within 30 days.[14] In 2003, the overall death rate for stroke was 54.3%.[1] Death rates were 51.9% for white men, 78.8% for black men, 50.5% for white women, and 69.1% for black women.[1]

For Hispanic or Latino persons, the 2002 age-adjusted death rate for strokes was 44.3% for men and 38.6% for women. Death rates were 50.8% for Asian or Pacific Islander men and 45.4% for women. Among American Indian or Alaska natives, death rates were 37.1% for men and 38.0% for women.[1]

Because women live longer than men, more women die of stroke each year. Women accounted for 61.0% of stroke deaths in the United States in 2003.[1] In 2002, the mean age of stroke death was 79.6 years; however, the mean age at death from stroke was lower in men than in women.[1]

In addition, a transient ischemic attack (TIA, a mini-stroke that lasts less than 24 hours), shows a prevalence of 2.7% in men 65 to 69 years of age and 3.6% for those age 75 to 79 years.[9] For women, the prevalence of TIA is 1.6% for those age 65 to 69 years and 4.1% for those age 75 to 79 years.[15] Approximately 50% of patients experiencing a TIA do not report it to their health care provider.[16] After a TIA, the 90-day risk of stroke is 3% to 17.3%, highest within the first 30 days.[17] Up to 25% of TIA victims die within 1 year,[18] with a 10-year stroke risk of 18.8%.[19] The combined 10-year risk of death from stroke, myocardial infarction, or vascular disease among TIA victims is 42.8%.[19]

■ CLASSIFICATION

CVA is usually classified by cause. Two major classes of stroke are occlusive and hemorrhagic; a lacunar infarction is a type of occlusive stroke. Hemorrhagic stroke may be either intracerebral hemorrhage or subarachnoid hemorrhage. Table 19-1 presents the various forms of CVA and their relative incidence. In addition to the forms of CVA presented in the table, a syndrome variously known *TIA, transient cerebral ischemia, incipient stroke,* or *mini-stroke* also exists. It consists of brief episodes of cerebral ischemia that result in no permanent neurologic damage (neurologic signs and symptoms resolve within 24 hours), whereas CVA victims almost always suffer some degree of permanent neurologic damage.

Lacunar infarction

Lacunar infarcts are among the most common cerebrovascular lesions. Small in size (<5 mm in diameter), lacunar infarcts often are associated with poorly controlled hypertension (80% to 90% of persons developing lacunar stroke have high blood pressure) or diabetes. They involve penetration of cerebral arterial branches that lie deep in the cerebrum or brain stem.[20,21] Prognosis for recovery from the deficits produced by

TABLE 19-1 Classification of cerebrovascular disease

Cause	Approximate % of all CVAs	Initial mortality rate (%)	Recurrence rate (%)
CEREBRAL ISCHEMIA AND INFARCTION	88	30	*
Atherosclerosis and thrombosis	81	*	20
Cerebral embolism	7	*	*
INTRACRANIAL HEMORRHAGE	12	80	*
Arterial aneurysms	*	45	33
Hypertensive vascular disease	*	50	rare

CVA, cerebrovascular accident; *, unknown.

lacunar infarction is usually good, with many individuals experiencing partial or complete resolution over the subsequent 4 to 6 weeks.[21]

Cerebral infarction

The most prevalent form of CVA is the occlusive stroke, accounting for approximately 88% of all CVAs. Occlusive stroke most commonly results from atherosclerotic disease and cardiac abnormalities. Thrombosis of intracranial and extracranial arteries and cerebral embolization from various sites throughout the body are the primary causes of cerebral infarction. *Cerebral infarction* may be defined as the death of neural (brain) tissue as a result of ischemia. The primary cause of ischemia is a prolonged decrease in blood flow to the brain. Cerebral infarction is most common in individuals 60 to 69 years of age and occurs more frequently in men (a 2:1 ratio).[22]

Cerebral infarction is usually accompanied by abnormalities in the arterial blood supply from the heart to the brain. In most instances, atherosclerosis (which is found commonly in certain anatomic areas) produces this alteration in arterial blood supply. Emboli most often originate in a heart in atrial fibrillation and after myocardial infarction,[23,24] and in neck veins, specifically in the internal carotid artery at the carotid bifurcation in the neck and the junction of the vertebral and basilar arteries (Figure 19-1). By the third decade of a normal adult's life, there is usually significant atherosclerotic plaque in arteries. However, in most cases, clinical evidence, in the form of acute myocardial infarction or cerebral infarction, does not develop until the individual reaches the fifth or sixth decade of life.

Narrowing of atherosclerotic vessels must be significant (a luminal reduction of approximately 80% to 90%) before blood flow drops to clinically significant levels. Normal cerebral blood flow is 40 to 60 mL/100 g of brain per minute. When the cerebral blood flow cerebral blood flow falls below 15 to 18 mL/100 g of

brain per minute, physiologic changes occur. The brain loses electrical activity and becomes electrically "silent," although neuronal integrity and function remain intact. Clinically, electrically silent areas of brain manifest a neurologic deficit even though the brain cells are still viable. When cerebral blood flow falls below 10 mL/100 g of brain per minute, cell membrane failure occurs.[8] A second important factor in atherosclerotic vessels is the formation of thrombi (blood clots). Thrombus formation is more likely to occur in atherosclerotic than in nonatherosclerotic vessels. In atherosclerosis or thrombosis, blood flow to the area of the brain distal to the vessel narrowing, or occlusion, is severely reduced so that a portion of brain tissue becomes ischemic, and its cells become necrotic and shrunken or infarcted, producing signs and symptoms of neurologic deficit. Patients with certain diseases have been shown to be more likely to develop atherosclerosis, especially at relatively early ages, and to experience more severe forms of the condition. Foremost among these diseases are high blood pressure and diabetes mellitus.[25,26] Acute episodes of cerebral ischemia and infarction may develop at any time; however, approximately 20% occur during sleep.

Cerebral embolization is a causative factor in approximately 7% of CVAs. Embolization of a mural thrombus in patients with atrial fibrillation is the most common source of these emboli, and patients who have atrial fibrillation are 5 to 17 times more likely to develop a stroke than those who do not have this condition.[23] Other causes include prosthetic heart valves, acute myocardial infarction, bacterial endocarditis, mitral valve prolapse, and thyrotoxicosis with atrial fibrillation.[27] Cerebral embolization occurs throughout the age spectrum of 20 to 70 years; however, it is most frequent in individuals older than 40 years.

Transient ischemic attack (TIA)

TIA, also termed *incipient stroke, transient cerebral ischemia,* or *mini-stroke,* is considered a "temporary

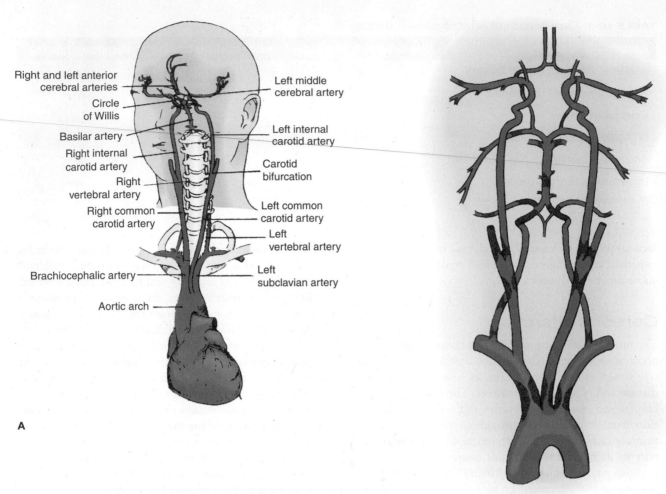

A

Right and left anterior cerebral arteries

Circle of Willis

Basilar artery

Right internal carotid artery

Right vertebral artery

Right common carotid artery

Brachiocephalic artery

Aortic arch

Left middle cerebral artery

Left internal carotid artery

Carotid bifurcation

Left common carotid artery

Left vertebral artery

Left subclavian artery

C

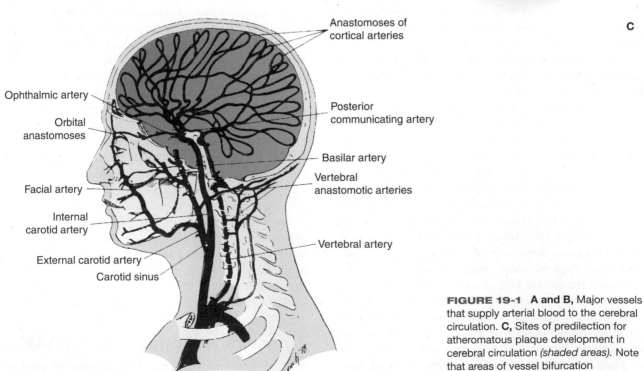

B

Anastomoses of cortical arteries

Ophthalmic artery

Orbital anastomoses

Facial artery

Internal carotid artery

External carotid artery

Carotid sinus

Posterior communicating artery

Basilar artery

Vertebral anastomotic arteries

Vertebral artery

FIGURE 19-1 **A and B,** Major vessels that supply arterial blood to the cerebral circulation. **C,** Sites of predilection for atheromatous plaque development in cerebral circulation *(shaded areas).* Note that areas of vessel bifurcation commonly are involved.

stroke" in much the same manner that angina pectoris is considered a "temporary heart attack." TIA is defined as a neurologic deficit that has complete clinical resolution within 24 hours.[8] TIAs rarely last more than 8 hours, and most last less than 30 minutes. Attacks may occur many times a day or at weekly or monthly intervals. Three or more TIAs occurring within 72 hours are termed *crescendo TIAs*. In the periods between episodes, the patient is asymptomatic. Platelet, fibrin, or other atherosclerotic embolic material from the neck or heart may lodge in a cerebral vessel and interfere transiently with blood flow, causing the TIA.[28]

Clinically, TIAs signal the existence of a significant degree of cerebrovascular disease and clearly demonstrate a potential danger of cerebral infarction.[29] Although clinical deficits resolve within 24 hours, studies demonstrate that up to 64% have computed tomography and 81% have magnetic resonance imaging evidence of an infarction.[30,31]

Hemorrhagic stroke: intracerebral hemorrhage and subarachnoid hemorrhage

The second major category of CVA is hemorrhagic stroke, classified according into the location of the bleed as intracerebral or subarachnoid hemorrhage. The latter occurs on the surface of the brain within the subarachnoid space, whereas the former occurs within the parenchyma of the brain.

Hemorrhagic stroke is responsible for approximately 10% of all acute cases of cerebrovascular disease and, regardless of the specific cause, represents a serious problem with a high mortality rate. The 30-day mortality rate for intracerebral hemorrhage is up to 50%, with half of the deaths occurring within the first 2 days.[32] It occurs most commonly in individuals older than 50 years of age. It may develop in any blood vessel, but the usual source of bleeding is arterial. Most victims have long-standing hypertension.[8]

The two major sources of intracerebral hemorrhage are ruptured arterial aneurysms and hypertensive vascular disease. In both cases the walls of the blood vessels involved are defective—congenital defects in the former and acquired defects in the latter—producing weakened areas. The cause of the actual vessel wall rupture is most likely an acute change or elevation in systolic blood pressure. Subarachnoid hemorrhage most commonly occurs when an aneurysm ruptures as a result of weakened vessel walls at arterial bifurcations.[33] Rupture occurs with a sudden increase in local pressure within a critically stretched aneurysm sac. Intracerebral hemorrhage occurs when weakened arterioles rupture as a result of chronic, systemic hypertension.[8]

Clinically, most cases of intracerebral hemorrhage occur while patients are engaged in normal activities, such as heavy lifting or straining while passing a stool, factors that are categorized as physical stress and are associated with elevations in blood pressure. Although intracerebral hemorrhage is responsible for only 10% of all CVAs, it represents more of a potential risk to the dental practitioner, who must manage acutely anxious patients during potentially painful dental procedures. Both anxiety and pain are associated with potentially significant increases in the heart rate and blood pressure (primarily systolic) of the patient, making development of a hemorrhagic CVA more likely in the dental environment than an ischemic stroke.

Survivors of episodes of cerebrovascular disease have a high risk of recurrence (see Table 19-1). Within 12 to 24 months, 20% of individuals who have suffered CVAs as a result of atherosclerotic vascular disease experience repeat attacks; more than 33% of patients with ruptured aneurysms develop recurrent episodes.[34] However, the risk of recurrent CVA is not the major threat to survival of these patients. Cardiovascular disease is *the* major limiting factor for the patient who has had a CVA.

More than 50% of post-CVA victims die of acute myocardial infarction or heart failure.[35] These patients represent an increased risk during dental treatment. Thorough evaluation of such patients before the start of dental treatment and special considerations during treatment can minimize potential risk.

■ PREDISPOSING FACTORS

Many factors have been shown to significantly increase the risk of having a CVA (Table 19-2). Factors include high blood pressure (hypertension), diabetes mellitus, cardiac enlargement (as determined with electrocardiography), hypercholesterolemia, use of oral contraceptives, and cigarette smoking. Some early reports associated the use of birth control pills with a ninefold increased risk of thrombotic stroke,[36] but more recent analyses suggest that this risk is confined to women on oral contraceptives who also smoke cigarettes.[37–39]

Consistently elevated blood pressure is a major risk factor in the development of both occlusive and hemorrhagic stroke. Evidence from the National Heart, Lung, and Blood Institute's Framingham Heart study has led to the believe that high blood pressure may be the major predisposing factor in the development of a hemorrhagic CVA.[40] The risk that an individual may develop a hemorrhagic CVA increases an estimated 30% for every 10–mm Hg elevation of the systolic blood pressure above 160 mm Hg.[41] Prolonged periods of elevated

TABLE 19-2 Types of stroke and associated risk factors

Stroke syndrome	Risk factors
OCCLUSIVE	
Emboli	Atrial fibrillation
Thrombi	Acute myocardial infarction
TIA	Abnormal valves
Reversible ischemic neurologic deficit	Hypertension
	Smoking
Progressive	Lipids
Completed	Age
	Diabetes
	Prior TIA
Lacunar	Hypertension (90%)
HEMORRHAGIC	
Subarachnoid	None
Intracerebral	Hypertension (50%)
Cerebellar	Hypertension (50%)

TIA, transient ischemic attack.

blood pressure also produce thickening and fibrinoid degeneration of cerebral arteries. Atherosclerosis develops at earlier ages and to more severe degrees in patients with elevated blood pressure.

The normal response of cerebral arteries to elevations in blood pressure is yet another mechanism by which high blood pressure promotes an increased incidence of CVA. Cerebral arteries, primarily smaller ones, constrict in response to blood pressure elevations. Constriction reduces local cerebral blood flow, leading to ischemia of localized areas of the brain that may produce infarction if prolonged.

It is worth repeating that high blood pressure is the single greatest risk factor in the development of all forms of cerebrovascular disease. Fortunately, however, high blood pressure is also the only major risk factor that, if reversed, is associated with a decreased incidence of CVA. This fact is of particular importance to the dental profession because so many dental treatments are associated with pain, either real or imagined, which increases the patient's fear. A significant percentage of dental patients will exhibit signs of increased cardiovascular activity. Clinical manifestations of such increases include elevated blood pressure and increased heart rate. In patients with evidence of other CVA risk factors, such as diabetes and atherosclerosis, this increase in cardiovascular activity might precipitate an acute CVA, more likely the more ominous hemorrhagic type.

The patient who has had a CVA represents an even greater risk in the dental office. Chances are good that CVA survivors may recover some degree of function. According to 2002 National Heart, Lung, and Blood Institute statistics for ischemic stroke survivors, 50% had some degree of hemiparesis, 30% were unable to walk without some assistance, 26% were dependent in activities of daily living, 19% had aphasia, 35% had depressive symptoms, and 26% were living in a nursing home.[42]

CVA is the leading cause of serious, long-term disability in the United States, and survivors may be correctly termed "the walking wounded." As McCarthy[43] stated, CVA survivors are "accidents waiting to happen." An independently mobile post-CVA patient expects to receive dental treatment; however, a point worth stressing is that the recurrence rate for CVA is high (see Table 19-1) and that factors such as pain and anxiety only add to the risk such a patient presents. Proper management of pain and anxiety are of the utmost importance in the treatment of a patient who has had a CVA.

■ PREVENTION

Prevention of the occurrence or recurrence of CVA is based on the recognition of the risk factors discussed and possible modifications in dental treatment that accommodate the diminished ability of the patient to effectively handle stress. The medical history questionnaire contains many questions that may prompt the patient to discuss problems that may indicate cerebrovascular complications. In addition, the dialogue history may help in the determination of what modifications if any are needed.

✎ MEDICAL HISTORY QUESTIONNAIRE

Section I, Circle Appropriate Answer:

Question 1: Is your general health good?

Question 2: Has there been a change in your health within the last year?

Question 3: Have you been hospitalized or had a serious illness in the last three years?

Question 4: Are you being treated by a physician now? For what?

  Comment: These are general survey question designed to detect known diseases and other significant medical problems. If stroke is mentioned, then a thorough dialogue history must follow.

Section II, Have You Experienced:

Question 18: Dizziness?

Question 19: Ringing in the ears?

Question 20: Headaches?

Question 21: Fainting spells?

Question 22: Blurred vision?

Question 23: Seizures?

Comment: The clinical signs and symptoms presented in these questions may indicate the prior occurrence of TIA. In such cases, further patient evaluation is warranted through dialogue history.

Section III, Do You Have or Have You Had:

Question 33: Stroke, hardening of the arteries?

Comment: A positive response to a history of stroke requires that a dialogue history be conducted to determine the degree to which that individual is at risk during dental treatment.

Question 34: High blood pressure?

Comment: High blood pressure is the single most important risk factor in causing CVA and the only risk factor that if managed decreases the risk of CVA. High blood pressure is present in more than two thirds of patients who have had a CVA. Routine blood pressure screening of all prospective dental patients and all medically compromised individuals has significantly helped to minimize the development of CVA and other acute high blood pressure sequelae, such as acute myocardial infarction and renal dysfunction, in dental patients.

Section IV, Do You Have or Have You Had:

Question 56: Hospitalization?

Question 58: Surgeries?

Comment: Persons having a stroke are hospitalized for varying lengths of time. Seek to determine the cause of hospitalization and if any surgical procedure was performed.

Section V, Are You Taking:

Question 62: Drugs, medications, over-the-counter medicines (including aspirin), natural remedies?

Comment: In the past, all CVA patients received anticoagulant therapy. Today, these drugs are used more cautiously in light of data from several studies demonstrating that there is little benefit to be gained from their administration in most forms of stroke and that they may, in fact, increase the risk of hemorrhage.[44,45] Anticoagulant therapy is valuable, however, in the treatment of patients who have had an embolic stroke when there is a cardiac source for the embolization, such as atrial fibrillation or valvular disease.[46] Antiplatelet therapy using dipyridamole (Persantine) or aspirin has been successful in the reduction of recurrent TIAs, but has not yet been demonstrated to decrease the long-term risk of stroke.[47]

Antihypertensive drugs are prescribed for the 66% of patients who have had a CVA whose blood pressures are elevated. The treating dentist must be aware of the potential side effects associated with each drug and possible interactions with commonly used dental drugs (e.g., propranolol and epinephrine).[48] Postural hypotension is a common side effect of many antihypertensive drugs. In addition, the doctor should have available

a variety of drug references, including ePocrates.com and the *ADA Guide to Dental Therapeutics.*[49,50]

Dialogue history

Question: When did you have your stroke (CVA)?

Question: What type of stroke did you suffer?

Question: Were you hospitalized? If so, for how long?

Comment: These questions seek basic information about the nature and severity of the CVA (ischemic [occlusive] or hemorrhagic). Following a stroke, a degree of recovery from neurologic deficit occurs. Although the length of time varies from patient to patient, considerable improvement usually occurs within the first 6 months. All but emergency dental treatment should be withheld during this period. Patients are routinely classified according to the American Society of Anesthesiologists (ASA) as a type for 6 months, at which time the risk is reevaluated.[51]

Question: What degree of neurologic deficit (paralysis) did you suffer after the CVA, and what degree of function have you recovered?

Comment: Although motor deficit (hemiplegia) may be fairly obvious in a CVA survivor, minor degrees of neurologic deficit may be less obvious. Patients are normally willing to discuss these problems with their doctor.

Question: What medications are you currently taking?

Comment: Question 62 of the medical history questionnaire should be referred to for discussion. Many patients who have had a CVA receive antihypertensive and antiplatelet drugs in their long-term management.

Question: If you experienced high blood pressure at the time of the CVA, how high or low was your blood pressure when you suffered the CVA?

Question: How often do you measure your blood pressure, and what is the normal reading?

Comment: A large percentage of patients had previously undetected high blood pressure before their stroke. Patients who are aware of their high blood pressure and seek to lower it monitor their blood pressures regularly. These recordings may serve as reference points to compare with the recordings obtained in the dental office environment. In general, the blood pressure of a patient who has had a CVA should not be elevated significantly.

Question: Have you ever experienced episodes of unexplained dizziness, numbness of the extremities, or speech defects?

Comment: Transient episodes of cerebral ischemia may produce fainting or dizzy spells. These episodes may occur daily or more infrequently. In many instances the patient is aware of the TIA and is receiving drug therapy (e.g., anticoagulant, antihypertensive, or antiplatelet drugs) to reduce the risk of CVA. Such patients should be managed as though they have suffered a CVA (ASA II or III). If a patient with no history of CVA experiences signs and symptoms of unexplained dizziness, numbness of the extremities, or speech defects, immediate consultation with the patient's primary care physician is warranted prior to the start of any dental treatment.

Physical examination

Physical evaluation of patients who have had a CVA should include a thorough visual examination to determine the extent of any residual neurologic deficit. The exam should include the recording of vital signs, including blood pressure, heart rate and rhythm, and respiratory rate.

Vital signs

Proper technique is essential for the accurate measurement of blood pressure (see Chapter 2). The medical risk associated with elevated blood pressure increases steadily with each millimeter of mercury that the blood pressure rises; no blood pressure exists below which risk is absent and above which risk increases. Therefore, guidelines for clinical use must be provided (see Table 2-3).

At the start of each dental appointment the doctor should be aware of the current blood pressure of the post-CVA patient. Because marked elevations in blood pressure increase the risk of recurrent CVAs, such elevations may be life-threatening. Guidelines indicate that any adult patient with a blood pressure of 200 mm Hg systolic or 115 mm Hg diastolic or above should not receive elective dental treatment until the blood pressure is brought under better control (for example, an ASA IV patient becoming an ASA III or II). This usually necessitates immediate medical consultation and delaying dental care while antihypertensive therapy is begun or corrected. Physical status (ASA) III blood pressure (between 160 and 199 mm Hg systolic and between 95 and 114 mm Hg diastolic) in a patient who has had a CVA warrants immediate medical consultation prior to the start of any dental treatment.

Apprehension

The presence of dentally induced fear should be determined. Anxiety leads to an increase in circulating blood levels of the catecholamines epinephrine and norepinephrine, which increase the heart rate and blood pressure.

Dental therapy considerations

The post-CVA patient represents an increased risk during dental treatment. Several basic factors must be considered in the management of such patients.

Length of time elapsed since the CVA

These patients should not undergo elective dental care within 6 months of the episode. The risk of recurrence is presumably greater during this time. Emergency care for pain or infection should be managed, if at all possible, noninvasively with medications. All invasive dental treatments should be delayed, if possible, or carried out in a controlled environment, if absolutely necessary. The clinic of a hospital or teaching institution (e.g., a dental school or hospital training program) might prove to be a more appropriate site for invasive dental treatment in the higher-risk patient.

Minimization of stress

The stress reduction protocol is ideal for use on patients who have had a CVA. Of importance are the following:

- Short, morning appointments that do not exceed the patient's limit of tolerance
- Effective pain control (e.g., local anesthetics with epinephrine in 1:200,000 or 1:100,000 concentrations used in the smallest appropriate volumes)
- Psychosedation during treatment (e.g., with nitrous oxide and oxygen inhalation sedation or light oral sedation)

NOTE: *All CNS depressants are relatively contraindicated in post-CVA patients. Any such depressant may pro-duce hypoxia, leading to the aggravation of confusion, aphasia, and other complications associated with CVA. In my experience, light levels of sedation, such as those produced with nitrous oxide and O_2 or the oral benzodiazepines, have proved safe and highly effective in the reduction of stress in post-CVA patients. These techniques should be used only if a particular condition warrants them.*

- Avoidance of the epinephrine-impregnated gingival retraction cord

Assessment of when the post-CVA patient is too great a risk for treatment

Blood pressure and heart rate are indicators of the patient's cardiovascular status at the time of dental treatment. Marked elevation in blood pressure should be viewed with great concern and dental treatment withheld until consultation with the patients primary care physician is obtained or corrective therapy achieved.

Recommended patient management for ASA adult blood pressure categories is modified in patients have had a CVA. It is this author's recommendation that medical consultation with the patient's primary care physician be sought when blood pressure increases significantly compared with previous measurements or when it exceeds 160 mm Hg (systolic) in the post-CVA patient (when no previous blood pressure readings are available). These patients should not receive elective dental treatment for 6 months after the episode.

NOTE: *Routine preoperative monitoring of blood pressure in all post-CVA patients is of utmost importance in the prevention of recurrent episodes.*

Assessment of bleeding

Most CVA survivors and those who suffer TIAs receive antiplatelet (aspirin) or anticoagulant therapy to reduce the morbidity and mortality associated with recurrent strokes. If a patient is receiving such drugs, medical consultation is indicated before any dental procedures that may be associated with significant bleeding are undertaken. Although excessive hemorrhage in the post-CVA patient rarely presents a clinical problem in dentistry, both the dentist and the physician must consider the possibility and take safeguards against it:

- Proceed with dental treatment without altering the anticoagulant blood level, which may increase postoperative bleeding.
- Lower the prothrombin time (i.e., decrease anticoagulant levels) before the procedure to decrease the risk of excessive bleeding with a possible increased risk of CVA.
- Alter the dental treatment plan to avoid excessive bleeding in instances in which the risk of reducing the prothrombin time is too great.

In most situations, dental treatment may proceed without altering the patient's anticoagulant drug therapy or difficulty with excessive bleeding.

Prothrombin time measures vitamin K–dependent clotting ability and is used to screen for bleeding disorders and to monitor patients who are receiving anticoagulants. The international normalized ratio (INR) is used in place of prothrombin time because it reduces interlaboratory variability in prothrombin time reporting. Normal values for an adult are between 11 and 13 seconds. The INR target range for the prevention and treatment of nonvalvular thromboembolic disease is 2 to 3.[49] In addition, bleeding time should be determined for patients receiving antiplatelet therapy with aspirin or dipyridamole. Normal range for bleeding time is 3 to 8 minutes.[49]

When a patient with an elevated INR is treated, the doctor should consider several of the following precautionary steps to minimize the risk of significant postoperative bleeding:

- Advice to the patient and primary care physician on the possible need for vitamin K if excessive bleeding occurs
- Use of hemostatic agents, such as oxidized cellulose, in extraction sockets
- Use of multiple sutures in surgical extraction sites and periodontal surgery areas
- Use of pressure packs for 6 to 12 hours after surgery (longer if necessary)
- Availability of the treating doctor via telephone for 24 hours after treatment

The doctor called on to manage a patient who has previously experienced a CVA should not proceed with the contemplated dental care until there is no doubt about the physical ability of this patient to safely tolerate the planned treatment. Whenever doubt or concern persists, discussion of the contemplated dental procedures and the physical status of the patient with the physician is strongly recommended (Table 19-3).

NOTE: *Patients with a history of TIAs should be managed the same as those with a history of CVA.*

■ CLINICAL MANIFESTATIONS

Signs and symptoms of cerebrovascular disease vary, depending on the area of the brain and type of CVA (Box 19-1, Table 19-4). The onset may be violent; the patient may fall to the ground, unmoving, exhibiting

TABLE 19-3 Physical status classifications for CVA and TIA

History	Physical status (ASA)	Dental therapy considerations
One documented CVA at least 6 months before treatment; no residual neurologic deficit or history of TIA	II	ASA II considerations include the following: • Light levels of sedation only • Routine postoperative follow-up via telephone
One or more documented CVAs at least 6 months before treatment; some degree of neurologic deficit evident	III	ASA III considerations include the following: • Light levels of sedation only • Routine follow-up via telephone
Documented CVA within 6 months of treatment with or without residual neurologic deficit	IV	ASA IV considerations

ASA, American Society of Anesthesiologists; CVA, cerebrovascular accident; TIA, transient ischemic attack.

Box 19-1 Clinical manifestations of CVAs

INFARCTION
Gradual onset of signs and symptoms (minutes to hours to days)
TIA frequently preceding
Headache, usually mild
Neurologic signs and symptoms*
Transient monocular blindness—TIA

EMBOLISM
Abrupt onset of signs and symptoms (seconds)
Mild headache preceding neurologic signs and symptoms* by several hours

HEMORRHAGE
Abrupt onset of signs and symptoms (seconds)
Sudden, violent headache
Nausea and vomiting
Chills and sweating
Dizziness and vertigo
Neurologic signs and symptoms*
Loss of consciousness

CVA, cerebrovascular accident; TIA, transient ischemic attack.
*Neurologic signs and symptoms include the following: paralysis on one side of the body, difficulty in breathing and swallowing, inability to speak or slurring of speech, loss of bladder and bowel control, pupils that are unequal in size.

TABLE 19-4 Clinical findings associated with ischemic stroke, ICH, and SAH

Symptom	Ischemic stroke	ICH	SAH
Headache	11–17%	33–41%	78–87%
Vomiting	8–11%	29–46%	45–48%
Decreased level of consciousness	13–15%	39–57%	48–68%
Seizure	0.3–3%	6–7%	7%

ICH, intracerebral hemorrhage; SAH, subarachnoid hemorrhage.
Data from Bogousslavsky J, Van Melle G, Regli F: The Lausanne Stroke Registry: analysis of 1,000 consecutive patients with first stroke, *Stroke* 19:1083–1092, 1988; Foulkes MA, Wolf PA, Price TR, et al.: The Stroke Data Bank: design, methods, and baseline characteristics, *Stroke* 19:547–554, 1988; and Mohr JP, Caplan LR, Melski JW, et al.: The Harvard Cooperative Stroke Registry: a prospective registry, *Neurology* 28:754–762, 1978.

a flushed face and bounding pulse. Respiratory efforts may be slow, and one arm and leg may become flaccid. In some cases the onset may be more gradual, with no alteration in consciousness and only minimal impairments in speech, thought, motor, and sensory functions.

Commonly observed signs and symptoms of CVAs include headaches, dizziness and vertigo, drowsiness, sweating and chills, nausea, and vomiting. Loss of consciousness, a particularly ominous sign, and convulsive movements are much less common. Weakness or paralysis occurs in the extremities contralateral to the CVA. Speech defects (aphasia) also may be noted.

Transient ischemic attack

As with all CVAs, clinical manifestations of TIAs vary according to the area of the brain affected; however, the symptoms in any given individual tend to be constant. The onset is abrupt and without warning, and recovery usually is rapid, often within a few minutes. Most TIAs cause transient numbness or weakness of the contralateral extremities (legs, arms, hands), which many patients describe as a feeling of "pins and needles." Transient monocular blindness is a distinctive, common sign of TIA. A gray-black shade progressively obscures all or part of the vision in the involved eye. The shade later recedes painlessly as the tiny embolus dislodges

from the retinal artery.[8] During a TIA, consciousness is usually unimpaired, although the thought process may be dulled.

Transient ischemic episodes normally last about 2 to 10 minutes, though by definition they may last for up to 24 hours. The rate of frequency varies from patient to patient. Crescendo TIAs are three or more TIAs occurring within a 72-hour period.

Cerebral infarction

Patients who suffer cerebral infarction as a result of atherosclerotic changes in cerebral blood vessels or thrombosis may experience a sudden onset or may encounter a slow, insidious onset (neurologic signs and symptoms appearing over a period of hours to days). Headaches, if present, are usually mild and generally limited to the side of the infarction. Vomiting is rare, and significant obtundation is unusual unless the infarction involves a massive area of the brain or the brain stem or occurs in a previously diseased brain.

Cerebral embolism

A CVA that occurs as a result of embolism differs clinically from other CVAs in that the onset of symptoms is usually abrupt. A mild headache is the first symptom, and it normally precedes by several hours the onset of neurologic symptoms, which occur on the contralateral side of the body only. Seizures usually herald the onset of a thrombotic stroke but are not specific indicators for this condition.[52,53]

Lacunar strokes, a subtype of thrombotic stroke, occur almost exclusively in patients with high blood pressure. They are small, well-localized infarcts with resultant characteristic neurologic abnormalities. Lacunar strokes are abrupt in onset, stabilize over a period of a few days, and do not affect higher-language function or consciousness.[20]

Cerebral hemorrhage

Because of the stressful nature of dental treatment and its possible effects on cardiovascular function, intracerebral hemorrhage and subarachnoid hemorrhage are the more likely forms of CVA to develop in a dental setting. The classic presentation of signs and symptoms is the sudden onset of headache, vomiting, severely elevated blood pressure, and focal neurologic deficits that progress over minutes.[8] Victims have described the headache as "excruciating," "intense," and "the worst I have ever experienced." The headache is at first localized but gradually becomes generalized. Other clinical signs and symptoms include nausea and vomiting, chills and sweating, dizziness, and vertigo. Signs of neurologic deficit may occur at any time but usually occur several hours after the onset. Severe cases are characterized by confusion, coma, or death.[10]

Hemorrhagic CVAs most commonly occur during periods of exertion—sexual intercourse, Valsalva maneuver, and labor and delivery—or physical and psychological stress, which may occur during dental treatment.[8] Consciousness is lost or impaired in about half of all patients. This is an ominous sign that usually indicates the occurrence of a large hemorrhage.[54,55] Of conscious patients, 50% demonstrate marked deterioration in consciousness and lose consciousness at a later time. The initial mortality rate from all hemorrhagic CVAs is approximately 50%, but the rate for comatose patients rises to between 70% and 100%.[56]

■ PATHOPHYSIOLOGY

The following two important factors work together to produce a CVA:
1. The brain's continual requirement for large amounts of O_2 and energy substrate
2. The inability of the brain to expand within its confining bony space, the cranium

The brain cannot store O_2 or glucose in reserve for use in times of increased need or deprivation. Acute disruption of the O_2 supply to the brain (e.g., via embolism or hemorrhage) produces alterations in brain activity that can be detected by electroencephalography within 10 to 20 seconds and irreversible neurologic death after 5 minutes.[57] Gradual deprivation (atherosclerotic change) produces the same result over a longer period of time.

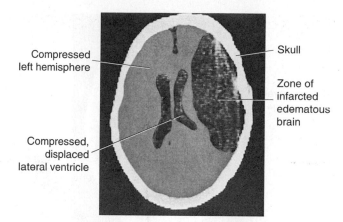

FIGURE 19-2 Computed tomographic (CT) scan of the cranium during cerebral vascular infarction.

Cerebrovascular ischemia and infarction

As ischemia develops, changes occur in the affected neural tissues. The ischemic tissue becomes soft, and the normally well-demarcated border between white and gray matter becomes less distinct. When viewed under a microscope, neurons in the ischemic area appear necrotic and shrunken. A second factor now emerges.

Edema is a normal occurrence following cerebral infarction. On a cellular level, ischemia results in anaerobic glycolysis with the production of lactate. Mitochondrial dysfunction develops, resulting in disruption of the membrane and vascular endothelium. Thus, the blood-brain barrier breaks down, and edema forms.[58]

The degree of edema is related to the size of the infarcted area. Edema increases the mass of the tissue within the cranium and causes the mild headache characteristic of atherosclerotic CVAs. In more severe CVAs the degree of edema may be so great as to force portions of the cerebral hemisphere into the tentorium cerebelli, further reducing blood and cerebrospinal fluid flow to the brain (Figure 19-2). The degree of ischemia and neurologic deficit therefore increases, potentially leading to ischemia and infarction of the upper brain stem (medulla), which produces a loss of consciousness and is invariably fatal.

The clinical significance of edema and of its management is that during the first 72 hours after a nonhemorrhagic CVA, a gradual increase in neurologic deficit and decrease in consciousness commonly occur. Cerebral edema in and around the infarcted area is the usual cause of these changes. A gradual return of some neurologic function normally follows as collateral circulation to the infarcted region improves. Maximal recovery normally occurs within 6 months.

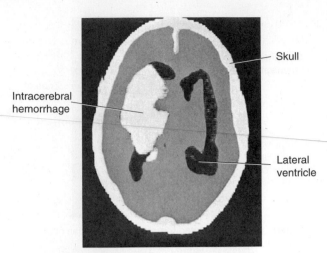

FIGURE 19-3　Computed tomographic (CT) scan of a hemorrhagic cerebrovascular accident.

Hemorrhagic CVA

Hemorrhagic CVAs differ clinically from nonhemorrhagic CVAs in that their onset is generally more rapid, the symptoms more intense, and the risk of death much greater. The most common source of blood in hemorrhagic CVAs is arterial. Two primary causes exist for this form of CVA—subarachnoid hemorrhage resulting from ruptured aneurysms and intracranial hemorrhage resulting from hypertensive vascular disease. Aneurysms, which are dilations in blood vessels in which the muscular walls have weakened and can rupture under increased pressure. In contrast, hypertensive vascular disease produces degenerative changes in blood vessel walls—usually smaller arterioles—over a longer period, weakening them and making them more susceptible to rupture. In addition, intracerebral hemorrhage may result from an idiopathic vascular disease, known as *amyloid angiopathy*, that occurs in older individuals.[8,59] Rupture of these vessels invariably occurs during periods of activity that produce blood pressure elevations.

Once vessels rupture, arterial blood rapidly fills the cranium, increasing intracerebral pressure, which may cause rapid displacement of the brain stem into the tentorium cerebelli and ultimately death. Cerebral edema, which always develops, only serves to increase the already high mortality rate for this type of CVA (Figure 19-3).

The intense headache noted in cases of hemorrhagic CVA is related to the irritating effects of blood and its breakdown products on blood vessels, meninges, and neural tissues of the brain. The headache is localized at first but becomes more generalized as meningeal irritation increases because of the spread of blood. The rapid increase in intracranial pressure brought on by hemorrhage and edema is responsible for the significant clinical differences noted between hemorrhagic and nonhemorrhagic CVAs. The area of neural tissue that loses its blood supply and becomes infarcted determines the neurologic deficits that the individual suffers.

■ MANAGEMENT

Management of the patient suffering an acute CVA depends on the rapidity of the onset of symptoms and the severity of the episode. In almost all cases supportive therapy and basic life support (BLS) are indicated.

The American Heart Association attached the term "brain attack" to the CVA to alert individuals to the immediate need for emergency management.[60-62] Until recently it was generally believed that little or nothing could be done to help the CVA victim or to minimize the degree of neurologic damage. With the advent of the neurointensive care unit and thrombolytic drugs, this is no longer true. The neurointensive care unit provides the monitoring and treatment for a progressing CVA and its complications. Patients who may be suitable for neurointensive care include the following:

- Patients with severe CVAs
- Patients receiving thrombolytic therapy
- Patients receiving hypervolemia-hypertensive-hemodilution therapy
- Patients at risk for and medical complications
- Patients experiencing in-hospital CVAs after medical and surgical procedures

In addition, thrombolysis has been demonstrated to be an effective treatment for ischemic stroke. Lack of awareness about this treatment, coupled with a short therapeutic window (<6 hours) are major obstacles to its use. Indiscriminate use of thrombolytic therapy can lead to an unacceptably high rate of hemorrhage. Early recognition of the onset of CVA, immediate transfer of the individual to a properly equipped facility, and careful screening of a computed tomographic scan of the head for signs of early infarction all are necessary for the safe administration of intravenous thrombolysis.[63,64]

The American Heart Association and the American Stroke Association have developed a community-oriented "Stroke Chain of Survival" (Box 19-2) for the management of acute ischemic stroke, in an effort to maximize stroke recovery.[65,66] The National Institute of Neurological Disorders and Stroke has developed recommended stroke evaluation targets for potential thrombolytic candidates[67] (Box 19-3).

Rapid recognition and reaction to stroke warning signs
Rapid emergency medical services (EMS) dispatch
Rapid EMS transport and hospital prenotification
Rapid diagnosis and treatment in the hospital

From Adams HP Jr., Adams RJ, del Zoppo GJ, Goldstein LB: Guidelines for the early management of patients with ischemic stroke: 2005 guidelines update: a scientific statement from the Stroke Council of the American Heart Association/American Stroke Association, *Stroke* 36:916–923, 2005; and Adams HP Jr, Adams RJ, del Zoppo GJ, et al.: Guidelines for the early management of patients with ischemic stroke: a scientific statement from the Stroke Council of the American Stroke Association, *Stroke* 34:1056–1083, 2003.

Box 19-3 National Institute of Neurological Disorders and Stroke time goals in treating stroke

TARGET TIME FRAME

ED arrival to doctor	10 minutes
ED arrival to CT completion	25 minutes
ED arrival to CT reading	45 minutes
ED arrival to treatment	60 minutes
Access to neurological expertise*	15 minutes
Access to neurosurgical expertise*	2 hours

ED, emergency department.
*By telephone or in person.
From Marler JR, Jones PW, Emr M, editors: *Setting new directions for stroke care: proceedings of a national symposium on rapid identification and treatment of acute stroke,* Bethesda, MD, National Institute of Neurological Disorders and Stroke, 1997.

Cerebrovascular accident and transient ischemic attack

In most instances of CVA and TIA, the victim remains conscious. Indeed, differentiating between a TIA and a CVA may initially be quite difficult. In such cases the duration of the episode becomes most important. Most TIAs last approximately 2 to 10 minutes, whereas the signs and symptoms of a CVA do not regress.

The following conditions provide diagnostic clues to the presence of CVA or TIA:[68]

- Hypertension (blood pressure above 140/90 mm Hg)
- Altered consciousness
- Hemiparesis, hemiparalysis
- Headache and blurred vision
- Asymmetry of face and pupils of eyes
- Incontinence
- Aphasia

Because of the uncertainty of diagnosis, initial management of any patient with signs and symptoms indicating cerebrovascular disease should be identical, regardless of the ultimate cause.

Prehospital management must focus on BLS, rapid identification of the problem, early hospital notification, and rapid transport.[69] Stroke victims can usually maintain their airway. Patients with intact protective airway reflexes should be administered O_2 if hypoxia is present with the head of the patient slightly elevated.[70,71] The patient should also be monitored and an intravenous (IV) line established, if possible.[70,71]

Step 1: discontinuation of the dental procedure.
Step 1a: activation of dental office emergency team

Step 2: P (position). A conscious patient reporting the aforementioned signs and symptoms should be placed in a comfortable position; most such patients prefer sitting upright or semiupright.

Step 3: A-B-C (airway-breathing-circulation), BLS as needed. The victim's airway, breathing, and circulation are assessed and the necessary steps implemented. When the victim is conscious, a rapid assessment can determine the adequacy of airway, breathing, and circulation.

Step 4: D (definitive care):
Step 4a: activation of emergency medical service (EMS). When signs and symptoms indicating possible cerebrovascular disease and an elevation in blood pressure appear, medical assistance should be sought immediately. Because thrombolytic therapy may help minimize residual neurologic deficit if it is begun early after the onset of a CVA, prompt access to emergency personnel is critical.

Step 4b: monitoring of vital signs. The blood pressure is usually elevated markedly during the episode, whereas the heart rate may be normal or elevated. In most cases either the radial or brachial arterial pulses, or both, are bounding. Comparison of vital signs with baseline values almost always demonstrates significant blood pressure elevation. The heart rate and rhythm and blood pressure should be monitored and recorded at least every 5 minutes during the acute episode.

Step 4c: management of signs and symptoms. Most TIA and CVA victims remain conscious throughout the episode. The patient should be allowed to remain seated upright (45 degrees, or semi-Fowler position, being recommended[68]), and attempt to maintain the patient's comfort. The semi-Fowler position slightly decreases the intracerebral blood pressure, whereas the supine position increases blood flow to the brain, a potentially dangerous situation during this time of significantly elevated blood pressure.

Step 4d: administration of O₂. O_2 may be administered via a nasal cannula or nasal hood. Do not administer any central nervous system (CNS) depressants to a patient believed to be suffering a stroke or TIA. Any drug producing CNS depression (e.g., analgesics, anti-anxiety agents, opioids, or inhalation sedatives) may adversely affect the patient's condition, masking any neurologic signs that might be present and making definitive diagnosis more difficult.

Conscious patient with resolution of signs and symptoms: transient ischemic attack

If clinical signs and symptoms resolve prior to arrival of emergency personnel, the episode was probably a TIA. When there is no history of cerebrovascular disease, emergency personnel are likely to transport that individual to the hospital for further neurologic evaluation. However, when a history of TIA is present, the victim should be hospitalized or immediately referred to the primary care physician.

Step 5: follow-up management. Following resolution of a TIA for which the individual does not require hospitalization, the patient's primary care physician should be contacted. Plans for medical examination of the patient and modifications in future dental treatment should be discussed. The patient should not be permitted to operate a motor vehicle or to depart from the dental office unescorted. An adult friend or relative, someone who has a vested interest in the health and safety of the patient, should be the person to escort the patient from the dental office.

Conscious patient with persistent signs and symptoms: cerebrovascular accident

If neurologic signs and symptoms do not resolve by the time emergency assistance arrives, the victim will be stabilized and transported to a hospital.

If at any time the victim loses consciousness management must continue. Loss of consciousness is associated with a poor clinical prognosis in CVA (70% to 100% initial mortality rate). Hemorrhagic CVA, the type most likely to occur during dental treatment, is also the most likely to produce unconsciousness. An intense headache is likely to precede the loss of consciousness, an additional clue to the presence of intracerebral hemorrhage or subarachnoid hemorrhage.

Step 1: P (position). The unconscious victim should be placed supine with the feet elevated slightly. Minor alterations in this position may be indicated later.

Step 2: A-B-C, BLS as needed. BLS is initiated immediately. Airway maintenance and respiratory support are particularly critical. O_2 should be administered as soon as it becomes available. Although cardiac arrest may occur at this time, the stroke victim is likely to require airway management only. Breathing is usually spontaneous, the carotid pulse strong and bounding.

Step 3: monitoring of vital signs. Vital signs (blood pressure, heart rate, and respiration) should be monitored and recorded. In most instances the heart rate is normal or slow and the pulse full and bounding. If heart rate, blood pressure, or both is absent, cardiopulmonary resuscitation should be initiated immediately. The blood pressure frequently is elevated significantly (systolic pressure >200 mm Hg).

Step 4: repositioning of the patient (if necessary). When the unconscious patient's blood pressure is markedly elevated, the position should be altered slightly from the normally recommended supine position. Because of the increase in cerebral blood flow in the supine position and the markedly elevated blood pressure observed in what is likely a hemorrhagic CVA, the patient should be placed in a semi-Fowler position, an almost-supine position with the head and chest elevated slightly. This new position must still allow for the maintenance of a patent airway and ventilation, if necessary. If cardiac arrest ensues and cardiopulmonary resuscitation becomes necessary, the patient must be repositioned into the supine position with the feet elevated.

Step 5: D (definitive care):
Step 5a: establishment of an IV line, if available. An IV infusion of 5% dextrose and water or normal saline may be started before the emergency personnel arrive. The availability of a patent vein will facilitate subsequent medical management.

Step 5b: definitive management. Once the patient is stabilized at the scene and transported to the hospital, immediate management of the hemorrhagic CVA patient is predicated upon preventing an increase in intracranial pressure. This requires terminating intracranial bleeding, surgical evacuation of blood from the cranium, and preventing or minimizing edema of the brain.

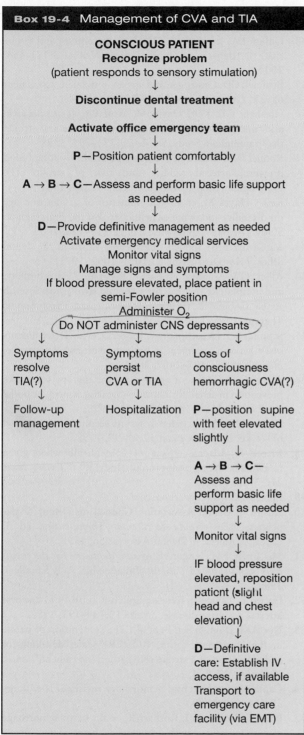

Box 19-4 Management of CVA and TIA

CONSCIOUS PATIENT
Recognize problem
(patient responds to sensory stimulation)
↓
Discontinue dental treatment
↓
Activate office emergency team
↓
P—Position patient comfortably
↓
A → B → C—Assess and perform basic life support
as needed
↓
D—Provide definitive management as needed
Activate emergency medical services
Monitor vital signs
Manage signs and symptoms
If blood pressure elevated, place patient in
semi-Fowler position
Administer O_2
Do NOT administer CNS depressants

Symptoms resolve TIA(?)	Symptoms persist CVA or TIA	Loss of consciousness hemorrhagic CVA(?)
↓	↓	↓
Follow-up management	Hospitalization	**P**—position supine with feet elevated slightly
		↓
		A → B → C—Assess and perform basic life support as needed
		↓
		Monitor vital signs
		↓
		IF blood pressure elevated, reposition patient (slight head and chest elevation)
		↓
		D—Definitive care: Establish IV access, if available Transport to emergency care facility (via EMT)

A, airway; **B,** breathing; **C,** circulation; CNS, central nervous system; **D,** definitive care; IV, intravenous; **P,** position.

Box 19-4 summarizes the management of CVAs and TIAs.
- **Drugs used in management:** O_2 is used to manage CVAs and TIAs.

- **Medical assistance required:** Patient suffering CVAs or TIAs require emergency assistance.

REFERENCES

1. American Heart Association: *Heart disease and stroke statistics—2006 update,* Dallas, American Heart Association, 2006.
2. Broderick J, Brott T, Kothari R, et al.: The Greater Cincinnati/Northern Kentucky Stroke Study: preliminary first-ever and total incidence rates of stroke among blacks, *Stroke* 29:415–421, 1998.
3. Williams GR, Jiang JG, Matchar DB, Samsa GP: Incidence and occurrence of total (first-ever and recurrent) stroke, *Stroke* 30:2523–2528, 1999.
4. Kolominsky-Rabas PL, Sarti C, Heuschmann PU, et al.: A prospective community-based study of stroke in Germany-The Erlangen Stroke Project (ESPro), *Stroke* 29:2501–2506, 1998.
5. Gresham GE, Phillips TF, Labi ML: ADL status in stroke: relative merits of three standard indexes, *Arch Phys Med Rehabil* 61:355–358, 1980.
6. Kothari RU, Brott T, Broderick JP, Hamilton CA: Emergency physicians: accuracy in the diagnosis of stroke, *Stroke* 26:2238–2241, 1995.
7. Kothari RU, Barsan W, Brott T, et al.: Frequency and accuracy of prehospital diagnosis of acute stroke, *Stroke* 26:937–941, 1995.
8. Kothari R, Barsan WG: Stroke. In: Marx JA, Hockberger RS, Walls RM, editors: *Rosen's emergency Medicine: concepts and clinical practice,* ed 5, St. Louis, Mosby, 2003, pp. 1433–1444.
9. Heros RC, Camarata PJ, Latchaw RE: Brain attack: introduction, *Neurosurg Clin North Am* 8:135–144, 1997.
10. American Heart Association: *Know the facts, get the stats: our guide to heart disease, stroke and risks,* Dallas, American Heart Association, 2003, Publication No. 55-0576 2003-04.
11. Farley CJ, Kittner SJ, Feeser BR, et al.: Stroke in children and sickle-cell disease. Baltimore-Washington Cooperative Young Stroke Study, *Neurology* 51:169–176, 1998.
12. Ferrera PC, Curran CB, Swanson H: Etiology of pediatric ischemic stroke, *Am J Emerg Med* 15:671–679, 1997.
13. Lynch JK, Hirtz DG, DeVeber G, Nelson KB: Report of the National Institute of Neurological Disorders and Stroke workshop on perinatal and childhood stroke, *Pediatrics* 109:116–123, 2002.
14. Rosamond WD, Folsom AR, Chambless LE, et al.: Stroke incidence and survival among middle-aged adults: 9-year follow-up of the Atherosclerotic Risk in Communities (ARIC) Cohort, *Stroke* 30:736–743, 1999.
15. Price TR, Psaty B, O'Leary D, et al.: Assessment of cerebrovascular disease in the Cardiovascular Health Study, *Ann Epidemiol* 3:504–507, 1993.
16. Johnston SC, Fayad PB, Gorelick PB, et al.: Prevalence and knowledge of transient ischemic attack among US adults, *Neurology* 60:1429–1434, 2003.

17. Lisbeth LD, Ireland JK, Risser JM, et al.: Stroke risk after transient ischemic attack in a population-based setting, *Stroke* 35:1842–1846, 2004.

18. Sherman DG: Reconsideration of TIA diagnostic criteria, *Neurology* 62:S20–S21, 2004.

19. Clark TG, Murphy MF, Rothwell PM: Long term risks of stroke, myocardial infarction, and vascular death in "low-risk" patients with a non-recent transient ischemic attack, *J Neurol Neurosurg Psychiatry* 74:577–580, 2003.

20. Norrving B: Long-term prognosis after lacunar infarction, *Lancet Neurol* 2:238–245, 2003.

21. Hermida RC: Hypertension—commentary, *Evidence-based Cardiovasc Med* 9:9–10, 2005.

22. Petty GW, Brown RD Jr, Whisnant JP, et al.: Ischemic stroke subtypes: a population-based study of incidence and risk factors, *Stroke* 30:2513–2516, 1999.

23. Jorgensen HS, Nakayama H, Reith J, et al.: Acute stroke with atrial fibrillation: the Copenhagen Stroke study, *Stroke* 10:1765–1769, 1996.

24. Mooe T, Eriksson P, Stegmayr B: Ischemic stroke after acute myocardial infarction: a population based study, *Stroke* 28:762–767, 1997.

25. Ezekowitz JA, Straus SE, Majumdar SR, McAlister FA: Stroke: strategies for primary prevention, *Am Fam Physician* 68:2379–2386.

26. Frohlich ED: Target organ involvement in hypertension: a realistic promise of prevention and reversal, *Med Clin North Am* 88:209–221, 2004.

27. Easton JD, Sherman DG: Management of cerebral embolism of cardiac origin, *Stroke* 11:433–442, 1980.

28. Levy DE: How transient are transient ischemic attacks? *Neurology* 38:674–677, 1988.

29. Earnest MP: Emergency diagnosis and management of brain infarctions and hemorrhages. In: Earnest MP, editor: *Neurologic emergencies,* New York, Churchill Livingstone, 1983.

30. Fazekas F, Fazekas G, Schmidt R, et al.: Magnetic resonance imaging correlates of transient ischemic attacks, *Stroke* 27:607–611, 1996.

31. Bhadelia RA, Anderson M, Polak JF, et al.: Prevalence and association of MRI-demonstrated brain infarcts in elderly subjects with a history of transient ischemic attack: the Cardiovascular Health Study, *Stroke* 30:383–388, 1999.

32. Broderick JP, Adams HP Jr, Barsan W, et al.: Guidelines for the management of spontaneous intracerebral hemorrhage: a statement for healthcare professionals from a special writing group of the Stroke Council, American Heart Association, *Stroke* 30:905–915, 1999.

33. Wiebers DO, Whisnant JP, O'Fallon WM: The natural history of unruptured intracranial aneurysms, *N Engl J Med* 304:696–698, 1981.

34. Barnett HJM: Progress towards stroke prevention: Robert Wartenberg lecture, *Neurology* 30:1212–1225, 1980.

35. Hennekens CH: Lessons from hypertension trials, *Am J Med* 104:50S–53S, 1998.

36. Collaborative Group for the Study of Stroke in Young Women: Oral contraceptives and stroke in young women. Associated risk factors, *JAMA* 231:718–722, 1975.

37. Bronner LL, Kanter DS, Manson JE: Primary prevention of stroke, *N Engl J Med* 333:1392–2000, 1995.

38. Gillum LA, Johnston SC: Oral contraceptives and stroke risk: the debate continues. *Lancet Neurol* 3:453–454, 2004.

39. Bushnell CD: Oestrogen and stroke in women: assessment of risk, *Lancet Neurol* 4:743–751, 2005.

40. Gresham GE, Kelly-Hayes M, Wolf PA, et al.: Survival and functional status 20 or more years after first stroke: the Framingham Study, *Stroke* 29:793–797, 1998.

41. Kannel WB, Wolf PA, McGee DL, et al.: Systolic blood pressure, arterial rigidity and risk of stroke. The Framingham Study, *JAMA* 245:1225–1229, 1981.

42. Kelley-Hayes M, et al. The influence of gender and age on disability following ischemic stroke: the Framingham Study. J Stroke Cerebrovasc Dis 12:119–126, 2003

43. McCarthy FM: Sudden, unexpected death in the dental office, *J Am Dent Assoc* 83:1091–1092, 1971.

44. Albers GW, Amarenco P, Easton JD, et al.: Antithrombotic and antiplatelet therapy for ischemic stroke: the Seventh ACCP Conference on Antithrombotic and Thrombolytic Therapy, *Chest* 126:483S–512S, 2004.

45. Schmidt WP, Heuschmann P, Taeger D, et al.: Determinants of IV heparin treatment in patients with ischemic stroke, *Neurology* 63:2407–2409, 2004.

46. Albers GW: Choice of antithrombotic therapy for stroke prevention in atrial fibrillation: warfarin, aspirin, or both? *Arch Intern Med* 158:1487–1491, 1998.

47. Diener HC: Antiplatelet drugs in secondary prevention of stroke, *Int J Clin Pract* 52:91–97, 1998.

48. Merck S: Adverse effects of epinephrine when given to patients taking propranolol (Inderal), *J Emerg Nurs* 21:27–32, 1995.

49. Epocrates. www.epocrates.com

50. American Dental Association Council on Dental Therapeutics: *ADA Guide to Dental Therapeutics,* ed 3, Chicago, American Dental Association, 1998.

51. McCarthy FM: *Essentials of safe dentistry for the medically compromised patient,* Philadelphia, WB Saunders, 1989.

52. Cocito L, Favale E, Reni K: Epileptic seizures in cerebral arterial occlusive disease, *Stroke* 13:189–195, 1982.

53. Nor AM, Davis J, Sen B, et al.: The recognition of stroke in the emergency room (ROSIER) scale: development and validation of a stroke recognition instrument, *Lancet Neurol* 4:727–734, 2005.

54. Caplan L: Intracerebral hemorrhage revisited, *Neurology* 38:624–627, 1988.

55. Brott T, Broderick J, Kothari R, et al.: Early hemorrhage growth in patients with intracerebral hemorrhage, *Stroke* 28:1–5, 1997.

56. Dennis MS: Outcome after brain hemorrhage, *Cerebrovasc Dis* 16:9–13, 2003.

57. White BC, Wiegenstein JG, Winegar CD: Brain ischemic anoxia: mechanisms of injury, *JAMA* 251:1586–1590, 1984.

58. Rehncrona S, Rosen I, Siesjo BK: Brain lactic acidosis and ischemic cell damage: biochemistry and neurophysiology, *J Cereb Blood Flow Metab* 1:297–311, 1981.

59. Drury I, Whisnant JP, Garraway WM: Primary intra-cerebral hemorrhage: impact of CT on incidences, *Neurology* 34:653–657, 1984.

60. Schellinger PD, Hacke W: Stroke: advances in therapy, *Lancet Neurol* 4:2, 2005.

61. Donnan GA: Stroke: prediction, prevention, and outcome, *Lancet Neurol* 3:9, 2004.

62. Holloway RG, Benesch CG, Burgin WS, Zentner JB: Prognosis and decision making in severe stroke, *JAMA* 294:725–733, 2005.

63. Fields MC, Levine SR: Patient page. Clot-busting therapy helps stroke victims—but only if they get treatment in time, *Neurology* 64:E1–E2, 2005.

64. Lee VH, Brown RD Jr.: Prevention of in-hospital mortality after stroke, *Lancet Neurol* 4:73–74, 2005.

65. Adams HP Jr., Adams RJ, del Zoppo GJ, Goldstein LB: Guidelines for the early management of patients with ischemic stroke: 2005 guidelines update: a scientific statement from the Stroke Council of the American Heart Association/American Stroke Association, *Stroke* 36:916–923, 2005.

66. Adams HP Jr, Adams RJ, del Zoppo GJ, et al.: Guidelines for the early management of patients with ischemic stroke: a scientific statement from the Stroke Council of the American Stroke Association, *Stroke* 34:1056–1083, 2003.

67. Marler JR, Jones PW, Emr M, editors: *Setting new directions for stroke care: proceedings of a national symposium on rapid identification and treatment of acute stroke*, Bethesda, MD, National Institute of Neurological Disorders and Stroke, 1997.

68. Pollakoff J, Pollakoff K: *EMT's guide to treatment*, Los Angeles, Jeff Gould, 1991.

69. American Heart Association: Adult stroke. *Circulation* 112:IV-111–IV-120, 2005.

70. Ronning OM, Guldvog B: Should stroke victims routinely receive supplemental oxygen? A quasi-randomized controlled trial, *Stroke* 30:2033–2037, 1999.

71. Elizabeth J, Singarayer J, Ellul J, et al.: Arterial oxygen saturation and posture in acute stroke, *Age Ageing* 22:269–272, 1993.

CHAPTER 20

Altered Consciousness:

Differential Diagnosis

A number of clinical conditions may cause alterations in an individual's state of consciousness (see Table 16-1). In almost all such situations the doctor must maintain the life of a patient who remains conscious but is exhibiting unusual behavior. If not recognized and managed promptly, several of these conditions may worsen, leading to the loss of consciousness. Basic management of each of these situations is similar (P→A→B→C) and is all that is required in some cases; however, others may require more definitive management, which can be performed only if the precise nature of the problem is known. The following is provided to aid in the determination of this diagnosis.

■ MEDICAL HISTORY

Several of the clinical conditions discussed in this section may become evident following review of the medical history questionnaire. The patient with diabetes mellitus or thyroid gland dysfunction or one who has had a cerebrovascular accident (CVA) is aware of the problem and normally indicates it on the questionnaire. A thorough dialogue history should enable the doctor to further determine the degree of risk this patient presents during dental care. Unless a previous episode is reported, neither hyperventilation nor drug overdose can be diagnosed from data on the medical history.

■ AGE

The age of the patient with altered consciousness may assist in the diagnosis. Hyperventilation occurs only rarely in children or in older individuals (>50 years); its greatest incidence is in those between 15 and 40 years. Hyperthyroidism most often occurs between the ages of 20 and 40, and more than 80% of diabetic patients develop the disease after age 35 years. Cerebrovascular disease is extremely rare in individuals under 40 years; its incidence increases with age. Drug overdose may occur at any age. In pediatric patients the most likely cause of altered consciousness is hypoglycemia secondary to type 1 diabetes.

■ SEX

Hyperthyroidism (thyrotoxicosis) occurs predominantly in females. However, hyperventilation and the other clinical conditions discussed in this section demonstrate little or no sex differentiation.

■ RELATED CIRCUMSTANCES

Undue stress resulting from anxiety and pain may predispose an individual to hyperventilation. Indeed, in the dental environment, hyperventilation is primarily a clinical expression of extreme fear. Stress may also be related to the onset of a hemorrhagic CVA. Additionally, persons who are hyperthyroid or hypoglycemic may appear acutely anxious, but specific clinical signs and symptoms associated with these problems usually permit an accurate differential diagnosis to be made.

■ ONSET OF SIGNS AND SYMPTOMS

The onset of clinical manifestations of altered consciousness is gradual in individuals suffering hyperglycemia (many hours to several days), hyperthyroidism and hypothyroidism (days to months), and CVAs produced by atherosclerotic changes in blood vessels (days to weeks). The patient will arrive in the dental office already exhibiting signs and symptoms. When the office staff members know the patient well, the alteration in consciousness may be quite obvious.

By contrast, hyperventilation, hypoglycemia, and CVAs produced by thrombosis, embolism, and especially intracerebral hemorrhage are accompanied by a more rapid onset of clinical manifestations (signs and symptoms developing more acutely within the dental office).

■ PRESENCE OF SYMPTOMS BETWEEN ACUTE EPISODES

The patient with undiagnosed thyroid dysfunction or inadequately managed thyroid dysfunction exhibits clinical evidence at all times. Post-CVA patients usually demonstrate some residual neurologic deficit, the severity of which ranges from flaccid paralysis to barely perceptible motor or sensory changes. In contrast, patients who experience transient ischemic attacks (TIAs) remain clinically free of symptoms between acute episodes. Brittle adults with diabetes may manifest the signs and symptoms of hyperglycemia at all times.

■ LOSS OF CONSCIOUSNESS

Although all the clinical conditions discussed in this section manifest primarily as alterations in consciousness, several may lead to the loss of consciousness. CVA, particularly hemorrhagic stroke, may be associated with unconsciousness, a particularly ominous clinical sign.

Patients with clinical evidence of thyroid dysfunction may also lose consciousness if the condition is poorly controlled. Significant mortality rates accompany the two clinical situations in which unconsciousness occurs—myxedema coma (hypothyroid) and thyroid crisis or storm (hyperthyroid). In addition, hyperglycemic and hypoglycemic individuals may ultimately lose consciousness; however, the hypoglycemic patient is more likely to lose consciousness rapidly. Hyperventilation rarely leads to unconsciousness.

■ SIGNS AND SYMPTOMS
Appearance of the skin (face)

The presence or absence of perspiration and the temperature of the skin may assist in the determination of a differential diagnosis. The skin of a clinically hyperglycemic diabetic patient is hot and dry to the touch (produced by dehydration), whereas that of the hypoglycemic patient is cold and wet (clammy). The skin of the clinically hyperthyroid individual is hot and wet, whereas the hypothyroid individual has dry skin and may demonstrate a subnormal body temperature.

Obvious anxiety

The clinical signs of agitation, perspiration, and possibly a fine tremor of the extremities (hands) give the appearance of nervousness and are apparent in patients who are hypoglycemic, hyperthyroid, or hyperventilating, as well as in patients who are simply quite nervous but otherwise healthy.

Paresthesia

Paresthesia, a feeling of numbness or "pins and needles" in various portions of the body, occurs in several situations. If it accompanies a rapid respiratory rate, paresthesia of the perioral region, fingertips, and toes is diagnostic of hyperventilation. Patients with TIAs exhibit unilateral paresthesia or muscle weakness unaccompanied by a change in respiration, which often develops in the absence of anxiety. An ischemic or hemorrhagic CVA demonstrates the aforementioned signs of TIA but continues to progress, whereas signs and symptoms of TIA commonly subside within 10 minutes.

Headache

Individuals with hypothyroidism may suffer headaches, but those experiencing acute CVAs are more likely to have them. A severe, intense headache, the kind described by many individuals as "the worst headache I have ever experienced" is an important clinical finding in intracerebral hemorrhage, a form of CVA.

"Drunken" appearance

The clinical appearance of drunkenness is most commonly evident after a patient overindulges in alcohol or another drug that depresses their central nervous system. However, hypoglycemia may present a similar clinical picture. The patient demonstrates signs of mental confusion and bizarre behavioral patterns that may lead to a suspicion of alcohol or other drug abuse. A history of diabetes, especially type 1, or of not eating before dental appointments may assist in differential diagnosis.

Breath odor

The telltale odor of alcohol on the breath aids in a diagnosis of patient-administered "predmedication." Severely hyperglycemic patients may have the characteristic fruity, sweet smell of acetone on their breath.

■ VITAL SIGNS
Respiration

Respiratory rate increases when hyperventilation, hyperthyroidism, or hyperglycemia is present. In hyperglycemic patients, this increase is frequently associated with the previously discussed odor of acetone. Patients suffering CVAs (unconscious patients with slow but deep respirations), those who have ingested an overdose of CNS-depressant drugs (alcohol, sedatives, antianxiety drugs, or opioids), and some hypoglycemic patients may demonstrate respiratory depression.

Blood pressure

Elevated blood pressure is found in hyperventilation, hyperthyroidism, and many kinds of CVA (intracerebral hemorrhage, subarachnoid hemorrhage, and cerebral thrombosis). In hyperglycemia there may be a slight decrease in blood pressure, whereas the blood pressure of the hypothyroid patient changes very little.

Heart rate

Rapid heart rates (tachycardia) accompany hyperventilation, hypoglycemia, hyperglycemia, and hyperthyroidism. Hypothyroid patients often demonstrate slower than normal heart rates.

■ SUMMARY

Each of the clinical conditions that produces altered consciousness possesses certain relevant clinical features. The following statements summarize the distinctive characteristics of each:

Hyperventilation: The respiratory rate is rapid, and the individual demonstrates deep respiratory excursions, acute anxiety, and elevations in blood pressure and heart rate; some patients may experience paresthesia of the extremities and circumoral region. The condition occurs primarily in those 15 to 40 years of age and seldom results in unconsciousness.

Hypoglycemia: Most such individuals have histories of diabetes (usually type 1) or lack of food ingestion. The patient may appear drunk, their skin cold and wet to the touch. Heart rate is rapid, and the patient may exhibit hand tremors. The onset of symptoms may appear rapidly and lead quickly to the loss of consciousness.

Hyperglycemia: These individuals often have histories of inadequately controlled diabetes. In hyperglycemia the skin appears hot and dry; the breath may have an odor of acetone; breathing is rapid and deep, known as *Kussmaul's respirations*. Such patients experience more gradual onsets of symptoms and rarely lose consciousness.

Hypothyroidism: These patients are sensitive to cold, and their body temperatures are lowered (no sweating). Speech and mental capabilities appear slower than normal. Peripheral edema (nonpitting) is present, particularly around the face and eyelids, and skin color is carotenemic. Hypothyroid patients are overly sensitive to CNS-depressant drugs and often note a history of recent unexplained weight gain.

Hyperthyroidism: These individuals are nervous and hyperactive, with elevations in blood pressure, heart rate, and body temperature. Their skin is wet and warm to the touch and they are overly sensitive to heat. Most patients report recent unexplained weight loss accompanied by an increase in appetite.

CVA: Those individuals suffering hemorrhagic CVAs report unusually intense headaches. They experience unilateral neurologic deficits (e.g., flaccid paralysis, speech defects). The level of consciousness is normally unchanged, though unconsciousness may occur.

PART 5

SEIZURES

21   Seizures

CHAPTER 21

Seizures

For most people, witnessing a seizure is a traumatic experience. The belief persists that a seizure is a life-threatening emergency requiring prompt intervention from a trained individual to prevent death. Happily this is not normally the case. Although in no sense benign, most convulsive episodes are simply transient alterations in brain function characterized clinically by an abrupt onset of motor, sensory, or psychic symptoms. In these instances prevention of injury to the victim during the seizure and supportive therapy after the seizure stops constitute the essentials of management. Proper management helps ensure that significant morbidity and mortality are rare. Only when seizures follow one another closely or become continuous do they represent a life-threatening medical emergency. In these cases prompt action and specific drug therapy are required to prevent death or significant postseizure morbidity. Box 21-1 lists some relevant terms and definitions introduced in this section.

Box 21-1 Terms related to seizures

Clonic: Intermittent muscular contractions and relaxation; the clonic phase being the actual convulsive portion of a seizure.

Convulsion, seizure: Defined in 1870 by Hughlings Jackson as "a symptom...an occasional, an excessive, and a disorderly discharge of nerve tissue;"[1] a more modern definition emphasized the same essentials, stating that a seizure is "a paroxysmal disorder of cerebral function characterized by an attack involving changes in the state of consciousness, motor activity, or sensory phenomena; a seizure is sudden in onset and usually of brief duration"; the terms *convulsion* and *seizure* are synonymous.

Epilepsy: Derived from the Greek term *epilepsia,* meaning "to take hold of"; epilepsy is defined as "A recurrent paroxysmal disorder of cerebral function marked by sudden, brief attacks of altered consciousness, motor activity, or sensory phenomena. Convulsive seizures are the most common form of attack."[2]

Ictus: A seizure.

Status epilepticus: Condition in which seizures are so prolonged or so repeated that recovery does not occur between attacks; a life-threatening medical emergency.

Stertorous: Characterized by snoring; used to describe breathing.

Tonic: A sustained muscular contraction; patient appearing rigid or stiff during the tonic phase of a seizure.

Box 21-2 Clinical and electroencephalographic classification of epileptic seizures

PARTIAL SEIZURES (FOCAL, LOCAL)*
Simple partial seizures
Motor signs
Somatosensory or special sensory symptoms
Autonomic symptoms or signs
Psychic symptoms

Complex partial seizures (psychomotor, temporal lobe)
Simple partial onset followed by impairment of consciousness†
Impairment of consciousness at onset

Partial seizures evolving to generalized tonic-clonic convulsions (secondarily generalized)‡
Simple partial seizures evolving to generalized tonic-clonic convulsions
Complex partial seizures evolving to generalized tonic-clonic convulsions (including simple partial seizure to complex partial seizure to generalized tonic-clonic convulsion)

GENERALIZED SEIZURES (CONVULSIVE OR NONCONVULSIVE)§
Absence seizures (true petit mal)
Atypical absence seizures
Myoclonic seizures
Clonic seizures
Tonic seizures
Tonic-clonic seizures (grand mal)
Atonic seizures
Unclassified epileptic seizures

---

*Partial seizures have behavioral or electroencephalographic evidence showing that the ictal discharge begins in one area of the brain. Seizures that do not alter consciousness are called *simple partial;* those that do are called *complex partial.*

†Complex partial seizures are said to evolve from simple partial seizures when they begin without an alteration in consciousness (for example, an aura).

‡Partial seizures can progress to generalized tonic-clonic convulsions and are called *secondarily generalized seizures.*

§Behavioral and electroencephalographic manifestations of true generalized seizures are generalized from the start. Several types of generalized seizures are recognized; some have no known structural or chemical causes (for example, true petit mal), whereas others are associated with diffuse brain damage.

Modified from the Commission on Classification and Terminology of the International League Against Epilepsy: Proposal for revised clinical and electroencephalographic classification of epileptic seizures, *Epilepsia* 22:489–501, 1981.

■ TYPES OF SEIZURE DISORDERS

The clinical manifestations of paroxysmal excessive neuronal brain activity (seizures) span a wide range of sensory and motor activities that may involve any or all of the following:

- Altered visceral function
- Sensory, olfactory, auditory, visual, and gustatory phenomena
- Abnormal motor movements
- Changes in mental acuity and behavior
- Alterations in consciousness

Box 21-2 presents a classification of the types of epilepsies by the Commission on Classification and Terminology of the International League Against Epilepsy.[3]

It is estimated that, in the United States, 10% of the population will have at least one seizure in their lifetime. The overall incidence of epilepsy is less than 1%.[4] More than 2.7 million Americans have epilepsy, with an additional 300,000 having a first seizure each year (120,000 are under age 18 years) with 200,000 new cases of epilepsy diagnosed each year.[5]

When seizures are examined by age of onset, a pattern becomes evident. The highest rates of incidence occur in the under the age of 2 years and over age 65 years.[5] More than three quarters of patients with epilepsy experienced their first seizure before age 20 years. The cumulative risk of developing epilepsy (recurrent seizures) is that by age 20 years 1% of the population has diagnosed epilepsy, which steadily increases to 3% at age 75 years.[5] In addition, the risk that an individual may suffer a second seizure after an initial, unprovoked episode is 30%. The chance for remission of seizures in childhood epilepsy is 50%,[5,6] whereas the recurrence rate in children after withdrawal from anticonvulsant drug therapy is 30%.[7,8]

Whereas all patients with epilepsy have seizures, many more patients have a single seizure during life and are not considered to have epilepsy.[9]

The types of seizures that occur most frequently and possess the greatest potential for morbidity and death are known as *generalized seizures.* Included in this group are tonic-clonic convulsive episodes, known clinically as *grand mal epilepsy,* and petit mal epilepsy, also called *absence attacks.*

Partial seizures

Partial, or focal, seizures are epileptic seizures characterized by motor, sensory, autonomic, or psychic symptoms during which consciousness is preserved.[9] Clinical signs and symptoms of focal seizures relate to the affected area of the brain (the ictal focus). Signs and symptoms evident in individuals suffering partial seizures may include specific motor or sensory symptoms, or both; therefore they are called *simple partial seizures.* Such seizures may also appear as "spells" associated with more complex symptoms, including illusions, hallucinations, or déjà vu, known as *complex partial seizures.* Focal seizures commonly remain localized, in which case the individual's consciousness or awareness usually is somewhat disturbed, and variable degrees of amnesia may be evident. On the other hand, a focal seizure can turn into a generalized seizure, in which case the individual loses consciousness. Although all seizures are significant, generalized seizures are clinically more dangerous in the dental office because of their greater potential for injury and postseizure complications.

Generalized seizures

The majority of patients with recurrent, generalized seizures develop one of three major forms: grand mal, petit mal, or psychomotor. Of all persons with epilepsy, 70% have only one type of seizure disorder, whereas the remaining 30% have two or more types.[10]

Grand mal epilepsy

More properly known as a *tonic-clonic seizure,* grand mal epilepsy is the most common form of seizure disorder, present in 90% of epileptic patients. Tonic-clonic seizure is what most persons envision when thinking about epilepsy. Approximately 60% of epileptics have this form alone, whereas 30% experience additional seizure types. Grand mal epilepsy occurs equally in both sexes and in any age group, although more than two thirds of cases occur by the time the individual reaches puberty.[5]

Tonic-clonic seizure may be produced by neurologic disorders, including neoplasm, cerebrovascular accident, meningitis, and encephalitis, or may develop in a neurologically sound brain secondary to a systemic metabolic or toxic disturbance. Causes include drug withdrawal, photic stimulation, menstruation, fatigue, alcohol or other intoxications, and falling asleep or awakening.[10] Neurologically induced tonic-clonic seizures usually last about 2 to 3 minutes and seldom more than 5 minutes (clonic phase). The entire seizure, including the immediate postictal period, lasts 5 to 15 minutes, but a complete return to normal, preictal cerebral function may take up to 2 hours.[11] The tonic-clonic seizure forms the basis for the discussion of seizures in this section.

Absence seizures

Absence seizures, also known as petit mal epilepsy, is found in 25% of epileptic patients. Only 4% of those individuals, however, report absence seizures as their sole type of seizure disorder; the other 21% have absence seizures in addition to other forms, most commonly grand mal.[5] The incidence of absence seizures among those with childhood epilepsy is less than 5%;[12] such seizures almost always occur in children and adolescents between 3 and 15 years of age.[13] The incidence of absence seizures decreases with age, and its persistence beyond age 30 years is rare. However, 40% to 80% of individuals with absence seizures go on to develop tonic-clonic seizure.[14]

Absence seizures may occur frequently, and individuals may experience multiple daily episodes. These seizures tend to occur shortly after awakening or during periods of inactivity. Conversely, exercise reduces the incidence of absence seizures.[15] Typical absence seizures are characterized by sudden behavioral arrest and unresponsiveness that may be accompanied by eyelid or facial clonus; automatisms; and autonomic, tonic, or atonic features. The duration rarely exceeds 10 seconds, and no aura or postictal state is observed.[9] The individual exhibits no movement during the episode other than perhaps a cyclic blinking of the eyelids. The episode usually terminates just as abruptly as it began. If the individual is standing at the onset of the seizure, their posture usually remains erect throughout the episode. In addition, a petit mal triad is recognized, consisting of myoclonic jerks, akinetic seizures, and brief absences or blank spells without associated falling and body convulsions. Individuals also exhibit characteristic electroencephalographic patterns consisting of 3 cycles per second.

Jacksonian epilepsy

With Jacksonian epilepsy (simple partial seizure), the individual often remains conscious despite an obvious impairment of consciousness. The focal convulsions of Jacksonian epilepsy may be motor, sensory, or autonomic in nature. Commonly, this type of epilepsy begins in the distal muscles of one limb as convulsive jerking or as paresthesias or on the face as a localized chronic spasm that spreads (the classic "Jacksonian march") in a more or less orderly manner. For example, it may start in the great toe and extend to the leg, thigh, trunk, and shoulder, possibly involving the upper limb. If the seizure crosses to the opposite side, the individual usually loses consciousness.[11]

Psychomotor seizures

Also known as *complex partial seizures,* psychomotor seizures are present in approximately 2% to 25% of children and 15% to 50% of adults[13,16,17] (6% experience this type only and 12% experience them in combination with other forms[5]). These seizures involve extensive cortical regions and produce a variety of symptoms. They last longer than simple partial seizures (usually 1 to 2 minutes), their onset and termination are more gradual, and they involve an associated impairment of consciousness.[11] Such episodes often progress into generalized seizures.[16] Common causes of psychomotor seizures include birth injury, tumors, and trauma.[18] The usual age of onset extends from late childhood to early adulthood.[13]

Psychomotor seizures include most seizures that do not meet the criteria described previously for grand mal, petit mal, or Jacksonian seizures. Individuals with psychomotor epilepsy often exhibit automatisms, apparently purposeful movements, incoherent speech, turning of the head, shifting of the eyes, smacking of the lips, twisting and writhing movements of the extremities, clouding of consciousness, and amnesia.

Status epilepticus

Status epilepticus is a medical emergency that demands prompt diagnosis and treatment if severe neurologic sequelae and death are to be minimized.[9] An estimated 125,000 to 195,000 episodes of status epilepticus occur in the United States annually, resulting in 22,000 to 42,000 deaths.[19] Status epilepticus is defined as continuous clinical or electrical seizure activity or repetitive seizures with incomplete neurologic recovery interictally for a period of at least 30 minutes.[9] Since most seizures terminate spontaneously within 1 to 2 minutes, patients having continuous seizure activity for 10 minutes or longer should be treated as if in status epilepticus.[9]

In the dental office environment, the definition of the Academy of Orthopaedic Surgeons may be more practical, defining status epilepticus as a seizure that continues for more than 5 minutes or a repeated seizure that begins before the individual recovers from the initial episode.[20]

The incidence of status epilepticus among epileptic patients is about 5%, although the reported range varies from 1.3% to 10%.[21,22] Status epilepticus is usually is categorized as generalized or partial (focal) and convulsive or nonconvulsive. Convulsive (tonic-clonic) status is a true medical emergency and carries an acute mortality rate of 10%[23] and a long-term mortality rate of more than 20%.[24] Convulsive seizures typically are tonic-clonic seizures.[25]

The most common factor precipitating status epilepticus is failure of the epileptic patient to take antiepileptic drugs.[26] Status epilepticus is also more common in patients whose epileptic causes are known.[27] Of 2588 patients with epilepsy, only 1.8% of the 1885 with epilepsy of unknown cause (idiopathic) experienced status epilepticus compared with 9% of those with epilepsy of known cause. The most common causes in the latter group were tumor or trauma.[27]

Prolonged absence seizures and psychomotor seizures are examples of nonconvulsive status and include mild to severe alterations in the level of consciousness and confusion with or without automatisms.[21] Absence status may last hours or days and is usually precipitated by hyperventilation, photic stimulation, psychogenic stress, fatigue, or minor trauma, frequently terminating in a generalized seizure.[28] Nonconvulsive status does not constitute an acutely life-threatening medical emergency in the dental office.

■ CAUSES

Many known causes exist to explain seizures. The International League Against Epilepsy has established a systematic approach to epilepsy classification to help clinicians make appropriate decisions regarding the evaluation and treatment of patients with epilepsy. Seizures are divided into *partial* (or focal) and *generalized* classes. Consciousness is retained in partial seizures because only a small region of the brain is affected. Consciousness is lost in generalized seizures because the entire cortex is affected. Partial seizures may secondarily generalize. "Primary" generalized seizures involve the whole brain from the onset (Table 21-1).[3,29]

Epilepsy can further be subdivided into three categories: (1) *symptomatic* of an identified underlying brain

TABLE 21-1   Examples of epilepsy syndromes in adolescents and adults

	Focal (localization-related)	Generalized
Idiopathic	Benign childhood epilepsy with centrotemporal spikes	Childhood absence epilepsy
	Benign occipital epilepsy	Juvenile absence epilepsy
	Autosomal dominant nocturnal frontal lobe epilepsy	Juvenile myoclonic epilepsy
		Epilepsy with generalized tonic-clonic seizures on awakening
		Cortical malformations
Symptomatic	Temporal lobe	Cortical dysplasias
	Frontal lobe	Metabolic abnormalities
	Parietal lobe	West's syndrome
	Occipital lobe	Lennox-Gastaut syndrome
		West's syndrome (unidentified etiology)
Cryptogenic	Any occurrence of partial seizures without obvious pathology	Lennox-Gastaut syndrome (unidentified pathology)

lesion; (2) *cryptogenic,* in which an anatomic lesion is suspected, but cannot be identified with current technology; and (3) *idiopathic,* in which an identifiable lesion is neither identified nor suspected.[29]

Inherited abnormalities of neurotransmission without corresponding anatomic lesions are though to be the cause of the idiopathic syndromes. More than 65% of individuals with recurrent seizures (i.e., epileptic individuals) may suffer from idiopathic epilepsy. Symptomatic epilepsy is present in the remaining nearly 35% of individuals who experience recurrent seizures. Some possible causes of symptomatic epilepsy include the following:

- Congenital abnormalities
- Perinatal injuries
- Metabolic and toxic disorders
- Head trauma
- Tumors and other space-occupying lesions
- Vascular diseases
- Degenerative disorders
- Infectious diseases

Congenital and *perinatal* conditions include maternal infection (rubella), trauma, or hypoxia during delivery.

Metabolic disorders, such as hypocalcemia, hypoglycemia, phenylketonuria, and alcohol or drug withdrawal, may also produce seizures. Metabolic disorders account for between 10% and 15% of all cases of acute isolated seizures.[30,31] Drugs and toxic substances account for about 4% of acute seizures. Commonly used drugs associated with the ability to provoke seizures (epileptogenic) include penicillin, hypoglycemic agents, local anesthetics, physostigmine,[32] and phenothiazines.[33] Withdrawal from addictive drugs such as cocaine also may provoke seizures.[34]

Head trauma is of great importance at any age, but especially in young adults. Posttraumatic epilepsy is more likely to develop when the dura mater is penetrated; seizures manifest within 2 years after the injury, with 75% occurring within the first year.[35] Epilepsy caused by craniocerebral injuries accounts for 5% to 15% of all cases of acquired epilepsy,[36] with a peak incidence between 20 and 40 years.[37]

Tumors and other space-occupying lesions may occur at any age but are especially common from middle age on, when the incidence of neoplastic disease increases. Tumors are relatively uncommon in children (accounting for 0.5% to 1% of childhood epilepsy[38]) but represent the most common acquired cause of seizures between 35 and 55 years, accounting for 10% of all cases of adult-onset secondary epilepsy.[39] Approximately 35% of cerebral tumors are associated with seizures, which are the initial symptom in 40% of this percentage group.[39,40]

The importance of *vascular diseases* in the production of seizures increases with age; such diseases are the most common causes of seizures that develop after 60 years. Any disease that impairs blood flow to the brain can provoke a seizure, the likelihood varying with the severity of cerebral ischemia. Arteriosclerotic cerebrovascular insufficiency and cerebral infarction, both of which present increased risks with increased age, are the most common vascular disorders provoking seizures.[41] In elderly patients such diseases account for 25% to 70% of acquired epilepsy[42] and 10% to 24% of acute isolated seizures.[43]

Infectious diseases, which are considered reversible causes of seizures, can occur at any age. Central nervous system (CNS) infections, such as bacterial meningitis or herpes encephalitis, frequently cause seizures. Infections account for 3% of acquired epilepsy[44] and 4% to 12% of acute isolated seizures.[43]

A phenomenon exists in which children and adults who are exposed to television interference and to the flickering lights and geometric patterns of video games develop seizures.[45] This phenomenon, called *photosensitive epilepsy*, was recently responsible for the occurrence of seizure and seizure-like activity in thousands of Japanese children watching one television show that featured flickering colored lights.[46]

The introduction of new, noninvasive neurodiagnostic techniques—most significantly, computed tomography and nuclear magnetic resonance imaging—has improved detection of underlying lesions in individuals with epileptic disorders. Thus, newly diagnosed cases of seizures will increasingly be diagnosed in the symptomatic category.

Febrile convulsions are usually associated with and precipitated by marked elevations in body temperature. They occur almost exclusively in infants and young children, particularly during the first year of life. Criteria for febrile seizures include the following:

- Age 3 months to 5 years (most occurring between 6 months and 3 years)
- Fever of 38.8°C (102°F)
- Infection not associated with the CNS

Approximately 2% to 3% of children suffer febrile convulsions. Most such convulsions are short, lasting less than 5 minutes. Only 2% to 4% of children with febrile convulsions develop epilepsy in later childhood or as adults.[47] Febrile convulsions are not a significant issue in the dental setting.

Table 21-2 presents the most common causes of seizures according to the age of the patient. The most likely causes for any type of seizure in the dental office include the following:

- Seizure in an epileptic patient
- Hypoglycemia
- Hypoxia secondary to syncope
- Local anesthetic overdose

■ PREDISPOSING FACTORS

Management of most patients with a history of epilepsy is based on prevention, or minimizing the frequency, of acute seizures. In almost all cases this goal is accomplished through the use of long-term antiepileptic (anticonvulsant) drug therapy. Despite therapy, acute seizure activity may still develop. In some cases no apparent predisposing factor can be determined; the seizure episode develops suddenly without warning. However, factors exist that are known to increase the frequency with which seizure activity develops. For instance, the immature brain is much more susceptible to biochemical alteration in cerebral blood flow than the adult brain. Therefore convulsions caused by hypoxia, hypoglycemia, or hypocalcemia are more likely to occur in younger age groups.[48] In addition, a "breakthrough" of seizure activity in a well-managed adult patient may also occur. Many cases have demonstrated that such episodes are often correlated with sleep or menstrual cycles.[49]

In many instances of seizure activity an acute triggering disturbance is evident. Such triggering factors include flashing lights (especially prominent in precipi-

TABLE 21-2 Top causes of seizures by age

Neonatal (first month)	Infancy (1–6 mo)	Early childhood (6 mo–3 yr)	Childhood and adolescence	Early adult life	Late adult life
1. Hypoxia	Hypoxia	Febrile convulsions	No known cause	Trauma	Vascular disease
2. Metabolic disorder	Metabolic disorder	Birth injury	Infection	Tumor	Trauma
3. Infection	Infection	Infection	Trauma	No known cause	Tumor
4. Congenital deformity	Congenital deformity	Toxin	Cerebral degenerative disease	Birth injury	Cerebral degenerative disease
		Trauma		Infection	
		Metabolic disorder		Cerebral degenerative disease	
		Cerebral degenerative disease			

Data modified from Pollack CV Jr., Pollack ES: Seizure. In: Marx JA, Hockberger RS, Walls RM, editors: *Rosen's emergency medicine: concepts and clinical practice*, ed 5, St. Louis, Mosby, 2002, pp. 1445–1455.

tating absence seizures), fatigue or decreased physical health, a missed meal, alcohol ingestion, and physical or emotional stress. Therefore, seizures may be said to be precipitated by a combination of several factors. The genetic predisposition to seizures and the presence of a localized brain lesion are among these factors. One or more of the following factors also may induce acute seizure activity:

- A generalized metabolic or toxic disturbance that produces an increase in cerebral neuronal excitation
- A state of cerebrovascular insufficiency
- An acute triggering disturbance, such as sleep, menstrual cycle, fatigue, flickering lights, or physical or psychological stress

Each of these factors also may produce seizure activity individually.

■ PREVENTION
Nonepileptic causes

The prevention of acute seizure activity in the dental office may be difficult because of the idiopathic nature of most seizures. However, physical evaluation of the patient before treatment may facilitate the prevention of seizures produced by metabolic or toxic disturbances. (See Chapter 17 for a discussion of the prevention of hypoglycemic reactions.)

A local anesthetic overdose (e.g., toxic reaction) is the most likely nonepileptic cause of a seizure in the dental office. Adequate patient evaluation and preparation, care in selection of local anesthetic agents, and use of the proper administration technique go far in preventing toxic reaction (see Chapter 23).

Epileptic causes

The doctor's goal with epileptic patients (as it is with all patients) is to determine the likelihood of an acute seizure developing during dental treatment, and to take any of the steps necessary to minimize that possibility. In addition, the doctor and staff members should be prepared to manage any patient who has a seizure that may arise despite preventive techniques and should attempt to minimize any associated clinical complications (e.g., soft tissue injury or fractures).

 MEDICAL HISTORY QUESTIONNAIRE

Section I, Circle Appropriate Answer:

Question 2: Has there been a change in your health within the last year?

Question 3: Have you been hospitalized or had a serious illness in the last 3 years?

Question 4: Are you being treated by a physician now? For what?
Comment: These are general survey question designed to pick of known diseases and other significant medical problems. If epilepsy is mentioned then a thorough dialogue history must follow.

Section II, Have You Experienced:

Question 21: Fainting spells?
Comment: An affirmative response to fainting spells should prompt dialogue history into the cause of the syncopal event.

Question 23: Seizures?
Comment: A thorough dialogue history is necessary to determine the type of seizure, manner of control, degree of control, and clinical manifestations associated with acute seizure activity in the patient.

Section V: Are You Taking:

Question 62: Drugs, medications, over-the-counter medicines (including aspirin), natural remedies?
Comment: Dialogue history is required to determine significant information regarding all drugs being taken by the patient.

A basic principle in the use of anticonvulsants is to select a single drug (monotherapy) rather than a combination (polytherapy), and use it until it becomes ineffective or until toxic signs become evident (Table 21-3).[50] If seizure control proves effective (i.e., no seizures for at least 4 years), the patient usually asks about drug therapy termination. Some physicians withdraw anticonvulsant medications gradually over a period of weeks to months, one drug at a time, if the patient is free of seizures for 2 to 4 years.

However, seizures recur in many such cases. Sudden withdrawal of anticonvulsant therapy is a common cause of status epilepticus. In a study of 68 children who were free of seizures for 4 years, more than two thirds successfully terminated drug therapy without seizure recurrence.[51] Callaghan et al.[8] reported that only 33% of patients—both adults and children—had a relapse after being free of seizures for 2 years. (The patients were followed for 3 years after discontinuation of drug therapy.) Withdrawal rarely is attempted in patients at the age of puberty, especially females, who usually continue drug therapy through adolescence.

Box 21-3 lists commonly used antiepileptic drugs.

Dialogue history

In response to a positive history of seizures, the following information should be sought:

What type of seizures (epilepsy) do you suffer?

How often do you experience (acute) seizures? When was your last seizure?
Comment: Generalized tonic-clonic seizures are controlled effectively in many patients. Proper drug therapy helps prevent seizures in more than 70% of epileptic patients. Such patients may be free of seizures for several years, or seizures may

TABLE 21-3 Drugs used for long-term anticonvulsant therapy in adults

Drug (brand name)	Indication	Dose (mg/ kg per day)	Daily doses
Carbamazepine (Tegretol, Carbatrol, Equetro)	Partial, GCS	15–25	3–4
Phenytoin (Dilantin, Phenytek)	Partial, GCS	3–8	1–3
Phenobarbital	Partial, GCS	2–4	1
Primidone* (Mysoline)	Partial, GCS	10–20	4
Ethosuximide (Zarontin)	Absence	10–30	2
Clonazepam (Klonopin)	Absence	0.03–0.3	2
Valproate (Depacon)	All	15–60	4
Felbamate (Felbatol)	Partial, GCS, atonic	3600 mg/ day	3

GCS, generalized convulsive seizure.
*Primidone is a congener of phenobarbital.
From Pollack CV Jr, Pollack ES: Seizures. In: Marx JA, Hockberger RS, Walls RA, editors: *Hosen's emergency medicine: concepts and clinical practice,* ed 5, St. Louis, Mosby, 2002, pp. 1445–1455.

occur only infrequently (e.g., once or twice per year). Others, however, may suffer seizures several times per week or even daily. Absence seizures may occur as frequently as every several days or in clusters of 100 or more per day. If an individual experiences seizures frequently (decreased seizure control), the likelihood that a seizure may develop during dental treatment is increased.

What signals the onset of your seizures? (What is your aura?)

Comment: Patients with tonic-clonic seizures (grand mal epilepsy) have a specific aura, or premonition, that heralds the onset of the seizure. The aura is a subjective sensation that may precede the seizure by several hours or only a few seconds. The aura commonly lasts a few seconds and relates to the specific region of the brain in which the abnormal electrical discharge originates. The aura may be stereotyped for a particular patient. Some common auras include an odd sensation in the epigastric region; an unpleasant taste or smell; various visual or auditory hallucinations; a sense of fear; strange sensations, such as numbness in the limbs; and motor phenomena, such as turning of the head or eyes or the spasm of a limb. Because the aura is part of the seizure, the signs may alert the dental team to the onset of a seizure, enabling them to initiate proper management quickly.

How long do your seizures normally last?

Comment: Seizures, except for status epilepticus, are self-limiting. The clonic phase of a tonic-clonic seizure usually lasts not more than 2 to 5 minutes; the immediate recovery period lasts about 10 to 15 minutes, with a complete return to preictal cerebral function in about 2 hours.[11] The duration of the convulsive phase has important implications in clinical management. Once completed, seizures do not normally recur during the immediate postseizure period; however, recurrent seizures may occur (as in status epilepticus).

Have you ever been hospitalized as a result of your seizures?

Comment: This question helps determine whether status epilepticus ever occurred and whether previous seizures resulted in serious injury. In addition, most epileptic patients most likely have been hospitalized on one or more occasions when bystanders in a public area summoned emergency medical personnel. Paramedical personnel must follow strict treatment protocol; when the postictal epileptic patient does not meet certain recovery criteria, a brief period of hospitalization is required.

Physical examination

If an epileptic patient is examined between seizures, no specific clinical signs or symptoms exist that lead to a diagnosis of epilepsy; however, more than 50% of patients with recurring seizures demonstrate electroencephalogram abnormalities during the interictal period. No specific dental treatment modifications are indicated, aside from possible psychosedation necessitated by obvious anxiety. Because most anticonvulsants are CNS depressants, such as the benzodiazepines (e.g., diazepam, oxazepam, and midazolam), special care must be taken to avoid oversedation when conscious sedation techniques are used.

Psychological implications of epilepsy

Folklore and myth have tried to connect epilepsy to violent behavior.[52] Although little evidence exists to support this link, many physicians and lay individuals believe that epileptic patients are dangerous, potentially violent people.[53] The incidence of epilepsy among prisoners in U.S. jails is approximately 1.8%, compared with an incidence between 0.5% and 1% in the general population.[54,55] Patients with psychomotor or grand mal seizures may exhibit signs of fright and in fact struggle irrationally with any individual who tries to help during the seizure.

Most patients with recurrent seizures can and do adapt in the work force and society despite occasional periods of disability because of seizures and their immediate consequences. The most serious feature of epileptic disability is social ostracism, which is especially damaging to the school-age child who is embarrassed by seizures and may be set apart from other children because of fear and ignorance.[56] Many such

---

Box 21-3 Drugs used in the long-term management of epilepsy

CONVENTIONAL	NEW	UNCONVENTIONAL	EXPERIMENTAL
Carbamazepine (Tegretol)	Felbamate (Felbatol)	Adrenocorticotrophic hormone (ACTH)[†]	Clobazam (Frisium)[*,§]
Ethosuximide (Zarontin)	Gabapentin (Neurontin)	Acetazolamide (Diamox)	Eterobarb[§]
Phenobarbital	Lamotrigine (Lamictal)	Amantadine (Symmetrel)[†]	Ganaxolone[§]
Phenytoin (Dilantin)	Levetiracetam (Keppra)	Bromides[†,‡]	Losigamone[§]
Primidone (Mysoline)	Oxcarbazepine (Trileptal)	Clomiphene (Clomid)[†]	Nitrazepam (Mogadon)[*,§]
Valproic acid (Depakene)	Tiagabine (Gabitril)	Ethotoin (Peganone)	Piracetam (Nootropil)[§]
	Topiramate (Topamax)	Mephenytoin (Mesantoin)	Pregabalin[§]
	Zonisamide (Zonegran)	Mephobarbital (Mebaral)	Progabide[§]
		Methsuximide (Celontin)	Remacemide[§]
		Trimethadione (Tridione)	Rotigotine[§]
			Retinamide[§]
			SPM927 (Harkoseride)[§]
			Stiripentol[§]
			Vigabatrin (Sabril)[*,§]

[*]Approved in other countries.
[†]Not FDA approved for this indication.
[‡]May be compounded by pharmacists.
[§]Investigational drug in the United States.
Data from Ranta A, Fountain NB: Seizures in adolescents and adults. In: Rakel RE, Bope ET, editors: *Conn's current therapy 2005,* ed 57, Philadelphia, WB Saunders, 2005.

---

epileptic patients feel rejected and subsequently withdraw from others. This withdrawal, combined with the prejudice that many such children and adolescents may experience, can lead to inadequate educational, matrimonial, and employment opportunities. Because of low self-esteem, many epileptic individuals may choose companions with emotional, physical, or mental handicaps of their own. Alcoholism and substance abuse may follow.

The overall risk of death among epileptic patients ranges from that of the general population to a rate 200% greater; this rate is significantly higher for the patient with poorly controlled epilepsy. Various factors contribute to the increased risk to the life and health of the epileptic patient, including ictal brain injury, medication side effects, trauma during seizure episodes, and an increased rate of suicide.[57]

Dental therapy considerations

The major consideration in the dental treatment of persons with epilepsy is to prepare to manage a seizure, if it should occur. Specific modifications in dental treatment should be considered only if warranted. Psychological stress and fatigue increase the likelihood of a seizure developing. If the individual exhibits dentistry-related fear, conscious sedation should be considered during treatment.

Conscious sedation

Inhalation sedation with nitrous oxide and oxygen is a highly recommended route of sedation for the apprehensive epileptic patient because it allows the administrator a great degree of control over its actions. When administered with at least 20% O_2, no medical contraindications exist to the administration of nitrous oxide.[58] Oral conscious sedation may also be effective in the management of the less apprehensive epileptic patient. Benzodiazepines (e.g., diazepam, oxazepam, triazolam, flurazepam) are highly recommended for adult patients, whereas promethazine, hydroxyzine, and midazolam are suggested for children.

More profound levels of CNS depression (parenteral conscious sedation or deep sedation) may be employed safely via the intravenous (IV) or intramuscular routes in the more phobic epileptic patient. The usual precautions

TABLE 21-4 Physical status classification of seizure disorders

Description	ASA physical status	Treatment considerations
History of seizures well controlled by medications (no acute seizures within past 3 months)	II	Usual ASA II considerations
History of seizure activity controlled by medication, yet seizures occurring more often than once per month	III	ASA III considerations, including preparation for seizure management
History of status epilepticus	III–IV	Medical consultation before treatment
History of seizure activity poorly controlled by medication; frequency of acute seizures (more than once per week)	IV	Medical consultation and better control of seizures, if possible, before routine dental treatment

ASA, American Society of Anesthesiologists.

associated with parenteral sedation techniques must be applied. Hypoxia or anoxia can induce seizures in any patient but is more likely to do so in those with pre-existing seizure disorders. The use of supplemental O_2 during treatment and the pulse oximeter is strongly suggested whenever greater levels of CNS depression are sought.[58]

The use of alcohol is definitely contraindicated in epileptic patients because it may precipitate seizures.[59] Therefore, epileptic patients should not undergo dental treatment if recent alcohol ingestion is obvious. In addition, the doctor should not consider the use of alcohol as a sedative agent for an epileptic patient.

Table 21-4 presents the physical status classifications for epileptic patients based on the American Society of Anesthesiologists (ASA) physical status classification system. A typical patient with well-controlled epilepsy represents an ASA II risk, whereas those with less well-controlled epilepsy may represent ASA III or IV risks.

■ CLINICAL MANIFESTATIONS

Partial seizures

Partial seizures begin in a localized area of the brain and involve only one hemisphere. The seizure is called a *simple partial seizure* when consciousness is unaltered. For example, a focal motor seizure is a simple partial seizure during which the individual remains fully alert and conscious while a limb jerks for several seconds.

However, if the abnormal neuronal discharge spreads to the opposite hemisphere, consciousness is altered and the patient's ability to respond is impaired. This is called a *complex partial seizure* and is associated with complex behavior patterns called *automatisms*. An example of a typical complex partial seizure is the sudden onset of a bad taste in the mouth (the aura), followed by a lack of responsiveness, fumbling of the hands, and smacking of the lips. The patient slowly becomes reoriented in about 1 minute and is back to normal except for slight lethargy within 3 minutes.

The automatic behavior that occurs is associated with impaired consciousness and a loss of higher voluntary control. The nature of the automatic behavior is related to the degree and duration of the confusion and to the psychological and environmental conditions existing at the time of the episode. Primitive, unco-ordinated, purposeless activities, such as lip smacking or chewing and sucking movements, occur in patients with moderate levels of impaired consciousness. On the other hand, the automatism may manifest as a mechanical continuation of activities initiated before the onset of the seizure in mildly confused patients. The patient may continue to move a spoon toward the mouth in an eating movement or pace around a room if either activity began before the seizure began. The entire seizure lasts a few minutes, and the individual experiences only momentary postictal confusion and amnesia for ictal events.[60]

Focal status epilepticus, a rare condition, resists anticonvulsant drug therapy. Characteristically, seizure activity lasts over a period of weeks despite vigorous treatment. Fortunately, this type of seizure is does not threaten the individual's life. Both simple and complex partial seizures may progress to generalized tonic-clonic seizures.

Absence seizure (petit mal)

Absence attacks occur primarily in children, with an onset between 3 and 15 years. The seizure has an abrupt onset, characterized by a complete suppression of all mental functions, manifested by sudden immobility and a blank stare. The individual may exhibit simple automatisms and minor facial clonic movements, such as intermittent blinking at three cycles per second and mouthing movements. Such attacks may last 5 to 30 seconds, whereas petit mal status may persist for hours or days. Individuals exhibit no prodromal or postictal periods, and the episodes terminate as abruptly as they began. The blank stare is followed by the immediate resumption of normal activity. If the attack occurs during conversation, the patient may miss a few words or break off in midsentence for a few seconds; however, the impairment of external awareness is so brief that the patient is unaware of it. Amnesia for ictal events is common, and the individual may experience a subjective sense of lost time.[61]

Commonly, a young child may be diagnosed informally with petit mal epilepsy when the child first enters school. After a few weeks or months, the child's teacher may advise the parents that the child daydreams frequently or goes off into "another world" for brief periods of time. Medical evaluation usually provides definitive evidence of petit mal epilepsy.

Tonic-clonic seizure

The tonic-clonic seizure may be divided into three distinct clinical phases: a prodromal phase, including a preictal phase; a convulsive, or ictal, phase; and a postseizure, or postictal, phase.

Prodromal phase

For a variable period of time (several minutes to several hours) before a tonic-clonic seizure occurs, the epileptic patient exhibits subtle to obvious changes in emotional reactivity, including increases in anxiety or depression. These changes are usually not evident to dental staff members, but a close friend or relative may notice them. If such changes appear in an epileptic patient before a dental appointment, dental treatment should be postponed and preparation for a seizure is warranted.

The immediate onset of a tonic-clonic seizure is marked in most patients by the appearance of an aura.[62] The aura is not really a warning sign; instead, it is an actual part of the seizure. Most epileptic patients exhibit the same recurrent aura before each episode. The aura usually lasts only a few seconds, and its clinical manifestations relate to the specific area of the brain in which the seizure originates. The aura itself, which may be olfactory, visual, gustatory, or auditory in nature, may be considered a simple partial seizure that progresses to a tonic-clonic seizure.

Unfortunately, many patients are unaware of their auras because of the amnesia that occurs during this period. Most patients with tonic-clonic seizure remember nothing from the time immediately preceding the onset of the seizure until they fully recover, perhaps 15 or more minutes. To explain their own auras, patients must seek bystanders who can relate to them the specific manifestations.

Preictal phase

Soon after the appearance of the aura, the individual loses consciousness and, if standing, falls to the floor. It is at this time that most seizure-related injuries are sustained. Simultaneously, a series of generalized bilateral, major myoclonic jerks occur, usually in flexion, and last for several seconds. The so-called *epileptic cry* occurs at this time. This is a sudden vocalization produced as air is expelled through a partially closed glottis while the diaphragmatic muscles go into spasm. Autonomic changes are associated with this initial phase, including an increase in the heart rate and blood pressure up to twice the baseline value, a marked increase in bladder pressure, cutaneous vascular congestion and piloerection, glandular hypersecretion, superior ocular deviation with mydriasis, and apnea.[63]

Ictal phase

Tonic component. A series of sustained generalized skeletal muscle contractions occur, first in flexion, which then progress to a tonic extensor rigidity of the extremities and trunk (Figure 21-1). During the ictal phase of the seizure, the muscles of respiration are also involved, and dyspnea and cyanosis may be evident, indicating inadequate ventilation. This period of tonic rigidity usually lasts from 10 to 20 seconds.

Clonic component. The tonic phase evolves into the clonic component, which is characterized by generalized clonic movements of the body accompanied by heavy, stertorous breathing. Alternating muscular relaxation and violent flexor contractions characterize clonic activity (Figure 21-2). During this phase the

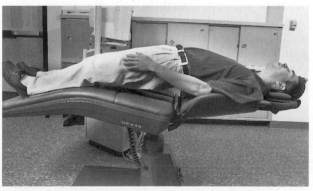

FIGURE 21-1 A victim during the tonic phase of a generalized tonic-clonic seizure (grand mal).

FIGURE 21-2　A victim during the clonic phase of a generalized tonic-clonic seizure (grand mal).

patient may froth at the mouth because air and saliva are mixed. Blood may also appear in the mouth because the victim may bite the lateral side of the tongue and cheek during the clonic portion of the seizure, injuring intraoral soft tissues.[64] This activity usually lasts about 2 to 5 minutes, after which clonic movements become less frequent, the relaxation portions become prolonged, and the individual exhibits a final flexor jerk. The ictal phase ends as respiratory movements return to normal and tonic-clonic movements cease.

Postictal phase

When tonic-clonic movements cease and breathing returns to normal, the patient enters the postictal phase, during which consciousness gradually returns. The clinical manifestations of this phase largely depend on the severity of the ictal phase.

In the first several minutes of the immediate postictal phase the patient exhibits a momentary period of muscular flaccidity during which urinary or fecal incontinence may occur because of sphincter relaxation. With termination of seizure, the patient relaxes and sleeps deeply. If the seizure was severe, the patient may initially be comatose or nonresponsive. As consciousness gradually returns, the patient is initially disoriented and confused, unaware of the surroundings or the day of the week and unable to count backward from 10 to 1 or complete other simple mathematical calculations. Alertness increases with time. Patients may then fall into a deep, but rousable, recuperative sleep and report headache and muscle soreness when they awaken.

After most episodes of tonic-clonic seizure, individuals usually exhibit almost total amnesia of the ictal and postictal phases. Some, however, may retain memory of the prodromal phase. Full recovery of preseizure cerebral functioning takes approximately 2 hours.[65]

Tonic-clonic seizure status (grand mal status)

Status epilepticus is defined as a continuous seizure or the repetitive recurrence of any type of seizure without recovery between attacks.[66,67] In this discussion, it is considered to be a direct continuation of the tonic-clonic seizure previously described. Grand mal status

is life-threatening. Patients in status epilepticus exhibit the same clinical signs and symptoms as those in the convulsive phase of a tonic-clonic seizure; the one major difference is duration. Tonic-clonic seizures normally last 2 to 5 minutes. Grand mal status may persist for hours or days and is the major cause of death directly related to seizure disorders. Mortality rates range from 3% to 23%, depending on the study cited.[68,69] The incidence of grand mal status has increased since the introduction of effective anticonvulsants; most cases result from drug or alcohol withdrawal (barbiturate withdrawal being particularly severe), severe head injury, or metabolic derangements.[70–72]

Clinically, any continuous tonic-clonic seizure that lasts 5 or more minutes is classified as grand mal status.[73] The patient is nonresponsive (unconscious), cyanotic, and diaphoretic and demonstrates generalized clonic contractions with a brief or entirely absent tonic phase. As grand mal status progresses, the patient becomes hyperthermic, the body temperature rising to 41°C. (106°F). The cardiovascular system is overworked, with tachycardia and dysrhythmias noted, and the blood pressure is elevated, with measurements of 300/150 mm Hg not infrequently reported. Unterminated grand mal status may progress until one of the following occurs:[68,74]

- Death as a result of cardiac arrest
- Irreversible neuronal damage from cerebral hypoxia, which occurs secondary to inadequate ventilation and the increased metabolic requirements of the entire body (the CNS in particular)
- A decrease in cerebral blood flow in response to increased intracranial pressure
- A significant decrease in blood glucose levels as the brain uses large volumes for metabolism

■ PATHOPHYSIOLOGY

Epilepsy is not a disease; it is a symptom that normally represents a primary form of brain dysfunction. However, detection of such a lesion is not possible in approximately 75% of patients with recurrent seizure disorders (idiopathic epilepsy).[75] Epileptic patients should be viewed as individuals with brains that malfunction periodically.

Although initial examination may fail to demonstrate it, adult-onset epilepsy most often occurs in response to the presence of a structural brain lesion. Small tumors may take considerable time to enlarge to a size at which they become detectable even with the diagnostic tools available today. Epileptic patients should undergo periodic medical examination (every 4 to 6 months), and annual electroencephalograms are recommended. The use of computed tomography and magnetic resonance imaging have significantly aided in the detection of previously undetectable lesions.

Though incompletely understood, experimental drug models of epilepsy presume that intrinsic intracellular and extracellular metabolic disturbances exist in the neurons of epileptic patients and produce excessive and prolonged membrane depolarization. What prompts such activity is unclear. Proposed mechanisms include disruption of normal structure—whether congenital, maturational, or acquired (e.g., scar tissue)—and disruption of local metabolic or biochemical function.[4,76,77]

The common denominator among epileptic patients is an increased permeability of the neuronal cell membrane with changes in sodium and potassium movement that affect the resting membrane potential and membrane excitability.[33,63,78] Subtle changes in the local concentrations of two neurotransmitters, acetylcholine (which is excitatory to cortical neurons) and gamma-aminobutyric acid (GABA) (which is inhibitory), in sensitive neurons, such as those at the ictogenic focus, produce sustained membrane depolarization, ultimately followed by local hyperpolarization and then recruitment.[33,63,78]

These hyperexcitable neurons are located in aggregates in an epileptogenic focus (the site of origin of the seizure) somewhere within the brain and tend toward recurrent, high-frequency bursts of action potentials.

Clinical seizure activity develops if the abnormal discharge is propagated along neural pathways or if local neuron recruitment occurs (if additional neighboring neurons are stimulated to discharge). Once a critical mass of neurons is recruited and a sustained excitation occurs, the seizure is propagated along conducting pathways to subcortical areas and thalamic centers. If this discharge remains localized within the focal area, a partial seizure develops, with clinical signs and symptoms related to the specific focal area. If the discharge continues to spread through normal neuronal tissue and recruitment continues, generalized seizures occur. Clinical manifestations of the seizure depend on the focus of origin and the region of the brain into which the discharge subsequently spreads.

Clinical seizures caused by systemic metabolic and toxic disorders provide evidence that seizures also can arise in normal neurologic tissues. Deficiencies in O_2, as in the hypoxia that develops during vasodepressor syncope;[79] or of glucose, which result in hypoglycemia;[80] or in calcium ions, which result in hypocalcemia, create a membrane instability that predisposes otherwise normal neurons to paroxysmal discharge. Adequate electrical stimulation may also produce clinical seizures in normal neurologic tissues (e.g., electroconvulsive therapy).

Significant alterations occur in both cerebral and systemic physiology during generalized motor seizures.

Cerebral changes include marked increases in blood flow, O_2 and glucose use, and carbon dioxide production. These changes are associated with cerebral hypoxia and carbon dioxide retention, resulting in acidosis and lactic acid accumulation.[80–82] After 20 minutes of continuous seizure activity, cerebral metabolic demands may exceed the available supply, leading to potential neuronal destruction.[82,83]

The systemic effects of prolonged seizures are believed to be secondary to the massive autonomic discharge that produces tachycardia, hypertension, and hyperglycemia.[84] Other adverse systemic effects are produced secondary to massive skeletal muscle metabolism and disturbances in pulmonary ventilation, leading to lactic acidosis, hypoxia, hypoglycemia, and hyperpyrexia.[85,86]

■ MANAGEMENT

Management of a patient during the ictal phase of a tonic-clonic seizure focuses on prevention of injury and maintenance of adequate ventilation. With almost all seizures, there is no need for anticonvulsant drug administration because most seizures are self-limiting. If a seizure persists for an unusually long period of time (>5 minutes), however, anticonvulsant drug therapy must be seriously considered.

After the convulsive phase ends, the patient exhibits varying degrees of CNS, cardiovascular, and respiratory depression, all of which require additional supportive management.[66,73] There will almost always be a prior knowledge of seizure activity in this patient, so it is highly unlikely that the dental office staff will be surprised if a seizure occurs.

Absence seizures and partial seizures

Management of absence seizures and partial seizures is protective in nature; the rescuer acts to protect the victim from injury. In each of these seizure types, there is little or no danger to the victim, for even with no assistance from staff members, death is rare. Indeed many such seizures are so brief that staff members may be unaware that an episode even occurred. However, if these seizures persist for a significant length of time (average absence seizure being 5 to 30 seconds; average partial seizure lasting 1 to 2 minutes), emergency medical assistance should be summoned immediately.

Diagnostic clues to the presence of an absence seizure or partial seizure are as follows:

- Sudden onset of immobility and blank stare
- Simple automatic behavior
- Slow blinking of eyelids

- Short duration (seconds to minutes)
- Rapid recovery

Step 1: recognition of the problem.   Lack of response to sensory stimulation.

Step 2: termination the procedure.

Step 3: activation of office emergency team, if needed.

Step 4: P (position).   In most cases of absence seizure or simple partial seizure, neither the time nor the need exists to modify patient positioning.

Step 5: reassurance of the patient.   After the seizure, the doctor should speak with the patient to determine the level of alertness and seek to determine whether the episode was related to the dental treatment. If it is felt that the seizure was related to dental phobia, appropriate steps in the stress reduction protocol should be used for all future appointments (see Chapter 2).

In addition, consultation with the patient's primary care physician is indicated if seizures have increased recently in either frequency or severity. In most cases no need exists to seek outside emergency medical assistance or administer anticonvulsant drugs.

Step 6: discharge of the patient and subsequent dental care.   The patient who suffers seizures is unlikely to be permitted to operate a motor vehicle. All states maintain requirements that prohibit epileptic individuals from operating motor vehicles until they can document control over seizures for at least 1 year (states vary on time requirements).[87,88] Therefore, such patients are usually discharged from the office in the care of an adult companion or guardian who has a vested interest in their health and safety.

Any dental-related factors that may have helped precipitate the episode should be taken into consideration and steps taken to prevent a recurrence in future treatments. Box 21-4 outlines the steps to follow in the management of petit mal and partial seizures.

Tonic-clonic seizures (grand mal)

Diagnostic clues that may prompt a suspicion of tonic-clonic seizure are as follows:[89]

- Presence of aura prior to loss of consciousness
- Loss of consciousness
- Tonic-clonic muscle contraction
- Clenched teeth; tongue biting
- Incontinence

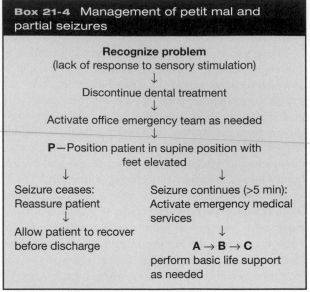

Box 21-4   Management of petit mal and partial seizures

Recognize problem
(lack of response to sensory stimulation)
↓
Discontinue dental treatment
↓
Activate office emergency team as needed
↓
P—Position patient in supine position with feet elevated
↓   ↓
Seizure ceases: Seizure continues (>5 min):
Reassure patient   Activate emergency medical services
↓   ↓
Allow patient to recover   **A → B → C**
before discharge   perform basic life support as needed

A, airway; **B,** breathing; **C,** circulation; **P,** position.

Prodromal (preictal) phase
Step 1: recognition of the problem (aura) and termination of the dental procedure.   When a patient with a history of tonic-clonic seizure exhibits the aura, treatment should cease immediately. A variable period of time is available for the removal of as much dental equipment from the patient's mouth as possible before the individual loses consciousness and progresses to the ictal phase. In addition, any dental appliances should be removed from the patient's mouth. Documented reports exist of individuals aspirating removable dental appliances during seizures.[90]

Ictal phase
Step 2: activation of the dental office emergency team.

Step 3: P (position).   When a seizure develops and the victim is not seated in the dental chair, gently place the victim on the floor in the supine position. If it occurs while the patient is seated in the dental chair, moving the patient will be difficult. Leave the patient in the dental chair, which should then be placed in the supine position.

Step 4: consideration of summoning emergency medical services (EMS).   Although most tonic-clonic seizures are of brief duration (~2 minutes), seeking medical assistance should be considered for the following reasons:
1. If the seizure is still ongoing when emergency personnel arrive, a patent vein and IV

administration of anticonvulsant drug therapy may be easier to achieve.

2. If the seizure has terminated by the time emergency personnel arrive (a much more likely occurrence), emergency workers can help evaluate the patient's postictal state, including the need for possible hospitalization or discharge.

That said, however, there are occasions when it might be more prudent to delay seeking medical assistance—for example, when the epileptic patient is accompanied by a spouse, parent, or guardian. That individual may be able to provide guidance about the nature of the patient's seizures. However, if ever the doctor believes that the summoning of emergency medical assistance is warranted, it should be done immediately.

Step 5: A-B-C (airway-breathing-circulation), or basic life support, as needed.

During the seizure, especially during the tonic phase, respiration may be inadequate. Indeed, brief periods of apnea may occur in association with obvious cyanosis. Secretions may also accumulate in the oral cavity and, if in large enough amounts, produce a degree of airway obstruction. Saliva and blood are the most common secretions. During the clonic phase, respiration improves but may still require the rescuer's assistance via airway maintenance (e.g., head tilt–chin lift). The heart rate and blood pressure are significantly elevated above baseline values.

The victim's head should be extended (head tilt) to ensure airway patency, and, if possible, the oral cavity suctioned carefully to remove excessive secretions. However, suctioning is a difficult task and, fortunately, not always necessary. Soft rubber or plastic suction catheters are preferable to metal ones, which produce more soft and hard tissue damage (bleeding, trauma). In either case the suction apparatus should be inserted between the buccal surface of the teeth and the cheek (Figure 21-3), not between the teeth of the patient.

Step 6: D (definitive care):

Step 6a: prevention of injury. If the victim is on a bed or a well-padded, carpeted floor in an area devoid of hard objects that may cause injury, the rescuer may permit the patient to seize, with little risk of injury to the victim. Gently restraining the victim's arms and legs from gross, exaggerated movements (allowing for minor movements) prevents injury resulting from joint overextension or dislocation. No attempt should be made to hold the patient's extremities in a fixed position because of the risk of bony fractures.[20,66,73] If the floor is not padded, however, the head must be protected from traumatic injury through placement of a thin, soft

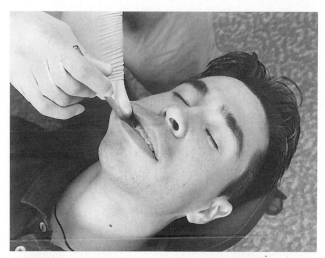

FIGURE 21-3 The suction apparatus should be inserted between the buccal surface of the teeth and the cheek.

item (a blanket or jacket) beneath the head, ensuring that the head is not flexed forward, obstructing the airway.

In addition, when the victim has a seizure in the dental chair, the danger is that the victim may fall from the chair or be injured by nearby dental equipment. Fortunately, the typical dental chair is a good site on which to have a seizure. The headrests on most dental units are normally well padded so that no additional protection is necessary for the head. Any additional pillow or doughnut device atop the headrest should be removed, leaving a bare but padded headrest. The doughnut or pillow may throw the patient's head forward, increasing the likelihood of partial or complete airway obstruction. Removing the headrest permits extending the neck, lifting the tongue, and creating greater airway patency (Figure 21-4).

Our concern is that patients not impale their arms or legs on equipment such as burs and hand instruments. One member of the office emergency team should move as much equipment as possible away from the victim while two other members stand by the patient to minimize the risk of injury. In addition, one member should be positioned at the victim's chest to protect the head and arms; the second member should stand astride the feet (Figure 21-5).[91]

NOTE: *Placement of any object in the oral cavity is usually not indicated during a tonic-clonic seizure. Many dentists, physicians, and nurses have been trained to attempt to place objects into the mouth of the seizing patient to prevent injury to intraoral tissues and prevent the patient from "swallowing their tongue." Soft items, such as handkerchiefs, towels, and gauze pads, have*

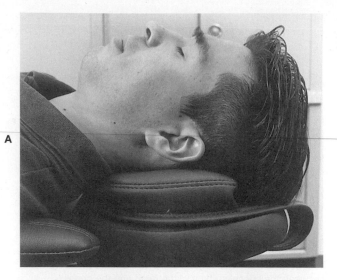

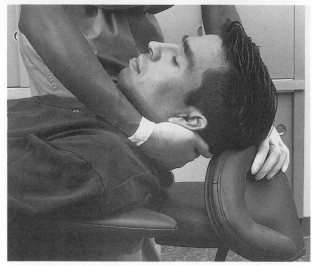

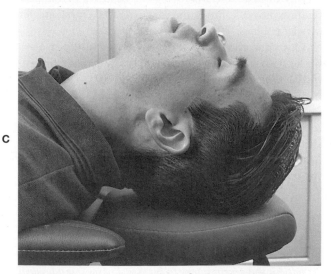

FIGURE 21-4 **A,** The headrest of a dental chair with a doughnut or pillow; head thrown forward results in partial or complete airway obstruction. **B,** A bare headrest. **C,** Head extended; increased airway patency.

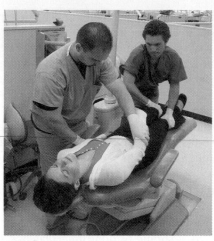

FIGURE 21-5 To prevent the victim from injury, one dental office team member should be positioned at the patient's chest while the second member should stand astride the victim's feet.

also been recommended, as have ratchet-type (Molt) and rubber mouth props, wooden tongue depressors wrapped in gauze, and even teaspoons. The forcible insertion of objects into the patient's mouth does not improve airway maintenance. Indeed the patient's muscles of mastication are in tetany during the seizure, and the patient's mouth must be forced open, greatly increasing the risk of injury to both the soft and hard tissues. Teeth have been fractured and aspirated during these attempts to help seizing patients.[92] The possibility of injury to the rescuer also exists when attempts are made to place protective objects into the convulsing patient's mouth. Under no circumstances should a rescuer place the fingers between the teeth of a convulsing patient.

In most grand mal seizures, little to no bleeding occurs. Roberge and Maciera-Rodriguez[64] studied the incidence of seizure-related intraoral lacerations in 100 patients. They found that 44% of seizing patients suffered intraoral lacerations, primarily on the lateral border of the tongue. Only 2 of these 44 patients subsequently required surgical repair of the laceration. My experience has been that attempting to place any object into the mouth of a patient during the ictal phase of a tonic-clonic seizure is unnecessary, difficult to do, and fraught with possible danger to both patient and rescuer.

In addition, tight, binding clothes should be loosened to prevent possible injury by the straining patient and as an aid in breathing.

Postictal phase

With cessation of seizures the postictal phase begins, a period of generalized depression involving the central nervous, cardiovascular, and respiratory systems. The degree of depression is related to the degree of stimulation experienced during the preceding ictal phase.[65] During the postictal phase, significant morbidity and even death may occur. The ictal phase is a highly dramatic and emotionally charged event for eyewitnesses, and attention is quickly focused on the patient. Once convulsions end, the patient relaxes and so, unfortunately, do the rescuers. This response is premature because the patient may demonstrate significant CNS and respiratory depression during the postictal phase to a degree that respiratory depression and airway obstruction may become evident.

Step 7: P (position).

The victim should remain in the supine position with the feet elevated slightly.

Step 8: A-B-C, or basic life support, as needed.

Postictal patients almost always require airway management. On rare occasion they also require assisted or controlled ventilation. O_2 may be administered via a full mask or nasal cannula, if indicated. Airway maintenance and adequacy of ventilation remain primary considerations at this time.

Step 9: monitoring of vital signs.

Vital signs should be monitored and recorded at regular intervals (at least every 5 minutes). Blood pressure and respiration may be depressed in the immediate postictal period; their return to baseline values is gradual. The heart rate may be near the baseline level, slightly depressed, or slightly elevated.

Step 10: reassurance of the patient and recovery.

Recovery from a seizure occurs slowly, with the patient initially somnolent, but rousable, and gradually becoming increasingly alert. Return to normal preseizure cerebral functioning may require as long as 2 hours. The patient also experiences significant confusion and disorientation. At this point the patient should be reassured that all is right. For example, I tell my patients the following: "This is Doctor Malamed. You are in the dental office. You had a seizure, and everything is all right." Patients respond more promptly when a familiar voice speaks to them. If a spouse, family member, relative, or friend is available, that individual should be asked to speak with and reassure the patient. Recovery includes a return of the vital signs to approximately baseline levels and a disappearance of the confusion and disorientation of the early postictal period.

Step 11: discharge.

This step is very difficult for me and represents the primary reason I recommend

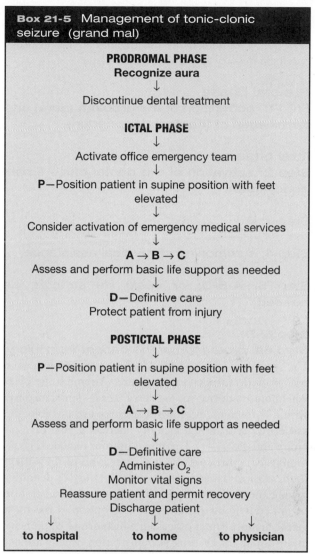

Box 21-5   Management of tonic-clonic seizure (grand mal)

PRODROMAL PHASE
Recognize aura
↓
Discontinue dental treatment

ICTAL PHASE
↓
Activate office emergency team
↓
P—Position patient in supine position with feet elevated
↓
Consider activation of emergency medical services
↓
A → B → C
Assess and perform basic life support as needed
↓
D—Definitive care
Protect patient from injury

POSTICTAL PHASE
↓
P—Position patient in supine position with feet elevated
↓
A → B → C
Assess and perform basic life support as needed
↓
D—Definitive care
Administer O_2
Monitor vital signs
Reassure patient and permit recovery
Discharge patient
↓   ↓   ↓
to hospital   to home   to physician

A, airway; B, breathing; C, circulation; D, definitive care; P, position.

considering calling for emergency medical assistance at the onset of a seizure. After the seizure has ended, should the patient be hospitalized, sent to the primary care physician, or sent home, and, if so, how?

Paramedical personnel follow strict protocols established for the management of specific emergency situations. In many jurisdictions, criteria for hospitalization of the postseizure victim who has a history of epilepsy include a lack of orientation to space and time. Emergency personnel make this decision quickly and, if necessary, transport the patient to the hospital for additional evaluation. If the patient recovers more completely and hospitalization is not warranted, discharge from the dental office occurs in the custody of a responsible adult relative or close friend (who has a vested interest in the health and safety of the patient).

Box 21-5 outlines the protocol for the management of a tonic-clonic seizure.

Grand mal status

If the tonic-clonic seizure persists for unusually long periods (>5 minutes), the use of anticonvulsant drugs may be necessary to terminate the seizure.

Preictal phase

Step 1: recognition of the problem (aura) and termination of the dental procedure.

Ictal phase

Step 2: activation of the dental office emergency team.

Step 3: P.

Step 4: summoning of medical assistance.

Step 5: A-B-C, or basic life support, as needed.

Step 6: D.
Step 6a: protection of the patient from injury.
The previous steps detailed the management of a patient with a tonic-clonic seizure. Although the overwhelming majority of seizures cease spontaneously within 5 minutes, prolonged seizures are possible and associated with a significantly increased risk of morbidity and death.[68,74] Treatment options include (1) continuing basic life support and protection of the patient until medical assistance is available and (2) definitive management of the seizure through the administration of anticonvulsant drugs. The first option is the most viable in most dental offices, in which drugs, equipment, and training for IV drug administration usually are not available. The administration of anticonvulsant drugs should be considered only when both the doctor and the office staff members are well versed in the pharmacology of these drugs; and possess the knowledge, ability, and equipment necessary to perform venipuncture; and are able to ventilate the apneic patient.

Step 7: venipuncture and administration of the anticonvulsant drug.   Various anticonvulsant drugs are used to terminate seizures. The ideal drug should produce a rapid onset of action and last only briefly.[93,94] Effectiveness depends on IV administration; the intramuscular route is too slow and unpredictable, and the oral route is contraindicated in unconscious, convulsing patients. Intranasal administration of midazolam has demonstrated efficacy in management of pediatric status epilepticus.[95,96] An IV infusion should be established or the drug injected directly into the patient's vein. Because blood pressure is elevated significantly during a seizure, superficial peripheral veins

usually are visible, which makes injection relatively easy for the experienced doctor who has an assistant to restrain the arm. However, IV injections should not be attempted if proper equipment and adequately trained staff members are not immediately available. In such instances supportive care should be continued until more highly trained personnel arrive.

The anticonvulsant drug of choice for the abortive treatment of tonic-clonic seizure is a benzodiazepine, either diazepam (Valium)[63,97,98] or midazolam (Versed, Hypnovel, Dormicum).[98] Diazepam is more than 90% effective in instances of primary convulsive status.[98,99] A 5- to 10-mg dose should be administered via the IV route at a rate of 5 mg per minute and repeated every 10 to 15 minutes, as necessary, to a maximum cumulative dose of 30 mg.[100] Children 5 to 12 years receive diazepam in doses of 0.2 to 0.5 mg/kg intravenously, a dose that can be repeated every 15 to 30 minutes, as necessary, to a maximum cumulative dose of 10 mg.[100] The diazepam dose for children over 12 years of age is 5 to 10 mg, administered via the IV route at a rate of 5 mg per minute and repeated every 15 to 30 minutes, as necessary, to a maximum cumulative dose of 30 mg.[100] Potentially serious side effects of diazepam are related to excessively rapid injection and include transient hypotension, bradycardia, respiratory depression, and cardiac arrest.[100] If the dose is titrated slowly, side effects are rare. In general, the total dose should not exceed 0.5 mg/kg for short-term therapy.[100] Midazolam, a water-soluble benzodiazepine, has also proven its effectiveness as an anticonvulsant when administered via an IV, intranasal, or intramuscular route.[101–104] Lorazepam may be as effective as diazepam, but its onset is slower and its effect longer.[98,105]

Step 8: administration of a 50% dextrose solution.   The IV administration of 25 to 50 mL of a 50% dextrose solution is recommended to rule out hypoglycemia as a possible cause of the seizure. This solution also helps the patient maintain blood sugar levels because the brain uses large quantities of glucose during the ictal state.[63]

Step 9: subsequent management.   All patients with tonic-clonic seizure status require hospitalization after the episode for neurologic evaluation and initiation of a treatment protocol to minimize further episodes. If the previously mentioned drugs do not terminate the seizure, other agents may be required. These include phenytoin (20 mg/kg IV) for long-term seizure control and phenobarbital (20 mg/kg) for continuing seizures.[63]

Box 21-6 outlines the management of patients with tonic-clonic status epilepticus.

In addition, the following information may prove useful:

- **Drugs used in management:** O₂ may be used during management of any seizure. If status epilepticus occurs, an anticonvulsant, preferably diazepam or midazolam, may be administered.
- **Medical assistance required:** Treatment of patients with seizures frequently requires the summoning of emergency personnel.

Box 21-6 Management of tonic-clonic status

PRODROMAL PHASE
Recognize aura
↓
Discontinue dental treatment

ICTAL PHASE
↓
Activate office emergency team
↓
P—Position patient in supine position
with feet elevated
↓
Consider activation of emergency medical services
↓
A → B → C
Assess and perform basic life support as needed
↓
D—Definitive care
Protect patient from injury

IF SEIZURE PERSISTS FOR MORE THAN 5 MINUTES

↓	If available
A → B → C	Perform venipuncture
Assess and perform basic	and administer IV
life support as needed	anticonvulsant
Protect patient from injury	↓
↓	Administer 50% IV
D—Definitive care	dextrose solution
Protect patient from injury	
until emergency assistance	
arrives	

A, airway; **B,** breathing; **C,** circulation; **D,** definitive care; IV, intravenous; **P,** position.

DIFFERENTIAL DIAGNOSIS

Seizures are not often confused with other systemic medical conditions. However, seizures may be part of the clinical manifestation of several other systemic disorders (Table 21-5). This section is designed to aid in the diagnosis of possible causes of seizure activity.

Vasodepressor syncope is the most common cause of unconsciousness in the dental office. If hypoxia or anoxia persist, brief periods of seizure activity may occur.[79] One distinguishing factor that indicates vasodepressor syncope is the presence of a definite precipitating factor, such as fear. Individuals suffering vasodepressor syncope usually exhibit prodromal signs, such as lightheadedness, nausea, or vomiting and diaphoresis, before losing consciousness; epileptic patients do not exhibit such signs. The duration of unconsciousness in cases of vasodepressor syncope normally is quite brief, and recovery begins once blood flow to the brain increases. Muscles are flaccid, and no convulsive movements are present initially. Blood pressure and heart rate are also depressed, and bladder and bowel incontinence are rare. When syncopal patients regain consciousness, they do not experience disorientation or confusion; they are alert and can perform simple mental calculations. The primary cause of seizure activity in vasodepressor syncope is hypoxia, which is reversible with proper positioning (supine) and/or airway management.

Cerebrovascular accident may also lead to the loss of consciousness and possible convulsions.[106] Aids in differential diagnosis include the possible presence of an intense headache before the loss of consciousness and of signs of neurologic dysfunction (e.g., muscle weakness or paralysis).

Lastly, hypoglycemia may progress to the loss of consciousness, and seizures may develop.[107] The patient's medical history and clinical signs and symptoms can usually provide evidence (see Chapter 17). Additional management in this situation requires the administration of IV dextrose, either 50% (adult) or 25% (pediatric) solution.

TABLE 21-5 Possible causes of seizure disorders

Cause	Frequency	Text discussion
Epilepsy (tonic-clonic seizure)	Most common	Seizures (Part Five)
Local anesthetic overdose (toxic reaction)	Less common	Drug-related emergencies (Part Six)
Hyperventilation	Rare	Respiratory distress (Part Three)
Cerebrovascular accident	Rare	Altered consciousness (Part Four)
Hypoglycemia	Rare	Altered consciousness (Part Four)
Vasodepressor syncope	Rare	Unconsciousness (Part Two)

REFERENCES

1. Taylor J, editor: *Selected writings of John Hughlings Jackson,* vol 1, *On epilepsy and epileptiform convulsions,* London, Hodder and Stoughton, 1931. Reprinted 1958, New York, Basic Books.
2. Thomas CL, editor: *Taber's cyclopedic medical dictionary,* ed 18, Philadelphia, F.A. Davis, 1997.
3. Commission on Classification and Terminology of the International League Against Epilepsy: Proposal for revised clinical and electroencephalographic classification of epileptic seizures, *Epilepsia* 22:489–501, 1981.
4. Hauser WA, Hesdorffer DC: Epilepsy: frequency, causes and consequences, New York, Demos, 1990.
5. Epilepsy Foundation of America. www.epilepsyfoundation. org
6. Camfield PR, Camfield CS, Dooley JM, et al.: Epilepsy after a first unprovoked seizure in childhood, *Neurology* 35:1657–1660, 1985.
7. Shinnar S, Vining EP, Mellits ED, et al.: Discontinuing antiepileptic medication in children with epilepsy after two years without seizures: a prospective study, *N Engl J Med* 313:976–980, 1985.
8. Callaghan N, Garrett A, Goggin T: Withdrawal of anticonvulsant drugs in patients free of seizures for two years: a prospective study, *N Engl J Med* 318:942–946, 1988.
9. Foldvary-Schaefer N, Wyllie E: Epilepsy. In: Goetz CG, editor: *Textbook of clinical neurology,* ed 2, Philadelphia, WB Saunders, 2003, pp. 1059–1088.
10. Bazil CW, Morrell MJ, Pedley TA: Epilepsy. In: Rowland LP, editor: *Merritt's neurology,* ed 11, Philadelphia, Lippincott Williams & Wilkins, 2005, pp. 990–1014.
11. Gastaut H: *Epileptic seizures,* Springfield, IL, Charles C Thomas, 1972.
12. Panayiotopoulos CP: Syndromes of idiopathic generalized epilepsies not recognized by the International League Against Epilepsy, *Epilepsia* 46:57–66, 2005.
13. Grosso S, Galimberti D, Vezzosi P, et al.: Childhood absence epilepsy: evolution and prognostic factors, *Epilepsia* 46:1796–1801, 2005.
14. Janz D: The idiopathic generalized epilepsies of adolescence with childhood and juvenile age of onset, *Epilepsia* 38:4–11, 1997.
15. Kaplan PW: No, some types of nonconvulsive status epilepticus cause little permanent neurologic sequelae (or: "the cure may be worse than the disease"), *Neurophysiologie Clin* 30:377–382, 2000.
16. Guerrini R: Epilepsy in children, *Lancet* 367:499–504, 2006.
17. Malow BA: Sleep and epilepsy, *Neurol Clin* 23:1127–1147, 2005.
18. Uijl SG, Leijten FS, Parra J, et al.: What is the current evidence on decision-making after referral for temporal lobe epilepsy surgery? A review of the literature, *Seizure* 14:534–540, 2005.
19. De Lorenzo RJ, Hauser WA, Townes AR, et al.: A prospective, population-based epidemiologic study of status epilepticus in Richmond, Virginia, *Neurology* 46:1029–1035, 1996.
20. American Academy of Orthopaedic Surgeons: *Emergency care and transportation for the sick and injured,* ed 4, Orco, IL, American Academy of Orthopaedic Surgeons, 1987.
21. Young GB: Status epilepticus and brain damage: pathology and pathophysiology, *Adv Neurol* 97:217–220, 2006.
22. Young GB: Status epilepticus and refractory status epilepticus: introductory and summary statements, *Adv Neurol* 97:183–185, 2006.
23. Lhatoo SD, Sander JW: Sudden unexpected death in epilepsy, *Hong Kong Med J* 8:354–358, 2002.
24. Jallon P: Mortality in patients with epilepsy, *Curr Opin Neurol* 17:141–146, 2004.
25. Shorvon S, Walker M: Status epilepticus in idiopathic generalized epilepsy, *Epilepsia* 46:73–79, 2005.
26. Gumnit RJ, Sell MA, editors: *Epilepsy: a handbook for physicians,* ed 4, Minneapolis, MN, University of Minnesota Comprehensive Epilepsy Program, 1981.
27. Janz D: Etiology of convulsive status epilepticus. In: Delgado-Escueta AV, Wasterlain CG, Treiman DM, Porter RJ, editors: *Advances in neurology,* vol 34, New York, Raven Press, 1983.
28. Kaplan PW: Prognosis in nonconvulsive status epilepticus, *Epileptic Disorders* 2:185–193, 2000.
29. Ranta A, Fountain NB: Seizures and epilepsy in adolescents and adults. In: Rakel RE, Bope ET, editors: *Conn's current therapy 2005,* ed 57. Philadephia, WB Saunders, 2005.
30. Morrell MJ: Reproductive and metabolic disorders in women with epilepsy, *Epilepsia* 44:11–20, 2003.
31. Vigevano F, Bartuli A: Infantile epileptic syndromes and metabolic etiologies, *J Childhood Neurol* 17:S9–S13, 2002.
32. Newton R: Physostigmine salicylate in the treatment of tricyclic antidepressant overdosage, *JAMA* 231:941–943, 1975.
33. Lipka LJ, Lathers CM: Psychoactive agents, seizure production, and sudden death in epilepsy, *J Clin Pharmacol* 27:169–183, 1987.
34. Macedo DS, Santos RS, Belchior LD, et al.: Effect of anxiolytics, antidepressant, and antipsychotic drugs on cocaine-induced seizures and mortality, *Epilepsy Behav* 5:852–856, 2004.
35. Benardo LS: Prevention of epilepsy after head trauma: do we need new drugs or a new approach? *Epilepsia* 44:27–33, 2003.
36. Herman ST: Epilepsy after brain insult: targeting epileptogenesis, *Neurology* 59:S21–S26, 2002.
37. Dugan EM, Howell JM: Posttraumatic seizures, *Emerg Med Clin North Am* 12:1081–1087, 1994.
38. Holmes GL: *Diagnosis and management of seizures in childhood,* Philadelphia, WB Saunders, 1987.
39. Bromfield EB: Epilepsy in patients with brain tumors and other cancers, *Rev Neurol Dis* 1:S27–S33, 2004.
40. Reinikainen KJ, Keranen T, Lehtinen JM, et al.: CT brain scan and EEG in the diagnosis of adult onset seizures, *Epilepsy Res* 1:178–184, 1987.
41. Waterhouse E, Towne A: Seizures in the elderly: nuances in presentation and treatment, *Cleve Clin J Med* 72:S26–S37, 2005.

42. Ferro JM, Pinto F: Poststroke epilepsy: epidemiology, pathophysiology and management, *Drugs Aging* 21:639–653, 2004.

43. Sander JW, Perucca E: Epilepsy and comorbidity: infections and antimicrobials usage in relation to epilepsy management, *Acta Neurol Scand* 180:16–22, 2003.

44. Preux PM, Druet-Cabanac M: Epidemiology and aetiology of epilepsy in sub-Saharan Africa, *Lancet Neurol* 4:21–31, 2005.

45. Dahlquist NR, Mellinger JF, Klass DW: Hazard of video games in patients with light-sensitive epilepsy, *JAMA* 249:776–777, 1983.

46. Millett CJ, Fish DR, Thompson PJ: A survey of epilepsy-patient perceptions of video-game material/electronic screens and other factors as seizure precipitants, *Seizure* 6:457–459, 1997.

47. Annegers JF, Hauser WA, Shirts SB, Kurland LT: Factors prognostic of unprovoked seizures after febrile convulsions, *N Engl J Med* 316:493–498, 1987.

48. Rubin DH, Conway EE Jr, Caplen SM, et al.: Neurologic disorders. In: Marx JA, Hockberger RS, Walls RM, editors: *Rosen's emergency medicine: concepts and clinical practice*, ed 5, St. Louis, Mosby, 2002, pp. 2344–2369.

49. Aminoff MJ: Neurology. In: Tierney LM Jr., McPhee SJ, Papadakis MA, editors: *Current medical diagnosis and treatment 2007*, Stamford, CT, Appleton & Lange, 2007.

50. Porter RJ: How to use antiepileptic drugs. In: Levy RH, Dreifuss FE, Matlson RH, et al., editors: *Antiepileptic drugs*, ed 3, New York, Raven Press, 1989.

51. Emerson R, D'Souza BJ, Vining EP, et al.: Stopping medication in children with epilepsy: predictors of outcome, *N Engl J Med* 304:1125–1129, 1981.

52. Treiman DM: Violence and the epilepsy defense, *Neurol Clin* 17:245–255, 1999.

53. Tsopelas ND, Saintfort R, Fricchione GL: The relationship of psychiatric illness and seizures, *Curr Psychiatry Rep* 3:235–242, 2001.

54. Fearnley D, Zaatar A: A cross-sectional study which measures the prevalence and characteristics of prisoners who report a family history of epilepsy, *Med Sci Law* 41:305–308, 2001.

55. Whitman S, Coleman TE, Patmon C, et al.: Epilepsy in prison: elevated prevalence and no relationship to violence, *Neurology* 34:775–782, 1984.

56. Living with epilepsy, *New York Times*, February 23, 1982.

57. Elwes R, Johnson AL, Shorvon SD, Reynolds EH: The prognosis for seizure control in newly diagnosed epilepsy, *N Engl J Med* 311:944–947, 1984.

58. Malamed SF: *Sedation: a guide to patient management*, ed 4, St. Louis, Mosby, 2003.

59. Shaw G: Alcohol and the nervous system, *Clin Endocrinol Metab* 7:385–404, 1978.

60. Muszkat M, Rizzuti S: New focal epileptic seizures according to the ILAE Task Force on Classification and Terminology, *Arq Neuropsiquiatr* 61:47–53, 2003.

61. Blumenfeld H: Consciousness and epilepsy: why are patients with absence seizures absent? *Prog Brain Res* 150:271–286, 2005.

62. Shneker BF, Fountain NB: Epilepsy, *Dis Mon* 49:426–478, 2003.

63. Pollack CV Jr., Pollack ES: Seizures. In: Marx JA, Hockberger RS, Walls RM, editors: *Rosen's emergency medicine: concepts and clinical practice*, ed 5, St. Louis, Mosby, 2002, pp. 1445–1455.

64. Roberge RJ, Maciera-Rodriguez L: Seizure-related oral lacerations: incidence and distribution, *J Am Dent Assoc* 111:279–280, 1985.

65. Schachter SC: Seizure disorders, *Prim Care* 31:85–94, 2004.

66. Sirven JI, Waterhouse E: Management of status epilepticus, *Am Fam Physician* 68:469–476, 2003.

67. Chen JWY, Wasterlain CG: Status epilepticus: pathophysiology and management in adults, *Lancet Neurol* 5:246–256, 2006.

68. Logroscino G, Hesdorffer DC, Cascino G, et al.: Mortality after a first episode of status epilepticus in the United States and Europe, *Epilepsia* 46:46–48, 2005.

69. Maytal J, Shinnar S, Moshe SL, Alvarez LA: Low morbidity and mortality of status epilepticus in children, *Pediatrics* 83:323–331, 1989.

70. Sanya EO: Status epilepticus—a review article, *Niger J Med* 13:89–97, 2004.

71. Patwardhan RV, Dellabadia J Jr, Rashidi M, et al.: Control of refractory status epilepticus precipitated by anticonvulsant withdrawal using left vagal nerve stimulation: a case report, *Surg Neurol* 64:170–173, 2005.

72. Legriel S, Mentec H: Status epilepticus during acute hypercarbia: a case report (letter), *Intensive Care Med* 31:314, 2005.

73. Marik PE, Varon J: The management of status epilepticus, *Chest* 126:582–591, 2004.

74. Chin RF, Neville BG, Scott RC: A systematic review of the epidemiology of status epilepticus, *Eur J Neurol* 11:800–810, 2004.

75. Blume WT: Diagnosis and management of epilepsy, *CMAJ* 168:441–448, 2003.

76. Engel J, Starkman S: Overview of seizures, *Emerg Med Clin North Am* 12:895–923, 1994.

77. Engel J: *Seizures and epilepsy*, Philadelphia, FA Davis, 1989.

78. Reynolds EH: Water, electrolytes and epilepsy, *J Neurol Sci* 11:327–358, 1970.

79. McKeon A, Vaughan C, Delanty N: Seizure versus syncope, *Lancet Neurol* 5:171–180, 2006.

80. Sperling MA, Menon RK: Differential diagnosis and management of neonatal hypoglycemia, *Pediatr Clin North Am* 51:703–723, 2004.

81. Chapman AG, Meldrum BS, Siesjo BK: Cerebral metabolic changes during prolonged epileptic seizures in rats, *J Neurochem* 28:1025–1035, 1977.

82. Holmes GL: Effects of seizures on brain development: lessons from the laboratory, *Pediatr Neurol* 33:1–11, 2005.

83. Kreisman NR, Rosenthal M, Lamanna JC, Sick TJ: Cerebral oxygenation during recurrent seizures. In: Delgado-Escueta AV, Wasterlain CG, Treiman DM, Porter RJ, editors: *Advances in neurology*, vol 34, New York, Raven Press, 1983.

84. Laidlaw J, Richens A: *A textbook of epilepsy,* Edinburgh, Scotland, Churchill Livingstone, 1976.

85. Orringer CE, Eustace JC, Wunsch CD, Gardner LB: Natural history of lactic acidosis after grand mal seizures. A model for the study of an anion-gap acidosis not assoiated with hyperkalemia, *N Engl J Med* 297:796–799, 1977.

86. Meldrum BS, Vigouroux RA, Brierly JB: Systemic factors and epileptic brain damage: prolonged seizures in paralyzed artificially ventilated baboons, *Arch Neurol* 29:82–87, 1973.

87. Richards KC: Patient page: The risk of fatal car crashes in people with epilepsy, *Neurology* 63:E12–E13, 2004.

88. Sheth SG, Krauss G, Krumholz A, Li G: Mortality in epilepsy: driving fatalities vs other causes of death in patients with epilepsy, *Neurology* 63:1002–1007, 2004.

89. Pollakoff J, Pollakoff K: *EMT's guide to treatment,* Los Angeles, Jeff Gould, 1991.

90. Giovannitti JA Jr: Aspiration of a partial denture during an epileptic seizure, *J Am Dent Assoc* 103:895, 1981.

91. Stoopler ET, Sollecito TP, Greenberg MS: Seizure disorders: update on medical and dental considerations, *Gen Dent* 51:361–366, 2003.

92. Scheuer ML, Pedley TA: The evaluation and treatment of seizures, *N Engl J Med* 323:1468–1474, 1990.

93. Prasad K, Al-Roomi K, Krishnan PR, Sequeria R: Anticonvulsant therapy for status epilepticus, *Cochrane Database Syst Rev* 4: CD003723, 2005.

94. Bleck TP: Refractory status epilepticus, *Curr Opin Crit Care* 11:117–120, 2005.

95. Mahmoudian T, Zadeh MM: Comparison of intranasal midazolam with intravenous diazepam for treating acute seizures in children, *Epilepsy Behav* 5:253–255, 2004.

96. Wilson MT, Macleod S, O'Regan ME: Nasal/buccal midazolam use in the community, *Arch Dis Child* 89: 50–51, 2004.

97. Sankar R: Initial treatment of epilepsy with antiepileptic drugs: pediatric issues, *Neurology* 63:S30–S39, 2004.

98. ACEP Clinical Policies Committee Clinical Policies Subcommittee on Seizures. Clinical policy: Critical issues in the evaluation and management of adult patients presenting in the emergency department with seizures, *Ann Emerg Med* 43:605–625, 2004.

99. Pitkanen A, Kharatishvili I, Narkilahti S, et al.: Administration of diazepam during status epilepticus reduces development and severity of epilepsy in rat, *Epilepsy Res* 63:27–42, 2005.

100. ePocrates. Diazepam. www.ePocrates.com

101. Jaimovich DG, Shabino CL, Noorani PA, et al.: Intravenous midazolam suppression of pentyl-enetetrazol-induced epileptogenic activity in a porcine model, *Crit Care Med* 18:313–316, 1990.

102. Nordt SP, Clark RF: Midazolam: a review of therapeutic uses and toxicity, *J Emerg Med* 15:357–365, 1997.

103. Chamberlain JM, Altieri MA, Futterman C, et al.: A prospective, randomized study comparing intramuscular midazolam with intravenous diazepam for the treatment of seizures in children, *Pediatr Emerg Care* 13:92–94, 1997.

104. Kendall JL, Reynolds M, Goldberg R: Intranasal midazolam in patients with status epilepticus, *Ann Emerg Med* 29:415–417, 1997.

105. Dachs R: Responding to an in-flight emergency, *Am Fam Physician* 68:975–976, 2003.

106. Devuyst G, Karapanayiotides T, Hottinger I, et al.: Prodromal and early epileptic seizures in acute stroke: does higher serum cholesterol protect? *Neurology* 61:249–252, 2003.

107. Freedman SB, Powell EC: Pediatric seizures and their management in the emergency department, *Clin Ped Emerg Med* 4:195–206, 2003.

PART 6

DRUG-RELATED EMERGENCIES

22 Drug-Related Emergencies: General Considerations

23 Drug Overdose Reactions

24 Allergy

25 Drug-Related Emergencies: Differential Diagnosis

Drug-Related Emergencies:

General Considerations

The administration of drugs is commonplace in the practice of dentistry. *Local anesthetics* are an integral part of the dental treatment plan whenever potentially painful procedures are considered. *Analgesics* are prescribed for relief of preexisting pain or alleviation of potential post-operative pain, *antibiotics* are used in management of infections, and *central nervous system (CNS) depressants* are prescribed for all phases of the dental treatment (before, during, and after) for the prevention and management of dentistry-related fears. These four drug categories constitute the overwhelming majority of all drugs used in the practice of dentistry.

Whenever a drug is administered to a patient, a rational purpose should exist for its use. Indiscriminate administration of drugs is one of the major reasons the number of incidents of serious drug-related, life-threatening emergencies reported in the medical and dental literature has increased.[1-4] Most drug-related emergencies are classified as one aspect of iatrogenic disease, a category that encompasses an entire spectrum of adverse effects that physicians or dentists produce unintentionally during patient management.

The high incidence of reports of adverse drug reactions (ADRs) in medical literature accounts for 3% to 20% of all hospital admissions.[4-6] An additional 5% to 40% of patients hospitalized for other reasons experience ADRs during their hospitalization. Furthermore, 10% to 18% of those patients admitted to the hospital because of an ADR have yet another ADR during their time in the hospital, resulting in the length of hospitalization being doubled.[5] In most cases, careful prescribing habits or care in the administration of drugs might have prevented the occurrence of an ADR. A recent report noted than more than 106,000 individuals died in U.S. hospitals because of adverse reactions to drugs they received while undergoing medical treatment for a primary disorder. An additional 2.2 million suffered serious but nonfatal ADRs.[7]

Some general principles of toxicology are presented here so that the following material may be better understood (Box 22-1). Toxicology is the study of the harmful effects of chemicals (drugs) on biological systems. These harmful effects range from those that may prove inconsequential to the patient and are reversible entirely once the chemical is withdrawn, to those that prove uncomfortable but are not seriously harmful, to those that seriously may incapacitate the patient or cause death.[8] Whenever a drug is administered, two types of reactions may be noted: (1) desirable drug actions, those that are sought clinically and usually are beneficial, and (2) side effects, which are often undesirable drug actions.

An example of a desired drug action is the relief of anxiety through the administration of diazepam to a fearful dental patient (anxiolysis). A side effect of diazepam used in this manner that is normally not desired but does not usually harm the patient is drowsiness. However, drowsiness may prove beneficial under certain circumstances, such as when the patient is extremely apprehensive. However, the same degree of drowsiness while that patient is driving an automobile may prove hazardous. A side effect or undesirable drug action may also prove harmful to the patient. Respiratory and cardiovascular depression, although they rarely accompany proper administration of diazepam, can occur after either parenteral (intramuscular [IM] or intravenous [IV]) or oral administration.[9]

A general principle of toxicology is that no drug ever exerts a single action. All chemicals exert many actions, some desirable and others undesirable. Ideally, the correct drug is administered in the correct dose via the correct route to the correct patient at the correct time for the correct reason, and this drug does not produce unwanted effects.[8] This clinical situation rarely if ever occurs because no drug is so specific that it produces only the desired effects in all patients. No clinically useful drug is entirely devoid of toxicity. In addition, ADRs may occur when the wrong drug is administered to the wrong patient in the wrong dose via the wrong route at the wrong time for the wrong reason.

■ PREVENTION

Although the preceding discussion may seem unduly pessimistic, it has not been presented with the intention of scaring dental practitioners away from administering drugs to their patients. Indeed, my firm conviction is that drug use is absolutely essential in dentistry for the safe and proper management of most patients. Thus, it is important that every doctor become familiar with the pharmacologic properties of all drugs he or she uses and prescribes. Several excellent references may serve as readily available sources of information.[10-13]

Pallasch[8] stated the following:

> In most cases it is possible with sound clinical and pharmacological judgment to prevent serious toxicity from occurring. The aim of rational therapeutics is to maximize the therapeutic and minimize the toxic effects of a given drug. No drug is "completely safe" or "completely harmful." All drugs are capable of producing harm if handled improperly, and conversely, any drug may be handled safely if proper precautions are observed. The potential toxicity of a drug rests in the hands of the user.

Another factor in the safe use of drugs is a consideration of the patient who is to receive the drug. Individuals react in very different ways to the same stimulus; it should not be surprising that patients will vary markedly in their reactions to drugs. Before administering any drug or prescribing any medication, the doctor must ask specific questions about the patient's past and present drug history.

Box 22-1 General principles of toxicology

1. No drug ever exerts a single action.
2. No clinically useful drug is entirely devoid of toxicity.
3. The potential toxicity of a drug rests in the hands of the user.

✎ **MEDICAL HISTORY QUESTIONNAIRE**

Question 38 on the University of the Pacific School of Dentistry medical history refers specifically to adverse drug reactions. Section

V, questions 61 to 64, relates to substances being "taken" by the patient: recreational drugs; drugs, medications, over-the-counter medicines (including aspirin); and natural remedies.

Patients, especially older persons, frequently make a significant mental distinction between the words "drug" and "medicine." In their thought process, medicines are prescribed to you to take by your doctor while (illicit) drugs are "done." You "take" medicine and you "do" drugs. It is therefore necessary for the doctor, hygienist, or assistant who is reviewing the medical history to use these words carefully.

In the following discussion, the term "drugs" will be used to connote any and all medicines being taken by the patient, licit or illicit.

Section I, Circle Appropriate Answer:

Question 4: Are you being treated by a physician now? For what?
Comment: Patients under a physician's care might well be receiving prescription or nonprescription drugs. Determination of the reason for being under a physician's care can help in the determination of drug administration.

Section III, Do You Have or Have You Had:

Question 38: Allergies to: drugs, foods, medications, latex?
Comment: Common signs and symptoms of allergy are presented in this section along with the names of drugs that commonly are associated with ADRs. A report of allergy is an alleged history until such time as it can be proved or disproved. Any allegation of allergy to any drug must lead the doctor to an in-depth dialogue history seeking the precise nature of the previous "allergy" (see Chapters 23 and 24). Unfortunately, most patients, as well many physicians and dentists, label themselves as "allergic" to a drug whenever they experience any ADR.[14] It is the duty of the primary health care provider to seek to determine the true nature of the ADR prior to administering the same, or closely related, drug to the patient.

Section V, Are You Taking:

Question 61: Recreational drugs?

Question 62: Drugs, medications, over-the-counter medicines (including aspirin), natural remedies?

Question 63: Tobacco in any form?

Question 64: Alcohol?
Comment: Determination of current, or recent, drug use by the patient provides a plethora of information regarding the medical condition of the patient, as well as the potential for drug-drug interactions with dentally administered drugs. An in-depth dialogue history must follow to determine why each drug is being taken by the patient and whether it is being taken correctly (patient nonadherence is a major problem with drugs taken long term, such as antihypertensive agents).[15]

Dialogue history

Whenever a patient mentions that they are taking one or more drugs, the dentist must determine: (1) the name of the drug; (2) reason for which it is being taken; (3) dosage of the drug; (4) dosage schedule

(e.g., two, three, four times daily); (5) whether the patient adheres strictly to the dosage schedule or whether nonadherence is an issue; (6) whether there have been any adverse effects noted by the patient, and if so, what they are; and (7) the potential for drug-drug interactions with drugs being considered for administration by the dentist.

If a patient responds positively to an allergy or ADR (question 38), the doctor should obtain the following information from the patient concerning the incident:

What drug did you take?

Were you taking any other medications at the time of the allergic reaction or ADR?

Did the individual who administered the drug record your vital signs?

What was the time sequence of events during the reaction?

Where were you when the reaction occurred (e.g., at home or in a medical or dental office)?

What clinical manifestations (signs and symptoms) did you exhibit?

What acute treatment did you receive?

Have you received the offending agent or any chemical related to it since the incident; if so, what was your reaction?
Most patients respond affirmatively to "allergy" if they have ever experienced any adverse reaction to a drug. (This will be discussed in detail in the remaining chapters in this section.) Actually, the incidence of allergic phenomena is low, despite the high incidence of reports of allergy in dental and medical histories. The reason for this variance lies in the fact that to the patient, any ADR is an allergy; the lay individual often is not familiar with the classification of drug reactions.

Notations such as "allergy to Novocain" and "allergy to codeine" are commonly found on medical history questionnaires. Although allergies to these drugs are possible, the ADR in question was, most likely, not an allergy. Careful questioning through dialogue history usually reveals that "allergy to Novocain" was, in fact, a psychogenic reaction, such as hyperventilation or vasodepressor syncope, or a mild overdose (toxic) reaction to the drug. "Allergy to codeine" most likely consisted of stomach upset, nausea, or vomiting, all of which are undesirable side effects of the drug, not an allergic reaction.

Questions that reveal the precise nature of the ADR are important. However, patients may often provide vague answers, which do not allow the doctor to distinguish a harmless ADR from a true allergic reaction. At such times the doctor should attempt to locate and speak to the individual who observed or managed the "allergic" reaction and who may be able to provide more precise details of the event.

In addition, reactions often thought of as ADRs in fact may be unrelated to the administered drug. In an article entitled "Adverse Nondrug Reactions," Reidenberg and Lowenthal[16] demonstrated the occurrence of common drug side effects in persons who had not received any medications for 2 weeks. If they had been taking medications at the time that the reaction occurred, they might have been reported as ADRs.

Whenever doubt remains as to the potential safety of a drug, it is prudent to initially assume that the patient *is* allergic and avoid its use until the question of allergy is answered definitively. This process may require referral of the patient to an allergist or other individual for evaluation. In most cases of alleged allergy, alternative drugs are available that possess the same beneficial clinical properties without the same potential for allergy as the drug in question. These "safer" alternatives should be used until allergy is ruled out conclusively.

Even in the absence of a history of ADR, it is still recommended that the patient be questioned directly before any new drugs are administered. Therefore the doctor may ask the patient: "Have you ever taken Valium before?" If the answer is "yes," the next question may be, "What effect did it produce?" Common, proprietary names should also be used (e.g., Valium) because few non–health care professionals are familiar with generic names of drugs (e.g., diazepam). If the individual does not report any ADRs, the doctor may feel more confident when administering the drug but must always be aware that ADRs (including allergy) may still occur despite prior administration of the same drug without complication.

Care in drug administration

About 85% of ADRs are related to the administration of a drug overdose.[5] Drug overdose (also known as a *toxic reaction*) may be absolute (too many milligrams) or relative (a normal therapeutic dose leading to overdose in a particular patient). Regardless of the type of overdose, most such reactions can be prevented through careful dose determination (in nontitratable routes of drug administration such as oral, IM, and intranasal [IN]) or careful administration (titration via IV and inhalation routes). Clinical response to drugs is related to dose (dose dependent); however, even minute quantities of a drug may precipitate a severe allergic reaction (anaphylaxis) in a previously sensitized individual.

The route of drug administration also influences the number and severity of ADRs. Two major routes—enteral and parenteral—are considered. Enteral routes of administration are those in which the drug is administered in the gastrointestinal tract and subsequently absorbed into the circulatory system; it includes the oral and rectal routes. In parenteral administration the drug bypasses the gastrointestinal tract; techniques of parenteral drug administration include IM, IN, transdermal, submucosal, subcutaneous (SC), IV, intraspinal, and intracapsular injections. Inhalation and topical application comprise additional routes of administration that may be classified as parenteral.

In general, serious ADRs occur more frequently following parenteral drug administration than after administration via enteral routes. IV drug administration is the most effective route because it provides a rapid onset and a high degree of reliability; it also carries a greater potential for serious ADRs. However, when used properly (e.g., titrated), the IV route remains a safe and important option in the practice of dentistry.

ADRs associated with enteral drug administration are usually less serious. Enterally administered drugs are much less clinically effective than those administered parenterally. A general rule in drug administration states that if a drug is clinically effective when administered enterally, this route is preferable to its parenteral administration.

In drug administration the route of administration must be considered carefully. Not all drugs may be administered via every route, and the degree of effectiveness for some drugs may vary considerably on the basis of the route. For example, 10 mg of diazepam administered intravenously usually provides a level of sedation adequate to permit a phobic patient to tolerate dental treatment; in contrast, the level of sedation achieved through oral administration of 10 mg of diazepam will probably be inadequate to allow comfortable dental treatment for the same patient. On the other hand, antibiotic prophylaxis for the patient with rheumatic heart disease may be achieved with either IM injection or oral administration of penicillin or amoxicillin 1 hour before treatment. In both instances the antibiotic blood level is adequate to prevent transient bacteremia from producing bacterial endocarditis. In this instance, however, the oral route is preferred over the parenteral. Penicillin has a high potential for provoking allergy, and its route of administration has a bearing on the severity of any reaction that might arise.

Most drug-related emergency situations are preventable. Careful questioning of the patient regarding any prior exposure and subsequent reaction to a drug before its administration, careful selection of the most appropriate route of administration, use of the proper technique, and familiarity with the pharmacology of all drugs prescribed to patients or used in the dental office can significantly reduce the incidence of ADRs.

■ CLASSIFICATION

Classifying ADRs has become confusing. In the past a variety of terms, such as *side effect, adverse experience, drug-induced disease, disease of medical progress, secondary effect,* and *intolerance,* described such a reaction. Today's approach is simpler; most reactions are classified simply as ADRs.

The classification proposed by Pallasch[8] represents a simplified approach to the classification of ADRs (Box 22-2). This classification presents the following three major methods by which drugs may produce ADRs:

1. Direct extension of a drug's pharmacologic actions

Box 22-2 Classification of ADRs
TOXICITY RESULTING FROM DIRECT EXTENSION OF PHARMACOLOGIC EFFECTS
Side effects
Abnormal dose (overdose)
Local toxic effects
TOXICITY RESULTING FROM ALTERED RECIPIENT (PATIENT)
Presence of pathologic processes
Emotional disturbances
Genetic aberrations (idiosyncrasy)
Teratogenicity
Drug-drug interactions
TOXICITY RESULTING FROM DRUG ALLERGY

ADR, adverse drug reaction.
Modified from Pallasch TJ: *Pharmacology for dental students and practitioners,* Philadelphia, Lea & Febiger, 1980.

2. Deleterious effect on a chemically, genetically, metabolically, or morphologically altered recipient (the patient)
3. Initiation of an immune (allergic) response

Approximately 85% of ADRs result from the pharmacologic effects of the drug, whereas 15% result from immunologic reactions.[5]

Most ADRs are merely annoying and do not pose a threat to the patient's life. However, several potential responses to drugs exist that are life-threatening and require immediate effective management if the patient is to recover to full function. Such responses include the *overdose reaction* (a direct extension of the usual pharmacologic properties of the drug) and the *allergic reaction.* (Because of the critical nature of these responses and their importance in dentistry, subsequent chapters will discuss these responses in more detail.) *Idiosyncrasy,* the last of the critical drug-related situations, is discussed fully in this chapter.

Overdose reaction

Overdose (toxic reaction) is a condition that results from exposure to toxic amounts of a substance that does not cause adverse effects when administered in smaller amounts.[17] It refers to those clinical signs and symptoms resulting from an absolute or a relative over-administration of a drug that leads to elevated blood levels of the drug in its target organs and tissues.*

---

*Target organs and tissues are those sites in the body in which a specific drug exerts a pharmacologic action. For example, the brain is a target organ for alcohol.

Clinical signs and symptoms of overdose are related to a direct extension of the normal pharmacologic actions of the drug. For example, with therapeutic blood levels in the CNS, barbiturates mildly depress the CNS, resulting in sedation or hypnosis (both potentially desirable effects). Barbiturate overdose (higher blood levels of the barbiturate in the CNS) produces a more profound CNS depression, increasing the likelihood of significant respiratory and cardiovascular depression.

Further elevation in barbiturate blood levels results in loss of consciousness (general anesthesia or a medical emergency, depending on the clinical situation) and increasing degrees of respiratory depression, which results eventually in respiratory arrest (apnea). Local anesthetics are also CNS depressants. When these drugs are administered properly and in therapeutic doses, little or no evidence of CNS depression is evident; however, increased blood levels (in the CNS and myocardium) evoke signs and symptoms of selective CNS depression (see Chapter 23).

Allergy

Allergy is defined as a hypersensitive response to an allergen to which the individual has been previously exposed and to which that individual has developed antibodies.[17] Clinically, an allergy can manifest itself in a variety of ways, including drug fever, angioedema, urticaria, dermatitis, depression of blood-forming organs, photosensitivity, and anaphylaxis (the latter being an acute systemic reaction that may result in respiratory distress or cardiovascular collapse). Certain drugs and substances are much more likely than others to cause allergic reactions (e.g., penicillin, aspirin, latex, bisulfites, peanuts, and bee stings). An allergic reaction is potentially possible with any drug or chemical.

In marked contrast to an overdose, in which clinical manifestations relate directly to the normal pharmacology of the drug, the observed clinical response in allergy is always a result of an exaggerated response by the immune system. The degree of heightened response determines the acuteness and severity of the observed allergy.

Allergic responses to a barbiturate, local anesthetic, and an antibiotic are caused by the same mechanism and clinically may appear identical. Indeed allergic responses to peanuts, bananas, shellfish, and bee stings are similar to each other and to those produced by drug allergy. All responses require the same basic emergency management, whereas overdose reactions to the same three items are clinically quite dissimilar, requiring entirely different modes of treatment.

A third factor when comparing overdose and allergic reactions is the amount, or dose, of the drug administered. Overdose requires that a dose of the drug or substance be of sufficient size to produce a blood level high enough to produce an ADR. Overdose reactions are dose related. Allergy, in contrast, is not dose dependent. If a person is not allergic to penicillin, that person can tolerate extremely large doses safely; however, if allergy exists, exposure to even a minute volume (<1 mg) may result in death.[18] Consider the volume of venom injected into an individual by a stinging insect, such as a bee. Acutely allergic individuals may experience clinical death (cardiopulmonary arrest) within seconds of being stung.

Idiosyncrasy

Idiosyncrasy, or an idiosyncratic reaction, may be defined alternatively as an individual's unique hypersensitivity to a particular drug, food, or other substance;[17] ADRs that cannot be explained by any known pharmacologic or biochemical mechanism; or any ADR that is neither an overdose nor an allergic reaction. An example of idiosyncratic reaction is CNS stimulation (e.g., excitation or agitation) that occurs after the administration of a known CNS depressant, such as a barbiturate or histamine-blocker.

Idiosyncratic reactions cover an extremely wide range of clinical expression. Almost any type of reaction may be seen. Examples include depression that follows the administration of a stimulant, stimulation that follows the administration of a depressant, and hyperpyrexia (markedly elevated body temperature) that follows the administration of a muscle relaxant, such as succinylcholine. It is difficult to predict in advance which persons may experience idiosyncratic reactions or the nature of the resulting reactions.

Management of idiosyncratic reactions

Because of the unpredictability of the nature and occurrence of idiosyncratic reactions, their management is of necessity symptomatic. The essentials of basic life support—P→A→B→C (position-airway-breathing-circulation)—are vital.

If an idiosyncratic reaction manifests itself as a seizure, the treatment protocol for seizures should be followed (see Chapter 21). Prevention of injury and airway management are the primary considerations. Knowledge of the steps of basic management for the various emergency situations in this text should enable the doctor to successfully treat most idiosyncratic reactions.

Current wisdom proposes that almost all instances of idiosyncrasy are associated with underlying genetic mechanisms. Such genetic aberrations remain undetected until the individual receives a specific drug, which then produces the bizarre (nonpharmacologic) clinical expression. For example, an idiosyncratic reaction to succinylcholine may produce malignant hyperthermia.

■ DRUG-RELATED EMERGENCIES

Before the primary drugs used in dentistry and their major ADRs are discussed, it is important to discuss the factor responsible for more drug-related emergencies than any other. In the preceding discussion of ADRs, all responses were related directly to the action of a drug on a biological system. However, many "drug" reactions are associated with the administration of the drug, not by the clinical actions of that drug. The major cause of drug-related emergency situations in the dental office is the *administration* of local anesthetics. Although true ADRs in response to local anesthetics may occur, most ADRs associated with local anesthetics are related to the act of administering the drug—the injection.

Psychogenic reactions, most notably vasodepressor syncope and hyperventilation, are the most common "drug-related" emergencies in dentistry. Both usually result from the extreme emotional stress occurring when a person receives the local anesthetic injection, not from the drug itself. Psychogenic reactions may also occur with parenteral administration of a drug.[*] The potential for a psychogenic reaction increases whenever a needle and syringe are involved. It is extremely rare for someone to experience a psychogenic reaction in response to enteral drug administration.

Drug use in dentistry

Dental practitioners use four categories of drugs in patient management to the virtual exclusion of all others (Table 22-1): local anesthetics, antibiotics, analgesics, and antianxiety drugs. Local anesthetics are dentistry's most commonly used, and important, drugs; they are administered routinely whenever a dental procedure might produce pain. This chapter discusses examples of commonly prescribed or administered drugs and their potential for ADRs. It is strongly recommended that the reader consult the drug's package insert, a pharmacology textbook, or other drug information source (e.g., www.ePocrates.com) when considering the use of any drug.

---

*This author has seen, on four occasions, fathers of pediatric patients faint as their children were receiving IM injections of a sedative drug.

TABLE 22-1 Commonly used local anesthetics

Generic	Proprietary (North America)	Group
Articaine	Astracaine, Septanest, Septocaine, Ultracaine, Zorcaine	Amide
Benzocaine	Many (topical anesthetic)	Ester
Bupivacaine	Marcaine	Amide
Lidocaine	Alphacaine, Lignospan, Octocaine, Xylocaine	Amide
Mepivacaine	Arestocaine, Carbocaine, Isocaine, Polocaine, Scandanest	Amide
Prilocaine	Citanest	Amide

Local anesthetics

Local anesthetics, the most widely used drugs in dentistry (an estimated 300 million dental cartridges injected in the United States each year), are the safest and the most effective drugs in all of medicine for the prevention and management of pain. Table 22-1 lists the available local anesthetics in the United States, Canada, Europe, and Asia today. Articaine, bupivacaine, etidocaine, lidocaine, mepivacaine, and prilocaine are amide local anesthetics, whereas benzocaine, tetracaine, propoxycaine, and procaine are ester-type drugs.

Before the introduction of the first amide, lidocaine, in the late 1940s, esters were used exclusively. Although effective local anesthetics, esters carry a significant risk for allergy.[19] This potential was one of the reasons for the development and introduction of the amide local anesthetics. Allergy to amide local anesthetics, although not impossible,[20,21] is extremely rare.[22] Reports occasionally appear in the medical and dental literature of an "allergic reaction" to an amide local anesthetic. However, careful documentation proves that essentially all incidents were psychogenic or idiosyncratic reactions or the result of overdose or allergy to some other component of the injected solution.[22] (Chapter 24 discusses in detail allergy to local anesthetics.)

The most commonly observed ADRs to amide local anesthetics are associated with their administration. Psychogenic responses (vasodepressor syncope and hyperventilation) make up the greatest number of local anesthetic reactions observed today. The next most common cause (a very, very distant second) of ADRs to local anesthetics is the overdose (toxic) reaction, which in many instances is produced by a relative overdose (secondary to inadvertent intravascular injection) of the drug rather than by absolute overdose (secondary to administration of too large a total dose).[23] True

documented and reproducible allergy is an extremely rare and unlikely cause of an ADR resulting from amide local anesthetic administration.

Topically applied local anesthetics may also produce ADRs. Psychogenic responses rarely occur; indeed, topical anesthetics are usually used to help minimize the occurrence of psychogenic responses during the injection of local anesthetics. However, topical anesthetics do have the potential to produce two ADRs. The first, allergy, occurs because most topical anesthetics, in addition to being ester-type local anesthetics (e.g., benzocaine), also contain many other ingredients (e.g., methylparaben), which possess a relatively high degree of allergenicity. Allergic responses, such as erythema or angioedema of the mucous membranes and lips, are not uncommon after topical application of these drugs. The second, much less common, ADR associated with topically applied local anesthetics is overdose, which occurs because of the rapid absorption of some topical anesthetics through mucous membranes of the oral cavity. When the local anesthetic is absorbed rapidly, its blood level rises rapidly.[24]

I strongly recommend the use of topical anesthetics before intraoral injection of any local anesthetic.[25] The benefits of topical anesthetics clearly outweigh any associated risk. Safer use of topical anesthetics may be achieved through the use of either amide-type topical anesthetics or benzocaine (an ester) combined with their judicious administration to mucous membranes.

Antibiotics

Dental professionals also prescribe antibiotics frequently to treat established active infection. Antibiotics should not be prescribed prophylactically to prevent the development of infections except in special circumstances, such as the prevention of bacterial endocarditis. Because of the development of resistant bacterial strains[26] and allergy, antibiotics should be used only when therapeutic indications exist. As a group, antibiotics possess a low incidence of adverse effects, a fact that most likely is responsible for their overadministration and the subsequent development of antibiotic-resistant bacterial strains (e.g., tubercular bacilli and penicillin-resistant gonococcus).[26] In addition, medical and dental practitioners are also developing an increasing unease when administering parenteral antibiotics because of their potential for allergic reaction.

Within dentistry, there is little need for the parenteral administration of antibiotics (Table 22-2). Most protocols for the prophylactic administration of antibiotics recommend enteral administration.[27] If the dose and sequence of antibiotic administration are monitored closely, the resulting blood levels and therapeutic efficacy of these drugs should appear similar following

TABLE 22-2 Commonly prescribed antibiotics

Generic	Proprietary
Penicillin G	Bicillin LA
Penicillin V	Pen-Vee K
	Veetids
Ampicillin	Principen
Erythromycin	e-Mycin
	Ery-tab
	Eryc
	E.E.S.
	EryPed
	Erythrocin
Clindamycin	Cleocin
Cephalosporins, first generation	Ancef
	Duricef
	Keflex
	Kefzol
	Velosef
Cephalosporins, second generation	Ceclor
	Cefotan
	Ceftin
	Lorabid
	Mefoxin
Cephalosporins, third generation	Cedax
	Cefizox
	Cefobid
	Claforan
	Fortaz
	Omnicef
	Rocephin
	Spectracef
Cephalosporins, fourth generation	Maxipime
Amoxicillin	Amoxil
	DisperMox
	Trimox
Azithromycin	Zithromax
	Zmax

either parenteral or oral administration. One major advantage of oral administration is the decreased likelihood of ADRs. If ADRs occur following oral administration, they are more likely to be less acute than those that follow parenteral administration; however, serious reactions can develop in either case.[28] If parenteral administration of antibiotics, particularly penicillin, is required, the drug should not be administered in the dental office but rather in a hospital emergency department, where the patient can be maintained under observation for about 1 hour. The major ADR for which the doctor must be prepared when antibiotics are administered is allergy.

Analgesics

Pain-relieving drugs make up a significant portion of prescriptions written by dentists. Two major categories of analgesics are considered: mild (nonopioid) and strong (opioids) analgesics (Table 22-3).

Nonsteroidal antiinflammatory drugs (NSAIDs), such as ibuprofen and naproxen, have become extremely popular and are relatively safe. Most ADRs to NSAIDs are related to the gastrointestinal tract; examples include gastrointestinal upset, nausea, and constipation.[29] Other ADRs include headache, dizziness, and pruritus.[29]

Aspirin, acetaminophen, and codeine remain the most commonly prescribed analgesics in dentistry. Major ADRs associated with aspirin include a significant potential for allergy, with symptoms ranging from mild urticaria to bronchospasm to fatal anaphylaxis (see Chapter 24), and overdose (salicylism). Acetaminophen is most often associated with CNS depression or excitation, allergy, and overdose.[30]

Codeine is an opioid agonist analgesic; however, it is a mild analgesic compared with other opioids, such as morphine and meperidine. Although codeine allergy is possible, its incidence is actually quite low. Primary ADRs to codeine include nausea, vomiting, drowsiness, and constipation, all of which occur more often in ambulatory than in nonambulatory patients.[30] After a 60-mg oral dose, approximately 22% of patients become nauseated. A significantly lower incidence of nausea accompanies smaller doses, such as 30 mg. If codeine is administered in large amounts or to sensitive (hyperresponsive) patients, it may produce the same clinical signs and symptoms of severe overdose—respiratory and cardiovascular depression—as other, more potent opioids. Generally, 30 mg administered orally is a highly effective analgesic dose of codeine associated with a minimal incidence of ADRs. The most likely ADR noted with codeine is gastrointestinal upset, which is almost always a dose-related response.

Meperidine (Demerol), hydromorphone (Dilaudid), hydrocodone (Vicodin), oxycodone (OxyContin), and other opioid agonists occasionally are used to manage more severe dental pain. As with codeine, the major ADRs to these drugs are more annoying than life-threatening; most frequently, they include nausea and vomiting, dizziness, ataxia, sweating, and orthostatic hypotension.[30] Again, these ADRs are more likely to

TABLE 22-3 Common analgesic drugs used in dentistry

Generic	Proprietary
NONOPIOID	
Acetylsalicylic acid (aspirin)	Numerous
Acetaminophen	Tylenol
	Ultracet
Ibuprofen	Motrin
Naproxen	Anaprox
	Aleve
	Naprelan
Flurbiprofen	Ansaid
Ketoprofen	Orudis KT
	Actron
	Oruvail
Ketorolac	Toradol
OPIOID	
Codeine	
Hydrocodone	Vicodin (with acetaminophen)
Oxycodone	ETH-Oxydose
	OxyContin
	OxyFast
	OxyIR
	Roxicodone

TABLE 22-4 Common antianxiety agents and sedative-hypnotics

Generic	Proprietary
BENZODIAZEPINES	
Midazolam	Versed, Hypnovel, Dormicum
Diazepam	Valium
Oxazepam	Serax
Lorazepam	Ativan
Triazolam	Halcion
Flurazepam	Dalmane
Alprazolam	Niravam, Xanax
NONBENZODIAZEPINE ANXIOLYTIC/HYPNOTICS	
Zolpidem	Ambien
Zaleplon	Sonata
OTHERS	
Chloral hydrate	Aquachloral
Hydroxyzine	Atarax, Vistaril

occur in ambulatory patients than in nonambulatory patients (most dental patients being ambulatory). Overdose may occur and, as with all opioids, results in significant respiratory depression. Allergy, although possible, is rare.

Antianxiety drugs

The use of drugs for the relief of anxiety during all phases of dental treatment has increased significantly in recent years. Enteral routes, primarily oral, have experienced a renewed interest. Parenteral routes (inhalation, IM, and IV) have also gained popularity. With this increase in usage has come an increased potential for ADRs because of the increased effectiveness of parenterally administered drugs. Although many drugs are available for management of dental anxiety, most frequently used are the benzodiazepines (orally and parenterally) and inhalation agents (primarily nitrous oxide and oxygen). Happily, the use of barbiturates

(administered orally and parenterally) has declined significantly.

Benzodiazepines were developed to manage anxiety effectively without the unpleasant and dangerous ADRs associated with barbiturates. Table 22-4 lists major nonbarbiturate antianxiety and sedative-hypnotic agents. The benzodiazepines represented a major advance in the management of anxiety. The first—chlordiazepoxide (Librium)—was introduced in 1960. Others—diazepam (Valium), oxazepam (Serax), and clorazepate (Tranxene)—are commonly prescribed drugs and are the most effective and most widely used antianxiety drugs in dentistry.

Benzodiazepines, which may be administered orally or parenterally, are a decided improvement over barbiturates because of their remarkably lower incidence of side effects and overdose. Most likely because of their ease of availability, benzodiazepines are associated with more reported overdoses than any other class of drugs. However, there are extremely few well-documented reports of death associated solely with the ingestion of benzodiazepines.[31]

Overdose of benzodiazepines (even when administered via the IV route) usually consists of oversedation, drowsiness, and ataxia. Respiratory depression, though possible, is infrequent. Flurazepam (Dalmane) and triazolam (Halcion) are benzodiazepines marketed as nonbarbiturate sedative-hypnotics. Triazolam has recently become a favored orally administered sedative in dentistry in the United States.[32] Flurazepam and triazolam are highly effective substitutes for barbiturates when used as "sleeping pills." Although long-term administration of triazolam has been criticized, the use of either drug for specific indications in dentistry (e.g., pretreatment sedation both the evening before and the morning of treatment) is recommended.[33]

Inhalation sedation

Nitrous oxide (N_2O) and oxygen (O_2) inhalation sedation is another method of anxiety control that has garnered increasing interest among dental practitioners. An estimated 35% of dentists in the United States use N_2O–O_2.[34] Discovered in 1776 and first used clinically in 1844, N_2O is a highly effective antianxiety drug that, when properly administered, is remarkably free of unpleasant and potentially dangerous ADRs. Unwanted side effects associated with inhalation sedation include nausea, vomiting, and oversedation. If inhalation sedation is administered with less than 20% oxygen, unconsciousness may ensue, with cellular damage resulting from hypoxia (but not from N_2O).

With the development of a new generation of inhalation-sedation machines and the increased awareness of dental educators and manufacturers, safety features have been incorporated into current sedation units that make administration with less than 20% O_2 difficult, if not impossible.[35] In addition, no reports exist of allergy to N_2O. Overdose consists of excessive

TABLE 22-5 Drugs commonly used in dentistry and their most common ADRs

Drug	Allergy	Overdose	Side effects
LOCAL ANESTHETICS			
Esters	Common, especially with topical anesthetics; manifested as localized erythema and edema	Unlikely with esters unless genetic deficiency present (e.g., atypical plasma cholinesterase)	Rare; sedation (drowsiness) most common
Amides	Rare, virtually nonexistent; most clinical reports prove "alleged" allergy to be psychogenic reaction, overdose, or allergy to other component of solution	Most common ADR; CNS depression; manifested as drowsiness, tremor, tonic-clonic seizures	Rare; sedation most common
ANTIBIOTICS			
	Common; high allergic potential to many antibiotics; manifested clinically over entire spectrum of allergic phenomena	Rare; virtually nonexistent with penicillin	Rare; GI upset most common
ANALGESICS			
Nonopioid	Common; high allergy potential (aspirin)	Common; salicylism	Common
Opioid	Uncommon	Common; manifested as CNS depression (drowsiness) and respiratory depression	Most common ADR; manifested clinically as nausea or vomiting, orthostatic hypotension
ANXIOLYTICS/SEDATIVE-HYPNOTICS			
Benzodiazepines	Uncommon	Uncommon; CNS depression manifested as oversedation (excessive drowsiness)	Drowsiness most common
Nonbenzodiazepines			
N_2O-O_2	Rare; to date, never reported	Common; manifested as oversedation (excessive drowsiness)	Most common ADR; manifested as nausea; rarely vomiting

ADR, adverse drug event; CNS, central nervous system; GI, gastrointestinal.

sedation, which may manifest as rousable sleep or the loss of consciousness; however, the latter is extremely unlikely. Management of oversedation focuses on a decrease in the percentage of N_2O through an increase in the volume flow of O_2, coupled with the steps of basic life support—$P \rightarrow A \rightarrow B \rightarrow C$ (position-airway-breathing-circulation)—until the patient regains consciousness.

Table 22-5 lists the drug categories most frequently used in dentistry and their most common ADRs. Most important in drug use is the realization that all drugs can produce virtually any of the three serious ADRs—allergy, overdose, and idiosyncrasy.

REFERENCES

1. Kelly WN: Can the frequency and risks of fatal adverse drug events be determined? *Pharmacotherapy* 21:521–527, 2001.
2. Easton KL, Chapman CB, Brien JA: Frequency and characteristics of hospital admissions associated with drug-related problems in paediatrics, *Br J Clin Pharmacol* 57:611–615, 2004.
3. Phillips DP, Jarvinen JR, Phillips RR: A spike in fatal medication errors at the beginning of each month, *Pharmacotherapy* 25:1–9, 2005.
4. Winterstein AG, Almut G, Sauer BC, et al.: Preventable drug-related hospital admissions, *Ann Pharmacother* 36:1238–1248, 2002.
5. Nelson KM, Talbert RL: Drug-related hospital admissions, *Pharmacotherapy* 16:701–707, 1996.
6. Hallas J, Jensen KB, Grodum E, et al.: Drug-related admissions to a department of medical gastroenterology: the role of self-medicated and prescribed drugs, *Scand J Gastroenterol* 26:174–180, 1991.
7. Lazarou L, Pomeranz BH, Corey PN: Incidence of adverse drug reactions in hospitalized patients: meta-analysis of prospective studies, *JAMA* 279:1200–1205, 1998.
8. Pallasch TJ: *Pharmacology for dental students and practitioners,* Philadelphia, Lea & Febiger, 1980.
9. Arcangeli A, Antonelli M, Mignani V, Sandroni C: Sedation in PACU: the role of benzodiazepines, *Curr Drug Targets* 6:745–748, 2005.
10. www.ePocrates.com
11. MD Consult. www.MDConsult.com. Elsevier, 2006.
12. Physicians' Desk References. www.pdr.net
13. American Dental Association: *ADA guide to dental therapeutics,* ed 3, Chicago, American Dental Association, 2006.
14. Golembiewski JA: Allergic reactions to drugs: implications for perioperative care, *J Perianesth Nurs* 17:393–398, 2002.
15. Giles TD, Sander GE: Beyond the usual strategies for blood pressure reduction: therapeutic considerations and combination therapies, *J Clin Hypertens* 3:346–353, 2001.
16. Reidenberg MM, Lowenthal DT: Adverse nondrug reactions, *N Engl J Med* 279:678–679, 1968.
17. *Mosby's medical, nursing, and allied health dictionary,* ed 5, St. Louis, Mosby, 1998.
18. Steensma DP: The kiss of death: a severe allergic reaction to a shellfish induced by a good-night kiss, *Mayo Clin Proc* 78:221–222, 2003.
19. Criep LH, Castilho-Ribeiro C: Allergy to procaine hydrochloride with three fatalities, *JAMA* 151:1185–1187, 1955.
20. Brown DT, Beamish D, Wildsmith JA: Allergic reaction to an amide local anesthetic, *Br J Anaesth* 53:435–437, 1981.
21. Bateman PP: Multiple allergies to local anesthetics including prilocaine, *Med J Aust* 2:449–450, 1974.
22. Aldrete JA, Johnson DA: Allergy to local anesthetics, *JAMA* 207:356–357, 1969.
23. Adatia AK: Intravascular injection of local anesthetics (letter), *Br Dent J* 138:328, 1975.
24. Adriani J: Reactions to local anesthetics, *JAMA* 196:405–408, 1955.
25. Malamed SF: *Handbook of local anesthesia,* ed 5, St. Louis, Mosby, 2004.
26. Rice LB: Antimicrobial resistance in gram-positive bacteria, *Am J Infect Control* 34(5 Suppl 1):s11–s19; discussion s64–s73, 2006.
27. Dajani AS, Taubert KA, Wilson W, et al.: Prevention of bacterial endocarditis: recommendations by the American Heart Association, *JAMA* 277:1794–1801, 1997.
28. Gill CJ, Michaelides PL: Dental drugs and anaphylactic reactions: report of a case, *Oral Surg Oral Med Oral Pathol* 50:30–32, 1980.
29. Anaprox drug package insert, Syntex, Humacao, Puerto Rico, Inc., 1990.
30. Tylenol with codeine drug package insert, McNeil Pharmaceutical Products, Raritan, New Jersey, 1990.
31. Iserson KV: Tranquilizer overdose. In: Rosen P, Barkin RM, editors: *Emergency medicine,* ed 2, St. Louis, Mosby, 1988, p. 2105.
32. Dionne RA, Yagiela JA, Cote CJ, et al.: Balancing efficacy and safety in the use of oral sedation in dental outpatients, *J Am Dent Assoc* 137:502–513, 2006.
33. Gorman C: The dark side of Halcion (banned in Britain), *Time* October 4, 1991, p. 65.
34. ADA Survey Center: Nitrous oxide use, *ADA News* September 15, 1997, p. 6.
35. American Dental Association Council on Dental Materials, Instruments, and Equipment: *Dentists' desk reference materials, instruments, and equipment,* Chicago, American Dental Association, 1981.

CHAPTER 23

Drug Overdose Reactions

Drug overdose reactions have been defined previously as those clinical signs and symptoms that result from overly high blood levels of a drug in various target organs and tissues. Overdose reactions, also called *toxic reactions,* are the most common of all adverse drug reactions (ADRs), accounting for up to 85% by some estimates.[1] Overdose reactions represent a direct extension of the normal pharmacologic actions of the involved drug. For an overdose to occur, the drug must gain access to the body's circulation in quantities sufficient to produce adverse effects in the target organs.

Under normal circumstances there is a constant absorption of the drug from its site of administration (e.g., gastrointestinal tract [oral], muscles [intramuscular (IM)]) into the body's circulation, and a steady removal of the same drug from the blood as it is redistribution (e.g., to skeletal muscle) and biotransformation (also known as *metabolism* and *detoxification*) in other parts of the body, primarily the liver. In this situation, overly high blood levels of drugs seldom develop (Figure 23-1). However, a number of ways exist in which this steady state may be altered, leading to either a rapid elevation in blood level of the drug, producing a sudden onset of signs and symptoms of overdose, or a more gradual elevation of a drug's blood level, leading to a slower onset of signs and symptoms. In either case an overdose reaction is caused by a blood (plasma) level of a drug sufficiently high to produce adverse effects in the various organs and tissues of the body that are influenced by the administered drug. The clinical reaction continues only as long as the blood level remains above the threshold for overdose in that target organ or tissue.

In dentistry, four commonly used drug categories possess significant potentials for overdose: local anesthetics; vasoconstrictors, such as epinephrine; sedative-hypnotics; and opioid analgesics. Of these, local anesthetics are by far the most used drugs. A severe overdose reaction to a local anesthetic manifests as either a generalized tonic-clonic seizure or unconsciousness. The most commonly observed overdose reaction to sedative-hypnotics and opioid analgesics is varying degrees of central nervous system (CNS) and respiratory depression, whereas vasoconstrictor overdose produces an "anxiety" reaction accompanied by significant increases in cardiovascular function (blood pressure and heart rate).

Because the usual route of administration of these drugs and the clinical nature and management of the overdose reaction differ so markedly between these groups, this chapter divides overdose reactions into the following three sections:

1. Overdose reaction from local anesthetics
2. Overdose reaction from vasodepressor drugs
3. Overdose reaction from sedative-hypnotic and opioid analgesic drugs

■ LOCAL ANESTHETIC OVERDOSE REACTION

Local anesthetics are the most commonly used drugs in dentistry. The number of local anesthetic cartridges injected by dentists in the United States is conservatively estimated at 6 million per week, or more than 300 million per year. Actual numbers probably greatly exceed this figure. In addition, physicians, podiatrists, and other health care professionals also administer local anesthetics. Considering the frequency of administration, the fact that more ADRs are not reported is remarkable. I believe that local anesthetics are the safest and most effective drugs for the prevention and management of pain.

In all likelihood, however, a great many ADRs go unreported because they were transitory and innocuous enough that the doctor either did not recognize the reaction or deem it serious enough to report. Patients and, all too frequently, doctors commonly label any ADR to a local anesthetic an *allergic reaction*; however, on careful scrutiny most reactions to local anesthetics are revealed to be either overdose or, more likely, psychogenic responses.[2]

Predisposing factors

An overdose reaction to a local anesthetic is related to the blood level of the local anesthetic in certain tissues and organs (the myocardium and CNS). Several factors may profoundly influence the rate at which this blood level increases and the length of time for which it remains elevated. The presence of one or more of these factors predisposes the patient to the development of an overdose reaction. The first group of factors is related to the patient receiving the drug, whereas the second group relates to the drug itself and the area into which it is administered.

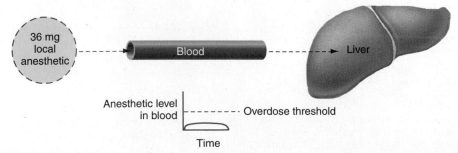

FIGURE 23-1 Under normal circumstances the body constantly absorbs the local anesthetic from the site of deposition while the liver removes the agent from the blood. Thus, local anesthetic levels in the blood remain low. (From Malamed SF: *Handbook of local anesthesia,* ed 5, St. Louis, Mosby, 2004.)

Patient factors

Normal distribution curve. Predisposing patient factors are those that modify the patient's response to the usual dose of a drug. This occurrence is referred to commonly as *biological,* or *individual variation.* The normal distribution curve illustrates this variable response to drugs (Figure 23-2). For a given "normal" or "usual" dose of a drug, approximately 68% of patients respond appropriately; 16% are less responsive (hyporesponsive), and 16% are overly responsive (hyperresponsive). Additional predisposing patient factors that influence drug responsiveness include age, body weight, pathologic processes, genetics, attitude and environment, and sex.

Age. At either end of the age spectrum, individuals report a higher incidence of ADRs. Many reasons exist for this finding, several of which are relevant to this discussion. Drug absorption, metabolism, and excretion may be imperfectly developed in younger age groups or be diminished in older age groups. Underdeveloped or decreased liver functioning may result in higher blood levels of drugs because the individual cannot biotransform the local anesthetic into a biologically inactive substance. In addition, renal dysfunction may prohibit the patient from excreting the local anesthetic. In patients 61 to 71 years of age, the half-life of lidocaine increased by approximately 70% over the value in a control group composed of patients age 22 to 26 years.[3] As a general rule of thumb, drug doses should be decreased for patients under 6 years and over 65 years.

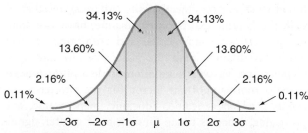

FIGURE 23-2 A normal, bell-shaped distribution curve. For any given drug, approximately 68% of patients experience desirable clinical effects with the usual adult dose, and 95% exhibit desirable effects with a slightly lower or higher dose. A small percentage of patients are hyporesponsive (right side of curve), requiring doses that exceed the "normal" before clinically desirable results occur. More important, however, are those hyperresponsive individuals (left side of curve) who exhibit clinically desirable results at lower-than-normal doses. Such patients are more likely to experience drug overdoses. (From Freilich JD, Bennett CR: Conscious-sedation in a patient on combined tranylcypromine and lithium therapy: a case report, *Anesth Prog* 30:86–88, 1983. Also in Malamed SF: *Handbook of local anesthesia,* ed 5, St. Louis, Mosby, 2004.)

Body weight. In general, the greater the lean body weight (within limits), the larger the dose of a drug the individual can tolerate before an overdose develops. This relates primarily to the greater blood volume in larger, heavier, nonobese individuals. This relationship does not apply to obese persons since the blood supply to adipose tissues is sparse compared with that supplying muscle. Therefore a 200-pound obese patient is less likely to tolerate the same dose of local anesthetic as safely as a 200-pound muscular individual. Because most drugs are distributed evenly throughout the body, the larger the individual, the greater their blood volume and the lower the blood level of the drug per milliliter of blood. For example, a dose of a local anesthetic administered to a 67.5-kg (150-pound) adult produces a lower blood level than the same dose administered to a 22.5-kg (50-pound) child (assuming nonintravascular administration). Drug doses are normally calculated on the basis of milligrams of drug per kilogram (mg/kg) or pound (mg/lb) of body weight. Such considerations are especially important in younger pediatric and frail older patients; a lack of consideration of body weight is one of the major causes of overdose reactions.

Drug doses calculated in terms of mg/lb or mg/kg of body weight are based on the response of the normal responding patient, which is calculated from the responses of large numbers of patients. Thus, individual patient response to drug administration can demonstrate significant variation, a fact that the normal distribution curve plainly illustrates (see Figure 23-2). The usual blood level of lidocaine in the brain required to induce seizure activity is 7.5 µg lidocaine per milliliter of blood (µg/mL). Hyporesponsive patients may not exhibit seizures until the brain's blood level attains a significantly higher level of lidocaine, whereas hyperresponsive patients may exhibit seizures at a brain blood level of lidocaine considerably below 7.5 µg/mL.[4] Therefore, a drug overdose reaction can occur even where the dose is within the normal range for that patient.

Pathologic process. The presence of preexisting disease may alter the body's ability to biotransform a drug into a biologically inactive substance. Most amide local anesthetics undergo biotransformation in the liver, with a small percentage of the drug excreted unchanged through the kidneys. Any disease state that reduces or increases hepatic blood flow is likely to alter various pharmacokinetic parameters of the amide local anesthetics.[5] Renal dysfunction, however, appears to have little effect on local anesthetic toxicity.

Patients with cardiovascular disease, especially congestive heart failure, demonstrate blood levels of local anesthetics almost twice those found in healthy patients receiving the same doses.[6,7] This difference results from several factors, including a reduced blood volume for drug distribution and a diminished hepatic blood flow secondary to low cardiac output. Pulmonary disease states, especially those associated with carbon dioxide retention, are associated with an increased risk of local anesthetic overdose. Carbon dioxide retention (increased $PaCO_2$) leads to respiratory acidosis, which results in a decrease in the seizure threshold for a local anesthetic.[8,9] An increase in $PaCO_2$ from 25 to 40 torr to 65 to 81 torr lowers the convulsive threshold for lidocaine by 53%.[8]

Genetics. It has been reported with increasing frequency that certain individuals possess genetic deficiencies that alter their response to certain drugs. A genetic deficiency in the enzyme serum cholinesterase is an important example. Produced in the liver, this enzyme circulates in the blood and is responsible for the biotransformation of two important drugs: succinylcholine[10] and the ester-type local anesthetics.[11,12] Succinylcholine is a short-acting, neuromuscular-blocking agent frequently administered during the induction of general anesthesia to produce skeletal muscle relaxation (as well as respiratory arrest) during tracheal intubation. In normal individuals the action of succinylcholine is approximately 3 minutes, the drug being metabolized by serum cholinesterase. In contrast, individuals with deficient or atypical serum cholinesterase biotransform succinylcholine at an extremely slow rate, producing a period of apnea that may persist up to several hours.[10] This same enzyme is responsible for the biotransformation of the ester local anesthetics. If an individual possesses atypical or deficient serum cholinesterase, the blood level of the ester local anesthetic increases and remains elevated longer than normal, increasing the likelihood of an overdose reaction.[12]

Attitude and environment. The psychological attitude of a patient greatly influences the ultimate effect of a drug. This factor is considerably important with sedative-hypnotic and opioid analgesics; what an individual expects a drug to do greatly influences the clinical efficacy of that agent. This expectation is called the *placebo response* and may be used to benefit by the doctor. With regard to local anesthetics, it has been shown that the convulsive threshold for local anesthetics is lowered in patients who are overly stressed (frightened). In addition, a patient's psychological attitude affects the response to stimulation. All dental practitioners have encountered apprehensive patients who overreact to stimuli, noting pain when only gentle pressure is applied to tissues. Additional local anesthetic is then administered, increasing the total dose received.

Sex. Differences between male and female animals regarding drug distribution, response, and metabolism have been described that are not of major importance to humans. The only instance of sexual difference in the human species occurs in the female during pregnancy, at which time renal function may be altered, leading to impaired excretion of certain drugs and their accumulation in the blood, potentially increasing the risk of overdose. Although not normally of clinical significance, this disturbance of renal function is a potential cause of local anesthetic overdose.

Drug factors

The second group of factors that may predispose an individual to overdose relates to the drugs themselves and to their site of administration. The drug's vasoactivity, dose and route of administration, speed of administration, vascularity of the injection site, and the presence of vasoconstrictors influence the risk of overdose.

Vasoactivity. Several factors relating to the physicochemical properties of local anesthetics may help determine whether the drug's blood level after injection is low or high. These include lipid solubility, protein binding, and vascular activity.

Local anesthetics that are more lipid soluble and more highly protein bound, such as etidocaine and bupivacaine, are retained in the fat and tissues at the site of injection and therefore exhibit a slower net systemic absorption rate compared to lidocaine and mepivacaine. This slower systemic absorption rate is associated with increased margins of safety. The rate of absorption of local anesthetics also depends on their direct actions on blood vessels at the injection site. All local anesthetics, with the notable exception of cocaine, have vasodilating properties.[13] Bupivacaine and etidocaine produce more vasodilation than do prilocaine, lidocaine, or mepivacaine. Vascular regulation of absorption appears to be a more important factor for the shorter-acting agents, such as articaine, lidocaine, mepivacaine, and prilocaine, whereas tissue binding is of greater significance for the longer-acting drugs, bupivacaine and etidocaine. Table 23-1 compares the lipid solubility, protein-binding, and vasodilating properties of commonly used local anesthetics. The greater the degree of vasodilation, the more rapidly the local anesthetic is absorbed into the circulation.

Dose. For many years it was thought that the concentration of an injected solution was of major importance in determining overdose potential, even though the total milligram dose remained the same. This thinking is incorrect. Braid and Scott[14] demonstrated that

TABLE 23-1 Comparison of physicochemical properties of local anesthetics

Drug	Lipid or buffer partition coefficient*	Protein binding (%)*	Relative vasodilating values†
Articaine	0.0	95	1.0
Bupivacaine	28	95	2.5
Etidocaine	141	94	2.5
Lidocaine	2.9	64	1.0
Mepivacaine	1.0	77	0.8
Prilocaine	0.8	55	0.5
Procaine	0.6	5.8	>2.5

*The body absorbs more lipid-soluble drugs slower; slower action is associated with an increased margin of safety.
†The greater the degree of vasodilation a drug produces, the more rapidly the drug is absorbed into the circulatory system.

TABLE 23-2 Concentrations of commonly used local anesthetics

Drug	Group	Available concentrations (%)
Articaine	Amide	4
Bupivacaine	Amide	0.5
Etidocaine	Amide	1
Lidocaine	Amide	2
Mepivacaine	Amide	2 (with vasoconstrictor)
		3 (without vasoconstrictor)
Prilocaine	Amide	3 or 4 (with vasoconstrictor)
		4 (without vasoconstrictor)

2% and 3% solutions of prilocaine yield the same blood level as an equivalent dose of a 1% solution if the same number of milligrams is administered. Jebson[15] proved the same theory, using 10% and 2% lidocaine.

Dosage, on the other hand, is a highly significant factor. Within the clinical dose range for most local anesthetics, a linear relationship exists between dose and peak blood concentration. The larger the dose of local anesthetic injected, the higher the peak blood level of the drug (Table 23-2).

Route of administration. Local anesthetics, when used to control pain, produce their clinical actions at the site of administration. Unlike most other drugs, local anesthetics (when used for pain prevention or control) need not enter the circulation and reach a certain minimal therapeutic blood level. The greater the length of time a local anesthetic remains in the area where pain control is desired and the greater its concentration at that site, the longer is the duration of anesthesia. As drug is absorbed into the circulatory system, pain control becomes less effective. When sufficient volume has been removed from the area (e.g., redistributed), the individual may again experience painful stimuli. At the same time, the more rapidly the local anesthetic is removed from the site of injection, the more rapidly the drug's blood level increases (toward overdose levels).

One factor frequently noted in overdose reactions to local anesthetics is inadvertent intravascular injection. In this instance, extremely high blood levels may be achieved in a very brief time, producing acute and severe overdose reactions; peak anesthetic blood level is dependent on the rate of intravascular administration. Absorption of (some) topical anesthetics through the oral mucous membrane and absorption of solutions from multiple intraoral injection sites may also produce overdose reactions (some topical anesthetics are absorbed rapidly through the oral mucous membrane).

Rate of injection. The rate of injection is vital in the cause or prevention of overdose reactions to all drugs. Intravenous (IV) injection of a local anesthetic drug may or may not produce signs and symptoms of overdose. Indeed, lidocaine is frequently administered via the IV route in doses of 1.0 to 1.5 mg/kg (70 mg to 105 mg in the typical 70-kg man) in the emergency management of several ventricular dysrhythmias.[16] A major deciding factor in whether intravascular administration is clinically safe or hazardous is the rate at which the drug is injected. A 36-mg dose of lidocaine (one dental cartridge in the United States) administered via an IV route in less than 15 seconds produces markedly elevated blood levels and a virtual guarantee of a serious overdose reaction. On the other hand, 100 mg of lidocaine administered intravenously over several minutes (as recommended in the management of cardiac dysrhythmias,* produces a significantly lower lidocaine blood level (because greater distribution has occurred) with a subsequent decreased risk of overdose.

Figure 23-3 illustrates representative blood levels following administration of 30 mg of tetracaine via various routes. The blood levels for the slow and rapid IV administration of tetracaine are especially significant.[18] Local anesthetic overdose reactions can result from the combination of inadvertent intravascular injection, combined with too rapid a rate of injection. Both causes are almost 100% preventable.

Vascularity of injection site. The greater the vascularity at the site of injection, the more rapidly the

---

*The drug package insert for intravenous cardiac lidocaine.[17]

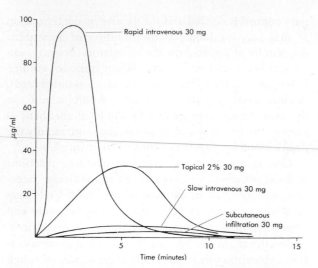

FIGURE 23-3 Blood levels of local anesthetic after administration via various routes. Note particularly the blood levels after the rapid and slow intravenous administrations. (Modified from Adriani J, Campbell B, Yardberry OH Jr.: Influence of absorption on systemic toxicity of local anesthetic agents. *Anesth Analg* 38:370–377, 1959.)

drug is absorbed into the circulation. Although rapid absorption is desirable with most parenterally administered drugs when therapeutic blood levels need to be achieved, it is a decided disadvantage in the use of local anesthetics administered for pain control. Local anesthetics must remain in the area of injection in order to block nerve conduction. Unfortunately for dentistry (at least as far as local anesthetic administration is concerned), the oral cavity is one of the more highly vascular areas of the body. A drug injected into the oral cavity is usually absorbed into the blood more rapidly than the same drug injected elsewhere in the body. This factor, plus the inherent vasodilating properties of most local anesthetics, is a major reason for the addition of vasoconstrictors to local anesthetic solutions.

Presence of vasoconstrictors. The addition of a vasoconstrictor to a local anesthetic results in a decrease in the rate of systemic absorption of the drug. The use of vasoconstrictors, along with adherence to proper injection technique, has greatly reduced the clinical toxicity of local anesthetics. Box 23-1 summarizes risk factors for local anesthetic overdose.

Prevention

Almost all overdose reactions to local anesthetics are preventable. Careful evaluation of the patient before the start of treatment along with careful drug administration can minimize the risk of overdose in all but a few situations. Two sets of predisposing factors were presented in the previous section of this chapter (see

---

Box 23-1 Predisposing factors for drug overdose

PATIENT FACTORS
Age (under 6 years; over 65 years)
Body weight (lower body weight increasing risk)
Pathologic processes (e.g., liver disease, congestive heart failure, pulmonary disease)
Genetics (e.g., atypical plasma cholinesterase)
Mental attitude (anxiety decreasing seizure threshold)
Sex (slight increase in risk during pregnancy)

DRUG FACTORS
Vasoactivity (vasodilation increasing risk)
Dose (higher dose increasing risk)
Route of administration (intravascular route increasing risk)
Rate of injection (rapid injection increasing risk)
Vascularity of injection site (increased vascularity increasing risk)
Presence of vasoconstrictor (decreasing risk)

Box 23–1). The first set, patient factors, are those that cannot be eliminated but that, when present, may require specific modifications to dental care to prevent drug-related problems from developing. The second set of factors is related to the drugs themselves or to their administration. These factors are usually avoidable through proper drug selection and local anesthetic injection technique.

Medical history questionnaire and dialogue history

The only questions directly related to the use of local anesthetics are included in the questionnaire's general drug use discussion, section V (see Figure 2-1). The doctor should carefully examine any ADRs to a local anesthetic to determine their precise nature. (Chapter 24 presents a detailed dialogue history for this type of questioning.)

In the absence of a history of ADRs to local anesthetics, a series of questions about experiences with dental injections should be posed to that patient. Question 5, which focuses on dental experiences in general, may provide relevant information about drug use and be useful in an evaluation of the patient's psychological status. A thorough medical history evaluation enables the doctor to eliminate two potential causes of local anesthetic overdose: unusually slow biotransformation of the local anesthetic and unusually slow elimination of the drug from the body.

Causes of overdose reactions

Consideration of the various mechanisms by which blood levels of local anesthetics may become increased is necessary before a discussion about prevention can commence. Moore[19] stated that high blood levels of local anesthetics may occur in one or more of the ways listed in Box 23-2. These factors form the basis for a discussion of the methods through which overdose reactions to local anesthetics may be prevented. As in any discussion of prevention, the patient-completed medical history questionnaire is a vital element.

Biotransformation and elimination. Ester local anesthetics undergo rapid biotransformation in the blood and liver. The major portion of this biotransformation process occurs within the blood through hydrolysis to paraaminobenzoic acid by the enzyme pseudocholinesterase.[20] A patient with a familial history of atypical pseudocholinesterase is unable to biotransform ester-type local anesthetics at a normal rate, thereby increasing the likelihood of elevated local anesthetic blood levels.[12] Atypical pseudocholinesterase is believed to occur in 1 of 2820 individuals.[21] Any patient with a questionable history should be referred to a physician for diagnostic tests, which may confirm or deny its existence. Atypical pseudocholinesterase, if present, is a *relative contraindication* to administration of an ester local anesthetic.

Amide local anesthetics may be administered to patients with atypical plasma cholinesterase without increased risk of overdose. Microsomal enzymes in the liver biotransform these anesthetics.[5] A history of liver disease (e.g., previous or present hepatitis or cirrhosis) does not absolutely contraindicate the use of amides but it may indicate that a degree of residual hepatic dysfunction exists, which can influence the ability of the liver to biotransform amide local anesthetics.

An ambulatory patient with a history of liver disease may receive amide local anesthetics; however, these drugs should be used judiciously (hepatic dysfunction is a *relative contraindication* to their administration). Minimal volumes should be employed for local anesthesia, bearing in mind that one cartridge may be able to produce an overdose in this patient if liver function is compromised significantly. In my experience, however,

such degrees of compromised liver function are more commonly present in hospitalized than in ambulatory patients. Whenever doubt exists, medical consultation should be sought before any drugs are injected. When a greater degree of liver function is present (American Society of Anesthesiologists [ASA] risk IV or V), the use of an ester local anesthetic is also a *relative contraindication* because the liver produces the hydrolytic enzyme cholinesterase, and liver dysfunction might also disturb the biotransformation of the esters as well.

A small percentage of an administered local anesthetic dose is eliminated from the blood unchanged, in its active form, through the kidneys. Reports have cited values for urinary excretion as 3% for lidocaine,[22] less than 1% for prilocaine,[23] 1% for mepivacaine,[24] less than 1% for etidocaine,[25] and less than 1% for bupivacaine.[26] Renal dysfunction does not usually result in excessive blood levels of local anesthetics. As with liver dysfunction, however, the dose of anesthetic should be limited to the absolute minimum required for clinically effective pain control.

The functionally anephric patient receiving renal dialysis also represents a *relative contraindication* to the administration of large doses of local anesthetics. Such patients are ambulatory between dialysis appointments and can visit the dental office for treatment. Undetoxified local anesthetic may accumulate in the blood of the patient, producing clinical signs and symptoms (usually mild) of local anesthetic overdose.

Too large a total dose. Administered to excess, any drug can produce signs and symptoms of overdose. The precise milligram dose at which the individual experiences toxic effects is impossible to predict. The principle of biological variability greatly influences the manner in which individuals respond to drugs. Most parenterally administered drugs are commonly administered in doses based on many factors, including age and physical status. A third consideration in dose determination is weight, a factor especially important in lighter-weight patients. Usually the larger the individual receiving the drug (within certain limits), the greater the drug distribution; therefore, the resulting blood level of the drug is lower, and the milligram dose for "safe" administration is larger.*

In the recent past, manufacturers of local anesthetic cartridges for dental use did not indicate maximum doses based on body weight. Instead, generations of dentists were taught that the maximum dose of lidocaine, for example, was 300 mg (without epinephrine) or

---

*Although generally valid, exceptions to this rule do exist. Biological variability and pathologic states may dramatically alter a patient's responsiveness to a drug; therefore, doctors must use special care when administering all drugs.

500 mg (with epinephrine) for any adult patient.[27] Unfortunately, instances arose in which these maximum doses proved too high for an individual patient's ability to tolerate, leading to illness or even death. Such arbitrary doses for adult patients are meaningless; one adult may weigh 200 pounds, whereas another may weigh 100 pounds. According to the old way of thinking, both patients should be able to safely tolerate the same milligram dose of local anesthetic.

It becomes obvious that such thinking is erroneous. Distribution of the local anesthetic throughout the circulatory system of a muscular 200-pound adult results in a lower blood concentration than the same drug in a 100-pound adult. When all other potential factors are equal, the smaller adult has a greater risk of overdose than the larger adult when both receive the same dose. Overdose develops when the rate of absorption of the local anesthetic into the cardiovascular system exceeds the rate at which the body removes that drug. Maximum doses of local anesthetics should be calculated on a milligram-per-weight basis (Table 23-3).[28]

In the adult patient, it is highly unlikely that the doses indicated in Table 23-3 will be reached. Conservative dental treatment rarely calls for the administration of more than two or three cartridges. Indeed, if indicated, full-mouth anesthesia (palatal, maxillary, and mandibular, bilaterally) may be achieved in the adult with fewer than six cartridges of local anesthetic. Exceptions do exist, however, such as with surgical procedures and prolonged treatments.

It is strongly suggested that doctors think in terms of "milligrams of local anesthetic" injected instead of the number of cartridges. Therefore, reviewing the relationship between percentage solution and number of milligrams contained in that solution becomes necessary (Table 23-4). A 1% solution contains 10 mg/mL; 2% solution, 20 mg/mL; 3% solution, 30 mg/mL, 4% solution, 40 mg/mL, and so on. If a typical dental cartridge in the United States contains 1.8 mL of solution, the number of milligrams of anesthetic is the volume of solution (1.8 mL) multiplied by the number of milligrams per milliliter of solution (e.g., 20 for a 2% solution). The result (36) is the number of milligrams of anesthetic in the dental cartridge. Cartridges in some countries contain 2.2 mL of anesthetic; thus, a cartridge of a 2% solution would contain 44 mg of anesthetic drug.

Rapid absorption of drug into circulation. The addition of vasoconstrictors to local anesthetics has proved to be of great benefit. Not only do vasoconstrictors increase the duration of action of most local anesthetics by enabling them to remain at the site of injection for a greater length of time in a concentration adequate to produce conduction blockade,[29] but they also reduce their systemic toxicity by retarding their absorption into the cardiovascular system (Table 23-5).[30] Peak local anesthetic blood levels of nonvasoconstrictor-containing solutions ("plain" drugs) develop 5 to 10 minutes after injection. With addition of a vasopressor, such as epinephrine, peak blood levels do not occur for approximately 30 minutes and they are lower.[31] Vasoconstrictors are integral components of all local anesthetic solutions whenever depth and duration of anesthesia are important. There are very few indications in dentistry in which local anesthetics should be used without vasoconstrictors.

The addition of vasoconstrictors to local anesthetics has brought with it a potential problem—vasoconstrictor overdose.[32] In most instances, the vasoconstrictor is epinephrine; thus, this potential toxic reaction cannot be taken lightly. (Vasoconstrictor overdose is discussed later in this chapter.)

Clinical experience with vasoconstrictors has led to the use of more and more dilute solutions with equally effective clinical applications. Early local anesthetics (procaine) contained epinephrine in 1:50,000 concentrations. Later combinations were produced with 1:80,000 and 1:100,000 concentrations. Recent dental local anesthetic additions—prilocaine, etidocaine, bupivacaine, and articaine—all contain epinephrine in 1:200,000 concentrations. Mepivacaine is available in some countries in a 1:200,000 epinephrine concentration, and lidocaine with a 1:300,000 epinephrine concentration is available in dental cartridges in some countries (not in the United States as of 2006). Use of the minimum effective concentrations of both the local anesthetic and the vasoconstrictor increase the safety of any drug.

Topical application of some local anesthetics to oral mucous membrane may also produce a rapid uptake of the drug. Absorption of some local anesthetics into the circulation after topical application is rapid, exceeded only by direct IV injection (see Figure 23-3).[18] Another important factor increasing overdose potential of topically applied local anesthetics is the need for administration in higher concentrations than injectable formulations of the same drug in order to anesthetize the mucous membrane adequately. For example, injectable lidocaine is effective as a 2% solution, whereas lidocaine for topical application requires a 5% or 10% concentration for effectiveness. Thus, the imprudent use of topical anesthetics may produce signs and symptoms of local anesthetic overdose.

Fortunately, many topical anesthetics are used as the base form of the drug (e.g., lidocaine, not lidocaine hydrochloride [HCl]), which is relatively insoluble in water and poorly absorbed into the circulation, thereby increasing the safety of this topical form of the drug.

TABLE 23-3 Maximum recommended doses of commonly used local anesthetics*

Patient weight		Articaine 4% with vasoconstrictor (3.2 mg/lb, 7.0 mg/kg)		Lidocaine 2% with or without vasoconstrictor (2.0 mg/lb, 4.4 mg/kg)		Mepivacaine 2% or 3% (2.0 mg/lb, 4.4 mg/kg)			Prilocaine 4% with or without vasoconstrictor (2.7 mg/lb, 6.0 mg/kg)	
lb	kg	mg	No. of cartridges	mg	No. of cartridges	mg	No. of cartridges 2%	No. of cartridges 3%	mg	No. of cartridges
20	9	64	0.9	40	1.1	40	1.1	0.8	54	0.75
40	18	128	1.8	80	2.2	80	2.2	1.5	108	1.5
60	27	192	2.7	120	3.3	120	3.3	2.2	162	2.25
80	36	256	3.6	160	4.4	160	4.4	3.0	216	3.0
100	45	320	4.4	200	5.5†	200	5.5	3.7	270	3.75
120	54	384	5.33	240	6.5	240	6.5	4.4	324	4.5
140	63	448	6.2	280	7.5	280	7.5	5.2	378	5.25
160	72	500	7.0	300	8.0	300	8.0	5.5	400	5.5
180	81	500	7.0	300	8.0	300	8.0	5.5	400	5.5
200	90	500	7.0	300	8.0	300	8.0	5.5	400	5.5

*Indicated doses are recommended for normal, healthy patients and should be decreased for debilitated or older individuals.
†The 0.2-mg epinephrine dose is a limiting factor for 1:50,000 epinephrine.
Modified from Malamed SF: *Handbook of local anesthesia*, ed 5, S: Louis, Mosby, 2004.

Articaine 4%. 3.2 mg/lb 500 mRD

Lido 2%. 2 mg/lb 300 mRD

Mepivacaine 2%. 3%. 2 mg/lb 300 mRD

Prilocaine 4%. 2.7 mg/lb 400 mRD

TABLE 23-4 Milligrams of local anesthetic per cartridge

Concentration = (%)	mg/mL	×1.8 mL = Total cartridge (US)	× 2.2 mL = Total cartridge (UK)	Drug(s)
1	10			
0.5	5	9	11	Bupivacaine
1.5	15	27	33	Etidocaine
2	20	36	44	Lidocaine, mepivacaine
3	30	54	66	Mepivacaine, prilocaine
4	40	72	88	Articaine, prilocaine

TABLE 23-5 Effect of vasoconstrictor (epinephrine 1:200,000) on peak local anesthetic level in blood

Local anesthetic	Dose (mg)	Peak level (μg/mL)		Decrease (%)
		No vasoconstrictor	Vasoconstrictor	
Etidocaine	300	1.4	1.3	7
Lidocaine	400	4.3	3.0	30
Mepivacaine	500	4.7	3.0	36
Prilocaine	400	2.8	2.6	7

Modified from Malamed SF: *Handbook of local anesthesia,* ed 5, St. Louis, Mosby, 2004.

An example is the DentiPatch (Noven Pharmaceuticals, Inc., Miami, FL), a topical anesthetic bandage. It contains 46.1 mg of the base form of lidocaine, more than a single cartridge of injectable lidocaine HCl. The maximum blood level of lidocaine after a 15-minute application is 12.8 μg/mL, compared with 220 μg/mL after injection of 36 mg of lidocaine HCl.[33]

Other local anesthetics commonly used topically include benzocaine and tetracaine, both of which are esters rapidly detoxified by plasma pseudocholinesterase. Tetracaine is absorbed rapidly from mucous membranes, whereas benzocaine is poorly absorbed.[18] Overdose reactions to benzocaine are virtually unknown.[34] Tetracaine, on the other hand, has a significant toxicity potential and must therefore be used judiciously. In addition, as esters, both drugs are more likely to produce allergic reactions and localized tissue reactions (irritation) than are the amide topical anesthetics.

Topical anesthetics are important components in the management of pain and anxiety. They are applied commonly to the site of needle penetration before intraoral injections. When used in small, localized areas, topical anesthetics carry only a small chance for significant increases in anesthetic blood levels. Unfortunately, these anesthetics are also commonly applied over large areas (quadrants, or whole arches) before soft tissue procedures, such as scaling and curettage, when an injection of local anesthetic is not planned. Used in this manner, some topical anesthetics may produce significant blood levels, increasing the possibility of clinical overdose, particularly if this topical application is then followed by the injection of local anesthetics.

This information must not be used to justify discontinuation of topical anesthetic use. Indeed, I feel that topical anesthetics are an extremely important component of every local anesthetic injection. However, the dentist and dental hygienist must be aware of potential complications and take care to prevent them. The following suggestions are offered to aid in the wise administration of topical anesthetics:

- Amide-type topical anesthetics should be used whenever possible. Although the potential for overdose exists with all local anesthetics, other ADRs (e.g., local tissue reaction and allergy) occur more frequently with ester-type topical anesthetics, such as benzocaine and tetracaine.
- The area of application should be small. Only rarely is application over a full quadrant warranted. The application of topical anesthetics to a full quadrant requires larger quantities of drug, increasing the risk of overdose. I feel that whenever larger areas (e.g., three or more teeth) require soft tissue anesthesia, injection of a local anesthetic should be seriously considered.

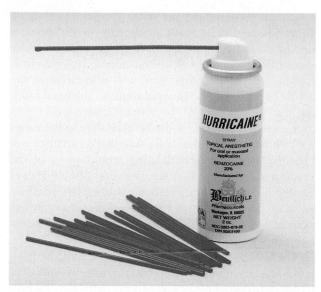

FIGURE 23-4 A topical anesthetic spray with a metered applicator. Depression of the nozzle releases a 10-mg dose of lidocaine. (From Malamed SF: *Handbook of local anesthesia,* ed 5, St. Louis, Mosby, 2004.)

■ Metered-dose forms of topical anesthetics should be used. Local anesthetics in the form of ointments and especially sprays are difficult to monitor during application, and overdose may occur inadvertently. A spray form of an amide anesthetic (e.g., lidocaine 10%) is available that delivers a metered 10-mg dose with each application is recommended (Figure 23-4).[35]

Intravascular injection. Intravascular injection is possible with any intraoral injection but is more likely to occur in certain anatomic areas (Table 23-6). Nerve block techniques possess a greater potential for intravascular injection; 11% of aspiration test results were positive in inferior alveolar nerve block, 5% in mental nerve block, and 3% in posterior superior alveolar nerve block, indicating that the needle bevel lay within the lumen of a blood vessel (vein or artery).[36]

Both IV and intraarterial administration may produce overdose reactions. Past wisdom stated that only IV injection of a local anesthetic could produce an overdose reaction and that intraarterial injection would not elevate blood levels since arterial blood travels away from the heart, not toward it, like venous blood. Aldrete et al.[37,38] theorized that intraarterial administration of local anesthetics may produce an overdose as rapidly as (or more rapidly than) IV injection. The suggested mechanism is a reversal of blood flow within the artery when local anesthetic is injected rapidly. If occurring during an inferior alveolar nerve block, blood would flow retrograde from the inferior alveolar artery

TABLE 23-6 Percentage of positive aspiration for intraoral injections

Injection	Positive aspiration (%)
Inferior alveolar nerve block	11.7
Mental (incisive) nerve block	5.7
Posterior superior alveolar nerve block	3.1
Anterior superior alveolar nerve block	0.7
Buccal nerve block	0.5

From Barlett SZ: Clinical observations on the effects of injections of local anesthetics preceded by aspiration, *Oral Surg Oral Med Oral Pathol* 33:520–526, 1972.

to the internal maxillary artery, back to the external carotid, then to the common carotid, and finally to the internal carotid and to the brain, a distance of only several inches in a human.

Intravascular injection of local anesthetics in the practice of dentistry should almost never occur. Careful injection technique and knowledge of the anatomy of the area to be anesthetized should minimize the occurrence of overdose reactions. Factors necessary to prevent this complication include the use of an aspirating syringe, use of a needle no smaller than 27-gauge, aspiration in at least two planes before injection, and slow administration of the local anesthetic.

Recommending the use of an aspirating syringe for all injections should seem unnecessary; all North American dental schools teach its use to their students. However, in a survey of the injection practices of dentists, 21% of those surveyed voluntarily admitted using nonaspirating syringes.[28] No justification exists for the use of such devices for any local anesthetic injection because a nonaspirating syringe makes aspiration to determine the location of the needle bevel impossible.

Needle gauge is important in determining whether the needle tip is located within a vessel before drug injection. The needles most commonly available in dentistry are 25-, 27-, and 30-gauge, with the 27-gauge being used most frequently.[28] Needle gauge is of importance in several respects during local anesthetic injection. Accuracy in injection technique is one critical point. For a local anesthetic to control pain, it must be deposited near the nerve. As the needle passes through tissue toward the target nerve, it is deflected to varying degrees by its bevel. The extent of deflection has been tested and is related to the caliber or gauge of the needle. Needles with greater rigidity (i.e., larger gauge) deflect less when passed through tissues to the depth required for an inferior alveolar nerve block.[39,40]

The second critical point relating to needle gauge is reliability of aspiration. In other words, if the needle tip is located within the lumen of a blood vessel, do results of aspiration tests always prove positive? Several studies have demonstrated that it is not possible to aspirate consistently with a needle gauge smaller than 25.[41,42] However, Trapp and Davies[43] reported that in vivo human blood may be aspirated through 23-, 25-, 27-, and 30-gauge needles without clinically significant differences in flow resistance.

Small-gauge needles occlude more easily with tissue plugs or with the wall of the blood vessel than do larger needles, leading to false-negative aspirations. For injection techniques with a greater likelihood of positive aspiration, a 25-gauge needle should be used. These techniques include all block injections, especially inferior alveolar nerve block. Unfortunately, the majority of practicing dentists surveyed favor the 27-gauge needle for inferior alveolar nerve block (64% using the 27-gauge needle and 34% using the 25-gauge needle).[28]

The technique of aspiration is yet another factor of importance in preventing intravascular injection. All local anesthetic needles are beveled at their tips (Figure 23-5A). The bevel of the needle may be within a vein with its bevel lying against the inner wall of the vessel. When negative pressure is created in the aspirating syringe (harpoon-type or self-aspirating syringe) during aspiration, the wall of the blood vessel may be sucked up against the bevel of the needle, preventing the return of blood into the needle and cartridge (Figure 23-5B). Clinically, absence of blood return is interpreted as a "negative" aspiration, and the injection of the anesthetic solution proceeds. Injection of the local anesthetic requires that positive pressure be placed on the plunger to expel the anesthetic from the cartridge through the needle and into the tissues. However, where the bevel of the needle lies against the inner wall of the vessel, the positive pressure of the anesthetic solution pushes the vessel wall away from the needle bevel and the local anesthetic, following a negative aspiration test result, is deposited intravascularly (Figure 23-5C).

On the basis of the preceding discussion, a single aspiration test may prove inadequate in the prevention of intravascular injection. A minimum of two tests should be performed before and during drug administration. During each aspiration test, orientation of the needle bevel should be changed slightly. The hand holding the syringe should be turned approximately 45 degrees to reorient the needle bevel relative to the vessel wall. Return of blood into the anesthetic cartridge is a "positive" aspiration, mandating repositioning of the needle and reaspiration. A negative result should always be obtained before local anesthetic is administered. Only 60% of dentists surveyed indicated that they always aspirate before mandibular block; 25% said they rarely aspirate, and 15% said they never aspirate.[28]

The last factor related to prevention of overdose from intravascular injection concerns the rate of injection. Rapid intravascular injection of a full cartridge (1.8 mL) of a 2% local anesthetic solution (36 mg) produces anesthetic blood levels that significantly exceed those required for overdose. In addition, the anesthetic blood level rises so rapidly that the onset of signs and symptoms is noted within seconds. Rapid injection may be defined as the administration of the contents (1.8 mL) of a dental anesthetic cartridge in 30 seconds or less. The same quantity of anesthetic injected intravascularly at a slower rate (at least 60 seconds) produces blood levels below the minimum for overdose (see Figure 23-3).[18] If the ensuing anesthetic blood level does exceed this minimum, the onset of the reaction is slower, with signs and symptoms less severe than those observed after rapid injection.

Slow injection of drugs is perhaps the most important factor in the prevention of ADRs. It is difficult to inject a drug too slowly, but quite easy to inject too rapidly. The administration of a full 1.8-mL cartridge of local anesthetic should take a minimum of 60 seconds.[28] Such efforts significantly reduce the risk of a serious overdose reaction from intravascular injection. Of doctors

FIGURE 23-5 Intravascular injection of a local anesthetic. **A,** The needle is inserted in the lumen of the blood vessel. **B,** An aspiration test should then be performed. Negative pressure pulls the vessel wall against the bevel of the needle; therefore, no blood enters the syringe, indicating a negative aspiration. **C,** The drug is injected. Positive pressure on the plunger of the syringe forces the local anesthetic solution out via the needle. The wall of the vessel is forced from the bevel, and the anesthetic solution is deposited directly into the lumen of the blood vessel. (From Malamed SF: *Handbook of local anesthesia,* ed 5, St. Louis, Mosby, 2004.)

surveyed, 46% administered a full cartridge of solution for the inferior alveolar nerve block in fewer than 30 seconds. Only 15% responded that they spent 60 seconds or longer on the same injection.[28]

Administration technique. Overdose reactions, and indeed all ADRs related to local anesthesia, may be minimized through proper administration of local anesthetics, described as follows:

1. A preliminary medical evaluation should be completed before local anesthetic administration.
2. Anxiety, fear, and apprehension should be recognized and managed before administration of a local anesthetic.
3. Whenever possible, the patient should receive injections while in a supine or semisupine position. An upright position should only be used if necessary, as with patients with severe cardiorespiratory disease.
4. Topical anesthetics should be applied to the site of needle penetration for at least 1 minute before all injections.
5. The weakest effective concentration of local anesthetic solution should be injected in the smallest volume compatible with successful anesthesia.
6. The anesthetic solution should be appropriate for the patient and for the planned dental treatment (e.g., appropriate duration of effect).
7. Vasoconstrictors should be included in all local anesthetics, if not specifically contraindicated.
8. Aspirating syringes must always be used for all local anesthetic injections.
9. Needles should be disposable, sharp, rigid, capable of reliable aspiration, and of adequate length for the contemplated injection technique. Most nerve blocks require the use of long (approximately 32 mm) 25-gauge needles. Short 27-gauge needles (20 mm) may be used for other injection techniques.
10. Aspiration should be performed in at least two planes before injection.
11. Injection should be slow; at least 60 seconds should be spent on each 1.8-mL dental cartridge.
12. A member of the dental office staff who is trained in the recognition of life-threatening situations should remain with the patient after the administration of the anesthetic. Most local anesthetic overdose reactions occur within the first 5 minutes after injection. All too often, incidents are reported in which the doctor returns to the treatment room only to find the

patient in the throes of a life-threatening ADR. Continuous observation permits prompt recognition and management with a high probability of complete recovery.

NOTE: *Variations may exist in needle selection for some regional nerve blocks. Textbooks on local anesthesia should be consulted for more specific information.*

Clinical manifestations

Signs and symptoms of overdose appear when the local anesthetic blood level in its target organ, such as the brain or heart (myocardium), rises above the critical level at which adverse effects of the drug develop. The brain responds to the concentration of local anesthetic delivered by the circulatory system regardless of the way in which the local anesthetic initially entered into the blood. The blood or plasma level of local anesthetic dictates the degree of severity and the duration of the response. The rate of onset of signs and symptoms corresponds to the blood level. Various causes of local anesthetic overdose produce a range of rates of onset.

Onset, intensity, and duration

Rapid intravascular injection produces clinical signs and symptoms of overdose rapidly, with seizures or unconsciousness developing within seconds. This type of overdose reaction, assuming the patient receives proper management, is usually of shorter duration than other forms because of continued drug redistribution (lowering cerebral blood levels) and, to a lesser extent, the biotransformation of the local anesthetic by the liver or by serum cholinesterase while the reaction continues. Overdose due to rapid intravascular injection may occur with all local anesthetics (Table 23-7).

Signs and symptoms of local anesthetic overdose resulting from *too large a total dose* or *unusually rapid absorption* into the cardiovascular system do not develop as rapidly as those produced by intravascular injection. In these two situations, signs and symptoms usually appear approximately 5 to 10 minutes after drug administration if a "plain" anesthetic solution was administered or approximately 30 minutes after injection if vasopressors were included; such signs and symptoms are initially mild.[31] Signs and symptoms may manifest as obvious agitation, increasing in intensity and progression over the next few minutes or longer if the blood level continues to rise. Clinically, the severity of these reactions may be as great as that of reactions associated with direct intravascular injection or may not progress beyond mild reactions. Like intravascular injection, these reactions are also self-limiting because of continued redistribution and biotransformation of

TABLE 23-7 Comparison of forms of local anesthetic overdose

Method of overdose	Likelihood of occurrence	Onset of signs and symptoms	Intensity of signs and symptoms	Duration of signs and symptoms	Primary prevention	Drug groups
Rapid intravascular	Common	Most rapid (seconds); intraarterial faster than IV	Usually most intense	2–3 minutes	Aspiration; slow injection	Amides and esters
Too large a total dose	Most common	5–30 minutes	Gradual onset with increased intensity; may prove severe	Usually 5–30 minutes (depends on dose and ability to metabolize and excrete)	Administration of minimal doses	Amides; esters only rarely
Rapid absorption	Likely with "high normal" doses if no vasoconstrictor used	5–30 minutes	Gradual onset with increased intensity; may prove severe	Usually 5–30 minutes (depends on dose and ability to metabolize and excrete)	Use of vasoconstrictor; limit on topical anesthetic use or use of nonabsorbed type (base form of drug)	Amides; esters only rarely
Slow biotransformation	Uncommon	1–3 hours	Gradual onset with slow increase in intensity	Potential for longest duration because of inability to metabolize agents	Adequate pretreatment physical evaluation of patient	Amides and esters
Slow elimination	Least common	Several hours	Gradual onset with slow increase in intensity	Potential for longest duration because of inability to excrete agents	Adequate pretreatment physical evaluation of patient	Amides and esters

IV, intravenous.

the local anesthetic. However, they do last significantly longer than the intravascular responses.

In two cases I have witnessed, the patients received adequate mandibular anesthesia (following multiple injections) and were undergoing restorative procedures for 20 and 25 minutes, respectively, when clinical manifestations of overdose became obvious. These included mild tremor, which progressed slowly into a "mild" seizure over the next 30 minutes.

Unusually slow biotransformation or *elimination* of local anesthetics rarely produces signs and symptoms of overdose while the patient is still in the dental office. In situations in which the patient has received a large dose of local anesthetic, signs and symptoms of mild overdose may develop 90 or more minutes later. In most situations this patient has usually left the dental office.

Signs and symptoms

Local anesthetics depress excitable membranes. The cardiovascular system and CNS are especially sensitive and are considered "target organs" for local anesthetic drugs. The usual clinical expression of local anesthetic overdose is one of apparent stimulation followed by a period of depression.

Minimal to moderate blood levels. The initial clinical signs of overdose in the CNS are usually excitatory. At low overdose blood levels, the patient usually becomes confused, talkative, apprehensive, and excited; speech may be slurred. A generalized stuttering follows, which may progress to muscular twitching and tremor, commonly noted in the muscles of the face and the distal parts of the extremities. The patient may also exhibit nystagmus. The blood pressure, heart rate, and respiratory rate increase.[44]

Headache may also be a symptom of overdose (secondary to local anesthetic induced dilation of cerebral blood vessels). In addition, many patients initially report feeling a generalized feeling of lightheadedness and dizziness, that is, "different" from that associated with alcohol. These symptoms then progress to visual and auditory disturbances (e.g., difficulty in focusing, blurred vision, and ringing in the ears [tinnitus]). Numbness of the tongue and perioral tissues commonly develops, as does a feeling of being either flushed or chilled. As the reaction progresses, and if the anesthetic blood level rises, the patient experiences drowsiness and disorientation and may eventually lose consciousness. Signs and symptoms of mild local anesthetic overdose may resemble psychomotor or temporal lobe epilepsy (see Chapter 21).

Moderate to high blood levels. As the local anesthetic blood level continues to rise, clinical manifes-

tations of overdose progress to a generalized convulsive state with tonic-clonic seizures. After this "stimulatory" or "excitatory" phase, a period of generalized CNS depression ensues, characteristically of a degree of severity related to the degree of stimulation preceding it. Therefore, if the patient suffered intensive tonic-clonic seizures, postseizure depression is more profound, probably characterized by unconsciousness and respiratory depression or respiratory arrest. If the stimulatory phase was mild (e.g., talkativeness or agitation), the depressant phase will also be mild, perhaps consisting of only a period of disorientation and lethargy. Blood pressure, heart rate, and respiratory rate are usually depressed during this phase, again to a degree proportionate to the degree of previous stimulation (Box 23-3).

Although the sequence just described represents the usual clinical expression of local anesthetic overdose, the excitatory phase of the reaction may be extremely brief or even absent. This is especially true with lidocaine and mepivacaine, in which overdose may appear

---

Box 23-3 Clinical manifestations of local anesthetic overdose

SIGNS

Low to moderate overdose levels
Confusion
Talkativeness
Apprehension
Excitedness
Slurred speech
Generalized stutter
Muscular twitching and tremor of the face and extremities
Nystagmus
Elevated blood pressure
Elevated heart rate
Elevated respiratory rate

Moderate to high blood levels
Generalized tonic-clonic seizure, followed by:
Generalized central nervous system depression
Depressed blood pressure, heart rate, and respiratory rate

SYMPTOMS
Headache
Lightheadedness
Dizziness
Blurred vision, inability to focus
Ringing in ears
Numbness of tongue and perioral tissues
Flushed or chilled feeling
Drowsiness
Disorientation
Loss of consciousness

initially as drowsiness and nystagmus, leading directly to either unconsciousness or generalized tonic-clonic seizure activity.[45] Etidocaine and bupivacaine do not normally cause drowsiness before seizures;[46] progression from the preseizure state of alertness to seizures with these drugs is much more abrupt.

The overdose reaction continues until the cerebral blood level of the drug falls below the minimal blood level for overdose or until the reaction is terminated through appropriate management, including possible drug therapy.

Pathophysiology

Local anesthetic overdose is produced by overly high blood levels of a drug in its target organs and tissues. When the drug's entry into the blood exceeds its rate of removal, overdose levels may be reached. The period of time required for clinical signs and symptoms to appear varies considerably depending on the cause of the elevated blood level. Drugs do not merely affect a single organ or tissue, and all drugs have multiple actions. Local anesthetics are typical of all drugs in this regard.

Although the primary pharmacologic action of a local anesthetic is inhibition of the excitation conduction process in peripheral nerves, its ability to stabilize membranes is not limited solely to peripheral nerves. Any excitable membranes, such as those in the heart, brain, and neuromuscular junction, are altered by local anesthetics if they reach a sufficient tissue concentration.[47] The following section discusses both the desirable and the undesirable systemic actions of local anesthetics.

A sample of blood may be drawn from the patient to determine the amount of local anesthetic present per milliliter of blood. This is referred to commonly as the *blood level,* or *plasma level,* of a local anesthetic. Blood levels of drugs are measured in micrograms (μg) per milliliter (1000 μg = 1 mg).

An additional factor to consider when discussing blood levels of drugs is that although ranges are mentioned for various systemic actions, patients will differ in their responses to drugs. Even though seizure activity may occur at a blood level of 7.5 μg/mL of lidocaine for most individuals, others may exhibit seizures at lower blood levels, whereas others may be able to tolerate blood levels that are greatly in excess of those listed without experiencing ADRs. In addition, different local anesthetics have different threshold levels at which signs and symptoms of overdose usually appear (Table 23-8). Drugs associated with higher plasma levels for overdose are not necessarily less toxic because these drugs are usually less potent local anesthetics and must therefore

TABLE 23-8 Clinical manifestations of local anesthetic overdose

Agent	Usual threshold for CNS signs and symptoms
Bupivacaine, etidocaine	1–2 μg/mL
Prilocaine	4 μg/mL
Lidocaine, mepivacaine	5 μg/mL

CNS, central nervous system.

be injected at higher concentrations to be effective. For example, the ratio of CNS toxicity of bupivacaine, etidocaine, and lidocaine is approximately 4:2:1, which is similar to the relative potency of these drugs for the production of regional anesthesia in humans.[48]

Local anesthetic blood levels

Following intraoral injection, the drug slowly enters the blood. Circulating blood levels of lidocaine have been monitored and recorded after such injections; these documented levels form the basis of the following discussion (Figure 23-6). Blood levels of other anesthetics differ from those reported for lidocaine. Cannell et al.[49] demonstrated that blood levels rise to a maximum of approximately 1.0 μg/mL after the administration of 40 to 160 mg lidocaine (the equivalent of 1 to 4.5 cartridges) via intraoral injection. No ADRs were reported at those levels.

As the lidocaine blood level increases, systemic actions are noted, some of which have considerable therapeutic value. With lidocaine blood levels between 4.5 and 7.0 μg/mL, signs of CNS irritability are noted. When this increases to 7.5 μg/mL or greater, tonic-clonic seizure activity develops. A blood level of 10 μg/mL is characterized by marked CNS depression. In addition, at overdose levels adverse actions on the cardiovascular system are noted. Most adverse effects on the cardiovascular system do not develop until higher levels of local anesthetic occur. (See Figure 23-3 for the effect of the various routes of administration on the blood level of the anesthetic.)

Systemic activity of local anesthetics

Local anesthetics inhibit the function of all excitable membranes. In dentistry these drugs are normally applied to a very specific region of the body, where they perform their primary function—a reversible blockade or depression of peripheral nerve conduction. Other actions of local anesthetics relate to their absorption into the cardiovascular system and their systemic actions on other excitable membranes, including smooth

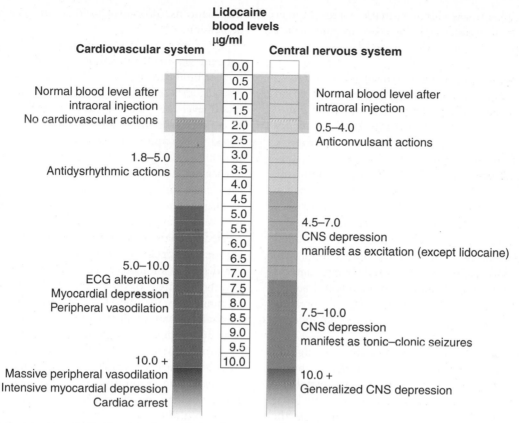

Lidocaine blood levels µg/ml

Cardiovascular system

Normal blood level after intraoral injection
No cardiovascular actions

1.8–5.0
Antidysrhythmic actions

5.0–10.0
ECG alterations
Myocardial depression
Peripheral vasodilation

10.0 +
Massive peripheral vasodilation
Intensive myocardial depression
Cardiac arrest

0.0
0.5
1.0
1.5
2.0
2.5
3.0
3.5
4.0
4.5
5.0
5.5
6.0
6.5
7.0
7.5
8.0
8.5
9.0
9.5
10.0

Central nervous system

Normal blood level after intraoral injection

0.5–4.0
Anticonvulsant actions

4.5–7.0
CNS depression
manifest as excitation (except lidocaine)

7.5–10.0
CNS depression
manifest as tonic–clonic seizures

10.0 +
Generalized CNS depression

FIGURE 23-6 Local anesthetic blood levels and their actions on cardiovascular and central nervous systems. CNS, central nervous system. (From Malamed SF: *Handbook of local anesthesia,* ed 5, St. Louis, Mosby, 2004.)

muscle, the myocardium, and the CNS. Although high blood levels of local anesthetics produce undesirable systemic responses, some desirable actions may occur at nonoverdose levels.

Cardiovascular actions. Local anesthetics, particularly lidocaine, are frequently used in the management of various ventricular dysrhythmias, especially ventricular extrasystole (premature ventricular contractions) and ventricular tachycardia. Considerable data today illustrate the alterations that occur in the myocardium as blood levels of lidocaine increase.[50,51] In general, the minimal effective blood level of lidocaine for antidysrhythmic activity is 1.8 (µg/mL).[52] In the range from approximately 2 to 5 (µg/mL), the action of lidocaine on the myocardium includes electrophysiologic changes only. These include a prolongation or abolition of the slow phase of depolarization during diastole in Purkinje fibers and a shortening of the action potential duration and of the effective refractory period. At this therapeutic level, no alterations in myocardial contractility, diastolic volume, intraventricular pressure, or cardiac output are evident.[46,51] The healthy

as well as the diseased myocardium tolerate mildly elevated blood levels of local anesthetic without deleterious effects.

When used to treat dysrhythmias, lidocaine is administered intravenously (slowly!) in a 50- to 100-mg bolus (1.0 to 1.5 mg/kg).[53] Overdose is a potential concern, but the benefit-to-risk ratio allows for the judicious use of IV lidocaine. Further elevation of the lidocaine blood level (5 to 10 µg/mL) produces a prolongation of conduction time through various portions of the heart and an increase in the diastolic threshold. This may be noted on the electrocardiogram as an increased P-R interval and QRS duration and sinus bradycardia. In addition, decreased myocardial contractility, increased diastolic volume, decreased intraventricular pressure, and decreased cardiac output are evident.[50,54] Peripheral vascular effects observed at this level include vasodilation, which produces a drop in blood pressure and occurs as a result of the direct relaxant effect of lidocaine on peripheral vascular smooth muscle.[55]

Further increases in blood levels of lidocaine (>10 µg/mL) lead to an accentuation of the aforementioned electrophysiologic and hemodynamic effects, in particular massive peripheral vasodilation, marked reduction in myocardial contractility, and slowed heart rate, which may ultimately result in cardiac arrest.[50,55]

CNS actions. The CNS is extremely sensitive to the actions of local anesthetics.[56] As cerebral blood levels of local anesthetics rise, clinical signs and symptoms develop. Local anesthetics readily cross the blood-brain barrier, progressively depressing CNS function.[47] At nonoverdose levels of lidocaine (<5 µg/mL), no clinical signs of adverse effects on the CNS exist; however, a CNS-depressant action that has potential therapeutic value is observed. At cerebral blood levels between 0.5 and 4.0 µg/mL, lidocaine can terminate various forms of seizure.[57,58] Most clinically useful local anesthetics possess this anticonvulsant property (both procaine and lidocaine having been used to terminate or decrease the duration of grand mal or petit mal seizures). This anticonvulsant action may be related to a depression of hyperexcitable cortical neurons present in epileptic patients.

As the blood level of lidocaine rises above 4.5 µg/mL, early signs and symptoms of CNS alteration appear. These are usually related to increased cortical irritability (e.g., agitation, talkativeness, and tremor). Numbness of the tongue and perioral tissues may result from the rich blood supply to these tissues, allowing the drugs to produce a blockade of the nerve endings.[54]

With further increase in cerebral blood level to 7.5 µg/mL or greater (lidocaine), generalized tonic-clonic seizures develop. Following this period of CNS stimulation, a further increase in cerebral blood level of the local anesthetic results in termination of seizure activity and an electroencephalographic pattern consistent with generalized CNS depression.[54] Respiratory depression and arrest are also noted.

The fact that local anesthetics are CNS depressants on the one hand but that CNS stimulation is the first clinical manifestation of this depression may seem contradictory. The stimulation and subsequent depression produced by high blood levels of local anesthetics result *solely* from depression of neuronal activity. The cerebral cortex receives inhibitory and facilitory (stimulatory) impulses. If it is considered that these two groups of neurons are depressed selectively by different blood levels of local anesthetics, this seeming contradiction is explained. At anesthetic blood levels capable of producing seizures, the inhibitory pathways in the cerebral cortex are depressed, not the stimulatory pathways. This depression of inhibitory pathways allows facilitory neurons to function unopposed, leading to increased excitation of the CNS and ultimately to seizures.[59] As the local anesthetic blood level increases still further, stimulatory neurons are depressed along with inhibitory neurons, producing a state of generalized CNS depression.

The duration of the seizure, although primarily dependent on the local anesthetic blood level, can be further modified by the acid-base status of the patient. The higher the $PaCO_2$, the lower the local anesthetic blood level required to precipitate generalized seizures. In contrast, the lower the $PaCO_2$, the greater the drug blood level required to produce seizures.[8] Lowering a patient's $PaCO_2$ through hyperventilation raises the cortical seizure threshold to local anesthetics and lessens the chance that a drug may cause seizures.

Drug-induced seizures, in and of themselves, are not necessarily fatal. However, the mortality rate in untreated animals is more than 60%.[60] The duration of the seizure appears to be a critical factor in determining the degree of morbidity. The convulsing brain requires greatly elevated oxygen (O_2) and glucose levels to continue functioning. To a degree, the body's own mechanisms can compensate for this; however, respiratory and circulatory support can enhance the chances of survival significantly. If blood levels of the local anesthetic rise even further, cardiovascular depression is produced and respiration is increasingly impaired by uncoordinated muscle spasm during the seizure. Brain function is affected even more through reduced cerebral blood flow and hypoxia (see Figure 23-6).[61]

Management

Management of local anesthetic overdose is based on its severity. In most cases the reaction is mild and transitory, requiring little or no specific treatment. However, when the reaction is more severe and of longer duration, prompt management is necessary. Most local anesthetic overdoses are self-limiting; the blood level of the local anesthetic decreases over time as the reaction progresses because of redistribution (primarily) and biotransformation (secondarily) of the drug. Rare indeed is the occasion on which drugs other than O_2 need be administered to terminate a local anesthetic overdose.

Overtreatment of a local anesthetic overdose is a potential problem. In the rush of excitement that follows this unexpected reaction, emergency drugs, such as anticonvulsants, may be administered too freely. All anticonvulsants are CNS depressants and will delay the return of consciousness. The time for aggressive IV management of the local anesthetic overdose comes when simpler measures fail to terminate the seizure. However, by ending the seizure, anticonvulsants may give the rescuer a false sense of accomplishment; no anticonvulsant is wholly innocuous.

It is well worth repeating that during and after administration of a local anesthetic the patient should remain under continual observation. Careful observation for any change in behavior after the administration of a local anesthetic allows for prompt recognition and management, thus minimizing potential hazard for the patient.

Mild overdose reaction with rapid onset

An overdose in which signs and symptoms develop within 5 to 10 minutes following drug administration is considered rapid in onset. Possible causes include intravascular injection, unusually rapid absorption, or administration of too large a total dose. If clinical manifestations do not progress beyond mild CNS excitation and consciousness is retained, significant definitive care is not necessary. The local anesthetic undergoes redistribution and biotransformation, with the blood level falling below the overdose level in a relatively short time.

The following are diagnostic clues to the presence of mild local anesthetic overdose:

- Onset approximately 5 to 10 minutes following drug administration
- Talkativeness
- Increased anxiety
- Facial muscle twitching
- Increased heart rate, blood pressure, and respiration

Step 1: termination of the dental procedure.

Step 2: P (position). The conscious patient is placed in a comfortable position.

Step 3: reassurance of the patient.

Step 4: A-B-C (airway-breathing-circulation), basic life support (BLS) as needed. Patency of the airway, breathing, and circulation must be assessed and implemented, as needed. In mild local anesthetic overdose, the victim's airway, breathing, and circulation remain adequate, with no intervention necessary.

Step 5: D (definitive care):
Step 5a: administration of O_2. At this point the fact that a lowered $PaCO_2$ level elevates the seizure threshold of a local anesthetic may be used to the patient's advantage. The patient should be asked to purposefully hyperventilate by deep breathing on room air or O_2 via a full-face mask or nasal hood. This can decrease the likelihood of seizures.

Step 5b: monitoring of vital signs. The stage of postexcitation depression is mild in this form of reaction, with little or no definitive treatment required.

O_2 may be administered and the patient's vital signs monitored and recorded regularly (e.g., every 5 minutes).

Step 5c: administration of an anticonvulsant drug, if needed. The administration of an anticonvulsant, such as diazepam or midazolam, usually is not indicated in the mild overdose reaction described here. However, if the doctor is proficient in venipuncture and has little difficulty in accessing a vein, diazepam or midazolam may be administered via the IV route, titrated at a rate of 1 mL per minute until the clinical reaction abates. Doses of IV drugs should always be titrated to clinical effect (in this case the cessation of muscular twitching). Small doses of IV diazepam or midazolam may prove effective.[62] Diazepam doses as little as 2.5 to 5 mg have been known to terminate seizures. It must be emphasized, however, that for a mild reaction to a local anesthetic, anticonvulsant drug therapy normally is not indicated.

Step 5d: summoning of emergency medical assistance. If the doctor deems emergency assistance necessary, such assistance should be sought immediately. The decision to seek help is based solely on the doctor's instinct. My feeling is that emergency assistance should be sought whenever an anticonvulsant drug has been administered to terminate the reaction. In addition, if signs and symptoms appear to be increasing in intensity and venous access is not available, emergency assistance is indicated.

Step 6: recovery and discharge. The patient should be permitted to recover for as long as is necessary. The scheduled treatment may continue or be postponed after a thorough evaluation of the patient's physical and emotional status. If the treating doctor harbors any doubts or concerns about the patient's condition following the reaction, medical evaluation, preferably by an emergency department physician, is indicated before that patient is discharged. If an anticonvulsant drug was administered, the patient should receive medical evaluation before discharge and must not leave the office unescorted.

Box 23-4 outlines the steps in the management of a mild local anesthetic overdose with rapid onset.

Mild overdose reaction with delayed onset (>10 minutes)

If a patient exhibits signs and symptoms of a mild overdose after local anesthetic administration in the recommended manner, if adequate pain control has resulted, and if dental treatment has begun, the most likely causes are unusually rapid absorption or administration of too large a total dose of the drug.

Box 23-4 Management of mild local anesthetic overdose with rapid onset

Recognize problem
(Onset 5–10 minutes after local anesthetic administration, talkativeness, increased anxiety, facial muscle twitching, increased heart and respiratory rates, elevated blood pressure)
↓
Discontinue dental treatment
↓
P—Position patient comfortably
↓
Reassure the patient
↓
A → B → C—Assess airway, breathing, circulation, and administer as needed basic life support as needed
↓
D—Provide definitive management as needed
Administer O_2
Monitor vital signs
Administer anticonvulsant drug as needed
Activate emergency medical service as needed
Permit patient to recover
Discharge of patient

A, airway; **B**, breathing; **C**, circulation; **D**, definitive care; **P**, position.

Step 1: termination of the procedure.

Step 2: P (position).
The patient should be allowed to assume a comfortable position.

Step 3: reassurance of the patient.

Step 4: A-B-C (airway, breathing, circulation) or BLS, as needed.
If the patient is conscious, the steps of BLS are not necessary.

Step 5: D (definitive care):

Step 5a: administration of O_2 and instruction of patient to hyperventilate.

Step 5b: monitoring of vital signs.

Step 5c: administration of anticonvulsant, if needed.
Overdose reactions resulting from either unusually rapid absorption or administration of too large a total dose of the drug usually progress in intensity gradually and last longer than those caused by intravascular drug administration. If venous access is possible, an IV infusion may be established and an anticonvulsant, such as diazepam or midazolam, administered via titration until clinical signs and symptoms abate.

Step 5d: summoning of medical assistance (optional).
When venipuncture is not practical, medical assistance should be sought immediately.

Postexcitement depression is relatively mild after a mild excitement phase. The use of an anticonvulsant to help terminate the reaction may increase the level of postexcitation depression. Monitoring the patient and adhering to the steps of BLS are normally entirely adequate to successfully manage a mild overdose reaction with delayed onset. In addition, O_2 should be administered. Whenever an anticonvulsant is administered, medical assistance should be sought.

Step 5e: medical consultation.
After successful management of a mild overdose with slow onset, a physician should evaluate the patient to seek possible causes of the reaction.

Step 6: recovery and discharge.
The patient should be allowed to recover for as long as necessary and escorted to a local hospital or their primary care physician's office by an adult companion, such as a spouse, relative, or friend. When emergency personnel are present, they will suggest a decision on patient disposition.

Step 7: subsequent dental treatment.
Before scheduling further dental treatment in which local anesthetics may be necessary, a complete evaluation of the patient should be performed to help determine the cause of the overdose reaction.

Box 23-5 outlines the protocol for the management of a mild local anesthetic overdose with delayed onset.

Severe overdose reaction with rapid onset
If signs and symptoms of overdose appear almost immediately (within seconds to 1 minute) following local anesthetic administration (e.g., while the anesthetic syringe is still in the patient's mouth or within a few seconds after the injection), intravascular injection—either via the IV or intraarterial route—is the most likely cause of the overdose reaction. Because of the extremely rapid increase in anesthetic blood level, clinical manifestations are likely to be severe. Unconsciousness, possibly accompanied by seizures, may mark the initial clinical manifestation.

The following are diagnostic clues to the presence of severe overdose to a local anesthetic:

- Signs and symptoms appearing either during injection or seconds after its completion
- Generalized tonic-clonic seizures
- Loss of consciousness

> **Box 23-5** Management of mild overdose reaction with delayed onset
>
> **Recognize problem**
> (Onset >10 minutes after local anesthetic administration, talkativeness, increased anxiety, facial muscle twitching, increased heart and respiratory rates, elevated blood pressure)
> ↓
> Discontinue dental treatment
> ↓
> **P**—Position patient comfortably
> ↓
> Reassure the patient
> ↓
> **A → B → C**—Assess airway, breathing, circulation, and administer basic life support as needed
> ↓
> **D**—Provide definitive management as needed
> Administer O_2
> Monitor vital signs
> Administer anticonvulsant drug as needed
> Activate emergency medical service as needed
> Medical consultation prior to subsequent dental care
> Permit patient to recover
> Discharge of patient

A, airway; **B**, breathing; **C**, circulation; **D**, definitive care; **P**, position.

Step 1: P (position). The syringe should be removed from the patient's mouth (if applicable) and the patient placed in the supine position with the feet elevated slightly. Subsequent management is based on the presence or absence of seizures.

Step 2: summoning of emergency medical assistance. Whenever a seizure develops during or after local anesthetic injection, emergency assistance should be sought immediately.

When loss of consciousness is the sole clinical sign present, the patient should be placed in the supine position with their feet elevated slightly and managed as described in Chapter 5. If consciousness rapidly returns, vasodepressor syncope was the likely cause and medical assistance is usually not required. If the patient does not respond rapidly, emergency assistance should be sought as soon as possible.

Step 3: A-B-C (airway, breathing, circulation) or BLS, as needed.

Step 4: D (definitive care):
Step 4a: administration of O_2. Adequate oxygenation and ventilation during local anesthetic-induced seizures is extremely important in terminating seizures

and minimizing associated morbidity. O_2 should be administered as soon as it becomes available.

Ensuring adequacy of ventilation—the removal of carbon dioxide and the administration of O_2—helps minimize and prevent hypercarbia and hypoxia and maintains the seizure threshold of the anesthetic drug (local anesthetic seizure threshold is lowered if the patient becomes acidotic). In most instances of local anesthetic-induced seizures, airway maintenance and assisted ventilation are necessary (**A + B**), but the heart should remain functional (blood pressure and heart rate are present).

Step 4b: protection of the patient. If seizures occur, which are common, management follows the protocol outlined in the discussion on seizures (see Chapter 21). Recommended management includes the prevention of injury through protection of the arms, legs, and head. Do not attempt to place any object between the teeth of a convulsing patient. Tight, binding articles of clothing, such as ties, collars, and belts, should be loosened. Prevention of injury is a primary objective of seizure management.

Step 4c: monitoring of vital signs. The blood level of local anesthetic decreases as it is redistributed. Assuming ventilation of the victim is adequate, the anesthetic blood level should fall below the seizure threshold and the seizure ceases (unless the patient has become acidotic). In most cases of local anesthetic-induced seizure, definitive drug therapy to terminate the seizure is unnecessary.

Step 4d: venipuncture and IV anticonvulsant administration. IV anticonvulsant administration should not be considered unless the doctor is well trained in venipuncture, has the appropriate drugs available, and can manage an unconscious, apneic patient during the postseizure period. If possible, the dose of either diazepam or midazolam is titrated slowly until the seizure ends. In certain cases, however, securing of a vein in a convulsing patient may prove difficult. In such situations BLS should continue until assistance arrives.

Step 5: postictal management. Following the seizure comes a period of generalized CNS depression that is usually equal in intensity to the previous degree of excitation. During this period the patient may be drowsy or even unconscious, breathing may be shallow or absent, the airway may be partially or totally obstructed, and blood pressure and heart rate may be depressed or absent. Management is predicated upon the signs and symptoms present.

The use of anticonvulsants to terminate seizures only increases postictal depression. Barbiturates have greater respiratory depressant actions than the benzodiazepines diazepam and midazolam, although all are equally effective as anticonvulsants; thus, benzodiazepines are the drugs of choice in seizure management.

Step 5a: A-B-C (airway, breathing, circulation) or BLS, as needed.

Step 5b: monitoring of vital signs.
Management in the postictal period requires adherence to the steps of BLS. A patent airway must be maintained and O$_2$ or artificial ventilation administered, as needed. In addition, vital signs are monitored and recorded (every 5 minutes). If either blood pressure or heart beat is absent, chest compressions are started immediately (see Chapter 30). Most commonly, however, the blood pressure and heart rate generally are depressed in the immediate postictal period, gradually returning toward baseline levels as the patient recovers.

Step 5c: additional management considerations.
If the patient's blood pressure remains depressed for an extended period (>30 minutes) and medical assistance is not yet available, administration of a vasopressor to elevate blood pressure should be considered. Once again, this step should be considered only when the doctor is well trained in the administration of vasopressors and in the management of any complications associated with their administration. A vasopressor, such as ephedrine (25 to 50 mg intramuscularly), produces a mild elevation in blood pressure, the effect lasting 1 hour or more. Administration of 1000 mL of either normal saline or a 5% dextrose and water solution via IV infusion is another means of elevating blood pressure.

Step 6: recovery and discharge.
Emergency medical personnel will stabilize the patient's condition before transferring the patient, via ambulance, to the emergency department of a local hospital for definitive management, observation, and recovery.

> NOTE: As previously discussed, the first clinical sign of a rapid rise in the local anesthetic blood level may be unconsciousness. When this occurs, management follows the protocol outlined in Chapter 5. Follow-up therapy is identical to that suggested for the postseizure patient.

Severe overdose reaction with slow onset
Local anesthetic overdose that evolves slowly (over 10 minutes or more) is unlikely to progress to a point at which severe clinical signs and symptoms develop if that individual is observed continuously and prompt management initiated. Clinical signs and symptoms of overdose usually progress from mild to tonic-clonic seizures over a relatively brief period of time (5 minutes or less); in some cases the progression may be much less pronounced. In all cases dental treatment must cease as soon as signs and symptoms of overdose become evident.

Step 1: termination of dental treatment.
Treatment is likely to have begun before the signs and symptoms of overdose become evident. Immediately cease the procedure and initiate emergency care.

Step 2: P (positioning).
Positioning depends on the status of the patient. If conscious, initial positioning is based on comfort; however, the unconscious patient is placed into the supine position with the legs elevated slightly.

Step 3: A-B-C (airway, breathing, circulation) or BLS, as needed.

Step 4: D (definitive care):
Step 4a: summoning of medical assistance.

Step 4b: protection of the patient.

Step 4c: administration of O$_2$.

Step 4d: monitoring of vital signs.

Step 4e: venipuncture and administration of IV anticonvulsant.
If symptoms are mild at the onset but become more severe, administration of an anticonvulsant drug should be considered. IV titration of a suitable anticonvulsant is indicated.

Step 5: postictal management:
Step 5a: A-B-C (airway, breathing, circulation), or BLS, as needed.

Step 5b: monitoring of vital signs.
Management in the postictal period of CNS, respiratory, and cardiovascular depression requires adherence to the steps of BLS. Airway patency is assured and O$_2$ or artificial ventilation administered, as needed. Vital signs continue to be monitored and recorded (every 5 minutes). If blood pressure or heart rate are absent, chest compression is initiated immediately (see Chapter 30). In general, blood pressure and heart rate are depressed in the immediate postictal period, gradually returning to baseline levels as recovery progresses.

Step 5c: additional management considerations. A mild vasopressor (e.g., ephedrine) or infusion of IV fluids may be indicated if the blood pressure remains depressed for a prolonged period.

Step 6: recovery and discharge.

Emergency personnel stabilize the patient and prepare for transport to the emergency department of a local hospital for definitive management, recovery, and discharge.

Local anesthetic–induced seizures need not lead to significant morbidity or death if the patient is properly prepared for the injection; if the individual administering the local anesthetic is well trained in the recognition and management of complications, including seizures; and if appropriate resuscitation equipment is readily available. Administration of local anesthetics without such precautions is contraindicated.

Box 23-6 outlines the protocol for the management of severe local anesthetic drug overdose with slow or rapid onset.

- **Drugs used in management:** O_2, anticonvulsants (e.g., diazepam or midazolam), and vasopressors, such as ephedrine (optional), may be administered in the management of an overdose reaction.

Box 23-6 Management of a severe local anesthetic overdose with slow or rapid onset

Recognize problem
(Onset seconds to 1 minute after local anesthetic administration, generalized tonic-clonic seizures; loss of consciousness)
↓
P—Position patient supine with legs elevated slightly
↓
Activate emergency medical service
↓
A → B → C—Assess airway, breathing, circulation, and administer basic life support as needed
↓
D—Provide definitive management as needed
Administer O_2
Protect the patient from injury
Monitor vital signs
Administer venipuncture and administer anticonvulsant drug as needed
↓
Postictal management
A → B → C—Assess airway, breathing, circulation, and administer basic life support as needed
↓
D—Provide definitive management as needed
Administer O_2
Monitor vital signs
Recovery and discharge

A, airway; **B,** breathing; **C,** circulation; **D,** definitive care; **P,** position.

- **Medical assistance required:** If the reaction is mild, assistance is recommended but not necessary; if, however, the reaction is severe or if an anticonvulsant is administered to terminate the episode, emergency personnel should be sought immediately.

■ EPINEPHRINE (VASOCONSTRICTOR) OVERDOSE REACTION

Precipitating factors and prevention

The increased use of vasoconstrictors in local anesthetic solutions has introduced a potentially new ADR-vasoconstrictor overdose. Although a variety of vasoconstrictors currently are used in dentistry (Table 23-9), the most effective and widely used is epinephrine (Adrenalin). Overdose reactions with drugs other than epinephrine are uncommon because of the lower potencies of the other drugs. These reactions are more likely to occur when greater concentrations of epinephrine are used (Table 23-10).

The optimum concentration of epinephrine for the prolongation of anesthesia with lidocaine is a 1:250,000 dilution.[63] No apparent reason exists for the use of the 1:50,000 dilution frequently used today for pain control in the United States; it contains twice as much epinephrine per milliliter as a 1:100,000 dilution and four times that found in a 1:200,000 dilution while not providing the anesthetic with any positive attributes. The only benefit of the 1:50,000 concentration of epinephrine lesser other concentrations is the control of bleeding (hemostasis). However, when used for this purpose, epinephrine must be applied directly at the site where the bleeding occurs or may occur. Only small volumes of the solution are required, and only small quantities are feasible in many surgical sites because larger volumes may actually interfere with the procedure. Overdose reactions from this use of 1:50,000 epinephrine are rare.

Another form of epinephrine used in dentistry is more likely to produce an overdose or precipitate other life-threatening situations. Some doctors use racemic epinephrine gingival retraction cord before taking impressions for crown and bridge procedures. Currently available epinephrine-impregnated retraction cord contains 310 to 1000 μg of racemic epinephrine per inch of cord.[64] Racemic epinephrine is a combination of the levorotatory and dextrorotatory forms of epinephrine, the latter being about one twelfth to one eighteenth as potent as the former.

TABLE 23-9 Vasoconstrictors commonly used in dentistry

Agent	Available Concentrations	Maximum dose	Local anesthetics used with agent
Epinephrine	1:50,000	Healthy adult: 0.2 mg	Lidocaine 2%
	1:100,000	Patient with CVD and ASA III, IV: 0.04 mg	Lidocaine 2%
	1:200,000		Articaine 4%
			Articaine 4%
			Bupivacaine 0.5%
			Prilocaine 4%
Levonordefrin (Neo-Cobefrin)	1:20,000	Healthy adult: 1.0 mg	Mepivacaine 2%
		Patient with CVD and ASA III, IV: 0.2 mg	

ASA, American Society of Anesthesiologists; CVD, cardiovascular disease.

TABLE 23-10 Dilutions of vasoconstrictors used in dentistry

Dilution	Available drug	Dose (mg/mL)	mg/cartridge (1.8 mL)	Maximum no. of cartridges
1:1000	Epinephrine SC, IM Anaphylaxis	1.0	N/A	N/A
1:10,000	Epinephrine IV, ET Cardiac arrest	0.1	N/A	N/A
1:20,000	Levonordefrin	0.05	0.09	10 (H), 2 (C)
1:50,000	Epinephrine	0.02	0.036	5 (H), 1 (C)
1:80,000	Epinephrine	0.0125	0.0275 (2.2 mL cartridge)	10 (H), 2 (C)
1:100,000	Epinephrine	0.01	0.018	10 (H), 2 (C)
1:200,000	Epinephrine	0.005	0.009	10 (H)*, 2 (C)
1:300,000	Epinephrine	0.0033	0.006	10 (H)*, 4 (C)

*Maximum number of cartridges determined by local anesthetic dose.
C, cardiac patient; ET, endotracheal; H, healthy patient; IM, intramuscular; IV, intravenous; N/A, not applicable; SC, subcutaneous.

Because of the high epinephrine concentration in this preparation, retraction cord is a potential danger to all patients, especially at-risk cardiovascular patients. The gingival epithelium, already disturbed (i.e., abraded) by dental procedures such as cavity preparation, absorbs the epinephrine from the retraction cord rapidly, whereas intact oral epithelium absorbs little epinephrine into the systemic circulation. Studies have demonstrated that from 24% to 92% of the applied epinephrine is absorbed into the CVS;[64] the extreme variability is believed to result from the degree of vascular exposure (bleeding) and the duration of the exposure.

When gingival retraction is necessary, as is frequently the case, other, nonvasoactive retraction materials should be used. Effective hemostatics that do not possess the cardiovascular actions of epinephrine are available and recommended. Commercial preparations of hemostatics that do not contain vasoactive substances include Hemodent, Gingi-Aid, Hemodettes, Hemogin-L, Rastringent, Styptin, and Ultradent (containing aluminum chloride); Gel-Cord (with aluminum sulfate); many generics containing potassium aluminum sulfate; and Astringedent, Hemodent-FS, Stasis, and ViscoStat (containing ferric sulfate).[64] The American Dental Association states that "epinephrine cord is contraindicated in patients with a history of cardiovascular diseases, diabetes and hyperthyroidism, and in those taking monoamine-oxidase inhibitors, rauwolfias, and ganglionic blocking agents."[64]

Clinical manifestations and pathophysiology

The clinical manifestations of epinephrine (vasoconstrictor) overdose are similar in many ways to an acute anxiety response. Most signs and symptoms of an acute

---

Box 23-7 Clinical manifestations of epinephrine overdose

SIGNS
Elevated blood pressure
Elevated heart rate

SYMPTOMS
Fear
Anxiety
Tenseness
Restlessness
Throbbing headache
Tremor
Perspiration
Weakness
Dizziness
Pallor
Respiratory difficulty
Palpitations

---

anxiety response are produced by the release of large amounts of endogenous catecholamines (epinephrine and norepinephrine) from the adrenal medulla. As with all drug overdose reactions, clinical signs and symptoms relate to the normal pharmacology of the administered drug (Box 23-7). The patient may report some symptoms, such as "My heart is pounding" or "I feel nervous." Signs of epinephrine overdose include a sharp rise in both the blood pressures—especially the systolic—and heart rate. The elevation in blood pressure creates potential hazards, especially when it follows inadvertent intravascular injection. Epinephrine overdose may produce cerebral hemorrhage and cardiac dysrhythmias.

Cases of subarachnoid hemorrhage have been recorded after subcutaneous administration of 0.5 mg epinephrine, and blood pressures of more than 400/300 mm Hg have been recorded for short periods.[65] Epinephrine, a powerful cardiac stimulant, may predispose a patient to ventricular dysrhythmias. The heart rate increases (140 to 160 beats per minute or faster is common), and the rhythm may be altered. Premature ventricular contractions occur first, followed by ventricular tachycardia. Ventricular fibrillation may follow and is universally fatal unless immediate recognition and management ensue (see Chapter 30). Patients with preexisting cardiovascular disease are at greater risk for such adverse actions. Increasing the workload of an already impaired cardiovascular system is likely to precipitate an acute exacerbation of the preexisting problem, such as anginal pain, myocardial infarction, heart failure, or cerebrovascular accident.[66-68]

Epinephrine overdose reactions are transitory, the acute phase rarely lasting for more than a few minutes;

however, the patient may feel tired and depressed ("washed out") for prolonged periods after the episode. The normally short duration of an epinephrine reaction is related to the body's rapid biotransformation of the drug. The liver produces the enzymes monoamine oxidase and catecholamine-O-methyltransferase, which are necessary for the biotransformation of epinephrine. Patients receiving monoamine oxidase inhibitors to manage depression cannot eliminate epinephrine from their bodies at the normal rate and are more susceptible to epinephrine overdose.[69] In addition, drug-drug interactions between epinephrine and noncardioselective β-blockers increase the risk of overdose.[69,70] Propranolol (Inderal) is the most commonly used member of this group. The reaction is a hypertensive crisis. Both systolic and the diastolic blood pressures rise dramatically, with a compensatory decrease in the heart rate (bradycardia). Though a dose-related response, such as this, usually requires administration of a considerably large dose of epinephrine, this has occurred in individuals who received small doses (for example, one or two cartridges of local anesthetic with epinephrine 1:100,000).[71,72]

Management

Most instances of epinephrine overdose are of such short duration that little or no formal management is necessary. On occasion, however, the reaction may last longer and thus require some action. Management parallels that of a cerebrovascular accident associated with markedly elevated blood pressure (see Chapter 19).

The following signs and symptoms provide diagnostic clues to the presence of an overdose of vasoconstrictor:

- Increased anxiety after injection
- Tremor of limbs
- Diaphoresis (sweating)
- Headache
- Florid appearance
- Possible increased or decreased heart rate (tachycardia [palpitation] and bradycardia, respectively)
- Elevated blood pressure

Step 1: termination of the procedure. As soon as clinical manifestations of overdose appear, the procedure should be halted and the source of epinephrine removed. Obviously, removal is impossible after injection of a local anesthetic; however, if present, gingival retraction cord should be removed immediately.

Step 2: P (position). The conscious patient is positioned comfortably (patient determines the position). However, the supine position is *not* recommended since it accentuates the cardiovascular effects of epinephrine, particularly increased cerebral blood flow. A semi-seated or upright position minimizes, to a slight degree, this elevation in cerebral blood pressure.

Step 3: A-B-C (airway, breathing, circulation) or BLS, as needed.

Airway, breathing, and circulation are assessed and implemented as needed. Assessment usually demonstrates a patient who is conscious with patent airway and adequate circulation.

Step 4: D (definitive care):

Step 4a: reassurance of the patient. Patients experiencing this reaction usually exhibit increased anxiety and restlessness accompanied by other signs and symptoms, such as palpitation and respiratory distress, which further increase their apprehension and exacerbate the clinical problem. The doctor should attempt to reassure these patients.

Step 4b: monitoring of vital signs. Blood pressure and heart rate should be monitored and recorded every 5 minutes during the episode. Striking elevations may be noted in both, but they should decline gradually toward baseline levels over time. This statement is especially true when epinephrine-impregnated gingival retraction cord has been applied and then removed from the gingival tissues.

Step 4c: summoning of medical assistance. When a patient exhibits a marked elevation in blood pressure and heart rate, as well as signs and symptoms associated with cerebrovascular problems (e.g., headache and flushing), medical assistance should be sought immediately.

Step 4d: administration of O_2. If available, O_2 may be administered. If the patient reports difficulty in breathing, a nasal cannula, nasal hood, or full-face mask should be used.

Step 4e: recovery. Vital signs gradually return to baseline levels. Blood pressure and heart rate should be monitored and recorded every 5 minutes during this time, and the patient should remain seated in the dental chair for as long as is necessary after the episode. Patients invariably feel fatigued and depressed ("washed out") for considerable lengths of time following epinephrine overdose.

Step 4f: administration of a vasodilator (optional). If the patient's blood pressure does not begin to return toward the baseline level, administration of a drug designed to lower blood pressure may become necessary. Nitroglycerin, available in the office emergency drug kit, is a potent vasodilator used primarily in the management of anginal pain. However, a side effect of the drug is postural hypotension; the administration of a dose (two sprays translingually) to a patient who is seated upright takes advantage of this fact. Blood pressure should be monitored continually at this time.

Step 5: discharge.

When emergency personnel arrive, they can more thoroughly evaluate the patient's cardiovascular status. When blood pressure is still considerably elevated, IV antihypertensive drugs, such as labetalol or atenolol, may be administered. A decision is then made as to the patient's disposition after consultation with the emergency medical team, dentist, and emergency department physicians. In most situations in which the intensity of cardiovascular symptoms and signs was not great, the patient will not require hospitalization. However, when signs and symptoms of cardiovascular stimulation persist, a period of hospitalization for evaluation may be recommended.

Box 23-8 outlines the steps in the protocol for the management of an epinephrine overdose.

- **Drugs used in management:** O_2 is used to manage this reaction.
- **Medical assistance required:** If the reaction is minor, no assistance is necessary. If, however, the reaction proves severe, emergency personnel should be summoned.

Box 23-8 Management of an epinephrine (vasopressor) overdose

Recognize problem
(Increased anxiety after injection, tremor of limbs, diaphoresis, headache, florid appearance, possible increased or decreased heart rate, elevated blood pressure)
↓
Discontinue dental treatment
↓
P—Position patient comfortably
↓
A → B → C—Assess airway, breathing, circulation, and administer basic life support as needed
↓
D—Provide definitive management as needed
Reassure the patient
Monitor vital signs
Activate emergency medical service as needed
Administer O_2
Permit patient to recover
Administer vasodilator as needed
Discharge of patient

A, airway; **B**, breathing; **C**, circulation; **D**, definitive care; **P**, Position.

■ CENTRAL NERVOUS SYSTEM DEPRESSANT OVERDOSE REACTIONS

Whenever CNS-depressant drugs are administered, the possibility exists that an exaggerated degree of CNS depression may develop. Clinically, this reaction may be noted in a range from slight oversedation to unconsciousness and respiratory arrest. Barbiturates are the most likely drug group to produce an overdose.[73] Barbiturates represented the first major breakthrough in drug management of anxiety, and because of this, many associated ADRs, such as allergy, addiction, and overdose, were tolerated. However, with the introduction of newer antianxiety drugs, such as benzodiazepines, that do not possess the same potential for abuse and overdose, barbiturate use has declined.[73]

Although the barbiturates possess the greatest potential for ADR, opioid agonist analgesics are responsible for a greater number of clinically significant episodes of overdose and respiratory depression in dentistry. This is simply because opioids are used today to a much greater extent than barbiturates. The administration of opioids is popular in the management of uncooperative or precooperative pediatric patients.[74] In addition, opioids are often used intravenously in conjunction with other sedative drugs to help achieve sedation and pain control in fearful patients. Goodson and Moore[75] reported 14 cases in pediatric dentistry in which the administration of opioids and other drugs led to seven deaths and three cases of brain damage. Several opioids were implicated in these reactions—alphaprodine (seven cases), meperidine (six cases), and pentazocine (one case).

Predisposing factors and prevention

The clinical efficacy of a drug depends in large part on its absorption into the cardiovascular system and its subsequent blood level in different target organs. In the case of CNS depressants, the brain is the target organ. Only the inhalation and IV routes of drug administration, with their rapid onsets of action, permit titration of the drug to a precise clinical effect.[76] Drug absorption via oral and IM administration is erratic, demonstrated by a wide range of variability in clinical effectiveness.

The normal distribution curve becomes important when drugs are administered via routes in which titration is not possible. Average drug doses are based on this curve. For example, an oral dose of 5 mg diazepam produces the desired effect (anxiolysis) in the majority of patients (about 70%). For some (about 15%), however, these doses are ineffective. Such individuals require larger doses to attain the same clinical level of sedation. Patients like this, termed *hyporesponders,* are not at risk for overdose when they receive "average" doses since the clinical result of this dose is a lack of adequate response. Potential danger lies with the remaining 15% of patients, for whom average doses of diazepam are too great. These individuals are sensitive (a term that differs in meaning with, and must not be mistaken for, *allergy*) to the drug, requiring smaller doses to obtain clinically effective sedation. They are known as *hyperresponders.*

Predicting a patient's response to a drug is impossible; only a history of an ADR can provide a clue. The medical history questionnaire should be examined carefully regarding all drug reactions. If the patient reports a history of CNS drug sensitivity, great care must be exercised whenever the administration of any CNS depressant, especially an opioid, is considered. The administration of lower than usual doses or the substitution of different drug categories, such as nonsteroidal antiinflammatory drugs (NSAIDs) or opioid agonist/antagonists, should be considered.

Although the nature of an overdose cannot be easily predicted in advance, one cause of overdose is preventable. It relates to the clinical goal that the doctor seeks through drug administration. Some doctors use CNS depressants to achieve deep levels of sedation in fearful patients. When CNS-depressant drugs are administered for this purpose via nontitratable routes (e.g., oral or IM), the potential for overdose increases.

The use of a CNS depressant to obtain deep sedation via a route of administration in which titration is not possible is an invitation to overdose and cannot be recommended. Only those techniques that permit titration—IV and inhalation—can be safely employed to achieve deeper levels of sedation, and then only when the doctor is thoroughly familiar with both the technique of administration and the drugs to be administered and is prepared to manage all possible complications associated with the procedure. One point worth stressing, however, is that absorption of drugs administered via inhalation and IV sedation into the systemic circulation occurs rapidly; thus, drug responses, both therapeutic and adverse, may occur suddenly. Titration therefore remains the greatest safety feature that these techniques possess (Table 23-11).

Clinical manifestations

Barbiturate and nonbarbiturate sedative-hypnotics

Though the use of barbiturates in dentistry has declined, they are still used, thus their inclusion in the following discussion. Benzodiazepines are the most used

TABLE 23-11 Routes of drug administration

Route of administration	Control		Recommended safe sedative levels
	Titration	Rapid reversal	
Oral, rectal	No	No	Light only
IM, IN	No	No	Adults: light, moderate
			Children: light, moderate, deep
IV	Yes	Yes (opioids, benzodiazepines)	Adults, children: light, moderate, deep*
Inhalation	Yes	Yes	Light, moderate

IM, intramuscular; IN, intranasal; IV, intravenous.

*Usually, little need exists for IV sedation in normal, healthy children. Most children who can tolerate venipuncture can also receive intraorally administered local anesthetics. IV sedation, however, remains important in the management of disabled children and adults.

orally administered drugs for anxiolysis and (conscious) sedation. Although these drugs are capable of producing the responses described here, it is highly unlikely that this will occur when benzodiazepines are used.

Barbiturates *depress* a number of physiologic properties, including neurons, respiration, and muscle (skeletal, smooth, and cardiac). The mechanism of action (sedation and hypnosis) is depression at the level of the hypothalamus and ascending reticular activating system, which decreases the transmission of impulses to the cerebral cortex. Further elevation of the barbiturate blood level produces depression at other CNS levels, including profound cortical depression, depression of motor function, and depression of the medulla.[77] The following diagram illustrates this decline:

Sedation (calming) → hypnosis (sleep) → general anesthesia (unconsciousness with progressive respiratory and cardiovascular depression) → respiratory arrest

Sedation and oversedation. At low (therapeutic) blood levels, the patient appears calm and cooperative (sedated). As the barbiturate blood level increases, the patient falls into a rousable sleep (hypnosis). The doctor then notices the patient's inability to keep the mouth open in spite of constant reminders. In addition, patients at this level of barbiturate-induced CNS depression tend to overrespond to stimulation, especially noxious stimulation. The unsedated adult patient, or a patient sedated with benzodiazepines, may grimace in response to pain, but the oversedated (with barbiturates) adult exhibits an exaggerated response, perhaps yelling or jumping. This reflects the loss of self-control over emotion produced by the generalized CNS-depressant action of the barbiturate.[77]

Hypnosis. As the barbiturate blood level continues to increase, hypnosis (sleep) ensues and the patient experiences a minor depression of respiratory function (decreased depth and increased rate of ventilation). This

barbiturate blood level produces virtually no adverse action on the cardiovascular system, only a slight decrease in blood pressure and heart rate similar to that seen in normal sleep. However, dental care cannot be continued at this level of CNS depression since the patient cannot cooperate in keeping the mouth open and may require assistance in the maintenance of a patent airway (e.g., head tilt). The patient can still respond to noxious stimulation but in a sluggish yet still exaggerated manner.

General anesthesia. Further increase in barbiturate blood level broadens the degree of CNS depression to the point at which the patient loses consciousness (i.e., does not respond to sensory stimulation, loses protective reflexes, and cannot maintain a patent airway). Spontaneous respiratory movements remain; however, with additional increase in barbiturate blood level medullary depression occurs, clinically evidenced as respiratory and cardiovascular depression. Respiratory depression is clinically evident as shallow breathing movements at slow or, more commonly, rapid rates. Expansive movements of the chest do not guarantee that air is entering or leaving the lungs, only that the patient is attempting to bring air into the lungs. Airway obstruction may occur as the muscular tongue relaxes and falls into the hypopharynx.

Cardiovascular depression is noted by a continued decrease in blood pressure, caused by medullary depression, direct depression of the myocardium and vascular smooth muscle, along with an increase in heart rate. The patient develops a shock-like appearance, with a weak and rapid pulse and cold, moist skin.

Respiratory arrest. If the barbiturate blood level continues to increase or the patient does not receive adequate treatment in the general anesthesia stage, respiratory arrest may occur. This condition can be diagnosed readily and managed through assessment of the airway and breathing. However, delays in management or inadequate management will cause the condition to progress to cardiac arrest.

Other nonbarbiturate sedative-hypnotic drugs, such as hydroxyzine, chloral hydrate, and promethazine, also possess the potential to produce overdose; however, overdose is not as likely to occur as with the bariturates.[78,79] The potential for overdose varies significantly from drug to drug, but all sedative-hypnotics harbor this potential to varying degrees.

Opioid agonists

Meperidine, morphine, and fentanyl (and its congeners alfentanil, sufentanil, and remifentanil) are the most frequently used parenteral opioids. Meperidine and fentanyl are the most popular in dentistry.

Meperidine, like most opioid agonists, exerts its primary pharmacologic actions on the CNS. Therapeutic doses of meperidine produce analgesia, sedation, euphoria, and a degree of respiratory depression. Of principle concern is the respiratory depressant effect of opioid agonists. These drugs directly depress the medullary respiratory center. Individuals demonstrate respiratory depression from opioid agonists even at doses that do not disturb their level of consciousness. The degree of respiratory depression is dose dependent—the greater the dose of the drug, the more significant the level of respiratory depression.[76] The opioid agonist/antagonists—nalbuphine and butorphanol—provide analgesia and sedation with minimal respiratory depression.[80,81]

Death from opioid overdose almost always is the result of respiratory arrest.[82] All phases of respiration are depressed—rate, minute volume, and tidal volume.[83] Respiratory rate may fall below 10 breaths per minute; rates of 5 to 6 breaths per minute are common. The cause of the decreased respiratory activity is a reduction in responsiveness of the medullary respiratory centers to increased $PaCO_2$ and a depression of the pontine and medullary centers responsible for respiratory rhythm.[82]

The cardiovascular effects of meperidine are not clinically significant when the drug is administered within the usual therapeutic dose range. After IV administration of meperidine, however, the heart rate normally increases, produced by its atropine-like, vagolytic properties. At overdose levels blood pressure remains stable until late in the course of the reaction, when it drops, primarily as a result of hypoxia. At this point the administration of O_2 will produce an increase in blood pressure despite continued medullary depression. Higher blood levels of opioid agonists may lead to the loss of consciousness (e.g., general anesthesia in a controlled situation; a complication when seeking sedation).

Overdose reactions to both sedative-hypnotics and opioid agonists are produced by a progressive depression of the CNS manifested by alterations in the level of consciousness and respiratory depression that ends in respiratory arrest. The loss of consciousness produced by barbiturates or opioid agonists is not always due to overdose; in other words, loss of consciousness is sometimes desirable. For example, these drugs are administered commonly as primary agents in general anesthesia. However, when sedation is the goal, the loss of consciousness and respiratory depression must be considered to be serious, though not always preventable, complications of drug administration.

The duration and degree of this clinical reaction vary according to the route of administration, the dose, and the patient's individual sensitivity to the drug. Oral or rectal administration normally results in less CNS depression; however, this depression tends to last longer. IM and submucosal administration result in more profound levels of CNS depression that last relatively long periods of time, whereas IV administration produces a rapid onset of a profound level of depression that lasts for a shorter period than the levels produced by other routes. The onset of respiratory depression after IV administration may be rapid, whereas after oral or rectal administration it is slower. Onset is intermediate for IM and subcutaneous drug administration.

Management
Sedative-hypnotic drugs

Management of an overdose of sedative-hypnotic drugs is predicated on correction of the clinical manifestations of CNS depression. Of primary importance is the recognition and management of respiratory depression through the administration of BLS. Unfortunately, no effective antagonist exists to reverse the CNS-depressant properties of the barbiturate sedative-hypnotics. Benzodiazepines, however, can be reversed through administration of flumazenil.

Diagnostic clues to an overdose of a sedative-hypnotic drug include the following:[84]

- Recent administration of sedative-hypnotic drug
- Decreased level of consciousness
- Sleepy → unconscious
- Respiratory depression (rapid rate, shallow depth)
- Loss of motor coordination (ataxia)
- Slurred speech

Step 1: termination of the dental procedure.
The rate at which clinical signs and symptoms of overdose develop will vary with route of administration. Onset occurs within minutes after IV administration;

within 10 to 30 minutes after IM administration; and within 45 minutes to 1 hour after oral administration.

Step 2: P (position).
The semiconscious or unconscious patient is placed in the supine position with their legs elevated slightly. The goal in this situation, regardless of the level of consciousness, is maintenance of adequate cerebral blood flow.

Step 3: A-B-C (airway, breathing, circulation) or BLS, as needed.
A patent airway must be ensured and the adequacy of breathing assessed. Head tilt or head tilt–chin lift may be needed to maintain airway patency. The rescuer must next assess the presence or adequacy of the patient's spontaneous ventilatory efforts by placing their ear 1 inch from the patient's mouth and nose and listening and feeling for exhaled air while looking at the patient's chest to determine whether spontaneous respiratory efforts are present. Maintenance of a patent airway is the most important step in management of this patient. Step 4b, the provision of adequate oxygenation, is contingent on successful maintenance of a patent airway.

Step 4: D (definitive care):
Step 4a: summoning of medical assistance, if needed.
When a patient loses consciousness following administration of a barbiturate for sedative purposes, seeking medical assistance should be considered. The requirement for medical assistance will vary according to the doctor's training in airway management and anesthesiology. Where the patient remains conscious but overly sedated, seeking medical assistance is more of a judgment call by the doctor. When in doubt it is always wiser to seek assistance sooner rather than later.

Step 4b: administration of O₂.
The patient may exhibit different types of breathing. They may be conscious but overly sedated, responding slowly to painful stimuli. In this situation patients most likely can maintain their own airway and breathe spontaneously and somewhat effectively. The rescuer need only monitor the patient, assist with airway maintenance (e.g., the head tilt–chin lift procedure) and administer O_2 through a demand valve or nasal cannula, if desired.

However, the patient may be more deeply sedated and poorly responsive to stimulation, with a partially or totally obstructed airway. In this situation assisted ventilation is essential in addition to airway maintenance. With airway patency ensured, the patient should receive O_2 via full-face mask. If spontaneous breathing is present but shallow, assisted positive-pressure ventilation is indicated. Such ventilation is accomplished through activation of the positive-pressure mask just as the patient begins each respiratory movement (as the chest begins to expand). The positive-pressure mask is activated by pressing the button on top of the mask until the patient's chest rises, at which point the button is released. When a self-inflating bag-valve-mask device is used, the bellows bag is squeezed at the start of each inhalation. An air-tight seal and head tilt must be maintained at all times when either device is used.

If respiratory arrest has occurred, controlled artificial ventilation is started immediately. The recommended rate for the adult is one breath every 5 to 6 seconds (10 to 12 per minute). For the child (1 year of age to the onset of puberty) and the infant, one breath every 3 to 5 seconds (12 to 20 per minute) is recommended.[85] Expansion of the patient's chest with every ventilation is the only sure sign of a successful ventilation. Overinflation is to be avoided because this leads to abdominal distention, resulting in inadequate ventilation and increased risk of regurgitation.

Step 4c: monitoring of vital signs.
The patient's vital signs must be monitored throughout the episode. A member of the office emergency team should monitor and record the blood pressure, heart rate and rhythm, and respiratory rate every 5 minutes. If the blood level of the sedative-hypnotic drug increases significantly, the blood pressure decreases as the heart rate increases.[86] If blood pressure and pulse disappear, cardiopulmonary resuscitation (P→A→B→C) must be instituted immediately.

In most cases of barbiturate or nonbarbiturate sedative-hypnotic drug overdose, the patient can be maintained in this manner until the cerebral blood level of the drug decreases and the patient recovers consciousness, or emergency assistance arrives. Recovery results from redistribution of the drug within compartments in the body, not from biotransformation. The patient appears more alert and responsive, breathing improves (becomes deeper), and blood pressure returns to near baseline levels. The length of time for recovery depends on the drug administered (short-acting versus long-acting) and its route of administration.

Step 4d: establishment of an IV line, if possible.
If an IV infusion has not previously been established, one should be set up at this time, if proper training and equipment are available. Although no effective antidotal drugs exist for barbiturate and some other sedative-hypnotic drug (e.g., chloral hydrate) overdoses, hypotension may be treated effectively through intravenously administered fluids or drugs. As blood pressure decreases, however, veins become progressively

more difficult to locate and cannulate. Securing venous access at the earliest possible time may prove invaluable later.

Only the doctor possessing the necessary training and equipment for venipuncture, and can ensure that the patient continues to receive adequate care from other personnel, should attempt venipuncture. *A patent airway is more important than a patent vein.*

Step 4e: definitive management. Definitive management of sedative-hypnotic overdose produced by a barbiturate is based on maintenance of a patent airway and adequacy of ventilation until the patient recovers. Signs and symptoms of hypotension are checked by monitoring vital signs and determining the adequacy of tissue perfusion.*

The IV administration of flumazenil, a specific benzodiazepine antagonist, reverses benzodiazepine overdose. Flumazenil is administered intravenously in a 0.2-mg dose over 15 seconds; recovery is evaluated at 45 seconds. If recovery is not adequate at 1 minute, an additional dose of 0.2 mg may be administered. This is repeated every 5 minutes until recovery occurs or a dose of 1.0 mg is administered.[87]

Step 5: recovery and discharge. If the overdose is profound, requiring assistance of emergency personnel, the patient may require stabilization and transportation to a hospital for observation and full recovery. If hospitalization is necessary, the doctor should accompany their patient to the hospital.

Box 23-9 outlines the steps in the management of sedative-hypnotic overdose.

- **Drugs used in management:** O_2, flumazenil (for benzodiazepine overdose).
- **Medical assistance required:** If the patient's level of consciousness is altered, the training and experience of the doctor dictates the need for assistance. If the patient is unconscious, assistance should likely be sought.

In most cases, however, sedative-hypnotic overdose is significantly less severe, with diminished responsiveness and minimal respiratory depression. Management consists of positioning, airway maintenance, and assisted ventilation until the individual recovers. Emergency medical assistance is usually not required. Before being discharged into the custody of a responsible adult, the patient must be able to stand and walk without assis-

---

*Adequacy of tissue perfusion may be determined by pressing on a nail-bed or skin and releasing the pressure. Adequate perfusion is present when color returns in not more than 3 seconds. If 4 or more seconds are required, tissue perfusion is inadequate and consideration must be given to the immediate infusion of intravenous fluids.

Box 23-9 Management of sedative-hypnotic overdose

Recognize problem
(Recent administration of CNS-depressant drug; decreased level of consciousness; respiratory depression; loss of motor coordination; slurred speech)
↓
Discontinue dental treatment
↓
P—Position patient in supine position with feet elevated
↓
A → B → C—Assess airway and breathing, palpate carotid pulse for up to 10 seconds
↓
D—Provide definitive management as needed
Activate emergency medical service if recovery not immediate
Administer O_2
Monitor vital signs
Establish IV line, if possible
Provide definitive management:
- Administer intravenous flumazenil for benzodiazepine overdose
- Continue **P-A-B-C**—for barbiturate overdose

Permit recovery and discharge patient

A, airway; **B,** breathing; **C,** circulation; CNS, central nervous system; **D,** definitive care; IV, intravenous; **P,** position.

tance. Under no circumstances should the patient be discharged alone or before adequate recovery has occurred.

Opioid analgesics

Oversedation and respiratory depression are the primary clinical manifestations of opioid overdose. Cardiovascular depression normally does not develop until late in the overdose reaction, especially in a supine patient. Management of the patient who has received an absolute or relative overdose of an opioid is the same as that described for the sedative-hypnotic drugs with one major addition-specific antagonists are available that reverse the clinical actions of opioid agonists. The clinical picture may vary from minor alterations in consciousness with minimal respiratory depression to unconsciousness and apnea.

Diagnostic clues to the presence of an opioid overdose include the following:[82]

- Altered level of consciousness
- Respiratory depression (slow rate; normal to deep depth)
- Miosis (contraction of pupils of the eyes)

Step 1: termination of the dental procedure.

Step 2: P (position). The patient should be placed in the supine position with the legs elevated slightly.

Step 3: A-B-C (airway, breathing, circulation) or BLS, as needed. A patent airway must be ensured and breathing monitored. Opioids produce decreased rates of respiration with little change in tidal volume; therefore, the depth of ventilation is increased.[83]

In most cases of opioid overdose the patient remains conscious, though not fully alert and responsive. Assistance in airway maintenance may be desirable (e.g., head tilt–chin lift). With more profound depression, unconsciousness and respiratory arrest may occur, necessitating assessment of the airway and breathing. Because the cardiovascular system is relatively unaffected by opioid overdose, blood pressure and heart rate remain close to baseline values if the patient receives adequate oxygenation (especially if the patient remains in the supine position).[88]

Step 4: D (definitive care):
Step 4a: summoning of medical assistance, if needed. Depending on the level of consciousness, the degree of respiratory depression, the training of the doctor in emergency care and anesthesiology, and the availability of equipment and drugs, seeking emergency medical assistance may be indicated at this time. When the patient is unconscious and in respiratory arrest, emergency medical assistance should be summoned immediately if the doctor is not well trained in anesthesiology. In the hands of a doctor well trained in emergency care and anesthesiology (e.g., a dentist anesthesiologist), management may continue to include the administration of antidotal drugs.

Step 4b: administration of O₂. O_2 and/or artificial ventilation should be administered, if necessary. The administration of O_2 is especially important in the early management of opioid overdose. Minimal cardiovascular depression is normally present and occurs as a result of hypoxia secondary to respiratory depression. The administration of O_2 to a patient with a patent airway prevents or reverses opioid-induced cardiovascular depression.[89]

Step 4c: monitoring and recording of vital signs. Vital signs should be monitored every 5 minutes and entered on a record sheet. If pulse and blood pressure are absent, cardiopulmonary resuscitation ($P \rightarrow A \rightarrow B \rightarrow C$) must be initiated immediately.

Step 4d: establishment of an IV line, if possible. Because the cardiovascular system is minimally affected by opioid overdose (with the patient in the supine position), establishing an IV infusion is possible in most patients. The availability of IV access expedites definitive therapy.

Step 4e: antidotal drug administration. Definitive management is available when an opioid is the likely cause of the overdose. Even when what normally is considered a small opioid dose is administered (in a hyperresponding patient), an opioid antagonist should be administered if excessive respiratory depression or apnea develops. However, no drug should be administered until airway patency and adequate ventilation are ensured and vital signs monitored ($P \rightarrow A \rightarrow B \rightarrow C$). At this time an opioid antagonist should be administered. The drug of choice, naloxone, should be administered intravenously, if possible, to take advantage of a more rapid onset of action.

If an IV route is unavailable, IM administration is acceptable. The onset of action is slower, but naloxone will be just as effective if an opioid is responsible for the respiratory depression. Regardless of the route of administration, the emergency team must continue to provide the necessary steps of BLS from the time of naloxone administration until its onset of action, a point that becomes evident through increased patient responsiveness and more adequate and rapid ventilatory efforts. After IV administration, naloxone's actions are observed within 1 to 2 minutes (if not faster), and within 10 minutes after IM administration if the blood pressure is near its baseline value.

Naloxone is available in a 1-mL ampule containing 0.4 mg (adult) and 0.02 mg (pediatric). The drug is loaded into a plastic disposable syringe, and when the IV route is available, 3 mL of diluent (any IV fluid) is added to the syringe, producing a final concentration of 0.1 mg/mL of naloxone (adult) or 0.005 mg/mL (pediatric). The drug is administered intravenously to the adult at a rate of 1 mL per minute until the ventilatory rate and alertness increase. In children the IV dose is 0.01 mg/kg.[90] If administered intramuscularly, a dose of 0.4 mg (adult) or 0.01 mg/kg (pediatric) is injected into a suitable muscle mass, such as the mid-deltoid (adult) or vastus lateralis (child or adult); if the patient is unconscious, the drug may also be administered sublingually.

One potential problem with naloxone is that its duration of clinical activity may be shorter than that of the opioid it is used to reverse. This fact is especially true in cases in which longer-acting opioid agonists, such as morphine, are administered; it is less likely to occur with meperidine and even less likely with fentanyl and its analogues alfentanil,[91] sufentanil,[92] and remifentanil.[93] When the opioid action is of greater duration than the naloxone administered via an IV route, the doctor and staff would notice an initial improvement in the patient's clinical picture as the naloxone begins to act followed by a recurrence of CNS depression approximately 10 or more minutes later (after IV administration of naloxone). The opioid producing the overdose continues to undergo redistribution and biotransformation during this time; thus, if such a rebound effect does occur, the effect is more likely to be much less intense than the initial response.

In cases in which longer-acting opioids, such as morphine, are administered via an IM or submucosal route, the initial IV dose of naloxone should be followed with an IM dose (0.4 mg [adult] or 0.01 mg/kg [pediatric]). In this way, as the clinical action of the IV naloxone dose wanes, the level of naloxone from the IM dose reaches a peak, minimizing the likelihood of a relapse of significant respiratory or CNS depression. The administration of naloxone in opioid overdose is important but not the most critical step in overall patient management.

Step 5: recovery. Continuously observe and monitor the patient after naloxone administration. The patient may be transported to a recovery area within the dental office but should remain under constant supervision for at least 1 hour. On the other hand, the planned dental treatment may continue if the doctor deems it safe. Once again, whether to continue dental care is a judgment that can be made by the doctor only after both the status of the patient and the level of expertise of the doctor and staff in recognizing and managing this problem are considered. If any doubt exists, treatment should not continue. Vital signs should be recorded every 5 minutes during the recovery period; O_2 and suction must be available; and trained personnel must be present.

Step 6: discharge. Patient discharge may require transport to a hospital facility for observation or follow-up care. Usually, hospitalization is unnecessary. After an adequate period of recovery (minimum of 1-hour observation) in the dental or medical office, the patient may be discharged into the custody of a responsible adult companion through use of the same recovery criteria established for parenteral sedation and general anesthesia.[76]

Box 23-10 outlines the steps to follow in management of opioid overdose.

- **Drugs used in management:** O_2 and naloxone are used to manage opioid overdose.
- **Medical assistance required:** In cases in which the patient's level of consciousness is altered or the patient is unconscious, the doctor's training and

Box 23-10 Management of opioid overdose

Recognize problem
(Altered level of consciousness; respiratory depression; miosis)
↓
Discontinue dental treatment
↓
P—Position patient in supine position with feet elevated
↓
A → B → C—Assess airway, breathing, and circulation
↓
D—Provide definitive management as needed
Activate emergency medical service as needed
Administer O_2
Monitor vital signs
Establish IV line, if possible

Provide definitive management:
- Administer IV or IM naloxone
- Continue **P-A-B-C as needed**

Permit recovery and discharge patient

A, airway; **B,** breathing; **C,** circulation; **D,** definitive care; IM, intramuscular; IV, intravenous; **P,** position.

expertise should determine whether emergency personnel are necessary.

■ SUMMARY

The previous discussions dealt with overdose reactions of varying degrees of severity that occur following administration of a single drug. Although single-drug overdose can and does occur, especially after IM or submucosal administration (e.g., because of the inability to titrate to effect), a majority of overdose reactions involve the administration of more than one drug. In many of these cases, for example, an antianxiety drug may be combined with an opioid to provide a level of sedation and some analgesia. To these, a local anesthetic is added for pain control. Drugs in all three categories are CNS depressants. Added to this combination, in many cases, is nitrous oxide and O_2, yet another CNS depressant.

Whenever more than one CNS-depressant drug is administered, the doses of both drugs must be reduced to prevent exaggerated, undesirable clinical responses. As Table 23-12 illustrates, most of the cases reported by Goodson and Moore[75] did not take this step, with disastrous consequences.

Another factor must be considered, one to which most health professionals do not, as a rule, give much thought in the use of sedative techniques. Local anesthetics

TABLE 23-12   Dose administered relative to recommended maximum dose

Case	Opioid analgesic (%)*	Antiemetic sedatives (%)*	Local anesthetics (%)*	N₂O-O₂	Result
1	216	36	172	–	Death
2	173	145	237	–	Death
3	336	0	342	–	Death
4	127	27	267	+	Death
5	309	372	230	+	Brain damage
6	436	?	?	–	Death
7	100	136	107	–	Death
8	167	300	219	+	Brain damage
9	66	0	60	–	Recovery
10	66	92	?	+	Recovery
11	183	0	?	–	Recovery
12	200	558	0	–	Recovery
13	250	136	127	–	Brain damage
14	50	0	370	+	Death

+, N_2O-O_2 was used; –, N_2O-O_2 was not used.

*Expressed as percentage of maximal recommended dose for that patient.

From Goodson JM, Moore PA: Life-threatening reactions after pedodontic sedation: an assessment of narcotic, local anesthetic, and antiemetic drug interaction, *J Am Dent Assoc* 107:239–245, 1983.

TABLE 23-13   Maximum recommended doses of local anesthetics

Drug	Dose mg/kg	Dose mg/lb	Absolute maximum dose
Articaine	7.0	3.2	500
Bupivacaine	2.0	0.9	90
Lidocaine	4.4	2.0	300
Mepivacaine	4.4	2.0	300
Prilocaine	6.0	2.7	400

themselves are CNS depressants and may produce additive actions when administered in conjunction with the drugs commonly used for sedation. The maximum dose of local anesthetic administered to any patient, but especially to a child or lighter-weight or older adult, should be based on body weight in kilograms or pounds. When no other CNS depressants are to be administered, this maximum dose may usually be administered without adverse effect if the patient is an ASA I risk and falls within the normal responding range on the bell-shaped curve. Table 23-13 lists the maximum recommended doses of the most commonly used local anesthetics. When administered in conjunction with other CNS depressants, the dose of the local anesthetic should be minimized.

Ensuring a cooperative patient who maintains protective reflexes (e.g., swallowing, coughing, and maintaining the airway) is the primary goal of sedation. Whenever possible, this goal should be achieved through use of the simplest technique available and the fewest drugs possible. Polypharmacy, the administration of multiple drugs, is necessary in many patients to achieve the desired level of sedation or analgesia; however, if reaching this desired effect is possible with one drug, the combination need not be used. The use of drug combinations simply increases the opportunity for ADRs as well as making it less obvious which drug may be responsible for the problem, thereby making management more difficult.

Single-drug regimens are preferable to combinations of drugs. Rational drug combinations are available for use in cases in which they are specifically indicated. Severe ADRs should not develop after IV drug administration if titration is strictly adhered to at all times. Titration is not possible with the IM and oral routes of administration, and the doctor therefore must modify individual drug doses prior to their administration. Serious ADRs are more likely to occur in techniques where titration is not possible.

Consideration must also be given to the use of multiple techniques of sedation, as opposed to multiple drugs via one technique of administration. During the course of treatment, a hard-to-manage patient may receive oral antianxiety drugs for pretreatment, followed by IM, submucosal, or IV sedation, as well as inhalation sedation and local anesthesia. Whenever oral sedation with CNS depressants has been used, the doses of all subsequent CNS depressants should be carefully evaluated before their administration. This step is critical when the IM or submucosal route is used because they do not permit titration. With inhalation and IV sedation, careful titration of CNS-depressant drugs to the patient who has previously received oral premedication usually produces the desired level of clinical sedation with a minimal risk of ADRs.

How, then, may overdose reactions best be prevented? Goodson and Moore[75] made the following recommendations on the use of sedative techniques in which opioids are being administered:

- *Be prepared for emergencies.* Continuous monitoring of the cardiovascular and respiratory systems is necessary. An emergency kit containing epinephrine, O_2, naloxone, and flumazenil should be readily available, as should equipment and trained personnel. In their article, Goodson and Moore[75] state that "because multiple sedative drug techniques can easily induce unconsciousness, respiratory arrest, and convulsions, practitioners should be prepared and trained to recognize and control these occurrences."
- *Individualize drug doses.* When drugs are used in combination, the dose of each drug must be selected carefully. The toxic effects of drug combinations appear to be additive. Drug selection must be based on the patient's general health history. The presence of systemic disease (ASA II, III, or IV) usually indicates the need for a dose reduction. Because most sedative drugs are available in concentrated forms and because children require such small doses, extreme care must be taken when these drugs are prepared for administration. Fixed-dose administration of drugs based on a range of ages (e.g., children 4 to 6 years all receiving 50 mg) is not recommended. Doses should be based on the patient's body weight or surface area whenever possible.[94]

If the selected drug dose fails to produce the desired clinical effect, it is prudent to consider a change in the sedation technique or in the drug (at a subsequent appointment), rather than increasing the drug dose to a higher and potentially more dangerous level at the same visit.

- *Recognize and expect adverse drug effects.* When combinations of CNS depressants are administered, the potential for excessive CNS and respiration depression is increased and should be expected.

The Dentists Insurance Company, in a retrospective study of deaths and morbidity in dental practices over a 3-year period, concluded that in most of those incidents related to drug administration, three common factors were present:[95]

1. Improper preoperative evaluation of the patient
2. Lack of knowledge of drug pharmacology by the doctor
3. Lack of adequate monitoring during the procedure

These three factors increased the risk of serious ADRs significantly, with a negative outcome as the usual result.

An overdose reaction to the administration of CNS-depressant drugs may not always be preventable; however, proper care on the part of the doctor can minimize their occurrence, with a successful outcome almost every time. With techniques such as IV and inhalation sedation, in which titration is possible, overdose should be rare. With oral, IM, and submucosal drug administration, the doctor has little control over the drug's ultimate effect because of the inability to titrate. The doctor must therefore exercise greater care in the preoperative evaluation of the patient, determination of the appropriate drug dose, and monitoring throughout the procedure.

When the oral, submucosal, or IM route of administration is used, the onset of adverse reactions may be delayed. The adverse reaction may not develop until after the rubber dam is in place and the dental procedure has begun. Monitoring throughout the procedure therefore becomes extremely important in patient safety. As of May 2006, my preferences in monitoring during parenteral sedation are as follows:[76]

1. CNS
   Direct verbal contact with patient
2. Respiratory system
   Pretracheal stethoscope
   Pulse oximetry
3. Cardiovascular system
   Continuous monitoring of vital signs
   Electrocardiogram

REFERENCES

1. Caranasos GJ: Drug reactions. In: Schwartz GR, editor: *Principles and practice of emergency medicine,* ed 4, Baltimore, Williams & Wilkins, 1999.
2. Berkun Y, Ben-Zvi A, Levy Y, et al.: Evaluation of adverse reactions to local anesthetics: experience with 236 patients, *Ann Allergy Asthma Immunol* 91:342–345, 2003.
3. Nation RL, Triggs EJ, Selig M: Lignocaine kinetics in cardiac patients and aged subjects, *Br J Clin Pharmacol* 4:439–448, 1977.

4. Demetrescu M, Julien RM: Local anesthesia and experimental epilepsy, *Epilepsia* 15:235–248, 1974.

5. Arthur GR: Pharmacokinetics of local anesthetics. In: Strichartz GR, editor: *Local anesthetics: handbook of experimental pharmacology,* vol 81, Berlin, Springer-Verlag, 1987.

6. Bax ND, Tucker GT, Woods HF: Lignocaine and indocyanine green kinetics in patients following myocardial infarction, *Br J Clin Pharmacol* 10:353–361, 1980.

7. Sawyer DR, Ludden TM, Crawford MH: Continuous infusion of lidocaine in patients with cardiac arrhythmias: unpredictability of plasma concentrations, *Arch Intern Med* 141:43–45, 1981.

8. Englesson S: The influence of acid-base changes on central nervous system toxicity of local anaesthetic agents. I. An experimental study in cats, *Acta Anaesthesiol Scand* 18:79–87, 1974.

9. DeJong RH, Wagman IH, Prince DA: Effect of carbon dioxide on the cortical seizure threshold to lidocaine, *Exp Neurol* 17:221–232, 1982.

10. Maiorana A, Roach RB Jr.: Heterozygous pseudocholinesterase deficiency: a case report and review of the literature, *J Oral Maxillofac Surg* 61:845–847, 2003.

11. Lanks KW, Sklar GS: Pseudocholinesterase levels and rates of chloroprocaine hydrolysis in patients receiving adequate doses of phospholine iodide, *Anesthesiology* 52:434–435, 1980.

12. Zsigmond EK, Eilderton TE: Survey of local anesthetic toxicity in the families of patients with atypical plasma cholinesterase, *J Oral Surg* 33:833–837, 1975.

13. Lindorf HH, Ganssen A, Mayer P: Thermographic representation of the vascular effects of local anesthetics, *Electromedica* 4:106–109, 1974.

14. Braid DP, Scott DB: The systemic absorption of local analgesic drugs, *Br J Anaesth* 37:394–404, 1965.

15. Jebson PR: Intramuscular lignocaine 2 and 10. *Br Med J* 3:566–567, 1971.

16. Kudenchuk PJ, Racht EM: Pharmacologic treatment of cardiac arrest, *Prehosp Emerg Care* 3:279–282, 1999.

17. Drug package insert, lidocaine hydrochloride, *Physician's GenRx,* St. Louis, Mosby, 1996.

18. Adriani J: Toxicity of local anesthetics. *Postgrad Med* 24:95–100, 1958.

19. Moore DC: *Complications of regional anesthesia,* Springfield, IL, Charles C. Thomas, 1955.

20. du Souich P, Erill S: Metabolism of procainamide in patients with chronic heart failure, chronic respiratory failure, and chronic renal failure. *Eur J Clin Pharmacol* 14: 21–27, 1978.

21. Downs JR: Atypical cholinesterase activity: its importance in dentistry, *J Oral Surg* 24:256–257, 1966.

22. Keenaghan JB, Boyes RN: The tissue distribution, metabolism and excretion of lidocaine in rats, guinea pigs, dogs and man, *J Pharmacol Exp Ther* 180:454–463, 1972.

23. Mather LE, Tucker GT: Pharmacokinetics and biotransformation of local anesthetics, *Anesthesiol Clin* 16:23–51, 1978.

24. Meffin P, Robertson AV, Thomas J, Winkler J: Neutral metabolites of mepivacaine in humans, *Xenobiotica* 3:191–196, 1973.

25. Thomas J, Morgan D, Vine J: Metabolism of etidocaine in man, *Xenobiotica* 6:39–48, 1976.

26. Friedman GA, Rowlingson JC. DiFazio CA. Donegan MF: Evaluation of the analgesic effect and urinary excretion of systemic bupivacaine in man, *Anesth Analg* 61: 23–27, 1982.

27. Monheim LM: *Local anesthesia and pain control in dental practice,* St. Louis, Mosby, 1957.

28. Malamed SF: *Handbook of local anesthesia,* ed 5, St. Louis, Mosby, 2004.

29. Bieter RN: Applied pharmacology of local anesthetics, *Am J Surg* 34:500–510, 1936.

30. Vandam LD: Some aspects of the history of local anesthesia. In: Strichartz GR, editor: *Local anesthetics: handbook of experimental pharmacology,* vol 81, Berlin, Springer-Verlag, 1987.

31. Jastak JT, Yagiela JA, Donaldson D: *Local anesthesia of the oral cavity,* Philadelphia, WB Saunders, 1995.

32. Larsen LS, Larsen A: Labetalol in the treatment of epinephrine overdose, *Ann Emerg Med* 19:680–682, 1990.

33. Houpt MI, Heins P, Lamster I, et al.: An evaluation of intraoral lidocaine patches in reducing needle-insertion pain, *Compendium* 18:309–318, 1997.

34. Marcovitz PA, Williamson BD, Armstrong WF: Toxic methemoglobinemia caused by topical anesthetic given before transesophageal echocardiography, *J Am Soc Echocardiogr* 4:615–618, 1991.

35. Xylocaine 10% oral spray, drug package insert, Westboro, MA, Astra Pharmaceutical Products,1996.

36. Bartlett SZ: Clinical observations on the effects of injections of local anesthetics preceded by aspiration, *Oral Surg* 33:520–526, 1972.

37. Aldrete JA, Romo-Salas F, Arora S, et al.: Reverse arterial blood flow as a pathway for central nervous system toxic responses following injection of local anesthetics. *Anesth Analg* 57:428–433, 1978.

38. Aldrete JA, Narang R. Sada T, et al.: Reverse carotid blood flow—a possible explanation for some reactions to local anesthetics, *J Am Dent Assoc* 94:1142–1145, 1977.

39. Jeske AH, Boshart BF: Deflection of conventional versus nondeflecting dental needles in vitro, *Anesth Prog* 32: 62–64, 1985.

40. Blanton PL, Jeske AH: Misconceptions involving dental local anesthesia. Part 1: Anatomy, *Tex Dent J* 119: 296–300, 302–304, 306–307, 2002.

41. Foldes FF, Molloy R, McNall PG, Koukal LR: Comparison of toxicity of intravenously given local anesthetic agents in man. *JAMA* 172: 1493–1498, 1960.

42. Kramer HS Jr, Mitton V: Complications of local anesthesia, *Dent Clin North Am* 17:443–460, 1973.

43. Trapp LD, Davies RO: Aspiration as a function of hypodermic needle internal diameter in the in-vivo human upper limb, *Anesth Prog* 27:49–51, 1980.

44. Covino BG, Vassallo HG: *Local anesthetics: mechanisms of action and clinical use,* New York, Grune & Stratton, 1976.

45. Scott DB, Cousins MJ: Clinical pharmacology of local anesthetic agents. In: Cousins MJ, Bridenbaugh PO, editors: *Neural blockade,* ed 3, Philadelphia, Lippincott-Raven, 1998.

46. Munson ES, Tucker WK, Ausinsch B, Malagodi MH: Etidocaine, bupivacaine, and lidocaine seizure thresholds in monkeys, *Anesthesiology* 42:471–478, 1975.

47. Covino BG: Toxic and systemic effects of local anesthetic agents. In: Strichartz GR, editor: *Local anesthetics: handbook of experimental pharmacology,* vol 81, Berlin, Springer-Verlag, 1987.

48. Liu PL, Feldman HS, Giasi R, et al.: Comparative CNS toxicity of lidocaine, etidocaine, bupivcaine, and tetracaine in awake dogs following rapid IV administration, *Anesth Analg* 62:375–379, 1983.

49. Cannell H, Walters H, Beckett AH, Saunders A: Circulating levels of lignocaine after peri-oral injections, *Br Dent J* 138:87–93, 1975.

50. Moller RA, Covino, BG: Cardiac electrophysiologic effects of lidocaine and bupivacaine. *Anesth Analg* 67:107–114, 1988.

51. Liu PL, Feldman HS, Giasi R, et al.: Comparative CNS toxicity of lidocaine, etidocaine, bupivacaine, and tetracaine in awake dogs following rapid intravenous administration, *Anesth Analg* 62:375–379, 1983.

52. Harrison DC, Alderman FL: Relation of blood levels to clinical effectiveness of lidocaine. In: Scott DB, Julian DC, editors: *Lidocaine in the treatment of ventricular arrhythmias,* Edinburgh, E & S Livingstone, 1971.

53. American Heart Association: *Textbook of Advanced Cardiac Life Support,* Dallas, American Heart Association, 1997.

54. Strichartz GR, Covino BG: Local anesthetics. In: Stoelting RK, Miller RD, editors: *Basics of anesthesia,* ed 4, New York, Churchill-Livingstone, 2000, pp. 80–88.

55. Liu P, Feldman HS, Covino BM, et al.: Acute cardiovascular toxicity of intravenous amide local anesthetics in anesthetized ventilated dogs. *Anesth Analg* 61:317–322, 1982.

56. Scott DB: Toxicity caused by local anaesthetic drugs, *Br J Anaesth* 53:553–554, 1981.

57. DeToledo JC: Lidocaine and seizures, *Ther Drug Monit* 22:320–322, 2000.

58. Capek R, Esplin B: Effects of lidocaine on hippocampal pyramidal cells: depression of repetitive firing, *Neuroreport* 5:681–684, 1994.

59. Pascual J, Ciudad J, Berciano J: Role of lidocaine (lignocaine) in managing status epilepticus, *J Neurol Neurosurg Psychiatry* 55:49–51, 1992.

60. Adatia AK: Intravascular injection of local anesthetics (letter), *Br Dent J* 138:328, 1975.

61. Ingvar M, Siesjo BK: Local blood flow and glucose consumption in the rat brain during sustained bicuculline-induced seizures, *Acta Neurol Scand* 68:129–144, 1983.

62. Jaimovich DG, Shabino CL, Noorani PA, et al.: Intravenous midazolam suppression of pentylene tetrazol-induced epileptogenic activity in a porcine model, *Crit Care Med* 18:313–316, 1990.

63. Jakob W: Local anaesthesia and vasoconstrictive additional components, *Newslett Int Fed Dent Anesthesiol Soc* 2:1–3, 1989.

64. American Dental Association: *ADA Guide to Dental Therapeutics,* ed 3, Chicago, American Dental Association, 2003.

65. Kademani D, Voiner JL, Quinn PD: Acute hypertensive crisis resulting in pulmonary edema and myocardial ischemia during orthognathic surgery, *J Oral Maxillofac Surg* 62:240–243, 2004.

66. Bader JD, Bonito AJ, Shugars DA: A systematic review of cardiovascular effects of epinephrine on hypertensive dental patients, *Oral Surg Oral Med Oral Pathol Oral Radiol Endod* 93:647–653, 2002.

67. Campbell RL: Cardiovascular effects of epinephrine overdose: case report, *Anesth Prog* 24:190–193, 1977.

68. Jacobsen G: Stung postman gets $2.6m for wrong help, *Sydney Morning Herald* February 5, 2005. www.smh.com.au

69. Wynn RL: Epinephrine interactions with beta-blockers, *Gen Dent* 42:116–117, 1994.

70. Merck S: Adverse effects of epinephrine when given to patients taking propranolol (Inderal), *J Emerg Nurs* 21:27–32, 1995.

71. Centeno RF, Yu YL: The propanolol-epinephrine interaction revisited: a serious and potentially catastrophic adverse drug interaction in facial plastic surgery, *Plast Reconstr Surg* 111:944–945, 2003.

72. Mann SJ, Krakoff LR: Hypertensive crisis caused by hypoglycemia and propranolol, *Arch Intern Med* 144:2427–2428, 1984.

73. Baltarowich LL: Sedative-hypnotics. In: Marx JA, Hockberger RS, Walls RM, editors: *Rosen's emergency medicine: concepts and clinical practice,* ed 5, St. Louis, Mosby, 2002, pp. 2207–2217.

74. Braham RL: *Textbook of pediatric dentistry,* Baltimore, Williams & Wilkins, 1985.

75. Goodson JM, Moore PA: Life-threatening reactions after pedodontic sedation: an assessment of opioid, local anesthetic, and antiemetic drug interaction, *J Am Dent Assoc* 107:239–245, 1983.

76. Malamed SF: *Sedation: a guide to patient management,* ed 4, St. Louis, Mosby, 2003.

77. Harvey SC: Hypnotics and sedatives: the barbiturates. In: Goodman IS, Gilman A, Hardman JG, et al., editors: *Pharmacological basis of therapeutics,* ed 9, New York, McGraw-Hill, 1996.

78. Zendell E: Chloral hydrate overdose: a case report, *Anesth Prog* 19:165–168, 1972.

79. Sams DR, Thornton JB, Wright JT: The assessment of two oral sedation drug regimens in pediatric dental patients, *J Dent Child* 59:306–312, 1992.

80. Gal TJ, DiFazio CA, Moscicki J: Analgesic and respiratory depressant activity of nalbuphine: a comparison with morphine, *Anesthesiology* 57:367–374, 1982.

81. Bowdle TA: Clinical pharmacology of antagonists of narcotic-induced respiratory depression. A brief review, *Acute Care* 12:70–76, 1988.

82. Jaffe JH, Martin WR: Opioid analgesics and antagonists. In: Goodman IS, Gilman A, Hardman JG, et al., editors:

Pharmacological basis of therapeutics, ed 9, New York, McGraw-Hill, 1996.

83. Allen T: Opioids. In: Marx JA, Hockberger RS, Walls RM, editors: *Rosen's emergency medicine: concepts and clinical practice,* ed 5, St. Louis, Mosby, 2002, pp. 2180–2286.

84. Pollakoff J, Pollakoff K: *EMT's guide to signs and symptoms,* Los Angeles, Jeff Gould, 1991.

85. International Liaison Committee on Resuscitation. 2005 International Consensus on Cardiopulmonary Resuscitation and Emergency Cardiovascular Care Science with Treatment Recommendations, *Circulation* 112: III-1–III-136, 2005.

86. Coupey SM: Barbiturates, *Pediatr Rev* 18:260–264, 1997.

87. Romazicon, drug package insert, Roche Laboratories, October 1994.

88. Lowenstein E: Morphine "anesthesia"—a perspective, *Anesthesiology* 35:563–565, 1971.

89. Duberstein JL, Kaufman DM: A clinical study of an epidemic of heroin-induced pulmonary edema, *Am J Med* 51:704–714, 1971.

90. Narcan, drug package insert, DuPont Pharmaceuticals, July 1996.

91. Janssens F, Torremans J, Janssen PA: Synthetic 1,4-disubstituted-1,4-dihydro-5H-tetrazol-5-one derivatives of fentanil: alfentanil (R 39209), a potent, extremely short-acting opioid analgesic, *J Med Chem* 29:2290–2297, 1986.

92. Clotz MA, Nahata MC: Clinical uses of fentanyl, sufentanil, and alfentanil, *Clin Pharmacy* 10:581–593, 1991.

93. Servin F: Remifentanil: when and how to use it, *Eur J Anaesthesiol* 15:41–44, 1997.

94. Modell W: *Modell's drugs in current use and new drugs.* New York, Springer, 1988.

95. deJulien LE Jr.: TDIC update: Causes of severe morbidity/mortality cases. *J Calif Dent Assoc* 11:45–48, 1983.

CHAPTER 24

Allergy

Allergy has previously been defined as a hypersensitive state acquired through exposure to a particular allergen, reexposure to which produces a heightened capacity to react.[1] Allergic reactions cover a broad range of clinical manifestations, from mild, delayed reactions developing as long as 48 hours after exposure to the antigen, to immediate and life-threatening reactions developing within seconds of exposure. A classification of allergic reactions is presented in Table 24-1.[2] Although all allergic phenomena are important, two forms of allergy are of particular consequence in the practice of dentistry. The type I, or anaphylactic (immediate), reaction may present the dental office staff with the most acutely life-threatening situation of any discussed in this textbook. The type IV, or delayed, allergic reaction, seen clinically as contact dermatitis, is particularly relevant because of the significant number of dental personnel who develop this form of allergy. Allergic reactions to latex among health workers are being reported with increasing frequency,[3,4] as are reports of allergy in patients to latex gloves worn by their doctors.[5]

TABLE 24-1   Classification of allergic diseases (after Gell and Coombs)

Type	Mechanism	Principal antibody or cell	Time of reactions	Clinical examples
I	Anaphylaxis (immediate, homocytochromic, antigenic-induced, antibody-mediated)	IgE	Seconds to minutes	Anaphylaxis (drugs, insect venom, antisera)
				Atopic bronchial asthma
				Allergic rhinitis
				Urticaria
				Angioedema
				Hay fever
II	Cytotoxic (antimembrane)	IgG IgM (activate complement)	–	Transfusion reactions
				Goodpasture's syndrome
				Autoimmune hemolysis
				Hemolytic anemia
				Certain drug reactions
III	Immune complex (serum sickness–like)	IgG (form complexes with complement)	6 to 8 hours	Membranous glomerulonephritis
				Serum sickness
				Lupus nephritis
				Occupational allergic alveolitis
				Acute viral hepatitis
IV	Cell-mediated (delayed) or tuberculin-type response	–	48 hours	Allergic contact dermatitis
				Infectious granulomas (tuberculosis, mycoses)
				Tissue graft rejection
				Chronic hepatitis

Modified from Krupp MA, Chatton MJ: *Current medical diagnosis and treatment,* Los Altos, CA, Lange Medical, 1984.

Latex-induced anaphylaxis can present in the operating room in patients, surgeons, nurses, or anesthesiologists. Latex has been reported to account for up to 17% of cases of intraoperative anaphylaxis.[4]

Immediate allergic reactions are of primary concern and receive major emphasis in the following discussion. The type I reaction may be subdivided into several forms of response, including generalized and localized anaphylaxis.[2] A list of type I allergic reactions follows:

Type I immediate hypersensitivity:
- Generalized (systemic) anaphylaxis
- Localized anaphylaxis
- Urticaria (in the skin)
- Bronchospasm (in the respiratory tract)
- Food allergy (in the gastrointestinal tract and other organs)

Terms relevant to allergy are listed in Box 24-1.

All allergic reactions are mediated through immunologic mechanisms that are similar, regardless of the specific antigen responsible for initiating the reaction. Therefore it is possible, and likely, that an allergic reaction to the venom of a stinging insect, such as a wasp, may be identical to the reaction to eating a strawberry, or after aspirin or penicillin administration to a previously sensitized individual. This must be differentiated from the overdose or toxic drug reaction that represents a direct extension of the normal pharmacologic properties of the drug involved.

Overdose reactions are much more frequently encountered than are allergic drug reactions (85% of adverse drug reactions [ADRs] result from the pharmacologic actions of a drug; 15% are immunologic reactions[6]), even though to the nonmedical individual *any* ADR is assumed to be allergy. It is hoped that after the discussions in this section, the reader will be able to fully evaluate an alleged history allergy to determine what really occurred and will be able to differentiate between these two important ADRs—allergy and overdose.

Chapter 25 presents a differential diagnosis of the several ADRs and other clinically similar reactions.

Allergy is a frightening word to those health professionals involved in primary patient care. In the dental profession, many drugs possessing a significant potential for provoking allergy are regularly administered or

> **Box 24-1 Terms relevant to allergy**
>
> **Allergen:** An antigen that can elicit allergic symptoms.
> **Anaphylactic:** From the Greek *ana* = against or backward; *phylax* = guard or protect, meaning "without protection"; to be distinguished from prophylaxis, as in "for protection."[7]
> **Anaphylactoid:** Anaphylactoid reactions, which mimic true IgE mediated anaphylaxis, are idiosyncratic reactions that occur generally when the patient is first exposed to a particular drug or agent. Although they are not immunologically mediated, their emergency management is the same as that of immunologically mediated reactions.
> **Angioedema:** (angioneurotic edema) Noninflammatory edema involving the skin, subcutaneous tissue, underlying muscle, and mucous membranes, especially those of the gastrointestinal and upper respiratory tracts; occurs in response to exposure to an allergen; the most critical area of involvement is the larynx (laryngeal edema).
> **Antibody:** Those substances found in the blood or tissues that respond to the administration of, or react with, an antigen; they differ in structure (e.g., IgE and IgG) and are capable of eliciting distinctly different responses (e.g., anaphylaxis or serum sickness).
> **Antigen:** Any substance foreign to the host that is capable of activating an immune (e.g., allergic) response by stimulating the development of a specific antibody.
> **Atopy:** A "strange disease"; a clinical hypersensitivity state subject to hereditary influences; examples include asthma, hay fever, and eczema.
> **Pruritus:** Itching.
> **Urticaria:** A vascular reaction of the skin marked by the transient appearance of smooth, slightly elevated patches that are redder or paler than the surrounding skin and are often accompanied by severe itching.

prescribed. Although prevention has been emphasized repeatedly throughout this book, in no other situation is this concept of greater significance than in allergy.

Though not the most common ADR, allergy is oftentimes associated with the most serious of these reactions. Emphasis will be placed on the more immediate allergic reaction and on those specific drugs and chemicals in common use in dental practice.

■ PREDISPOSING FACTORS

The number of persons with significant allergy is not small. In the United States, 15% have allergic conditions severe enough to require medical management. Thirty-three percent of all chronic disease in children is allergic in nature.[8,9] Individuals with allergy represent a potentially serious risk when they receive drugs during their dental care. Although never risk-free, drug administration is commonly accomplished without any significant frequency of adverse reactions (indeed, if ADRs occurred with great frequency, dentists would avoid using many drugs in their dental practice). However, in the individual genetically predisposed to allergy (e.g., the atopic patient), great care must be taken when considering the use of any drug. Patients with multiple allergies (e.g., hay fever, asthma, or allergy to numerous foods) are much more likely to have an allergic response to drugs used in dentistry than is a patient with no history of allergy.

Although a patient's history is the major factor in determining the risk of allergy, the specific drug to be employed is also of extreme importance. In allergy, as opposed to overdose, prior contact (a sensitizing dose) is almost always necessary for allergy to develop. Such is not the case in anaphylactoid reactions, however. In the "usual" allergic reaction, signs and symptoms appear only after a subsequent (challenge) dose is administered. Without the sensitizing and challenge doses, allergy will not occur.

Certain drug groups possess a higher rate of allergenicity than others. In one survey, barbiturates, penicillins, meprobamate, codeine, and thiazide diuretics were responsible for over 70% of the allergic reactions encountered.[10] Laryngeal edema, acute bronchospasm with respiratory failure, and circulatory collapse, occurring alone or in combination, are responsible for 400 to 800 anaphylactic deaths annually in the United States.[11] Leading causes of death from anaphylaxis are parenterally administered penicillin (100 to 500 deaths per year) and stings from insects in the Hymenoptera order (bees, wasps, hornets, and yellow jackets)—40 to 100 deaths per year.[12,13] Medications frequently involved in anaphylactoid deaths include radiopaque contrast media (up to 50 deaths per year)[14] and the iatrogenic administration of common medications, such as aspirin and other nonsteroidal antiinflammatory drugs (NSAIDs).[15,16] Other leading causes of death from anaphylaxis are peanuts[17] and latex.[18] Box 24-2 lists the more commonly used drugs in dental practice that possess a significant potential for allergy.

Antibiotics

Probably the most significant ADR associated with antibiotics is their ability to provoke allergic reactions. Some antibiotics, such as erythromycin, are associated with a very low incidence of allergy, whereas others, particularly the sulfonamides and penicillins, provoke allergic responses more frequently. In the majority of cases, an allergic reaction associated with antibiotic therapy is not life-threatening. The penicillins, the most

Box 24-2 Drugs used in dental practice that may potentially cause an allergic reaction
ANTIBIOTICS Penicillins Cephalosporins Tetracyclines Sulfonamides
ANALGESICS Acetylsalicylic acid (ASA; aspirin) Nonsteroidal antiinflammatory drugs (NSAIDs)
OPIOIDS Fentanyl Morphine Meperidine Codeine
ANTIANXIETY DRUGS Barbiturates

LOCAL ANESTHETICS
Esters
   Procaine
   Propoxycaine
   Benzocaine
   Tetracaine
Antioxidant
   Sodium (meta)bisulfite
Parabens
   Methylparaben

OTHER AGENTS Acrylic monomer (methyl methacrylate)

commonly used antibiotics in dentistry, are a major exception. The first anaphylactic-induced death caused by penicillin was reported in 1949.[19] Penicillin has remained the leading cause of fatal anaphylaxis since that time.[20,21]

The incidence of allergy to penicillin ranges anywhere from 0.7% to 10% of those receiving the drug.[12] Approximately 2.5 million persons in the United States are allergic to penicillin. Of patients receiving penicillin, 0.015% to 0.04% will develop anaphylaxis, with a fatality rate of 0.0015% to 0.002%.[12] This accounts for 100 to 500 deaths per year.

In a survey on the nature and extent of penicillin side reactions, 150 cases of anaphylaxis were studied. Of the patients observed, 14% had a history of other allergies, 70% had previously received penicillin, and over 33% had previously experienced an immediate allergic reaction to the drug. When the patient died, death usually occurred within 15 minutes.[22] Allergy to penicillin may be induced by any route of administration. The topical route is most likely to sensitize (5%

to 12% sensitized); the oral route least likely (0.1% sensitized). However, it is also possible to be sensitized to penicillin without knowledge of prior exposure because penicillin is a natural contaminant of the environment. Penicillin mold is airborne and may be found in bread, cheese, milk, and fruit. Parenterally administered penicillin is responsible for the vast majority of severe anaphylactic reactions, with only a small number of deaths reported from oral penicillin.[10] Cephalosporins, structurally similar to penicillin, have been reported to be cross-allergenic in 5% to 16% of patients.[23]

Analgesics

Allergy may develop to any of the pain-relieving drugs commonly used in dentistry. This is somewhat true regarding the opioid agonist analgesics, such as codeine, but the incidence of true allergy to the opioids is quite low, even though "allergic to codeine" is frequently listed on medical history questionnaires. A thorough dialogue history is needed to determine the precise nature of the ADR. In most instances, "allergy to codeine" turns out to be merely annoying (dose-related) side effects such as nausea, vomiting, drowsiness, dysphoria (restlessness), or constipation.

The incidence of allergy to aspirin is relatively high (estimated to be from 0.2% to 0.9%), with symptoms ranging from mild urticaria to anaphylaxis.[24,25] Previous ingestion of aspirin without ill effect is no guarantee against subsequent allergic reaction to the drug. Allergic reactions to aspirin also take the form of angioedema and bronchospasm. Bronchospasm is the chief allergic manifestation in most persons sensitive to aspirin, but especially in the middle-aged woman who also has nasal polyps, pansinusitis, and rhinitis.[26,27] Anaphylaxis may also occur.[28] Other NSAIDs also carry a risk of allergy.[15,16,29]

Antianxiety drugs

Of the many drugs used for the management of fear in dentistry, the barbiturates probably possess the greatest potential for sensitization of patients. Although not as common as allergy to penicillin or aspirin, barbiturate allergy usually manifests itself in the form of skin lesions such as hives and urticaria or, less frequently, in the form of blood dyscrasias such as agranulocytosis or thrombocytopenia.[30] Allergy to barbiturates occurs much more frequently in persons with a history of asthma, urticaria, and angioedema. A history of allergy to any of the barbiturates represents an absolute contraindication to the use of any other barbiturate. Other drug groups frequently used for anxiolysis and sedation, such as the benzodiazepines, have a much lower risk of allergenicity than the barbiturates.[31]

Local anesthetics

Local anesthetics are the most important as well as the most commonly used drugs in dentistry. Without their availability, dentistry would revert back to the days when all dental procedures were associated with pain. Though uncommon, adverse drug reactions are seen with the use of local anesthetics. The overwhelming majority of these ADRs are not allergic in nature, but are related to a direct effect of the drug.[32,33] Allergy to local anesthetics can occur; however, the incidence of such reactions has markedly decreased with the introduction of amide-type local anesthetics in the 1940s. Allergic manifestations of local anesthetics may range from an allergic dermatitis (commonly occurring among dental office personnel) to typical bronchospasm to fatal systemic anaphylaxis.

Allergy to local anesthetics occurs much more frequently in response to the ester local anesthetics such as procaine, propoxycaine, benzocaine, tetracaine, and compounds related to them, such as procaine penicillin G and procainamide (an antidysrhythmic drug).[32,34] Amide-type local anesthetics are essentially free of this problem, yet the frequency of reports of allergy to amide local anesthetics in the dental and medical literature and on the medical history questionnaire seems to be increasing.[35–39] This seeming contradiction may be cleared up with careful evaluation of these alleged allergies. Several investigators, most notably Aldrete and Johnson,[40] have investigated these reports and extensively evaluated each case, seeking to determine the nature of the reaction. In most cases the reaction was

the result of either psychogenic factors or drug overdose (see Chapter 23); in other cases, reactions were of an allergic nature. When an ester local anesthetic is involved, a true allergic reaction is frequently elicited; however, with use of an amide local anesthetic, a purported allergic reaction is frequently shown to be another type of response (e.g., overdose, idiosyncrasy, or psychogenic). Malamed examined 229 patients referred for evaluation of "local anesthetic allergy" (Malamed SF: Evaluation of 229 patients with presumed "allergy to local anesthesia," unpublished data, 2006). Careful dialogue history and intracutaneous testing found no patient to be allergic to an amide local anesthetic and four patients with allergy to the paraben preservative. Esters were not evaluated in these patients.

Although true allergy to amide local anesthetics is rare, patients are more likely to demonstrate true allergy to components of the dental cartridge. The dental cartridge contains a number of items besides the local anesthetic (Table 24-2). Of special interest with respect to allergy are two items: methylparaben and sodium metabisulfite. The parabens—methyl, ethyl, and propyl—are bacteriostatic agents and are added to many drugs, foods, and cosmetics that are meant for multiple use. Parabens are structurally related to the ester local anesthetics, thus their increased allergenicity. It is difficult if not impossible to avoid contact with parabens. Because of their increasing use, the frequency of sensitization to the parabens has greatly increased. Parabens are used increasingly in nondrug items, such as skin creams, hair lotions, suntan preparations, face powder, soaps, lipsticks, toothpastes, syrups, soft drinks, and candies. In response to the increasing incidence of allergic reactions to these products, certain products have been marked as "hypoallergenic" and do not contain any parabens. Although anaphylaxis has been reported, paraben allergy

TABLE 24-2 Contents of local anesthetic cartridge

Ingredient	Function	"Plain" cartridge	Vasoconstrictor-containing cartridge
Local anesthetic	Conduction blockade	✔	✔
Vasoconstrictor	Decrease absorption of local anesthetic into blood, thus increasing duration of anesthesia and decreasing local anesthetic toxicity	✘	✔
Sodium (meta)bisulfite	Antioxidant for vasoconstrictor	✘	✔
Sodium chloride	Isotonicity of solution	✔	✔
Sterile water	Diluent	✔	✔
Methylparaben*	Bacteriostatic agent (to increase shelf life by maintaining sterility)	✘	✘

*Methylparaben has been excluded from all local anesthetic cartridges manufactured in the United States since January 1984. It is still found in multidose vials of medications and in some local anesthetic cartridges manufactured outside of the United States.

is rarely systemic, most commonly appearing as a localized skin eruption or as localized edema.

Patients with a history of allergy to an amide local anesthetic were tested by using the anesthetic without methylparaben and with the preservative alone.[40] In every instance the patient reacted to the preservative but did not react to the same anesthetic without methylparaben. Paraben allergy is almost exclusively limited to a dermatologic-type response. In 1984, the Food and Drug Administration ordered the removal of paraben preservatives from all single-use local anesthetic cartridges manufactured in the United States. Methylparaben is still included in dental cartridges of local anesthetics in some countries and is found in all multiple-dose containers of injectable drugs.

Allergy to sodium bisulfite or metabisulfite is being reported with increasing frequency.[41-43] Bisulfites are antioxidants and are commonly used in restaurants where they are sprayed on fruits and vegetables as an antioxidant to prevent discoloration. For example, sliced apples sprayed with bisulfite do not turn brown (i.e., become oxidized). Bisulfites are also used to prevent bacterial contamination of wines, beers, and distilled beverages.[44] Persons with bisulfite allergy frequently respond to contact with bisulfite with severe respiratory allergy, commonly bronchospasm. Within the asthmatic population, reports demonstrate that up to 10% are allergic to bisulfites.[41,45] It is not known whether bisulfites are triggers of anaphylaxis.[41,45,46] A history of bisulfite allergy should alert the doctor to the possibility of this same type of response if sodium bisulfite or metabisulfite is included in the local anesthetic cartridge.

Box 24-3 Sulfite-containing agents

Restaurant salads (e.g., lettuce, tomatoes, carrots, peppers, dressings)
Fresh fruits
Dried fruits
Wine, beer, cordials
Alcohol
All sparkling grape juices, including nonalcoholic
Potatoes (e.g., french fries, chips)
Sausage meats
Cider and vinegar
Pickles
Dehydrated vegetables
Cheese and cheese mixtures
Bottled lemon and lime juice
Gelatin
Corn bread or muffin mix
Shrimp and other seafood
Fresh fish
Avocados (e.g., guacamole)
Soups (canned or dried)
Sauces and gravies used on meats and fish

Bisulfites are present in all local anesthetic cartridges that contain a vasoconstrictor. Local anesthetic solutions not containing vasoconstrictor additives do not contain bisulfites. Common sources of exposure to bisulfites are presented in Box 24-3.

Topical anesthetics are also potential allergens. Many topical anesthetics are esters, with benzocaine and tetracaine most commonly employed. Many topical anesthetics, even amides (e.g., lidocaine), contain preservatives such as the parabens (methyl, ethyl, propyl), so that allergy must always be a consideration when these drugs are used.

Clinical manifestations of allergy related to topical anesthetic application may span the entire spectrum of allergic responses; however, the most common response is allergic contact stomatitis, which may include mild erythema, edema, and ulcerations. If widespread and severe, the edema may lead to difficulty in swallowing and breathing.

Other agents

"Denture sore mouth" is a name commonly given to inflammatory changes of mucous membranes developing beneath dentures. Most frequently the palatal oral mucosa and maxillary ridges are involved, with the tissue appearing bright red and edematous and the patient reporting soreness, rawness, dryness, and burning.

Acrylic resins can produce allergy. This is much more likely to occur when self-cured acrylics are used instead of heat-cured acrylics. In addition, dental personnel and laboratory technicians may develop contact dermatitis to these materials. These reactions occur most frequently on the fingers and hands and are almost always caused by the acrylic monomer (the liquid), methyl methacrylate.

Heat-cured acrylics are less frequently associated with allergy because the monomer is used more thoroughly in the polymerization process. In cold-cured or self-cured acrylics, it is likely that small amounts of monomer remain unpolymerized, and it is this that produces the allergic response in the previously sensitized individual. Cold-curing or self-curing acrylics are employed in denture repair and relining procedures, as well as in the fabrication of temporary crowns, bridges, and splints.

■ PREVENTION

 MEDICAL HISTORY QUESTIONNAIRE

The medical history questionnaire contains several questions relating to allergy.

Section II, Have You Experienced:

Question 13. Sinus problems?

Section III, Do You Have or Have You Had:

Question 35. Asthma, tuberculosis, emphysema, other lung diseases?

Comment: Sinus problems, though not always associated with allergy, frequently are.

The cause of the sinus problem should be determined.

Question 38. Allergies to: food, drugs, medications, latex?

Comment: A thorough dialogue history must be obtained to determine the precise nature of the reported "allergy."

Adverse drug reactions are not uncommon; those most frequently reported are usually labeled "allergy." Any positive response to these questions must be thoroughly evaluated through the dialogue history. In all instances in which the possibility of allergy does exist, it is prudent for the doctor to assume that the allergy is "real" and to continue to do so until the exact nature of the reaction can be determined. The dialogue history is a vital part of this process, as is medical consultation in the event that any doubt remains concerning the allergy following the dentist's evaluation of the patient. The drug or drugs in question, as well as any closely related drugs, should *not* be used until the alleged allergy has been thoroughly evaluated and disproved (to the satisfaction of both the doctor and patient).

Fortunately, substitute drugs exist and may be employed in place of most of those that commonly cause allergy. These substitute drugs possess most of the same desirable clinical actions as the primary drugs, but are not as allergenic. The only group in which substitute drugs are not as effective as the primary agents is local anesthetics. Because these are also the most important drugs employed in dentistry, much of the following discussion is related to the question of local anesthetic "allergy."

Dialogue history

Following a positive response to the question about a previous allergies (question 38), the doctor should seek as much information as possible directly from the patient. The following questions should be asked, modified where appropriate, in the evaluation of an alleged drug allergy.

What drug was used?

Comment: A patient who is truly allergic to a drug should know the generic name of that drug. Many persons with documented allergic histories wear a Medic Alert bracelet (Figure 24-1) that lists those items to which they are allergic as well as other medical conditions that might exist.

However, the most common responses to this question are, *"I'm allergic to local anesthetics," "I'm allergic to Novocain,"* or *"I'm allergic to all '-caine' drugs."* Novocain (procaine), an ester, is no longer used today as a local anesthetic in dentistry (though in some rare situations in medicine, it may still be used), the amides having virtually replaced the esters. Yet patients routinely refer to the local anesthetics they receive as *"shots of Novocain."* There are two reasons for this: first, the name Novocain is virtually synonymous with dental injections. Second, despite the fact that the ester local anesthetics are no longer available in dental cartridges, many doctors still refer to all local anesthetics as Novocain, even though they use amide local anesthetics exclusively. Therefore, the usual response to the question remains, *"I'm allergic to Novocain."* This response, if received from a patient who has truly been managed properly (see text that follows) in the past after an adverse reaction to a local anesthetic, indicates that the patient was sensitive to an ester local anesthetic but not to the amide local anesthetic. However, the answers received are usually too general and too vague to allow conclusions to be drawn without further questioning.

What amount of drug was administered?

Comment: This question seeks to determine whether or not there was a definite dose-response relationship, as might, or might not, be seen in an overdose reaction. The problem is that the patient rarely knows these clinical details and can provide little or no assistance.

Did the solution contain vasoconstrictors or preservatives?

Comment: The reaction may have been an overdose or over-reaction to the vasoconstrictor in the solution. If an allergic reaction did occur, perhaps it was related to the antioxidant, sodium (meta)bisulfite, and not to the local anesthetic. Unfortunately, most patients are unable to furnish this information.

Were you taking any other medication at the time?

Comment: This question seeks to determine the possibility that drug interaction or another drug was responsible for the reported adverse reaction.

Describe the time sequence of events?

Comment: When, in relation to the administration of the drug, did the reaction occur? Most ADRs associated with local anesthetic administration occur during or immediately following their injection. Syncope, hyperventilation, overdose, and anaphylaxis are most likely to develop at the time of injection or within seconds or minutes after, although any of these reactions might also occur later during dental therapy. Try to determine how long the episode lasted. How long was it until the patient was discharged from the office? Was dental treatment continued after the episode?

FIGURE 24-1 Medical alert bracelet. (From Chapleau W: *Emergency first responder: making the difference,* St. Louis, Mosby, 2004.)

Dental treatment that continued following the episode indicates that the reaction was probably not an allergic response.

What position were you in when the reaction took place?

Comment: Injection of local anesthetics with the patient in an upright position is most likely to produce a psychogenic response (e.g., vasodepressor syncope). This does not exclude the possibility that other reactions might have occurred; however, if the patient was in a supine position during injection, vasodepressor syncope seems less likely to be the cause of the reaction, even though loss of consciousness may occur on rare occasion in these circumstances.

How did the reaction manifest itself?

"What happened?"

Comment: This may be the most important question because it asks the patient to describe what actually happened. The "allergy" in many instances is explained by the answer to this question. Signs and symptoms described by the patient should be recorded and evaluated to make a tentative diagnosis of the ADR. See the chapters on overdose reaction (Chapter 23), vasodepressor syncope (Chapter 6), and the differential diagnosis of drug reactions (Chapter 25), as well as this chapter, for complete listings of clinical signs and symptoms of each of these responses.

Did the patient lose consciousness?

Did seizures occur?

Was there a skin reaction or respiratory distress?

Comment: Allergic reactions normally involve one or more of the following systems: skin (e.g., itching, edema, rash), the gastrointestinal system (e.g., diarrhea, nausea and vomiting, cramping), exocrine glands (e.g., running nose, watery eyes), respiratory system (e.g., bronchospasm, laryngeal edema), and cardiovascular (e.g., hypotension, tachycardia) or genitourinary system. Most often, patients describe their allergy as one in which they suffered palpitations, severe headache, sweating, and mild shaking (tremor). These reactions are usually of psychogenic origin or are related to the administration of overly large doses of vasoconstrictors, not allergy. Hyperventilation, an anxiety-induced response in which the patient loses control of his or her breathing—breathing rapidly and deeply—leads to signs and symptoms of dizziness, light-headedness, and peripheral (e.g., fingers, toes, lips) paresthesia.

What treatment was given?

Comment: Where the patient is able to describe the management of the reaction, the doctor can usually determine its cause.

Were drugs administered? If so, what drugs?

Comment: Epinephrine, histamine-blockers, anticonvulsants, aromatic ammonia? Knowledge of definitive management of each of these situations can lead to an accurate diagnosis.

Drugs employed in the management of allergy include three drug types or categories: *epinephrine* (Adrenalin); *histamine-blockers*, such as diphenhydramine (Benadryl); and *corticosteroids*, including hydrocortisone sodium succinate (Solu-Cortef). The use of one or more of these drugs greatly increases the likelihood that an allergic reaction did, in fact, occur.

Anticonvulsants, such as diazepam (Valium), midazolam (Versed, Hypnovel, Dormicum), or the injectable barbiturates, including pentobarbital (Nembutal), are administered to manage seizures, either generalized tonic-clonic or those induced by local anesthetics. *Aromatic ammonia* is frequently used in the treatment of syncopal episodes. *Oxygen* may be administered in any or all of these reactions.

Were the services of a physician or paramedical personnel required? Were you hospitalized?

Comment: A positive response indicates the likelihood that a more serious reaction occurred. Most psychogenic responses can be ruled out in this instance.

What is the name and address of the doctor (dentist, physician, or hospital) who was treating you at the time the adverse reaction took place?

Comment: Whenever possible, it is usually valuable to speak to the doctor who managed the previous acute episode. He or she is, in most instances, able to locate the patient's records and to describe in detail what really happened. Direct discussion with the dentist or physician normally provides a wealth of information with which the knowledgeable practitioner can determine the precise nature of the previous reaction.

It is unlikely that a health care professional will ever forget a case of anaphylaxis occurring during patient management. It is much more likely that details of a syncopal episode will be forgotten with time.

Medical consultation

If doubt remains concerning the nature of the problem after completion of the dialogue history, allergy must still be considered a possibility and the drug(s) in question not used. At this point, referral of the patient should be considered, looking for a doctor who will be able to more fully evaluate the nature of their prior reaction. Physicians, primarily allergists and anesthesiologists, and some dentists (dentist anesthesiologists) are likely to be willing and able to completely evaluate this patient. This doctor will also be able to perform certain tests that will prove more reliable in assessing the patient's alleged local anesthetic allergy.

Among the more commonly used tests are skin testing; passive transfer methods; and blood tests, such as the basophil degranulation test.[47]

Skin testing is still the primary means of testing for local anesthetic allergy. Although several types of skin test are used, the *intracutaneous test* is considered to be among the most reliable.[40] Intracutaneous testing involves the injection of 0.1 mL of the test solution and is thought to be 100 times more sensitive than a cutaneous test. It is, however, more unpleasant because it requires multiple needle punctures. Other problems associated with its use involve false-positive results produced by the localized release of histamine in response to skin puncture by the needle. However, intracutaneous testing is clinically useful because a negative response probably means that the patient can safely receive the local anesthetic tested. No instance of an immediate allergic reaction has been reported in a patient with a previously negative intracutaneous response for a given agent.[40]

In all instances in which skin testing is employed, the anesthetic solutions should not contain any preservative (methyl paraben, sodium [meta]bisulfite). Tests for allergy to methylparaben may be done separately, if considered necessary. If a positive response to paraben occurs, local anesthetics to which the patient is not allergic should be used during the patient's dental treatment, provided they do not contain any preservative. Dental cartridges manufactured in the United States since January 1984 do not contain methylparaben.

The protocol for intracutaneous testing for local anesthetic allergy currently in use at the University of Southern California School of Dentistry is summarized as follows: After an extensive dialogue history, review of the patient's medical history, informed consent, and establishment of an intravenous line, 0.1 mL of each of the following is deposited intracutaneously: 0.9% normal saline solution, 1% or 2% lidocaine, 3% mepivacaine, and 4% prilocaine, all without methylparaben or sodium [meta]bisulfite, followed, if considered necessary, by 0.1 mL of bacteriostatic water and/or one or more local anesthetics containing methylparaben. The patient's vital signs (blood pressure, heart rate and rhythm, PaO_2) are monitored throughout the procedure. After successful completion of this phase of the testing (60 minutes), 1 mL of one of the preceding local anesthetic solutions that tested negative is administered intraorally by means of supraperiosteal (infiltration) injection, atraumatically, but without using a topical anesthetic, above a maxillary anterior tooth. This is the *challenge test,* and it frequently provokes the so-called allergic reaction, that is, signs and symptoms of a psychogenic response (Malamed SF: Evaluation of 229 patients with presumed "allergy to local anesthesia," unpublished data, 2006).

After having completed 229 local anesthetic allergy test procedures, I have encountered four allergic responses to the paraben preservative (all in the early 1980s) but none to the local anesthetic itself. Numerous psychogenic responses have developed during either the intracutaneous or the intraoral testing procedures (Malamed SF: Evaluation of 229 patients with presumed "allergy to local anesthesia," unpublished data, 2006).

Skin testing is not without risk. Severe, immediate allergic reactions may be precipitated by the administration of as little as 0.1 mL of a drug to a sensitized patient. Emergency drugs, equipment, and personnel for resuscitation must always be readily available when contemplating allergy testing.

Allergy testing in the dental office

It is occasionally suggested that in an emergency situation (such as a toothache or infection), the doctor should carry out the aforementioned testing procedure in the dental office. It is my firm conviction that dental office allergy testing should not be considered for the following reasons. First, skin testing, although potentially valuable, is not foolproof. Localized histamine release (false-positive reactions) may result from the trauma of needle insertion. A negative reaction, although commonly taken to indicate that a drug may be injected safely, may also prove unreliable. In some cases the drug itself is not the agent to which the patient is sensitive. Instead, a metabolite resulting from biotransformation of the drug may be responsible. The skin test would be negative or a positive response would be delayed for many hours under these circumstances. A second and even more compelling factor for not using skin testing in the dental office is the possibility (though remote) that even the minute quantity of local anesthetic injected (0.1 mL) could precipitate an immediate and acute systemic anaphylaxis in a truly allergic patient. Drugs, equipment, and personnel needed for the management of anaphylaxis and cardiopulmonary arrest must always be available when allergy testing is undertaken.

Dental therapy modifications
Allergy to drugs other than local anesthetics

When a patient is proved to be truly allergic to a drug, precautions must be taken to prevent the individual from receiving that substance. The outside of the dental chart should be marked with a medical alert sign that is easily visible, alerting dental office staff to look at the medical history carefully. Inside the chart it should be noted that the patient "is allergic to."* For all of the more highly allergenic drugs prescribed in dentistry, substitute drugs are available that are usually equipotent in therapeutic effect but that pose less of a risk of allergy.

Penicillin allergy may be circumvented through the use of erythromycin; it is a drug possessing virtually

---

*Health Insurance Portability and Accountability Act (HIPAA) regulations preclude writing a patient's medical information on the outside of the chart where it might be seen by other persons. A general notice on the outside, "Medical Alert," is adequate to alert staff to check the patient's medical history prior to the start of treatment.

the same clinical spectrum of effectiveness as penicillin G, but with a lower incidence of allergy. Sensitization reactions to erythromycin, including skin lesions, fever, and anaphylaxis, have been reported but are much less frequent than penicillin allergy.[48] Erythromycin remains the classic substitute drug for penicillin G.

Acetaminophen can be administered in cases of allergy to aspirin or NSAIDs. Although as effective an analgesic as aspirin, acetaminophen is not as effective an antipyretic. However, it is not cross-allergenic with aspirin and may be administered to the salicylate-sensitive patient. NSAIDs may also be substituted for aspirin if cross-sensitivity does not exist.

Allergy to *opioid analgesics* is rare, with the unpleasant side effects of nausea and vomiting the most commonly encountered adverse reactions. However, in the presence of true opioid allergy, no opioid should be used because cross-allergenicity occurs. Nonopioid analgesics, such as NSAIDs, may be of value in this situation.

Though rarely used today in dentistry, *barbiturate allergy* represents an absolute contraindication to administration of any barbiturate since cross-allergenicity exists. However, the chemical structures of the nonbarbiturate sedative-hypnotics are sufficiently different so that cross-allergenicity does not occur. These drugs may safely be employed in patients with barbiturate allergy. Included in this group of drugs are the benzodiazepines flurazepam, diazepam, midazolam, oxazepam, and triazolam, as well as chloral hydrate, and hydroxyzine.

Allergy to methyl methacrylate monomer is most readily avoided by not employing acrylic resins. If, however, acrylic resins must be used, heat-cured acrylic is much less allergenic than cold-cured or self-cured acrylic.

Another potential cause of allergy involves the (bi)sulfites. Sulfites are included, as antioxidants, in every dental local anesthetic cartridge with a vasopressor. Although sulfite allergy can occur in any person, the patient with allergic-type asthma is most likely to demonstrate this problem. When sulfite allergy exists, local anesthetics without a vasopressor can be substituted (e.g., prilocaine "plain" and mepivacaine "plain").

Latex sensitivity has become a significant problem among health care professionals and their patients. The use of vinyl as a latex substitute has minimized the occurrence of allergic reactions. When latex allergy exists, the use of local anesthetic cartridges should be avoided. The thin diaphragm through which the needle enters the cartridge is trilayered, the middle portion of which is latex. Although highly unlikely, it is possible for this latex to be injected into the sensitive patient, inducing a serious allergic reaction.[49–52] In January 2006, a "latex-free" dental local anesthetic cartridge was introduced into the U.S. market.[53]

Table 24-3 summarizes the substitute drugs discussed here. In all cases it is possible for a patient to be allergic to one of the substitute drugs. Therefore the doctor must specifically question the patient about any drug before it is administered. When considering the use of these or any other drugs, several additional factors must be considered. The likelihood of an allergic reaction to a drug increases with the duration and the number of courses of drug therapy. One remarkable example is a patient who had received 16 courses of penicillin therapy without adverse reaction over many years but developed anaphylactic shock with the 17th. Although long-term drug therapy is rarely necessary in dentistry, acute allergic reactions may occur even in the absence of a previous history of allergy.

The route of drug administration is also important. Allergic symptoms can arise with any route of administration. The site of administration is frequently the main target area for the allergy, especially with topical application of drugs. Of significance, however, is the finding that anaphylactic reactions occur much less commonly after enteral rather than parenteral administration of drugs. The frequency of other types of allergy may also be decreased through the use of the oral route. It is important therefore to consider the route of drug administration and, if possible, to administer a drug orally rather than parenterally. Penicillin is an example of a highly allergenic drug. There are few, if any, indications today for the parenteral administration of penicillin in a dental office since oral administration has been shown to result in therapeutic blood levels of penicillin in a relatively short time.[54] However, anaphylaxis has been reported after the oral administration of penicillin.[10,55] Drugs for the management of anxiety may require parenteral administration when used in the fearful patient. The risk of allergy to the drug must be weighed against the potential benefit to be gained from its use by this route. Local anesthetics, however, are a drug group that must be administered parenterally. Allergic reactions observed after parenteral drug administration tend to occur more rapidly and to become more intense than those following enteral administration.

■ MANAGEMENT
Alleged allergy to local anesthetics
Elective dental care

When there is a questionable history of allergy, local anesthetics should not be administered. Elective dental

TABLE 24-3 Allergenic drugs and possible substitutes

Category	Drug	Usual substitute	
		Generic	Proprietary
Antibiotics	Penicillin	Erythromycin	Ilosone
			Erythrocin
Analgesics	Acetylsalicylic acid (aspirin)	Acetaminophen	Tylenol
	Opioid	NSAIDs	Tempra
			Datril
			Naproxen
			Ibuprofen
			Many available
Sedative-hypnotics	Barbiturates	Flurazepam	Dalmane
		Diazepam	Valium
		Triazolam	Halcion
		Chloral hydrate	Noctec
		Hydroxyzine	Atarax, Vistaril
Acrylic	Methyl methacrylate	Avoid use if possible, otherwise use heat-cured acrylic	
Antioxidants	Sodium (meta)bisulfite	Non-vasopressor-containing local anesthetic	Mepivacaine
			Prilocaine

NSAID, nonsteroidal anti-inflammatory drug.

care requiring local anesthesia, either topical or injectable, should be postponed until a thorough evaluation has been completed by a competent individual. Dental care not requiring injectable or topical anesthesia may be carried out during this period.

Emergency dental care

The patient in pain or with an oral infection presents a more difficult situation. In many cases the patient will be new to the office, has a tooth requiring extraction or pulpal extirpation, and has a satisfactory medical history except for an alleged "allergy to Novocain." After questioning, the allergy seems most likely to have been of psychogenic origin (e.g., vasodepressor syncope), but a degree of doubt remains. How might this patient be managed?

Option 1: consultation. The most practical approach to this situation is immediate consultation with a person able to test the patient for allergy to local anesthetics. Treatment should be postponed if at all possible. If present, pain may be managed with orally administered analgesics and infection controlled with antibiotics. These represent temporary measures only. Following evaluation of the patient's claim of allergy, definitive dental care may proceed.

Option 2: general anesthesia. A second approach might be to use general anesthesia in place of local anesthesia to manage the dental emergency. Although general anesthesia is highly useful and a relatively safe technique when properly performed, there are complications and problems associated with it, not the least of which is the fact that it is unavailable in most dental offices. However, general anesthesia remains a viable alternative to local anesthesia in the management of the "allergic" patient, provided adequate facilities and well-trained personnel are available.

Option 3: histamine-blocker. A third option to consider when emergency treatment is necessary and general anesthesia is not available is the use of a histamine-blocker, such as diphenhydramine, as a local anesthetic for the management of pain during treatment. Most injectable histamine-blockers possess local anesthetic properties. Several are more potent local anesthetics than procaine. Diphenhydramine has been the most commonly used histamine-blocker in this regard. Used as a 1% solution with 1:100,000 epinephrine, diphenhydramine produces pulpal anesthesia of up to 30 minutes' duration.[56-58] An unwanted side effect frequently noted during intraoral administration of diphenhydramine is a burning or stinging sensation.

Concurrent administration of N_2O-O_2 along with diphenhydramine minimizes discomfort. Another possible unwanted result of the use of a histamine-blocker as a local anesthetic is postoperative tissue swelling and soreness. These unpleasant actions must be considered before these agents are used. For these reasons, the use of diphenhydramine as a local anesthetic is usually limited to those circumstances in which (1) there is a questionable history of local anesthetic allergy, (2) the patient has a dental emergency requiring immediate physical intervention, and (3) general anesthesia is not a reasonable alternative. It must again be kept in mind that allergy may develop to any drug, including the histamine-blockers.[59] The patient must be questioned about prior exposure to histamine-blockers or other drugs before they are used.

It is also important to remember that there are almost no dental emergency situations (short of hemorrhage and infection involving airway obstruction) in which immediate physical intervention is absolutely required. Appropriate drug therapy with immediate medical consultation *(option 1)* remains the most reasonable mode of action in these cases of alleged local anesthetic allergy coupled with a dental emergency.

Confirmed allergy to local anesthetics

Management of a patient with true, documented, and reproducible allergy to local anesthetics varies according to the nature of the allergy. If the allergy is limited to the ester drugs (e.g., procaine, propoxycaine, benzocaine, or tetracaine), the amides (e.g., articaine, lidocaine, mepivacaine, or prilocaine) may be used because cross-allergenicity, although possible, is quite rare. If the local anesthetic allergy was actually an allergy to the paraben preservative, an amide local anesthetic may be injected if it does not contain any preservative. Dental cartridges in the United States have not contained parabens since 1984; however, if the local anesthetic was administered by a nondental health care professional, it is possible that the drug contained paraben since multiple-dose vials of local anesthetics (all of which contain paraben) are frequently used by medical personnel. Documented sulfite allergy, though rarely associated with dental local anesthetics, mandates serious consideration of a local anesthetic that does not contain a vasopressor.[46]

On occasion, however, it is reported that a patient is allergic to all "-caine" drugs. The author recommends that this report undergo careful scrutiny and that the method by which this conclusion was reached be re-examined (What tests, if any, were carried out? By whom? Were pure solutions used? Or were preservatives present?). All too often patients are labeled "allergic to all local anesthetics" when in reality they are not. These patients often have their dental treatment carried out in a hospital setting under general anesthesia, when proper evaluation might have prevented this, saving the patient much time and money in addition to decreasing both the operative and anesthetic risk.

The following statement on local anesthetic allergy by Aldrete and Johnson[40] concludes this important section on the prevention of allergy:

> A strong plea is made for a thorough evaluation of the circumstances surrounding an adverse reaction to a local anesthetic before the label of "allergic to procaine," "allergic to lidocaine," or "allergic to all 'caine' drugs" is entered on the front of the patient's chart. We believe that untoward reactions observed during the use of local anesthetic agents are quite frequently the result of over-dosage.... The benefits obtained from the use of local anesthetic agents should not be denied to a patient just because of an untoward response during a previous exposure to one of them. Instead, details of the circumstances surrounding the incident, such as sequence of events, other drugs administered, and the type of procedure, must be evaluated.

■ CLINICAL MANIFESTATIONS

The various forms that allergic reactions may take are listed in Table 24-1. In addition to this classification, it is also possible to list reactions according to the length of time that elapses between contact with the antigen and appearance of clinical signs and symptoms. The two categories in this grouping are *immediate* and *delayed* reactions.

Immediate allergic reactions are those that occur within seconds to hours of exposure and include types I, II, and III of the Gell and Coombs classification system (see Table 24-1), whereas delayed allergic reactions develop hours to days after antigenic exposure. The type IV reaction is an example of delayed response.

Of greatest significance are immediate reactions, in particular the type I, or anaphylactic, reaction. Most allergic drug reactions are immediate. A number of organs and tissues are affected during immediate allergic reactions, particularly the skin, cardiovascular system, respiratory system, eyes, and gastrointestinal tract. Generalized (systemic) anaphylaxis by definition affects all of these systems. When hypotension occurs as a part of the reaction, resulting in the loss of consciousness, the term *anaphylactic shock* is employed.

Immediate allergic reactions also manifest themselves through any number of combinations involving these systems. Reactions involving one organ system are referred to as *localized anaphylaxis.* Examples of localized anaphylaxis include bronchial asthma, in which the respiratory system is the target, and urticaria, in which skin is the target organ. Skin and respiratory reactions are discussed individually, followed by a description of generalized anaphylaxis.

Onset

The time elapsing between antigenic exposure of the patient and development of clinical symptoms is of great importance. In general, the more rapidly signs and symptoms of allergy occur after exposure to an allergen, the more intense the ultimate reaction.[60] Conversely, the greater the amount of time elapsing between exposure and onset, the less intense the reaction. However, rare cases have been reported of systemic anaphylaxis developing up to several hours after antigenic exposure.[61] Of importance, too, is the rate at which signs and symptoms progress once they appear. If they appear and rapidly increase in intensity, the reaction is more likely to be life-threatening than is one that progresses slowly or not at all once initial signs and symptoms appear. These time factors have a bearing on the management of allergic reactions.

NOTE: *In general, the more rapidly signs and symptoms of allergy occur after exposure, the more intense is the ultimate reaction and the more aggressive its management.*

Skin reaction

Allergic skin reactions are the most common sensitization reaction to drug administration. Many types of allergic skin reaction occur; the three most important types of which are localized anaphylaxis, contact dermatitis, and drug eruption. Drug eruption constitutes the most common group of skin manifestations of drug allergy. Included in this category are urticaria (itching, hives), erythema (rash), and angioedema (localized swelling measuring several centimeters in diameter). Urticaria is associated with wheals (smooth, slightly elevated patches of skin) and frequently with intense itching (pruritus). In angioedema, localized swelling occurs in response to an allergen. Several forms of angioedema exist, but they are clinically similar.[62,63] Skin is usually of normal temperature and color, unless the reaction is accompanied by urticaria or erythema. Pain and itching are uncommon. The areas most frequently involved include the periorbital, perioral, and intraoral regions of the face, as well as the extremities. Of special interest in dentistry is the potential involvement of the lips, tongue, pharynx, and larynx, which can lead to significant airway obstruction.

The preceding group of signs and symptoms are most often noted in *hereditary angioneurotic edema.*[63] Angioedema is observed most frequently after administration of topical anesthetics (e.g., ester local anesthetics or methylparaben) to the oral mucosa. Within 30 to 60 minutes, the tissue in contact with the allergen appears quite swollen and erythematous.

Allergic skin reactions, if the sole manifestation of an allergic response, are normally not considered life-threatening. Yet a skin reaction developing rapidly after drug administration may be only the first indication of a more generalized reaction to follow.

Contact dermatitis is an allergic reaction more often observed in members of the dental profession than in dental patients. The sensitization process may require years of constant exposure to the allergen before clinical symptoms occur. These include erythema, induration (hardness), edema, and vesicle formation. Long-term exposure to a specific antigen results in dry, scaly lesions resembling eczema. Signs and symptoms related to allergic skin reactions are presented in Table 24-4.

Respiratory reactions

Clinical signs and symptoms of allergy may be limited exclusively to the respiratory tract, or signs and symptoms of respiratory tract involvement may occur along with other systemic responses. In a slowly evolving generalized allergic reaction, respiratory reactions normally follow skin, exocrine, and gastrointestinal responses, but precede cardiovascular signs and symptoms. *Bronchospasm* is the classic respiratory manifestation

TABLE 24-4 Clinical manifestations of allergic skin reactions

Reaction	Symptoms	Signs	Pathophysiology
Urticaria	Pruritus, tingling and warmth, flushing, hives	Urticaria, diffuse erythema	Increased vascular permeability, vasodilation
Angioedema	Nonpruritic extremity, periorbital and perioral swelling	Nonpitting edema, frequently asymmetric	Increased vascular permeability, vasodilation

From Lindzon RD, Silvers WS: Anaphylaxis. In: Marx JA, Hockberger RS, Walls RM, editors: *Rosen's emergency medicine: concepts and clinical practice,* ed 5, St. Louis, Mosby, 2002.

of allergy. It represents the clinical result of bronchial smooth muscle constriction. Signs and symptoms of an acute episode of allergic asthma are identical to nonallergic asthma. They include respiratory distress, dyspnea, wheezing, flushing, possible cyanosis, perspiration, tachycardia, greatly increased anxiety, and the use of accessory muscles of respiration. Asthma is described fully in Chapter 13.

A second respiratory manifestation of allergy may be the extension of angioedema to the larynx, which produces swelling of the vocal apparatus with subsequent obstruction of the airway. Clinical signs and symptoms of this acutely life-threatening situation include little or no exchange of air from the lungs (*look* to see if the chest is moving; *listen* for wheezing, indicative of a partial airway obstruction, or no sound, indicating complete airway obstruction; *feel* that there is little or no air exchange).

The occurrence of significant angioedema represents an ominous clinical sign. Acute airway obstruction leads rapidly to death unless corrected immediately. Laryngeal edema represents the effects of allergy on the upper airway. Asthma represents the actions of allergy on the lower airway.

Table 24-5 summarizes the clinical signs and symptoms of allergy on the respiratory system.

Generalized anaphylaxis

Anaphylactic reactions are often life-threatening and almost always unanticipated. Even when there are mild symptoms initially, the potential for progression to a severe and even irreversible outcome must be recognized. Any delay in the recognition of the initial signs and symptoms of anaphylaxis can result in a fatal outcome because of airway obstruction or vascular collapse.[64]

Generalized anaphylaxis is a most dramatic and acutely life-threatening allergic reaction and may cause death within a few minutes. Most deaths from anaph-

ylaxis occur within the first 30 minutes after antigenic exposure, although many victims succumb up to 120 minutes after the onset of the anaphylactic reaction.[65] It may develop after the administration of an antigen by any route, but is most likely to occur after parenteral administration. The time from antigenic challenge to onset of signs and symptoms is quite variable, but typically the reaction develops rapidly, reaching a maximal intensity within 5 to 30 minutes. Delayed responses of an hour or more have also been reported. It is thought that this results from the rate at which the antigen enters the circulatory system.

Signs and symptoms of generalized anaphylaxis are highly variable.[11] Four major clinical syndromes are recognized: skin reactions, smooth muscle spasm (gastrointestinal and genitourinary tracts and respiratory smooth muscle), respiratory distress, and cardiovascular collapse (Box 24-4). In typical generalized anaphylaxis, the symptoms progressively evolve through these four areas; however, in cases of fatal anaphylaxis, respiratory and cardiovascular disturbances predominate and are evident early in the reaction. In a typical generalized anaphylactic reaction, the first involvement is with the skin. The patient experiences a generalized warmth and tingling of the face, mouth, upper chest, palms, soles, or the site of antigenic exposure. Pruritus is a universal feature and may be accompanied by generalized flushing and urticaria, whereas nonpruritic angioedema may also be evident initially. Other reactions noted during

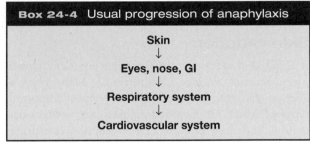

Box 24-4 Usual progression of anaphylaxis

Skin
↓
Eyes, nose, GI
↓
Respiratory system
↓
Cardiovascular system

GI, gastrointestinal tract.

TABLE 24-5 Clinical manifestations of respiratory allergic reactions

Reaction	Symptoms	Signs	Pathophysiology
Rhinitis	Nasal congestion, nasal itching, sneezing	Nasal mucosal edema, rhinorrhea	Increased vascular permeability, vasodilation, stimulation of nerve endings
Laryngeal edema	Dyspnea, hoarseness, tight throat	Laryngeal stridor, supraglottic and glottic edema	As above, plus increased exocrine gland secretions
Bronchospasm	Cough, wheezing, retrosternal tightness, dyspnea	Cough, wheeze (bronchi), tachypnea, respiratory distress, cyanosis	As above, plus bronchiole smooth-muscle contraction

From Lindzon RD, Silvers WS: Anaphylaxis. In: Marx JA, Hockberger RS, Walls RM, editors: *Rosen's emergency medicine: concepts and clinical practice,* ed 5, St. Louis, Mosby, 2002.

the early phase of the reaction include conjunctivitis, vasomotor rhinitis (inflammation of the mucous membranes of the nose, marked by increased mucous secretion), and pilomotor erection (the feeling of "hair standing on end"). Cramping abdominal pain with nausea, vomiting, diarrhea, and tenesmus (persistent, ineffectual spasms of the rectum or bladder, accompanied by the desire to empty the bowel or bladder), incontinence, pelvic pain, headache, a sense of impending doom, or a decrease in the level of consciousness also occur.

These manifestations may soon be followed by mild to severe respiratory distress. The patient may describe a cough, a sense of pressure on the chest, dyspnea, and wheeze from bronchospasm, or throat tightness, odynophagia (a severe sensation of burning, squeezing pain while swallowing), or hoarseness associated with laryngeal edema or oropharyngeal angioedema. In rapidly developing anaphylaxis, symptoms may occur within a very short time with considerable overlap. In particularly severe reactions, respiratory and cardiovascular symptoms may be the only signs present.

Signs and symptoms of cardiovascular involvement occur next and include pallor, lightheadedness, palpitation, tachycardia, hypotension, and cardiac dysrhythmias, followed by loss of consciousness and cardiac arrest. With loss of consciousness the anaphylactic reaction may more properly be called anaphylactic shock.

Cardiovascular signs and symptoms of allergy are summarized in Table 24-6. Any of these patterns may occur singly or in combination.[11] The duration of the anaphylactic reaction or any part of it may vary from minutes to a day or more. With prompt and appropriate therapy the entire reaction may be terminated rapidly; however, the two most serious sequelae, hypotension and laryngeal edema, may persist for hours or days despite therapy. Death may occur at any time, the usual cause (from autopsy reports) being upper airway obstruction secondary to laryngeal edema. Table 24-7 lists signs and symptoms of anaphylaxis and the percentage of cases in which they are noted.

■ PATHOPHYSIOLOGY

The clinical manifestations of allergy result from an antigen-antibody reaction. Such reactions are a part of the body's defense mechanisms (i.e., immune system), described in the following section to provide a better understanding of the processes involved in allergy.

For acute, immediate allergy or for anaphylaxis to occur, three conditions must be met:[11]

1. An antigen-induced stimulation of the immune system with specific immunoglobulin E (IgE) antibody formation
2. A latent period after the initial antigenic exposure for sensitization of mast cells and basophils
3. Subsequent reexposure to that specific antigen

Anaphylactoid reactions are those reactions that produce the same clinical picture as anaphylaxis but are not IgE mediated.[64] Anaphylactoid reactions may occur

TABLE 24-6 Clinical manifestations of allergic cardiovascular reactions

Reaction	Symptoms	Signs	Pathophysiology
Circulatory collapse	Light-headedness, generalized weakness, syncope, ischemic chest pain	Tachycardia, hypotension, shock	Increased vascular permeability, vasodilation a. Loss of vasomotor tone b. Increased venous capacitance
Dysrhythmias	As above, plus palpitations	ECG changes: tachycardia, nonspecific and ischemic ST-T wave changes, premature atrial and ventricular contractions, nodal rhythm, atrial fibrillation	Decreased cardiac output a. Direct mediator-induced myocardial suppression b. Decreased effective plasma volume c. Decreased preload d. Decreased afterload e. Dysrhythmias g. Iatrogenic effects of drugs used in treatment h. Preexisting heart disease
Cardiac arrest		Pulselessness; ECG changes: ventricular fibrillation, asystole	

ECG, electrocardiographic.

From Lindzon RD, Silvers WS: Anaphylaxis. In: Marx JA, Hockberger RS, Walls RM, editors: *Rosen's emergency medicine: concepts and clinical practice,* ed 5, St. Louis, Mosby, 2002.

TABLE 24-7 Frequency of occurrence of signs and symptoms of anaphylaxis

Signs and symptoms	Cases (%)*
CUTANEOUS	>90
Urticaria and angioedema	85–90
Flush	45–55
Pruritus without rash	2–5
RESPIRATORY	40–60
Dyspnea, wheeze	45–50
Upper airway angioedema	50–60
Rhinitis	15–20
CNS	
Dizziness, syncope, hypotension	30–35
ABDOMINAL	
Nausea, vomiting, diarrhea, cramping pain	25–30
MISCELLANEOUS	
Headache	5–8
Substernal pain	4–6
Seizure	1–2

*Percentages are approximations.
CNS, central nervous system.
Modified from Lieberman PL: Anaphylaxis and anaphylactoid reactions. Also in Church MK, Shute JK, Sampson AP: Mast cell-derived mediators. In: Adkinson NF Jr, Yunginger JW, Busse WW, et al., editors: *Middleton's allergy: principles and practice,* ed 6, St. Louis, Mosby, 2003, pp. 186–209.

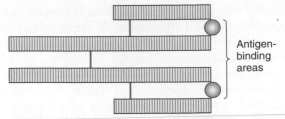

FIGURE 24-2 The basic structure of an antibody molecule. (From Ibsen OAC, Phelan JA: *Oral pathology for the dental hygienist,* ed 4, St. Louis, WB Saunders, 2004.)

after a single, first-time exposure to certain substances (such as drugs).

Antigens, haptens, and allergens

An antigen is any substance capable of inducing the formation of an antibody. Antigens are foreign to the species into which they are injected or ingested and may be harmful or harmless. Most antigens are proteins with a molecular weight between 5000 and 40,000. Materials with a molecular weight less than 5000 are usually not allergenic or antigenic. Virtually all proteins, whether of animal, plant, or microbial origin, possess antigenic potential.

Drugs, however, are not proteins and commonly possess a very low molecular weight (500 to 1000), making them unlikely antigens. The hapten theory of drug allergy explains the mechanism through which drugs may act as antigens. A hapten is a specific, protein-free substance that can combine to form a hapten-protein complex with a carrier protein-circulating albumin. The hapten itself is not antigenic; however, when coupled with the carrier protein, an immune response may be provoked. The hapten may combine with the carrier protein outside the body and then be injected into the individual, or the hapten may combine with tissue proteins of the host after administration into the body. The latter mechanism is the one by which most drugs become antigens and thus capable of inducing antibody formation and causing an allergic reaction.[11] Penicillin and aspirin are examples of haptens. Haptens are also called *incomplete antigens.*

An allergen is an antigen that can elicit allergic symptoms. It is obvious that not every antigen is an allergen. An antigen or allergen may stimulate the production of several classes of immunoglobulins, each of which possesses different functions.

NOTE: *All drugs must be viewed as potential antigens and should be administered only when clinically indicated.*[66]

Antibodies (immunoglobulins)

An antibody is a substance found in the blood or tissues that responds to the administration of an antigen or that reacts with it. The molecular weights of antibodies range from 150,000 (immunoglobulin G [IgG]) to 900,000 (IgM). The basic structure of an antibody molecule consists of two heavy and two light polypeptide chains linked in a Y configuration by covalent disulfide bonds. The base of the heavy chain (called *Fc* for crystallizable unit) binds the antibody to the surface of a cell, while the arms of the antibody bind with receptor sites on the antigen (Figure 24-2).

Immunoglobulins are produced by B lymphocytes (which constitute 10% to 15% of the circulating lymphocyte population) and are classified as IgA, IgD, IgE, IgG, and IgM according to structural differences in the heavy chains. Each immunoglobulin differs in its biological functions and in the type of allergic response it may elicit (Table 24-8; see Table 24-1).[68]

TABLE 24-8 Properties of human immunoglobulins

	IgA	IgD	IgE	IgG	IgM
Molecular weight	180,000	150,000	200,000	150,000	900,000
Normal serum concentration (mg/100 mL)	275	5	0.03	1200	120
Primary function	Local or mucosal reactions or infections	Antigen receptor on β lymphocytes	Type I hypersensitivity	Infection; type III hypersensitivity	Possible role in particular antigens

IgA is found principally in the serum and in external secretions such as saliva and sputum. It represents 10% to 15% of all immunoglobulins. It plays a role in the defense mechanisms of the external surfaces of the body, including mucous membranes. Fetal production of IgA begins during the last 6 months in utero, and adult levels are reached by 5 years of age.

IgD is found in serum only in small amounts, representing but 0.2% of immunoglobulins. IgD is probably important as an antigen receptor on B lymphocytes.

IgE, the antibody responsible for immediate hypersensitivity, is synthesized by plasma cells in the nasal mucosa, respiratory tract, gastrointestinal tract, and lymphoid tissues. It is only found in trace amounts in the serum. It binds to tissue mast cells and basophils. When mast cell–bound IgE combines with an antigen, the mast cell releases histamine and other vasoactive substances. The half-life of IgE is approximately 2 days, serum levels normally being quite low—0.03 mg/100 mL.

IgG represents approximately 75% to 80% of antibodies in normal serum. Its chief biological functions are the binding to and enhancement of phagocytosis of bacteria and the neutralization of bacterial toxins. IgG also crosses the placenta and imparts immune protection to the fetus, continuing for the first 6 months after birth. Shortly after birth, the infant begins to synthesize IgG, and by the age of 4 to 5 years, IgG levels approach adult levels.

IgM, the heaviest antibody, is active in both agglutinating and cytolytic reactions, accounting for 5% to 10% of all immunoglobulins. Production of IgM begins during the final 6 months of fetal life, and adult levels are reached by 1 year of age.

Antibodies possess the ability to bind with the specific antigen that induces their production. This immunologic specificity is based on similarities in the structures of the antigen and antibody. Antibodies possess at least two specific antigen-binding sites per molecule (the Fab fragments). IgM possesses five, and IgA probably has more than two. Antibodies are not entirely specific, and cross-sensitivity is possible between chemically similar substances.

Defense mechanisms of the body

When exposed to a foreign substance, the body protects itself through a number of mechanisms (Box 24-5). These include anatomic barriers, which attempt to exclude entry of the antigen into the body. Examples of barriers include the epithelium of the gastrointestinal tract, the sneeze and cough mechanisms, and the mucociliary blanket of the tracheobronchial tree. Once the foreign substance gains entry to the body, two other nonspecific defense mechanisms are brought into play. These include mobilization of phagocytic blood cells, such as leukocytes, histiocytes, and macrophages, and the production of nonspecific chemical substances, such as lysozymes and proteolytic enzymes, which assist in removal of the foreign substance. A more specific defense mechanism is also employed. IgA antibody is produced by plasma cells in response to the antigen. IgA then aids in the removal or detoxification of the antigen from the host.

Through these processes of anatomic localization, phagocytosis, and destruction, the antigen is usually eliminated, resulting in little or no damage to the host. If, however, the antigen survives because of genetic defects in the patient, such as atopy, or because of the nature of the antigen itself, additional defense mechanisms may be called into play that may ultimately prove harmful to the host. These include reactions resulting in the formation of antibodies that, on subsequent exposure to the antigen, may induce the formation of precipitates of antigen-antibody complexes within cells or blood vessels (type III response) or may result in the subsequent release of the chemical mediators of the type I allergic response.

Box 24-5 Defense mechanisms of the body

Anatomic barriers
Mobilization of phagocytotic blood cells
Production of enzymes
IgA antibody production

There are at least three possible results of an antigen-antibody reaction:

1. Antibodies are produced that combine with the antigen to neutralize it or change it so that it becomes innocuous.
2. The antigen-antibody combination occurs within blood vessels in a magnitude sufficient to produce actual precipitates within small blood vessels, resulting in vascular occlusions with subsequent ischemic necrosis (e.g., the Arthus reaction type III).
3. The antigen-antibody union activates proteolytic enzymes that release certain chemicals from cells, which in turn act to produce the anaphylactic response.

The first response is of benefit to the host, leading to elimination of the foreign material; the second and third responses can produce injury and death.

Type I allergic reaction— anaphylaxis

The type I (anaphylactic or immediate) allergic reaction is of great concern to all health professionals. For any true allergic reaction to occur, the patient must have previously been exposed to the antigen. This is called the *sensitizing dose,* with subsequent exposure to the antigen called the *challenge dose.*

Sensitizing dose

During the sensitization phase, the patient is initially exposed to the antigen. In response to the antigen, β lymphocytes are stimulated to develop into mature plasma cells that produce increasing amounts of immuno-globins specific for that antigen. When a susceptible (atopic) individual is exposed, antigen-specific IgE antibodies are formed, which interact only with that particular antigen (or with very closely related antigens, i.e., cross-sensitivity). IgE antibodies are cytophilic and selectively attach themselves to the cell membranes of circulating basophils and tissue mast cells.

Sensitization occurs when the complement-fixing (Fc) portion of the IgE antibody affixes to receptor sites on the cell membrane of mast cells in the interstitial space and circulating basophils in the vascular space.[68,69] A latent period of variable duration (several days to possibly years) ensues, during which time IgE antibody continues to be produced (attaching to basophils and mast cells) while the level of antigen progressively decreases. After this latent period, antigen is no longer present, but high levels of IgE sensitized basophils and mast cells remain. The patient has been sensitized to the specific antigen.

Challenge (allergic) dose

Reexposure to the antigen results in an antigen-antibody interaction thought to be initiated by the antigen bridging the antibody fixing (Fab) arms of two adjacent IgE antibodies on the surface of sensitized mast cells or basophils.[70] In the presence of calcium, this bridging initiates a complex series of intramembrane and intracellular events that culminate in structural and functional membrane changes, granule solubilization, exocytosis, and the release of preformed chemical mediators of allergy into the circulation.[71] The primary preformed mediators of allergy are histamine, eosinophilic chemotactic factor of anaphylaxis (ECF-A), high-molecular-weight-neutrophil chemotactic factor (HMW-NCF), and the kallikreins.[72] Other preformed chemical mediators include enzymatic proteases (e.g., tryptase), acid hydrolases, and proteoglycans. These preformed mediators in turn may directly produce local and systemic pharmacologic effects, cause the release of other spontaneously generated mediators, or activate reflexes that ultimately produce the clinical picture of anaphylaxis. Spontaneously generated mediators include the leukotrienes, prostaglandins, and platelet aggregating factor (PAF).[73]

Chemical mediators of anaphylaxis

The endogenous chemicals released from tissue mast cells and circulating basophils act on the primary target tissues, including the vascular, bronchial, and gastrointestinal smooth muscles; vascular endothelium; and exocrine glands, and are ultimately responsible for the clinical picture of allergy. That these chemicals are responsible for the signs and symptoms of allergy explains the similarity in allergic reactions regardless of the antigen inducing the response (e.g., penicillin, aspirin, procaine, shellfish, strawberries, peanuts, bisulfites, stinging insects). The level of intensity of an allergic reaction may vary greatly (e.g., anaphylaxis, mild urticaria) from patient to patient. Factors involved in determining the level of magnitude of an allergic response include (1) the amount of antigen or antibody present, (2) the affinity of the antibody for the antigen, (3) the concentration of chemical mediators, (4) the concentration of receptors for mediators, and (5) the affinity of the mediators for receptors. All these factors, except for the antigen, are endogenous, which explains the wide variation in individual susceptibility. The major chemical mediators of allergy are briefly described along with their primary biological functions.

Histamine.   Histamine is a widely distributed normal constituent of many tissues, including the skin, lungs, nervous system, and gastrointestinal tract. In many tissues histamine is stored in preformed granules within the mast cell (a fixed-tissue cell) or in circulating blood in basophils.[74] It is stored in a physiologically inactive form and is electrostatically bound to heparin in granule form. When an IgE-induced antigen-antibody reaction occurs, these granules undergo a process in which they are activated and released from the basophils and mast cells without damaging the cell. The actions of histamine within the body (described in the following paragraphs) are mediated by two different tissue histamine receptors called H_1 and H_2.[75,76] The clinical manifestations of histamine are influenced by the ratio of H_1 and H_2 activation.[73]

Particularly important pharmacologic actions of histamine include those on the cardiovascular system, smooth muscle, and glands. Cardiovascular actions of histamine include capillary dilation and increased capillary permeability. The action of capillary dilation, an H_1 and H_2 effect, is probably the most important action effected by histamine. All capillaries are involved after histamine administration. The effect is most obvious in the skin of the face and upper chest, the so-called *blushing area,* which becomes hot and flushed. Increased capillary permeability also leads to an outward passage of plasma protein and fluid into extracellular spaces, resulting in the formation of edema.

Other cardiovascular responses to histamine include the *triple response.* When administered subcutaneously or released in the skin, histamine produces (1) a localized red spot extending a few millimeters around the site of injection, (2) a brighter red flush or flare that is irregular in outline and extends for about 1 cm beyond the original red spot, and (3) localized edema fluid, which forms a wheal that is noted in about 1.5 minutes and occupies the same area as the original red spot. Histamine is also the chemical mediator of pain and itch.

Because of histamine's cardiovascular actions, venous return decreases and systemic blood pressure and cardiac output are significantly reduced. The resulting hypotension is normally of short duration because of the rapid inactivation of histamine and because of other compensatory reflexes that are activated in response to histamine release, including increased catecholamine release from the adrenal medulla. Histamine relaxes vascular smooth muscle in humans; however, most non-vascular smooth muscle is contracted (H_1). Smooth-muscle constriction is most prominent in the uterus and bronchi. Bronchiolar smooth-muscle constriction leads to the clinical syndrome of bronchospasm.

Smooth muscle of the gastrointestinal tract is moderately constricted, whereas that of the urinary bladder and gallbladder is only slightly constricted.

Actions of histamine on exocrine glands involve stimulation of secretions. Stimulated glands include the gastric, salivary, lacrimal, pancreatic, and intestinal glands. Increased secretion from mucous glands leads to the clinical syndrome of rhinitis, which is prominent in many allergic reactions.

Histamine is considered to be *the* major chemical mediator of anaphylaxis. Many of the physiologic responses to histamine may be moderated or blocked by the administration of pharmacologic doses of histamine-blockers before histamine has been released.

Slow-reacting substance of anaphylaxis. Slow-reacting substance of anaphylaxis (SRS-A) is a spontaneously generated mediator thought to be produced from the interaction of the antigen-IgE-mast cell and the subsequent transformation of cell membrane lipids to arachidonic acid. Arachidonic acid is then metabolized to the prostaglandins, thromboxanes, and prostacyclins, or to the leukotrienes. SRS-A is a mixture of leukotrienes (LTC_4, LTD_4, LTE_4).[77] Leukotrienes produce a marked and prolonged bronchial smooth-muscle contraction. This effect is 6000 times as potent as that of histamine.[78] This bronchoconstrictive action is slower in onset (thus its original name, SRS-A) and of longer duration than that of histamine. Leukotrienes also increase vascular permeability and potentiate the effects of histamine.[79] The actions of leukotrienes are not diminished or reversed by histamine-blocking drugs.

Eosinophilic chemotactic factor of anaphylaxis. Eosinophilic chemotactic factor of anaphylaxis (ECF-A) is a preformed mediator that has the ability to attract eosinophils to the target organ involved in the allergic reaction.[80] Eosinophils, through their release of secondary enzymatic mediators, are major regulatory leukocytes of anaphylaxis.

Another preformed mediator, *HMW-NCF* (neutrophil chemotactic factor), is released rapidly into the circulation, has a half-life of several hours, and has a second peak level that correlates with the late-phase asthmatic response.[81]

Basophil kallikreins, preformed mediators, are responsible for the generation of kinins. Bradykinins have been implicated as the mediators responsible for cardiovascular collapse in clinical situations where no other manifestations of anaphylaxis are present.[82] The pharmacologic actions of the bradykinins include vasodilation, increased permeability of blood vessels, and production of pain. Blood levels of bradykinin are significantly increased during anaphylaxis.

Prostaglandins (PGs) are spontaneously generated mediators that are metabolites of arachidonic acid. Almost all cells can produce these potent mediators. PGD_2 causes smooth-muscle contraction and increased vascular permeability; PGE_1 and PGE_2 produce bronchodilation, whereas PGF_2 is a potent bronchoconstrictor.[83]

PAF is the most potent compound known to cause the aggregation of human platelets.[84,85] It produces many important clinical findings in anaphylaxis, including cardiovascular collapse, pulmonary edema, and a prolonged increase in total pulmonary resistance.[86]

The chemical mediators described here act on the primary target organs to produce the clinical picture (signs and symptoms) of allergy and anaphylaxis.

Respiratory signs and symptoms

Vasodilation and increased vascular permeability result in transudation of plasma and proteins into interstitial spaces, which, along with increases in mucus secretion, laryngeal edema, and angioedema, may result in asphyxia from upper respiratory tract obstruction.[87] Bronchospasm resulting from bronchial smooth-muscle constriction, respiratory mucosal edema, and increased mucus production can produce coughing, chest tightness, dyspnea, and wheezing.[11]

Cardiovascular signs and symptoms

Decreased vasomotor tone and increases in venous capacitance secondary to vasodilation can provoke cardiovascular collapse. Increased vascular permeability, a characteristic feature of anaphylaxis, allows transfer of as much as 50% of the intravascular fluid into the extravascular space within 10 minutes. As a result, hemodynamic collapse might occur rapidly with little or no cutaneous or respiratory manifestations.[64,88]

Lightheadedness and syncope, tachycardia, dysrhythmia, orthostatic hypotension, and shock all results from these cardiovascular responses.

Gastrointestinal signs and symptoms

Cramping, abdominal pain, nausea and vomiting, diarrhea, and tenesmus are produced by gastrointestinal mucosal edema and smooth muscle contraction.[89]

Urticaria, rhinitis, and conjunctivitis

These are endpoints of increased vascular permeability and vasodilation.[11] In cases of fatal anaphylaxis, the most prominent clinical pathologic features are observed in the respiratory and cardiovascular systems and include laryngeal edema, pulmonary hyperinflation, peribronchial vascular congestion, intraalveolar hemor-

rhage, pulmonary edema, increased tracheobronchial secretions, eosinophilic infiltration of the bronchial walls, and varying degrees of myocardial damage.[90]

■ MANAGEMENT

The clinical picture of allergy may be quite varied. Of special concern to the doctor are signs and symptoms of immediate allergy, which range from mild skin lesions to angioedema to generalized anaphylaxis. The speed with which symptoms of allergy appear and the rate at which they progress determine the mode of management of the reaction. Preparedness, prompt recognition, and appropriate and aggressive treatment are integral to parts of successful management of anaphylaxis.[64]

Skin reactions

Skin lesions may range from localized angioedema to diffuse erythema, urticaria, and pruritus. Management of these reactions is based on the speed with which they appear after antigenic challenge (e.g., drug administration).

Delayed reactions

Skin reactions that appear a considerable time after antigenic exposure (60 minutes or more) and do not progress may be considered, at least initially, to be non–life-threatening. These include a mild skin reaction or a localized mucous membrane reaction after the application of topical anesthesia.

Diagnostic clues to the presence of an allergic skin reaction include the following:[91]
- Hives, itching
- Edema
- Flushed skin

Step 1: termination of the dental procedure and activate dental office emergency team. Stop treatment immediately upon recognizing the clinical manifestations of an allergic skin reaction.

Step 2: P (position). Because this patient is not in distress except for a degree of discomfort produced by any itching that might be present, positioning is based on comfort.

Step 3: A-B-C (airway-breathing-circulation) or basic life support (BLS), as needed. Assess airway, breathing, and circulation, implementing basic life support as needed. At this juncture, airway, breathing, and circulation will be adequately maintained by the patient.

Step 4: D (definitive care):

Step 4a: administration of histamine-blocker.
Immediate management of a mild, delayed-onset skin reaction is to *consider* administration of a histamine blocker. In the presence of a very localized response, such as a small area of the lower lip appearing slightly swollen and erythematous, with some itching of the overlying skin after topical anesthetic application, observation might be considered initially. The patient, or parent or guardian, should be advised to call the dental office immediately if the involved area appears to increase so that a suitable drug (histamine-blocker) may be prescribed. An alternative in this case of a very mild, localized reaction is to give the patient a prescription for an orally administered histamine-blocker and advise the patient either to not take the drug unless the reaction becomes bothersome or to begin taking the drug immediately. When the histamine-blocker is taken orally, administer it as recommended for 2 to 3 days. The oral dose of diphenhydramine is 50 mg (for adults) three to four times a day, and 25 mg for children over 20 pounds.

There is rarely a need to summon outside medical assistance for this type of response. When a more generalized slow-onset skin reaction develops, recommended management is somewhat more aggressive. This situation is most likely to occur in a patient who has received oral antibiotic prophylaxis about 1 hour before the onset of symptoms and has developed a more generalized allergic skin reaction. Examination of the patient demonstrates no involvement, as yet, of other systems. Management of this patient should involve the intravenous (IV) or intramuscular (IM) administration of a histamine-blocker such as diphenhydramine (50 mg for adults; 25 mg for children). Onset of action of an IV histamine-blocker is a few minutes, whereas 10 to 30 minutes are required for the relief of symptoms following IM administration. The patient is then given a prescription for diphenhydramine or chlorpheniramine to be taken orally every 4 to 6 hours for 2 to 3 days.

Do not allow this patient to leave the dental office until the clinical signs and symptoms have resolved. In addition, do not allow a patient who has received a parenteral histamine-blocker to leave the dental office alone or to operate a motor vehicle. Varying degrees of central nervous system (CNS) depression (e.g., drowsiness, fatigue, sedation) are noted after histamine-blocker administration by any route, but this is much more likely when the agent is administered parenterally.

Step 4b: medical consultation. Consultation with the patient's primary care physician or an allergist should follow, with a thorough evaluation of the allergic reaction completed before any further dental treatment is started. Compile a complete list of all drugs and chemicals administered to the patient for evaluation by the allergist.

If the skin reaction does not develop until the patient has left the dental office, request that the patient return to the office,* if possible, where one of the management therapies described above will be employed.

Should the reaction occur but the patient is unable to return to the dental office, strongly advise the patient to see his or her physician or to report to the emergency department of a local hospital.

Histamine-blockers reverse the actions of histamine by occupying H_1 receptor sites on the effector cell (competitive antagonism). Histamine-blockers thereby prevent the agonist molecules (histamine) from occupying these sites, without initiating a response themselves. The protective responses of histamine-blockers include the control of edema formation and pruritus. Other allergic responses such as hypotension and bronchospasm are influenced little, if at all, by histamine-blockers. It can be seen therefore that histamine-blockers are of value only in mild allergic responses where small quantities of histamine have been released or in the prevention of allergic reactions in allergic individuals.

Box 24-6 outlines the steps in management of the delayed-onset, allergic skin reaction.

- **Drugs used in management:** Histamine-blocker administered orally or parenterally.
- **Medical assistance required:** None is usually required.

Rapid-onset skin reaction

Allergic skin reactions arising in less than 60 minutes are managed more aggressively. Other allergic symptoms of a relatively minor nature included in this section are conjunctivitis, rhinitis, urticaria, pruritus, and erythema.

Diagnostic clues to the presence of an allergic skin reaction include the following:[84]

- Same as for delayed skin reaction
- Conjunctivitis
- Rhinitis

Step 1: termination of the dental procedure and activation of dental office emergency team. Stop treatment immediately upon recognition of the clinical manifestations of allergy.

---

*Although most delayed-onset localized skin reactions do not progress to systemic involvement and anaphylaxis, extreme caution must be observed with all allergic reactions. It is impossible to effectively evaluate a patient by telephone.

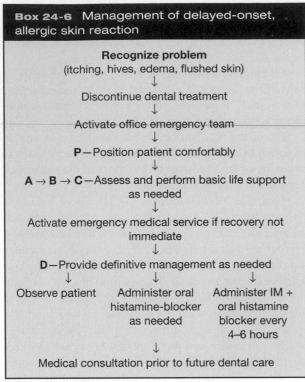

Box 24-6 Management of delayed-onset, allergic skin reaction

Recognize problem
(itching, hives, edema, flushed skin)
↓
Discontinue dental treatment
↓
Activate office emergency team
↓
P—Position patient comfortably
↓
A → B → C—Assess and perform basic life support as needed
↓
Activate emergency medical service if recovery not immediate
↓
D—Provide definitive management as needed
↓   ↓   ↓
Observe patient   Administer oral   Administer IM +
                   histamine-blocker   oral histamine
                   as needed   blocker every
                                      4–6 hours
↓
Medical consultation prior to future dental care

A, airway; B, breathing; C, circulation; D, definitive care;
IM, intramuscular; P, position.

Step 2: P (position).
Because this patient is not in acute distress, positioning is based on comfort.

Step 3: A-B-C (airway, breathing, circulation) or BLS, as needed.
Assess airway, breathing, and circulation and implement basic life support as needed. At this juncture, airway, breathing, and circulation will be adequate.

Step 4: D (definitive care):
Management of the more rapid-onset allergic reaction is predicated on the presence or absence of signs of respiratory or cardiovascular involvement. Allergy that appears shortly after antigenic challenge is more likely to progress rapidly and to be more intense than a delayed-onset reaction. Treatment is necessarily more aggressive the more rapid the onset.

Step 4a: monitoring of vital signs.
Monitor and record vital signs—heart rate and rhythm, blood pressure, and respirations—every 5 minutes.

Step 4b: administration of histamine-blocker.
In the absence of signs of cardiovascular and respiratory involvement (no tachycardia, hypotension, dizziness, lightheadedness, dyspnea, or wheezing), definitive management involves the administration of a parenteral histamine-blocker. Diphenhydramine is administered via the IV or IM route as described in the previous section. With resolution of clinical signs and symptoms, prescribe an oral histamine-blocker for 2 to 3 days. Do not allow the patient to leave the office alone or to operate a motor vehicle. Medical evaluation should be completed before any further dental treatment is considered.

Step 4c: repositioning of patient.
In the presence of signs of either cardiovascular (tachycardia, hypotension, dizziness, lightheadedness) or respiratory (dyspnea, wheezing) involvement, additional steps are necessary. If *hypotension* is evident, position the patient in the supine position with the legs elevated. With *respiratory distress* in the absence of cardiovascular involvement, position is determined by patient comfort.

Step 4d: oxygen and venipuncture, if available.
Administer oxygen via nasal cannula, nasal hood, or face mask as soon as available. In addition, if equipment and trained personnel are available, establish an IV line.

Step 4e: administration of epinephrine.
Recommended management of this mild anaphylactic reaction involving the cardiovascular or respiratory systems requires immediate administration of IM epinephrine 1:1000 in a dose of 0.3 mL (0.3 mg adult), 0.15 mg (child), or 0.075 mg (infant). Epinephrine may be administered every 5 to 20 minutes as needed, to a total of three doses. If the IV route is available, administer 1 mL of 1:10,000 (0.1 mg) by slow IV push over 3 to 5 minutes. Observe the patient for either the desired therapeutic effect or the development of complications. Additional 0.1-mg (1-mL) doses may be administered over a 15- to 30-minute period to a maximum dose of 5 mL.

Step 4f: summoning of medical assistance.
Any allergic reaction requiring the administration of epinephrine also requires additional medical assistance.

Step 4g: administration of histamine-blocker.
With resolution of the cardiovascular or respiratory signs and symptoms of the allergic reaction, administer a histamine-blocker (diphenhydramine, 50 mg) intramuscularly. The pediatric dose of diphenhydramine is 25 mg. Histamine-blockers are administered intramuscularly to provide a more prolonged duration of clinical activity.

Step 4h: monitoring of cardiovascular and respiratory systems.
Continue monitoring and

recording of the cardiovascular and respiratory responses of the patient throughout the episode. The need for additional drug therapy (e.g., epinephrine) will be based on these findings.

Step 4i: recovery and discharge. With arrival of emergency medical personnel, an IV infusion will be started, if not done previously, and appropriate drug therapy administered. The patient who has had a mild anaphylactic reaction (e.g., urticaria, rhinitis, conjunctivitis, with respiratory or cardiovascular involvement) will be stabilized and transported to the emergency department of a hospital for observation and possible additional treatment.

Box 24-7 outlines the steps in management of a rapid-onset skin reaction.

- **Drugs used in management:** Oxygen, a histamine-blocker (IM), and epinephrine (IM or IV).
- **Medical assistance required:** None is required if skin only; it is needed if there is respiratory or cardiovascular involvement.

Respiratory reactions

Bronchospasm

The most likely populations in dentistry in which an allergic reaction will manifest itself as a respiratory problem (bronchospasm) are (1) asthmatic patients allergic to bisulfites and comes into contact with them during dental care and (2) patients allergic to aspirin.

Diagnostic clues to the presence of an allergy involving bronchospasm include the following:

- Wheezing
- Use of accessory muscles of respiration

Bronchial smooth muscle constriction results in asthma-like reactions. Management of the acute asthmatic episode was described in depth in Chapter 13 and includes the following steps.

Step 1: termination of the dental procedure and activation of dental office emergency team.

Step 2: P (position). An upright or semierect position is usually preferred by the conscious patient exhibiting difficulty breathing.

Step 3: A-B-C (airway, breathing, circulation) or BLS, as needed. Assessment of airway, breathing, and circulation initially proves adequate. Breathing may show varying degrees of inadequacy, ranging from mild bronchospasm to almost complete obstruction, and cyanosis.

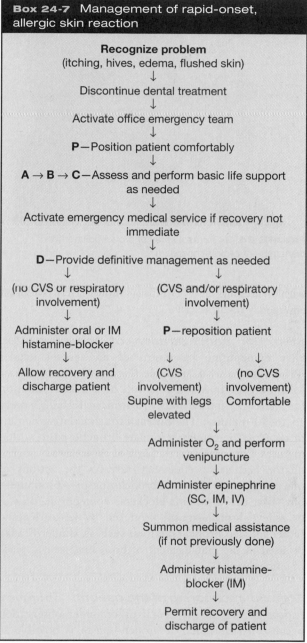

Box 24-7 Management of rapid-onset, allergic skin reaction

Recognize problem
(itching, hives, edema, flushed skin)
↓
Discontinue dental treatment
↓
Activate office emergency team
↓
P—Position patient comfortably
↓
A → B → C—Assess and perform basic life support as needed
↓
Activate emergency medical service if recovery not immediate
↓
D—Provide definitive management as needed
↓   ↓
(no CVS or respiratory   (CVS and/or respiratory
involvement)   involvement)
↓   ↓
Administer oral or IM   **P**—reposition patient
histamine-blocker
↓   ↓   ↓
Allow recovery and   (CVS   (no CVS
discharge patient   involvement)   involvement)
                        Supine with legs Comfortable
                        elevated
                                    ↓
                        Administer O$_2$ and perform
                        venipuncture
                                    ↓
                        Administer epinephrine
                        (SC, IM, IV)
                                    ↓
                        Summon medical assistance
                        (if not previously done)
                                    ↓
                        Administer histamine-
                        blocker (IM)
                                    ↓
                        Permit recovery and
                        discharge of patient

A, airway; *B,* breathing; *C,* circulation; *D,* definitive care; *IM,* intramuscular; *IV,* intravenous; *P,* position; *SC,* subcutaneous.

Step 4: removal of materials from the patient's mouth.

Step 5: calming of the patient. The conscious patient experiencing respiratory distress may become quite fearful. Try to allay any apprehensions.

Step 6: D (definitive care):
Step 6a: summoning of medical assistance: With clinically evident respiratory distress associated

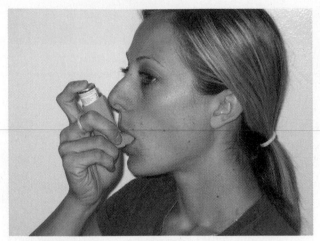

FIGURE 24-3 Aerosol spray of bronchodilator for management of bronchospasm.

with wheezing and cyanosis, immediately summon emergency medical care.

Step 6b: administration of bronchodilator.

Give epinephrine by means of an aerosol inhaler (Primatene Mist, if available [Figure 24-3]), by IM or subcutaneous injection (0.3 mL of a 1:1000 dilution for adults), or intravenously (0.1 mL of 1:10,000) every 15 to 30 minutes. The potent bronchodilating actions of epinephrine usually terminate bronchospasm within minutes. Epinephrine is the drug of choice as a bronchodilator because it effectively reverses the actions of one of the major causes of bronchospasm—histamine—but, like the histamine-blockers, epinephrine does n ot relieve bronchospasm produced by leukotrienes.[92] Other inhaled bronchodilators, such as albuterol, may be used in the management of bronchospasm in place of epinephrine.

Step 6c: monitoring of the patient.

The patient should remain in the dental office under observation because a recurrence of bronchospasm is possible as the epinephrine undergoes rapid biotransformation. Should bronchospasm reappear, readminister epinephrine intramuscularly, subcutaneously, or by inhalation (aerosol).

Step 6d: administration of histamine-blocker.

IM administration of a histamine-blocker minimizes the likelihood of recurrence of bronchospasm because the histamine-blocker occupies the histamine receptor site, preventing a relapse. Diphenhydramine, 50 mg IM (adults), or 2 mg/kg IM or IV (children), is recommended.

Step 6e: recovery and discharge.

With arrival of emergency medical personnel the victim will be

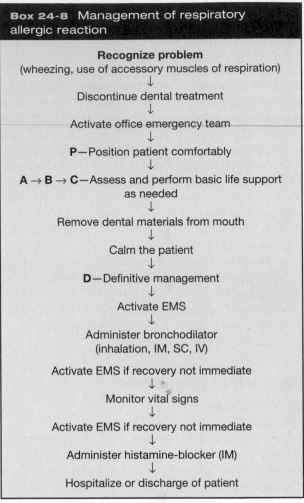

Box 24-8 Management of respiratory allergic reaction

Recognize problem
(wheezing, use of accessory muscles of respiration)
↓
Discontinue dental treatment
↓
Activate office emergency team
↓
P—Position patient comfortably
↓
A → **B** → **C**—Assess and perform basic life support as needed
↓
Remove dental materials from mouth
↓
Calm the patient
↓
D—Definitive management
↓
Activate EMS
↓
Administer bronchodilator
(inhalation, IM, SC, IV)

Activate EMS if recovery not immediate
↓
Monitor vital signs
↓
Activate EMS if recovery not immediate
↓
Administer histamine-blocker (IM)
↓
Hospitalize or discharge of patient

A, airway; **B,** breathing; **C,** circulation; **D,** definitive care; EMS, emergency medical service; IM, intramuscular; IV, intravenous; **P,** position; SC, subcutaneous.

stabilized and additional treatment started, if necessary. Additional treatment may involve the administration of one or more of the following: intravenous bronchodilators; atropine, steroids (methylprednisolone), and intubation and ventilation if bronchospasm is persistent and severe. In most cases a patient exhibiting an allergic reaction consisting primarily of respiratory signs and symptoms will require a variable period of hospitalization.

Box 24-8 outlines the steps to take in managing the respiratory allergic reaction.

- **Drugs used in management:** Oxygen; bronchodilators, specifically, epinephrine (inhalation, IV, IM, or subcutaneous); and a histamine-blocker (IM).
- **Medical assistance required:** Assistance is needed if there is significant respiratory distress.

Laryngeal edema

A second, and usually more life-threatening, respiratory allergic manifestation is the development of laryngeal edema. Laryngeal edema may be diagnosed when little or no air movement can be heard or felt through the mouth and nose despite exaggerated spontaneous respiratory movements by the patient, or when a patent airway cannot be obtained. A partially obstructed larynx in the presence of spontaneous respiratory movements produces the characteristically high-pitched crowing sound of stridor, in contrast to the wheezing characteristic of bronchospasm, whereas total obstruction is accompanied by silence in the presence of spontaneous chest movement. The patient soon loses consciousness from lack of oxygen (e.g., hypoxia or anoxia). Fortunately, laryngeal edema is not common, but may arise in any acute allergic reaction that involves the airway.

Diagnostic clues to the presence of laryngeal edema include the following:

- Respiratory distress
- Exaggerated chest movements
- High-pitched crowing sound (stridor; partial obstruction), no sound (total obstruction)
- Cyanosis
- Loss of consciousness

Step 1: termination of the dental procedure and activation of dental office emergency team.

Step 2: P (position).
An upright or semierect position is usually preferred by the conscious patient exhibiting difficulty breathing. If the degree of laryngeal edema is significant, the level of consciousness will be altered and the supine position with feet elevated is more appropriate. Should the patient be unwilling or unable to tolerate the supine position, then position based on comfort is recommended.

Step 3: A-B-C (airway, breathing, circulation) or BLS, as needed.
Airway will be the most critical factor in management of laryngeal edema. Initial management should include extension of the neck via head tilt–chin lift, or jaw thrust–chin lift, followed by the insertion of a nasopharyngeal tube or oropharyngeal airway. The conscious patient is usually able to tolerate a nasopharyngeal airway, whereas an oropharyngeal airway is likely to produce a gag reflex.

Step 4: D (definitive care):
Step 4a: summoning of medical assistance.

Step 4b: administration of epinephrine.
Immediate administration of 0.3 mL of 1:1000 epinephrine IM (0.15 mL for child, 0.075 for infant) or 10 mL of 1:10,000 epinephrine IV titrated over 5 minutes (adult), repeated every 3 to 5 minutes as necessary, is recommended. Do not exceed a maximum dose for 1:10,000 epinephrine of 5.0 mL every 15 to 30 minutes.

Step 4c: maintenance of airway.
In the presence of a partially obstructed airway, epinephrine administration may halt or even reverse the progress of laryngeal edema. Use of airway maneuvers or devices, such as oropharyngeal or nasopharyngeal airways, should be considered if available and if doctor is trained in their use.

Step 4d: administration of oxygen.
Administer oxygen as soon as it becomes available.

Step 4e: additional drug management.
Administer a histamine-blocker (diphenhydramine, 50 mg for adults, 25 mg for children) and corticosteroid (hydrocortisone, 100 mg) IM or IV after clinical recovery, as noted by airway improvement: normal, or at least improved, breath sounds; absence of cyanosis; and less exaggerated chest excursions. Corticosteroids inhibit edema and capillary dilation by stabilizing basement membranes. They are of little immediate value because of their slow onset of action, even when administered intravenously. Corticosteroids have an onset of action approximately 6 hours after their administration.[93] Corticosteroids function to prevent a relapse, whereas the function of epinephrine, a more rapidly acting drug employed during the acute phase of anaphylaxis, is to halt or reverse the deleterious actions of histamine and other mediators of allergy.

These procedures (steps 1 through 4e) are normally adequate to maintain the patient. With arrival of medical assistance, the patient will be stabilized and transferred to a hospital for further observation and treatment.

Step 4f: cricothyrotomy.
A totally obstructed airway may not be reopened at all or not in time by the administration of epinephrine and other drugs. In this case it becomes necessary to create an emergency airway to maintain the patient's life. Time is of the essence, and it is not possible to delay action until medical assistance arrives. A cricothyrotomy is the procedure of choice to establish an airway in this situation. (Cricothyrotomy was described in Chapter 11.) Once an airway is obtained administer oxygen, using artificial ventilation if needed, and monitor vital signs.

Prior to arrival of emergency medical assistance, the drugs previously administered may halt the progress of the laryngeal edema and might even reverse it to

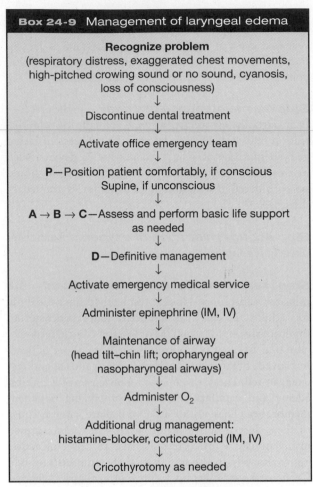

> **Box 24-9**   Management of laryngeal edema
>
> **Recognize problem**
> (respiratory distress, exaggerated chest movements,
> high-pitched crowing sound or no sound, cyanosis,
> loss of consciousness)
> ↓
> Discontinue dental treatment
> ↓
> Activate office emergency team
> ↓
> **P**—Position patient comfortably, if conscious
> Supine, if unconscious
> ↓
> **A → B → C**—Assess and perform basic life support
> as needed
> ↓
> **D**—Definitive management
> ↓
> Activate emergency medical service
> ↓
> Administer epinephrine (IM, IV)
> ↓
> Maintenance of airway
> (head tilt–chin lift; oropharyngeal or
> nasopharyngeal airways)
> ↓
> Administer O₂
> ↓
> Additional drug management:
> histamine-blocker, corticosteroid (IM, IV)
> ↓
> Cricothyrotomy as needed

A, airway; **B,** breathing; **C,** circulation; **D,** definitive care;
IM, intramuscular; IV, intravenous; **P,** position; SC, subcutaneous.

a degree. The patient will require hospitalization after stabilization and transfer from the dental office by the paramedics.

Box 24-9 outlines the steps in the management of laryngeal edema.

- **Drugs used in management:** Oxygen, epinephrine (IV, IM), histamine-blocker (IM), and a corticosteroid (IV, IM).
- **Medical assistance required:** Assistance is required.

Epinephrine and allergy

Epinephrine is the most important drug in the initial management of all immediate allergic reactions involving either the respiratory or cardiovascular system. Its actions effectively counteract those of histamine and the other chemical mediators of allergy. Although histamine-blockers reverse several allergic symptoms, especially edema and itch, they are of little value with others

such as bronchospasm and hypotension. Epinephrine possesses properties to reverse all of these actions and has a more rapid onset of action than do histamine-blockers. The actions of epinephrine are classified as β-adrenergic and α-adrenergic agonist effects. The β-adrenergic effects of epinephrine mimic those produced by efferent sympathetic (adrenergic) nerve activity on the heart (β_1) and lungs (β_2), whereas β-adrenergic properties mimic those of the sympathetic nerves on the peripheral vasculature. Useful β-adrenergic actions of epinephrine include bronchodilation, increased myocardial contractility, increased heart rate, and constriction of arterioles with a redistribution of blood to the systemic circulation. Useful β-adrenergic actions include cutaneous, mucosal, and splanchnic vasoconstriction, with a total increase in systemic vascular resistance. This action, in addition to the β_1-adrenergic actions (e.g., increased heart rate and myocardial contractility), leads to increased cardiac output. Increased cardiac output, along with the increased systemic vascular resistance, produces an increased systemic blood pressure. Epinephrine also reverses rhinitis and urticaria.

Although epinephrine is rapid acting because of its rapid biotransformation, it is also a relatively short-acting drug. Therefore, whenever epinephrine is used in an emergency situation, the patient should be observed for a long enough period to ensure that symptoms of allergy do not recur. In addition, care must be taken when considering the readministration of epinephrine. Epinephrine produces dramatic increases in heart rate and blood pressure (epinephrine injection has produced cerebrovascular hemorrhage) and increases the risk of developing dysrhythmias.[94] Before readministering epinephrine (0.3 mL of 1:1000 in adults, 0.15 mL in children, 0.0075 mL in infants), the cardiovascular status of the patient must be evaluated and the risk of readministration carefully weighed against its benefits.

Epinephrine is relatively contraindicated in elderly patients and in those with known coronary artery disease and hypertension, and it must be avoided in those patients with life-threatening tachydysrhythmias.[11] In these situations it may be prudent to delay the (re)administration of epinephrine and to administer a histamine-blocker and/or corticosteroid (whichever is appropriate) in its place. However, in the presence of continued deterioration of the patient, epinephrine must be (re)administered.

The route of epinephrine administration depends on the severity of the clinical situation. Epinephrine may be given through the subcutaneous (SC) route when the reaction is mild and the patient normotensive. However, when generalized urticaria or hypotension exists, SC absorption may be variable and slow; IM administration is preferred.[11] Whenever possible, the IV route should be used in more acute and life-threatening allergic reactions. It is important to remember that epinephrine 1:1000 is not meant for IV administration.[94] One milliliter should always be diluted with 9 mL of diluent to produce a 1:10,000 concentration, which is administered intravenously at a rate of 1 mL (0.1 mg) per minute.

Generalized anaphylaxis

In generalized anaphylaxis a wide range of clinical manifestations may develop; however, the cardiovascular system is involved in virtually all systemic allergic reactions. In rapidly progressing anaphylaxis, cardiovascular collapse may occur within minutes of the onset of symptoms. Immediate and aggressive management of this situation is imperative if the victim is to have a chance of survival. In the dental office this reaction is most likely to occur during or immediately after the administration of penicillin or aspirin to a previously sensitized patient. A more remote, although increasingly possible, cause might be latex sensitivity.[3–5,18]

Two other life-threatening situations may develop during the injection of a local anesthetic that might on occasion mimic anaphylaxis: vasodepressor syncope and a local anesthetic overdose. In the immediate management of this situation, there must be an attempt to diagnose the actual cause of the problem.

Epinephrine and oxygen are the most important therapeutic agents administered in anaphylaxis. Epinephrine is the drug of choice, and the appropriate dose should be administered promptly at the onset of apparent anaphylaxis.[64] Respiratory compromise and cardiovascular collapse cause the most concern because they are the most frequent causes of death from anaphylaxis.[95]

Signs of allergy present

Should any clinical signs, such as urticaria, erythema, pruritus, or wheezing, be noted before or after the patient's collapse, the diagnosis is obvious—allergy—and management proceeds accordingly.

Step 1: termination of the dental procedure and activation of dental office emergency team.

Step 2: P (position).
Place the unconscious, or conscious but hypotensive, patient into a supine position with the legs elevated slightly.

Step 3: A-B-C (airway, breathing, circulation) or BLS, as needed.
Maintain the airway via head tilt–chin lift, and carry out the steps of BLS as needed.

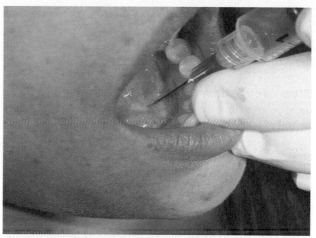

FIGURE 24-4 Sublingual epinephrine injection.

Step 4: D (definitive care):
Step 4a: summoning of medical assistance.
As soon as systemic allergy is considered a possibility, summon emergency medical care.

Step 4b: administration of epinephrine.
Administer epinephrine from the emergency kit (0.3 mL of 1:1000 for adults, 0.15 mL for children, 0.075 mL for infants) via the IM route as quickly as possible. Because of the immediate need for epinephrine, a preloaded syringe of epinephrine is recommended for the emergency kit. Epinephrine is the only injectable drug that needs to be kept in a preloaded form, which minimizes confusion when looking for it in this near-panic situation.

The site for IM injection should be based on muscle perfusion in the presence of what is likely to be profound hypotension. With decreased perfusion, the absorption of epinephrine from a muscle will be delayed. It is recommended that consideration be given to the administration of epinephrine in this situation into the body of the tongue (intralingual) or the floor of the mouth (sublingual) (Figure 24-4). The needle may enter from either an extraoral or an intraoral puncture site. The vascularity of the oral cavity, even in the presence of hypotension, will provide a more rapid onset of activity than that seen in the more traditional IM sites (mid-deltoid, vastus lateralis).

Epinephrine, in one or more doses, usually produces clinical improvement in the patient. Respiratory and cardiovascular signs and symptoms should decrease in severity; breath sounds improve as bronchospasm decreases and blood pressure increases.

Should the clinical picture fail to improve or continue to deteriorate (i.e., increasing severity of symptoms) within 5 minutes of the initial epinephrine dose, a second dose is administered. Subsequent doses may be administered as needed every 5 to 10 minutes, if the potential risk of epinephrine administration (e.g., excessive cardiovascular stimulation) is kept in mind and the patient is adequately monitored.

Step 4c: administration of oxygen. Deliver oxygen at a flow of 5 to 6 L per minute via nasal hood or full face mask at any time during the episode.

Step 4d: monitoring of vital signs. Continuously monitor the patient's cardiovascular and respiratory status. Record blood pressure and heart rate (at the carotid artery) at least every 5 minutes, and start chest compressions if cardiac arrest occurs. During this acute, life-threatening phase of what is obviously an anaphylactic reaction, management consists of BLS, the administration of oxygen and epinephrine, activation of EMS, and continual monitoring of vital signs. Until the patient's status improves, no additional drug therapy is indicated.

Step 4e: additional drug therapy. Once clinical improvement is noted (e.g., increased blood pressure, decreased bronchospasm, return of consciousness), additional drug therapy is required. This includes the administration of a histamine-blocker and corticosteroid (both drugs delivered through the IM or, when possible, IV route). They function to prevent a recurrence of symptoms and to obviate the need for further administration of epinephrine. They are not administered during the acute phase of the reaction because they are too slow in onset and they do not do enough immediate good to justify their use while the victim's life remains in danger. Epinephrine and oxygen are the only drugs to administer during the life-threatening phase of the anaphylactic reaction.

Throughout this text it has been stressed that definitive treatment of emergencies with drugs is of secondary importance to the **P-A-B-Cs** of basic life support. Drugs need not be administered in all emergency situations. Anaphylaxis is the exception. Once a diagnosis of acute, generalized anaphylaxis has been made, it is imperative that drug therapy (i.e., epinephrine) be initiated as soon as possible after the start of BLS. Review of clinical reports demonstrates the effectiveness of immediate drug therapy in anaphylaxis. Recovery from anaphylaxis is related to the rapidity with which effective treatment is instituted. Delay in treatment increases the mortality rate. Eighty-seven percent of those experiencing anaphylaxis provoked by bee stings survived if treated within the first hour, but only 67% of dying patients were treated in this first hour.[96]

On arrival in the office, emergency personnel will establish intravenous access, administer appropriate

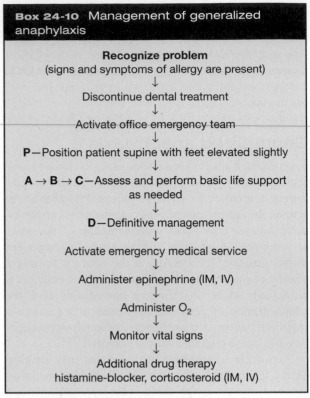

Box 24-10 Management of generalized anaphylaxis

Recognize problem
(signs and symptoms of allergy are present)
↓
Discontinue dental treatment
↓
Activate office emergency team
↓
P—Position patient supine with feet elevated slightly
↓
A → B → C—Assess and perform basic life support as needed
↓
D—Definitive management
↓
Activate emergency medical service
↓
Administer epinephrine (IM, IV)
↓
Administer O₂
↓
Monitor vital signs
↓
Additional drug therapy
histamine-blocker, corticosteroid (IM, IV)

A, airway; **B**, breathing; **C**, circulation; **D**, definitive care; IM, intramuscular; IV, intravenous; **P**, position.

drugs (histamine-blocker, corticosteroid), stabilize the victim, and transport him or her to the hospital emergency department for definitive care.

Box 24-10 outlines the steps to take to manage generalized anaphylaxis.

- **Drugs used in management:** Oxygen, epinephrine (IV, IM, or sublingually), a histamine blocker (IM), and a corticosteroid (IV, IM).
- **Medical assistance required:** Emergency medical assistance is required.

No clinical signs of allergy present

A second clinical picture of anaphylaxis might well be one in which the patient receiving a potential allergen loses consciousness without any obvious signs of allergy being observed.[89,98] This clinical picture is disturbing because in the absence of any obvious clinical signs and symptoms of allergy, drug management of anaphylaxis is not indicated.

Step 1: termination of the dental procedure and activation of dental office emergency team.

Step 2: P (position). Management of this situation, which might prove to result from any of a number

of causes, requires immediate positioning of the patient supine with the legs elevated slightly.

Step 3: A-B-C or BLS, as needed.

Victims of vasodepressor syncope or postural hypotension rapidly recover consciousness once properly positioned with airway patency ensured. Patients who do not recover at this point should continue to have the appropriate elements of BLS applied (breathing, circulation).

Step 4: D (definitive care):

Step 4a: summoning of emergency medical assistance. If consciousness does not return promptly after BLS, seek emergency medical assistance immediately.

Step 4b: administration of oxygen.

Step 4c: monitoring of vital signs. Monitor blood pressure, heart rate and rhythm, and respiration at least every 5 minutes, and start the elements of BLS at any time they are required.

Step 4d: definitive management. On arrival, emergency medical personnel will seek to diagnose the cause of the loss of consciousness. If a diagnosis is forthcoming, appropriate drug therapy will be started and the patient will be stabilized and transferred to a local hospital emergency department.

Absent any definitive signs and symptoms of allergy, such as edema, urticaria, or bronchospasm, epinephrine and other drug therapies are usually not indicated. Any of a number of other situations may be the cause of the unconsciousness, for example, drug overdose, hypoglycemia, cerebrovascular accident, acute adrenal insufficiency, myocardial infarction, or cardiopulmonary arrest.

Continued application of BLS until medical assistance arrives is the most prudent management of this situation.

Box 24-11 outlines the steps to take to manage generalized anaphylaxis without obvious signs of allergy being present.

- **Drugs used in management:** Oxygen.
- **Medical assistance required:** Emergency medical assistance is required.

Laryngeal edema

Laryngeal edema is yet another possible development during the generalized anaphylactic reaction. Should a patent airway be difficult to maintain despite adequate head tilt and a clear pharynx (obtained by suctioning), it may become necessary to perform cricothyrotomy.

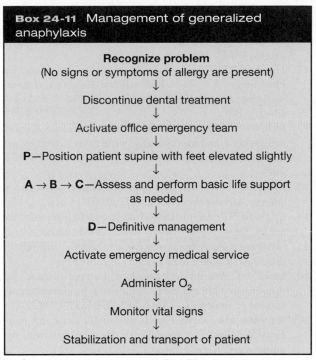

Box 24-11 Management of generalized anaphylaxis

Recognize problem
(No signs or symptoms of allergy are present)
↓
Discontinue dental treatment
↓
Activate office emergency team
↓
P—Position patient supine with feet elevated slightly
↓
A → B → C—Assess and perform basic life support as needed
↓
D—Definitive management
↓
Activate emergency medical service
↓
Administer O₂
↓
Monitor vital signs
↓
Stabilization and transport of patient

A, airway; *B,* breathing; *C,* circulation; *D,* definitive care; *P,* position.

Laryngeal edema is a very serious manifestation of allergy. Once airway patency has been ensured by cricothyrotomy, epinephrine may be administered (0.3 mL of 1:1000 solution IM), followed by administration of a histamine-blocker and corticosteroid, as described earlier. Once stabilized, the patient will be transferred to a hospital for definitive management and observation.

REFERENCES

1. *Mosby's dictionary of medicine, nursing & health professions,* ed 7, St. Louis, Mosby, 2006.
2. Lachmann PJ, editor: *Clinical aspects of immunology,* ed 5, Boston, Blackwell Scientific, 1993.
3. Chen MD, Greenspoon JS, Long TL: Latex anaphylaxis in an obstetrics and gynecology physician, *Am J Obstet Gynecol* 166:968–969, 1992.
4. Alenius H, Kurup V, Kelly K, et al.: Latex allergy: frequent occurrence of IgE antibodies to a cluster of 11 latex proteins in patients with spina bifida and histories of anaphylaxis, *J Lab Clin Med* 123:712–720, 1994.
5. Leynadier F, Dry J: Allergy to latex, *Clin Rev Allergy* 9:371–377, 1991.
6. Caranasos GJ: Drug reactions. In: Schwartz GR, editor: *Principles and practice of emergency medicine,* ed 4, Baltimore, Williams & Wilkins, 1999.
7. Portier P, Richet C: De l'action anaphylactique des certain venins, *CR Soc Biol (Paris)* 54:170–172, 1902.
8. Buisseret PD: Allergy, *Sci Am* 247:86–95, 1982.
9. Pascoe DJ: Anaphylaxis. In: Pascoe DJ, Grossman J,

editors: *Quick reference to pediatric emergencies,* ed 3, Philadelphia, JB Lippincott, 1984.

10. Anderson JA: Allergic reactions to drugs and biologic agents, *JAMA* 268:2844–2857, 1992.
11. Lindzon RD, Silvers WS: Anaphylaxis. In: Marx JA, Hockberger RS, Walls RM, editors: *Rosen's emergency medicine: concepts and clinical practice,* ed 5, St. Louis, Mosby, 2002.
12. Sicherer SH, Leung DY: Advances in allergic skin disease, anaphylaxis, and hypersensitivity reactions to food, drugs, and insect stings, *J Allergy Clin Immunol* 114:118–124, 2004.
13. Hoffman DR: Fatal reactions to hymenoptera stings, *Allergy Asthma Proc* 24:123–127, 2003.
14. Cochran ST: Anaphylactoid reactions to radiocontrast media, *Curr Allergy Asthma Rep* 5:28–31, 2005.
15. Settipane GA: Adverse reactions to aspirin and related drugs, *Arch Intern Med* 141:328–332, 1981.
16. Smith VT: Anaphylactic shock, acute renal failure, and disseminated intravascular coagulation: suspected complications of zomepirac, *JAMA* 247:1172–1173, 1982.
17. Sampson HA, Mendelson L, Rosen JP: Fatal and near-fatal anaphylactic reactions to food in children and adolescents, *N Engl J Med* 327:380–384, 1992.
18. Simms J: Latex allergy alert, *Can Nurse* 91:27–30, 1995.
19. Waldbott GL: Anaphylactic death from penicillin, *JAMA* 139:526–527, 1949.
20. Shepherd GM: Hypersensitivity reactions to drugs: evaluation and management, *Mt Sinai J Med* 70:113–125, 2003.
21. Bennett AT, Collins KA: An unusual case of anaphylaxis. Mold in pancake mix, *Am J Forensic Med Pathol* 22: 292–295, 2001.
22. Spark RP: Fatal anaphylaxis to oral penicillin, *Am J Clin Pathol* 56:407–411, 1971.
23. Fonacier L, Hirschberg R, Gerson S: Adverse drug reactions to a cephalosporins in hospitalized patients with a history of penicillin allergy, *Allergy Asthma Proc* 26:135–141, 2005.
24. Stevenson DD: Aspirin and NSAID sensitivity, *Immunol Allergy Clin North Am* 24:491–505, 2004.
25. Berkes EA: Anaphylactic and anaphylactoid reactions to aspirin and other NSAIDs, *Clin Rev Allergy Immunol* 24:137–148, 2003.
26. Grattan CE: Aspirin sensitivity and urticaria, *Clin Exp Dermatol* 28:123–127, 2003.
27. Namazy JA, Simon RA: Sensitivity to nonsteroidal anti-inflammatory drugs, *Ann Allergy Asthma Immunol* 89:542–650, 2002.
28. Ross JE: Naproxen-induced anaphylaxis: a case report, *Am J Forensic Med Pathol* 15:180–181, 1994.
29. Simon RA, Namazy J: Adverse reactions to aspirin and nonsteroidal antiinflammatory drugs (NSAIDs), *Clin Rev Allergy Immunol* 24:239–252, 2003.
30. Wasserman SI: Anaphylaxis. In: Middleton E, Ellis FF, Reed CE, editors: *Allergy: principles and practice,* ed 5, St. Louis, Mosby, 1998.
31. Chiu AM, Kelly KJ: Anaphylaxis: drug allergy, insect stings, and latex, *Immunol Allergy Clin North Am* 25:389–405, 2005.
32. Aldrete JA, Johnson DA: Allergy to local anesthetics, *JAMA* 207:356–357, 1969.
33. Baluga JC: Allergy to local anesthetics in dentistry. Myth or reality? *Rev Alerg Mex* 50:176–181, 2003.
34. Berkun Y, Ben-Zvi A, Levy Y, et al.: Evaluation of adverse reactions to local anesthetics: experience with 236 patients, *Ann Allergy Asthma Immunol* 91:342–345, 2003.
35. Ogunsalu CO: Anaphylactic reaction following administration of lignocaine hydrochloride infiltration: case report, *Aust Dent J* 43:170–171, 1998.
36. Ismail K, Simpson PJ: Anaphylactic shock following intravenous administration of lignocaine, *Acta Anaesthesiol Scand* 41:1071–1072 1997.
37. Seng GF, Kraus K, Cartwright G, et al.: Confirmed allergic reactions to amide local anesthetics, *Gen Dent* 44:52–54, 1996.
38. Malanin K, Kalimo K: Hypersensitivity to the local anesthetic articaine hydrochloride, *Anesth Prog* 42:144–145, 1995.
39. Jackson D, Chen AH, Bennett CR: Identifying true lidocaine allergy, *J Am Dent Assoc* 125:1362–1366, 1994.
40. Aldrete JA, Johnson DA: Evaluation of intracutaneous testing for investigation of allergy to local anesthetic agents, *Anesth Analg* 49:173–183, 1970.
41. Vandenbossche LE, Hop WC, de Jongste JC: Bronchial responsiveness to inhaled metabisulfite in asthmatic children increases with age, *Pediatr Pulmonol* 16:236–242, 1993.
42. Stevenson DD, Simon RA: Sensitivity to ingested metabisulfites in asthmatic subjects, *J Allergy Clin Immunol* 68:26–32, 1981.
43. Sher TH, Schwartz HJ: Bisulfite sensitivity manifesting as an allergic reaction to aerosol therapy, *Ann Allergy* 54:224–226, 1985.
44. Borghesan F, Basso D, Chieco Bianchi F, et al.: Allergy to wine, *Allergy* 59:1135–1136, 2004.
45. Twarog FJ, Leung DYM: Anaphylaxis to a component of isoetharine (sodium bisulfite), *JAMA* 248:2030–2031, 1982.
46. Haas DA: An update on local anesthetics in dentistry, *J Can Dent Assoc* 68:546–551, 2002.
47. Sogn DD, Evans R 3rd, Shepherd GM, et al.: Results of the National Institute of Allergy and Infectious Diseases Collaborative Clinical Trial to test the predictive value of skin testing with major and minor penicillin derivatives in hospitalized adults, *Arch Intern Med* 152:1025–1032, 1992.
48. Kamada MM, Twarog F, Leung DY: Multiple antibiotic sensitivity in a pediatric population, *Allergy Proceed* 12:347–350, 1991.
49. Perusse R, Goulet JP, Turcotte JY: Contraindications to vasoconstrictors in dentistry: Part II. Hyperthyroidism, diabetes, sulfite sensitivity, cortico-dependent asthma, and pheochromocytoma, *Oral Surg Oral Med Oral Pathol* 74:687–691, 1992.
50. Schwartz HJ, Gilbert IA, Lenner KA, et al.: Metabisulfite sensitivity and local dental anesthesia, *Ann Allergy* 62: 83–86, 1989.

51. Schwartz HJ, Sher TH: Bisulfite sensitivity manifesting as allergy to local dental anesthesia, *J Allergy Clin Immunol* 75:525–527, 1985.

52. Shojaei AR, Haas DA: Local anesthetic cartridges and latex allergy: a literature review, *J Can Dent Assoc* 68: 622–626, 2002.

53. Septodontic. www.septodontinc.com/site.html

54. Dajani AS, Taubert KA, Wilson W, et al.: Prevention of bacterial endocarditis. Recommendations by the American Heart Association, *JAMA* 277:1794–1801, 1997.

55. Sorensen HT, Nielsen B, Ostergaard Nielsen J: Anaphylactic shock occurring outside hospitals, *Allergy* 44: 288–290, 1989.

56. Malamed SF: Diphenhydramine hydrochloride; its use as a local anesthetic in dentistry, *Anesth Prog* 20:76–82, 1973.

57. Uckan S, Guler N, Sumer M, Ungor M: Local anesthetic efficacy for oral surgery. Comparison of diphenhydramine and prilocaine, *Oral Surg Oral Med Oral Pathol Oral Radiol Endod* 86:26–30, 1998.

58. Ernst AA, Marvez-Valls E, Mall G, et al.: 1% lidocaine versus 0.5% diphenhydramine for local anesthesia in minor laceration repair, *Ann Emerg Med* 23:1328–1332, 1994.

59. Benadryl, package insert, Morris Plains, New Jersey, Parke-Davis, 1990.

60. Ewan PW: Anaphylaxis, *BMJ* 316: 1442–1445, 1998.

61. Brazil E, MacNamara AF: Not so immediate hypersensitivity—the danger of biphasic allergic reactions, *J Accid Emerg Med* 15:252–253, 1998.

62. Lipozencic J, Wolf R: Life-threatening severe allergic reactions: urticaria, angioedema, and anaphylaxis, *Clin Dermatol* 23:193–205, 2005.

63. Kim JS, Pongracic JA: Hereditary and acquired angioedema, *Allergy Asthma Proc* 25:S47–S49, 2004.

64. Lieberman P, Kemp SF, Oppenheimer J, et al.: The diagnosis and management of anaphylaxis: an updated practice parameter, *J Allergy Clin Immunol* 115:S483–S523, 2005.

65. Gavalas M, Sadana A, Metcalf S: Guidelines for the management of anaphylaxis in the emergency department, *J Accid Emerg Med* 15:96–98, 1998.

66. Demoly P, Gomes ER: Drug hypersensitivities: definition, epidemiology and risk factors, *Allerg Immunol (Paris)* 37:202–206, 2005.

67. Katz WA, Kaye D: Immunologic principles. In: Rose LF, Kaye D, editors: *Internal medicine for dentistry*, ed 2, St. Louis, Mosby, 1990.

68. Ishizaka K, Tomioka H, Ishizaka T: Mechanisms of passive sensitization. I. Presence of IgE and IgG molecules on human leukocytes, *J Immunol* 105:1459–1467, 1970.

69. Ishizaka T, Soto CS, Ishizaka K: Mechanisms of passive sensitization. III. Number of IgE molecules and their receptor sites on human basophil granulocytes, *J Immunol* 111:500–511, 1973.

70. Sullivan TJ, Kulcyzcki A Jr: Immediate hypersensitivity responses. In: Parker CW, editor: *Clinical immunology*, vol 1, Philadelphia, WB Saunders, 1980, pp. 115–142.

71. Ishizaka T, Ishizaka K, Tomioka H: Release of histamine and slow reacting substance of anaphylaxis (SRS-A) by IgE-anti-IgE reactions on monkey mast cells, *J Immunol* 108:513–534, 1972.

72. Kaliner M, Austen KF: A sequence of biochemical events in the antigen-induced release of chemical mediator from sensitized human lung tissue, *J Exp Med* 138:1077–1094, 1973.

73. Wasserman SI: Mediators of immediate hypersensitivity, *J Allergy Clin Immunol* 72:101–109, 1983.

74. Piper PJ: Mediators of anaphylactic hypersensitivity. In: Brent L, Holborow J, editors: *Progress in immunology II*, vol 4, London, North-Holland, 1974.

75. Church MK, Shute JK, Sampson AP: Mast cell-derived mediators. In: Adkinson NF Jr, Yunginger JW, Busse WW et al., editors: *Middleton's allergy: principles and practice*, ed 6, St. Louis, Mosby, 2003, pp. 186–209.

76. Beaven MA: Histamine, the classic histamine-blockers (H_1 inhibitors), *N Engl J Med* 294:320–325, 1976.

77. Samuelsson B: Leukotrienes: mediators of allergic reactions and inflammation, *Int Arch Allergy Appl Immunol* 66:98–106, 1981.

78. Israel E, Drazen JM: Leukotrienes and asthma: a basic review, *Curr Concepts Aller Clin Immunol* 14:11–16, 1983.

79. Levi R, Burke JA: Cardiac anaphylaxis: SRS-A potentiates and extends the effects of released histamine, *Eur J Pharmacol* 62:41–49, 1980.

80. Goetzl EJ, Austen KF: Purification and synthesis of eosinophilotactic tetrapeptides of human lung tissue: identification as eosinophil chemotactic factor of anaphylaxis, *Proc Natl Acad Sci USA* 72:4123–4127, 1975.

81. Nagy L, Lee TH, Kay AB: Neutrophil chemotactic activity in antigen-induced late asthmatic reactions, *N Engl J Med* 306:497–501, 1982.

82. Newball HH, Berninger RW, Talamo RC, Lichtenstein LM: Anaphylactic release of a basophil kallikrein-like activity. I. Purification and characterization, *J Clin Invest* 64:457–465, 1979.

83. Schulman ES, Newball HH, Demers LM, et al.: Anaphylactic release of thromboxane A_2, prostaglandin D_2, and prostacyclin from human lung parenchyma, *Am Rev Respir Dis* 124:402–406, 1981.

84. Wanderer AA, Grandel KE, Wasserman SI, Farr RS: Clinical characteristics of cold-induced systemic reactions in acquired cold urticaria syndromes: recommendations for prevention of this complication and a proposal for a diagnostic classification of cold urticaria, *J Allergy Clin Immunol* 78:417–423, 1986.

85. Hanahan DJ, Demopoulos CA, Liehr J, Pinckard RN: Identification of platelet activating factor isolated from rabbit basophils as acetyl glyceryl ether phosphorylcholine, *J Biol Chem* 255:5514–5516, 1980.

86. Pinkard RN, Halonen M, Palmer JD, et al.: Intravascular aggregation and pulmonary sequestration of platelets during IgE-induced systemic anaphylaxis in the rabbit: abrogation of lethal anaphylactic shock by platelet depletion, *J Immunol* 119:2185–2193, 1977.

87. Orange RP, Donsky GJ: Anaphylaxis. In: Adkinson NF, Middleton E, editors: *Middleton's allergy: principles and practice*, ed 6, St. Louis, Mosby, 2003.

88. Matasar MJ, Neugut AI: Epidemiology of anaphylaxis in the United States, *Curr Allergy Asthma Rep* 3:30–35, 2003.

89. Muelleman RL, Tran TP: Allergy, hypersensitivity, and anaphylaxis. In: Marx JA, Hockberger RS, Walls RM, editors: *Rosen's emergency medicine: concepts and clinical practice*, ed 5, St. Louis, Mosby, 2002, pp. 1619–1634.

90. Tang AW: A practical guide to anaphylaxis, *Am Fam Physician* 68:1325–1332, 2003.

91. Pollakoff J, Pollakoff K: *EMT's guide to signs and symptoms*, Los Angeles, Jeff Gould, 1991.

92. Higgins JC: The "crashing astimatic," *Am Fam Physician* 69:1045–1046, 2004.

93. Morris HG: Pharmacology of corticosteroids in asthma. In: Middleton E, Ellis FF, Reed CE, editors: *Allergy: principles and practice*, ed 5, St. Louis, Mosby, 1998.

94. Jacobsen G: Stung postman gets $2.6m for wrong help, *Sydney Morning Herald*, February 1, 2005.

95. Kemp SF, Lockey RF: Anaphylaxis: a review of causes and mechanisms, *J Allergy Clin Immunol* 110:341–348, 2002.

96. Peters GA, Karnes WE, Bastron JA: Near fatal and fatal reactions to insect sting, *Ann Allergy* 41:268–273, 1978.

97. Hanashiro PK, Weil MH: Anaphylactic shock in man: report of two cases with detailed hemodynamic and metabolic studies, *Arch Intern Med* 119:129–140, 1967.

Drug-Related Emergencies:

Differential Diagnosis

Drugs are never used without risk. In this section, potentially life-threatening systemic adverse drug reactions (ADRs) were discussed. These reactions are compared here to better enable the clinician to rapidly diagnose the precise cause of the reaction and initiate appropriate therapy. Included in the differential diagnosis is vasodepressor syncope because it is a common "drug-related" reaction.

■ MEDICAL HISTORY

Medical history is of significance in the prevention of ADRs. Thorough evaluation of a patient's prior response to drugs is a major factor in prevention of these reactions. *Allergy* must be documented; however, the drug or drugs provoking the reaction must be avoided until the patient undergoes definitive evaluation. When documented allergy exists, alternative drugs must be used. History of drug exposure without adverse response does not, however, preclude the occurrence of allergy with a subsequent exposure.

Drug overdose (toxic reaction) is more difficult to evaluate from the medical history. Patients (and sometimes their health care providers) commonly refer to all ADRs as "allergy." Only a thorough dialogue history and knowledge of the pharmacology of the drug in question can lead to a diagnosis of prior overdose reaction.

Vasodepressor syncope is commonly associated with parenteral drug administration, particularly local anesthetics. A history of "blacking out" whenever an injection is administered should lead the doctor to suspect vasodepressor syncope and take measures to prevent its recurrence.

■ AGE

Allergy and overdose may occur at any age. Children appear to have a greater potential to develop allergy than do adults; however, many children outgrow their childhood allergies, especially food allergies. Interestingly, over 90% of deaths from anaphylaxis occur in patients older than 19 years of age.[1,2]

Drug overdose may also develop in any patient, but patients on either end of the age spectrum, children and the elderly, represent a greater risk, especially with central nervous system (CNS)–depressant drugs such as sedative-hypnotics, opioid agonist analgesics, and local anesthetics. Adult dosages of these drugs should not be administered to children.

Vasodepressor syncope, on the other hand, is only rarely observed in younger patients or in patients over the age of 40 years. It is an axiom that "healthy children do not faint." They act like children, not keeping their fears inside, but loudly and visibly expressing them. The age span from late teens to late thirties, primarily in males, represents the high occurrence category for vasodepressor syncope.

■ SEX

Drug overdose and allergy do not occur with greater frequency in either sex. However, vasodepressor syncope is much more common in males. The most likely candidate for vasodepressor syncope is a male under the age of 35 years.

■ POSITION

The patient's position at the time clinical signs and symptoms appear is relevant primarily during the administration of local anesthetics. Position has no bearing on the development of allergy or overdose. Both may develop with the patient in any position. Vasodepressor syncope, however, is rarely observed if local anesthetics are administered with the patient supine. Injection of local anesthetics into a patient seated upright is much more likely to lead to vasodepressor syncope.

Positioning of the patient once clinical symptoms develop also aids in diagnosis of the reaction if loss of consciousness develops. Placing the unconscious patient into a supine position leads to rapid improvement in the case of vasodepressor syncope (assuming the airway is patent) but produces no significant improvement in the patient suffering from drug overdose or allergy.

■ ONSET OF SIGNS AND SYMPTOMS

Vasodepressor syncope, drug overdose, and allergy may develop immediately after drug administration, or they may develop more slowly. Vasodepressor syncope most often occurs immediately prior to the actual administration of a drug (it is most often a response to the "needle"), but may also develop during or after its administration. Loss of consciousness (syncope) occurring *just before* drug administration is caused neither by allergy nor overdose; it is most often related to fear. Clinical symptoms developing *during* drug administration may be related to any of these reactions; however, in this situation the dose of drug administered is of great importance (see text that follows). Signs and symptoms that appear *after* drug administration most likely represent drug overdose or allergy. Vasodepressor syncope may also occur at this time, but in this situation the acute precipitating factor is most probably related to a different stimulus, such as the sight of blood or of dental instruments.

■ PRIOR EXPOSURE TO DRUG

Prior exposure to a specific drug or to a closely related drug is essential for allergy to occur.

Vasodepressor syncope is not truly a drug-related situation except in the sense that the psychological aspect of receiving a drug may precipitate the reaction. (The injection of sterile water might just as readily precipitate vasodepressor syncope as a local anesthetic in the fearful patient. The main factor in the reaction is the injection.)

Prior exposure to a drug is not relevant in drug overdose. It may occur with the first exposure to the drug or at any subsequent exposure.

■ DOSE OF DRUG ADMINISTERED

The occurrence of vasodepressor syncope is unrelated to the dose of drug administered, whereas drug overdose is, in most instances, related to the quantity of drug administered. Overdose represents an extension of the normal pharmacologic actions of a drug beyond its desired therapeutic effect and is related to elevated blood levels of the drug in its specific target organs. Relative overdose may develop in patients for whom a normal therapeutic dose produces adverse effects (hyperresponders), illustrating the phenomenon of biological variability as represented by the normal distribution curve.

Allergy is not normally related to the absolute dosage of drug administered. Allergy testing using 0.1 mL of an agent may produce fatal systemic anaphylaxis in a previously sensitized patient.

■ OVERALL INCIDENCE OF OCCURRENCE

Vasodepressor syncope is the most commonly occurring adverse reaction in dental offices. Of "true" adverse drug reactions, minor side effects (nonlethal, undesirable drug actions that develop at therapeutic levels, e.g., nausea or sedation) are encountered most frequently. Drug overdose represents the most common of the potentially life-threatening situations that occur, whereas only 15% of ADRs are truly allergic in nature.[3]

■ SIGNS AND SYMPTOMS

Duration of reaction

Overdose reactions to local anesthetics are normally self-limiting, if managed effectively. Rapid intravascular injection of one dental cartridge of local anesthetic may lead to acute clinical symptoms (e.g., seizures) for 1 to 2 minutes before the drugs blood level falls below

overdose levels (provided airway patency and oxygenation are maintained). Epinephrine overdose is of short duration because of the rapid biotransformation of epinephrine into inactive forms.

Vasodepressor syncope is commonly self-limiting once the victim is placed into a supine position.

Allergy, on the other hand, may persist for extended periods. As long as any of the chemical mediators, released in response to the allergen, remain in the patient's body, signs and symptoms of allergy may continue. It is not uncommon for allergic reactions to persist for hours or days despite aggressive treatment.

Changes in appearance of skin

Allergy most often presents as a skin reaction. One of its clinical signs, flushing (i.e., erythema) may occur in other emergency situations as well; however, when flushing is accompanied by urticaria, pruritus (itching), or both, a clinical diagnosis of allergy is appropriate.

Epinephrine overdose may also produce erythema, yet other clinical signs allow for the ready differentiation of this reaction from allergy. Signs of epinephrine overdose include intense headache, tremor, increased anxiety, tachycardia, and significantly elevated blood pressure.

Pallor and cold, clammy skin are observed in vasodepressor syncope and possibly in *local anesthetic overdose* as hypotension develops. Pallor may also be noted in epinephrine overdose. Edema is noted only in allergic reactions.

Appearance of nervousness

An increase in outward nervousness, described as fear, apprehension, or agitation, after completion of the injection may be observed in both local anesthetic and epinephrine overdose. The patient with vasodepressor syncope may appear nervous before and during the administration of the drug, but does not usually become progressively more nervous during the postinjection period. This patient's major reported symptom is one of "feeling bad" or "feeling faint." Allergic patients do not develop marked nervousness; most of these patients simply complain of "feeling terrible."

Loss of consciousness

Local anesthetic overdose, *acute systemic anaphylaxis*, and vasodepressor syncope may all lead to the loss of consciousness. All may also produce milder reactions that do not evolve to this degree.

Epinephrine overdose seldom produces unconsciousness unless serious cardiovascular complications develop (cerebrovascular accident, cardiac arrest).

Presence of seizures

Local anesthetic overdose is most likely to produce generalized tonic-clonic seizures, whereas milder convulsive movement (e.g., individual muscles such as a finger or facial muscle twitching) may occur in vasodepressor syncope. A mild, generalized tremor of the extremities is normally observed in epinephrine overdose. Seizures do not usually occur with allergy in the absence of hypoxia.

Respiratory symptoms

Dyspnea, or difficulty in breathing, may be present in any of these situations. Respiratory symptoms are most marked in allergy. Wheezing, a product of bronchial smooth-muscle constriction, leads to a presumptive diagnosis of asthma or allergy. Because management of both of these clinical entities is identical, precise diagnosis is not immediately required.

Stridor, a high-pitched crowing sound, should lead the doctor to consider laryngeal obstruction. This may be produced by a foreign object in the posterior pharynx or by laryngeal edema resulting from allergy. In the absence of other signs of allergy, such as a skin reaction, the airway should be suctioned to remove any foreign material before further management is considered.

Total airway obstruction is most often produced by the tongue in an unconscious patient. If, following airway maneuvers (head tilt–chin lift) and suctioning, the obstruction persists, lower airway obstruction should be considered. Regardless of the cause (e.g., edema or foreign object), a patent airway must be established rapidly through the abdominal thrust (Heimlich maneuver) or cricothyrotomy.

■ VITAL SIGNS
Heart rate

The heart rate increases during the presyncopal phase of vasodepressor syncope, but decreases dramatically to approximately 40 beats per minute with the loss of consciousness, remaining low throughout the postsyncopal period.

Local anesthetic overdose and allergy are also associated with increased heart rate; however, unlike vasodepressor syncope, bradycardia does not occur when consciousness is lost. A shock reaction develops that is characterized by rapid heart rate (tachycardia) and low blood pressure (hypotension), producing a pulse that is described as "weak and thready."

Epinephrine overdose, on the other hand, produces a dramatic increase in heart rate *and* blood pressure, leading to a "full and bounding" pulse. In addition, the heart rate may become irregular during the epinephrine reaction, owing to the effects of the drug on the myocardium.

Blood pressure

Blood pressure remains at or near baseline level during the presyncopal phase of vasodepressor syncope. With loss of consciousness, however, blood pressure decreases significantly. In acute allergic reactions blood pressure may fall precipitously because of massive vasodilation. Indeed, this reaction (acute systemic anaphylaxis) is one of the most likely of all the ADRs to lead to cardiovascular collapse (cardiac arrest).

During the early phase of local anesthetic overdose, blood pressure is usually slightly elevated. As the reaction progresses, blood pressure returns to baseline or falls below this level. Blood pressure during an epinephrine overdose reaction is dramatically increased. Pressures greatly in excess of 200 mm Hg systolic and 120 mm Hg diastolic may be observed during this reaction.

■ SUMMARY

Each of these clinical syndromes is presented with several outstanding features.

Vasodepressor syncope has a presyncopal phase of relatively long duration. The patient feels faint and lightheaded, the skin loses color, and perspiration is evident. Consciousness is regained rapidly with placement of the victim in the supine position. This reaction commonly results from fear and is the most frequent (drug-related) emergency noted in dentistry.

Local anesthetic overdose is related to high blood levels of local anesthetic in its target organs, the CNS and myocardium. It is commonly produced by the administration of too large a dose, overly rapid absorption, or rapid intravascular injection. Commonly, signs and symptoms of CNS stimulation (e.g., agitation, increased heart rate and blood pressure, and possibly seizures) are followed by depression (e.g., lethargy, cardiovascular depression, respiratory depression, and loss of consciousness).

Epinephrine overdose is most frequently the product of fear of injections, particularly intraoral. It also results from the use of excessive concentrations of epinephrine, such as those found in gingival retraction cord. The least likely cause of epinephrine overdose is the epinephrine contained in vasopressor-containing local anesthetics. The most prominent clinical signs and symptoms include greatly increased nervousness; mild tremor; an intense, throbbing headache; and significant elevations

TABLE 25-1 Comparison of drug-related emergencies (by common factor)

Related (common) factors	Vasodepressor syncope	Overdose: local anesthetic or epinephrine	Drug allergy
Age of patient	18 to 40 years most common	Any age—more likely in children than in adults	Any age
Sex of patient	More common in males	No sexual difference in occurrence	No sexual difference in occurrence
Position of patient	Unlikely in supine position	Not related to position	Not related to position
Onset of symptoms	Before, during, or immediately after administration	During or after administration	During or after administration
Prior exposure to drug	Not related	May occur with any drug; any administration	Prior exposure, "sensitizing dose" required
Dose of drug administered	Not related	Dose-related	Not dose-related
Overall incidence of occurrence	Most common "drug-related" emergency	Overdose is the most common true drug-related emergency (85% of all ADRs)	Rare—represent 15% of all ADRs

TABLE 25-2 Comparison of drug-related emergencies (by signs and symptoms)

Signs and symptoms	Vasodepressor syncope	Overdose		Drug allergy
		Local anesthetic	Epinephrine	
Duration of acute symptoms	Brief, following positioning	Self-limiting (2 to 30 minutes)	Extremely brief (usually seconds)	Long—hours to days
Appearance of skin	Pale, cold, moist	Not relevant	Erythematous	Erythematous, presence of urticartia, pruritus, edema
Appearance of nervousness	No drastic increase	Increased anxiety, agitation	Fear, anxiety present	Not present
Loss of consciousness	Yes—vasodepressor syncope is most common cause of loss of consciousness	Yes—in severe reaction	No—rarely, if ever	Yes—in severe reaction
Presence of seizures	Rare—limited to mild, localized	Yes—tonic-clonic seizure	Mild tremor	No—unless hypoxia present
Respiratory symptoms	Not diagnostic	Not diagnostic	Not diagnostic	Wheezing, laryngeal edema
CARDIOVASCULAR SYMPTOMS				
Heart rate (pulse)	Initial elevation (presyncope), then depression (syncope)	Increased Weak and thready	Dramatic increase in palpitations Full and bounding	Increased Weak and thready
Blood pressure	Initially normal (presyncope), then depression	Initial increase, then depression	Dramatic increase	Significant depression
Most significant diagnostic criteria	Presyncopal manifestations, rapid recovery following positioning	CNS "stimulation" after drug administration	Palpitations, intense headache, brief duration	Erythematous, urticaria, and pruritus; bronchospasm

of blood pressure and heart rate. Epinephrine reactions are usually brief. Consciousness is seldom lost unless significant cardiovascular complications arise.

Allergy may manifest itself in a variety of ways. However, obvious clinical signs of allergy include the skin reactions of flushing, urticaria, and itching. Edema may also occur. The presence of wheezing with increased respiratory efforts also signifies allergy. Allergy is the least common of these three ADRs, but potentially the most dangerous.

Tables 25-1 and 25-2 compare the different types of adverse drug reactions.

REFERENCES

1. Parrish HM: Analysis of 460 fatalities from venomous animals in the United States, *Am J Med Sci* 245:129–141, 1963.
2. Reisman RE: Insect allergy. In: Middleton E Jr., Reed CE, Ellis EF, editors: *Allergy: principles and practice*, St. Louis, Mosby, 1978.
3. Caranasos GJ: Drug reactions. In: Schwartz GR, Hanke BK, Mayer TA, et al., editors: *Principles and practice of emergency medicine*, ed 4, Philadelphia, Lippincott Williams & Wilkins, 1999.

PART 7

CHEST PAIN

26 Chest Pain: General Considerations

27 Angina Pectoris

28 Acute Myocardial Infarction

29 Chest Pain: Differential Diagnosis

CHAPTER 26

Chest Pain:

General Considerations

There are many specific causes for the clinical symptom of chest pain that are noncardiac in origin. Yet the sudden onset of chest pain invariably is a frightening experience as it immediately invokes thoughts of "heart attack" in the mind of the victim. Because cardiovascular disease is *the* major cause of death in the United States today, this concern is not entirely unfounded. The almost universal presence of signs of cardiovascular disease in adults means that we all are potential victims of one or more of its clinical manifestations. If we add to this the stresses involved in dental treatment, it becomes evident that many medically compromised patients will represent an increased risk during their treatment. Recognition of these potentially high-risk patients and incorporation of specific treatment modifications go far to diminish the chances of life-threatening situations developing.

TABLE 26-1 Potential causes of chest pain

Cause	Frequency	Text discussion
Angina pectoris	Most common	Chest pain (Part Seven)
Hyperventilation	Common	Respiratory difficulty (Part Three)
Myocardial infarction	Less common	Chest pain (Part Seven)

Box 26-1 Important terms and definitions

Acute coronary syndrome: Term used to describe patients with unstable angina or myocardial infarction
Acute MI: Acute myocardial infarction
Anoxia: Absence of oxygen supply to tissue despite adequate perfusion
Angina pectoris: *Angina* is a Latin word describing a spasmodic, cramplike, choking feeling of suffocating pain; *pectoris* is the Latin word for chest
CAD: Coronary artery disease
CHD: Coronary heart disease
CVD: Cardiovascular disease
Hypoxia: Reduced oxygen supply to tissue despite adequate perfusion
Ischemic heart disease: Heart disease secondary to insufficient blood supply to the myocardium
Infarction: Area of coagulation necrosis in a tissue caused by local ischemia, resulting from obstruction of circulation to the area
Ischemia: Oxygen deprivation accompanied by inadequate removal of metabolites consequent to inadequate perfusion
Unstable angina pectoris: Angina that has changed to a more frequent and more severe form; can occur during rest and may be an indication of impending myocardial infarction

Although chest pain is a major clue to the possible presence of ischemic heart disease, the underlying disease process has normally been present for considerable time prior to the appearance of clinical symptoms. Indeed, chest pain is not always the presenting symptom of ischemic heart disease. Previous chapters have discussed two other clinical expressions of cardiovascular disease (CVD): heart failure, presenting as respiratory distress (Chapter 14), and cerebrovascular ischemia and infarction (Chapter 19), presenting as alterations in consciousness. In this section, three additional clinical manifestations of heart disease are discussed. Two of these, angina pectoris (Chapter 27) and myocardial infarction (MI) (Chapter 28), most commonly present as chest pain. Another clinical syndrome, cardiac arrest, is discussed in Chapter 30. Cardiac arrest is a possible acute complication of all forms of CVD, or it may be the initial indication of the presence of cardiovascular disease.[1]

The most common causes of acute chest pain encountered in dental situations include angina pectoris, hyperventilation, and MI (Table 26-1). There are numerous other causes, both cardiac and noncardiac, that present as chest pain and must be differentiated from true cardiac pain. These include hiatal hernia, esophageal spasm, peptic ulcer, cholecystitis, musculoskeletal pain associated with the chest wall syndrome, pulmonary embolism, pneumothorax, mitral valve prolapse, pericarditis, cocaine use, and acute dissecting aortic aneurysm.[2-7] A differential diagnosis of chest pain, both cardiac and noncardiac, is presented in Chapter 29.

A major etiologic factor underlying virtually all forms of cardiovascular disease is atherosclerosis. Atherosclerosis represents a special type of thickening and hardening of medium- and large-size arteries that accounts for a very large proportion of acute myocardial infarctions and cases of ischemic heart disease. It is also responsible for many strokes (those caused by cerebral ischemia and infarction[8]), numerous instances of peripheral vascular disease, and most aneurysms of the lower abdominal aorta, which can rupture, causing sudden fatal hemorrhage.[9] Atherosclerosis is present in approximately 90% of patients with significant non-congenital heart disease.[10] When present in arteries that supply the myocardium, the disease state is called coronary artery disease (CAD). Other common names include coronary heart disease (CHD), ischemic heart disease, and atherosclerotic heart disease. CAD may be defined as a narrowing or an occlusion of the coronary arteries, usually by atherosclerosis, that results in an imbalance between the requirement for and the supply of oxygen to the myocardium, leading to myocardial ischemia. An understanding of CAD and atherosclerosis leads to a greater knowledge of their clinical manifestations. The remainder of this chapter discusses important factors involved in cardiovascular disease, a disease responsible for 37.3% of all deaths in the United States in 2003.[11]

Definitions of terms to be used in this section are listed in Box 26-1.

■ PREDISPOSING FACTORS

In 2003, diseases of the heart and blood vessels were responsible for an estimated 910,614 deaths in the United States.[11] In 2006, 565,000 Americans will have had a new MI and about 300,000 will have had a recurrent attack.[12] It is estimated that an additional 175,000 silent first heart attacks occur each year.[11,12]

Coronary heart disease caused 1 in every 5 deaths in the United States in 2003, cited as an underlying or contributing cause of death in 653,000 persons. MI

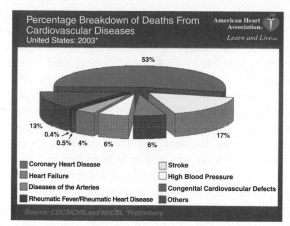

FIGURE 26-1 Percentage breakdown of deaths from cardiovascular disease. (From American Heart Association: Heart disease and stroke statistics—2006 update. Dallas, American Heart Association, 2006.)

TABLE 26-2 Prevalence of cardiovascular disease*

Condition	Prevalence (estimated)
High blood pressure	65,000,000
Coronary heart disease	13,200,000
Myocardial infarction	7,200,000
Angina pectoris	6,500,000
Stroke	5,500,000
Heart failure	5,000,000
Congenital cardiovascular defects	1,000,000

*Because patients may have more than one cardiovascular disease, it is not possible to add these conditions to arrive at a total.
From Thom T, Haase N, Rosamond W, et al.: Heart disease and stroke statistics—2006 update: a report from the American Heart Association Statistics Committee and Stroke Statistics Committee, *Circulation* 113:85–151, 2006.

was a contributing or underlying cause of death in 221,000 of these persons.[11] The remainder died of cerebrovascular accident, high blood pressure, rheumatic heart disease, and other causes such as aneurysms and pulmonary emboli (Figure 26-1).[11]

CVD has been the leading cause of death in the United States since 1900 (except for 1918 [influenza]). Nearly 2500 Americans die daily, an average of one CVD death every 35 seconds. CVD is responsible for more deaths annually than the next four leading causes of death combined (cancer, chronic lower respiratory tract diseases, accidents, and diabetes mellitus).[11] The death rate resulting from cardiovascular disease increased in each decade in the United States until the 1970s, from which time the death rate from myocardial ischemia and its complications has declined dramatically (see Figure 26-1).[13] A decline of 20.7% in the death rate was noted between 1968 and 1976.[13] Analysis of data from the Framingham Heart Study from 1950 to 1999 showed that overall death rates from CHD declined by 59%.[14] This decline occurred each year and was noted in both sexes, in all age groups, and in the three major ethnic groups (white, black, and Hispanic). This decline continues at the present time, with the death rate from CVD declining by 22.1% between 1993 and 2003.[11] Reasons for the decline in CVD mortality are not well understood, but are thought to result from factors including the following:[15-17]

- Improved detection and treatment of high blood pressure
- Decreased cigarette use
- A change toward a more prudent diet
- Improvements in the medical and surgical care of cardiovascular disease

These modifications in CVD risk factors are thought to account for only half of the decline in mortality for men and one third of the decline in mortality for younger women.[13] In addition, the impact of emergency medical services and coronary artery bypass surgery is not believed to account for this decline in cardiovascular mortality.[13]

Despite these advances and the unexplained decline in cardiovascular mortality, death from cardiovascular disease is still a formidable problem. Cardiovascular disease remains the leading cause of death in the United States (see Figure 26-1). Of an estimated 2,440,000 deaths that occurred in the United States in 2003, 37.3% (1 in every 2.7 deaths) were caused by cardiovascular disease. CVD as a contributing cause of death accounted for 58% of deaths in 2002.[11]

An even more disturbing figure, however, is the overall prevalence* of cardiovascular disease in the United States. According to the American Heart Association, 71,300,000 persons have one or more forms of CVD[11] (Table 26-2). These persons represent a great potential risk during dental treatment. Most of them are ambulatory, and a significant number may be asymptomatic, perhaps even unaware of their CVD, when appearing for routine dental care. As is evident, any procedure or incident that results in an increase in the workload of such an individual's cardiovascular system is potentially dangerous.

In 2003 it was estimated that 879,000 persons were discharged from U.S. hospitals with a diagnosis of acute coronary syndrome. This is the term increasingly used to describe patients who present with either acute MI or unstable angina. Of these, 767,000 persons were diagnosed on discharge with myocardial infarction, and the remainder (112,000) with unstable angina.[11]

---

*Prevalence is an estimate of how many people have a disease at a given time. Incidence is an estimate of the number of new cases of a disease that develop in a population in a specific period of time.

Advances in emergency cardiac care have decreased mortality for patients with acute coronary syndromes suffering acute MI who reach the hospital.[18,19] Additional decreases in mortality from acute coronary syndromes have occurred from the increased use of aspirin in the prehospital phase of acute MI,[20,21] thrombolytic therapy, or percutaneous transluminal angioplasty.[22,23] Yet when cardiopulmonary arrest occurs outside of the hospital, the survival rate for those victims who are not resuscitated before their arrival at the hospital remains dismal (6.4%).[24] The introduction of the automatic external defibrillator shows a yet unfulfilled promise of increasing this rate of survival.[25,26]

Statistics from the Framingham Heart Study over a 44-year follow-up of its participants and a 20-year follow-up of their offspring demonstrate an annual incidence of first major cardiovascular events rising from 7 per 1000 men at age 35 to 44 to 68 per 1000 at age 85 to 94.[27] In general, the female rate lags behind the male rate by about 10 years for total CHD and by 20 years for more serious clinical events such as MI and sudden death.[11,28,29] The lifetime risk for development of CVD is 2 in 3 for men and more than 1 in 2 for women at age 40.[11,30]

The prevalence of cardiovascular diseases demonstrates some significant differences among ethnic groups (Table 26-3).[11] Among Americans age 40 to 74 years, MI is more common in males and angina is more common in women.[11] Between 1971 and 1994, age-adjusted rates of self-reported MI increased among African-American men and women and Mexican-American men, but decreased among white men and women.[31]

The average life expectancy in 2003 of persons born in the United States is 77.6 years.[32] Over 152,000 Americans killed by CVD annually are under age 65 years.[11] In 2002, 32% of deaths from CVD occurred prematurely (e.g., prior to age 75 [which is close to the average life expectancy]).[11]

It is estimated that 700,000 Americans will have a new coronary attack (acute coronary syndrome, MI, angina pectoris) each year and about 500,000 will have a recurrent attack.[12] An additional 175,000 will have silent first MIs each year.[12] The average age of a person having a first MI is 65.8 years for men and 70.4 for women.[12,33] Data show that 2% of clinically significant CAD occurs before the age of 30 years. This incidence increases with age; 80% of CAD occurs between the sixth and eighth decades of life (age 50 to 70 years), with the peak incidence in men occurring between 50 and 60 years of age and in women between 60 and 70 years of age.[34,35] Once having a recognized MI, 25% of men and 38% of women die within 1 year. Because women have MIs at a later age than men, they are more likely to die from them earlier. Almost 50% of men and women having an MI under age 65 years die within 8 years.[27]

The widespread occurrence and incidence of CAD has prompted much research into its causes. In addition, researchers are studying possible methods of preventing CAD from progressing to the point of clinical morbidity and death. A number factors have been identified that, when present, increase the probability of an individual's exhibiting clinical manifestations of CAD.[36,37] Major risk factors for heart disease are listed in Box 26-2. Although the evidence relating these factors to a significant increase in morbidity and mortality from CAD is obvious, uncertainty remains about the degree of benefit to be obtained by removing or managing these factors.[1,14,15]

Box 26-2 Risk factors for atherosclerotic disease

Dyslipidemia
Smoking
Hypertension
Insulin resistance and diabetes
Exercise and obesity
Mental stress and cardiovascular risk
Estrogen status

TABLE 26-3 Prevalence of cardiovascular disease by ethnicity

Group	Heart disease (%)	Coronary heart disease (%)	Hypertension (%)	Previous stroke (%)
Asian	5.6	3.8	16.1	1.8
Hispanic/Latino	7.7	4.5	19.0	2.2
White	11.4	5.9	20.5	2.3
Hawaiians/Pacific Islander	16.6	4.9	18.2	–
American Indian/Alaska Native	13.8	8.2	23.9	3.1
Black/African American	9.9	5.3	31.6	3.5

Risk factors for atherosclerotic disease

From an epidemiologic perspective, a "risk factor" is a characteristic or feature of an individual or population that is present early in life and is associated with an increased risk of developing future disease.[37] The risk factor may be a behavior (e.g., smoking), an inherited trait (e.g., family history), or a laboratory measurement (e.g., cholesterol). For a risk factor to be considered causal, the marker of interest must predate the onset of disease and must have biological plausibility.[37] Several risk factors, such as hyperlipidemia and hypertension are modifiable; trials have demonstrated that lowering these factors reduces vascular risk.[37,38] Conventional atherosclerotic risk factors include hyperlipidemia, smoking, hypertension, insulin resistance and diabetes, physical activity, obesity, and hormone status.[37]

Dyslipidemia (lipoprotein disorders)

Among the recognized risk factors for the development of atherosclerosis, one of the most well documented is the relationship between blood lipid levels and CAD.[39,40] Evidence associating increased serum cholesterol levels with increased incidence of CAD is extensive and unequivocal.[37–39] Stated quite simply, persons with the highest cholesterol levels are at greatest risk of developing CAD, but even those with lower serum cholesterol levels are not completely free of risk.

A number of lipoproteins have been identified, including chylomicrons, very-low-density lipoproteins, intermediate-density lipoprotein, low-density lipoprotein (LDL), high-density lipoprotein (HDL) and lipoprotein(a). LDL is known to be atherogenic and is the lipoprotein most directly associated with CAD, while HDL levels demonstrate an inverse association with risk of CAD (higher HDL levels equate with lower risk of development of CAD).[41–43] There is, however, no cutoff point in serum cholesterol levels below which there is no risk.[34] Persons with blood cholesterol levels in excess of 300 mg/dL have a risk of developing CAD four times greater than do those with blood cholesterol levels less than 200 mg/dL. Mean levels for total plasma cholesterol in white males are 200 mg/dL between the ages of 35 and 39, 213 mg/dL between the ages of 45 and 49, and 221 mg/dL between the ages of 65 and 69, whereas plasma LDL cholesterol levels in these same groups are 133, 143, and 150 mg/dL, respectively.[37]

The American Heart Association recommendations for cholesterol levels are found in Table 26-4.

Smoking

Cigarette smoking is the single most important modifiable risk factor for coronary artery disease and the leading preventable cause of death in the United States, where it is responsible for over 400,000 deaths annually.[44] Tobacco smoking is a major risk factor for acute MI and death from CAD. Results of numerous studies demonstrate that total mortality (all causes), total cardiovascular morbidity and mortality, and the incidence of CAD are significantly higher in male smokers than in male nonsmokers. Compared with nonsmokers, those who smoke 20 or more cigarettes daily (1 pack) have a twofold to threefold increase in total CHD.[45] There is also a direct relationship between these events and the number of cigarettes smoked daily.[37,46] Consumption of as few as one to four cigarettes daily increases CAD risk.[45]

Cessation of cigarette smoking constitutes the single most important intervention in preventive cardiology.[37]

TABLE 26-4 Initial classification based on total cholesterol and HDL cholesterol

Lipid level	Category
TOTAL CHOLESTEROL	
<200 mg/dL	Desirable level associated with a lower risk for CHD
200–239 mg/dL	Borderline high
≥240 mg/dL	High blood cholesterol; person with this number has twice the risk of CHD as a person with a level <200 mg/dL
HDL CHOLESTEROL	
<40 mg/dL (men) <50 mg/dL (women)	Low HDL cholesterol; major risk factor for heart disease
≥60 mg/dL	High HDL cholesterol
	Considered to protect against heart disease
LDL CHOLESTEROL	
<100 mg/dL	Optimal
100–129 mg/dL	Near or above optimal
130–159 mg/dL	Borderline high
160–189 mg/dL	High
≥190 mg/dL	Very high
TRIGLYCERIDE LEVEL	
<150 mg/dL	Normal
150–199 mg/dL	Borderline high
200–499 mg/dL	High
≥500 mg/dL	Very high

CHD, coronary heart disease; HDL, high-density lipoprotein; LDL, low-density lipoprotein.
Data modified from www.americanheart.org

The risk of a first heart attack (MI) is reduced by nearly 65% with smoking cessation.[47] Although elevated cardiovascular risks associated with smoking decrease significantly following cessation, the risks of cancer of the lungs, pancreas, and stomach persist for more than a decade, as do the risks of developing chronic obstructive pulmonary disease.[37]

Hypertension

The risks of morbidity and death from CAD, as well as the risk of other diseases produced or exacerbated by atherosclerosis, show a smooth, direct relationship to blood pressure levels over the entire range of values. As with blood lipids, there is no cutoff point at which risk suddenly changes from low to high.[48]

Of an estimated 50 million Americans with high blood pressure, the hypertension evades diagnosis in almost one third; and only one fourth receive effective treatment.[49] Meta-analysis evaluating more than 5500 cardiovascular events found a 27% increase in risk of CHD and a 42% increase in the risk of ischemic stroke for every 7–mm Hg elevation of diastolic blood pressure.[50]

Reduction of blood pressure greatly reduces risk.[51] Pharmacologic reductions in diastolic blood pressure of 5 to 6 mm Hg appear to reduce the risk of stroke by over 40%, the risk of vascular death by 21%, and the risk of CHD by 14%.[52] Damage that has developed within arteries over the years because of high blood pressure cannot be undone (see section on pathophysiology); however, the atherosclerotic process will be slowed if the patient's blood pressure is lowered.

Insulin resistance and diabetes

Three fourths of all deaths among diabetic patients result from CHD.[53] Compared to persons without diabetes, diabetic patients have greater degrees of atherosclerosis in both major arteries and in the microvascular circulation.[37] Diabetic patients have substantially increased rates of atherosclerotic complications both in the settings of primary intervention and after coronary interventional procedures.[54]

Persons with diabetes have threefold to fivefold increased rates of future cardiovascular events.[55] Hyperglycemia is associated closely with microvascular disease; however, insulin resistance itself promotes atherosclerosis even before it produces frank evidence of diabetes.[56,57]

Despite evidence demonstrating increased cardiovascular risk with diabetes and insulin resistance, few trials have evaluated whether improved glycemic control improves cardiovascular risk.[58,59] Results of these two trials demonstrated only marginal benefit on coronary event rates. Therefore, exercise, diet, avoidance of obesity, and aggressive control of other risk factors remain primary targets for risk reduction in patients with type 2 diabetes.[60]

Exercise and obesity

Mortality data suggest that over 200,000 deaths from physical inactivity occur in the United States annually.[61] Prospective studies have demonstrated the relationship between levels of physical activity and reduced rates of cardiovascular morbidity and overall mortality.[62,63] Regular physical exercise decreases myocardial oxygen demand and increases exercise capacity, both of which are associated with decreased coronary risk.[64]

In a study of men free of apparent CVD, those with the highest levels of activity had a 40% reduction in nonfatal cardiovascular events and a 24% reduction in cardiovascular death compared with those with sedentary lifestyles.[62] Significant reductions were also noted for persons with originally sedentary lifestyles but who later increased exercise levels.[65] Thus, increasing exercise levels even in mid- to late life reduces coronary risk in men[66] and women.[67] Rates of stroke also declined among those with lifelong exercise habits.[68]

The mechanism by which exercise lowers cardiovascular risk is uncertain but is likely to include favorable effects on blood pressure,[69] weight control, lipid profiles,[70] and improved glucose tolerance.[71] Exercise also reduces propensity for in situ thrombosis.[72]

Mental stress and cardiovascular risk

Mental stress produces an adrenergic stimulation that augments myocardial oxygen requirements and can aggravate myocardial ischemia. Mental stress may also produce coronary vasoconstriction, particularly in atherosclerotic coronary arteries, and therefore can influence myocardial oxygen supply as well.[73] Catecholamines can also promote alterations in thrombosis and coagulation that might favor clot formation and stability. These factors might trigger complications of preexisting atherosclerotic lesions.[74]

Because the dental office environment is mentally stressful for many patients, this factor must be considered whenever a fearful patient is seen.

Estrogen status

Prior to menopause, women have lower age-adjusted incidence and mortality rates for coronary heart disease than men. These rates converge after menopause, suggesting a major role for estrogen in delaying the progression of atherosclerosis. Much of this is the result of the beneficial actions of estrogen on lipid fractions.[75,76] Other potentially beneficial effects of estrogen probably include direct vascular mechanisms,[77] reduced LDL oxidation,[78] altered adhesion molecule levels,[79]

TABLE 26-5 Risk factors for the prevention of cardiovascular disease

Factor	Effect	Intervention	Comment
Smoking	Twofold to threefold increased risk	Smoking cessation with behavior modification	Smoking cessation results in 60% decrease in CHD risk by 3 years
About half of benefit occurs in first 3 to 6 months
Hypercholesterolemia	10% increase in serum cholesterol decreases risk of CVD by 20% to 30%	Dietary changes; lipid-lowering medications	Decrease in serum cholesterol by 10% reduces CVD death by 10% and CVD events by 18%
Hypertension	7–mm Hg increase in BP over baseline increases risk of CVD by 27%	Lifestyle modifications, weight loss, limited alcohol intake, aerobic exercise, and medications	5 to 6–mm Hg reduction in BP results in 42% decrease in risk of stroke and 16% decrease in risk of CVD
Aspirin in secondary prevention	Decrease CVD events by 25%	Daily low-dose aspirin	Reduces risk among those with any form of CVD

BP, blood pressure; CHD, coronary heart disease; CVD, cardiovascular disease.
Modified from Gaziano JM, Manson JE: Primary and secondary prevention of coronary heart disease. In: Zipes D, Libby P, Bonow R, Braunwald E, editors: *Braunwald's heart disease: a textbook of cardiovascular medicine*, ed 7, Philadelphia, WB Saunders, 2005, pp. 1040–1065.

increased fibrinolytic capacity,[80] and enhanced glucose metabolism.[81]

Exogenous estrogen use among young women for oral contraceptive purposes is associated with increased rates of intravascular thrombosis, including deep-vein thrombosis and pulmonary embolism as well as MI and stroke.[37] By contrast, estrogen use in postmenopausal women, for hormone replacement therapy, reduces cardiovascular risk by 35% to 45%.[82] In one study, estrogen users had a relative risk of CAD 40% lower than nonusers,[83] as well as reduced rates of all-cause mortality.[84]

The clinical use of hormone replacement therapy remains controversial for a number of reasons, including potential study bias;[85] other risks associated with estrogen, including endometrial cancer, gallstones, venous thrombosis, and possibly breast cancer;[86] and data from studies finding no evidence of a difference in risk for nonfatal MI or cardiovascular death between women assigned to hormone replacement therapy or placebo.[87] Data from available randomized trials are at odds with observational evidence, underscoring the need for successful completion of additional studies.

Table 26-5 summarizes modifiable risk factors for the prevention of cardiovascular disease.

■ PREVENTION

Unfortunately, primary prevention (i.e., prevention of initial development) of atherosclerosis and CAD has not yet been effectively demonstrated. Research into the known risk factors may, some day, demonstrate

the feasibility of prevention of clinical CAD. To date, however, secondary prevention (i.e., prevention of death after the onset of clinical symptoms) is the norm. In too many cases this effort proves to be too late to prevent death or significant morbidity.

Emphasis is placed on the elimination of any known risk factors that may be present. Smoking is discouraged, optimal weight and physical fitness encouraged, and special diets and medications recommended for those with elevated blood cholesterol levels. Uncontrolled hyperthyroidism or diabetes mellitus is brought under control and blood pressure elevations corrected. However, conflicting evidence has been gathered concerning the effectiveness of some of these therapies in preventing morbidity and death.

Management of elevated blood pressure has been effectively demonstrated to produce a significant decrease in morbidity and mortality rates from CAD. The classic Veterans Administration studies proved conclusively that reduction of elevated blood pressure led to a highly significant decrease in the incidence of fatal and nonfatal cardiovascular events.[88] The Hypertension Detection and Follow-up Program Cooperative Group demonstrated that vigorous drug management of even mild elevations in blood pressure (diastolic blood pressure 90 to 104 mm Hg) led to significant reductions (a decline of 20.3%) in cardiovascular morbidity and mortality.[89]

It stands to reason that monitoring and recording blood pressure of *all* dental patients prior to the start of any dental treatment might well prove to be a life-saving procedure. A suggested protocol for the management of dental patients with elevated blood pressure was presented in Chapter 2.

Another significant factor that may be applied to the dental office setting is the reduction of stress related to the planned dental care through treatment modification. As described previously, physical and mental (psychological) stress increases myocardial workload and therefore the oxygen utilization of the myocardium. In a patient with impaired coronary blood flow, this increased requirement for oxygen may not be met, leading to an acute exacerbation of some form of CHD. The stress reduction protocol (see Chapter 2) is invaluable in the management of most patients with CHD. Of particular importance will be the administration of supplemental oxygen through a nasal cannula or nasal hood to higher-risk patients during dental treatment.

■ CLINICAL MANIFESTATIONS

Atherosclerosis, by itself, does not produce clinical manifestations of disease. Only when the degree of atherosclerosis becomes great enough to produce a deficit in the blood supply and ischemia to an area of the body do signs and symptoms become apparent. The nature of the subsequent clinical syndrome depends on these factors:

1. The size and location of the tissue inadequately supplied with blood
2. The severity of the deficiency
3. The rate of development of the deficiency
4. The duration of the deficiency

For example, cerebrovascular ischemia is a manifestation of atherosclerosis occurring in the brain. If the deficit is mild and of short duration, a transient ischemic attack (TIA) may be the sole clinical manifestation, whereas a cerebrovascular accident (CVA) develops with infarction of neuronal tissues if the ischemia is of greater duration and more complete. A TIA is normally of short duration, resolving without residual neuronal deficiency, whereas CVA produces permanent neuronal damage. The clinical manifestations of atherosclerosis in coronary blood vessels (e.g., angina pectoris, MI, heart failure, cardiac dysrhythmias, and sudden death) are summarized in Table 26-6.

Angina pectoris (see Chapter 27) is a transient, localized ischemia of the myocardium (similar to TIA), whereas an MI (see Chapter 28) is a result of more prolonged arterial occlusion (akin to CVA). Heart failure and cardiac dysrhythmias quite frequently develop after MI as chronic complications, but they may also occur through a process of gradual fibrosis of the myocardium and the cardiac conduction system in the absence of myocardial infarction. Sudden death (e.g., cardiopulmonary arrest) may develop after any of the aforementioned mechanisms or through the occurrence of ventricular fibrillation (see Chapter 30).

TABLE 26-6 Clinical manifestations of atherosclerosis

	Manifestation	Mechanism
NONCARDIAC		
Diabetes mellitus	Diabetic retinopathy and blindness	Atherosclerosis of retinal blood vessels
	Increased infection and poor healing of lower limb, with possible amputation of toes or feet	Atherosclerosis of arteries to leg
Cerebral arteries	Transient ischemic attack	Transient occlusion of vessels
	Cerebrovascular accident	Prolonged occlusion of vessels
CARDIAC		
Coronary artery disease	Angina pectoris	Transient, localized myocardial ischemia
	Unstable angina	Prolonged myocardial ischemia, with or without myocardial necrosis
	MI	Prolonged arterial occlusion
	Heart failure	Gradual fibrosis of myocardium; occurs commonly after MI
	Dysrhythmias	Gradual fibrosis of myocardium; occurs commonly after MI
	Sudden cardiac arrest	Any of the above and/or ventricular fibrillation

MI, myocardial infarction.

■ PATHOPHYSIOLOGY
Atherosclerosis

Atherosclerosis is an ongoing process that starts in utero as soon as blood begins to flow in rudimentary blood vessels. It occurs in all individuals at certain sites of predilection. Atherosclerosis is therefore considered to be a reactive biological response of arteries to the forces being generated by the flow of blood. Texon[90] described atherosclerosis as "the price we pay for blood flow as a requirement of life."

Atherosclerosis affects certain regions of the arterial tree preferentially. It can involve both large and medium-sized arteries diffusely. Postmortem and intravascular ultrasonographic studies have revealed widespread intimal thickening in patients with atherosclerosis and,

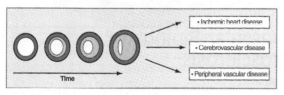

FIGURE 26-2 A schematic life history of an atherosclerotic lesion. In Western societies, and increasingly in developing countries, atherogenesis begins in early life. Lesions usually evolve slowly over decades, often progressing in an asymptomatic manner or eventually causing stable symptoms related to embarrassment of flow, such as angina pectoris or intermittent claudication. For the first part of the life history of the lesion, growth proceeds abluminally, in an outward direction, preserving the lumen (compensatory enlargement or "positive remodeling"). A minority of lesions will produce thrombotic complications, leading to clinical manifestations such as the unstable coronary syndromes, thrombotic stroke, or critical limb ischemia. (From Braunwald E, Zipes DP, Libby P, editors: *Braunwald's heart disease: a textbook of cardiovascular medicine,* ed 6, vol 1, Philadelphia, WB Saunders, 2001.)

indeed, in many asymptomatic human adults.[91,92] At the same time, atherosclerosis is a focal disease that constricts some areas of affected blood vessels much more than others.[91]

Atherosclerosis is a disease with both chronic and acute manifestations. Libby has stated that "few human diseases have a longer 'incubation' period than atherosclerosis, which begins to affect arteries in many North Americans in the 2nd and 3rd decades of life"[91] (Figure 26-2). Yet typically, symptoms of atherosclerosis do not occur until several decades later, even later in women. Despite this time course and prolonged period of clinical inactivity, the dreaded complications of atheroma, such as MI, unstable angina, or stroke typically occur suddenly.[91,93]

The basic factor in the development of an atherosclerotic lesion (called an *atheroma*) is multiplication of the smooth-muscle cells of the intimal layer of the blood vessel in response to pressure changes within the vessel (Figure 26-3 and Box 26-3). In a normal blood vessel, there is constant movement of lipids into and out of the intimal layer. However, when proliferative

---

Box 26-3 Pathophysiology of atherosclerosis

INITIATION OF ATHEROSCLEROSIS
Extracellular lipid accumulation
Leukocyte recruitment
Intracellular lipid accumulation: foam cell formation

EVOLUTION OF ATHEROMA
Smooth-muscle migration and proliferation
Smooth-muscle cell death during atherogenesis
Angiogenesis in plaques
Plaque mineralization

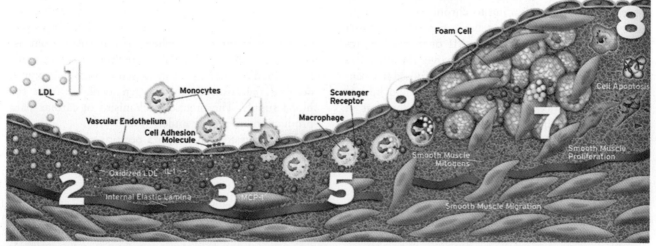

FIGURE 26-3 Schematic of the evolution of atherosclerotic plaque. (From Braunwald E, Zipes DP, Libby P, editors: *Braunwald's heart disease: a textbook of cardiovascular medicine,* ed 6, vol 1, Philadelphia, WB Saunders, 2001.)

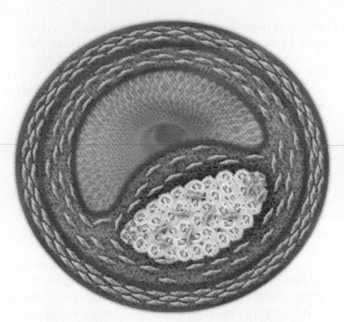

FIGURE 26-4 Typical atherosclerosis. (From Braunwald E, Zipes DP, Libby P, editors: *Braunwald's heart disease: a textbook of cardiovascular medicine,* ed 6, vol 1, Philadelphia, WB Saunders, 2001.)

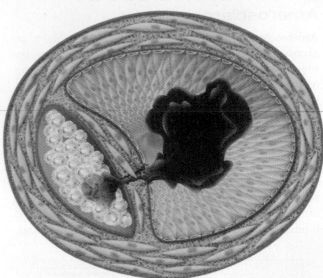

FIGURE 26-5 Ruptured fibrous cap. (From Braunwald E, Zipes DP, Libby P, editors: *Braunwald's heart disease: a textbook of cardiovascular medicine,* ed 6, vol 1, Philadelphia, WB Saunders, 2001.)

changes occur within the intimal smooth muscle cells, the ability of these cells to maintain a steady level of lipids is altered, and the influx of lipids into the intima becomes predominant. This influx is initially made up of cholesterol, triglycerides, and phospholipids and appears as a yellowish streak or plaque that is visible within the lumen of the artery.[94] As the lesion progresses, cholesterol becomes the predominant lipid. Fibrous tissue next grows into and around the atheroma, and finally, calcium is deposited into the lesion. The atheroma, which began as a soft fatty lesion, becomes a larger, harder lesion.[95–97] With increased size, obstruction of blood flow through the vessel at the point of the lesion may occur, leading to chronic ischemia (e.g., heart failure, dysrhythmias), acute ischemia (e.g., angina pectoris, TIA), or infarction (e.g., MI or cerebral infarction) (Figure 26-4). If the fibrous cap over the atheroma ruptures, the atheromatous material is exposed to circulating blood platelets, which then clump and initiate thrombus formation with subsequent development of acute clinical manifestations (e.g., MI, CVA, or cardiac arrest) (Figure 26-5).[98,99]

Location

Atherosclerosis of the coronary arteries occurs predominantly in the proximal segments of medium-size coronary arteries, especially where they bifurcate. Interestingly, only those vessels that run over the surface of the myocardium appear to be susceptible to the devel-

opment of atheromatous lesions.[100] Vessels that enter the myocardium (the penetrating or muscular branches) do not demonstrate atheromata. The explanation for this is not yet known. The most common site in which clinically significant atherosclerosis develops in the heart, leading to major morbidity and death, is the anterior descending branch of the left coronary artery. Occlusion of this vessel leads to infarction of the anterior portion of the left ventricle. The blood supply to the myocardium is shown in Figure 26-6.

Chest pain

The basic mechanism of cardiac pain is a decrease or cessation of blood flow to the myocardium. Episodes of cardiac pain occur when critical myocardial ischemia is produced by an absolute decrease of the coronary blood flow or by an increased myocardial oxygen demand that exceeds the oxygen available from the blood supply. The precise mechanisms of cardiac pain production are poorly understood.[101]

It is suggested that angina pectoris results from ischemic episodes that excite chemosensitive and mechanosensitive receptors in the heart. Stimulation of these receptors results in release of adenosine, bradykinin, and other substances that excite the sensory ends of the sympathetic and vagal afferent nerves, which connect to the upper five thoracic sympathetic ganglia and upper five distal thoracic roots of the spinal cord.[102,103] Positron-emission tomographic (PET) findings on changes

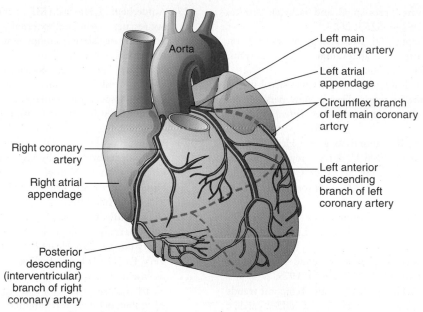

FIGURE 26-6   Coronary arteries. (From Copstead-Kirkhorn LE, Banasik JL: *Pathophysiology*, ed 3, St. Louis, WB Saunders, 2005.)

in regional cerebral blood flow associated with angina pectoris have led to the proposed mechanism that cortical activation is necessary for pain sensation and that the thalamus acts as a gate for afferent pain signals.[104]

Sudden obstruction of a major coronary vessel, primarily by thrombosis, and the occurrence of MI are often associated with violent pain, yet if the vessel occlusion develops gradually, there may be no clinically evident signs. This is primarily because of the gradual development of an effective collateral circulation between the left and right coronary arteries.[105] In the presence of adequate collateral circulation, occlusion of the right coronary artery may not lead to infarction of that part of the tissue that is also supplied by the left coronary artery. Unfortunately, in the normal heart there is usually a minimally developed collateral circulation, which in part explains the greater incidence of acute episodes of cardiac disease.[106]

■ MANAGEMENT

Management of acute clinical manifestations of ischemic heart disease is directed toward the specific clinical entity that develops. In the patient with heart failure, primary management of the acute episode (acute pulmonary edema) is based on alleviating respiratory distress, which is the major immediate symptom. Angina and acute MI produce acute paroxysms of chest pain of varying intensity and duration. Immediate management of these clinical entities is directed at alleviating this pain. In all instances of clinical ischemic heart disease,

the goals of management include (1) decreasing the myocardial workload, thereby decreasing myocardial oxygen requirement, and (2) providing the victim with an increased supply of oxygen. When clinical death occurs (cardiopulmonary arrest), the goal of immediate therapy is, of course, the prevention of permanent or biological death. The principles of basic life support must be applied as rapidly and as effectively as possible. Cardiac arrest is a possible complication of all forms of CAD.

REFERENCES

1. Aufderheide TP, Brady WJ, Gibler WB: Acute ischemic coronary syndromes. In: Marx JA, Hockberger RS, Walls RN, editors: *Rosen's emergency medicine: concepts and clinical practice*, ed 5, St. Louis, Mosby, 2002, pp. 1011–1052.
2. Braunwald E: Valvular heart disease. In: Fauci AS, editor: *Harrison's principles of internal medicine*, ed 14, New York, McGraw-Hill, Health Professions Division, 1998, pp. 1311–1323.
3. Fisch S: On the origin of cardiac pain: a new hypothesis, *Arch Intern Med* 140:754–755, 1980.
4. Eslick GD, Fass R: Noncardiac chest pain: evaluation and treatment, *Gastroenterol Clin North Am* 32: 531–552, 2003.
5. Hendrickson M, Naparist TR: Abdominal surgical emergencies in the elderly, *Emerg Med Clin North Am* 21:937–969, 2003.
6. Perron AD: Chest pain in athletes, *Clin Sports Med* 22:37–50, 2003.
7. Hoey J: Cocaine-associated chest pain in the emergency department, *CMAJ* 168:1017–1018, 2003.

8. Griffin JH: Activated protein C and ischemic stroke, *Crit Care Med* 32:S247–S253, 2004.

9. Nunnelee JD, Spaner SD: The quality of research on physical examination for abdominal aortic aneurysm, *J Vasc Nurs* 22:14–18, 2004.

10. Kannel WB, Castell WP, Gordon T: Cholesterol in the prediction of atherosclerotic disease: new perspectives based on the Framingham study, *Ann Intern Med* 90: 85–91, 1979.

11. Thom T, Haase N, Rosamond W, et al.: Heart Disease and Stroke Statistics—2006 Update: a report from the American Heart Association Statistics Committee and Stroke Statistics Committee, *Circulation* 113:85–151, 2006.

12. Atherosclerosis Risk in Communities (ARIC, 1987–2000). Bethesda, MD, National Heart, Lung, and Blood Institute, 2006.

13. Stern MP: The recent decline in ischemic heart disease mortality, *Ann Intern Med* 91:630–640, 1979.

14. Fox CS, Evans JC, Larson MG, et al.: Temporal trends in coronary heart disease, mortality and sudden cardiac death from 1950–1999: the Framingham Heart Study, *Circulation* 110:522–527, 2004.

15. Kannel WB, Thom TJ: Implication of the recent decline in cardiovascular mortality, *Cardiovasc Med* 4:983–988, 1979.

16. Goldman L, Cook EF: The decline in ischemic heart disease mortality rates: an analysis of the comparative effects of medical interventions and changes in lifestyle, *Ann Intern Med* 101:825–836, 1984.

17. TIMI Study Group: The thrombolysis in myocardial infarction (TIMI) trial: phase I findings, *N Engl J Med* 312:932–936, 1985.

18. Nordmann AJ, Hengstler P, Harr T, et al.: Clinical outcomes of primary stenting versus balloon angioplasty in patients with myocardial infarction: a meta-analysis of randomized controlled trials, *Am J Med* 116:253–262, 2004.

19. Cohen M, Arjomand H, Pollack CV Jr.: The evolution of thrombolytic therapy and adjunctive antithrombotic regimens in acute ST-segment elevation myocardial infarction, *Am J Emerg Med* 22:14–23, 2004.

20. Maggioni AP, Sessa F, Latini R, Tognoni G: Treatment of acute myocardial infarction today, *Am Heart J* 134: S9–S14, 1997.

21. Deeks J, Watt I, Freemantle N: Aspirin and acute myocardial infarction: clarifying the message, *Br J Gen Pract* 45:395–396, 1995.

22. Welsh RC, Ornato J, Armstrong PW: Prehospital management of acute ST-elevation myocardial infarction: a time for reappraisal in North America, *Am Heart J* 145:1–8, 2003.

23. Haro LH, Decker WW, Boie ET, Wright RS: Initial approach to the patient who has chest pain, *Cardiol Clin* 24:1–17, 2006.

24. Nichol G, Stiell IG, Laupacis A, et al.: A cumulative meta-analysis of the effectiveness of defibrillator-capable emergency medical services for victims of out-of-hospital cardiac arrest, *Ann Emerg Med* 34:517–525, 1999.

25. Aufderheide T, Hazinski MF, Nichol G, et al.: Community lay rescuer automated external defibrillation programs: key state legislative components and implementation strategies: a summary of a decade of experience for healthcare providers, policymakers, legislators, employers, and community leaders from the American Heart Association Emergency Cardiovascular Care Committee, Council on Clinical Cardiology, and Office of State Advocacy, *Circulation* 113:1260–1270, 2006.

26. Valenzuela TD, Roe DJ, Nichol G, et al.: Outcomes of rapid defibrillation by security officers after cardiac arrest in casinos, *N Engl J Med* 343:1206–1209, 2000.

27. Hurst W: *The heart, arteries and veins*, ed 10, New York, McGraw-Hill, 2002.

28. Gensini GF, Comeglio M, Colella A: Classical risk factors and emerging elements in the risk profile for coronary artery disease, *Eur Heart J* 19:A53–A61, 1998.

29. Levy RI, Feinleib M: Risk factors for coronary artery disease and their management. In: Braunwald E, editor: *Heart disease: a textbook of cardiovascular medicine*, ed 5, Philadelphia, WB Saunders, 1997.

30. Lloyd-Jones DM, Larson MG, Beiser A, Levy D: Lifetime risk of developing coronary artery disease, *Lancet* 353:89–92, 1999.

31. Ford ES, Giles WH: Changes in prevalence of non-fatal coronary heart disease in the United States from 1971–1994, *Ethn Dis* 13:85–93, 2003.

32. National Center for Health Statistics: Preliminary data for 2003, *NSVR*, Hyattsville, MD, National Center for Health Statistics, 53: 2005.

33. Cardiovascular Health Study, Bethesda, MD, National Heart Lung and Blood Institute, 2005.

34. Stamler J: Lifestyles, major risk factors, proof, and public policy, *Circulation* 58:3–19, 1978.

35. National Center for Health Statistics. Health, United States, 2006. www.cdc.gov/nchs/hus.htm

36. Feinleib M, Williams RR: Relative risks of myocardial infarction, cardiovascular disease, and peripheral vascular disease by type of smoking, *Proc Third World Conf Smoking Health* I:243–256, 1976.

37. Ridker PM, Genest J, Libby P: Risk factors for atherosclerotic disease. In: Zipes D, Libby P, Bonow R, Braunwald E, editors: *Braunwald's heart disease: a textbook of cardiovascular medicine*, ed 7, Philadelphia, WB Saunders, 2005.

38. Pearson T, Fuster V: 27th Bethesda Conference: Matching the intensity of risk factor management with the hazard for coronary disease events, *J Am Coll Cardiol* 27: 957–1047, 1996.

39. Steinberg D: The cholesterol controversy is over: why did it take so long? *Circulation* 80:1070–1078, 1989.

40. Assman G, Schulte H, von Eckardstein A, Huang Y: High-density lipoprotein cholesterol as a predictor of coronary heart disease risk. The PROCAM experience and pathophysiological implications for reverse cholesterol transport, *Atherosclerosis* 124:S11–S20, 1996.

41. Genest JJ, Marcil M, Denis M, et al.: High density lipoproteins in health and in disease, *J Invest Med* 47:31–42, 1999.

42. Young SG, Fielding CJ: The ABCs of cholesterol efflux, *Nat Genet* 22:316–318, 1999.

43. Castelli WP, Doyle JT, Gordon T, et al.: HDL cholesterol and other lipids in coronary heart disease: the cooperative lipoprotein phenotyping study, *Circulation* 55:767–772, 1977.

44. Centers for Disease Control: *The health consequences of smoking: nicotine addiction. A Report of the Surgeon General.* Rockville, MD, U.S. Department of Health and Human Services, Public Health Service, Centers for Disease Control, 1988.

45. Willett WC, Green A, Stampfer MJ, et al.: Relative and absolute excess risks of coronary heart disease among women who smoke cigarettes, *N Engl J Med* 317:1303–1309, 1987.

46. Ball K, Turner R: Smoking and the heart: the basis for action, *Lancet* 2:822–826, 1974.

47. Manson JE, Tosteson H, Ridker PM, et al.: The primary prevention of myocardial infarction, *N Engl J Med* 326:1406–1416, 1992.

48. Lembo G, Morisco C, Lanni F, et al.: Systemic hypertension and coronary artery disease: the link. *Am J Cardiol* 82:2H–7H, 1998.

49. The Sixth Report of the Joint National Committee on Prevention, Detection, Evaluation, and Treatment of High Blood Pressure, *Arch Intern Med* 157:2413–2446, 1997.

50. MacMahon S, Peto R, Cutler J, et al.: Blood pressure, stroke, and coronary heart disease: I. Prolonged differences in blood pressure: prospective observational studies corrected for the regression dilution bias, *Lancet* 335:765–774, 1990.

51. Wassertheil-Smoller S, Oberman A, Blaufox MD, et al.: The Trial of Antihypertensive Interventions and Management (TAIM) Study: final results with regard to blood pressure, cardiovascular risk, and quality of life, *Am J Hypertension* 5:37–44, 1992.

52. Collins R, Peto R, MacMahon S, et al.: Blood pressure, stroke, and coronary heart disease: II. Short-term reductions in blood pressure: Overview of randomised drug trials in their epidemiological context, *Lancet* 335:827–838, 1990.

53. Gu K, Cowie CC, Harris MI: Mortality in adults with and without diabetes in a national cohort of the U.S. population, 1971–1993, *Diabetes Care* 21:1138–1145, 1998.

54. Stein B, Weintraub WS, Gebhart SP, et al.: Influence of diabetes mellitus on early and late outcome after percutaneous transluminal coronary angioplasty, *Circulation* 91:979–989, 1995.

55. Kannel W, McGee D: Diabetes and glucose tolerance as risk factors for cardiovascular disease. The Framingham Study, *Diabetes Care* 2:120–126, 1979.

56. Nathan DM: Long-term complications of diabetes mellitus, *N Engl J Med* 328:1676–1685, 1993.

57. Despres JP, Lamarche B, Mauriege P, et al.: Hyperinsulinemia as an independent risk factor for ischemic heart disease, *N Engl J Med* 334:952–957, 1993.

58. The effect of intensive treatment of diabetes on the development and progression of long-term complications in insulin-dependent diabetes mellitus. The Diabetes Control and Complications Trial Research Group, *N Engl J Med* 329:977–986, 1993.

59. Intensive blood-glucose control with sulphonylureas or insulin compared with conventional treatment and risk of complications in patients with type-2 diabetes (UKPDS 33). UK Prospective Diabetes Study (UKPDS) Group, *Lancet* 352:837–853, 1998.

60. Liu S, Stampfer M, Manson JE, et al.: A prospective study of dietary intake of carbohydrate, glycemic load, and risk of myocardial infarction in US women, *Am J Clin Nutr* 71:1455–1461, 2000.

61. Hahn RA, Teutsch SM, Rothenberg RB, et al.: Excess deaths from nine chronic diseases in the United States, 1986, *JAMA* 264:2654–2659, 1990.

62. Paffenbarger RS Jr, Hyde RT, Wing AL, et al.: Physical activity, all-cause mortality, and longevity of college alumni, *N Engl J Med* 314:605–613, 1986.

63. Rosengren A, Wilhelmsen L: Physical activity protects against coronary death and deaths from all causes in middle-aged men: evidence from a 20-year follow-up of the primary prevention study in Goteborg, *Ann Epidemiol* 7:69–75, 1997.

64. Fletcher GF, Blair SN, Blumenthal J, et al.: Statement on exercise: benefits and recommendations for physical activity programs for all Americans: a statement for health professionals by the Committee on Exercise and Cardiac Rehabilitation of the Council on Clinical Cardiology, American Heart Association, *Circulation* 86:340–344, 1992.

65. Paffenbarger RS Jr, Hyde RT, Wing AL, et al.: The association of changes in physical-activity level and other lifestyle characteristics with mortality among men, *N Engl J Med* 328:538–545, 1993.

66. Wannamethee SG, Shaper AG, Walker M: Changes in physical activity, mortality, and incidence of coronary heart disease in older men, *Lancet* 351:1603–1608, 1998.

67. Manson JE, Hu FB, Rich-Edwards JW, et al.: A prospective study of walking as compared with vigorous exercise in the prevention of coronary heart disease in women, *N Engl J Med* 341:650–658, 1999.

68. Lee IM, Hennekens CH, Berger K, et al.: Exercise and risk of stroke in male physicians, *Stroke* 30:1–6, 1999.

69. Kokkinos PF, Narayan P, Colleran JA, et al.: Effects of regular exercise on blood pressure and left ventricular hypertrophy in African-American men with severe hypertension, *N Engl J Med* 333:1462–1467, 1995.

70. King AC, Haskell WL, Young DR, et al.: Long-term effects of varyhing intensities and formats of physical activity on participation rates, fitness, and lipoproteins in men and women aged 50 to 65 years, *Circulation* 91:2596–2604, 1995.

71. Lynch J, Helmrich SP, Lakka TA, et al.: Moderately intense physical activities and high levels of cardiorespiratory fitness reduce the risk of non-insulin-dependent diabetes mellitus in middle-aged men, *Arch Intern Med* 156:1307–1314, 1996.

72. Kestin AS, Ellis PA, Barnard MR, et al.: Effect of

strenuous exercise on platelet activation state and reactivity, *Circulation* 88:1502–1511, 1993.

73. Yeung AC, Vekshtein VI, Krantz DS, et al.: The effect of atherosclerosis on the vasomotor response of coronary arteries to mental stress, *N Engl J Med* 325:1551–1556, 1991.

74. Leor J, Poole WK, Kloner RA: Sudden cardiac death triggered by an earthquake, *N Engl J Med* 334:413–419, 1996.

75. Effects of estrogen/progestin regimens on heart disease risk factors in postmenopausal women. The Postmenopausal Estrogen/Progestin Interventions (PEPI) Trial. The Writing Group for the PEPI Trial, *JAMA* 273: 199–208, 1995.

76. Walsh BW, Schiff I, Rosner B, et al.: Effects of postmenopausal estrogen replacement on the concentrations and metabolism of plasma lipoproteins, *N Engl J Med* 325:1196–1204, 1991.

77. Reis SE, Gloth ST, Blumenthal RS, et al.: Ethinyl estradiol acutely attenuates abnormal coronary vasomotor responses to acetylcholine in postmenopausal women, *Circulation* 89:52–60, 1994.

78. Shwaery GT, Vita JA, Kenney JF Jr.: Antioxidant protection of LDL by physiologic concentrations of estrogens is specific for 17-beta-estradiol, *Atherosclerosis* 138:255–262, 1998.

79. Caulin-Glaser T, Farrell WJ, Pfau SE, et al.: Modulation of circulating cellular adhesion molecules in postmenopausal women with coronary artery disease, *J Am Coll Cardiol* 31:1555–1560, 1998.

80. Koh KK, Mincemoyer R, Bui MN, et al.: Effects of hormone-replacement therapy on fibrinolysis in postmenopausal women, *N Engl J Med* 336:683–690, 1997.

81. Espeland MA, Hogan PE, Fineberg SE, et al.: Effect of postmenopausal hormone therapy on glucose and insulin concentrations: PEPI Investigators. Postmenopausal Estrogen/Progestin Interventions, *Diabetes Care* 21:1589–1595, 1998.

82. Grodstein F, Stampfer M: The epidemiology of coronary artery disease and estrogen replacement in postmenopausal women, *Prog Cardiovasc Dis* 38:199–210, 1995.

83. Grodstein F, Stampfer MJ, Manson JE, et al.: Postmenopausal estrogen and progestin use and the risk of cardiovascular disease, *N Engl J Med* 335:453–461, 1996.

84. Grodstein F, Stampfer MJ, Colditz GA, et al.: Postmenopausal hormone therapy and mortality, *N Engl J Med* 336:1769–1775, 1997.

85. Matthews KA, Kuller LH, Wing RR, et al.: Prior use of estrogen replacement therapy: are users healthier than nonusers? *Am J Epidemiol* 143:971–978, 1996.

86. Colditz GA, Hankinson SE, Hunter DJ, et al.: The use of estrogens and progestins and the risk of breast cancer in postmenopausal women, *N Engl J Med* 332:1589–1593, 1995.

87. Hulley S, Grady D, Bush T, et al.: Randomized trial of estrogen plus progestin for secondary prevention of coronary heart disease in postmenopausal women. Heart and Estrogen/progestin Replacement Study (HERS) Research Group, *JAMA* 280:605–613, 1998.

88. Veterans Administration Cooperative Study Group on Antihypertensive Agents: 1970. II. Results in patients with diastolic blood pressure averaging 90–114 mm Hg, *JAMA* 215:1143–1152, 1970.

89. Hypertension Detection and Follow-up Program Cooperative Group: Five-year findings of the hypertension detection and follow-up program. I. Reduction in mortality of persons with high blood pressure, including mild hypertension, *JAMA* 242:2562–2271, 1979.

90. Texon M: Atherosclerosis, its hemodynamic basis and implications, *Med Clin North Am* 58:257–268, 1974.

91. Libby P: The vascular biology of atherosclerosis. In: Zipes D, Libby P, Bonow R, et al., editors: *Braunwald's heart disease: a textbook of cardiovascular medicine*, ed 7, Philadelphia, WB Saunders, 2005, pp. 995–1009.

92. Tuzcu EM, Hobbs RE, Rincon G, et al.: Occult and frequent transmission of atherosclerotic coronary disease with cardiac transplantation: insights from intravascular ultrasound, *Circulation* 91:1706–1713, 1995.

93. McGill HC Jr, McMahan CA, Zieske AW, et al.: Association of coronary heart disease risk factors with microscopic qualities of coronary atherosclerosis in youth, *Circulation* 102:374–379, 2000.

94. Stamler J, Daviglus ML, Garside DB, et al.: Relationship of baseline serum cholesterol levels in 3 large cohorts of younger men to long-term coronary, cardiovascular, and all-cause mortality and to longevity, *JAMA* 284: 311–318, 2000.

95. Ross R: Atherosclerosis—an inflammatory disease, *N Engl J Med* 340:115–126, 1999.

96. Libby P: The molecular bases of the acute coronary syndromes, *Circulation* 91:2844–2850, 1995.

97. Isner JM, Kearney M, Bortman S, et al.: Apoptosis in human atherosclerosis and restenosis, *Circulation* 91: 2703–2711, 1995.

98. Falk E, Shah P, Fuster V: Coronary plaque disruption, *Circulation* 92:657–671, 1995.

99. Lee R, Libby P: The unstable atheroma, *Arterioscler Thromb Vasc Biol* 17:1859–1867, 1997.

100. Mitchell JRA, Schwartz CJ: *Arterial disease*, Oxford, Blackwell Scientific, 1965.

101. Gersh BJ, Braunwald E, Bonow RO: Chronic coronary artery disease. In: Zipes D, Libby P, Bonow R, et al., editors: *Braunwald's heart disease: a textbook of cardiovascular medicine*, ed 7, Philadelphia, WB Saunders, 2005.

102. Maseri A: *Ischemic heart disease: a rational basis for clinical practice and clinical research*, New York, Churchill Livingstone, 1995.

103. Foreman RD: Mechanisms of cardiac pain, *Annu Rev Physiol* 61:143–167, 1999.

104. Rosen RD, Paulesu E, Frith CD, et al.: Central nervous pathways mediating angina pectoris. *Lancet* 344: 147–150, 1994.

105. Schaper W, Ito WD: Molecular mechanisms of coronary collateral vessel growth, *Circ Res* 79:911–919, 1996.

106. Firoozan S, Forfar JC: Exercise training and the coronary collateral circulation: is its value underestimated in man? *Eur Heart J* 17:1791–1795, 1996.

Angina Pectoris

Angina is a Latin word describing a spasmodic, cramplike, choking feeling or suffocating pain; *pectoris* is the Latin word for chest.[1] These words aptly describe the basic clinical manifestations of angina pectoris, commonly called angina, the classic expression of ischemic heart disease. The term *angina pectoris* was first used in 1768 in a lecture by Dr. William Heberden to distinguish the "strangling" sensation of angina from the word *dolor,* which means pain.[2] A definition of angina is "a characteristic thoracic pain, usually substernal; precipitated chiefly by exercise, emotion, or a heavy meal; relieved by vasodilator drugs and a few minutes' rest; and a result of a moderate inadequacy of the coronary circulation."[1] Another description of angina states that it is a "discomfort in the chest or adjacent areas caused by myocardial ischemia. It is usually brought on by exertion and associated with a disturbance in myocardial function, but without myocardial necrosis."[3] The major clinical characteristic of angina is chest pain. However, the word "pain" is seldom used by the victim. Much more commonly, the sensation is described as a dull, aching discomfort, "viselike," "constricting," "suffocating," "crushing," "heavy," and "squeezing."[4]

TABLE 27-1 Clinical characteristics of angina

Characteristic	More likely to be angina	Less likely to be angina
Type of pain	Dull, pressure	Sharp, stabbing
Duration	2–5 min; always <15–20 min	Seconds or hours
Onset	Gradual	Rapid
Location	Substernal	Lateral chest wall; back
Reproducible	With exertion	With inspiration
Associated symptoms	Present	Absent
Palpation of chest wall	Not painful	Painful; exactly reproduces pain complaint

Modified from Zink BJ: Angina and unstable angina. In: Gibler WB, Aufderheide TP, editors: *Emergency cardiac care*, St. Louis, Mosby, 1994.

Angina is clinically important to dentistry because it is usually a sign indicating the presence of a significant degree of coronary artery disease (CAD). However, anginal pain is not specific for CAD; it may also be found with aortic stenosis, hypertensive heart disease, or even in the absence of demonstrable heart disease.[4] The onset of anginal pain indicates that the myocardium is not receiving an adequate oxygen supply and that myocardial ischemia has developed. If prolonged, infarction of the myocardium may occur. The patient with a history of angina represents an increased risk during dental care. Any factor increasing myocardial oxygen requirements can precipitate an acute episode of chest pain, which, although usually readily managed with vasodilator drug therapy, can ultimately lead to myocardial infarction (MI), acute dysrhythmias, or cardiac arrest. The prevention of acute episodes of chest pain proves ultimately more satisfactory than management of the episode after it develops.

It is important to distinguish chest "pain" associated with angina with pain located in the chest region that is not associated with myocardial ischemia (e.g., intercostal muscle spasm). Table 27-1 distinguishes between chest "pain" that is more or less likely to be anginal in origin. Chest "pain" described as a "sharp, knife-like pain, that hurts 'whenever I breathe,' that can be localized to a specific area" is normally not of ischemic origin. Anginal pain is described in the terms presented above, is constant (not associated with breathing), and is not localized; rather, it is described as covering a larger "region."

■ PREDISPOSING FACTORS

Factors leading to the initial development of angina are discussed in Chapter 26 (see Box 26-2). In most patients, acute anginal episodes are precipitated by factors that produce a relative inability of the coronary arteries to supply the myocardium with adequate volumes of

Box 27-1 Precipitating factors in angina pectoris

Physical activity
Hot, humid environment
Cold weather
Large meals
Emotional stress (argument, anxiety, or sexual excitement)
Caffeine ingestion
Fever, anemia, or thyrotoxicosis
Cigarette smoking
Smog
High altitudes
Second-hand smoke

oxygenated blood. Common precipitating factors are listed in Box 27-1.

The most common type of angina is *stable angina*. Synonyms include chronic, classic, or exertional angina. Stable angina is usually the result of chronic CAD due to obstruction of the coronary arteries by atheromatous plaque.[5,6] An estimated 13,200,000 Americans have CAD, of which 6,500,000 have angina and 7,200,000 have had MI.[7,8] Among Americans age 40 to 74 years, the age-adjusted prevalence of angina pectoris is higher among women than men.[9]

The prevalence of CAD in groups of patients with stable angina, atypical angina, and nonanginal chest pain has been reported as 90%, 50%, and 16%, respectively,[10] whereas the incidence of CAD in asymptomatic adults has been estimated at 3% to 4%. Stable angina is commonly triggered by one of the "four 'E's": exercise, emotion, exposure to cold, and eating. The "pain" of stable angina normally lasts from 1 to 15 minutes, builds gradually, and reaches maximum intensity quickly. This "pain" is usually relieved by rest or the administration of nitroglycerin. Two other forms of angina are described: variant angina and unstable angina.

TABLE 27-2 Comparison of anginal syndromes

Anginal syndrome	Synonyms	Precipitating factors	Duration	Response to nitroglycerin
Stable	Chronic, classic, exertional	Emotional stress, physical exertion, cold weather	1–15 minutes	Good
Variant	Prinzmetal's, atypical, vasospastic	Coronary artery spasm	Variable (duration of coronary artery spasm)	Good
Unstable	Preinfarction, crescendo, acute coronary insufficiency, intermediate coronary syndrome, impending myocardial infarction	Any factor or no factor	Up to 30 minutes	Questionable

Variant angina, also termed *Prinzmetal's angina*, *atypical angina*, or *vasospastic angina*, is more likely to occur with the patient at rest than during physical exertion or emotional stress; it may develop at odd times during the day or night (even awakening patients from sleep); and it is often associated with dysrhythmias or conduction defects. Coronary artery spasm is the cause of variant angina. Spasm of a coronary artery produces a sudden, brief occlusion of an epicardial or large septal coronary artery. Normal or diseased coronary arteries may become constricted. Variant angina may recur at the same time each day in an individual. It is thought that diurnal fluctuations in circulating endogenous catecholamine levels, highest during the early morning hours, are partially responsible for nocturnal angina. Variant angina is more common in women under the age of 50 years, whereas stable angina is uncommon in women in this age group in the absence of severe hypercholesterolemia, high blood pressure, or diabetes mellitus. Signs and symptoms of variant angina include syncope, dyspnea, and palpitation. Nitroglycerin usually promptly relieves pain, while calcium-channel blockers form the mainstay of treatment for variant angina, significantly reducing the incidence of acute events.[11]

Another syndrome, *unstable angina*, is described. Other names for this syndrome are preinfarction angina, crescendo angina, intermediate coronary syndrome, premature or impending MI, and coronary insufficiency. Unstable angina is a syndrome that lies intermediate between stable angina and acute MI. It is quite significant because of its adverse prognosis and for the unpredictability of sudden onset of acute MI in some patients with unstable angina. Unstable angina is the result of the progression of atherosclerosis. The percentage of patients with unstable angina progressing to acute MI is high.[12] Episodes of pain associated with unstable angina may persist for up to 30 minutes and may be precipitated by any of the factors mentioned for the other forms of angina, or for no apparent reason.

Unstable angina is defined as angina pectoris with at least one of three features:[13]
1. It occurs at rest (or with minimal exertion) usually lasting more than 20 minutes (if not interrupted by nitroglycerin)
2. It is severe and described as frank pain and of new onset (i.e., within 1 month)
3. It occurs with a crescendo pattern (i.e., more severe, prolonged, or frequent than previously).

Unstable angina has been classified based on clinical features:[14] Patients are divided into three groups according to the clinical circumstances of the acute ischemic episode: primary unstable angina, secondary unstable angina, and post-MI angina. Table 27-2 compares these three anginal syndromes. Patients are also classified according to the severity of the ischemia (acute rest pain, subacute rest pain, or new-onset severe angina) (Table 27-3). This classification has been demonstrated to be predictive or risk stratification.[15]

About 1.5 million patients are hospitalized in the United States annually with unstable angina. It is more common in older people, in persons with a history of CAD, and in people with atherosclerosis known to be present in other vascular beds or with multiple coronary risk factors.[16]

■ PREVENTION

As has been stressed previously, the prevention of life-threatening situations is much preferred to their management after they occur. In no category is this truer than that of chest pain because the outcome all too often is death. With the multitude of stresses placed on both the doctor and the dental patient, it is probable that most persons (doctor as well as patient) experience an increase in their cardiac workload during dental treatment. Identification of the at-risk patient permits modification in dental care that, in most instances,

TABLE 27-3 Braunwald's clinical classification of unstable angina

Class	Definition	Death or MI to 1 year (%)
Severity		
Class I	New onset of severe angina or accelerated angina; no pain at rest	7.3
Class II	Angina at rest within past month but not within preceding 48 hours (angina at rest, subacute)	10.3
Class III	Angina at rest within 48 hours (angina at rest, acute)	10.8
Clinical circumstances		
A (secondary angina)	Develops in presence of extracardiac condition that intensifies myocardial ischemia	14.1
B (primary angina)	Develops in the absence of extracardiac conditions	8.5
C (postinfarction angina)	Develops within 2 weeks after acute MI	18.5

MI, myocardial infarction.
Modified from Braunwald E: Unstable angina: a classification, *Circulation* 80:410–414, 1989.

will prevent the development of chest pain. Because emotional and physical stress are major elements known to precipitate chest pain, the elimination of stress is a primary preventive measure.

 MEDICAL HISTORY QUESTIONNAIRE

Section II, Have You Experienced:

Question 7: Chest pain (angina)?

Question 9: Shortness of breath?
Comment: A history of chest pain or shortness of breath should lead to a dialogue history seeking to determine the underlying cause of the problem(s).

Section III, Do You Have or Have You Had:

Question 29: Heart disease?

Question 30: Heart attack, heart defects?

Question 31: Heart murmurs?

Question 33: Stroke, hardening of the arteries?

Question 34: High blood pressure?

Question 39: Family history of diabetes, heart problems, tumors?

Question 49: Thyroid, adrenal disease?

Question 50: Diabetes?
Comment: A positive response to any of these questions should elicit an in-depth dialogue history seeking to determine whether chest pain on exertion (anginal-type pain) is present. The problems listed in the preceding questions are frequently associated with either a higher incidence of atherosclerosis or angina.

Section IV, Do You Have or Have You Had:

Question 56: Hospitalization?

Question 58: Surgeries?
Comment: A positive response should elicit questioning about the cause of hospitalization or surgery. Patients with persistent symptoms despite adequate medical therapy and patients with high-risk coronary anatomy are considered for coronary revascularization. Percutaneous transluminal coronary angioplasty (PTCA) or coronary artery bypass graft (CABG) surgery is frequently indicated for patients with severe angina pectoris as a means of providing myocardial revascularization in the presence of significant CAD.[17,18]

Section V, Are You Taking:

Question 62: Drugs, medications, over-the-counter medicines (including aspirin), natural remedies?
Comment: Patients with angina pectoris may take various drugs to either decrease the frequency of acute episodes of chest pain or terminate the acute episode. Commonly employed drugs include *antiplatelet agents*, such as aspirin (80 to 325 mg daily). Aspirin decreased cardiovascular mortality by 30% (Physicians' Health Study[19]) and 50%.[20] In a more recent trial, the addition of 75 mg of clopidogrel (Plavix) resulted in a 16% reduction in cardiovascular events above that obtained with aspirin.[21] *Antianginal medications*, such as β-blockers and nitrates (i.e., nitroglycerin), are used for the initial treatment of stable angina. Calcium-channel blockers are considered if there are contraindications or adverse responses to either β-blockers or nitrates or if symptoms are not well controlled with a combination of these agents.[11] *Nitrates*, such as nitroglycerin, both increase myocardial blood flow by coronary vasodilation and reduce myocardial oxygen demand. The latter effect is produced by venodilation, leading to decreased myocardial preload and reduction in ventricular wall stress, thereby reducing myocardial oxygen demand. Nitroglycerin is administered sublingually or by buccal spray (0.3 to 0.6 mg) if the patient is experiencing

TABLE 27-4 Drugs used to prevent or treat anginal episodes (nitrates)

Generic name	Route of administration	Dosage	Onset of action	Duration of action
Nitroglycerin	Sublingual tablet	0.15–0.9 mg	2–5 min	15–30 min
	Sublingual spray (Nitrolingual)	0.4 mg	2–5 min	15–30 min
	Transdermal patch	0.2–0.8 mg every 12 h	30 min	8–14 h
	Intravenous	5–200 µg/min	2–5 min	During infusion, tolerance develops after 7–8 h
Isosorbide dinitrate (Isordil)	Oral	5–80 mg twice or thrice daily	30 min	8 h
Isosorbide mononitrate (Imdur)	Oral	20–40 mg twice daily	30 min	12–24 h

TABLE 27-5 Drugs used to prevent or treat anginal episodes (other)

Generic name	Proprietary name	Side effects
β-blockers: (cardioselective)		For all β-blockers: severe bradycardia, AV conduction defects, left ventricular failure
Atenolol	Tenormin	
Metoprolol	Lopressor	
Carvedilol	Coreg	
β-blockers: (nonselective)		For nonselective β-blockers: bronchospasm
Nadolol	Corgard	For all β-blockers: severe bradycardia, AV conduction defects, left ventricular failure
Propranolol	Inderal	
Calcium-channel blockers		For all calcium-channel blockers: peripheral edema, hypotension, dizziness, lightheadedness, headache, weakness, nausea, constipation
Nifedipine	Adalat	
Amlodipine	Norvasc	
Nicardipine	Cardene	
Nitrendipine	Baypress	
Verapamil	Verelan	
Diltiazem	Cardizem	

AV, atrioventricular.

Ischemic chest pain. If, following three doses at 5-minute intervals, the episode has not terminated, additional, more aggressive measures are indicated, including activating emergency medical services.[22] *Cardioselective β-blockers* are frequently used since they offer the advantage of not interfering with bronchodilation or peripheral vasodilation. Their dosage is titrated to reduce the resting heart rate to 55 to 60 beats per minute. β-blockers are ineffective in patients with vasospastic angina. *Calcium-channel blockers* cause coronary vasodilation and decrease blood pressure. Used in conjunction with β-blockers patients with chronic stable angina reduces symptomatic and asymptomatic ischemic events even further. In patients with vasospastic (Prinzmetal's) angina, calcium-channel blockers significantly reduce the incidence of angina.

Although the frequency of anginal episodes may be decreased with *long-acting nitrates,* there is no convincing evidence that they prolong life. Drugs such as isosorbide dinitrate, mononitrates, transdermal nitroglycerin patches, and nitroglycerin ointment are used to prevent recurrence of angina. Sublingual (or oral spray) nitroglycerin is the agent of choice in acute anginal episodes.

Tables 27-4 and 27-5 list drugs used in the prevention or management of anginal episodes.

Dialogue history

For patients with a history of angina, dialogue history should seek to determine the following information concerning their anginal episodes:

Describe a typical anginal episode.

Comment: The quality of chest discomfort of anginal episodes should be determined by asking the patient to describe, in his or her own words, the nature of the episode and the usual radiation pattern associated with it. In place of the word *pain,* many patients describe their anginal attacks as "an unpleasant sensation," "squeezing," "pressing," "strangling," "constricting," "bursting," and "burning." If the patient describes the episodes with terms such as "shooting," "knifelike," "sharp," "stabbing," "fleeting," or "tingling," the pain is probably not anginal (see Table 27-1).[5] Observe the patient as he or she describes the pain. Clenching of the fist in front of the chest while describing the sensation is a very strong indication of an ischemic origin for the pain (the Levine sign).[23,24]

Where does the "pain" hurt or radiate?

Comment: Determine the location of the pain. Anginal pain is usually substernal, across both sides of the chest. Pain may radiate to various regions. Common sites of radiation of ischemic chest pain include the neck and jaw; the upper epigastric region (stomach); intrascapular (between the shoulder blades); substernal radiating to the left arm; epigastric radiating to the neck, jaw, and both arms; and the left shoulder and the inner aspect of both arms (Figure 27-1).[5]

If the pain or discomfort can be localized (i.e., the patient can point to a spot where it hurts), the origin is usually not ischemic, but from the skin or the chest wall. Ischemic pain, arising from the deeper structures (e.g., the heart) tends to be more generalized in location, hurting over a larger area, as opposed to a more well-defined spot.[23]

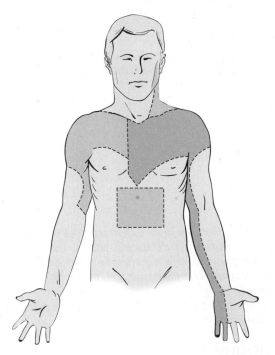

Substernal pain projected to left shoulder and arm (ulanar nerve distribution)

Less frequent referred sites including right shoulder and arm, left jaw, neck, and epigastrium

FIGURE 27-1 Radiation patterns of chest pain. (Modified from Jastak JT, Cowan EF Jr: Patients at risk, *Dent Clin North Am* 17:363–377, 1973.)

How long do your anginal episodes last?

Comment: Determine the duration of the typical episode. Angina is, by definition, of short duration. If the episode is precipitated by exertion and the patient stops and rests, the discomfort normally ceases within 2 to 10 minutes. Chest pain lasting less than 30 minutes is usually not anginal. This brief duration commonly points to a noncardiac origin, such as musculoskeletal pain, hiatal hernia, or functional pain. Chest pain lasting for hours suggests acute MI, pericarditis, dissecting aortic aneurysm, musculoskeletal disease, herpes zoster, or anxiety. Anginal episodes developing after a large meal or emotional stress tend to be longer lasting and more difficult to treat. The longer the duration of ischemia, the greater is the risk of irreversible myocardial damage.

What precipitates your anginal episode?

Comment: Determine the precipitating factors in the anginal episode. Typically, anginal pain arises during exertion. The level of exertion required to precipitate angina varies from patient to patient and may vary from day to day and throughout the day in the same patient, but is usually relatively constant for each patient. *Can the patient walk two level city blocks or climb one flight of stairs without developing chest pain?* This question will provide helpful information. Of particular importance for the doctor is the relationship of emotional factors to anginal episodes and the patient's attitude toward dentistry.

How frequently do you suffer anginal attacks?

Comment: The frequency of anginal episodes varies from patient to patient. Attacks may occur infrequently, perhaps once a week or once a month, or the patient may experience acute episodes several times a day. On average, the patient with stable angina experiences one or two episodes per week. The risk of an episode being precipitated in the dental office is obviously increased in a patient with a greater frequency of episodes under normal conditions or in a patient with dental phobia.

How does nitroglycerin affect the anginal episode?

Comment: Determine what the patient does to relieve the pain. Nitroglycerin and rest characteristically relieve the discomfort of angina in approximately 2 to 4 minutes. Nitroglycerin in the form of a tablet, spray, or ointment greatly shortens the duration of the anginal episode. Definitive management of chest pain in the dental patient is initiated by the administration of nitroglycerin, with any subsequent treatment based on the patient's response or lack of response to this antianginal drug. Chest pain lasting 10 minutes or more may prove to be acute MI or unstable angina and requires immediate activation of emergency medical service (EMS). Pain of *esophageal spasm* or *esophagitis* may also be relieved by nitroglycerin; however, pain of esophagitis and peptic ulcer is also relieved by ingestion of food and antacids, whereas anginal pain is not. Chest pain relieved by leaning forward is secondary to acute pericarditis, whereas chest pain relieved by holding the breath in deep expiration is commonly caused by pleurisy.[23]

Describe any symptoms, other than chest pain, that are associated with your anginal attacks.

Comment: The presence of other accompanying signs and symptoms may help the doctor to determine the cause of the patient's chest pain. For example, severe chest pain accompanied by *nausea and vomiting* is often caused by myocardial infarction. Chest pain associated with *palpitation* may be produced by ischemia secondary to a tachydysrhythmia in a patient with underlying CAD. Chest pain accompanied by *hemoptysis* (coughing up of blood from the respiratory tract) may be produced by a pulmonary embolism or lung tumor. Pain associated with *fever* is noted in pneumonia and pericarditis.[23] Medical consultation is suggested if any accompanying symptoms appear disturbing to the doctor or patient.

The diagnosis of angina pectoris depends almost entirely on the dialogue history, and it is quite important to permit the patient sufficient time to describe the symptoms without interruption. Patients frequently use gestures to describe the location and quality of the symptom, such as placing a closed fist against the sternum—the Levine sign."[23]

Physical examination

Physical examination of a patient with a history of angina will yield essentially normal findings during the period *between* episodes. Physical findings *during* the acute episode are described on p. 461.

Unstable angina pectoris

Unstable angina pectoris is extremely significant to dentistry because the associated increased risk of MI. Patients with unstable angina should be managed in the dental environment as though they had recently had an MI (within the past 6 months). They represent an American Society of Anesthesiologists (ASA) physical status IV risk and are not considered candidates for elective dental care.

Unstable angina may be recognized from the dialogue history obtained from the anginal patient. As mentioned previously, the characteristics of the acute anginal episode for a given patient (with stable angina) have some degree of consistency from episode to episode. In unstable angina the "pain" differs in character, frequency, duration, radiation, and severity—in which the pain, over a period of hours or days, demonstrates a crescendo or increasing quality, or occurs at rest, or during the night.

Not all patients with unstable angina progress to MI, but they are considered to be in a precarious balance between myocardial oxygen supply and demand, and prudence dictates that they be treated as if they had had a minor MI.

Medical management of unstable angina includes bed rest; the administration of nitrates (including intravenous nitroglycerin), β-blockers, and calcium-channel blockers; and psychological rest and reassurance. Nitroglycerin ointment or transdermal nitroglycerin is frequently employed.

When medical treatment has not improved or eliminated the patient's symptoms, or if they become worse, surgical intervention may be indicated. Surgical options include PTCA, CABG surgery, atherectomy, and laser angioplasty.

Evidence shows that patients who are admitted to a coronary care unit (CCU) because of unstable angina suggestive of MI, but in whom infarction is never demonstrated, have a higher death rate over the next 1 to 2 years than patients with ordinary angina.[24,25] Only emergency dental care should be considered for patients with unstable angina and then only after consultation with their physician. Preferable location of dental treatment is within a hospital environment.

■ DENTAL THERAPY CONSIDERATIONS

Prevention of acute episodes of angina during dental treatment is predicated on minimizing stress so that the myocardial oxygen demand of the patient is met. The stress reduction protocol is particularly important to the anginal patient. Specific consideration must be given to the intraoperative components of the protocol, particularly the length of the appointment, pain control during treatment, and the use of psychosedation. The typical anginal patient (stable angina) represents an ASA III risk (Table 27-6). Patients with unstable or daily anginal episodes should be considered ASA IV risks, with dental care limited to emergency treatment and then only after consultation with the patient's physician.

Length of appointment

An important factor in preventing the occurrence of anginal episodes during dental treatment is to avoid overstressing the patient. No absolute time limit for treatment can be given because individual patient tolerance to stress varies considerably. However, treatment should cease when the anginal patient demonstrates signs or symptoms of fatigue, such as sweating, fidgety movements, or increased anxiety. If vital signs are being monitored, blood pressure and heart rate may become elevated. Allow the patient to rest before discharge.

Supplemental oxygen

Anginal patients are excellent candidates for supplemental oxygen via nasal cannula or nasal hood during dental treatment. A flow of 3 to 5 L/min via cannula or 5 to 7 L/min via nasal hood minimizes the possible development of myocardial ischemia.

TABLE 27-6   Dental therapy considerations in angina pectoris

Frequency of angina	Patient's abilities	ASA physical status	Considerations
0–1/month	Patient can walk two level city blocks or climb one flight of stairs without distress*	II	Usual ASA II considerations and supplemental O_2
2–4/month	Patient can walk two level city blocks or climb one flight of stairs without distress*	II	Usual ASA II considerations to include supplemental O_2 and possible premedication with nitroglycerin 5 minutes prior to start of dental treatment
2–3/week	Pain develops before patient walks two level city blocks or climbs one flight of stairs	III	Usual ASA III considerations to include supplemental O_2 and possible premedication with nitroglycerin 5 minutes prior to start of dental treatment
Daily episodes or recent (within past 2–3 weeks) changes in character of episodes: ↑ frequency, ↑ duration, or ↑ severity; Radiation to new site; Precipitated by less activity; Decreased response to usual nitroglycerin dose	Patient unable to walk 2 level city blocks or climb one flight of stairs	IV	Usual ASA IV considerations

*Distress—shortness of breath, chest pain, undue fatigue.
ASA, American Society of Anesthesiologists.

Pain control during therapy

Pain, especially when acute, is quite stressful; therefore its control in the anginal patient is important. The prevention of pain during dental treatment can best be ensured through the appropriate use of local anesthesia. The question that arises all too frequently concerns the advisability of using a vasoconstrictor in conjunction with the local anesthetic in a patient at cardiac risk.

Clinical evidence has accumulated supporting the statement that, for most patients at cardiac risk, local anesthetics containing a vasoconstrictor (e.g., epinephrine or levonordefrin) are indicated for pain control during dental treatment.[26] The American Dental Association, in conjunction with the American Heart Association (originally the New York Heart Association), published the findings of joint committees that researched this question in 1955 and again in 1964.[26,27]

Benefits to be gained from addition of a vasoconstrictor to local anesthetic solution include longer duration of anesthesia; more profound anesthesia; reduction of bleeding in the operative field; and reduction of the local anesthetic's peak plasma level, which thereby reduces the risk of adverse systemic reactions.[28] Epinephrine is also used to aid in gingival retraction in prosthodontic and surgical procedures.

During periods of stress, normal epinephrine release from the adrenal medulla can increase 20- to 40-fold.[28,29] Treatment-associated pain can act as such a stressor. Local anesthetics that do not contain a vasopressor (in the United States: 3% mepivacaine hydrochloride [HCl], 4% prilocaine HCl; 2% lidocaine HCl), provide a short duration of not-so-profound pain control leading to a greater probability of a patient's experiencing pain during dental treatment and, in turn, significant endogenous catecholamine (epinephrine and norepinephrine) release.

Human studies examining cardiovascular variables after dental injection of 1.8 to 5.4 mL of local anesthetic with epinephrine (1:100,000) have found no significant changes in mean arterial blood pressure, blood pressure, or heart rate in healthy persons or in persons with mild to moderate cardiovascular disease.[29-33]

Vasopressor administration should be minimized in patients at increased risk (i.e., patients with CVD; ASA III and above). Plasma concentrations of epinephrine in persons standing are similar to those achieved after intraoral injection of 3.6 mL (two dental cartridges [United States]) of lidocaine with 1:100,000 epinephrine (~0.04 mg epinephrine); it is assumed that this dosage should be safe in ambulatory patients with CVD.[28]

Adequate depth of anesthesia to permit tooth manipulation (e.g., extraction, cavity preparation) without the patient's experiencing pain is the major factor determining the ultimate blood level of catecholamines. Local anesthetics that contain no vasoconstrictor (e.g., "plain" lidocaine, prilocaine, and mepivacaine) are less likely to provide pulpal anesthesia of sufficient depth and duration to permit completion of the planned dental care before the patient experiences pain. The addition of minimal concentrations of epinephrine (1:200,000 and 1:100,000) to the local anesthetic prolongs the duration of pulpal anesthesia in most cases well beyond the time required for treatment, so that the anginal patient does not experience any pain and the release of endogenous catecholamines is minimized.

Though there are no officially recognized maximum doses of vasoconstrictors when the drug is used in local anesthetics, it is widely accepted that vasoconstrictor usage be minimized in patients with increased risk of vasoconstrictor toxicity.[28] Therefore, the unofficially recognized maximum dose of epinephrine recommended for administration in a patient at cardiac risk (ASA III) at one appointment is 0.04 mg.[28] In terms of commonly used epinephrine concentrations, this is the equivalent of approximately one cartridge (1.8 mL) of a local anesthetic containing a 1:50,000 concentration of epinephrine (0.02 mg/mL), two cartridges with 1:100,000 epinephrine (0.01 mg/mL), or four cartridges with 1:200,000 epinephrine (0.005 mg/mL). Patients with poorly controlled ischemic heart disease (ASA IV) should not receive local anesthetics with vasoconstrictors (nor should elective dental procedures be considered.[29,30]

Local anesthetic should always be administered in the smallest dosage compatible with effective pain control, following aspiration and slow administration.

If confronted with a patient who states that he or she cannot receive epinephrine, consultation with the patient's physician should be completed before initiating dental treatment. If considerable doubt still remains concerning a particular patient after medical consultation about the inclusion of epinephrine in local anesthetics, it is recommended that a second opinion be obtained or that a local anesthetic with a different vasoconstrictor (e.g., mepivacaine HCl with levonordefrin), or a drug that provides sufficient duration of pulpal anesthesia without a vasoconstrictor (e.g., 4% prilocaine HCl and 3% mepivacaine HCl), be employed. A textbook on local anesthesia or the drug package insert should be consulted before selecting a local anesthetic. Absolute contraindications to the inclusion of vasoconstrictors in local anesthetics are the presence of cardiac dysrhythmias that persist despite antidysrhythmic therapy, unstable angina, recent MI, severe hypertension, and severe untreated heart failure.[29] These conditions also,

as a rule, represent absolute contraindications to elective dental treatment.

Patients receiving noncardiospecific β-adrenergic blockers (e.g., nadolol, propranolol) for the management of angina or other cardiovascular disorders are at potential risk when receiving vasoconstrictors. Acute hypertensive episodes have been reported after the administration of local anesthetics containing vasoconstrictors.[34,35]

One additional factor must be mentioned regarding the use of epinephrine in a patient at cardiac risk: 8% racemic epinephrine, a combination of the dextrorotatory and levorotatory forms commonly used in gingival retraction cord prior to taking impressions, contains approximately 4% (40 mg/mL) of the pharmacologically active levo form of epinephrine, which is 40 times the epinephrine concentration used in acute emergency situations (e.g., 1 mg/mL in anaphylaxis). Absorption of epinephrine through unbraided mucous membranes into the cardiovascular system is of little concern; however, where gingival abrasion and active bleeding are present (as occurs after subgingival tooth preparation), epinephrine is more rapidly absorbed. Plasma levels of epinephrine may rise rapidly in this situation, leading to manifestations (primarily cardiovascular) of epinephrine overdose (see Chapter 23).[36,37] Tachycardia, palpitation, sweating, tremor, and headache are the usual clinical symptoms. In the patient with preexisting, clinically evident, or subclinical CVD, this increase in cardiovascular activity may prove dangerous (e.g., lead to myocardial ischemia). The American Dental Association states

> Although epinephrine cord is used by a majority of practitioners rather than astringent cord for gingival retraction and hemostasis, epinephrine cord is contraindicated in patients with a history of cardiovascular diseases and dysrhythmias, diabetes and hyperthyroidism and in those taking rauwolfias and ganglionic blocking agents. Caution is advised in patients taking monoamine oxidase inhibitors.[38]

Psychosedation

The use of sedation during the dental appointment is indicated for the patient who experiences acute anginal episodes once a week or more often, or for any anginal patient fearful of dentistry. Of the various techniques of conscious sedation currently in use, inhalation sedation with nitrous oxide (N_2O) and oxygen (O_2) is my preferred technique for all patients at cardiac risk.[39] Reasons for this preference include (1) the increased percentage of O_2 that the patient always receives along with the N_2O (most sedation units available in the

United States do not deliver less than 27% to 30% O_2); (2) the anxiolytic properties of N_2O, which successfully eliminate or reduce the stress of dental therapy, thereby minimizing endogenous catecholamine release; and (3) the minor but potentially highly significant analgesic properties of N_2O. As discussed in Chapter 28, N_2O and O_2 are commonly employed *during* the emergency management of MI in many countries, including the United States.

Additional considerations

Vital signs
Patients with a history of angina should have their vital signs monitored and recorded before the start of treatment at each visit to the dental office. Minimally, these recordings should include blood pressure, heart rate and rhythm, and respiratory rate. It is suggested that measurements also be taken upon completion of the treatment, prior to patient discharge.

Nitroglycerin premedication
It has been suggested by some authorities that nitroglycerin be administered on a routine basis (prophylactically) to all anginal patients 5 minutes before the start of dental treatment.[40,41] Nitroglycerin exerts a clinical action within 2 to 4 minutes, with a duration of action of approximately 30 minutes. Being somewhat conservative in the administration of drugs, I suggest that nitroglycerin prophylaxis be reserved for the anginal patient who experiences episodes of anginal pain more than once a week and who exhibits fear of dentistry (ASA III). However, I do feel that before beginning dental treatment on the higher-risk anginal patient, the doctor should request that the patient's nitroglycerin spray or tablets be placed where they will be immediately accessible if needed. Although nitroglycerin is present in the dental office emergency kit, the patient's own nitroglycerin is used preferentially.

■ CLINICAL MANIFESTATIONS

The primary clinical manifestation of angina is chest pain. The doctor managing the anginal patient usually has been forewarned about this medical condition through the medical history questionnaire and is prepared to manage it. Although most instances of anginal pain are easily terminated, it is always possible that a supposed anginal attack is actually a more severe manifestation of ischemic heart disease-unstable angina or an acute MI. The initial clinical manifestations of all of these cardiovascular problems are quite similar; there-

fore, the immediate management of chest pain is based on the patient's response to certain initial steps in treatment.

Signs and symptoms

Pain
The patient becomes acutely aware of the sudden onset of chest pain and stops any activities. In the dental chair the patient will normally sit upright and press a fist against the chest. Since these patients have a history of angina they will almost always volunteer that they are having "an angina attack." If questioned about the pain, it is commonly described as a sensation of squeezing, burning, pressing, choking, aching, bursting, tightness, or "gas." In fact, on many occasions episodes of cardiac pain are mistaken for indigestion—not infrequently with a fatal outcome (see Chapter 28). The patient may state that it feels as if there were a heavy weight on the chest. In describing this sensation, many anginal victims hold a clenched fist to their chest as they describe their attacks (the Levine sign).

Sharp pains are not typical of angina. In addition, respiratory movements (inspiration) do not exaggerate the discomfort. The sensation is more of a dull, aching, heavy pain than a searing hot or knifelike pain. The pain is located substernally, most commonly in the middle of the sternum, but it may also appear just to the left of the sternum. Finally, pain of cardiac origin tends to be more generalized than noncardiac pain, which can often be localized to one specific site (see discussion of radiation of pain that follows).

Radiation of pain
Chest pain normally spreads or radiates to other locations in the body distant from the chest. Figure 27-1 shows the more common pathways of radiation. Typically, the sensation radiates to the left shoulder and distally down the medial surface of the left arm, occasionally as far as the hand and fingers, following the distribution of the ulnar nerve. The sensation felt is that of an ache, numbness, or tingling discomfort. Less commonly, the pain may radiate to the right shoulder only or to both shoulders. Other sites of radiation include the left side of the neck (usually described as a constricting sensation), with continuation up into the left side of the face and mandible. Mandibular pain, for which the victim sought dental care, was reported as the sole clinical manifestation of chest pain in one case of angina.[42] Another possible, yet relatively uncommon, area of radiation is the upper epigastrium.

Patient reaction to anginal pain varies. In some individuals the discomfort of angina subsides without having to stop activities. Other individuals experience moderate pain that persists but does not become more intense. The victim is able to tolerate this level of discomfort and is not forced to stop activities. In most anginal patients, however, the clinical progression is of a different nature. In these persons the pain becomes progressively more intense, eventually forcing them to seek relief by terminating activities, taking medication, or both. It must always be kept in mind that the clinical characteristics of acute anginal episodes are reasonably consistent for each patient from episode to episode. The intensity, frequency, radiation, and duration of the episodes demonstrate little variation. Recent changes in the usual pattern of the disease, with increased frequency, duration, or intensity, are signs of unstable angina and should be reported immediately to the patient's physician. If the patient is in the dental office and unstable angina is suspected, EMS should immediately be activated. This is commonly associated with recent obstructive disease of the coronary arteries and frequently precedes acute MI or sudden death.

Physical examination

During acute anginal episodes, the following signs and symptoms may be noted: the patient is apprehensive, is usually sweating, may press a fist to the sternum, and appears anxious to take nitroglycerin. The heart rate is markedly elevated, as is blood pressure, with values of 200/150 mm Hg having been recorded in normotensive patients during acute anginal episodes. Respiratory difficulty (dyspnea) and a feeling of faintness may also be noted during the episode.

Complications

Although most anginal episodes resolve without residual complication, it is possible for more acute situations to develop. Acute cardiac dysrhythmias occurring during the episode are the most common. Although normally not life-threatening, significant ventricular dysrhythmias such as premature ventricular contractions, ventricular tachycardia, or ventricular fibrillation may occur. Another potential complication of angina is MI.

Prognosis

Only a small number of deaths due to CHD are listed as being related to angina. These are usually recorded as a portion of total deaths from CHD.[7]

The prognosis for the anginal patient depends largely on the severity of the underlying disorder (e.g., ischemic heart disease, CAD) and the presence or absence of additional risk factors.[43,45] Data from the Framingham study obtained before the widespread use of aspirin, β-blockers, and aggressive modification of risk factors showed that the annual mortality rate of patients with chronic stable angina was 4%.[46] In men with angina, the annual mortality is 1.4% if they have no history of MI, a normal electrocardiogram, and normal blood pressure. This rate increases to 7.4% annually among men with elevated blood pressure, to 8.4% among those with abnormal electrocardiogram, and to 12% among those with elevated blood pressure abnormal electrocardiogram. Other factors, such as the presence of diabetes mellitus, heart failure, cardiac dysrhythmias, and cardiac hypertrophy, tend to decrease life expectancy even further. Fifty percent of all anginal patients die suddenly (cardiac arrest). Thirty-three percent die after MI, and most of the remainder die of heart failure.[46–48] The combination of treatments described previously has improved prognosis. However, a more recent study in the United Kingdom of patients evaluated for the first time with typical angina demonstrated (over a 15-month period) a 4% mortality rate and a 7% rate of nonfatal MI, with only an 11% rate of spontaneous remission of angina.[49]

■ PATHOPHYSIOLOGY

Angina pectoris results from myocardial ischemia, which is caused by an imbalance between myocardial O_2 requirements and myocardial O_2 supply.[6] The patient with ischemic heart disease or CAD may be asymptomatic at rest or during moderate exertion because, under these circumstances, their coronary arteries are able to deliver an adequate supply of oxygen to the myocardium. Any additional increase in O_2 requirement of the myocardium above this critical level, which varies from patient to patient, results in a degree of O_2 deficiency, development of myocardial ischemia, with the subsequent appearance of clinical manifestations of anginal pains (or of other ischemic heart disease syndromes, such as acute MI and dysrhythmias).

The pain of angina may be related to the metabolic changes produced in the ischemic myocardium. Chemicals such as adenosine, bradykinin, histamine, and serotonin are released from ischemic cells. They act on intracardiac sympathetic nerves that go to the cardiac plexus and to sympathetic ganglia at the C7 to T4 level. Impulses are then transmitted through the spinal cord to the thalamus and the cerebral cortex.[50] Further evidence for this theory comes from patients with spontaneous angina (i.e., onset of anginal pain while the patient is at rest). Increases in blood pressure and heart rate seen during acute anginal episodes are consistently observed *before* the onset of pain. Changes in the electrocardiogram also occur from 1 to 3 minutes before the onset of pain. These factors indicate that a buildup of the metabolic products of ischemia occurs before the stimulation of pain fibers.

Some of the most dangerous occurrences observed during the anginal episode include the continuing elevation in blood pressure and tachycardia. Both produce a potentially dangerous feedback system. Myocardial O_2 requirement increases as the workload of the heart continues to rise (with increasing blood pressure and rapid heart rate). If the coronary arteries are unable to deliver the required oxygen, myocardial ischemia increases, which in turn increases the chances of acute, possibly fatal, ventricular dysrhythmias and MI. Rapid management of the anginal episode becomes quite important.

Coronary artery spasm (Prinzmetal's variant angina) has been demonstrated to occur either spontaneously or on exposure to cold, by exposure to ergot-derivative drugs used to treat migraine headaches, or by mechanical irritation from a cardiac catheter.[44,50-53] Spasm has been observed in the large coronary arteries, whether healthy or atherosclerotic, resulting in decreased coronary blood flow.[53] Prolonged spasm of the coronary arteries in angina may result in documented episodes of myocardial infarction—even in the absence of visible CAD.

In order to treat a patient with chest pain for angina, they **MUST** have a prior history of angina pectoris.

ALL instances of first time chest pain occurring in a dental setting require **IMMEDIATE** activation of emergency medical services (EMS).

■ MANAGEMENT

The primary goal in the management of the acute anginal episode is to eliminate myocardial ischemia by either decreasing the myocardial oxygen requirement or increasing O_2 delivery to the heart. Diagnostic clues to the presence of angina include the following:[54]

- Patient history of angina pectoris
- Onset with exercise, activity, or stress
- Symptoms that include pressure, tightness, or a heavy weight
- Substernal, epigastric, or jaw pain
- Mild to moderate discomfort

Patient with a history of angina pectoris

Step 1: termination of the dental procedure and activation of office emergency team. With the onset of chest pain, immediately stop all dental procedures. In many instances the precipitating factor may be related to the dental treatment, such as the sight of a local anesthetic syringe, scalpel, or hand piece, and simply by terminating the procedure the acute episode of chest pain ends. Activate the office emergency team.

Step 2: P (position). The anginal patient is conscious and usually apprehensive. Allow patients to position themselves in the most comfortable manner. Commonly this will be sitting or standing upright.[55] The supine position is rarely preferred by patients with chest "pain" and, in fact, commonly makes the pain subjectively seem to be more intense.

Step 3: A-B-C (airway-breathing-circulation) or basic life support (BLS), as needed. The anginal patient is conscious; breathes spontaneously; and has a palpable pulse in the wrist, antecubital fossa, and carotid artery.

Step 4: D (definitive care):
Step 4a: administration of vasodilator and oxygen. A member of the emergency team should immediately get the emergency kit and O_2. Oxygen may be administered at any time to the anginal patient. A nasal cannula or nasal hood is preferred. As soon as possible (even before O_2 is available), give nitroglycerin transmucosally (e.g., nitrolingual spray) or sublingually (e.g., tablet). Initially the patient's own nitroglycerin supply is preferred as the dosage will be correct for the patient. The number of sprays or tablets administered is determined by the patient's usual requirement (0.3 to 0.6 mg is the usual dose). One or two metered sprays are recommended initially, with no more than three metered doses within a 15-minute period,[56] whereas sublingual nitroglycerin tablets are recommended at 0.3 to 0.6 mg every 5 minutes as needed, with no more than three tablets every 15 minutes.[57] In the dental office, the use of nitrolingual spray is preferred to the sublingual tablets because of the relative instability of the tablets (Figure 27-2).[58]

Effects and side effects of nitroglycerin. Nitroglycerin normally reduces or eliminates anginal discomfort dramatically within 2 to 4 minutes. Commonly observed side effects of nitroglycerin administration include a fullness or pounding in the head, flushing, tachycardia, and possible hypotension (if the patient is sitting upright). The presence of hypotension represents a contraindication to nitroglycerin administration.[56,57]

Action of nitroglycerin. Nitroglycerin is the single most effective drug available for the management of acute anginal episodes. Its action is to relax vascular smooth muscle.[59] In normal individuals the administration of

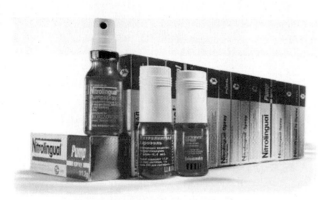

FIGURE 27-2 Nitrolingual spray.

nitroglycerin decreases coronary artery resistance and increases coronary blood flow. This mechanism is probably of little consequence in patients with significant CAD, however. The probable mechanism of action of nitroglycerin in anginal patients is its ability to produce a decrease in the systemic vascular resistance through arterial and, primarily, venous dilation.[60] This leads to a decrease in return of venous blood to the heart and a decrease in cardiac output, which results in a lessened cardiac workload. A decrease in cardiac work produces a lower oxygen requirement of the myocardium and a reversal of the oxygen insufficiency that existed during the episode.[60]

Step 4b: administration of additional vasodilators, if necessary.
If the patient's nitroglycerin tablets are ineffective in relieving anginal pain within 5 minutes, administer a second dose from the patient's drug supply or, preferably, from the dental office emergency kit, which will be fresher than the patient's. Nitroglycerin tablets lose potency unless stored in tightly sealed glass containers.[58] This is one possible explanation for the failure of the patient's nitroglycerin to relieve anginal pains. Nitroglycerin spray is considerably more stable than sublingual tablets and is preferred in this situation. A test for nitroglycerin potency is to place a tablet on the tongue; the drug is still potent if a tingling sensation is felt as the tablet dissolves, with a feeling of coolness throughout the mouth similar to that associated with mint candy but without the taste. A second possible explanation for the failure of nitroglycerin to provide relief is that the etiology of the chest pain is not angina but MI. Administration of nitroglycerin and the patient's subsequent response to it is a major factor in the differential diagnosis of these two important cardiovascular syndromes.

The American Heart Association recommends that in a patient known to have angina pectoris, emergency medical care be sought if chest pain is not relieved by three nitroglycerin tablets or spray doses over a 10-minute period. In a person with previously unrecognized coronary disease, the persistence of chest pain for 2 minutes or longer is an indication for emergency medical assistance.[61]

Step 4c: summoning of medical assistance, if necessary.
If an episode of chest pain in a patient known to have angina has not been terminated after the administration of O_2 and the suggested three doses of nitroglycerin, seek medical assistance immediately. This step will usually be unnecessary for patients with angina pectoris. The management of continued or increasing chest pain will be discussed in Chapter 28.

If nitroglycerin is unavailable or proves ineffective in terminating an episode of chest pain, consider administration of a calcium-channel blocker, such as nifedipine, verapamil, or diltiazem.

If ever a patient with a history of angina pectoris asks that EMS be summoned, do so immediately. Patients know "their angina" and when something about it is "different" they become frightened, convinced that this is the "big one" (MI).

Another indication for activating EMS is anginal pain that is initially relieved by nitroglycerin but which subsequently returns. This is an indication for immediate activation of EMS.

Effects and side effects of calcium slow-channel blockers. Patients known to have coronary artery spasm as a component of their anginal episodes usually respond well to the administration of nifedipine (10 to 20 mg) sublingually. Nifedipine, verapamil, and diltiazem are calcium entry–blocking agents.

Verapamil has been the most extensively studied drug in this group of agents for emergency cardiac care. Its actions are representative of the other drugs in the group. The therapeutic usefulness of verapamil is based on its slow channel-blocking properties, particularly the inward flow of calcium ions in cardiac and vascular smooth muscle. By blocking calcium influx and supply to the myocardial contractile mechanism, verapamil exerts a direct depressant effect on the inotropic state and therefore on the myocardial oxygen requirement. Verapamil also reduces contractile tone in vascular smooth muscle, which results in coronary and peripheral vasodilation, which in turn reduces systemic vascular resistance. Additionally, the calcium-channel blockers exhibit antidysrhythmic effects, specifically by slowing conduction and prolonging refractoriness in the atrioventricular node. The current primary use of verapamil and other calcium-channel blockers is as an antidysrhythmic drug. (It is highly effective in the management of paroxysmal supraventricular ventricular tachycardia.) Its hemodynamic properties account for its beneficial actions in managing angina induced by coronary artery spasm.[62,63]

Opioids, such as morphine and meperidine, are not indicated because they do not treat the cause of pain (i.e., inadequate oxygen supply). The only indication for opioid administration is MI (see Chapter 28).

Step 5: modification of future dental therapy.

After termination of the anginal episode, determine what factors might have caused it to occur. Consider modification of future dental treatment to prevent chest pain from recurring.

Dental treatment may resume at any time (at the same visit if considered necessary) after termination of the anginal pain. Allow the patient to rest until he or she is comfortable before resuming dental care or discharge. Monitor and record vital signs before discharging the patient. The patient may be permitted to leave the office unescorted and to operate a motor vehicle if, in the opinion of the dentist, he or she is able to do so. In the unlikely situation that doubt persists about the degree of recovery, seek medical assistance or a medical consultation, or contact a friend or relative of the patient (a person with a vested interest in the patient's health and safety) to serve as an escort.

No history of chest pain

With no history of chest pain, EMS (9-1-1) should be activated immediately along with the implementation, as needed, of the steps of basic life support (P → A→ B→ C→ D).

The preceding steps described for management of angina are appropriate: the administration of nitroglycerin and oxygen, unless contraindications exist (hypotension).

Even if this initial episode of chest pain is relieved by nitroglycerin and oxygen, a thorough evaluation of such patients, who are probably very frightened, is in order, thus the recommendation for seeking medical assistance immediately. Box 27-2 outlines the steps to follow to manage chest pain in a patient with a history of angina pectoris.

- **Drugs used in management:** Nitroglycerin and oxygen.
- **Medical assistance required:** Assistance is not needed if there is a history of angina and relief of pain. If ever a patient with a history of angina wishes EMS to be contacted, DO NOT HESITATE to do so. Contacting EMS is also required if this is the initial episode of chest pain or if pain is not relieved with three doses of nitroglycerin.

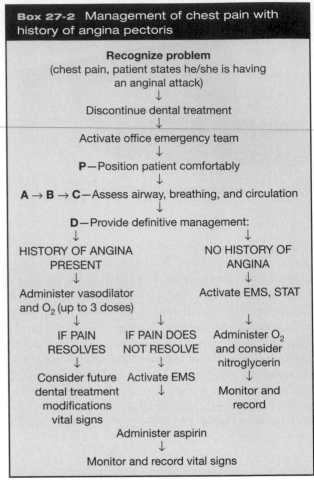

Box 27-2 Management of chest pain with history of angina pectoris

A, airway; **B,** breathing; **C,** circulation; **D,** definitive care; EMS, emergency medical service; **P,** position.

REFERENCES

1. *Mosby's dictionary of medicine, nursing, and health professions,* ed 7, St. Louis, Mosby, 2006.
2. Heberden W: Some account of a disorder of the breast, *Med Trans Coll Physic (London)* 2:59–67, 1772.
3. Matthews MB, Julian DG: Angina pectoris: definition and description. In: Julkian DG, editor: *Angina pectoris,* ed 2, New York, Churchill Livingstone, 1985.
4. Gersh BJ, Braunwald E, Bonow RO: Chronic coronary artery disease. In: Braunwald E, Zipes DP, Libby P, editors: *Braunwald's heart disease: a textbook of cardiovascular medicine,* ed 6, Philadelphia, WB Saunders, 2001.
5. Angst DM, Bensinger DA: Angina. In: Forbes S, editor: *Cardiopulmonary emergencies,* Springhouse, PA, Springhouse, 1991.
6. Maseri A: *Ischemic heart disease: a rational basis for clinical practice and clinical research,* New York, Churchill Livingstone, 1995.
7. Thom T, Haase N, Rosamond W, et al.: Heart disease and stroke statistics—2006 update: a report from the

American Heart Association Statistics Committee and Stroke Statistics Committee, *Circulation* 113:85–151, 2006.

8. Atherosclerosis Risk in Communities (ARIC, 1987–2000). Bethesda, MD, National Heart, Lung, and Blood Institute, 2006.
9. Ford ES, Giles WH: Changes in prevalence of nonfatal coronary heart disease in the United States from 1971–1994, *Ethn Dis* 13:85–93, 2003.
10. Diamond GA, Forrester JS: Analysis of probability as an aid in the clinical diagnosis of coronary heart disease, *N Engl J Med* 300:1350–1358, 1979.
11. Ramachandrundi S, Sheps DS: Management of angina pectoris. In: Rakel RE, Bope ET, editors: *Conn's current therapy,* ed 57, Philadelphia, WB Saunders, 2005.
12. Waters D, Lam J, Theroux P: Newer concepts in the treatment of unstable angina pectoris, *Am J Cardiol* 68:34C–41C, 1991.
13. Cannon CP, Braunwald E: Unstable angina. In: Braunwald E, Zipes DP, Libby P, editors: *Braunwald's heart disease: a textbook of cardiovascular medicine,* ed 6, Philadelphia, WB Saunders, 2001.
14. Braunwald E: Unstable angina: a classification, *Circulation* 80:410–414, 1989.
15. Calvin JE, Klein LW, VandenBerg BJ, et al.: Risk stratification in unstable angina: prospective validation of the Braunwald classification, *JAMA* 273:136–144, 1996.
16. Waters DD: Acute coronary syndrome: unstable angina and non-ST segment elevation myocardial infarction. In: Goldman L, Ausiello D, editors: *Cecil textbook of medicine,* ed 22, Philadelphia, WB Saunders, 2004.
17. McCullough PA, O'Neill WW, Graham M, et al.: A prospective randomized trial of triage angiography in acute coronary syndromes ineligible for thrombolytic therapy: results of the Medicine Versus Angiography in Thrombolytic Exclusion (MATE) trial, *J Am Coll Cardiol* 32:596–605, 1998.
18. Boden WE, O'Rourke RA, Crawford MH, et al.: Outcomes in patients with acute non-Q-wave myocardial infarction randomly assigned to an invasive as compared with a conservative strategy, *N Engl J Med* 338:1785–1792, 1998.
19. Sesso HD, Gaziano JM, VanDenburgh M, et al.: Comparison of baseline characteristics and mortality experience of participants and nonparticipants in a randomized clinical trial: the Physicians' Health Study, *Control Clin Trials* 23:686–702, 2002.
20. The RISC Group: risk of myocardial infarction and death during treatment with low dose aspirin and intravenous heparin in men with unstable coronary artery disease, *Lancet* 336:827–830, 1990.
21. Gerschutz GP, Bhatt DL: The Clopidogrel in Unstable Angina to Prevent Recurrent Events (CURE) study: to what extent should the results be generalizable? *Am Heart J* 145:595–601, 2003.
22. Braunwald E, Antman EM, Beasley JW, et al.: ACC/AHA guidelines for the management of patients with unstable angina/non-ST-segment elevation myocardial infarction:

a report of the American College of Cardiology/American Heart Association Task Force on Practice Guidelines (Committee on the Management of Unstable Angina and Non-ST-segment Elevation Myocardial Infarction), *J Am Coll Cardiol* 36:970–1062, 2000.
23. Braunwald E: The history. In: Braunwald E, Zipes DP, Libby P, editors: *Braunwald's heart disease: a textbook of cardiovascular medicine,* ed 6, Philadelphia, WB Saunders, 2001.
24. Wehrmacher WH, Bellows R: Unstable angina, *Comprehens Ther* 30:6–9, 2004.
25. Hasdai D, Topol EJ, Califf RM, et al.: Cardiogenic shock complicating acute coronary syndromes, *Lancet* 356:749–756, 2000.
26. New York Heart Association: Report of the special committee of the New York Heart Association, Inc., on the use of epinephrine in connection with procaine in dental procedures, *J Am Dent Assoc* 50:108, 1955.
27. American Dental Association Council on Dental Therapeutics: American Dental Association and American Heart Association joint report: management of dental problems in patients with cardiovascular disease, *J Am Dent Assoc* 68:533, 1964.
28. Yagiela JA: Injectable and topical local anesthetics. In: Ciancio SG, editor, *ADA guide to dental therapeutics,* ed 3, Chicago, American Dental Association, 2003, pp. 1–16.
29. Perusse R, Goulet JP, Turcotte JY: Contraindications to vasoconstrictors in dentistry. Part I: cardiovascular diseases, *Oral Surg Oral Med Oral Pathol* 74:687–691, 1992.
30. Rose LF, Mealey B, Minsk L, Cohen DW: Oral care for patients with cardiovascular disease and stroke, *J Am Dent Assoc* 133:37S–44S, 2002.
31. Findler M, Galili D, Meidan Z, et al.: Dental treatment in very high risk patients with active ischemic heart disease, *Oral Surg Oral Med Oral Pathol* 76:298–300, 1993.
32. Meyer FU: Haemodynamic changes under emotional stress following a minor surgical procedure under local anesthesia, *Int J Oral Maxiollofac Surg* 16:688–694, 1987.
33. Levine E, Tzukert AA, Mosseri M, et al.: Perioperative hemodynamic changes in ischemic heart disease patients undergoing dental treatment, *Spec Care Dentist* 12:84–88, 1992.
34. Brummett RE: Warning to otolaryngologists using local anesthetics containing epinephrine: potential serious reaction occurring in patients treated with beta-adrenergic receptor blockers, *Arch Otolaryngol* 110:561, 1984.
35. Yagiela JA: *Deadfalls in drug interactions. 6th annual review course in dental anesthesiology,* Chicago, American Dental Society of Anesthesiology, 1990.
36. Houston JB, Appleby RC, DeCounter L, et al.: Effect of r-epinephrine impregnated retraction cord on the cardiovascular system, *J Prosthet Dent* 24:373–376, 1970.
37. Pogue WL, Harrison JD: Absorption of epinephrine during tissue retraction, *J Prosthet Dent* 18:242–247, 1967.
38. Burrell KH, Glick M: Hemostatics, astringents and gingival retraction products. In: Ciancio SG, editor: *ADA*

guide to dental therapeutics, ed 3, Chicago, American Dental Association, 2003, pp. 104–118.

39. Malamed SF: *Sedation: a guide to patient management,* ed 4, St. Louis, Mosby, 2003.

40. McCarthy FM: *Essentials of safe dentistry for the medically compromised patient,* Philadelphia, WB Saunders, 1989.

41. Winsor T, Berger HJ: Oral nitroglycerin as a prophylactic antianginal drug: clinical, physiologic, and statistical evidence of efficacy based on a three-phase experimental design, *Am Heart J* 90:611–626, 1975.

42. Godefroy JN, Batisse JP: Dental pain and cardiac pain, *Revue Française d'Endodontie* 9:17–21, 1991.

43. Kelemen MD: Angina pectoris: evaluation in the office, *Med Clin North Am* 90:391–416, 2006.

44. Yang EH, Lerman A: Management of the patient with chest pain and a normal coronary angiogram, *Cardiol Clin* 23:559–568, 2005.

45. Kent RI: Prognosis of symptomatic or mildly symptomatic patients with coronary artery disease, *Am J Cardiol* 49:1823–1831, 1982.

46. Kannel WB, Feinleib M: Natural history of angina pectoris in the Framingham study: prognosis and survival, *Am J Cardiol* 29:154–163, 1972

47. Frank CW, Weinblatt E, Shapiro S: Angina pectoris in men: prognostic significance of selected medical factors, *Circulation* 47:509–517, 1973.

48. Brand FN, Larson M, Friedman LM, et al.: Epidemiologic assessment of angina before and after myocardial infarction: the Framingham study. *Am Heart J* 132:174–178, 1996.

49. Gandhi MM, Lampe FC, Wood DA: Incidence, clinical characteristics, and short-term prognosis of angina pectoris, *Br Heart J* 73:193–198, 1995.

50. Cannon RO III: Microvascular angina: cardiovascular investigations regarding pathophysiology and management, *Med Clin North Am* 75:1097–1108, 1991.

51. Soares-Costa JT, Soares-Costa TJ: Prinzmetal's variant angina, *Rev Port Cardiol* 23:1337–1356, 2004.

52. Vandergoten P, Benit E, Dendale P: Prinzmetal's variant angina: three case reports and a review of the literature, *Acta Cardiol* 54:71–76, 1999.

53. Maseri A, Crea F, Lanza GA: Coronary vasoconstriction: where do we stand in 1999? An important, multifaceted but elusive role (editorial), *Cardiologia* 44:115–118, 1999.

54. Pollakoff J, Pollakoff K: *EMT's guide to signs and symptoms,* Los Angeles, Jeff Gould, 1991.

55. Pollakoff J, Pollakoff K: *EMT's guide to treatment,* Los Angeles, Jeff Gould, 1991.

56. Nitrolingual spray. www.ePocrates.com

57. Nitrostat sublingual tablets. www.ePocrates.com

58. Mayer GA: Instability of nitroglycerin tablets, *Can Med Assoc J* 110:788–789, 1974.

59. Robertson RM, Robertson D: Drugs used for the treatment of myocardial ischemia. In: Goodman LS, Gilman A, Hardman JG, et al., editors: *Goodman & Gilman's the pharmacological basis of therapeutics,* ed 9, New York, McGraw-Hill, 1996.

60. Parker JD, Parker JO: Nitrate therapy for stable angina pectoris, *N Engl J Med* 338:520–531, 1998.

61. American Heart Association: *Warning signs and actions: our guide to quick action for heart attack, cardiac arrest and stroke emergencies,* Dallas, American Heart Association, 2005.

62. Gerstenblith G, Ouyang P, Achuff SC, et al.: Nifedipine in unstable angina: a double-blind, randomized trial, *N Engl J Med* 306:885–889, 1982.

63. Ellrodt AG, Singh BN: Clinical applications of slow channel blocking compounds. *Pharmacol Ther* 23:1–43, 1983.

CHAPTER 28

Acute Myocardial Infarction

Myocardial infarction (MI) is a clinical syndrome caused by a deficient coronary arterial blood supply to a region of myocardium that results in cellular death and necrosis. The syndrome is usually characterized by severe and prolonged substernal pain similar to, but more intense and of longer duration than, that of angina pectoris. Complications associated with MI include shock, heart failure, and cardiac arrest. Synonyms for MI include *coronary occlusion* and *heart attack*.

In 2006, 565,000 Americans will have a new acute MI and about 300,000 will have a recurrent attack.[1] It is estimated that an additional 175,000 silent first heart attacks occur each year.[1,2] Another 1 million patients with suggested acute MI are admitted yearly to coronary care units in the United States.[1] The average age of a person having a first MI is 65.8 years for males and 70.4 years for women.[2] Though the death rate from acute MI has declined 30% since the early 1990s, it is still a fatal event in approximately one third of patients.[3] About 50% of deaths associated with acute MI occur within the first hour of the event and result from the development of fatal dysrhythmias, most often ventricular fibrillation.

MI is the single leading cause of death in the United States. Over 83% of people who die of acute MI are age 65 or older.[4] Yet acute MI is responsible for 35% of deaths in men between the ages of 35 and 50 years. A man living in North America has a 20% chance of suffering an acute MI or sudden death before the age of 65 years; for women the risk is 10%.[2]

Although a relatively common clinical occurrence, acute MI unfortunately still has a high mortality rate; approximately 36% of acute MI victims (540,000) die, 250,000 of those before reaching a hospital.[3] To increase the chance for survival after acute MI, the dentist must know ways to prevent its occurrence, how to recognize its signs and symptoms, and how to manage it effectively. Killip[5] has stated that, "once admitted to a hospital, the patient has already survived a significant risk," a statement as true today as it was in 1976. Indeed, recent advances in resuscitation and in management of acute MI have substantially reduced the mortality rate among victims who reach the hospital.[6,7]

In addition to recognizing and treating MI, dentists are asked to manage the dental needs of patients who have survived an MI (status post-MI). The American Heart Association estimates that 7,200,000 victims of MI in the United States are still alive.[1] Most patients who survive an MI are able to resume their normal activities within 6 to 8 weeks.[8] As with patients who have experienced cerebral vascular accident or those with angina, patients who have had an MI are at greater risk of reinfarction during dental care.

About 25% of men and 38% of women who experience an MI in a given year die of it.[9] Major risk factors associated with these deaths include the severity of left ventricular damage,[10] continued myocardial ischemia,[11] and a predisposition to ventricular dysrhythmias.[12] Of MI survivors, 30% develop significant angina pectoris.[13] Compared with the general population, survivors of acute MI face a 10-fold risk of heart failure and a fourfold to sixfold risk of sudden death.[1]

In MI, a portion of myocardium dies. Depending on the extent of myocardial damage and the presence or absence of acute complications such as dysrhythmias, heart failure, and cardiac arrest, the victim either survives or dies during the acute phase of the disease. After this acute phase, further complications, such as continued myocardial ischemia or heart failure, may develop. The latter decreases the ability of the heart to carry out its primary mechanical function—that of a pump—because of the size of the infarcted area of myocardium. Varying degrees of heart failure are common after MI. Knowledge of the presence of a compromised myocardium enables the dentist to modify dental treatment to decrease potential risk to the patient.

■ PREDISPOSING FACTORS

The cause of acute MI in more than 90% of all cases is coronary artery disease (atherosclerosis; CAD).[3] Other risk factors include obesity, being male (especially during the fifth to seventh decades of life), and undue stress (see Chapter 26). Friedman[14] and Friedman and Rosenman[15] described the cardiac risk patient as a "coronary prone" individual. This person is further characterized as having a type A behavior pattern, described as follows:[16]

> Foremost is a frightening and often obsessive sense of time urgency. He is determined to accomplish too much in too little time. He struggles both with his environment and with himself, but mainly with the latter. He is alert, very intense, and usually hostile. He is very competitive and ambitious; he wants recognition and seeks advancement. He tends to speed up his ordinary activities by looking at his watch often, by being on time, by hating to wait in line at the bank, movie, or restaurant. He is usually in occupations subject to deadlines.

These patients themselves have labeled the type A behavior pattern as the "hurry-up" disease.[16,17] In addition, a strong family history of cardiovascular disease, an abnormal electrocardiogram, elevated blood pressure, enlarged heart size, or an elevated blood cholesterol level add to the risk of suffering an MI.

Immediate predisposing factors for MI include a significant decrease in blood flow through the coronary arteries as occurs with coronary thrombosis, or an increase in the level of cardiac work load without a corresponding increase in the supply of oxygen to the myocardium as occurs with extreme stress.

The situation of decreased perfusion is called *myocardial ischemia*. Factors other than severe CAD that are implicated in the pathogenesis of acute MI include rupture (fissuring or hemorrhage) of atherosclerotic plaque[18] and arterial spasm.[19] On rare occasion, acute MI can occur in the absence of coronary artery narrowing if there is a marked disparity between myocardial O_2 supply and demand. The abuse of cocaine has been implicated as a cause of such a disparity.[20,21]

Location and extent of infarction

The anterior descending branch of the left coronary artery is the most common site of clinically significant atherosclerosis within the heart. Not surprisingly, this vessel is the most common site of thrombosis leading to MI. With occlusion of this vessel, the anterior portion of the left ventricle becomes ischemic, and in the absence of adequate collateral circulation, infarction occurs with subsequent myocardial necrosis throughout the distribution of the occluded artery (Figure 28-1). Occlusion of the left circumflex artery produces anterolateral infarction. Thrombosis of the right coronary artery leads to infarction of the posteroinferior portion of the left ventricle and might also involve the right

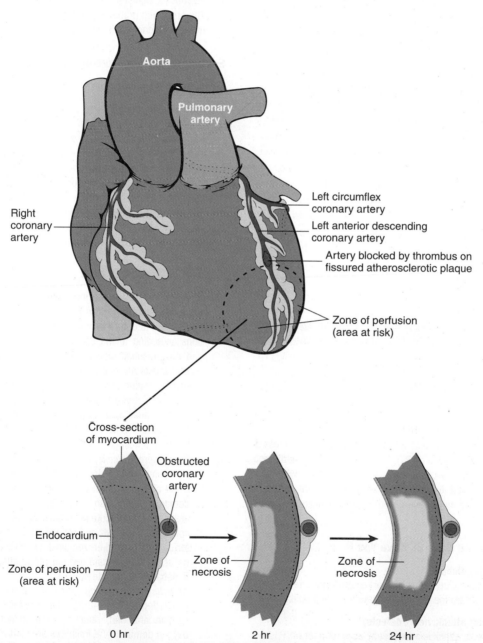

FIGURE 28-1 Occlusion of anterior descending branch of left coronary artery and area of infarction. (From Kumar V, Cotran RS, Robbins SL: *Basic pathology,* ed 7, St. Louis, WB Saunders, 2005.)

ventricular myocardium.[22] The extent of infarction therefore is related to several factors, including the anatomic distribution of the occluded vessel, the adequacy of collateral circulation, the extent of existing CAD throughout the myocardium (one vessel versus multivessel involvement), and whether or not previous infarction has occurred.[23]

■ PREVENTION

Prevention of a first MI in a high-risk patient, although a seemingly impossible task, may be attempted by the dentist through strict adherence to the stress reduction protocol. The stress reduction protocol minimizes potentially adverse effects of undue stress on the workload and O_2 requirement of the myocardium, thereby reducing the risk from one of the immediate predisposing factors of acute MI (i.e., increased cardiac workload). Other immediate predisposing factors, including thrombosis, occlusion, or spasm of a coronary blood vessel, cannot be prevented.

The dental patient with a history of MI must be identified, and the doctor must attempt to obtain as much information regarding the current physical status of this patient as possible so that risk may be determined before starting dental treatment. This necessitates the use of the medical history questionnaire, physical examination, and dialogue history.

 MEDICAL HISTORY QUESTIONNAIRE

Section II, Have You Experienced:

Question 7: Chest pain (angina)?

Question 8: Swollen ankles?

Question 9: Shortness of breath?

Comment: A history of chest pain, swollen ankles, or shortness of breath should provoke a dialogue history seeking to determine the underlying cause of the problem(s). In patients who have had an MI and have experienced loss of a significant portion of their myocardium, heart failure and respiratory distress may be evident.

Section III, Do You Have or Have You Had:

Question 29: Heart disease?

Comment: "Heart disease" is a catch-all term. If the response is YES, seek to determine the precise nature of the problem.

Question 30: Heart attack, heart defects?

Comment: Heart attack is a frequently used term for MI. Positive reply to this question requires an in-depth dialogue history to determine the level of significance of the MI to the proposed dental treatment plan.

Question 31: Heart murmurs?

Question 33: Stroke, hardening of the arteries?

Question 34: High blood pressure?

Question 39: Family history of diabetes, heart problems, tumors?

Question 49: Thyroid, adrenal disease?

Question 50: Diabetes?

Comment: A positive response to any of these questions should elicit an in-depth dialogue history seeking to determine whether clinical evidence of cardiovascular disease is present, and if present its significance to the proposed dental treatment plan. The preceding problems are frequently associated with either a higher incidence of atherosclerosis or cardiovascular disease.

Section IV, Do You Have or Have You Had:

Question 56: Hospitalization?

Question 58: Surgeries?

Comment: A positive response should elicit questioning to seek the cause of hospitalization or surgery. Patients with persistent symptoms despite adequate medical therapy and patients with high-risk coronary anatomy are considered for coronary revascularization. Percutaneous coronary revascularization, coronary artery bypass graft surgery, and intraaortic balloon counterpulsation are frequently indicated for patients with unstable angina or who have had an MI as a means of providing myocardial revascularization in the presence of significant CAD.[24–26]

Section V, Are You Taking:

Question 62: Drugs, medications, over-the-counter medicines (including aspirin), natural remedies?

Comment: Patients who have had an MI receive various medications according to the degree of residual myocardial damage and the presence of complications. These patients frequently receive one or more of the following drug groups:

- *Aspirin:* Aspirin (325 mg) and/or clopidogrel (Plavix, 75 mg/d) are administered to patients in the immediate post-MI period and continued upon hospital discharge for periods of from 3 to 12 months.[27] If the patient is concurrently taking clopidogrel, the aspirin dosage is reduced to 81 mg/d.[28]
- *β-adrenergic-blockers:* β-adrenergic blockers are important as adjunct therapy during acute MI as they reduce heart rate, blood pressure, cardiac contractility, and myocardial oxygen demand.[29] They also reduce infarct size, alleviate the pain associated with acute MI, reduce the likelihood of developing complications of MI, and reduce mortality from acute MI. Unfortunately, β-blockers remain underutilized in clinical practice despite definitive data demonstrating efficacy from their use in patients with acute MI.[30]
- *Angiotensin-converting enzyme inhibitors:* Angiotensin-converting enzyme (ACE) inhibitors reduce blood pressure and cardiac afterload, resulting in a reduction of myocardial oxygen demand. ACE inhibitors are started on the first day of hospitalization for acute MI and should be continued in all patients who have had an MI for 6 weeks and permanently in patients with reduced left ventricular function.[31] Some experts

now recommend use of ACE inhibitors in all patients who have had an MI, given recent data on secondary prevention of MIs.[32,33]

- *Lipid-lowering treatment:* Hyperlipidemia is a recognized risk factor for CAD, and most victims of acute MI have elevated low-density lipoprotein cholesterol (>100 mg/dL).[34] Initiating the administration of statin agents to patients with hyperlipidemia and CAD within 3 months of hospital discharge has been demonstrated to be associated with improved long-term survival.[35,36]

- *Nitrates:* Nitrates, such as nitroglycerin, dilate coronary arteries; improve coronary and collateral blood flow to the ischemic area of the myocardium; and reduce cardiac preload, which, in turn, results in a reduced myocardial oxygen requirement. Nitroglycerin also controls hypertension associated with acute anxiety response during acute MI.[37] Despite these beneficial findings, several studies failed to demonstrate any reduction in mortality from the use of nitroglycerin during acute MI.[38,39] Nitrates are indicated for patients who have had an MI and still exhibit anginal-type pains.

- *Calcium-channel blockers:* Calcium-channel blockers have been widely tested in acute MI but have not demonstrated any long-term benefit in prognosis overall.[28]

- *Anticoagulation:* Warfarin reduces the incidence of arterial emboli during the first 3 months after large anterior infarctions.

- *Other drugs categories:* Diuretics are used to manage heart failure and high blood pressure; digitalis or dopamine is also helpful for heart failure.

Table 28-1 summarizes drugs used in the post-MI period.

Dialogue history

In the presence of a positive history of cardiovascular disease (e.g., angina, MI), the following dialogue history should be pursued:

Has the pattern of your episodes of angina changed in the last month?

Comment: As discussed in Chapter 27, anginal episodes are usually fairly consistent for each patient. Increased frequency, duration, or severity or decrease in the level of precipitating factors or effectiveness of nitroglycerin may be an indication of unstable angina.[40] Immediate consultation with the patient's physician is desirable.

When did you have your last myocardial infarction?

Comment: Following MI, risk of reinfarction is increased. A patient who has had an MI is at increased risk during dental therapy regardless of the amount of time elapsed since the initial episode.[13] In the immediate postinfarction period, however, there is a considerably higher risk of reinfarction. In a study of surgical patients by Weinblatt et al.,[41] the reinfarction rate (MI recurring during surgery or in the immediate postoperative period [4 hours]) was 37% if the surgical procedure occurred within 3 months of the initial episode, 16% if the procedure was performed within 4 to 6 months of the episode, and 5% if the procedure was performed more than 6 months after the episode, compared with 0.1% in persons with no history of MI. During the period of recovery from acute MI, collateral circulation to the infarcted area improves, thereby allowing the myocardium to heal and minimizing the size of the residual infarct.[42,43] This process of healing and myocardial stabilization is usually

TABLE 28-1 Medications used for patients who have had myocardial infarction

Drug category	Examples	Rationale
β-blockers	Propranolol Timolol Metoprolol	Studies demonstrate that β-blockers decrease the likelihood of sudden death and reinfarction in months following acute MI
Calcium-channel blockers	Diltiazem Verapamil	Prevent reinfarction and reduce mortality rate
Antiplatelet agents	Aspirin Clopidogrel	Shown to reduce incidence of sudden death and recurrent MI
Anticoagulants	Warfarin	Reduce incidence of arterial emboli in initial 3 months following acute MI
ACE inhibitors	Captopril	Prevent left ventricular dilation and onset of heart failure
Diuretics	Hydrochlorothiazide	High blood pressure, heart failure
Inotropic drugs	Digitalis Dopamine Dobutamine Amrinone	Heart failure
Nitrates	Nitroglycerin—ointment, transdermal, sublingual tablet, or spray Long-acting nitrates (see Table 27-4)	Anginal pains

ACE, angiotensin-converting enzyme; MI, myocardial infarction.

complete in 6 months.[44] The increased risk for the patient who has had an MI is illustrated by an overall mortality rate of 30% within the first month after the infarction.[8,13] A majority of these deaths are associated with the onset of significant dysrhythmias (e.g., ventricular tachycardia and ventricular fibrillation).[45,46] Although this high mortality rate does decrease with time, after 10 years the postinfarction mortality rate is still 10 times that for those with no history of MI.[13]

What medications and drugs are you currently taking?

Comment: Refer to Medical History Questionnaire question 62 for a list of drugs frequently prescribed to patients who have had an MI. This information indicates the degree of residual myocardial damage, the presence of any significant signs and symptoms (e.g., chest pain, shortness of breath, undue fatigue), and damage to the cardiac conduction system (e.g., presence of dysrhythmias).

Physical examination

Vital signs should be recorded before and immediately after all dental appointments in the patient who has had an MI (see Table 2-1 for suggested management of patients according to their blood pressure readings). Additional examination of this patient may not provide any reliable indication of previous MI. Many survivors of a mild MI (e.g., minimal residual damage) appear to be in extremely fine physical and mental condition. Researchers have investigated the role of physical exercise in the rehabilitation of the myocardium after infarction. Findings have led to comprehensive physical training programs for many of these patients.[47–49] Patients are permitted to resume normal activities, such as walking and sexual activity, in a graded manner during convalescence. Such programs result in both subjective and objective improvement, recorded as decreases in heart rate and blood pressure, as well as a return to a normal or near-normal lifestyle and improved morale. Unfortunately, there is much less evidence for improvement in ventricular function and little convincing evidence that these programs decrease the recurrence rate of MI or the mortality rate.[50] It must always be remembered, therefore, that regardless of the apparent state of physical fitness of patients who have had an MI, they must still be considered at increased risk during all dental procedures.

Patients who have a significant degree of ventricular damage may present with clinical signs and symptoms of heart failure (see Chapter 14). Visual examination of these patients may reveal a degree of peripheral cyanosis (e.g., noted in nail beds, mucous membranes), coolness of the extremities, peripheral edema (in ankles), and possible orthopnea (difficulty in breathing that is relieved by sitting upright). These patients are at considerable risk during dental treatment.

■ DENTAL THERAPY CONSIDERATIONS

Dental therapy considerations for the patient who has had an MI include reducing dental-related stress with possible alteration in drug therapy, dental therapy, or both. These patients are classified by the American Society of Anesthesiologists (ASA) as an ASA II, III, or IV risk depending on the time elapsed since the previous infarction, the number of prior infarcts, and the presence of continued signs or symptoms of cardiovascular disease (e.g., dyspnea, chest pain, dysrhythmias). Table 28-2 presents the ASA classification of the patient who has had an MI.

TABLE 28-2   Dental therapy considerations for patients who have had a myocardial infarction

Number of episodes of MI	ASA physical status	Considerations
One documented MI at least 6 months previously; no residual cardiovascular complications	II or III	Usual ASA II considerations to include supplemental O_2 during treatment and follow-up telephone call after therapy
One documented episode at least 6 months previously; angina, heart failure, or dysrhythmia present	III or IV	Use dialogue history to determine level of risk (ASA); usual ASA III considerations, including possible premedication with nitroglycerin 5 minutes before surgery (if history of angina present); O_2 through nasal canula or nasal hood; and follow-up telephone call after therapy
More than one documented episode, most recent one at least 6 months previously; no further cardiovascular complications	III	Usual ASA III considerations to include supplemental O_2 during treatment and follow-up telephone call after therapy
Documented episode less than 6 months previously, or severe post-MI complications	IV	Usual ASA IV considerations

ASA, American Society of Anesthesiologists; MI, myocardial infarction.

Stress reduction

The degree of stress intolerance, although present in all patients who have had an MI, varies from person to person. Use of the stress reduction protocol should be seriously consideration. Of special importance are intra-operative stress reduction and adequate pain control.

Supplemental oxygen

The administration of supplemental O_2 to the patients who have had an MI minimizes the risk of hypoxia and myocardial ischemia. An O_2 flow of 3 to 5 L/min through a nasal cannula (humidified) or nasal hood (5 to 7 L/min) is recommended.

Sedation

Oxygen may also be delivered in conjunction with nitrous oxide (N_2O). N_2O-O_2 inhalation sedation is the most recommended sedation technique for the patient at cardiac risk. Its value in the management of acute MI is discussed later in this chapter. Other sedation techniques may be used as deemed necessary by the doctor. Hypoxia should be avoided in all sedation techniques through administration of supplemental O_2.

Pain control

Adequate pain control during treatment is a critical factor in increasing safety during dental treatment of the cardiac risk patient. As discussed in Chapter 27, endogenous catecholamine release potentially is more dangerous to the patient at cardiac risk than the 0.01 mg/mL of exogenous epinephrine introduced into the tissues with a properly administered local anesthetic containing epinephrine in a 1:100,000 concentration. Vasoconstrictors are contraindicated in patients with intractable ventricular dysrhythmias or any ASA IV patient at cardiac risk (elective dental care, likewise, is contraindicated in such patients). The use of vasoconstrictor-containing local anesthetics is relatively contraindicated in patients receiving noncardiospecific β-blockers, such as propranolol.[51]

Duration of treatment

The duration of the dental appointment for the patient who has had an MI varies but *should not exceed the patient's level of tolerance.* Patients demonstrating signs of discomfort, such as dyspnea, diaphoresis, and increased anxiety, should be queried to determine a cause with further treatment modified, or possibly terminated.

Six months after MI

It is strongly recommended that elective dental care, even procedures as seemingly innocuous as prophylaxis, be avoided until at least 6 months after MI.[52,53] Invasive emergency care, such as that for infection and pain, is not recommended in the dental office during this time, if possible. Acute dental problems (e.g., infection, pain) may at first be managed pharmacologically, through administration of oral drugs (e.g., antibiotics or analgesics) alone; any necessary invasive treatment, such as extraction or pulpal extirpation, should proceed in a more controlled environment, such as a hospital dental clinic.

Only emergency procedures should be considered less than 6 months after an MI. Even in these cases, immediate invasive care is warranted only after medications have been ineffective in resolving the problem and a hospital setting (a controlled environment) is available for the planned treatment.

Medical consultation

Medical consultation should be considered before commencing dental treatment of a patient who has had an MI when, after a full dental, medical, and psychological evaluation of the patient, the doctor has any doubt regarding the patient's status (e.g., ability to safely handle dental stress). If emergency dental treatment is scheduled for this patient within the recommended 6-month waiting period, medical consultation is strongly suggested before treatment begins.

Anticoagulant or antiplatelet therapy

Medical consultation is also indicated before any treatment involving a risk of hemorrhage (e.g., periodontal surgery, oral surgery, implant placement, or local anesthetic nerve block with a significant positive aspiration risk [e.g., inferior alveolar nerve block]) if the patient is currently receiving anticoagulant or antiplatelet therapy. The post-MI use of anticoagulants is less common today than in the recent past.

Elective dental surgery is frequently performed in patients whose international normalized ratio (prothrombin time or protime) is 2 to 3 without the development of bleeding problems.[52] In most instances, therefore, the proposed dental procedure need not be postponed, and the patient's anticoagulant medication need not be altered. However, the doctor should take precautions to prevent postoperative hemorrhage. Possible steps include a hemostatic dressing placed within an extraction site, multiple sutures in the surgical area, intraoral pressure packs, ice packs (extraoral), avoidance of mouth rinses, and a soft diet for 48 hours after the procedure. Additionally, inferior alveolar and posterior superior alveolar nerve block injections are associated with increased risk of hemorrhage and therefore should be avoided, if possible, in some cases.

■ CLINICAL MANIFESTATIONS
Pain

The chief clinical manifestation of acute MI is the sudden onset of severe, anginal-type pain, which is experienced in 80% of cases. Because acute MI most often develops from thrombus formation in a coronary artery, it may occur without an obvious precipitating cause. Acute MI often develops during a period of rest or sleep, but it may also occur during or immediately after a period of unusually strong exercise (Table 28-3).[54-56] A high percentage of MIs occur in the early morning, most commonly between 6 AM and noon (most frequently on Monday [where the weekend is Saturday/Sunday]), perhaps associated with circadian elevations in plasma catecholamines and cortisol and increases in platelet aggrability.[57-59] Emotional stress may be a precipitating factor.[60,61] The pain builds rapidly to maximal intensity, lasting for prolonged periods (30 minutes to several hours) if unmanaged.

Pain associated with acute MI is described as an intense sensation, much like a pressure or weight on the chest or like a deep ache within the chest. The victim may state "it feels like there is a heavy rock or someone sitting on my chest."[62] Rarely is the pain described as sharp or stabbing. It is located substernally, over the middle to upper third of the sternum and, much less commonly, over the lower third of the epigastrium.[63] Unfortunately, when the pain of acute MI occurs in the epigastrium and is associated with nausea and vomit-

ing (see next section), the clinical picture may easily be confused with that of acute gastritis, cholecystitis, or peptic ulcer.

Neither rest nor nitroglycerin reduces the pain. The pain of MI is most effectively relieved through the administration of opioids such as morphine. Radiation of pain occurs in the same pattern as that for angina (see Figure 27-2).

In 20% to 25% of cases, pain is either absent or minor and is overshadowed by immediate complications, such as acute pulmonary edema, heart failure, profound weakness, shock, syncope, or cerebral thrombosis. This type of infarction is called a silent (painless) infarction and is more commonly noted in women, the elderly, and diabetic patients.[64-66]

Other clinical signs and symptoms

The patient suffering an MI may appear in acute distress. A cold sweat is usually present; the patient feels quite weak and appears apprehensive, expressing an intense fear of impending doom. Although "intense fear of impending doom" may appear to the reader to be an overly dramatic statement, many victims of acute MI do indeed report this. In contrast to anginal patients, who lie, sit, or stand still, realizing that any activity might increase their discomfort, patients with acute MI are frequently quite restless, moving about in a futile attempt to find a more comfortable position. They may clutch at their chest with a fist, the *Levine sign* (a sign of ischemic pain popularized by Dr. Samuel A. Levine). Dyspnea is usually present; with the patient reporting that the crushing pressure on the chest prevents normal breathing. Respiratory movements do not intensify the painful sensation. Nausea and vomiting frequently occur, especially if the pain is severe. Other clinical signs and symptoms associated with acute MI can include a feeling of light-headedness or faintness, coughing, wheezing, and abdominal bloating. This last symptom leads some victims to think (hope?) that they are suffering from upset stomach or indigestion, thereby delaying the initiation of proper treatment and increasing the risk of death.

Acute MI should be suspected in the following three situations:
1. A first episode of chest pain suggestive of acute MI that occurs either at rest or with ordinary activity. Although it is possible for a first episode of chest pain that develops during dental treatment to be anginal (especially if the patient is dental phobic), it may also indicate coronary artery occlusion.
2. Change in a previously stable pattern of anginal pain. This may involve either increased frequency or

TABLE 28-3 Patient activity at onset of myocardial infarction

Activity	Percentage
At rest	51
Modest or usual exertion	18
Physical exertion	13
Sleep	8
During surgical procedure	6
Other	4

Data from Phipps C: Contributory causes of coronary thrombosis, *JAMA* 106:761, 1936.

severity, or the occurrence of rest (unstable) angina for the first time.

3. Chest pain suggestive of myocardial ischemia in a patient with known CAD if unrelieved by rest or nitroglycerin.

Physical findings

Patients appear restless and apprehensive and may be in severe pain. Their color may be poor: the face an ashen gray, with nailbeds and other mucous membranes cyanotic. Skin is cool, pale, and moist. Heart rate (pulse) may be weak, thready, and rapid (tachycardic), although a slow rate (bradycardia) may occasionally be present. Dysrhythmias are often present: premature ventricular contractions are seen in 93% of patients within the first 4 hours after acute MI.[67] Blood pressure may be normal but much more commonly is low, decreasing dramatically over the first few hours and possibly falling to shock levels. Respirations are rapid and shallow. If the left ventricle is the major site of infarction, left ventricular failure may become clinically evident, with labored breathing, frothy sputum, and other signs of heart failure (dependent edema); or pulmonary edema may gradually develop (Box 28-1).

Acute complications

The greatest risk of death from MI occurs during the first 4 to 6 hours after coronary artery occlusion and the onset of signs and symptoms. Complications such as acute dysrhythmias and cardiac arrest can occur abruptly during this time. More than 60% of deaths associated with acute MI occur within an hour of the event and are associated with acute fatal dysrhythmias, such as pulseless ventricular tachycardia and ventricular fibrillation.[45] Premature ventricular contractions are common (93%). Their presence indicates increased irritability of the damaged myocardium and may presage the development of potentially fatal dysrhythmias: ventricular tachycardia or ventricular fibrillation.

Ventricular fibrillation is 15 times more likely to occur in the first hour after the onset of signs and symptoms than in the next 12 hours;[68,69] it develops in the first hour in approximately 36% of persons with acute MI.[70] The significant mortality rate associated with MI is in part based on the average delay (4.9 hours) between the onset of signs and symptoms and intervention by the emergency medical system.[71] The doctor must mentally prepare for the development of acute complications. Survival through the prehospitalization period is indeed a good omen because once the patient is hospitalized in the emergency department and then in a specialized cardiac care unit, the chances for ultimate survival increase significantly. The most dangerous period is the time spent waiting for medical assistance to arrive.[68–70] Adequate preparation by the dental office staff can improve the chances for a successful outcome in this situation.

Box 28-1   Clinical manifestations of acute myocardial infarction

SYMPTOMS
Pain
Severe to intolerable
Prolonged, 30 min
Crushing, choking
Retrosternal
Radiates: left arm, hand, epigastrium, shoulders, neck, jaw
Nausea and vomiting
Weakness
Dizziness
Palpitations
Cold perspiration
Sense of impending doom

SIGNS
Restlessness
Acute distress
Skin—cool, pale, moist
Heart rate—bradycardia to tachycardia; PVCs common

PVC, premature ventricular contraction.

■ PATHOPHYSIOLOGY

Acute MI is usually the direct result of a sudden occlusion of a major coronary vessel. The obstruction may result from acute thrombosis, subintimal hemorrhage, or rupture of an atheromatous plaque, which leads to platelet aggregation and thrombus formation. The resulting thrombus can occlude more than 50% of the vessel lumen, which can lead to myocardial ischemia, hypoxia, acidosis, and eventually infarction.[72] The consequences of the occlusion depend upon the extent of the thrombotic process, the characteristics of the preexisting plaque, and the availability of collateral circulation.[72] The artery most often involved in coronary occlusion is the anterior descending branch of the left coronary artery, which supplies the anterior left ventricle. There are two major types of acute MI are STE (ST-segment elevation acute MI, also known as STEMI, and formerly called Q-wave acute MI) and non-STE (formerly non–Q-wave). The latter generally results from incomplete occlusion or spontaneous lysis of the thrombus and often signifies the presence of additional jeopardized myocardium; it is associated with a higher incidence of reinfarction and recurrent ischemia.[73] Patients with non-STEMI often benefit most from an aggressive management strategy.[74]

Occlusion may occur rapidly, or develop over a prolonged period. In either case it is possible that even 100% occlusion of a coronary vessel may not lead to ischemia and infarction. In the presence of adequate collateral circulation, the myocardium supplied by the occluded vessel will still receive an adequate blood supply. Unfortunately, collateral circulation in the normal heart is usually poorly developed. Angiographically apparent collateral arteries are usually not seen until the coronary obstruction is greater than 90%.[75] Collateral circulation may provide up to 50% of coronary blood flow in chronic total occlusions. Because these vessels enlarge over the next 3 to 4 weeks following occlusion, the size of the area of myocardial necrosis is usually smaller than would be expected.[76]

Acute MI may occur even though a blood vessel is not totally occluded. In an area dependent for its blood supply on collateral circulation (e.g., a previously infarcted area with now adequate collateral circulation), a minimal change in blood supply through the vessel may lead to infarction. This may come about through a partial occlusion of the vessel or from a change in vascular resistance in the vessel (e.g., spasm).

Infarction of myocardium produces alterations in the contractility of the heart owing to loss of functioning myocardial segments. The degree of depression of cardiac function in acute MI is directly related to the extent of left ventricular damage.[77] Because the left ventricle is most commonly involved in acute MI, the blood supply leaving the heart may be diminished, leading to many of the clinical signs and symptoms observed in acute MI, such as cool, moist skin; peripheral cyanosis; and tachycardia. The larger the infarct, the greater the degree of circulatory inadequacy (e.g., signs and symptoms of heart failure). Left ventricular filling pressures increase significantly, even in the presence of a small infarct. With a larger infarct there is a greater increase in left ventricular filling pressure and clinical evidence of left ventricular failure. Infarction of 40% or more of left ventricular mass leads to clinical evidence of hypotension, decreased cardiac output, and cardiogenic shock, which is often fatal.[78,79]

Cardiogenic shock occurs in approximately 10% to 15% of patients with acute MI who survive long enough to reach the hospital.[79,80] Cardiogenic shock is an ominous sign associated with a high mortality rate. Developing approximately 10 hours after the onset of the infarction, it results from cardiac dysrhythmias, the continued presence of severe pain, the onset of acute pulmonary edema, or pulmonary embolism. Clinical evidence of cardiogenic shock includes hypotension (systolic blood pressure below 80 mm Hg) and signs of an inadequate peripheral circulation (e.g., mental confusion, cool skin, peripheral cyanosis, tachycardia, and decreased urinary output).[80,81]

Probably the most threatening feature in the early postinfarction period (1 to 2 hours) is the presence of cardiac dysrhythmias. Most patients with cardiogenic shock (95%) exhibit abnormalities in heart rhythm. These abnormalities are significant because they may produce alterations in the normal sequence of atrial and ventricular contraction, thereby leading to inadequate cardiac output, or they may produce an aberrant focus of electrical depolarization in the myocardium. They also may adversely affect the ventricular rate, producing *bradycardia* (slow heart rate), *ventricular tachycardia* (extremely rapid contraction rate with insufficient time for ventricular filling), *ventricular fibrillation* (irregular, uncoordinated, ineffective contraction of individual muscle bundles), or, less commonly, asystole (complete absence of contractions). Commonly observed dysrhythmias are shown in Figure 30-1.

Death in the early postinfarction period usually is a result of acute dysrhythmia, although it may be produced by the infarction of a large mass of myocardium.[69,70] Patient survival after MI depends on many factors, the most important of which are the state of left ventricular function and the severity of obstructive lesions in the coronary vascular bed. Complete clinical recovery (i.e., no chronic complications) and a normal electrocardiogram are compatible with a 10- to 20-year period of survival. However, patients who exhibit residual heart failure usually die within 1 to 5 years.[82,83]

■ MANAGEMENT

Clinical management of acute MI is based on recognition of signs and symptoms and implementation of the required steps of basic life support. Initially it may be difficult to distinguish between the discomfort of angina and that of acute MI. Although there are subtle differences initially, the doctor may find it difficult to determine which of these clinical entities is present at the onset of the episode of acute chest pain.

As stressed in the discussion of angina pectoris (Chapter 27), a dental office diagnosis of angina will occur only when a patient presents in the office with a history of angina pectoris and confirms to the doctor that the "pain" is consistent with the usual angina. In all other situations, especially where there is no history of angina, emergency medical assistance is summoned immediately and the patient managed initially as though he or she were indeed suffering an acute MI.

Diagnostic clues to the presence of acute MI include the following:[84]

- Symptoms of pressure, tightness, a heavy weight
- Substernal, epigastric pain that may radiate to the jaw
- Moderate to severe discomfort
- Longer duration (>30 minutes) than anginal pain
- Nausea and vomiting
- Diaphoresis
- Dyspnea
- Irregular pulse
- Generalized weakness

Atypical signs and symptoms develop in approximately 10% to 30% of acute MI cases. Factors contributing to this include patient age, alternate chief complaints, atypical discomfort; and certain comorbid states.[72,85-90] Table 28-4 presents various typical and atypical symptoms of acute MI.

TABLE 28-4 Symptoms of acute myocardial infarction

Symptom	Bayer et al.[†]	Tinker	Uretsky et al.	Pathy
TYPICAL				
Chest pain	515	51	75	75
ATYPICAL				
Dyspnea	118	19	14	77
Syncope	72	4	1	27
Confusion	46	1	–	51
Stroke	32	6	–	26
Fatigue	36	2	4	10
Nausea/emesis	28	–	1	10
Sudden death	–	–	–	31
Giddiness	18	3	–	22
Diaphoresis	18	–	–	2
Arterial embolus	3	–	–	19
Palpitation	4	–	–	14
Renal failure	–	–	–	11
Pulmonary embolus	–	–	–	8
Restlessness	–	–	–	4
Abdominal pain	–	–	5	–
Arm pain only	–	–	1	–
Cough	–	–	1	–
SILENT				
No symptoms	17	1	–	–
Total	777[*]	87[†]	102[‡]	387[†]

*Patients able to report multiple symptoms; therefore, total exceeds 777.
†Patients classified by principal symptom, although all patients reporting chest or epigastric discomfort were placed in typical group.
‡Same as †, except patients with epigastric symptoms were placed in atypical group.
Data obtained from Aufderheide TP, Brady WJ, Gibler WB: Acute ischemic coronary syndromes. In: Marx JA, Hockberger RS, Walls RM, editors: *Rosen's emergency medicine: concepts and clinical practice*, ed 5, St. Louis, Mosby, 2002, pp. 1011–1052.
Citations for studies reported in table are as follows:
Bayer AJ, Chadha JS, Farag RR, Pathy MS: Changing presentation of myocardial infarction with increasing old age, *J Am Geriatr Soc* 34:263–266, 1986; Tinker GM: Clinical presentation of myocardial infarction in the elderly, *Age Ageing* 10:237–240, 1981; Uretsky BF, Farquhar DS, Berezin AF, Hood WB Jr.: Symptomatic myocardial infarction without chest pain: prevalence and clinical course, *Am J Cardiol* 40:498–503, 1977; Pathy MS: Clinical presentation of myocardial infarction in the elderly, *Br Heart J* 29:190–199, 1967.

If these symptoms occur, these steps should be followed.

Step 1: termination of the dental procedure; activation of office emergency team.
With the onset of chest pain, immediately stop treatment and activate the dental office emergency team.

Step 2: diagnosis.
Although, at the outset, it may prove difficult to distinguish between the pain of angina and acute MI, it is immediately apparent that the patient (victim) is in acute distress and must be treated accordingly.

Three potential clinical situations follow:

- *Anginal patient—acute anginal attack*: A patient with a history of angina is usually able to tell if the current episode of pain is anginal. If angina is felt to be the problem, the steps described in Chapter 27 are to be followed. The patient with angina, who is accustomed to treating this condition, will oftentimes be calmer about the situation than will the doctor, who is probably unaccustomed to patients experiencing acute chest pain during dental treatment.

- *Anginal patient—not angina*: A patient with angina in whom the chest pain is more intense than usual will become frightened, convinced that "the big one" is happening. If ever a patient with angina wishes emergency medical service (EMS) to be summoned, do so immediately. Recommended management follows the steps outlined later for acute MI.

- No *history of chest pain*: ACTIVATE EMS, immediately. Chest pain developing with no history of chest pain is frightening to patients, who may be convinced that a "heart attack" is occurring and that they are going to die. Management of this situation is presented below.

Step 3: P (position).
Conscious patients experiencing chest pain can be positioned in any position comfortable for them. Upright is usually preferred.

Step 4: A-B-C (airway-breathing-circulation) or basic life support (BLS), as needed.
At this point in the acute MI, the patient will be experiencing more intense discomfort and may be demonstrating clinical signs of decreased cardiac output (i.e., diaphoresis; cool, moist extremities; ashen gray pallor; cyanosis of mucous membranes and nailbeds). Airway, breathing, and circulation are assessed and are usually adequate.

Step 5: D (definitive care).
Prehospital management of the suspected MI victim adheres to the MONA acronym: M is morphine; O, oxygen; N, nitroglycerin; and A, aspirin. Suspected victims include persons with potential unstable angina pectoris or MI. Treatment involves the following approaches: (1) increase myocardial O_2 supply through supplemental inhaled O_2 and thrombolytic therapy, which restores coronary blood flow; (2) use of β-adrenergic blockade to decrease the force of myocardial contraction and therefore oxygen demand; (3) increase metabolic substrate availability to the myocardium through nitroglycerin, morphine, thrombolytic agents, and percutaneous transluminal coronary angioplasty (PTCA); (4) protect injured myocardial cell function by decreasing inflammation or toxic injury through antiinflammatory drugs and perfluorochemicals; and (5) prevent reocclusion of the coronary artery through inhibition of platelet aggregation and thrombus formation through the use of antiplatelet agents such as aspirin and antithrombins, including heparin.[72]

Step 5a: administration of oxygen.
Administer O_2 as soon as it is available. Evidence suggests that increased arterial oxygen tension (PaO_2) may decrease the size of the infarct.[91,92] Oxygen should be delivered through a nasal cannula or nasal hood at a flow rate of 4 to 6 L/min.

Step 5b: summoning of medical assistance.
When there is strong suspicion that chest pain is not of anginal origin but is likely to be a MI, or in the instance of a first episode of chest pain, the EMS system should be activated as soon as possible. Do not hesitate to activate EMS.

More than 60% of all deaths from acute MI occur within the first few hours after the onset of symptoms, usually before the victim is hospitalized. It is reported that more than two thirds of cases of out-of-hospital sudden cardiac arrest occurred in the patient's home.[93-95] Three fourths of all deaths occur within the first 24 hours. Most prehospital cardiac arrest deaths result from the development of life-threatening dysrhythmias that are common in the immediate postinfarction period, as well as from misinterpretation or denial of signs and symptoms by the patient or medical personnel. Early entry into the EMS system is often vital for patient survival, yet 26% to 44% of patients having an acute MI delay more than 4 hours before seeking medical care.[72]

Data support the conclusions that (1) time is critical to optimal outcome for patients with acute MI; (2) major trials of thrombolytic therapy document that maximum treatment benefit occurs during the first 1 to 2 hours following symptom onset; and (3) only a small percentage of patients with acute MI receive treatment within 1 hour of onset of symptoms.[72] Among the most significant factors delaying entry into the EMS system is patient/bystander factors. Median patient delays range from 2 to 6.5 hours in numerous studies, well beyond the critical first hour during which more than 50% of acute MI deaths occur.[72]

Step 5c: administration of nitroglycerin. Administer nitroglycerin. If the victim has a history of angina, nitroglycerin, which should always be available, is used at this time unless contraindications to its administration exist. Nitroglycerin from the emergency kit is used when the patient does not have a personal supply or if the patient's supply does not relieve the pain. The patient's vital signs should be recorded before administering nitroglycerin. *Nitroglycerin should not be administered in the presence of hypotension* (if systolic blood pressure is below 90 mm Hg) since it can further decrease mean arterial pressure. Nitroglycerin normally acts within 2 to 4 minutes to dramatically reduce or terminate the discomfort of angina. If angina is the cause, symptoms resolve and the acute episode is terminated. Dental care may resume if both the doctor and patient so desire, or the treatment is terminated and the patient dismissed from the office (see discussion in Chapter 27). If, despite the administration of O₂ and nitroglycerin, the pain continues or increases, or if nitroglycerin relieves the pain, but the pain returns in a few minutes, a presumptive diagnosis of acute MI must be seriously considered.

> NOTE: *Chest pain that is alleviated by nitroglycerin but returns should be managed as though it were acute MI.*

Step 5d: antiplatelet therapy. Platelets play a major role in thrombus formation following rupture of coronary artery plaque and are integrally involved in the pathophysiology of acute MI.[72] In patients with unstable angina pectoris, antiplatelet therapy has led to dramatic reductions in its progression to acute MI. Additionally, patients experiencing acute MI also experience significant benefit from antiplatelet therapy, with decreases in mortality ranging from 25% to 50%.[96] Therefore, there is a sound scientific basis for recommending antiplatelet therapy in all patients with acute MI.[72]

Administration of aspirin is a part of the MONA acronym used during the prehospital management of out-of-hospital acute MI victims.[97,98] Aspirin irreversibly acetylates platelet cyclooxygenase for the life span of the platelet (8 to 10 days). Aspirin therefore halts production of proaggregatory thromboxane A2 and is also an indirect antithrombotic agent.[72,99] Standard doses range from 160 to 325 mg given orally. Minimal side effects are noted with 160 mg.

A dose of 325 mg should be administered orally, chewed, and swallowed by all patients with suspected acute MI or unstable angina unless significant allergy or life-threatening hemorrhage contraindicates its administration.[72,100-103]

Aspirin therapy confers conclusive net benefits in the acute phase of evolving acute MI and should be administered routinely in these cases. In the Second International Study of Infarct Survival (ISIS-2),[96] more than 17,000 men and women were randomly assigned within 24 hours of onset of symptoms of suspected acute MI to one of two treatment groups: 162 mg of aspirin or placebo daily for 30 days. After 5 weeks, patients who received aspirin had statistically significant reductions in risk of vascular death (23%), nonfatal reinfarction (49%), and nonfatal stroke (46%). Hemorrhagic stroke or gastrointestinal bleeding did not increase in the treated group, and minor bleeding increased only slightly. Thus, aspirin has perhaps the best benefit/risk ratio of any proven therapy for acute MI. The benefits of aspirin for risk of subsequent acute MI, stroke, or vascular death are substantial. The risks of serious bleeding and sensitivity reactions are low and are amenable to treatment in an acute care setting, even when the patient has a history of bleeding or other sensitivity to aspirin. Thus, contraindications to use of aspirin in acute MI are relative, not absolute.

To achieve an immediate clinical antithrombotic effect, an initial minimum loading dose of 162 mg should be used in acute MI. If an enteric-coated aspirin is the only preparation available, the first tablet should be chewed or crushed before administration. In 1996 the, U.S. Food and Drug Administration[104] proposed a professional labeling indication for aspirin in patients with acute MI: an initial dose of 160 to 162.5 mg continued daily for at least 30 days.[105]

Clopidogrel (Plavix), at an initial dose of 300 mg orally, may be used in place of, or along with, aspirin. Clopidogrel inhibits adenosine diphosphate binding to platelet receptors. Platelets exposed to clopidogrel are affected for the remainder of their lifespan.[106]

Clopidogrel has been demonstrated to decrease the rate of a combined endpoint of cardiovascular death, MI, or stroke.[107,108] Like aspirin, clopidogrel is contraindicated in patients allergic to any component of the drug and in the presence of active pathologic bleeding, such as peptic ulcer or intracranial hemorrhage.[106]

Step 5e: monitoring of vital signs. Monitor vital signs. Vital signs (e.g., blood pressure, heart rate and rhythm, respiration) should be monitored on a regular basis (every 5 minutes) and recorded.

Step 5f: relief of pain. Relieve pain. Prolonged pain during acute MI is potentially life-threatening. It leads to increased patient anxiety and contributes to

excessive activity of the autonomic nervous system, producing an increase in cardiovascular workload and oxygen requirement. In addition, prolonged, intense pain is one of the causative factors of cardiogenic shock, which is associated with a high mortality rate. Where nitroglycerin fails to alleviate the discomfort associated with acute MI, morphine sulfate administration is appropriate.[109]

Morphine is a potent analgesic that also has anxiolytic actions, both of which may be beneficial to patients experiencing chest discomfort. Intravenous (IV) administration of 2 to 5 mg of morphine sulfate repeated every 5 to 30 minutes adequately relieves pain and allays apprehension.[72,110] Morphine also increases venous capacitance and systemic vascular resistance, relieving pulmonary congestion and thereby decreasing myocardial oxygen requirements.[110] *Morphine should not be readministered if the respiratory rate is less than 12 breaths per minute.* Naloxone, an opioid antagonist, should always be available when opioids are administered.

Another useful analgesic for administration in acute MI may already be present in the dental office. A mixture of N_2O and O_2, more commonly indicated as an inhalation sedation technique in dental practice, has been used in Great Britain and an increasing number of countries since 1967 in premixed cylinders containing 50% N_2O and 50% O_2 (Entonox)[111] (see Figure 28-1). Premixed cylinders of N_2O (35%) and O_2 (65%) (Dolonox) have also been used in the United States in the treatment of MI.[65] In Great Britain, the N_2O-O_2 mixture is used on emergency ambulances and is the primary agent for pain relief in acute cardiovascular emergency situations. The primary advantage of N_2O-O_2 is that it provides the patient with a gaseous analgesic agent that by itself has little effect on blood pressure. This contrasts with the use of parenteral analgesics, which are more likely to reduce blood pressure and produce adverse side effects (e.g., excessive central nervous system depression, respiratory depression, nausea, and vomiting). The use of this mixture also provides the patient with a source of enriched O_2 (50% to 65% vs. 21% in atmospheric air).[111–117]

A 35% to 40% concentration of N_2O is administered through the nasal hood or by means of a full face mask. When the patient is ready to be transported from the dental office to the hospital, the medical or paramedical personnel administer a parenteral analgesic (e.g., morphine sulfate) to provide continuing pain relief during the journey if portable sources of N_2O-O_2 are unavailable.

Step 6: preparation to manage complications. The major complications of acute MI likely to develop while awaiting the arrival of emergency medical assistance are acute dysrhythmias, heart failure, and cardiac arrest. Management of *acute dysrhythmias* requires IV administration of various drugs. In addition, the presence of an electrocardiogram and training to interpret the electrocardiogram are essential. Drugs that may be administered in the management of dysrhythmias include lidocaine and atropine.[118] Without an electrocardiographic monitor, no antidysrhythmic drug (other than O_2) should be administered to a patient with dysrhythmias. O_2 administration must be continued.

Left ventricular failure may develop if a significant portion of the myocardium has been infarcted. Respiratory symptoms are most prominent, with dyspnea and acute pulmonary edema noted. (Management of acute pulmonary edema is discussed fully in Chapter 14.)

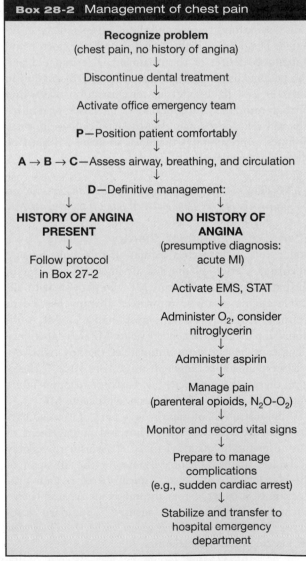

Box 28-2   Management of chest pain

Recognize problem
(chest pain, no history of angina)
↓
Discontinue dental treatment
↓
Activate office emergency team
↓
P—Position patient comfortably
↓
A → **B** → **C**—Assess airway, breathing, and circulation
↓
D—Definitive management:

HISTORY OF ANGINA PRESENT	**NO HISTORY OF ANGINA**
↓	(presumptive diagnosis: acute MI)
Follow protocol in Box 27-2	↓

Activate EMS, STAT
↓
Administer O_2, consider nitroglycerin
↓
Administer aspirin
↓
Manage pain
(parenteral opioids, N_2O-O_2)
↓
Monitor and record vital signs
↓
Prepare to manage complications
(e.g., sudden cardiac arrest)
↓
Stabilize and transfer to hospital emergency department

A, airway; **B**, breathing; **C**, circulation; **D**, definitive care; EMS, emergency medical service; **P**, position; MI, myocardial infarction.

Essentials of management include positioning the patient and a reduction in circulating blood volume through the use of a bloodless phlebotomy. O_2 should continue to be administered to this patient. *Cardiac arrest,* indicative of acute cardiorespiratory collapse, requires immediate effective management. Chapter 30 discusses this important subject in depth.

Step 7: transportation of patient to hospital.

After the victim's condition has been stabilized (i.e., relief of pain and stabilization of heart rhythm and blood pressure), the patient will be transported to a primary care facility (e.g., emergency department of a hospital). The dentist should accompany the patient to the hospital in the ambulance, if permitted, or follow by car and should remain with the patient until a physician is in attendance. Box 28-2 outlines the steps to follow in the management of chest pain thought to be acute MI.

Immediate in-hospital management

Although immediate in-hospital management is not entirely germane to the discussion of dental office management of medical emergencies, it is prudent to discuss the importance of seeking emergency medical assistance as soon as possible whenever an acute MI is suspected.

The initial treatment of suspected acute MI should be standardized at all hospitals.[28] Myocardial necrosis and salvage are time dependent. Delays in diagnosis and initial management of acute MI result in greater myocardial necrosis and elevated mortality rates.[28]

Table 28-5 presents suggested goals to be sought in every patient within 30 minutes of arrival in the hospital emergency department.

Initial treatment therapies include, but are not limited to, administration of aspirin, oxygen, analgesia, fibrinolytic therapy, β-blockers, and ACE inhibitors.[28,72]

Great strides have been made in myocardial salvation in the prevention of cellular death of myocardium acutely deprived of blood during the infarction. Two procedures, IV fibrinolytic therapy[119,120] and primary PTCA,[121-123] permit revascularization of the damaged myocardium. These procedures must be initiated as soon as possible following injury, before irreversible myocardium damage occurs (usually within the first 5 to 6 hours of occlusion).

Thrombolytic therapy

Thrombolytic therapy greatly reduces mortality and limits infarct size. Its greatest benefit is noted if therapy is initiated within the first 1 to 3 hours of infarct, when a 50% or greater reduction in mortality is observed.[124] The degree of benefit rapidly diminishes thereafter, but a 10% reduction in mortality may be noted up to 10 hours after the onset of pain.[125] Serious bleeding complications develop in 0.5% to 5.0% of patients.[125] Contraindications to thrombolytic therapy include known bleeding diatheses, a history of any cerebrovascular disease, uncontrolled high blood pressure (>190/110 mm Hg), pregnancy, and recent trauma or surgery of the head or spine.

Several thrombolytic agents are used: tissue plasminogen activator (t-PA, alteplase [Activase]), streptokinase

TABLE 28-5 Initial hospital management of suspected acute myocardial infarction

Time frame	Goal to achieve in management of suspected acute MI in emergency department
10 min	Obtain 12-lead ECG
	Administer supplemental O_2 (2–4 L by nasal cannula)
	Administer aspirin (four 81-mg tablets, chewed)
	Obtain focused history and physical examination
20 min	Review 12-lead ECG
	Review chest radiograph
	Obtain blood chemistries (complete blood count, lipids, and cardiac biomarkers)
	Administer heparin
	Administer β-blockers
	Consider intravenous nitroglycerin
30 min	Initiate reperfusion therapy
	Administer narcotic analgesic
	Transfer to coronary care unit

ECG, electrocardiogram; MI, myocardial infarction.
From Wright RS: Treatment of acute myocardial infarction. In: Rakel RE, Bope ET, editors: *Conn's current therapy 2005*, ed 57, Philadelphia, WB Saunders, 2005.

(Streptase), reteplase (Retavase) and tenecteplase (TNK-tPA, TNKase).[28,72]

PTCA

An increasing number of acute care centers manage acute MI with primary PTCA (immediate angiography and PTCA of the "infarct-related" vessel), rather than thrombolysis.[126] Results have been excellent, but because the number of centers performing this procedure is limited, these results may not hold true when more patients are studied.[127,128]

When a patient is in cardiogenic shock, PTCA is the preferred management (along with coronary artery bypass graft surgery) because thrombolysis has not improved the dismal prognosis for this group of patients.[129]

- **Drugs used in management:** Nitroglycerin; oxygen; morphine or N_2O-O_2
- **Medical assistance required:** Yes

REFERENCES

1. Thom T, Haase N, Rosamond W et al.: Heart Disease and Stroke Statistics—2006 Update: a report from the American Heart Association Statistics Committee and Stroke Statistics Committee, *Circulation* 113:85–151, 2006.
2. U.S. Department of Health and Human Services: Atherosclerosis Risk in Communities (ARIC, 1987–2000). Bethesda, MD, National Heart, Lung, and Blood Institute, 2006.
3. Antman EM, Braunwald E: Acute myocardial infarction. In: Zipes D, Libby P, Bonow R, Braunwald E, editors: *Braunwald's heart disease: a textbook of cardiovascular medicine,* ed 7, Philadelphia, WB Saunders, 2005.
4. Centers for Disease Control and Prevention/National Center for Health Statistics. 2006.
5. Killip T: Arrhythmias in myocardial infarction, *Med Clin North Am* 60:233–244, 1976.
6. Smith SM: Current management of acute myocardial infarction, *Dis Mon* 41:363–433, 1995.
7. Tunstall-Pedoe H, Vanuzzo D, Hobbs M, et al.: Estimation of contribution of changes in coronary care to improving survival, event rates, and coronary heart disease mortality across the WHO MONICA Project populations, *Lancet* 355:688–700, 2000.
8. American Heart Association: *Coronary heart disease and angina pectoris,* Dallas, American Heart Association, 1998.
9. Hurst W: *The heart, arteries and veins,* ed 10, New York, McGraw-Hill, 2002.
10. Scognamiglio R, Fasoli G, Nistri S, et al.: Left ventricular function and prognosis after myocardial infarction: rationale for therapeutic strategies, *Cardiovasc Drugs Ther* 8 Suppl 2:319–325, 1994.
11. Norris RM, Barnaby PF, Brandt PW, et al.: Prognosis after recovery from first acute myocardial infarction:

12. determinants of reinfarction and sudden death, *Am J Cardiol* 53:408–413, 1984.
12. Hedblad B, Janzon L, Johansson BW, Juul-Moller S: Survival and incidence of myocardial infarction in men with ambulatory ECG-detected frequent and complex ventricular arrhythmias. 10 year follow-up of the "Men born 1914" study in Malmö, Sweden, *Eur Heart J* 18:1787–1795, 1997.
13. Kannel WB: Some lessons in cardiovascular epidemiology from Framingham, *Am J Cardiol* 37:269–282, 1976.
14. Friedman EH: Type A or B behavior (letter), *JAMA* 228:1369, 1974.
15. Friedman M, Rosenman RH: *Type A behavior and your heart,* New York, Alfred A. Knopf, 1974.
16. Kawachi I, Sparrow D, Kubzansky LD, et al.: Prospective study of a self-report type A scale and risk of coronary heart disease: test of the MMPI-2 type A scale, *Circulation* 98:405–412, 1998.
17. Pickering T, Clemow L, Davidson K, Gerin W: Behavioral cardiology—has its time finally arrived? *Mt Sinai J Med* 70:101–112, 2003.
18. Kolodgie FD, Burke AP, Farb A, et al.: The thin-cap fibroatheroma: a type of vulnerable plaque: the major precursor lesion to acute coronary syndromes, *Curr Opin Cardiol* 16:285–292, 2001.
19. Szatjzel J, Mach F, Righetti A: Role of the vascular epithelium in patients with angina pectoris or acute myocardial infarction with normal coronary arteries, *Postgrad Med J* 76:16–21, 2000.
20. Feldman JA, Bui LD, Mitchell PM, et al.: The evaluation of cocaine-induced chest pain with acute myocardial perfusion imaging, *Acad Emerg Med J* 6:103–109, 1999.
21. Benzaquen BS, Cohen V, Eisenberg MJ: Effects of cocaine on the coronary arteries, *Am Heart J* 402–410, 2001.
22. Dolter K: Myocardial infarction. In: Forbes S, editor: *Cardiopulmonary emergencies,* Springhouse, PA, Springhouse, 1990.
23. Little WC, Downes TR, Applegate RJ: The underlying coronary lesion in myocardial infarction: implications for coronary angiography, *Clin Cardiol* 14:868–874, 1991.
24. O'Rourke DJ, Quinton HB, Piper W, et al.: Survival in patients with peripheral vascular disease after percutaneous coronary intervention and coronary artery bypass graft surgery, *Ann Thorac Surg* 78:466–470, 2004.
25. Sedrakyan A: Improving clinical outcomes in coronary artery bypass graft surgery, *Am J Health Syst Pharm* 62:S19–S23, 2005.
26. Sitzer VA, Atkins PJ: Developing and implementing a standard of care for intra-aortic balloon counterpulsation, *Crit Care Nurs Clin North Am* 8:451–457, 1996.
27. Reiffel JA: Practical algorithms for pharmacologic management of the post myocardial infarction patient. American Heart Association. American College of Cardiology, *Clin Cardiol* 28:I28–I37, 2005.
28. Wright RS: Treatment of acute myocardial infarction.

In: Rakel RE, Bope ET, editors: *Conn's current therapy 2005*, ed 57, Philadelphia, WB Saunders, 2005.

29. Fonarow GC: Beta-blockers for the post-myocardial infarction patient: current clinical evidence and practical considerations, *Rev Cardiovasc Med* 7:1–9, 2006.

30. Mendelson G, Aronow WS: Underutilization of beta-blockers in older patients with prior myocardial infarction or coronary artery disease in an academic, hospital-based geriatrics practice, *J Am Geriatr Soc* 45:1360–1361, 1997.

31. van der Elst ME, Bouvy ML, de Blaey CJ, de Boer A: Preventive drug use in patients with a history of nonfatal myocardial infarction during 12-year follow-up in The Netherlands: a retrospective analysis, *Clin Ther* 27:1806–1814, 2005.

32. de Kam PJ, Voors AA, Fici F, et al.: The revised role of ACE-inhibition after myocardial infarction in the thrombolytic/primary PCI era, *J Renin Angiotensin Aldosterone Syst* 5:161–168, 2004.

33. Lee VC, Rhew DC, Dylan M, et al.: Meta-analysis: angiotensin-receptor blockers in chronic heart failure and high-risk acute myocardial infarction, *Ann Intern Med* 141:693–704, 2004.

34. von Eckardstein A: Risk factors for atherosclerotic vascular disease, *Handb Exp Pharmacol* 170:71–105, 2005.

35. Sackner-Bernstein J: Reducing the risks of sudden death and heart failure post myocardial infarction: utility of optimized pharmacotherapy, *Clin Cardiol* 28:I19–I27, 2005.

36. Zhou Z, Rahme E, Pilote L: Association between time of statin initiation after hospital discharge from acute myocardial infarction and risk of recurrence and mortality in patients > or =65 years of age, *Am J Cardiol* 97:155–159, 2006.

37. Shannon AW, Harrigan RA: General pharmacologic treatment of acute myocardial infarction, *Emerg Med Clin North Am* 19:417–431, 2001.

38. Six-month effects of early treatment with lisinopril and transdermal glyceryl trinitrate singly and together withdrawn six weeks after acute myocardial infarction: the GISSI-3 trial. Gruppo Italiano per lo Studio della Sopravvivenza nell'Infarto Miocardico, *J Am Coll Cardiol* 27:337–344, 1996.

39. Hayes OW: Emergency management of acute myocardial infarction. Focus on pharmacologic therapy, *Emerg Med Clin North Am* 16:541–563, vii–viii, 1998.

40. Natarajan M: Angina (unstable), *Clin Evid* 14:60–70, 2005.

41. Weinblatt E, Shapiro S, Frank CW, Sager RV: Prognosis of men after first myocardial infarction: mortality and first recurrence in relation to selected parameters, *Am J Public Health* 58:1329–1347, 1968.

42. Gorlin R: Coronary collaterals. In: Gorlin R, editor: *Coronary artery disease*, Philadelphia, WB Saunders, 1976, pp. 69.

43. Bolooki H: Myocardial revascularization after acute infarction, *Am J Cardiol* 36:395–406, 1975.

44. Fishbein MC, Maclean D, Maroko PR: The histo-pathological evolution of myocardial infarction, *Chest* 73:843–849, 1978.

45. Boersma E, Maas AC, Deckers JW, Simoons ML: Early thrombolytic treatment in acute myocardial infarction: reappraisal of the golden hour, *Lancet* 348:771–775, 1996.

46. Perron AD, Sweeney T: Arrhythmic complications of acute coronary syndromes, *Emerg Med Clin North Am* 23:1065–1082, 2005.

47. Paramo JA, Olavide I, Barba J, et al.: Long-term cardiac rehabilitation program favorably influences fibrinolysis and lipid concentrations in myocardial infarction, *Haematologica* 83:519–524, 1998.

48. Miller TD, Balady GJ, Fletcher GF: Exercise and its role in the prevention and rehabilitation of cardiovascular disease, *Ann Behav Med* 19:220–229, 1997.

49. Datoe W, Huston P: Current trends in cardiac rehabilitation, *CMAJ* 156:527–532, 1997.

50. Neill WA, Oxendine JM: Exercise can promote coronary collateral development without improving perfusion of ischemic myocardium, *Circulation* 60:1513–1519, 1979.

51. Brummett RE: Warning to otolaryngologists using local anesthetics containing epinephrine: potential serious reaction occurring in patients treated with beta-adrenergic receptor blockers, *Arch Otolaryngol* 110:561, 1984.

52. Little J, Miller C, Phodus N, Falace D: Bleeding disorders. In: Little J, Miller C, Phodus N, Falace D, editors: *Dental management of the medically compromised patient*, ed 6, St. Louis, Mosby, 2002, pp. 332–364.

53. Little JW, Falace DA, Miller CS, Rodus NL, editors: *Dental management of the medically compromised patient*, ed 5, St. Louis, Mosby, 1997.

54. Phipps C: Contributory causes of coronary thrombosis, *JAMA* 106:761–762, 1936.

55. Kasikcioglu E: Cardiac response to prolonged strenuous exercise: a physiologic model for stunning myocardium (letter), *Am J Cardiol* 95:707, 2005.

56. Junker-Neff A, Eberle R, V Arnim T, et al.: Is there an association between the sleep apnea syndrome and the circadian peak of myocardial infarction in the morning hours? *Dtsch Med Wochenschr* 130:2818–2822, 2005.

57. Arntz HR, Willich SN, Schreiber C, et al.: Diurnal, weekly, and seasonal variation of sudden death. Population-based analysis of 24,061 consecutive cases, *Eur Heart J* 21:315–320, 2000.

58. Singh JP, Muller JE: Triggers to acute coronary syndrome. In: Therouox P, editor: *Acute coronary syndromes: a companion to Braunwald's heart disease*. Philadelphia, WB Saunders, 2003, pp. 108–118.

59. Muller JE, Abela GS, Nestow RW, et al.: Triggers, acute risk factors and vulnerable plaques: the lexicon of a new frontier, *J Am Coll Cardiol* 23:809–813, 1994.

60. Ueyama T, Senba E, Kasamatsu K, et al.: Molecular mechanism of emotional stress-induced and catecholamine-induced heart attack, *J Cardiovasc Pharmacol* 41:S115–S118, 2003.

61. Parmar MS, Luque-Coqui AF: Killer dreams, *Can J Cardiol* 14:1389–1391, 1998.

62. Achar SA, Kundu S, Norcross WA: Diagnosis of acute coronary syndrome, *Am Fam Physician* 72:119–126, 2005.

63. Ornato JP: Critical decision making in the management of patients with acute myocardial infarction and other acute coronary syndromes, *Emerg Med Clin North Am* 19:283–293, 2001.

64. Aronow WS, Silent MI: Prevalence and prognosis in older patients diagnosed by routine electrocardiograms, *Geriatrics* 58:24–26, 36–38, 40, 2003.

65. Kulbertus H, Legrand V: Women and cardiovascular diseases, particularly coronaropathies, *Rev Med Liege* 54:244–250, 1999.

66. McGuire DK, Granger CB: Diabetes and ischemic heart disease, *Am Heart J* 138:S366–S375, 1999.

67. Iribarren C, Crow RS, Hannan PJ, et al.: Validation of death certificate diagnosis of out-of-hospital sudden cardiac death, *Am J Cardiol* 82:50–53, 1998.

68. Pantridge JF, Geddes JS: A mobile intensive care unit in the management of myocardial infarction, *Lancet* 2: 271–273, 1967.

69. Chatterjee K: Complications of acute myocardial infarction, *Curr Probl Cardiol* 18:1–79, 1993.

70 Brugada P, Andries EW: Early post-myocardial infarction ventricular arrhythmias, *Cardiovasc Clin* 22:165–180, 1992.

71. Ridker PM, Manson JE, Goldhaber SZ, et al.: Comparison of delay times to hospital presentation for physicians and nonphysicians with acute myocardial infarction, *Am J Cardiol* 70:10–13, 1992.

72. Aufderheide TP, Brady WJ, Gibler WB: Acute ischemic coronary syndromes. In: Marx JA, Hockberger RS, Walls RM, editors: *Rosen's emergency medicine: concepts and clinical practice*, ed 5, St. Louis, Mosby, 2002, pp. 1011–1052.

73. Alpert JS, Francis GS: *Handbook of coronary care*, ed 5, Boston, Little, Brown, 1993.

74. Bybee KA, Kopecky SL: Acute myocardial infarction. In: Rakel RE, Bope ET, editors: *Conn's current therapy 2006*, Philadelphia, WB Saunders, 2006.

75. Popma JJ: Coronary angiography and intravascular ultrasound imaging. In: Zipes D, Libby P, Bonow R, Braunwald E, editors: *Braunwald's heart disease: a textbook of cardiovascular medicine*, ed 7, Philadelphia, WB Saunders, 2005.

76. Fujita M, Nakae I, Kihara Y, et al.: Determinants of collateral development in patients with acute myocardial infarction, *Clin Cardiol* 22:595–599, 1999.

77. Anavekar NS, Anavekar NS. Clinical modifiers for heart failure following myocardial infarction, *Curr Heart Fail Rep* 2:165–173, 2005.

78. Duvernoy CS, Bates ER: Management of cardiogenic shock attributable to acute myocardial infarction in the reperfusion era, *J Intensive Care Med* 20:188–198, 2005.

79. Kline JA: Shock. In: Marx JA, Hockberger RS, Walls RM, editors: *Rosen's emergency medicine: concepts and clinical practice*, ed 5, St. Louis, Mosby, 2002, pp. 33–47.

80. Wernly JA: Ischemia, reperfusion, and the role of surgery in the treatment of cardiogenic shock secondary to acute myocardial infarction: an interpretative review, *J Surg Res* 117:6–21, 2004.

81. Krost WS: Cardiogenic shock, *Emerg Med Serv* 33: 69–73, 78, 2004.

82. Sharpe N: Correlations of left ventricular hypertrophy with cardiovascular mortality, *Int J Clin Pract* Suppl: 16–22, 2000.

83. Kannel WB: Incidence and epidemiology of heart failure, *Heart Fail Rev* 5:167–173, 2000.

84. Pollakoff J, Pollakoff K: *EMT's guide to signs and symptoms*, Los Angeles, Jeff Gould, 1991.

85. Canto JG, Shlipak MG, Rogers WJ, et al.: Prevalence, clinical characteristics, and mortality among patients with acute myocardial infarction presenting without chest pain, *JAMA* 283:3223–3229, 2000.

86. Lusiani L, Perrone A, Pesavento R, Conte G: Prevalence, clinical features, and acute course of atypical myocardial infarction, *Angiology* 45:49–55, 1994.

87. Uretsky BF, Farquhar DS, Berezin AF, Hood WB Jr.: Symptomatic myocardial infarction without chest pain: prevalence and clinical course, *Am J Cardiol* 40: 498–503, 1977.

88. Bayer AJ, Chadha JS, Farag RR, Pathy MS: Changing presentation of myocardial infarction with increasing old age, *J Am Geriatr Soc* 34:263–266, 1986.

89. Jacoby RM, Nesto RW: Acute myocardial infarction in the diabetic patient: pathophysiology, clinical course, and prognosis, *J Am Coll Cardiol* 20:736–744, 1992.

90. Bertolet BD, Hill JA: Unrecognized myocardial infarction, *Cardiovasc Clin* 20:173–182, 1989.

91. Maroko PR, Radvany P, Braunwald E, Hale SL: Reduction of infarct size by oxygen inhalation following acute coronary occlusion, *Circulation* 52:360–368, 1975.

92. Ribeiro LG, Louie EK, Davis MA, Moroko PR: Augmentation of collateral blood flow to the ischaemic myocardium by oxygen inhalation following experimental coronary artery occlusion, *Cardiovasc Res* 13:160–166, 1979.

93. Holmberg M, Holmberg S, Herlitz J, Gardelov B: Survival after cardiac arrest outside hospital in Sweden. Swedish Cardiac Arrest Registry, *Resuscitation* 36:29–36, 1998.

94. Becker L, Eisenberg M, Fahrenbruch C, Cobb L: Public locations of cardiac arrest. Implications for public access defibrillation, *Circulation* 97:2106–2109, 1998.

95. Litwin PE, Eisenberg MS, Hallstrom AP, Cummins RO: The location of collapse and its effect on survival from cardiac arrest, *Ann Emerg Med* 16:787–791, 1987.

96. ISIS-2 (Second International Study of Infarct Survival) Collaborative Group: Randomised trial of intravenous streptokinase, oral aspirin, both, or neither among 17,187 cases of suspected acute myocardial infarction: ISIS-2, *Lancet* 2:349–360, 1988.

97. Haro LH: Initial approach to the patient who has chest pain, *Cardiol Clin* 24:1–17, v, 2006.

98. Schiff JH: Acute coronary syndrome in the prehospital phase, *Anaesthesist* 54:957–974, 2005.

99. Fitzgerald GA: Prostaglandins, aspirin, and related compounds. In: Arend WP, Armitage JO, Drazen JM,

et al., editors: *Cecil textbook of medicine*, ed 22, Philadelphia, WB Saunders, 2004.

100. Ayala TH: Pathogenesis and early management of non-ST-segment elevation acute coronary syndrome, *Cardiol Clin* 24:19–35, 2006.

101. Harrrington RA: Antithrombotic therapy for coronary artery disease: the Seventh ACCP Conference on Antithrombotic and Thrombolytic Therapy, *Chest* 126:513S–548S, 2004.

102. Pollack CV Jr.: 2002 update to the ACC/AHA guidelines for the management of patients with unstable angina and non-ST-segment elevation myocardial infarction: implications for emergency department management, *Ann Emerg Med* 41:355–369, 2003.

103. Messmore HL Jr.: Antiplatelet agents: current drugs and future trends, *Hematol Oncol Clin North Am* 19:87–117, vi, 2005.

104. US Food and Drug Administration: Internal analgesic, antipyretic, and antirheumatic drug products for over-the-counter human use: proposed amendment to the tentative final monograph, *Fed Reg* 61:30002, 1996.

105. American Heart Association Science Advisory and Coordinating Committee: *Aspirin as a therapeutic agent in cardiovascular disease*, Dallas, American Heart Association, 1997.

106. Clopidogrel bisulfate. www.MDConsult.com

107. A randomized, blinded, trial of clopidogrel versus aspirin in patients at risk of ischaemic events (CAPRIE). CAPRIE Steering Committee, *Lancet* 348:1329–1339, 1996

108. Mehta SR, Yusef S, Peters RJ, et al.: Clopidogrel in Unstable angina to prevent Recurrent Events trial (CURE) Investigators, *Lancet* 358:527–533, 2001.

109. O'Conner R, Persse D, Zachariah B, et al.: Acute coronary syndrome: pharmacotherapy, *Prehosp Emerg Care* 5:58–64, 2001.

110. Todres D: The role of morphine in acute myocardial infarction, *Am Heart J* 81:566–570, 1971.

111. Nancekievill D: Apparatus for the administration of Entonox (50% N_2O: 50% O_2 mixture) by intermittent positive pressure, *Anaesthesia* 29:736–739, 1974.

112. Thompson PL, Lown B: Nitrous oxide as an analgesic in acute myocardial infarction, *JAMA* 235:924–927, 1976.

113. Eisele JH, Reitan JA, Massumi RA, et al.: Myocardial performance and N_2O analgesia in coronary artery disease, *Anesthesiology* 44:16–20, 1976.

114. Kerr F, Brown MG, Irving JB, et al.: A double blind trial of patient-controlled nitrous oxide/oxygen analgesia in myocardial infarction, *Lancet* 1:397–400, 1975.

115. Stern MS, Shine KI: Nitrous oxide and oxygen in coronary artery disease, *JAMA* 245:129, 1981.

116. Fridlund B, Carlsson B: Acute myocardial infarction patients' chest pain as monitored and evaluated by ambulance personnel, *Intensive Crit Care Nurs* 8:113–117, 1992.

117. O'Leary U, Puglia C, Friehling TD, Kowey PR: Nitrous oxide anesthesia in patients with ischemic chest discomfort: effect on beta-endorphins, *J Clin Pharmacol* 27:957–961, 1987.

118. International Liaison Committee on Resuscitation. 2005 International Consensus on Cardiopulmonary Resuscitation and Emergency Cardiovascular Care Science with Treatment Recommendations, *Circulation* 112:III1–III136, 2005.

119. GISSI-2. A factorial randomised trial of alteplase versus streptokinase and heparin versus no heparin among 12,490 patients with acute myocardial infarction, *Lancet* 336:65–71, 1990.

120. The International Study Group: In-hospital mortality and clinical course of 20,891 patients with suspected myocardial infarction randomised between alteplase and streptokinase with or without heparin, *Lancet* 336:71–75, 1990.

121. Grines CL, Browne KF, Marco J, et al.: A comparison of immediate angioplasty with thrombolytic therapy for acute myocardial infarction, *N Engl J Med* 328:673–679, 1993.

122. Zijlstra F, de Boer MJ, Hoorntje JC, et al.: A comparison of immediate coronary angioplasty with intravenous streptokinase in acute myocardial infarction, *N Engl J Med* 328:680–684, 1993.

123. The GUSTO IIb Angioplasty Substudy Investigators. A clinical trial comparing primary coronary angioplasty with tissue plasminogen activator for acute myocardial infarction, *N Engl J Med* 336:1621–1628, 1997.

124. Raitt MH, Maynard C, Wagner GS, et al.: Relation between symptom duration before thrombolytic therapy and final myocardial infarct size, *Circulation* 93:48–53, 1996.

125. Mahaffey KW, Granger CB, Sloan MA, et al.: Risk factors for in-hospital nonhemorrhagic stroke in patients with acute myocardial infarction treated with: results from GUSTO-I, *Circulation* 97:757–764, 1998.

126. Michel MB, Yusuf S: Does PTCA in acute myocardial infarction affect mortality and reinfarction rates? *Circulation* 91:476–485, 1995.

127. Terrin ML, Williams DO, Kleiman NS, et al.: Two- and three-year results of the thrombolysis in myocardial infarction (TIMI) phase II clinical trial, *J Am Coll Cardiol* 22:1763–1772, 1993.

128. Zahn R, Koch A, Rustige J, et al.: Primary angioplasty versus thrombolysis in the treatment of acute myocardial infarction, *Am J Cardiol* 79:264–269, 1997.

129. Mueller HS, Cohen LS, Braunwald E, et al.: Predictors of early morbidity and mortality after thrombolytic therapy in acute myocardial infarction: analyses of patient subgroups in the Thrombolysis in Myocardial Infarction (TIMI) trial, phase II, *Circulation* 85:1254–1264, 1992.

CHAPTER 29

Chest Pain:

Differential Diagnosis

Two major clinical syndromes presenting as chest pain are angina pectoris and myocardial infarction (MI). Yet sometimes chest pain may not be cardiac in origin. Indeed, everybody experiences various forms of chest pain on occasion. Fortunately, most of these pains are unrelated to ischemic heart disease and are, for the most part, innocuous or, at the least, not acutely life-threatening. However, many of those experiencing any form of chest pain have stopped and thought, "This pain I am feeling now is the *real* thing." This chapter describes the differences between chest pain associated with ischemic heart disease and that which is noncardiac in origin.[1] Following that the differential diagnosis of the two major forms of cardiac (ischemic) chest pain, angina pectoris and acute myocardial infarction, is presented. Box 29-1 lists some of the many possible causes of chest pain.

Box 29-1 Causes of chest pain

CARDIAC RELATED
Angina pectoris
Myocardial infarction

NOT CARDIAC RELATED
Muscle strain (musculoskeletal)
Pericarditis
Esophagitis
Hiatal hernia
Pulmonary embolism
Dissecting aortic aneurysm
Acute indigestion
Intestinal "gas"

■ NONCARDIAC CHEST PAIN

Noncardiac chest pain may usually be differentiated from the ischemia-induced pain of angina and myocardial infarction because the sharp, knifelike chest pain that increases in intensity with inspiration and diminishes with exhalation is usually not related to cardiac syndromes.

Chest pain aggravated by movement (e.g., twisting, turning, or stretching of the sore area) is most often related to muscle or nerve injuries, not cardiac disease. I use the word *usually* when describing "typical" chest pains as there are instances in which patients are aware of sharp, knifelike pains that may in fact be related to cardiac disease. Variations from the typical are expected, and the dental health professional is well advised to take note of this.

Probably the most common cause of noncardiac chest pain is *musculoskeletal,* resulting from muscle strain that occurs after exercise or physical exertion.[2] This form of pain is normally localized (the patient can point to a specific site of discomfort), does not radiate, and is made worse by breathing and movement. A heating pad or mild analgesic medication may give relief.

Pericarditis is an inflammation of the outer membrane covering the heart (the pericardium) and most commonly results from viral infection. The pain of pericarditis is similar to that of angina or myocardial infarction, occurs in the midsternum, and is described as "oppressive." Clues to its differential diagnosis include aggravation of the pain of pericarditis when breathing and swallowing, characteristic relief of the pain when the patient bends forward from the waist, and often the presence of a fever before the onset of pain.[3]

Esophagitis, with or without *hiatal hernia,* produces a substernal or epigastric burning pain precipitated by eating or lying down after a meal. Pain is relieved by antacids. There often is an acid reflux into the mouth.[4]

Pulmonary embolism usually indicates the sudden occlusion of a blood vessel within the lungs by an embolus that has been "thrown" (broken loose) from the legs. The patient experiences a sudden severe chest pain that is commonly associated with the coughing up of blood-tinged sputum.[5] Pulmonary embolism represents an acutely life-threatening situation.

A less common cause of acute chest pain is *dissecting aortic aneurysm.* The patient experiences sudden, acute, severe chest pain that is often greatest at onset. Typically, it spreads up and down the chest and back over a period of hours. The dissecting aortic aneurysm may lead rapidly to death.[6]

Two other common causes of chest pain often make it difficult to differentiate between cardiac and noncardiac pain. These are the pains of acute indigestion and "gas," occurring primarily in the upper epigastric region. A major factor responsible for the high initial mortality rate associated with MI is misinterpretation or denial of clinical symptoms by the patient or the attending physician. Symptoms commonly attributed to indigestion or gas are only later discovered to have been produced by MI. Gas pain is normally sharp and knifelike, increasing in intensity with breathing. This fact should assist in differentiating gas pain from the pain of ischemic heart disease. Acute indigestion is similar to the pain of angina or myocardial infarction; therefore, all patients with this symptom should be carefully evaluated. *Epigastric discomfort* can be a manifestation of myocardial ischemia or infarction and must not be dismissed lightly. Unusual or prolonged indigestion should rouse suspicion, particularly in a high-risk individual. The American Heart Association recommends that a patient with previously unrecognized CAD seek medical assistance if suspicious chest pain persists for 2 minutes or longer.[7]

■ CARDIAC CHEST PAIN

Angina and MI are the two most common causes of ischemic heart disease–related chest pain in the dental environment. Differential diagnosis is essential because these two syndromes represent quite different risks to the patient and are ultimately managed differently. The following discussion is offered to assist in making this differential diagnosis.

Medical history

The patient with angina is aware of its existence and possesses drugs to manage acute anginal episodes. It is possible that a patient with a negative history of heart problems will suffer a first episode of angina in the dental office setting. Because of the stress associated with many dental procedures, at least in the minds of dental patients, there is frequently an increase in myocardial workload in the dental office setting. It is not unlikely that episodes of anginal-type chest pain may develop in this situation, especially in patients with a history of angina. However, absent a history of chest pain, the possibility also exists that this first episode of chest pain might be an MI. For this reason, it is highly recommended that a first episode of chest pain be managed as though it were an MI, until proven otherwise. The patient's medical history may indicate a prior MI. Many patients who survive MI later develop episodes of angina and will have nitroglycerin available.

In the absence of a history of angina pectoris, always assume that a first episode of chest pain is MI and active emergency medical service (EMS) immediately!

Age

Coronary artery disease (CAD) can be found in all age groups. There is little clinical difference between the age of patients developing angina and those sustaining an MI. Clinical evidence of CAD is most commonly observed between the ages of 50 and 60 years in men and 60 and 70 years in women.

Sex

CAD is primarily a disease of males. The overall male: female ratio is 4:1. Before the age of 40 years, the ratio is 8:1.

Related circumstances

The clinical symptoms of angina are usually associated with some form of exertion, whether physical or mental. On the other hand, although MI may occur during or immediately after a period of exertion, it frequently occurs during periods of rest. Angina rarely occurs during rest, although coronary artery spasm may provoke anginal pain at any time. Unstable angina, by definition, may occur at rest. When chest pain develops at rest in the dental environment, activation of EMS should be seriously considered.

Clinical symptoms and signs
Location of chest pain

Location of chest pain is not a reliable indicator of the nature of the pain. Both anginal pain and the pain of MI occur substernally or just to the left of the midsternal region.

Description of chest pain

Chest "pain" associated with angina or MI is usually not described as pain by the patient. More commonly the sensation is described as "squeezing," "pressing," "tightness," "heaviness," "as though there were a heavy weight on my chest," or "crushing." The pain associated with MI is more intense than that of angina and is more commonly described as painful or intolerable.

Radiation of chest pain

Differentiation between angina and MI is difficult to make by using radiation of pain as a criterion because both have similar radiation patterns. Radiation pain commonly occurs to the left shoulder and medial aspect of the left arm, following the distribution of the ulnar nerve. Less frequently pain may radiate to the right shoulder, the mandibular region, or the epigastrium.

Duration of chest pain

The pain associated with MI is normally of long duration, lasting from 30 minutes to several hours if untreated. As mentioned in Chapter 28, untreated cardiac pain may induce cardiogenic shock. Pain associated with angina is almost always brief. Merely terminating the activity that induced the episode brings relief within 3 to 5 minutes. Anginal episodes precipitated by eating a large meal or anger may persist longer, lasting perhaps 30 minutes or more.

Response to medication

Probably the most reliable diagnostic tool is the patient's response to the administration of medications. A vasodilator, usually nitroglycerin, is administered. Anginal pain will be relieved approximately 2 to 4 minutes after administration of nitroglycerin. Nitroglycerin may temporarily diminish the pain of myocardial infarction, but more commonly it has no effect. The pain of MI is commonly managed through administration of opioid analgesics, such as morphine, or nitrous oxide and oxygen.

Administration of a vasodilator to the patient with presumed cardiac-related chest pain offers a reliable method of differentiating between the pain of angina and that of MI. For this reason, the administration of nitroglycerin is one of the initial steps in the clinical drug management (along with O_2) of chest pain in the dental office.

Vital signs
Heart rate

Heart rate during acute episodes of angina increases and may feel full or bounding. A rapid heart rate may also occur during MI, however, because blood pressure is usually decreased, the pulse may feel weak or thready. The heart rate during MI may also be slow (bradycardia).

Blood pressure

Episodes of angina are normally accompanied by marked elevations in blood pressure, whereas blood pressure in MI may be normal but more commonly is decreased.

Respiration

Patients with either acute coronary syndrome may exhibit respiratory distress. Respiratory rate is increased while the depth of respiration may be more shallow than usual. During MI, clinical evidence of left ventricular failure may be noted.

Other signs and symptoms

Most patients with MI and some patients with angina appear quite apprehensive, bathed in cold sweat. Anginal patients can compare the present episode with previous ones, which can give a clue as to the seriousness of the present attack. Anginal episodes tend to be similar in an individual patient. Changes in severity, duration, or frequency may indicate the occurrence of unstable angina or MI. Patients with MI often express a fear of impending doom.

During MI, facial skin may appear ashen gray. Nailbeds and other visible mucous membranes may appear cyanotic. These changes rarely occur during episodes of angina.

Nausea and vomiting are common during MI, especially in the presence of severe pain. Nausea and vomiting are uncommon with anginal pain.

■ SUMMARY

The clinical diagnosis of chest pain is difficult. However, the response of the patient to the administration of nitroglycerin invariably leads to an accurate diagnosis. Acute anginal episodes are usually similar from episode to episode for a given patient. Any change in the nature of acute angina producing a more severe episode may indicate the occurrence of MI.

Noncardiac chest pain usually is easy to differentiate from ischemic heart pain because of the nature of the

TABLE 29-1 Comparison of cardiac and noncardiac pain

Noncardiac chest pain	Cardiac chest pain
Sharp, knifelike	Dull
Stabbing sensation	Aching
Aggravated by movement	Heaviness, oppressive feeling
Present only with breathing	Present at all times
Localized (patient able to point to one spot)	Generalized (occurs over a wider area)

Data obtained from Malamed SF: Beyond the basics: emergency medicine in dentistry, *J Am Dent Assoc* 128:843–854, 1997.

pain. However, two common forms of substernal, upper epigastric, discomfort—acute indigestion and gas—are quite difficult to differentiate from ischemic heart pain. These symptoms cannot be ignored. Careful evaluation is required, and medical consultation considered if there is any doubt as to the cause of a patient's chest pain.

Table 29-1 differentiates cardiac from noncardiac pain.

REFERENCES

1. Malamed SF: Beyond the basics: emergency medicine in dentistry, *J Am Dent Assoc* 128:843–854, 1997.
2. Brown JE, Hamilton GC: Chest pain. In: Marx JA, Hockberger RS, Walls RM, editors: *Rosen's emergency medicine: concepts and clinical practice*, ed 5, St. Louis, Mosby, 2002.
3. Fallon EM, Roques J: Acute chest pain, *AACN Clin Issues* 8:383–397, 1997.
4. Lemire S: Assessment of clinical severity and investigation of uncomplicated gastroesophageal reflux disease and noncardiac angina-like chest pain, *Can J Gastroenterol* 11:37B–40B, 1997.
5. Favretto G, Stritoni P: Pulmonary embolism: diagnostic algorithms, *Ital Heart J* 6:799–804, 2005.
6. Chen K, Varon J, Wenker OC, et al.: Acute thoracic aortic dissection: the basics, *J Emerg Med* 15:859–867, 1997.
7. *Heart attack, stroke & cardiac arrest warning signs,* Dallas, American Heart Association, 2005.

PART 8

CARDIAC ARREST

30   Cardiac Arrest

31   Pediatric Considerations

CHAPTER 30

Cardiac Arrest

Angina pectoris, myocardial infarction, and heart failure represent clinical manifestations of ischemic heart disease. Associated with each of these entities is the possible development of acute complications, including cardiac dysrhythmias and cardiopulmonary collapse. The latter is also called *cardiac arrest, sudden cardiac arrest (SCA),* or *sudden death.* Sudden cardiac arrest may also occur as an acute clinical entity in the absence of overt cardiovascular manifestations. Of all victims of SCA, 25% did not exhibit clinical signs or symptoms before the onset of SCA.[1] Stated another way, the first clinical indication of the presence of ischemic heart disease may be the (clinical) death of the patient.

Death, as previously described, implies *clinical* death as opposed to *biological* or *cellular* death. Clinical death occurs at the moment the victim collapses in cardiopulmonary arrest. The victim "looks dead"—they are clinically dead (they are unconscious, are not breathing, and have no pulse). Clinical death may, on occasion, be reversed if recognized promptly and managed effectively, thereby preventing biological death, which is irreversible. Biological death follows when permanent cellular damage occurs, primarily from a lack of oxygen. At the moment of SCA (clinical death), oxygenated blood remains in the tissues throughout the body. Cells in these tissues are not yet dead as they still have "fuel" to live off of (O_2 and "sugar"). When these fuels are fully consumed, cellular death ensues. The rate at which cells consume O_2 and sugar determines the rate at which they die. Cells with higher metabolic rates will suffer irreversible damage sooner than those with slower rates. Because of their high metabolic rate, biological or cellular death of neuronal (brain) tissue occurs approximately 4 to 6 minutes after SCA (in the absence of basic life support [BLS]).[2]

Because neurons are exquisitely sensitive to anoxia, cerebral resuscitation becomes *the* most important goal in saving a life in cardiac arrest. To reach that goal, rescuers must first restart the victim's heart. Cerebral resuscitation—return of the victim to the prearrest level of neurologic functioning—is the ultimate goal of emergency cardiac care.[3] Safar and Bircher[4] have proposed the term *cardiopulmonary-cerebral resuscitation* (CPCR) to replace the more familiar term, cardiopulmonary resuscitation (CPR). Clinicians should always remember the term *cerebral,* for it is a reminder of our primary purpose: to return the patient to his or her best neurologic outcome.[3] Unless spontaneous ventilation and circulation are restored quickly, successful cerebral resuscitation cannot occur.[5]

In 2002 in the United States, more than 927,448 deaths were attributed to cardiovascular disease.[6] Of these, 53% or 491,547 were due to coronary artery disease. Data from the Centers for Disease Control and Prevention estimates that in the United States approximately 400,000 to 460,000 people die of heart disease in an emergency department or before reaching a hospital, which accounts for over 60% of all cardiac deaths.[7] About 250,000 of these deaths occur in the out-of-hospital setting.[7–9] The annual incidence of SCA in North America is 0.55 per 1000 population.[10,11]

With the introduction of closed chest cardiac compression by Kouwenhoven et al.,[12] in 1960, a new era in cardiac resuscitation began. SCA, previously irreversible, became reversible in many instances with the effective application of this new technique. Although the rate of successful resuscitation from out-of-hospital

SCA has shown only modest gains since the 1960s, it must be remembered that before emergency medical services (EMS) became available, SCA was almost universally fatal. Given the circumstances necessary for resuscitation to be successful, it is remarkable that anyone survives.[13]

The rationale for cardiac resuscitation outside the hospital is that, in most cases, cardiac arrest is unexpected and cannot be predicted accurately in individual patients; thus, effective preventive measures are lacking. Immediate efforts at resuscitation offer the only realistic hope for most victims.[13] In some communities, such as Seattle, Washington, where advanced EMS systems exist, the rate of successful resuscitation and ultimate discharge home has more than doubled during the 1990s.[14] Response time from dispatch to arrival of a BLS team averages less than 3 minutes in Seattle, with a paramedic unit capable of administering advanced cardiac life support (ACLS) arriving 4 minutes later. A result of this expeditious response is that up to 60% of patients with ventricular fibrillation are successfully resuscitated at the scene, and 25% survive to leave the hospital.[14] In addition to Seattle's advanced EMS system, more than 33% of the population of King County, Washington, are trained in CPR (Table 30-1).[15]

Unfortunately, Seattle's experience with out-of-hospital cardiac arrest has not been duplicated in most cities, although cities with equivalent programs do have similar survival rates. Gray et al.[16] found that in several New England communities, rates of resuscitation from out-of-hospital cardiac arrest average 20%, with even fewer patients surviving until hospital discharge. Other studies have reported discharge rates of 2% to 33% after cardiac arrests outside the hospital.[17] Higher rates of successful resuscitation and survival to discharge from hospital have occurred in specific environments, including airports,[18] airlines,[19] and casinos.[20] Well-organized police CPR and automatic external defibrillator (AED) rescue programs have also demonstrated improved survival from out-of-hospital SCA.[21]

■ SURVIVAL FROM SUDDEN CARDIAC ARREST

Poor survival rates after resuscitation efforts from out-of-hospital SCA result from several factors, some of which are related to fate (Was the event witnessed or unwitnessed? What is the cardiac rhythm when first recorded?) and others to the emergency response itself (length of time from collapse to the initiation of resuscitation efforts and defibrillation).[17,22,23] The absence of any single favorable condition in the "chain of survival" (see below) results in an unsuccessful resuscitation.[24]

TABLE 30-1 Effectiveness of early defibrillation programs*

Location	Before early defibrillation	After early defibrillation	Odds ratio for improved survival
King County, WA	7 (N/A)	26 (10/38)	3.7
Iowa	3 (1/31)	19 (12/64)	6.3
SE Minnesota	4 (1/27)	17 (6/36)	4.3
NE Minnesota	2 (3/118)	10 (8/81)	5.0
Wisconsin	4 (32/893)	11 (33/304)	2.8

*Values in second and third columns are percentage of patients surviving and, in parentheses, number of patients surviving/number of patients with ventricular fibrillation.
N/A, not available.
Data from Cummins RO: From concept to standard-of-care? Review of the clinical experience with automated external defibrillators, *Ann Emerg Med* 18:1269–1275, 1989.

Some of the factors considered when trying to estimate the likelihood of survival from out-of-hospital SCA include[25]

- Was the arrest witnessed or unwitnessed?
- Was the original cardiac rhythm documented by the paramedics upon arrival?
- Was lay bystander CPR performed?
- How long did it take for help to arrive (i.e., speed of paramedic response)?

Witnessed versus unwitnessed

During a 3-year period, 28% of 380 patients whose cardiac arrests were witnessed were ultimately discharged from the hospital compared with only 3% of 231 victims of unwitnessed arrest.[25-27]

Initial rhythm

When the initial heart rhythm on electrocardiography (ECG) was either ventricular tachycardia (Figure 30-1B) or ventricular fibrillation (Figure 30-1C and D), survival rates were higher: 28% of 389 patients survived,[25,28,29] compared with 3% of 222 patients in asystole.[25] Survival is unusual (<5% of patients) when either pulseless electrical activity or asystole (Figure 30-1E) is initially recorded.[13,30,31] In a series of nearly 1100 attempted resuscitations of patients in asystole, only 13 survived (0.012%).[32]

It is unlikely that pulseless electrical activity or asystole is the initial rhythm precipitating SCA. In patients sustaining SCA while undergoing continuous cardiac monitoring (Holter monitoring), ventricular tachycardia of varying duration was frequently noted as the precipitating mechanism of arrest, deteriorating with time into coarse, and then fine, ventricular fibrillation.[10,11,33] Pulseless electrical activity and asystole are probably secondary dysrhythmias developing after ventricular

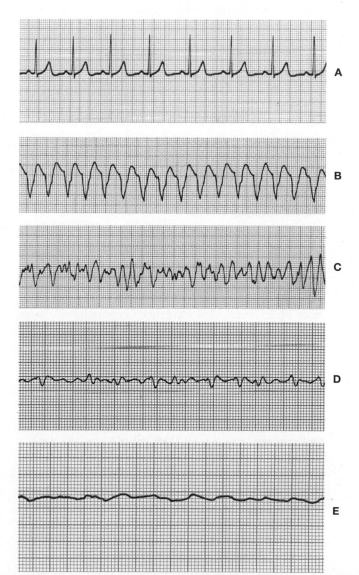

FIGURE 30-1 **A,** Normal sinus rhythm (or pulseless electrical activity). **B,** Ventricular tachycardia. **C,** Coarse ventricular fibrillation. **D,** Fine ventricular fibrillation. **E,** Asystole.

© American Heart Association

FIGURE 30-2 Basic Life Support (BLS) for Healthcare Providers. (Reproduced with permission. *Basic Life Support for Healthcare Providers* © 2006, American Heart Association.)

tachycardia and ventricular fibrillation, during the time from patient collapse to EMS arrival.

Bystander CPR

Bystander-initiated CPR increases survival rates.[14,34–36] When bystander CPR was initiated, a 32% survival rate was noted.[14] The survival rate fell to 14% when BLS was delayed until the arrival of EMS.[14] In Japan, it was estimated that if the occurrence of bystander-initiated CPR increased from its present level, an additional 1800 persons a year would be successfully resuscitated.[35]

Response time

When paramedics were able to initiate ACLS within 4 minutes, 56% of patients survived.[13] This rate fell to 35% when response time was 4 to 8 minutes and to 17% if response time exceeded 8 minutes.[13] In cities with response times as short as 3 to 5 minutes, survival rates of 25% to 33% have been reported.[37,38] Large U.S. cities, such as New York and Chicago, have EMS response times of 11.4 minutes and 16 minutes, respectively.[39–41] Not surprisingly, survival rates from out-of-hospital cardiac arrest are quite low, 1.4% and 2.0%, respectively.

■ THE CHAIN OF SURVIVAL

Survival after cardiac arrest depends on a series of critical interventions. The absence of any one intervention or delay in its implementation minimizes the likelihood of survival. The *chain of survival* is used to describe this emergency cardiac care concept (Figure 30-2).[24,42] The four links in the *adult chain of survival** are:

(1) early access to the EMS system, (2) early BLS, (3) early defibrillation, and (4) early ACLS.

Several important principles are underscored by the chain of survival. If any one link in the chain is inadequate, survival rates will be poor. This factor is the major explanation for the extreme variability in survival rates reported over the last 20 years.[43] All links must be strong to ensure rapid defibrillation. A major problem has been that call-to-defibrillation intervals are too long. To increase survival rates, shorter intervals are necessary.[24]

The first link: early access

Early recognition of the emergency and activation of the EMS or local emergency response system involves calling "9-1-1." Events that occur from the time that the victim collapses to arrival of EMS personnel are included in early access.[24,41,44–47] These events are (1) recognition of unconsciousness, (2) rapid notification of EMS via telephone *before* the start of BLS in adults and *after providing about five cycles* of BLS in children and infants, (3) rapid dispatch of EMS responders, and (4) rapid responder arrival at victim's side with all necessary equipment. All these must occur before defibrillation or ACLS can begin.

The second link: early BLS (CPR)

Early bystander CPR can double or triple the victim's chance of survival from SCA from ventricular fibrillation.[48,49] BLS is most effective when started immediately after a victim collapses. In almost all studies, bystander CPR has a significantly positive effect on survival.[48–51] Bystander CPR is the best treatment a cardiac arrest victim can receive until the arrival of a defibrillator and ACLS.[48–51]

BLS is not a substitute for definitive treatment. Without defibrillation and the administration of adjunctive drugs, such as epinephrine or vasopressin, BLS will not result in adequate perfusion of vital organs such

---

*The Pediatric Chain of Survival will be introduced and discussed in Chapter 31.

as the heart and brain.[52] BLS simply buys some time until definitive therapy can be provided.[53] BLS cannot prevent ventricular tachycardia or ventricular fibrillation from deteriorating into pulseless electrical activity or asystole.[54] Remember, however, that BLS *is* essential to prevent irreversible cerebral damage.

A single, unassisted rescuer with an adult victim should activate EMS after establishing unresponsiveness, but before commencing BLS ("Phone First"). In a pediatric arrest victim, the EMS system should be activated after five cycles of BLS have been provided ("Phone Fast").

The third link: early defibrillation

The interval from collapse to defibrillation is one of the most important determinants of survival from SCA.[18,48,55] Resuscitation is most successful with BLS if defibrillation is performed within 3 to 5 minutes of collapse, with survival rates as high as 49% to 75% (see Table 30-1).[18–20,56–59]

Widespread introduction of the AED has enabled nonmedical personnel trained in its use to improve survival chances for out-of-hospital cardiac arrest victims. The American Heart Association has endorsed the position that every emergency vehicle that may transport cardiac arrest victims be equipped with a defibrillator and that emergency personnel be trained to operate this device.[60]

Manual, automatic, or semiautomatic external defibrillators may be used for rapid defibrillation. The *manual defibrillator* requires interpretation of a monitor or cardiac rhythm strip by a trained rescuer and careful adherence to proper protocol. Use of this device by trained physicians, emergency medical technicians, dentists, and other health care personnel has led to improved survival.[61] Defibrillation using a *fully automated AED* does not require the operator to press buttons to activate either the "analyze" or "shock" mode.[62] Most available AEDs in North America in 2006 technically are *semiautomated external defibrillators*. These devices analyze cardiac rhythm and advise the operator to defibrillate if ventricular tachycardia or ventricular fibrillation ("shockable" rhythms) is recognized, or to "check airway, check breathing, check pulse and continue CPR if no pulse present" if a shockable rhythm is not detected. The widespread effectiveness and proven safety of AEDs have made it acceptable for nonmedical professionals to operate the device for use with adult and child victims.[62,63]

In October 2004, the U.S. Food and Drug Administration approved the over-the-counter sale of AEDs.

All AEDs can be operated by following four simple steps: (1) turn on the power, (2) attach the device, (3) initiate rhythm analysis, and (4) deliver the shock if indicated and if safe.

Different brands and models of AED have varying features, such as paper strip and voice recorders, rhythm display methods, energy levels, and messages to the operator. Many newer devices (as of 2006) have a BLS prompt system that talks the rescuer through the steps of BLS (P→A→B→C→D) in real time.

In the latter part of the 1990s, the availability of AEDs greatly increased. Airlines, public buses, taxicabs, factories, office buildings, and other places where large numbers of persons congregate have included AEDs in their emergency preparedness protocols.[64–66]

The advent, in the 1960s, of EMS systems involving mobile coronary care units staffed by trained paramedical personnel increased the likelihood that the chain of survival could remain intact. Early use of definitive therapy (defibrillation) led to a more than doubling of survival rates from out-of-hospital cardiac arrest.[17]

In February 2006, the state of Florida became the first state in the United States to mandate the presence of an AED in every dental office location, stating in an Office Safety requirement rule that "As part of the minimum standard of care, every dental office location shall be required to have an automatic external defibrillator by February 28, 2006. Any dentist practicing after February 28, 2006 without an automatic external defibrillator on site shall be considered to be practicing below the minimum standard of care."[67]

The fourth link: early ACLS

Early ACLS provided at the scene by the dentist (if trained) or paramedics is another critical link in the management of cardiac arrest. ACLS brings to the scene equipment for the support of ventilation, establishes venous access permitting the administration of drugs, controls dysrhythmias, and stabilizes the victim for transport.

The one factor that unites all four links of the chain of survival is time. The more quickly cardiac arrest is recognized, resuscitation efforts are instituted by a bystander, and advanced management started (defibrillation and ACLS), the greater the likelihood that the initial rhythm will be either ventricular tachycardia or ventricular fibrillation, and the greater the likelihood of a successful resuscitation.

■ THE DENTAL OFFICE

It is highly unlikely that cardiac arrest occurring in a dental office would go unwitnessed for more than a few seconds. BLS would probably be initiated by members of a prepared office emergency team within a minute or so of the collapse, thereby providing extra time for the initiation of advanced resuscitative techniques. The presence of an AED in the dental office could significantly increase the likelihood of survival from cardiac arrest in this environment.

As has been stressed throughout this text, the ability to effectively implement the steps of BLS—position, airway, breathing, circulation—is absolutely critical in saving a life in any emergency situation. The emergencies presented thus far, however, have been limited to situations in which only one, two, or three steps (position + airway *or* position + airway + breathing) of BLS were required for effective patient management. Chest compression has not been necessary. In the unlikely event that cardiopulmonary arrest does occur, rapid action by the entire dental office emergency team is required if the victim is to be successfully resuscitated.

BLS is readily carried out without the use of any adjunctive equipment or drug therapy. BLS consists of airway management, artificial ventilation, and external chest compression to ensure delivery of a continuous supply of oxygenated blood to the brain and heart, thereby preventing irreversible (biological) death and providing some additional time until advanced resuscitation procedures can be initiated.

In 2000 the International Liaison Committee on Resuscitation and the American Heart Association redefined BLS for healthcare providers to include defibrillaton.[68]

■ CARDIOPULMONARY ARREST

Although disease of the cardiovascular system is the most common cause of SCA, other life-threatening situations may also culminate this way (Table 30-2).

Regardless of the precise nature of its cause, SCA must be recognized and managed as quickly as possible, minimizing the period of anoxia to the brain and myocardium and increasing the likelihood for a successful outcome without neurologic damage.

Cardiopulmonary arrest is composed of two specific entities: pulmonary arrest and cardiac arrest. Pulmonary, or respiratory, arrest occurs with cessation of effective respiratory movement, whereas cardiac arrest refers to the cessation of circulation or to circulation that is inadequate to sustain life.

Respiratory arrest may develop in the absence of cardiac arrest (such as occurs with an overdose of opioids). However, if respiratory arrest is unrecognized, unmanaged, or managed ineffectively, cardiac function deteriorates, with cardiac arrest supervening in a short time, depending in part on the degree of oxygen deprivation and the underlying status of the victim's myocardium and coronary arteries. The most common cause of cardiac arrest in healthy children is anoxia due to airway obstruction or respiratory arrest (see Chapter 31).[69,70] Cardiac arrest may also occur in the absence of respiratory arrest (e.g., with electric shock); however, this is quite rare, especially within the dental environment. In such circumstances respiratory arrest inevitably follows within a few seconds. *In most instances, respiratory arrest precedes cardiac arrest.*

Pulmonary (respiratory) arrest

Recognition and management of respiratory arrest have been described previously (see Chapter 5).

Cardiac arrest

The term *cardiac arrest* must be defined to avoid possible confusion. At one time, the term was used to indicate that the heart had stopped beating, a situation

TABLE 30-2 Possible causes of cardiac arrest*

Cause	Frequency	Where discussed in text
Myocardial infarction	Most common	Chest pain (Part Seven)
Sudden cardiac arrest (no prior symptoms)	Most common	Cardiac arrest (Chapter 30)
Airway obstruction	Less common	Respiratory distress (Part Three)
Drug overdose	Less common	Drug-related emergencies (Part Six)
Anaphylaxis	Less common	Drug-related emergencies (Part Six)
Seizure disorders	Rare	Seizure disorders (Part Five)
Acute adrenal insufficiency	Rare	Unconsciousness (Part Two)

*All medical emergency situations may ultimately lead to cardiac arrest. In most instances prompt recognition and initiation of effective management of the specific situation prevent cardiac arrest.

referred to today as *ventricular standstill* or *asystole*. In fact, cardiac arrest occurs when the heart ceases to carry out its primary mechanical function: that of pumping blood. When circulation of blood is absent or, if present, is inadequate to maintain life, the victim is in cardiac arrest. Cardiac arrest, as defined today, may result from any of the following: pulseless electrical activity, (pulseless) ventricular tachycardia, ventricular fibrillation, or ventricular standstill (asystole).

In pulseless electrical activity, the heart continues to beat in a coordinated manner (normal QRS complexes are noted on ECG), but so weakly that effective circulation of blood throughout the cardiovascular system is not accomplished (see Figure 30-1A). This situation may result from drug overdose (toxic reaction), including local anesthetics, barbiturates, and opioids, all of which are used in dentistry (see Chapter 23). Pulseless electrical activity most commonly results from hypovolemia, hypoxia, acidosis, hypo- or hyperkalemia, hypoglycemia, hypothermia, cardiac tamponade, tension pneumothorax, thrombosis, or trauma.[71] Pulseless electrical activity was formerly called electromechanical dissociation. Victims of SCA who are in pulseless electrical activity do not benefit from defibrillation. *Pulseless electrical activity is NOT a shockable rhythm.*

Ventricular tachycardia is an accelerated beating of the ventricles. Each contraction represents an organized heartbeat termed a premature ventricular contraction. The victim with ventricular tachycardia may be conscious with a palpable pulse or may be unconscious without palpable pulse (see Figure 30-1B). These two entities are treated quite differently. In ventricular tachycardia with pulse, drugs such as amiodarone are administered in an attempt to stabilize the myocardium, or synchronized cardioversion is performed. *Ventricular tachycardia with a pulse is NOT a "shockable rhythm."* However, absent a palpable pulse, the indicated treatment is identical to that for ventricular fibrillation—defibrillation. *Pulseless ventricular tachycardia is a shockable rhythm.*

Ventricular fibrillation is a dysrhythmia in which individual myocardial bundles contract chaotically and independently of each other in contradistinction to the normal, regular, coordinated, and synchronized contraction of myocardial fibers, as occurs in a normal sinus rhythm (see Figure 30-1A). Although myocardial elements are still contracting, little or no effective circulation is present. Most victims of SCA demonstrate ventricular fibrillation at some point during their arrest.[10,11,33] Ventricular fibrillation is a common occurrence in the period immediately after acute myocardial infarction (within the first 2 to 4 hours) and is the leading cause of death from ischemic heart disease. In humans, ventricular fibrillation occurs 15 times more frequently during the first hour after the onset of signs and symptoms of acute myocardial infarction than during the next 12 hours. Ventricular tachycardia normally deteriorates into coarse ventricular fibrillation. As myocardial fibers weaken, coarse ventricular fibrillation becomes fine ventricular fibrillation and eventually, as the myocardium dies, asystole.[72] *Ventricular fibrillation (both coarse and fine) is a shockable rhythm.*

Ventricular asystole refers to the absence of contractile movements of myocardial fibers. Cardiac arrest in its strictest sense refers to ventricular asystole. A severe lack of oxygen to myocardial muscle is the most common cause of this situation. *Asystole is NOT a shockable rhythm.*

Although there are four cardiac arrest rhythms (pulseless ventricular tachycardia, ventricular fibrillation, asystole, and pulseless electrical activity), in an emergency situation, the precise rhythm present is not immediately known. The clinical picture of all four is the same: an unconscious victim in whom respiration, blood pressure, and pulse are absent. Time is critical; every second that passes without effective circulation adds to the degree of hypoxia or anoxia in the tissues of the body, to the development of respiratory and metabolic acidosis, and to rhythms such as asystole and pulseless electrical activity, from which effective resuscitation is unlikely.

The immediate clinical management of cardiopulmonary arrest is based on the need to furnish the victim's tissues (primarily the brain and myocardium) with a supply of oxygenated blood that is adequate to maintain life (prevent biological or cellular death) until definitive management (ACLS) can be initiated.

■ BASIC LIFE SUPPORT (CPR)

The technique of CPR has undergone intensive scrutiny by various segments of the medical community. Standardization of technique is being sought so that teaching the procedures will not lead to confusion among those called on to use them.

In May 1973, the American Heart Association and the National Academy of Sciences National Research Council cosponsored a National Conference on Standards of Cardiopulmonary Resuscitation and Emergency Cardiac Care, which for the first time presented standardized procedures for basic and advanced life support.[73] Since then a significant body of research has added to our understanding of the phenomenon of cardiac arrest and CPR. In 1979, 1985, 1992, and 1999 subsequent conferences were held to update these standards.[68,74–77]

Until the 2000 revision, the definition of basic life support for health care providers was P→A→B→C. In the 2000 guidelines, a major change occurred with the inclusion of defibrillation (**D**) as a part of BLS for health care providers.[68] The technique of BLS described throughout this text was recommended by the 2005 conference.[77]

Several broad areas of training in life support were established at these conferences. BLS and ACLS represent different degrees of training and responsibility in the management of the cardiac arrest victim and implementation of BLS to maintain life until the victim recovers sufficiently to be transported to a hospital or ACLS becomes available. Guidelines for the emergency management of infants and children were established as pediatric advanced life support. BLS includes the P→A→B→C→D steps of CPR, which are discussed later (Figure 30-3). ACLS consists of training in the following areas: BLS, use of adjunctive equipment and techniques (such as endotracheal intubation and open chest internal cardiac compression), cardiac monitoring (ECG) for dysrhythmia recognition, establishment of an intravenous infusion, stabilization of the victim's condition, and the use of definitive therapy (administration of drugs to assist in establishing and maintaining an effective cardiac rhythm and circulation).

The level of training in life support varies according to an individual's requirements. *All* dental office personnel should be certified at least at the level of BLS for the health care provider. More frequently today, dentists are receiving training and certification in ACLS (provider level). ACLS provider-level training is invaluable because of the potential for complications associated with the administration of drugs, such as local anesthetics, antibiotics, analgesics, and sedatives. All other dental office personnel (dental hygienists, dental assistants, and nonchairside personnel) should be knowledgeable in and capable of proper application of the techniques of BLS for the health care provider.

Training in BLS should be repeated at least annually by all office personnel and more frequently if possible. Weaver et al.[78] showed that retention of skills by trainees who do not perform CPR regularly is quite limited. Only 11.7% of 61 trainees were capable of properly performing one-person CPR on mannequins, compared with 85% of the same group 6 months earlier. Subsequent reports by Sternbach et al.[79] and Woollard et al.[80] have confirmed the findings of Weaver et al.

BLS courses are sponsored by many organizations, including the American Heart Association, American Red Cross, dental societies, and fire departments. Most major dental meetings now offer BLS training courses. The BLS health care provider program involves train-

ing in four areas: (1) single-rescuer CPR, (2) two-rescuer CPR, (3) obstructed airway, and (4) pediatric (infant and child) BLS. Additionally, and of great significance for dentistry, the health care provider program can provide training in ventilation with a mask (mouth-to-mask, bag-valve-mask, and positive pressure oxygen). This will overcome the "yuck factor" of performing mouth-to-mouth ventilation (on a dental patient).[81]

Team approach

With the possible exception of anaphylaxis, in no other life-threatening situation is prompt recognition and management of greater importance than in cardiac arrest. Although a single rescuer can effectively perform BLS, the procedure becomes more efficient when a trained team of rescuers is available. The team approach (one rescuer compressing the chest, the other ventilating) to BLS is described next. All dental office personnel should receive their training together so that they may interact effectively as a team when necessary.

BLS

As mentioned previously, BLS consists of the application, as needed, of the procedures of positioning (**P**), airway maintenance (**A**), breathing (**B**), and circulation by means of chest compression (**C**) to the victim of any medical emergency, including cardiac arrest, until recovery, or until the victim can be stabilized and transported to an emergency care facility or until advanced life support is available.

Three of the four components of cardiopulmonary resuscitation have previously been discussed. Positioning, airway maintenance, and ventilation in the unconscious patient are discussed in Chapter 5; lower airway obstruction is discussed in Chapter 11. Together these make up the **P**, **A**, and **B** portions of CPR. Figure 30-3 summarizes these important steps of BLS.

Cardiac arrest in the dental office

Cardiac arrest, as well as any other life-threatening situation, may occur anywhere within the dental office. Medical emergencies have occurred in the waiting room, rest room, laboratory, doctor's office, and treatment room.[82] In all situations the unconscious victim must be placed in the supine position so that BLS may be initiated. The victim of cardiopulmonary arrest may be seated in the dental chair at the time of collapse. The question that must then be asked is: "*Can effective CPR be performed with the victim still in the dental chair?*" The answer is yes; however, in many BLS (CPR)

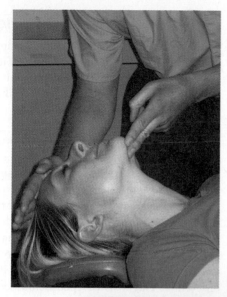

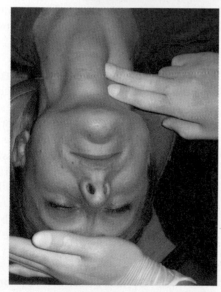

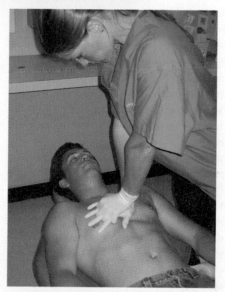

FIGURE 30-3 Summary of basic life support for adult victim.

courses, it is recommended by the lead instructor (especially when this person is not a dentist) that the cardiac arrest victim be moved from the dental chair onto the floor, if at all possible, so that more effective chest compression may be performed. In most dental treatment rooms, however, little or no room is available on the floor adjacent to the dental chair to accommodate both the victim and one or two rescuers.

Lepere et al.[83] demonstrated that chest compression between 41 and 50 mm could successfully be achieved with the victim on either a dental chair or the floor. In addition, ventilation was found to be more effective with the victim in the dental chair (37% too shallow on floor, 15% in dental chair). BLS should be initiated with the patient in the chair.

If possible, a hard object such as a solid board (e.g., a removable cabinet top or a molded CPR backboard) should be placed under the victim to support the spinal column. Under no circumstances should BLS be withheld or delayed because of the inability to move the victim to a more suitable location.

In all of the following sequences, it is assumed that the patient (victim) has suffered cardiac arrest; that is, the victim is unconscious and both respiration and pulse are absent. These basic steps (P→A→B→C) are equally important in the management of all emergency situations—not just cardiac arrest.

The first step in the management of all emergency situations is the implementation, as needed, of BLS. This means that in every situation considered an emergency by the doctor or by any rescuer, the steps listed in Figure 30-3 must be assessed and performed as needed.

Patient response to these steps will guide rescuers in their management. In many instances in which the victim is conscious (e.g., with respiratory distress, altered consciousness, or chest pain), the rescuer need only position the victim (P) comfortably, and assess A, B, and C—a process requiring but a few seconds. The patient will be effectively maintaining A, B, and C by himself or herself, allowing the rescuer to continue to step D, definitive management.

In another situation the rescuer may determine that the victim is unconscious (lack of response to sensory stimulation; e.g., "shake and shout"). Positioning (supine with feet elevated slightly), assessment of the airway, and head tilt–chin lift are required; however, assessment of B and C may demonstrate the adequacy of spontaneous breathing and the presence of an effective pulse. In this situation, the rescuer need only maintain an airway (A) while contemplating definitive management.

Although P, A, B, and C are always assessed in every emergency situation, only those elements deemed necessary for the victim's survival are instituted.

CPR sequence—adult victim

Implementation of the links in the chain of survival are crucial to successful resuscitation (see Figure 30-2). Survival from out-of-hospital SCA most often occurs when "good" BLS is administered and defibrillation occurs within 3 to 5 minutes of collapse.[19–21]

Step 1: recognition of unconsciousness. Stimulate the victim by gently shaking the shoulders and shouting the victim's name. Lack of response to sensory stimulation establishes a diagnosis of unconsciousness Many factors may be responsible for the loss of consciousness (see Table 5-1), most of which do not lead immediately to respiratory and cardiac arrest. However, prompt management of unconsciousness from any cause follows the identical format—P→A→B→C. A differential diagnosis of unconsciousness is reached by assessing patient response or lack of response to each of these steps.

Step 2: summon assistance and P—position the patient. The rescuer will not want to treat the victim alone; therefore, assistance should be sought as soon as unconsciousness is recognized. Members of the office emergency team should report to the scene of the emergency, bringing the emergency drug kit, oxygen, and the AED. They should be prepared to assist in any manner deemed necessary. As we have not yet determined whether cardiac arrest has occurred, this step does not require activation of the EMS system, just the dental office emergency team.

The patient is placed in the supine position. The head and chest of the victim are placed parallel to the floor and the feet elevated slightly (10 degrees) to facilitate return of blood from the periphery.

Step 3: A—assessment and maintenance of airway. Head tilt combined with chin lift may be used to obtain a patent airway. The rescuer places one hand on the victim's forehead and the other hand on the bony prominence of the chin (symphysis). The head is extended backward, stretching the tissues in the neck and lifting the tongue off the posterior wall of the pharynx (Figure 30-4). Head tilt–chin lift is the single most important procedure in airway maintenance. If head tilt–chin lift is ineffective in establishing a patent airway, the jaw-thrust maneuver can be used.

Step 4: B—breathing.
Step 4a: B—assessment of breathing and ventilation, if needed. While maintaining head tilt–chin lift, the rescuer places his or her ear approximately 1 inch from the victim's mouth and nose so that

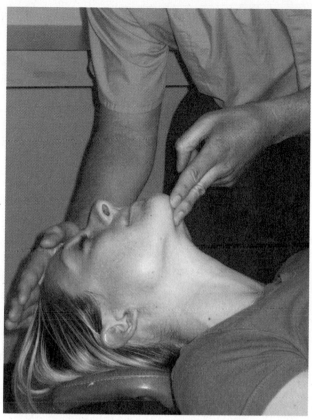

FIGURE 30-4 Head tilt–chin lift.

FIGURE 30-5 Assess breathing: look, listen, and feel while maintaining head tilt–chin lift.

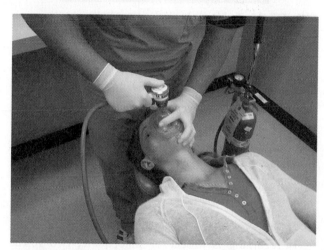

FIGURE 30-6 Mouth-to-mask ventilation. Holding mask (wide—nose; narrow—cleft).

any exhaled air from the victim may be felt and heard. The rescuer looks toward the chest of the victim to see whether spontaneous respiratory efforts are present (Figure 30-5). Breathing is assessed for at least 5 seconds and no more than 10 seconds. With SCA, respiratory efforts are absent or are so weak as to be essentially nonexistent (agonal breaths).

Step 4b: rescue breathing. In the absence of effective respiratory movement, rescue breathing is started. Several techniques of rescue breathing are discussed in Chapter 5; however, in this section only one—mouth-to-mask ventilation—is considered. Other techniques may also be used, but no technique of rescue breathing is effective unless a patent airway is maintained throughout the ventilatory process. Most devices employed in rescue breathing require advanced training.

To perform *mouth-to-mask ventilation*, head tilt–chin lift must be maintained. The mask is held in position with one or two hands as needed, maintaining both an airtight seal and patent airway. The rescuer's mouth is placed on the breathing port of the mask and air is forced into the victim until the chest is seen to rise. Masks usually have a one-way valve that directs exhaled air away from the rescuer. The rescuer positions himself

or herself at the victim's side, enabling a lone rescuer to both give breaths and perform chest compressions. The mask is placed on the victim's face with the narrow portion over the bridge of the nose and the wider part in the cleft of the chin (Figure 30-6). Seal the mask against the victim's face: using the hand that is closer to the top of the victim's head, place the index finger and thumb along the border of the mask while placing the thumb of the other hand along the lower margin of the mask (Figure 30-7). The remaining fingers of the hand closer to the victim's neck are placed along the bony inferior border of the mandible, which is then lifted. Head tilt–chin lift is then performed to establish a patent airway. While head tilt–chin lift is maintained, press firmly and completely around the outside margin of the mask to obtain an airtight seal. Deliver air over 1 second to make the victim's chest rise.

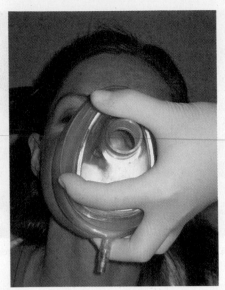

FIGURE 30-7 Mouth-to-mask demonstrating finger positioning.

Rescue breathing for the adult victim:
• Give 1 breath every 5 to 6 seconds (10–12 breaths per minute).
• Give each breath in 1 second.
• Each breath must result in a visible chest rise.
• Check the pulse again in about 2 minutes.

Modified from American Heart Association: *BLS for healthcare providers student manual,* Dallas, American Heart Association, 2006.

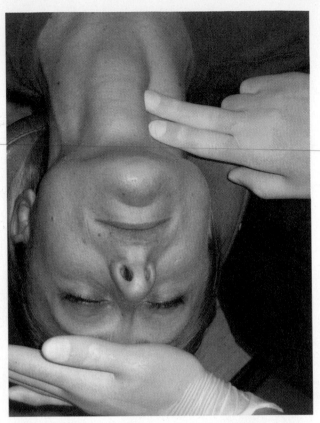

FIGURE 30-8 Carotid artery is located in groove between the trachea and the sternocleidomastoid muscle. Head tilt must be maintained.

If breathing is absent or inadequate, two rescue breaths are delivered with the chest rising with each breath. Effective rescue breathing is noted by expansion of the victim's chest. In a normal adult, the minimal volume of air should be 800 mL/breath but need not exceed 1200 mL/breath for adequate ventilation. Exhalation is passive, with the rescuer removing his or her mouth from that of the victim, taking in a breath of fresh air, and watching the chest fall.

Following assessment of breathing and delivery of two breaths, if necessary, the pulse is checked (see step 5, below). If an apneic victim has a palpable pulse, it is necessary to continue with rescue breathing only (P→A→B). In the adult victim, rescue breathing is delivered at a rate of one breath every 5 to 6 seconds (10 to 12 breaths per minute).

The pulse is rechecked every 2 minutes.

Step 5: C—circulation.
Step 5a: C—assessment of circulation. Having delivered oxygen to the blood, the health care provider must next determine whether that blood is being circu-

lated to the tissues and organs of the body, primarily to the brain, which is composed of cells (neurons) that are exquisitely sensitive to anoxia, and the heart. A large artery must be located and carefully palpated.[84] The femoral artery in the groin and the carotid artery in the neck are two large, central arteries. Although either may be palpated, the carotid artery is much preferred. Since it is located in the neck, the rescuer can access it easily without having to disrobe the victim. In addition, the carotid artery transports oxygenated blood to the victim's brain, the organ that must be adequately perfused for resuscitation to be successful with no, or with minimal, neurologic damage.

The carotid artery is located in a groove between the trachea and the sternocleidomastoid muscle on the anterolateral aspect of the neck (Figure 30-8). The fleshy portions of the first and second fingers of the rescuer are used to feel for a pulse. The artery should be palpated for not less than 5 seconds and no more than 10 seconds. The thumb should never be used to monitor a pulse because the thumb contains a medium-sized artery, and the palpated pulse may be that of the rescuer. (This is not uncommon, especially when the rescuer is "pumped up" as is common during administration of BLS.) Unless the carotid pulse is unquestionably present, external chest compression is initiated immediately.

Pulse check is an important part of BLS for health care providers. However, studies have shown that lay rescuers fail to recognize the absence of a pulse in 10% of pulseless victims and fail to detect a pulse in 40% of victims with a pulse.[85] Health care providers may take too long to do pulse check and also have difficulty determining whether a pulse is present or absent.[86,87]

The pulse should be checked for at least 5 seconds but not for more than 10 seconds.[85]

Pulse check

- If the rescuer is unsure whether or not the victim has a pulse, chest compression should be started.
- Unnecessary cardiopulmonary resuscitation is less harmful than not performing chest compression when the victim truly needs it.

Modified from American Heart Association: *BLS for healthcare providers student manual,* Dallas, American Heart Association, 2006.

Step 5b: activation of EMS. EMS should be activated after the pulse check, if not already done. Most communities in the United States use the emergency number 9-1-1*, however, the appropriate telephone number for a given locality should be called. Information given to the EMS dispatcher should include the following:

1. Location of the emergency (with names of cross streets, if possible)
2. Number of telephone from which the call is made
3. What happened (e.g., heart attack, seizure, accident)
4. Number of persons who need help
5. Condition of the victim(s)
6. Aid being given to the victim(s)
7. Any other information requested

To ensure that EMS personnel have no more questions, the caller should hang up only when told to do so by the EMS operator. If more than one rescuer is available, one person is sent immediately to activate the EMS, returning with the emergency drug kit, oxygen, and AED. Eisenberg et al.[88] showed that the shorter the time interval between collapse and the initiation of BLS and ACLS, the greater the likelihood of survival for the victim of cardiac arrest (Table 30-3). The likelihood of survival from out-of-hospital SCA decreases at a rate of approximately 10% per minute from time of collapse to delivery of defibrillation.[89,90]

---

*9-1-1 is the EMS number in the United States and Canada, but other EMS numbers exist, for example, 0-0-0 in Australia; 1-1-9 in Japan; 1-1-2 or 9-9-9 in the United Kingdom; and 1-1-2 in most of Europe and standard on GSM mobile phones.

TABLE 30-3 Rate of survival from cardiac arrest resulting from ventricular fibrillation, as related to promptness of initiation of CPR and ACLS

Initiation of CPR (minutes)	Arrival of ACLS (minutes)	Survival rate (%)
0–4	0–8	43
0–4	16+	10
8–12	8–16	6
8–12	16+	0
12+	12+	0

ACLS, advanced cardiac life support; CPR, cardiopulmonary resuscitation.
Data from Eisenberg MS, Bergner L, Hallstrom A: Cardiac resuscitation in the community: importance of rapid provision and implications for program planning, *JAMA* 241:1905–1907, 1979.

With but one rescuer present and an adult victim, the rescuer, on determining unresponsiveness, activates EMS immediately and returns to the victim, bringing the AED, O_2 cylinder, and emergency drug kit, then commences BLS. This action brings the third (early defibrillation) and fourth (early ACLS) links of the chain of survival to the victim more quickly. If the rescuer is alone with no telephone, the only option is to continue BLS.

Step 5c: chest compression. External chest compression consists of the rhythmic application of pressure over the lower half of the sternum. The heart lies under and just to the left of the midline under the lower half of the sternum and above the spinal column. Chest compressions create blood flow by increasing intrathoracic pressure and by direct compression of the heart. Properly performed chest compressions can produce systolic arterial pressure peaks of 60 to 80 mm Hg; however, diastolic pressure is low and mean arterial pressure in the carotid artery rarely exceeds 40 mm Hg.[85,91]

Blood flow produced by chest compression delivers a small but critical supply of O_2 and other substrates to the brain and myocardium.[85] The more oxygenated the myocardium when defibrillation is performed, the greater the likelihood that the shock will be successful (the greater the likelihood of coarse ventricular fibrillation being present than either fine ventricular fibrillation or asystole). If the shock is delivered more than 4 minutes after collapse, chest compression prior to defibrillation is especially important.[92–94]

When the sternum is compressed, intrathoracic pressure is increased. This increased pressure produces cardiac output by compressing the vessels within the chest cavity and forcing blood back to, and through, the heart. When this pressure is released, venous blood from the periphery flows back into the heart to refill its chambers.[95] The volume of blood in the ventricles and the volume ejected from the heart with compression increases with succeeding compression/recoil. Two to three compression/recoils are necessary in order to sufficiently fill the ventricles to enable a decent cardiac output to occur. The adult sternum is properly compressed to a depth of 4 to 5 cm (1.5 to 2 inches) and then allowed to fully return to its normal position before the next compression is delivered. Venous blood returns to the heart during recoil of the chest wall. Complete chest recoil is necessary for CPR to be effective.[96] Incomplete chest recoil is associated with increased intrathoracic pressures, decreased coronary perfusion, and decreased cerebral perfusion.[96] Assessment of CPR in humans, performed by health care providers, illustrates that incomplete recoil is quite common, especially when rescuers are fatigued.[97] Half of all chest compressions were too shallow, and no compressions were provided during 24% to 49% of CPR time.[98,99] Without chest compression there is no blood flow and coronary artery perfusion pressure quickly falls. Prolonged interruptions in chest compression are associated with a reduced return of spontaneous circulation, reduced survival rates, and reduced postresuscitation myocardial function.[99–102]

Location of compression point

To perform effective chest compression while minimizing injury to other organs (lungs, liver, heart), the rescuer's hands must be properly positioned. The 2005 guidelines from the American Heart Association recommend the procedure in Box 30-1 for locating the proper position and delivering effective chest compression.[62]

The rescuer compresses the lower half of the sternum in the middle of the chest, between the nipples.[103] The heel of one hand is placed on the middle of the sternum between the nipples with the heel of the other hand placed on top of the first so that they are overlapped and parallel.[103–105] The fingers of the two hands are then interlaced, with the fingers of the top hand pulling the fingers of the lower hand upward. In this manner, only the heel of the lower hand remains in contact with the victim's chest (Figure 30-9). These procedures are important to follow because if the fingers of the hand contact the chest wall, the pressures exerted in chest compression will be delivered over a larger area and will therefore be less effective in increasing intrathoracic pressure. In addition, this pressure will be extended to the ribs, not just to the sternum, increasing the likelihood of costochondral separation or rib fracture, with possible contusion and laceration of the heart and lungs.

Application of pressure

Having determined the proper location for chest compression and hand positioning, the rescuer can begin

Box 30-1 Technique of chest compression—adult

Position yourself at victim's side.
Make sure victim is lying on his or her back on a firm, flat surface. If victim is lying facedown, carefully roll victim onto the back.
Move or remove all clothing covering the victim's chest. Skin must be visible.
Place the heel of one hand on the center of the victim's bare chest between the nipples.
Put the heel of the other hand on top of the first.
Straighten your arms and position your shoulders directly over your hands.
Push hard and fast. Press down 1.5 to 2 inches with each compression. For each chest compression, make sure you push straight down on the victim's sternum.
At the end of each compression make sure you allow the chest to recoil or re-expand completely. Full chest recoil allows more blood to refill the heart between chest compressions. Incomplete chest recoil will reduce the blood flow created by chest compressions.
Deliver compressions in a smooth fashion at a rate of 100 compressions per minute.

From American Heart Association: *BLS for healthcare providers student manual,* Dallas, American Heart Association, 2006.

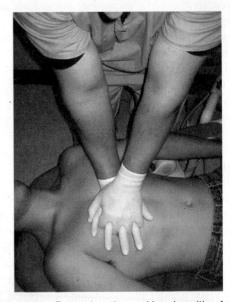

FIGURE 30-9 Proper location and hand position for adult chest compression.

chest compression. Chest compression is strenuous, and recent evidence demonstrates that rescuers become fatigued within 1 minute of CPR, resulting in inadequate compression depth or rates.[97]

The following points facilitate implementation of chest compression with maximal effectiveness: The shoulders

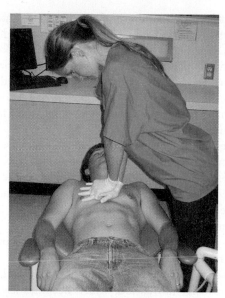

FIGURE 30-10 Proper rescuer position for adult chest compression.

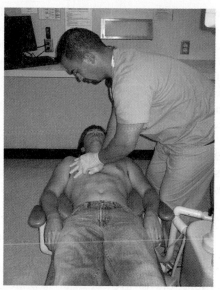

FIGURE 30-12 Improper positioning (elbows bent, shoulders at angle to chest).

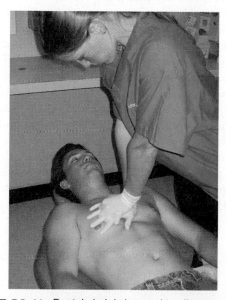

FIGURE 30-11 Dental chair is lowered to allow rescuer to bring shoulders directly over sternum of victim.

of the rescuer must be located directly over the sternum of the victim, and the rescuer's elbows should be locked straight, not bent (Figure 30-10). If the victim is lying on the floor, the rescuer kneels at the victim's side, close enough to the body so that the rescuer's shoulders are directly over the victim's sternum. If the victim is in the dental chair, the rescuer stands astride the victim, with the chair lowered so that proper positioning can be achieved (Figure 30-11).[83] Downward compression should take 50% of the entire compression cycle.[106]

Improper positioning of the shoulders (at an angle to the sternum) decreases effectiveness of chest compressions while increasing the likelihood of complications related to costochondral separation from stretching of ribs on one side, and fracture of ribs from bending ribs on the opposite side (Figure 30-12). Bending of the elbows greatly decreases effectiveness of emergency cardiac care and leads to rapid fatigue of the rescuer.

Rate of chest compression

The 2005 American Heart Association guidelines recommend a compression rate of about 100 per minute.[85] Interruption of chest compressions is associated with decreased survival,[100–102] yet several studies reported that compressions are interrupted between 25% and 49% of total arrest time.[98–100] The new guidelines recommend that health care providers should interrupt chest compressions as infrequently as possible and try to limit interruptions to no longer than 10 seconds except for specific interventions, such as insertion of an advanced airway or use of a defibrillator.[85]

Compression–ventilation ratio

A compression–ventilation ratio of 30:2 is currently recommended for all single-rescuer resuscitations (adult, child, infant).[85] The 30:2 ratio is not based on clinical science. Rather, it represents a consensus of experts.[85] The 30:2 ratio replaces the 15:2 and 5:1 from previous guidelines and is designed to increase the number of compressions, reduce the likelihood of hyperventilation, minimize interruptions in chest compressions for ventilation, and simplify instruction for teaching and skills retention.[85] A 30:2 compression–ventilation ratio is more tiring than 15:2,[97] leading to inadequate compression depth or rate. Therefore, when two or more rescuers are available, it is recommended to switch the compressor every 2 minutes (or after five cycles of compressions and ventilations at a ratio of 30:2).[85] Every effort should be made to accomplish the switch in less than 5 seconds.[85]

Step 6: *defibrillation.* When a single rescuer encounters a nonresponsive victim, he or she immediately activates EMS (9-1-1) [Phone First] (steps 1 and 5b) and returns to the victim with the AED. The single rescuer starts with 2 minutes (four to five cycles) of CPR. The AED is used only if the victim does not respond, is not breathing, and is pulseless. In the dental office it is likely that more than one person will be available. In this situation, four to five cycles of BLS are provided prior to use of the AED. The effect of BLS prior to the delivery of a shock has been demonstrated to be largely positive. With arrival of EMS more than 4 to 5 minutes after dispatch, a brief period of CPR (1.5 to 3 minutes) before defibrillation improved return of spontaneous circulation and survival rates for adults with out-of-hospital ventricular fibrillation or pulseless ventricular tachycardia.[92,93]

Health care providers in facilities with AEDs available on-site should administer CPR until the AED arrives. It should then be used as soon as it is available.[107]

In many communities the time interval from EMS call to EMS arrival is 7 to 8 minutes or longer.[17] This means that in the first minutes after collapse, the victim's chance of survival is in the hands of bystanders.[85]

Victims of SCA require immediate CPR, which provides circulation of a small but critical volume of oxygenated blood to the brain and myocardium. CPR prolongs the period of time that the myocardium remains in ventricular fibrillation, increasing the likelihood that defibrillation will terminate ventricular fibrillation and allow the heart to resume an effective rhythm and effective systemic perfusion. A period of CPR is especially important if the shock is not delivered for 4 or more minutes after collapse.[92,93]

Defibrillation does not "restart" the heart. Defibrillation "stuns" the myocardium, producing a period of asystole. If the myocardium is still viable, the heart's normal pacemakers may resume firing producing an effective ECG rhythm that ultimately may produce adequate blood flow (Figure 30-13).[85]

Figure 30-14 illustrates the result of SCA in which BLS is not initiated until arrival of EMS, 10 minutes after collapse. Coarse ventricular fibrillation becomes fine ventricular fibrillation, which becomes asystole as the available O_2 supply in the myocardium is exhausted. The ECG records asystole, a rhythm with an extremely poor survival rate. In addition, without BLS performed it is extremely likely that if the victim survives SCA he or she will exhibit permanent neurologic damage.

In Figure 30-15A, BLS is started within several minutes of collapse and EMS is activated but does not arrive until 10 minutes after the collapse. It is noted that BLS does not convert ventricular fibrillation into a more functional rhythm. By circulating oxygenated blood to the myocardium the duration of time the heart stays in ventricular fibrillation (coarse then fine) is prolonged. On arrival at 10 minutes after collapse, EMS encounters a patient in fine ventricular fibrillation, a rhythm with a poor prognosis but one better than asystole. Compare Figure 30-14 with Figure 30-15A. If BLS→defibrillation→BLS→defibrillation is ineffective, drugs such as

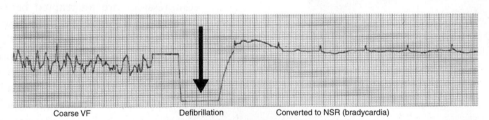

Coarse VF   Defibrillation   Converted to NSR (bradycardia)

FIGURE 30-13 Coarse VF (left) is successfully converted to a normal sinus rhythm (NSR [sinus bradycardia]) (right). *Arrow* indicates time of defibrillation.

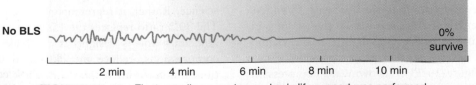

No BLS   0% survive

2 min   4 min   6 min   8 min   10 min

FIGURE 30-14 Electrocardiogram when no basic life support was performed.

epinephrine or vasopressin will be administered, followed by BLS→defibrillation.[108,109] The goal in administering these drugs is to convert fine ventricular fibrillation into a more coarse ventricular fibrillation, where the myocardium will be more receptive to subsequent shocks.[109] Survival rates are approximately 5% to 6%, with a lesser likelihood of the survivor suffering significant permanent neurologic damage.

In the presence of bystander-initiated BLS, more rapid arrival of EMS and earlier defibrillation results in significantly improved survival rates. In Figure 30-15B, BLS is started promptly and EMS arrives in 7 minutes and delivers the shock. The cardiac rhythm is more likely to be coarse ventricular fibrillation at this time, a rhythm that is more responsive to defibrillation. Neurologic damage is unlikely in this scenario.

Figure 30-15C illustrates the most optimal situation, one in which BLS is initiated promptly (by the dental office staff) and an AED is readily available in the office. Following a period of BLS (four to five cycles of 30:2 in 2 minutes) the shock is delivered to a myocardium that is more likely to be in coarse ventricular fibrillation or even ventricular tachycardia, rhythms with higher rates of successful defibrillation. Neurologic damage is highly unlikely in this scenario.

It can be seen in Figure 30-15 that with BLS performed, the primary determinant of survival from SCA is the speed with which defibrillation is delivered after collapse. It is estimated that, with BLS administered, survival rates from SCA decrease at approximately 10% per minute.[89,90] When bystander CPR is started, the decrease in survival is more gradual, averaging 3% to 4% per minute from collapse to defibrillation.[48,90]

Immediately following successful conversion of ventricular fibrillation/ventricular tachycardia, the heart may demonstrate asystole or bradycardia, and the heart may pump ineffectively. In one study of SCA with ventricular fibrillation, only 20% to 40% of victims demonstrated an organized rhythm (e.g., normal sinus rhythm, bradycardia) 60 seconds after delivery of a shock. It is likely that even fewer had effective perfusion at that point.[111] Therefore, new American Heart Association guidelines recommend delivery of CPR for several minutes following defibrillation until adequate perfusion is present.[85,110,112]

AED technique (adult). While chest compressions are being performed by the first rescuer, the second rescuer prepares to use the AED.

- Minimize interruptions in chest compression.
- Try to keep interruptions to 10 seconds or less.
- Remove or move clothing covering the victim's chest to allow rescuers to provide chest compressions and to apply the AED electrode pads.
- Place the AED at the victim's side near the rescuer who will be operating it. In most instances this will on the side of the victim opposite the rescuer performing chest compressions.
- Operator POWERS ON the AED and follows voice prompts.
- ATTACH adult AED electrode pads.
- Do NOT use child pads (or child key or switch)
- Remove the backing from the adhesive electrode pads.
- ATTACH the adhesive electrode pads to the bare skin of the victim as per diagrams on electrodes.
- ATTACH the electrode cable to the AED (if not preconnected).

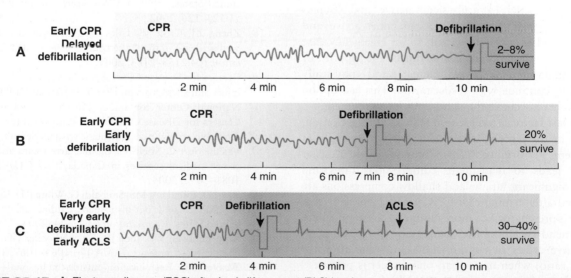

FIGURE 30-15 **A,** Electrocardiogram (ECG) after basic life support (BLS) has been started; defibrillation at 10 minutes. **B,** ECG after BLS has been started; defibrillation at 7 minutes. **C,** ECG after BLS has been started; defibrillation at 4 minutes.

- ANALYZE. Ensure that no one is touching the victim and allow the AED to check the heart rhythm (or push ANALYZE button if needed).
- SHOCK. Be sure that no one is touching the victim and deliver a shock (following AED prompts).
- Start CPR immediately (beginning with chest compressions) after delivery of shock.
- If no shock is indicated, as per AED voice prompts, resume CPR, beginning with chest compressions.

The Appendix summarizes the management of cardiac arrest in the adult.

Beginning and terminating BLS

BLS is most effective if begun immediately after SCA has occurred. If cardiac arrest continues for 10 minutes or more, survival is highly unlikely and if the victim survives it is extremely unlikely that the victim's central nervous system will be restored to its precardiac arrest status. In their study of unsuccessful resuscitation attempts, Gray et al.[16] found improved outcome with a total resuscitation time (collapse to recovery) of less than 15 minutes, confirming the ineffectiveness of prolonged resuscitation. However, individual cases of effective resuscitation with little or no residual central nervous system deficit after long periods (1 hour and longer) have been reported, usually in situations of hypothermia (submergence in cold water).[113]

In the dental office environment, BLS should be started on all victims of cardiac arrest.

Once started, CPR should be continued until one of the following occurs: (1) the victim recovers, demonstrating adequate spontaneous respiratory exchange and circulation (2) a second rescuer, equally well trained in BLS, becomes available to assist or take over the efforts of the first rescuer; (3) a physician arrives and assumes overall responsibility; (4) EMS personnel arrive and stabilize and transfer the victim to an emergency care facility that is able to provide advanced life support; or (5) the single rescuer becomes exhausted and is physically unable to continue with resuscitation. This last option is unlikely to occur in the dental office environment.

The last factor listed for termination of resuscitation, fatigue of the rescuer, is not as unlikely as it might at first seem. Performing BLS is strenuous work. Rescuer fatigue leads to inadequate compressions rates and depth. Significant fatigue and shallow compressions are observed after 1 minute of CPR, yet rescuers deny that fatigue is present for 5 or more minutes.[96] New guidelines recommend switching the compressor every 2 minutes (after five cycles of compressions and ventilations at a 30:2 ratio) when more than one rescuer is present.[85] Cases have been reported in which the rescuer has suffered cardiac arrest or myocardial infarction while performing BLS, with one or both persons dying.[82] This factor alone should motivate the doctor to ensure that all members of the dental office staff are fully trained in BLS procedures.

Transport of victim

The victim of cardiac arrest is ultimately transferred from the scene of the incident (e.g., the dental office) to the emergency department of a hospital, where further management is available. If permitted, the doctor should accompany the victim in the ambulance to the hospital.

REFERENCES

1. Cobb LA, Werner JA, Trobaugh GB: Sudden cardiac arrest. I. A decade's experience with out-of-hospital resuscitation, *Mod Concepts Cardiovasc Dis* 49:31–36, 1980.
2. Rabkin SW, Mathewson FAL, Tate RB: Chronobiology of cardiac sudden death in men, *JAMA* 244:1357–1358, 1980.
3. American Heart Association: *Manual of advanced cardiac life support,* Dallas, American Heart Association, 1997.
4. Safar P, Bircher N: *Cardiopulmonary cerebral resuscitation: World Federation of Societies of Anaesthesiologists International CPCR guidelines,* ed 3, Philadelphia, WB Saunders, 1988.
5. Abramson NS, Safar P, Detre K, et al.: Neurologic recovery after cardiac arrest: effect of duration of ischemia. Brain Resuscitation Clinical Trial I Study Group, *Crit Care Med* 13:930–931, 1985.
6. Centers for Disease Control and Prevention/National Center for Health Statistics, Bethesda, MD, 2005.
7. State-specific mortality from sudden cardiac death—United States, 1999, *MMWR Morb Mortal Wkly Rep* 51:123–126, 2002.
8. Zheng ZJ, Croft JB, Giles WH, Mensah GA: Sudden cardiac death in the United States, 1989 to 1998, *Circulation* 104:2158–2163, 2001.
9. Centers for Disease Control and Prevention: Web-based Injury Statistics Query and Reporting System (WISQARS). National Center for Injury Prevention and Control, Centers for Disease Control and Prevention (producer). Available at: www.cdc.gov/ncipc/wisqars/default.htm
10. Vaillancourt C, Stiell IG: Cardiac arrest care and emergency medical services in Canada, *Can J Cardiol* 20: 1081–1090, 2004.
11. Rea TD, Eisenberg MS, Sinibaldi G, White RD: Incidence of EMS treated out-of-hospital cardiac arrest in the United States, *Resuscitation* 63:17–24, 2004.
12. Kouwenhoven WB, Jude JR, Knickerbocker GG: Closed chest cardiac massage, *JAMA* 173:1064–1067, 1960.
13. Weaver WD: Resuscitation outside the hospital—what's lacking (editorial), *N Engl J Med* 325:1437–1439, 1991.

14. Cobb LA, Werner JA: Predictors and prevention of sudden cardiac death. In Alexander RW, Schlant RC, Fuster V, editors: *Hurst's the heart, arteries and veins,* ed 9, New York, McGraw-Hill, 1998.

15. Cummins RO: From concept to standard-of-care? Review of the clinical experience with automated external defibrillators, *Ann Emerg Med* 18:1269–1275, 1989.

16. Gray WA, Capone RJ, Most AS: Unsuccessful emergency medical resuscitation: are continued efforts in the emergency department justified? *N Engl J Med* 325:1393–1398, 1991.

17. Eisenberg MS, Horwood BT, Cummins RO, et al.: Cardiac arrest and resuscitation: a tale of 29 cities, *Ann Emerg Med* 19:179–186, 1990.

18. Caffrey SL, Willoughby PJ, Pepe PE, Becker LB: Public use of automated external defibrillators, *N Engl J Med* 347:1242–1247, 2002.

19. Page RI, Joglar JA, Kowal RC, et al.: Use of automated external defibrillators by a US airline, *N Engl J Med* 343:1210–1216, 2000.

20. Valenzuela TD, Roe DJ, Nichol G, et al.: Outcomes of rapid defibrillation by security officers after cardiac arrest in casinos, *N Engl J Med* 343:1206–1209, 2000.

21. White RD, Bunch TJ, Hankins DG: Evolution of a community-wide early defibrillation programme experience over 13 years using police/fire personnel and paramedics as responders, *Resuscitation* 65:279–283, 2005.

22. Kida M, Kawamura T, Fukuoka T, et al.: Out-of-hospital cardiac arrest and survival: an epidemiological analysis of emergency service reports in a large city in Japan. *Circ J* 68:603–609, 2004.

23. Hollenberg J, Bang A, Lindqvist J, et al.: Difference in survival after out-of-hospital cardiac arrest between the two largest cities in Sweden: a matter of time? *J Intern Med* 257:247–254, 2005.

24. Cummins RO, Omato JP, Thies WH, Pepes PE: Improving survival from sudden cardiac arrest: the "chain of survival" concept. A statement for health professionals from the Advanced Cardiac Life Support Subcommittee and the Emergency Cardiac Care Committee, American Heart Association, *Circulation* 83:1832–1847, 1991

25. Eisenberg MS, Hallstrom A, Bergner L: The ACLS score predicting survival from out-of-hospital cardiac arrest, *JAMA* 246:50–52, 1981.

26. Wilcox-Gok VL: Survival from out-of-hospital cardiac arrest. A multivariate analysis, *Med Care* 29:104–114, 1991.

27. Fan KL, Leung LP: Prognosis of patients with ventricular fibrillation in out-of-hospital cardiac arrest in Hong Kong: prospective study, *Hong Kong Med J* 8:318–321, 2002.

28. Myerburg RJ, Kessler KM, Zaman L, et al.: Survivors of prehospital cardiac arrest, *JAMA* 247:1485–1490, 1982.

29. DeMaio VJ, Stiell IG, Spaite DW, et al.: CPR—only survivors of out-of-hospital cardiac arrest: implications for out-of-hospital care and cardiac arrest research methodology, *Ann Emerg Med* 37:602–608, 2001.

30. Parish DC, Dinesh Chandra KM, Dane FC: Success changes the problem: why ventricular fibrillation is declining, why pulseless electrical activity is emerging and what to do about it, *Resuscitation* 58:31–35, 2003.

31. Herlitz J, Estrom L, Wennerblom B, et al.: Survival among patients with out-of-hospital cardiac arrest found in electromechanical dissociation, *Resuscitation* 29:97–106, 1995.

32. Weaver WD, Cobb LA, Hallstrom AP, et al.: Considerations for improving survival from out-of-hospital cardiac arrest, *Ann Emerg Med* 15:1181–1186, 1986.

33. Cobb LA, Farenbruch CE, Olsufka M, Copass MK: Changing incidence of out-of-hospital ventricular fibrillation, 1980–2000, *JAMA* 288:3008–3013, 2002.

34. Dorph E, Wik K, Steen PA: Dispatcher-assisted cardiopulmonary resuscitation. An evaluation of efficacy amongst elderly, *Resuscitation* 56:265–273, 2003.

35. Sekimoto M, Noguchi Y, Rahman M, et al.: Estimating the effect of bystander-initiated cardiopulmonary resuscitation in Japan, *Resuscitation* 50:153–160, 2001.

36. Troiano P, Masaryk J, Stueven HA, et al.: The effect of bystander CPR on neurologic outcome in survivors of prehospital cardiac arrests, *Resuscitation* 17:91–98, 1989.

37. Cummins RO, Eisenberg MS, Litwin PE, et al.: Automatic external defibrillators used by emergency medical technicians: a controlled clinical trial, *JAMA* 257:1605–1610, 1987.

38. Weaver WD, Hill D, Farenbruch CE, et al.: Use of the automatic external defibrillator in the management of out-of-hospital cardiac arrest, *N Engl J Med* 319: 661–666, 1988.

39. Lombardi G, Gallagher E, Gennis P: Outcome of out-of-hospital cardiac arrest in New York City: the pre-hospital arrest survival evaluation (PHASE) study, *JAMA* 271: 678–683, 1994.

40. Westal RE, Reissman S, Doering G: Out-of-hospital cardiac arrests: an 8-year New York City experience, *Am J Emerg Med* 14:364–368, 1996.

41. Becker LB, Ostrander MP, Barrett J, Kondos GT: Outcome of CPR in a large metropolitan area—where are the survivors? *Ann Emerg Med* 20:355–361, 1991.

42. Cummins RO: The "chain of survival" concept: how it can save lives, *Heart Dis Stroke* 1:43–45, 1992.

43. Eisenberg MS, Cummins RO, Damon S, et al.: Survival rates from out-of-hospital cardiac arrest: recommendations for uniform definitions and data to report, *Ann Emerg Med* 19:1249–1259, 1990.

44. Calle PA, Lagaert I, Vanhaute O, Buylaert WA: Do victims of an out-of-hospital cardiac arrest benefit from a training program for emergency medical dispatchers? *Resuscitation* 35:213–218, 1997.

45. Curka PA, Pepe PE, Ginger ventricular fibrillation, et al.: Emergency medical services priority dispatch, *Ann Emerg Med* 22:1688–1695, 1993.

46. Smaha LA: Dialing 911: a call to action, *Prev Cardiol* 5:37–41, 2002.

47. Fedoruk JC, Currie WL, Gobet M: Locations of cardiac arrest: affirmation for community, Public Access Defibrillation (PAD) Program, *Prehospital Disaster Med* 17:202–205, 2002.

48. Valenzuela TD, Roe DJ, Cretin S, et al.: Estimating effectiveness of cardiac arrest interventions: a logistic regression survival model, *Circulation* 96:3308–3313, 1997.

49. Holmberg M, Holmberg S, Herlitz J: Factors modifying the effect of bystander cardiopulmonary resuscitation on survival in out-of-hospital cardiac arrest patients in Sweden, *Eur Heart J* 22:511–519, 2001.

50. Cummins RO, Eisenberg MS: Prehospital cardiopulmonary resuscitation: is it effective? *JAMA* 253:2408–2412, 1985.

51. Bossaert L, Van Hoeyweghen R: Bystander cardiopulmonary resuscitation (CPR) in out-of-hospital cardiac arrest: the Cerebral Resuscitation Study Group, *Resuscitation* 17:S55–S69, 1989.

52. Weil MH; Tang W: Cardiopulmonary resuscitation: a promise as yet largely unfulfilled, *Dis Mon* 43:429–501, 1997.

53. Stueven H, Troiano P, Thompson B, et al.: Bystander/first responder CPR: ten years experience in a paramedic system, *Ann Emerg Med* 15:707–710, 1986.

54. Enns J, Tween WA, Donen N: Prehospital cardiac rhythm deterioration in a system providing only basic life support, *Ann Emerg Med* 12:478–481, 1983.

55. Nichol G, Stiell IG, Laupacis A, et al.: A cumulative meta-analysis of the effectiveness of defibrillator-capable emergency medical services for victims of out-of-hospital cardiac arrest, *N Engl J Med* 34:517–525, 1999.

56. Weaver WD, Hill D, Farenbruch CE, et al.: Use of the automatic external defibrillator in the management of out-of-hospital cardiac arrest, *N Engl J Med* 319:661–666, 1988.

57. Auble TE, Menegazzi H, Paris PM: Effect of out-of-hospital defibrillation by basic life support providers on cardiac arrest mortality: a metaanalysis, *Ann Emerg Med* 25:642–658, 1995.

58. O'Rourke MF, Donaldson E, Geddes JS: An airline cardiac arrest program, *Circulation* 96:2849–2853, 1997.

59. Page RL, Hamdan MH, McKenas DK: Defibrillation aboard a commercial aircraft, *Circulation* 97:1429–1430, 1998.

60. Cobb LA, Eliastam M, Kerber RE, et al.: Report of the American Heart Association Task Force on the Future of Cardiopulmonary Resuscitation, *Circulation* 85:2346–2355, 1992.

61. O'Hearn P: Early defibrillation: lessons learned, *J Cardiovasc Nurs* 10:24–36, 1996.

62. American Heart Association: *BLS for healthcare providers student manual,* Dallas, American Heart Association, 2006.

63. Samson R, Berg R, Bingham R: Pediatric Advanced Life Support Task Force ILCOR. Use of automated external defibrillators for children: an update. An advisory statement from the Pediatric Advanced Life Support Task Force, International Liaison Committee on Resuscitation, *Resuscitation* 57:237–243, 2003.

64. Eisenberg MS, Pantridge JF, Cobb LA, Geddes JS: The revolution and evolution of prehospital cardiac care, *Arch Intern Med* 156:1611–1619, 1996.

65. Fromm RE Jr, Varon J: Automated external versus blind manual defibrillation by untrained lay rescuers, *Resuscitation* 33:219–221, 1997.

66. Kerber RE, Becker LB, Bourland JD, et al.: Automatic external defibrillators for public access defibrillation: recommendations for specifying and reporting arrhythmia analysis algorithm performance, incorporating new waveforms, and enhancing safety. A statement for health professionals from the American Heart Association Task Force on Automatic External Defibrillation, Subcommittee on AED Safety and Efficacy, *Circulation* 95:1677–1682, 1997.

67. Rule 64B5-17.015, Department of Health, Board of Dentistry, volume 29, number 42, Tallahassee, FL, Office Safety Requirement, October 17, 2003.

68. American Heart Association in collaboration with International Liaison Committee on Resuscitation: Guidelines 2000 for Cardiopulmonary Resuscitation and Emergency Cardiovascular Care, *Circulation* 102:I1–I384, 2000.

69. Young KD, Seidel JS: Pediatric cardiopulmonary resuscitation: a collective review, *Ann Emerg Med* 33:195–205, 1999.

70. Richman PB, Nashed AH: The etiology of cardiac arrest in children and young adults: special considerations for ED management, *Am J Emerg Med* 17:264–270, 1999.

71. International Liaison Committee on Resuscitation: 2005 International Consensus on Cardiopulmonary Resuscitation and Emergency Cardiovascular Care Science with Treatment Recommendations, *Circulation* 112:IV-50–IV-66, 2005.

72. Weisfeldt ML, Becker IB: Resuscitation after cardiac arrest: a 3-phase time-sensitive model, *JAMA* 288:3035–3038, 2002.

73. Standards for cardiopulmonary resuscitation (CPR) and emergency cardiac care (ECC), *JAMA* 227:852–860, 1974.

74. Standards and guidelines for cardiopulmonary resuscitation (CPR) and emergency cardiac care (ECC), *JAMA* 244:453–509, 1980.

75. Standards and guidelines for cardiopulmonary resuscitation (CPR) and emergency cardiac care (ECC), National Academy of Sciences, National Research Council, *JAMA* 255:2905–2989, 1986.

76. Guidelines for cardiopulmonary resuscitation (CPR) and emergency cardiac care (ECC). *JAMA* 286:2135–2302, 1992.

77. International Liaison Committee on Resuscitation. 2005 International Consensus on Cardiopulmonary Resuscitation and Emergency Cardiovascular Care Science with Treatment Recommendations, *Circulation* 112:I-1–I-187, 2005.

78. Weaver FJ, Ramirez AG, Dorfman SB, et al.: Trainees' retention of cardiopulmonary resuscitation, *JAMA* 241:901–903, 1979.

79. Sternbach GL, Kiskaddon RT, Fossel M, Eliastam M: The retention of cardiopulmonary resuscitation skills, *J Emerg Med* 2:33–36, 1984.

80. Woollard M, Whitfeild R, Smith A, et al.: Skill acquisition and retention in automated external defibrillator (AED)

use and CPR by lay responders: a prospective study, *Resuscitation* 60:17–28, 2004.

81. Becker LB, Berg RA, Pepe PE, et al.: A reappraisal of mouth-to-mouth ventilation during bystander-initiated cardiopulmonary resuscitation. A statement for healthcare professionals from the Ventilation Working Group of the Basic Life Support and Pediatric Life Support Subcommittees, American Heart Association, *Resuscitation* 35:189–201, 1997.

82. Brown D: Patient has heart attack, dies; dentist also stricken, *Los Angeles Times*, February 7, 1988.

83. Lepere AJ, Finn J, Jacobs I: Efficacy of cardiopulmonary resuscitation performed in a dental chair, *Aust Dent J* 48:244–247, 2003.

84. Mather C, O'Kelly S: The palpation of pulses, *Anaesthesia* 51:189–191, 1996.

85. American Heart Association: 2005 American Heart Association guidelines for cardiopulmonary resuscitation and emergency cardiovascular care. International Consensus on Science. Part 4: Adult basic life support, *Circulation* 112: IV1–IV203, 2005.

86. Kidwell CS, Starkman S, Eckstein M, et al.: Identifying stroke in the field: prospective validation of the Los Angeles prehospital stroke screen (LAPSS), *Stroke* 31: 71–76, 2000.

87. Moule P: Checking the carotid pulse: diagnostic accuracy in students of the healthcare professions, *Resuscitation* 44:195–201, 2000.

88. Eisenberg MS, Bergner L, Hallstrom A: Cardiac resuscitation in the community: importance of rapid provision and implications for program planning, *JAMA* 241:1905–1907, 1979.

89. McIntyre KM: Cardiopulmonary resuscitation and the ultimate coronary care unit (editorial), *JAMA* 244: 510–511, 1980.

90. Larsen MP, Eisenberg MS, Cummins RO, Hallstrom AP: Predicting survival from out-of-hospital cardiac arrest: a graphic model, *Ann Emerg Med* 22:1652–1658, 1993.

91. Paradis NA, Martin GB, Goetting MG, et al.: Simultaneous aortic, jugular bulb, and right atrial pressures during cardiopulmonary resuscitation in humans: insights into mechanisms, *Circulation* 80;361–368, 1989.

92. Cobb LA, Fahrenbruch CE, Walsh TR, et al.: Influence of cardiopulmonary resuscitation prior to defibrillation in patients with out-of-hospital ventricular fibrillation, *JAMA* 281:1182–1188, 1999.

93. Wik L, Hansen TB, Flylling F, et al.: Delaying defibrillation to give basic cardiopulmonary resuscitation to patients with out-of-hospital ventricular fibrillation: a randomized trial, *JAMA* 289:1389–1395, 2003.

94. Stiell I, Nichol G, Wells G, et al.: Health-related quality of life is better for cardiac arrest survivors who received citizen cardiopulmonary resuscitation, *Circulation* 108: 1939–1944, 2003.

95. Aufderheide TP, Pirrallo RG, Yannopoulos D, et al.: Incomplete chest wall decompression: a clinical evaluation of CPR performance by EMS personnel and assessment of alternative manual compression-decompression techniques, *Resuscitation* 64:353–362, 2005.

96. Yannopoulos D, McKnite S, Aufderheide TP, et al.: Effects of incomplete chest wall decompression during cardiopulmonary resuscitation on coronary and cerebral perfusion pressures in a porcine model of cardiac arrest, *Resuscitation* 64:363–372, 2005.

97. Greingor JL: Quality of cardiac massage with ratio compression-ventilation 5/1 and 15/2, *Resuscitation* 55:263–267, 2002.

98. Wik L, Kramer-Johansen J, Myklebust H, et al.: Quality of cardiopulmonary resuscitation during out-of-hospital cardiac arrest, *JAMA* 293:299–304, 2005.

99. Abella BS, Alvarado JP, Myklebust H, et al.: Quality of cardiopulmonary resuscitation during in-hospital cardiac arrest, *JAMA* 293:305–310, 2005.

100. Kern KB, Hilwig RW, Berg RA, et al.: Importance of continuous chest compressions during cardiopulmonary resuscitation: improved outcome during simulated single lay-rescuer scenario, *Circulation* 105:645–649, 2002.

101. Yu T, Weil MH, Tang W, et al.: Adverse outcomes of interrupted precordial compression during automated defibrillation, *Circulation* 106:368–372, 2002.

102. Berg RA, Hilwig RW, Kern KB, et al.: Automated external defibrillation versus manual defibrillation for prolonged ventricular fibrillation: lethal delays of chest compression before and after countershocks, *Ann Emerg Med* 42:458–467, 2003.

103. Handley AJ. Teaching hand placement for chest compression—a simpler technique, *Resuscitation* 53:29–36, 2002.

104. Liberman M, Lavoie A, Mulder D, Sampalis J: Cardiopulmonary resuscitation: errors made by prehospital emergency medical personnel, *Resuscitation* 42:47–55, 1999.

105. Kundra P, Dey S, Ravishankar M: Role of dominant hand position during external cardiac compression, *Br J Anaesth* 84:491–493, 2000.

106. Handley AJ, Handley JA: The relationship between rate of chest compression and compression:relaxation ratio, *Resuscitation* 30:237–241, 1995.

107. American Heart Association. *BLS for healthcare providers student manual*, Dallas, American Heart Association, 2005.

108. Choux C, Gueugniaud PY, Barbieux, et al.: Standard dose versus repeated high doses of epinephrine in cardiac arrest outside the hospital, *Resuscitation* 29:3–9, 1995.

109. Ong ME, Lim SH, Anantharaman V: Intravenous adrenaline or vasopressin in sudden cardiac arrest: a literature review, *Ann Acad Med Singapore* 31:785–792, 2002.

110. American Heart Association: 2005 American Heart Association guidelines for cardiopulmonary resuscitation and emergency cardiovascular care. International Consensus on Science. Part 7.2: Management of cardiac arrest, *Circulation* 112: IV-58–IV-66, 2005.

111. Carpenter J, Rea TD, Murray JA, et al.: Defibrillation waveform and post-shock rhythm in out-of-hospital ventricular fibrillation cardiac arrest, *Resuscitation* 59:189–196, 2003.

112. White RD, Russell JK: Refibrillation, resuscitation and survival in out-of-hospital sudden cardiac arrest victims treated with biphasic automated external defibrillators, *Resuscitation* 55:17–23, 2002.

113. Walpoth BH, Locher T, Leupi F, et al.: Accidental deep hypothermia with cardiopulmonary arrest: extracorporeal blood rewarming in 11 patients, *Eur J Cardiothorac Surg* 4:390–393, 1990.

CHAPTER 31

PEDIATRIC CONSIDERATIONS

Medical emergencies can and do occur in the practice of dentistry. Most medical emergencies develop when the patient, commonly an adult, is fearful or has inadequate pain control. The most common emergencies noted in adult dental patients include syncope (~50%), non–life-threatening allergy, acute anginal episodes, postural hypotension, seizures, acute asthmatic attacks, and hyperventilation.[1] Previous sections of this text dealt with prevention, recognition, and management of the more common medical emergencies occurring in the dental environment in adult victims.

Medical emergencies can and do happen in pediatric patients as well (Table 31-1). As with adults, most emergencies observed in the pediatric dental environment were stress related (fainting [syncope], hysteria, seizures, hyperventilation, bronchospasm). Many of the medical emergencies encountered in the pediatric dental office happened to the parent of the child patient. In many instances the parent, sitting in the treatment room near the child, experienced the medical emergency while observing the child's dental treatment, the sight of blood, or the "needle," provoking a stress-induced emergency situation.

TABLE 31-1 Results of survey of incidence of specific emergency situations (over a 10-year period)*

Situation	Reported incidents (no.)	Comments by doctors
Fainting (syncope)	75	Mostly parents
Hysteria	23	"All the time, it's PEDO"
Allergy, mild	22	
Seizures	13	
Hypoglycemia	9	
Hyperventilation	7	
Aspiration	5	
Respiratory distress	4	
Bronchospasm	3	
Airway obstruction	3	
Cardiac arrest	1	
Allergy, anaphylaxis	1	
Drug overdose	1	
Local anesthesia overdose	1	

*n = 66 doctors responding to survey at 2004 American Academy of Pediatric Dentistry Pediatric Emergencies in the Dental Office (PEDO) course.

Box 31-1 Definitions of victims by age for health care providers

Infants during first 28 days of life = NEONATE
<1 year = INFANT (includes neonatal period)
1 year to puberty or adolescence = CHILD
Adolescence and older = ADULT

Signs of puberty include breast development on the female and underarm, chest, and facial hair on the male.

From ECC Committee, Subcommittees and Task Forces of the American Heart Association: 2005 American Heart Association Guidelines for Cardiopulmonary Resuscitation and Emergency Cardiovascular Care. *Circulation* 112(24 Suppl):IV1–IV203, 2005.

Emergencies associated with local anesthetic or central nervous system (CNS)–depressant drug administration occur more often in children than adults. The outcome of these situations oftentimes is less than optimal. It is this author's considered opinion that the most likely scenario for a serious drug-related emergency developing in dentistry is a younger, lighter-weight child receiving multiple quadrants of dental treatment in the office of a younger, less experienced, nonpediatric dentist (e.g., generalist).[2]

All dental practices must prepare to manage potentially life-threatening emergencies, be the victim a child or adult. The following sections review the preparation of the dental office and staff to successfully manage medical emergencies that might arise in younger patients in the dental office.

Table 31-2 presents the results of a self-assessment survey of 66 pediatric dentists participating in the PEDO (Pediatric Emergencies in the Dental Office) continuing dental education program sponsored by the American Academy of Pediatric Dentistry in 2004.[3] Doctors were asked to assess their level of confidence in recognizing and managing specific emergency situations. Levels of confidence in emergencies involving the cardiovascular, respiratory, and central nervous systems were rated as lowest.

For the purposes of basic life support (BLS) (cardiopulmonary resuscitation [CPR]), the child has been defined, by American Heart Association guidelines for BLS, as a person from 1 year of age to age 8 years (1 through 7 years).[4] The 2005 guidelines for emergency cardiovascular care redefined the child patient. For BLS purposes, an infant remains a person under the age of 1 year. The child is now defined, for health care providers, as a person from 1 year of age to the start of puberty. Puberty is defined in the guidelines as breast development in females and the presence of underarm, chest, and facial hair in males.[5,6] Once puberty is reached the victim is managed according to adult BLS guidelines (Box 31-1).

■ PREPARATION

Preparation to manage pediatric medical emergencies mimics that for adults. The following four steps are critical in preparing the office and staff to recognize and effectively manage medical emergencies: (1) the ability to properly perform BLS; (2) a functioning dental office emergency team; (3) ready access to emergency assistance; and (4) the availability of emergency drugs and equipment.

Basic life support

BLS or CPR is *the* single most important step in preparation of the office and staff to successfully manage medical emergencies. BLS for health care providers is defined as Position, Airway, Breathing, Circulation, and Defibrillation. Most U.S. states mandate BLS certification for licensure to practice as a dentist. A majority of states also require BLS certification for dental hygienists,

TABLE 31-2 PEDO 2004: Results of survey of incidence of and level of "confidence" in recognizing and managing specific emergency situations*

Situation	Recognition	Management	Confidence level
Cardiac arrest	81	104	Least
Local anesthetic overdose	81	97	
Allergy and anaphylaxis	74	95	
Bronchospasm	76	95	
Drug overdose	80	93	
Aspiration	69	91	
Respiratory distress	69	82	
Airway obstruction	61	81	
Seizures	60	77	
Hypoglycemia	83	76	
Hysteria	65	76	
Hyperventilation	63	70	
Mild allergy	62	63	
Syncope (faint)	54	54	Most

*n = 66 doctors responding to survey at 2004 American Academy of Pediatric Dentistry Pediatric Emergencies in the Dental Office (PEDO) course. Responses were: 1 = very confident; 2 = "so-so" confident; and 3 = not confident. Numbers in the table are the sum of all responses. Higher totals indicate a lesser degree of confidence.

while some mandate certification for dental assistants. The importance of BLS as preparation for managing pediatric medical emergencies is highlighted by the fact that the primary etiology of cardiac arrest in children is respiratory (airway or breathing) problems, usually airway obstruction or respiratory arrest (as might occur with overly deep "conscious" sedation).[7] The young child's heart is usually healthy, coronary artery disease being essentially nonexistent in young patients. However, a healthy young heart will cease to pump if deprived of oxygen for a period of time. At the moment of pediatric cardiac arrest little to no residual oxygen (O_2) remains in the victim's blood (almost all available O_2 has been utilized by the now dying cells). Acidosis and cellular (biological) death develop relatively rapidly. Survival rates (in the United States) from out-of-hospital sudden cardiac arrest in pediatric patients is from 2% to 10%, and survivors are frequently neurologically devastated.[8-10] By contrast, cardiac arrest in adults commonly develops secondary to advanced coronary artery disease. At the moment the adult heart goes into arrest there remains a reservoir of O_2 in the blood and tissues that can be consumed before cellular death occurs.

The very basic step of airway management (head tilt–chin lift) is critically important in saving the life of a child.

Pediatric advanced life support

Because children are different from adults, the dentist and staff in offices where significant numbers of young patients are treated should successfully complete a course in pediatric advanced life support (PALS).[11] Similar to BLS, PALS stresses basic and advanced life support techniques for younger patients (neonates, infants, and children). The course is offered through organizations such as hospitals and pediatric dental societies; the course outline is presented in Box 31-2.

PEDO

As mentioned previously, PEDO is a didactic and clinical course in emergency medicine designed for the entire staff of the pediatric dental office. Sponsored by the American Academy of Pediatric Dentistry, the course provides in-depth, hands-on training in the prevention and management of specific emergency situations that arise more commonly in children.[3]

Emergency team

Similar to the emergency team described in Chapter 3, the pediatric dental office team consists of three individuals, each assigned specific tasks to perform, as outlined in Table 31-3.

Box 31-2 Pediatric Advanced Life Support Course Outline[10]

The Chain of Survival and Emergency Medical Services for Children*
Basic Life Support for the PALS Healthcare Provider*
Airway, Ventilation, and Management of Respiratory Distress and Failure*
Fluid Therapy and Medications for Shock and Cardiac Arrest
Vascular Access*
Rhythm Disturbances
Postarrest Stabilization and Transport
Trauma Resuscitation and Spinal Immobilization
Children with Special Healthcare Needs*
Toxicology*
Neonatal Resuscitation
Rapid Sequence Intubation
Sedation Issues for the PALS Provider*
Coping with Death and Dying
Ethical and Legal Aspects of CPR in Children*

*Denotes subjects of special interest to dentists treating children.
CPR, cardiopulmonary resuscitation; PALS, pediatric advanced life support.
From the American Heart Association: 2005 American Heart Association (AHA) guidelines for cardiopulmonary resuscitation (CPR) and emergency cardiovascular care (ECC) of pediatric and neonatal patients: pediatric advanced life support, *Pediatrics* 117:e1005–e1028, 2006.

All members of the office emergency team should be interchangeable. Although the proper and effective management of the emergency situation is ultimately the doctor's responsibility, emergency management may be performed by any trained individual under supervision of the doctor.

Access to emergency medical services

Assistance in managing an emergency should be sought as soon as the treating (e.g., responsible) doctor feels it is warranted. Emergency medical services (EMS) should be sought if the doctor: (1) does not know what is happening; (2) knows, but does not like, what is happening; or (3) ever feels uncomfortable with the situation. Seek help as soon as possible in these situations. Do not delay. There is no loss of face when help arrives to find the victim recovered.

In virtually all situations, the most practical course for getting help is to activate the EMS system (e.g., 9-1-1 in the United States and Canada). In an emergency, the ultimate responsibility of the treating doctor is to keep the victim alive until: the victim recovers or help arrives to take over management of the situation, providing the "helper" is better able to manage the situation than the treating doctor.

TABLE 31-3 Office emergency team

Team member	Responsibilities
Member 1 (first person on scene of emergency)	1. Remain with victim 2. Activate office emergency system 3. BLS as necessary
Member 2	1. Bring emergency equipment* to scene

Member 3 (and other members of the dental office staff)	1. Assist as necessary
	   a. Activate EMS
	   b. Meet and escort EMS to office
	   c. Assist with BLS
	   d. Prepare emergency drugs for administration
	   e. Monitor and record vital signs

Emergency equipment includes oxygen supply, emergency drugs, and an automated external defibrillator.
BLS, basic life support; EMS, emergency medical service.

Emergency drugs and equipment

Every dental office must have emergency drugs and equipment, as recommended in Tables 31-4, 31-5, and 31-6. Minor modifications are necessary in offices where children are treated (shaded rows in Tables 31-4 and 31-6).

In offices where CNS depressants are employed for conscious sedation, specific antidotal drugs should be included in the emergency drug kit (see Table 31-5). For benzodiazepines (e.g., diazepam, midazolam, triazolam), flumazenil should be available, while naloxone is included in the drug kit if opioids are employed. Single doses of these antidotal drugs may prove ineffective when administered to manage overdose resulting from orally administered or longer-acting benzodiazepines (e.g., lorazepam) and opioids (e.g., morphine).

■ BASIC MANAGEMENT

As described throughout this text, basic management of *all* medical emergencies follows the $P \rightarrow A \rightarrow B \rightarrow C \rightarrow D$ acronym, where **P** is positioning, **A** is airway, **B** is breathing, **C** is circulation, and **D** is definitive care (in the BLS acronym, **D** is defibrillation).

Basic management of pediatric medical emergencies mimics that of the adult. It is first necessary to determine whether the patient is conscious or unconscious. Unconsciousness is defined as the lack of response to sensory stimulation (e.g., lack of response to the "shake and shout" maneuver).

TABLE 31-4 Recommended emergency drugs for pediatric office

Drug (brand name)	Indication	Availability	Recommended for kit
Epinephrine (Adrenalin)	Anaphylaxis	1:1000 (adult) (0.3 mg/dose)	1 preloaded syringe + 3 × 1 mL ampules of 1:1000
Epinephrine (Adrenalin)	Anaphylaxis	1:2000 (pediatric) (0.15 mg/dose)	1 preloaded syringe + 3 × 1 mL ampules of 1:1000
Diphenhydramine HCl (Benadryl)	Mild allergy	50 mg/mL	2–3 × 1 mL ampules of 50 mg/mL
Oxygen	All emergencies	"E" cylinder + delivery devices	Minimum 1, preferably 2, "E" cylinders
Albuterol (Proventil, Ventolin)	Bronchospasm	Metered aerosol inhaler	1 aerosol inhaler
Sugar	Hypoglycemia	Orange juice, Insta-Glucose	12-ounce bottle of orange juice and/or 1 tube of Insta-Glucose
Aspirin	Suspected myocardial infarction	325-mg tablets	1–2 sealed tablets
Nitroglycerin	Angina pectoris	Metered spray	1 nitrolingual spray

TABLE 31-5 Antidotal drugs

Drug	Indication	Availability	Recommended for kit
Flumazenil (Romazicon)	Benzodiazepine antagonist	0.1 mg/mL	1 × 10 mL multidose vial
Naloxone (Narcan)	Opioid antagonist	0.4 mg/mL	2 × 1 mL ampule of 0.4 mg/mL

TABLE 31-6 Dental office emergency equipment

Device	Availability	Recommended for kit
Automated external defibrillator (AED)	Many	1 AED (pediatric AEDs are available)[9]
Face masks	Various sizes for children and adults	Several pediatric masks + adult mask
Disposable syringes and needles	2-mL syringe with 20-gauge needle	2–3 sterile, disposable syringes
Spacer for bronchodilator inhaler	Various manufacturers	1 spacer

Position

The most common cause of loss of consciousness, in children as well as adults, is hypotension. All unconscious patients are placed, at least initially, in the supine position with the feet elevated slightly, increasing cerebral blood flow with minimum interference with ventilation.[12] Conscious persons experiencing a medical emergency are placed in whatever position they find most comfortable. As an example, most persons in acute respiratory distress (e.g., bronchospasm, hyperventilation) automatically assume an upright position to improve ventilation.

Airway and breathing

In the unconscious person, head tilt–chin lift must be performed (Figure 31-1), followed by an assessment of ventilation (look, listen, feel).

An important point to remember: seeing the victim's chest moving (e.g., spontaneous respiratory movements) does not always mean that the victim is breathing (exchanging air), but simply that he or she is *attempting* to breathe. Hearing and feeling the exchange of air against the rescuer's cheek is the only true indication of successful ventilation.

In the absence of spontaneous respiratory efforts (e.g., chest not moving, apnea), controlled ventilation

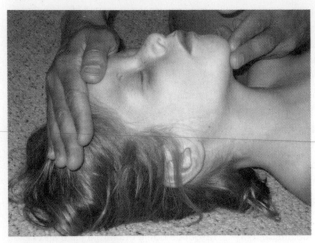

FIGURE 31-1 Head tilt–chin lift.

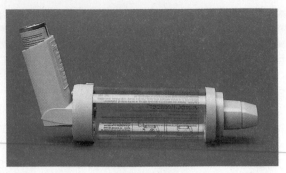

FIGURE 31-2 Bronchodilator with spacer. (From Chapleau W: *Emergency first responder: making the difference,* St. Louis, Mosby, 2004.)

must be performed as expeditiously as possible. With a full face mask or with positive pressure oxygen for the pubescent patient, rescue breaths are delivered at a rate of 10 to 12 breaths per minute, or one breath every 5 to 6 seconds, whereas a rate of 12 to 20 breaths per minute (1 breath every 3 to 5 seconds) is used for the infant and child victim.[13] Each breath is given over 1 second and should produce visible chest rise so as to prevent hyperventilation, which leads to gastric distention and regurgitation. Health care providers often deliver excessive ventilation during CPR, more so when the victim is a small child or an infant.[14,15] Respiratory arrest in children is reviewed in depth below.

Circulation

In pediatric medical emergencies, a palpable pulse will probably be present, especially where airway and breathing are adequately and rapidly assessed and supported.

Palpation of the carotid artery is preferred in children (>1 year) and adults, whereas the brachial pulse is preferred in infants (<1 year). A pulse is checked for at least 5 seconds but not more than 10 seconds. In the absence of a palpable pulse, chest compression must be commenced, with EMS summoned immediately. Cardiac arrest in children is reviewed in depth below.

Definitive care

Following assessment and implementation of the needed steps of BLS, the doctor seeks to determine the cause of the problem. When diagnosis is possible and appropriate treatment available, it should be implemented immediately. If a diagnosis is made but appropriate treatment is not available or if the cause of the problem

remains unknown, EMS should be sought immediately. Definitive management of several common pediatric emergencies follows.

■ SPECIFIC EMERGENCIES
Bronchospasm (acute asthmatic attack)

Recognition.

Conscious patient in acute respiratory distress, demonstrating wheezing, supraclavicular and intercostals retraction. Prior history of asthma usually present.

P. Position comfortably, usually upright.

A, B, C. Assessed as adequate (victim is conscious and able to speak, though not normally).

D (definitive care).

1. Administer bronchodilator

If the patient's inhaler is available, allow the patient to use it. If patient is younger and the parents or guardian is available, bring them into the treatment room to assist in administration of bronchodilator. Many younger children require the use of a spacer in order to obtain adequate relief with the inhaler (Figure 31-2).[2]

2. Administer O_2, via facemask or nasal cannula at a flow rate of 3 to 5 L/min.[3]

3. Summon EMS if the parent or guardian of the patient suggests it, or if the episode of bronchospasm does not terminate following two doses of the bronchodilator.

Management of bronchospasm is more fully discussed in Chapter 13.

Generalized tonic-clonic seizure (grand mal seizure)

Recognition.

Period of muscle rigidity (~20 seconds [tonic phase]) followed by alternating muscle contraction and relaxation lasting for about 1 to 2 minutes (clonic phase).

P. Position supine.

A, B, C. Assessed as adequate (respiratory and cardiovascular stimulation are noted during the seizure).

D (definitive care).

1. Protect victim from injury. Keep victim in the dental chair; gently hold arms and legs, preventing uncontrolled movements, but *do not* hold so tight as to prevent all movement.

2. If parent or guardian is available, bring them to the treatment room to assist in assessing the victim.

3. Summon EMS if the parent or guardian of patient suggests it, or if the seizure continues for more than 2 minutes.

Most tonic-clonic seizures stop within 1 minute and almost always within 2 minutes (thus the recommendation for EMS with prolonged seizure activity). At the conclusion of the seizure, $P \rightarrow A \rightarrow B \rightarrow C \rightarrow D$ must be reassessed, as follows:

P. Position supine.

A, B, C. Assessed and managed as needed. In most (but not all) postseizure situations, **A** must be managed, but **B** and **C** are assessed as adequate.

D (definitive care).

With assistance from the parent or guardian, try to communicate with the patient, who is probably in a state similar to a deep physiologic sleep. Following a tonic-clonic seizure, the victim is normally quite disoriented. As the parents or guardian has seen this situation before, allow them to talk with the patient to help reorient the patient to both space and time.

Seizure management is fully discussed in Chapter 21.

Sedation overdose

Recognition. Lack of response to sensory stimulation.

Consider.

An overdose of sedation is general anesthesia (though general anesthesia represents a "controlled state of unconsciousness"), whereby with oversedation unconsciousness is unintentionally achieved. Effective management of a patient receiving general anesthesia is predicated on airway management and ventilation. Oversedation should *not* represent an emergency in the hands of a doctor who has been adequately trained to administer general anesthesia or conscious sedation to children or adults.

P. Position supine.

A, B, C. Assessed and managed as necessary.

In most cases, **A** alone is required; **A** and **B** will be needed in a few situations. **C** will generally be present if **A** and **B** are properly assessed and adequately managed.

D (definitive care).

1. Monitor patient by using a pulse oximeter (and measurement of blood pressure and heart rate or rhythm).

> **Remember:**
> Do not place anything between the teeth of a convulsing person.

> **Remember:**
> Most morbidity and death associated with seizures occur in the postseizure period because the rescuer does not do enough for the victim.
> **(P→A→B→C→D)**

> **Remember:**
> 1. Specific antidotal therapy may not be effective following the oral administration of central nervous system depressants.
> 2. Antidotal therapy should be administered intravenously, if possible.
> 3. Naloxone may be administered intramuscularly.

2. Stimulate the patient periodically (verbally or by squeezing the trapezius muscle) seeking response.

3. Antidotal drug therapy: If benzodiazepines were administered parenterally, and if intravenous (IV) access is available, administer IV flumazenil in a dose of 0.2 mg (2 mL) in 15 seconds, waiting 45 seconds to evaluate recovery. If recovery is not adequate at 1 minute, an additional dose of 0.2 mg may be administered. Repeat every minute until patient recovers or a dose of 1.0 mg has been delivered. Titrate IV naloxone at 0.1 mg. (0.25 mL) per minute to a dose of 1.0 mg if an opioid was administered. Naloxone can be administered through an intramuscular (IM) route in a dosage of 0.01 mg/kg of body weight every 2 to 3 minutes until the patient becomes responsive. There is no evidence that flumazenil is effective following IM administration.

4. EMS may, or may not, be summoned, depending on the clinical situation. Sedation overdose is fully discussed in Chapter 23.

Local anesthetic overdose

A true overdose of local anesthetic should be always preventable.[2]

Recognition.

Generalized tonic-clonic seizure or unconsciousness, generally developing within seconds (following rapid intravascular administration) or in 5 to 40 minutes after local anesthetic administration. Following rapid intravascular administration, signs and symptoms of local anesthetic overdose may develop within seconds.

P. Position supine.

A, B, C. Assessed and administered as needed.

D (definitive care).

1. Generalized tonic-clonic seizure: follow protocol for seizures (above). With airway management and ventilation (as needed), the clonic phase of a local anesthetic–induced seizure usually ceases in less than 1 minute. In the absence of an adequate airway or adequate ventilation, CO_2 is retained and the patient becomes hypercarbic and acidotic, lowering the seizure threshold of the LA and leading to a more prolonged and more intense seizure.[16]

2. Unconsciousness: the basic protocol for management of the unconscious patient is followed when a local anesthetic overdose presents as loss of consciousness. Management of airway and breathing, as needed, minimizes the possible occurrence of cardiac arrest. As the cerebral blood level of the local anesthetic decreases (through redistribution of the drug), the seizure stops and consciousness returns.

3. Summon EMS if consciousness is not restored in 2 minutes or if the patient is not breathing.

Local anesthetic overdose is fully discussed in Chapter 23.

Respiratory arrest

In pediatric dentistry, respiratory depression or respiratory arrest (apnea) in the normal healthy child (American Society of Anesthesiology class I) most commonly occurs secondary to the administration of CNS-depressant drugs used for conscious sedation, deep sedation, or general anesthesia in conjunction with local anesthetic administration.[17]

Undiagnosed and improperly managed respiratory depression can lead to a dental office catastrophe: cardiac arrest and death, or survival with severe, permanent neurologic damage.

Safety in conscious sedation is predicated upon a number of items, including titration and monitoring.

The ability to *titrate** is the ultimate safety factor in drug administration. Only drugs administered intravenously or by inhalation (N_2O-O_2) possess this ability and therefore represent the most controllable (and therefore safest) routes of drug administration. Drugs administered through the oral, IM, or intranasal routes have a significantly slower onset of action and cannot be titrated. Pediatric dosages of drugs administered by these routes are determined by a formula of x mg of drug per kilogram of body weight. This is based on the response of approximately 70% of persons who

respond normally to a given drug dosage. Fifteen percent of patients do not achieve the desired level of sedation with this dosage (so-called hyporesponders), while the remaining 15% demonstrate exaggerated responses (the hyperresponders).

Monitoring of the sedated patient is the second essential element in safety. As the patient becomes progressively more CNS depressed (as sedation becomes deeper), the ability to respond to verbal and physical stimulation is increasingly impaired. Assessing the level of CNS depression is the most important monitor during conscious sedation. This is achieved by communicating with the patient and evaluating the response. A conscious patient must be capable of "an appropriate response to verbal and/or physical stimulation."[18] A conscious patient must also be able to maintain the patency of the airway.

Monitors such as the pulse oximeter and pretracheal stethoscope enable the doctor to quickly recognize the onset of respiratory depression or arrest and provide timely management.

Cardiac arrest, when it occurs in children, is rarely a sudden event, and noncardiac causes predominate.[6] Cardiac arrest in children typically represents the terminal event of prolonged respiratory failure, respiratory arrest, or airway management problems.[19,20] The heart of a healthy young child will cease to pump blood when it is deprived of oxygen for a period of time. Inadequate monitoring or inadequate airway management during conscious sedation is common in cases of pediatric cardiac arrest.[17]

In the dental environment, the unrecognized development of respiratory depression or respiratory arrest can lead to cardiac arrest. Survival rates from pediatric out-of-hospital cardiac arrest in the United States are low, are variously estimated at 2% to 10%.[7-9] Survivors are commonly neurologically devastated.[21] Conversely, survival rates from respiratory arrest in children are approximately 70%.[7] Neurologically intact survival rates of 70% or greater have been reported of children with respiratory arrest alone.[10,11]

Proper airway management and the ability to ventilate the apneic patient are prime considerations in the prevention of neurologic damage and pediatric cardiac arrest.[20]

The infant and child are at greater risk for the development of airway obstruction and respiratory arrest than the adult.[22] Compared with adults, the airway of infants and smaller children has relatively large adenoids and tonsils; a tongue that is proportionately large in relation to the size of the oropharynx; small nasal passageways; and a smaller, more compliant trachea that is easily collapsed in the presence of increased airway resistance.

---

*Titration: the administration of small incremental doses of a drug to a patient until the desired clinical effect is achieved.

Additional factors increasing the risk of respiratory or cardiac arrest in infants and smaller children include a metabolic rate with up to double the oxygen consumption of adults; a smaller functional residual lung capacity with limited oxygen reserve; physiologic collapse of smaller airways (atelectasis) with increases in airway resistance; and the rapid development of hypoxia with airway obstruction.[23] The following is meant as a *review* of the management of respiratory depression or arrest in the small child.

Management of respiratory distress

Recognition: It has been this author's experience that maintenance of a patent airway in the child receiving conscious sedation is not difficult and is commonly accomplished by the treating dentist. O_2 saturation is normally maintained in the range of 98% or 99% during treatment of maxillary teeth. Given the positioning of the doctor, usually seated behind the sedated patient, the very act of working on maxillary teeth extends the patient's neck into an almost ideal airway position known as head tilt (Figure 31-3). Difficulties in airway management most often develop with mandibular treatment. Regardless of the doctor's position (behind or in front of the sedated patient), the pressures placed onto the teeth and mandible force the jaw downwards toward the chest, moving the pliable soft tissues closer together and, in the much younger patient, potentially compromising the integrity of the tracheal rings (Figure 31-4). Though most pediatric conscious sedation cases are uneventful, O_2 saturation frequently drops slightly at the time of transition from maxillary to mandibular treatment. The quality of sound heard through the pretracheal stethoscope may change from the normal quiet and sometimes hard-to-hear, whooshing to that of "snoring," indicating partial airway obstruction, the cause of which most commonly is the tongue or other soft tissues.[24,25]

The audible alarm on the pulse oximeter for "low" oxygen saturation is commonly set at 90%. With compromise of the airway, O_2 saturation will decrease (either slowly or rapidly) until the alarm activates when the reading falls below 90%.

Management of respiratory depression

Management of this, and all, emergency situations follows the $P \rightarrow A \rightarrow B \rightarrow C \rightarrow D$ algorithm. On recognition of respiratory depression, immediately place the patient into the supine position (**P**) (if not already supine as per the sedation protocol). Extend the neck and tilt the head using the head tilt–chin lift maneuver (**A**). Place one hand on the child's forehead and gently tilt the head back. At the same time, place the fingertips of your other hand on the symphysis of the mandible and lift the chin to open the airway (see Figure 31-1). These simple and basic procedures stretch the soft tissues in the oropharynx and nasopharynx, thereby lifting the tongue and reestablishing airway patency. Snoring ceases, the patient's chest is seen to rhythmically move up and down, and the O_2 saturation returns to its previous level (**B**). This situation, in the hands of a pediatric dentist trained in conscious sedation and BLS, does not constitute an emergency.

Management of respiratory arrest

Recognition: Following administration of a CNS-depressant drug, it is noted that the patient is quiet and not moving. The assistant gently shakes the patient, eliciting no response. The patient is placed into the supine position (**P**) and the treating doctor notified.

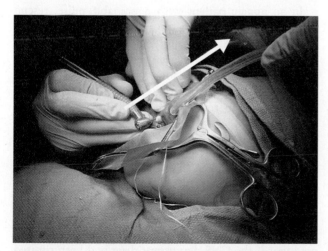

FIGURE 31-3 Upward pressure on teeth during dental treatment in maxilla aids in maintenance of airway during sedation.

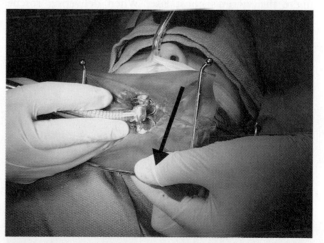

FIGURE 31-4 Downward pressure during dental treatment in the mandible acts to increase the likelihood of airway obstruction during sedation.

While maintaining head tilt–chin lift (**A**), the assistant places his or her ear 1 inch (2.5 cm) away from the patient's mouth and nose and *looks* for the rise and fall of the chest and abdomen, *listens* at the patient's mouth and nose for exhaled breath sounds, and *feels* for air movement from the patient's mouth against the cheek (**B**). This *look, listen, and feel* process should last no more than 10 seconds.

(As soon as it becomes available, the pulse oximeter should be placed on the patient [by a second person], if not already in place.)

Once recognized, respiratory arrest (apnea) must be managed immediately. Rescue breathing is started. All dental office personnel should undergo regular training (at least annually, if not more often) in BLS (**P→A→B→C→D**). This course should include training in the use of a face mask to aid in ventilation of an apneic victim.

Absent the immediate availability of positive pressure O_2, mouth-to-mask (or mouth-to-mouth) ventilation is provided. Rescue breathing should never be delayed while a rescuer searches for a device or tries to learn how to use it.[26]

Maintaining head tilt–chin lift, place the mask on the victim's face, using the bridge of the nose as a guide for correct position. Seal the mask against the face by using your hand that is closer to the top of the victim's head, place the index finger and thumb along the border of the mask, and place the thumb of your other hand along the lower margin of the mask. Place the remaining fingers of your hand closer to the victim's neck along the bony margin of the jaw and lift the jaw. Perform head tilt–chin lift to establish an open airway (Figure 31-5). While lifting the jaw, press firmly and completely around the outside margin of the mask to seal the mask against the face.

For the adult or child, deliver air over 1 second to make the victim's chest rise. When delivering rescue

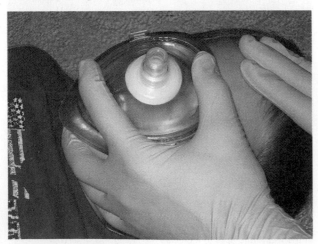

FIGURE 31-5 Mouth-to-mask resuscitation.

breaths to children, be sure to give only enough air to make the victim's chest visibly rise. For small children, less volume will be required than for larger children and adults.[27]

Initially, two breaths are delivered to the apneic victim, followed by one breath every 5 seconds (12 breaths per minute) for the adult and child, and one breath every 3 seconds (20 breaths per minute) for the infant and child victim.[13] Each breath is given over 1 second and should produce visible chest rise. Improper opening of the airway is the most common cause of airway obstruction and inadequate ventilation during resuscitation.[28]

Use of a mask (mouth-to-mask), a bag-valve-mask device, or positive-pressure oxygen is more efficient but requires training to be used effectively. Training can be obtained during a BLS health care provider or PALS provider course. A bag-valve-mask device delivers 21% oxygen, unless it is attached to a source of oxygen ("E" cylinder of oxygen) in which case oxygen concentrations of 30% to 80% can be delivered.[29] A positive-pressure oxygen delivery system enables 100% oxygen to be delivered to the patient.

Regardless of the device used for ventilation (mask, bag-valve-mask, positive pressure), the rescuer should use only the force and tidal volume necessary to cause the patient's chest to rise visibly.

Once rescue breathing has been successfully started, the circulatory status of the patient is assessed (**C**). The pulse is checked for not less than 5 seconds and no more than 10 seconds. In infants, the brachial artery (on the medial aspect of the antecubital fossa) is palpated, while the carotid artery is checked in children and adults.[30] In the absence of a palpable pulse cardiac arrest is diagnosed and chest compression started. Pediatric cardiac arrest is discussed in the following section.

In an apneic patient with a palpable pulse, rescue breathing is continued at the age- and size-appropriate rate with the patient being monitored (**D** [definitive care]). Whether EMS (9-1-1) needs to be activated will depend on the treating doctor's training and clinical experience, as well as the nature of the unfolding event. A simple maxim to remember: When in doubt, seek help!

Administration of a drug-specific reversal agent might also be considered at this time (**D** [definitive care]); however, the effectiveness of naloxone or flumazenil depends on the route by which it and the offending drugs are administered. If both are administered through the IV route, then reversal should produce an observable effect in approximately 1 minute. It is important to note that if the CNS-depressant drug had been titrated intravenously, it is highly unlikely that this event would have occurred. After oral, intranasal, or IM administration of the offending drug, the effect of the reversal agent will be both delayed and less pronounced.

Continue to support ventilation until spontaneous respirations return. Stimulate the patient during this time. Stimulation can be verbal, photic (by shining the surgical light in the patient's eyes), or physical (pinching the trapezius muscle is an excellent stimulus for breathing). A conscious patient responds to peripheral pain by grimacing and by taking in a deep breath.

With return of spontaneous breathing and consciousness, the situation is essentially over. Continue to monitor vital signs and determine (if EMS has not been summoned) when the patient has recovered adequately to permit him or her to be discharged home in the company of the parent or guardian. Where any degree of doubt remains in the mind of the treating doctor, medical consultation before dismissal from the office is warranted.

Respiratory depression, respiratory arrest, and airway management problems are the most common cause of cardiac arrest in healthy children.

Cardiac arrest

Cardiac arrest is an uncommon event within the pediatric population. However, when cardiac arrest does occur in this younger age group, its consequences are devastating: death of a previously healthy child or a successful resuscitation with the patient suffering massive permanent neurologic damage.

Cardiopulmonary arrest in healthy infants and children is rarely a sudden event and does not often result from a primary cardiac cause.[7] Undetected airway problems, prolonged respiratory depression, and apnea are frequent causes of pediatric cardiac arrest. In contrast, cardiopulmonary arrest in adults usually develops suddenly and is primarily cardiac in origin. Approximately 1000 adults die daily in the United States alone from sudden cardiac arrest.[31]

The heart functions to pump blood to all cells and tissues of the body. The myocardium contracts in a coordinated manner to achieve this effect, termed *normal sinus rhythm*. During contraction (systole), blood is pumped from the heart into the arterial circulation; during diastole, the ventricles refill.

Cardiac arrest is the "cessation of cardiac mechanical activity, determined by the inability to palpate a central pulse, unresponsiveness, and apnea (i.e., no signs of circulation or life)."[13]

Pediatric cardiac arrest in a dental situation is all too often associated with administration of CNS-depressant drugs, for either behavior management (oral, intranasal, or IM sedation) or pain control (local anesthetics). Respiratory depression and apnea, which usually develop

before, and are responsible for, pediatric cardiac arrest, were reviewed in the preceding section.

Once recognized, the management of cardiac arrest is the same regardless of the victim's age. The goal of BLS is to deliver oxygen-containing blood to all cells and organs of the body, particularly the brain and myocardium, so as to enable successful resuscitation with little or no permanent neurologic damage.

Management of all medical emergencies is predicated on the P→A→B→C→D algorithm.

Differences between adult and pediatric cardiac arrest

There exist several substantive differences in BLS depending on the size or age of the victim. These differences arise from the fact that the etiology of cardiopulmonary arrest differs in children and adults.

Adults. In the adult victim of sudden cardiac arrest, a history of coronary artery disease is usually present. The advanced age of the typical adult victim helps to explain the onset of sudden cardiac arrest. Coronary artery disease leading to the development of a thrombus within a coronary artery produces myocardial injury secondary to ischemia. Ischemic myocardium is predisposed to rhythm irregularities (dysrhythmias) some of which—pulseless ventricular tachycardia and coarse and fine ventricular fibrillation—are nonfunctional rhythms and are fatal if not treated promptly. Though no longer pumping blood, the myocardium is, initially, still "alive" (electrical activity exists) but is beating chaotically (ventricular fibrillation) or ineffectually (ventricular tachycardia).

Resuscitation (BLS) may prove successful in restoring a functional cardiac rhythm as long as any myocardial activity persists.

Survival rates decrease markedly as the cardiac rhythm deteriorates from ventricular tachycardia to coarse and then to fine ventricular fibrillation and finally to asystole.[32] Defibrillation, the delivery of an electric shock across the chest simultaneously depolarizing every myocardial fiber, is *the* most important intervention in adult resuscitation.[33]

The shorter the elapsed time from collapse of the victim to delivery of a shock, the greater the likelihood of the cardiac rhythm being either ventricular tachycardia or coarse ventricular fibrillation, both of which respond better to defibrillation than fine ventricular fibrillation or asystole.[34]

The automated external defibrillator (AED), a computerized, battery-operated device that detects the presence of a shockable rhythm (pulseless ventricular tachycardia or ventricular fibrillation) has been called "the greatest advance in life-saving since the introduction of CPR in

1960."[35] Success of AEDs is predicated on the fact that in the adult victim of sudden cardiac arrest, the myocardium contains oxygen and the heart is still "alive," though no blood is being circulated.

Children. Healthy children usually have no evidence of coronary artery disease. Cardiac arrest commonly results from undetected airway problems, prolonged respiratory depression, and apnea. A significant difference from the adult victim is that at the time of cardiac arrest the child's myocardium is already depleted of oxygen.[7,36] Ventricular tachycardia and ventricular fibrillation are not frequent findings in pediatric cardiac arrest; the latter occurs in approximately 20% of out-of-hospital pediatric cardiac arrests.[37] The occurrence of ventricular fibrillation increases with age of the victim—it is found in 3% of children 0 to 8 years of age but in 15% of victims age 8 to 30 years.[38] In monitored pediatric patients, the first dysrhythmia noted during prolonged respiratory depression or apnea is sinus bradycardia, a clinically significant slowing of the normally rapid pediatric heart rate.[39] Untreated or undetected bradycardia may become asystole ("silent heart").

Because of these findings, defibrillation is less important in pediatric cardiac arrest. Of prime importance is the implementation of basic life support (P→A→B→C→D) as soon as possible. The delivery of oxygenated blood to the myocardium and brain can, it is hoped, allow a functional cardiac rhythm to be restored and prevent brain damage.

Thus, a significant difference in the basic emergency protocol of BLS for adults and children: In adults, when a single rescuer is with the victim with no one within shouting distance, *phone first.* Activate EMS immediately (before starting BLS) to provide prompt access to defibrillation. In a pediatric situation, since the likely cause of cardiac arrest is anoxia, BLS is started immediately, and EMS is activated after delivery of BLS for 2 minutes (with 1 rescuer)—*phone fast.* With two rescuers present, one starts BLS while the other activates EMS and obtains the AED.

CPR sequence—child victim (age 1 year to the start of puberty)

The pediatric chain of survival (Figure 31-6) includes four links: prevention, BLS, prompt access to EMS, and prompt PALS.[5] The first three links make up pediatric BLS.

Step 1: recognition of unconsciousness. Establish unresponsiveness by gently tapping the victim and asking loudly "Are you okay?" Use the child's name if it is known.

Step 2: summoning of assistance and P (position the patient). If the child is unresponsive and not moving, shout for help and commence BLS. Place the victim in a supine position on a hard surface (the dental chair can support the victim during chest compression [if needed]).[40]

Step 3: A (assess and maintain the airway). Because the tongue is the most likely case of airway obstruction in the unconscious pediatric patient, the head tilt–chin lift procedure is used to establish a patent airway.

Step 4: B (breathing).
Step 4a: assessment of breathing and ventilate, if needed. While maintaining head tilt–chin lift, assess whether the victim is exchanging air (e.g., is breathing). *Look* at the victim's chest and abdomen for spontaneous respiratory efforts; *listen* for exhaled breath sounds at the nose and mouth; and *feel* for exhaled air against your cheek. Not more than 10 seconds should be taken to assess breathing.

Step 4b: rescue breathing. If the pulse of a child is greater than 60 beats per minute but there is no spontaneous breathing (or breathing is inadequate), rescue breaths are delivered at a rate of one breath every 3 to 5 seconds (12 to 20 breaths per minute), until spontaneous breathing resumes. Each breath is given

© American Heart Association

FIGURE 31-6 Pediatric chain of survival. (Reproduced with permission. *Basic Life Support for Healthcare Providers* © 2006, American Heart Association.)

Rescue breathing for the child victim:

- Give one breath every 3 to 5 seconds (12–20 breaths per minute).
- Give each breath in 1 second.
- Each breath must result in visible chest rise.
- Check the pulse again in about 2 minutes.

Modified from American Heart Association: *BLS for healthcare providers student manual*, Dallas, American Heart Association, 2006.

Pulse check

- If the rescuer is unsure whether the victim has a pulse, chest compression should be started.
- Unnecessary cardiopulmonary resuscitation is less harmful than not performing chest compression when the victim truly needs it.

Modified from American Heart Association: *BLS for healthcare providers student manual*, Dallas, American Heart Association, 2006.

Characteristics of good chest compressions—child:

- **Push hard:** Sufficient force is applied to compress the chest of the child; approximately one third to one half of its anterior–posterior diameter.
- **Push fast:** Compress at a rate of approximately 100 compressions per minute.
- **Full recoil:** Release pressure completely to permit chest to fully recoil.
- **Minimize interruptions:** Minimize interruptions in chest compressions.

From American Heart Association: 2005 American Heart Association guidelines for cardiopulmonary resuscitation and emergency cardiovascular care. International Consensus on Science. Part 11: pediatric basic life support, *Circulation* 112:IV1–IV203, 2005.

---

over 1 minute; each breath should cause visible chest rise. The pulse should be reevaluated every 2 minutes during rescue breathing. Not less than 5 seconds and not more than 10 seconds are spent checking the pulse.

Step 5: C (circulation).

Step 5a: assessment of circulation. In the child victim the carotid or femoral pulse should be palpated, taking no more than 10 seconds to do so. Studies have shown that health care providers are unable to reliably detect a pulse and will mistakenly believe a pulse is present when it is not.[41-43]

If a pulse is not definitely palpated (because there is no pulse or you are not certain about whether there is a pulse) chest compression should be started.

Step 5b: activate EMS. If not already done, EMS should be activated immediately. In a majority of children, cardiac arrest is asphyxial (airway involved). If a health care provider is present at the moment of collapse (unresponsive, apneic, "sedated" child patient in the dental chair), BLS is started immediately and five cycles (2 minutes) are delivered before EMS is activated; BLS is then resumed with as few interruptions in chest compressions as possible.[5]

Step 5c: chest compression.
Location of compression point. The lower half of the sternum is compressed, with care taken not to compress the xiphoid process. After each compression, the chest is permitted to recoil fully, permitting a greater volume of blood to flow into the heart.[44]

Application of pressure. The chest of the child should be compressed by using the heel of one hand (for a smaller child or a larger rescuer) or with two hands (as in the adult if a larger child or a smaller rescuer). The chest of the child must be compressed about one third to half its anterior-posterior depth.[5]

Rate of chest compression. The 2005 guidelines recommend a compression rate of about 100 per minute for the child victim.[5]

Compression–ventilation ratio. A compression ventilation ratio of 30:2 is employed for the single rescuer with a child victim. The pause in compression for ventilations should be as short as possible because coronary perfusion pressure drops with each pause for breathing, pulse check, or attachment of the AED.[45,46]

If a second trained rescuer is present, one rescuer provides chest compressions while the other maintains the airway (head tilt–chin lift) and performs ventilations at a ratio of 15:2 with as short a pause in compressions as possible for ventilation.[5] Do not simultaneously compress the chest and deliver ventilations with either mouth-to-mouth or mouth-to-mask ventilation. The 15:2 compression-ventilation ratio for two rescuers is used for children up to the start of puberty.[5]

With two or more rescuers present, they should rotate the role of compressor approximately every 2 minutes to minimize compressor fatigue and deterioration in the rate and quality of chest compression.[47,48]

Step 6: defibrillation. Pediatric dentists and other dentists who treat large numbers of children should have available an AED capable of detecting pediatric shockable rhythms (pulseless ventricular tachycardia and ventricular fibrillation) and are equipped to decrease the delivered energy to make it suitable for children 1 to 8 years of age.[49] Since publication of the 2000 BLS guidelines, data have demonstrated the safety and effectiveness of AEDs in children 1 year to 8 years of age.[50,51]

AED technique (child). Once the electrode pads are properly attached to the victim, the AED is turned on and voice prompts are followed. If the rhythm is shockable, one shock is delivered and BLS is resumed

immediately, starting with chest compression for five cycles.

If the rhythm is not shockable, then BLS is resumed immediately for five cycles, following which the rhythm is checked again. This is continued (five cycles, rhythm check) until EMS arrives and takes over or the victim starts to move spontaneously.

Figure 31-7 summarizes and illustrates pediatric BLS. Table 31-7 compares 2005 BLS guidelines for infants, children, and adults.

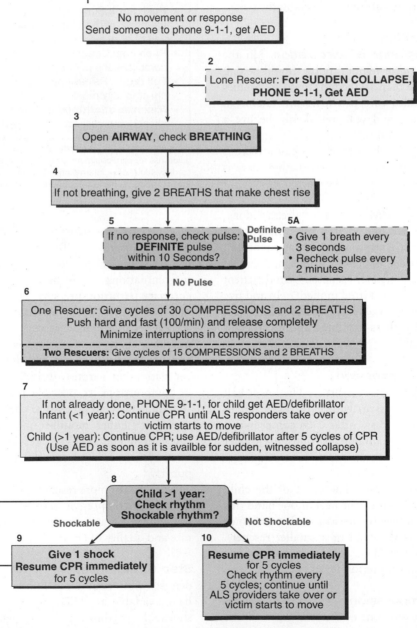

FIGURE 31-7 Pediatric BLS algorithm. (Reproduced with permission. *Basic Life Support for Healthcare Providers* © 2006, American Heart Association.)

TABLE 31-7 Summary of BLS techniques for infants, children, and adults

| Victim | Respirations per minute | Ratio of compression to ventilation | Compressions | | | |
			Rate/min	Depth	Hands	Site
Infant (<1 year of age)	12–20	30:2 (1 rescuer) 15:2 (2 rescuers)	Approximately 100	$1/3$–$1/2$ depth of chest	2–3 fingers	Just below nipple line (lower half of sternum)
Child (1 year to adolescent)	12–20	30:2 (1 rescuer) 15:2 (2 rescuers)	Approximately 100	$1/3$–$1/2$ depth of chest	Heel of one hand or as for adults	Lower half of sternum, between nipples
Adult (adolescent and older)	10–12	30:2 (1 or 2 rescuers)	Approximately 100	$1^1/_2$–2 in	Heel of one hand, other hand on top	Lower half of sternum, between nipples

REFERENCES

1. Malamed SF: Managing medical emergencies, *J Am Dent Assoc* 124:40–53, 1993.
2. Malamed SF: Allergic and toxic reactions to local anesthetics, *Dentistry Today* 22:114–121, 2003.
3. American Academy of Pediatric Dentistry. www.aapd.org
4. American Heart Association in collaboration with International Liaison Committee on Resuscitation. Guidelines 2000 for cardiopulmonary resuscitation and emergency cardiovascular care, *Circulation* 102:I1–I384, 2000.
5. American Heart Association: 2005 American Heart Association guidelines for cardiopulmonary resuscitation and emergency cardiovascular care. International Consensus on Science, *Circulation* 112:IV-1–IV-211, 2005.
6. ILCOR 2005 international consensus on cardiopulmonary resuscitation and emergency cardiovascular care science with treatment recommendations, *Circulation* 112:III-1–III-125, 2005.
7. Young KD, Seidel JS: Pediatric cardiopulmonary resuscitation: a collective review, *Ann Emerg Med* 33:195 205, 1999.
8. Pitetti R, Glustein JZ, Bhende MS: Prehospital care and outcome of pediatric out-of-hospital cardiac arrest, *Prehosp Emerg Care* 6:283–290, 2002.
9. Schindler MB, Bohn Desmond, Cox PN, et al.: Outcome of out-of-hospital cardiac or respiratory arrest in children, *N Engl J Med* 335:1473–1479, 1996.
10. Herlitz J, Engdahl J, Svensson L, et al.: Characteristics and outcome among children suffering from out of hospital cardiac arrest in Sweden, *Resuscitation* 64:37–40, 2005.
11. Lankster MA, Brasfield MS 3rd: Update on pediatric advanced life support guidelines, *Crit Care Nurs Clin North Am* 17:59–64, 2005.
12. Erie JK: Effect of position on ventilation. In: Faust RJ, editor: *Anesthesiology review*, New York, Churchill Livingstone, 1991.
13. American Heart Association: 2005 American Heart Association guidelines for cardiopulmonary resuscitation and emergency cardiovascular care. International Consensus on Science. Part 11: pediatric basic life support, *Circulation* 112:IV-156–IV-166, 2005.
14. Aufderheide TP, Sigurdsson G, Pirrallo RG, et al.: Hyperventilation-induced hypotension during cardiopulmonary resuscitation, *Circulation* 109:1960–1965, 2004.
15. Abella BS, Alvarado JP, Myklebust H, et al.: Quality of cardiopulmonary resuscitation during in-hospital cardiac arrest, *JAMA* 293:305–310, 2005.
16. Chin KL, Yagiela JA, Quinn CL, et al.: Serum mepivacaine concentrations after intraoral injection in young children, *J Calif Dent Assoc* 31:757–764, 2003.
17. Goodson JM, Moore PA: Life-threatening reactions after pediatric sedation: an assessment of opioid, local anesthetic, and antiemetic drug interaction, *J Am Dent Assoc* 107:239–245, 1983.
18. American Dental Association House of Delegates: Guidelines for the use of conscious sedation, deep sedation and general anesthesia for dentists. American Dental Association, October 2003.
19. Sirbaugh PE, Pepe PE, Shook JE, et al.: A prospective, population-based study on the demographics, epidemiology, management, and outcome of out-of-hospital pediatric cardiopulmonary arrest, *Ann Emerg Med* 33:174–184, 1999.
20. Kuisma M, Suominen P, Korpela R: Paediatric out-of-hospital cardiac arrests: epidemiology and outcome, *Resuscitation* 30:141–150, 1995.
21. Lopez-Herce J, Garcia C, Rodriquez-Nunez A, et al.: Long-term outcome of paediatric cardiorespiratory arrest in Spain, *Resuscitation* 64:79–85, 2005.
22. Cote CJ, Rodrea ID, Goudsouzian NG, et al.: *A practice of anesthesia for infants and children*, ed 3, Philadelphia, WB Saunders, 2001.
23. Nadkarni V: Ventricular fibrillation in the asphyxiated piglet model. In: Quan L, Franklin WH, editors: *Ventricular fibrillation: a pediatric problem*, Armonk, NY, Futura Publishers, 2000, pp. 43–54.

24. Guildner CW: Resuscitation: opening the airway: a comparative study of techniques for opening an airway obstructed by the tongue, *JACEP* 5:588–590, 1976.

25. Elam JO, Greene DG, Schneider MA, et al.: Head-tilt method of oral resuscitation, *JAMA* 172:812–815, 1960.

26. Emergency Cardiac Care Committee and Subcommittees, American Heart Association: Guidelines for cardio-pulmonary resuscitation and emergency cardiac care, VI: pediatric advanced life support, *Circulation* 102:I-253-I-290, 2000.

27. American Heart Association: *BLS for healthcare providers student manual,* Dallas, American Heart Association, 2006.

28. Zideman DA: Paediatric and neonatal life support, *Br J Anaesth* 79:179–187, 1997.

29. Finer NN, Barrington KJ, Al-Fadley F, Peters KL: Limita-tions of self-inflating resuscitators, *Paediatrics* 77:417–420, 1986.

30. Cavallaro DL, Melker RJ: Comparison on two techniques for detecting cardiac activity in infants, *Crit Care Med* 11:189–190, 1983.

31. Chugh SS, Jui J, Gunson K, et al.: Current burden of sudden cardiac death: multiple source surveillance versus retrospective death-certificate-based review in a large US community, *J Am Coll Cardiol* 44:1268–1275, 2004.

32. McIntyre KM: Cardiopulmonary resuscitation and the ultimate coronary care unit (editorial), *JAMA* 244:510–511, 1980.

33. Eisenberg MS, Horwood BT, Cummins RO, et al.: Cardiac arrest and resuscitation: a tale of 29 cities, *Ann Emerg Med* 19:179–186, 1990.

34. Kuisma M, Alaspaa A: Out-of-hospital cardiac arrests of non-cardiac origin: epidemiology and outcome, *Eur Heart J* 18:1122–1128, 1997.

35. Valenzuela T, Roe D, Nichol G, et al.: Outcomes of rapid defibrillation by security officers after cardiac arrest in casinos, *N Engl J Med* 343:1206–1209, 2000.

36. Richman PB, Nashed AH: The etiology of cardiac arrest in children and young adults: special considerations for ED management, *Am J Emerg Med* 17:264–270, 1999.

37. Mogayzel C, Quan L, Graves JR, et al.: Out-of-hospital ventricular fibrillation in children and adolescents: causes and outomes, *Ann Emerg Med* 25:484–491, 1999.

38. Appleton GO, Cummins RO, Larson MP, Graves JR: CPR and the single rescuer: at what age should you "call first" rather than "call fast"? *Ann Emerg Med* 25:492–494, 1995.

39. Sirbaugh PE, Pepe PE, Shook JE, et al.: A prospective, population-based study on the demographics, epidemi-ology, management and outcome of out-of-hospital pediatric cardiopulmonary arrest, *Ann Emerg Med* 33:174–184, 1999.

40. Lepere AJ, Finn J, Jacobs I: Efficacy of cardiopulmonary resuscitation performed in a dental chair, *Aust Dent J* 48:244–247, 2003.

41. Ochoa FJ, Ramalle-Gomara E, Carpintero JM, et al.: Competence of health professionals to check the carotid pulse, *Resuscitation* 37:173–175, 1998.

42. Lapostolle F, Le Toumelin P, Agostinucci JM, et al.: Basic cardiac life support providers checking the carotid pulse: performance, degree of conviction, and influencing factors, *Acad Emerg Med* 11:878–880, 2004.

43. Moule P: Checking the carotid pulse: diagnostic accuracy in students of healthcare professions, *Resuscitation* 44:195–201, 2000.

44. Aufderheide TP, Pirrallo RG, Yannopoulos D, et al.: Incomplete chest wall decompression: a clinical evaluation of CPR performance by EMS personnel and assessment of alternative manual chest compression-decompression techniques, *Resuscitation* 64:353–362, 2005.

45. Berg RA, Sanders AB, Kern KB, et al.: Adverse hemo-dynamic effects of interrupting chest compressions for rescue breathing during cardiopulmonary resuscitation for ventricular fibrillation cardiac arrest, *Circulation* 104:2465–2470, 2001.

46. Kern KB, Hilwig RW, Berg RA, Ewy GA: Efficacy of chest compression-only BLS CPR in the presence of an occluded airway, *Resuscitation* 39:179–188, 1998.

47. Ashton A, McCluskey A, Gwinnutt CL, Keenan AM: Effect of rescuer fatigue on the performance of continuous external cardiac compressions over 3 min, *Resuscitation* 55:151–155, 2002.

48. Ochoa FJ, Ramalle-Gomara E, Lisa V, Saralegui I: The effect of rescuer fatigue on the quality of chest compres-sions, *Resuscitation* 37:149–152, 1998.

49. Atkins DL, Jorgenson DB: Attenuated pediatric electrode pads for automated external defibrillator use in children, *Resuscitation* 66:31–37, 2005.

50. Atkinson E, Mikysa B, Conway JA, et al.: Specificity and sensitivity of automated external defibrillator rhythm analysis in infants and children, *Ann Emerg Med* 42:185–196, 2003.

51. Cecchin F, Jorgenson DB, Burul CI, et al.: Is arrhythmia detection by automatic external defibrillator accurate for children? Sensitivity and specificity of an automatic ex-ternal defibrillator algorithm in 696 pediatric arrhythmias, *Circulation* 103:2483–2488, 2001.

APPENDIX

QUICK-REFERENCE SECTION TO LIFE-THREATENING SITUATIONS

BLS for Healthcare Providers Course

2-Rescuer Adult CPR and AED Practice Sheet

Performance Guidelines	
Check for response • If there is no response, send someone to activate the emergency response system and get the AED	
Open the airway • Head tilt–chin lift **Check for adequate breathing** (take at least 5 and no more than 10 seconds) • Look, listen, and feel **If no adequate breathing, give 2 breaths** • Make the chest rise **Check pulse** • Take at least 5 seconds and no more than 10 seconds	Open airway Give 2 breaths
If no pulse, start cycles of 30 compressions and 2 breaths: • 30 compressions (push hard, push fast) • Rate of 100 per minute • 2 breaths AED arrives after 2 cycles of CPR *Minimize interruptions in chest compressions; try to keep interruptions to 10 seconds or less*	**30** **2**

Reproduced with permission. *Basic Life Support for Healthcare Providers* © 2006, American Heart Association.

Put the AED next to the victim and follow commands:

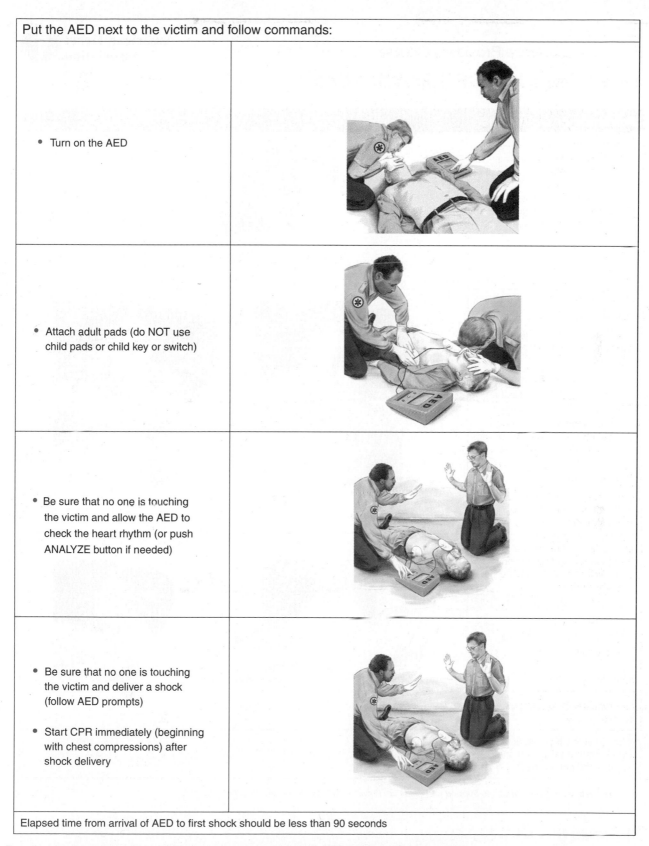

- Turn on the AED

- Attach adult pads (do NOT use child pads or child key or switch)

- Be sure that no one is touching the victim and allow the AED to check the heart rhythm (or push ANALYZE button if needed)

- Be sure that no one is touching the victim and deliver a shock (follow AED prompts)

- Start CPR immediately (beginning with chest compressions) after shock delivery

Elapsed time from arrival of AED to first shock should be less than 90 seconds

BLS for Healthcare Providers Course

1-Rescuer Child CPR Practice Sheet

American Heart Association®

Learn and Live sm

Performance Guidelines	
Check for response • If there is no response, shout for help Send someone to activate the emergency response system and get the AED	
Open the airway • Head tilt–chin lift **Check for breathing (take at least 5 and no more than 10 seconds)** • Look, listen, and feel **If no breathing, give 2 breaths** • Make the chest rise (you may need to try a couple of times to give a total of 2 breaths that make the chest rise) **Check pulse** • Take at least 5 seconds and no more than 10 seconds	Open airway, check breathing Give 2 breaths
If no pulse or if heart rate is less than 60 beats per minute start cycles of 30 compressions and 2 breaths: • 30 compressions (push hard, push fast) • Rate of 100 per minute • 2 breaths *Minimize interruptions in chest compressions; try to keep interruptions to 10 seconds or less*	**30** **2**
After 5 cycles, if alone, activate the emergency response system and get the AED	

Reproduced with permission. *Basic Life Support for Healthcare Providers* © 2006, American Heart Association.

BLS for Healthcare Providers Course

2-Rescuer Child CPR and AED Practice Sheet

American Heart Association®

Learn and Live ᴬᴹ

Performance Guidelines	
Check for response • If there is no response, send someone to activate the emergency response system and get the AED	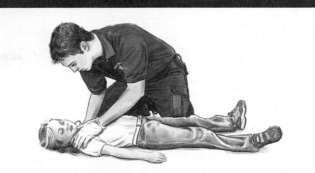
Open the airway • Head tilt–chin lift **Check for breathing (take at least 5 and no more than 10 seconds)** • Look, listen, and feel **If no breathing, give 2 breaths** • Make the chest rise (you may need to try a couple of times to give a total of 2 breaths that make the chest rise) **Check pulse** • Take at least 5 seconds and no more than 10 seconds	 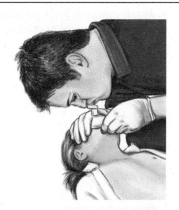 Open airway, check breathing Give 2 breaths
If no pulse or if heart rate is less than 60 beats per minute with signs of poor perfusion, start cycles of 15 compressions and 2 breaths: • 15 compressions (push hard, push fast) • Rate of 100 per minute • 2 breaths *Minimize interruptions in chest compressions; try to keep to less than 10 seconds*	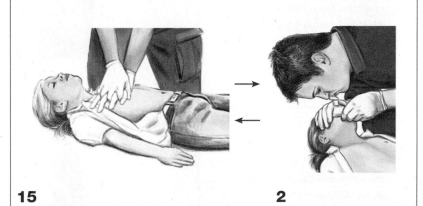 **15** **2**

After 5 cycles or about 2 minutes of CPR, use the AED.

Put the AED next to the victim and follow commands:

• Turn on the AED	
• Attach *child* pads if available; use a child key or switch if available • Use adult pads if child pads are not available	
• Be sure that no one is touching the victim and allow the AED to check the heart rhythm (or push ANALYZE button if needed)	
• Be sure that no one is touching the victim and deliver a shock (follow AED prompts) • Start CPR immediately (beginning with chest compressions) after shock delivery	

Reproduced with permission. *Basic Life Support for Healthcare Providers* © 2006, American Heart Association.

Part 2

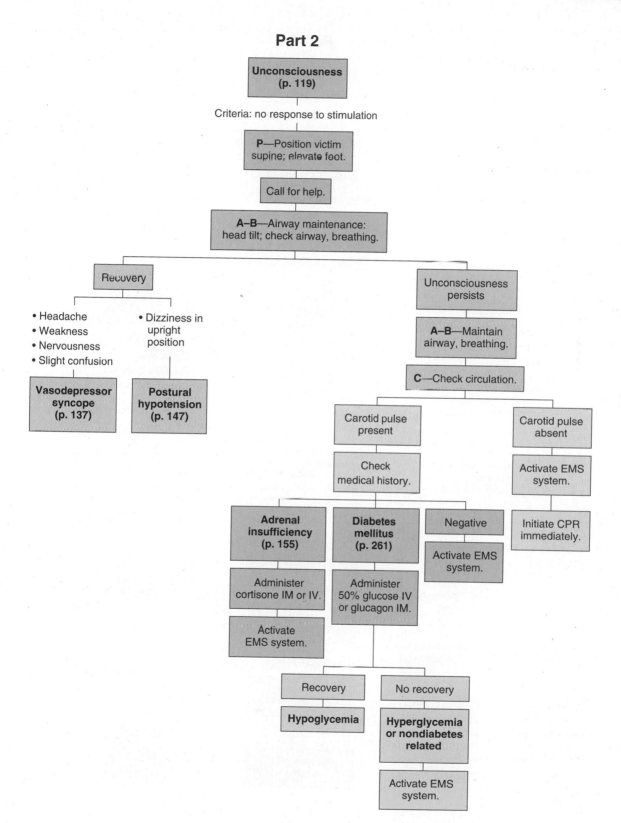

Unconsciousness (p. 119)

Criteria: no response to stimulation

P—Position victim supine; elevate foot.

Call for help.

A–B—Airway maintenance: head tilt; check airway, breathing.

Recovery

- Headache
- Weakness
- Nervousness
- Slight confusion

- Dizziness in upright position

Vasodepressor syncope (p. 137)

Postural hypotension (p. 147)

Unconsciousness persists

A–B—Maintain airway, breathing.

C—Check circulation.

Carotid pulse present

Carotid pulse absent

Check medical history.

Activate EMS system.

Adrenal insufficiency (p. 155)

Diabetes mellitus (p. 261)

Negative

Initiate CPR immediately.

Administer cortisone IM or IV.

Administer 50% glucose IV or glucagon IM.

Activate EMS system.

Activate EMS system.

Recovery

No recovery

Hypoglycemia

Hyperglycemia or nondiabetes related

Activate EMS system.

Part 3

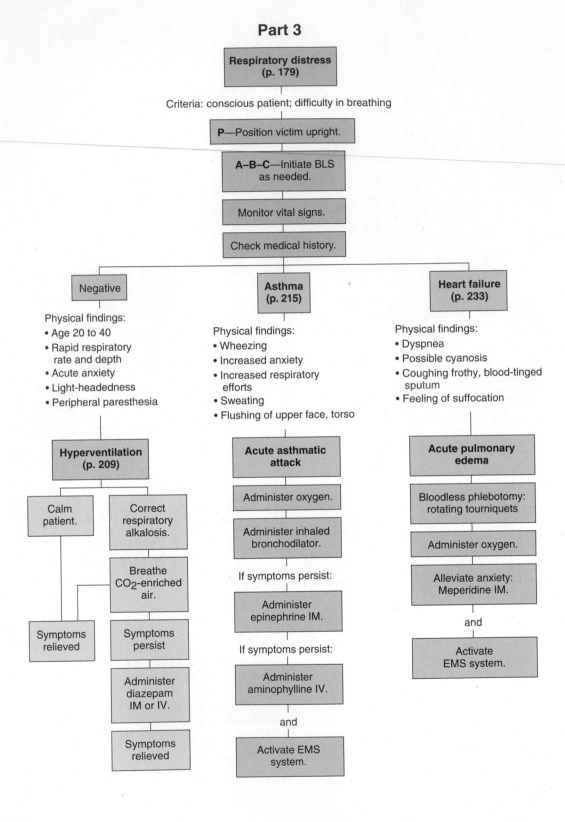

Respiratory distress
(p. 179)

Criteria: conscious patient; difficulty in breathing

P—Position victim upright.

A–B–C—Initiate BLS as needed.

Monitor vital signs.

Check medical history.

Negative

Asthma
(p. 215)

Heart failure
(p. 233)

Physical findings:
• Age 20 to 40
• Rapid respiratory rate and depth
• Acute anxiety
• Light-headedness
• Peripheral paresthesia

Physical findings:
• Wheezing
• Increased anxiety
• Increased respiratory efforts
• Sweating
• Flushing of upper face, torso

Physical findings:
• Dyspnea
• Possible cyanosis
• Coughing frothy, blood-tinged sputum
• Feeling of suffocation

Hyperventilation
(p. 209)

Acute asthmatic attack

Acute pulmonary edema

Calm patient.

Correct respiratory alkalosis.

Administer oxygen.

Bloodless phlebotomy: rotating tourniquets

Administer inhaled bronchodilator.

Administer oxygen.

Breathe CO_2-enriched air.

If symptoms persist:

Alleviate anxiety: Meperidine IM.

Symptoms relieved

Symptoms persist

Administer epinephrine IM.

and

If symptoms persist:

Activate EMS system.

Administer diazepam IM or IV.

Administer aminophylline IV.

and

Symptoms relieved

Activate EMS system.

Part 4

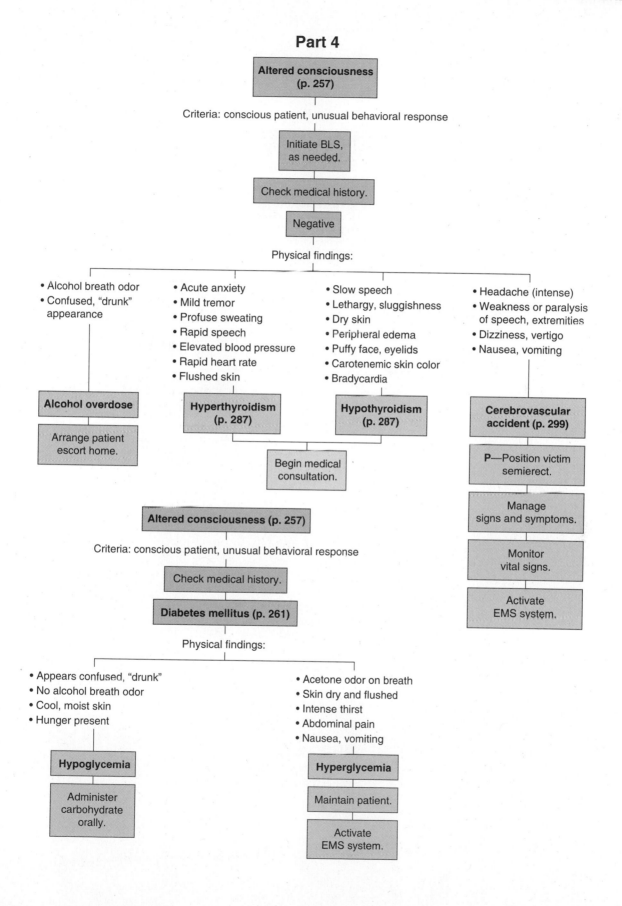

Altered consciousness (p. 257)

Criteria: conscious patient, unusual behavioral response

Initiate BLS, as needed.

Check medical history.

Negative

Physical findings:

- Alcohol breath odor
- Confused, "drunk" appearance

- Acute anxiety
- Mild tremor
- Profuse sweating
- Rapid speech
- Elevated blood pressure
- Rapid heart rate
- Flushed skin

- Slow speech
- Lethargy, sluggishness
- Dry skin
- Peripheral edema
- Puffy face, eyelids
- Carotenemic skin color
- Bradycardia

- Headache (intense)
- Weakness or paralysis of speech, extremities
- Dizziness, vertigo
- Nausea, vomiting

Alcohol overdose

Arrange patient escort home.

Hyperthyroidism (p. 287)

Hypothyroidism (p. 287)

Begin medical consultation.

Cerebrovascular accident (p. 299)

P—Position victim semierect.

Manage signs and symptoms.

Monitor vital signs.

Activate EMS system.

Altered consciousness (p. 257)

Criteria: conscious patient, unusual behavioral response

Check medical history.

Diabetes mellitus (p. 261)

Physical findings:

- Appears confused, "drunk"
- No alcohol breath odor
- Cool, moist skin
- Hunger present

- Acetone odor on breath
- Skin dry and flushed
- Intense thirst
- Abdominal pain
- Nausea, vomiting

Hypoglycemia

Administer carbohydrate orally.

Hyperglycemia

Maintain patient.

Activate EMS system.

Part 5

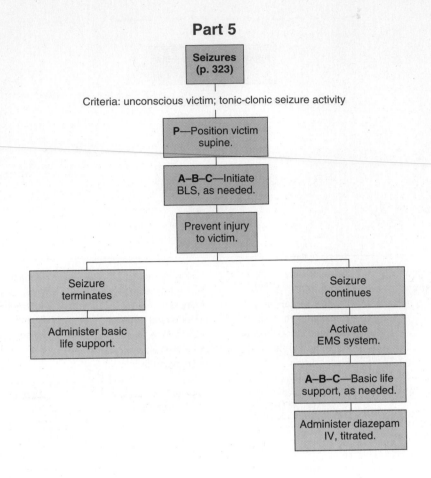

Seizures
(p. 323)

Criteria: unconscious victim; tonic-clonic seizure activity

P—Position victim supine.

A–B–C—Initiate BLS, as needed.

Prevent injury to victim.

Seizure terminates

Administer basic life support.

Seizure continues

Activate EMS system.

A–B–C—Basic life support, as needed.

Administer diazepam IV, titrated.

Part 6

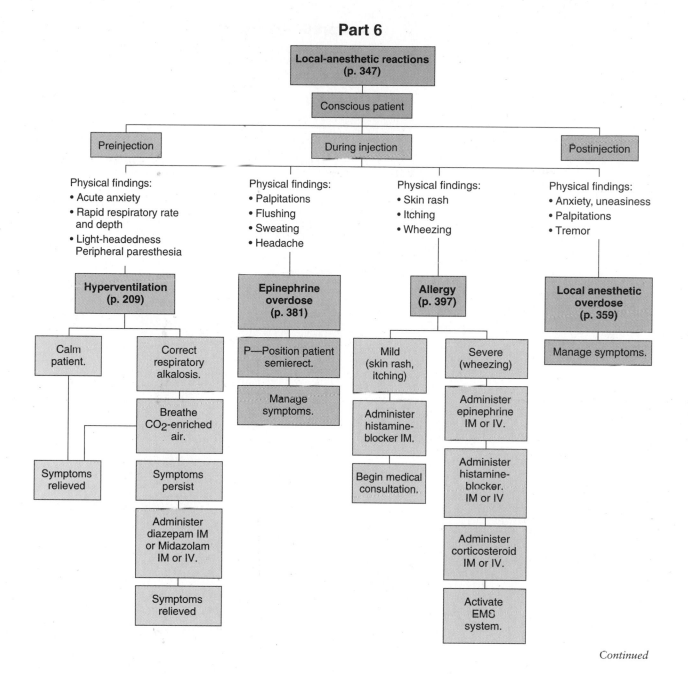

Continued

Part 6—cont'd

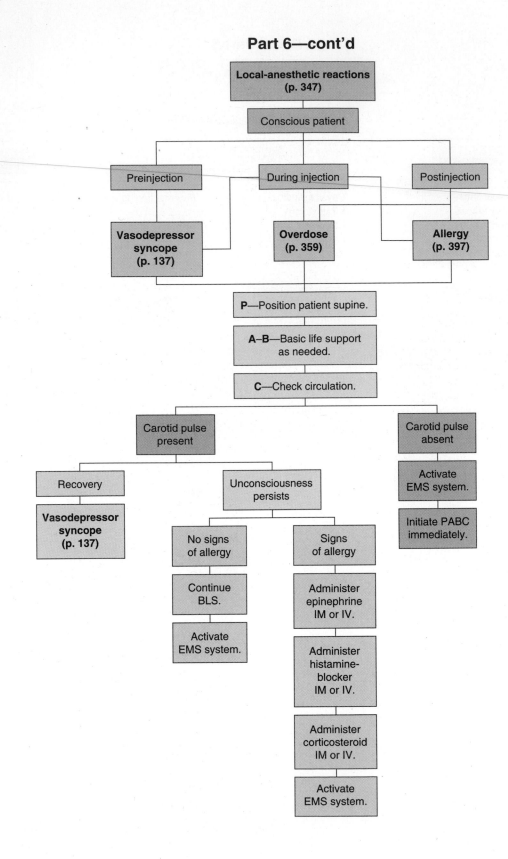

Part 7

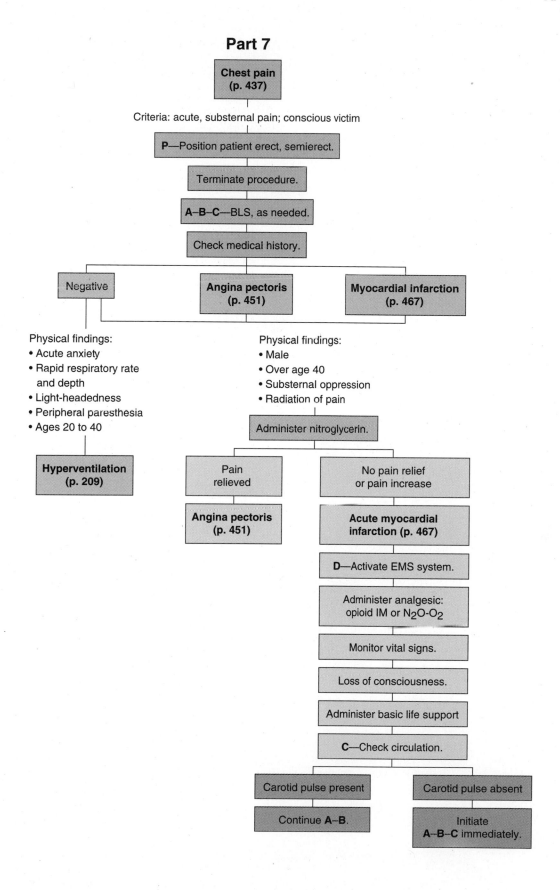

Chest pain
(p. 437)

Criteria: acute, substernal pain; conscious victim

P—Position patient erect, semierect.

Terminate procedure.

A–B–C—BLS, as needed.

Check medical history.

Negative

Angina pectoris
(p. 451)

Myocardial infarction
(p. 467)

Physical findings:
- Acute anxiety
- Rapid respiratory rate
  and depth
- Light-headedness
- Peripheral paresthesia
- Ages 20 to 40

Physical findings:
- Male
- Over age 40
- Substernal oppression
- Radiation of pain

Administer nitroglycerin.

Hyperventilation
(p. 209)

Pain
relieved

No pain relief
or pain increase

Angina pectoris
(p. 451)

Acute myocardial
infarction (p. 467)

D—Activate EMS system.

Administer analgesic:
opioid IM or N_2O-O_2

Monitor vital signs.

Loss of consciousness.

Administer basic life support

C—Check circulation.

Carotid pulse present

Carotid pulse absent

Continue **A–B**.

Initiate
A–B–C immediately.

INDEX

Page numbers followed by f refer to figures; page numbers followed by t refer to tables; page numbers followed by b refer to boxes.

A

Abdominal pain, in acute MI, 477t
Abdominal thrust. *See* Heimlich maneuver
Absence seizures
  clinical manifestations of, 332–333
  management of, 335–336
  overview of, 325–326
Acetaminophen
  ADRs to, 355t
  allergic reactions to, 406, 407t
Acetylsalicylic acid. *See* Aspirin
Acidosis
  metabolic, 279
  pathophysiology of, 279
ACLS. *See* Advanced cardiovascular life
    support
Acquired immunodeficiency syndrome
    (AIDS), 27
Acrylic monomer, allergic reactions to,
    400b, 402
ACTH. *See* Adrenocorticotropic hormone
Acute adrenal insufficiency. *See also*
    Addison's disease
  clinical features of, 161t
  in conscious patient, 165–166, 167b
  criteria for, 165b
  emergency drug kits for, 167
  hydrocortisone for, 158t
  medical history questionnaire for,
    158–160
  overview of, 155–156
  in unconscious person, 166–168, 168b
Acute coronary syndrome, 438b
Acute myocardial infarction. *See also*
    Myocardial infarction
  clinical manifestations, 474–475, 474t,
    475b
  management of, 476–482, 477t, 480b,
    481t
  overview of, 438b, 467–468
  pathophysiology, 475–476
  predisposing factors, 468–470, 469t
  prevention, 470–472, 471t
  therapy considerations, 472–473, 472t
Acute pulmonary edema
  clinical manifestations of, 242–243, 243t
  management of, 246–248, 247b
  overview of, 234

Addison's disease
  additional considerations of, 160
  incidence of, 156
  postural hypotension and, 150
  predisposing factors for, 156–158
Adipocytes, diabetes and, 265
Adrenal cortex, hypofunctioning of, 164f
Adrenal crisis. *See* Acute adrenal
    insufficiency
Adrenal gland
  anatomy of, 156
  dysfunction of, 28
  insufficiency, 156
  normal function of, 161–163, 162f
Adrenalin. *See* Epinephrine
β-adrenergic blockers, 470, 471t
Adrenocorticotropic hormone (ACTH),
    162–163, 163f
ADRs. *See* Adverse drug reactions
Adult chain of survival
  first link, 496
  forth link, 497
  second link, 496–497
  third link, 497
Advanced cardiovascular life support
    (ACLS). *See also* Basic life
    support; Cardiopulmonary
    resuscitation
  in chain of survival, 497
  drug kit essentials for
    atropine, 91t, 92
    epinephrine, 90, 91t
    lidocaine, 91–92, 91t
    morphine, 91t, 93
    oxygen, 91, 91t
    verapamil, 91t, 93
  geography and, 60
Advanced trauma life support (ATLS),
    geography and, 60
Adverse drug reactions (ADRs). *See also*
    Drug-related emergencies
  to analgesics, 354–355, 355t, 356t
  to antibiotics, 353–354, 354t, 356t
  to anxiolytics, 355–356, 355t
  classification of, 351–352, 351b
  in dental procedure, 31t–37t
  drug administration in, 350
  to inhalation sedation, 356–357

Adverse drug reactions (ADRs)—*cont'd*
  to LAs, 353
  to nitrous oxide, 356–357
  to NSAIDS, 385
  prevention of, 348
AED technique. *See also* Automated
      external defibrillators
  adult, 509–510
    practice sheet, 532–533
  pediatric, 528–529, 528f
    practice sheet, 535–536
AEDs. *See* Automated external defibrillators
Age
  altered consciousness and, 318
  CAD and, 489
  drug overdose and, 361
  drug-related emergencies and, 430
  heart failure by, 234f
  postural hypotension and, 149–150
  respiratory distress and, 252
  seizures by, 328t
  unconsciousness and, 172
AIDS. *See* Acquired immunodeficiency
      syndrome
Airway adjuncts, for unconscious patient,
      132, 133f
Airways. *See also* Breathing; Respiration;
      Ventilation
  adult *vs.* infant, 128t
  advanced devices for, 89–90, 89f
  artificial, 45, 88–89, 88f
  emergency
    invasive, 199–202
    noninvasive, 194–199
  inflammation of, 223
  neural control of, 222–223
  obstruction of
    causes, 129t
    in children, 516t
    in unconscious patient, 123, 123f,
      125–127, 126f, 127f
  patency of, 127–130, 128t
Albuterol
  in emergency kits, 74–75, 75f
  for pediatric emergencies, 519t
Alcohol
  medical history questions regarding, 30
  unconsciousness and, 174

Allergen, 412
  defined, 399
Allergic reactions, 397–425, 398t, 400b,
    409t, 410t
Allergy. *See also* Drug-related emergencies
  from ADRs, 351–352
  asthma and, 223
  in children, 516t
  clinical manifestations of, 408–411,
      409t, 410t, 411t
  corticosteroids for, 82t, 84–85
  epinephrine for, 71
  management of
    generalized anaphylaxis, 423–425,
        423f, 424b, 425b
    to local anesthetics, 406–408, 407t
    respiratory reactions, 419–423, 420b,
        420f, 422b
    skin reactions, 416–419, 418b, 419b
  medical history questionnaire regarding,
      27, 402–404, 403f
  overview of, 397–399, 398t, 399b
  pathophysiology of, 411–416, 412f,
      412t, 413b, 413t
  predisposing factors, 399–402, 400b,
      401t, 402b
  prevention, 402–406, 403f
Alprazolam
  ADRs to, 355t
  for anxiety, 55t
Altered consciousness
  causes of, 258t
  clinical manifestations, 259
  differential diagnosis, 317–320
  flow chart for, 539
  management of, 259–260, 260b
  overview of, 257
  pathophysiology, 259
  predisposing factors, 258–259
  prevention of, 259
American Society of Anesthesiologists
    (ASA), physical status
    classification system, 50–53
Amides, ADRs to, 356t
Amlodipine, 455t
Amoxicillin, 25t
  ADRs to, 355t
Ampicillin, 25t
  ADRs to, 355t
Amrinone, 471t
Amyl nitrate, in emergency kits, 73
Amyloid angiopathy, 310
Analgesics. *See also* specific agents
  ADRs to, 354–355, 355t, 356t
  allergic reactions to, 400, 400b
Anaphylactic reaction. *See also* Allergy
  defined, 397, 399
  overview of, 398
  pathophysiology of, 414–416
Anaphylactoid, 399
Anaphylaxis
  allergic reactions and, 410–411, 410b,
      411t, 412t
  chemical mediators of, 414–416

Anemia, 27–28
Anesthesia
  ASA risk classification, 50–53
  for stress, 56
Anesthetic cartridge, allergic reactions
      from, 401–402, 401t
Angina
  defined, 451
  medical history questionnaire regarding,
      19–20
Angina pectoris
  characteristics of, 452t
  chest pain and, 438, 438t
  clinical manifestations of, 444, 444t,
      460–461
  location of pain in, 489
  management of, 462–464, 463f, 464b
  overview of, 452
  pathophysiology, 461–462
  predisposing factors, 452–453, 452b,
      453t
  prevention, 453–457, 454t, 455t, 456f
  therapy considerations, 457–460
Angioedema
  in allergic reaction, 409, 409t
  defined, 399
Angiotensin-converting enzyme inhibitors,
      470–471, 471t
Ankles
  with edema, 239, 239f
  swollen, 21
Anoxia, 120b, 180b
  defined, 438b
Antianxiety drugs
  allergic reactions to, 400–401, 400b
  in drug-related emergencies, 355–356,
      356t
Antibiotics
  ADRs and, 353–354, 354t, 356t
  allergic reactions to, 399–400, 400b
Antibody
  antigen reaction, 414
  defined, 399
  pathophysiology of, 412–413, 412f,
      413b
  structure of, 412f
Anticoagulant, 473
Antidotal drugs
  emergency kit of, 93t, 94–96
  in pediatric office, 518, 519t
Antigen
  allergies and, 412
  antibody reaction, 414
  defined, 399
Antihistamine. *See* Histamine
Antihypertensives, in emergency kits, 82t,
      86–88
Antihypoglycemics, in emergency kits,
      75–76
Antiplatelet therapy, in acute MI, 473, 479
Anxiety. *See also* Antianxiety drugs; Stress
  altered consciousness and, 319
  ASA risk classification of, 48–50
  blood pressure and, 41–42

Anxiety—*cont'd*
  drugs for, 55t
  hyperventilation and, 210, 211–212
  postoperative pain control and, 57
  recognition of
    clinical signs in, 50b
    observation of patient, 48–50
    psychological examination, 48–50
    questionnaire, 48, 49b
    vasodepressor syncope and, 139–140
Anxiolytics, ADRs to, 355–356, 355t
Apnea, 180b
Appointments
  length of, 11
  scheduling of, 55–56
Apprehension
  in acute MI, 490
  in CVA, 306
Arm pain, in acute MI, 477t
Aromatic ammonia
  in emergency kits, 82t, 86–87, 87f
  for syncope, 142, 142f
Arterial embolus, in acute MI, 477t
Arthritis, 24
Articaine, 354t
  dosage, 367t
Artificial airways. *See also* Airway;
      Ventilation
  in emergency kits, 88–89, 88f
  indications for, 45
Artificial joints, 29
ASA. *See* American Society of
      Anesthesiologists
Aspiration
  in children, 516t
  of foreign bodies, 186–187, 187f
Aspirin
  ADRs to, 355t
  allergic reactions to, 400, 400b
  in CVA, 307
  in emergency drug kits, 76, 76f
  MI and, 470, 471t
  for pediatric emergencies, 519t
Asthma. *See also* Respiratory distress
  cardiac, 242
  classification of, 218f, 221t
  clinical manifestations of, 221–222,
      221b
  management of, 225–229, 225b, 226f,
      227f, 228b
    drug therapies for, 219f, 220f
  medical history questionnaire regarding,
      25, 26
  overview of, 215–216
  pathophysiology, 222–225, 225t
  predisposing factors, 216–217, 216b,
      217f
  prevention, 217–221, 218b
Asystole, 495–496, 495f, 498–499
Atenolol, 455t
Atheroma, 445, 445f
Atherosclerosis. *See also* Acute myocardial
      infarction; Coronary artery
      disease

Atherosclerosis—cont'd
 clinical manifestations of, 444, 444t
 pathophysiology of, 445–446, 445b, 445f
 risk factors for, 440b, 441–443
ATLS. See Advanced trauma life support
Atmospheric air ventilation, 131
Atopy, 399
Atropine
 in ACLS drug kit, 91t, 92
 in emergency kits, 82t, 86
Attitude, drug overdose and, 362
Auscultatory gap, 41, 42f
Autoimmune factors, in diabetes, 264
Automated external defibrillators (AEDs),
  in emergency kit, 114
 availability of, 497
 in chain of survival, 494, 497
Automatisms, 332
Azithromycin, 25t
 ADRs to, 355t

B
Baby boomers, life expectancy, 9f
Back blows, 195, 195f
Bag-valve-mask
 for emergency ventilation, 77–78, 77f
 for unconscious patient, 131–132, 132f
Banyan emergency kits, 66f
Barbiturates
 ADRs, 32t
 allergic reactions to, 400–401, 400b,
  406, 407t
 overdose of, 385
  clinical manifestations of, 385–387
Basedow's disease. See Thyrotoxicosis
Baseline vital signs, 38
Basic life support (BLS)
 beginning/terminating of, 510
 in cardiopulmonary arrest, 500
 in chain of survival, 496–497
 chest compression in, 502, 505–506
 for children, 516–518, 518b, 518t, 529t
 circulation in, 504–505, 504f, 520
 defibrillation in, 508–510, 508f, 509f
 by staff, 61
 summary of, 501f
 for syncope, 143–144
 training, 499–500
 in unconscious patient, 134–135, 135b,
  174–175, 175b
Basophil kallikreins, 415
Benzocaine, 354t
 allergic reactions to, 400b, 401
Benzodiazepines. See also Antianxiety
  drugs
 ADRs, 31t–32t
 ADRs to, 355–356, 355t, 356t
Biotransformation, 365
Birth control, 30
Bisulfites, allergic reactions to, 400b, 402
Bleeding disorders
 in CVA, 307
 medical history questionnaire regarding,
  21

Blood
 glucose, pathophysiology of, 278–279
 samples, 270–271, 271f
Blood level
 defined, 374
 in LAs overdose, 373–374, 375f
Blood pressure. See also Pulse; Vital signs
 in altered consciousness, 319
 average, 243f
 in chest pain, 490
 CVD and, 444
 diastolic, 40–41, 41f
 in drug-related emergencies, 432
 gravity and, 151–152, 152f
 measurement of
  anxiety and, 41–42
  baseline, 38, 39
  devices for, 39f, 40f
  errors in, 41–42
  guidelines for clinical evaluation, 42,
   43t, 44t
  in home, 39, 39f
  Korotkoff sounds, 40–41, 41f, 42f
  techniques in, 39
 preoperative monitoring of, 39–40
 in respiratory distress, 253
 systolic, 40, 41f
 unconsciousness and, 132, 134, 134f,
  174, 174t
Blood pressure cuff
 illustration of, 39f
 OR monitor, 39f
 proper placement of, 40f
 size of, 41, 41f
Blood sugar. See Hyperglycemia;
  Hypoglycemia
Bloodless phlebotomy, 247–248
BLS. See Basic life support
Blurred vision, 24
Blushing area, 415
Brachial artery, 40, 40f
Bradycardia
 in acute MI, 476
 atropine for, 91t, 92
 in syncope, 140
 treatment of, 86
Bradypnea, 44
"Brain attack," 25. See also
  Cerebrovascular accident
Breach of duty, 108
Breath odor
 in altered consciousness, 319
 unconsciousness and, 174
 in visual inspection, 47
Breathing. See also Airways;
  Ventilation
 in asthmatic patients, 224–225
 rescue, 503–504
 in unconsciousness patient, 127–130
Breathlessness, in LVF, 241
Bronchodilator
 administration of, 426–427, 428
 for allergic reaction, 420, 420f
 for children, 520, 520f

Bronchodilator—cont'd
 parenteral, 225f
 proper use of, 226f
Bronchospasm
 in allergic reaction, 409–410, 410t
 in children, 516t, 520
 management of
  in allergic reaction, 419–420, 420b,
   420f
  in asthma attack, 223–224
 severe, 227–229
Bruising, medical history questionnaire
  regarding, 21
Bupivacaine, 354t
Bystander CPR, 496

C
CAD. See Coronary artery disease
Calcium slow-channel blockers, 463–464
Cancer, 27
Captopril, 471t
Carbamazepine, for seizures, 330t
Cardiac arrest. See also Sudden cardiac
  arrest
 in acute MI, 475
 in cardiopulmonary arrest, 498–499,
  498t
 causes of, 498
 in children, 516t
 in dental office, 500, 502
 epinephrine for, 90, 91t
 overview of, 493–494
 pediatric, 525
  vs. adult, 525–526
 survival rates in, 505t
Cardiac asthma, 242
Cardiac-oriented classification, 13t
Cardiogenic shock, 476
Cardiopulmonary arrest, 498–499, 498t
Cardiopulmonary resuscitation (CPR)
 adult
  2-rescuer practice sheet, 532–533
  steps in, 502–506, 503f, 504f, 505t
 bystander, 496
 in cardiac arrest, 494
 in chain of survival, 496–497
 pediatric, 516–518, 518b, 518t,
  526–529, 528f, 529f
 rescuer practice sheets, 534–536
 training in, 499–500
Cardiopulmonary-cerebral resuscitation
  (CPCR), in cardiac arrest, 494
Cardiovascular disease (CVD)
 deaths from, 439f
 prevalence of, 439t
  by race, 440t
 risk factors for, 438b
Cardiovascular reactions, in allergies,
  410–411, 411t
Carotid artery, 504–505, 504f
Carvedilol, 455t
Causation, 108–109
Cefadroxil, 25t
Cefazolin, 25t

Central nervous system (CNS)
depressant overdose
clinical manifestations, 385–387
management, 387–391, 389b, 391b
predisposing factors/prevention, 385,
386t
in unconscious patient, 123
Cephalexin, 25t
Cephalosporins, ADRs to, 34t–35t, 355t
Cerebral apoplexy. *See* Cerebrovascular
accident
Cerebral circulation, in syncope,
122–123
Cerebral embolization
clinical manifestations of, 308–309
in CVA, 301
Cerebral hemorrhage, 309
Cerebral infarction
clinical manifestations of, 308
overview of, 301, 301t
sites of, 302f
Cerebral resuscitation, 494
Cerebral vascular infarction,
pathophysiology of, 309, 309f
Cerebrovascular accident (CVA)
classification
cerebral infarction, 301, 301t
hemorrhagic stroke, 301t, 303
lacunar infarction, 300–301, 301t
physical status, 307t
transient ischemic attack, 301, 301t,
303
clinical manifestations of, 307–309,
308b, 308t
differential diagnosis, 320
management of, 310–313, 311b, 313b
medical history questionnaire regarding,
25
overview of, 300
pathophysiology of, 309–310, 309f,
310f
Cerebrovascular ischemia
clinical manifestations of, 444, 444t
pathophysiology of, 309
Chain of survival
adult
first link, 496
forth link, 497
second link, 496–497
third link, 497
pediatric, 526–528, 526f
Chair position. *See also* Patient
positioning
airway obstruction and, 187, 188f
Challenge dose, 414
CHD. *See* Coronary heart disease
Chest compression
adult
in BLS, 502, 505–506
compression-ventilation ratio in, 507
hand position in, 506f
location of, 506
patient positioning in, 507, 507f
pressure application in, 506–507

Chest compression—*cont'd*
adult—*cont'd*
rate of, 507
technique of, 506b
pediatric, 527
Chest pain. *See also* Acute myocardial
infarction; Angina pectoris
angina. *See* Angina
atherosclerotic, 446–447
cardiac, 488–490
clinical manifestations of, 444, 444t
description of, 489
differential diagnosis, 487–490, 488b,
490t
duration of, 489
flow chart for, 543
location of, 489
management of, 447, 464b
medication response in, 489
noncardiac, 488
vs. cardiac, 490t
overview of, 437–438, 438b, 438t
pathophysiology, 445–447, 445b, 445f,
446f, 447f
predisposing factors, 438–443
prevention of, 443–444, 443t
radiation patterns of, 456f, 460–461, 489
in respiratory distress, 253
unconsciousness and, 173
Chest thrusts, in airway obstruction,
197–198, 198b, 198f
Children. *See also* Infants; Pediatric
airway obstruction in, 187f
anxiety in, 49
aspiration in, 516t
blood pressure ranges in, 44t
CPR in, 516–518, 518t, 526–529, 528f,
529f
heart rates in, 45t
hypothyroidism in, 292, 292f
petit mal epilepsy in, 332–333
Chloral hydrate, ADRs to, 33t, 355t
Chlorpheniramine, 72
Cholesterol, atherosclerotic disease and,
441t, 443t
Ciprofloxacin, ADRs, 37t
Circulation
assessment of, in BLS, 504–505, 504f
pediatric, in BLS, 520
Clarithromycin, 25t
Clindamycin, 25t
ADRs to, 36t, 355t
Clonazepam, 330t
Clonic, 324b
Clopidogrel, 471t
Closed chest cardiac compression, 494
CNS. *See* Central nervous system
Codeine
ADRs to, 355t
allergic reactions to, 400, 400b
Cold sweat, 474, 490
Collegiality, 114
Coma, 120b
Community, standards of, 114

Complex partial seizures. *See* Partial
seizures; Psychomotor seizures
Compression-ventilation ratio, 507
Confusion, 258b
in acute MI, 477t
Congenital heart lesions, 24–25
Congestive heart failure. *See also* Heart
failure
drug overdose and, 361–362
Conjunctivitis, in anaphylaxis, 416
Consciousness. *See also* Altered
consciousness
acute adrenal insufficiency during,
165–166, 167b
assessment of, 124, 124f
defined, 120b
drugs and, 121
loss of, 318, 431. *See also*
Unconsciousness
Consent, 109–110
in emergencies, 110–112
oral and maxillofacial, 111f
Constipation, medical history
questionnaire regarding, 21
Contact dermatitis, 397. *See also* Allergy
Contact lenses, 29
Contract law, 107
Convalescence, postural hypotension and,
149
Convulsion, 324b
Coronary artery disease (CAD)
age and, 489
angina and, 452
clinical manifestations of, 444t
MI and, 468
risk factors for, 438b
Coronary artery spasm, 462
Coronary heart disease (CHD), 438b
Coronary occlusion. *See* Myocardial
infarction
"Coronary prone," 468
Corticosteroids
in emergency kits, 82t, 84–85
levels of, 163f
systemic, 158t
Corticotrophin-releasing hormone (CRH),
163
Cortisol, hypersecretion of, 156
Cortisone, 158t
Cough
in acute MI, 477t
medical history questionnaire regarding,
21
CPCR. *See* Cardiopulmonary-cerebral
resuscitation
CPR. *See* Cardiopulmonary resuscitation
Cretinism, 288
clinical manifestations of, 292, 292f
CRH. *See* Corticotrophin-releasing
hormone
Cricothyrotomy
anatomic relationships in, 202–203,
202f
anatomy in, 202f

Cricothyrotomy—*cont'd*
contraindications to, 204
equipment, 203
scalpel use in, 202f, 203–204, 203f, 204f
tracheostomy *vs.*, 199–202
Cricothyrotomy device, 88, 88f
Criminal law, 107–108
Cushing's syndrome, 156
CVA. *See* Cerebrovascular accident
Cyanosis
in respiratory distress, 253
in RVF, 242

D
Dam. *See* Rubber dam
Damage, 109
Death, 7–9
in acute MI, 476, 477t
circumstances of, 8t
clinical, 494
top 5 causes of, 10b
Defense mechanisms, of body, 413–414, 413b
Defibrillation
in BLS, 508–510, 508f, 509f
in chain of survival, 497
in children, 526
effectiveness of, 495t
by staff, 61–62
Defibrillators
automated external. *See* Automated external defibrillators
in emergency kits, 78–80
manual, 497
medical history questions and, 29, 30f
PVCs and, 44
Delayed allergic reactions, 408–409
Delayed reaction, 397. *See also* Allergy
Delirium, 258b
Dental cartridge. *See* anesthetic cartridge
Dental floss, foreign body retrieval by, 188, 189f, 190
"Denture sore mouth," 402
Dexamethasone, 158t
Dextrose, 82t, 84
Diabetes mellitus. *See also* Hyperglycemia; Hypoglycemia; Insulin
acute complications of, 263
atherosclerotic disease and, 442
chronic complications of, 263–264, 263t
classification of, 275t
gestational, 267
impaired fasting glucose, 266
impaired glucose tolerance, 266
type 1, 265–266, 266b, 266f
type 2, 265b, 266, 266b, 266t
clinical manifestations of, 276–277, 277b, 277t
control of, 268–269, 269b
dental therapy considerations, 275–276, 276t
hyperglycemia, 263, 268
hypoglycemia, 263, 268, 268t, 269b
identification, 277, 278f

Diabetes mellitus—*cont'd*
management of, 280–284, 281b, 282f, 284b
type 1, 269–271, 270b, 270f
type 2, 271–273, 272t, 273f
medical history questions regarding, 28
multiple daily injection technique in, 270b
overview of, 261–262, 262f
pathophysiology, 277–280
predisposing factors, 264–265, 265b
prevention, 273–276, 275t
Diabetic coma, 276
Diabetic nephropathy, 264
Dialogue history, 47–48
Diaphoresis, 477t
Diarrhea, 21
Diazepam
ADRs to, 355t
for anxiety, 55t
Digitalis, 471t
Diltiazem, 455t
in MI, 471t
Diphenhydramine HCl, for pediatric emergencies, 519t
Dissecting aortic aneurysm, 488, 488b
Diuretics
in heart failure, 236, 236t
in MI, 471t
Diurnal variation, 163
Dizziness. *See also* Syncope
in altered consciousness, 258b
medical history questionnaire regarding, 21
Dobutamine, 471t
Dopamine, 471t
Drug(s). *See also* specific drug
administration of, 350, 363
altered consciousness from, 258
antidotal, 93t, 94–96, 518, 519t
consciousness and, 121
increased use of, 11–12
injectable
administration of, 68–69, 69b, 69f, 101–104, 101f, 102f, 103f, 104f
epinephrine, 68t
in module four, 93t, 94–96
in module one, 70–72, 71f
in module three, 90–93, 91t
in module two, 81—86, 82t
parenteral, 69–70
medical history questions regarding, 29–30
noninjectable
in module one, 73–76
in module three, 91t
in module two, 82t, 86–88, 87f
postural hypotension and, 148, 149b
vasoactivity of, 362, 363t
Drug interactions, 30, 31t–37t
medical emergencies and, 5
Drug kits. *See* Emergency drug kits
Drug overdose, 350
in children, 516t
reaction in, 351

Drug overdose reactions
CNS-depressants
clinical manifestations, 385–387, 386t
management of, 387–391, 389b, 391b
overview, 385
predisposing factors, 385
epinephrine, 381–384, 382t, 383b, 384b
local anesthetic
clinical manifestations, 371–374, 372t, 373b, 374t
drug factors, 362–364, 363t, 364b, 364f
management of, 376–381, 378b, 379b
pathophysiology, 374–376, 375f
predisposing factors, 360–362
prevention, 364–371, 365b, 367t, 368t, 369f, 370f
summary of, 391–393, 392t
Drug-related emergencies. *See also* Adverse drug reactions
analgesics, 354–355, 355t
antianxiety drugs, 355–356, 356t
antibiotics, 353–354, 354t
classification, 351–352, 351b
comparison of, 433t
differential diagnosis, 429–434, 433t
factors of, 352–353
inhalation sedation, 356–357
local anesthetics, 353, 353t
overview, 347–348, 348b, 352–353
prevention, 348–350
"Drunken" appearance, 319
Dry mouth, 24
Dyslipidemia, in atherosclerotic disease, 441
Dysphagia, 21
Dyspnea
in acute MI, 477t
defined, 178b
in drug-related emergencies, 432
in LVF, 241
paroxysmal nocturnal, 241–242
Dysrhythmia. *See also* Bradycardia; Ventricular fibrillation
in acute MI, 475
LAs overdose and, 375–376
lidocaine for, 91–92, 91t
management of, 480

E
ECF-a. *See* Eosinophilic chemotactic factor of anaphylaxis
ECG. *See* Electrocardiography
Edema
acute pulmonary
clinical manifestations of, 242–243, 243t
management of, 246–248, 247b
overview of, 234
in ankles, 239, 239f
hereditary angioneurotic, 409
laryngeal
in allergic reaction, 410, 410t, 421–422, 422b

Edema—*cont'd*
  laryngeal—*cont'd*
    in anaphylactic reaction, 425
  peripheral, 253
Ejection fraction, 244
Elastic recoil, 224
Elderly
  baby boomers, 9f
  life expectancy of, 9–11
  physical changes in, 10b
  postural hypotension in, 149–150
  pulmonary changes in, 11t
Electrocardiography (ECG)
  BLS and, 508f
  in cardiac arrest, 495–496, 495f
  in defibrillation, 509f
Emergencies. *See also* Drug-related
      emergencies
  cardiac-oriented classification, 13t
  common medical, 13b
  consent in, 110–112
  defined, 110–112
  drug kits for, 65–96
  legal responsibilities in, 112–116
  pediatric
    bronchospasm, 520–521
    cardiac arrest, 525–526
    LA overdose, 521–522
    overview of, 515–516, 516b, 516t
    preparation for, 516–518, 517t, 518b,
        518t
    respiratory arrest, 522–525, 524f
    sedation overdose, 521, 523f
    tonic-clonic seizure, 521
  philosophical aspects of, 114–116
Emergency drug kits
  in acute adrenal insufficiency, 167
  commercial *vs.* homemade, 65–67, 66f
  components of, 67–68
  drug checklist for, 97f
  equipment
    artificial airways, 88–89, 89f
    defibrillator, 78–80
    Magill intubation forceps, 80–81, 81f
    overview of, 76–77
    oxygen delivery system, 76–78, 77–78,
        77f, 78f
    suction apparatus, 80, 80f
    syringes, 80, 80f
    tourniquets, 80, 81f
  guidelines for, 60
  labeling for, 97b
  legality of, 115–116
  life-threatening, 3
  module four, 93–96, 93t
  module one, 70–81
    drugs in, 70–76, 70t
    equipment in, 76–80
  module three, 90–93, 91t
  module two
    drugs in, 81–86, 81t
    equipment in, 88–90, 88f, 89f
  organization of, 96–98, 96f
  in pediatric office, 518, 519t

Emergency drug kits—*cont'd*
  specific outline of, 13–14
  staff preparation for, 60–65
  studies regarding, 4t, 5t, 6t, 7t
  systems-oriented classification of, 12–13,
      12b
  telephone numbers in, 63–64
  training for, 60
  types of, 66f, 67f
Emergency team, 517, 518b. *See also* Staff
Emergency treatment record, 63, 64f
Emphysema, 25, 26–27
End-diastolic volume, 244
Endocarditis prophylaxis
  cardiac conditions associated with, 26b
  procedures that require, 26b
Endotracheal intubation, with
      laryngoscope, 89, 90f
Environmental factors
  in diabetes, 264
  drug overdose and, 362
Eosinophilic chemotactic factor of
      anaphylaxis (ECF-A), 415–416
Epigastric discomfort, 488
Epilepsy
  defined, 324b
  drugs for, 331b
  examples of, 327t
  prevention, 329
  psychological implications of, 330–331
Epileptic cry, 333
Epinephrine
  in ACLS drug kit, 90, 91t
  ADRs, 31t
  allergy and, 422–423, 423f
  availability of, 71
  dosages for, 68t, 71–72
  in emergency drug kits, 70–72, 71f
  overdose
    clinical manifestations/
        pathophysiology, 382–383, 383b
    management of, 383–384, 384b
    precipitating factors/prevention of,
        381–382, 382t
  for pediatric emergencies, 519t
  side effects of, 71
  therapeutic indications for, 71
EpiPen. *See* Epinephrine
Erythromycin, 355t
Esmolol, 82t, 85–86
Esophagitis, 488, 488b
Esters
  ADRs to, 356t
  allergic reactions to, 400b, 401
Estrogen status, CVD and, 442–443
Eszopiclone, 55t
Ethosuximide, 330t
Euthyroid, 291
Examination. *See* Physical examination
Exercise
  chest pain and, 488
  CVD and, 442
Exhaled air ventilation, 130–131, 130f,
      131f

Exophthalmos, 294f
Experience, lack of, 113
Extremities, tingling/numbness of, 173
  in respiratory distress, 253
Extrinsic asthma, 216

F
Fainting
  defined, 120, 120b. *See also* Syncope
  stress and, 16
Family history, 27
Fatigue
  in acute MI, 477t
  in LVF, 241
Fear-related emergencies, 16
  stress and, 16
Febrile convulsions, 328
Felbamate, 330t
Fentanyl, overdose of, 387
Fever
  medical history questionnaire regarding,
      21
  temperature during, 46
Finger sweep, 198–199, 198f, 199f
Fludrocortisone, 158t
Flumazenil
  in emergency kit, 93t, 94–95
  for pediatric emergencies, 519t
Flurazepam
  ADRs to, 355t
  for anxiety, 55t
Flurbiprofen, ADRs to, 355t
Foreign body airway obstruction
  invasive procedures for, 199–202
  management of, 190–191, 190b, 191b
  maneuvers, 193–195
    back blows, 195, 195f
    chest thrusts, 197–198, 198b, 198f
    finger sweep, 198–199, 198f, 199f
    Heimlich, 195–197, 196f
    manual thrusts, 195, 196f, 197f
  overview of, 186
  prevention of, 186–190
  recognition of, 191–193, 192b, 192f,
      192t, 193b
  removal sequences in, 200b
Foreseeability, 113
"Four E's," 452
Frank-Starling relationship, 244–245

G
"Gas," 488, 488b
Gender
  altered consciousness and, 318
  CAD and, 489
  drug overdose and, 362
  drug-related emergencies and, 430
  heart failure by, 234f
  respiratory distress and, 252
Generalized anaphylaxis. *See also*
      Anaphylaxis
  allergy and, 423–425, 424b, 425b
Generalized seizures, 324b, 325. *See also*
      Grand mal epilepsy

Genetic factors
  in diabetes, 264–265
  drug overdose and, 362
Geriatric patients. *See* Elderly
Giddiness, in acute MI, 477t
Glaucoma, 27
Glucagon, in emergency kits, 82t, 84
Glucocorticosteroids
  for adrenal insufficiency, 156
  adrenocortical function with, 157b
  clinical indications for, 157b
  coverage protocol for, 160, 160f
  equivalent doses of, 159t
  levels of, in secondary insufficiency,
    164f
  "rule of twos," 159t
Gluconeogenesis, 278–279
Glucose. *See also* Diabetes mellitus;
    Insulin
  monitoring of, 269–270, 270f, 271b
  pathophysiology of, 277–278
Glycogenolysis, 278–279
Glycosuria, 279
Good Samaritan statutes, 112
Grand mal epilepsy
  clinical manifestations of, 334
  management of, 340–341
  overview of, 325
Graves' disease, 288, 289. *See also*
    Thyrotoxicosis
Gravity, blood pressure and, 151–152,
    152f

H
Haptens, 412
Head tilt-chin lift technique
  in airway obstruction, 193, 193f
  in cardiac arrest, 503f
  in children, 519–520, 520f
  in unconsciousness patient, 125–127,
    125f, 127f
Head trauma, seizures and, 327
Headache
  in CVAs, 319
  medical history questionnaire regarding,
    24
  unconsciousness and, 173
Healthfirst emergency kits, 67f
Heart
  functioning of, 234, 243–244
  occlusion of, 469f
"Heart attack," 437. *See also* Cardiac
    arrest; Myocardial infarction
Heart disease, 24
Heart failure
  classification of, 237f, 239b
  clinical manifestations of, 240–243, 243t
  drug therapy for, 236t
  management of, 236t, 246–248, 247b
  medical history questionnaire regarding,
    24
  overview of, 234–235, 234f
  pathophysiology, 243–246, 244t

Heart failure—*cont'd*
  physical evaluation in, 238–239, 238f,
    239f
  predisposing factors of, 235
  prevalence of, 234f
  prevention, 235–238, 236t
  stages of, 241t
Heart murmurs, 25
Heart pain. *See* Chest pain
Heart rate. *See also* Pulse; Vital signs
  in altered consciousness, 319
  beats per minute in, 43
  in children, 45t
  guidelines for clinical evaluation, 43–44
  measurement of, 42–43
  in respiratory distress, 253
  unconsciousness and, 132, 134, 134f,
    174, 174t
Height and weight, 46
Heimlich maneuver, 195–197, 196f, 197f
Hematogenous total joint infection, 29
Hematuria, medical history questionnaire
    regarding, 21
Hemoglobin A$_{1c}$, 274t
Hemophilia, 21
Hemorrhagic stroke, 301t, 303
Hepatitis, 27
Hereditary angioneurotic edema, 409
Herpes, 27–28
Hiatal hernia, 488, 488b
High blood pressure, 25
Histamine
  anaphylaxis and, 414–415
  blocker, 407–408
HIV. *See* Human Immunodeficiency virus
Holter monitoring, 495
Human Immunodeficiency virus (HIV), 27
"Hurry-up" disease, 468
Hydrochlorothiazide, 471t
Hydrocodone, ADRs to, 355t
Hydrocortisone
  for acute adrenal insufficiency, 158t
  in emergency kits, 82t, 84–85
Hydroxyzine, ADRs to, 355t
Hypercarbia, signs and symptoms of, 224b
Hyperglycemia. *See also* Diabetes mellitus
  clinical manifestations of, 276, 277t
  in diabetes, 268
  differential diagnosis, 320
  management of, 280–281, 281b
  overview of, 263
  pathophysiology of, 279
Hyperpnea, 180b
Hyperresponders, 385
Hypertension. *See also* Postural
    hypotension
  atherosclerotic disease and, 442, 443t
  management of, 85–86
Hyperthyroidism. *See also* Thyrotoxicosis
  clinical manifestations of, 293–294,
    294f, 294t
  dental therapy considerations in,
    291–292
  differential diagnosis, 320

Hyperventilation. *See also* Breathing;
    Respiration
  altered consciousness from, 258, 319
  chest pain and, 438, 438t
  in children, 516t
  clinical manifestations, 210–211, 211t
  defined, 180b
  evaluation of, 44–45
  management of, 212–214, 213f, 214f
  overview, 209
  predisposing factors, 210
  prevention, 210
  stress and, 16
  unconsciousness and, 173
Hypnosis, 386
Hypoglycemia
  in children, 516t
  clinical manifestations of, 276–277,
    277b
  in diabetes, 268, 268t, 269b
  differential diagnosis, 320
  management of, 281–284, 284b
  overview of, 263
  pathophysiology of, 279–280
  treatment of, 84
Hyporesponders, 385
Hypotension
  dopamine for, 91t, 92–93
  treatment of, 84
Hypothyroidism
  causes of, 288b
  clinical manifestations of, 292–293, 293t
  dental therapy considerations in, 291
  differential diagnosis, 320
  management of, 295–296
  medications for, 290t
  overview of, 288
  pathophysiology of, 295
  predisposing factors, 288–289
Hypoventilation, 180b
Hypoxia
  defined, 120b, 180b, 438b
  signs and symptoms of, 224b
Hysteria, in children, 516t

I
Ibuprofen, ADRs to, 355t
Ictus, 324b
Idiosyncratic reaction, 352
Immediate allergic reactions, 408–409
Immunoglobulins. *See also* Antibody
  pathophysiology of, 412–413, 413t
Incontinence, unconsciousness and, 174
Indigestion, 488b
Infants. *See also* Children; Pediatric
  airways anatomy in, 128t
  CPR in, 526–529, 528f, 529f
  cretinism in, 288
  obstructed airways in, 199, 199f, 201b
  pulse measurement in, 43
  respiratory rate, 46t
Infarction, 438b
Infection, in diabetes, 263, 264
Infectious diseases, seizures and, 327–328

Inflammation, of airway, 223
Inhalation sedation
  ADRs to, 356–357
  in MI, 473
Inhaler. *See also* Albuterol; Bronchodilator
  for asthma, 226–227
  types of, 227f
  use of, 226f, 228f
Injections
  intramuscular
    sites, 101, 101f, 102f
    technique, 101–102, 101f, 102f
  intravascular
    equipment, 103f
    of LAs, 369–371, 370f
    patient positioning, 103, 103f
    technique, 103–104, 103f, 104f
Insulin. *See also* Diabetes mellitus
  pathophysiology of, 278
  pump, 273f
  resistance, 265
  secretion, 265
  for type 2 diabetes, 272–273
Insulin resistance, atherosclerotic disease
    and, 442
Insurance. *See* Liability
Intracerebral hemorrhage, 303
Intracranial hemorrhage, pathophysiology
    of, 310, 310f
Intracutaneous test, for allergy, 404–405
Intramuscular injections, administration of
  sites, 101, 101f, 102f
  technique, 101–102, 101f, 102f
Intravascular injections
  administration of
    equipment, 103f
    patient positioning, 103, 103f
    technique, 103–104, 103f, 104f
  of LAs, 369–371, 370f
Intrinsic asthma, 216–217
Intubation
  endotracheal, 89, 90f
  Magill forceps for, 80–81, 81f
Ischemia, 438b
Isosorbide dinitrate, for angina, 455t
Isosorbide mononitrate, for angina, 455t
Isovolemic period of systole, 244

J
Jacksonian epilepsy, 326
Jaundice, 24
Jaw-thrust technique, 126, 126f
  in airway obstruction, 193–194, 194f
Joints, artificial, 29. *See also*
      Hematogenous total joint
      infection

K
Ketoacidosis, 279
Ketoprofen, ADRs to, 355t
Ketorolac, ADRs to, 355t
Ketosis, 279
Korotkoff sounds, 40–41, 41f, 42f
Kussmaul's respirations, 279

L
Lacunar infarction, 300–301, 301t
Large blood vessel disease, 263
Laryngeal edema
  in allergic reaction, 410, 410t
    management of, 421–422, 422b
  in anaphylactic reaction, 425
Laryngeal mask airway (LMA), 89, 89f
Larynx, anatomy of, 202
LAs. *See* Local anesthetics
Latex, allergic reactions to, 397–398, 406,
    407t
Left ventricle, normal functioning of,
    244–245
Left ventricular failure (LVF)
  clinical manifestations of, 240–242
  management of, 480
Left-heart failure. *See* Acute pulmonary
      edema
Lesions
  atherosclerotic, 445f
  seizures and, 327
Levine sign, 474
Levothyroxine, 290t
Liability
  limiting, 113
  MICRA and, 106
  theories of
    breach of duty, 108
    causation, 108–109
    consent, 109–110
    contract law, 107
    criminal law, 107–108
    damage, 109
    duty, 108
    reasonableness, 109
    statute of limitations, 110
    statute violation, 106–107
    tort law, 108
"Liability crisis," 106
Lidocaine
  in ACLS drug kit, 91–92, 91t
  ADRs to, 354t
  dosage, 367t
Life expectancy, in US, 9t
Ligature, foreign body retrieval by, 188,
    189f
Liothyronine, 290t
Liotrix, 290t
Lipid-lowering treatment, 471
LMA. *See* Laryngeal mask airway
Local anesthetics (LAs). *See also* specific
      drug
  ADRs to, 31t, 353, 353t
  allergic reactions to, 400b, 401–402,
      401t, 402b, 405–408, 407t
    alleged, 406–408
    confirmed, 408
  comparison of forms, 372t
  dosages for, 365–366, 366t, 368t, 369f,
      369t
  overdose reactions
    in children, 516t, 521–522
    flow chart for, 541–542

Local anesthetics (LAs)—*cont'd*
  overdose reactions—*cont'd*
    overview, 360
    predisposing factors, 360–364, 361f,
        364b, 364f
Localized anaphylaxis, 409
Long-form medical history, 16–17
"Look-listen-and-feel" technique
  in airway obstruction, 193, 193f
  in cardiac arrest, 503f
  in children, 524
  in unconsciousness patient, 127, 128f
Lorazepam, ADRs to, 355t
Loss of consciousness. *See* Syncope;
      Unconsciousness
LVF. *See* Left ventricular failure

M
Macrolides, ADRs to, 35t–36t
Magill intubation forceps
  in emergency kits, 80–81, 81f
  foreign body retrieval by, 188, 188f
Malum in se, 107
Malum prohibitum, 107
Manual defibrillator, 497
Manual thrusts, for airway obstruction, 195
Medical alert bracelets, for allergy, 403f
Medical consultation, 53–54, 53b
Medical history questionnaire, 16–17
  for acute adrenal insufficiency, 158–160
  in acute MI, 470–472
  altered consciousness and, 318
  for angina pectoris, 454–457
  anxiety and, 48
  on asthma, 217–219
  consultation request in, 23f
  in CVA, 304–305
  in drug-related emergencies, 348–349
  on heart failure, 235–238
  interview sheet in, 22f
  pediatric, 17f
  physical examination and, 38–48
  question-based analysis, 17, 19, 21,
      24–30
  respiratory distress and, 252
  for seizures, 329–330
  in Spanish, 20f
  in thyroid dysfunction, 289–291
  updating of, 30, 38
  value of, 17
Medical Insurance Compensation Reform
      Act (MICRA), 106
Medically compromised patients, stress
      and, 16
Medications, 29–30
Mental stress. *See also* Stress
  CVD and, 442, 444
Meperidine, overdose of, 387
Mepivacaine, 354t
  dosage, 367t
Metabolic acidosis, 279
Metabolic disorders, seizures and, 327
Metabolic function, in unconscious
      patient, 123

Metaproterenol, in emergency kits, 74
Methyl methacrylate, allergic reactions to, 406, 407t
Methylparaben, allergic reactions to, 400b, 401–402
Methylprednisolone, 158t
Metoprolol, 455t
  in MI, 471t
Metronidazole, ADRs to, 37t
MI. *See* Myocardial infarction
MICRA. *See* Medical Insurance Compensation Reform Act
Microangiopathy, 263–264
Midazolam
  ADRs to, 355t
  for anxiety, 55t
  in emergency kits, 81–83, 82f, 82t
Minimally invasive glucose monitors, 271
Mixed asthma, 217
Morbidity, 4–7
Morphine
  in ACLS drug kit, 91t, 93
  in acute MI, 479–480
  overdose of, 387
Morphine sulfate, in emergency kits, 82t, 83
Mouth-to-mask ventilation
  in cardiac arrest, 503, 503f, 504f
  in children, 524, 524f
Mouth-to-mouth resuscitation, 130–131, 130f
Mouth-to-nose ventilation, 131, 131f
Multiple daily injection technique, 270b
Muscle strain, 488b
Musculoskeletal, chest pain, 488
Myocardial infarction (MI)
  acute
    clinical manifestations, 474–475, 474t, 475b
    management of, 476–482, 477t, 480b, 481t
    overview of, 467–468
    pathophysiology, 475–476
    predisposing factors, 468–470, 469f
    prevention, 470–472, 471t
    therapy considerations in, 472–473, 472t
  chest pain and, 438, 438t
  heart rate in, 489–490
  location of pain in, 489
  location/extent of infarction, 469–470, 469f
  medical history questionnaire regarding, 24–25
Myocardial ischemia, 468–469
Myocardium, 476
Myxedema
  clinical manifestations of, 293
  overview of, 288
  pathophysiology of, 295

N
Nadolol, 455t
Nalbuphine, 94

Naloxone
  in emergency kit, 93t, 94
  for pediatric emergencies, 519t
Naproxen, ADRs to, 355t
Nausea, in acute MI, 477t, 490
Nervousness, 431
Neurohumoral inhibitors, in heart failure, 236t, 237
Nicardipine, 455t
Nifedipine
  for angina, 455t
  in emergency kits, 82t, 87–88
Night sweats, 21
911 calls
  in cardiac arrest, 505
  in chain of survival, 496
  in pediatric emergency, 518
  preparedness for, 63–65
  responsibility and, 115
Nitrates, MI and, 471, 471t
Nitrendipine, 455t
Nitroglycerin
  action of, 462–463
  for angina, 455t, 460
  in emergency kits, 73–74, 74f
  for pediatric emergencies, 519t
  side effects of, 462
Nitrolingual spray, 463, 463f
Nitrous oxide
  ADRs to, 356–357
  for epileptic patients, 331
Nonsteroidal antiinflammatory drugs (NSAIDS), ADRs and, 34t, 385
Normal distribution curve, 361, 361f
Normal sinus rhythm (NSR)
  in clinical evaluation, 43–44, 45f
  pediatric, 525
NSAIDS. *See* Nonsteroidal antiinflammatory drugs
NSR. *See* Normal sinus rhythm

O
Obesity
  CVD and, 442
  in diabetes, 265
Obstructive airway disease, management of, 220f
Office personnel. *See* Staff
Older patients. *See* Elderly
Opioids
  ADRs and, 33t–34t, 385
  allergic reactions to, 406, 407t
  overdose of, 387
  management, 389–391, 391b
Oral packing, airway obstruction and, 187, 187f
Orthopnea
  defined, 180b
  in LVF, 241
Orthostatic hypotension. *See* Postural hypotension
Oxazepam
  ADRs to, 355t
  for anxiety, 55t

Oxycodone, ADRs to, 355t
Oxygen
  in ACLS drug kit, 91, 91t
  adult requirements of, 244t
  in angina pectoris, 457, 462–463
  deprivation of, 123
  in emergency drug kits, 73, 73f
  in MI, 473
  for pediatric emergencies, 519t
  for stress reduction, 57, 57f
  for unconscious patient, 132, 134f

P
Pacemaker
  diagram of, 29f
  medical history questions regarding, 29
$PaCO_2$, 180b
Pain
  control
    in angina, 458–459
    in MI, 473
    postoperative, 57
    during treatment, 56
  in MI, 474
  morphine for, 91t, 93
  sign/symptoms of, in angina, 460–461
Pallor
  during acute MI, 475, 490
  during unconsciousness, 173
Palpatory systolic pressure, 40
Palpitation, in acute MI, 477t
PaO_2, 180b
Parabens, allergic reactions to, 400b, 401–402
Paresthesias, 293, 319
Paroxysmal nocturnal dyspnea, in LVF, 241–242
Parry's disease. *See* Thyrotoxicosis
Partial seizures
  classification of, 324b
  clinical manifestations of, 332
  management of, 335–336, 336b
  overview of, 325
Patient positioning
  drug-related emergencies and, 430
  in heart failure, 240
  in postural hypotension, 151–152, 152f
  in respiratory distress, 252
  during seizure, 338f
  during unconsciousness, 172–173, 173b
Pediatric advanced life support, 517, 518b
Pediatric blood pressure ranges, 44t
Pediatric chain of survival, 526–528, 526f
Pediatric CPR, 516–518, 518t, 526–529, 528f, 529f
  rescuer practice sheets for, 534–536
Pediatric emergencies, 17f
  bronchospasm, 520–521
  cardiac arrest, 525–526
  LA overdose, 521–522
  management of, 17f, 518–520, 519t, 520f
  overview of, 515–516, 516b, 516t

Pediatric emergencies—cont'd
  preparation for, 516–518, 517t, 518b, 518t
  respiratory arrest, 522–525, 524f
  sedation overdose, 521, 523f
  tonic-clonic seizure, 521
Pediatric emergencies in the Dental Office (PEDO), 516, 517, 517t
PEDO. See Pediatric Emergencies in the Dental Office
Penicillin
  ADRs, 34t–35t
  allergic reactions to, 399–400, 400b, 405–406, 407t
Penicillin G, 355t
Penicillin V, 355t
Pericarditis, 488, 488b
Peripheral edema, in respiratory distress, 253
Personnel. See Staff
Petit mal epilepsy. See Absence seizures
Phenobarbital, for seizures, 330t
Phenylephrine, in emergency kits, 82t, 83–84
Phenytoin, for seizures, 330t
Phlebotomy, 247–248
Photosensitive epilepsy, 328
Physical evaluation
  goals of, 16b
  medical history questionnaire in. See Medical history questionnaire
Physical examination, 38–48
  consultation in, 53–54, 53b
  of diabetic, 275, 275t
  dialogue history and, 47–48
  overview of, 38
  in postural hypotension, 150–151, 151b
  in thyroid dysfunction, 291
  visual inspection, 46–47
  vital signs
    blood pressure, 39–42
    heart rate/rhythm, 42–44
    height and weight, 46
    respiratory rate, 44–46
    temperature, 46
Physical exhaustion, postural hypotension and, 150
Physical Status Classification System
  ASA I, 51
  ASA II, 51
  ASA III, 51–52
  ASA IV, 52
  ASA V, 52–53
  overview, 50–51
Physostigmine, in emergency kit, 93t, 95
"Pins and needles." See Paresthesias
Pitting, 242
Placebo response, 362
Plaque, atherosclerotic, 445f
Plasma level. See Blood level
Plummer's disease. See Thyrotoxicosis
Pocket mask, 78, 78f
Polydipsia, 24

Polyuria, 24
Poor decisions, examples of, 113
Positive inotropics agents, in heart failure, 236–237, 236t
Positron-emission tomograph, 446
Postsyncope
  clinical manifestations of, 141, 142
  management of, 144
Postural hypotension
  clinical manifestations, 151, 151b
  management of, 153–154, 154b
  overview of, 147–148
  pathophysiology, 151–152, 152f, 153t
  predisposing factors in, 148–150, 149b
  prevention, 150–151
Postural reflex, inadequate, 149
Practice drills, for emergencies, 62–63
Practice sheets
  child CPR, 534–536
  CPR and AED, 532–533
Prednisolone, 158t
Pregnancy, postural hypotension in, 149
Premature ventricular contractions (PVCs), in clinical evaluation, 43–44, 45f
Premedication, for stress-reduction, 54–55, 55t
Presyncope
  clinical manifestations, 140, 140b
  management, 142, 142f
  pathophysiology, 141
  signs/symptoms of, 173–175, 174t, 175b
Prilocaine, 354t, 367t
Primidone, for seizures, 330t
Prinzmetal's variant angina, 462
Private practice, emergencies in, 4t
Procaine
  allergic reactions to, 400b, 401
  in emergency kit, 93t, 95–96
Propoxycaine, allergic reactions to, 400b, 401
Propranolol, 455t
  in MI, 471t
Prostaglandins, 415–416
Prosthetic heart valve, 28–29
Pruritus, 399
Pseudomyotonic deep tendon reflexes, 293
Psychiatric care, 28
Psychic mechanisms, in unconscious patient, 123–124
Psychomotor seizures, 326
Psychosedation
  in angina, 459–460
  for stress, 16
PTCA, 481–482
Pulmonary arrest, in cardiopulmonary arrest, 498, 498t
Pulmonary embolism, chest pain and, 488
Pulmonary embolus
  in acute MI, 477t
  chest pain and, 488b
Pulse. See also Heart rate; Vital signs
  guidelines for clinical evaluation, 43–44

Pulse—cont'd
  measurement of, 42–43
  in infants, 43
  quality of, 44
Pulseless electrical activity, 495–496, 495f
  in cardiopulmonary arrest, 499
Pulsus alternans, 44
  in LVF, 242
PVCs. See Premature ventricular contractions

R
Race, CVD by, 440t
Radial artery, 40, 40f
Radial pulse, 40
Rapid intravascular injection, 371
Reasonableness, 109
Recreational drugs, 29
Recumbency, postural hypotension and, 149
Referral letter, 28b
Relationships
  doctor-patient, 112–113
  good samaritan, 112
  professional, 114
Relative contraindication, 365
Renal disease, in diabetes, 264
Renal failure
  in acute MI, 477t
  medical history questions regarding, 28
Rescue breathing, 503–504
Respiration
  in altered consciousness, 319
  in chest pain, 490
  defined, 180b
Respiratory alkalosis, 212
Respiratory arrest, 386–387
  in cardiopulmonary arrest, 498, 498t
  in children, 522–525, 523f, 524f
Respiratory depression, pediatric, 523
Respiratory distress
  age and, 252
  causes of, 180b
  in children, 516t
  clinical manifestations, 181
  differential diagnosis, 251–253
  duration of, 253
  flow chart for, 538
  management of, 181–183, 182b
  overview, 179
  pathophysiology, 181
  predisposing factors, 180
  prevention, 180–181
  sites of origin of, 182f
  terms related to, 180b
Respiratory rate
  guidelines for clinical evaluation, 44–46
  in infants, 46t
  overview of, 44
Respiratory reactions, allergic, 409–410, 410t
  management of, 419–422, 420b, 420f, 422b
Respondeat superior, 113–114

Resuscitation. *See also* Basic life support; Cardiopulmonary resuscitation; Cardiopulmonary-cerebral resuscitation
  in cardiac arrest, 78–79
  cerebral, 494
  mouth-to-mouth, 130–131
Rheumatic fever, 25
Rhinitis
  in allergic reaction, 410, 410t
  in anaphylaxis, 416
Right ventricular failure (RVF), clinical manifestations of, 242
Rubber dam
  airway obstruction and, 186, 187b, 187f
  in stress reduction, 57
"Rule of twos," 159b
RVF. *See* Right ventricular failure

S
Scalpel, in cricothyrotomy, 203–204, 204f
Sedation
  in MI, 473
  overdose, in children, 521
Sedative-hypnotics
  for anxiety, 54–55, 55t
  overdose management of, 387–389, 389b
Seizures. *See also* Absence seizures; Partial seizures; Tonic-clonic seizures
  causes of, 326–328, 327t, 328t
  in children, 516t
  clinical manifestations, 332–334, 333f, 334f
  differential diagnosis, 341, 341t
  in drug-related emergencies, 432
  flow chart for, 540
  management of, 335–341, 336b, 337f, 338f, 339b, 341b
  medical history questionnaire regarding, 24
  overview of, 323, 324b
  pathophysiology, 334–335
  predisposing factors, 328–329
  prevention, 329–332, 330t, 331, 332t
  treatment of, 81–83
  types of, 324–326, 324b
Semiautomated external defibrillators. *See* Automated external defibrillators
Sensitizing dose, 414
Sex. *See* Gender
"Shake and shout" maneuver, 122, 124f
Shock, cardiogenic, 476
"Shockable rhythm," 499
Short-form medical history, 16–17
Shortness of breath
  medical history questionnaire regarding, 21
  in respiratory distress, 252–253
Shy-Drager syndrome, postural hypotension and, 150
Simple consent, 109
Simple partial seizures. *See* Partial seizures

Skin
  allergic reactions, management of, 416–419, 417b, 418b
  allergy testing, 404–405
  appearance of, 319
  reactions, allergic, 409, 409t
  in visual inspection, 47
Skin disease, 27
Slow-reacting substance of anaphylaxis (SRS-A), 415
Smoking, atherosclerotic disease and, 441–442, 443t
Sodium bisulfite, allergic reactions to, 400b, 402
Spanish, 20f
Speech, in visual inspection, 47
SRS-A. *See* Slow-reacting substance of anaphylaxis
Stable angina, 452, 453t
Staff
  BLS training by, 4–99–500
  defibrillation by, 61–62
  emergency practice drills for, 62–63
  foreign body retrieval by, 188
  life support by, 61
  patient anxiety and, 49
  team management of, 62
  training of, 60–61
Standards, community, 114
Starvation, postural hypotension and, 150
Status asthmaticus
  clinical manifestations of, 222
  overview of, 217
Status epilepticus
  clinical manifestations of, 334
  defined, 324b
  overview of, 326
Statute violation, 106–107
  malum in se, 107
  malum prohibitum, 107
Sternum, 505
Stertorous, 324b
Stress. *See also* Anxiety
  in CVA, 306
  mental, CVD and, 442, 444
  psychosedation for, 56
  reduction of, 16
  in MI, 473
  respiratory distress and, 252
  syncope and, 139
  toleration of, 16
  unconsciousness and, 172, 173b
Stress-reduction protocols, 54–57, 160
  in acute MI, 470
  anxiety recognition and, 54
  hyperventilation and, 210
  medical consultation, 54
  premedication, 54–55, 55t
  types of, 54, 54b
Stridor, in drug-related emergencies, 432
Stroke. *See also* Cerebrovascular accident
  in acute MI, 477t
  medical history questionnaire regarding, 25

Stroke—*cont'd*
  prevalence of, 299
  time goals in treating, 311b
  types of, 304t
"Stroke Chain of Survival," 310, 311b
Subarachnoid hemorrhage, 303
  pathophysiology of, 310, 310f
Suction apparatus
  in emergency drug kits, 80, 80f
  foreign body retrieval by, 188
  in seizures, 337f
Sudden cardiac arrest (SCA)
  overview of, 493–494
  survival from, 397t, 494–496, 495f
Sudden death, 493
Sugar
  in emergency drug kits, 75–76, 76f
  for pediatric emergencies, 519t
Sulfamethoxazole, ADRs to, 37t
Supine hypotensive syndrome of pregnancy, 149
Supraventricular tachycardia, verapamil for, 91t, 93
Surgery, 29
Swallowed objects
  management of, 190b
  radiograph of, 190f
Sweating, thyroid dysfunction and, 293–294
Syncope. *See also* Unconsciousness; Vasodepressor syncope
  in acute MI, 477t
  basic life support in, 174–175, 175b
  in children, 516t
  classification by mechanism, 122, 122t
  clinical manifestations, 140
  defined, 120b
  differential diagnosis of, 120b
  management of, 143–144, 143f
  overview of, 137–138
  pathophysiology, 141–142
  synonyms for, 138b
Syringes, in emergency drug kits, 80, 80f
Systems-oriented classification, 12–13, 12b

T
Tachypnea, 180b
Team members. *See also* Staff
  BLS and, 500
  duties of, 62
  pediatric emergency, 517–518, 518t
Temperature
  guidelines for clinical evaluation, 46
  overview of, 46
Terminal illness, ASA classification of, 52–53
Tetracaine, allergic reactions to, 400b, 401
Tetracyclines, ADRs to, 36t
Thermometer, digital, 46f
Thrombolytic therapy, 481
Thyroid crisis, 288
Thyroid gland
  anatomy of, 202–203, 202f, 287
  medical history questions regarding, 28

Thyroid gland dysfunction
altered consciousness and, 259
causes of, 288b, 289b
clinical manifestations, 292–294, 292f, 293t, 294f, 294t
management, 295–297, 296b
overview of, 288
pathophysiology, 295
predisposing factors, 288–289
prevention, 289–292, 290t, 292t
Thyroid storm
clinical manifestations of, 288, 294
in hyperthyroidism, 289
pathophysiology of, 295
Thyroid USP, 290t
Thyrotoxicosis
causes of, 289b
clinical manifestations of, 293–294, 294f, 294t
management of, 296–297
medications for, 290t
overview of, 288
pathophysiology of, 295
predisposing factors, 289
TIA. *See* Transient ischemic attack
Time, in chain of survival, 497
Timolol, 471t
Tinnitus, 24
Titrate, 522
Tobacco, 30
Tongue
grasping forceps, foreign body retrieval by, 188, 189f
in unconscious patient, 123, 123f
Tonic-clonic seizures. *See also* Grand mal epilepsy
in children, 521
defined, 324b
ictal phase, 333–334, 333f, 334f
management of, 336–341, 337f, 338f, 339b, 341b
postictal phase, 334
preictal phase, 333
prodromal phase of, 333
unconsciousness and, 174
Torr, 180b
Tort law, 108
Tourniquets
in emergency kits, 80, 81f
placement of, 103–104, 103f
Toxic goiter. *See* Thyrotoxicosis
Toxic reaction. *See* Drug overdose
Toxicology, 348, 348b
Trachea, 202, 202f
Tracheostomy, cricothyrotomy *vs.*, 199–202
Transient ischemic attack (TIA)
classification, 300
clinical manifestations of, 308
management of, 311–313, 313b
overview of, 301, 301t, 303
physical status classifications, 307t
Tremor, in visual inspection, 47
Trendelenburg position, 129, 129f
Triamcinolone, 158t

Triazolam
ADRs to, 355t
for anxiety, 55t
Trimethoprim, ADRs, 37t
Triple response, 415
Tuberculosis, 25, 26
Tumors
medical history questionnaire regarding, 27
seizures and, 327

U
Ulcers, 27
Unconsciousness. *See also* Syncope
acute adrenal insufficiency during, 166–168, 168b
airways
adjuncts, 132, 133f
obstruction of, 123, 123f, 125–127, 126f, 127f
blood pressure and, 132, 134, 134f, 174, 174f
causes of, 121t, 172b
clinical manifestations, 122
defined, 120b
differential diagnosis, 171–175, 172b, 173b, 174t, 175b
duration of, 174–175, 175b
flow chart for, 537
heart rate and, 132, 134, 134f, 174
management of, 124–135, 172b
overview of, 119–120
pathophysiology of, 122–124, 123f
predisposing factors, 120–121, 121t
prevention, 121–122
terms of, 120b
United States, life expectancy in, 9t
University of the Pacific School of Dentistry
medical history questionnaire, 18f
website for, 17
Unstable angina
classification of, 454t
comparison of, 453, 453t
defined, 438b
prevention of, 457
related circumstances, 489
Urticaria
in allergies, 409, 409t
in anaphylaxis, 416
defined, 399

V
Valproate, for seizures, 330t
Variant angina, 453, 453t
Varicose veins, postural hypotension in, 150
Vascular disorders
postural hypotension and, 150
seizures and, 327
Vasoconstrictors, ADRs, 31t
Vasodepressor syncope, 122. *See also* Syncope; Unconsciousness
case study, 144–145
clinical manifestations, 140–141, 140b

Vasodepressor syncope—*cont'd*
management of, 142–145, 145b
overview of, 137–138
pathophysiology of, 141–142
predisposing factors, 138, 138b
prevention, 139–140
Vasodilator
in angina pectoris, 462–463
in emergency kits, 73–74, 74f
in heart failure, 236t, 237, 248
Vasovagal syncope. *See* Vasodepressor syncope
Ventilation
alveolar, 180b
artificial, 45
in unconscious patient, 130–132, 130f, 131f, 132f
methods of, 77–78, 77t
mouth-to-mask, 503, 503f, 504f
spontaneous, 45
Ventricular fibrillation
in acute MI, 475
in cardiopulmonary arrest, 499
in clinical diagnosis, 45f
Ventricular standstill, 498–499
Ventricular tachycardia
in acute MI, 476
in cardiopulmonary arrest, 499
Verapamil
in ACLS drug kit, 91t, 93
for angina, 455t
for angina pectoris, 463–464
in MI, 471t
Vision, blurred, 24
Visual inspection, 46–47
Vital signs. *See also* Heart rate; Pulse
in altered consciousness, 319
baseline, 38, 39
in chest pain, 489–490
in drug-related emergencies, 432
hyperventilation and, 211
in MI, 472
pre/postoperative, 56
Vomiting, 21

W
Waiting time, 56
Warfarin, 471t
Weakness, in LVF, 241
Websites, for University of the Pacific, 17
Weight
drug overdose and, 361
medical history questionnaire regarding, 21
Wheezing, in respiratory distress, 252

Z
Zaleplon
ADRs to, 31t–32t, 355t
for anxiety, 55t
Zolpidem
ADRs to, 31t–32t, 355t
for anxiety, 55t